KEY TO MAPS

1 SYMBOLS LEGEND

THE WORLD
MAPS 2 – 5

EUROPE
MAPS 6 – 45

By reference to this Key to Maps, and its continuation on the back endpaper, the most suitable map of a required area can be found.

The map pages of the core World Atlas section are keyed according to their continental subsections and scale category. There are three scale categories, as indicated below. All scales are quoted as representative ratios expressed in millions (as denoted by the abbreviation M).

Large scale: between 1:1M and 2½M

Medium scale: between 1:2½M and 1:7½M

Small scale: smaller than 1:7½M

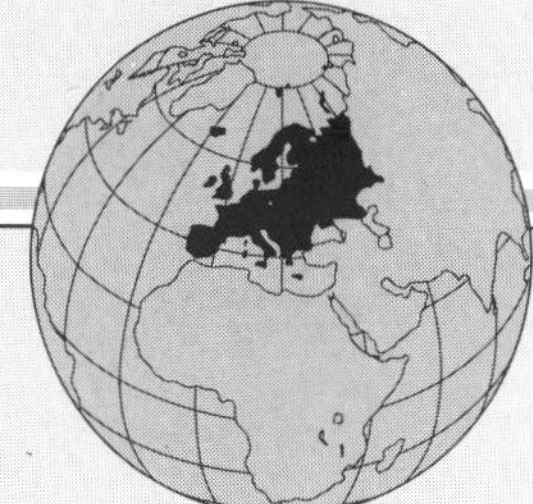

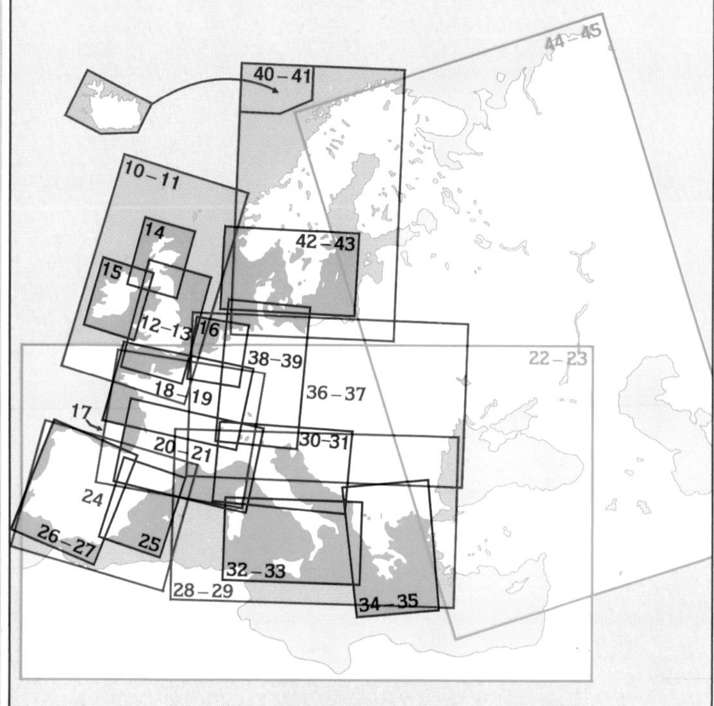

ASIA
MAPS 46 – 67

AFRICA
MAPS 68 – 81

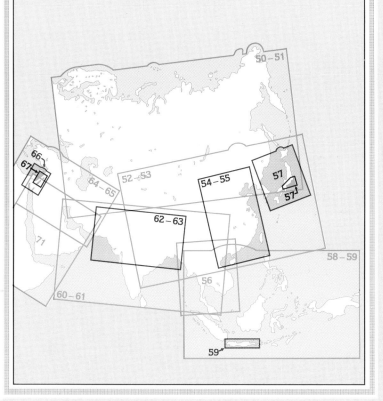

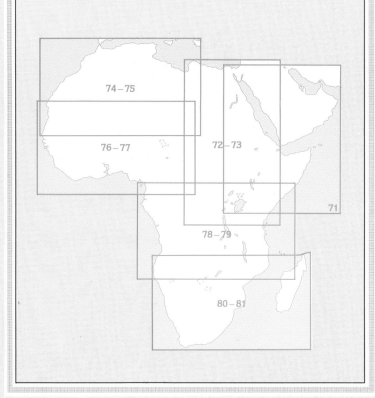

Continued on Back Endpaper

COLLINS

ATLAS

OF THE WORLD

COLLINS

ATLAS

OF THE WORLD

HarperCollins*Publishers*

Collins Atlas of the World
First published 1983 by William Collins Sons & Co. Ltd
Reprinted 1983, 1985, 1986, 1987
Revised 1988 Reprinted 1989, 1990

New Edition 1991
Reprinted 1992

Maps © Collins and Collins-Longman Atlases
Illustrated section and statistics © Bartholomew
Collins is an imprint of Bartholomew,
a division of HarperCollins Publishers

12 Duncan Street
Edinburgh
EH9 1TA

Printed in Scotland by HarperCollins Manufacturing, Glasgow

ISBN 0 00 447823 1

Photograph Credits
J. Allen Cash Photolibrary
Chalmers Clapperton, Aberdeen University
D. R. & P. Davies
Greenpeace
The Hutchison Library
The Image Bank
Frank Lane Picture Library
London Docklands Development Corporation
Meteorological Department, National Centre for Atmospheric Research/National Science Foundation, USA
National Oceanic And Atmospheric Administration, USA
Peter Newark's Pictures
Panos Pictures
Nigel Press
Science Photo Library
Sefton Photo Library
Spectrum Colour Library
Tropix Photographic Library
UNICEF Photo
United Nations Environment Programme

FOREWORD

MAPS, as essential aids in the understanding of the world around us, would appear to have been made ever since man first moved about the Earth. To begin with they were relatively primitive plans of very limited areas, carved in wood or painted on rock, bark or skins. Later, the highly organized peoples of the ancient civilizations, in conducting their everyday life, made many functional maps on such materials as clay tablets, papyrus and eventually paper.

However, the first attempt to map the whole of the known world, as opposed to producing local plans of small areas, is attributed to the famous Greek cosmographer, Ptolemy (AD 87 - 150). The many maps of the classical world that accompanied his celebrated manuscript *Geographia* - itself to be regarded as the standard geographical reference work for many centuries - represent the forerunner of the atlas as we know it today.

ATLASES, in the modern sense of systematic collections of maps of uniform size, were born, much later still, in the Netherlands of the 16th century, during the world's great age of exploration. Indeed, it was the eminent Flemish cartographer Mercator (1512 - 1594) who first so used the word Atlas; taking the name of the ancient Greek mythological titan who symbolically supported the world on his shoulders.

Since the time of these early atlases our knowledge of the world has been greatly increased through continued exploration and scientific discovery. Today, the fast developing space age technology allows man to survey our planet, and beyond, in the most precise detail. The resulting mass of geographical and astronomical data is such that the non-specialist atlas user could easily be overwhelmed. This current information explosion, combined with a new awareness of our world brought about by the views of our planet from space, improved communications, greater opportunity for leisure and travel, and increased media exposure, we believe, calls for a new type of atlas that presents to the general reader, not only an up-to-date collection of well-documented maps, but also an illuminating and readily accessible record of the latest findings and essential facts about our world.

COLLINS ATLAS OF THE WORLD is published with the explicit aim of meeting this need for a convenient and moderately priced reference atlas, that places at our fingertips an accurate, authoritative, comprehensive and clearly presented picture of the world as it is know today. To achieve this objective, Collins, building on its traditions and experience of over one hundred years' innovative atlas publishing, assembled a talented team of geographers, cartographers, designers, editors and writers. Working to a carefully devised plan, this team has brought together in a single volume a new and complete set of maps, a compendium of contemporary geographical data, and an informative and in-depth survey at contemporary world environmental issues.

As a result of the detailed process of research, compilation and design, together with the latest cartographic techniques, which have gone into the production of *Collins Atlas of the World*, we believe that our readers will have the best and most up-to-date atlas available in its class. In terms of cartographic presentation, geographical knowledge and visual elegance, the publication of *Collins Atlas of the World* represents a major step forward, which we hope will contribute to a better awareness and understanding of our fascinating and fast changing world as we approach the 21st century.

CONTENTS

OUR WORLD

WORLD ATLAS

GEOGRAPHICAL DATA

GUIDE TO THE ATLAS

COLLINS ATLAS OF THE WORLD consists of three self-contained but interrelated sections, as is clearly indicated in the preceding list of contents. First, under the title of OUR WORLD there is an informative and in-depth survey of contemporary world environmental issues. Next, the WORLD ATLAS section, comprising 128 pages of maps, using the most modern cartographic techniques and up-to-date sources, forms the core of this book. Finally, the maps, diagrams and text of these first two sections, are complemented by a detailed compendium of GEOGRAPHICAL DATA.

OUR WORLD

This concise encyclopaedia section, by use of stimulating illustrations, photographs, diagrams and informative text, brings together much of the current knowledge and thinking concerning world environmental issues. The first section covers the physical environment, dealing with natural hazards and their implications for mankind, and with the detrimental effects of human activity on the natural environment. The second section covers the human environment, dealing with the exploitation of natural resources and the need to seek renewable alternatives, the continuing need to improve the quality of life for all the peoples of the world through health programmes or universal education, the problems of overpopulation and urbanisation, and with development issues raised through the inequitable distribution of wealth.

WORLD ATLAS

The main section of 128 pages of maps has been carefully planned and designed to meet the contemporary needs of the atlas user. Full recognition has been given to the many different purposes that currently call for map reference.

Map coverage extends to every part of the world in a balanced scheme that avoids any individual country or regional bias. Map areas are chosen to reflect the social, economic, cultural or historical importance of a particular region. Each double spread or single page map has been planned deliberately to cover an entire physical or political unit. Generous map overlaps are included to maintain continuity. Following two world maps, giving separate coverage of the main political and physical features, each of the continents is treated systematically in a subsection of its own. Apart from being listed in the contents, full coverage of all regional maps of each continent is also clearly depicted in the Key to Maps to be found on the front and back endpapers. Also at the beginning of each continental subsection, alongside a special Global View political map, all map coverage, country by country, is identified in an additional handy page index. Finally, as a further aid to the reader in locating the required area, a postage stamp key map is incorporated into the title margin of each map page.

Map projections have been chosen to reflect the different requirements of particular areas. No map can be absolutely true on account of the impossibility of representing a spheroid accurately on a flat surface without some distortion in either area, distance, direction or shape. In a general world atlas it is the equal area property that is most important to retain for comparative map studies and feature size evaluation and this principle has

been followed wherever possible in this map section. As a special feature of this atlas, the Global View projections used for each continental political map have been specially devised to allow for a realistic area comparison between the land areas of each continent and also between land and sea.

Map scales, as expressions of the relationship which the distance between any two points of the map bears to the corresponding distance on the ground, are in the context of this atlas grouped into three distinct categories.

Large scales, of between 1:1 000 000 (1 centimetre to 10 kilometres or 1 inch to 16 miles) and 1:2 500 000 (1 centimetre to 25 kilometres or 1 inch to 40 miles), are used to cover particularly densely populated areas of Western Europe, United States, Canada and Japan, as well as a special detailed map of the Holy Land.

Medium scales, of between 1:2 500 000 and 1:7 500 000 are used for maps of important parts of Europe, North America, Australasia, India, China, etc.

Small scales, of less than 1:7 500 000 (e.g. 1:1 0 000 000, 1:15 000 000, 1:25 000 000 etc.) are selected for maps of the complete world, continents, oceans, polar regions and many of the larger countries.

The actual scale at which a particular area is mapped therefore reflects its shape, size and density of detail, and as a basic principle the more detail required to be shown of an area, the greater its scale. However, throughout this atlas, map scales have been limited in number, as far as possible, in order to facilitate comparison between maps.

Map measurements give preference to the metric system which is now used in nearly every country throughout the world. All spot heights and ocean depths are shown in metres and the relief and submarine layer delineation is based on metric contour levels. However, all linear scalebar and height reference column figures are given in metric and Imperial equivalents to facilitate conversion of measurements for the non-metric reader.

Map symbols used are fully explained in the legend to be found on the first page of the World Atlas section. Careful study and frequent reference to this legend will aid in the reader's ability to extract maximum information.

Topography is shown by the combined means of precise spot heights, contouring, layer tinting and three-dimensional hill shading. Similar techniques are also used to depict the sea bed on the World Physical map and those of the oceans and polar regions.

Hydrographic features such as coastlines, rivers, lakes, swamps and canals are clearly differentiated.

Communications are particularly well represented with the contemporary importance of airports and road networks duly emphasized.

International boundaries and national capitals are fully documented and internal administrative divisions are shown with the maximum detail that the scale will allow. Boundary delineation reflects the 'de facto' rather than the 'de jure' political interpretation and where relevant an undefined or disputed boundary is distinguished. However there is no intended implication that the publishers necessarily endorse or accept the status of any political entity recorded on the maps.

Settlements are shown by a series of graded town stamps from major cities down to tiny villages.

Other features, such as notable ancient monuments, oases, national parks, oil and gas fields, are selectively included on particular maps that merit their identification.

Lettering styles used in the maps have been chosen with great care to ensure maximum legibility and clear distinction of named feature categories. The size and weight of the various typefaces reflect the relative importance of the features. Town names are graded to correspond with the appropriate town stamp.

Map place names have been selected in accordance with maintaining legibility at a given scale and at the same time striking an appropriate balance between natural and man-made features worthy of note. Name forms have been standardized according to the widely accepted principle, now well established in international reference atlases, of including place names and geographical terms in the local language of the country in question. In the case of non-Roman scripts (e.g. Arabic), transliteration and transcription have either been based on the rules recommended by the Permanent Committee on Geographical Names and the United States Board of Geographical Names, or as in the case of the adopted Pinyin transcription of Chinese names, a system officially proposed by the country concerned. The diacritical signs used in each language or transliteration have been retained on all the maps and throughout the index. However the English language reader's requirements have also been recognised in that the names of all countries, oceans, major seas and land features as well as familiar alternative name versions of important towns are presented in English.

Map sources used in the compilation of this atlas were many and varied, but always of the latest available information. At each stage of their preparation the maps were submitted to a thorough process of research and continual revision to ensure that on publication all data would be as accurate as practicable. A well-documented data bank was created to ensure consistency and validity of all information represented on the maps.

GEOGRAPHICAL DATA

This detailed data section forms an appropriate complement to the preceding maps and illustrated texts. There are three parts, each providing a different type of essential geographical information.

World Facts and Figures Drawn from the latest available official sources, these tables present an easy reference profile of significant world physical, political and demographic as well as national data.

Glossary of Geographical Terms This explains most of the foreign language and geographical terms which are to be found incorporated in the place names on the maps and the index.

World Index This concluding part of the atlas lists in alphabetical order all individual place names to be found on the maps, which total about 40,000. Each entry in the index is referenced to the appropriate map page number, the country or region in which the name is located and the position of the name on the map, given by its co-ordinates of latitude and longitude. A full explanation of how to use the index is to be found on page 140.

OUR WORLD

While the earth formed about 4500 million years ago, life as we know it today has only evolved gradually over the last 45 million years. Human beings have inhabited the earth for less than half a million years, and a couple of hundred generations takes us back to the dawn of history. Within this time people have conquered the animal kingdom, learnt how to harness the forces of nature, and proliferated in such numbers that they have colonised nearly every corner of the earth. Even more stunning are the changes which have taken place within living memory. The use of electricity, nuclear fission and modern technology have now given us the power to alter the balance of life on earth.

The first astronauts reported that the earth hangs "like a blue pearl in space". Their experience has helped dispel the dangerous notion that the world is boundless in extent, with limitless resources. Ecologists have also shown that the earth is a self enclosed system in which all forms of life are interconnected. Disruption in one part of the ecosystem can have serious consequences elsewhere. It follows that all human activity has an effect on the natural environment, and that we misuse this fragile planet at our peril.

In recent years people have been putting the environment under increasing stress. Raw materials such as timber, water and minerals are beginning to run short. Pollution and the disposal of wastes are becoming critical issues, and global warming has highlighted the dangers that we face. Environmental problems have been compounded by inequalities of wealth, where rich nations control and exploit the bulk of available resources in a world in which large numbers of people are struggling for survival. Decisive and concerted action will be needed to confront the growing ecological crisis.

Despite these threats there are encouraging signs. Over the past few decades food production has more than matched the growth in population. In industry there is scope for much greater efficiency and more careful use of resources. Sustainable development holds one of the keys to the future. Improvements in social justice also offer great possibilities.

These are exciting times in which we live. In the next decade the state of the environment is set to become the most pressing issue confronting us all. The way we respond to the challenge will have a profound effect on the earth and its life support systems. We will only make balanced decisions on the basis of detailed and careful research. This illustrated encyclopaedia seeks to provide up-to-date information on the issues that confront us all.

EARTHQUAKES AND VOLCANOES

Plate boundaries, Earthquakes and Volcanoes

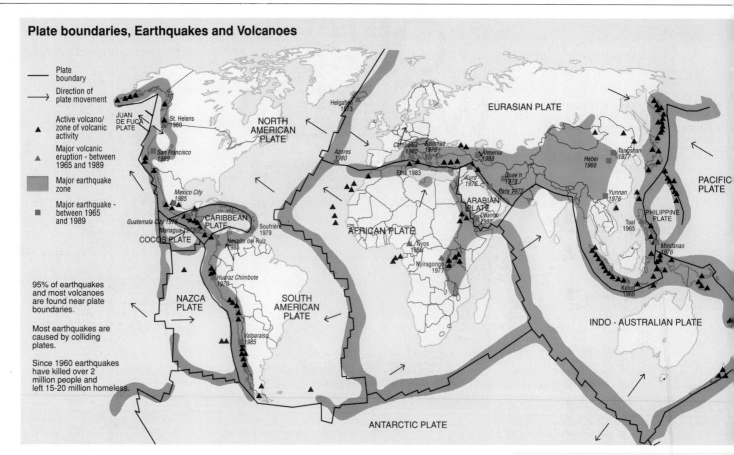

Legend:
- Plate boundary
- Direction of plate movement
- ▲ Active volcano/ zone of volcanic activity
- ▲ Major volcanic eruption - between 1965 and 1989
- Major earthquake zone
- ■ Major earthquake - between 1965 and 1989

95% of earthquakes and most volcanoes are found near plate boundaries.

Most earthquakes are caused by colliding plates.

Since 1960 earthquakes have killed over 2 million people and left 15-20 million homeless.

Map labels: JUAN DE FUCA PLATE, St. Helens 1980, NORTH AMERICAN PLATE, Helgafied 1973, EURASIAN PLATE, San Francisco 1989, Azores 1980, Campania 1980, Salonika 1975, Armenia 1988, Tangshan 1977, Hebei 1966, PACIFIC PLATE, Etna 1983, Skurd 1976, Quae'n 1978, Pats 1972, Yunnan 1976, Mexico City 1985, ARABIAN PLATE, Taal 1965, PHILIPPINE PLATE, Guatemala City 1976, CARIBBEAN PLATE, Soufrière 1979, Managua 1972, COCOS PLATE, Nevado del Ruiz 1985, Ghamar 1982, AFRICAN PLATE, Nyos 1986, Nyiragongo 1977, Mindanao 1976, Huaraz Chimbote 1978, NAZCA PLATE, SOUTH AMERICAN PLATE, Kelud 1966, INDO - AUSTRALIAN PLATE, Valparaiso 1985, ANTARCTIC PLATE

The Structure of the Earth

The earth's surface or crust forms a rigid layer of rock which varies in thickness from 6km to 40km. Beneath this there is a zone of semi-molten rock known as the aesthenosphere. Together with the upper mantle this reaches down to a depth of about 700km, below which there is the lower mantle and the core of the earth.

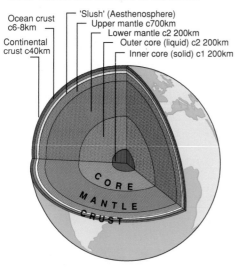

Labels:
- Ocean crust c6-8km
- Continental crust c40km
- 'Slush' (Aesthenosphere)
- Upper mantle c700km
- Lower mantle c2 200km
- Outer core (liquid) c2 200km
- Inner core (solid) c1 200km
- CORE
- MANTLE
- CRUST

The earth's interior consist of three layers - the crust on the surface, the mantle underneath and the core at the centre.

Types of Plates

The crust is broken into huge plates which fit together like the parts of a giant jigsaw. These float on the semi-molten rock below. The boundaries of the plates are marked by lines of volcanoes and earthquake activity.

There are three types of boundary:-

Diverging plates. When two plates move away from each other, molten rock wells up from the earth's core creating a ridge, eg the ridge down the Atlantic from Iceland to the Antarctic.

Converging plates. When two plates move towards each other a trench is formed as one slides beneath the other. It was a movement of this kind which created the Himalayas.

Shearing Plates. Sometimes neighbouring plates move horizontally in opposite directions from one another, eg the San Andreas fault in California

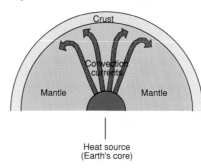

Labels: Crust, Convection currents, Mantle, Mantle, Heat source (Earth's core)

Convection and plate Movement

Plate movements cause continents to drift at about 2.5cm a year. They are carried by convection currents in the magma.

Diverging Plates

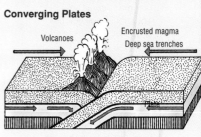

Labels: Encrusted magma forms a new ocean floor, Rift valley, Lava, Ocean ridge, Soft layer, Magma, Mantle, Plate

Diverging convection currents

Converging Plates

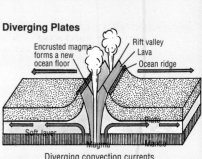

Labels: Volcanoes, Encrusted magma, Deep sea trenches, Plate

Converging convection currents

Shearing Plates

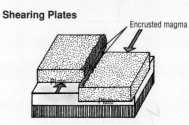

Labels: Encrusted magma, Plate, Plate

Currents moving past each other

Earthquakes

The shock from an earthquake spreads out from a point known as the epicentre. The amount of damage depends, among other things, on the depth of the epicentre.

The force of an earthquake is measured on a scale devised by an American, Dr Charles Richter. Each step on the scale represents a tenfold increase in intensity.

Parts of an earthquake

Shock waves reach surface — Epicentre — Normal fault
Origin or focus of pressure release
Shock waves travel outwards

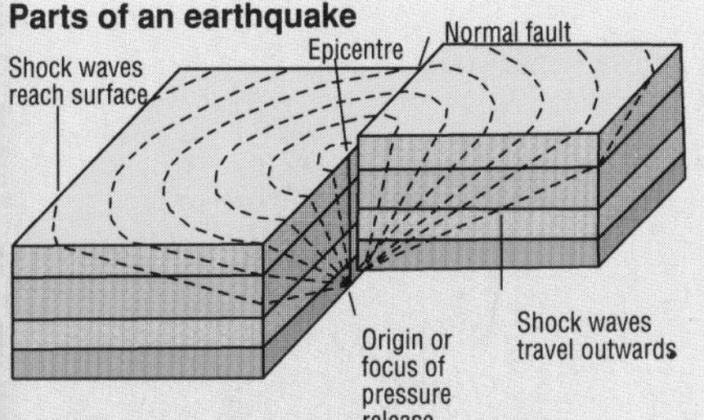

Major earthquakes since 1970

DATE	COUNTRY	FORCE (Richter scale)	DEATHS
31.5.70	Peru	7.7	66 800
23.12.72	Nicaragua	6.2	5 000
4.2.76	Guatemala	7.7	22 700
27.7.76	Tangshan, China	8.2	242 000
4.3.77	Romania	7.5	1 500
16.9.78	Iran	7.7	25 000
10.10.80	Algeria	7.5	2 600
23.11.80	Italy	6.8	3 000
13.12.82	Yemen	6.0	2 000
30.10.83	Turkey	7.1	1 200
19.9.85	Mexico	8.1	25 000
7.12.88	Armenia, USSR	6.9	25 000
17.10.89	California, USA	6.9	300

Volcanoes

There are about 500 active volcanoes in the world. The majority of them are found in two main zones: a 'Ring of Fire' around the Pacific Ocean and an east-west belt from Europe to Indonesia.

Volcanic eruptions can cause terrible damage. Molten rock pours out of the vent over the surrounding area, and rock dust and gas are blown high into the atmosphere.

Mt. St. Helens Volcano

DATE: May 18, 1980
LOCATION: Washington, USA
EXTENT OF DEBRIS: 57 000 sq km
DEATHS: 60

Rockies — Mt. St. Helens — Coastal Range — Lava flow
Subduction zone
Pacific Ocean
Magma
Earthquake focus
JUAN DE FUCA PLATE
NORTH AMERICAN PLATE

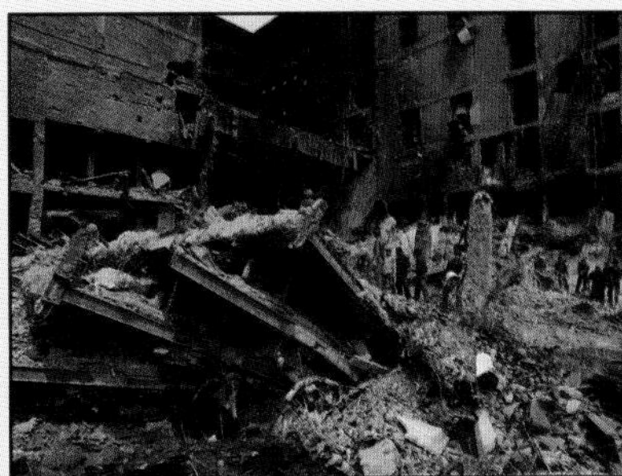

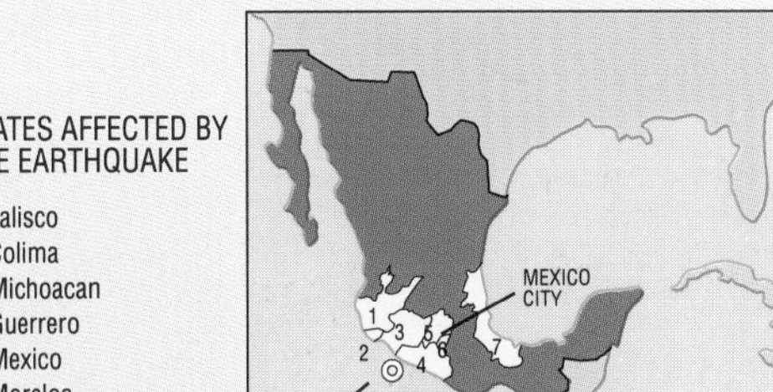

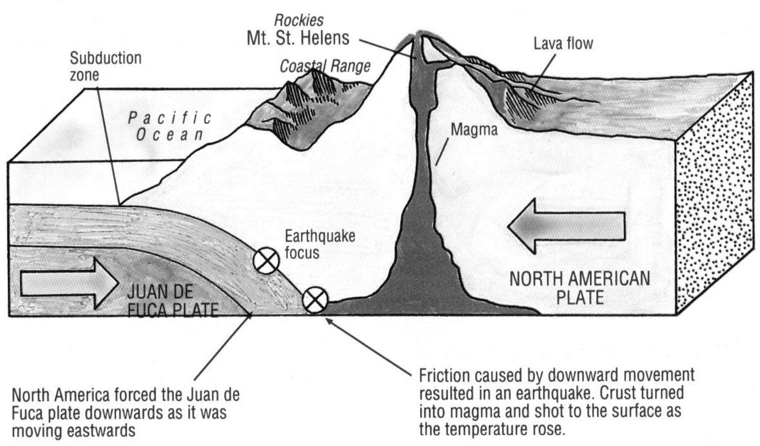

North America forced the Juan de Fuca plate downwards as it was moving eastwards

Friction caused by downward movement resulted in an earthquake. Crust turned into magma and shot to the surface as the temperature rose.

The Mexican Earthquake Disaster

Devastation in Mexico City. The photo shows a multi-storey building which has completely collapsed.

Seven states were affected by the earthquake. There were thousands of deaths and injuries and over 30 000 people were made homeless.

STATES AFFECTED BY THE EARTHQUAKE

1. Jalisco
2. Colima
3. Michoacan
4. Guerrero
5. Mexico
6. Morelos
7. Veracruz

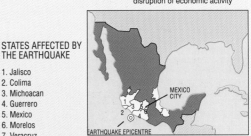

MEXICO CITY
EARTHQUAKE EPICENTRE

Mexico City
Epicentre
Pacific Ocean

Cocos Plate (Oceanic Crust) - Its downward movement created pressure
Focal point (where tension is released)
Earthquake waves
North American Plate (Continental Crust)

Mount St. Helens Eruption

The eruption of the Mount St. Helens in Washington, USA was one of the most dramatic in recent years. The explosion blew out of the side of the cone, and reduced the height of the mountain by 390m, creating a vast new crater. The blast also flattened half a million trees over a radius of 25km and blew dust high into the stratosphere across all of North America.

The volcano was in a remote area so only a small number of people were affected. It has given scientists an opportunity to find out more about what the early earth looked like. Plant life has returned quickly to the devastated areas. It seems that pockets survived in gulleys and under rocks enabling life to regenerate quickly.

How the volcano blew

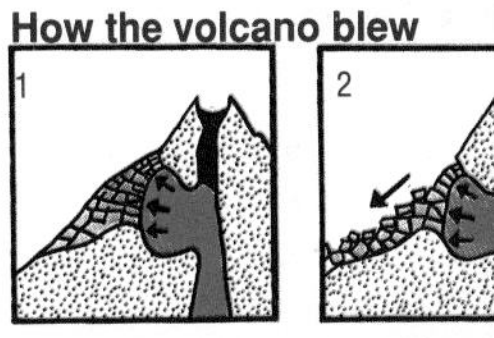

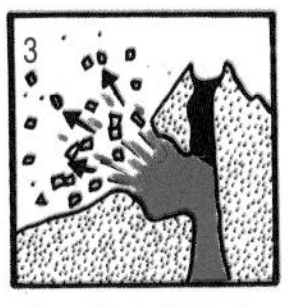

1. Build up of pressure
2. Landslide caused by stress
3. Eruption released magma

Results of the eruption

Davisson Lake
Turnwater Mt. 1600m
Green River
Black Mt. 1616m
Mt. Margaret 1786m
Spirit Lake
Elk Rock 1388m
N. Fk. Toutle Valley
S. Fk. Toutle Valley
2549m MT. ST. HELENS
1513m Goat Mt.
1258m Marble Mt.
Smith Creek

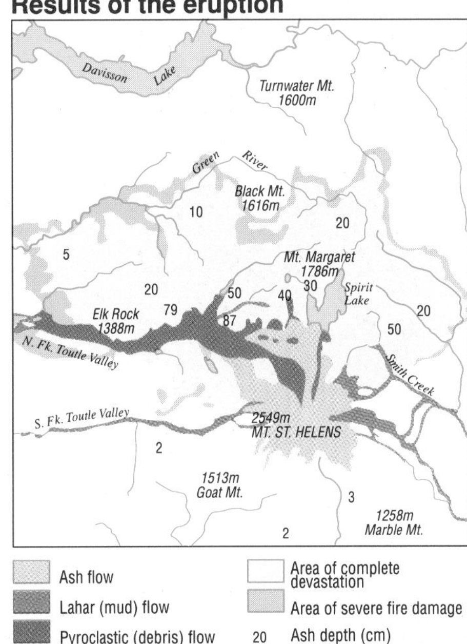

Ash flow
Lahar (mud) flow
Pyroclastic (debris) flow
Mud avalanche flow
Area of complete devastation
Area of severe fire damage
20 Ash depth (cm)

RIVERS AND FLOODS

Many important towns and cities are built on rivers. The Nile, Indus and Euphrates supported some of the earliest civilisations. The needs of agriculture, communication and trade have ensured that rivers remain important in the modern world. As population increases the demand on water resources is becoming greater. There is a pressing need for proper water management.

Major World Floods

Major river Basin

Country suffering severe flooding (1973-86). Floods recorded are those resulting in over 300 deaths and/or over 40 000 homeless and/or extensive property damage.

U.S.A. 1976, 1977, 1979, 1980, 1981, 1982, 1983, 1984, 1986

HONDURAS 1974

BRAZIL 1974, 1975, 1978, 1985

PERU 1974, 1982, 1983, 1986

BEN 198

Deforestation and Floods

Countries experiencing severe flooding(1963-85)
- ▲ Flood(s) causing over 1 000 deaths in any one year
- ▵ Flood(s) causing over 100 deaths in any one year

Annual rates of tropical forest clearance
- 1 250 000 - 2 500 000 acres
- 125 000 - 1 250 000 acres
- 0 -125 000 acres

(Source UNEP Data)

Forests can delay the release of flood water by trapping it in their roots. When the trees are cut down the result is often soil erosion and flooding.

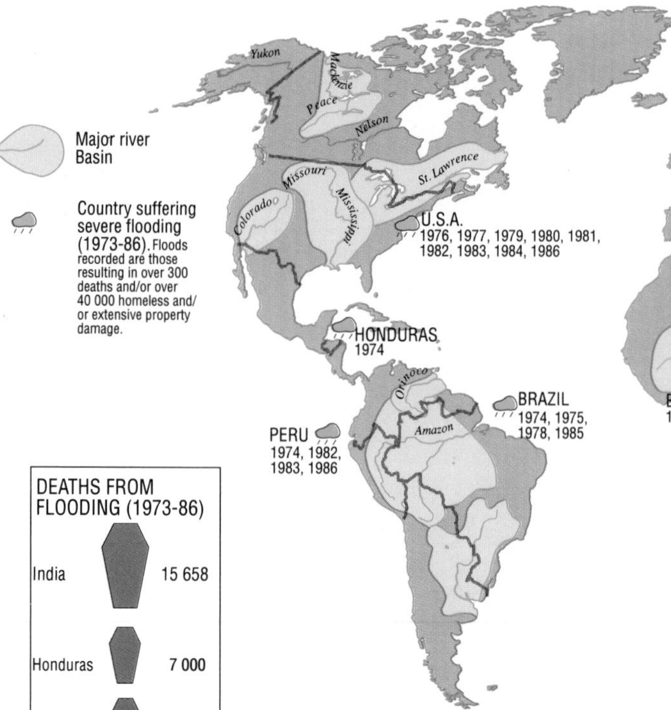

DEATHS FROM FLOODING (1973-86)	
India	15 658
Honduras	7 000
Brazil	5 601
Peru	3 257
Pakistan	1 850
China	1 550
Indonesia	1 501
Bangladesh	403
Japan	335
USA	305
Mozambique	300

Figs from UNEP Data Report

The Effects of Deforestation

FORESTED AREA

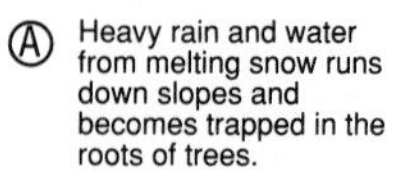

Ⓐ Heavy rain and water from melting snow runs down slopes and becomes trapped in the roots of trees.

Ⓑ Some fo the water evaporates, forms clouds and is carried on the wind to arid regions.

Ⓒ The water flows on towards the sea in a fairly steady flow, free of silt.

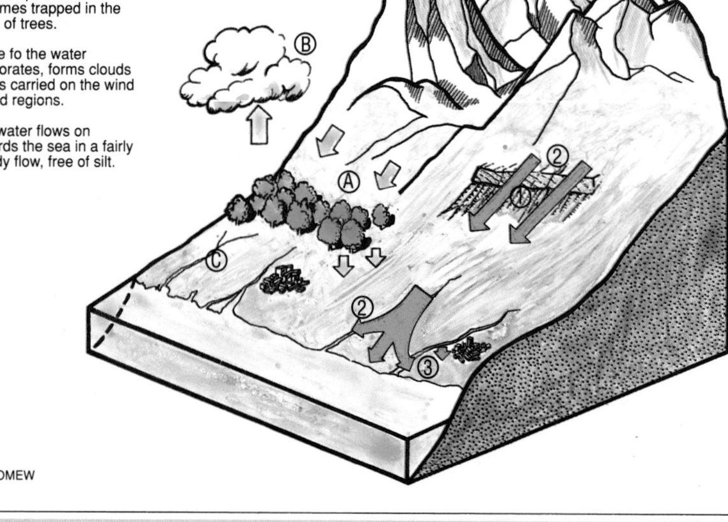

DEFORESTED AREA

① Without trees to hold it back, flood water rushes down mountain slopes.

② The swollen streams cut deep channels and carry away valuable top soil.

③ Further downstream the river channel becomes clogged with silt, causing floods.

Flooding in Bangladesh

In Bangladesh, the monsoon rains cause the rivers to flood each year. These floods are a normal part of life and help to renew the fertility of the soil. In recent years, however, the floods have become much more severe due to the clearance of forests in the Himalayas for fuelwood, farmland and logging. These floods have caused serious damage and loss of life.

Severe flooding as a result of deforestation in the Himalayas is also a problem in India. Each year it spends over a million US$ on river defences to control flooding.

SEPTEMBER 1987
671 dead
2 million homes washed away
4.3 million acres of land destroyed
3 million tonnes (10%) of rice and wheat crops lost

AUGUST 1988
Over 3 000 dead
75% of country flooded
250 bridges and 3 520 km of road destroyed
3 million tonnes of rice and other crops destroyed

© BARTHOLOMEW

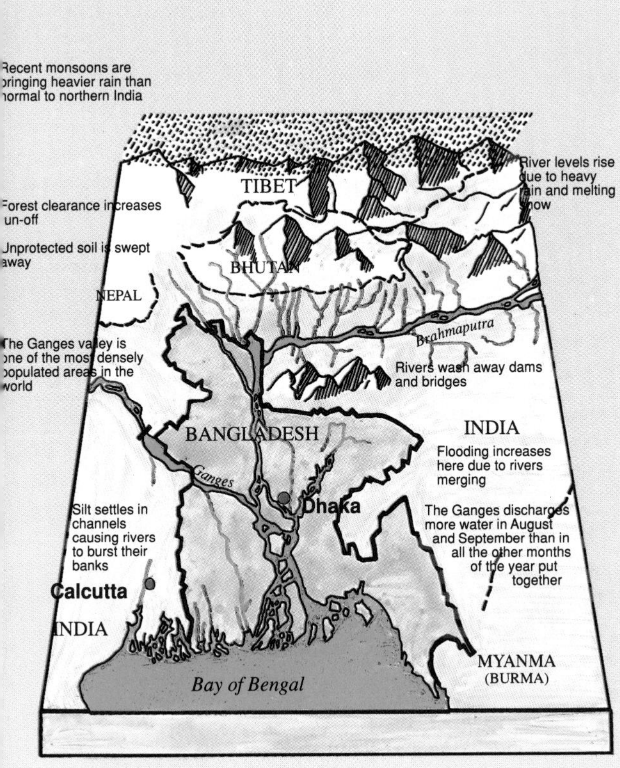

HOMELESS THROUGH FLOODING (1973-86)

INDIA	4 000 000
EGYPT	2 715 000
CHINA	2 600 000
HONDURAS	600 000
BRAZIL	350 000
BANGLADESH	200 000
KOREA	200 000
BENIN	200 000
SOMALI REP.	60 000
NEPAL	40 000

ANNUAL COST OF NATURAL HAZARDS WORLDWIDE

Floods	Tropical Cyclones	Earth-quakes	Drought	Others
40%	20%	15%	15%	10%

Total annual world costs = US $ 40 billion

Flood Damage

Flooding causes more damage than any other environmental hazard.

While all countries in the world are affected by floods, the impact on people in developing countries is greater. The number of deaths and homes destroyed is often much higher. This is partly because they cannot afford to protect themselves, and partly because shortage of land forces them to live in vulnerable areas. In addition any loss of food crops, export crops and employment can have a devastating effect.

Controlling Floods

Around the world there are plans for dams which will control floods and generate hydro-electric power.

Examples include:

Mekong dams on the Red river
Three Gorges dam on the Chang Jiang
Narmada dam in India

The problem with all these schemes is that they will flood large areas of land and attract industry which will put pressure on environmentally sensitive areas. Often local people do not benefit from them, foreign companies and banks taking most of the profits.

Many flood control measures only deal with the symptoms. The best solutions tackle the causes as well.

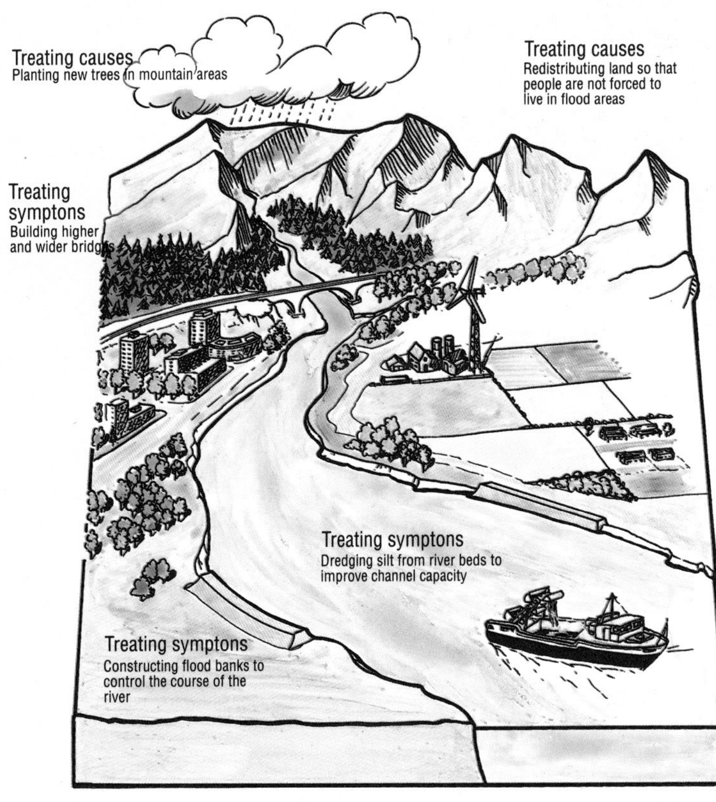

Treating causes
Planting new trees in mountain areas

Treating causes
Redistributing land so that people are not forced to live in flood areas

Treating symptons
Building higher and wider bridges

Treating symptons
Dredging silt from river beds to improve channel capacity

Treating symptons
Constructing flood banks to control the course of the river

TROPICAL STORMS

Tropical Storms

In the Tropics, intense storms form over the ocean in late summer and early autumn. The majority occur in the northern hemisphere. They are known as 'hurricanes' in the Caribbean, 'typhoons' in southeast Asia and 'cyclones' in the Bay of Bengal.

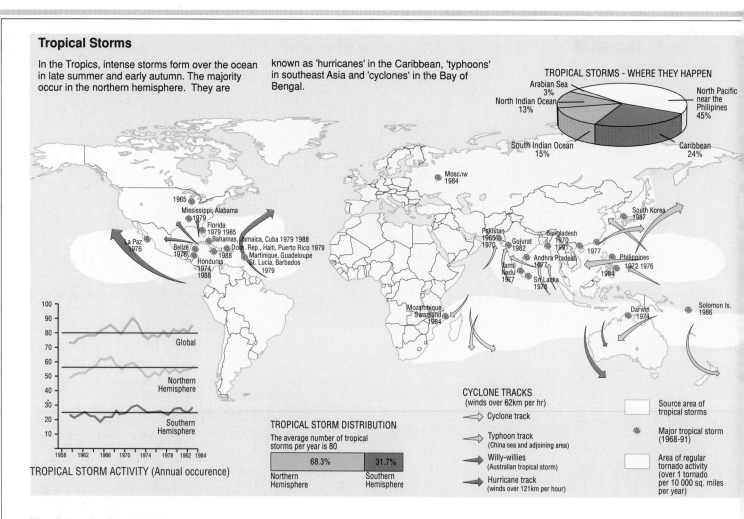

TROPICAL STORMS - WHERE THEY HAPPEN

- North Pacific near the Philipines 45%
- Caribbean 24%
- South Indian Ocean 15%
- North Indian Ocean 13%
- Arabian Sea 3%

TROPICAL STORM ACTIVITY (Annual occurence)
- Global
- Northern Hemisphere
- Southern Hemisphere

TROPICAL STORM DISTRIBUTION
The average number of tropical storms per year is 80

68.3%	31.7%
Northern Hemisphere	Southern Hemisphere

CYCLONE TRACKS
(winds over 62km per hr)
- Cyclone track
- Typhoon track (China sea and adjoining area)
- Willy-willies (Australian tropical storm)
- Hurricane track (winds over 121km per hour)

- Source area of tropical storms
- Major tropical storm (1968-91)
- Area of regular tornado activity (over 1 tornado per 10 000 sq. miles per year)

The Life of a Tropical Storm

Tropical storms can only begin if sea temperatures rise to 27°C or more. This allows large quantities of moisture to evaporate into the atmosphere creating unsettled weather conditions. As the pressure drops the storm begins to spin violently and is carried along by the trade winds. The storm sucks in more moisture as it passes over the warm ocean and becomes more intense. Eventually it comes to cooler areas, or passes over land, loses energy and breaks up.

Structure of a Tropical Storm

At the centre of a tropical storm there is an 'eye' of calm and cloudless skies. Around it, violent winds, often in excess of 100mph, bring torrential rain that may last for several days.

Naming Tropical Storms

Since the Second World War tropical storms have been named in alphabetical order. This means you can tell from the initial letter how many there have been in a season. Typhoons often use the full range af the alphabet. Hurricanes, being less frequent, tend to only use the first half.

Structure of a Hurricane

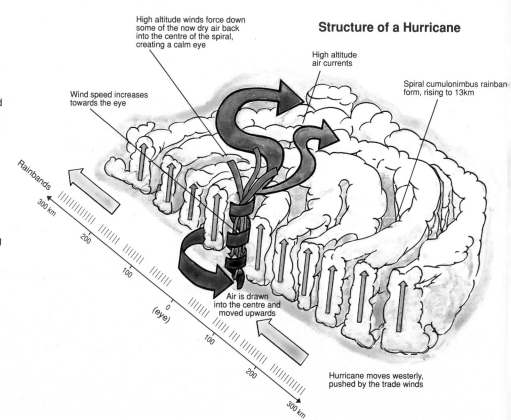

High altitude winds force down some of the now dry air back into the centre of the spiral, creating a calm eye

High altitude air currents

Spiral cumulonimbus rainbands form, rising to 13km

Wind speed increases towards the eye

Rainbands

Air is drawn into the centre and moved upwards

Hurricane moves westerly, pushed by the trade winds

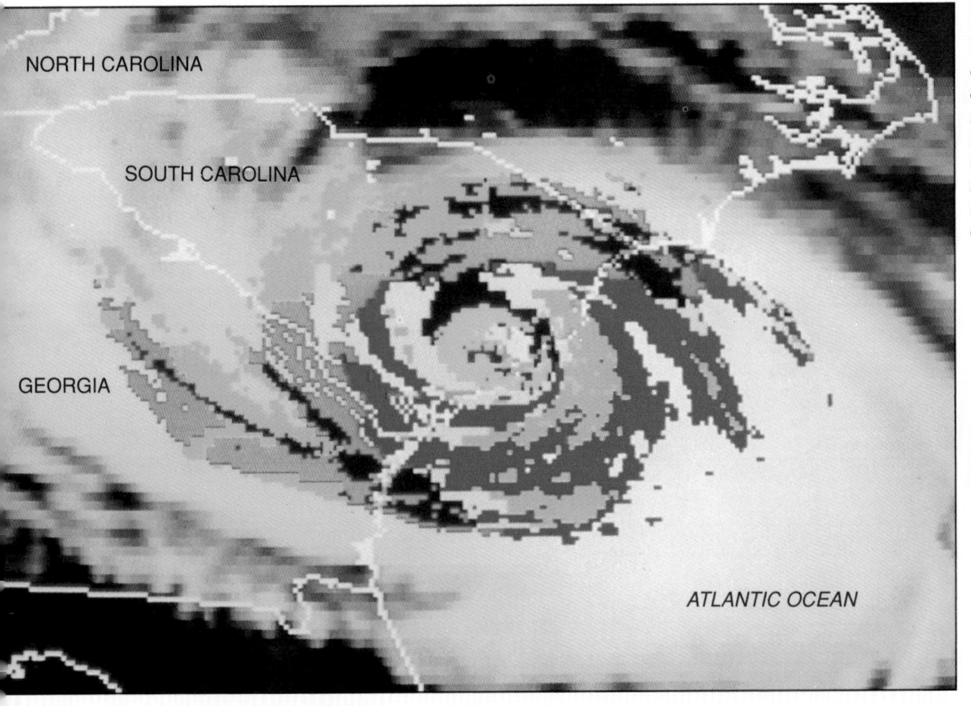

NORTH CAROLINA

SOUTH CAROLINA

GEORGIA

ATLANTIC OCEAN

Hurricane Hugo

First detected on the 9th September as a cluster of storms off the African coast, Hurricane Hugo developed into the strongest hurricane of 1989, sustaining wind speeds of 260km per hour. Hurricane Hugo left a trail of destruction across a number of Caribbean islands and in both North and South Carolina in the USA. The cost of the storm damage was estimated at 10 billion US dollars and 49 lives were lost.

False colour satellite image showing Hurricane Hugo as it struck the USA coast at South Carolina on 22nd September 1989.

The Effect of Hurricanes in the Caribbean

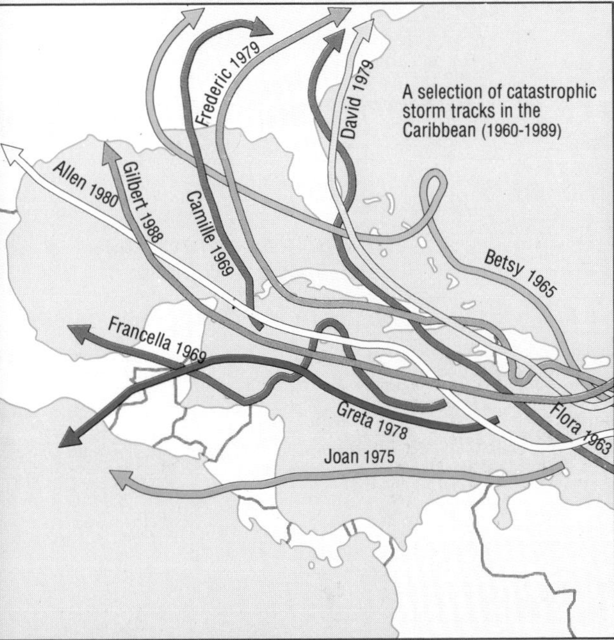

Frederic 1979

David 1979

Allen 1980

Gilbert 1988

Camille 1969

Betsy 1965

Francella 1969

Greta 1978

Flora 1963

Joan 1975

A selection of catastrophic storm tracks in the Caribbean (1960-1989)

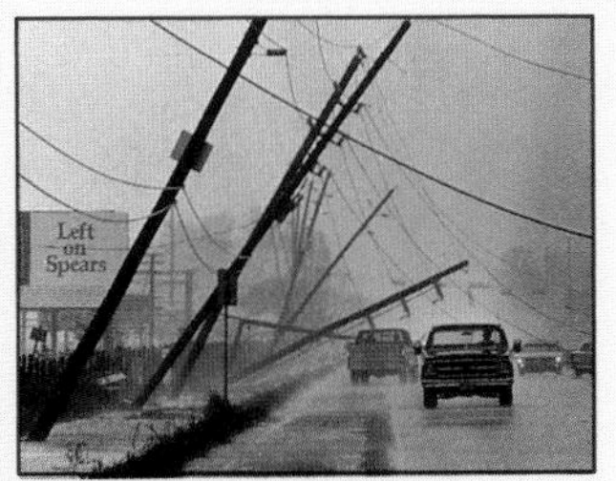

Vehicles, caught in a hurricane in Houston, Texas, dodge live power lines.

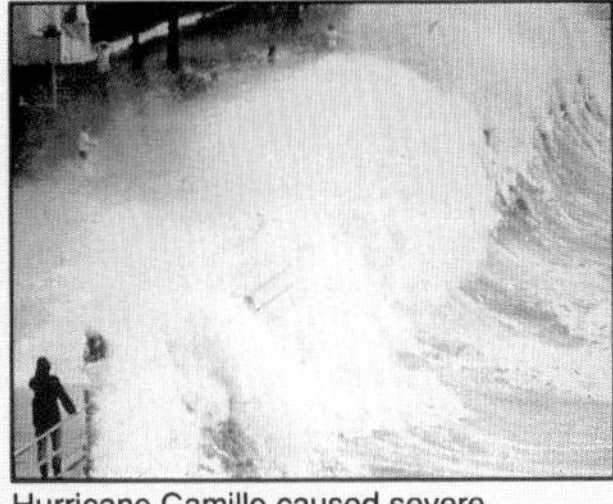

Hurricane Camille caused severe flooding in the USA. More than 300 people were killed.

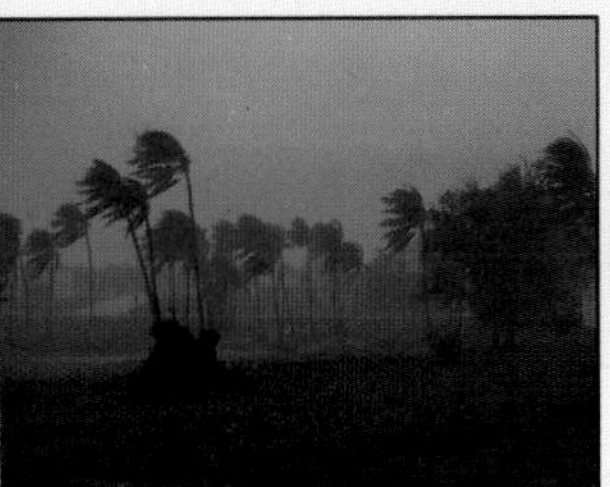

In 1988, Gilbert, the most powerful hurricane ever recorded, led to a national disaster being declared in Jamaica.

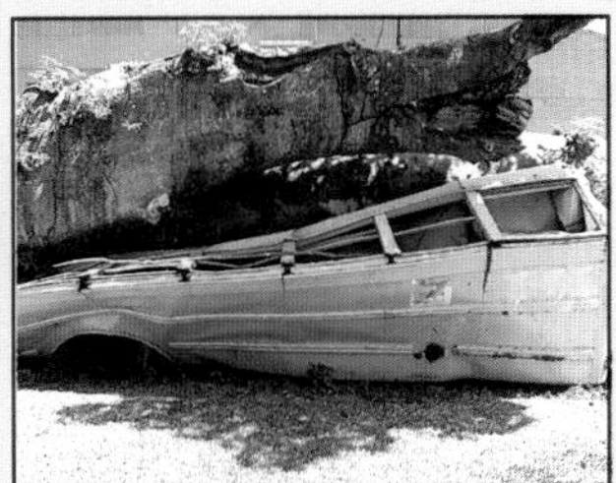

Hurricane David in 1979 caused widespread damage in Dominica. 1 300 people died and 100 000 were left homeless.

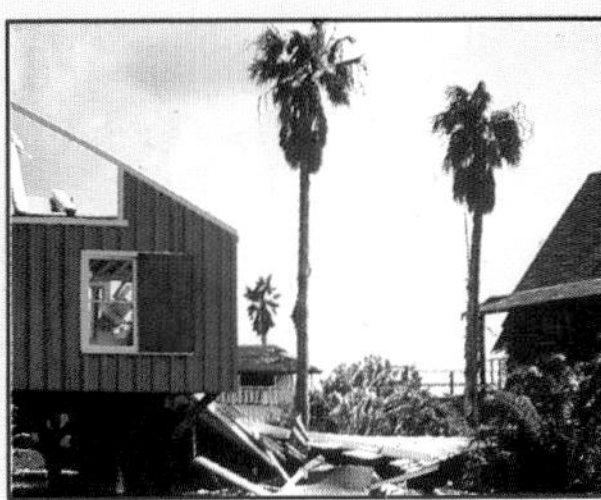

Hurricane Allen crossed Barbados and Jamaica causing death and destruction.

Hurricanes

Tropical storms can do terrible damage. Not only do the fierce winds tear buildings apart, but the low pressure can create a surge of seawater that floods coastal areas. The torrential rain adds to these problems.

In some parts of the world special emergency services and hurricane warning systems have been set up. It is in poorer countries that most lives are lost and the damage is worst. Here many buildings are badly constructed and people can not afford to take precautions.

Tornadoes

Tornadoes are violent whirling storms associated with rain and thunderstorms. Usually about 100 metres in width, and with only the most violent lasting longer than an hour, they are smaller and shorter lived than hurricanes. Wind speeds at the centre however can reach over 300 kph. At such high speed the tube of spinning air can cause loss of life and severe damage to property.

Tornadoes are particularly common in the Mississippi/Ohio basin where the warm humid air from the Gulf of Mexico meets the cool dry air from the north. They also occur, less frequently, in other parts of the world, including Australia and the Indian subcontinent.

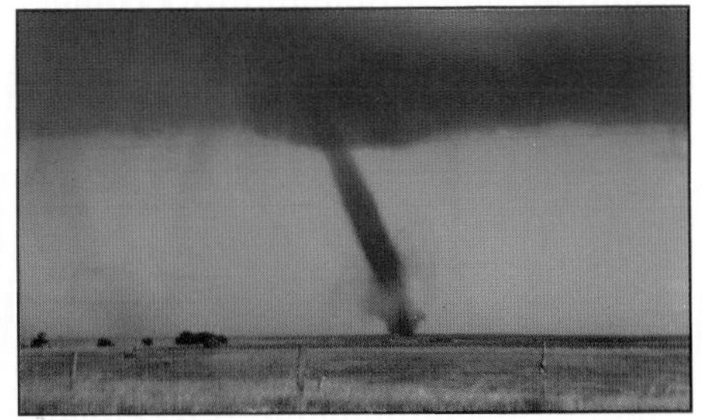

LANDSLIDES AND AVALANCHES

Major Landslides and Avalanches (1963 - 1986)

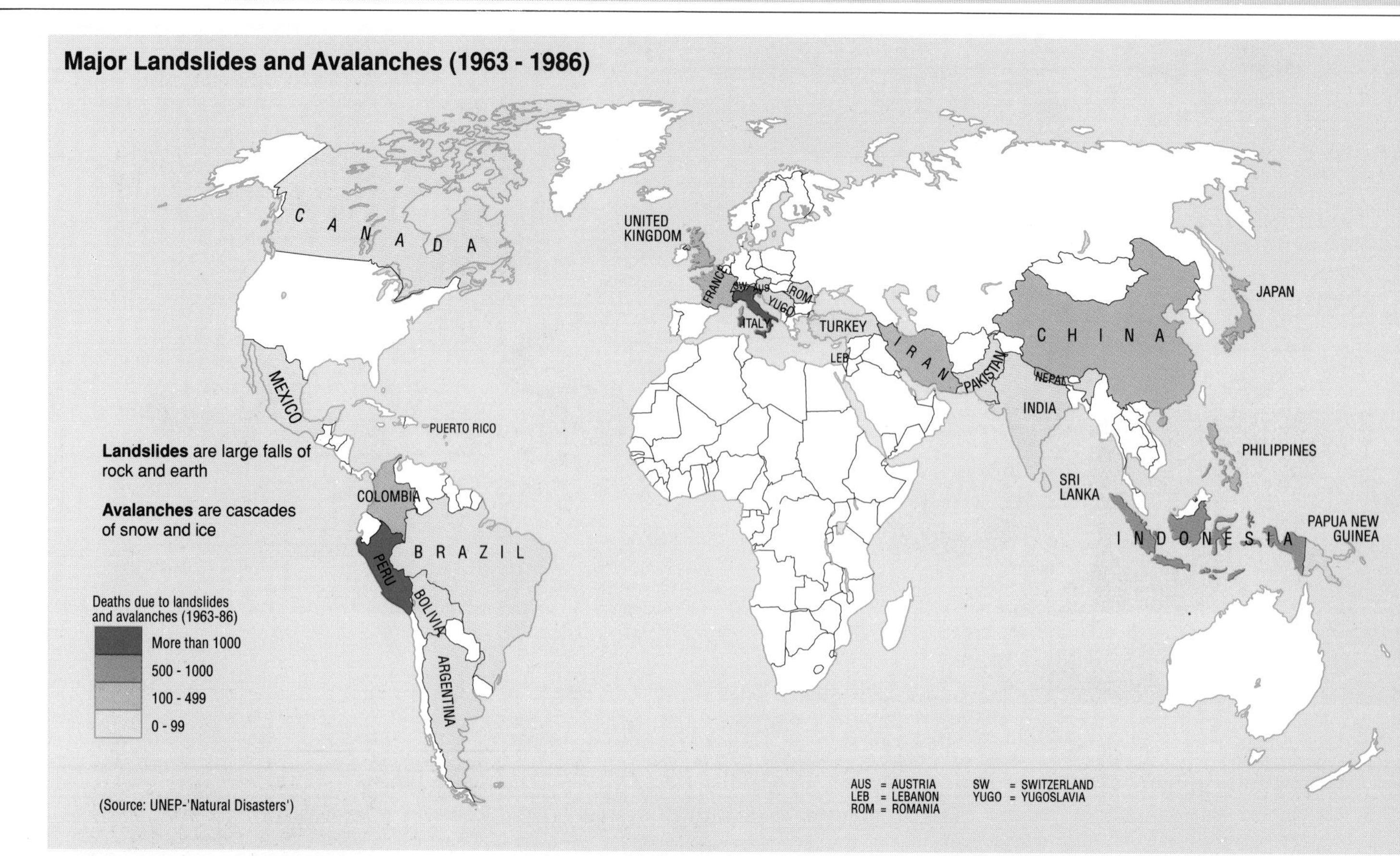

Landslides are large falls of rock and earth

Avalanches are cascades of snow and ice

Deaths due to landslides and avalanches (1963-86)

- More than 1000
- 500 - 1000
- 100 - 499
- 0 - 99

(Source: UNEP-'Natural Disasters')

AUS = AUSTRIA   SW = SWITZERLAND
LEB = LEBANON   YUGO = YUGOSLAVIA
ROM = ROMANIA

What Causes Landslides?

Wherever there are steep mountain slopes, there is the possibility of landslides and avalanches. Sometimes heavy rain can make the earth unstable. In other cases erosion causes dangerous undercutting.

Some of the the most damaging slips, however, are triggered by earthquakes and volcanoes. One single force, gravity, causes all these downhill movements.

Factors which Influence Landslides

A landslip occurs when a slope becomes too steep to resist the pull of gravity.

Buildings put pressure on the ground

Soil is loosened by alternate soaking and drying

Heavy rain makes the soil heavier and more fluid

Soil is disturbed by people and animals

Roads undercut the hillside

Water run-off carries soil downhill

Trees and plants hold the soil in place

Material from the banks is carried away as the river channel widens

Freezing and thawing causes soil to expand and contract

Water seeps into the ground

Water creeps downhill beneath the surface

Minor earthflows

Rivers cut back the bottom of the slope

© BARTHOLOMEW

Landslides and Avalanches in Italy

MAY 1985 - TRESENDA

A huge landslide killed 17 people and injured several others.

JULY 1987 - ADDA VALLEY

After heavy flooding, a landslide damned the River Adda and buried 2 villages, killing 44 people. Later 20 000 people were evacuated when the resulting lake was diverted back to its original course.

SARDINIA

Main Appennine landslide areas
- Light
- Serious
- Very serious

Main avalanche areas
- Low risk
- High risk

● Known epicentres of earthquakes occurring over the last 2 000 years

▲ Volcano

Mudflows

Colombia has many dormant volcanoes. In December 1984 one of them, Nevado del Ruiz began to show signs of life. After several minor incidents it erupted on 13th November 1985. The heat melted the ice cap at the top of the mountain and set off a mudflow. This swept downhill in a river 40 metres deep. The town of Armero was engulfed and about 25 000 people were killed.

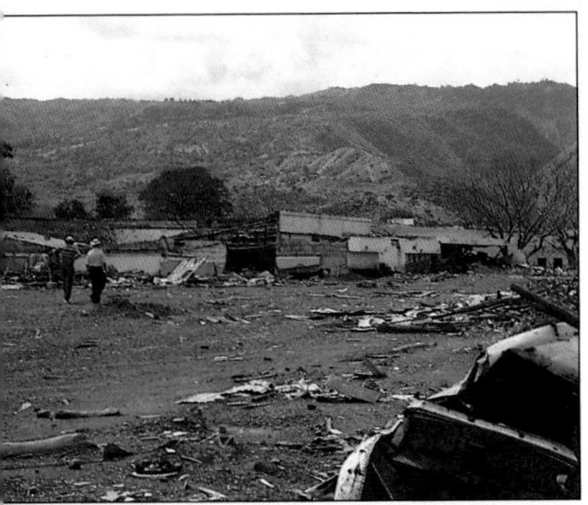

Nevado del Ruiz -
Hazard Assessment (1985)
- High lava flow hazard
- High pyroclastic flow hazard
- Moderate pyroclastic flow hazard
- High mudflow hazard

Nevado del Ruiz
Disaster (13th November 1985)
- Actual extent of mudflow
- Direction of Mudflow

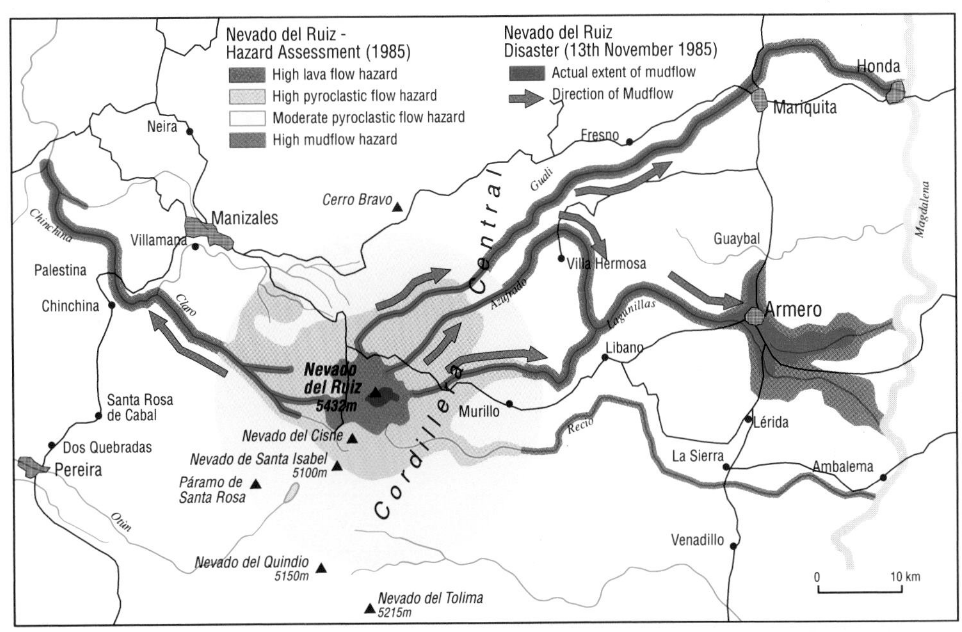

The worst avalanche to date happened on 31st May 1970 in Santa Valley in the Peruvian Andes. The avalanche travelled 17km down the mountain in only 15 minutes: an estimated 18 000 killed.

Cause, Effect and Prevention of Avalanches

Avalanches are most likely to happen in the spring as the snow melts. In the Alps the Föhn wind is especially dangerous as it is heated and dried as it blows over the mountains. One way of guarding against avalanches is to block gulleys with barriers to help break their force. However, the best solution of all is to avoid places exposed to falls from above. Avalanches often follow predictable routes.

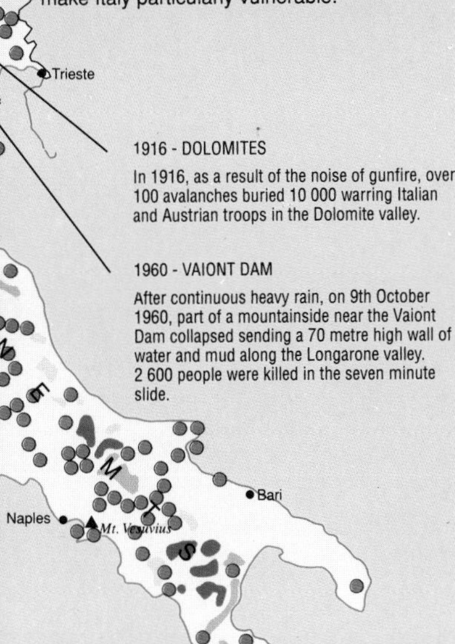

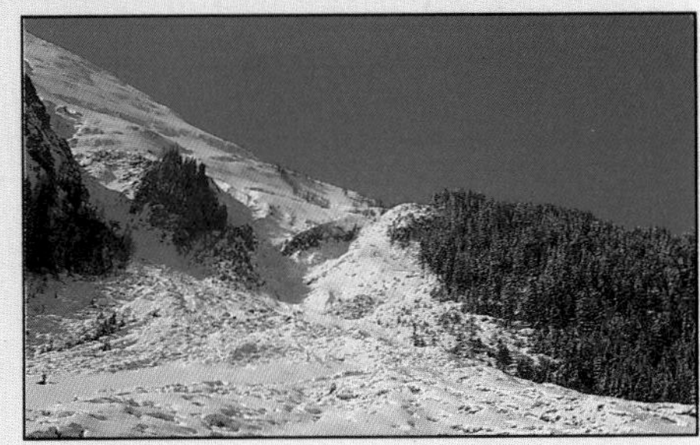

Twenty-five thousand Italians have been killed in landslides and avalanches in the last 25 years and thousands of others made homeless. The high mountains and frequent earthquakes make Italy particularly vulnerable.

1916 - DOLOMITES

In 1916, as a result of the noise of gunfire, over 100 avalanches buried 10 000 warring Italian and Austrian troops in the Dolomite valley.

1960 - VAIONT DAM

After continuous heavy rain, on 9th October 1960, part of a mountainside near the Vaiont Dam collapsed sending a 70 metre high wall of water and mud along the Longarone valley. 2 600 people were killed in the seven minute slide.

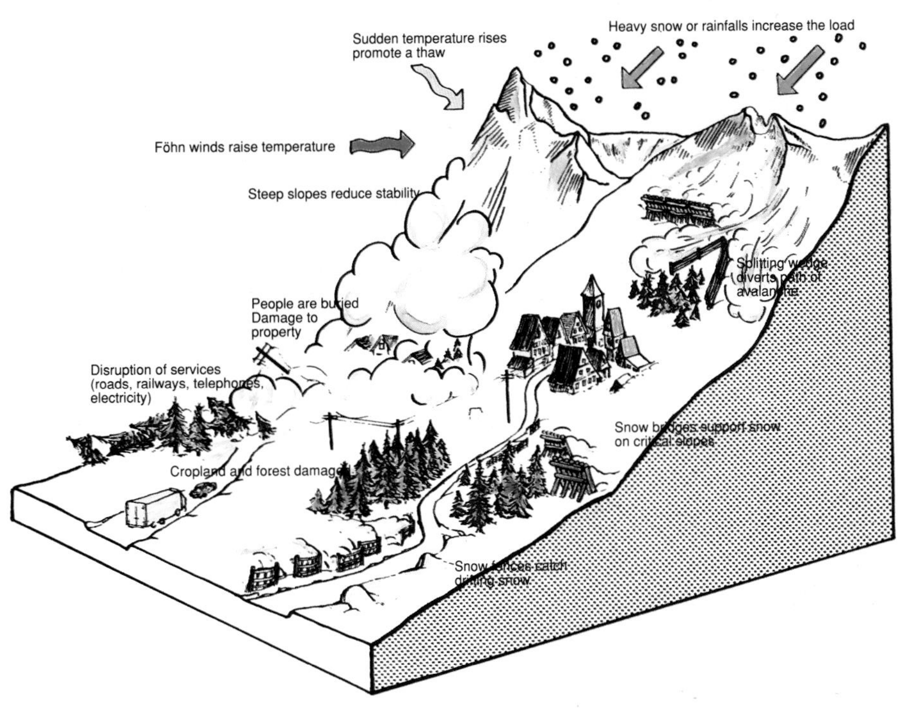

Sudden temperature rises promote a thaw

Heavy snow or rainfalls increase the load

Föhn winds raise temperature

Steep slopes reduce stability

Splitting wedge diverts path of avalanche

People are buried
Damage to property

Disruption of services (roads, railways, telephones, electricity)

Snow bridges support snow on critical slopes

Cropland and forest damage

Snow fences catch drifting snow

DROUGHT

Drought Affected Regions

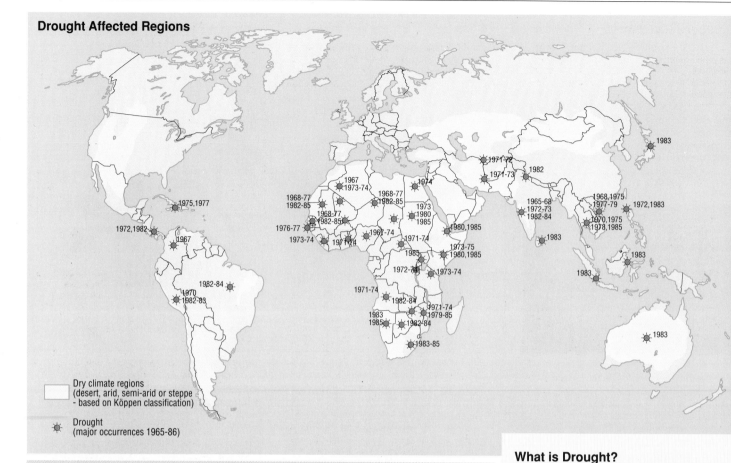

Dry climate regions
(desert, arid, semi-arid or steppe
- based on Köppen classification)

Drought
(major occurrences 1965-86)

Famine and War in Africa (1984-85)

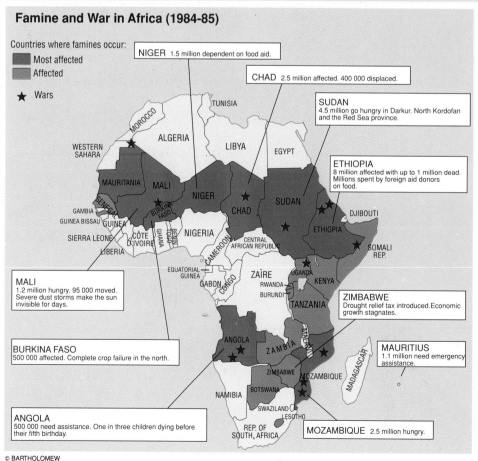

Countries where famines occur:

Most affected

Affected

★ Wars

NIGER 1.5 million dependent on food aid.

CHAD 2.5 million affected. 400 000 displaced.

SUDAN
4.5 million go hungry in Darkur. North Kordofan
and the Red Sea province.

ETHIOPIA
8 million affected with up to 1 million dead.
Millions spent by foreign aid donors
on food.

MALI
1.2 million hungry. 95 000 moved.
Severe dust storms make the sun
invisible for days.

BURKINA FASO
500 000 affected. Complete crop failure in the north.

ANGOLA
500 000 need assistance. One in three children dying before
their fifth birthday.

ZIMBABWE
Drought relief tax introduced. Economic
growth stagnates.

MAURITIUS
1.1 million need emergency
assistance.

MOZAMBIQUE 2.5 million hungry.

© BARTHOLOMEW

What is Drought?

A lack of rainfall over a long period is
known as drought. Droughts occur in
many parts of the world but they are
especially likely in places where the
climate is dry and variable. Desert
margins and monsoon lands suffer most.

The map shows where droughts have
occurred since the mid 1960's. Africa,
Southern Asia and parts of Latin America
have been particularly badly affected.

Famine and War

In the last twenty years there have been
wars in almost every country of Africa.
These have disrupted agriculture and
stopped farmers from planting and
harvesting crops properly. They have also
cost huge sums of money which could
have been spent on land improvement
schemes. These are the circumstances in
which droughts are much more likely to
lead to famine.

Drought in the Sahel

One of the worst droughts in the recent years has been in the Sahel. For the past 15 years rainfall has been very poor and human activities such as cutting trees and degrading the soil may have resulted in making the climate even drier.

Since 1970 rainfall in the Sahel has been well below average. No one can be certain if this is a temporary or permanent change. Scientists will need much more evidence before they can be sure what is happening to the climate.

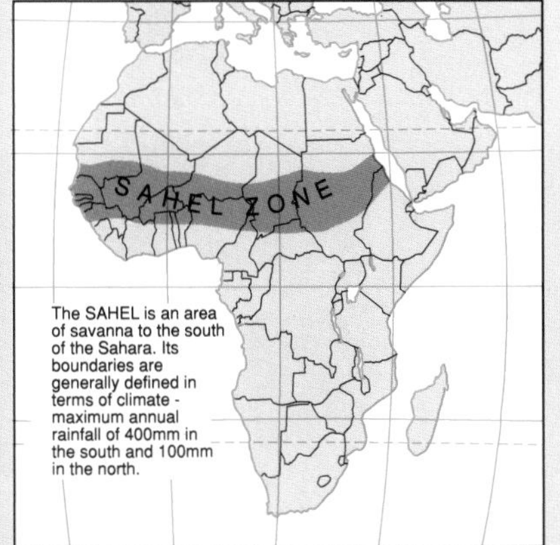

The SAHEL is an area of savanna to the south of the Sahara. Its boundaries are generally defined in terms of climate - maximum annual rainfall of 400mm in the south and 100mm in the north.

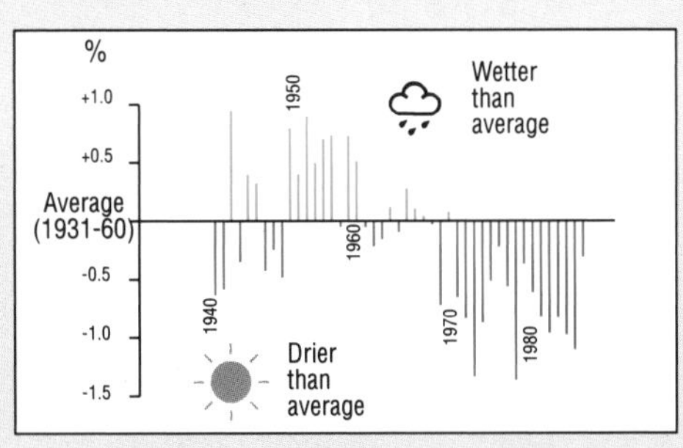

VARIATIONS IN THE ANNUAL RAINFALL AT 14 WEATHER STATIONS SINCE 1940

CARBON DIOXIDE LEVELS

1750 level = 100

Some scientists believe that pollution by gases such as carbon dioxide, CO_2, is causing the earth to heat up and cause the 'greenhouse' effect.

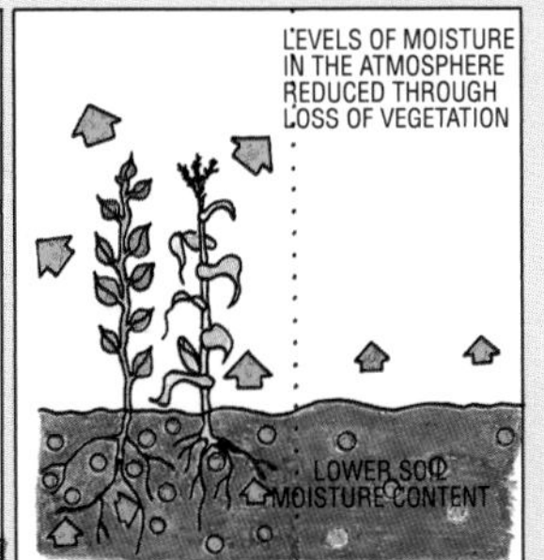

BARE GROUND REFLECTS MORE SOLAR RADIATION THAN VEGETATION

LEVELS OF MOISTURE IN THE ATMOSPHERE REDUCED THROUGH LOSS OF VEGETATION

LOWER SOIL MOISTURE CONTENT

Tree clearance increases the amount of radiation reflected from the ground. There is less evaporation and transpiration from plants, causing the climate to become drier.

Drought and Famine

Drought affects more people nowadays than any other natural disaster. The poor are especially vulnerable as they do not have the resources to protect themselves properly. Emergency food aid can help deal with the immediate food shortages.

In the longer term, famines will only be averted if people tackle the underlying causes. Land reform, fairer 'terms and trade' and peace could do much to solve the problem.

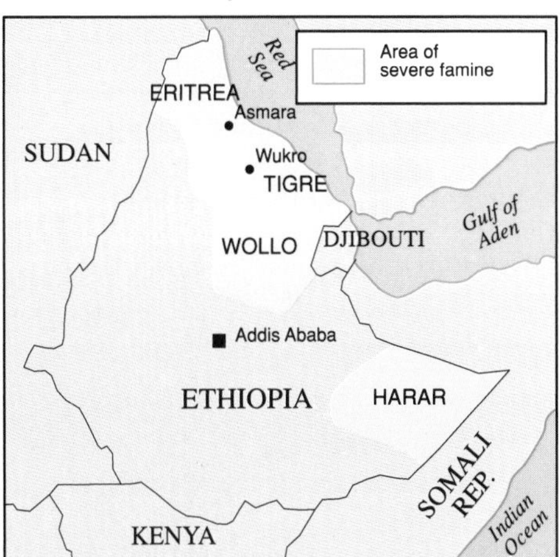

Famine occurence
- 10-13 years, in 33
- 7-9 years, in 33
- 4-8 years, in 33
- 1-3 years, in 33
- No record of large scale famine in the last 33 years

Numbers affected by drought

18.5m — 1960s
24.4m — 1970s
35m — 1985

Drought and famine in Ethiopia (1981-84)

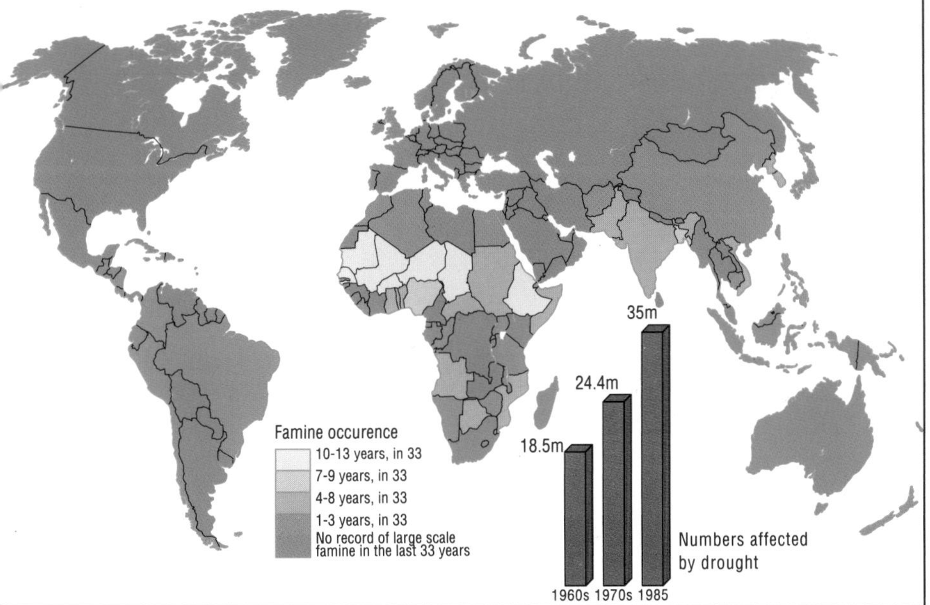

Area of severe famine

The famine in Ethiopia was one of the worst in the recent times. Eight million people were affected and a million lost their lives.

The famine was the result of a combination of factors:

- The population of Ethiopia is growing rapidly putting the land under pressure.
- Woods in the highlands have been cleared for fuel, leading to severe soil erosion and falling crop yields.
- In the lower areas dry grassland areas have been overgrazed.
- Since the 1960's some of the best land has been used to grow cash crops (sugar and coffee) for export.

The failure of rain for four consecutive years from 1981-1984 triggered a severe famine. However human action, not natural forces, was the underlying cause. Even at the height of the crisis, Ethiopia exported huge quantities of vegetables to Europe, while many people starved.

ECOLOGICAL CAUSES OF FAMINE	POLITICAL AND SOCIAL CAUSES OF FAMINE
increase in human population	land divided from one generation to another in small and scattered plots
forests cleared for fuel	government fails to put money into irrigation and land management schemes
animal manure used for fuel and not put back on the land	best grazing land taken from nomads to grow cash crops for export
overfarming of the grasslands	prolonged civil war costs huge sums of money
failure of the rains	countries overseas slow to give help in dealing with the famine

DEFORESTATION

Forests cover about one third of the world's land surface. Temperate and coniferous forest spreads across areas of Europe, Asia and North America. Further south, a band of tropical rainforest extending about ten degrees in latitude north and south of the equator forms the richest habitat on earth.

Temperate and coniferous forests are generally carefully managed and are quick to regrow. Rainforests take longer to grow and occupy a more fragile environment. They are also being destroyed at an alarming rate as people sell the wood and clear land for housing, crops and industry.

Shrinking Forests

1950
Rest of the earth
Temperate and coniferous forest
Tropical forest

1975

2000

Tropical Rainforest Under Threat

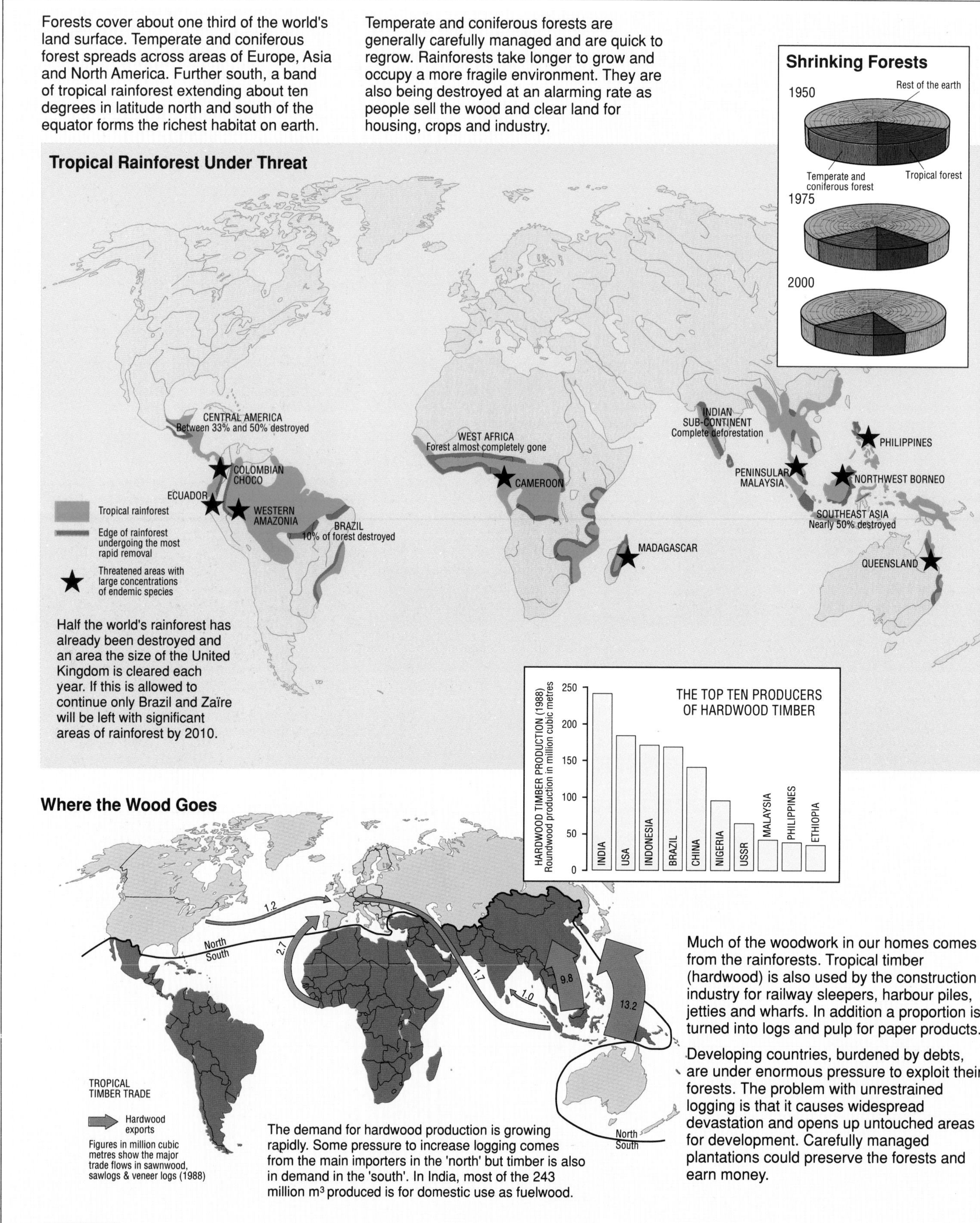

CENTRAL AMERICA
Between 33% and 50% destroyed

COLOMBIAN CHOCO

ECUADOR

WESTERN AMAZONIA

BRAZIL
10% of forest destroyed

WEST AFRICA
Forest almost completely gone

CAMEROON

MADAGASCAR

INDIAN SUB-CONTINENT
Complete deforestation

PHILIPPINES

PENINSULAR MALAYSIA

NORTHWEST BORNEO

SOUTHEAST ASIA
Nearly 50% destroyed

QUEENSLAND

Tropical rainforest

Edge of rainforest undergoing the most rapid removal

★ Threatened areas with large concentrations of endemic species

Half the world's rainforest has already been destroyed and an area the size of the United Kingdom is cleared each year. If this is allowed to continue only Brazil and Zaïre will be left with significant areas of rainforest by 2010.

Where the Wood Goes

North South

1.2

2.7

1.7

1.0

9.8

13.2

North South

TROPICAL TIMBER TRADE

➡ Hardwood exports

Figures in million cubic metres show the major trade flows in sawnwood, sawlogs & veneer logs (1988)

THE TOP TEN PRODUCERS OF HARDWOOD TIMBER

HARDWOOD TIMBER PRODUCTION (1988)
Roundwood production in million cubic metres

250 200 150 100 50 0

INDIA | USA | INDONESIA | BRAZIL | CHINA | NIGERIA | USSR | MALAYSIA | PHILIPPINES | ETHIOPIA

The demand for hardwood production is growing rapidly. Some pressure to increase logging comes from the main importers in the 'north' but timber is also in demand in the 'south'. In India, most of the 243 million m³ produced is for domestic use as fuelwood.

Much of the woodwork in our homes comes from the rainforests. Tropical timber (hardwood) is also used by the construction industry for railway sleepers, harbour piles, jetties and wharfs. In addition a proportion is turned into logs and pulp for paper products.

Developing countries, burdened by debts, are under enormous pressure to exploit their forests. The problem with unrestrained logging is that it causes widespread devastation and opens up untouched areas for development. Carefully managed plantations could preserve the forests and earn money.

The Real Costs of Rainforest Destruction

What we are losing?

People
In South America the rainforest is the home for tribal groups like the Yanomani. Rubber tappers also operate in many areas.

Plants
Many crops and medicines come from rainforest plants which are a unique and extremely valuable genetic resource.

Creatures
The rainforests are the richest and densest habitat on earth. They contain over half the world's insects, birds and animals.

The rainforests generally grow on very poor soils. The trees protect the soil from tropical storms and help to keep it moist during the dry season. Once the trees are cleared, the earth quickly washes away and the land, exposed to the hot sun, turns to desert.

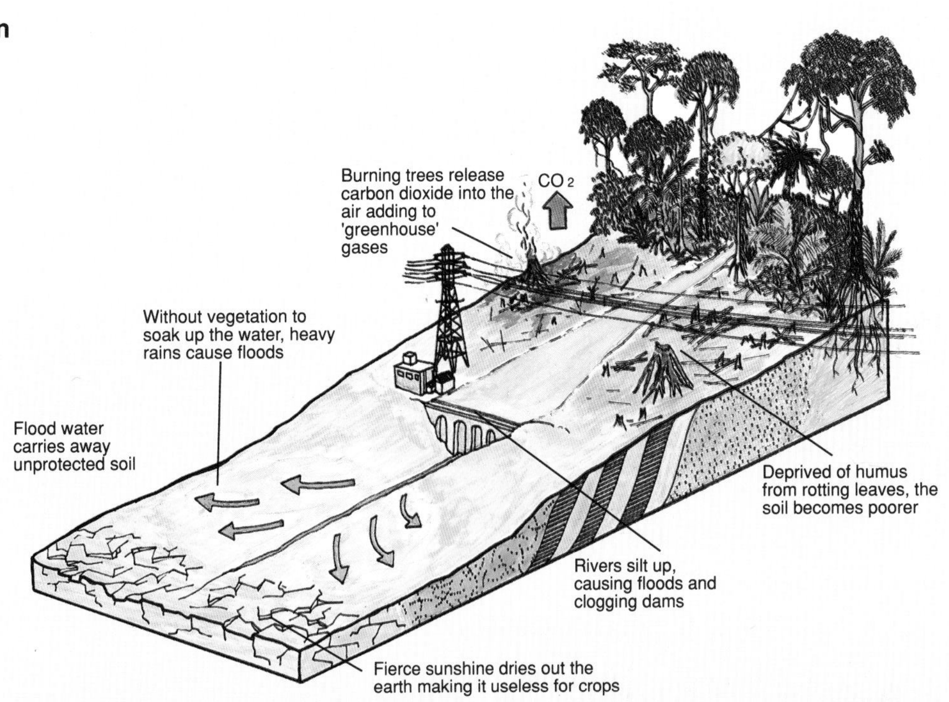

Burning trees release carbon dioxide into the air adding to 'greenhouse' gases CO_2

Without vegetation to soak up the water, heavy rains cause floods

Flood water carries away unprotected soil

Deprived of humus from rotting leaves, the soil becomes poorer

Rivers silt up, causing floods and clogging dams

Fierce sunshine dries out the earth making it useless for crops

Deforestation in Amazonia

About a third of the world's rainforest is in Amazonia. This area mostly belongs to Brazil, but also covers parts of neighbouring countries.

Brazilians are keen to open up Amazonia and exploit its riches. They see this as a way of developing industry and paying off debts. However, many projects take little account of the destruction which causes priceless areas of rainforest to literally go up in smoke.

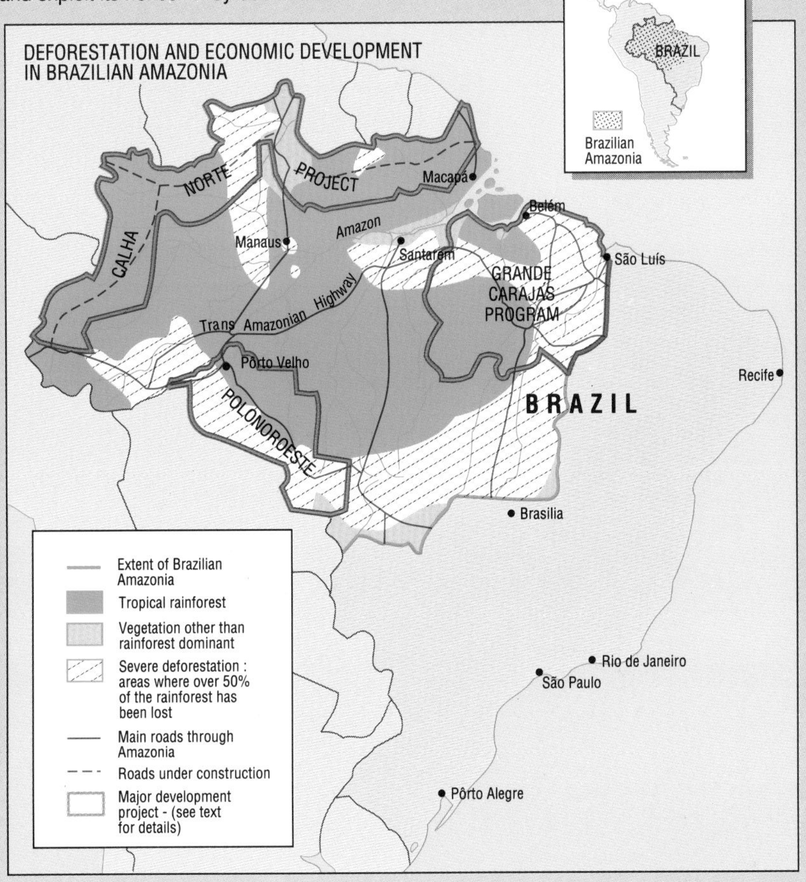

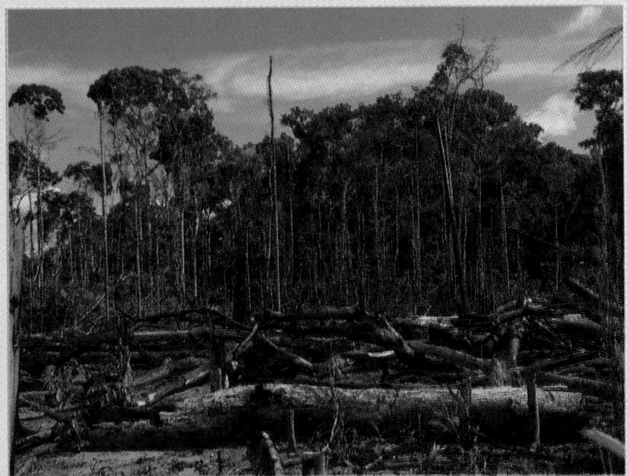

DEFORESTATION AND ECONOMIC DEVELOPMENT IN BRAZILIAN AMAZONIA

CALHA NORTE PROJECT
Macapá
Belém
Manaus
Amazon
Santarém
São Luís
GRANDE CARAJÁS PROGRAM
Trans Amazonian Highway
Pôrto Velho
Recife
POLONOROESTE
B R A Z I L
Brasilia
Rio de Janeiro
São Paulo
Pôrto Alegre

BRAZIL
Brazilian Amazonia

Legend:
- Extent of Brazilian Amazonia
- Tropical rainforest
- Vegetation other than rainforest dominant
- Severe deforestation: areas where over 50% of the rainforest has been lost
- Main roads through Amazonia
- Roads under construction
- Major development project - (see text for details)

A huge area along the northern border of Brazil has been set aside for the Calha Norte Project. Here companies have been granted mining concessions and permission to explore for oil. Hydro-electric power stations are being built to provide power for industrial development. The dams for these schemes will flood large areas of land, threatening the homes of fifty thousand Indians.

Further south, the Grand Carajás Program involves a massive open cast iron ore mine which will be linked by rail to a special port. Huge tracts of forest will also be cleared for a bauxite mine, cash crop plantations and cattle ranches.

In the west, the Polonoroeste Development Project has allowed thousands of immigrants to flood into the area. Originally it was intended to open up the area for agriculture, but the soil is so poor it cannot sustain crops.

DEMANDS ON LAND IN BRAZILIAN AMAZONIA

	$10^3 km^2$	% total
Already cleared	340	10%
Area to be flooded for HEP development	150	4.4%
Forest reserves maintained for timber production	500	15%
Colonised (up to 1989)	430	13%
Total officially earmarked for development	2 100	63.5%

SOIL EROSION

Soil Erosion

We depend on the soil for most of the food that we eat. Fruit, vegetables and cereal crops are grown directly in the soil. Even when we consume meat and poultry we are linked to the soil indirectly via the food chain. Without soil we would be unable to survive.

Soil erosion is a natural process. The action of wind and water is continually wearing away the surface of the earth. Human activity, however, can dramatically increase the rate at which it happens.

Soil erosion is an insidious process. It attracts little attention, yet it is happening all the time. Each year some 75 million tonnes of topsoil are lost around the world. This is causing harvests to fail and is blocking rivers and reservoirs with silt.

Factors Influencing Soil Erosion

TYPE OF SOIL

SLOPE OF THE LAND

VEGETATION COVER

FARMING PRACTICES

SOIL EROSION

All farming disturbs the soil but poor management can make the problem much worse. In some areas the removal of plants and trees exposes the land to heavy rain. Elsewhere dry soils are impoverished by overcultivation. Slopes are especially vulnerable. Once the soil is lost it can never be replaced.

Water Erosion

Water erosion is usually worst in areas of high rainfall. Here trees help to reduce the damage by trapping water in their roots and binding the soil together.

NORTH AMERICA	
Yukon	444
Mackenzie / Peace	256
Colombia / Snake	131
Mississippi / Missouri	256
Rio Grande	210

EUROPE	
Danube	133

ARCTIC OCEAN

ATLANTIC OCEAN

PACIFIC OCEAN

Annual precipitation (mm)
Over 3 000
2 000 - 3 000
1 000 - 2 000
Under 1 000

SOUTH AMERICA	
Amazon / Orinoco	1 438
São Francisco	28
Paranà / Paraguay	154

AFRICA	
Niger / Zaïre	113
Zambezi	290
Orange	17

Million tonnes of sediment carried annually to the oceans by a selection of river systems from around the world.

Soil Erosion in the USA

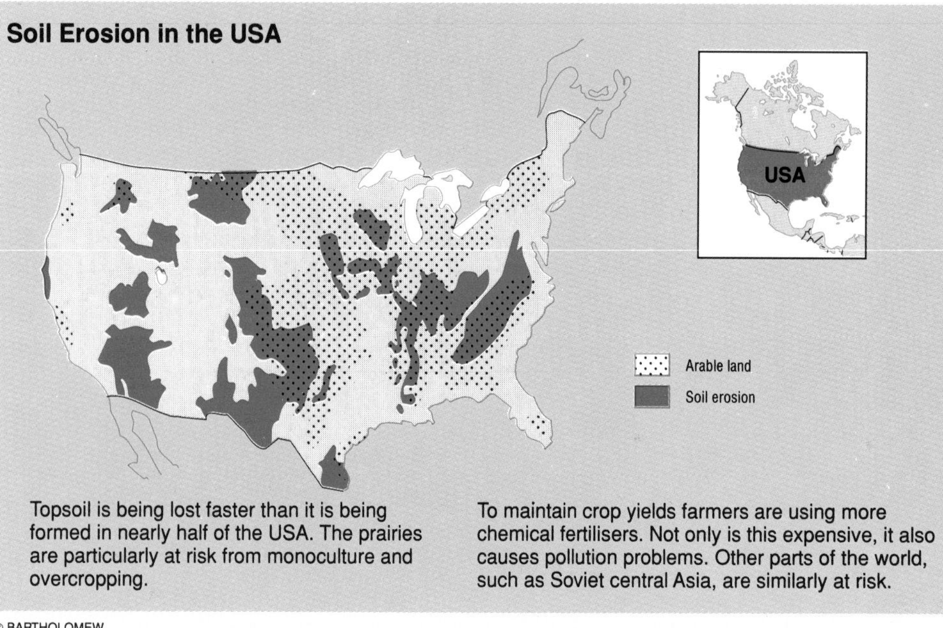

USA

Arable land

Soil erosion

Topsoil is being lost faster than it is being formed in nearly half of the USA. The prairies are particularly at risk from monoculture and overcropping.

To maintain crop yields farmers are using more chemical fertilisers. Not only is this expensive, it also causes pollution problems. Other parts of the world, such as Soviet central Asia, are similarly at risk.

The worst soil disaster of recent times occured in USA in the 1930's. Overcultivation of poor soil and the removal of hedges made the soil vulnerable. In prolonged drought, millions of tonnes of soil literall blew away, turning a large area of the Mid-west int Dust Bowl.

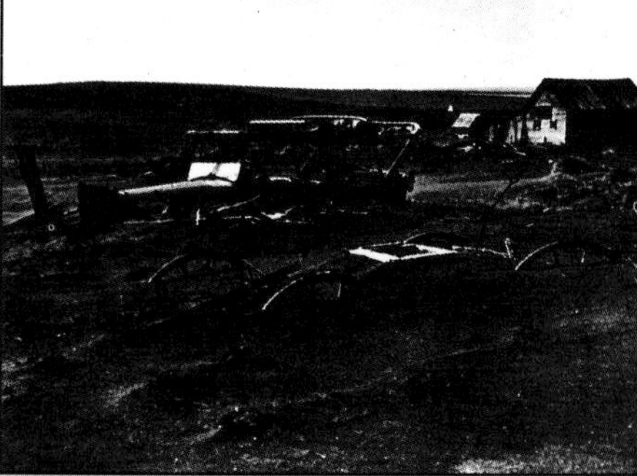

Dust Bowl in the USA - Farm machinery buried under du in South Dakota, 1936

f the trees are removed the effects can be devastating. The water rushes down the slopes, strips away the soil and causes flooding downstream.

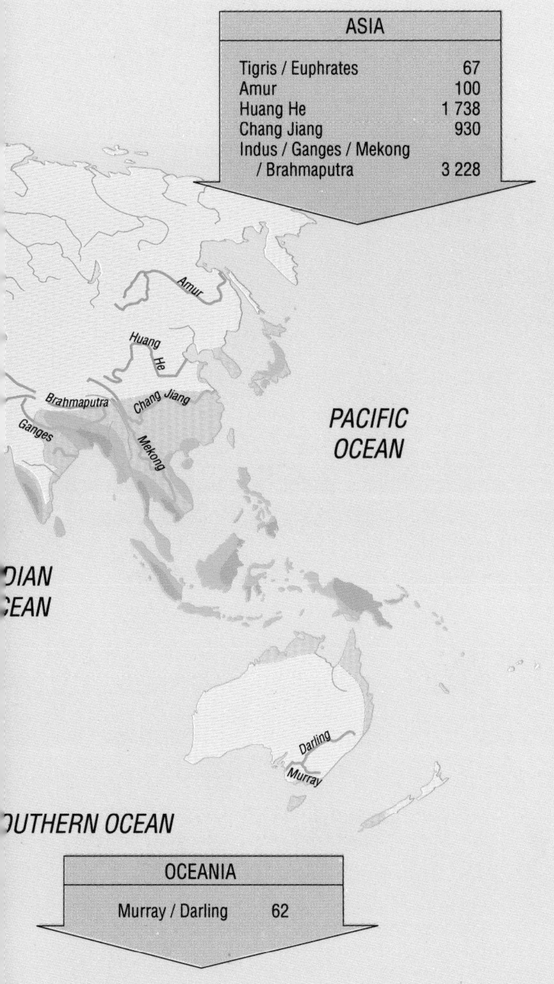

ASIA	
Tigris / Euphrates	67
Amur	100
Huang He	1 738
Chang Jiang	930
Indus / Ganges / Mekong / Brahmaputra	3 228

PACIFIC OCEAN

INDIAN OCEAN

SOUTHERN OCEAN

OCEANIA	
Murray / Darling	62

Halting Soil Erosion

There are many different ways of halting soil erosion.

- Terraces can be built across slopes to catch the soil as it washes down.

- Trees and grasses can be planted on grazing land.

- Farmers can be encouraged to leave the land fallow so as not to exhaust the soil.

One of the key problems is that more and more people are being forced to farm vulnerable land in order to survive. The solution lies in economic and political reforms. When local communities have enough money and power, they strive to protect their environment.

The Ganges Delta

Deltas are formed from the sediment which rivers carry down to the sea. They contain some of the most fertile soils in the world. However, they are also vulnerable to flooding and are liable to subside as the sediments compress.

The Ganges Delta receives about 3 million tonnes of sediment each year. This is creating a large new island in the Bay of Bengal. Silt deposits also block water channels causing floods. In recent years floods have become much more frequent as trees are cleared in the mountains allowing heavy monsoon rains to rush downstream.

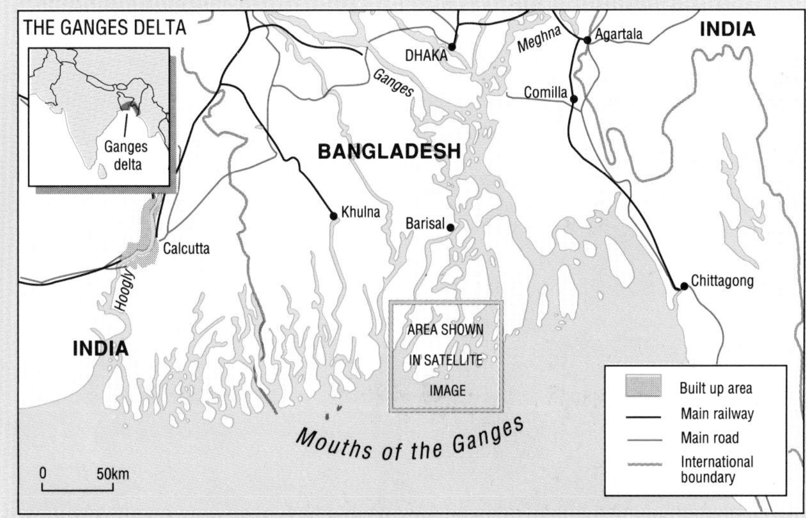

THE GANGES DELTA

Ganges delta

DHAKA
Meghna
Agartala
INDIA
Ganges
Comilla
BANGLADESH
Khulna
Barisal
Calcutta
Hooghly
INDIA
Chittagong

AREA SHOWN IN SATELLITE IMAGE

Mouths of the Ganges

0   50km

- Built up area
— Main railway
— Main road
— International boundary

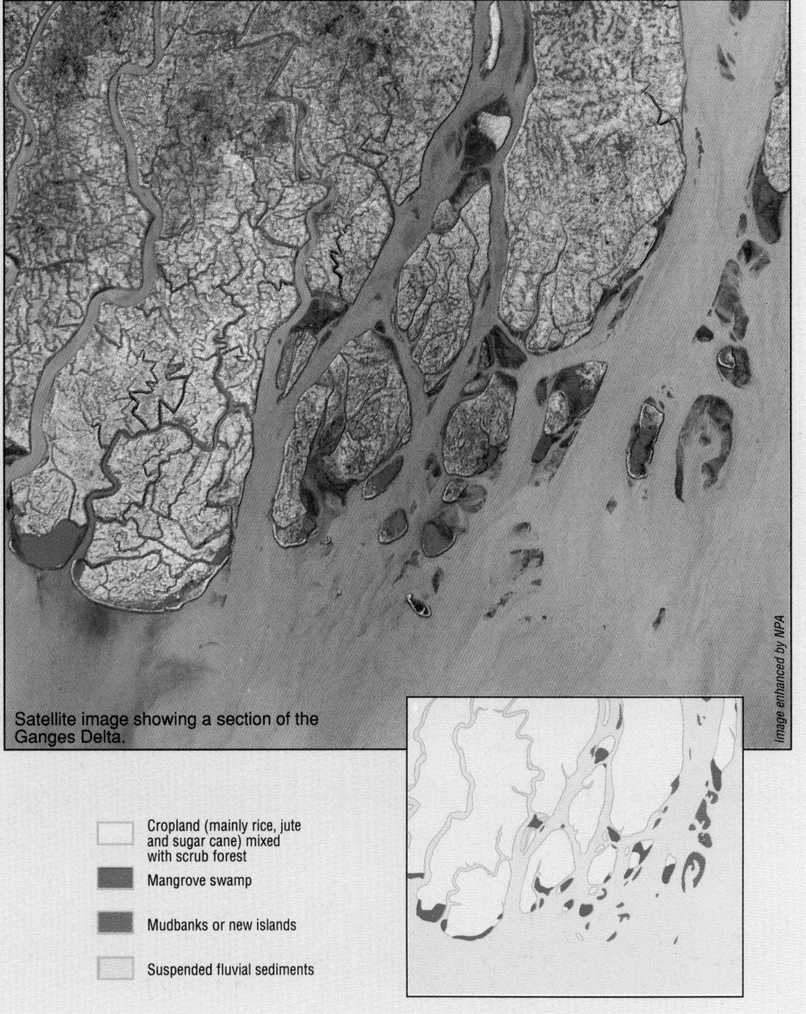

image enhanced by NPA

Satellite image showing a section of the Ganges Delta.

- Cropland (mainly rice, jute and sugar cane) mixed with scrub forest
- Mangrove swamp
- Mudbanks or new islands
- Suspended fluvial sediments

DESERTIFICATION

What is Desertification?

Desertification, or the spread of deserts, threatens over a third of the world's land surface. Severe deterioration and loss of soil can turn productive land into desert. Every year, an area the size of the United Kingdom is either lost or severely degraded. In some cases deserts appear to invade good land from the outside, but in fact it is deterioration of soil in the border regions which causes them to expand. By the year 2000 the situation is likely to become critical especially in the Sahel, the Andes and parts of South Asia.

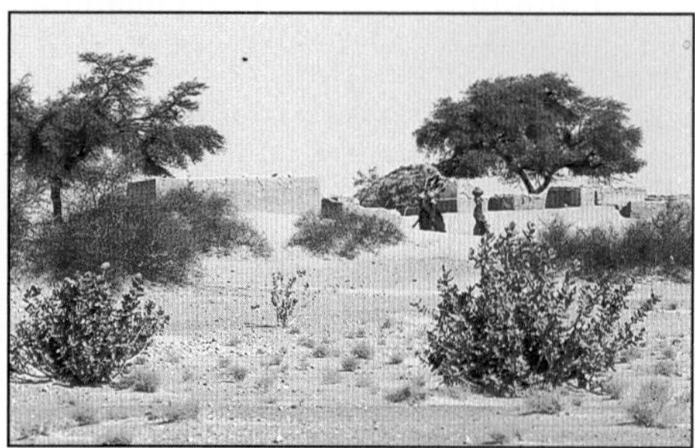

At one time lush trees and shrubs surrounded this Nile valley village.

The Causes

Desertification often begins when people decide or are forced to use land in dry areas too intensively. Overcultivation, overgrazing and the clearance of trees for fuelwood combine to degrade the soil. In other places, badly damaged irrigation schemes can make the land so salty it can no longer grow crops. The diagram below shows two ways in which desertification is triggered. Once desertification is started, natural factors, such as drought accelerate the process.

Where is Desertification Taking Place?

Fertile areas on the edge of existing deserts are most at risk. Here, harsh conditions mean that the land is only just able to grow crops and needs particularly careful management. Some 850 million people live in desert border regions and the population is growing rapidly.

WORLD LAND AT RISK

- Other land 66%
- Existing desert 6%
- Moderate 13%
- Severe 12%
- Very severe 3%

Land at risk of desertification

In Spain, ten percent of the land is affected by severe desertification.

Europe 2%

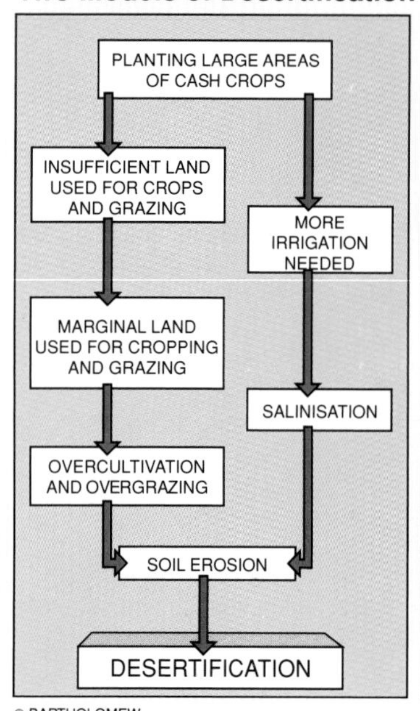

Southwest United States

Turkestan

Iranian

Sahara

Arabian

Thar

Somali

North and South America 19%

Atacama

Namib

Kalahari

Cattle ranching and overgrazing have degraded the soil in the western USA and parts of Mexico. Further south, unsuitable land is being cleared for crops in Brazil and Argentina.

Africa 34%

Overgrazing and the removal of trees threaten the Sahel, Mediterranean coast and southern Africa.

Two Models of Desertification

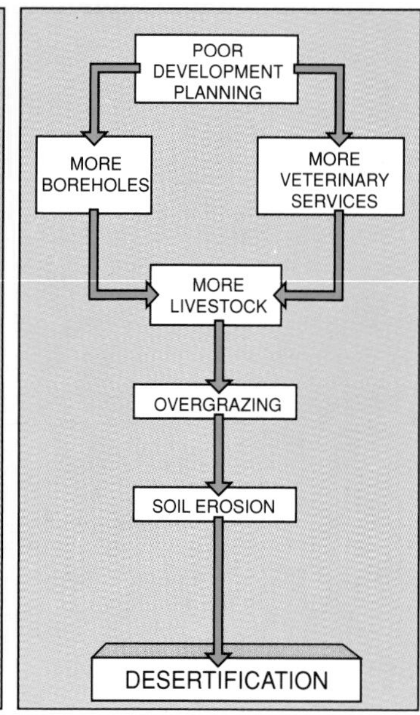

PLANTING LARGE AREAS OF CASH CROPS
→ INSUFFICIENT LAND USED FOR CROPS AND GRAZING
→ MORE IRRIGATION NEEDED
→ MARGINAL LAND USED FOR CROPPING AND GRAZING
→ SALINISATION
→ OVERCULTIVATION AND OVERGRAZING
→ SOIL EROSION
→ DESERTIFICATION

POOR DEVELOPMENT PLANNING
→ MORE BOREHOLES
→ MORE VETERINARY SERVICES
→ MORE LIVESTOCK
→ OVERGRAZING
→ SOIL EROSION
→ DESERTIFICATION

Effects of Desertification

Effects on People
Desertification is slow and insidious. Developing countries suffer most. Here, rural communities become trapped in a cycle of poverty which forces them to exploit the land beyond its capacity. This makes them very vulnerable to natural hazards, such as drought.

As crops fail and water sources dry up, people have no alternative but to leave the land. One sixth of the population of Burkina Faso fled the country in the drought of the early 1970's. In India and Brazil many victims of desertification have gone to live in the big cities, swelling the urban population.

Effects on Climate
Desertification can have a significant effect on the climate. The increase in dust prevents air from rising freely and forming clouds. In addition, the loss of vegetation reduces the amount of moisture in the air and allows temperatures to rise. Both these factors tend to make droughts worse.

...or irrigation schemes are causing ...esertification in the southern states of ...e USSR. Iran and many parts of the ...iddle East are also at risk.

Asia 31%

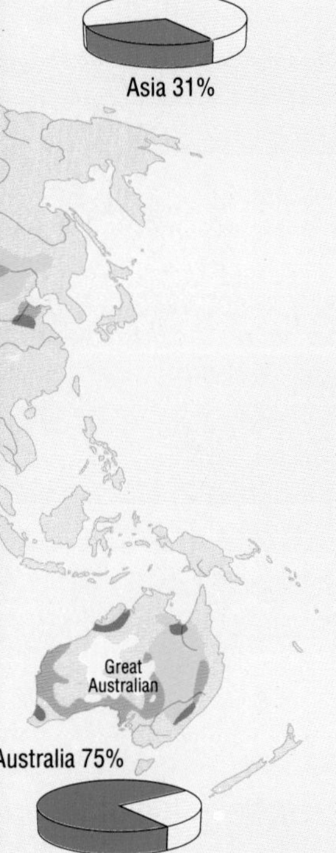

Australia 75%

Great Australian

Most of Australia is at risk due to poor stock raising.

Moderate desertification (Productivity reduced by up to 25%)

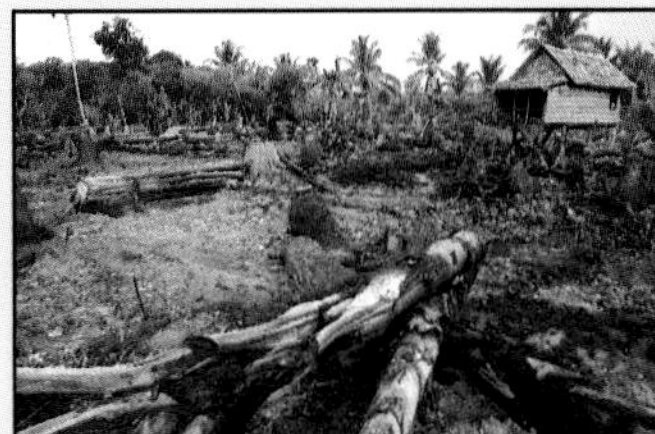

The removal of tree and plant cover exposes the soil. In irrigated areas, salts build up in the ground, killing crops.

Severe desertification (Productivity reduced by 25-50%)

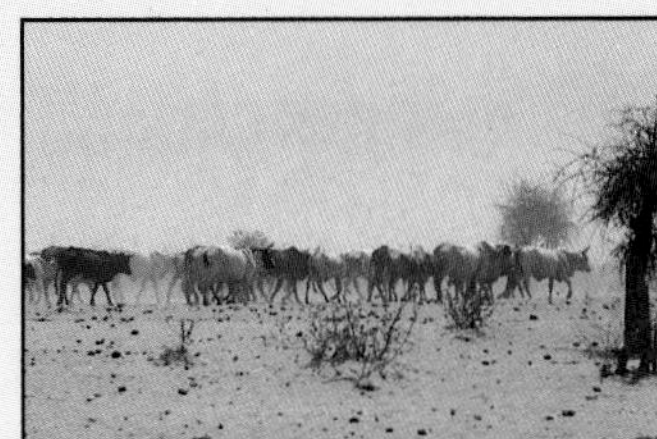

Dust storms and floods strip away much of the top soil. Plants struggle to survive.

Very severe desertification (Productivity reduced by over 50%)

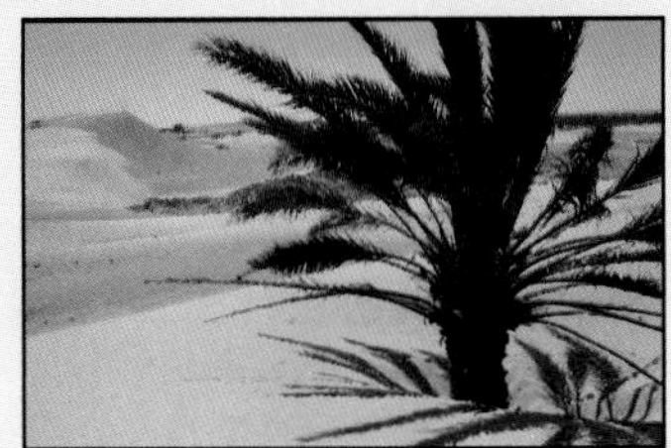

Bare ground is baked hard in the sun and plants wither. Sand, grit and dust storms are common.

Existing desert (Unproductive)

Combatting Desertification

There is nothing new about desertification. Before people cut them down, there were forests in the Sahara Desert which supported a good variety of wildlife. Desertification has played a role in the downfall of early civilisations, including the Roman Empire. What is new is the scale of the problem.

Human action causes desertification. By the same token it can also control and cure it. Reforestation, improved farming methods and better land use can halt the advance of the desert. There are many successful projects around the world.

- In Rajasthan, India, trees have been planted as shelter belts along roads.

- In Senegal coastal sand dunes have been stabilised.

- Lines of stones have been placed to follow the contours of the land to trap soil in fields in Burkina Faso.

- Watersheds have been terraced in Ethiopia.

- In northern China a forest 7 000 km long has been planted to protect the farmland from the Gobi Desert.

Where local people are given responsibility for the schemes and supported by their government the results have been particularly impressive. At the heart of the issue is the control of the land itself. If people feel secure and have a stake in the future they will act accordingly.

▲Africa - Population Affected by Desertification

Mediterranean Africa 8.5 million

Sahel 28.5 million

👤 1 milllion people

Africa South of the Sahel 25 million

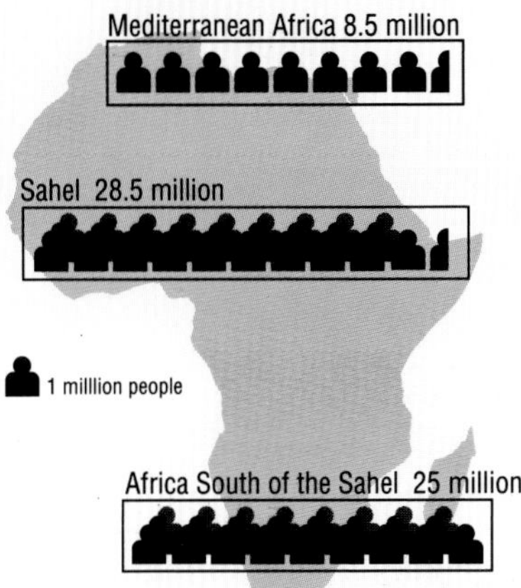

...During the 1960's and 1970's the Sahara ...Desert spread 100 km further south, forcing ...millions of people to leave their homes.

Preventative Measures

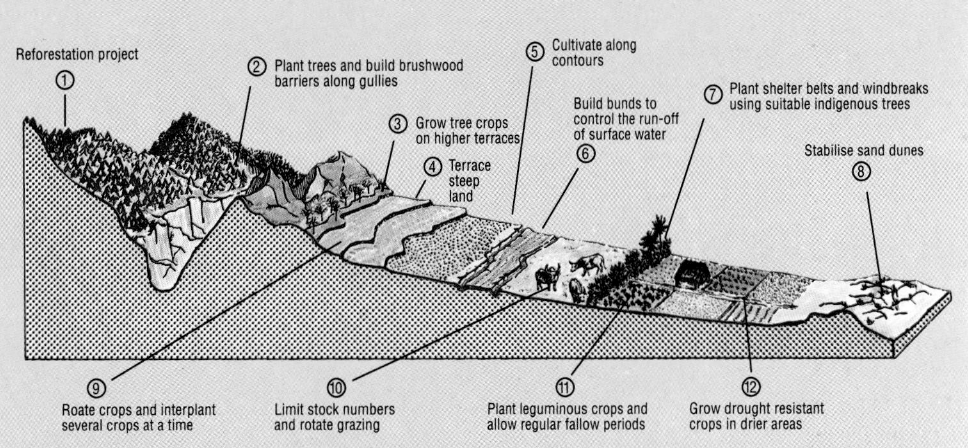

Reforestation project ①

② Plant trees and build brushwood barriers along gullies

③ Grow tree crops on higher terraces

④ Terrace steep land

⑤ Cultivate along contours

⑥ Build bunds to control the run-off of surface water

⑦ Plant shelter belts and windbreaks using suitable indigenous trees

⑧ Stabilise sand dunes

⑨ Roate crops and interplant several crops at a time

⑩ Limit stock numbers and rotate grazing

⑪ Plant leguminous crops and allow regular fallow periods

⑫ Grow drought resistant crops in drier areas

Although we know how to halt desertification, we are not winning the battle against it. Too little money is spent on preventative measures and there is a lack of long term planning. Many people are at risk and a massive effort will be needed to avoid famine in the years ahead.

AIR POLLUTION

What is Pollution?

All damage to the environment is known as pollution. Some pollution comes from natural sources. Volcanoes, for example, release poisonous gases into the atmosphere. Most pollution, however, is caused by human activity. As world population increases and technology advances pollution problems become more severe.

Air Pollution

The earth is covered by a layer of air which extends far into space. Only the lowest few kilometres can support life. As more fumes enter the atmosphere important changes begin to occur; if we go on using the atmosphere as a dustbin the earth will eventually become uninhabitable.

Ozone Destruction

The earth is surrounded by a layer of ozone, O_3, in the stratosphere about 25km above the surface. This filters out harmful ultra-violet light from the sun which can cause skin cancer. Recently scientists have noticed that the ozone layer is getting thinner. They were particularly alarmed to discover a hole opening up over Antarctica each spring.

Ozone destruction is caused by gases known as chlorofluorocarbons, CFC's. These are used in foams, refridgerators and aerosols. In 1987 many countries undertook to reduce their use of CFC's by signing an agreement called the Montreal Protocol.

The expanding hole in the ozone layer

1979

1986

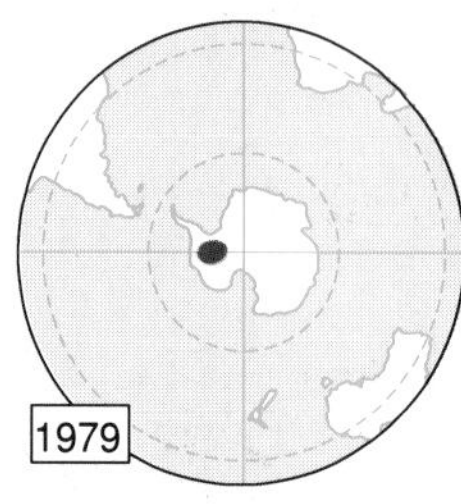

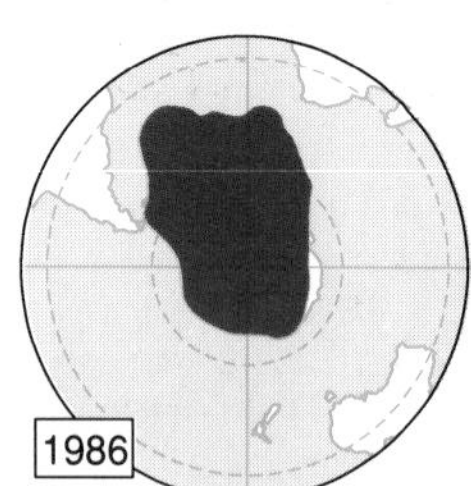

Each year the hole in the ozone layer over Antarctica gets larger. Places as far away as Australia and New Zealand are affected by the reduction in the ozone layer.

Atmospheric Pollution

AIR POLLUTION FROM SO_2
(1980-84 average in micrograms / m³ for selected urban areas)

☐ Under 40

☐ 40-60

■ 61-100

■ over 100

The WHO guidelines for sulphur dioxide concentration is 40-60 micrograms / m³

pH concentration in the northern hemisphere. (The pH scale ranges from 0-14 with LOWER values indicating GREATER acidity. Non acidified rainwater should have a pH value between 5.6 and 8.0)

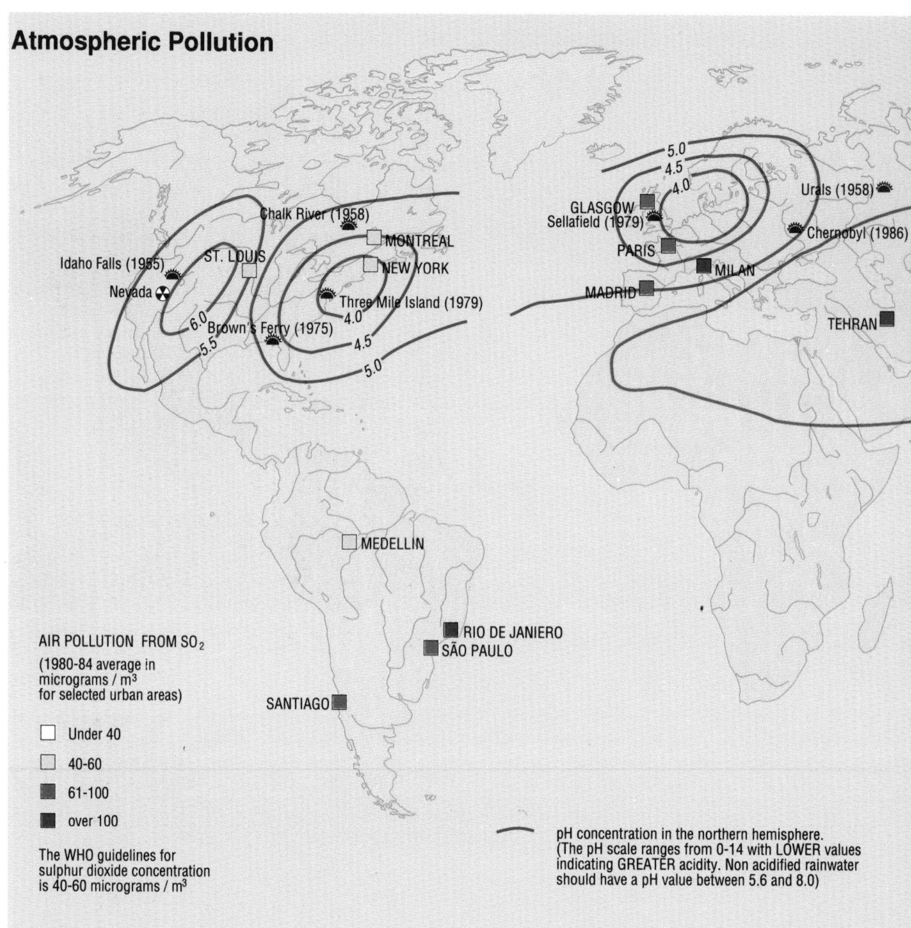

Global Warming

The world is now warmer than at any time since the last Ice Age. Scientists believe that in future temperatures will rise even faster. This is called global warming. Global warming is caused by a blanket of 'greenhouse gases' building up around the earth trapping heat from the sun. Carbon dioxode, CO_2, released by burning fossil fuels is one of the main causes.

CO_2 LEVELS
1750 level = 100 units

How the 'greenhouse effect' works

NITROUS OXIDE from fossil fuels, industry, households, cement manufacture and burning of rain forest.

METHANE from cattle ranching coal mines and paddy fields.

CARBON DIOXIDE from fossil fuels.

VISIBLE SHORTWAVE LIGHT passes trough the atmosphere to the earth's surface.

Some LONGWAVE HEAT RADIATION leaves the earth - but most is reflected back by 'greenhouse gases'.

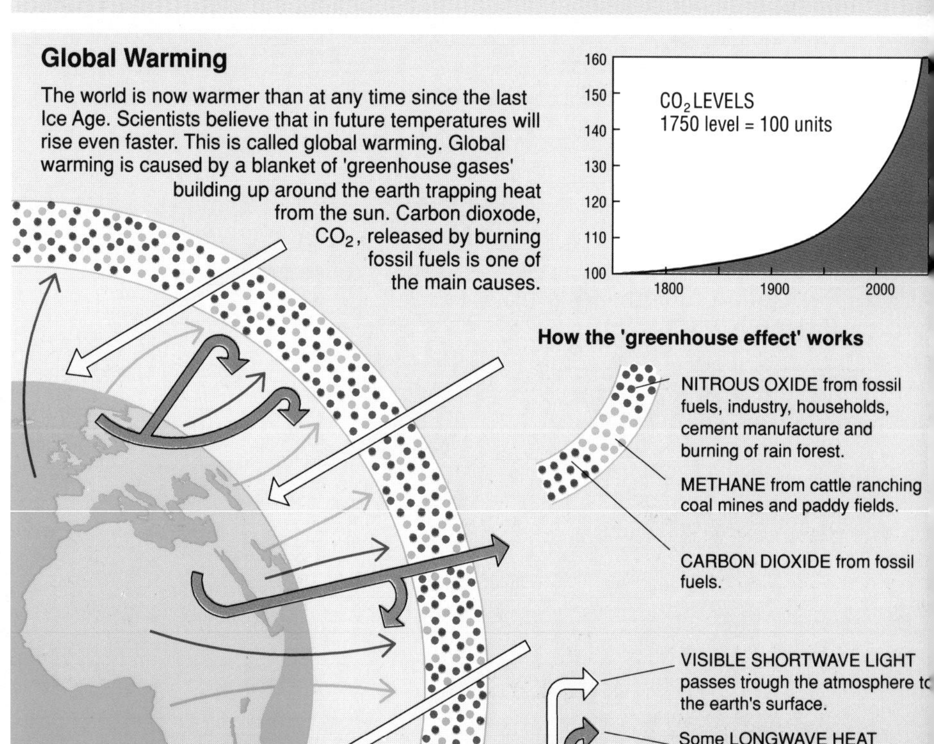

Acid Rain

Coal and oil release a mixture of gases as they burn. These gases combine with water vapour, sunlight and oxygen to form sulphuric acid and nitric acid which fall back to earth as acid rain. The effects of acid rain vary greatly, but areas with poor soil suffer most, especially in spring when melting snow pours contaminated water into rivers and lakes. One way of reducing the problem is to fit catalytic converters to cars and build flues in power stations. It would also help if we used energy more efficiently to reduce our consumption of fuel.

Acid rain in Europe

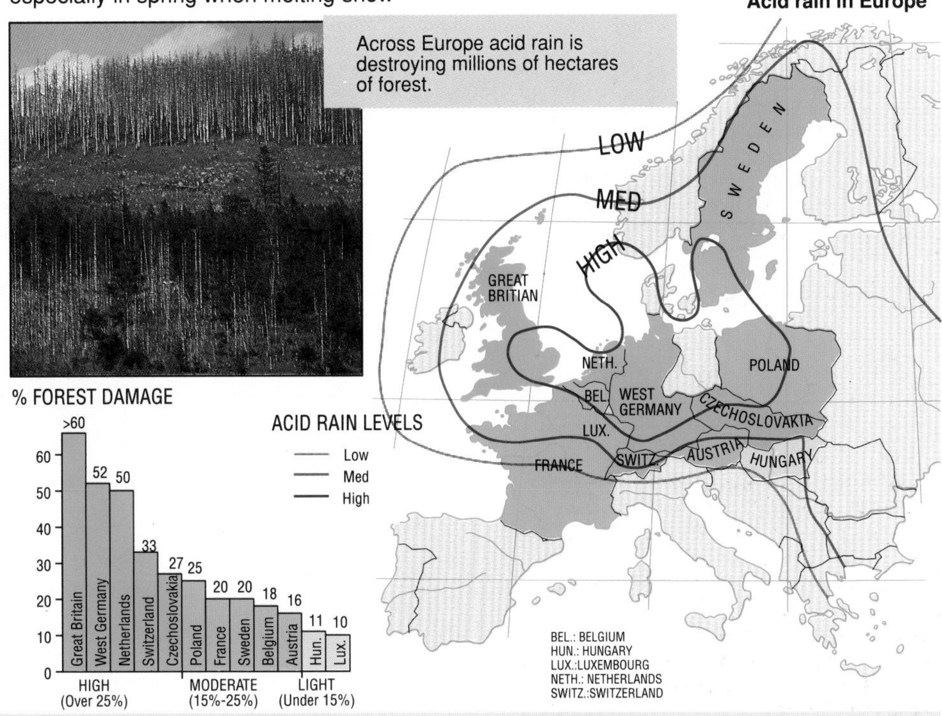

Across Europe acid rain is destroying millions of hectares of forest.

BEL.: BELGIUM
HUN.: HUNGARY
LUX.:LUXEMBOURG
NETH.:NETHERLANDS
SWITZ.:SWITZERLAND

% FOREST DAMAGE

ACID RAIN LEVELS

—— Low
—— Med
—— High

Country	%	Category
Great Britain	>60	HIGH (Over 25%)
West Germany	52	HIGH (Over 25%)
Netherlands	50	HIGH (Over 25%)
Switzerland	33	HIGH (Over 25%)
Czechoslovakia	27	MODERATE (15%-25%)
Poland	25	MODERATE (15%-25%)
France	20	MODERATE (15%-25%)
Sweden	20	MODERATE (15%-25%)
Belgium	18	MODERATE (15%-25%)
Austria	16	MODERATE (15%-25%)
Hun.	11	LIGHT (Under 15%)
Lux.	10	LIGHT (Under 15%)

☢ Current nuclear site

☢ Major accident at nuclear power station causing air pollution from radioactive discharge

---

What might happen if the earth's surface temperature increased, on average, by 1°C.

In an attempt to tackle the problem of global warming the European Community has agreed to freeze emissions of carbon dioxide at the current levels by the year 2000.

More humid than before

Drier than before

● Flooding through rise in sea level

Increase in surface temperature

Principal farming regions

It is impossible to predict the effect of global warming but these are some of the things which scientists expect:

flooding of low lying areas as the sea level rises

more violent storms and unpredictable weather

food shortage as crops fail

new pests and diseases

extinction of many plants and creatures as conditions change

c 3-4°C

c 1°C

MELTING ICECAPS LEADS TO HEAVY PACK ICE

SHORT WET WINTERS. LONG DRY SUMMERS

SHARP FALL IN GRAIN CROP YIELDS

SHARP FALL IN GRAIN CROP YIELDS

MORE DESTRUCTIVE HURRICANES

RISE IN SEA LEVEL

INCREASE IN FARMING

POOR RICE CROP

c 0.3°C-0.5°C

FAILURE OF ANCHOVY FISHERIES

MILLIONS MADE HOMELESS BY FLOODING

No data available

RISE IN SEA LEVEL

LAND POLLUTION

Hazardous Waste - Production and Trade

Hazardous and toxic waste damages the environment and poisons people and animals. Most toxic waste comes from the chemical industry. It is produced in increasing quantities each year.

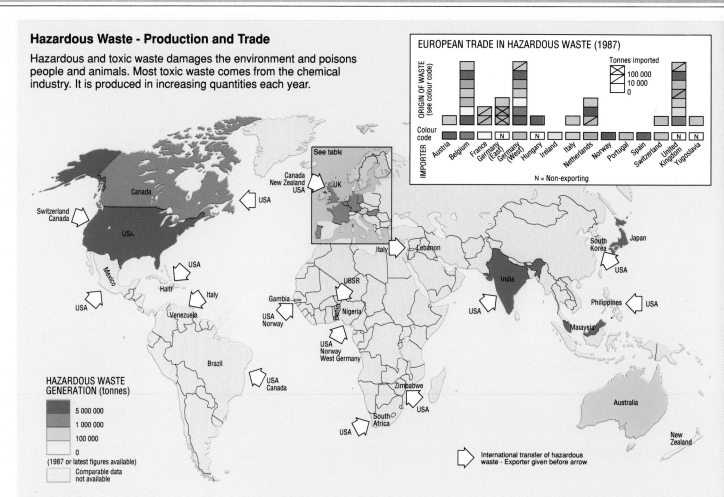

HAZARDOUS WASTE GENERATION (tonnes)

- 5 000 000
- 1 000 000
- 100 000
- 0

(1987 or latest figures available)

Comparable data not available

International transfer of hazardous waste - Exporter given before arrow

EUROPEAN TRADE IN HAZARDOUS WASTE (1987)

ORIGIN OF WASTE (see colour code)

Tonnes imported

- 100 000
- 10 000
- 0

Colour code

IMPORTER: Austria, Belgium, France, Germany (East), Germany (West), Hungary, Ireland, Italy, Netherlands, Norway, Portugal, Spain, Switzerland, United Kingdom, Yugoslavia

N = Non-exporting

Toxic Trade

It is very expensive to dispose of toxic waste properly so people are looking for cheap solutions. At the moment large quantities are shipped to developing countries, often illegally.

In 1988, for example, 10 000 drums of hazardous waste from Italy were discovered in a yard in the port of Koko, Nigeria. They were leaking acid and poisonous chemicals but local people had no idea what they contained. Nearly forty countries have now banned toxic waste imports but the regulations are difficult to enforce.

Waste Dumping

Some 350 million tonnes of hazardous waste are produced each year and there are over 70 000 different chemicals in regular use. Many of them have never been tested for their effect on the environment and nobody knows what happens when they are mixed together.

For years toxic waste has been dumped in landfill sites. If these are unlined, dangerous chemicals can seep into the soil and contaminate water supplies. The problem of indiscriminate dumping affects most industrialised countries and there are thousands of sites which need to be cleaned up.

% WASTE DISPOSAL BY LANDFILL
(selected countries - 1987 or latest figures available)

Australia, Canada, West Germany, Ireland, Italy, Japan, Netherlands, Spain, Sweden, Switzerland, United Kingdom

In Britain toxic waste is mixed with domestic rubbish in the controversial 'dilute and disperse' method. Many other countries favour the opposite approach and concentrate their most dangerous waste in specific places. Incineration is also increasingly favoured.

The best way of solving the problem of toxic waste is not to produce it in the first place. It is estimated that over the next decade industry could cut its production by a third. More waste could also be recycled or re-used.

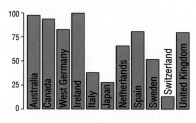

Toxic waste dump, Czechoslovakia.

© BARTHOLOMEW

DILUTE AND DISPERSE LANDFILL DISPOSAL

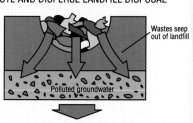

Wastes seep out of landfill

Polluted groundwater

Polluted streams and water supply

Agrochemicals

Around the world farmers are putting more and more chemicals on their land. This has led to great increases in crop yields but has also brought environmental problems. Nutrients from fertilisers are polluting rivers and lakes, while residues from pesticides have been detected in food and drinking water. In addition, pesticides are losing their effectiveness as insects develop immunity. In future agrochemicals will need to be used much more selectivley.

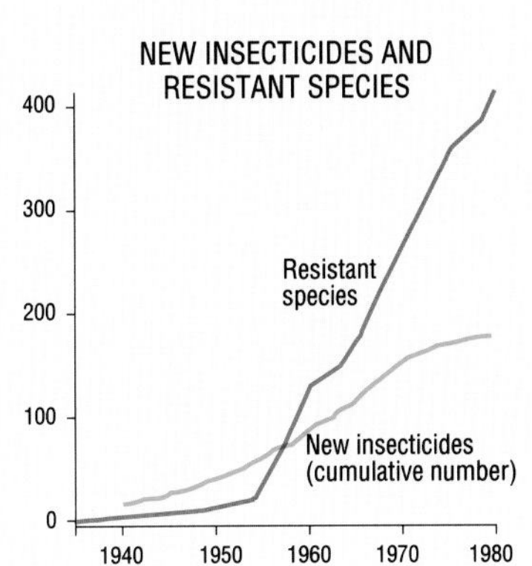

NEW INSECTICIDES AND RESISTANT SPECIES

Resistant species

New insecticides (cumulative number)

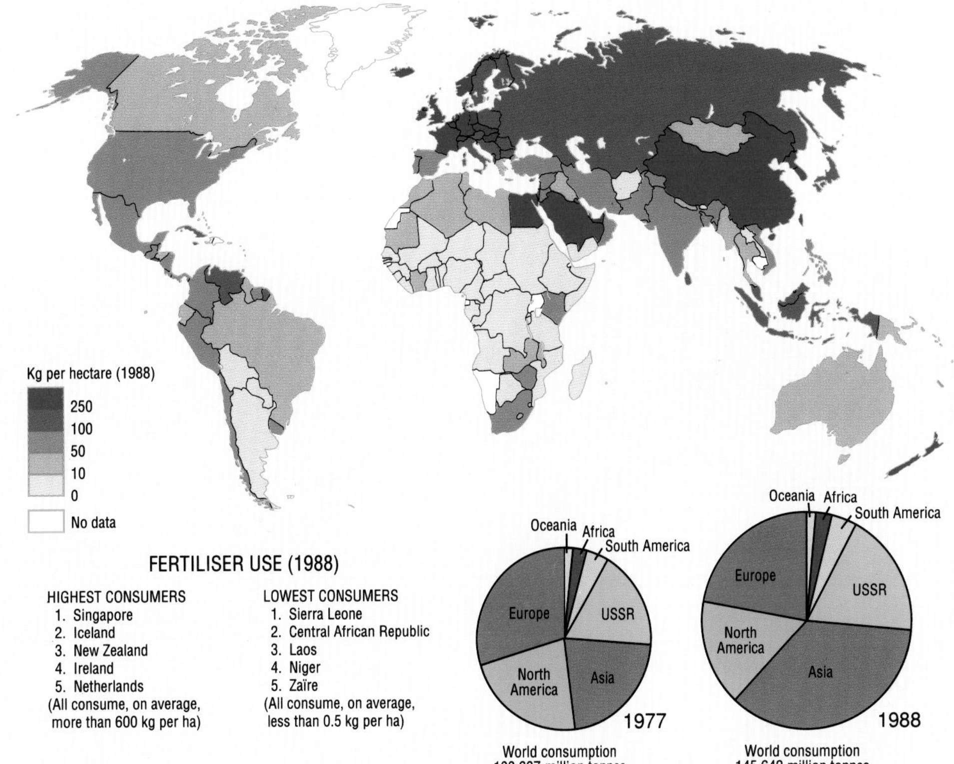

Kg per hectare (1988)

- 250
- 100
- 50
- 10
- 0
- No data

FERTILISER USE (1988)

HIGHEST CONSUMERS
1. Singapore
2. Iceland
3. New Zealand
4. Ireland
5. Netherlands

(All consume, on average, more than 600 kg per ha)

LOWEST CONSUMERS
1. Sierra Leone
2. Central African Republic
3. Laos
4. Niger
5. Zaïre

(All consume, on average, less than 0.5 kg per ha)

1977
World consumption
100 607 million tonnes

1988
World consumption
145 642 million tonnes

The Aral Sea Disaster

The Aral Sea in Soviet Central Asia used to be the fourth biggest lake in the world. It supported a thriving fishing industry, mixed agriculture and many species of plants and animals. Now the Aral Sea is drying up as water is diverted to irrigate cotton crops. Unless something is done it could disappear completely over the next thirty years.

Environmental Consequences

The dry sea bed has become a desert, poisoned by salt and residues from the chemicals sprayed on the cotton crop. Huge dust storms sweep up the contaminated soil and dump it back on the fields. Deposits have been found up to 5 000 km away on the shores of the Arctic Ocean.

The climate of the region has also begun to change. The Aral Sea used to act as a battery, storing heat in the summer and releasing it in the winter. Now temperatures have become more extreme and there is less rainfall.

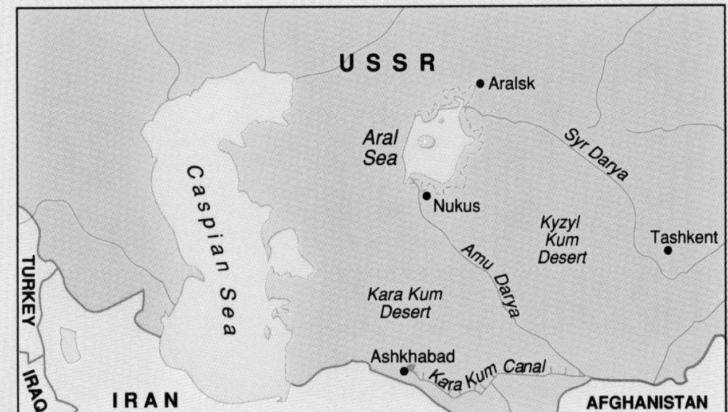

The location of the Aral Sea

The effect on the local community has been disasterous. Towns which used to depend on fishing are now up to 60 km from the shore. Disease and illness have multiplied among adults and one in ten babies die defore their first birthday.

ARAL SEA FACTS

▲ Only 4 out of 24 species of fish survive.

▲ The salinity of the water has increased from 10 to 27%.

▲ Surface area has decreased by 40% since 1960.

▲ 173 animal species have been cut to 38.

What could be done?

At present most of the irrigation canals leak a lot. If they were lined with plastic or concrete it would save large amounts of water. Also, the acreage under cotton could be reduced to cut down on irrigation. It will take massive changes to halt the present process and the Aral Sea will probably never be restored properly.

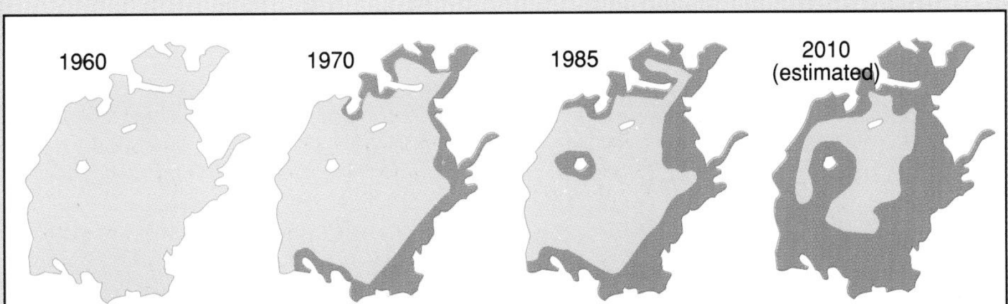

1960   1970   1985   2010 (estimated)

The changing shape of the Aral Sea

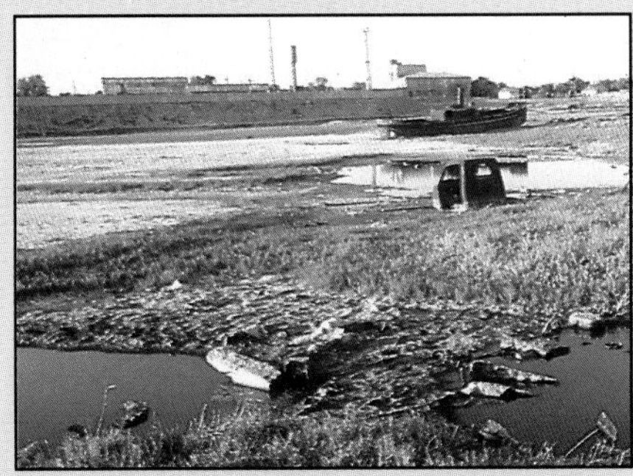

Aralsk, USSR - rusting boats lie in the wasteland that was once part of the Aral Sea.

WATER POLLUTION

The Water Budget

Seventy percent of the earth's surface is covered by water. Fresh water represents only 2.5% of the total. The rest is found in the oceans where the presence of salt makes it difficult to use.

Most of the fresh water lies deep underground or is frozen in the polar ice caps. Only a very small proportion is freely available. Nevertheless there is enough to meet our needs. The problems is that supplies are unevenly distributed around the world.

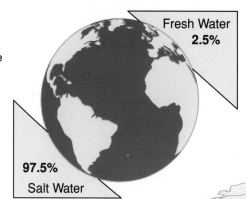

Fresh Water
2.5%

97.5%
Salt Water

Water Pollution

Water pollution is a worldwide problem. Waste from factories, farms and cities is poisoning rivers and seeping into groundwater. Lakes are particularly at risk as they allow pollutants to build up. Coastlines and shallow seas are highly vulnerable. The discharge of oil from tanker accidents and ships that wash out their tanks illegally is another problem. It is estimated that several million tonnes of oil are put into the sea each year.

Water Availability

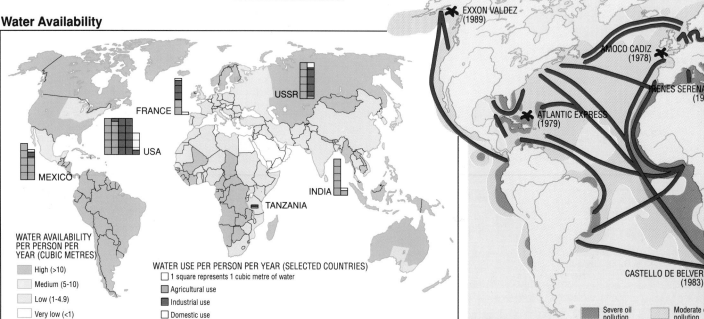

FRANCE
USSR
USA
MEXICO
INDIA
TANZANIA

WATER AVAILABILITY
PER PERSON PER
YEAR (CUBIC METRES)

- High (>10)
- Medium (5-10)
- Low (1-4.9)
- Very low (<1)

WATER USE PER PERSON PER YEAR (SELECTED COUNTRIES)
- □ 1 square represents 1 cubic metre of water
- Agricultural use
- Industrial use
- □ Domestic use

EXXON VALDEZ
(1989)

AMOCO CADIZ
(1978)

IRENES SERENA
(198

ATLANTIC EXPRESS
(1979)

CASTELLO DE BELVER
(1983)

- Severe oil pollution
- Moderate oil pollution

Pollution in the North Sea

North Sea Facts

- Average depth of water 95m.
- Rich variety of flora and fauna, including commercial fish stocks.
- 150 oil and gas platforms.
- 5 000 ships operating at any one time.
- Water replaced every 18 months on average.

B - BELGIUM
N - NETHERLANDS
D - DENMARK

NORWAY
North Sea
IRELAND UK
GERMANY

The North Sea receives much of the pollution that is generated in north-western Europe. Some is dumped directly into the water or absorbed from the atmosphere. Rivers are the single biggest source of pollution and contribute nearly half of the total.

Pollution has begun to have a serious effect on the ecology of the North Sea. Heavy metals from industry, sewage from towns and oil from ships have all added to the problem. In 1988, large numbers of seals were killed by a mystery virus. Countries bordering the North Sea have now agreed on various measures to control pollution. A lot more still needs to be done and many people would like to see stricter controls.

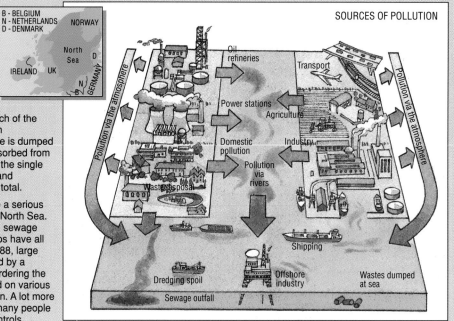

SOURCES OF POLLUTION

Pollution via the atmosphere

Oil refineries
Transport
Power stations
Agriculture
Domestic pollution
Industry
Pollution via rivers
Waste disposal
Shipping
Dredging spoil
Offshore industry
Wastes dumped at sea
Sewage outfall

SOURCES OF POLLUTION (1985)

Nitrogen
Total = 1 506 700 tonnes

Phosphorous
Total = 104 tonnes

Mercury & Cadmium
Total = 409 tonnes

Copper, Lead, Zinc, Chromium, Nickel & Arsenic
Total = 40 557 tonnes

- River Inputs
- Industrial Waste
- Sewage Sludge
- □ Dredging
- Atmospheric
- Direct Discharge

Source - North Sea Quality Status Report 1987

NUMBER OF ACCIDENTAL OIL SPILLS (1973-84)

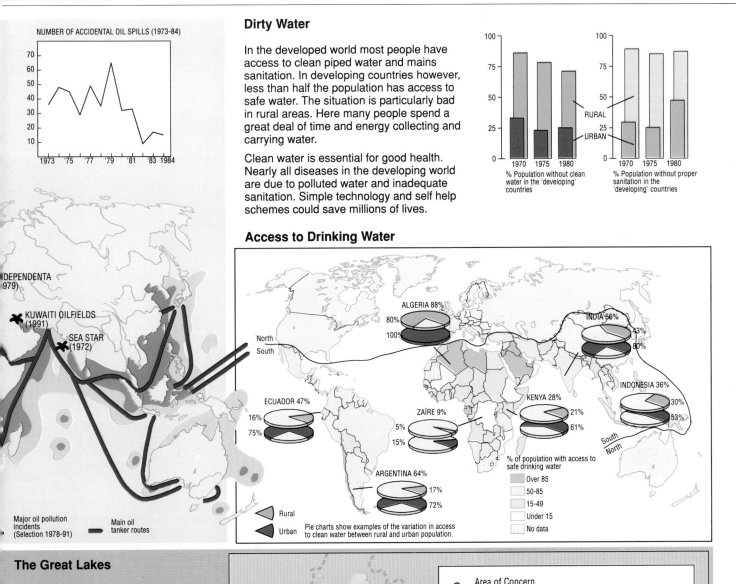

70
60
50
40
30
20
10

1973 '75 '77 '79 '81 '83 1984

...DEPENDENTA
...979)

✕ KUWAITI OILFIELDS
(1991)

✕ SEA STAR
(1972)

Major oil pollution
incidents
(Selection 1978-91)

━━ Main oil
tanker routes

Dirty Water

In the developed world most people have access to clean piped water and mains sanitation. In developing countries however, less than half the population has access to safe water. The situation is particularly bad in rural areas. Here many people spend a great deal of time and energy collecting and carrying water.

Clean water is essential for good health. Nearly all diseases in the developing world are due to polluted water and inadequate sanitation. Simple technology and self help schemes could save millions of lives.

RURAL

URBAN

% Population without clean water in the 'developing' countries

% Population without proper sanitation in the 'developing' countries

Access to Drinking Water

ALGERIA 88%
80%
100%

North
South

INDIA 56%
43%
80%

ECUADOR 47%
16%
75%

ZAÏRE 9%
5%
15%

KENYA 28%
21%
61%

INDONESIA 36%
30%
53%

South
North

ARGENTINA 64%
17%
72%

% of population with access to safe drinking water
- Over 85
- 50-85
- 15-49
- Under 15
- No data

Rural

Urban

Pie charts show examples of the variation in access to clean water between rural and urban population.

The Great Lakes

The Great Lakes in North America are the largest freshwater reservoir in the world. Some years ago they were threatened by large quantities of sewage and other pollution. Although this problem has been solved, the level of toxic chemicals in the water is now causing concern.

The chemicals come from a variety of sources. They are discharged into rivers, seep into the water from waste dumps, fall from the sky as toxic rain and wash off fields treated with fertilisers and pesticides. Sediments in some areas are so toxic they are unsafe to dredge. More than 360 chemicals have been identified in the Great Lakes which are the source of drinking water for 35 million people.

The International Joint Commission, which manages the Great Lakes, has designated forty two 'areas of concern' which need urgent attention. While this will help, it will not stop pollution from happening. In the longer term people need to alter their lifestyles so that they use less chemicals.

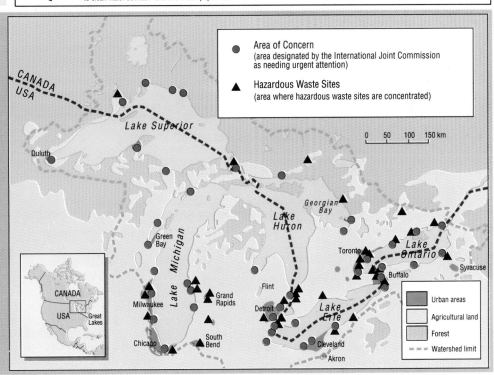

● Area of Concern
(area designated by the International Joint Commission as needing urgent attention)

▲ Hazardous Waste Sites
(area where hazardous waste sites are concentrated)

CANADA
USA

Lake Superior

Duluth

0   50   100   150 km

Georgian Bay

Lake Huron

Green Bay

Lake Michigan

Toronto

Lake Ontario

Syracuse

Buffalo

Flint

Grand Rapids

Detroit

Milwaukee

Lake Erie

CANADA

USA

Great Lakes

Chicago

South Bend

Cleveland

Akron

- Urban areas
- Agricultural land
- Forest
- Watershed limit

CONSERVING WILDLIFE

The Threat to Wildlife

Scientists believe there are between five and thirty million plant and animal species in the world. They estimate half of them could become extinct within the next sixty years. Thousands of plants and creatures are officially classed as endangered. There are many different threats to wildlife:

Pesticides pass through the food chain killing birds of prey and other higher forms of life

Toxic waste dumped in the sea builds up in the bodies of seals and dolphins making them vulnerable to disease

Hunting has devastated stocks of many valuable species such as elephants, whales and crocodiles

Habitat destruction has seriously affected many thousands of species as people claim new areas for farming and urban development.

Protected Areas

NUMBER OF PARKS AND PROTECTED AREAS DESIGNATED BY 1988

486	587	315	960	1 032		767

WORLD TOTAL = 4 320   168 / 5 /

- ☐ Africa
- ☐ Europe
- ☐ N. America
- ☐ USSR
- ☐ S. America
- ☐ Oceania
- ☐ Asia
- ☐ Antarctica

The world's first national park was created at Yellowstone in the USA in 1872. Now there are over four thousand all over the world. Many have been set up to protect areas of special wildlife and landscape value.

Endangered Wildlife
A selection of the world species at risk

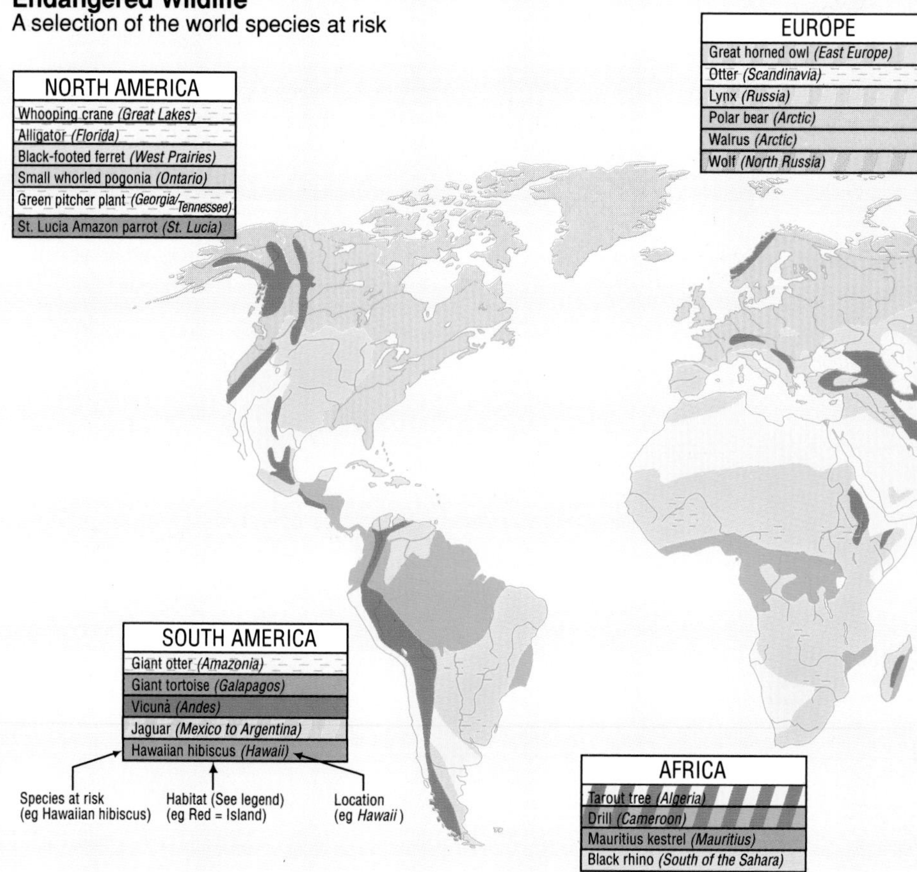

NORTH AMERICA

Whooping crane *(Great Lakes)*
Alligator *(Florida)*
Black-footed ferret *(West Prairies)*
Small whorled pogonia *(Ontario)*
Green pitcher plant *(Georgia/Tennessee)*
St. Lucia Amazon parrot *(St. Lucia)*

EUROPE

Great horned owl *(East Europe)*
Otter *(Scandinavia)*
Lynx *(Russia)*
Polar bear *(Arctic)*
Walrus *(Arctic)*
Wolf *(North Russia)*

SOUTH AMERICA

Giant otter *(Amazonia)*
Giant tortoise *(Galapagos)*
Vicuña *(Andes)*
Jaguar *(Mexico to Argentina)*
Hawaiian hibiscus *(Hawaii)*

Species at risk (eg Hawaiian hibiscus)   Habitat (See legend) (eg Red = Island)   Location (eg *Hawaii*)

AFRICA

Tarout tree *(Algeria)*
Drill *(Cameroon)*
Mauritius kestrel *(Mauritius)*
Black rhino *(South of the Sahara)*

National Parks: The Camargue Regional Park

The marshes and lakes in the Rhône delta in the Camargue in southern France form one of the most important coastal wetlands in Europe. The area has a complex ecology of salt steppe and freshwater lakes. It is famous for its bulls and wild horses, and is the home for many rare birds including bitterns, egrets and harriers.

Since 1942 a third of the natural habitat has been lost, mostly to agriculture, the salt industry and to create areas for hunting. Tourism is putting the area under particular pressure. Hotels and campsites have been set up and the visitors disturb the wildlife. Although most of the money they bring ends up in the hands of developers, some is invested in conservation and protecting wildlife.

LAND USE

- Agricultural land
- Woodland
- Sand
- Marsh
- Industrial salines
- Built-up areas
- Main road
- Railway

St-Gilles
Arles
Petit Rhône
Camargue Regional Park

0   5   10km

CAMARGUE REGIONAL PARK
Étang de Vaccarès
Petit Rhône
Étang de Malagroy
Étang dit l'Impérial
Saintes-Maries-de-la-Mer
Étang de Galabert
Grand Rhône
Port-St-Louis-du-Rhône
Mediterranean Sea

Regional Park boundary

THREATS TO NATURAL HABITAT
- ▲ Tourism
- ⬡ Agriculture
- ● Hunting

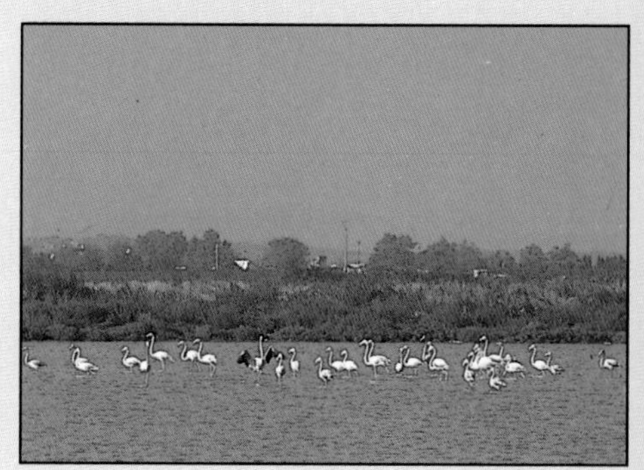

© BARTHOLOMEW

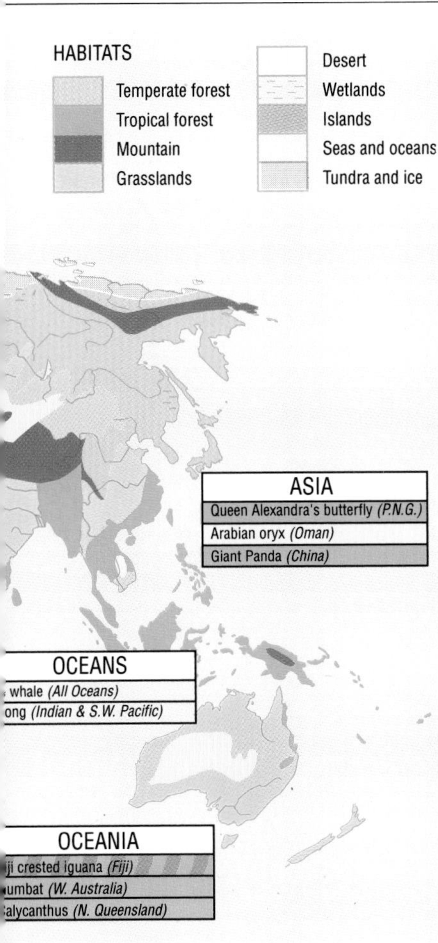

HABITATS

- Temperate forest
- Tropical forest
- Mountain
- Grasslands
- Desert
- Wetlands
- Islands
- Seas and oceans
- Tundra and ice

ASIA
Queen Alexandra's butterfly *(P.N.G.)*
Arabian oryx *(Oman)*
Giant Panda *(China)*

OCEANS
whale *(All Oceans)*
ong *(Indian & S.W. Pacific)*

OCEANIA
ji crested iguana *(Fiji)*
umbat *(W. Australia)*
alycanthus *(N. Queensland)*

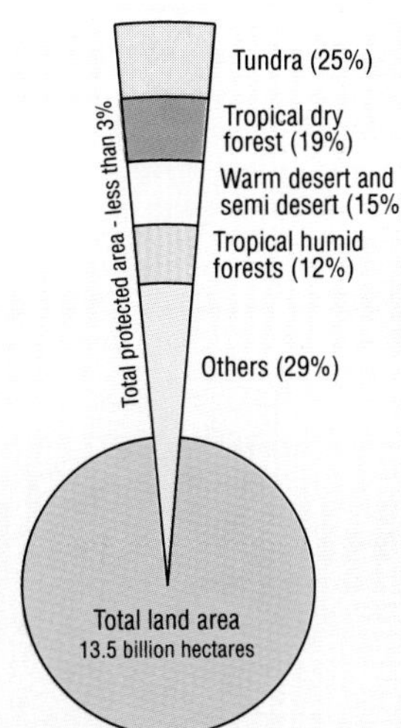

Tundra (25%)

Tropical dry forest (19%)

Warm desert and semi desert (15%)

Tropical humid forests (12%)

Others (29%)

Total protected area - less than 3%

Total land area
13.5 billion hectares

Habitat and Wildlife Protection

All over the world, wildlife is under enormous pressure. The loss of even a single species is a tragedy because it can never be recreated. As more become extinct, the environment is improverished, and unique genetic reserves are lost. Ultimately all life depends directly or indirectly on plants. The rainforests are specially important because they contain half of all known species. It seems certain that many species will disappear without ever being studied.

About 3% of the world's land surface has been made into protected areas. Major conservation initiatives have also been launched at national and international level. Some of them are shown on the maps below.

Biosphere Reserves

Biosphere reserves are a special kind of protected area. They consist of a core region surrounded by a buffer zone and transitional area. Ideally the core consists of a major ecosystem that is large enough to be self containing.

Biosphere reserves concentrate on scientific research and seek to involve local people wherever possible. There were 267 worldwide in 1988 overseen by UNESCO. One of the most successful is the Sierra de Manantlan Reserve in Mexico where scientists are studying a wild species of corn.

Wildlife Ranches

In Zimbabwe the government has set up a new wildlife project called CAMPFIRE. This aims to help local people get the most out of local resources such as trees, grazing land, water and wildlife. Instead of trying to rear cattle on rather unsuitable farmland, some communities now earn a living from managing wildlife.

The policy is paying dividends. It is based on the fact that wildlife is valuable and tourists, photographers and hunters will pay good prices. CAMPFIRE has succeeded by exploiting wildlife as an asset. Many plants and creatures have benefitted as a result.

Global conventions protecting species

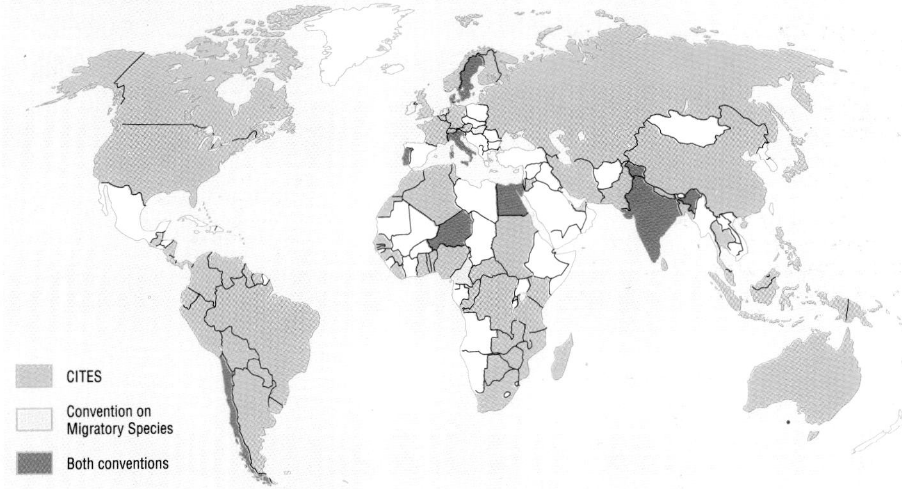

- CITES
- Convention on Migratory Species
- Both conventions

The Convention on International Trade in Endangered Species (CITES) controls world trade in wild plants and animals. The treaty came into force in 1975 and was signed by many countries. However it has proved difficult to stop illegal trade when some countries do not support a ban.

Global conventions protecting habitat

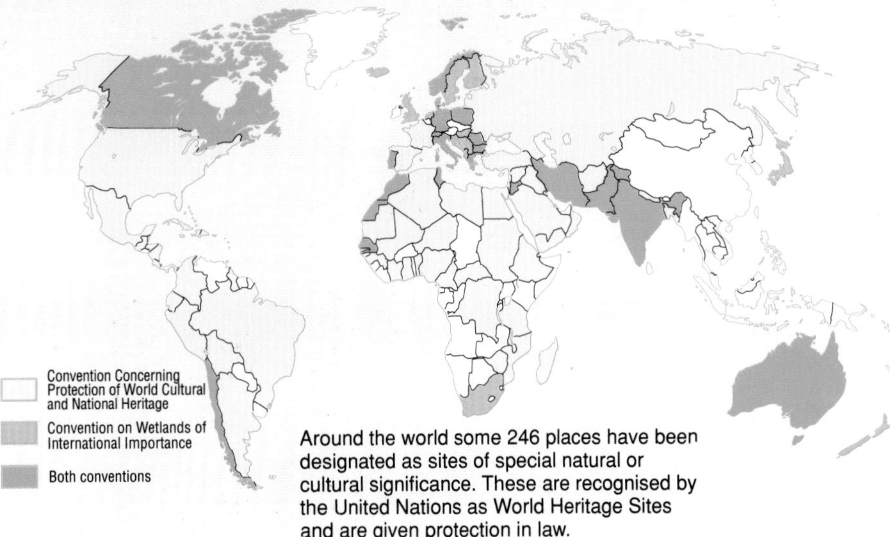

- Convention Concerning Protection of World Cultural and National Heritage
- Convention on Wetlands of International Importance
- Both conventions

Around the world some 246 places have been designated as sites of special natural or cultural significance. These are recognised by the United Nations as World Heritage Sites and are given protection in law.

POLAR ENVIRONMENTS

What are the Polar Regions?

The areas around the North and South Poles are known as the polar regions. They have the coldest and harshest climates on earth. The winters are long and dark and the summers are short. Snow and ice persist in most parts throughout the year.

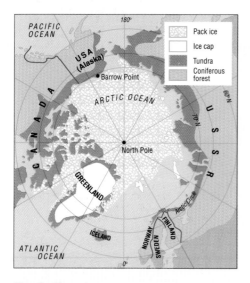

The Arctic

The Arctic consists of a relatively shallow ocean hemmed in by the coast of Asia, Europe and North America. It is covered by a mass of pack ice some three metres thick. To the south lies a frozen wilderness of lakes, marshes and peat bogs known as the tundra.

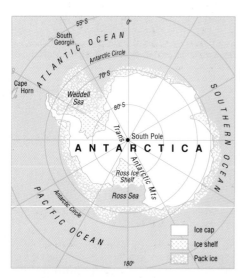

Antarctica

Antarctica is an isolated continent surrounded by oceans. It is covered by a great sheet of ice that extends nearly 1 000 km into the sea in the winter months. The intense cold is one of the mechanisms that drives the circulation of the atmosphere and oceans. In this way Antarctica has a profound influence on the world's climate.

© BARTHOLOMEW

Polar Habitats and Wildlife

Few plants and land creatures survive in the polar regions. The tundra is the only environment to support much life. Here the soil thaws briefly in the summer months allowing grass, moss and lichens to grow.

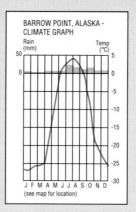

BARROW POINT, ALASKA - CLIMATE GRAPH
(see map for location)

The growing season is extremely short, as indicated on the temperature graph. Marine life is much more abundant. The Arctic Ocean is one of the world's richest fishing grounds, and around Antarctica, the Southern Ocean supports huge populations of krill, seals, whales and sea birds. However, despite the numbers, the food chain is very short and the balance of life delicate.

The Impact of Human Activity

Over the last few hundred years explorers and traders have brought a trail of destruction to the polar regions.

- The great auk, Labrador duck and other arctic species have been hunted to extinction.

- Inuit and other native communities have been disrupted and decimated by disease.

- In the Southern Ocean the survival of some types of whale is endangered by overfishing.

Nowadays more insidious pollution problems are beginning to take their toll.

- Pollution from industrial areas is drawn to the Arctic creating a white haze in the atmosphere.

- In Antarctica scientific bases dispoil their surroundings with huge quantities of rubbish.

- The ozone layer is thinning over polar regions as it is attacked by pollutants.

Waste dump at the US McMurdo base in Antarctica.

Polar regions need special protection because the environment is particularly fragile. In Antarctica, for example it can take ten years for a footprint in the moss to disappear. When life is so finely balanced, even a small disturbance can have a serious consequence.

The Exxon Valdez Disaster, Alaska

In March 1989 a supertanker, the Exxon Valdez, ran aground in Prince William Sound, off the coast of Alaska. It was loaded with 50 million gallons of crude oil. The accident produced a vast slick which eventually drifted 800 km along the coast before breaking up. It killed 32 000 birds, 950 sea otters and millions of fish. The polluted water in the sound is likely to affect fishing stocks for several years.

Sealions on an oil-covered rock after the Exxon Valdez oil spill.

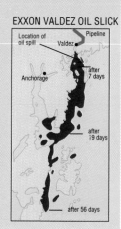

EXXON VALDEZ OIL SLICK

Natural Resources in the Arctic

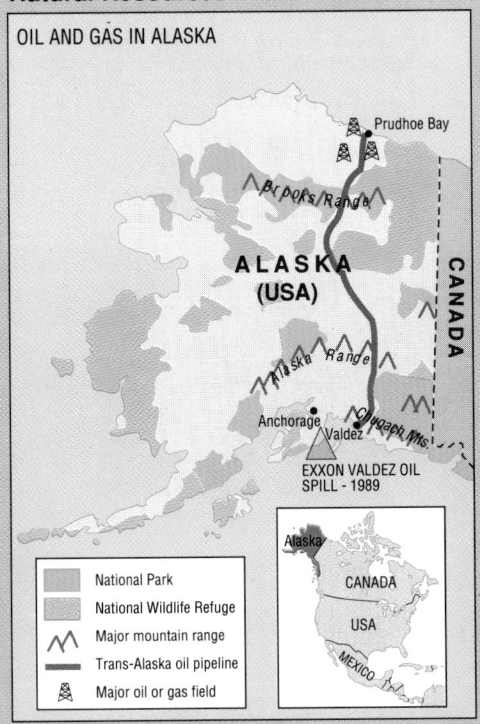

OIL AND GAS IN ALASKA

Prudhoe Bay
Brooks Range
ALASKA (USA)
CANADA
Alaska Range
Anchorage
Valdez
Chugach Mts.
EXXON VALDEZ OIL SPILL - 1989

Alaska
CANADA
USA
MEXICO

- National Park
- National Wildlife Refuge
- Major mountain range
- Trans-Alaska oil pipeline
- Major oil or gas field

Alaska

Oil was discovered in Prudhoe Bay on the north coast of Alaska in the late 1960's. Deciding how to transport it to the cities of the USA was a major problem. Eventually, the decision was made to build a pipeline to the ice-free port of Valdez 1 200 km to the south.

There was a great deal of opposition to the pipeline because of the unspoilt, fragile nature of the land to be crossed. When permission to build was finally given it was on condition that certain design specifications were met. For example, the pipeline was specially insulated and buried underground in places to protect the environment.

The Trans-Alaska pipeline currently delivers a quarter of the domestic oil used in the USA. Yet experts believe it will be operating at 25% capacity by the year 2000 as supplies run low. Other oil and gas reserves have been discovered in Alaska but many of these occur in conservation areas. Further development would conflict with the needs of wildlife which is protected in National Parks and Refuges.

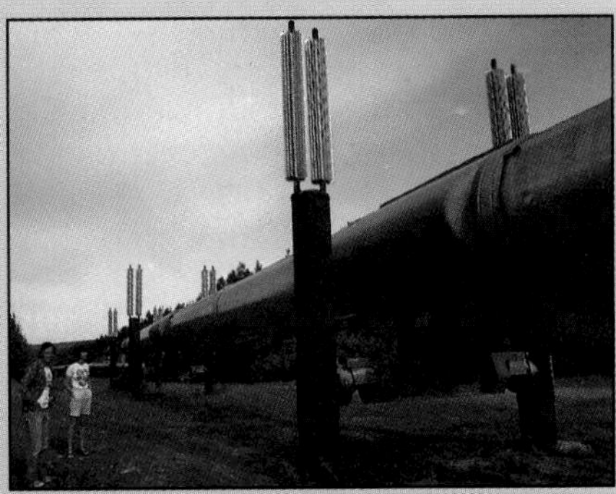

The Trans-Alaska Pipeline System connects North America's largest oil field at Prudhoe Bay to the port of Valdez.

Siberia

In the USSR, Siberia has huge fuel, mineral and timber reserves. Many of these are being exploited at a heavy cost to the environment. Pollution from a nickel works in the Kola Peninsula, for example, has destroyed several thousand square kilometres of forest. The question is how best to reconcile development and conservation.

Antarctica - Economic Resources and Territorial Claims

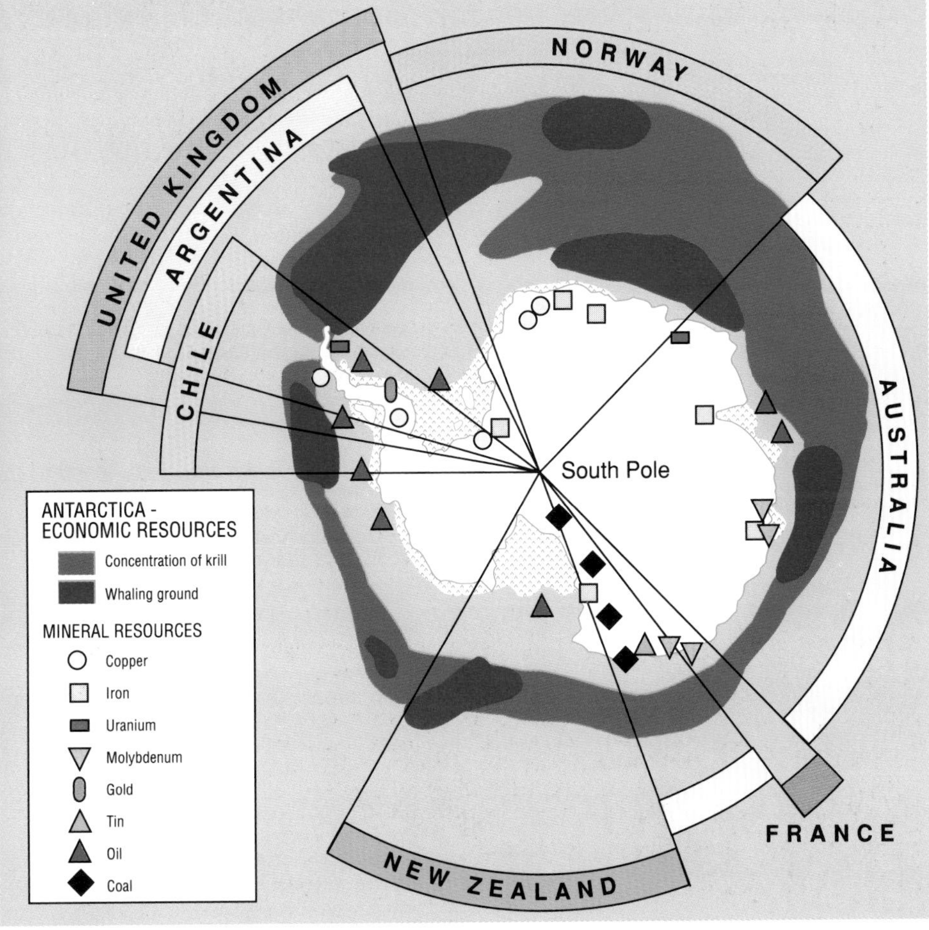

NORWAY
UNITED KINGDOM
ARGENTINA
CHILE
AUSTRALIA
South Pole
FRANCE
NEW ZEALAND

ANTARCTICA - ECONOMIC RESOURCES

- Concentration of krill
- Whaling ground

MINERAL RESOURCES
- ○ Copper
- □ Iron
- ▨ Uranium
- ▽ Molybdenum
- ◖ Gold
- △ Tin
- ▲ Oil
- ◆ Coal

Antarctica is the last great wilderness on earth. It is also rich in natural resources. It has large reserves of iron ore, oil off the coast and a huge coalfield under the Trans-Antarctic Mountains.

Various countries have laid claim to different parts of Antarctica. However, since 1961 the continent has been governed by a special Treaty which has set it aside for peaceful purposes such as scientific research.

Antarctica - World Park

The future of Antarctica hangs in the balance. In the years ahead it could:

- continue to be governed by a Treaty as at present,

- be governed by all nations of the world,

- be made into a world park with a ban on all commercial and military activity.

At a conference in 1991, it was proposed that mining in the continent be prohibited for the next 50 years. This would be an important step towards creating a world park.

NATURAL RESOURCES

What are Natural Resources?

Minerals, water, plants and animals are all natural resources. Human beings depend on exploiting them for their survival.

For thousands of years people only used natural resources in small quantities. With the growth of industry and population demand has escalated. The world now uses three times the amount of minerals that it did in1950. This is putting the environment under more and more pressure.

Renewable Resources

When we use resources we sometimes consume them completely. Many machines, for instance, burn up petrol in order to generate energy. Resources which are used up in this way are said to be non renewable. They include oil, chemicals and a variety of metals.

Other resources can be replaced. Timber, for example, is sometimes grown on plantations which are harvested at regular intervals, and is a renewable resource.

Renewable resources hold the key to the future. Sooner or later all the non renewable supplies will be used up. By contrast, we can go on using renewable resources for ever.

Exploitation of Natural Resources

Natural resources are unevenly distributed around the world. Large countries such as the USA, USSR, China and Australia have good supplies. Some smaller countries also have big reserves. Jamaica and Guinea, for example, have important bauxite mines which provide the raw material for aluminium.

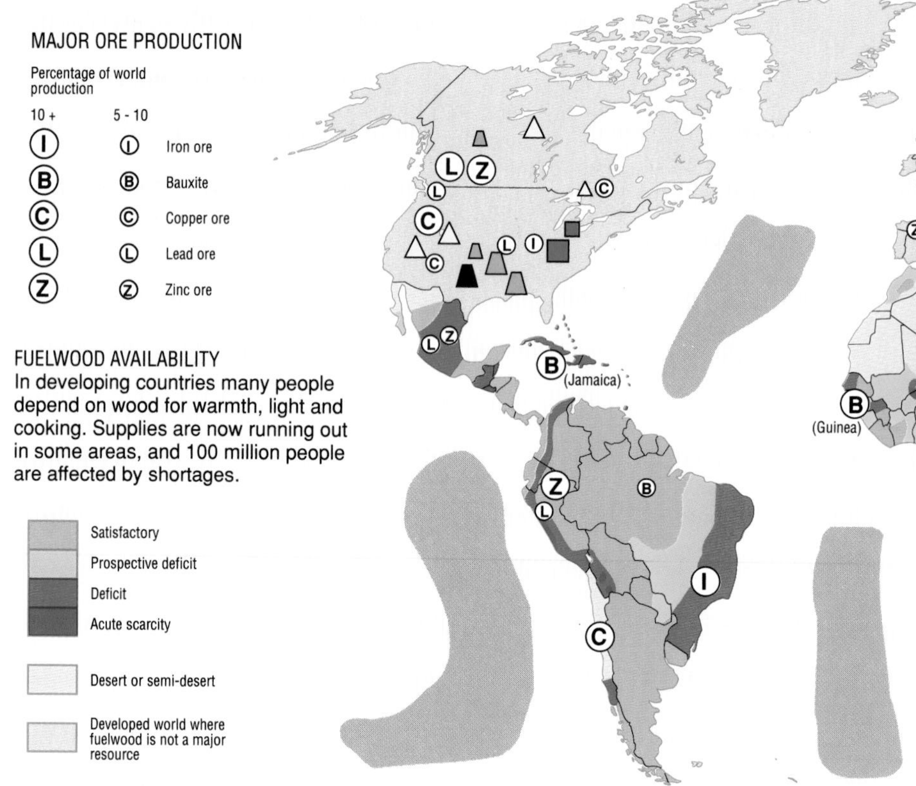

MAJOR ORE PRODUCTION

Percentage of world production

10 +	5 - 10	
I	I	Iron ore
B	B	Bauxite
C	C	Copper ore
L	L	Lead ore
Z	Z	Zinc ore

FUELWOOD AVAILABILITY
In developing countries many people depend on wood for warmth, light and cooking. Supplies are now running out in some areas, and 100 million people are affected by shortages.

- Satisfactory
- Prospective deficit
- Deficit
- Acute scarcity

- Desert or semi-desert

- Developed world where fuelwood is not a major resource

Environmental Issues in Mining

MIning is having a greater and greater effect on the environment. Ugly slag heaps and open pits have left scars in areas of scenic beauty. Subsidence and landslips can be a problem, but even more serious is the damage done to rivers as poisonous metals are washed into the water. This is a cause of concern in Brazil where prospectors are panning for gold in the tributaries of the Amazon.

Many countries have laws to control mining. Some old quarries have been restored to farmland or flooded to create attractive lakes.

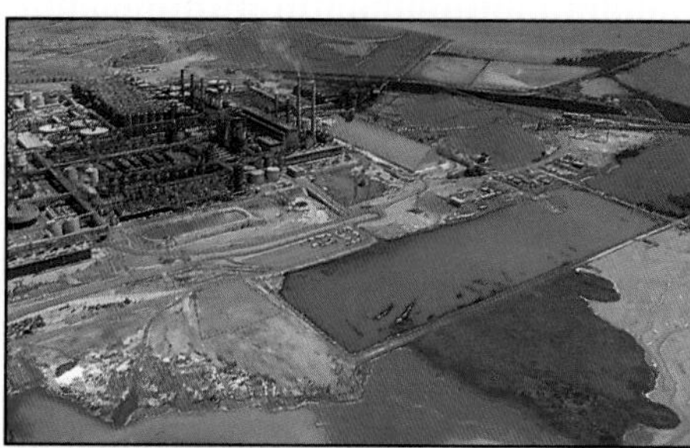

The environmental damage caused by extensive mining.

Uranium Mining in Australia

Australia possesses about one third of the world's economic reserves of uranium.This mineral has become important in the present century as the raw material for nuclear power stations and nuclear weapons. Most of the reserves are concentrated in the Northern Territory. The decision to exploit them was highly controversial.

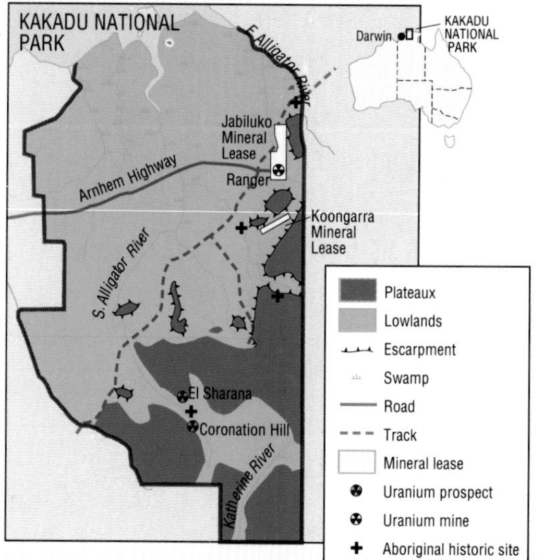

KAKADU NATIONAL PARK

Plateaux	
Lowlands	
Escarpment	
Swamp	
Road	
Track	
Mineral lease	
Uranium prospect	
Uranium mine	
Aboriginal historic site	

Arguments in favour

- The mines earn money and provide employment
- Nuclear power can help solve the world's energy crisis
- Strict safeguards control how the uranium is used

Arguments against

- Nuclear power stations are not safe
- The uranium could fall into the hands of terrorists
- The mines threatened a beautiful area where Aboriginees live

In 1977 the Australian government decided to go ahead with the mines. At the same time it created a National Park in the surrounding area and agreed to give some of the profits to the Aboriginees. Despite this compromise many people are still not satisfied.

NATURAL RESOURCES FROM THE OCEANS

There are large quantities of minerals deep on the ocean floor. Unfortunately these are difficult to get at and exploit.

Metal-rich sediments beneath ocean floor

MAJOR FUEL PRODUCTION

Percentage of world production

10 +	5 - 10	
▲	▲	Petroleum
▲	▲	Natural gas
■	■	Coal
△	△	Uranium

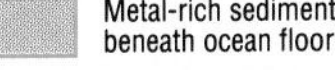

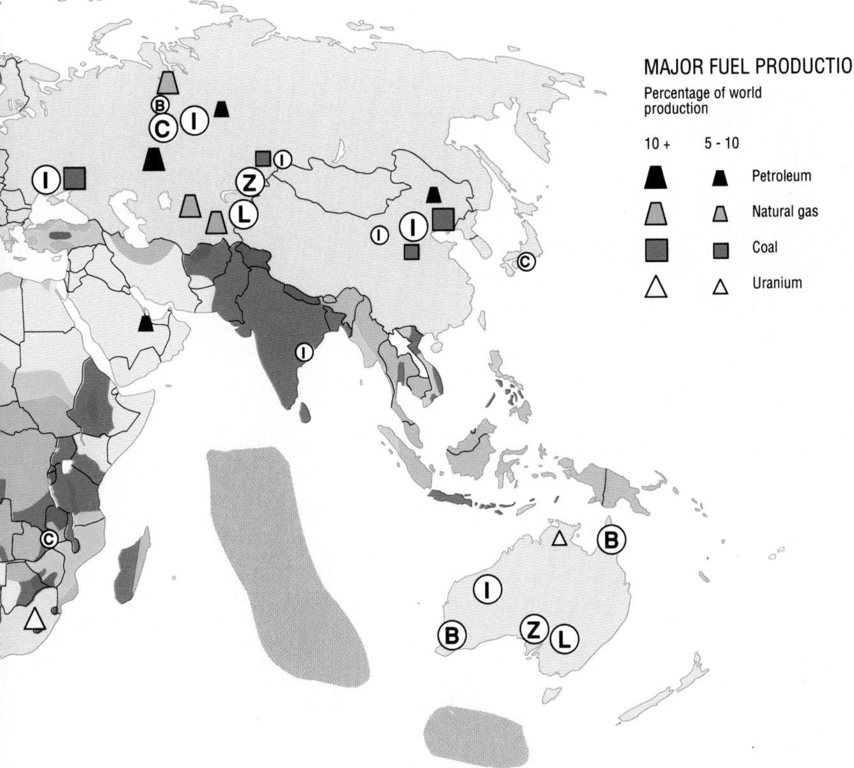

Depleting Resources

Some minerals are plentiful. Reserves of iron ore, for example, should last for 400 years at present rates of consumption. Other minerals are not so abundant and supplies may run low within our lifetime. These include diamonds, silver, gold, tin and zinc. One solution is to look for alternative materials. Another is to recycle waste products so the resources can be used again.

YEARS OF SUPPLY (WITH PRESENT PROVED RESERVES AND CONSUMPTION)

Diamonds, Silver, Gold, Tin, Zinc, Lead, Copper, Antimony, Nickel, Molybdenum, Cobalt, Platinum, Manganese, Bauxite, Chromium, Iron ore

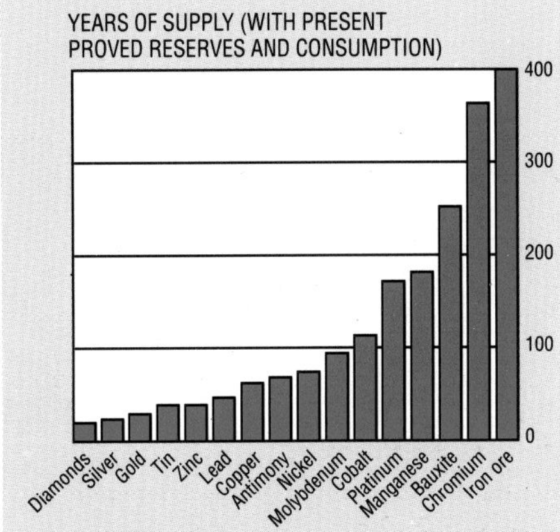

Substitution

In the past, tin was used extensively in the canning and packaging industry. Now that supplies are becoming scarcer alternative materials are being used. Glass, plastics, steel and aluminium have all proved suitable. However, the answer is not always this simple. Manganese is essential for high grade steel and there are no substitutes for chromium and platinum.

Recycling

Most waste products can be recycled. On a domestic level, many people now sort out paper and glass from their household rubbish. In industry, scrap metal provides almost half the iron needed for steel making.

Recycling not only reduces the demand on natural resources, it saves energy, conserves water and reduces pollution. It also helps to solve the problem of waste disposal.

Recycling has enormous scope. As individuals we can all play our part, but governments also need to help by putting taxes on pollution and encouraging conservation.

ENVIRONMENTAL BENEFITS OF RECYCLING

(Percentage reduction)

	ALUMINIUM	PAPER	GLASS
REDUCTION IN ENERGY USE	90-97	23-24	4-32
REDUCTION IN AIR POLLUTION	95	74	20
REDUCTION IN WATER POLLUTION	97	35	-
REDUCTION IN WATER USE	-	58	50

Recycling Aluminium Cans

Aluminium cans are cheap and easy to recycle. It takes twenty times more energy to make new aluminium from bauxite than to use scrap.

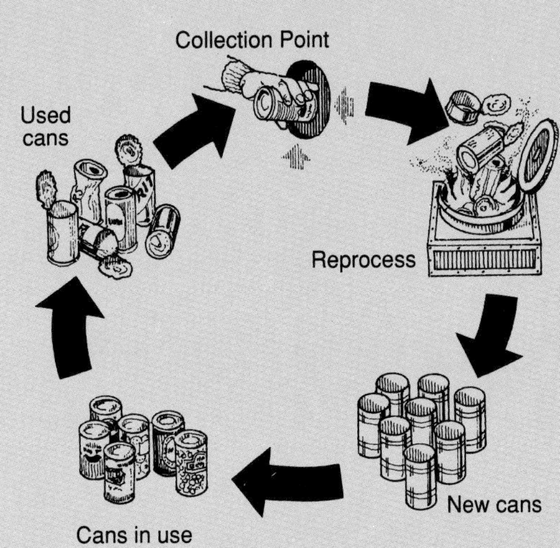

In the USA nearly 80% of aluminium cans are recycled. Other countries, especially in Europe, are beginning to follow suit.

RECYCLING PROCESS

Collection Point

Used cans

Reprocess

New cans

Cans in use

TRENDS IN ALUMINIUM CAN RECYCLING IN USA

Quantity recycled (10³t)

Cans consumed (%)

Quantity recycled

Percentage of consumption

1972 74 76 78 80 82 84 86 88

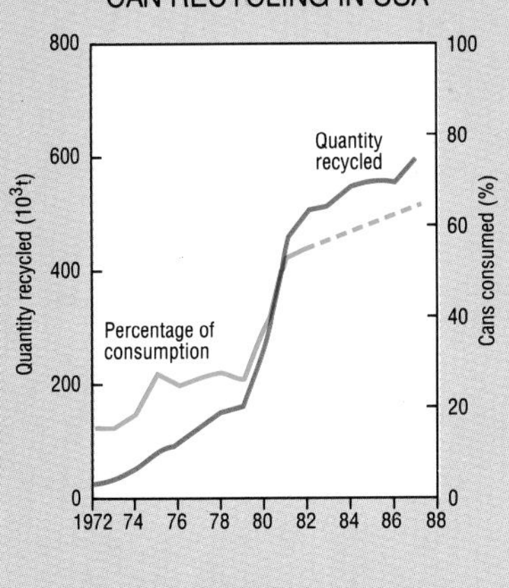

ENERGY

The Energy Problem

We depend on energy for almost everything that we do. Factories, farms, houses and vehicles all need power to make them work.

It was the discovery of new sources of power - chiefly wind, water and coal - which fuelled the Industrial Revolution. Since 1945 the boom in world economic activity has been based largely on oil.

Fossil fuels - coal, oil and gas - provide most of the world's energy. Consumption is very uneven. USA, Western Europe and Japan use nearly three quarters of the total. Africa and South Asia use only small quantities.

Fumes from fossil fuels are responsible for many pollution problems and are major factors in acid rain and global warming. This is one reason why plans to save energy are receiving so much attention. Energy conservation would also help to conserve supplies.

WORLD ENERGY PRODUCTION

Production of kilogram equivalents of all types of energy (Kg per person), 1988

- 30 000 - 120 000
- 2 014 - 29 999
- 300 - 2 013
- 0 - 299
- No data

WORLD ENERGY PRODUCTION

South America
Africa
Australasia
Asia
Europe (in USSR)
North America

Total : 9 350 954 thousand tonnes equivalent

WORLD ENERGY CONSUMPTION

Consumption of kilogram equivalents of all types of energy (Kg per person), 1988

- 8 000 - 20 000
- 1 894 - 7 999
- 500 - 1 893
- 0 - 499
- No data

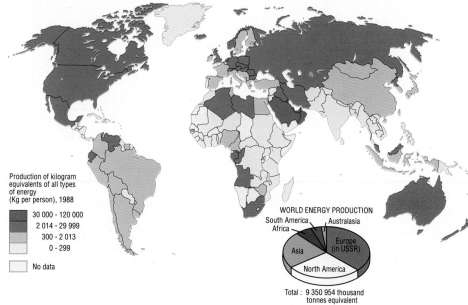

GROWTH IN CONSUMPTION (BY TYPE)

Million tonnes of oil equivalent

3 000 — Oil
2 000 — Coal
— Natural gas
1 000 — Hydro
— Nuclear
0
1972 74 76 78 80 82 84 86 88

© BARTHOLOMEW

Fuel Reserves

Fossil fuels will not last forever. It took a million years to create the fuel we now burn every twelve months. At present rates of consumption the known supplies of oil will be used up in about 45 years. Coal is much more plentiful and will last for several centuries.

WORLD RESERVES (BY TYPE), 1989

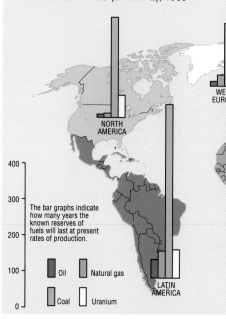

WEST EUROPE

NORTH AMERICA

400

300

The bar graphs indicate how many years the known reserves of fuels will last at present rates of production.

200

100

- Oil
- Natural gas
- Coal
- Uranium

LATIN AMERICA

0

Nuclear Energy

At one time nuclear power appeared to offer almost limitless supplies of cheap and clean electricity. However, there have always been doubts. There was the problem of disposing of nuclear waste and there was the risk of accidents. The catastrophe at Chernobyl in 1986, which spread radiation across the whole of Europe, made the dangers abundantly clear. We now know that electricity from nuclear power is expensive compared to electricity from coal.

In 1989 there were 426 commercial nuclear reactors producing one sixth of the world's electricity. The map shows the number of reactors in the European Community. Countries like France and the UK have invested heavily in nuclear power. Others, like Denmark, Ireland and Greece have never become involved.

NUCLEAR POWER IN THE EC

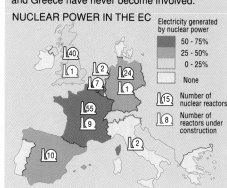

Electricity generated by nuclear power

- 50 - 75%
- 25 - 50%
- 0 - 25%
- None

- 15 Number of nuclear reactors
- 8 Number of reactors under construction

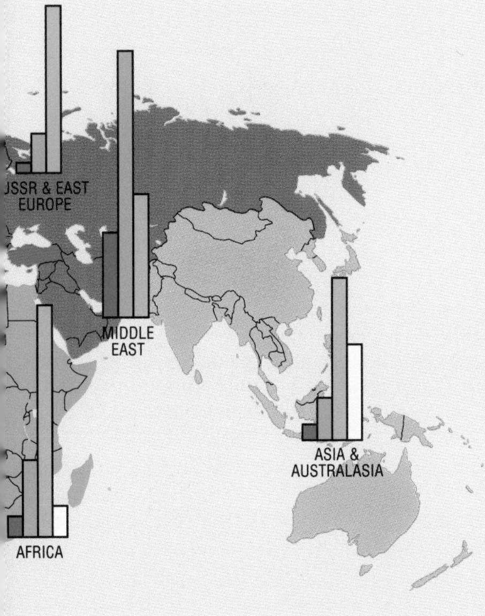

The search for new supplies will almost certainly result in valuable new finds. In addition, developments in technology will make it possible to exploit reserves that are currently uneconomic. The disadvantage is that many of these are likely to be in remote areas and difficult to extract.

Renewable Energy

Fossil fuels are likely to become more expensive as they get scarcer, and nuclear power is surrounded by questions. The alternative is to harness renewable energy from natural sources. This has the added advantage of avoiding the problem of air pollution.

Hydro Power
Hydro power works by storing water in dams to drive turbines. It now provides more than a fifth of the world's electricity. One of the drawbacks of hydro power is that the dams flood good farmland and in hot countries encourage the spread of waterborne diseases.

Solar Power
The simplest way of using the sun's rays is to heat water and buildings. Solar power can be converted into electricity using reflectors. The most promising areas are in the tropics where solar radiation is highest.

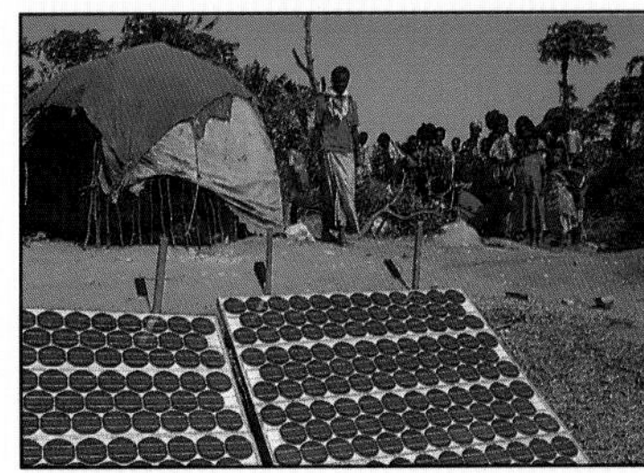

Solar panels for powering a borehole pump, Somali Republic.

Geothermal Power
Hot rocks beneath the earth's surface are a valuable source of energy. Most houses in Iceland are heated with water from underground reservoirs. In the UK experiments are being undertaken in Cornwall and Southampton.

Wind Power *see below*

Wave Power
The motion of the waves can be used to generate electricity. It is estimated that half the UK's supplies could come from an area off northwest Scotland. Much more research is needed but the world's first wave power scheme is operating off the coast of Norway.

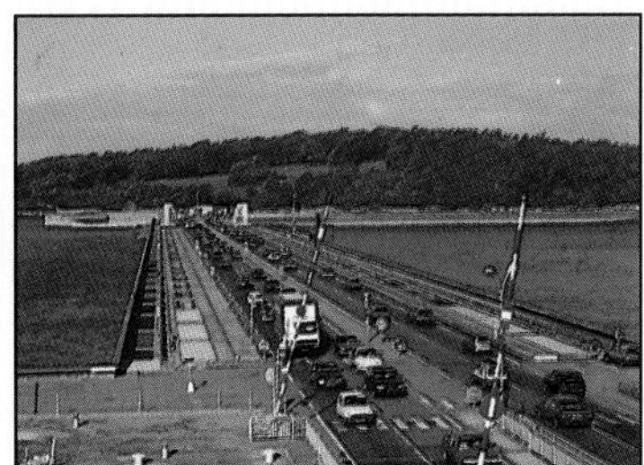

A tidal barrage on the River Rance, Brittany, France.

Tidal Power
Dams can trap sea water as it rises and falls with the tide. Estuaries make the best sites as they have a large tidal range. A dam on the Severn estuary could generate 5% of the UK's electricity but would cause ecological problems.

Biomass Power
Rotting waste matter from plants and animals produces methane which can be collected in tanks and used as fuel. In some places special power stations run on crop waste. India, Malaysia, the Philippines and the USA, for example, have power stations which burn rice husks.

Wind Power in the United Kingdom

LOCATION OF UK WIND DEVELOPMENTS

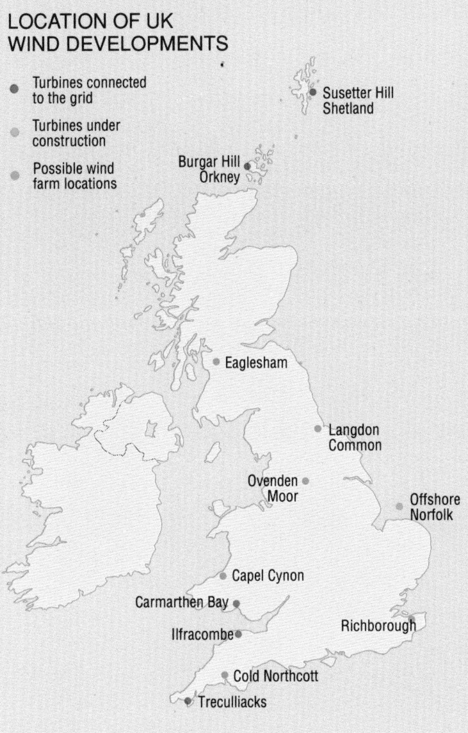

- Turbines connected to the grid
- Turbines under construction
- Possible wind farm locations

Susetter Hill Shetland
Burgar Hill Orkney
Eaglesham
Langdon Common
Ovenden Moor
Offshore Norfolk
Capel Cynon
Carmarthen Bay
Ilfracombe
Richborough
Cold Northcott
Treculliacks

Modern wind turbines can harness the power of the wind, much as windmills did in the past. Coasts and mountains are the best sites as the turbines need winds of over 25km per hour to make them work. Unfortunately, as shown on the map, these coincide with many of the UK's most scenic areas. Off shore locations might provide a solution.

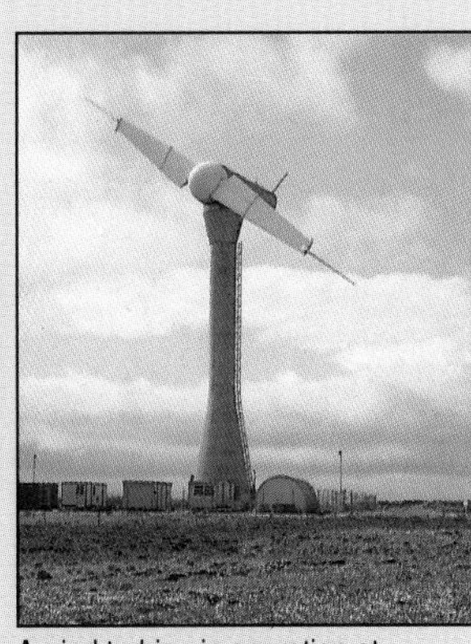

A wind turbine in operation at Burgar Hill, Orkney.

Ovenden Moor Wind Farm

At Ovenden Moor in West Yorkshire, a local company plans to build a wind farm with 35 turbines. The turbines will be about 30 metres high and painted so they blend in with the landscape. The site is on windy moorland remote from towns and villages.

Some people are worried about how the scheme will affect the landscape. They are also concerned about the disruption to a peaceful part of the country. A proposed wind farm in mid Wales has met with similar objections.

LOCATION MAP OF PROPOSED SITE

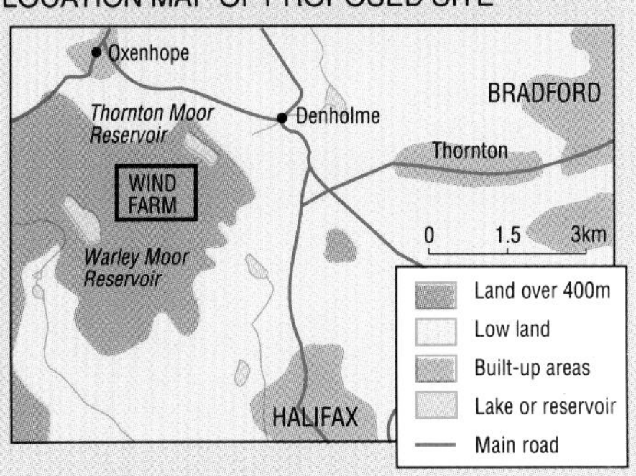

Oxenhope
Thornton Moor Reservoir
Denholme
BRADFORD
Thornton
WIND FARM
Warley Moor Reservoir
HALIFAX

0   1.5   3km

- Land over 400m
- Low land
- Built-up areas
- Lake or reservoir
- Main road

FOOD AND NUTRITION

Food Supply - A Problem of Poverty

There is enough food to feed all the people in the world. Production has more than doubled since the 1950's. Yet despite this, one person in five suffers from serious hunger. Most of the victims live in developing countries. They are either unable to grow the food they need, or too poor to buy it.

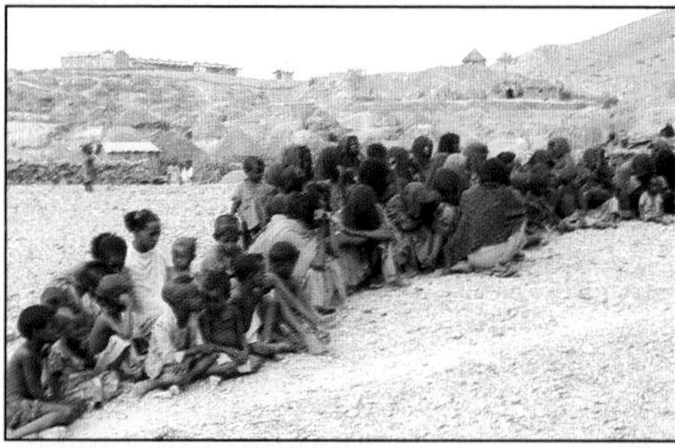

Queueing for food - Ethiopian famine

Thousands of people died in the Ethiopian famine of 1984, yet there was plenty of food in the area for those who could afford it.

Who Gets the Food?

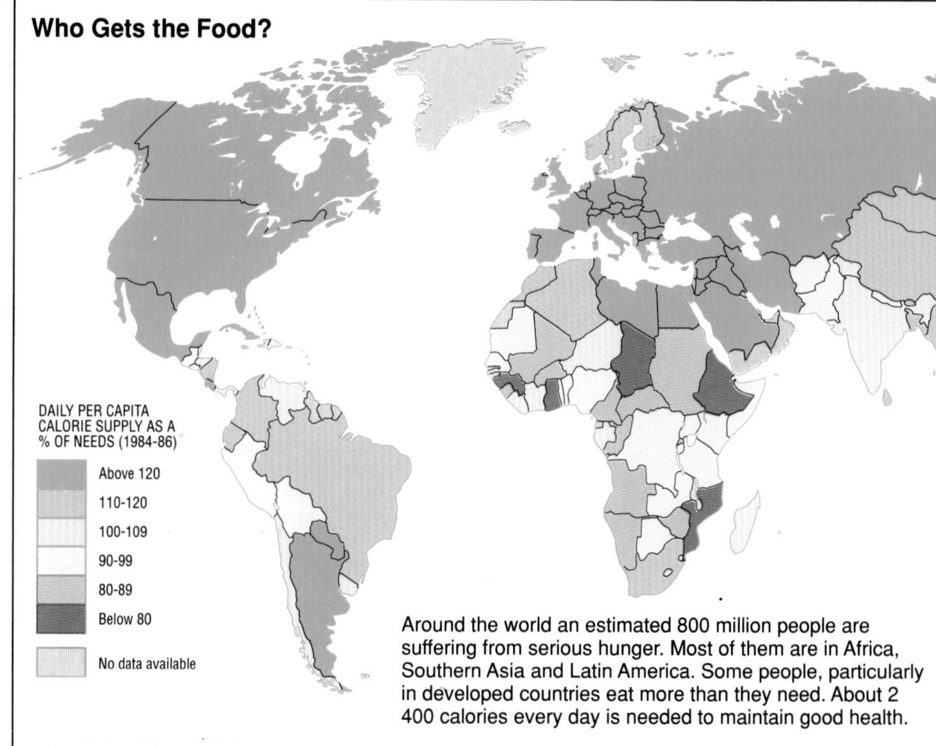

DAILY PER CAPITA CALORIE SUPPLY AS A % OF NEEDS (1984-86)

- Above 120
- 110-120
- 100-109
- 90-99
- 80-89
- Below 80
- No data available

Around the world an estimated 800 million people are suffering from serious hunger. Most of them are in Africa, Southern Asia and Latin America. Some people, particularly in developed countries eat more than they need. About 2 400 calories every day is needed to maintain good health.

The Real Causes of Hunger

Land Ownership
Farmland is distributed very unevenly. A few rich people and transnational companies own huge tracts but millions of peasants are landless and cannot support themselves.

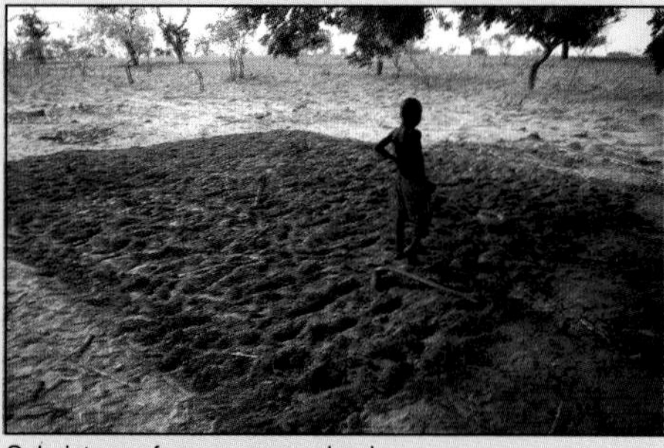

Subsistence farmer on poor land

Cash Crops
Some of the poorest countries in the world rely on selling cash crops, such as sugar and tea, to pay off their debts and buy machinery. These crops are grown on the best land, forcing local farmers to go elsewhere.

Natural Disasters
Natural disasters such as floods and famines seem inevitable. In fact they can be made worse by short-sighted farming and forestry policies.

Diet
More than a third of the grain in the world goes to feed animals. World hunger could be reduced immediately if some of this was fed directly to humans.

Mistaken Policies
In developing countries some governments supply city dwellers with cheap food. This keeps prices down and means that farmers have no incentive to grow more than they need for themselves.

War
War has disrupted agriculture in many parts of the developing world. The result is disasterous. Crops are left unharvested, villages abandoned and refugees flood into the cities.

Subsidies
In North America and Western Europe governments subsidise farmers. This causes surpluses, pushes prices down on world markets and forces people in poorer countries to overuse their land in order to survive. Food aid can have a similar effect. The photo below shows 'surplus' tomatoes being dumped on a farm in Italy.

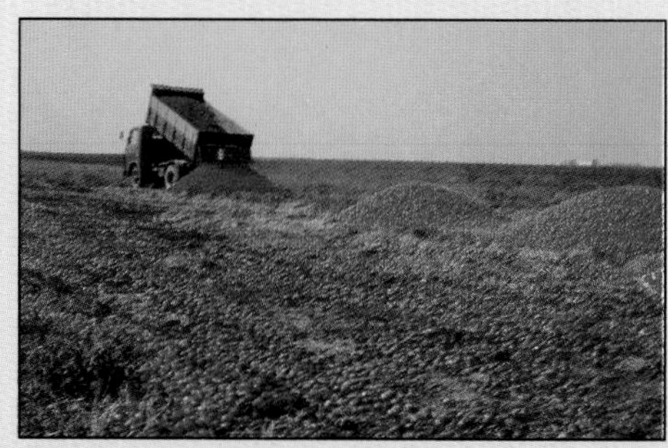

Zimbabwe - Improving Food Security

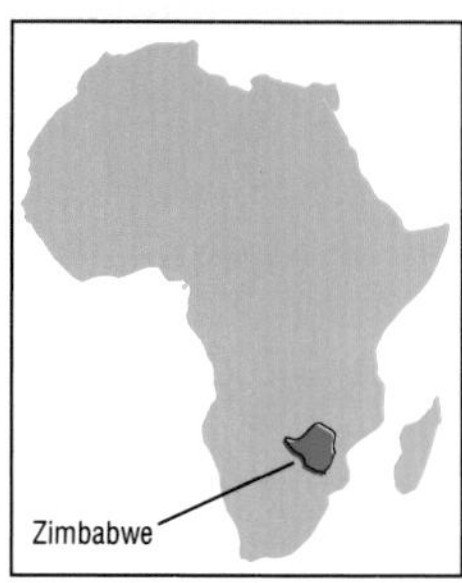

Zimbabwe

Since becoming independent in 1980, Zimbabwe has made agriculture one of its main priorities. The government has encouraged small farmers and reduced dependence on cash crops.

The measures taken include:

- redistributing land from large estates
- improving the status of women, many of whom run farms
- making more loans available
- promoting research into seeds and fertilisers
- putting up the price of crops

Advances in Agriculture

INDEX OF FOOD OUTPUT 1977-87

Average 1979-81 = 100

(Line graph showing indices from 1977 to 1987, with lines labelled Developing, World, Developed. Y-axis from 85 to 135.)

INDEX OF FOOD OUTPUT PER HEAD 1977-87

Average 1979-81 = 100

(Line graph showing indices from 1977 to 1987, with lines labelled Developing, World, Developed. Y-axis from 90 to 115.)

Remarkable changes have been made in agriculture over the last fifty years. Using new seeds and fertilisers, bumper crops have been produced in many parts of the world. The most dramatic results have been in Latin America and Asia. Here many countries have doubled production of three main cereal crops - wheat, rice and maize. This is known as the Green Revolution.

The graphs to the left show how food output in developing countries has increased dramatically since 1980 compared to the developed world. In the last few years however, the increase in output has tailed off. Since 1986, it has not kept pace with population growth.

The Green Revolution has only been achieved at a cost. The new seeds are expensive and can be vulnerable to disease. Fertilisers and pesticides are also expensive and cause pollution and soil degradation. For these reasons attention is now switching to organic methods which have been used with remarkable success by the Chinese.

Under this system crop wastes are recycled, weeds are kept down by biological methods and soil is conserved through terracing and forestry. Instead of trying to control natural forces, organic farming works with them. As the environment comes under more and more pressure, this approach appears increasingly attractive.

PROBLEMS OF ADVANCED AGRICULTURE

POLLUTION
- Agrochemicals reach and pollute water system

PESTICIDE POISONING
- Toxins build up in wildlife feeding on sprayed crops (and accumulate up the food chain)
- Farm workers may suffer effects of harmful chemicals

CONCENTRATION OF LAND OWNERSHIP
- New methods are more capital intensive and suited to farming large areas - small farms lose out

DEPLETION OF GROUNDWATER STOCKS
- New crop varieties require vast amounts of water for irrigation

EROSION AND DESERTIFICATION
- Monoculture, deforestation, ploughing and overcropping all encourage erosion

RESEARCH BIAS
- Research often funded by companies who produce and sell new hybrids and agrochemicals
- Traditional crops and farming methods rarely considered

LOSS OF GENETIC DIVERSITY
- Wide variety of traditional crops replaced by a few new hybrids
- Increase in use of monoculture

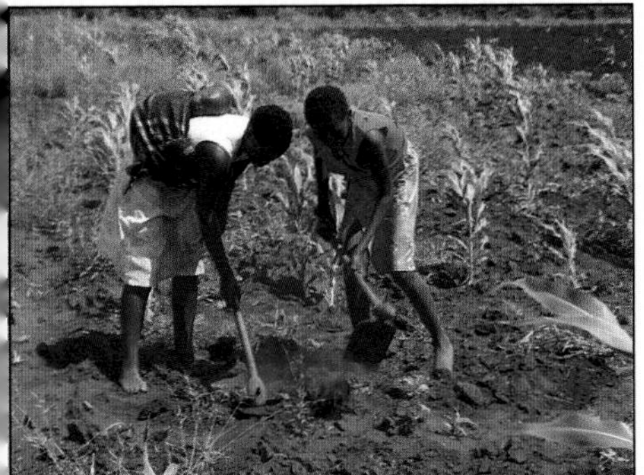

Women working the land

This policy has proved highly successful, particularly in cereal production. While most of Africa suffers from food shortages, Zimbabwe has produced record harvests. Not only is the country self sufficient, it also exports a surplus.

CROP YIELD - CEREALS

CEREALS	(a) 1964-66	1974-76	(b) 1984-86	a ›› b change
WORLD	1 549	1 952	2 552	65%
AFRICA	845	1 004	1 077	28%
ZIMBABWE	897	1 412	1 460	63%

Yield in kg per hectare

Unequal Shares

In rich countries many people eat more than they need. Elsewhere people go hungry. It is one of the scandals of modern times that poor nations, where people are starving, export food to nations that have too much.

The map shows the pattern of food and trade around the world. What it doesn't show is the vast differences within countries. Some sections of the population have access to many more resources than others. Even in a poor country a few rich people live very well indeed.

FOOD AND TRADE

- Enough food and net food exports
- Enough food due to net food imports
- Insufficient food and net food imports
- Insufficient food and net food exports
- No data available

(Enough/insufficient food = above/below recommended levels of protein intake)

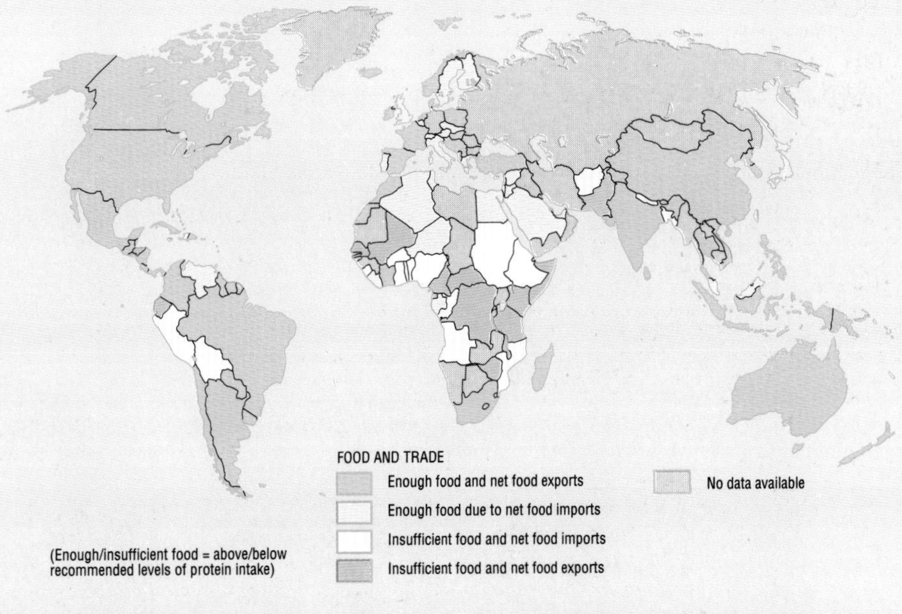

Improved methods of food farming are unlikely to solve the food crisis on their own. What are needed are political and economic reforms. Many developing countries are forced to sell cash crops to pay off their debts while people starve at home. Not only is this morally wrong, it is putting the environment under untold stress.

HEALTH AND DISEASE

Health for all?

We tend to take good health for granted. Yet we have only to become ill, to realise health is fundamental to our lives.

There is no simple way of measuring the health of a nation. One approach is to compare statistics. These show that in some rich countries people can expect to live nearly twice as long as in poor ones. Clearly health is very unevenly distributed around the world.

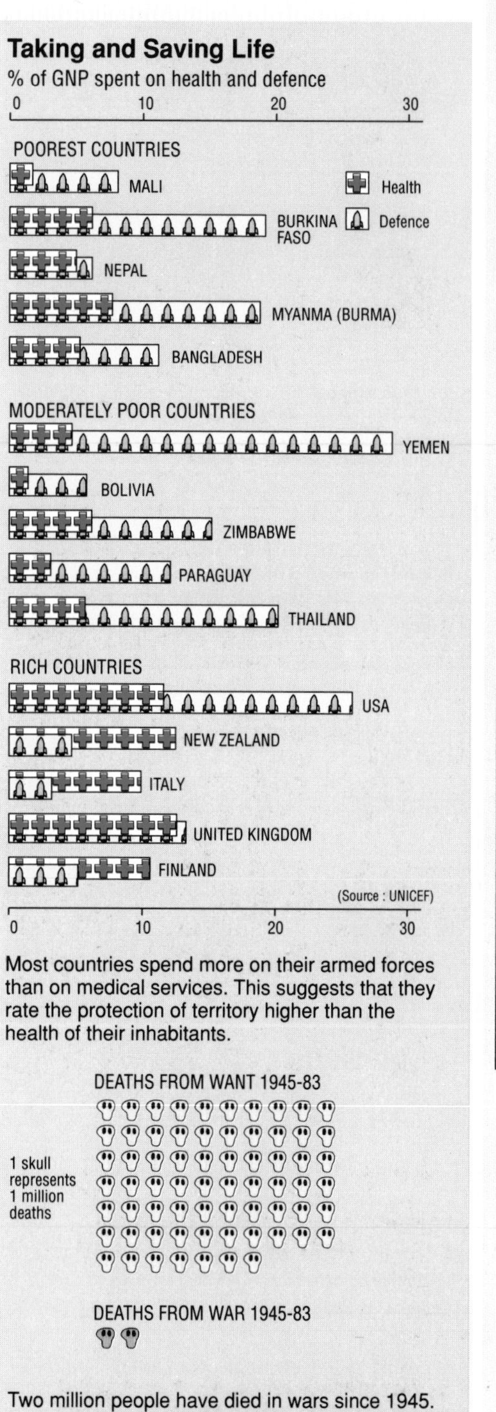

Taking and Saving Life
% of GNP spent on health and defence

POOREST COUNTRIES
MALI — Health
BURKINA FASO — Defence
NEPAL
MYANMA (BURMA)
BANGLADESH

MODERATELY POOR COUNTRIES
YEMEN
BOLIVIA
ZIMBABWE
PARAGUAY
THAILAND

RICH COUNTRIES
USA
NEW ZEALAND
ITALY
UNITED KINGDOM
FINLAND

(Source : UNICEF)

Most countries spend more on their armed forces than on medical services. This suggests that they rate the protection of territory higher than the health of their inhabitants.

DEATHS FROM WANT 1945-83

1 skull represents 1 million deaths

DEATHS FROM WAR 1945-83

Two million people have died in wars since 1945. Lack of food, water and sanitation have caused nearly twenty times that number of deaths.

Diseases of the Rich and Poor

In the rich countries of the 'North' most people can expect to live to a ripe old age. The most common diseases are heart disease and cancer, often brought on by stress, lack of exercise, smoking and bad diet. In the poor countries of the 'South' people are likely to die much earlier. Lack of food (malnutrition) and dirty water are the cause of many illnesses. Children are especially vulnerable.

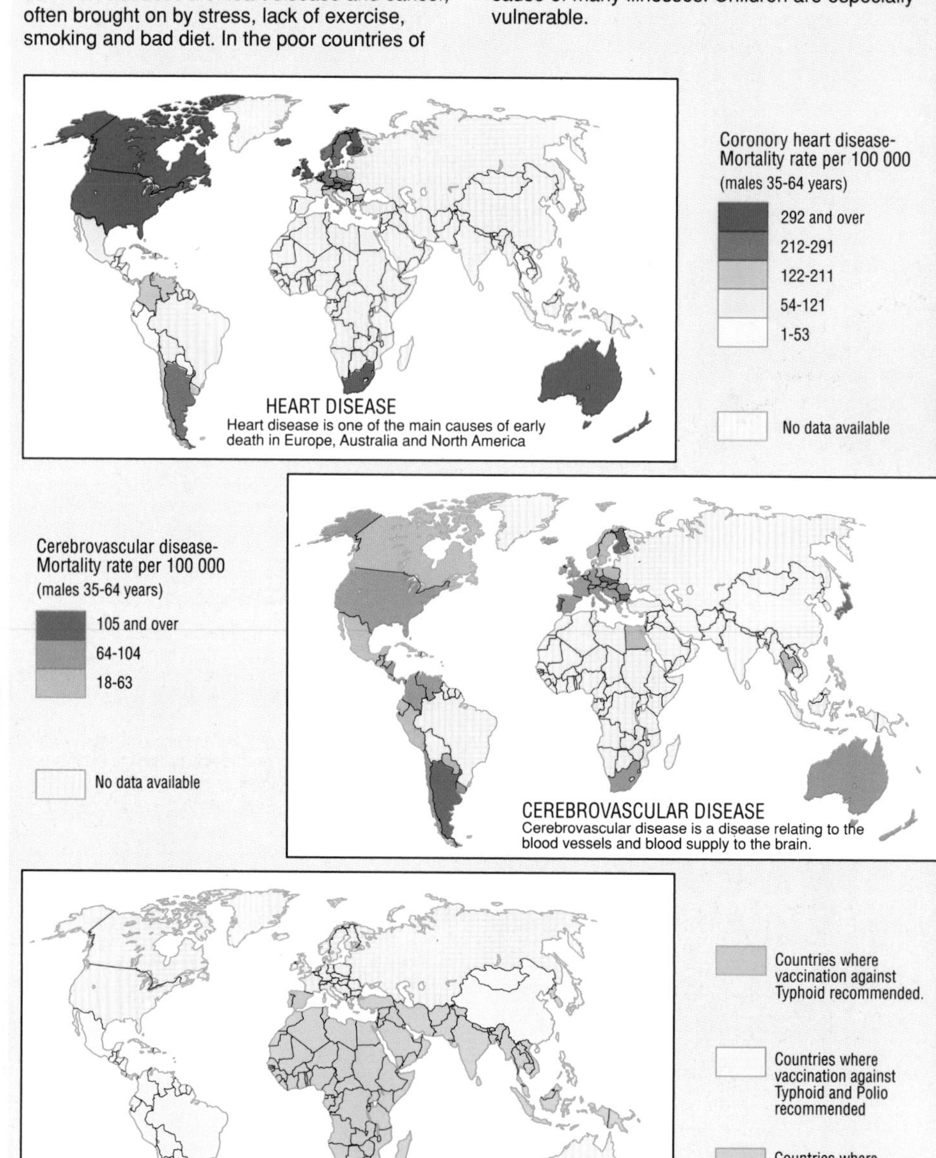

Coronory heart disease-
Mortality rate per 100 000
(males 35-64 years)

292 and over
212-291
122-211
54-121
1-53

No data available

HEART DISEASE
Heart disease is one of the main causes of early death in Europe, Australia and North America

Cerebrovascular disease-
Mortality rate per 100 000
(males 35-64 years)

105 and over
64-104
18-63

No data available

CEREBROVASCULAR DISEASE
Cerebrovascular disease is a disease relating to the blood vessels and blood supply to the brain.

Countries where vaccination against Typhoid recommended.

Countries where vaccination against Typhoid and Polio recommended

Countries where vaccination against Typhoid, Polio and Cholera recommended

TYPHOID, CHOLERA AND POLIO
Typhoid, cholera and polio are some of the diseases spread by dirty water.

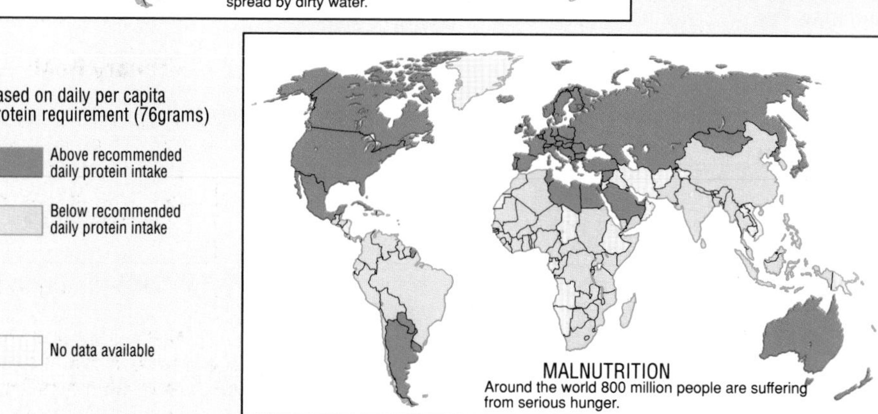

Based on daily per capita protein requirement (76grams)

Above recommended daily protein intake

Below recommended daily protein intake

No data available

MALNUTRITION
Around the world 800 million people are suffering from serious hunger.

Malaria

Malaria is a disease caused by a parasite and is spread from person to person by a mosquito. Half the world's population is at risk from malaria and 800 million suffer from it each year. Africa and the tropics are the worst affected. Recently cases have also been reported in the eastern Mediterranean.

Bilharzia

Bilharzia is an infection of the blood stream by parasites. It is carried by snails living in water and is passed to humans through dirty water. It affects 200 million people around the world sapping the energy of those who are infected.

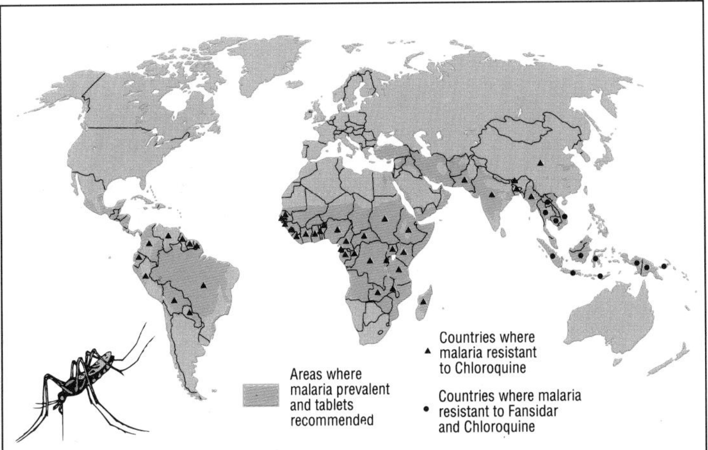

Areas where malaria prevalent and tablets recommended

▲ Countries where malaria resistant to Chloroquine

● Countries where malaria resistant to Fansidar and Chloroquine

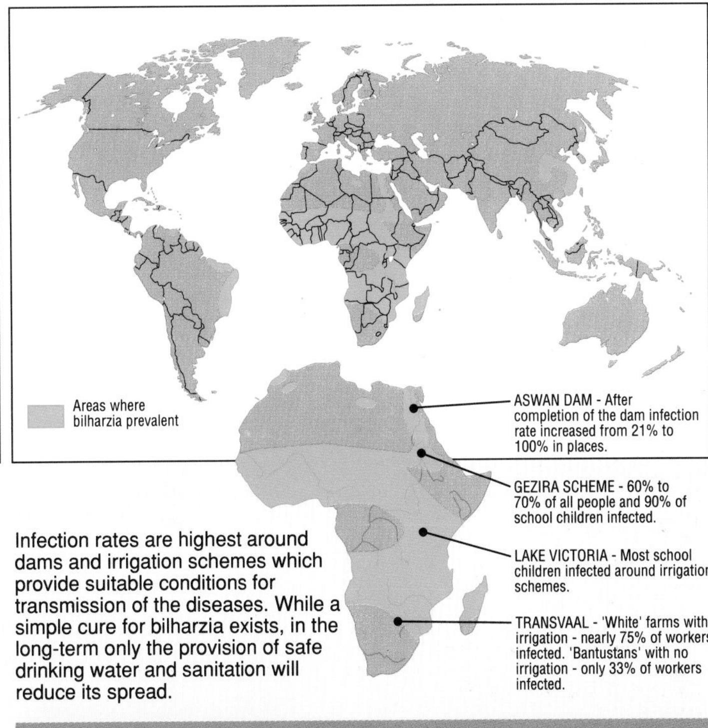

Areas where bilharzia prevalent

ASWAN DAM - After completion of the dam infection rate increased from 21% to 100% in places.

GEZIRA SCHEME - 60% to 70% of all people and 90% of school children infected.

LAKE VICTORIA - Most school children infected around irrigation schemes.

TRANSVAAL - 'White' farms with irrigation - nearly 75% of workers infected. 'Bantustans' with no irrigation - only 33% of workers infected.

Health Care

It is often more effective to put money into keeping people healthy than spending it on curing diseases. In the 'North' this means getting people to changes their life styles. Smoking, over-eating and the consumption of sugar, salt, fatty foods and alcohol are the main problems. Advertising campaigns can help spread the message.

In the 'South' most diseases are spread by dirty water. Better supplies and improved sanitation could save many lives. Better education and community health workers are also very effective. As it is, most governments spend their money on hospitals, doctors and expensive drugs. The diagram below shows how this only benefits a minority of people, most of them city dwellers.

Infection rates are highest around dams and irrigation schemes which provide suitable conditions for transmission of the diseases. While a simple cure for bilharzia exists, in the long-term only the provision of safe drinking water and sanitation will reduce its spread.

INVERTED VALUES
Public health expenditure and populations in poor countries 1985

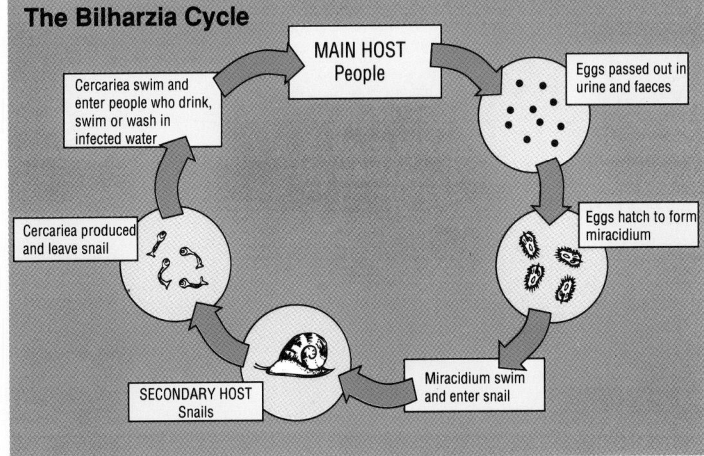

Percentage of national budget spent

Percentage of population served

Primary health care

Hospital care

The Bilharzia Cycle

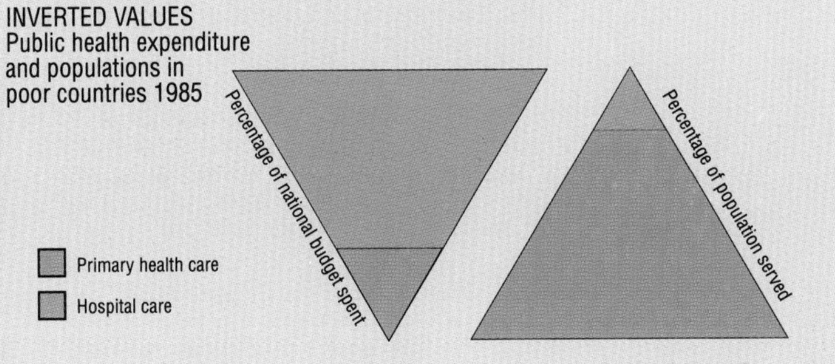

MAIN HOST People

Cercariea swim and enter people who drink, swim or wash in infected water

Eggs passed out in urine and faeces

Cercariea produced and leave snail

Eggs hatch to form miracidium

SECONDARY HOST Snails

Miracidium swim and enter snail

ORT

Every year five million children under the age of five die from dehydration caused by diarrhoea. A cheap and simple treatment has now been discovered which could save many of these lives. Known as Oral Rehydration Therapy (ORT), it consists of a mixture of sugar, water and salts. The challenge is to show parents how to use it. Already it may be preventing a million deaths a year.

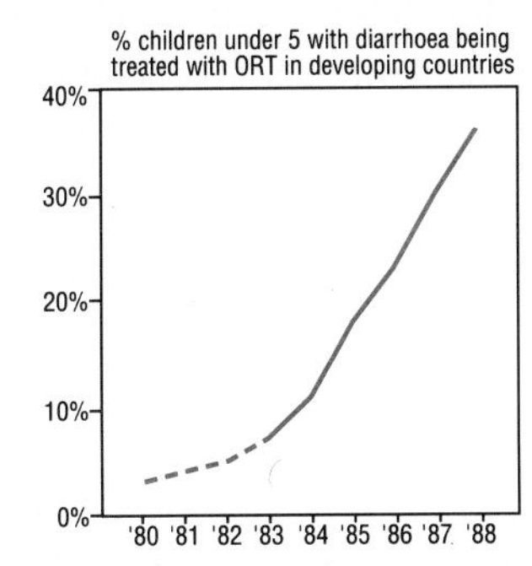

% children under 5 with diarrhoea being treated with ORT in developing countries

40%
30%
20%
10%
0%
'80 '81 '82 '83 '84 '85 '86 '87 '88

Primary Health Care

Many other diseases which affect poor countries can be treated without great expense. Immunisation, better education and simple methods of treatment could make an enormous difference. This approach, which works through the family and community, is known as primary health care.

The fight against disease

Some diseases have been eliminated. Smallpox, for example, has disappeared through vaccination. After the war great progress was made in controlling malaria. However the mosquito and bilharzia could increase if global warming is a reality.

EDUCATION

Education is more than just attending a class at school. It is a lifelong process which begins with what we learn as infants and continues into our old age. One of the chief values of schools is that it allows people to make sense of their experience.

The map shows how many children attend in schools around the world. There are many countries, especially in Africa, where less than half of all children receive a basic education. This is partly due to a shortage of schools in rural areas. Also, very poor families have to send their children to work from a very early age.

Changing Priorities

The best schools teach children about the modern world. In developing countries rural children need to know about soils, water and how to look after the environment. All too often the curriculum is based on the needs of city dwellers and is biased against village communities.

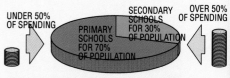

Many countries put money into higher education while the most pressing need is for basic primary teaching. However, the debt crisis has prompted many governments to cut back in this area.

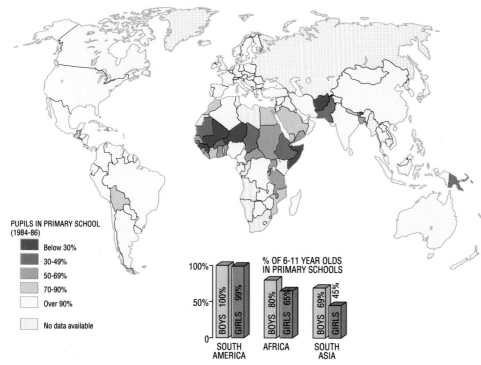

PUPILS IN PRIMARY SCHOOL (1984-86)

- Below 30%
- 30-49%
- 50-69%
- 70-90%
- Over 90%
- No data available

% OF 6-11 YEAR OLDS IN PRIMARY SCHOOLS

SOUTH AMERICA: BOYS 100%, GIRLS 99%
AFRICA: BOYS 80%, GIRLS 65%
SOUTH ASIA: BOYS 69%, GIRLS 45%

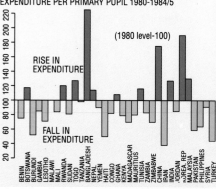

EXPENDITURE PER PRIMARY PUPIL 1980-1984/5

(1980 level-100)

RISE IN EXPENDITURE

FALL IN EXPENDITURE

BENIN, BOTSWANA, BURUNDI, GAMBIA, LESOTHO, MALAWI, MALI, RWANDA, SUDAN, TOGO, TANZANIA, BANGLADESH, NEPAL, YEMEN, HAITI, CONGO, GHANA, KENYA, MADAGASCAR, MAURITIUS, TUNISIA, ZAMBIA, ZIMBABWE, CHINA, IRAN, INDIA, JORDAN, KOREA, REP, MALAYSIA, PAKISTAN, PHILIPPINES, SYRIA, TURKEY

Education and Literacy

Literacy is the ability to read and write. Nowadays this is an essential skill which gives people the knowledge and power to take control of their lives. Around the world there are 900 million illiterate adults. Nearly all of them are in developing countries and two thirds of them are women.

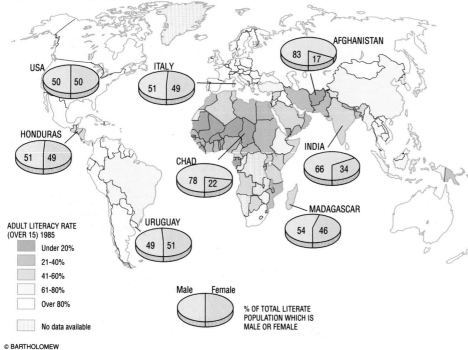

ADULT LITERACY RATE (OVER 15) 1985

- Under 20%
- 21-40%
- 41-60%
- 61-80%
- Over 80%
- No data available

USA 50 / 50
ITALY 51 / 49
AFGHANISTAN 83 / 17
HONDURAS 51 / 49
CHAD 78 / 22
INDIA 66 / 34
MADAGASCAR 54 / 46
URUGUAY 49 / 51

Male / Female

% OF TOTAL LITERATE POPULATION WHICH IS MALE OR FEMALE

Tertiary Education

The establishment of colleges and universities is a vital stage in the development of a country. It provides the opportunity for countries to break out from dependency on the developed world for skills and training, and can lead to a more independent and prosperous society.

However the cost of this is considerable, particularly for the poorer, less developed countries. Despite this, the numbers of students at this level has increased. In 1960 there were only 21 000 university students in the whole of Africa. Now there are over 400 000.

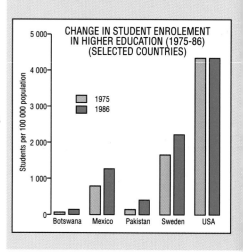

CHANGE IN STUDENT ENROLEMENT IN HIGHER EDUCATION (1975-86) (SELECTED COUNTRIES)

- 1975
- 1986

Students per 100 000 population

Botswana, Mexico, Pakistan, Sweden, USA

© BARTHOLOMEW

Equal Rights for Women

Educating girls is one of the best investments a country can make. To begin with, literate women have a better knowledge of food and nutrition which they pass on to their children and other members of the community. They also tend to have smaller families which reduces the pressure of population. In developing countries many girls never go to school. Those that do enrol often drop out before reaching secondary level. This is because girls are expected to take charge of household affairs or because of domestic reasons. Progress has been made recently but as the map shows many inequalities remain.

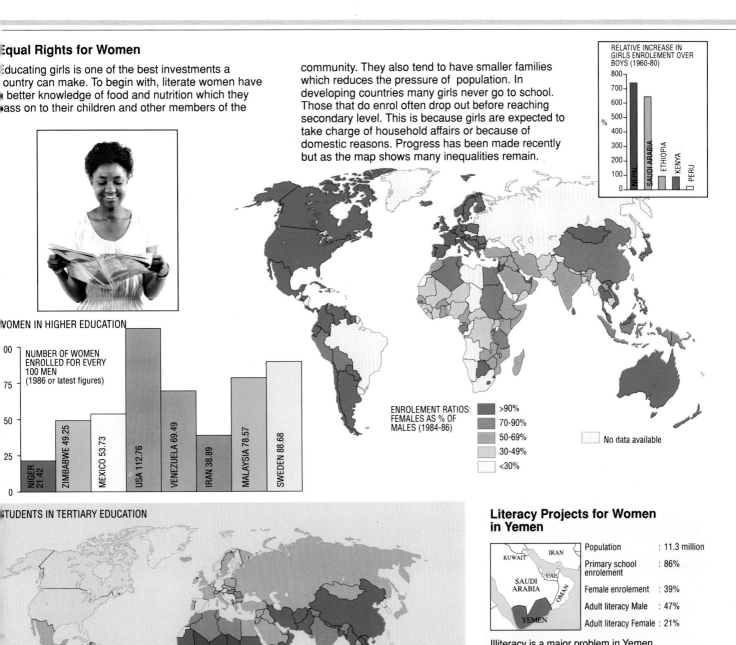

RELATIVE INCREASE IN GIRLS ENROLEMENT OVER BOYS (1960-80)

NEPAL · SAUDI ARABIA · ETHIOPIA · KENYA · PERU

ENROLEMENT RATIOS: FEMALES AS % OF MALES (1984-86)

- >90%
- 70-90%
- 50-69%
- 30-49%
- <30%
- No data available

WOMEN IN HIGHER EDUCATION

NUMBER OF WOMEN ENROLLED FOR EVERY 100 MEN (1986 or latest figures)

- NIGER 21.42
- ZIMBABWE 49.25
- MEXICO 53.73
- USA 112.76
- VENEZUELA 69.49
- IRAN 38.89
- MALAYSIA 78.57
- SWEDEN 88.68

STUDENTS IN TERTIARY EDUCATION

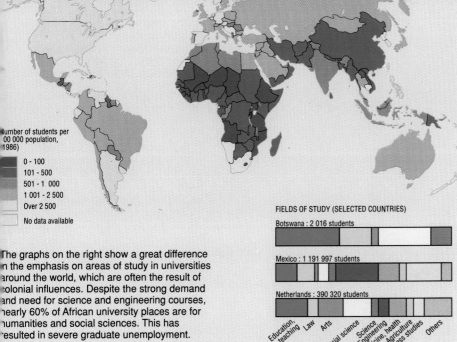

Number of students per 100 000 population, 1986

- 0 - 100
- 101 - 500
- 501 - 1 000
- 1 001 - 2 500
- Over 2 500
- No data available

The graphs on the right show a great difference in the emphasis on areas of study in universities around the world, which are often the result of colonial influences. Despite the strong demand and need for science and engineering courses, nearly 60% of African university places are for humanities and social sciences. This has resulted in severe graduate unemployment.

FIELDS OF STUDY (SELECTED COUNTRIES)

Botswana : 2 016 students

Mexico : 1 191 997 students

Netherlands : 390 320 students

Education, teaching · Law · Arts · Social science · Science · Engineering · Medicine, health · Agriculture · Business studies · Others

Literacy Projects for Women in Yemen

Population	: 11.3 million
Primary school enrolement	: 86%
Female enrolement	: 39%
Adult literacy Male	: 47%
Adult literacy Female	: 21%

Illiteracy is a major problem in Yemen where only about 40% of the total adult population can read. It is particularly high amongst women. Few women are able to complete even primary education because their traditional role is seen to be in the home. Once they are married it is very difficult for them to continue or restart education.

The Government of Yemen, working with aid agencies is attempting to improve the situation by various projects. The main aims are to:

- Introduce rights for women, including prohibiting marriage under 16
- Encourage more girls to attend school
- Set up literacy classes for women who left school early or never attended
- Enable women to maintain and improve reading and writing skills after leaving schools.

CITIES

The Growth of Cities

Cities were first built in the Middle East about 8 000 years ago. Here, the development of settled agriculture provided enough surplus food to support an urban population.

Today cities play a crucial role in human affairs. Athens, Rome and Venice, for example are famous for their contribution to European civilisation and culture. Administration and government is also organised from cities which explains their political importance.

The largest cities have vast populations. About 18 million people live in New York and Mexico City has now almost 20 million inhabitants. By the year 2000 over half the world's population will be living in urban areas. This rapid expansion of cities in the developing world is causing a crisis.

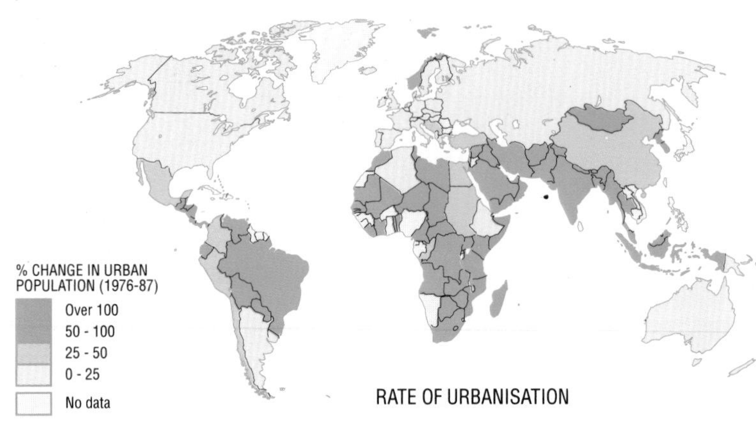

% CHANGE IN URBAN
POPULATION (1976-87)

- Over 100
- 50 - 100
- 25 - 50
- 0 - 25
- No data

RATE OF URBANISATION

The World's Largest Cities

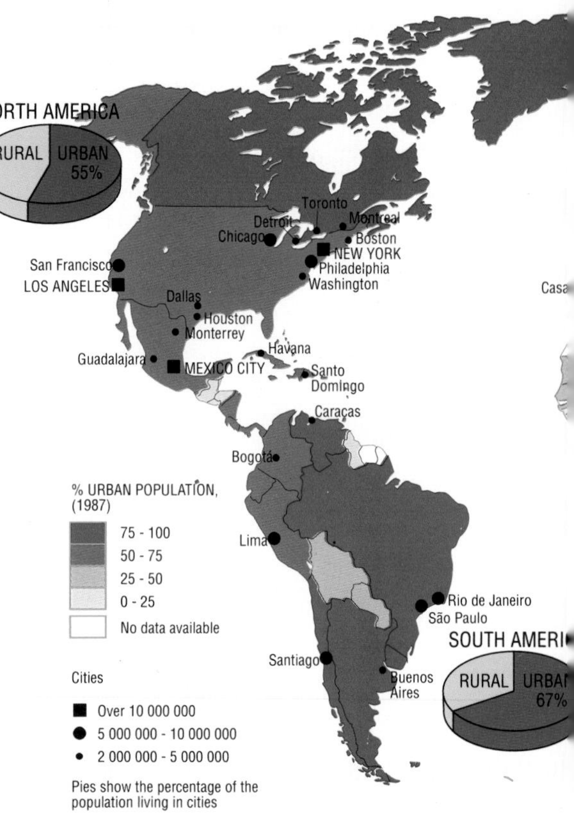

NORTH AMERICA

RURAL | URBAN 55%

Toronto
Detroit | Montreal
Chicago | Boston
San Francisco | NEW YORK
LOS ANGELES | Philadelphia
| Washington
Dallas
Houston
Monterrey | Havana
Guadalajara | MEXICO CITY | Santo
| Domingo
Caracas
Bogotá
Lima
| Rio de Janeiro
| São Paulo
Santiago | SOUTH AMERI
Buenos | RURAL | URBA
Aires | | 67%
Casa

% URBAN POPULATION,
(1987)

- 75 - 100
- 50 - 75
- 25 - 50
- 0 - 25
- No data available

Cities

- ■ Over 10 000 000
- ● 5 000 000 - 10 000 000
- • 2 000 000 - 5 000 000

Pies show the percentage of the
population living in cities

Planned Growth?
Developing World : Jakarta

Jakarta is one of the largest cities in the world. Almost half the population has no proper job but survives by providing services for others. This has created an underclass of people living in miserable shanties that sprawl along the surrounding roads. The population increases by a million every three years. Coping with such huge numbers is an immense challenge for the city authorities.

URBAN SPRAWL OF JAKARTA

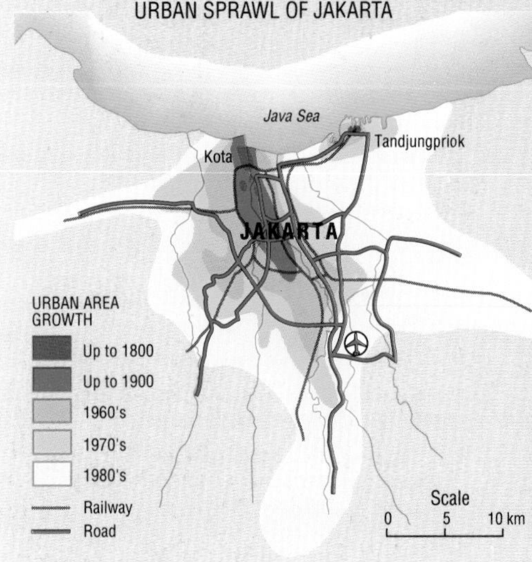

Java Sea
Kota | Tandjungpriok
JAKARTA

URBAN AREA
GROWTH

- Up to 1800
- Up to 1900
- 1960's
- 1970's
- 1980's

--- Railway
— Road

Scale
0   5   10 km

Developed World : Paris

Paris is another large city. It suffers from overcrowding, traffic congestion and poor housing. To tackle these problems, new buildings have been put up in the historic centre, satellite towns established round the edge and transport systems improved. These measures have helped to protect the city and maintain the quality of life for the people who live there.

URBAN GROWTH PLAN FOR PARIS

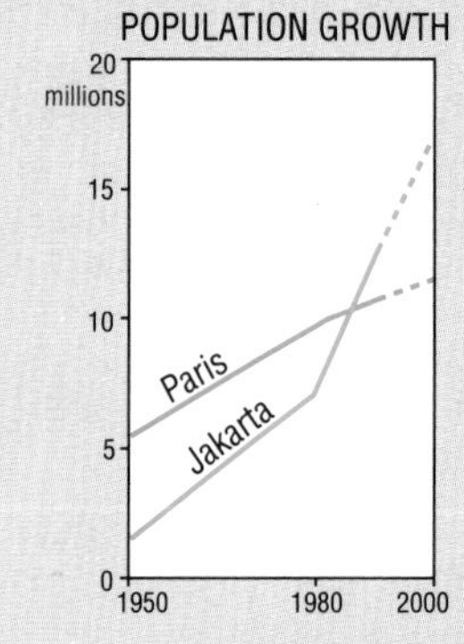

Cergy-Pontoise
Seine | Charles
| de Gaulle
| Marne
PARIS | Marne la Vallée
Saint-Quentin
| Orly
| Evry
| Melun
| Senart

0   15   30 Km

- Axis of growth
- Urban core
- Built-up area
- New town development
- ■ Urban centre developed within urban area
- • New urban centre
- — Road

POPULATION GROWTH

20
millions

15

10

5

Paris
Jakarta

0
1950   1980   2000

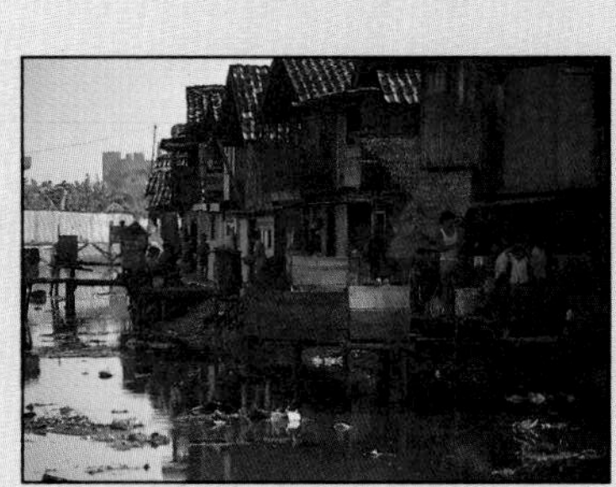

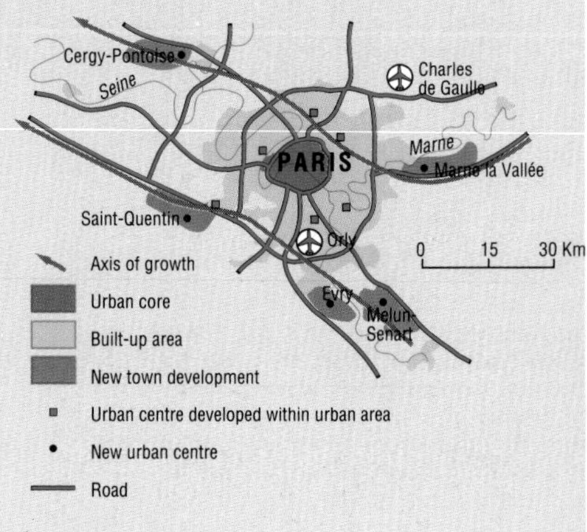

Sprawling slums of suburban Jakarta

© BARTHOLOMEW

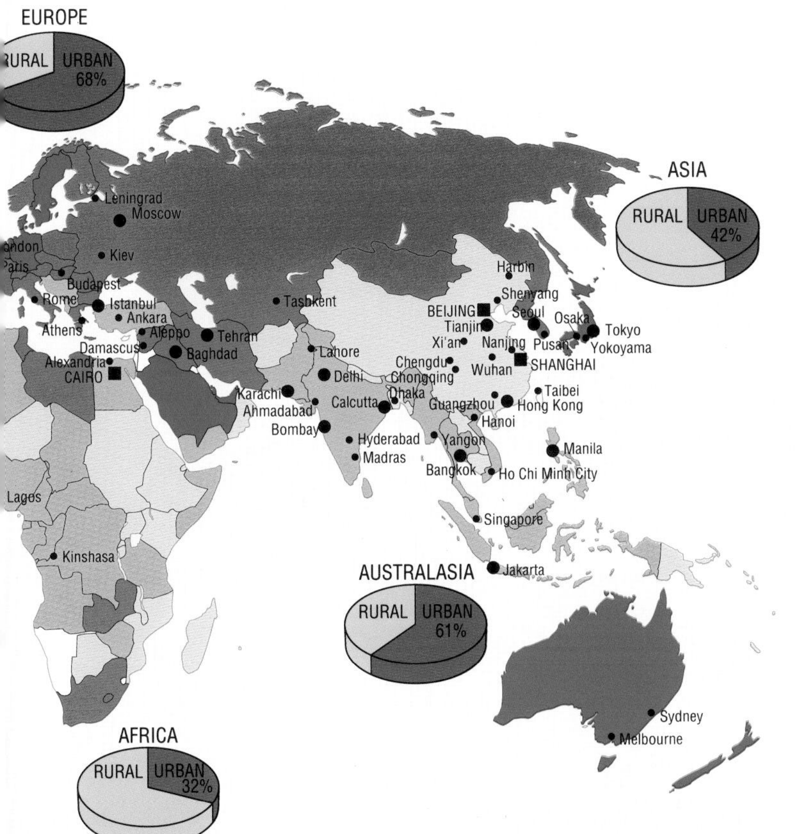

EUROPE
RURAL | URBAN 68%

ASIA
RURAL | URBAN 42%

AUSTRALASIA
RURAL | URBAN 61%

AFRICA
RURAL | URBAN 32%

Why do People come to Cities?

People come to cities for a variety of reasons. Some are attracted by the bright lights, greater freedom, better living conditions and the prospect of work. Others are driven off the land by wars, famines and development schemes.

This mixture of forces, which both encourages people to move and drives them forward, is known as the 'push-pull' process. It affects almost every country in the developing world.

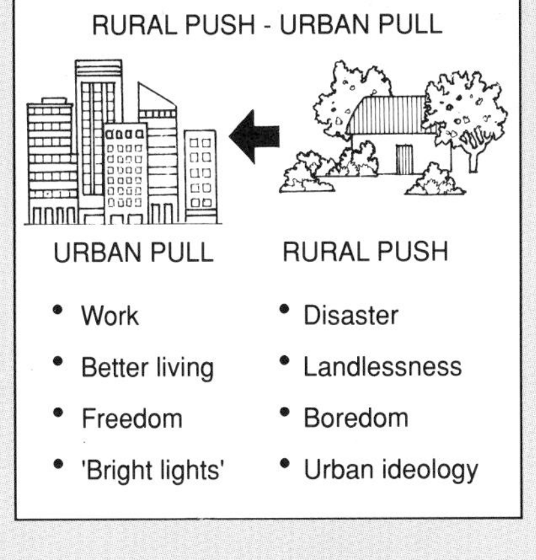

RURAL PUSH - URBAN PULL

URBAN PULL	RURAL PUSH
• Work	• Disaster
• Better living	• Landlessness
• Freedom	• Boredom
• 'Bright lights'	• Urban ideology

Urban Problems

Since 1950 the number of people living in cities has almost tripled.

Housing
All big cities have homeless people. In the developing world over half the city dwellers live in shanties where dirty water and poor sanitation cause disease. A quarter of all slum children die before the age of five.

Transport
Cities are busy, congested places and it is difficult to get about. In Athens traffic fumes are eating away the historic buildings.

Waste
New York produces so much garbage it has run out of places to dispose of it. Human sewage has helped make the Mediterranean the dirtiest sea in the world.

Resources
As they grow, cities cover valuable farmland, and make huge demands on the surrounding countryside for food, water and energy. Due to the shortage of firewood, Delhi is supplied from forests 700 km away.

Welfare
Overcrowding, noise and stress can have an adverse effect on the health of city dwellers. Levels of violent crime also tend to be higher.

Careful planning can help to provide better housing and services for city dwellers. Governments around the world could take a lead in tackling these issues.

Urban Regeneration : London Docklands

The London Docklands stretch down the Thames from Tower Bridge. A large community depended on the docks, but during the 1960's trade began to decline. This was due, to some extent to changing patterns of trade, larger ships, labour disputes, and poor management. By 1981 all the docks had closed.

People had different ideas about what to do. One suggestion was to try and halt the job losses. The alternative, adopted by the government, was to attract new companies to the area. An airport and light railway to the centre of London were built to encourage them.

The population of the area has now begun to increase. Fifteen thousand new homes have been built and a major office centre opened at Canary Wharfe. This may benefit newcomers but local people question if it has helped the old community.

HOUSING IN DOCKLANDS

1981   1991
Owner occupied
Council rented
Other

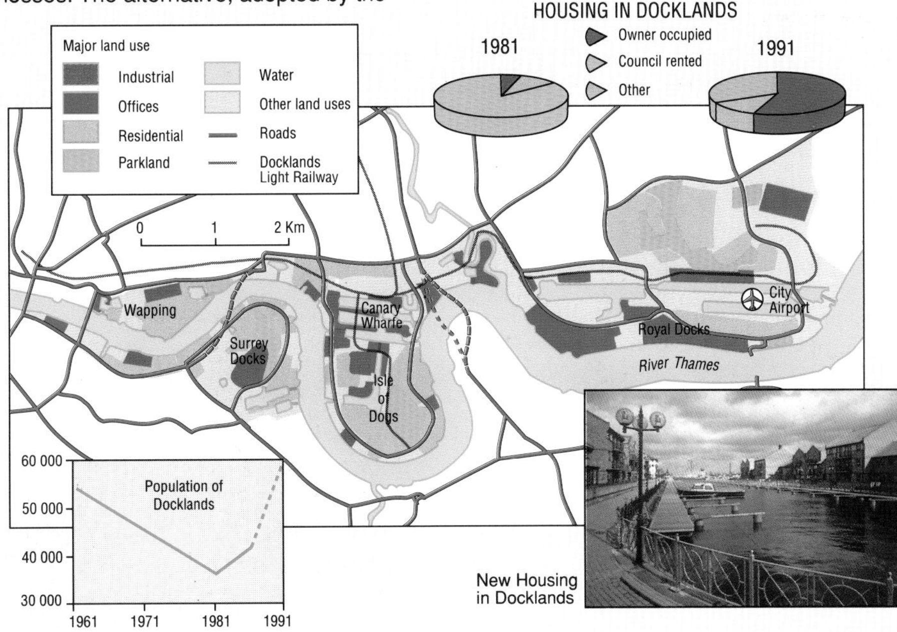

Major land use
Industrial
Offices
Residential
Parkland
Water
Other land uses
Roads
Docklands Light Railway

0   1   2 Km

Wapping
Surrey Docks
Canary Wharfe
Isle of Dogs
Royal Docks
City Airport
River Thames

New Housing in Docklands

Population of Docklands
60 000
50 000
40 000
30 000
1961   1971   1981   1991

PEOPLE ON THE MOVE

Ways of Travelling

For centuries the speed of travel depended on human effort or horse power. The Industrial Revolution changed all this. In the nineteenth century railways revolutionised land travel, linking in hours places which had previously been days apart. Now modern jet aircraft fly around the world at 1 000 km per hour. At this speed it takes less than 24 hours to reach the other side of the earth.

Some people have better access to travel than others. In industrialised countries extensive communications networks ensure that most of the people can move quickly from one place to another. In poorer countries many people do not have access to these facilities. There are also big variations between sections of the population. Men, for example, are more likely to drive cars than women. Children and the elderly also tend to be disadvantaged.

In general people are making more journeys than ever before. Some travel voluntarily for holidays or leisure. Others are forced to travel in search of work or to escape war and famine. This increase in mobility is having a profound effect on social customs and values.

Major International Migrations

Much of world history is the story of the migration of people from one place to another. Many of these movements have been marked by battles and conflicts. They have also tended to occur in waves over a period of time, rather than as single events.

The map shows how Europe's expansion in the past has affected many parts of the world. In the present century, poverty, war and famine have led to an unprecedented movement of people. As a result, many countries now have significant immigrant populations.

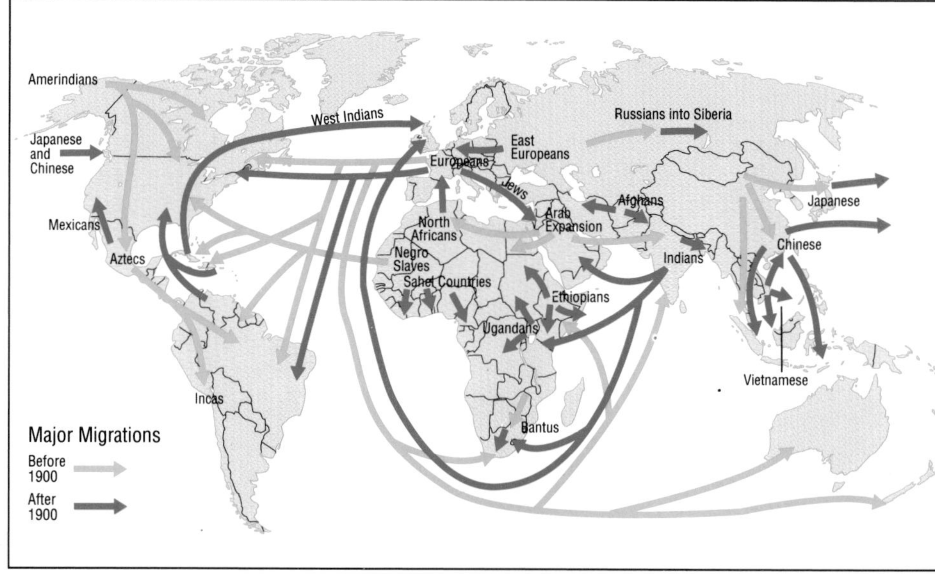

Major Migrations
Before 1900
After 1900

Car Culture

There are about 400 million cars in the world. Most of them are in industrialised countries. The USA, with 140 million, is still the home of car culture.

The number of cars in the world has doubled in the last twenty years. Car making is the largest industry in the world economy. It is dominated by a handful of powerful transnational companies.

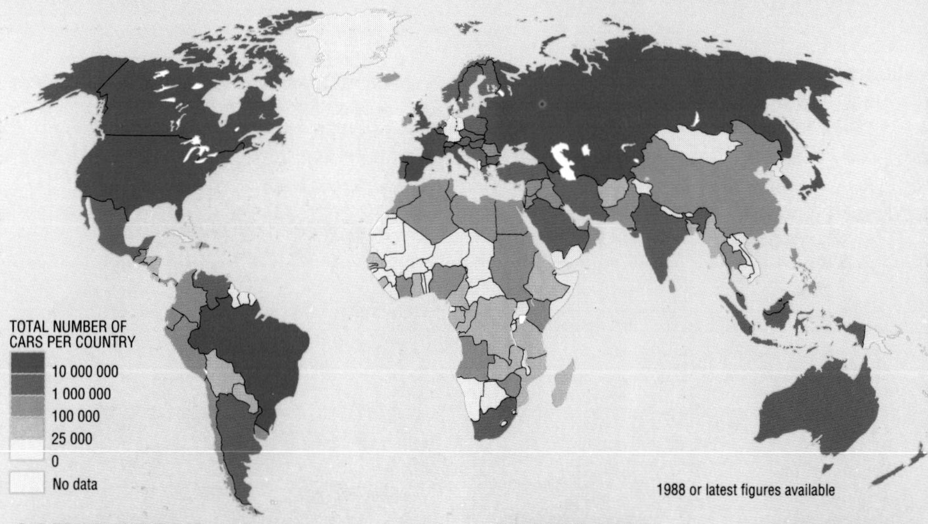

TOTAL NUMBER OF CARS PER COUNTRY

- 10 000 000
- 1 000 000
- 100 000
- 25 000
- 0
- No data

1988 or latest figures available

Cars may be convenient, but they cause widespread environmental damage. They are expensive to build, consume scarce resources and are difficult to dispose of when they wear out. In addition, car fumes make a major contribution to acid rain and greenhouse gases. About a third of the land in towns and cities is devoted to roads and car parking. Around the world, a quarter of a million people die each year in car accidents.

Many people believe that the car culture needs to be better controlled. In the UK, for example, traffic is expected to double over the next thirty years. The government is planning a massive road building programme. Yet new roads gobble up valuable land and quickly attract even more vehicles. One solution is to have more efficient public transport. The use of catalytic converters and lead free petrol is a positive trend as it reduces air pollution.

CAR TRAVEL IN THE USA

Population	246 330 000
Area	9 373 000 km^2
Total number of cars	140 655 000
Car ownership (per 1 000 people)	571
Total length of road network	6 233 308 km
Total length of motorways	82 214 km
Road density	0.68 km^2
Annual fuel consumption	358 744 000 tonnes of petrol
Average distance travelled per person per year	12 505 km

CAR TRAVEL IN ITALY

Population	57 440 000
Area	294 000 km^2
Total number of cars	25 490 000
Car ownership (per 1 000 people)	444
Total length of road network	301 846 km
Total length of motorways	5 997 km
Road density	1.03 km^2
Annual fuel consumption	12 445 000 tonnes of petrol
Average distance travelled per person per year	4 852 km

The Impact of Tourism

The Alps form a chain of mountains 1 000 km long. The snowy peaks, glaciers and beautiful alpine scenery are major tourist attractions. Every year 50 million people visit the Alps for their holidays, two thirds of them for winter skiing.

The tourist boom has led to tree clearance to make room for ski resorts, and encouraged development on steep and unsuitable slopes. As a result the risk of floods and avalanches has substantially increased. Areas above 2 000 metres are particularly at risk as their environment is delicately balanced.

Tourism and industry have caused an enormous increase in motor traffic and road building. Seven million vehicles cross the Alps each year contributing significantly to noise and air pollution. Acid rain affects 60% of the trees. Attempts are now being made to control vehicle fumes, replant trees and restore damaged landscapes. If there is enough public pressure much can be done to protect the Alps.

Around the world, tourism is on the increase. It creates jobs for local people, brings new community facilities and helps to preserve cultural and natural heritage. But it also puts pressure on the environment, undermines traditional values and tends to spoil the landscape. Careful planning can help to maximise the benefits and minimise the disturbance.

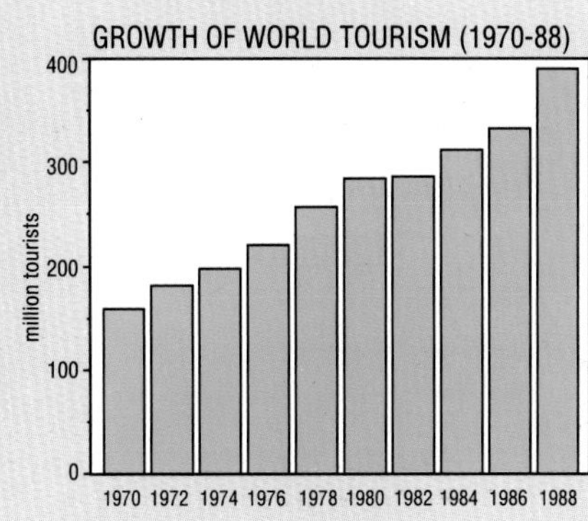

THE ALPS - ENVIRONMENT UNDER THREAT

GROWTH OF WORLD TOURISM (1970-88)

Refugees

There are about fifteen million refugees in the world. They are the victims of a variety of different forces. These include:

war and conflict
violence between different ethnic and religious groups
government repression
natural disasters such as floods, drought and earthquakes

Poor people tend to be worst affected as they do not have the means to protect themselves. The majority of refugees are women and children.

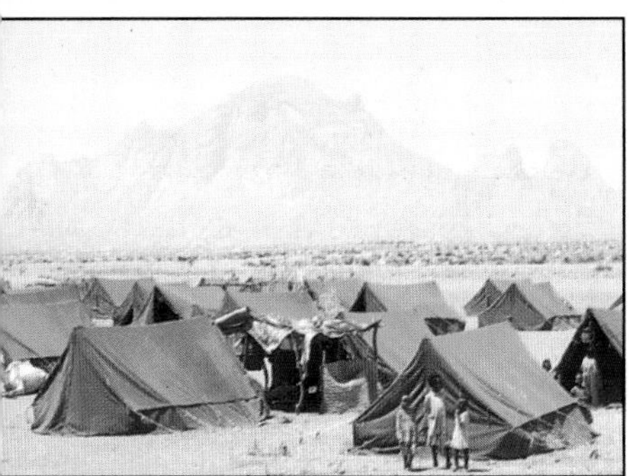

REFUGEE POPULATIONS

1 000 000
500 000
100 000
10 000
1 000
0
Source : UNHCR 1988

1.0 Countries receiving largest numbers of refugees (millions)

REFUGEE POPULATION BY CONTINENT

Africa 3 975 900
North America 1 353 000
Europe 711 500
Latin America 339 000
Asia 5 668 400
Oceania 91 800

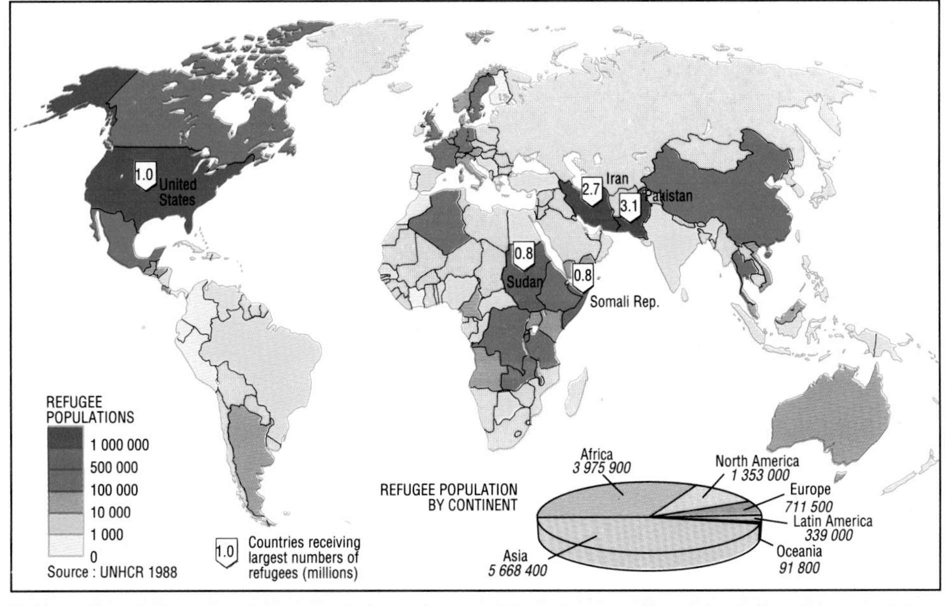

Refugee camp in Ethiopia

Pakistan has the largest refugee population in the world. It accommodates over three million refugees who fled from the Afghan War during the 1980's. In 1990 and 1991 the Gulf Crisis has caused the displacement of thousands of migrant workers, Kurds and other minorities from Iraq.

Although some refugees go to live permanently in Western Europe and North America, governments are often unwilling to accept large numbers of displaced people. The United Nations High Commission for Refugees (UNHCR) provides valuable international assistance. In the long term the best solution is for refugees to return to their homeland.

TRADE AND INTERNATIONAL DEBT

The Roots of Modern Trade

Modern trade dates back to the sixteenth century when early explorers began to make regular journeys to India and the Americas. It developed dramatically in the eighteenth and nineteenth centuries. By then Europe had extensive overseas colonies and the Industrial Revolution was gathering pace. These two factors created a world economic system with European needs and interests at its core. Present patterns of trade continue to reflect this. The income of many developing countries still depends on exporting products such as copper, coffee and tea. Manufacturing industries, by contrast, are concentrated in the developed countries of the 'North'. Machines, chemicals and consumer goods are produced here in large volumes. This accounts for the huge disparity in the value of trade between countries.

VALUE OF EXPORTS, 1988

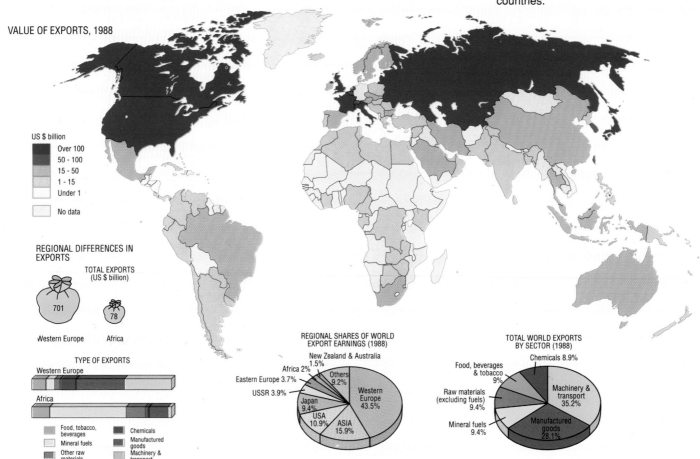

US $ billion

- Over 100
- 50 - 100
- 15 - 50
- 1 - 15
- Under 1
- No data

REGIONAL DIFFERENCES IN EXPORTS

TOTAL EXPORTS (US $ billion)

701 Western Europe   78 Africa

TYPE OF EXPORTS

Western Europe

Africa

- Food, tobacco, beverages
- Mineral fuels
- Other raw materials
- Chemicals
- Manufactured goods
- Machinery & transport

REGIONAL SHARES OF WORLD EXPORT EARNINGS (1988)

- New Zealand & Australia 1.5%
- Africa 2%
- Eastern Europe 3.7%
- USSR 3.9%
- Japan 9.4%
- USA 10.9%
- ASIA 15.9%
- Others 9.2%
- Western Europe 43.5%

TOTAL WORLD EXPORTS BY SECTOR (1988)

- Chemicals 8.9%
- Food, beverages & tobacco 9%
- Raw materials (excluding fuels) 9.4%
- Mineral fuels 9.4%
- Machinery & transport 35.2%
- Manufactured goods 28.1%

The Terms of Trade

One of the problems facing countries which export raw materials is that commodity prices fluctuate considerably. This is partly due to changing weather conditions. A bumper crop, for example, causes a glut and forces prices down.

The graph below shows how the terms of trade have changed. Between 1975 and 1983 most commodities halved their value in comparison with oil. Since then prices have to some extent recovered, but many producers are still struggling to recover from heavy losses in the early 1980's.

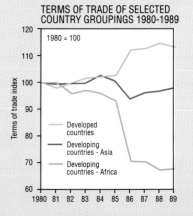

TERMS OF TRADE OF SELECTED COUNTRY GROUPINGS 1980-1989

1980 = 100

- Developed countries
- Developing countries - Asia
- Developing countries - Africa

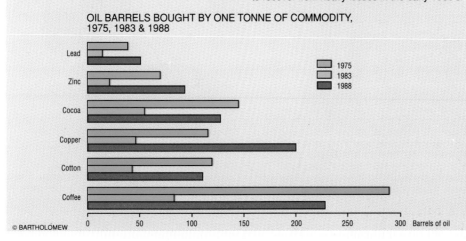

OIL BARRELS BOUGHT BY ONE TONNE OF COMMODITY, 1975, 1983 & 1988

- Lead
- Zinc
- Cocoa
- Copper
- Cotton
- Coffee

- 1975
- 1983
- 1988

Barrels of oil

Africa has been particularly hard hit by changes in the terms of trade. During the 1980's the value of its goods fell by a third. This has forced governments to borrow money, reducing economic and political independence.

© BARTHOLOMEW

Trade Dependency

Many developing countries depend on exporting one or two products which puts them in a very vulnerable position. Uganda, for example, earns 92% of its income from coffee. If the crops fails the results are disasterous. Also, the countries of the 'North' are often able to push prices down by playing one producer off against another.

To stop this happening, producers have formed themselves into associations called cartels. These have been largely unsuccessful, apart from OPEC (Organisation of Petroleum Exporting Countries) which managed to quadruple oil prices during the 1973 Middle East war.

Diversifying Production

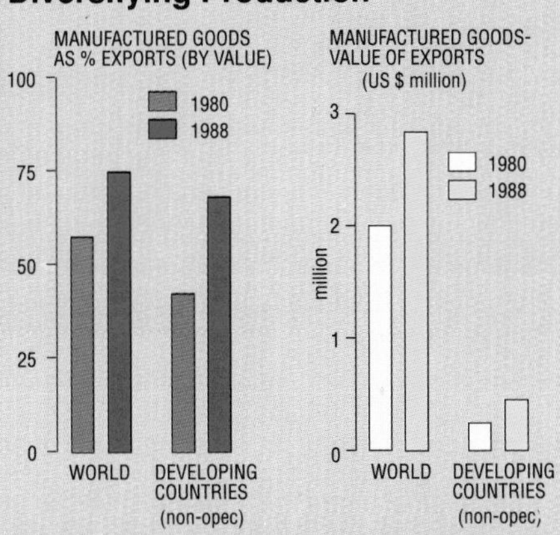

MANUFACTURED GOODS AS % EXPORTS (BY VALUE)

- 1980
- 1988

MANUFACTURED GOODS- VALUE OF EXPORTS (US $ million)

- 1980
- 1988

Developing countries are trying to diversify their economies to reduce trade dependency. More than half now have important manufacturing industries. As the graphs show, over the last decade the percentage of income from manufacturing has increased faster in the developing countries than in the rest of the world. In financial terms, however, these industries continue to be dwarfed by the developed countries of the 'North'.

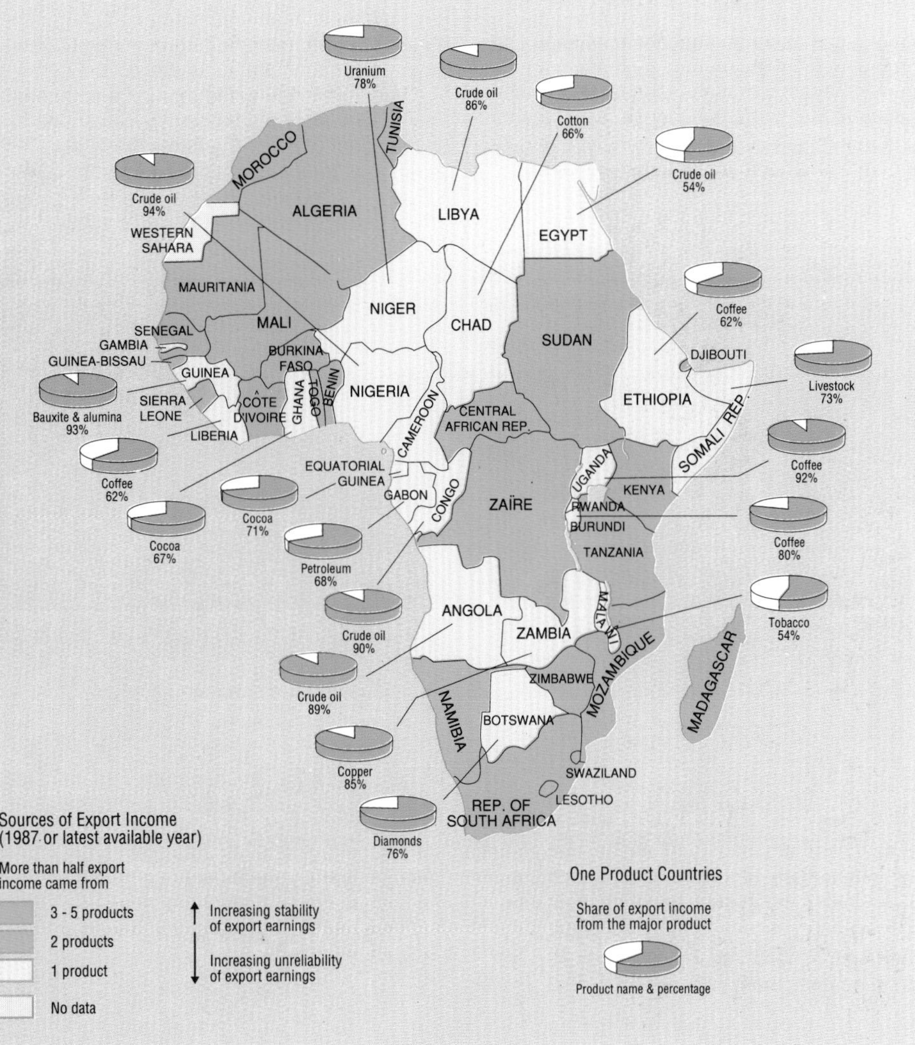

Sources of Export Income
(1987 or latest available year)

More than half export income came from

- 3 - 5 products
- 2 products
- 1 product
- No data

↑ Increasing stability of export earnings

↓ Increasing unreliability of export earnings

One Product Countries

Share of export income from the major product

Product name & percentage

Uranium 78%
Crude oil 86%
Cotton 66%
Crude oil 54%
Crude oil 94%
Coffee 62%
Livestock 73%
Bauxite & alumina 93%
Coffee 62%
Cocoa 71%
Coffee 92%
Cocoa 67%
Petroleum 68%
Coffee 80%
Crude oil 90%
Tobacco 54%
Crude oil 89%
Copper 85%
Diamonds 76%

The Debt Crisis

Unequal patterns of trade have driven many developing countries into debt. Repayments on loans often consume all their income.

As they struggle for survival, developing countries have to exploit their environment. Forests are cut down and the soil impoverished for short term gain.

One solution is to cancel all debts. Another is to exchange them for environmentally sound policies. It is clear that in many developing countries economic well-being and protection of the environment are inseparable.

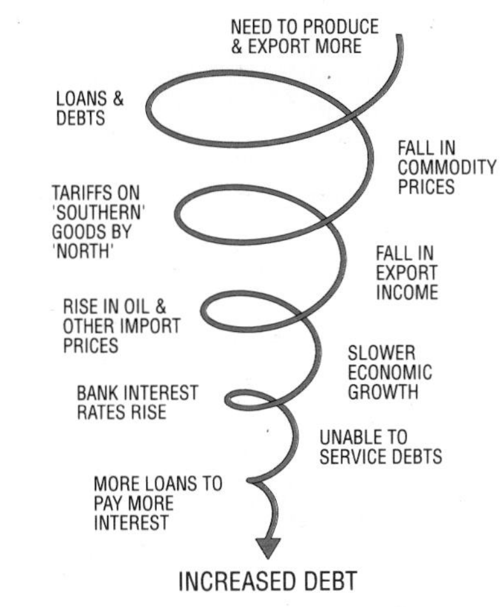

Repayment as a percentage of exports (1988)

- Over 40
- 30 - 40
- 20 - 30
- 10 - 20
- Under 10
- No data

INTERNATIONAL DEBT:
REPAYMENTS AS A PERCENTAGE OF EXPORTS

DEBT - THE DOWNWARD SPIRAL

NEED TO PRODUCE & EXPORT MORE
LOANS & DEBTS
FALL IN COMMODITY PRICES
TARIFFS ON 'SOUTHERN' GOODS BY 'NORTH'
FALL IN EXPORT INCOME
RISE IN OIL & OTHER IMPORT PRICES
SLOWER ECONOMIC GROWTH
BANK INTEREST RATES RISE
UNABLE TO SERVICE DEBTS
MORE LOANS TO PAY MORE INTEREST
INCREASED DEBT

INTERNATIONAL AID

Aid and Politics : The History of Aid

Aid was first given by the USA to help rebuild the countries of Western Europe after the Second World War and strengthen them against communism. Nowadays, most rich countries give some of their money to poorer parts of the world through international aid.

Britain's aid programme began in the 1960's as its colonies became independent. Over one hundred of the world's poorest countries now receive aid from Britain. However, the total amount of money given is relatively small. In 1989 the budget amounted to US$ 2.6 billion. Although this sounds a lot it is only a small proportion of Britain's wealth.

Aid, Trade and Debt

There are a number of different types of aid.

- emergency aid provides short term help during disasters such as wars, floods and famines.

- long term aid seeks to improve basic living conditions, so that people can sort out their own problems.

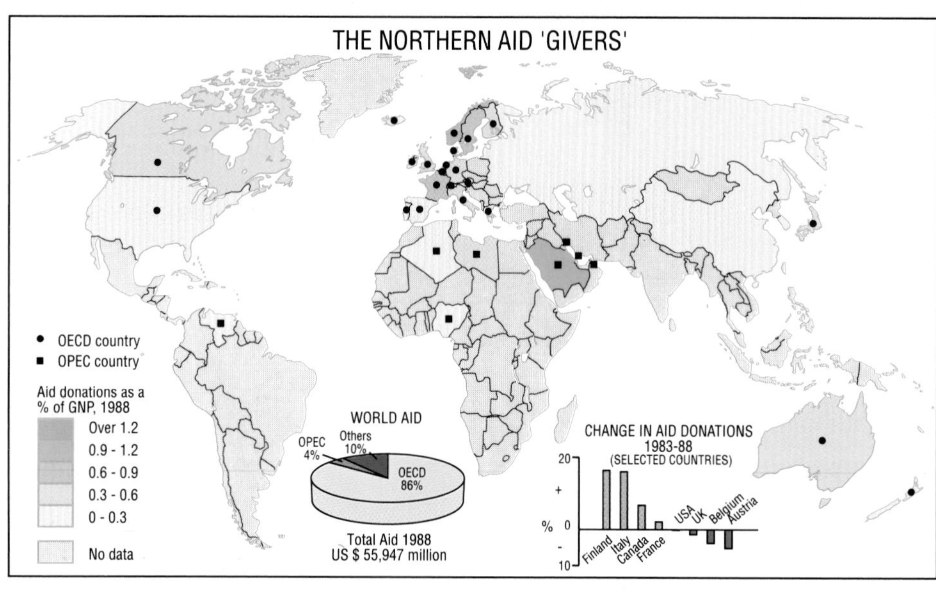

THE NORTHERN AID 'GIVERS'

- OECD country
- OPEC country

Aid donations as a % of GNP, 1988
- Over 1.2
- 0.9 - 1.2
- 0.6 - 0.9
- 0.3 - 0.6
- 0 - 0.3
- No data

WORLD AID
OPEC 4% Others 10% OECD 86%
Total Aid 1988 US $ 55,947 million

CHANGE IN AID DONATIONS 1983-88 (SELECTED COUNTRIES)
Finland Italy Canada France USA UK Belgium Austria

The United Nations has set rich countries the target of donating 0.7% of their GNP (Gross National Product) to aid. Only a few oil producers, France and the countries of Scandinavia actually achieve this.

Generally aid budgets, after reaching a peak in the 1970's have fallen back to lower levels. The UK gives only about 0.3% of its GNP and the USA 0.2%.

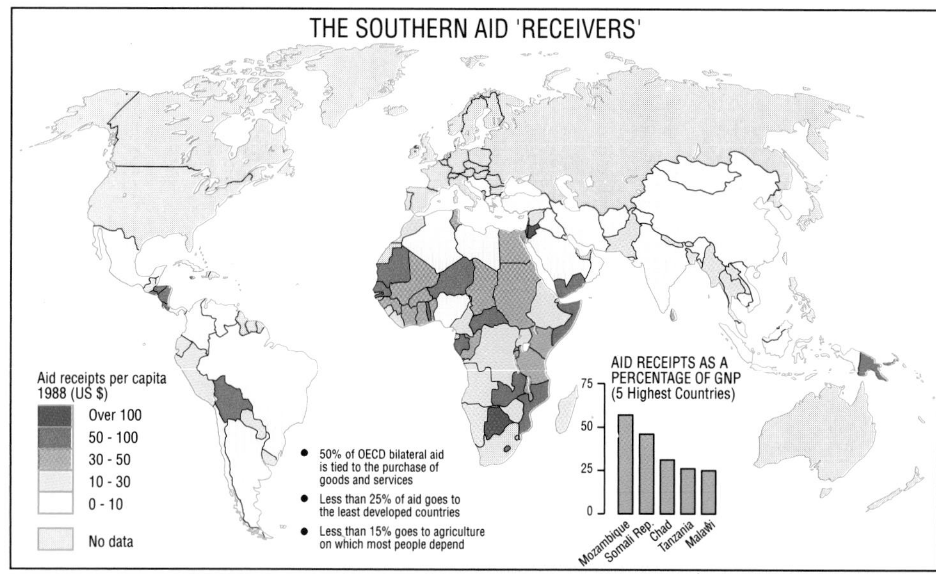

Sources of Money

GOVERNMENTS

Types of Aid

| BILATERAL given by one government directly to another | MULTILATERAL given through international organisations (World Bank, IMF etc) |

Problems

| Used to reward 'friendly' countries for political favours | Usually fails to benefit the poorest people but subsidises the rich |

| Often tied to goods and services from the donor country | Often used to finance large-scale prestige projects |

| Can take valuable markets from local industries | Take little or no account of environmental factors |

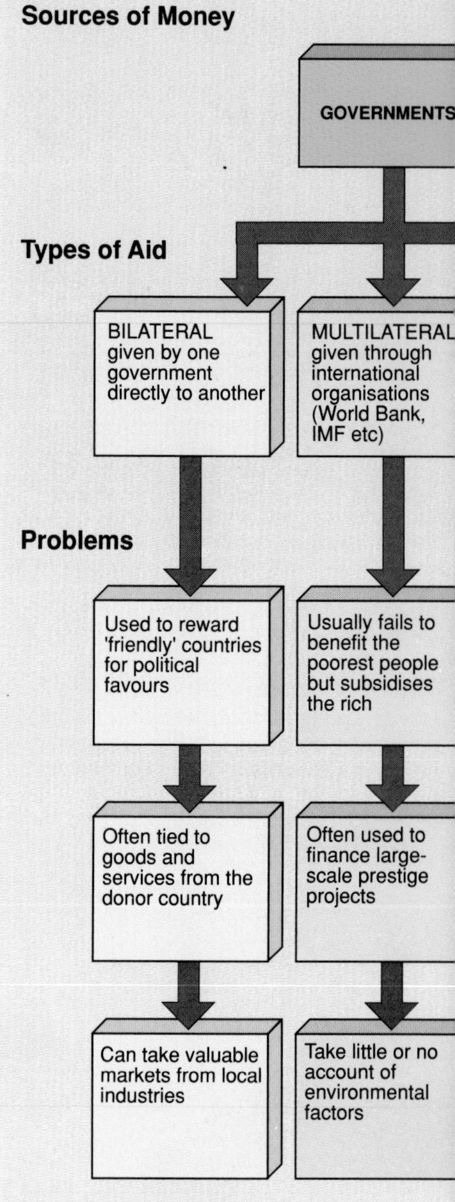

THE SOUTHERN AID 'RECEIVERS'

Aid receipts per capita 1988 (US $)
- Over 100
- 50 - 100
- 30 - 50
- 10 - 30
- 0 - 10
- No data

- 50% of OECD bilateral aid is tied to the purchase of goods and services
- Less than 25% of aid goes to the least developed countries
- Less than 15% goes to agriculture on which most people depend

AID RECEIPTS AS A PERCENTAGE OF GNP (5 Highest Countries)
Mozambique Somali Rep. Chad Tanzania Malawi

There are many reasons for giving aid. People believe that the rich have duty to help the poor. In addition, aid is a valuable way of reducing the great differences in wealth between the 'North' and 'South'.

However, self interest also plays a part. Donor nations often insist that the aid is spent on goods and services which they themselves provide. In this way the money that they give comes back to them as trade.

"We will give greater weight in allocation of our aid to political, industrial and commercial considerations."
UK government White Paper 1980.

Some aid projects are of dubious value. Large scale schemes, for example, tend to disrupt local people and damage the environment. It can also be difficult to ensure that goods and materials reach the people for whom they are intended.

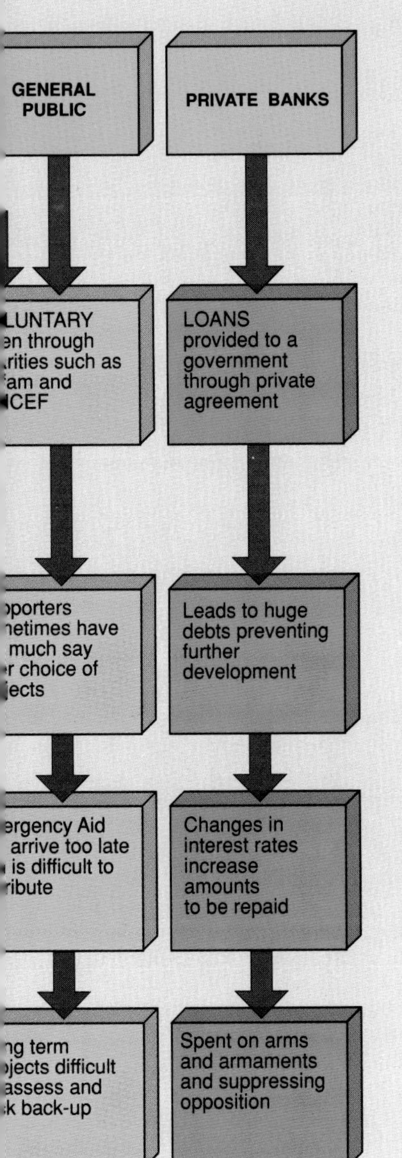

GENERAL PUBLIC	PRIVATE BANKS
...LUNTARY ...en through ...rities such as ...am and ...ICEF	LOANS provided to a government through private agreement
...pporters ...netimes have ...much say ...r choice of ...ects	Leads to huge debts preventing further development
...ergency Aid ...arrive too late ...is difficult to ...ribute	Changes in interest rates increase amounts to be repaid
...ng term ...jects difficult ...assess and ...k back-up	Spent on arms and armaments and suppressing opposition

"It's no use talking about aid when trade is unfair. What has been taken away from the poor in trade must be returned to the poor in aid."
Julius Nyere, ex-President of Tanzania.

Real Aid

In assessing an aid project the question to consider is whether it brings benefits to the poorest people.

The best schemes:

- encourage local decision making

- use simple technology

- involve small scale developments

- consider the circumstances which caused the problem

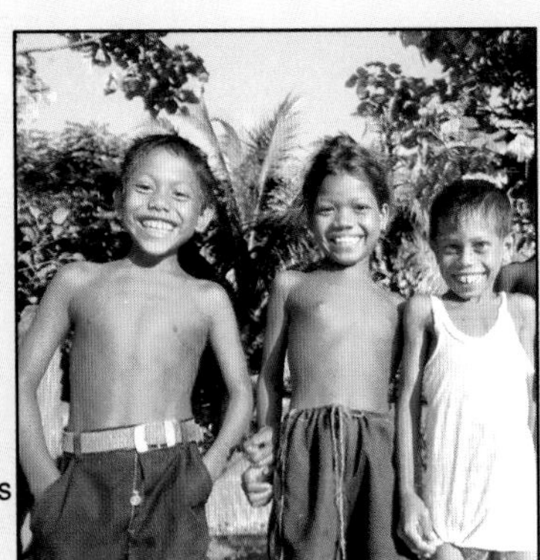

- enable communities to work together

- give people new knowledge and skills

- reduce the gap between rich and poor

- respect the environment

UNICEF Aid to the Philippines

Most of the sugar grown in the Philippines comes from the island of Negros. The plantations occupy the best land, so food has to be imported from elsewhere.

Conditions for sugar workers are harsh. They depend on the hacienderos or landlords for almost all their needs. Some villages have no running water or electricity.

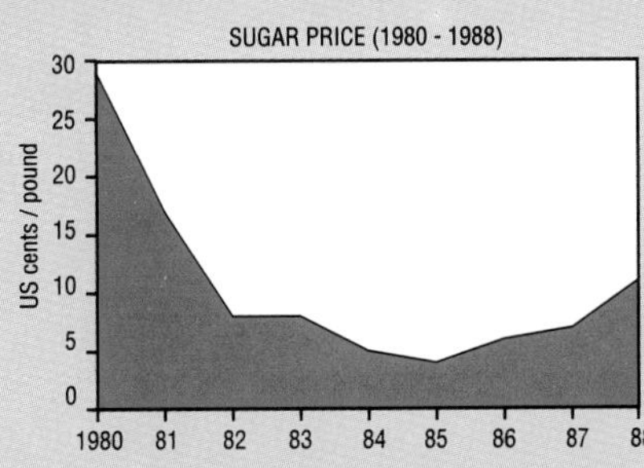

Between 1980 and 1985 the price of sugar fell from 29 US cents to 3 US cents a pound on world markets. This devastated the economy of Negros and threw many people out of work. One hundred and forty thousand children were affected by malnutrition.

The United Nations Children's Fund (UNICEF) and the Philippines government are now working together to solve the problem. Feeding centres have been set up across the island to provide children with a daily protein-rich 'supersnack'. In addition, health workers provide basic health care, innoculations and advice to parents.

So that children will have a more balanced diet in the future, community groups are being encouraged to grow vegetables on small plots of land. The aim is to establish 3 000 model gardens in villages throughout Negros.

UNICEF is contributing £2.5 million to the project. This will help to pay for food, seeds equipment and workers.

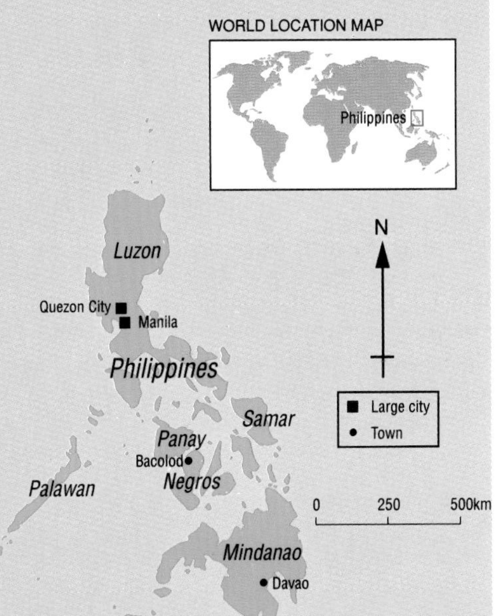

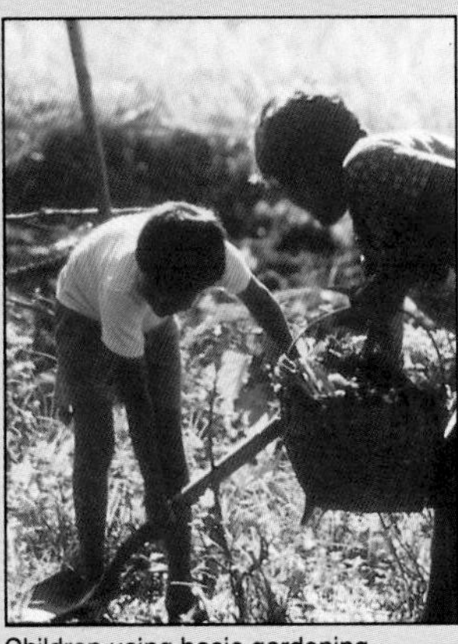

Children using basic gardening techniques to grow vegetables.

DIVIDED WORLD - INTERDEPENDENT WORLD

How is the World Divided?

We live in a very unequal world. In North America, Europe, Australia and Japan people are generally prosperous, eat plenty of food and have good housing. In Latin America, Africa and southern Asia conditions are very different. Here many people are trapped in a cycle of poverty, malnutrition and disease which reduces their expectation of life by many years.

The differences between 'North' and 'South' were drawn to public attention by the Brandt Report in 1980. The same basic pattern of wealth and poverty shows up on the maps below. It is important to remember, though, that there are rich and poor people in all countries. Also, the present pattern of inequality is relatively recent. For centuries the 'South' was the centre of world civilisation.

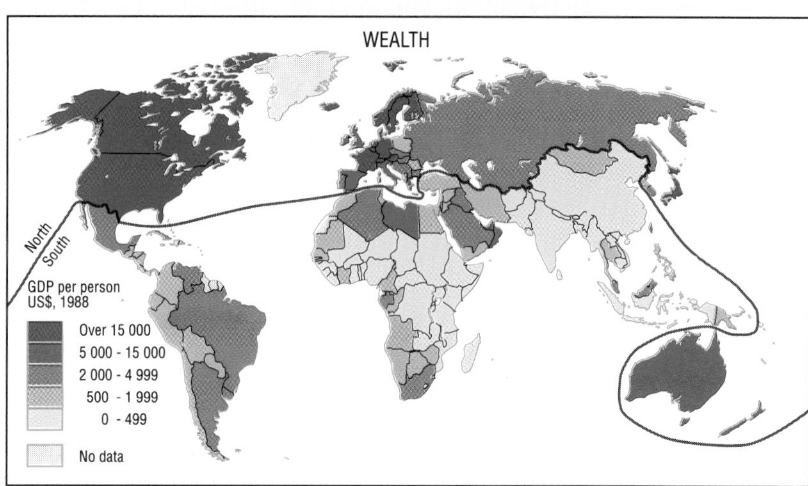

WEALTH

GDP per person
US$, 1988

- Over 15 000
- 5 000 - 15 000
- 2 000 - 4 999
- 500 - 1 999
- 0 - 499
- No data

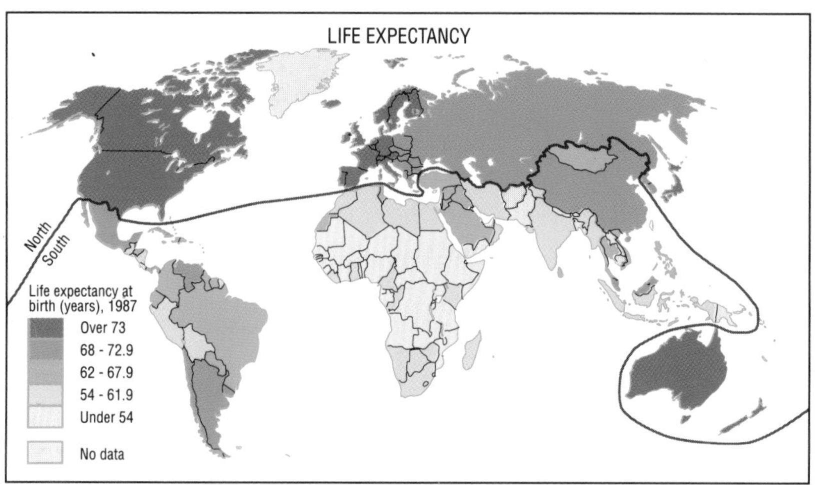

LIFE EXPECTANCY

Life expectancy at birth (years), 1987

- Over 73
- 68 - 72.9
- 62 - 67.9
- 54 - 61.9
- Under 54
- No data

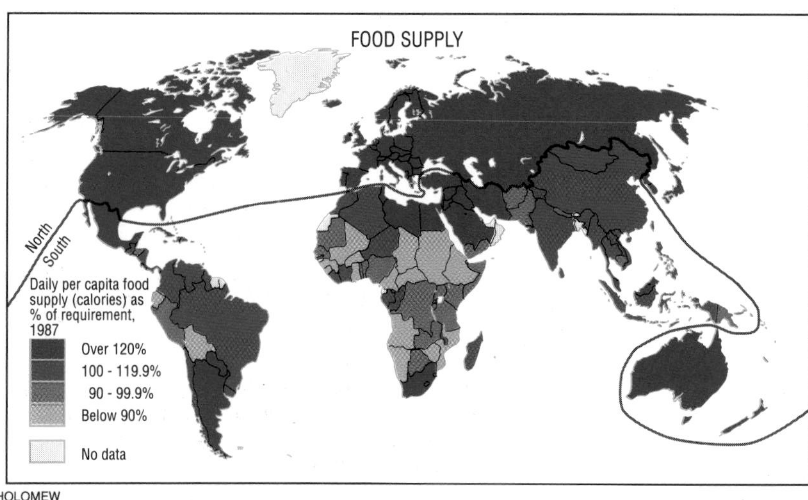

	North	South
Population	25%	75%
Life Expectancy	70 years	50 years

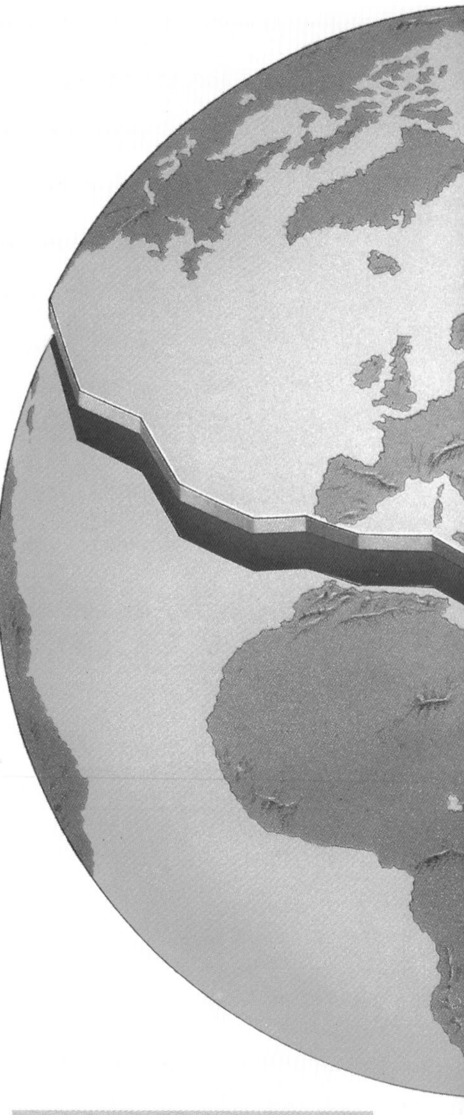

FOOD SUPPLY

Daily per capita food supply (calories) as % of requirement, 1987

- Over 120%
- 100 - 119.9%
- 90 - 99.9%
- Below 90%
- No data

© BARTHOLOMEW

Why are there Divisions?

The rise of capitalism, and the expansion of Europe since the sixteenth century, has created the present world economic system. It is geared to supplying the needs of Europe and North America. In general the 'South' provides raw materials for industries and consumers in the 'North'.

This trading system was re-inforced by the European colonial empires. Nowadays nearly all the countries of the world are politically independent. However, it has proved much more difficult to set up new economic structures. Indeed, over the last decade, many countries of the 'South' have become even more dependent on raw materials.

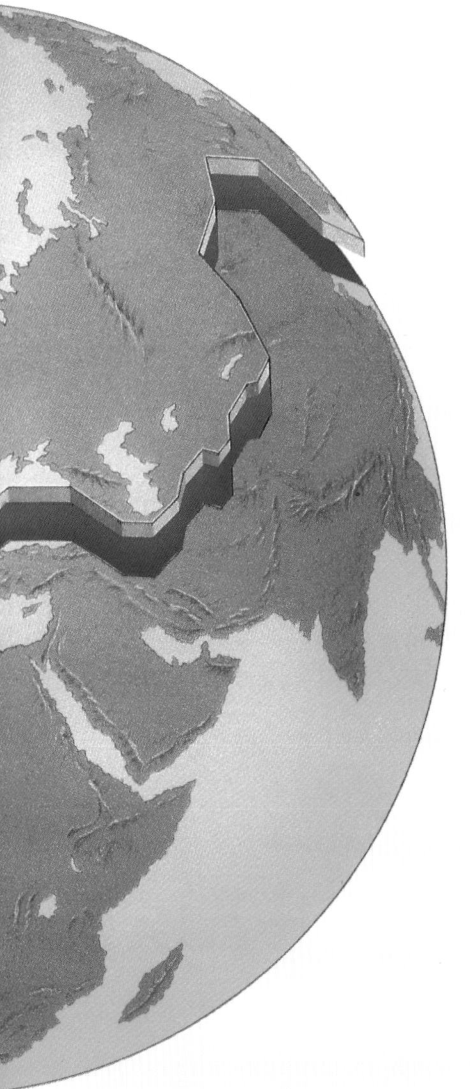

What is Interdependence?

'North' and 'South' are linked together in the same economic system. This means that economic growth in one part of the world depends on prosperity in another. Great differences in wealth affects the well being of us all and creates massive political and social tensions.

In recent years, environmental problems have demonstrated how the planet operates as a single ecosystem. Acid rain and global warming take no account of political frontiers. People are beginning to understand that we are all inhabitants of spaceship earth and we have to co-operate in looking after our home.

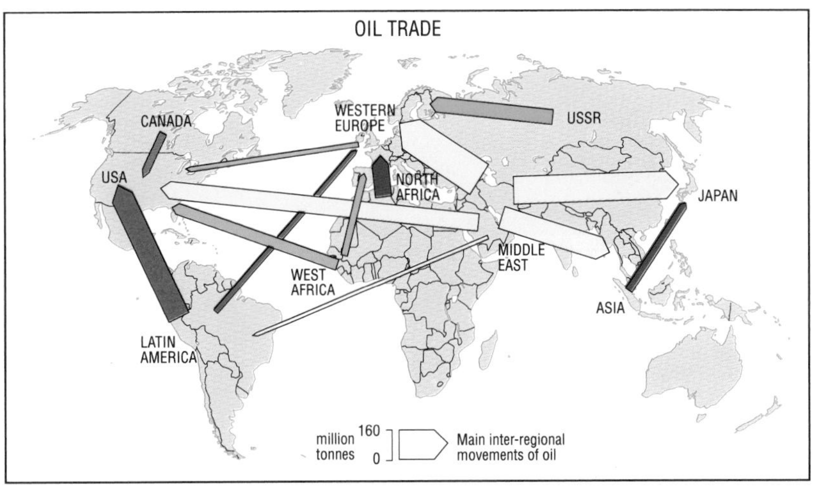

OIL TRADE

CANADA • WESTERN EUROPE • USSR • USA • NORTH AFRICA • JAPAN • WEST AFRICA • MIDDLE EAST • ASIA • LATIN AMERICA

million tonnes 160 0 → Main inter-regional movements of oil

	North	South
Income	80%	20%
Industry	90%	10%

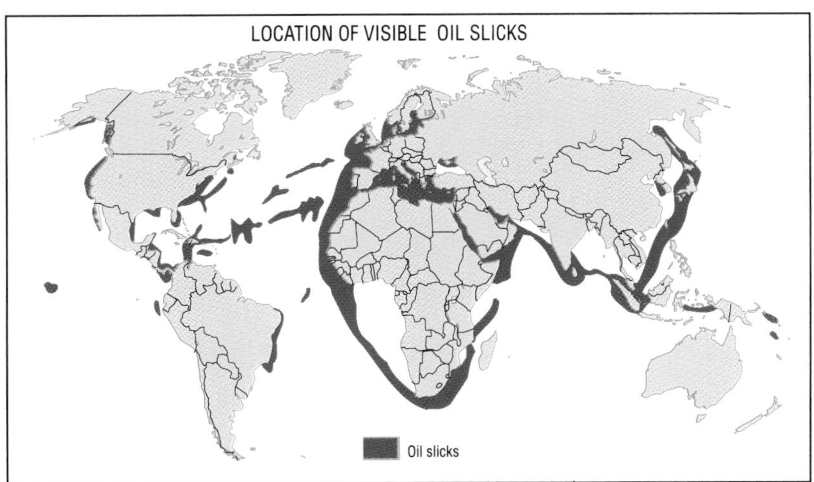

LOCATION OF VISIBLE OIL SLICKS

■ Oil slicks

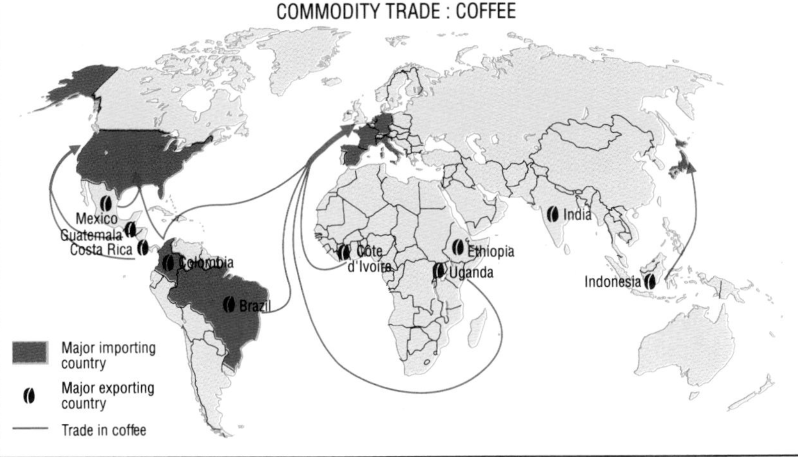

COMMODITY TRADE : COFFEE

Mexico
Guatemala
Costa Rica
Colombia
Brazil
Côte d'Ivoire
Ethiopia
Uganda
India
Indonesia

■ Major importing country

◖ Major exporting country

— Trade in coffee

What can be done?

It makes no sense to plunder the resources of the planet so rich get richer while the poor die of hunger. We need to look again at our social and economic priorities. The Brundtland Report identified two main ways to deal with current problems:

- sustainable development based on activities that respect and preserve the environment

- a new economic order that narrows the gap between developed and developing countries and makes world trade fairer

The only way of achieving these aims is through international action. We now realise that most major issues are globally connected. Yet public opinion and individual action can have an effect on government policy. Everyone has a part to play.

HEALING THE WOUNDS

Environmental problems are often complex and interconnected. Deforestation in the Himalayas, for example, is contributing to flooding in Bangladesh; pollution from factories in north west Europe is threatening fish stocks in the North Sea, and the debt crisis is forcing many developing countries to overuse their farmland.

Natural processes usually follow predictable patterns, but on occasions extreme events such as droughts, floods and earthquakes can pose a major threat in certain parts of the world. Often human activity has tended to exacerbate these natural hazards. Deforestation and overgrazing, for example, makes fragile environments even more vulnerable.

Economic activity has had a major impact on the environment, especially in the last fifty years. It is largely responsible for land, air and sea pollution and this is leading to widespread environmental degradation. The accumulation of pollutants is now reaching crisis proportions, and the nuclear accident at Chernobyl illustrated how a single incident can affect an entire continent. It is clear that major problems such as acid rain and global warming can only be solved by international action.

As world population has grown and living standards improve, there has been an increasing demand for raw materials. Yet the earth's resources are finite and need to be carefully conserved. One solution is to make use of sustainable sources such as renewable energy. Another is to recycle waste and use material more economically.

Concern has also been focused on contrasts in human welfare. In developing countries large numbers of people are trapped by poverty. Bad housing, lack of food, poor education and disease create a cycle of deprivation. Not only is this indefensible on humanitarian grounds, it is also putting the environment under unnecessary stress.

The world is undergoing an urban revolution, and everywhere people are moving into cities. The sheer pressure of numbers is threatening to swamp improvements in living conditions, and as populations continue to grow the difficulties increase. Development could help to alleviate these problems. However, the present pattern of world trade favours a few rich nations at the expense of the rest. A fairer world would be better for us all.

The environment crisis is a pressing concern. We need to ensure that economic growth is based on sustainable technologies. We need to address the problem of poverty and give genuine respect to human rights. The earth is the only home we have. Either we look after it properly, or we risk setting in motion a train of events that we will be unable to control.

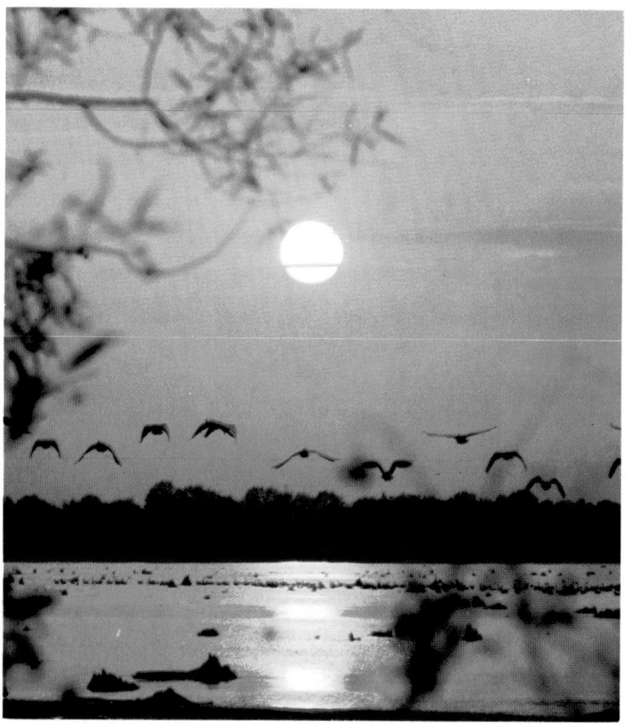

WORLD ATLAS

SYMBOLS

Relief

- ⬭ Land contour
- ▲ *8848* Spot height (metres)
- ⋈ Pass
- ▭ Permanent ice cap

Feet	Relief	Metres
16404		5000
9843		3000
6562		2000
3281		1000
1640		500
656		200
0		Sea Level
Land Dep. 656		200
13123		4000
22966		7000

Hydrography

- ⬭ Submarine contour
- ▼*11034* Ocean depth (metres)
- *(217)* Lake level
- Reef
- River
- Intermittent river
- Falls
- Dam
- Gorge
- Canal
- Lake/Reservoir
- Intermittent lake
- Marsh/Swamp

Communications

- Tunnel ⸺ Main railway
- ⊕ Main airport
- − − − Track

Road representation varies with the scale category.

- ═══ Principal road ⎫
- ─── Other main road ⎬ 1:1M-1:2½M

- ─── Principal road ⎫
- ─── Other main road ⎬ 1:2½M-1:7½M

- ─── Principal road   1:7½M or smaller

Administration

- ——— International boundary
- – – – Undefined/Disputed international boundary
- ········ Cease-fire line
- –·–·– Internal division : First order
- –··–··– Internal division : Second order
- ⊠ ⊙ ◎ / ◉ ◻ ▪ National capitals

Settlement

Each settlement is given a town stamp according to its relative importance and scale category.

	1:1M-1:2½M	1:2½M-1:7½M	1:7½M or smaller
⊠	Major City	Major City	Major City
◉	City	City	City
◎	Large Town	Large Town	Large Town
⊙	Town	Town	Town
○	Small Town	Small Town	—
•	Village	—	—
◆	Urban area (1:1M-1:2½M only)		

The size of type used for each settlement is graded to correspond with the appropriate town stamp.

Other features

- ∴ Ancient monument
- ◡ Oasis
- ⬭ National Park
- ▲ Oil field
- △ Gas field
- –·–·– Oil/Gas pipeline

Lettering

Various styles of lettering are used-each one representing a different type of feature.

ALPS	Physical feature	KENYA	Country name
Red Sea	Hydrographic feature	IOWA	Internal division
Paris	Settlement name	*(Fr.)*	Territorial administration

© Collins

THE WORLD : Political

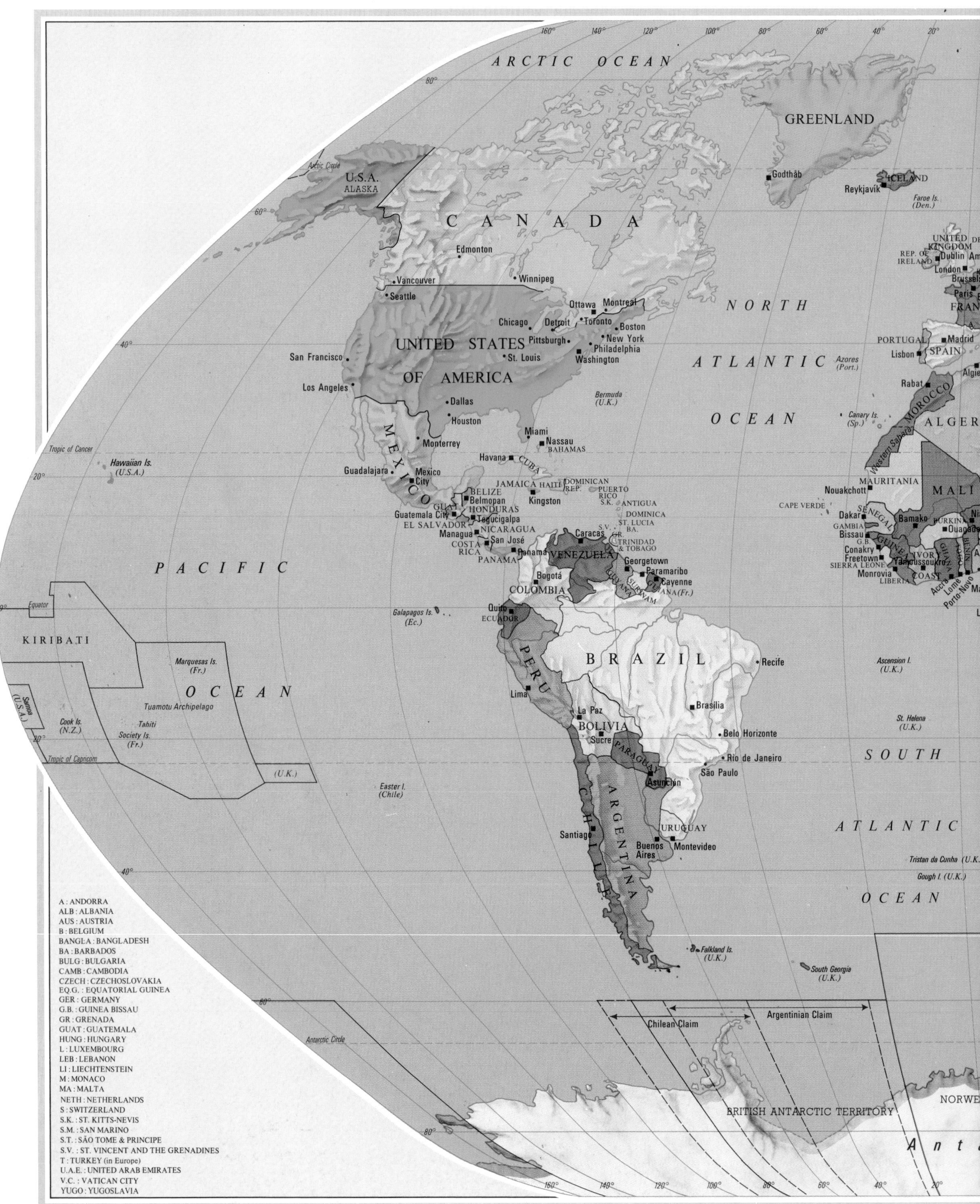

ARCTIC OCEAN

GREENLAND

Godthåb

ICELAND

Reykjavík

Faroe Is.
(Den.)

Arctic Circle

U.S.A.
ALASKA

C A N A D A

Edmonton

Vancouver   Winnipeg

Seattle

Ottawa Montreal

Chicago Detroit Toronto Boston

Pittsburgh New York

San Francisco

UNITED STATES

OF AMERICA

St. Louis Philadelphia

Washington

Los Angeles

Dallas

Houston

Miami

Monterrey

Nassau

BAHAMAS

Havana CUBA

Guadalajara Mexico

City

JAMAICA HAITI DOMINICAN

REP.

BELIZE Kingston PUERTO

RICO

S.K. ANTIGUA

Belmopan DOMINICA

Guatemala City HONDURAS ST. LUCIA

Tegucigalpa BA.

EL SALVADOR S.V.

Managua NICARAGUA

San José TRINIDAD

COSTA & TOBAGO

RICA Panama Caracas Georgetown

PANAMA VENEZUELA Paramaribo

Bogotá Cayenne

GUIANA (Fr.)

COLOMBIA SURINAM

Quito

ECUADOR

Galapagos Is.
(Ec.)

B R A Z I L

Recife

PERU

Lima

La Paz Brasilia

BOLIVIA

Sucre Belo Horizonte

PARAGUAY Rio de Janeiro

São Paulo

Asunción

C H I L E

ARGENTINA

URUGUAY

Santiago Montevideo

Buenos

Aires

Falkland Is.
(U.K.)

South Georgia
(U.K.)

NORTH

ATLANTIC

OCEAN

Bermuda
(U.K.)

PORTUGAL Madrid

Lisbon SPAIN

Azores
(Port.)

Rabat

Canary Is.
(Sp.)

MOROCCO ALGER

Western Sahara

MAURITANIA MALI

Nouakchott

CAPE VERDE SENEGAL Bamako BURKINA

Dakar Ouagad

GAMBIA GUINEA IVORY GHANA BENI

Bissau Conakry Yamoussoukro Lomé

G.B. Freetown COAST Accra Porto-Novo

SIERRA LEONE Monrovia

LIBERIA

Ascension I.
(U.K.)

St. Helena
(U.K.)

S O U T H

ATLANTIC

OCEAN

Tristan da Cunha (U.K.)

Gough I. (U.K.)

UNITED
KINGDOM Dublin Am

REP. OF London

IRELAND Brussel

Paris FRAN

P A C I F I C

O C E A N

Equator

KIRIBATI

Samoa
(U.S.A.)

Marquesas Is.
(Fr.)

Cook Is.
(N.Z.)

Tahiti

Society Is.
(Fr.)

Tuamotu Archipelago

Easter I.
(Chile)

(U.K.)

Tropic of Cancer

Hawaiian Is.
(U.S.A.)

Tropic of Capricorn

Antarctic Circle

Chilean Claim Argentinian Claim

BRITISH ANTARCTIC TERRITORY NORWE

A n t a

A : ANDORRA
ALB : ALBANIA
AUS : AUSTRIA
B : BELGIUM
BANGLA : BANGLADESH
BA : BARBADOS
BULG : BULGARIA
CAMB : CAMBODIA
CZECH : CZECHOSLOVAKIA
EQ.G. : EQUATORIAL GUINEA
GER : GERMANY
G.B. : GUINEA BISSAU
GR : GRENADA
GUAT : GUATEMALA
HUNG : HUNGARY
L : LUXEMBOURG
LEB : LEBANON
LI : LIECHTENSTEIN
M : MONACO
MA : MALTA
NETH : NETHERLANDS
S : SWITZERLAND
S.K. : ST. KITTS-NEVIS
S.M. : SAN MARINO
S.T. : SÃO TOME & PRINCIPE
S.V. : ST. VINCENT AND THE GRENADINES
T : TURKEY (in Europe)
U.A.E. : UNITED ARAB EMIRATES
V.C. : VATICAN CITY
YUGO : YUGOSLAVIA

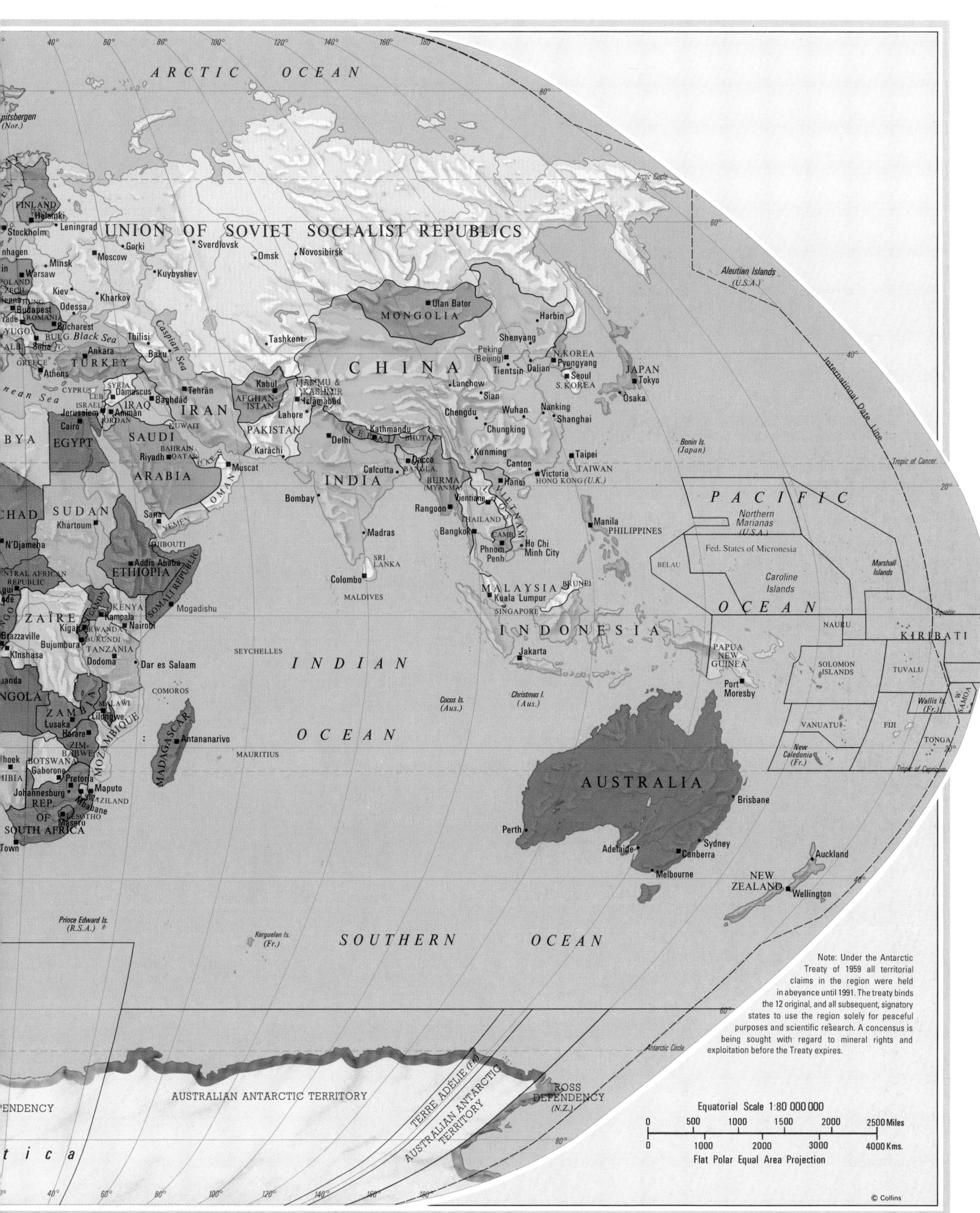

ARCTIC OCEAN

Arctic Circle

FINLAND
Helsinki
Stockholm • Leningrad
phagen • Minsk • Gorki • Sverdlovsk
• Moscow • Omsk • Novosibirsk
POLAND • Warsaw • Kuybyshev
• Kiev • Kharkov
Budapest • Odessa
YUGO- Bucharest • Thilisi
• ROMANIA • Caspian Sea
Sofia Black Sea • Baku
GREECE • Ankara • Tashkent
Athens TURKEY

UNION OF SOVIET SOCIALIST REPUBLICS

60°

Aleutian Islands (U.S.A.)

40°

MONGOLIA
• Ulan Bator
• Harbin
• Shenyang
Peking N.KOREA
(Beijing) Pyongyang • JAPAN
• Tientsin Dalian • Seoul • Tokyo
CHINA S.KOREA
CYPRUS SYRIA Tehrān Kabul JAMMU & • Lanchow • Osaka
ISRAEL Damascus AFGHAN- KASHMIR • Sian
Jerusalem Baghdād IRAQ ISTAN Islamabad • Chengdu • Wuhan Nanking
JORDAN Amman IRAN Lahore • Chungking • Shanghai
KUWAIT PAKISTAN Kathmandu
BAHRAIN Karāchi NEPAL BHUTAN • Kunming Canton
EGYPT Riyadh QATAR Delhi • Victoria
SAUDI U.A.E. BANGLA. Calcutta DACCA • Taipei
Muscat INDIA BURMA Hanoi HONG KONG (U.K.) TAIWAN
ARABIA OMAN (MYANMA) Vientiane
SUDAN YEMEN Bombay Rangoon
Sana PACIFIC
Khartoum Madras THAILAND Manila
N'Djamena DJIBOUTI Bangkok CAMB. PHILIPPINES Northern
Addis Ababa SRI Phnom Ho Chi Marianas
ETHIOPIA SOMALI REPUBLIC LANKA Penh Minh City (U.S.A.)
Colombo Fed. States of Micronesia
KENYA Mogadishu MALDIVES MALAYSIA BRUNEI BELAU OCEAN Caroline Marshall
Kampala Nairobi Kuala Lumpur Islands Islands
ZAÏRE RWANDA SINGAPORE NAURU
Kigali
BURUNDI INDONESIA
Bujumbura TANZANIA SEYCHELLES INDIAN PAPUA KIRIBATI
Dodoma NEW SOLOMON
Dar es Salaam Jakarta GUINEA ISLANDS TUVALU
COMOROS
ANGOLA OCEAN Cocos Is. Christmas I. Port VANUATU Wallis Is. W.
ZAMBIA MALAWI (Aus.) (Aus.) Moresby FIJI (Fr.) SAMOA
Lusaka Lilongwe New TONGA
Harare MADAGASCAR Caledonia
BOTSWANA ZIM- Antananarivo (Fr.)
hoek Gaborone BABWE
NIBIA Pretoria MAURITIUS AUSTRALIA
Johannesburg Maputo Brisbane
REP. SWAZILAND
OF LESOTHO Perth
SOUTH AFRICA Maseru Adelaide Sydney
Town Melbourne Canberra Auckland
NEW
ZEALAND Wellington

Prince Edward Is.
(R.S.A.)

Kerguelen Is.
(Fr.) SOUTHERN OCEAN

Note: Under the Antarctic
Treaty of 1959 all territorial
claims in the region were held
in abeyance until 1991. The treaty binds
the 12 original, and all subsequent, signatory
states to use the region solely for peaceful
purposes and scientific research. A concensus is
being sought with regard to mineral rights and
exploitation before the Treaty expires.

Antarctic Circle

ENDENCY AUSTRALIAN ANTARCTIC TERRITORY TERRE ADÉLIE (Fr.) ROSS
AUSTRALIAN ANTARCTIC DEPENDENCY
TERRITORY (N.Z.)
tica

Equatorial Scale 1:80 000 000

0 500 1000 1500 2000 2500 Miles
0 1000 2000 3000 4000 Kms.

Flat Polar Equal Area Projection

© Collins

3

THE WORLD : Physical

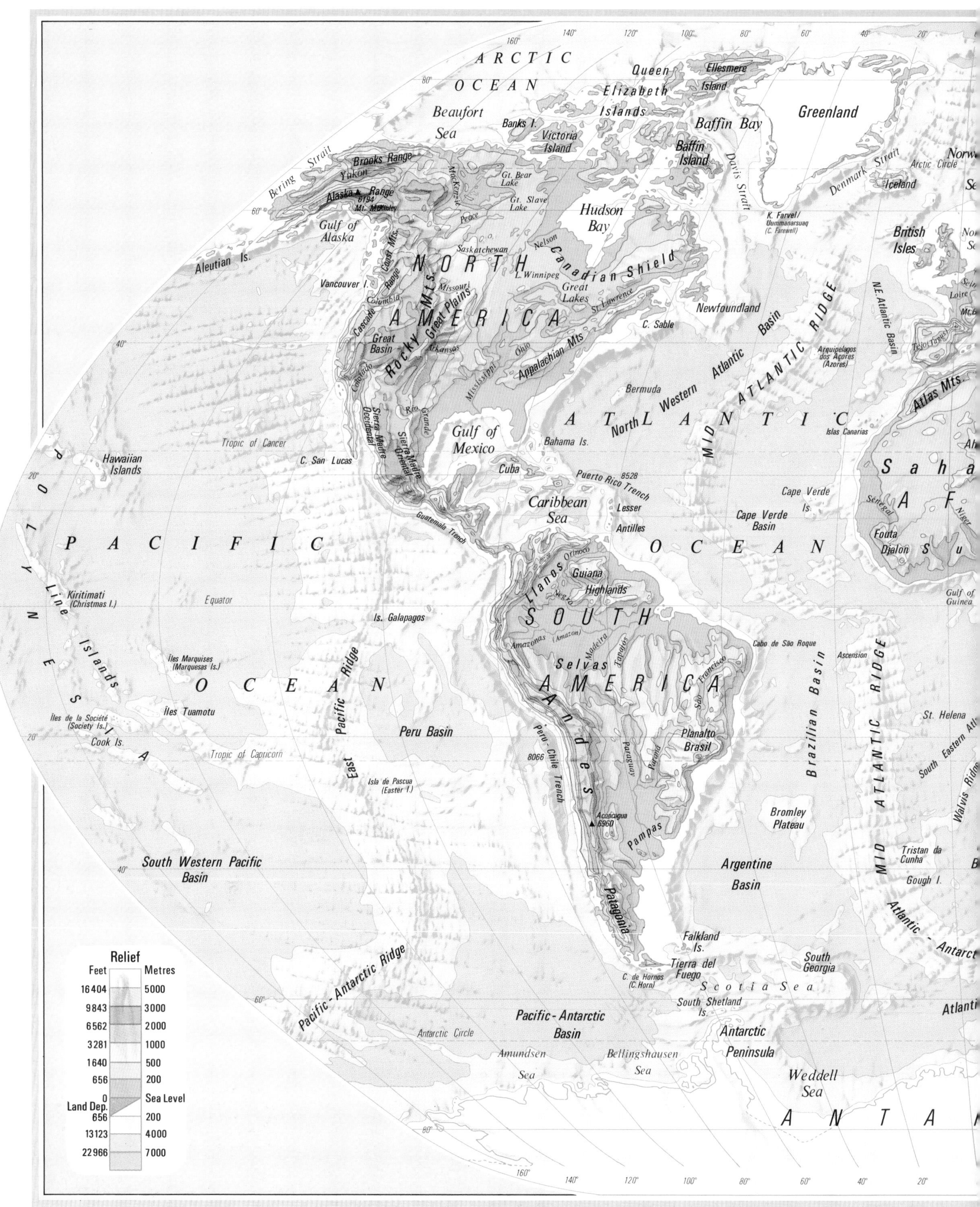

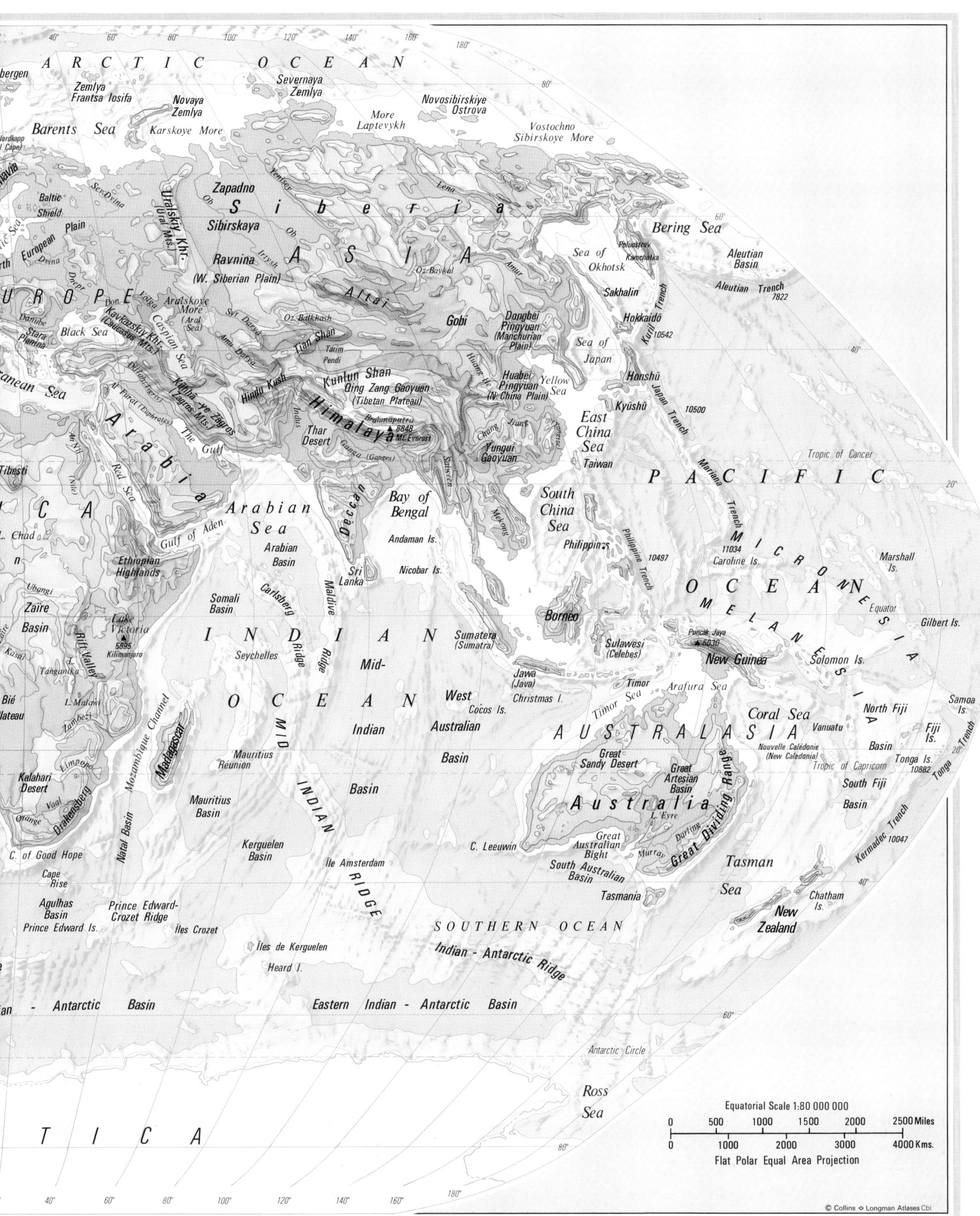

ARCTIC OCEAN

Spitsbergen
Zemlya
Frantsa Iosifa
Severnaya
Zemlya
Novosibirskiye
Ostrova
Nordkapp
N. Cape
Barents Sea
Novaya
Zemlya
More
Laptevykh
Vostochno
Sibirskoye More
80°

Karskoye More

Baltic
Shield
SevDvina
Zapadno
Sibirskaya
Siberia
ASIA
Bering Sea
60°

European
Plain
Dvina
Ob
Yenisey
Lena
Poluostrov
Kamchatka
Aleutian
Basin

UROPE
Don
Volga
Aral'skoye
More
(Aral Sea)
Ravnina
(W. Siberian Plain)
Irtysh
Oz. Baykal
Amur
Sea of
Okhotsk
Aleutian Trench
7822

Danube
Stara
Planina
Black Sea
Caspian Sea
Oz. Balkhash
Altai
Gobi
Dongbei
Pingyuan
(Manchurian
Plain)
Sakhalin
Hokkaidō
Kuril Trench
10542

Kavkazskiy Khr.
(Caucasus)
Syr Darya
Tian Shan
Tarim
Pendi
Huang He
Huabei
Pingyuan
(N.China Plain)
Sea of
Japan
Honshū
Japan Trench
40°

ranean Sea
Kizilya-ye Zagros
Zagros Mts.
Hindu Kush
Amu Darya
Kunlun Shan
Qing Zang Gaoyuan
(Tibetan Plateau)
Yellow
Sea
Kyūshū
Japan Trench
10500

Al Furat (Euphrates)
The Gulf
Arabia
Indus
Himalaya
Brahmaputra
9848
Mt.Everest
Thar
Desert
Ganga (Ganges)
Chang
Yungui
Gaoyuan
Jiang
East
China
Sea
Taiwan
Tropic of Cancer

Tibesti
Nile
Red Sea
An Nafd
Arabian
Sea
Deccan
Bay of
Bengal
Mekong
Xi Jiang
South
China
Sea
PACIFIC
Mariana Trench
20°

L. Chad
Gulf of Aden
Arabian
Basin
Andaman Is.
Philippines
11034
Caroline Is.
Marshall
Is.

ICA
Ethiopian
Highlands
Somali
Basin
Carlsberg
Maldive
Sri
Lanka
Nicobar Is.
Philippine Trench
10497
OCEAN
MICRONESIA

Ubangi
Zaire
Basin
Lake
Victoria
Kilimanjaro
5895
Ridge
Mid-
Seychelles
Sumatera
(Sumatra)
Borneo
Sulawesi
(Celebes)
Puncak Jaya
5030
New Guinea
Solomon Is.
MELANESIA
Equator
Gilbert Is.
0°

Kasai
Tanganyika
Rift Valley
INDIAN
Indian
West
Australian
Jawa
(Java)
Christmas I.
Timor
Sea
Arafura Sea
Coral Sea
Samoa
Is.
North Fiji

Bié
Plateau
L. Malawi
Zambezi
Mozambique Channel
Madagascar
OCEAN
Basin
Cocos Is.
AUSTRALASIA
Vanuatu
Nouvelle Calédonie
(New Caledonia)
Fiji
Is.
Tropic of Capricorn
20°

Kalahari
Desert
Limpopo
Mauritius
Réunion
MID
Basin
Great
Sandy Desert
Australia
Great
Artesian
Basin
Great Dividing Range
South Fiji
Basin
Tonga Is.
10882

C. of Good Hope
Orange
Vaal
Drakensberg
Mauritius
Basin
INDIAN
Kerguelen
Basin
Île Amsterdam
L. Eyre
Darling
Murray
South Australian
Basin
Tasman
Sea
Chatham
Is.
40°

Cape
Rise
C. Leeuwin
Great
Australian
Bight
Tasmania
New
Zealand

Agulhas
Basin
Prince Edward-
Crozet Ridge
Prince Edward Is.
Îles Crozet
RIDGE
Îles de Kerguelen
Heard I.
SOUTHERN OCEAN
Indian - Antarctic Ridge

ian - Antarctic Basin
Eastern Indian - Antarctic Basin
60°

Antarctic Circle

Ross
Sea
80°

TICA

Equatorial Scale 1:80 000 000

| 0 | 500 | 1000 | 1500 | 2000 | 2500 Miles |
| 0 | 1000 | 2000 | 3000 | 4000 Kms. |

Flat Polar Equal Area Projection

40°   60°   80°   100°   120°   140°   160°   180°

© Collins ◇ Longman Atlases Cbi

5

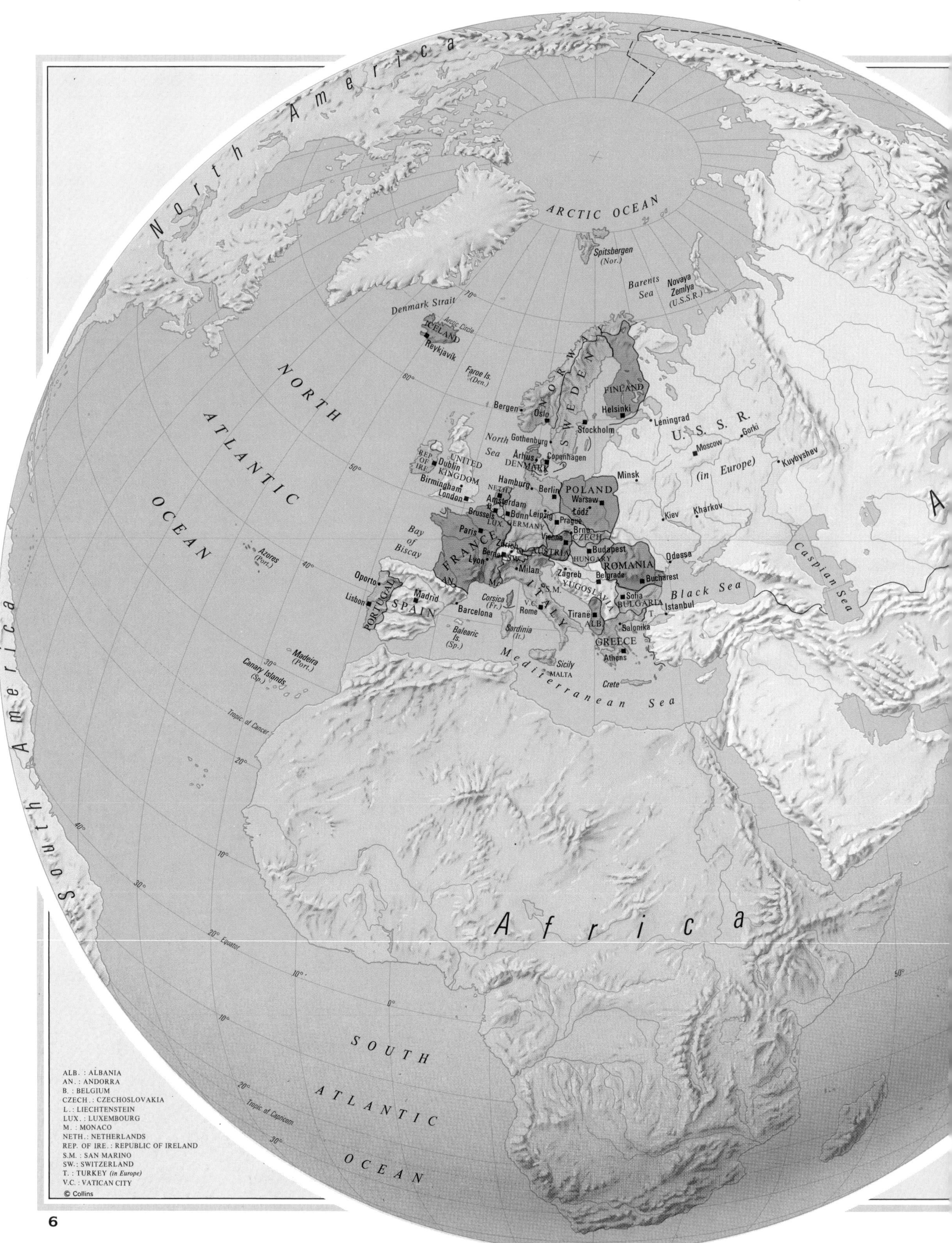

North America

ARCTIC OCEAN

Spitsbergen
(Nor.)

Barents
Sea

Novaya
Zemlya
(U.S.S.R.)

Denmark Strait

Arctic Circle
ICELAND
Reykjavik

70°

Faroe Is.
(Den.)

60°

NORWAY

SWEDEN

FINLAND
Helsinki

Bergen

Oslo

Leningrad

NORTH

Gothenburg
Stockholm

U.S.S.R.

ATLANTIC

North
Sea

Århus
DENMARK

Copenhagen

Minsk

Moscow

Gorki

(in Europe)

Kuybyshev

ATLANTIC

50°

REP.
OF
IRE.
Dublin

UNITED
KINGDOM

Hamburg
Berlin

POLAND
Warsaw

Kiev

Kharkov

OCEAN

Birmingham

NETH.

Amsterdam

Leipzig

Łódź

London

Brussels

Bonn
GERMANY

Prague

Brno

LUX.

Paris

Berne

Zürich

Vienna

CZECH.

Bay
of
Biscay

40°

FRANCE

Lyon

SW.

AUSTRIA

Budapest

HUNGARY

ROMANIA

Odessa

A

Azores
(Port.)

AN.

M.

Milan

Zagreb

Belgrade

Bucharest

Caspian Sea

Oporto

Madrid

Barcelona

Corsica
(Fr.)

S.M.

ITALY

YUGOSLAVIA

Sofia

BULGARIA

Black Sea

Istanbul

A

Lisbon

PORTUGAL

SPAIN

V.C.
Rome

Tiranë

ALB.

Salonika

T.

30°

Balearic
Is.
(Sp.)

Sardinia
(It.)

GREECE

Athens

Madeira
(Port.)

Canary Islands
(Sp.)

Sicily

MALTA

Crete

Mediterranean   Sea

Tropic of Cancer

20°

10°

Africa

0°   Equator

10°

50°

SOUTH

20°

ATLANTIC

Tropic of Capricorn

South America

30°

OCEAN

South America

ALB. : ALBANIA
AN. : ANDORRA
B. : BELGIUM
CZECH. : CZECHOSLOVAKIA
L. : LIECHTENSTEIN
LUX. : LUXEMBOURG
M. : MONACO
NETH. : NETHERLANDS
REP. OF IRE. : REPUBLIC OF IRELAND
S.M. : SAN MARINO
SW. : SWITZERLAND
T. : TURKEY (in Europe)
V.C. : VATICAN CITY

© Collins

EUROPE

EUROPE

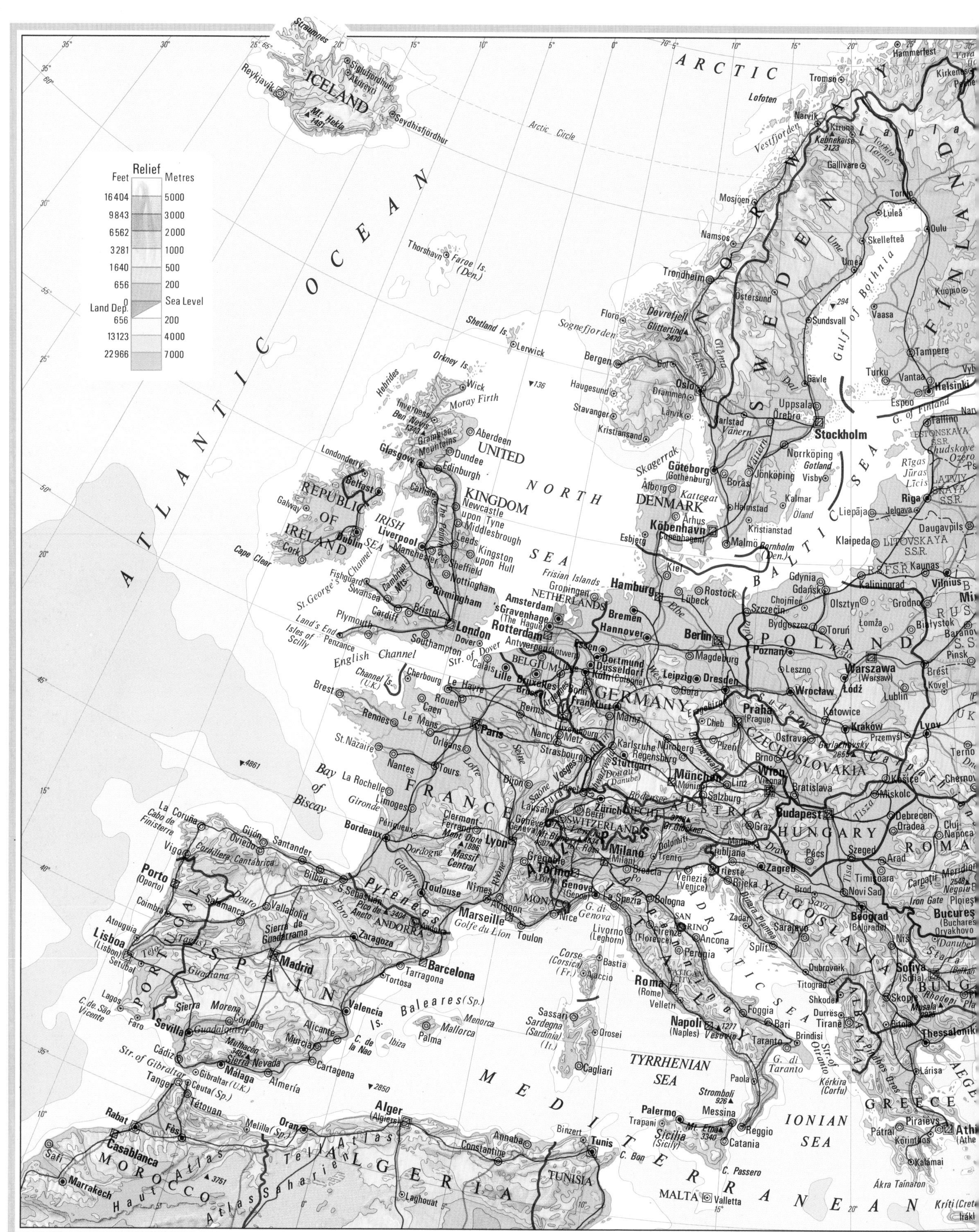

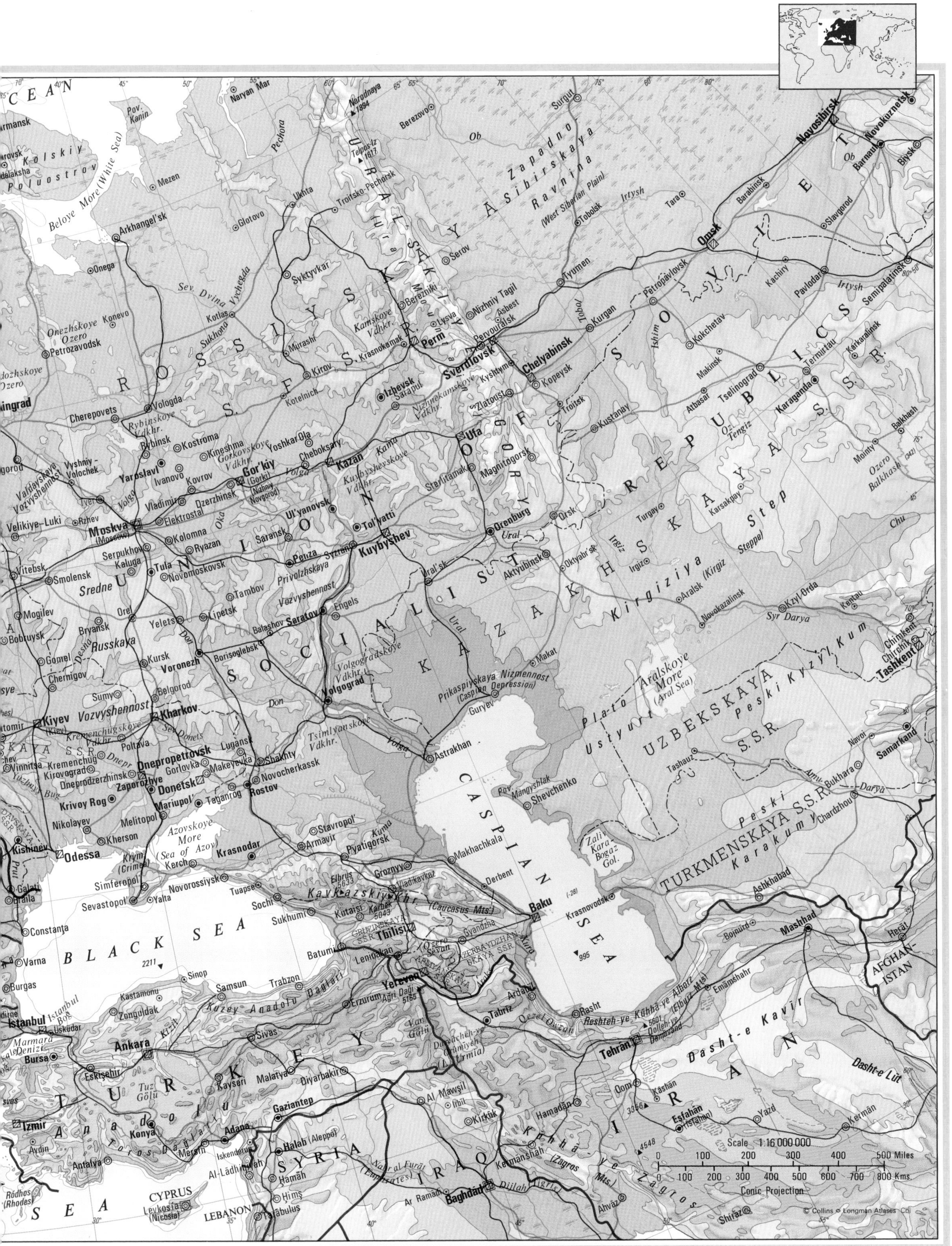
BLACK SEA
CASPIAN SEA
UNION OF SOVIET SOCIALIST REPUBLICS
ROSSIYSKAYA S.F.S.R.
KAZAKHSKAYA S.S.R.
UZBEKSKAYA S.S.R.
TURKMENSKAYA S.S.R.
TURKEY
IRAN
IRAQ
SYRIA
CYPRUS
LEBANON
AFGHANISTAN
Moskva
Kiyev
Volgograd
Tashkent
Tehrān
Baghdād
Ankara
Scale 1:16 000 000
Conic Projection
© Collins-Longman Atlases

BRITISH ISLES

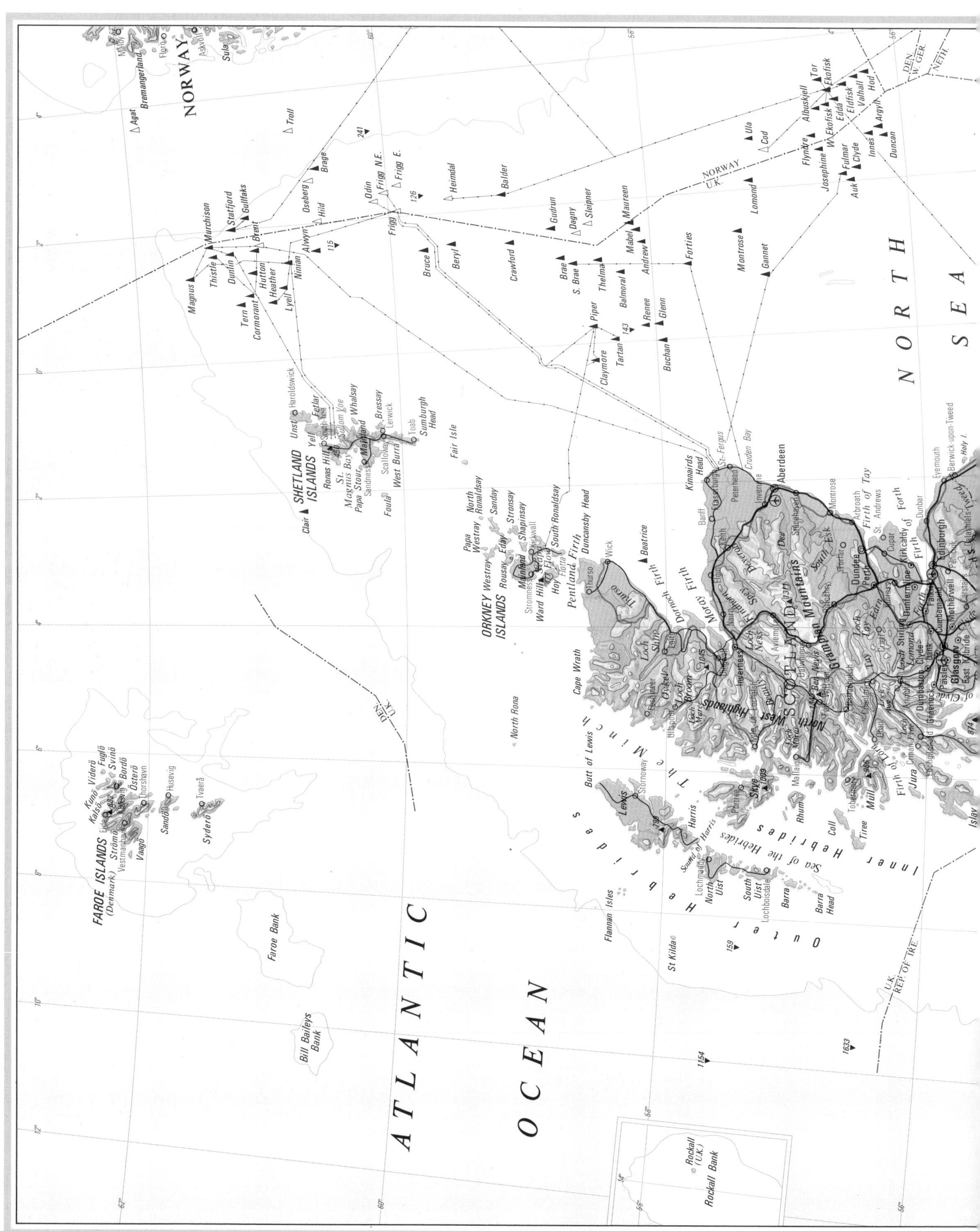

NORWAY

△ Mary
△ Bremangerland
△ Agat
Frigö
Askøll
Sula

△ Troll

NORTH SEA

DEN.
W.GER.
NETH.

241
▲ Brage

NORWAY
UK.

DEN.
UK.

△ Tor
▲ Albuskjell ▲ Ekofisk
Eldfisk △ Valhall ▲ Hod
Flyndre W. Ekofisk Edda
Josephine ▲ Fulmar Clyde
Auk △ Innes Argyll ▲ Duncan

Ula
△ Cod
Lomond

△ Odin △ Frigg N.E.
△ Frigg E.
126
△ Heimdal
Balder
Frigg

Gudrun
△ Dagny
○ Sleipner

△ Murchison
Statfjord ▲ Gullfaks
Oseberg △ Hild
Alwyn
115

Maureen
Mabel
▲ Andrew
Montrose
Gannet

▲ Magnus
▲ Thistle
Dunlin
Tern
Cormorant
Hutton
Heather
Lyell
Ninian
Bruce ▲
Beryl ▲
Crawford ▲
Brae ▲
S. Brae Thelma ▲
Balmoral
Renee
Glenn

Forties

Piper
Claymore
Tartan 143
Buchan

Harold swick
Unst
Fetlar
Yell South Yoe Whalsay
Bressay
Ronas Hill Sullom Voe
St. Mainland Lerwick
Magnus Bay
Papa Stour Scalloway
Sandness West Burra
Foula Toab
Sumburgh
Head

Clair ▲

Fair Isle

SHETLAND
ISLANDS

Westray North Ronaldsay
Papa Sanday
Westray Rousay Stronsay
Eday
Mainland Shapinsay
Ward Hill Kirkwall
Hoy Holm
Stromness
Hoxa
Flotta South Ronaldsay

ORKNEY
ISLANDS

Duncansby Head
Pentland Firth

Wick

Kinnairds
Head
Cruden Bay

Aberdeen

Fraserburgh St-Fergus
Peterhead

Inverurie Dee
Banff
Beatrice ▲
Thurso
Cape Wrath

Dornoch Firth
Moray Firth
Elgin
Spey

Nairn
Inverness

Montrose
Arbroath
Firth of Tay
St. Andrews
Dundee
Perth
Forfar

NORTH
SEA

North Rona

SCOTTISH
HIGHLANDS

GRAMPIAN
MOUNTAINS

Firth of Forth
Dunbar

Ullapool Loch
Broom

North West
Highlands

Loch Ness
Fort William

Loch
Lomond
Glasgow
Paisley
Clyde

Berwick-upon-Tweed
Eyemouth
Holy I.

Butt of Lewis
Stornoway

The Minch

Lewis

Harris

Skye

Sound of Harris
Lochmaddy
North
Uist
South
Uist
Lochboisdale

Mallaig
Rhum
Tobermory
Mull
Coll
Tiree

Firth of Lorn
Jura

Inner Hebrides

Firth of Clyde

FAROE ISLANDS
(Denmark)
Kuno Viderö Fuglö
Kalsö Svinö
Vestmanna Österö Bordö
Ström
Vaagö Thorshavn

Sandö Husavig
Ivaerö
Syderö

ATLANTIC
OCEAN

Flannan Isles
159

St Kilda

Barra
Barra
Head

Sound of Harris
Sea of the Hebrides

Outer Hebrides

Faroe
Bank

Bill Baileys
Bank

1154

1633

U.K.
REP. OF IRE.

Rockall
(U.K.)
Rockall Bank

10

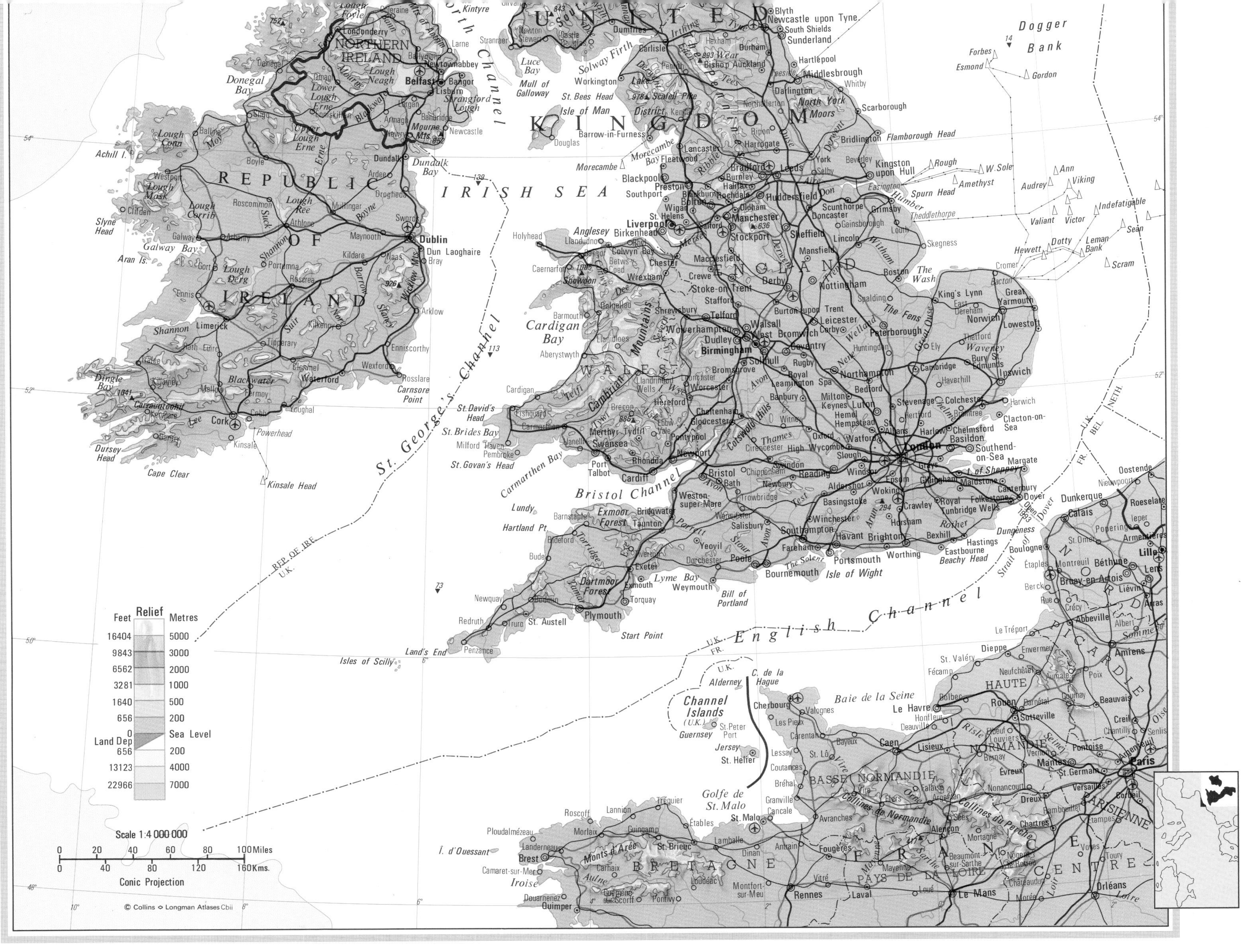
UNITED KINGDOM
ENGLAND
WALES
NORTHERN IRELAND
REPUBLIC OF IRELAND
FRANCE
PICARDIE
HAUTE NORMANDIE
BASSE NORMANDIE
BRETAGNE
PAYS DE LA LOIRE
CENTRE
PARISIENNE
IRISH SEA
North Channel
St. George's Channel
Bristol Channel
English Channel
Strait of Dover
Dogger Bank
Channel Islands (U.K.)
Isles of Scilly
Land's End
Cardigan Bay
Baie de la Seine
Golfe de St. Malo
Dublin
Belfast
London
Birmingham
Manchester
Liverpool
Leeds
Sheffield
Bristol
Cardiff
Plymouth
Southampton
Cork
Limerick
Galway
Paris
Rouen
Le Havre
Caen
Cherbourg
Rennes
Brest
Le Mans
Orléans
Amiens
Lille
Relief
Feet
Metres
16404 5000
9843 3000
6562 2000
3281 1000
1640 500
656 200
0 Sea Level
Land Dep 656 200
13123 4000
22966 7000
Scale 1:4 000 000
0 20 40 60 80 100 Miles
0 40 80 120 160 Kms.
Conic Projection
© Collins ◇ Longman Atlases Cbii

ENGLAND AND WALES

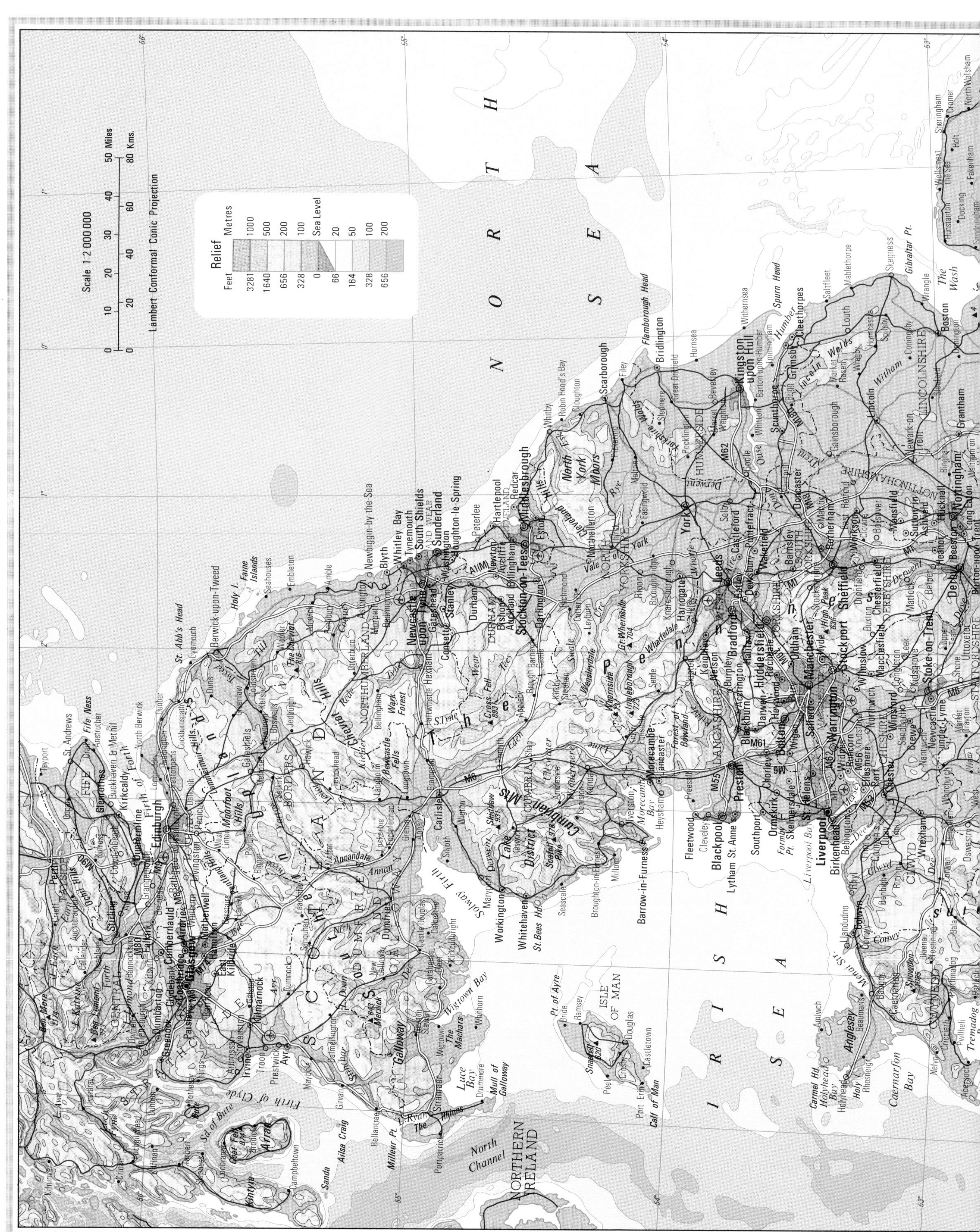

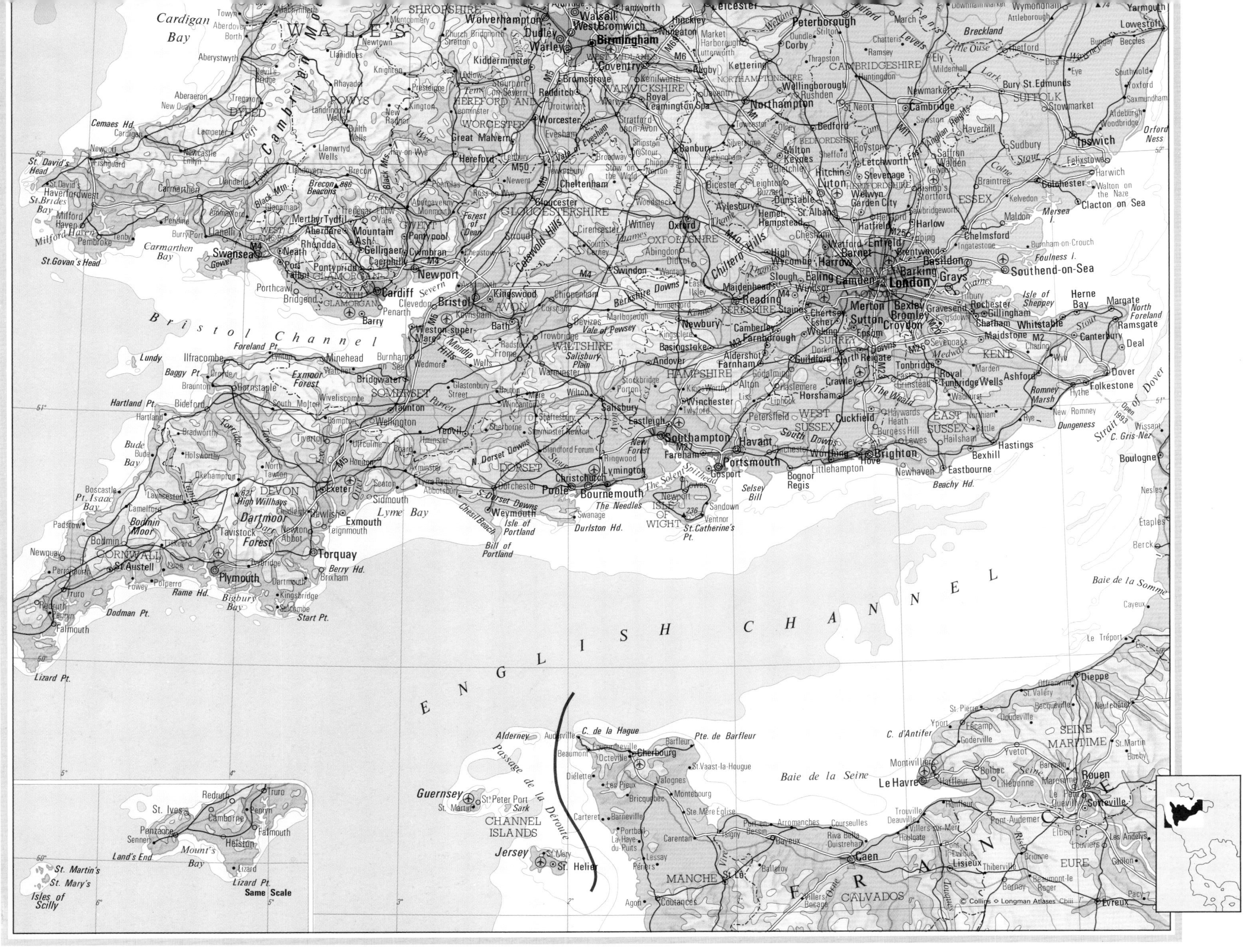

ENGLISH CHANNEL
Bristol Channel
Cardigan Bay
Carmarthen Bay
Lyme Bay
Baie de la Seine
Baie de la Somme
Strait of Dover
WALES
FRANCE
CHANNEL ISLANDS
Passage de la Déroute
Alderney
Guernsey
Sark
Jersey
ISLE OF WIGHT
Isles of Scilly
Land's End
Lizard Pt.
Start Pt.
Dodman Pt.
Hartland Pt.
St. David's Head
St. Govan's Head
Lundy
Dartmoor Forest
Exmoor Forest
Bodmin Moor
Mendip Hills
Cotswold Hills
Chiltern Hills
Salisbury Plain
South Downs
The Weald
Beachy Hd.
Dungeness
Selsey Bill
Bill of Portland
C. de la Hague
Pte. de Barfleur
C. d'Antifer
C. Gris-Nez
London
Birmingham
Bristol
Cardiff
Swansea
Newport
Plymouth
Exeter
Torquay
Bournemouth
Southampton
Portsmouth
Brighton
Hastings
Dover
Folkestone
Canterbury
Margate
Ramsgate
Southend-on-Sea
Chelmsford
Colchester
Ipswich
Cambridge
Oxford
Reading
Swindon
Gloucester
Cheltenham
Worcester
Hereford
Coventry
Northampton
Peterborough
Bedford
Luton
Wolverhampton
Walsall
Dudley
Lowestoft
Yarmouth
Cherbourg
Le Havre
Rouen
Caen
Dieppe
Boulogne
St. Helier
St. Peter Port
Penzance
Truro
Falmouth
Newquay
St. Austell
CORNWALL
DEVON
SOMERSET
DORSET
HAMPSHIRE
WILTSHIRE
KENT
ESSEX
SUFFOLK
SURREY
EAST SUSSEX
WEST SUSSEX
OXFORDSHIRE
GLOUCESTERSHIRE
CALVADOS
MANCHE
EURE
SEINE MARITIME
Same Scale
© Collins ◇ Longman Atlases

SCOTLAND

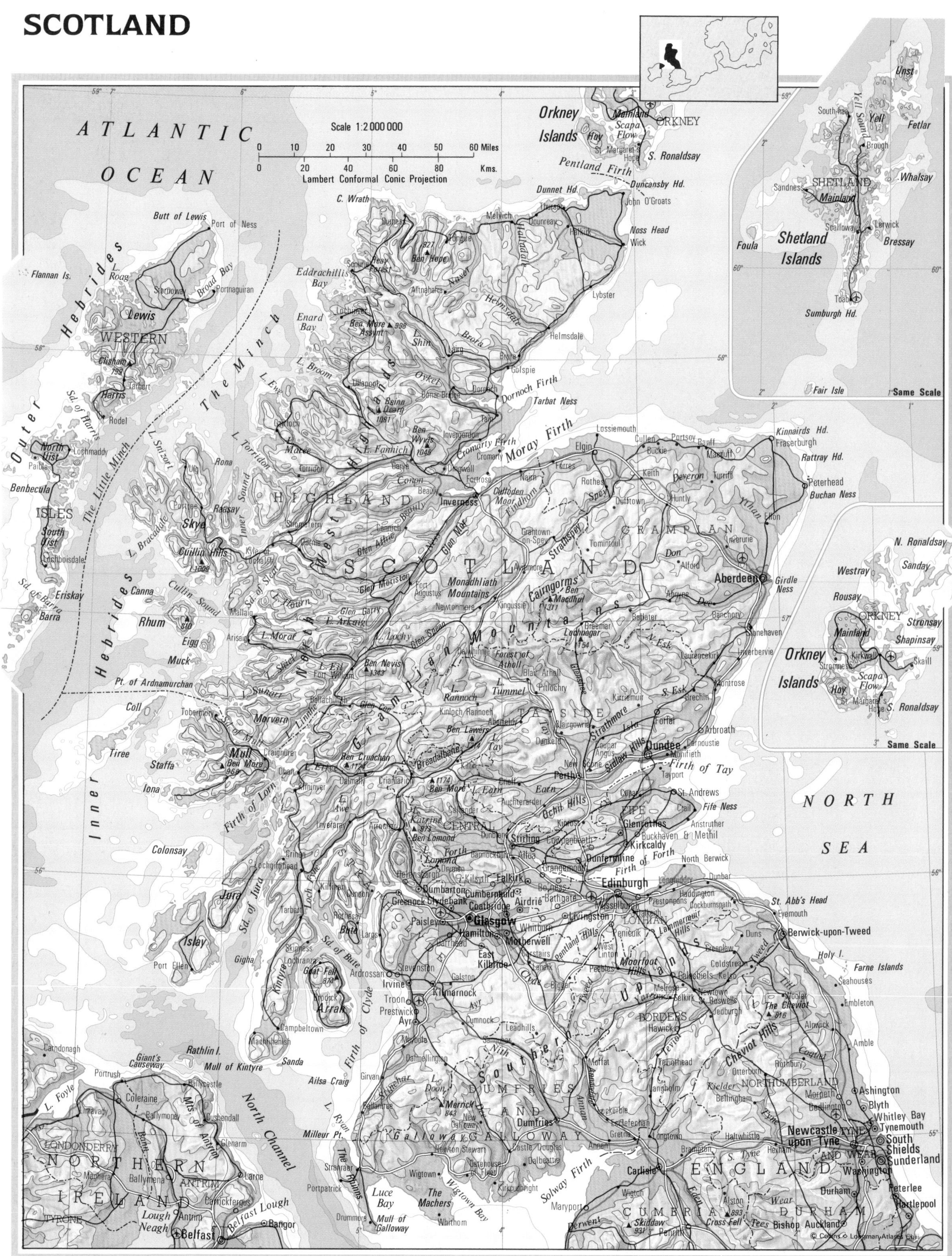

IRELAND

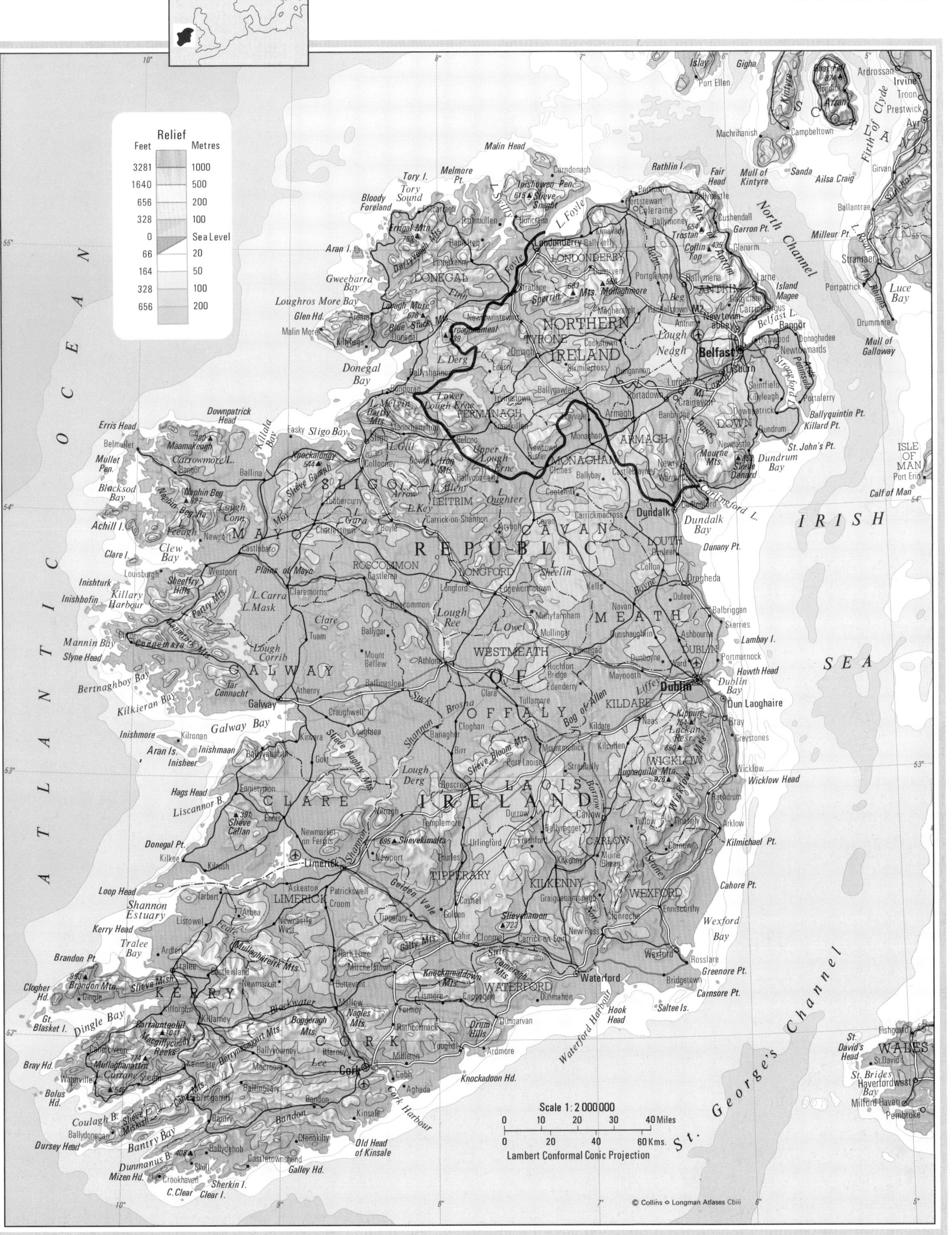

Relief

Feet		Metres
3281		1000
1640		500
656		200
328		100
0	Sea Level	0
66		20
164		50
328		100
656		200

Scale 1:2 000 000

0 10 20 30 40 Miles

0 20 40 60 Kms.

Lambert Conformal Conic Projection

© Collins ◇ Longman Atlases Cbiii

THE LOW COUNTRIES

Scale 1:2 000 000

0 10 20 30 40 50 60 Miles
0 20 40 60 80 Kms.

Conic Projection

Relief

Feet	Metres
16 404	5000
9843	3000
6562	2000
3281	1000
1640	500
656	200
0	Sea Level
Land Dep.	
656	200
13123	4000
22966	7000

NORTH SEA

NETHERLANDS

BELGIUM

GERMANY

FRANCE

LUXEMBOURG

Amsterdam
Rotterdam
's Gravenhage (The Hague)
Utrecht
Groningen
Eindhoven
Antwerpen
Bruxelles (Brussel)
Luxembourg
Köln
Düsseldorf
Essen
Dortmund
Bonn

© Collins ◇ Longman Atlases Cbill

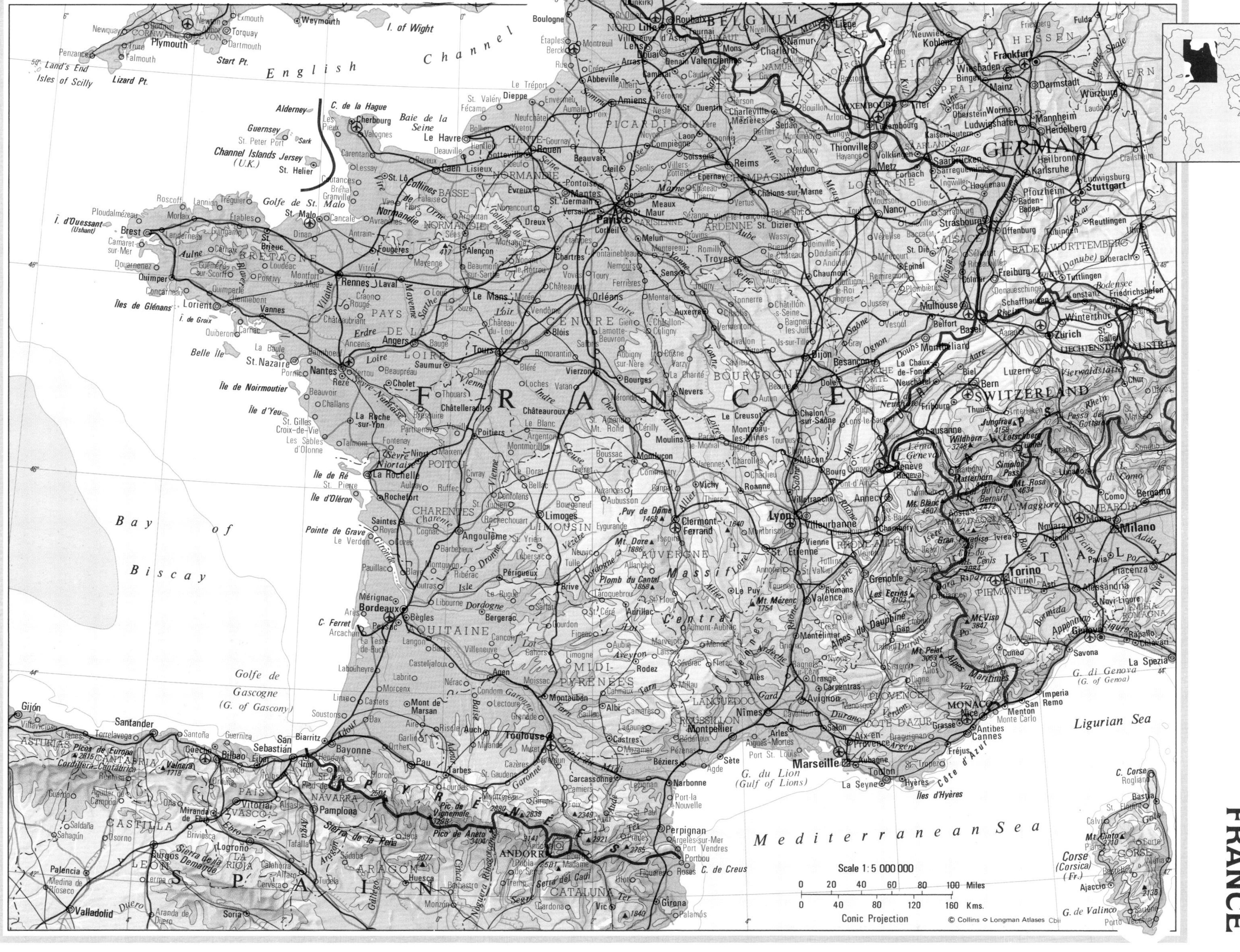

English Channel
I. of Wight
Bay of Biscay
Golfe de Gascogne
(G. of Gascony)
Mediterranean Sea
Ligurian Sea
G. du Lion
(Gulf of Lions)
G. di Genova
(G. of Genoa)
Channel Islands Jersey
(U.K.)
Corse
(Corsica)
(Fr.)
FRANCE
BELGIUM
GERMANY
SWITZERLAND
SPAIN
ANDORRA
MONACO
Paris
Lyon
Marseille
Bordeaux
Toulouse
Nantes
Brest
Strasbourg
Lille
Rennes
Orléans
Limoges
Grenoble
Nice
Montpellier
Scale 1: 5 000 000
0 20 40 60 80 100 Miles
0 40 80 120 160 Kms.
Conic Projection
© Collins ○ Longman Atlases

NORTHERN FRANCE

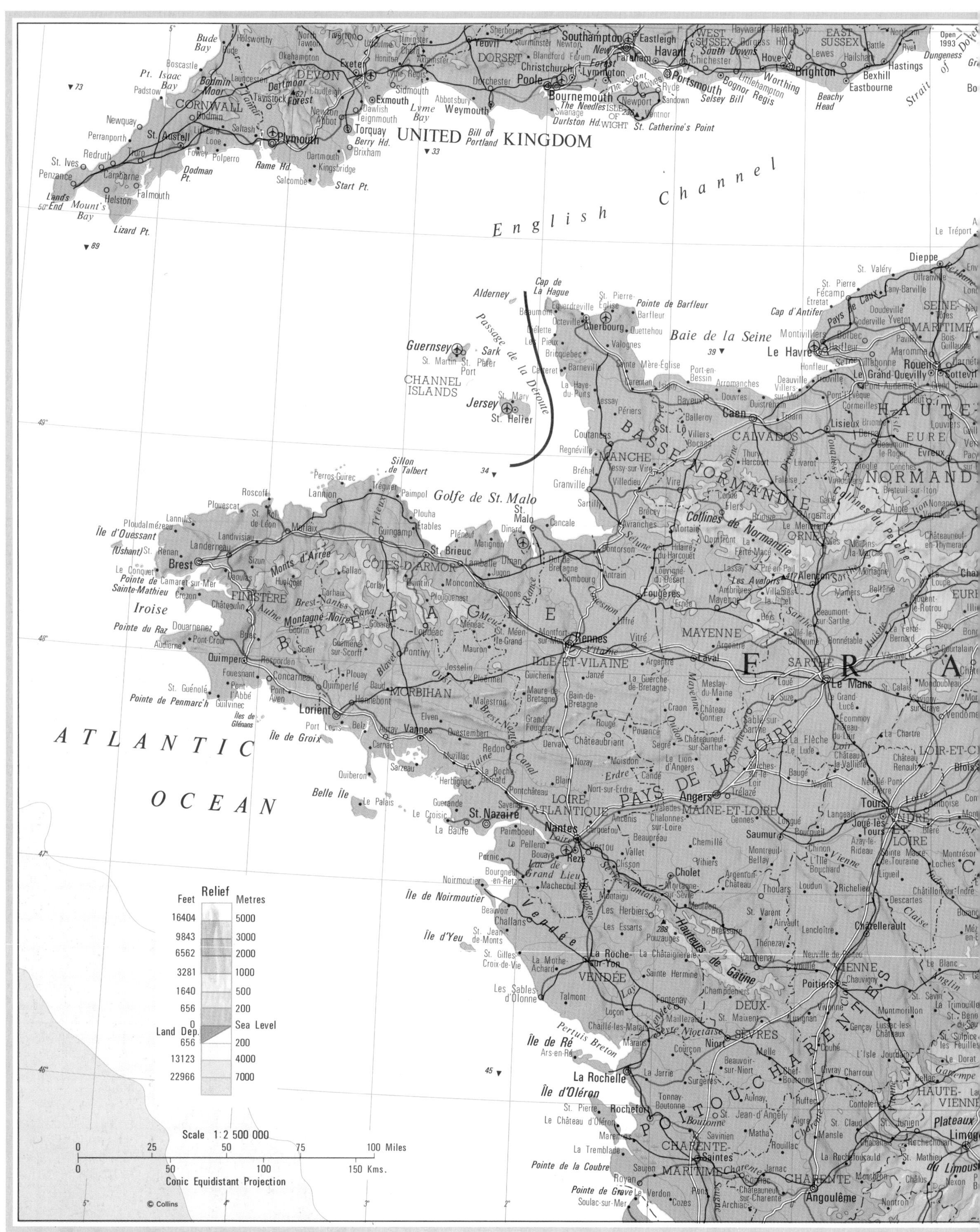

Relief

Feet		Metres
16404		5000
9843		3000
6562		2000
3281		1000
1640		500
656		200
0		Sea Level
Land Dep.		
656		200
13123		4000
22966		7000

Scale 1:2 500 000

0	25	50	75	100 Miles
0	50	100	150 Kms.	

Conic Equidistant Projection

© Collins

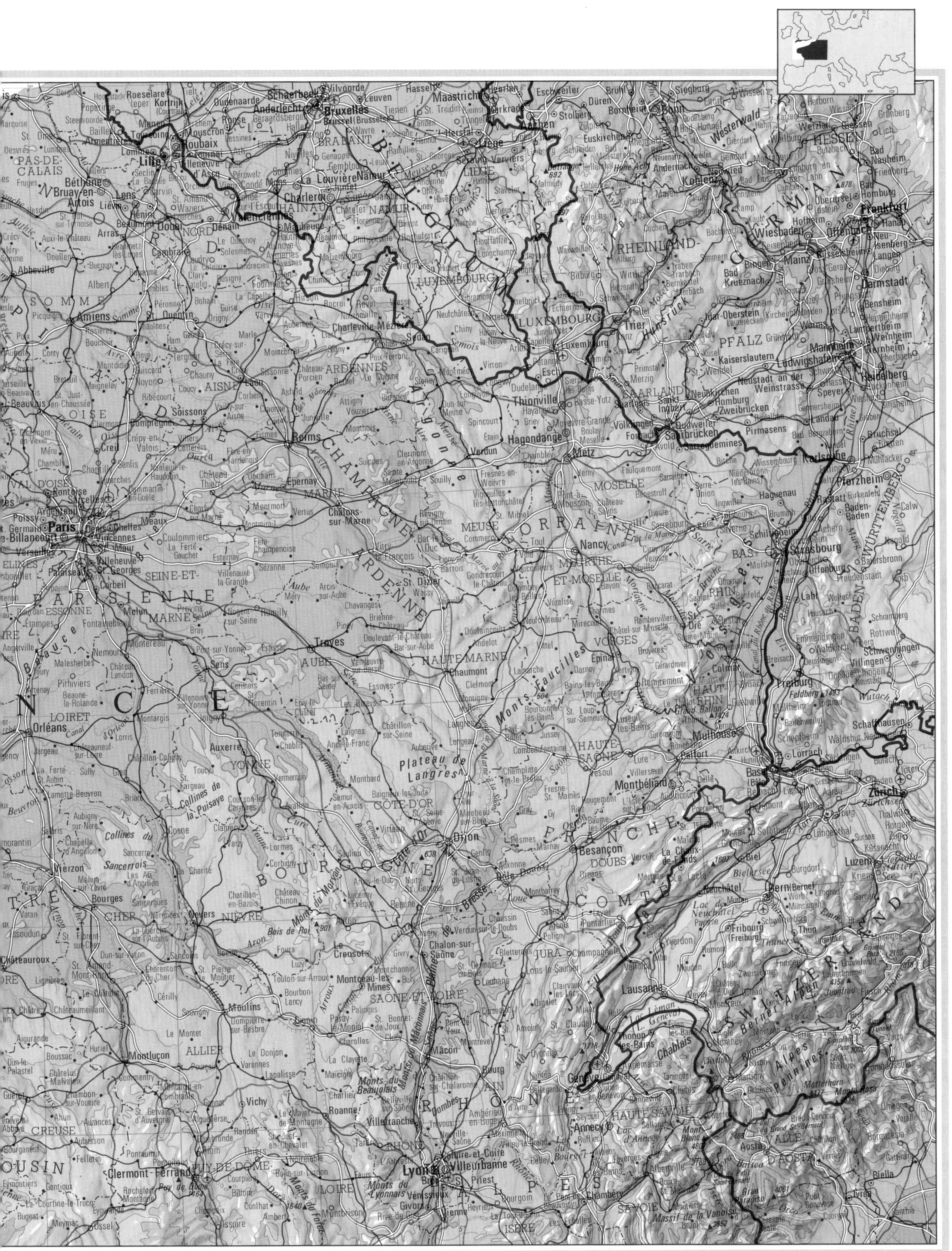

Bruxelles
Brussel (Brussels)
Maastricht
Aachen
Bonn
Liège
Namur
Charleroi
Lille
Roubaix
Koblenz
Westerwald
Wiesbaden
Mainz
Frankfurt
Offenbach
Darmstadt
HESSEN
RHEINLAND-
PFALZ
Trier
LUXEMBOURG
Luxembourg
SAARLAND
Saarbrücken
Kaiserslautern
Ludwigshafen
Mannheim
Heidelberg
Karlsruhe
Pforzheim
Thionville
Metz
Nancy
Strasbourg
Freiburg
Basel
Mulhouse
Zürich
Bern
Lausanne
Genève
Amiens
Reims
Paris
Versailles
Orléans
Troyes
Dijon
Besançon
Lyon
Villeurbanne
Clermont-Ferrand
Vichy
Moulins
Nevers
Bourges
Auxerre
Chaumont
Épinal
Verdun
Soissons
Sedan
Charleville-Mézières
Châlons-sur-Marne
Mâcon
Bourg
Annecy
Chambéry
Aosta
Chalon-sur-Saône
Le Creusot
PAS-DE-CALAIS
NORD
SOMME
AISNE
OISE
ARDENNES
MARNE
MEUSE
MOSELLE
VOSGES
AUBE
YONNE
NIÈVRE
CHER
ALLIER
LOIRE
RHÔNE
AIN
JURA
DOUBS
SAVOIE
HAUTE-SAVOIE
ISÈRE
CREUSE
PUY-DE-DÔME
CÔTE-D'OR
SAÔNE-ET-LOIRE
HAUTE-MARNE
HAUTE-SAÔNE
BRABANT
HAINAUT
NAMUR
LIÈGE
CHAMPAGNE
LORRAINE
BOURGOGNE
FRANCHE-COMTÉ
ALSACE
BADEN-WÜRTTEMBERG
SWITZERLAND
Plateau de Langres
Collines de la Puisaye
Monts Faucilles
Argonne
Massif de la Vanoise
Alpes Pennines
Berner Alpen
Lac Léman (L. Geneva)
Monts du Lyonnais
Monts du Beaujolais
Mont Blanc
Matterhorn
Monte Rosa
Feldberg 1493

SOUTHERN FRANCE

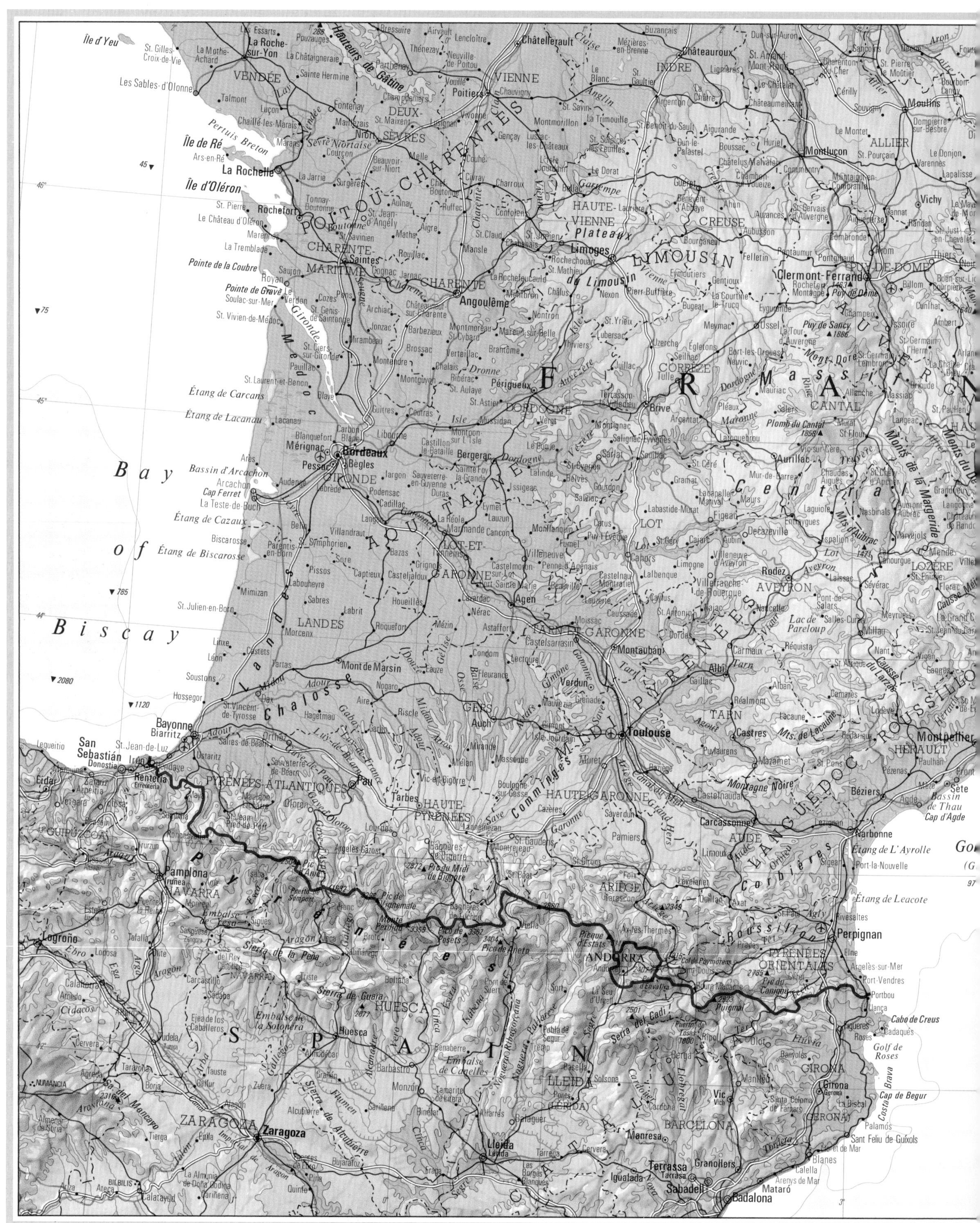

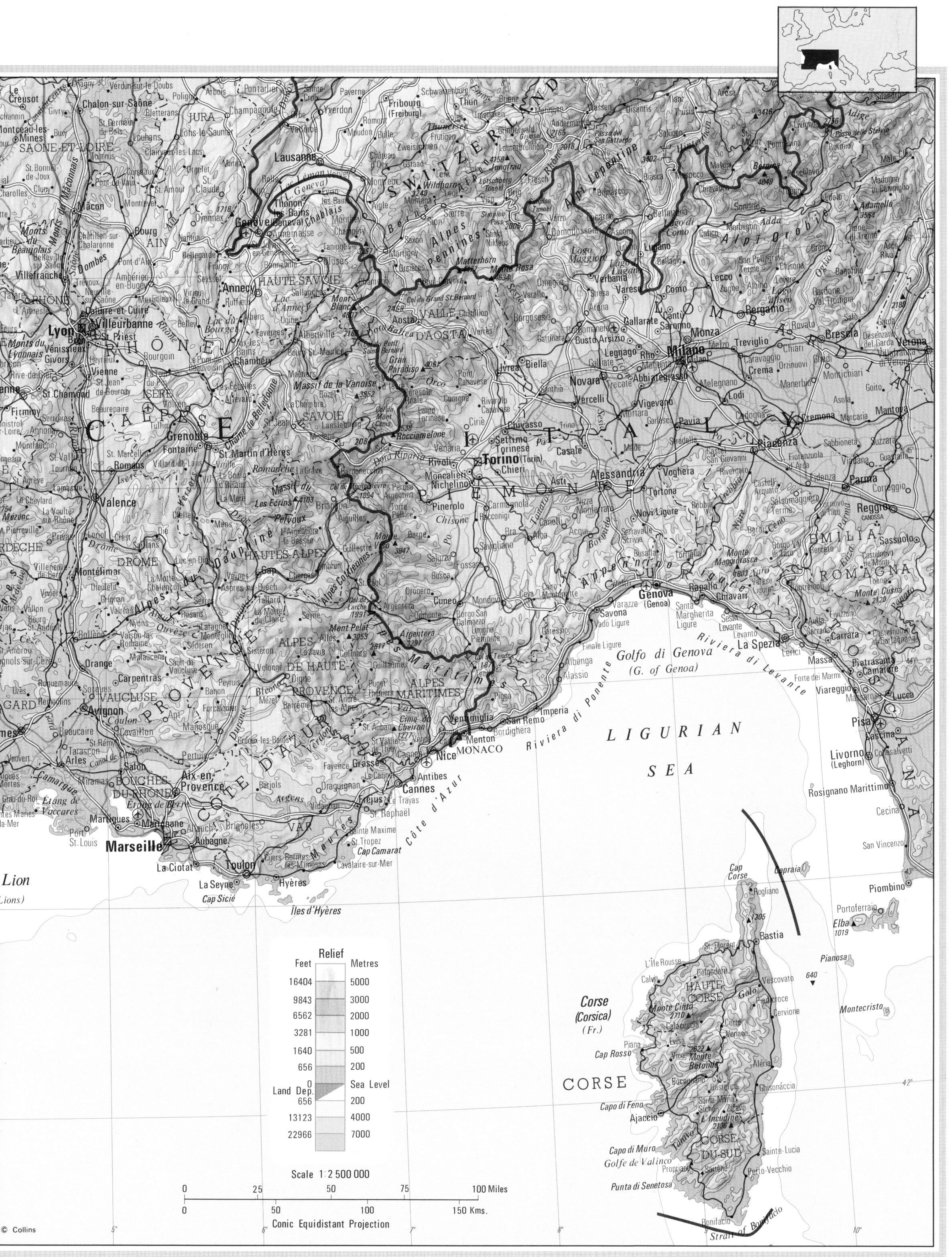

Relief

Feet	Metres
16404	5000
9843	3000
6562	2000
3281	1000
1640	500
656	200
0	Sea Level

Land Dep.

656	200
13123	4000
22966	7000

Scale 1 : 2 500 000

```
0        25        50        75      100 Miles
0       50       100           150 Kms.
```

Conic Equidistant Projection

MEDITERRANEAN LANDS

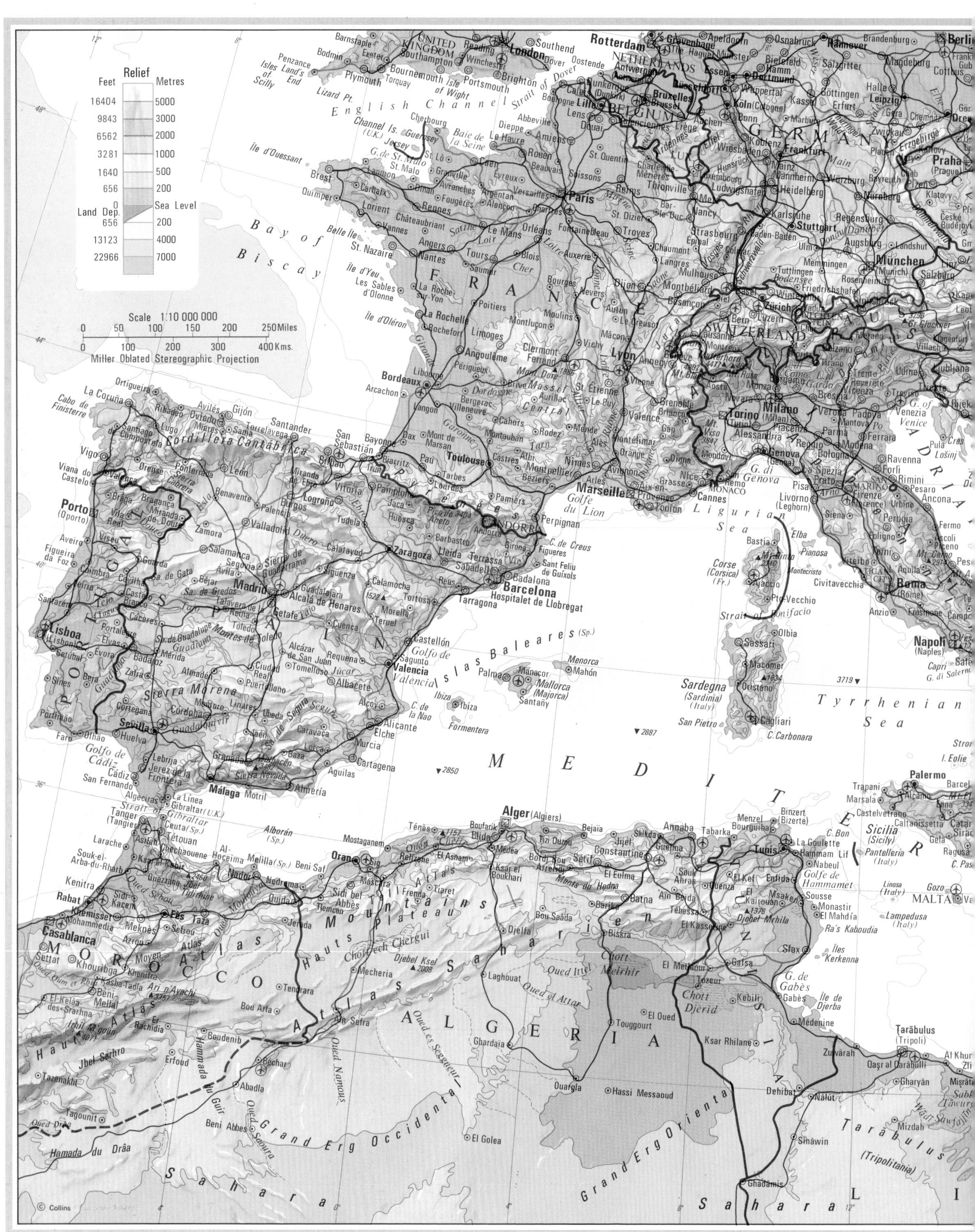

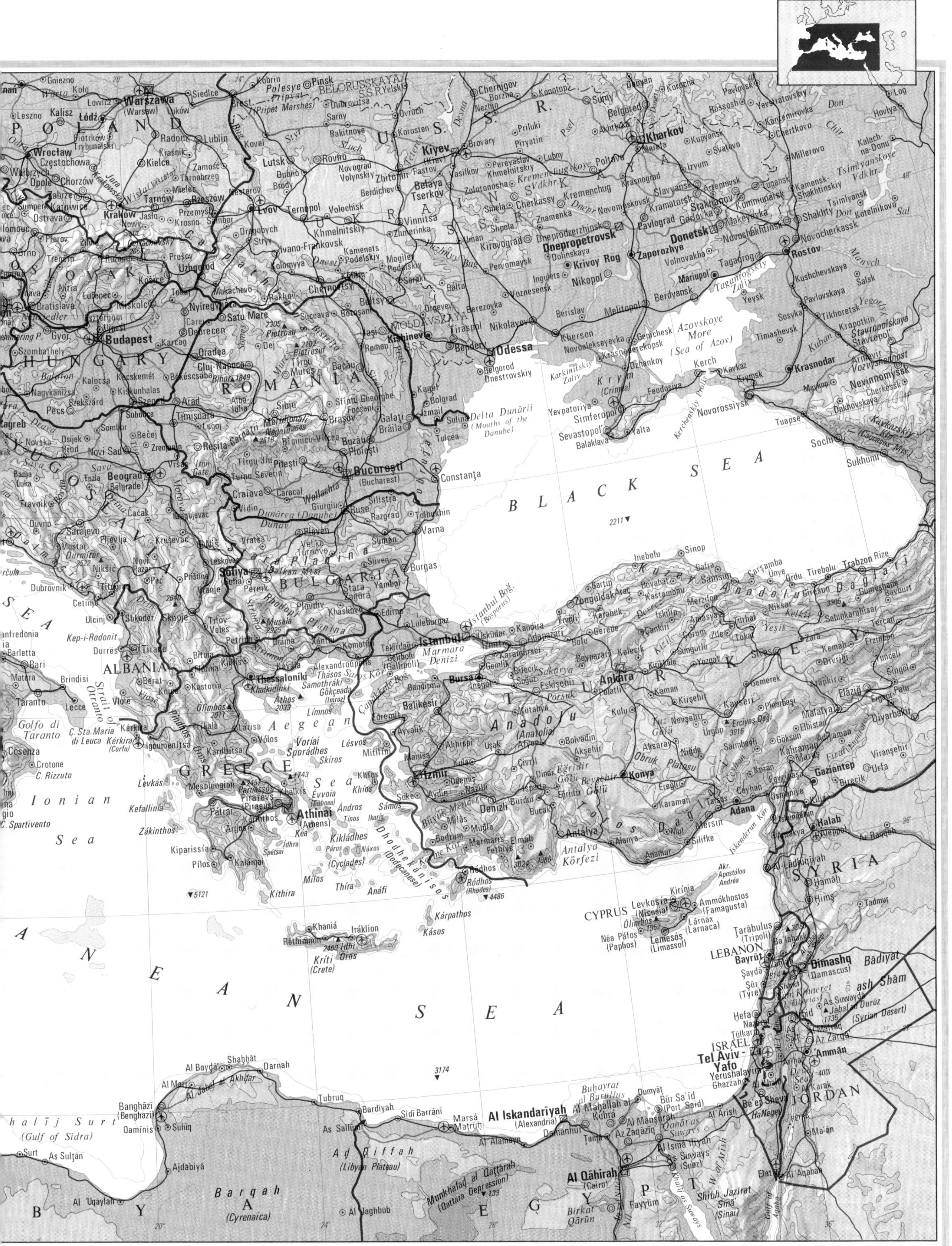

IBERIAN PENINSULA

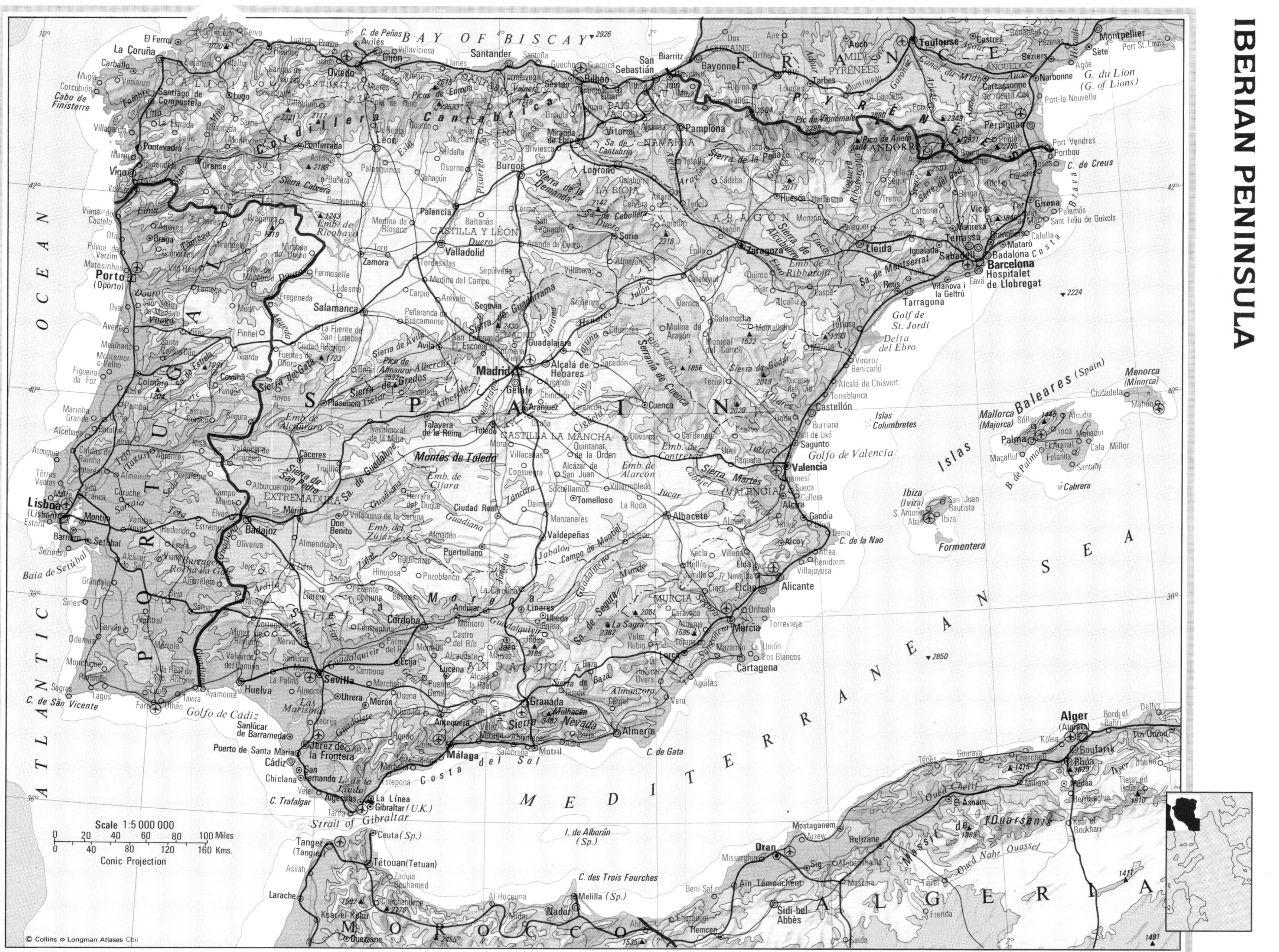

EASTERN SPAIN

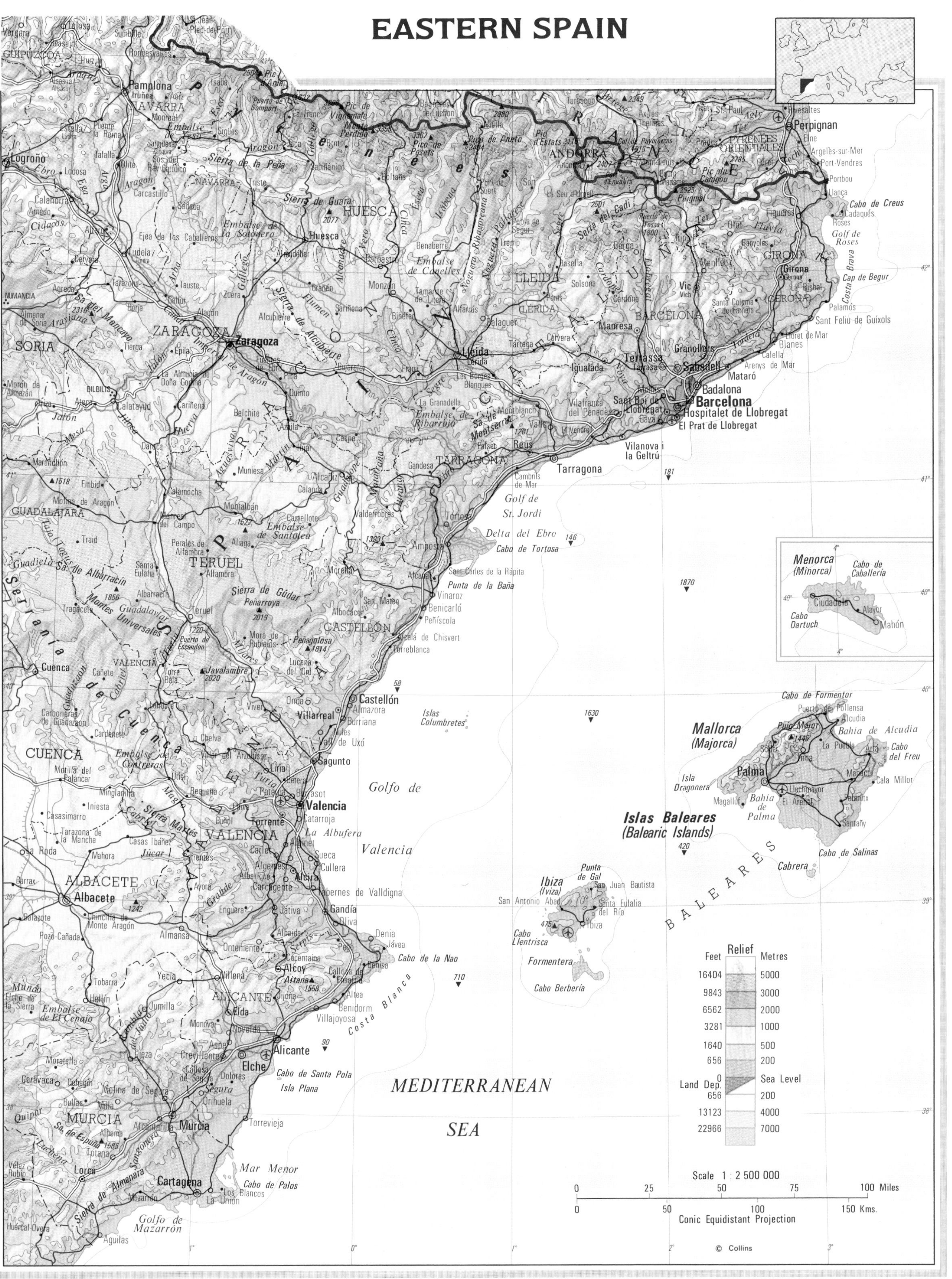

MEDITERRANEAN

SEA

Menorca
(Minorca)

Mallorca
(Majorca)

Islas Baleares
(Balearic Islands)

Ibiza
(Iviza)

Feet	Relief	Metres
16404		5000
9843		3000
6562		2000
3281		1000
1640		500
656		200
0		Sea Level
Land Dep.		
656		200
13123		4000
22966		7000

Scale 1 : 2 500 000

0   25   50   75   100 Miles

0   50   100   150 Kms.

Conic Equidistant Projection

© Collins

25

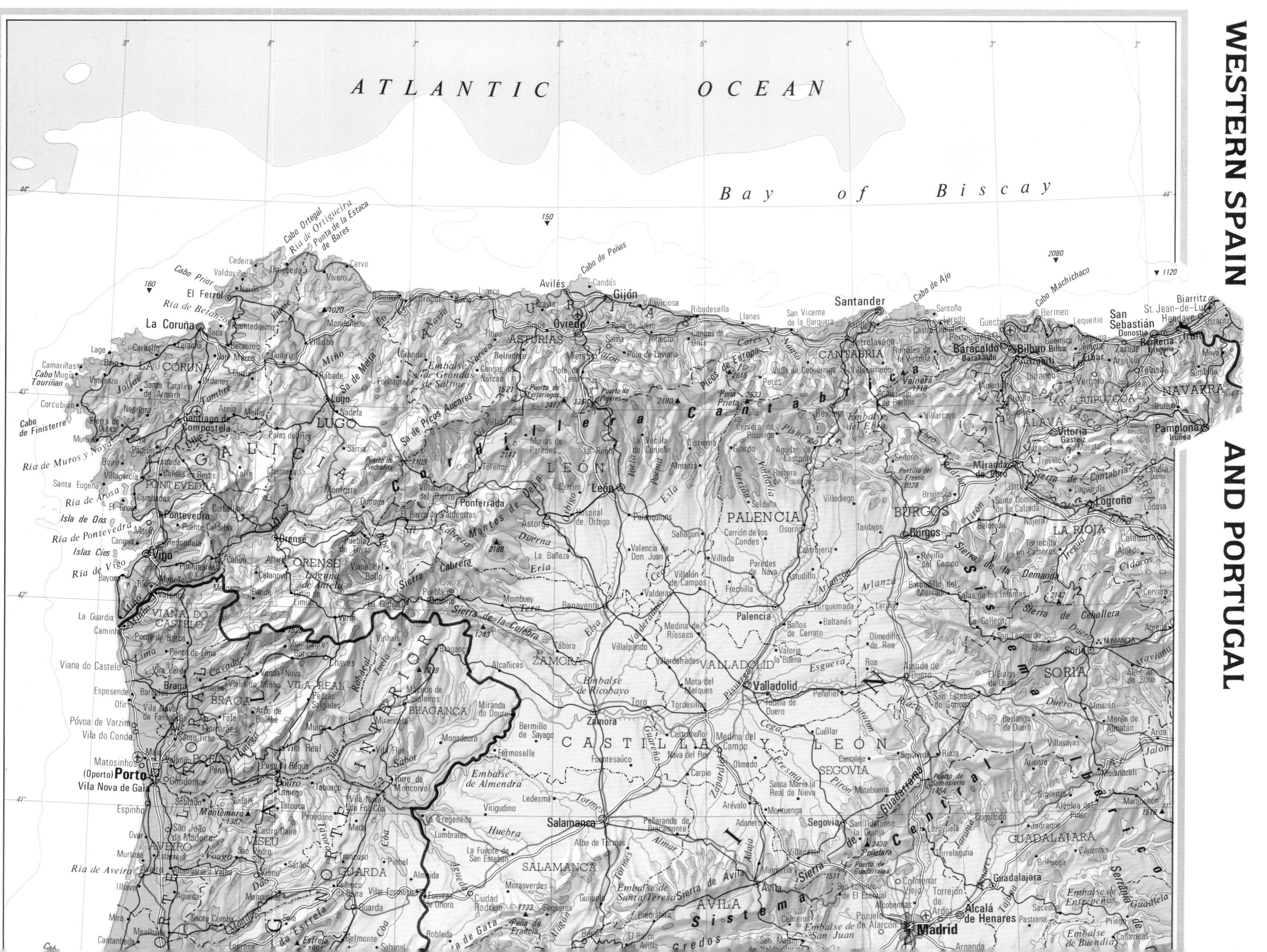

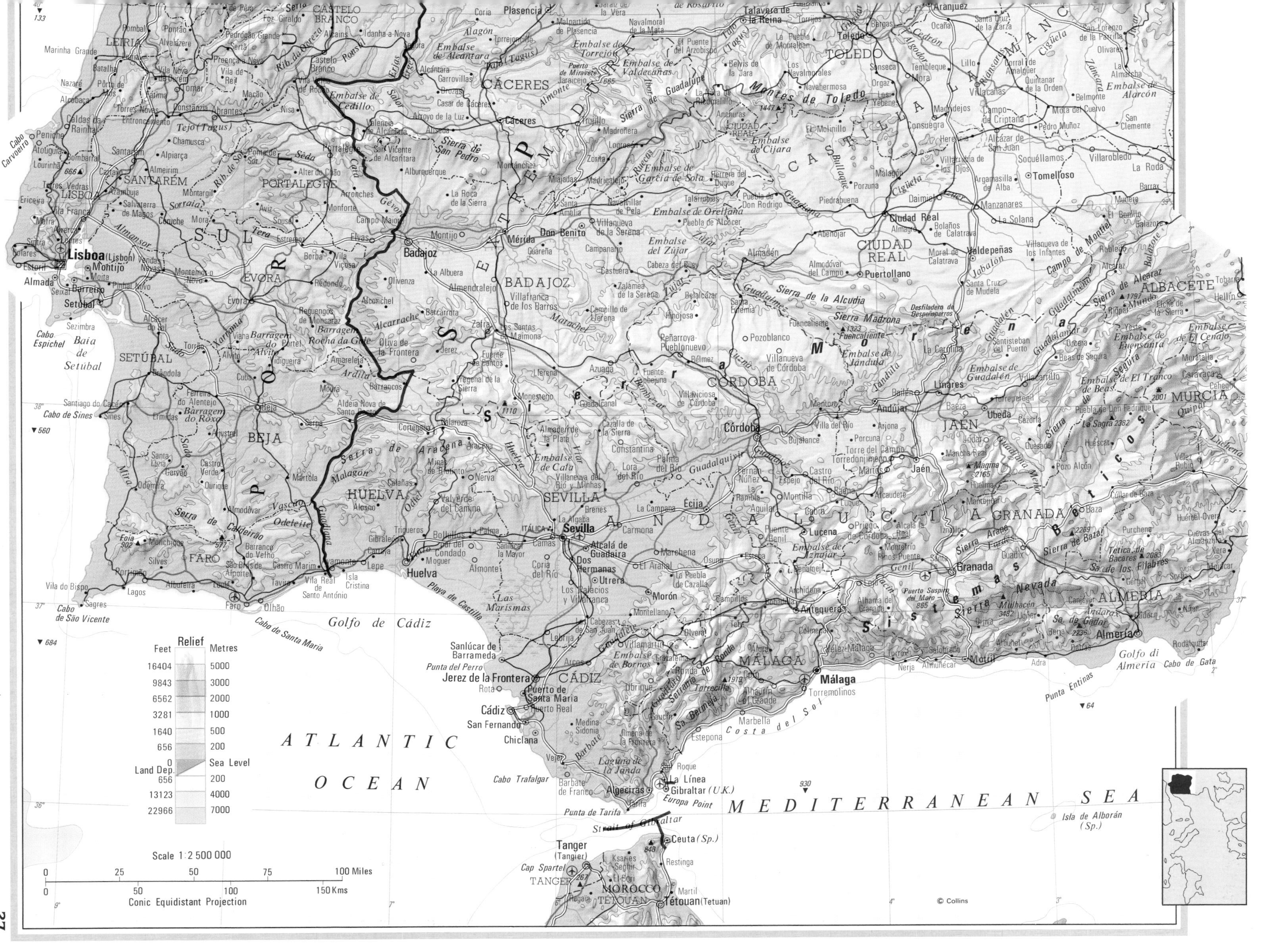
ATLANTIC OCEAN
MEDITERRANEAN SEA
Golfo de Cádiz
Golfo di Almería
Costa del Sol
Strait of Gibraltar
Isla de Alborán (Sp.)
Cabo de São Vicente
Cabo de Santa Maria
Cabo Trafalgar
Cabo de Gata
Cabo Espichel
Cabo de Sines
Cabo Carvoeiro
Baía de Setúbal
Lisboa (Lisbon)
Setúbal
Santarém
Portalegre
Évora
Beja
Faro
Sagres
Lagos
Olhão
Castelo Branco
Leiria
Badajoz
Cáceres
Mérida
Plasencia
Don Benito
Sevilla
Huelva
Cádiz
Jerez de la Frontera
Algeciras
La Línea
Gibraltar (U.K.)
Europa Point
Punta de Tarifa
Ceuta (Sp.)
Tanger (Tangier)
Tetouan (Tetuan)
MOROCCO
Córdoba
Málaga
Torremolinos
Marbella
Granada
Jaén
Úbeda
Linares
Almería
Motril
Murcia
Albacete
Ciudad Real
Puertollano
Valdepeñas
Toledo
Talavera de la Reina
Tomelloso
Mulhacén 3482
Sierra Nevada
Sierra Morena
Guadalquivir
Guadiana
Montes de Toledo
Relief
Feet Metres
16404 5000
9843 3000
6562 2000
3281 1000
1640 500
656 200
0 Sea Level
Land Dep. 656 200
13123 4000
22966 7000
Scale 1:2 500 000
0 25 50 75 100 Miles
0 50 100 150 Kms
Conic Equidistant Projection
© Collins

ITALY AND THE BALKANS

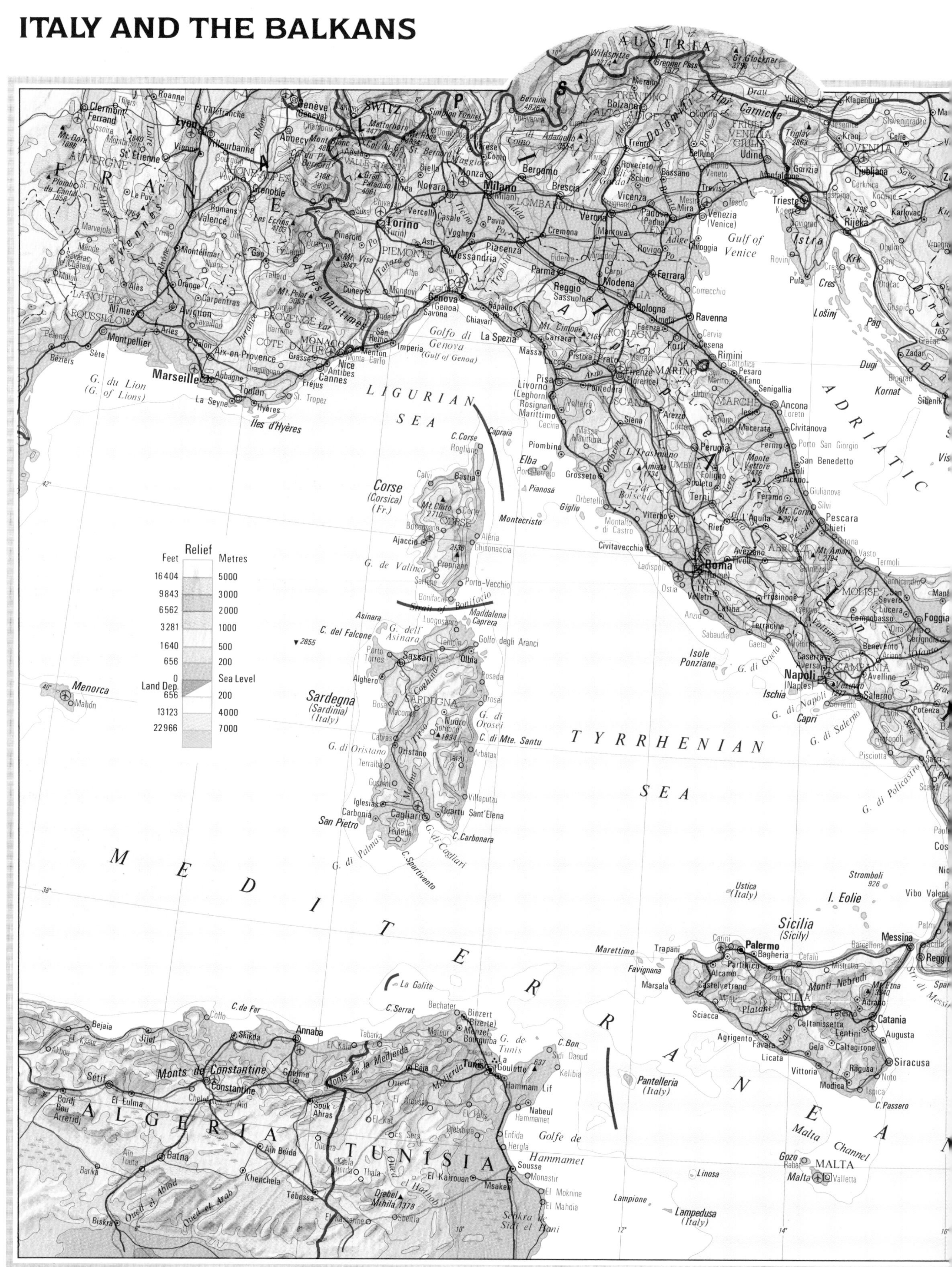

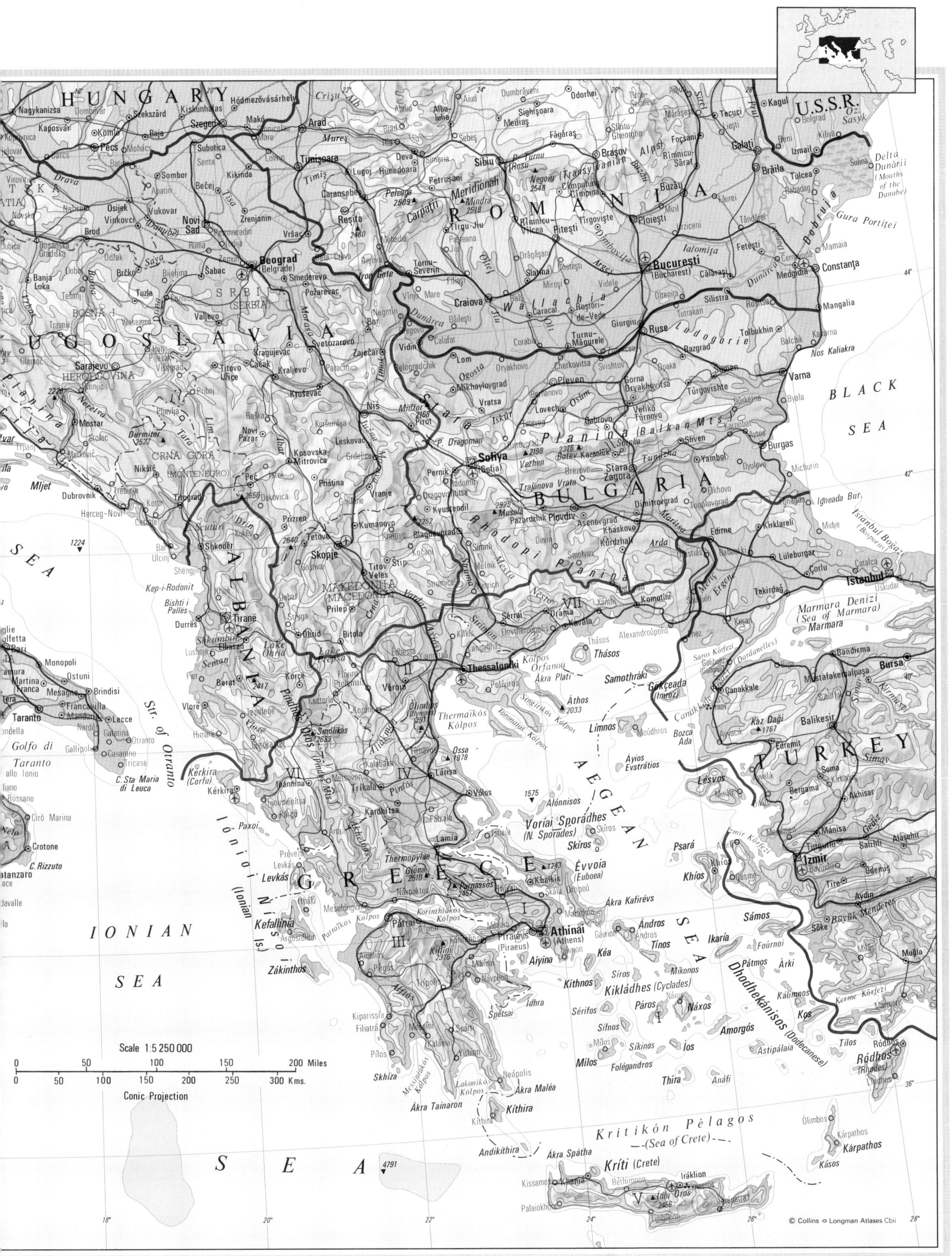

HUNGARY
ROMANIA
U.S.S.R.
YUGOSLAVIA
ALBANIA
BULGARIA
GREECE
TURKEY
BLACK SEA
AEGEAN SEA
IONIAN SEA
SEA
Marmara Denizi (Sea of Marmara)
Kritikón Pélagos (Sea of Crete)
Str. of Otranto
Golfo di Taranto
Delta Dunării (Mouths of the Danube)
Stara Planina (Balkan Mts.)
Rhodopi Planina
Wallachia
Carpaţii Meridionali
Alpi Transilvaniei
Dobrogea
Ludogorie
Pindhos Óros
Beograd (Belgrade)
Bucureşti (Bucharest)
Sofiya (Sofia)
Tiranë
Skopje
Athínai (Athens)
Piraiévs (Piraeus)
Thessaloníki
Istanbul
Izmir
Bursa
Constanţa
Varna
Burgas
Sarajevo
Titograd
Dubrovnik
Kérkira (Corfu)
Kefallinía
Zákinthos
Levkás
Évvoia (Euboea)
Kríti (Crete)
Ródhos (Rhodes)
Kárpathos
Kikládhes (Cyclades)
Dhodhekánisos (Dodecanese)
Vóriai Sporádhes (N. Sporades)
Límnos
Lésvos
Khíos
Sámos
Thásos
Samothráki
Gökçeada (Imroz)
Kíthira
Scale 1:5 250 000
0 50 100 150 200 Miles
0 50 100 150 200 250 300 Kms.
Conic Projection
© Collins ◇ Longman Atlases Cbii

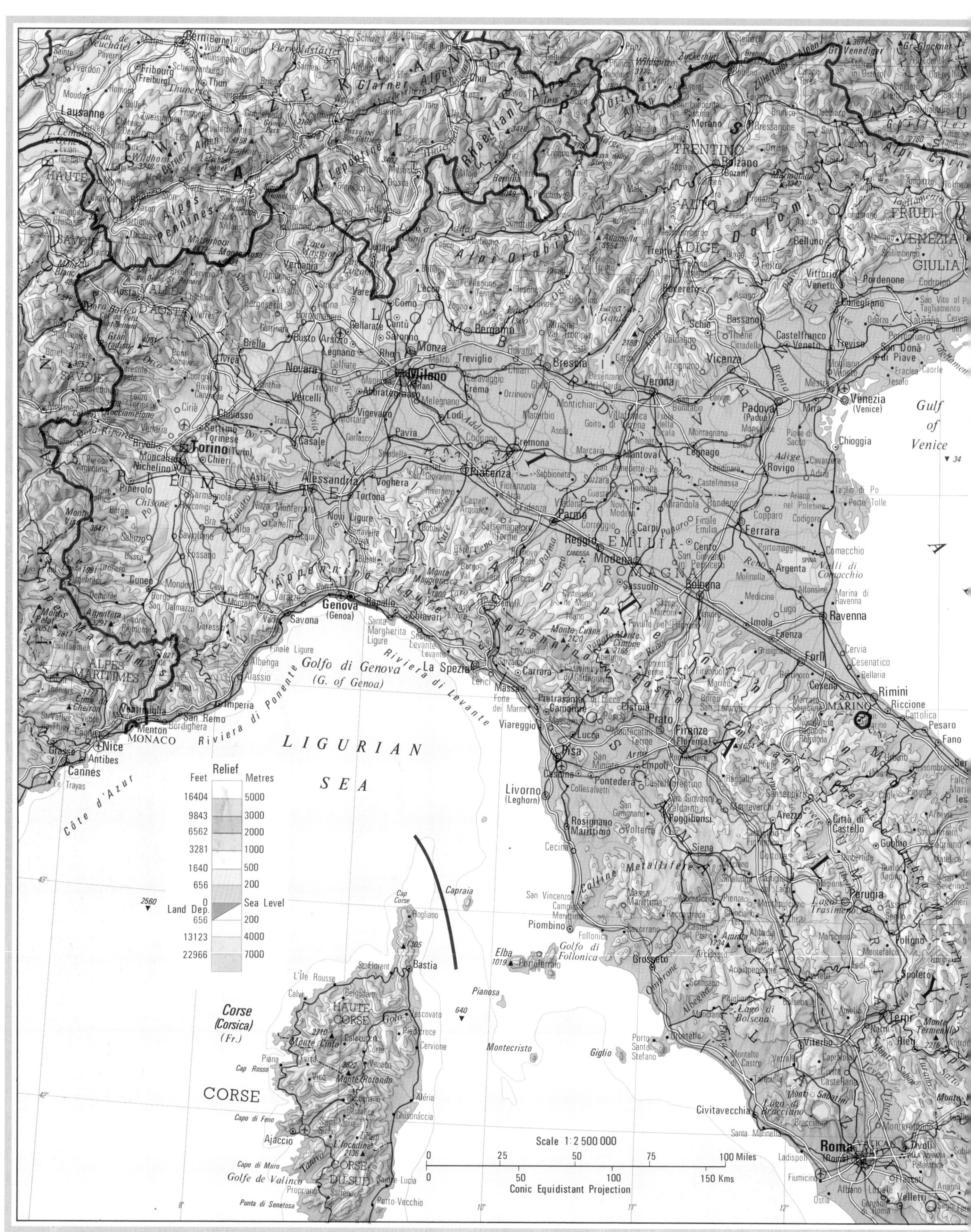

LIGURIAN SEA

Golfo di Genova
(G. of Genoa)

Riviera di Ponente

Riviera di Levante

Gulf of Venice

EMILIA-ROMAGNA

PIEMONTE

LOMBARDIA

TRENTINO ALTO ADIGE

FRIULI VENEZIA GIULIA

VENETO

Corse
(Corsica)
(Fr.)

HAUTE CORSE

CORSE

CORSE DU SUD

Golfe de Valinco

ALPES MARITIMES

Côte d'Azur

Relief	
Feet	Metres
16404	5000
9843	3000
6562	2000
3281	1000
1640	500
656	200
0	Sea Level
Land Dep.	
656	200
13123	4000
22966	7000

Scale 1: 2 500 000

0   25   50   75   100 Miles

0   50   100   150 Kms

Conic Equidistant Projection

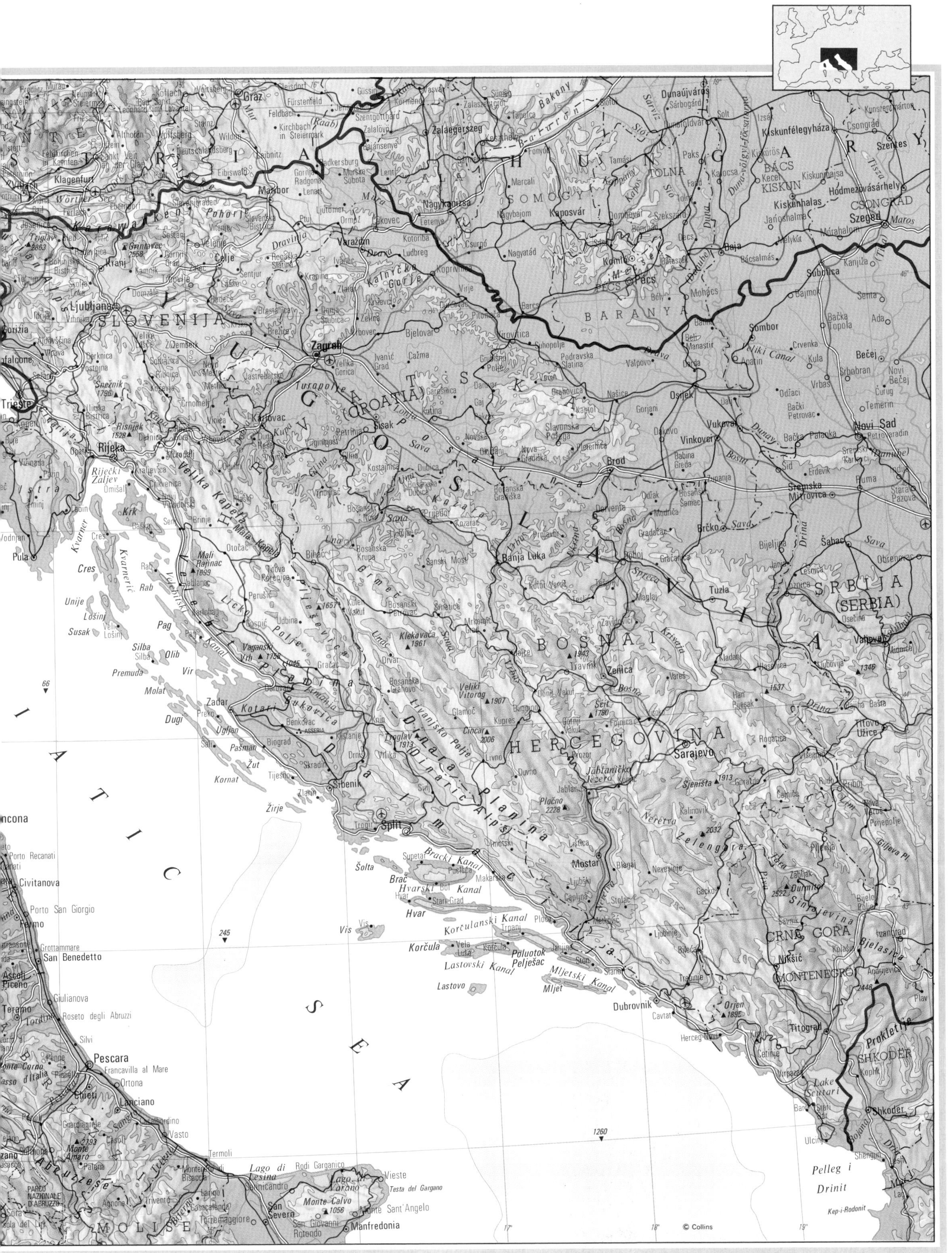

AUSTRIA
HUNGARY
YUGOSLAVIA
SLOVENIJA
HRVATSKA (CROATIA)
BOSNA I HERCEGOVINA
SRBIJA (SERBIA)
CRNA GORA (MONTENEGRO)
ADRIATIC SEA
Graz
Klagenfurt
Maribor
Ljubljana
Zagreb
Trieste
Rijeka
Karlovac
Sisak
Zadar
Šibenik
Split
Dubrovnik
Mostar
Sarajevo
Banja Luka
Zenica
Tuzla
Osijek
Novi Sad
Subotica
Szeged
Pécs
Kaposvár
Zalaegerszeg
Nagykanizsa
Kecskemét
Kiskunfélegyháza
Titograd
Shkodër
Pescara
Chieti
San Benedetto
Ancona
Manfredonia
Vieste
Termoli
Vasto
Lanciano
Ortona
Teramo
Fermo
Civitanova
Balaton
Bakony
Drava
Sava
Dunav
Tisza
Drina
Bosna
Una
Neretva
Istra
Krk
Cres
Lošinj
Rab
Pag
Dugi
Brač
Hvar
Vis
Korčula
Lastovo
Mljet
Velika Kapela
Dinara
Dinaric Alps
Triglav 2863
Monte Calvo 1056
Lake Scutari
MOLISE
ABRUZZI
© Collins

SOUTHERN ITALY

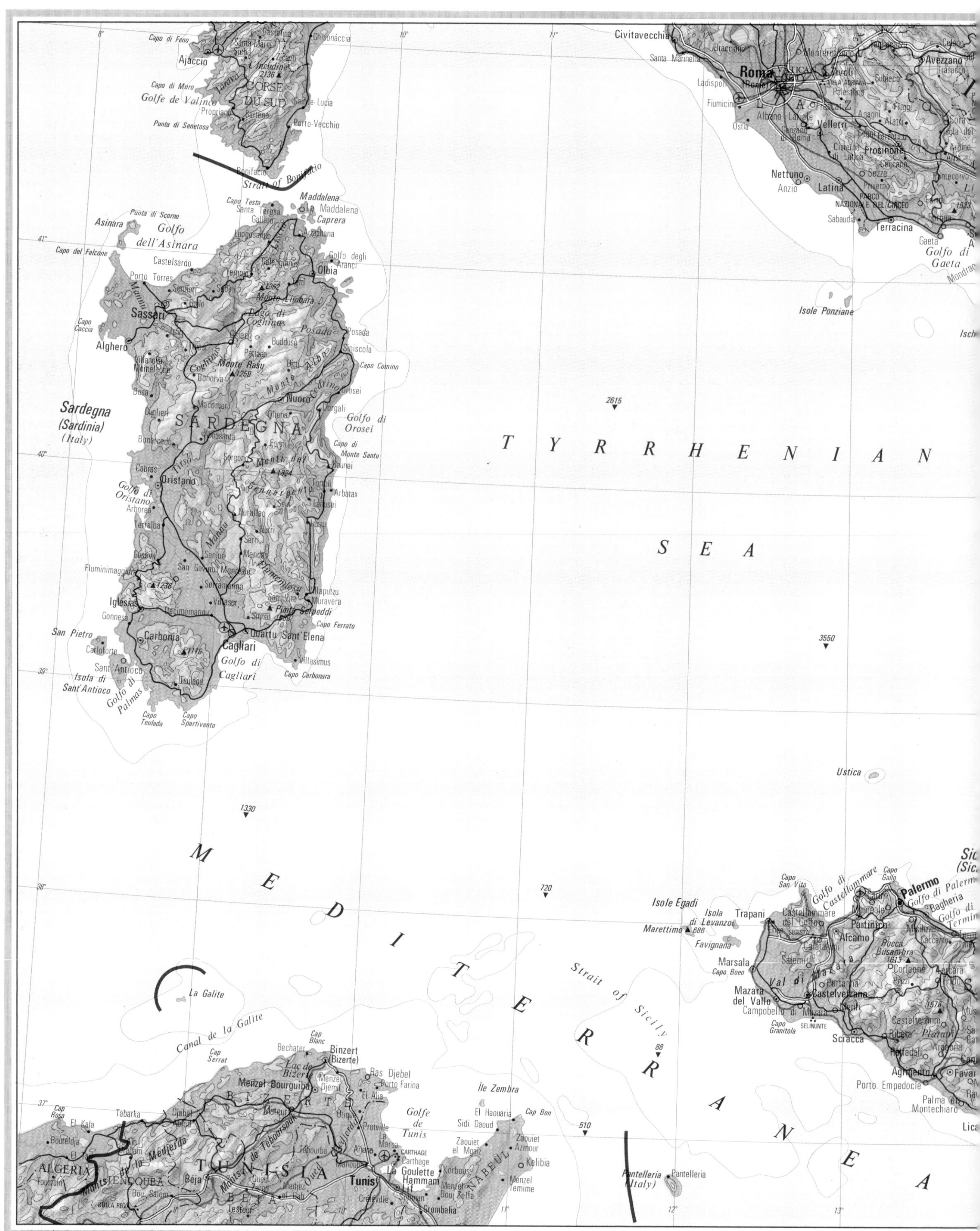

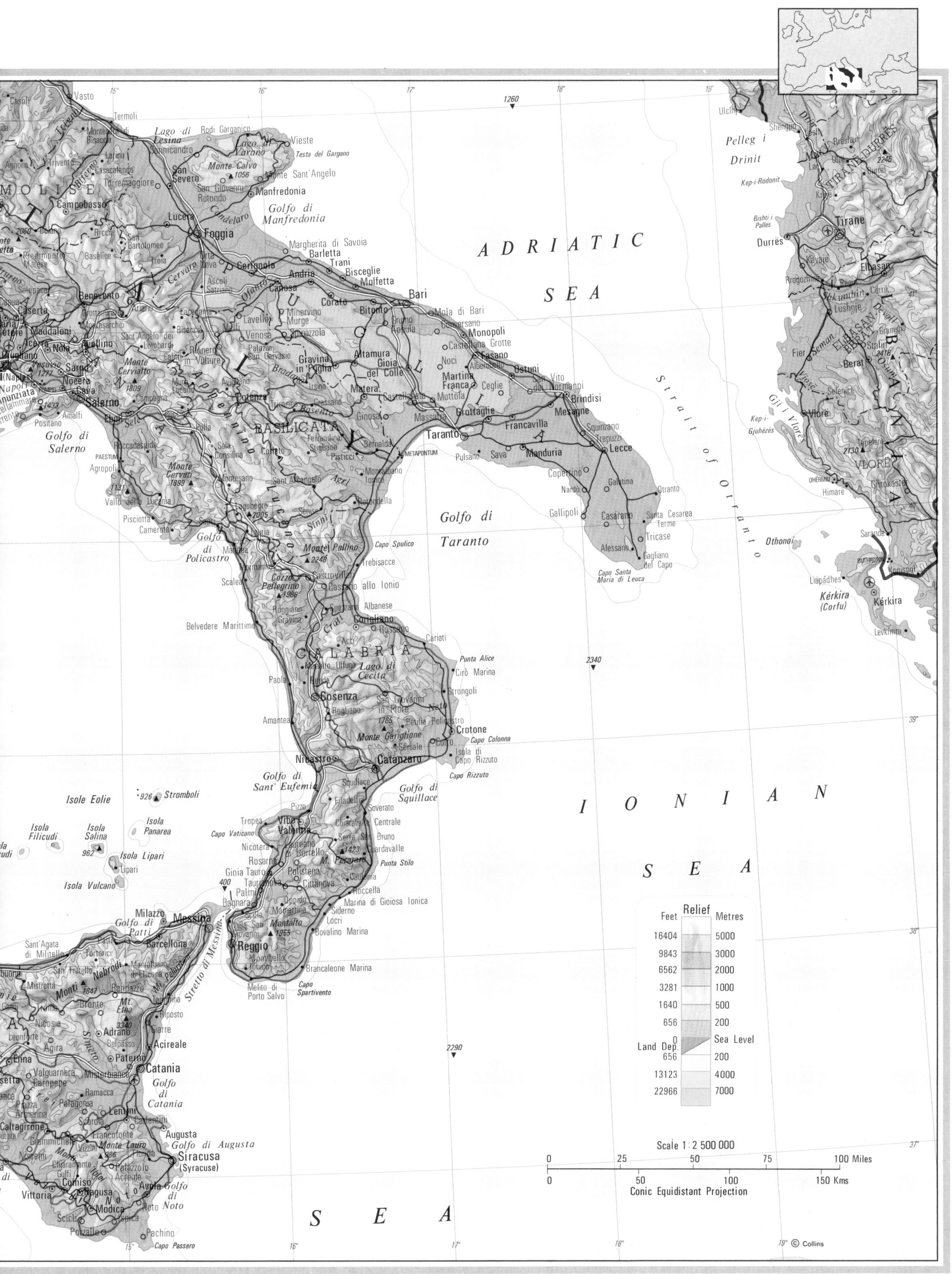

MOLISE

Vasto
Termoli
Lago di Lesina
Rodi Garganico
Lago di Varano
Vieste
Testa del Gargano
Monte Calvo
1056
Monte Sant'Angelo
San Severo
San Giovanni Rotondo
Manfredonia
Lucera
Foggia
Golfo di Manfredonia
Candelaro
Margherita di Savoia
Barletta
Trani
Bisceglie
Molfetta
Corato
Bari
Andria
Mola di Bari
Bitonto
Monopoli
Castellana Grotte
Noci
Alberobello
Fasano
Ostuni
Martina Franca
Ceglie
Brindisi
Mesagne
Francavilla
Grottaglie
TARANTO
Squinzano
Lecce
Manduria
Copertino
Galatina
Otranto
Nardo
Gallipoli
Casarano
Santa Cesarea Terme
Tricase
Alessano
Gagliano del Capo
Capo Santa Maria di Leuca

ADRIATIC SEA

Strait of Otranto

Pelleg i Drinit
Kep-i-Rodonit
Tirane
Durrës
Bishti i Palles
Gji i Vlorë
Vlorë

BASILICATA

Potenza
Matera

Golfo di Salerno
PAESTUM
Agropoli
Monte Cervati 1899
Vallo della Lucania
Golfo di Policastro
Monte Pollino 2248
Cozzo Pellegrino 1986
Golfo di Taranto

CALABRIA
Cosenza
Lago di Cecita
Crotone
Capo Colonna
Catanzaro
Capo Rizzuto

Golfo di Sant'Eufemia
Nicastro
Golfo di Squillace

IONIAN SEA

Isole Eolie
Stromboli 926
Isola Panarea
Isola Salina 962
Isola Filicudi
Isola Lipari
Lipari
Isola Vulcano

Milazzo
Golfo di Patti
Messina
Reggio
Capo Spartivento

Catania
Golfo di Catania
Siracusa (Syracuse)

SEA

Kérkira (Corfu)
Kérkira
Liapádhes
Levkími

Relief		
Feet		Metres
16404		5000
9843		3000
6562		2000
3281		1000
1640		500
656		200
0		Sea Level
Land Dep.		
656		200
13123		4000
22966		7000

Scale 1:2 500 000

0   25   50   75   100 Miles

0   50   100   150 Kms

Conic Equidistant Projection

© Collins

33

GREECE AND ALBANIA

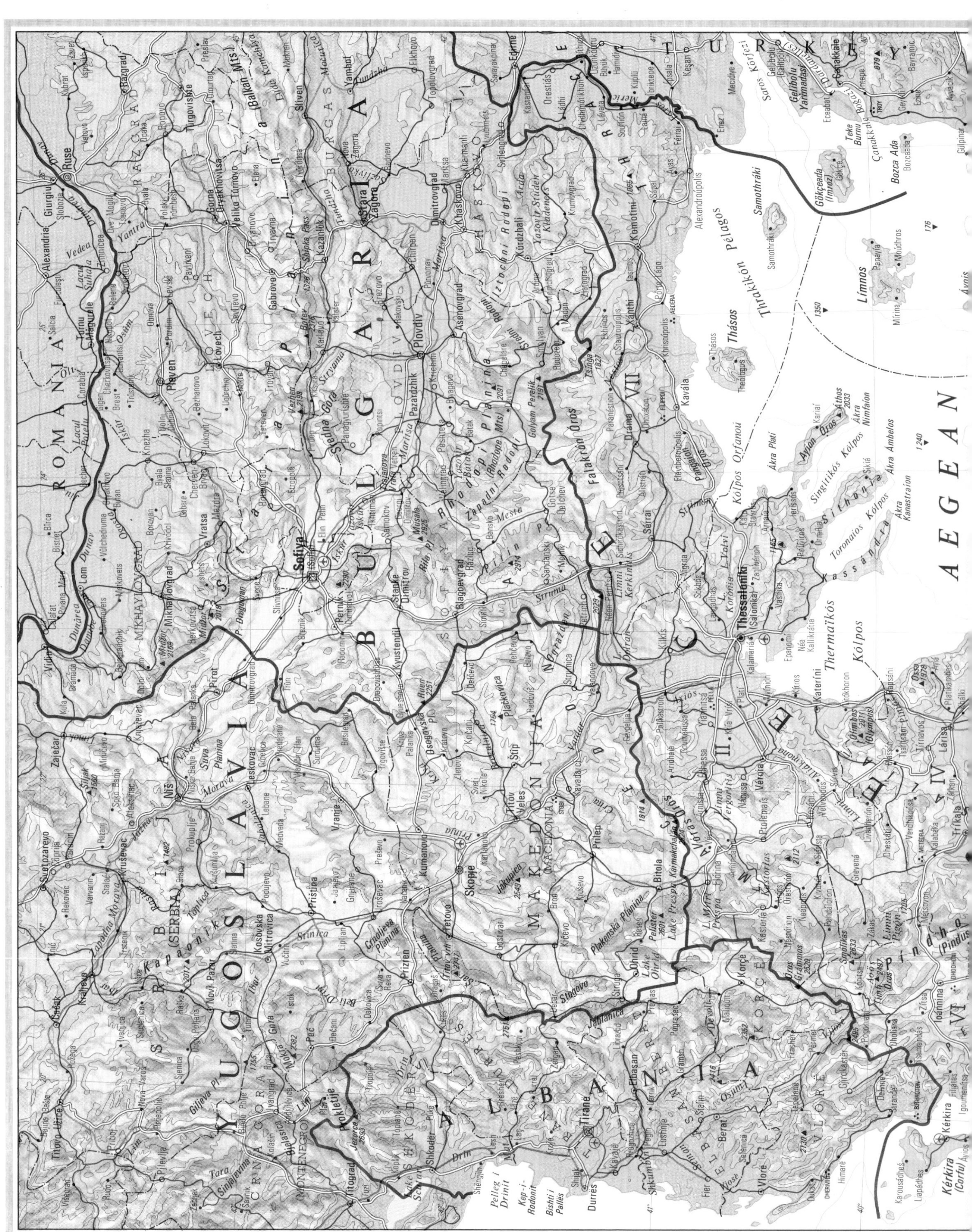

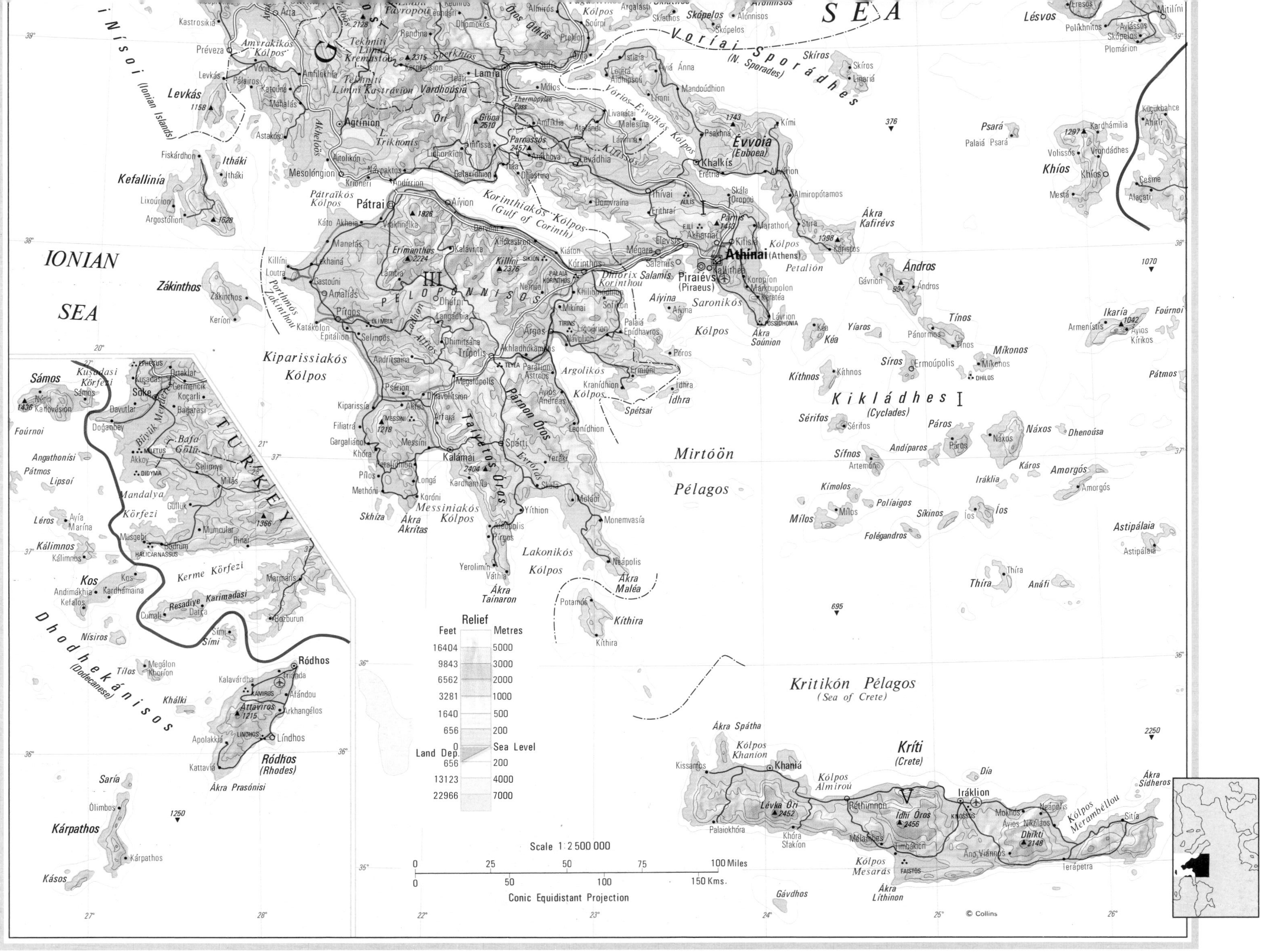

IONIAN SEA
SEA
Iónioi Nísoi (Ionian Islands)
Levkás
Itháki
Kefallinía
Zákinthos
Kiparissiakós Kólpos
Pátraïkós Kólpos
Korinthiakós Kólpos (Gulf of Corinth)
Pátrai
PELOPÓNNISOS
Athínai (Athens)
Piraiévs (Piraeus)
Saronikós Kólpos
Argolikós Kólpos
Lakonikós Kólpos
Messiniakós Kólpos
Kíthira
Évvoia (Euboea)
Vóriai Sporádhes (N. Sporades)
Skíros
Lésvos
Khíos
Psará
Ándros
Tínos
Míkonos
Kikládhes (Cyclades)
Náxos
Páros
Amorgós
Thíra
Mílos
Astipálaia
Ikaría
Mirtóön Pélagos
Kritikón Pélagos (Sea of Crete)
Kríti (Crete)
Iráklion
Khaniá
Réthimnon
TURKEY
Sámos
Kos
Ródhos (Rhodes)
Kárpathos
Dhodhekánisos (Dodecanese)
Relief
Feet
Metres
16404
5000
9843
3000
6562
2000
3281
1000
1640
500
656
200
0
Sea Level
Land Dep.
656
200
13123
4000
22966
7000
Scale 1:2 500 000
0 25 50 75 100 Miles
0 50 100 150 Kms.
Conic Equidistant Projection
© Collins

CENTRAL EUROPE

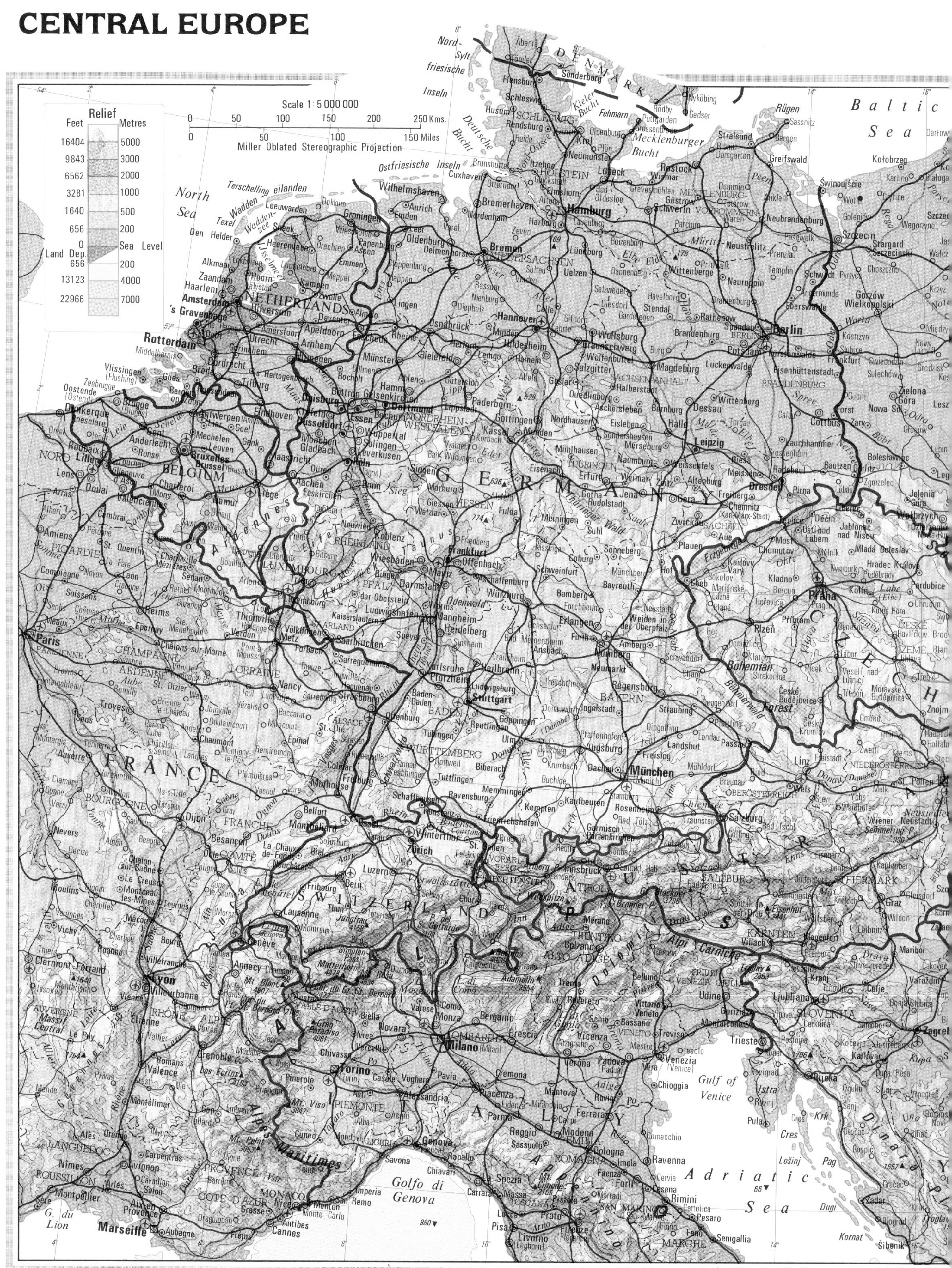

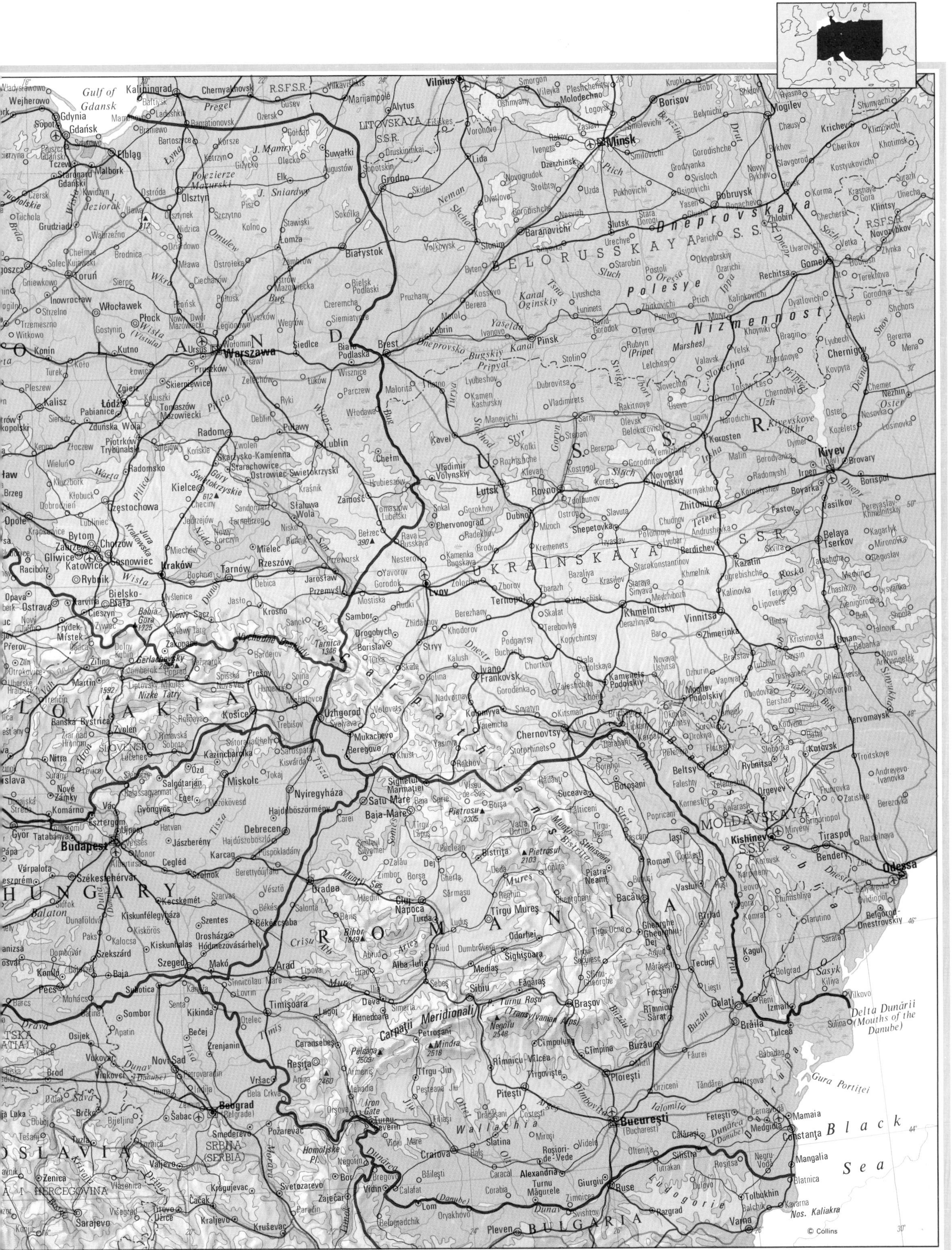

Gulf of Gdansk
Kaliningrad
Gdynia
Gdańsk
Sopot
Elbląg
Malbork
Tczew
Chernyakhovsk
R.S.F.S.R.
Vilnius
Marijampolė
Alytus
Molodechno
Borisov
Mogilev
Minsk
LITOVSKAYA S.S.R.
Suwałki
Augustów
Grodno
Olsztyn
Pojezierze Mazurskie
J. Mamry
J. Śniardwy
Lida
Baranovichi
Slutsk
Bobruysk
Zhlobin
Gomel
Dneprovskaya
BELORUSSKAYA S.S.R.
Polesye
Nizmennost
Pinsk
Brest
Kobrin
Białystok
Łomża
Toruń
Grudziądz
Włocławek
Płock
Inowrocław
Warszawa (Warsaw)
POLAND
Kutno
Łódź
Konin
Kalisz
Siedlce
Biała Podlaska
Lublin
Radom
Kielce
Częstochowa
Opole
Bytom
Chorzów
Gliwice
Katowice
Sosnowiec
Kraków
Tarnów
Rzeszów
Przemyśl
Nowy Sącz
Bielsko-Biała
Ostrava
Wisła
Chełm
Zamość
Kovel
Lutsk
Rovno
Dubno
Zhitomir
Korosten
Kiyev
Chernigov
Belaya Tserkov
Berdichev
Vinnitsa
Khmelnitskiy
Ternopol
Lvov
UKRAINSKAYA S.S.R.
Drogobych
Stryy
Ivano-Frankovsk
Kolomyya
Chernovtsy
Uzhgorod
Mukachevo
Beregovo
Košice
Prešov
SLOVAKIA
Nízke Tatry
Gerlachovský štít 2655
Tarnica 1346
Babia Góra 1725
Żilina
Banská Bystrica
Zvolen
Nitra
Komárno
Miskolc
Nyíregyháza
Debrecen
Budapest
Győr
Székesfehérvár
HUNGARY
Balaton
Kecskemét
Szeged
Pécs
Baja
Oradea
Cluj-Napoca
Satu Mare
Baia Mare
Suceava
Botoşani
Iaşi
Kishinev
MOLDAVSKAYA S.S.R.
Beltsy
Tiraspol
Bendery
Odessa
Izmail
Galati
Brăila
Tulcea
Delta Dunării (Mouths of the Danube)
Constanţa
Mangalia
Black Sea
Bacău
Piatra Neamţ
Tîrgu Mureş
Braşov
Sibiu
Arad
Timişoara
ROMANIA
Carpaţii Meridionali (Transylvanian Alps)
Negoiu 2548
Ploieşti
Piteşti
Bucureşti (Bucharest)
Craiova
Drobeta-Turnu Severin
Iron Gate
Beograd (Belgrade)
Novi Sad
Subotica
SRBIJA (SERBIA)
Niš
Sarajevo
Vidin
Lom
Pleven
Ruse
Varna
BULGARIA
Dunav (Danube)
Dunărea
Tisza
Prut
Dnestr
Dnepr
Pripyat
Bug
Desna
Nos. Kaliakra
© Collins

GERMANY AND SWITZERLAND

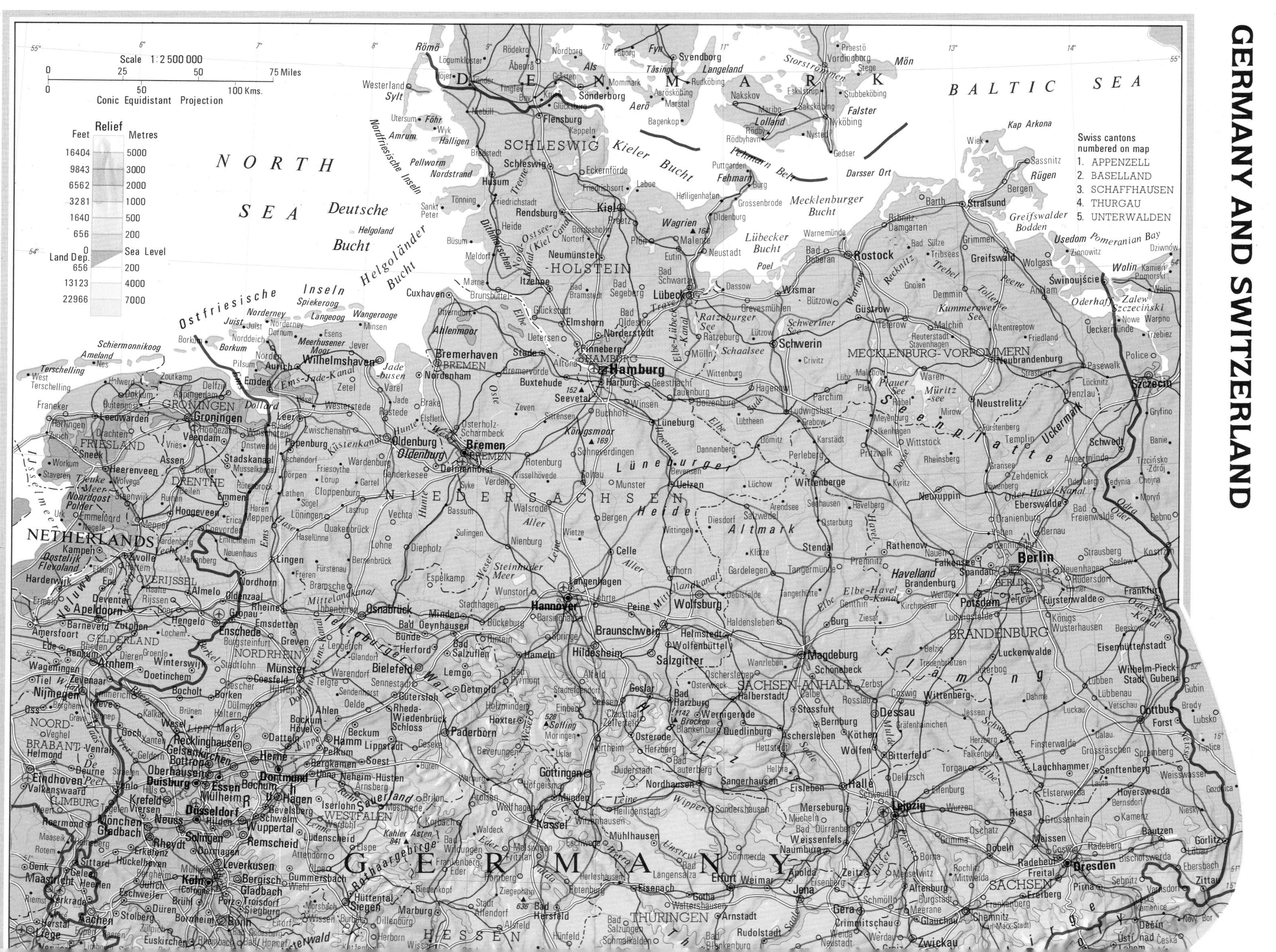

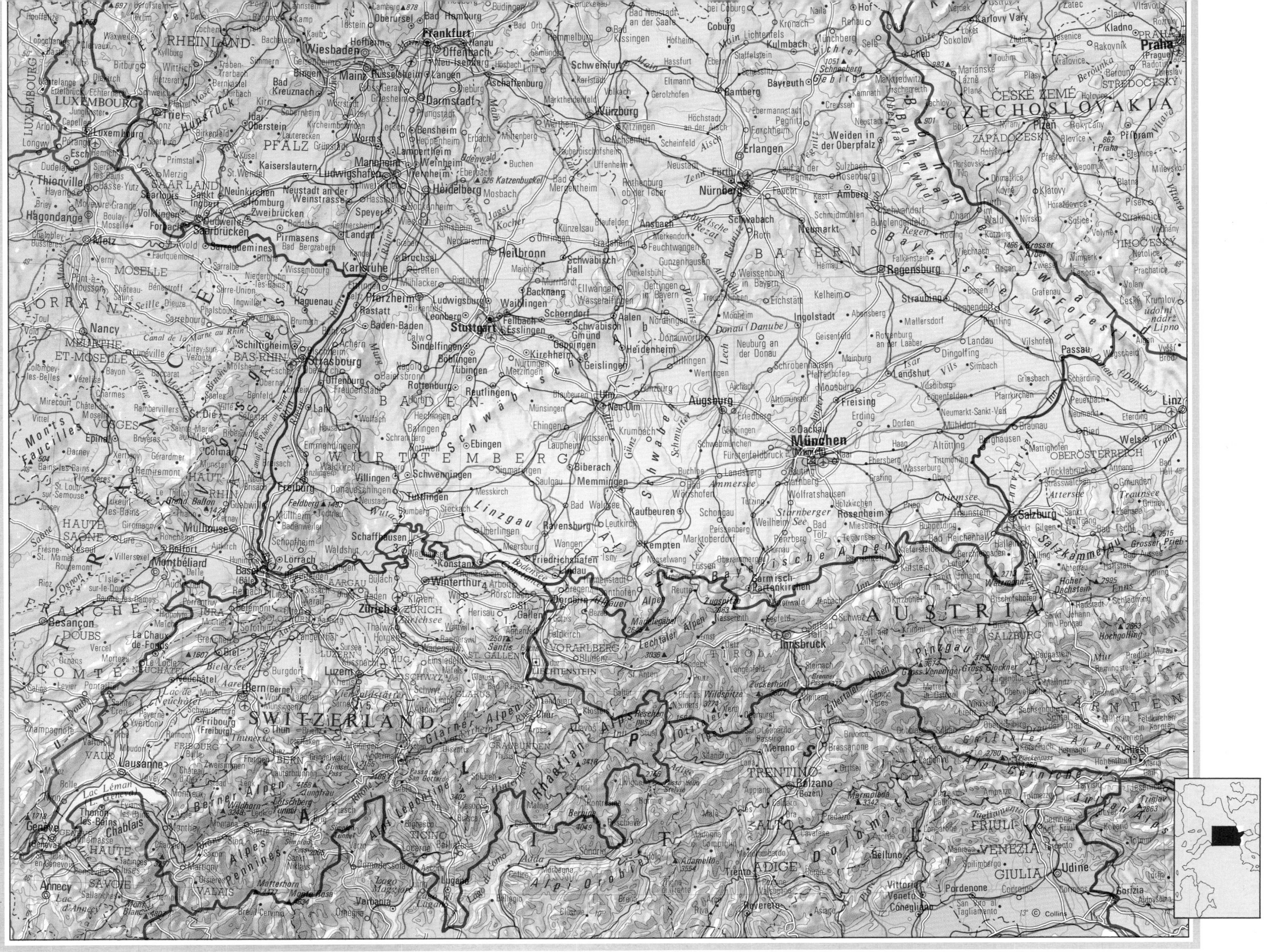
CZECHOSLOVAKIA
AUSTRIA
SWITZERLAND
BAYERN
BADEN-WÜRTTEMBERG
RHEINLAND
PFALZ
SAARLAND
LUXEMBOURG
LORRAINE
FRANCHE-COMTÉ
TRENTINO
ALTO ADIGE
FRIULI-VENEZIA GIULIA
TIROL
SALZBURG
KÄRNTEN
OBERÖSTERREICH
Praha
München
Nürnberg
Stuttgart
Frankfurt
Strasbourg
Zürich
Bern
Innsbruck
Salzburg
Linz
Augsburg
Regensburg
Würzburg
Karlsruhe
Mannheim
Heidelberg
Saarbrücken
Nancy
Metz
Besançon
Lausanne
Genève
Bolzano
Trento
Udine
Basel
Freiburg
Ulm
Kempten
Passau
Plzeň
Luzern
Annecy
Bodensee
Chiemsee
Ammersee
Starnberger See
Lac Léman
Schwäbische Alb
Bayerischer Wald
Bayerische Alpen
Dolomiti
© Collins

SCANDINAVIA AND BALTIC LANDS

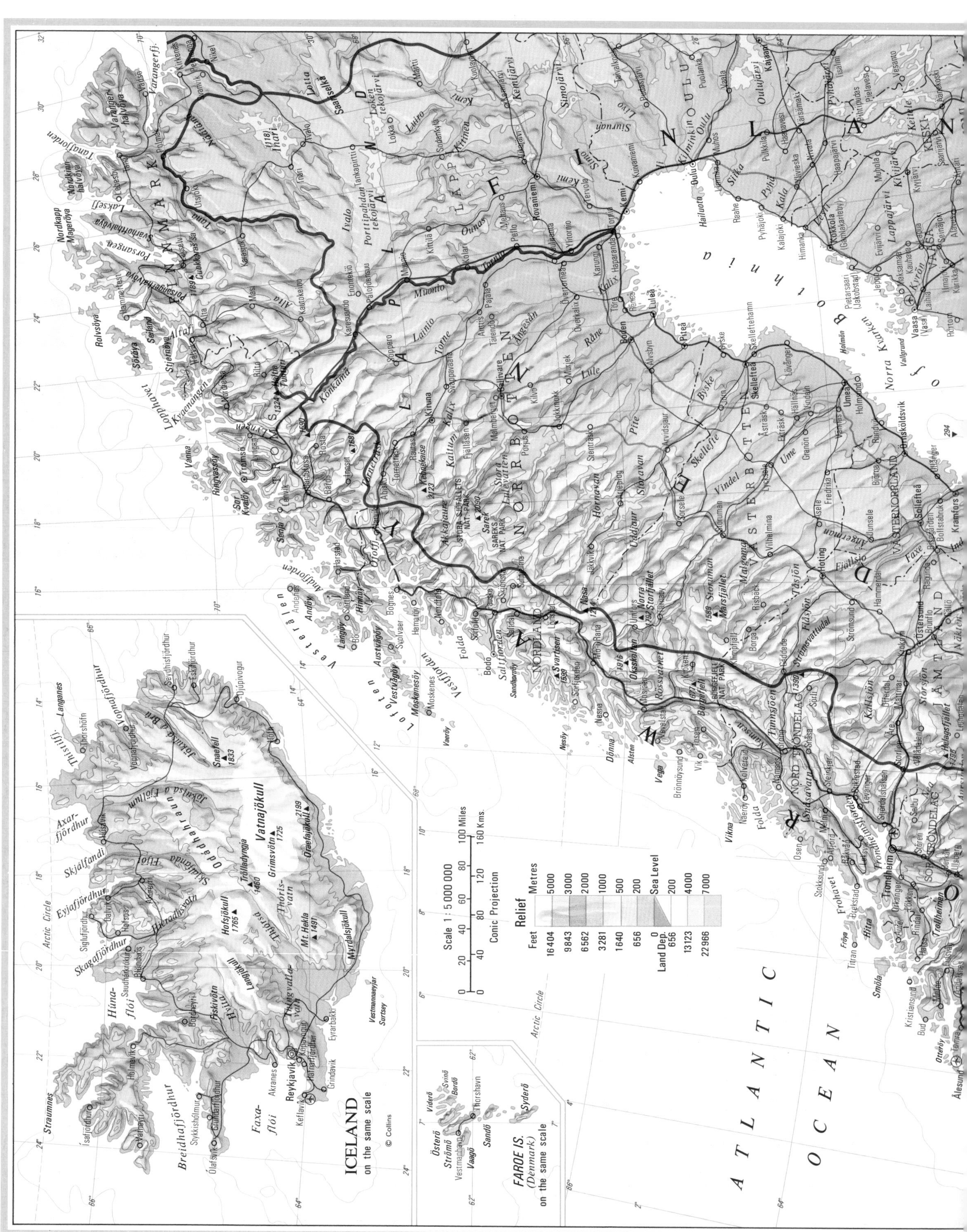

ICELAND
on the same scale

© Collins

FAROE IS.
(Denmark)
on the same scale

Scale 1 : 5 000 000

Conic Projection

Relief

Metres	
5000	
3000	
2000	
1000	
500	
200	
Sea Level	
200	
4000	
7000	

Feet	
16404	
9843	
6562	
3281	
1640	
656	
0	
Land Dep.	
656	
13123	
22966	

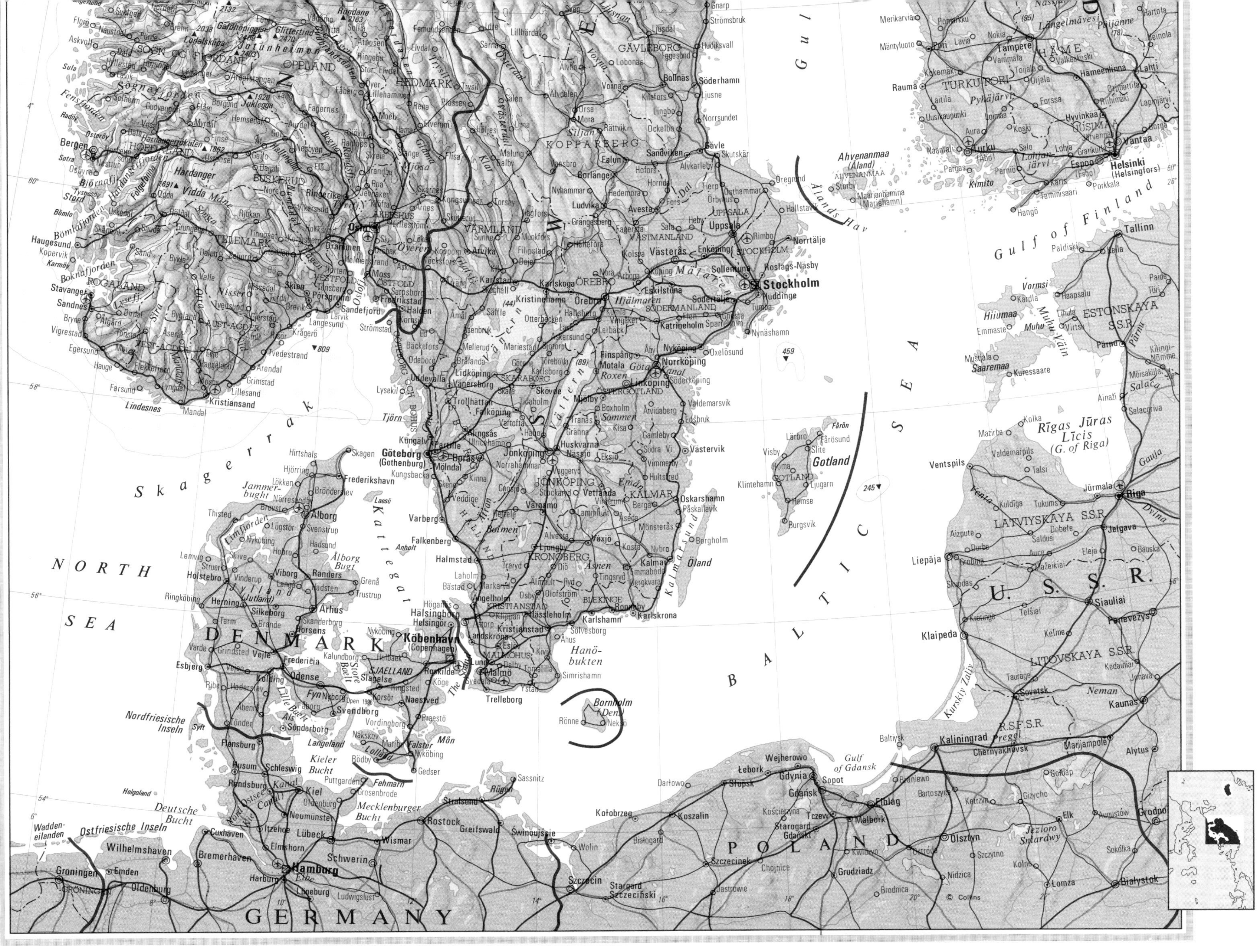

NORTH SEA
Skagerrak
Kattegat
BALTIC SEA
Gulf of Finland
Rīgas Jūras Līcis (G. of Riga)
Ålands Hav
Gulf of Gdansk
DENMARK
POLAND
GERMANY
U. S. S. R.
ESTONSKAYA S.S.R.
LATVIYSKAYA S.S.R.
LITOVSKAYA S.S.R.
Stockholm
Helsinki (Helsingfors)
Tallinn
Riga
København (Copenhagen)
Göteborg (Gothenburg)
Oslo
Bergen
Stavanger
Kristiansand
Gotland
Öland
Bornholm (Den.)
Saaremaa
Hiiumaa
Ahvenanmaa (Åland)
Malmö
Århus
Ålborg
Odense
Esbjerg
Turku
Tampere
Uppsala
Västerås
Örebro
Norrköping
Linköping
Jönköping
Kalmar
Karlskrona
Visby
Hamburg
Kiel
Lübeck
Flensburg
Rostock
Wismar
Schwerin
Bremerhaven
Wilhelmshaven
Emden
Groningen
Szczecin
Koszalin
Gdańsk
Gdynia
Elbląg
Olsztyn
Kaliningrad
Klaipeda
Liepāja
Ventspils
Siauliai
Jelgava
Kaunas
Pärnu
Białystok
Grodno
© Collins

SOUTHERN SCANDINAVIA

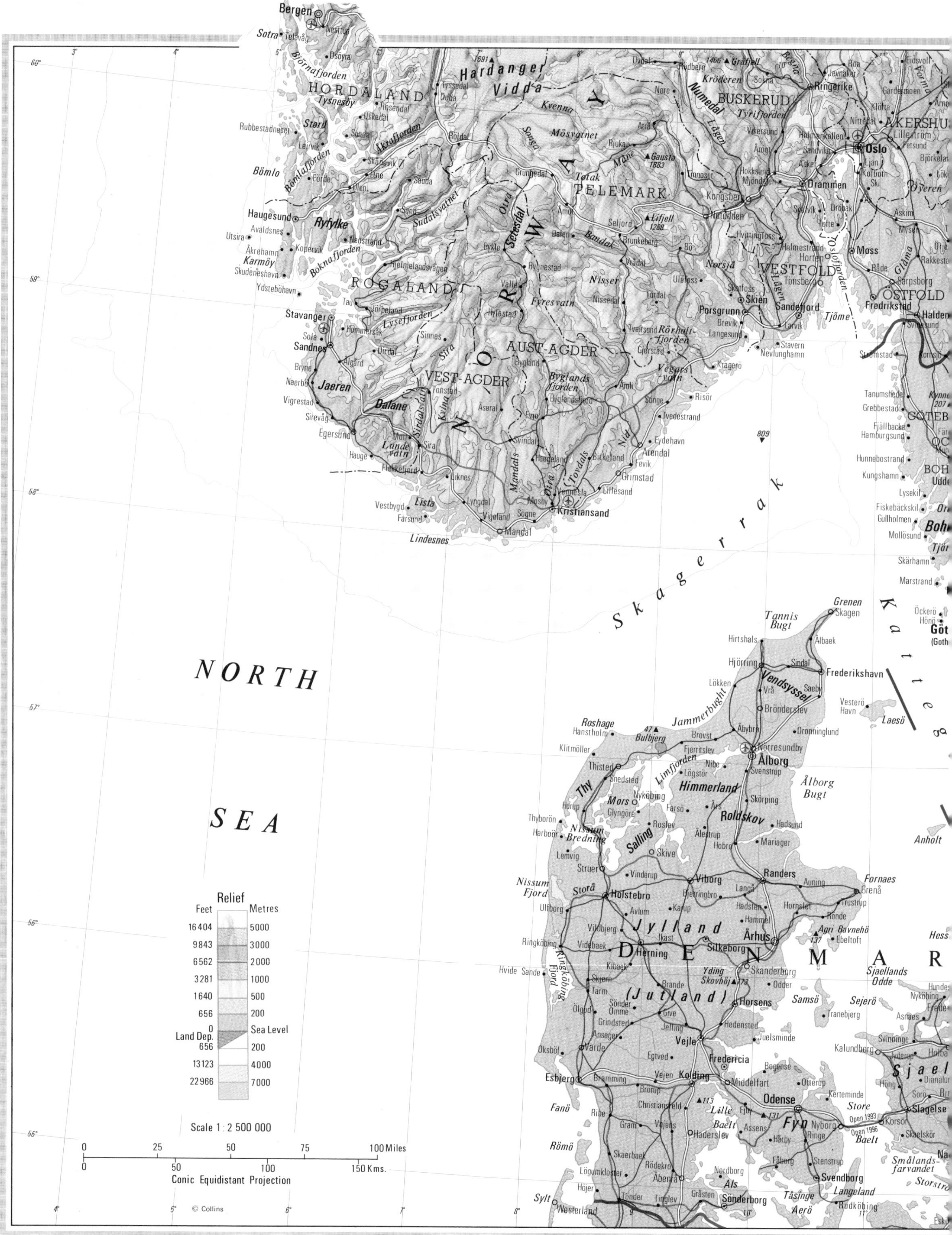

Relief

Feet		Metres
16 404		5000
9843		3000
6562		2000
3281		1000
1640		500
656		200
0	Sea Level	
Land Dep.		200
656		4000
13 123		4000
22 966		7000

Scale 1 : 2 500 000

Conic Equidistant Projection

© Collins

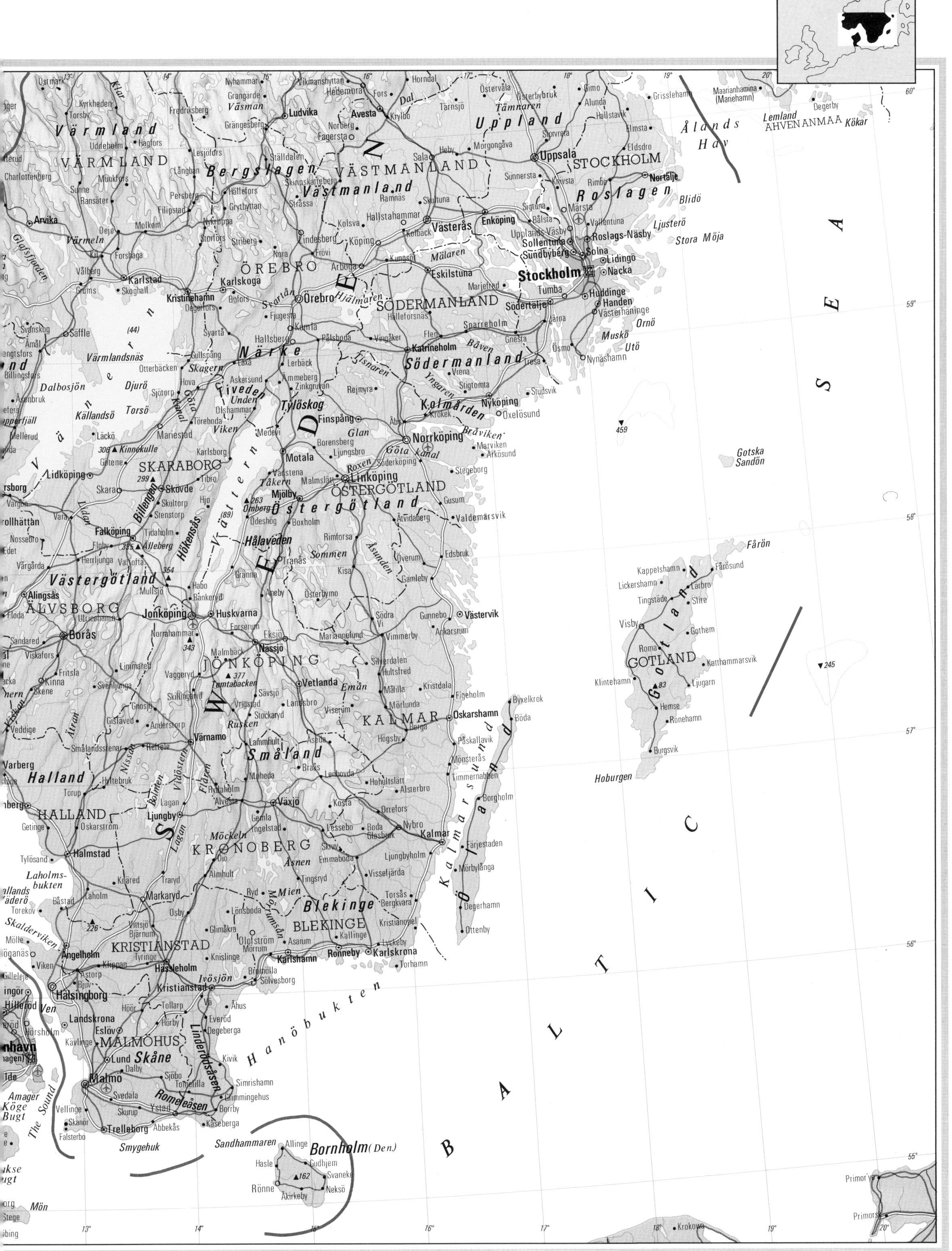

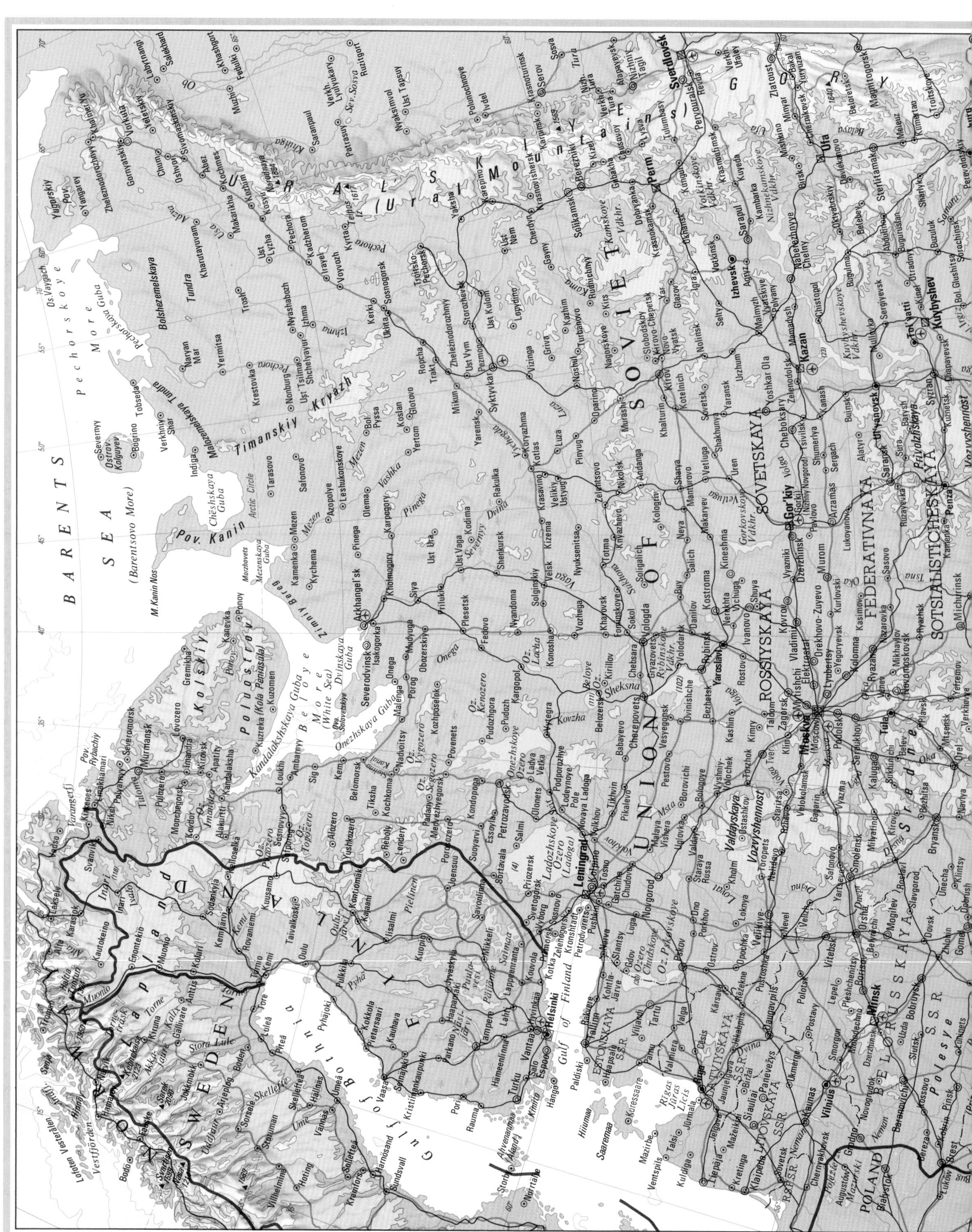

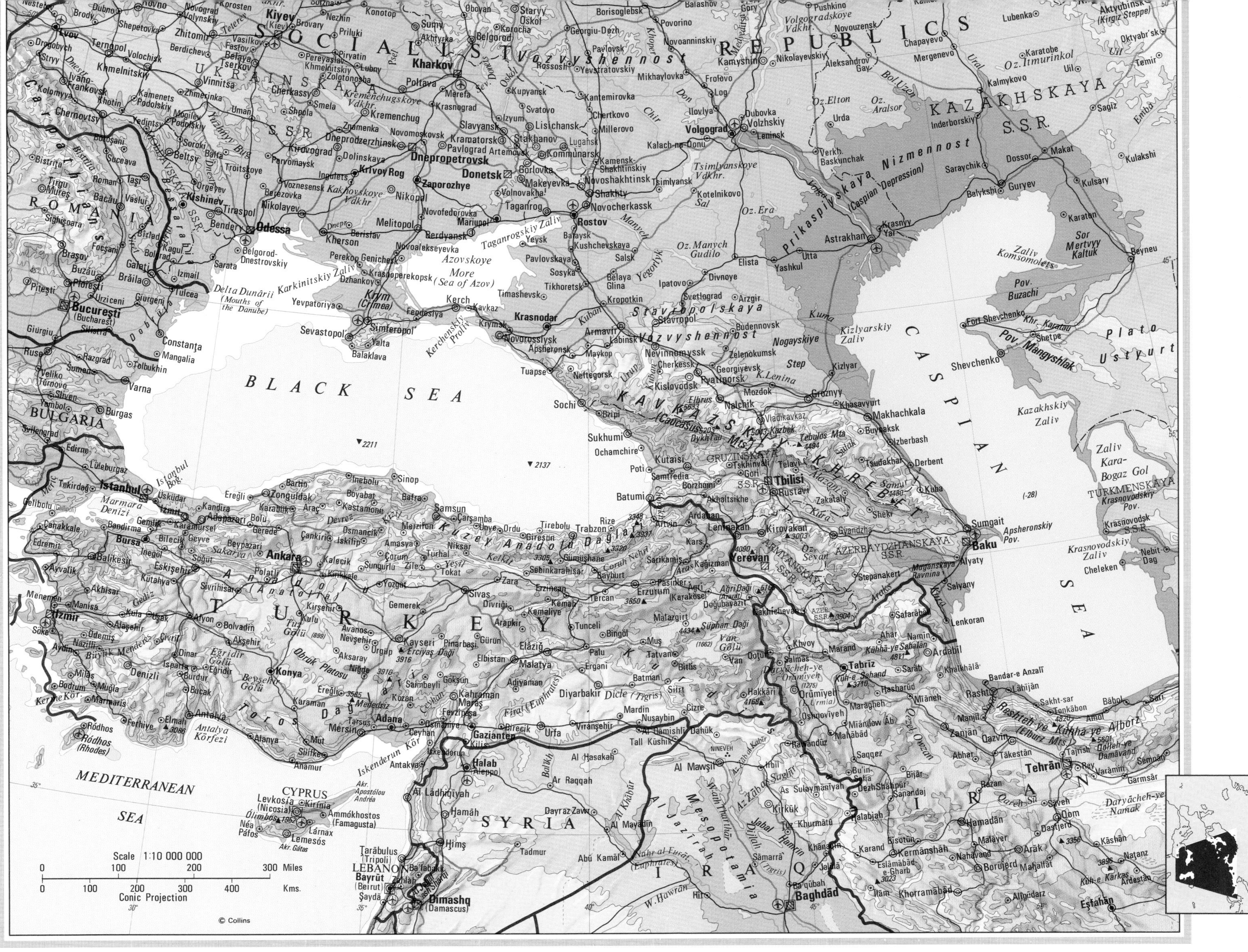

SOCIALIST REPUBLICS
UKRAINSKAYA S.S.R.
KAZAKHSKAYA S.S.R.
ROMANIA
BULGARIA
BLACK SEA
CASPIAN SEA
MEDITERRANEAN SEA
TURKEY
SYRIA
IRAQ
IRAN
CYPRUS
LEBANON
GRUZINSKAYA S.S.R.
ARMYANSKAYA S.S.R.
AZERBAYDZHANSKAYA S.S.R.
TURKMENSKAYA S.S.R.
Prikaspiyskaya Nizmennost (Caspian Depression)
Stavropolskaya Vozvyshennost
Nogayskiye Step
Kavkaz (Caucasus) Mts.
Bol'shoy Kavkaz
Kuzey Anadolu Dağları
Anadolu (Anatolia)
Toros Dağları
Mesopotamia
Al Jazirah
Azovskoye More (Sea of Azov)
Delta Dunării (Mouths of the Danube)
Plato Ustyurt
Reshteh-ye Kūhhā-ye Alborz (Elburz Mts.)
Kiyev
Kharkov
Dnepropetrovsk
Donetsk
Zaporozhye
Odessa
Kishinev
Rostov
Volgograd
Astrakhan
Krasnodar
Tbilisi
Yerevan
Baku
Tabriz
Tehrān
Baghdād
Dimashq (Damascus)
Bayrūt (Beirut)
Halab (Aleppo)
Ankara
Istanbul
Izmir
Bursa
Adana
Konya
Bucureşti (Bucharest)
Levkosía (Nicosia)
Scale 1:10 000 000
0 100 200 300 Miles
0 100 200 300 400 Kms.
Conic Projection
© Collins

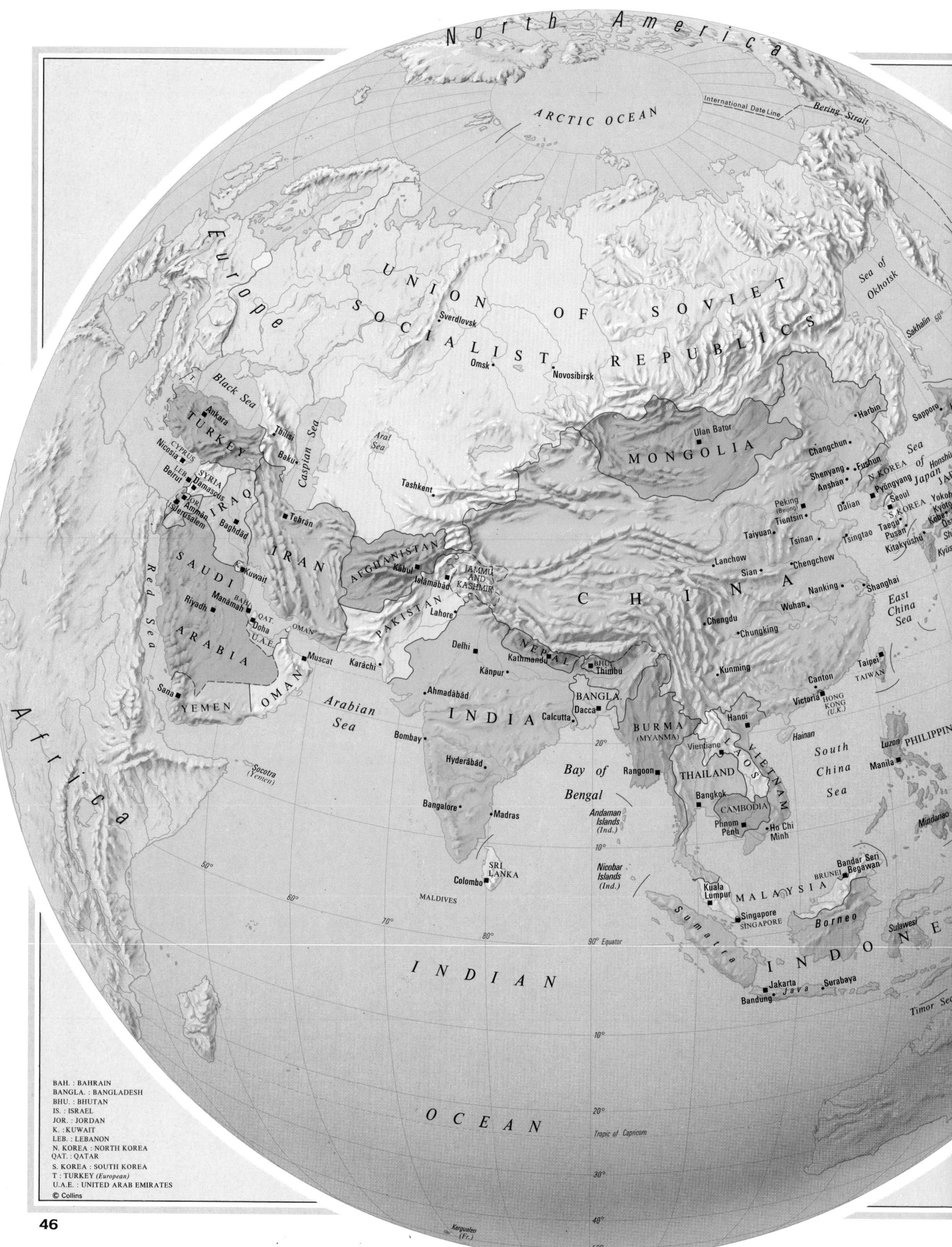

North America

ARCTIC OCEAN

International Date Line   Bering Strait

Europe

UNION   OF   SOVIET

SOCIALIST   REPUBLICS

Sverdlovsk

Omsk   Novosibirsk

Sea of
Okhotsk

Sakhalin

Black Sea

Ankara

TURKEY
Nicosia CYPRUS
LEB. SYRIA
Beirut Damascus
JOR. Amman
Jerusalem IS.
IRAQ
Baghdād

Tbilisi

Baku

Caspian Sea

Aral
Sea

Tashkent

MONGOLIA

Ulan Bator

Harbin

Sapporo

Changchun

Shenyang Fushun
Anshan N.KOREA
Peking Pyŏngyang
(Beijing) Seoul
Tientsin S.KOREA
Dalian Taegu

Sea
of Honshū
Japan JAP
Yokoh
Kyoto Kabe
Osa
Shi
Kyūs
Kitakyūshū

Tehrān

IRAN

AFGHANISTAN
Kābul

JAMMU
AND
KASHMIR

Taiyuan
Tsinan Tsingtao
Lanchow
Sian Chengchow

Nanking Shanghai
East
China
Sea

SAUDI

Kuwait

Riyadh Manāmah
BAH.
QAT. OMAN
Doha
U.A.E.

ARABIA

Islāmābād
PAKISTAN
Lahore

Delhi

CHINA

Wuhan

Chengdu
Chungking

Red Sea

Sana

YEMEN

OMAN

Muscat Karāchi

Arabian
Sea

Socotra
(Yemen)

Ahmadābād

Bombay

Hyderābād

Kānpur

NEPAL
Kathmandu
BHU.
Thimbu

INDIA

BANGLA.
Dacca

Calcutta

Kunming

BURMA
(MYANMA)

Hanoi

Hainan

Canton

Taipei
TAIWAN

Victoria HONG
KONG
(U.K.)

South
China
Sea

Luzon PHILIPPIN

Manila

Africa

Bay of
Bengal

Rangoon

Vientiane

THAILAND

LAOS

VIETNAM

Bangalore

Madras

Andaman
Islands
(Ind.)

Bangkok
CAMBODIA

Phnom
Penh

Ho Chi
Minh

Mindanao

SRI
LANKA

Colombo

Nicobar
Islands
(Ind.)

MALDIVES

Kuala
Lumpur

MALAYSIA

Bandar Seri
Begawan
BRUNEI

Singapore
SINGAPORE

Sumatra

Borneo

Sulawesi

INDONE

INDIAN

Jakarta Surabaya
Bandung Java

Timor Sea

OCEAN

20°

Tropic of Capricorn

30°

40°

50°

Kerguelen
(Fr.)

ASIA

COUNTRY	PAGE
AFGHANISTAN	48; 60
BAHRAIN	65
BANGLADESH	63
BHUTAN	63
BRUNEI	58
BURMA	56
CAMBODIA	56
CHINA	52-53; 54-55
CYPRUS	66
HONG KONG	55
INDIA	60-61; 62-63
INDONESIA	58-59
IRAN	65
IRAQ	64-65
ISRAEL	66; 67
JAPAN	57
JORDAN	64; 66; 67
KUWAIT	65
LAOS	56
LEBANON	66
MACAU	55
MALAYSIA	58
MALDIVES	60
MONGOLIA	52-53; 54
NEPAL	63
NORTH KOREA	53
OMAN	60
PAKISTAN	60; 62
PHILIPPINES	58-59
QATAR	65
SAUDI ARABIA	71; 64-65
SINGAPORE	58
SOUTH KOREA	53
SRI LANKA	61
SYRIA	64; 66; 67
TAIWAN	55
THAILAND	56
TURKEY	64
U.S.S.R.	50-51
UNITED ARAB EMIRATES	65
VIETNAM	56
YEMEN	71

ASIA AND INDIAN OCEAN

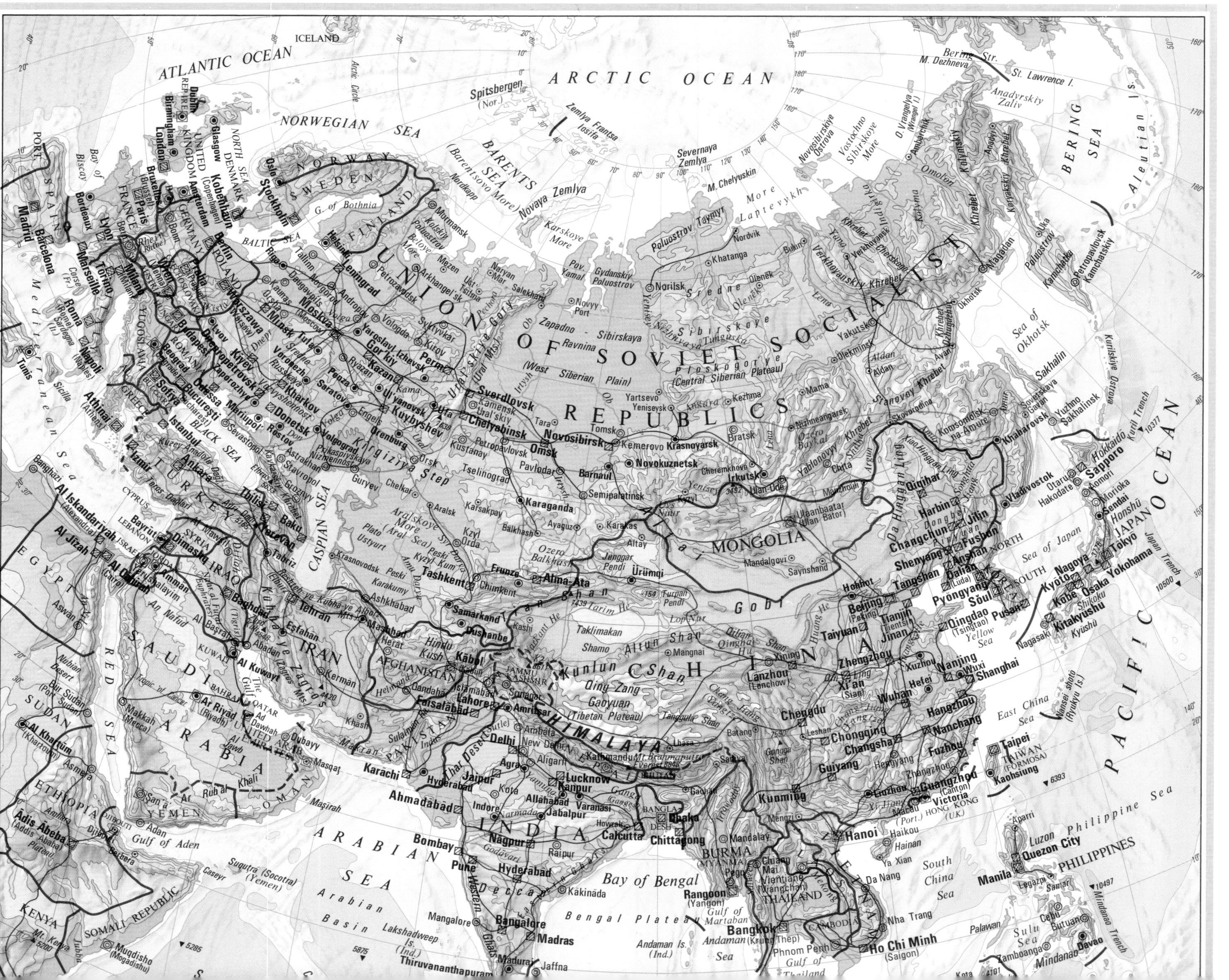

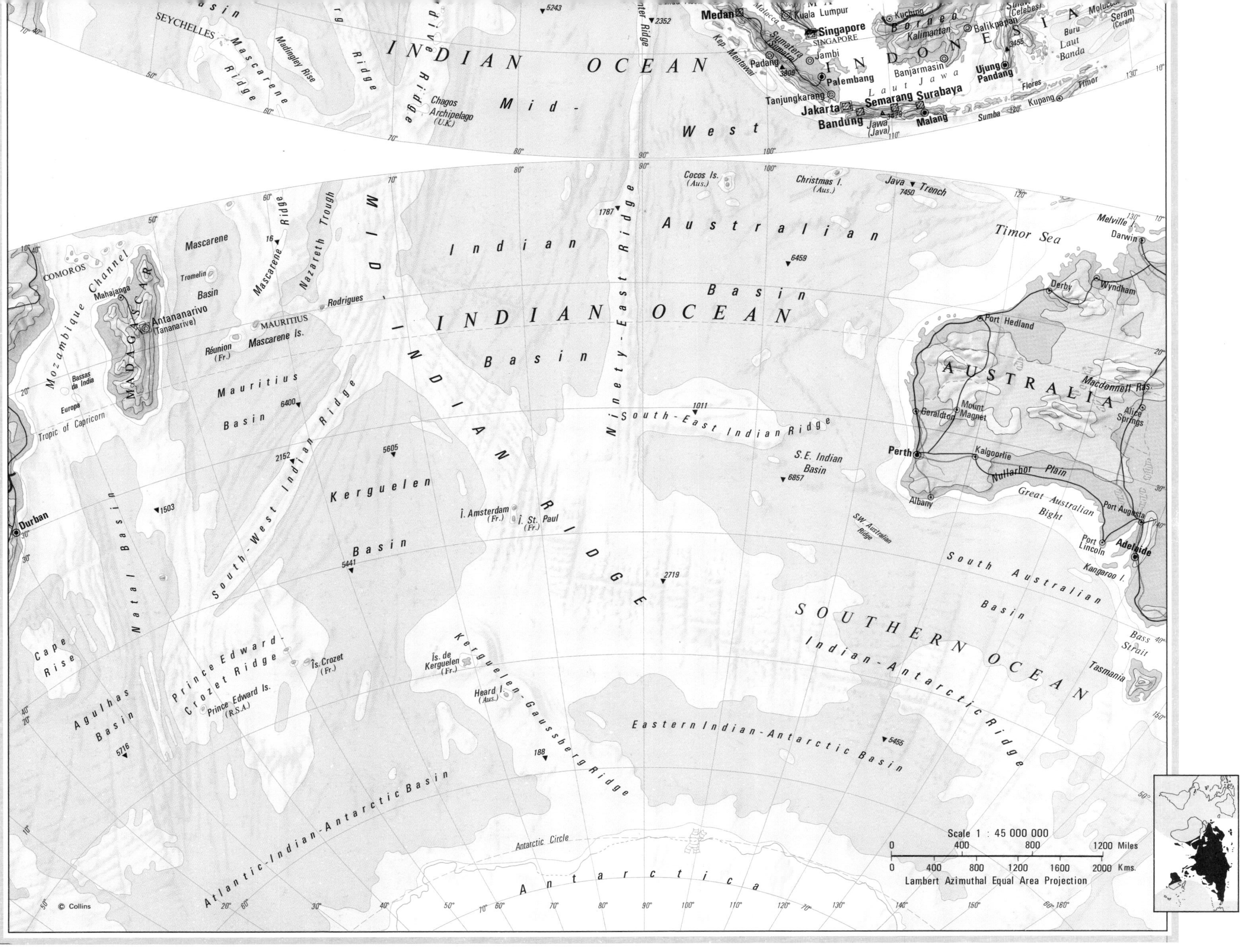

Moluccas
Seram
(Ceram)
Buru
Laut
Banda
Timor
Flores
Kupang
Sumba
Laut Banda
Sulawesi
(Celebes)
Ujung Pandang
Semarang Surabaya
Malang
Jawa
Jawa (Java)
Laut Jawa

Singapore
SINGAPORE
Jambi
Palembang
Tanjungkarang
Jakarta
Bandung

Kuala Lumpur
Padang
Kep. Mentawai

Medan
Sumatera
(Sumatra)

MELVILLE
Darwin
Wyndham
Derby
Port Hedland
Mount Magnet
Geraldton

AUSTRALIA

Alice Springs
Macdonnell Ras.

Adelaide
Port Augusta
Port Lincoln
Kangaroo I.
Bass. 40°
Bass Strait
Tasmania

Great Australian Bight
Nullarbor Plain
Kalgoorlie
Albany
Perth

South Australian Basin

SOUTHERN OCEAN

Indian–Antarctic Ridge

▼5465

Scale 1 : 45 000 000

0   400   800   1200 Miles
0   400   800   1200   1600   2000 Kms.

Lambert Azimuthal Equal Area Projection

Timor Sea

Java Trench 7450

Christmas I. (Aus.)
▼6459

Cocos Is. (Aus.)
1011

S.W. Australian Ridge

S.E. Indian Basin
▼6857

▼2719

INDONESIA

I N D I A N   O C E A N

West Australian Basin

M I D – I N D I A N   O C E A N

Ninety-east Ridge

South-East Indian Ridge

Indian Basin

N I N E T Y – E A S T   R I D G E

Eastern Indian–Antarctic Basin

Antarctica

Antarctic Circle

▼1787

enter Ridge ▼2352

▼5243

Chagos Archipelago (U.K.)

ve Ridge

rg Ridge

Maldive Ridge

SEYCHELLES

Basin

Mascarene Ridge

Madingley Rise

Mascarene Ridge

Nazareth Trough

Rodrigues

Ridge
16

Mascarene Is.
MAURITIUS
Mascarene Is.

Réunion (Fr.)
6400

Mauritius Basin
2152

Mascarene Basin
Tromelin

Antananarivo
Tananarive
▼1503

MADAGASCAR
Mahajanga

Mahajanga

COMOROS

Mozambique Channel

Bassas da India
Europa

Tropic of Capricorn

Durban

Kerguelen Basin
▼5605
▼5441

South-West Indian Ridge

i. Amsterdam (Fr.)
i. St. Paul (Fr.)

Kerguelen–Gaussberg Ridge

Is. de Kerguelen (Fr.)
Heard I. (Aus.) ▼188

Is. Crozet (Fr.)

Prince Edward Is.
Prince Edward (R.S.A.)
Crozet Ridge

Atlantic–Indian–Antarctic Basin

Natal Basin

Agulhas Basin
▼5716

Cape Rise

© Collins

49

U.S.S.R.

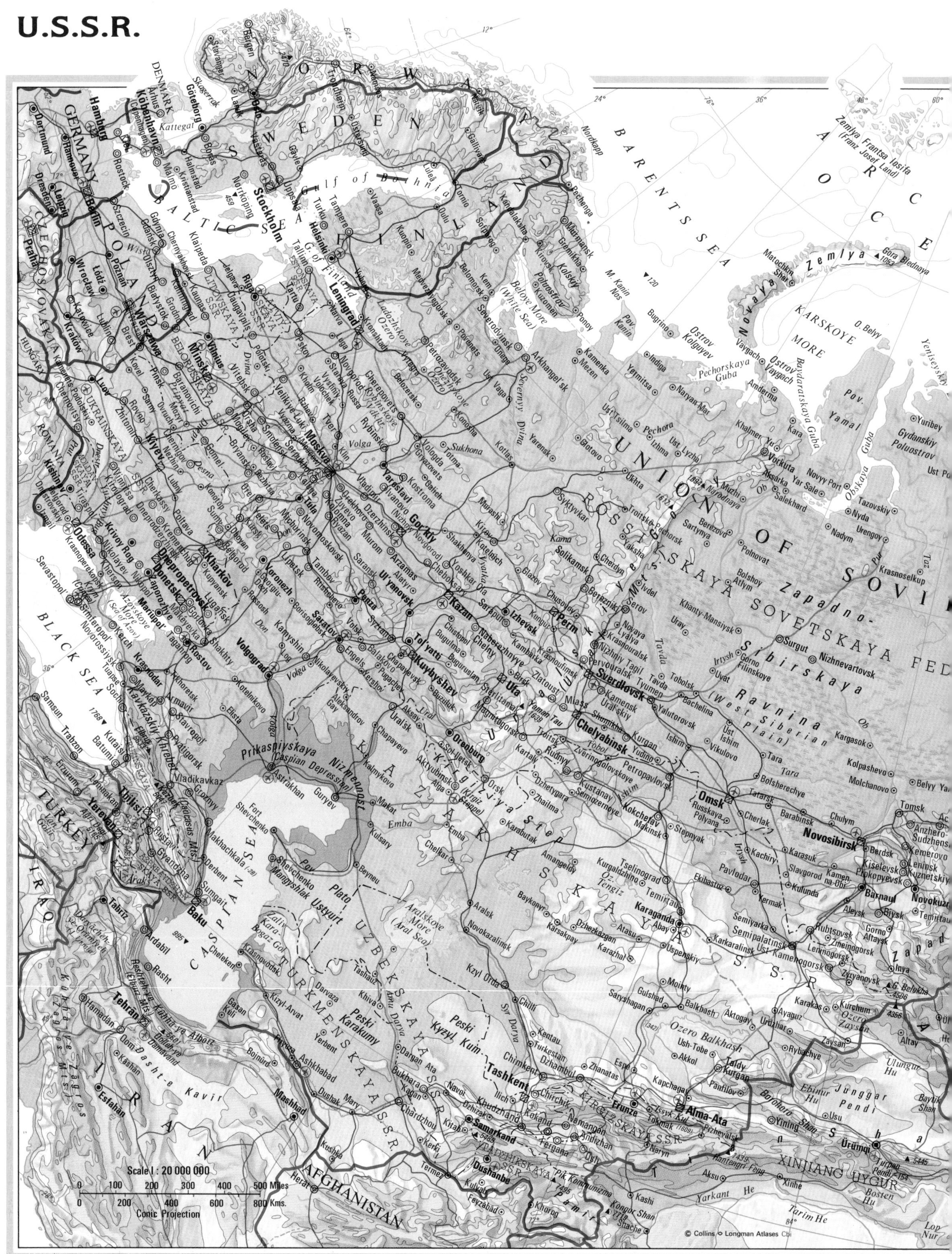

Scale 1 : 20 000 000
0 100 200 300 400 500 Miles
0 200 400 600 800 Kms.
Conic Projection
© Collins ◇ Longman Atlases

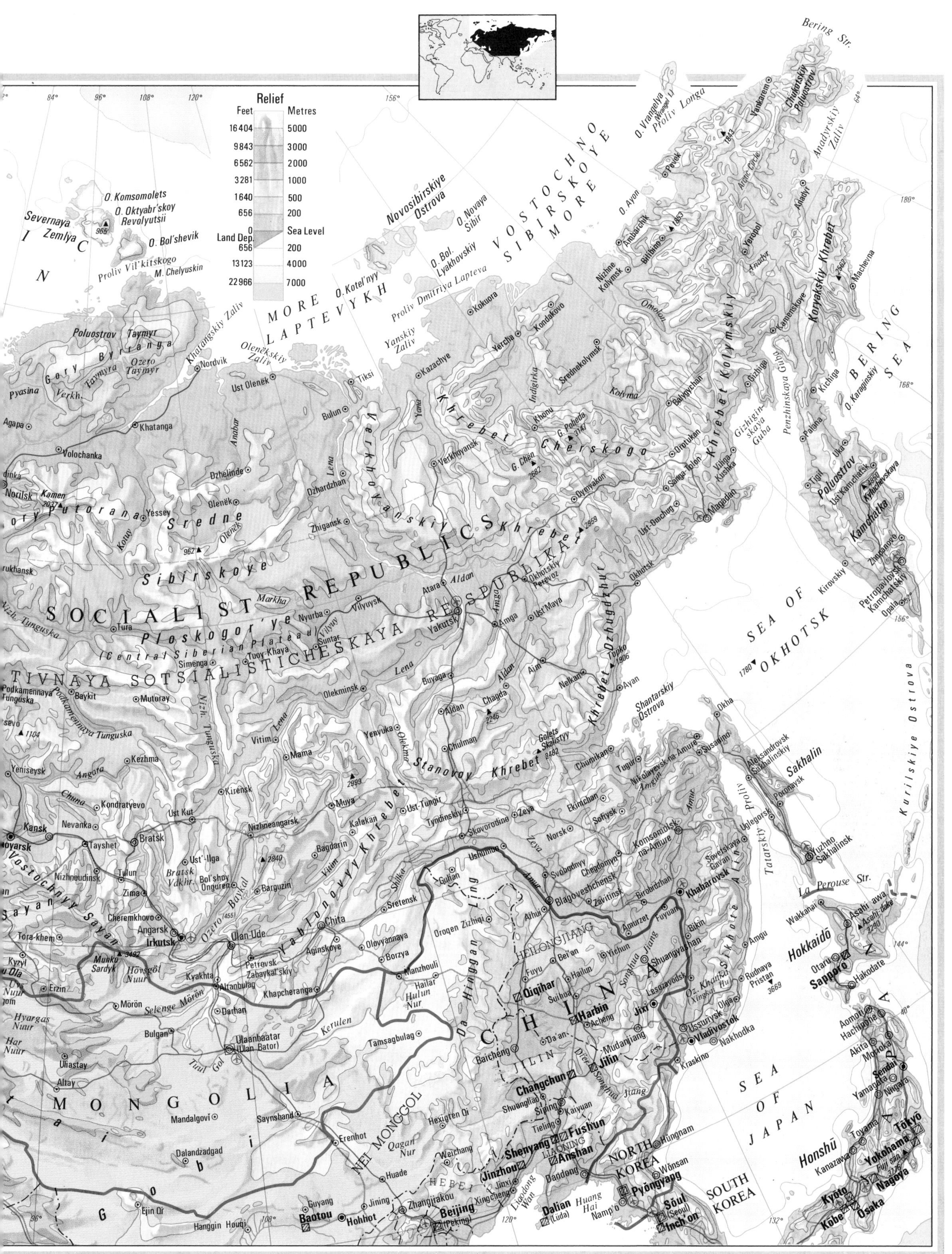
Relief
Feet Metres
16404 5000
9843 3000
6562 2000
3281 1000
1640 500
656 200
0 Sea Level
Land Dep.
656 200
13123 4000
22966 7000

EAST ASIA

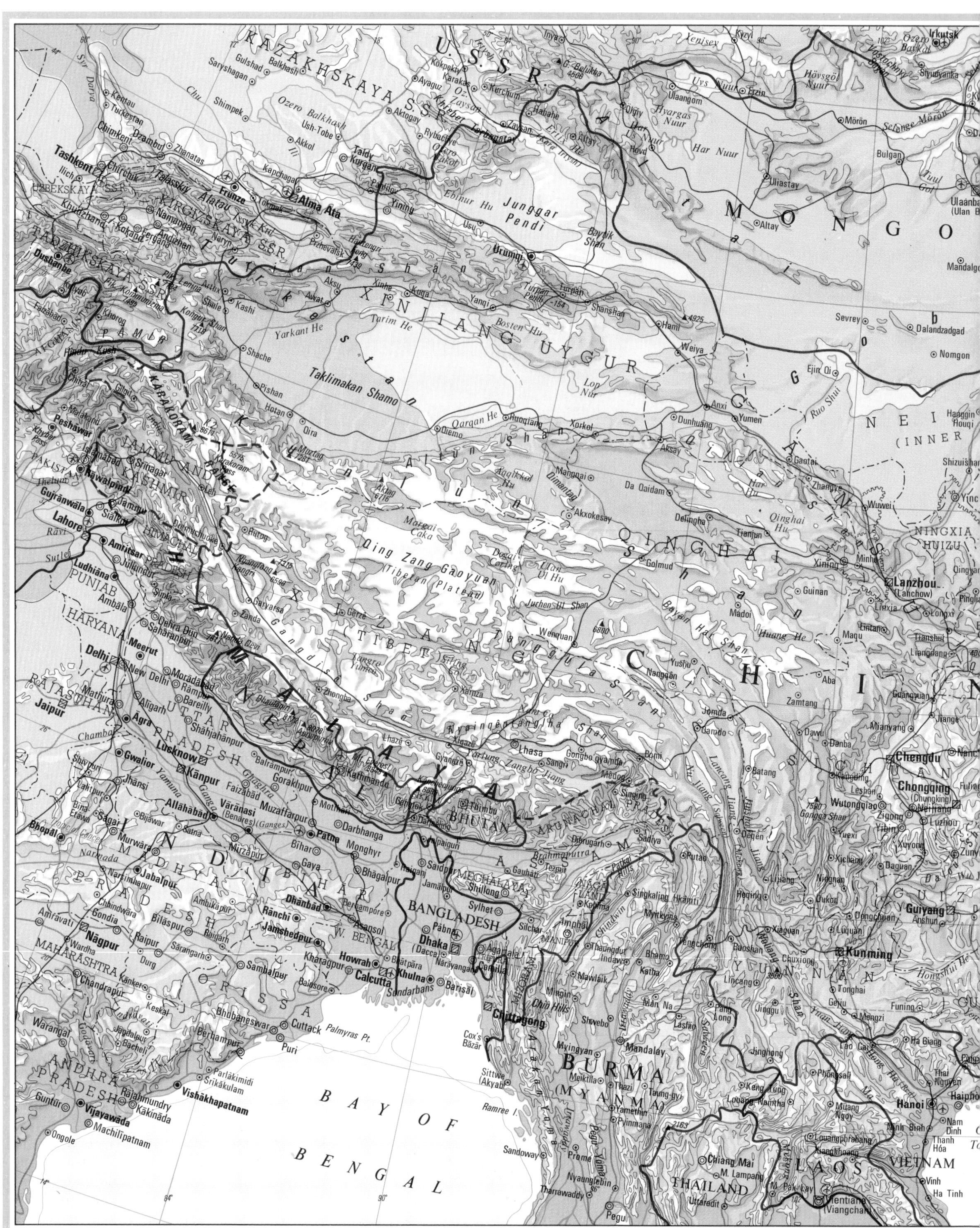
U.S.S.R.
KAZAKHSKAYA S.S.R.
KIRGIZSKAYA S.S.R.
UZBEKSKAYA S.S.R.
TADZHIKSKAYA S.S.R.
AFGHANISTAN
PAKISTAN
JAMMU AND KASHMIR
HIMACHAL PRADESH
PUNJAB
HARYANA
RAJASTHAN
UTTAR PRADESH
MADHYA PRADESH
MAHARASHTRA
ANDHRA PRADESH
ORISSA
BIHAR
W. BENGAL
INDIA
NEPAL
BHUTAN
ARUNACHAL PRADESH
ASSAM
MEGHALAYA
MANIPUR
BANGLADESH
BURMA
(MYANMA)
THAILAND
LAOS
VIETNAM
MONGOLIA
CHINA
XINJIANG UYGUR
XIZANG
QINGHAI
SICHUAN
YUNNAN
NINGXIA HUIZU
NEI MONGOL
(INNER
BAY OF BENGAL
Taklimakan Shamo
Qing Zang Gaoyuan
(Tibetan Plateau)
Junggar Pendi
KARAKORAM
HIMALAYA
Altun Shan
Kunlun Shan
Tian Shan
Gobi
Altai
Tashkent
Frunze
Alma Ata
Dushanbe
Urumqi
Kashi
Lhasa
Kathmandu
Thimbu
Delhi
New Delhi
Lahore
Peshawar
Rawalpindi
Srinagar
Agra
Lucknow
Kanpur
Varanasi
Allahabad
Patna
Calcutta
Howrah
Dhaka
(Dacca)
Chittagong
Mandalay
Lanzhou
(Lanchow)
Chengdu
Chongqing
(Chungking)
Kunming
Guiyang
Hanoi
Vientiane
(Viangchan)
Chiang Mai
Irkutsk
Ulaanbaatar
Xining
Golmud
Nagpur
Jaipur
Vishakhapatnam
Vijayawada

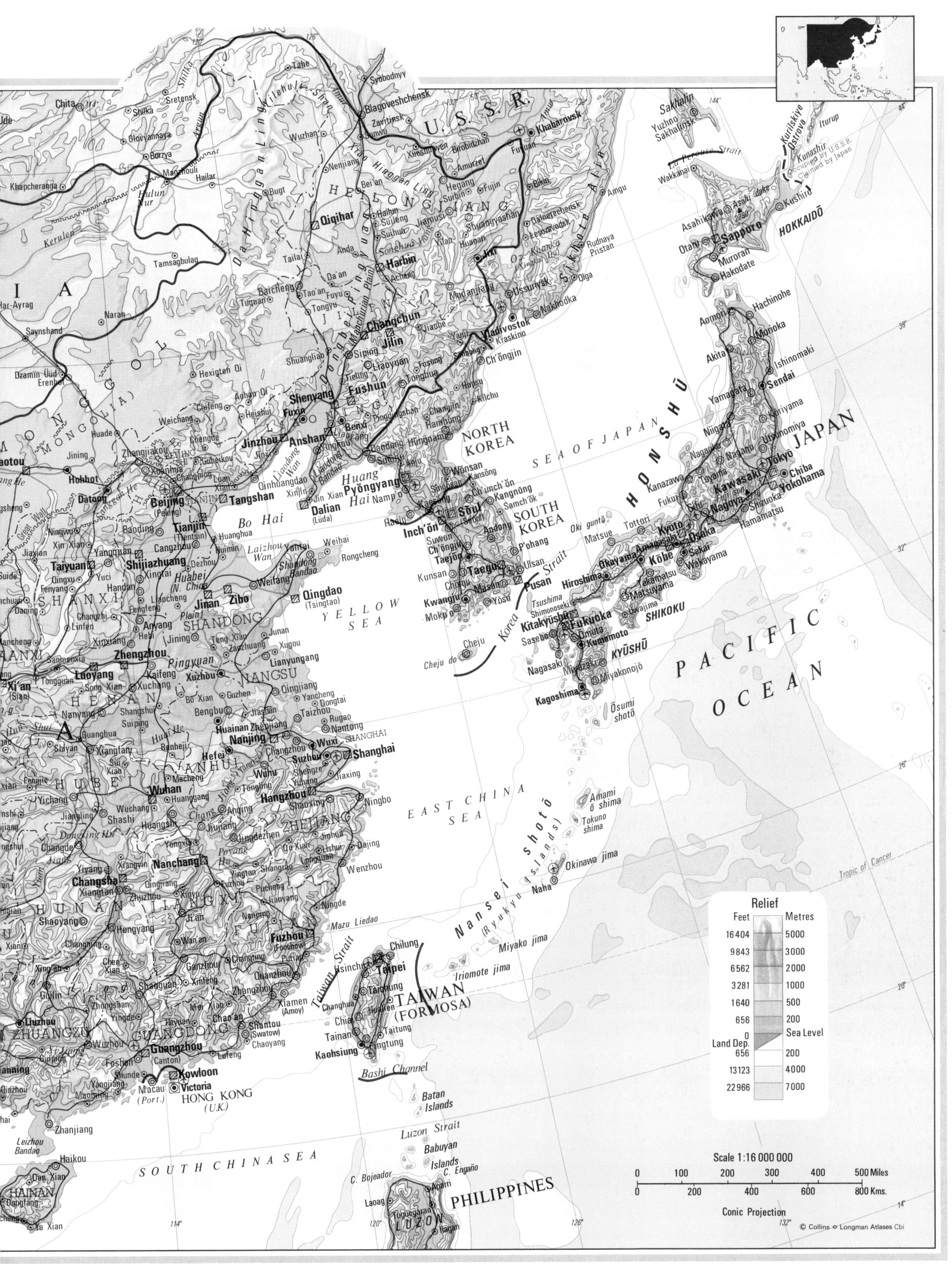
U. S. S. R.
HEILONGJIANG
JILIN
NORTH KOREA
SOUTH KOREA
JAPAN
HONSHŪ
HOKKAIDŌ
KYŪSHŪ
SHIKOKU
SEA OF JAPAN
PACIFIC OCEAN
YELLOW SEA
EAST CHINA SEA
SOUTH CHINA SEA
Bo Hai
Huang Hai
Korea Strait
Taiwan Strait
Bashi Channel
Luzon Strait
La Perouse Strait
TAIWAN (FORMOSA)
PHILIPPINES
LUZON
HAINAN
HONG KONG (U.K.)
Macau (Port.)
SHANDONG
JIANGSU
HENAN
ANHUI
HUBEI
ZHEJIANG
HUNAN
JIANGXI
FUJIAN
GUANGDONG
ZHUANGZU
SHANXI
MONGOLIA
Nansei shotō (Ryukyu Islands)
Ōsumi shotō
Amami ō shima
Tokuno shima
Okinawa jima
Miyako jima
Iriomote jima
Cheju do
Oki guntō
Tsushima
Batan Islands
Babuyan Islands
Kurilskiye Ostrova
Kunashir
Occupied by U.S.S.R. Claimed by Japan
Iturup
Sakhalin
Tropic of Cancer
Beijing (Peking)
Tianjin (Tientsin)
Shanghai
Nanjing
Wuhan
Shenyang
Harbin
Changchun
Qiqihar
Dalian (Lüda)
Qingdao (Tsingtao)
Pyŏngyang
Sŏul
Pusan
Tokyo
Osaka
Kyoto
Kōbe
Yokohama
Kawasaki
Nagoya
Sapporo
Fukuoka
Kitakyūshū
Hiroshima
Sendai
Taipei
Kaohsiung
Guangzhou (Canton)
Kowloon
Victoria
Fuzhou (Foochow)
Hangzhou
Vladivostok
Khabarovsk
Blagoveshchensk
Chita
Relief
Feet
Metres
16404 5000
9843 3000
6562 2000
3281 1000
1640 500
656 200
0 Sea Level
Land Dep.
656 200
13123 4000
22966 7000
Scale 1:16 000 000
0 100 200 300 400 500 Miles
0 200 400 600 800 Kms.
Conic Projection
© Collins - Longman Atlases Cbi

EAST CHINA

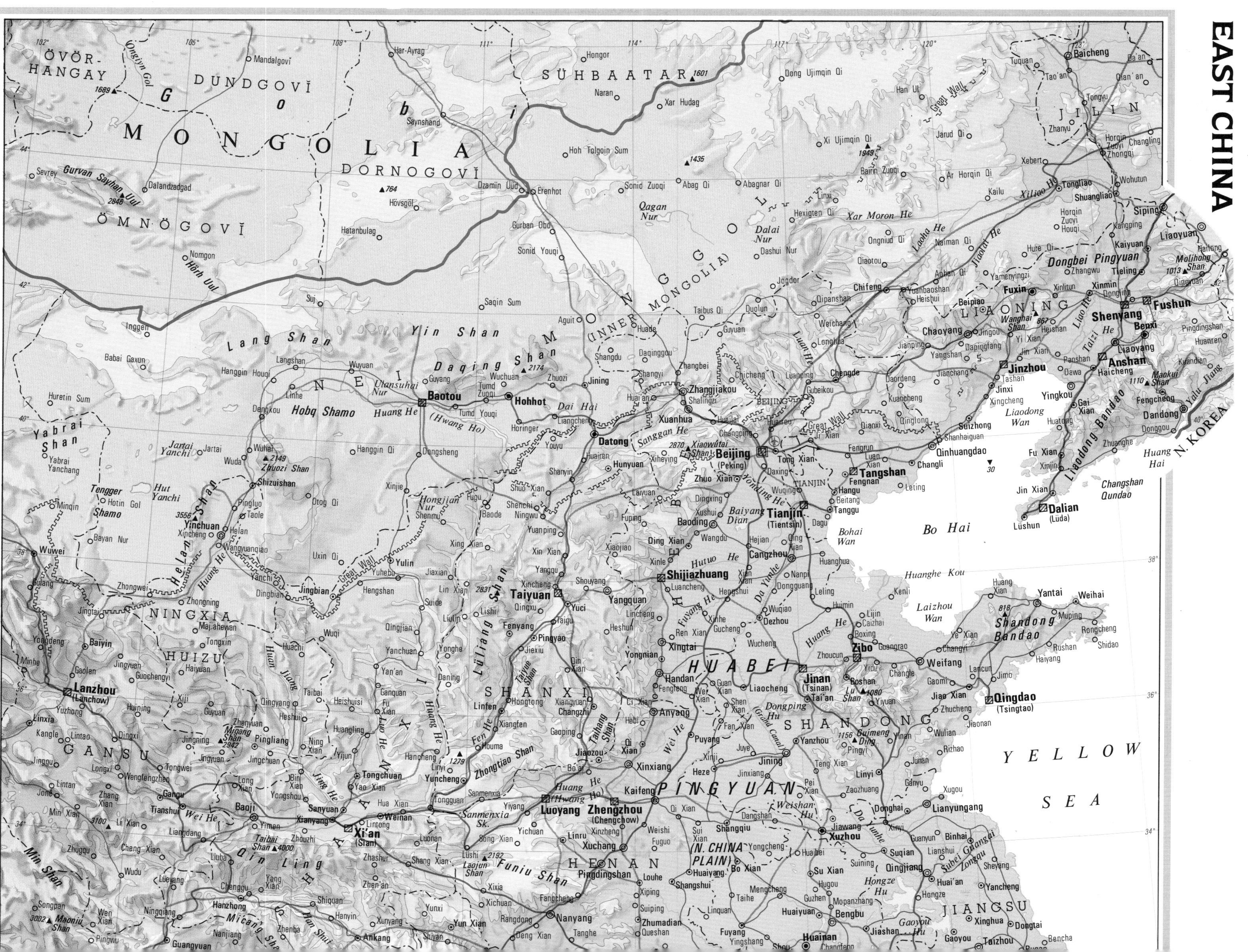

N. KOREA
YELLOW SEA
Bo Hai
Liaodong Wan
Liaodong Bandao
Shandong Bandao
Bohai Wan
Laizhou Wan
Huang Hai
LIAONING
JILIN
HUABEI PINGYUAN
(N. CHINA PLAIN)
SHANDONG
JIANGSU
HENAN
SHANXI
SHAANXI
NINGXIA HUIZU
GANSU
MONGOLIA
NEI MONGOL (INNER MONGOLIA)
DORNOGOVĬ
ÖMNÖGOVĬ
DUNDGOVĬ
SÜHBAATAR
ÖVÖR-HANGAY
Gobi
Beijing (Peking)
Tianjin (Tientsin)
Shenyang
Dalian (Lüda)
Qingdao (Tsingtao)
Jinan (Tsinan)
Shijiazhuang
Taiyuan
Zhengzhou (Chengchow)
Xi'an (Sian)
Lanzhou (Lanchow)
Baotou
Hohhot
Datong
Yinchuan
Luoyang
Kaifeng
Xuzhou
Tangshan
Anshan
Fushun
Jinzhou
Zibo
Huang He (Hwang Ho)
Yin Shan
Lang Shan
Daqing Shan
Lüliang Shan
Qin Ling
Funiu Shan
Hobq Shamo
Tengger Shamo
Great Wall

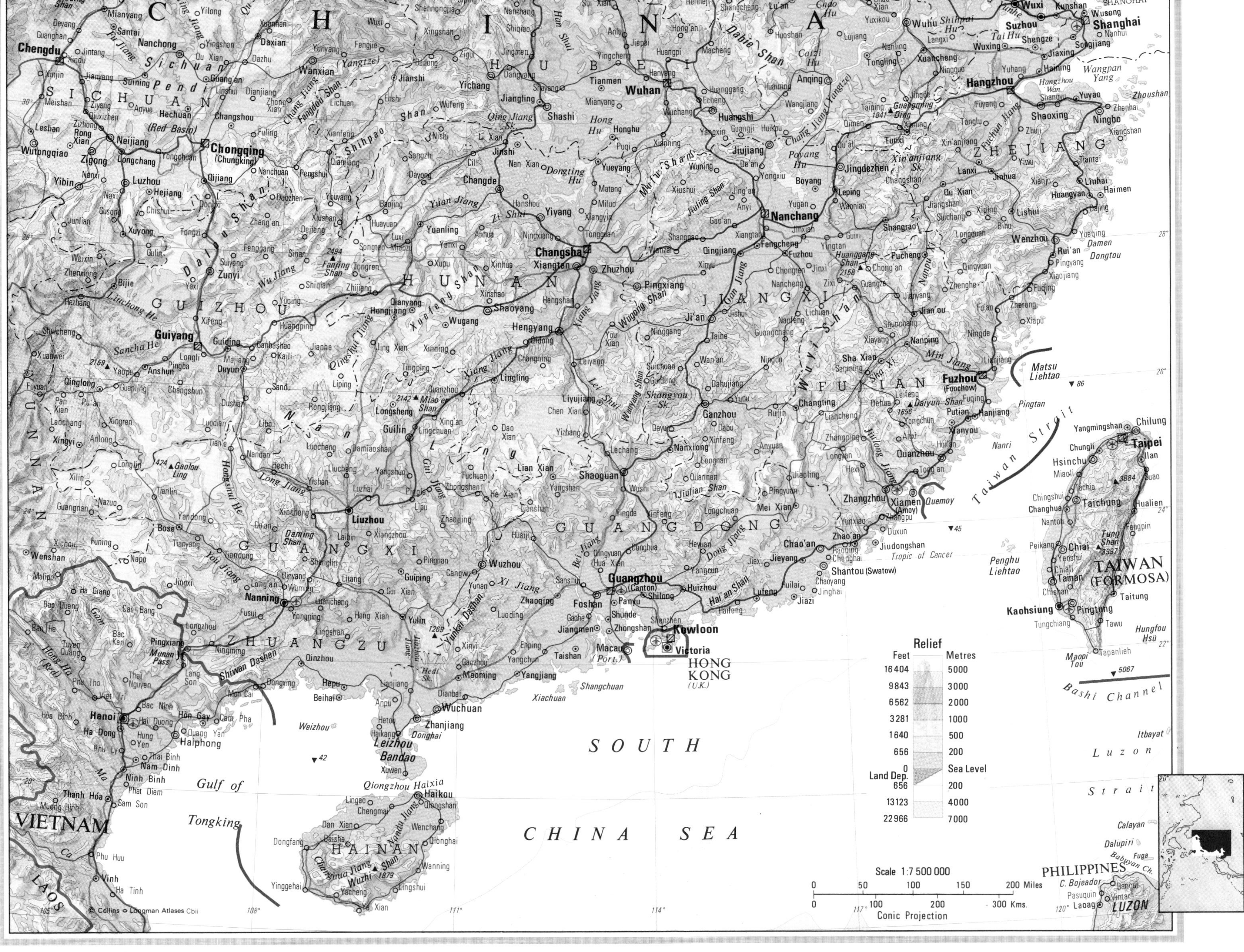

CHINA
SICHUAN
Sichuan Pendi (Red Basin)
HUBEI
HUNAN
GUIZHOU
JIANGXI
FUJIAN
ZHEJIANG
GUANGDONG
GUANGXI ZHUANGZU
HAINAN
YUNNAN
TAIWAN (FORMOSA)
HONG KONG (U.K.)
VIETNAM
LAOS
PHILIPPINES
LUZON
SOUTH CHINA SEA
Gulf of Tongking
Taiwan Strait
Bashi Channel
Luzon Strait
Tropic of Cancer
Shanghai
Hangzhou
Wuhan
Changsha
Nanchang
Fuzhou (Foochow)
Guangzhou (Canton)
Kowloon
Victoria
Macau (Port.)
Chongqing (Chungking)
Chengdu
Guiyang
Nanning
Hanoi
Haiphong
Taipei
Kaohsiung
Xiamen (Amoy)
Shantou (Swatow)
Relief
Feet
Metres
16404
5000
9843
3000
6562
2000
3281
1000
1640
500
656
200
0
Sea Level
Land Dep.
656
200
13123
4000
22966
7000
Scale 1:7 500 000
0 50 100 150 200 Miles
0 100 200 300 Kms.
Conic Projection
© Collins - Longman Atlases Cbii

INDO-CHINA

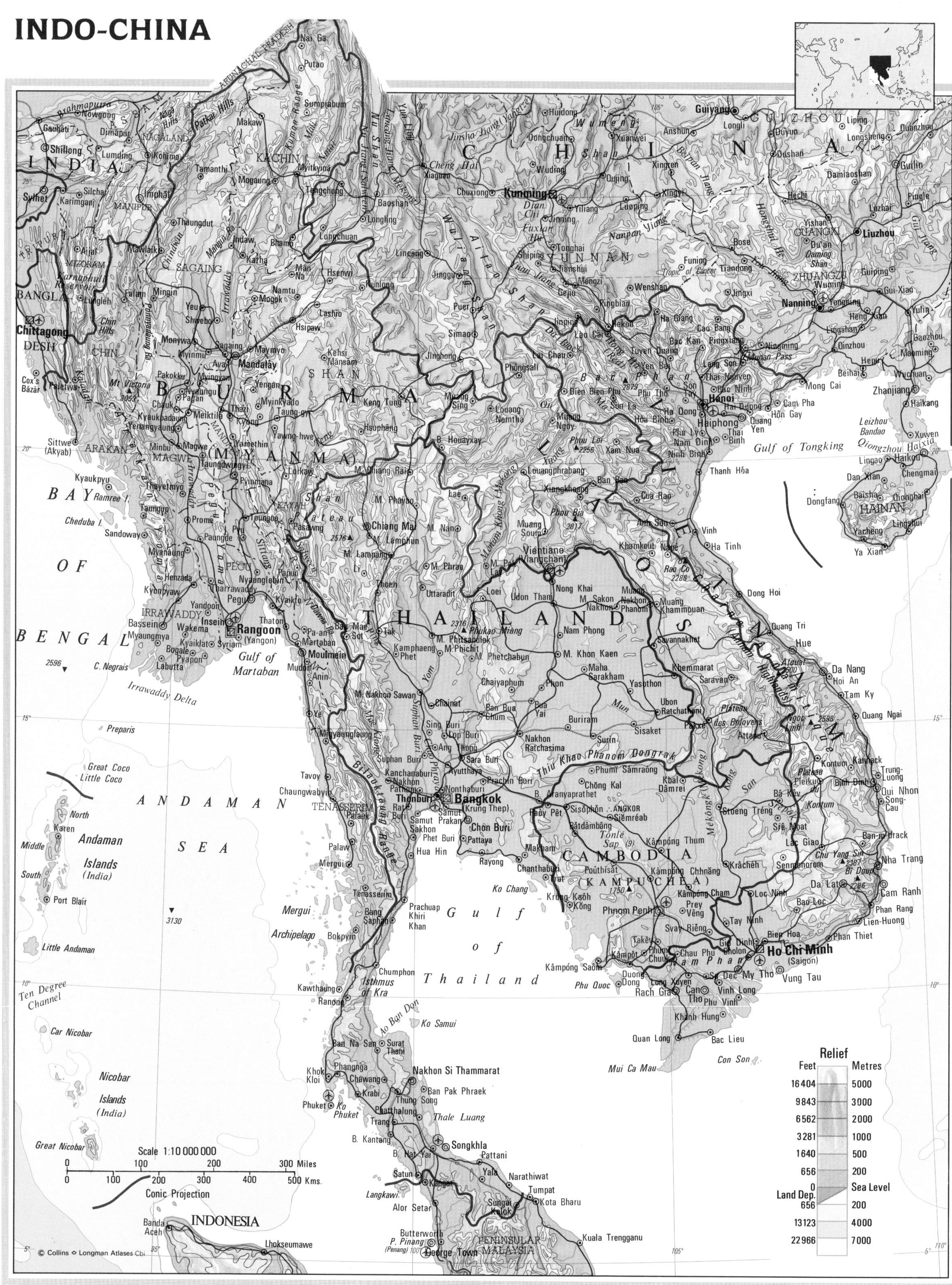

INDIA
BANGLADESH
BURMA (MYANMA)
CHINA
LAOS
THAILAND
CAMBODIA (KAMPUCHEA)
VIETNAM
INDONESIA
PENINSULAR MALAYSIA
YUNNAN
GUANGXI ZHUANGZU
GUIZHOU
HAINAN
SHAN
KACHIN
SAGAING
MANDALAY
MAGWE
ARAKAN
PEGU
IRRAWADDY
TENASSERIM
CHIN
MIZORAM
MANIPUR
NAGALAND
TRIPURA
BAY OF BENGAL
ANDAMAN SEA
Gulf of Martaban
Gulf of Thailand
Gulf of Tongking
Andaman Islands (India)
Nicobar Islands (India)
Mergui Archipelago
Isthmus of Kra
Shan Plateau
Irrawaddy Delta
Ten Degree Channel
Preparis
Great Coco
Little Coco
North
Middle
South
Little Andaman
Car Nicobar
Great Nicobar
Port Blair
Rangoon (Yangon)
Mandalay
Moulmein
Bangkok (Krung Thep)
Thonburi
Hanoi
Haiphong
Ho Chi Minh (Saigon)
Phnom Penh
Vientiane (Viangchan)
Kunming
Nanning
Guiyang
Liuzhou
Chittagong
Sylhet
Shillong
Imphal
Chiang Mai
Nakhon Si Thammarat
Songkhla
Phuket
George Town
Kota Bharu
Kuala Trengganu
Da Nang
Hue
Nha Trang
Cam Ranh
Qui Nhon
Vung Tau
Tonlé Sap
ANGKOR
Siĕmréab
Bătdâmbâng
Mekong
Con Son
Ko Samui
Ko Chang
Phu Quoc
Mui Ca Mau
Scale 1:10 000 000
0 100 200 300 Miles
0 100 200 300 400 500 Kms.
Conic Projection
Relief
Feet Metres
16404 5000
9843 3000
6562 2000
3281 1000
1640 500
656 200
0 Sea Level
Land Dep.
656 200
13123 4000
22966 7000
© Collins ◇ Longman Atlases Cbi

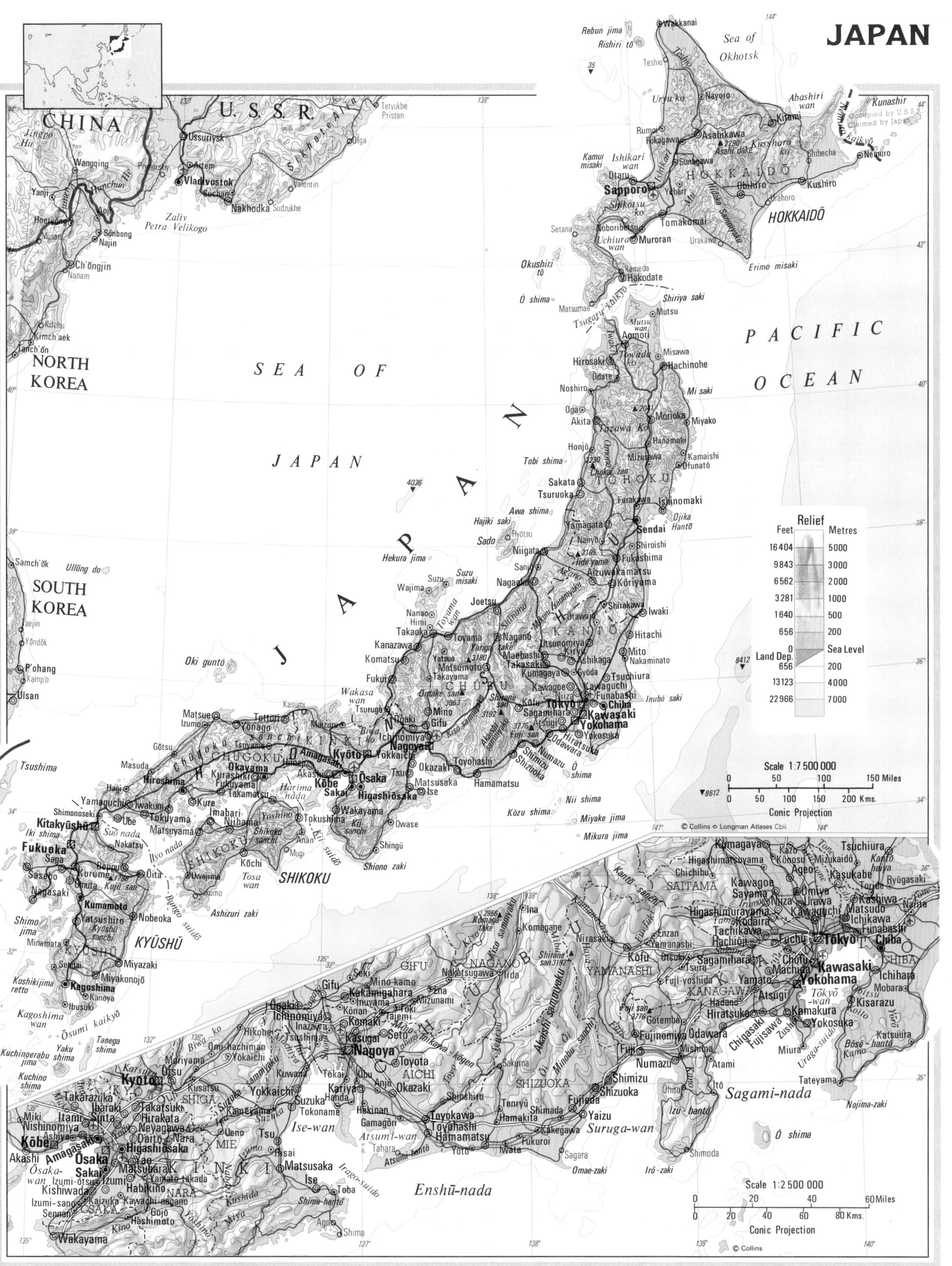

JAPAN
CHINA
U.S.S.R.
NORTH KOREA
SOUTH KOREA
SEA OF JAPAN
PACIFIC OCEAN
Sea of Okhotsk
HOKKAIDŌ
HONSHU
SHIKOKU
KYŪSHŪ
TŌHOKU
KANTŌ
CHŪBU
KINKI
CHŪGOKU
Wakkanai
Rebun jima
Rishiri tō
Teshio
Nayoro
Abashiri wan
Kitami
Kunashir
Occupied by U.S.S.R. Claimed by Japan
Nemuro
Asahikawa
Asahi dake
Rumoi
Ishikari wan
Otaru
Sapporo
Obihiro
Kushiro
Tomakomai
Muroran
Uchiura wan
Urakawa
Erimo misaki
Okushiri tō
Hakodate
Ō shima
Shiriya saki
Tsugaru kaikyō
Mutsu
Aomori
Hirosaki
Misawa
Hachinohe
Noshiro
Akita
Morioka
Miyako
Kamaishi
Ōfunatō
Tobi shima
Sakata
Tsuruoka
Ishinomaki
Yamagata
Sendai
Sado
Niigata
Fukushima
Aizuwakamatsu
Kōriyama
Iwaki
Hitachi
Mito
Joetsu
Nagano
Toyama
Kanazawa
Komatsu
Fukui
Utsunomiya
Maebashi
Takasaki
Tsuchiura
Kawaguchi
Chiba
Tōkyō
Kawasaki
Yokohama
Yokosuka
Inubō saki
Matsue
Tottori
Kyōto
Nagoya
Ōsaka
Kōbe
Sakai
Higashiōsaka
Wakayama
Okayama
Hiroshima
Kurashiki
Fukuyama
Takamatsu
Tokushima
Matsuyama
Kōchi
Shiono zaki
Tsushima
Kitakyūshū
Fukuoka
Saga
Nagasaki
Kumamoto
Ōita
Miyazaki
Kagoshima
Hamamatsu
Toyohashi
Shizuoka
Numazu
Relief
Feet
Metres
16 404 5000
9843 3000
6562 2000
3281 1000
1640 500
656 200
0 Sea Level
Land Dep.
656 200
13123 4000
22966 7000
Scale 1:7 500 000
0 50 100 150 Miles
0 50 100 150 200 Kms.
Conic Projection
© Collins – Longman Atlases Cbii
Kumagaya
Saitama
Kawagoe
Hachiōji
Kōfu
Sagamihara
Yamanashi
Kanagawa
Sagami-nada
Suruga-wan
Izu-hantō
Shimoda
Ō shima
Enshū-nada
Ise-wan
Tsu
Matsusaka
Toba
Shima
Gifu
Aichi
Toyota
Okazaki
Yokkaichi
Shiga
Mie
Nara
Scale 1:2 500 000
0 20 40 60 Miles
0 20 40 60 80 Kms.
Conic Projection
© Collins

SOUTHEAST ASIA

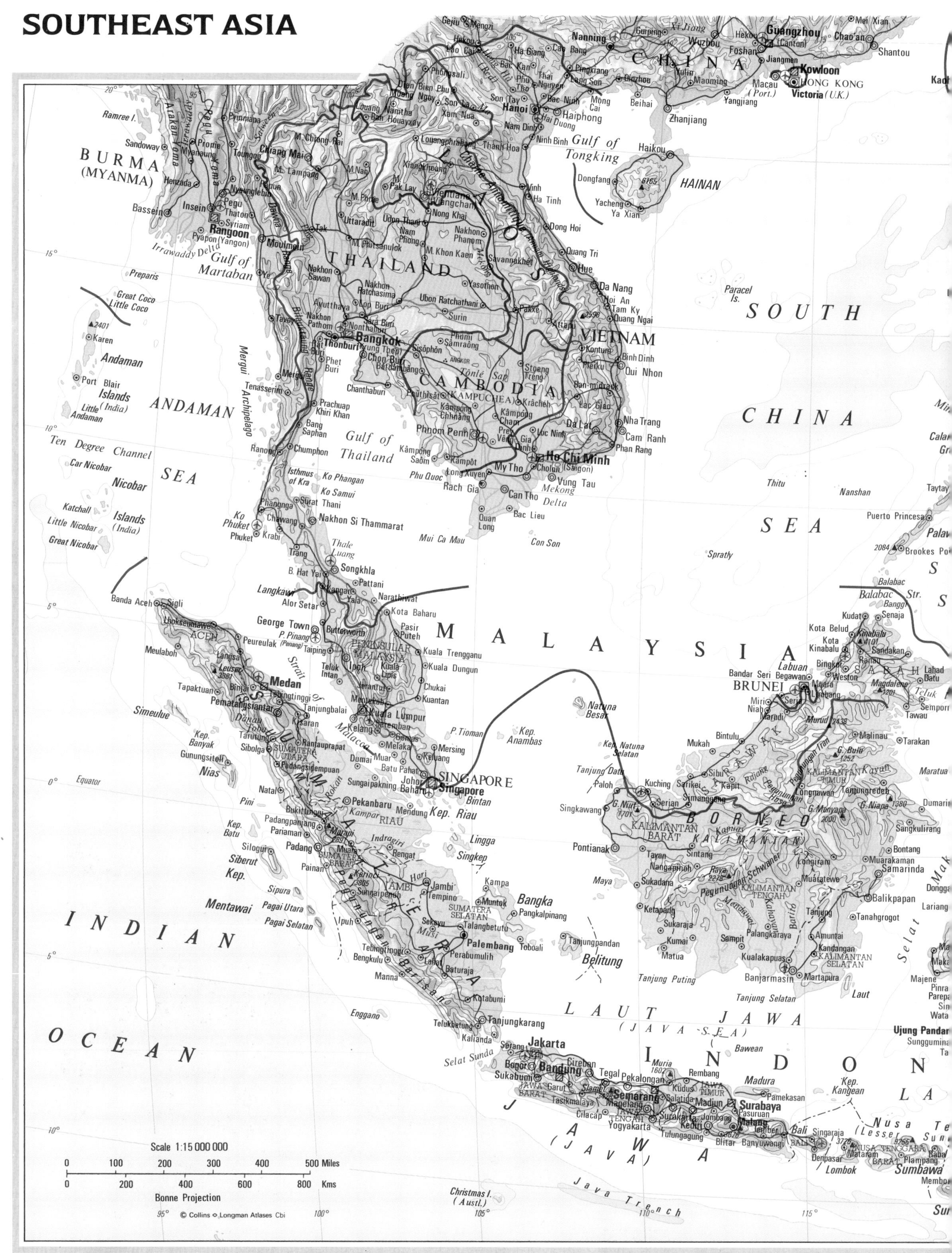

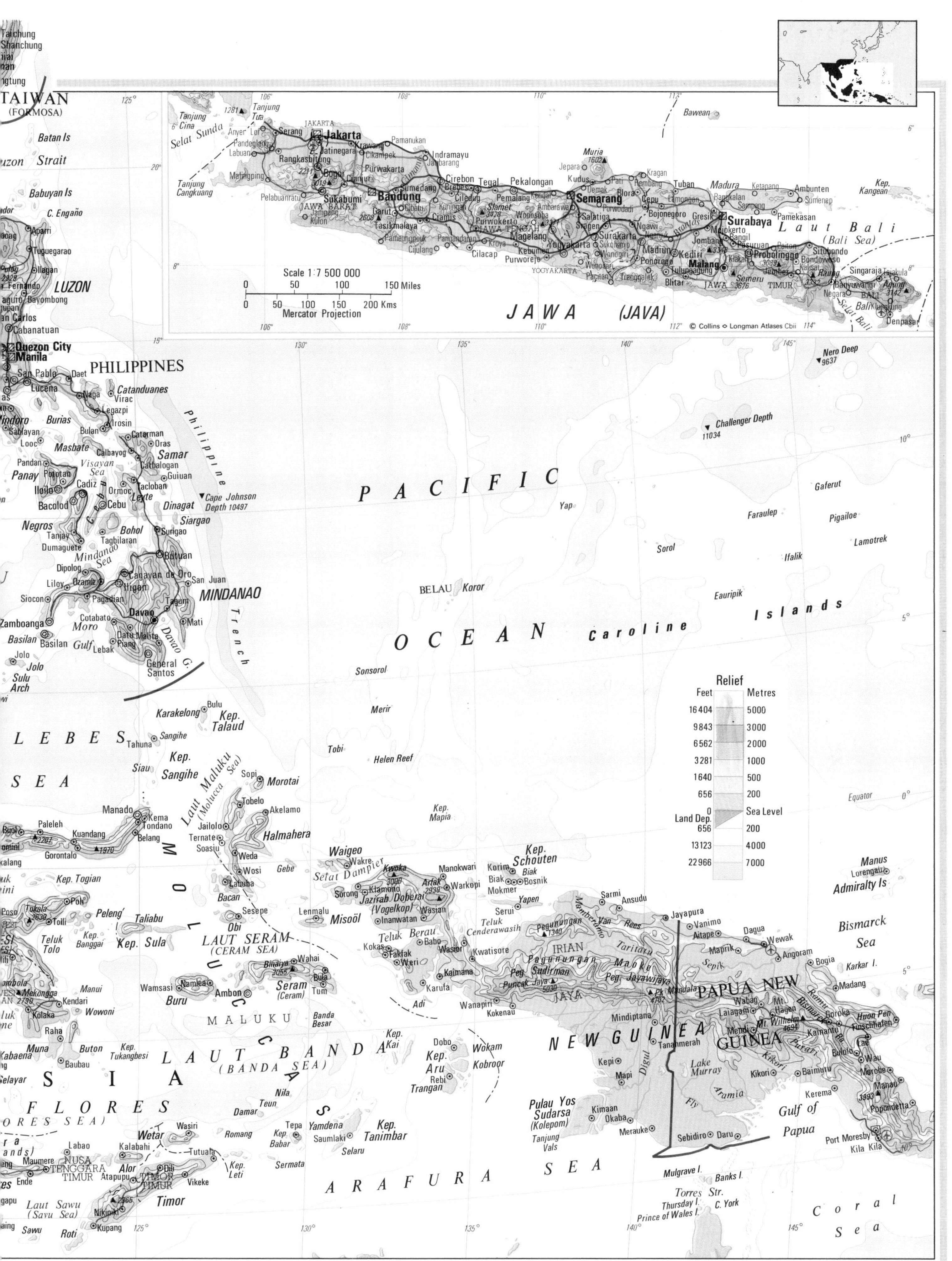

TAIWAN (FORMOSA)

Batan Is

Luzon Strait

Babuyan Is

C. Engaño

Aparri

Tuguegarao

LUZON

Fernando

Bayombong

Carlos

Cabanatuan

Quezon City

Manila

PHILIPPINES

San Pablo · Daet

Lucena

Naga · Catanduanes

Virac

Indoro · Legazpi

Burias · Irosin

Sablayan · Catarman

Looc · Bulan · Oras

Masbate · Calbayog · **Samar**

Panay · Iloilo · Catbalogan

Visayan Sea · Guiuan

Iloilo · Cadiz · Ormoc · Tacloban

Bacolod · Cebu · Leyte

Negros · Bohol · Siargao

Tanjay · Tagbilaran · Surigao

Dumaguete · Dinagat

Mindanao Sea · Butuan

Liloy · Ozamiz · Cagayan de Oro · San Juan

Dipolog · Iligan

Siocon · Pagadian · Tagum

Zamboanga · **MINDANAO** · **Davao**

Moro · Cotabato · Datu Piang · Mati

Basilan · Lebak

Jolo · Gulf · General Santos

Sulu Arch

Cape Johnson Depth 10497

Philippine Trench

Davao Trench

P A C I F I C

O C E A N

Yap

Faraulep

Sorol

Ifalik

Belau · Koror

Eauripik

Sonsorol

Merir

Tobi

Helen Reef

Gaferut

Pigailoe

Lamotrek

Caroline Islands

Challenger Depth 11034

Nero Deep 9637

Equator 0°

5°

L E B E S

S E A

Karakelong · Bulu

Kep. Talaud

Tahuna

Sangihe

Siau

Kep. Sangihe

Manado · Kema · Tondano

Palaleh · Tobelo

Kuandang · Belang · Akelamo

Gorontalo · Jailolo · Morotai

Ternate · Soasiu

Weda · Halmahera

Waigeo · Wakre

Setat Dampier

Sopi

Kwoka

Manokwari · Korim · Biak

Arfak · Warkopi · Bosnik

Sorong · Klamono · Mokmer

Jazirah Doberai (Vogelkop) · Wasian · Yapen

Lenmalu · Inanwatan

Misoöl · Serui · Sarmi · Ansudu

Teluk Berau · Babo · Teluk Cenderawasih

Kokas · Fakfak · Weri · Wastor

Binaiya · Wahai · Kwatisore

Namlea · Bula · Kaimana

Seram (Ceram) · Karufa

Wamsasi · Ambon · Tum

Buru · MALUKU · Adi · Wanapiri · Kokenau

Banda Besar

Wowoni

Raha

Kendari

Kolaka

Muna · Buton

Kabaena

Selayar

S I A

F L O R E S

(ORES SEA)

Kep. Togian

Poso · Tokala

Peleng' · Taliabu

Kep. Banggai · Kep. Sula

Teluk Tolo · Obi · Sesepe

Manui · **LAUT SERAM (CERAM SEA)**

M O L U C C A S

LAUT BANDA (BANDA SEA)

Nila · Damar

Teun

Romang · Babar

Wasiri · Yamdena · Kep. Tanimbar

Labao · Kalabahi · Saumlaki · Selaru

Tutuala · Kep. Leti · Sermata

NUSA TENGGARA TIMUR

Atapupu · TIMOR TIMUR · Dili · Vikeke

Alor · Timor

Ende · Nikiniki

Laut Sawu (Savu Sea)

Sawu · Kupang · Roti

Dobo · Kep. Kai · Wokam · Kep. Aru · Kobroor

Rebi · Trangan

Pulau Yos Sudarsa (Kolepom)

Kepi · Mapi · Kimaan · Okaba

Tanjung Vals · Merauke · Sebidiro · Daru

A R A F U R A   S E A

Mulgrave I. · Banks I.

Torres Str. · C. York

Thursday I. · Prince of Wales I.

Setat Dampier

Serui · Nabire

Pegunungan · Membramo · Jayapura · Vanimo

IRIN JAYA · Taritatu · Aitape · Wewak

Pegunungan Sudirman · Maoke · Pk. Mandala · Maprik · Dagua

Puncak Jaya 5030 · Peg. Jayawijaya · Angoram

Pk. Mandala 4702 · Sepik

Mindiptana · **PAPUA NEW**

N E W   G U I N E A · **GUINEA**

Wabag · Mt. Hagen 4694 · Mt. Wilhelm 4693

Tanahmerah · Laiagam · Mendi

Lake Murray · Kikori

Digul · Aramia

Fly · Kerema

Kila Kila · Port Moresby

Gulf of Papua

C o r a l   S e a

JAKARTA

Tanjung Cina · Tanjung Tua

Serang · Karawang · Pamanukan

Anyer Lor · **Jakarta** · Cikampek · Indramayu

Pandeglang · Jatinegara · Purwakarta

Labuan · Rangkasbitung · Cirebon · Tegal · Pekalongan

Matingping · Bogor · Cianjur · Purwakarta

Tanjung Cangkuang · **Bandung** · Kuningan · Pemalang

Pelabuanratu · **Sukabumi** · Ciledug · Brebes

JAWA BARAT · Garut · Cilacap · Pekalongan

Jampang · Pameungpeuk · Tasikmalaya · Cilamaya · Kebumen

Cijulang · Pamanukan · Pangandaran · Cilacap · Purworejo

Slamet · Woonosobo · Ambarawa · **Semarang**

JAWA TENGAH · Magelang · Salatiga

Kudus · Jepara · Pati · Kragan · Tuban

Demak · Blora · Rembang · **Surabaya**

Bojonegoro · Gresik · Madura · Bangkalan

Yogyakarta · Surakarta · Ngawi · Madiun · Jombang · Pasuruan

Sukoharjo · Sragen · Ponorogo · **Malang**

Wonogiri · Pacitan · Trenggalek · Blitar · Semeru 3676

YOGYAKARTA · JAWA TIMUR

Muria 1602

Bawean

Kep. Kangean

Sumenep

Pamekasan · Sampang

Sitobondo · Bondowoso

Jamber · Probolinggo

Banyuwangi · Singaraja · Jajakula

Negara · **BALI** · Denpasar · Agung 3142

Laut Bali (Bali Sea)

Selat Bali

J A W A   (J A V A)

Scale 1:7 500 000

0   50   100   150 Miles

0   50 100 150 200 Kms

Mercator Projection

© Collins · Longman Atlases Cbii

Relief

Feet	Metres
16 404	5000
9843	3000
6562	2000
3281	1000
1640	500
656	200
0	Sea Level
Land Dep.	
656	200
13123	4000
22966	7000

Kep. Mapia

Manus

Lorengau

Admiralty Is

Bismarck Sea

Karkar I.

Bogia · Madang

Huon Pen.

Fuschhafen

Kamantu · Lae

Bismarck Range

Morobe · Manari

Popondetta

59

SOUTH ASIA

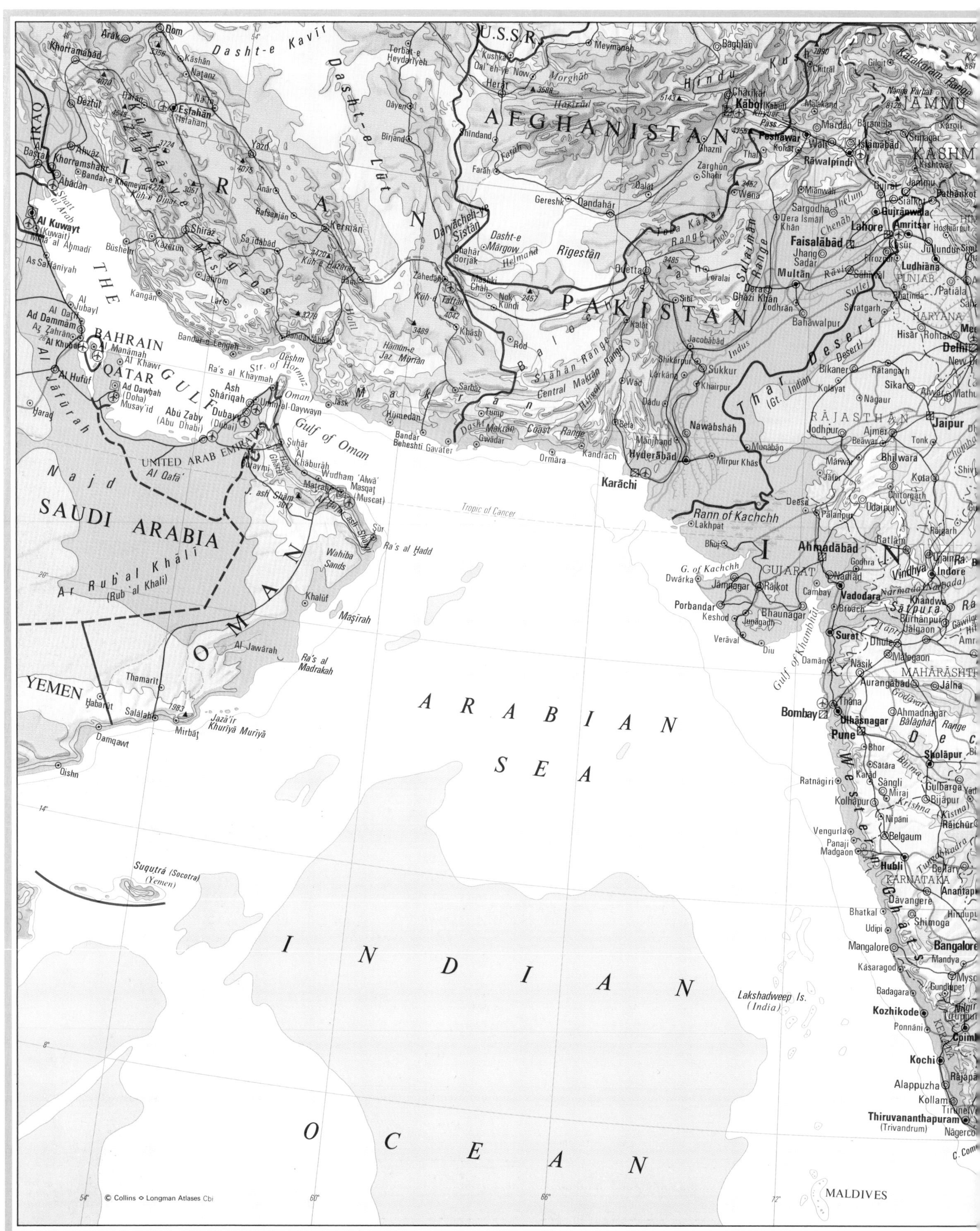

IRAN
AFGHANISTAN
PAKISTAN
INDIA
SAUDI ARABIA
OMAN
YEMEN
QATAR
BAHRAIN
UNITED ARAB EMIRATES
U.S.S.R.
IRAQ
JAMMU
KASHMIR
THE GULF
Gulf of Oman
Str. of Hormuz
ARABIAN SEA
INDIAN OCEAN
Tropic of Cancer
Rann of Kachchh
G. of Kachchh
Gulf of Khambhat
Lakshadweep Is. (India)
MALDIVES
Suquṭrá (Socotra) (Yemen)
Dasht-e Kavīr
Dasht-e Lūt
Hindu Kush
Karakoram Range
Ar Rub`al Khālī (Rub`al Khali)
Thar Desert (Gt. Indian Desert)
Rāwalpindi
Islāmābād
Lahore
Karāchi
Bombay
Ahmadābād
Jaipur
Delhi
Kābol
Kermān
Eṣfahān
Shīrāz
Quetta
Hyderābād
Multān
Faisalābād
Muscat
Pune
Bangalore
Kochi
Thiruvananthapuram (Trivandrum)
© Collins ◇ Longman Atlases Cbi

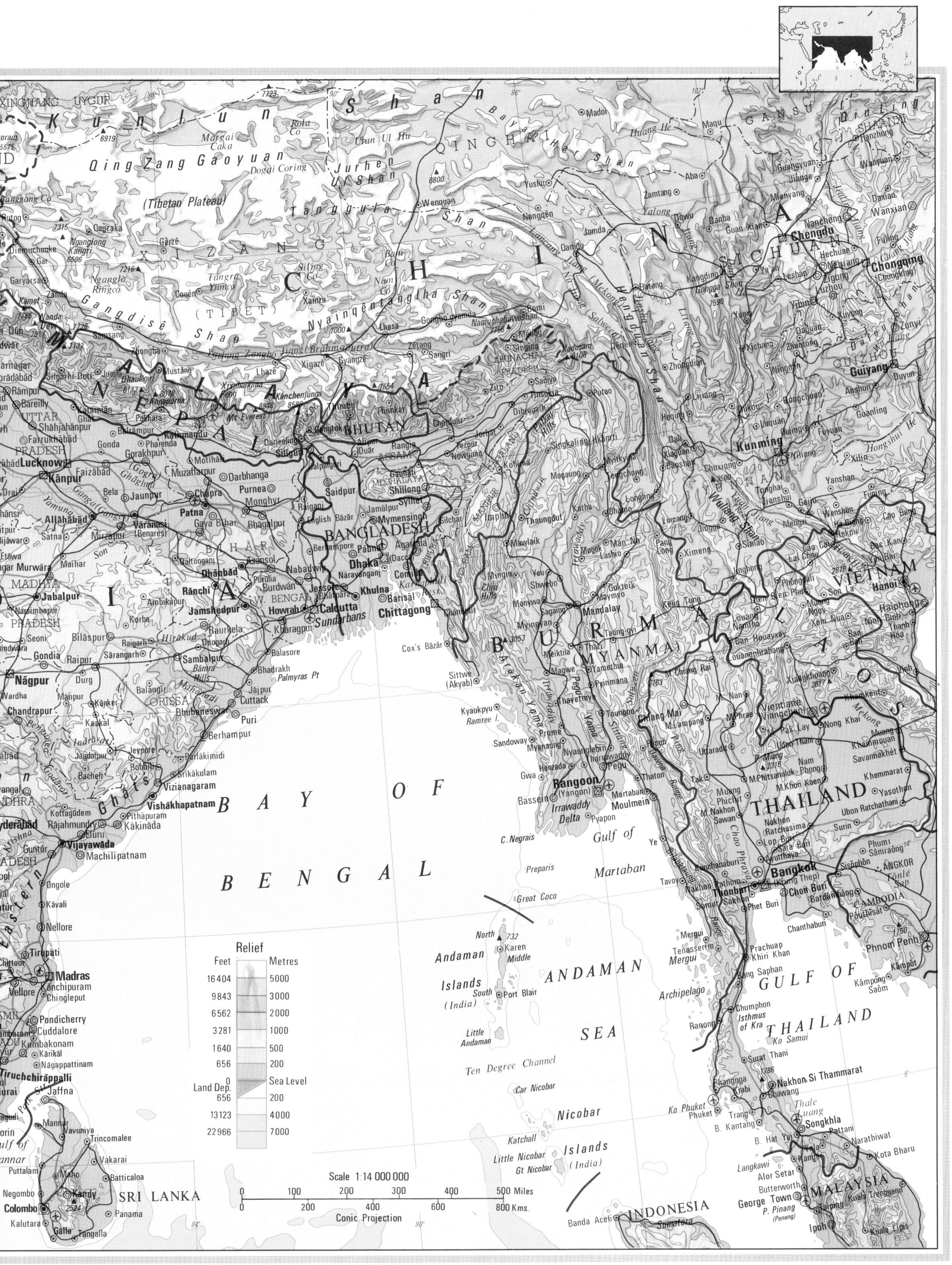
BAY OF BENGAL
ANDAMAN SEA
GULF OF THAILAND
Gulf of Martaban
CHINA
INDIA
NEPAL
BHUTAN
BANGLADESH
BURMA (MYANMA)
THAILAND
LAOS
VIETNAM
CAMBODIA
MALAYSIA
INDONESIA
SRI LANKA
Kunlun Shan
Qing Zang Gaoyuan (Tibetan Plateau)
XIZANG (TIBET)
Tanggula Shan
Gangdisê Shan
Nyainqêntanglha Shan
HIMALAYA
QINGHAI
SICHUAN
YUNNAN
GUIZHOU
Lhasa
Kathmandu
Mt Everest 8848
Thimphu
Calcutta
Dhaka
Chittagong
Rangoon (Yangon)
Mandalay
Bangkok (Krung Thep)
Vientiane (Viangchan)
Hanoi
Phnom Penh
Kunming
Chengdu
Chongqing (Chungking)
Guiyang
Madras
Colombo
Kandy
Lucknow
Kanpur
Patna
Jabalpur
Nagpur
Vishakhapatnam
Vijayawada
Andaman Islands (India)
Port Blair
Nicobar Islands (India)
Ten Degree Channel
Mergui Archipelago
Isthmus of Kra
Irrawaddy Delta
Relief
Feet
Metres
16404 5000
9843 3000
6562 2000
3281 1000
1640 500
656 200
0 Sea Level
Land Dep.
656 200
13123 4000
22966 7000
Scale 1:14 000 000
0 100 200 300 400 500 Miles
0 200 400 600 800 Kms.
Conic Projection

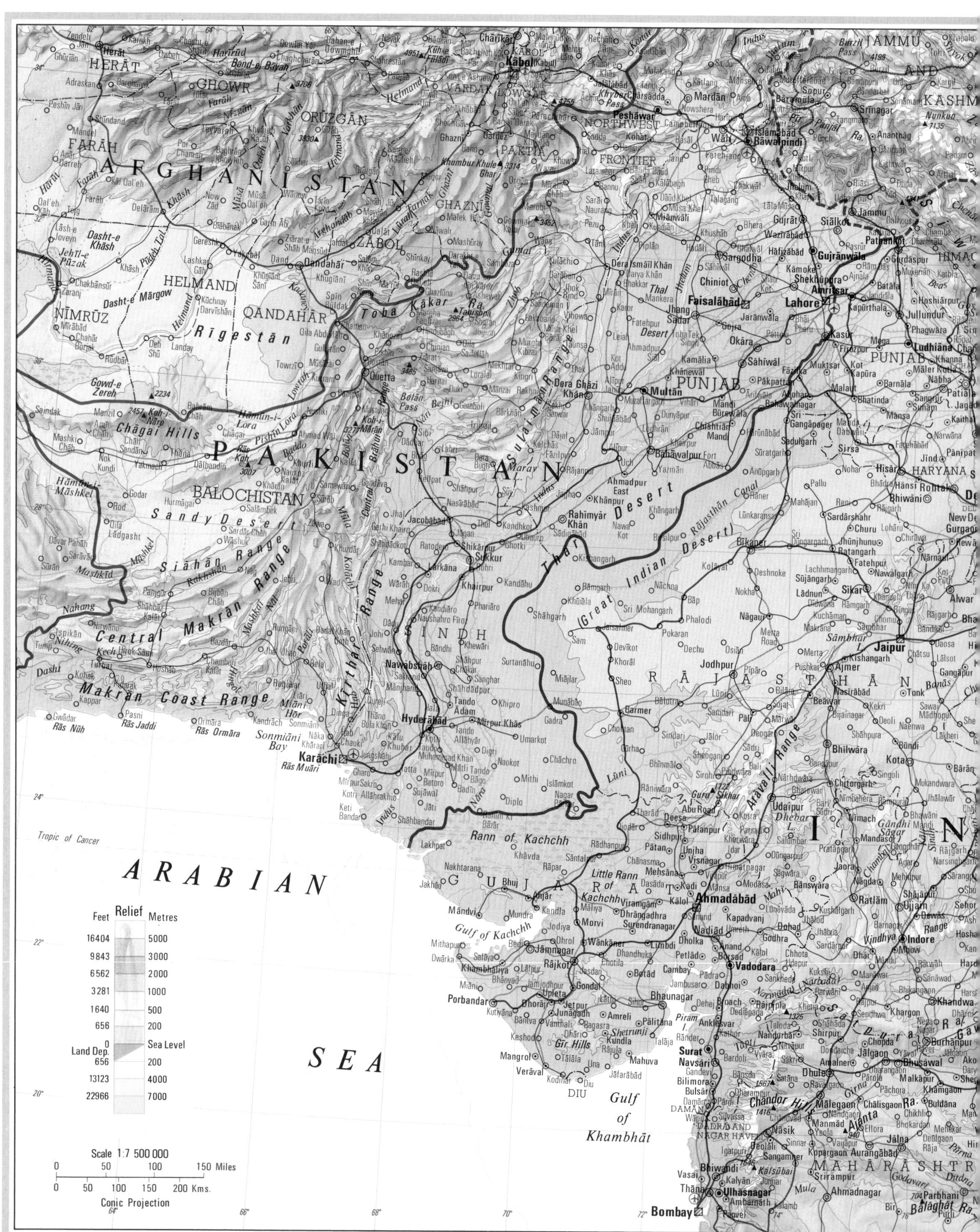

ARABIAN

SEA

Feet	Relief	Metres
16404		5000
9843		3000
6562		2000
3281		1000
1640		500
656		200
0		Sea Level
Land Dep.		
656		200
13123		4000
22966		7000

Scale 1:7 500 000

0   50   100   150 Miles

0   50   100   150   200 Kms.

Conic Projection

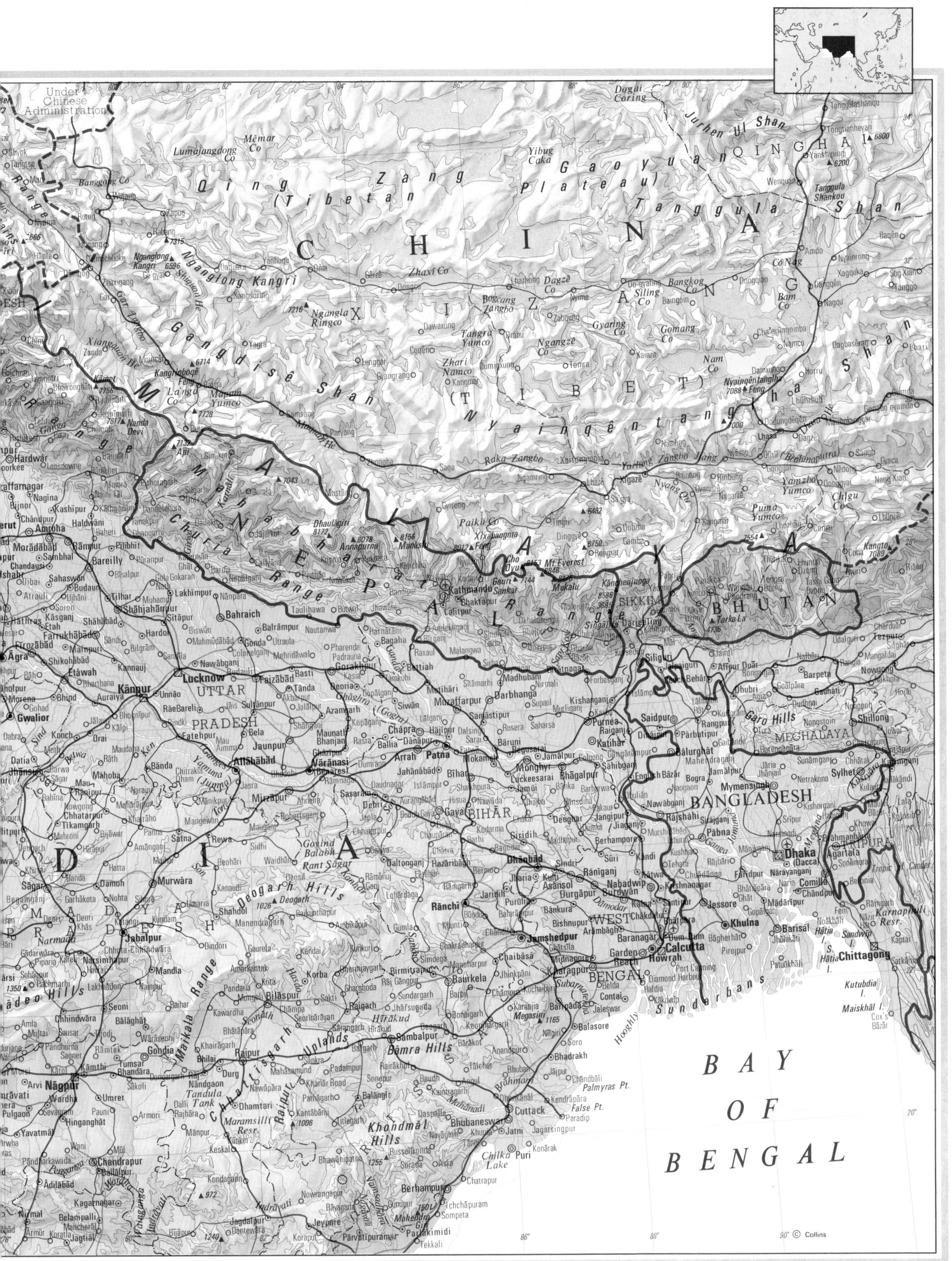

Under Chinese Administration

CHINA

Qing Zang Gaoyuan (Tibetan Plateau)

QINGHAI

Lumajangdong Co
Mêmar Co
Yibug Caka

X I Z A N G

(T I B E T)

Nyainqêntanglha Shan

Tanggula Shan

Ngglong Kangri

Gangdisê Shan

Ngangla Ringco

Tangra Yumco

Zhari Namco

Nam Co

Siling Co

Gomang Co

Gyaring Co

Ngangzê Co

Puma Yumco

Chigu Co

Yamzho Yumco

Brahmaputra

Lhasa

Raka Zangbo

Yarlung Zangbo Jiang

Xigazê

Kangto 7089

N E P A L

Mahabharat Range

Churia Range

Dhaulagiri 8172
Annapurna 8078
Manaslu 8156
Cho Oyu 8153
Mt. Everest 8848
Makalu 8586
Kanchenjunga 8586

Kathmandu
Bhaktapur
Lalitpur

SIKKIM
Darjeeling

BHUTAN
Torsa La

Pokhara

Gauri Sankar

H I M A L A Y A

Hardwār
Morādābād
Rāmpur
Bareilly

U T T A R

P R A D E S H

Lucknow
Kānpur
Allāhābad
Vārānasi
(Benares)

Gwalior

Gorakhpur
Patna

B I H Ā R

Gaya

Dhānbād

Rānchi

Jamshedpur

Siliguri

Cooch Behār

Garo Hills

MEGHALAYA

Shillong

Sylhet

BANGLADESH

Mymensingh

Dhaka (Dacca)

TRIPURA

Agartala

Comilla

Chittagong

Karnaphuli Resr.

I N D I A

M A D H Y A

P R A D E S H

Jabalpur

Nāgpur

Maikala Range

Deogarh Hills

Chhota Nāgpur

Rourkela

Sambalpur

Bilāspur

Raipur

Durg
Bhilai

WEST

BENGAL

Asansol
Durgāpur
Burdwān

Calcutta
Howrah

Khulna

Barisāl

Sundarbans

Bhubaneswar

Cuttack

Khondmāl Hills

Chilka Lake

Puri

Konārak

Berhampur

Balasore

Hooghly

B A Y

O F

B E N G A L

Kutubdia I.
Maiskhāl I.
Cox's Bāzār

© Collins

63

SOUTHWEST ASIA

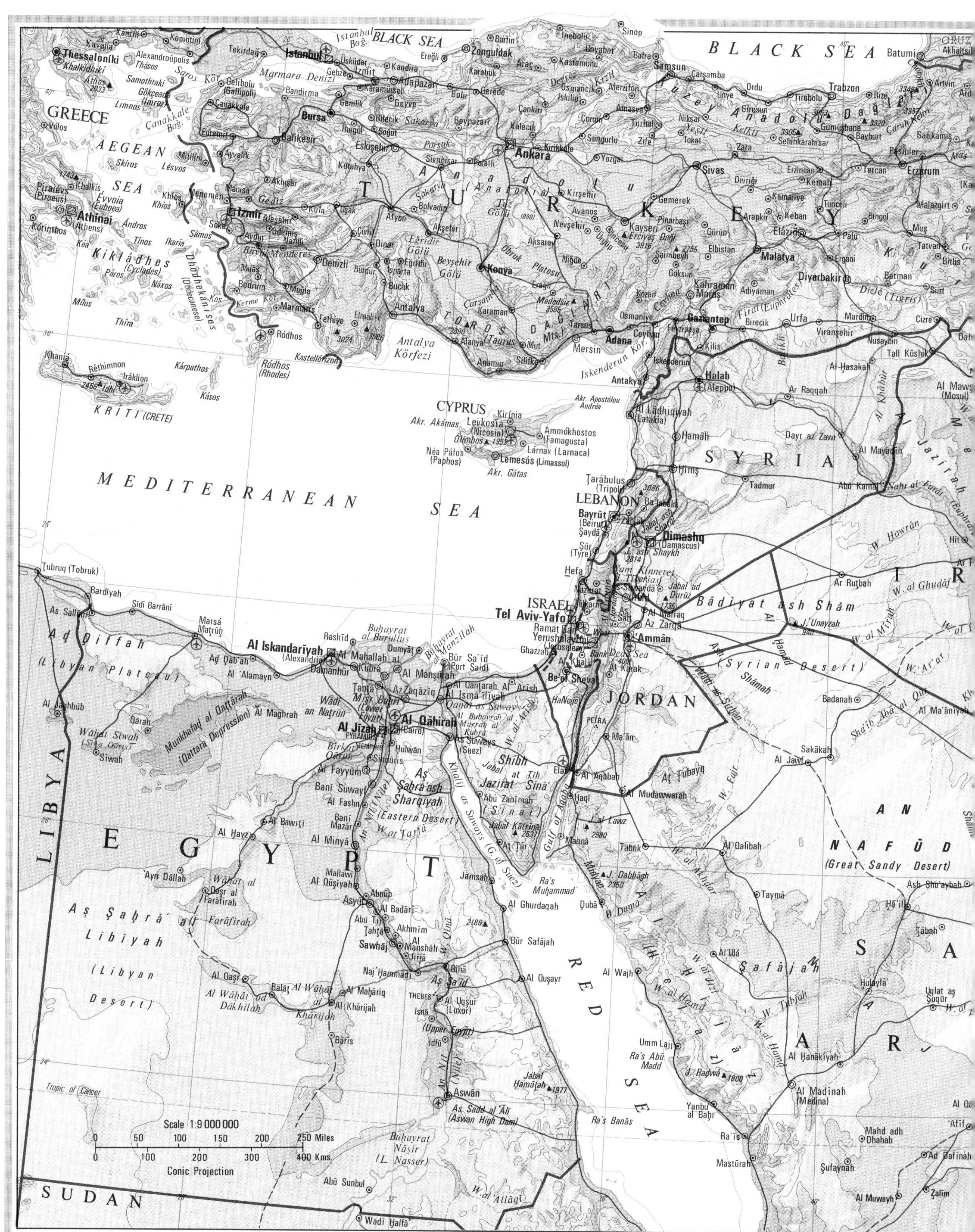

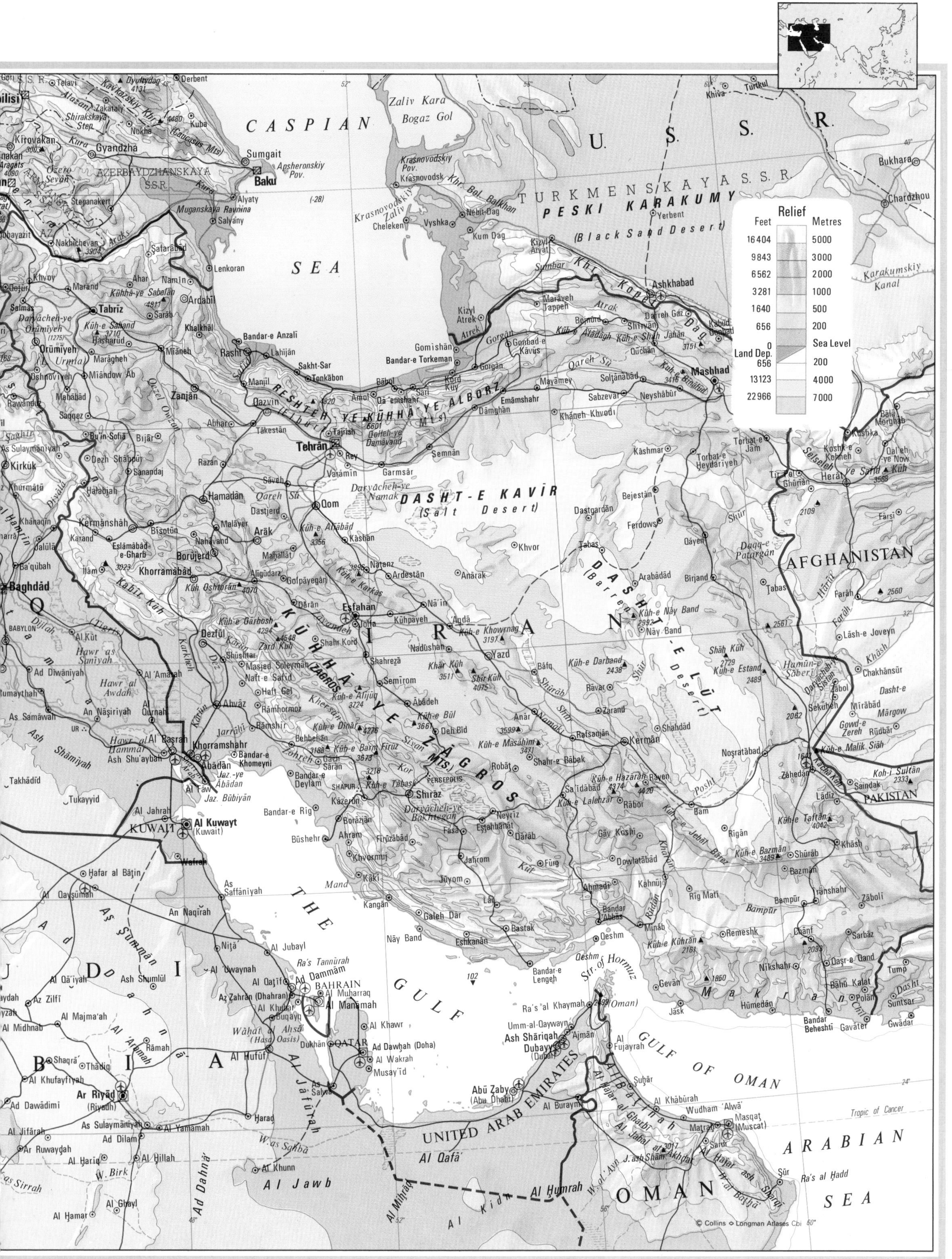

CASPIAN
SEA
U. S. S. R.
TURKMENSKAYA S.S.R.
PESKI KARAKUMY
(Black Sand Desert)
AZERBAYDZHANSKAYA S.S.R.
Relief
Feet
Metres
16404
5000
9843
3000
6562
2000
3281
1000
1640
500
656
200
0
Sea Level
Land Dep.
656
200
13123
4000
22966
7000
RESHTEH-YE KŪHHĀ-YE ALBORZ
DASHT-E KAVĪR
(Salt Desert)
DASHT-E LŪT
(Barren Desert)
IRAN
KŪHHĀ-YE ZĀGROS
AFGHANISTAN
PAKISTAN
KUWAIT
BAHRAIN
QATAR
UNITED ARAB EMIRATES
OMAN
THE GULF
GULF OF OMAN
ARABIAN SEA
Tehrān
Esfahān
Shīrāz
Mashhad
Tabrīz
Baku
Baghdād
Al Kuwayt
Ar Riyāḑ
Al Manāmah
Ad Dawḩah (Doha)
Abū Z̧aby
Masqaţ (Muscat)
Kermān
Yazd
Qom
Hamadān
Tropic of Cancer
© Collins ◇ Longman Atlases Cbi

THE LEVANT

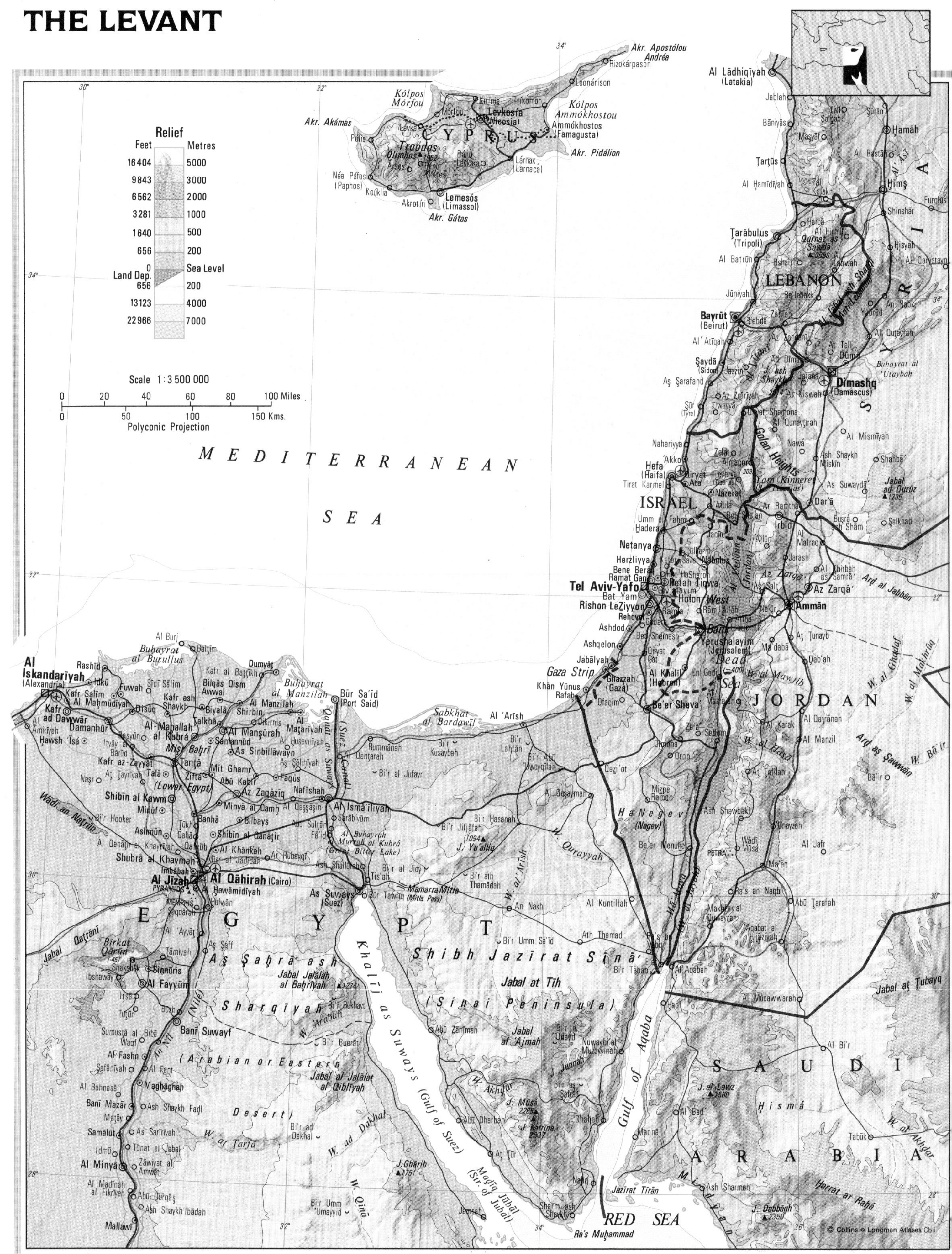

Relief

Feet	Metres
16 404	5000
9 843	3000
6 562	2000
3 281	1000
1 640	500
656	200
0	Sea Level
Land Dep.	
656	200
13 123	4000
22 966	7000

Scale 1:3 500 000

0   20   40   60   80   100 Miles
0   50   100   150 Kms.
Polyconic Projection

M E D I T E R R A N E A N

S E A

C Y P R U S

Kólpos
Mórfou

Kólpos
Ammókhostou

Akr. Apostólou
Andréa
Rizokárpason

Akr. Akámas

Leonárison

Levkosía
(Nicosia)

Ammókhostos
(Famagusta)

Akr. Pidálion

Néa Páfos
(Paphos)

Lárnax
(Larnaca)

Traóðos
Ólimbos

Lemesós
(Limassol)

Akr. Gátas

Akrotíri

SYRIA

Al Ládhiqiyah
(Latakia)

LEBANON

Bayrūt
(Beirut)

Dimashq
(Damascus)

Golan Heights

ISRAEL

Tel Aviv-Yafo

Yerushalayim
(Jerusalem)

Gaza Strip

West
Bank

Dead
Sea

Amman

JORDAN

HaNegev
(Negev)

Be'er Sheva

EGYPT

Al Iskandarīyah
(Alexandria)

Al Qāhirah (Cairo)

Al Jīzah

Lower Egypt

Khalīj as Suways (Gulf of Suez)

Shibh Jazīrat Sīnā'
(Sinai Peninsula)

Jabal at Tīh

Gulf of Aqaba

SAUDI

ARABIA

RED SEA

© Collins ● Longman Atlases Cbi

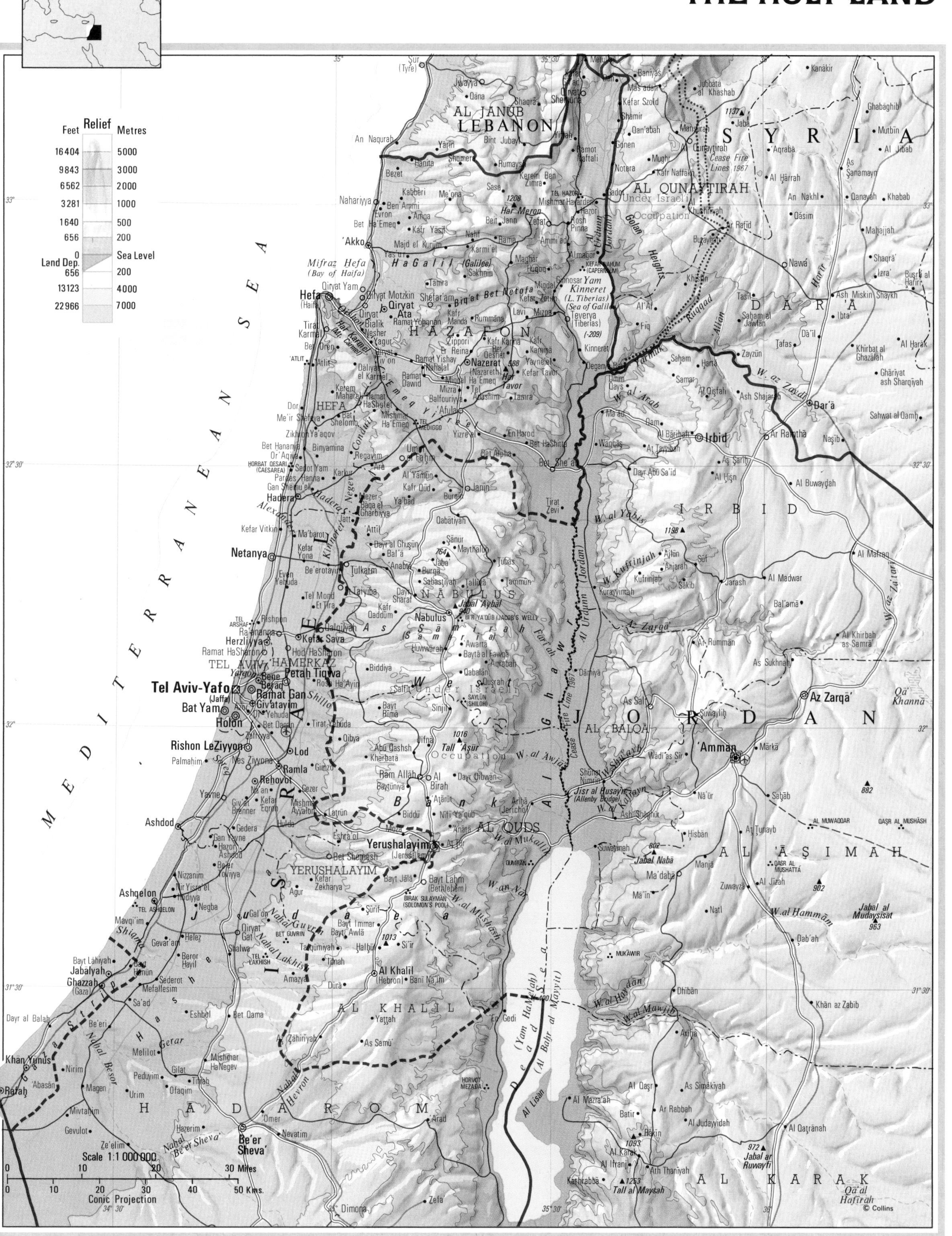

THE HOLY LAND

67

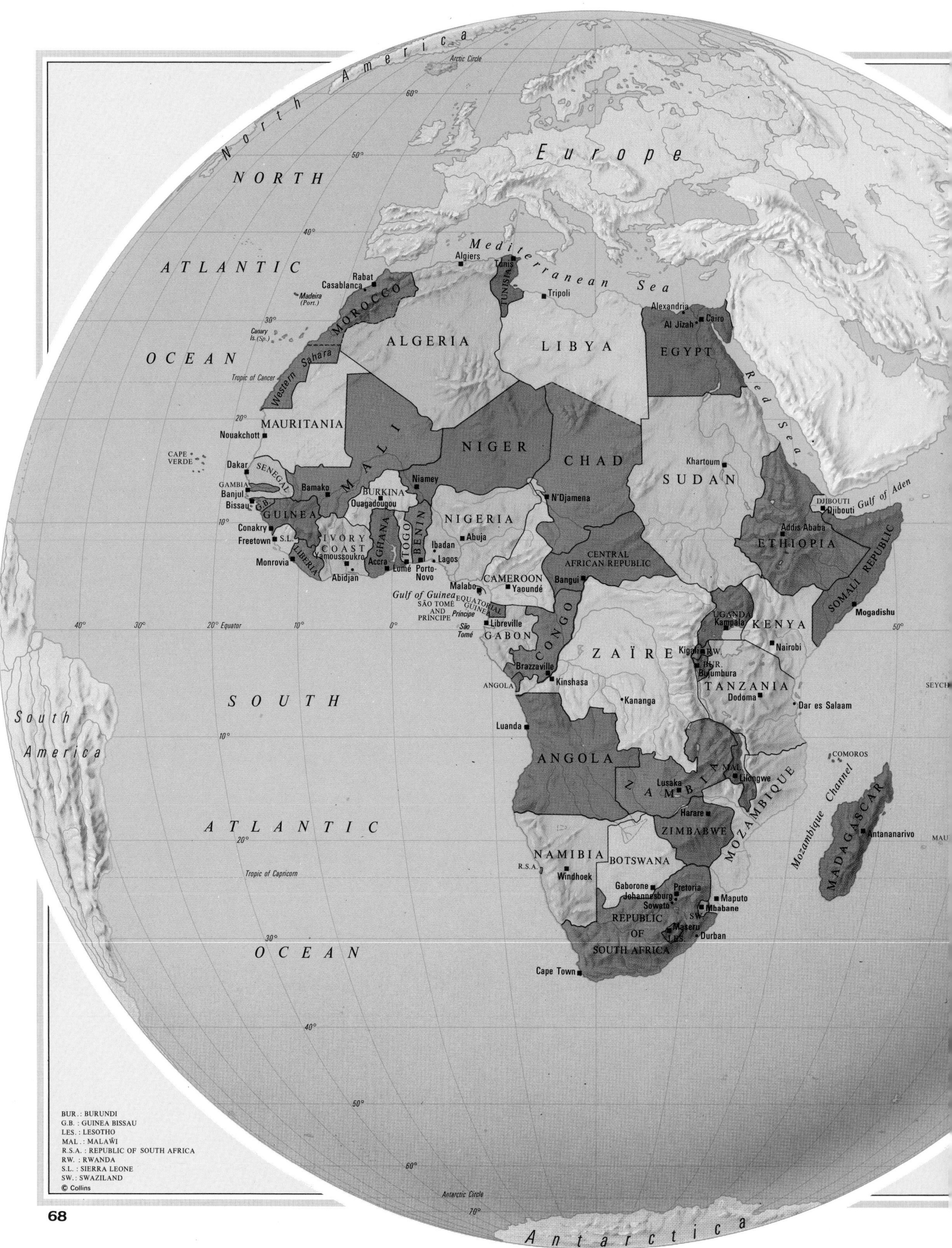

North America

Arctic Circle

NORTH

Europe

ATLANTIC

Mediterranean Sea

Algiers

Tunis

OCEAN

Rabat
Casablanca

MOROCCO

TUNISIA

Tripoli

Alexandria

Al Jīzah   Cairo

Madeira
(Port.)

Canary
Is.(Sp.)

Tropic of Cancer

Western Sahara

ALGERIA

LIBYA

EGYPT

Red Sea

MAURITANIA

Nouakchott

M A L I

NIGER

CHAD

Khartoum

SUDAN

CAPE
VERDE

Dakar

SENEGAL

Bamako

Niamey

BURKINA

N'Djamena

DJIBOUTI Gulf of Aden

GAMBIA

Banjul

Bissau

G.B.

GUINEA

Ouagadougou

Djibouti

Conakry

Freetown

S.L.

IVORY
COAST

GHANA

TOGO

BENIN

NIGERIA

Ibadan

Abuja

Addis Ababa

ETHIOPIA

Monrovia

LIBERIA

Yamoussoukro

Accra

Lomé

Porto-
Novo

Lagos

Abidjan

Malabo

CAMEROON

Bangui

SOMALI REPUBLIC

Gulf of Guinea

SÃO TOME
AND
PRINCIPE

EQUATORIAL
GUINEA

Yaoundé

CENTRAL
AFRICAN REPUBLIC

UGANDA

Mogadishu

Príncipe

*São
Tomé*

Libreville

GABON

CONGO

ZAÏRE

Kampala

KENYA

SEYCH

Kigali RW.

Nairobi

BUR.

Brazzaville

Bujumbura

SOUTH

ANGOLA

Kinshasa

TANZANIA

Dodoma

Dar es Salaam

Equator

America

Luanda

Kananga

COMOROS

ATLANTIC

South

ANGOLA

ZAMBIA

Lusaka

MAL.

Lilongwe

MADAGASCAR

Mozambique Channel

MAU

Harare

MOZAMBIQUE

Antananarivo

Tropic of Capricorn

NAMIBIA

BOTSWANA

ZIMBABWE

R.S.A.

Windhoek

Gaborone

Pretoria

Johannesburg

Maputo

Soweto

Mbabane

SW.

REPUBLIC
OF
SOUTH AFRICA

Maseru

Durban

L.S.

OCEAN

Cape Town

Antarctic Circle

Antarctica

AFRICA

INDIAN

OCEAN

AFRICA

FRANCE
ITALY
Beograd (Belgrade)
ROMANIA
YUGOSLAVIA
BULGARIA
Sofiya (Sofia)
Istanbul
Batumi
Black Sea
U.S.S.R.
Corse (Fr.)
Roma (Rome)
Tiranë
ALBANIA
GREECE
Samsun
Caspian Sea
Madrid
Barcelona
Napoli (Naples)
Sardegna (It.)
Athínai (Athens)
Bursa
Ankara
TURKEY
Yerevan
Lisboa (Lisbon)
SPAIN
Palermo
Sicilia
Izmir
Kríti
Halab (Aleppo)
SYRIA
Baghdād
Tehrān
Islas Baleares (Sp.)
MALTA
Mediterranean Sea
CYPRUS
LEBANON
Bayrūt
Dimashq (Damascus)
'Ammān
IRAQ
IRAN
Esfahān
Str. of Tanger (Tangier)
Gibraltar
Oran
Alger (Algiers)
Skikda
Annaba
Constantine
Tunis
Sfax
Tarābulus (Tripoli)
Al Bayda'
Al Iskandarīyah (Alexandria)
Yerushalayim
ISRAEL
Būr Sa'īd
JORDAN
Ar Riyād (Riyadh)
QATAR
Casablanca
Rabat
Oujda
Fès
Sidi bel Abbès
Meknes
Al Qāhirah (Cairo)
Al Jīzah
As Suways (Suez)
Madeira (Port.)
MOROCCO
Safi
Atlas Mts
Atlas Saharien
TUNISIA
Aswān
Al Madinah (Medina)
UNITED ARAB EMIRATES
Marrakech
Foukal 4165
El Golea
Touggourt
Nālūt
As Sahrā' al Lībīyah (Libyan Desert)
Buhayrat Nasir (L. Nasser)
Wādī Halfā
Nubian Desert
SAUDI ARABIA
BAHRAIN
Islas Canarias (Sp.)
Sta. Cruz
Tenerife
El Aaiún (Laâyoune)
In-Salah
Al Jawf
Tropic of Cancer
Jiddah (Jedda)
RED SEA
Dakhla
WESTERN SAHARA
ALGERIA
LIBYA
EGYPT
Makkah (Mecca)
ARABIA
Fdérik
Ahaggar 2918
Marzūq
Tibesti 3415
Dunqulah
Būr Sūdān
'Asmera
San'ā'
YEMEN
Nouadhibou
Sahara
Umm Durmān
4620
Adan (Aden)
Gulf of Aden
MAURITANIA
Tidjikdja
Kidal
Bodélé
Al Khartūm (Khartoum)
Mits'iwa
Nouakchott
St. Louis
Tombouctou (Timbuktu)
Gao
L. Chad
Abéché
Nyala
3071
SUDAN
Al Bahr al Azraq (Blue Nile)
DJIBOUTI
Djibouti
Berbera
MALI
NIGER
CHAD
Kayes
Nioro
Mopti
Niger
Agadez
N'Djamena
Al Muglad
Amhara
ETHIOPIA
Senegal
Bamako
San
Katsina
Kano
N'Djamena
Sarh
'Adīs Ābeba
Plateau
SENEGAL
Dakar
Banjul
GAMBIA
BURKINA
Ouagadougou
Sikasso
Sokoto
Kaduna
Gombe
Baûchi
Wāw
Al Bahr al Jabal (White Nile)
Wabe Shebele
SOMALI REPUBLIC
GUINEA BISSAU
Bissau
GUINEA
Labé
Kankan
Bobo Dioulasso
Tamale
NIGERIA
Abuja
Benue
Massif de l'Adamaoua 4070
CENTRAL AFRICAN REPUBLIC
Bangassou
Juba
Gulu
Wajir
Conakry
SIERRA LEONE
Freetown
Beyla
Mt Nimba 1768
Daloa
Bouaké
Oshogbo
Ibadan
Enugu
Onitsha
CAMEROON
Carnot
Bangui
Ubangi
Pakwach
L. Albert
Ruwenzori 5119
Mt Elgon
KENYA
Mt Kenya 5200
Baardheere
Muqdisho (Mogadishu)
Monrovia
LIBERIA
IVORY COAST
Yamoussoukro
GHANA
Kumasi
TOGO
BENIN
Porto-Novo
Lagos
Port Harcourt
Mt Cameroun 4070
Yaoundé
Congo
Kisangani
UGANDA
Kampala
RWANDA
Kigali
Lake Victoria
Nairobi
Konza
Kismaayo
Equator
Sassandra
Abidjan
Sekondi-Takoradi
Accra
Lomé
Malabo
EQUATORIAL GUINEA
Douala
Bata
GABON
Libreville
Congo Basin
ZAIRE
Bukavu
BURUNDI
Bujumbura
Kigoma
Kilimanjaro 5895
Arusha
Moshi
Korogwe
Pemba I.
INDIAN OCEAN
São Tomé & Príncipe
São Tomé
Port Gentil
Kutu
Inongo
Kindu
Tabora
Mombasa
ATLANTIC OCEAN
Pointe Noire
Cabinda
Brazzaville
Kikwit
Kasai
Ilebo
Kananga
Kalemie
Mbuji Mayi
Lake Tanganyika
TANZANIA
Dodoma
Zanzibar
Dar es Salaam
Matadi
Kinshasa
Pweto
Mweru
Manda
Lindi
Mtwara
Luanda
Catete
Luau
Likasi
Lubumbashi
Mpika
Mohoro
Rufiji
Aldabra Is.
Lobito
Benguela
Bié 2610
Huambo
Plateau
Kitwe
Ndola
Lake Malawi
Ruvuma
Pemba
COMOROS
Antsiranana
ANGOLA
Namibe
Zambezi
Lubango
Menongue
Mongu
ZAMBIA
Lusaka
Kabwe
Chipata
Lilongwe
Blantyre
Angoche
Moçambique
Mahajanga
Cuito
Cuando
Cubango
Zambezi
Kariba
L. Kariba
Harare
ZIMBABWE
MOZAMBIQUE
Quelimane
Namutoni
Tsumeb
Victoria Falls
Bulawayo
Beira
Nova Sofala
MADAGASCAR
Antananarivo (Tananarive)
NAMIBIA
Windhoek
Francistown
BOTSWANA
Kalahari Desert
Limpopo
Tropic of Capricorn
Fianarantsoa
WALVIS BAY
Walvisbaai (Walvis Bay)
Gaborone
Inhambane
Toliara
Lüderitz
Pretoria
Maputo
Mbabane
SWAZILAND
Tj. Vohimena
Orange
Kimberley
Hopetown
Johannesburg
Soweto
Maseru
LESOTHO
Durban
Springbok
Colesberg
REP. OF SOUTH AFRICA
Umzimvubu
Bitterfontein
Cradock
Cape Town
Kaapstad
C. of Good Hope
Piketberg
Worcester
Port Elizabeth
East London
C. Agulhas

Relief

Feet		Metres
16 404		5000
9843		3000
6562		2000
3281		1000
1640		500
656		200
0	Sea Level	
Land Dep.		
656		200
13 123		4000
22 966		7000

Scale 1:37 000 000

0 200 400 600 800 1000 Miles

0 400 800 1200 1600 Kms.

Lambert Azimuthal Equal Area Projection

© Collins • Longman Atlases Cbi

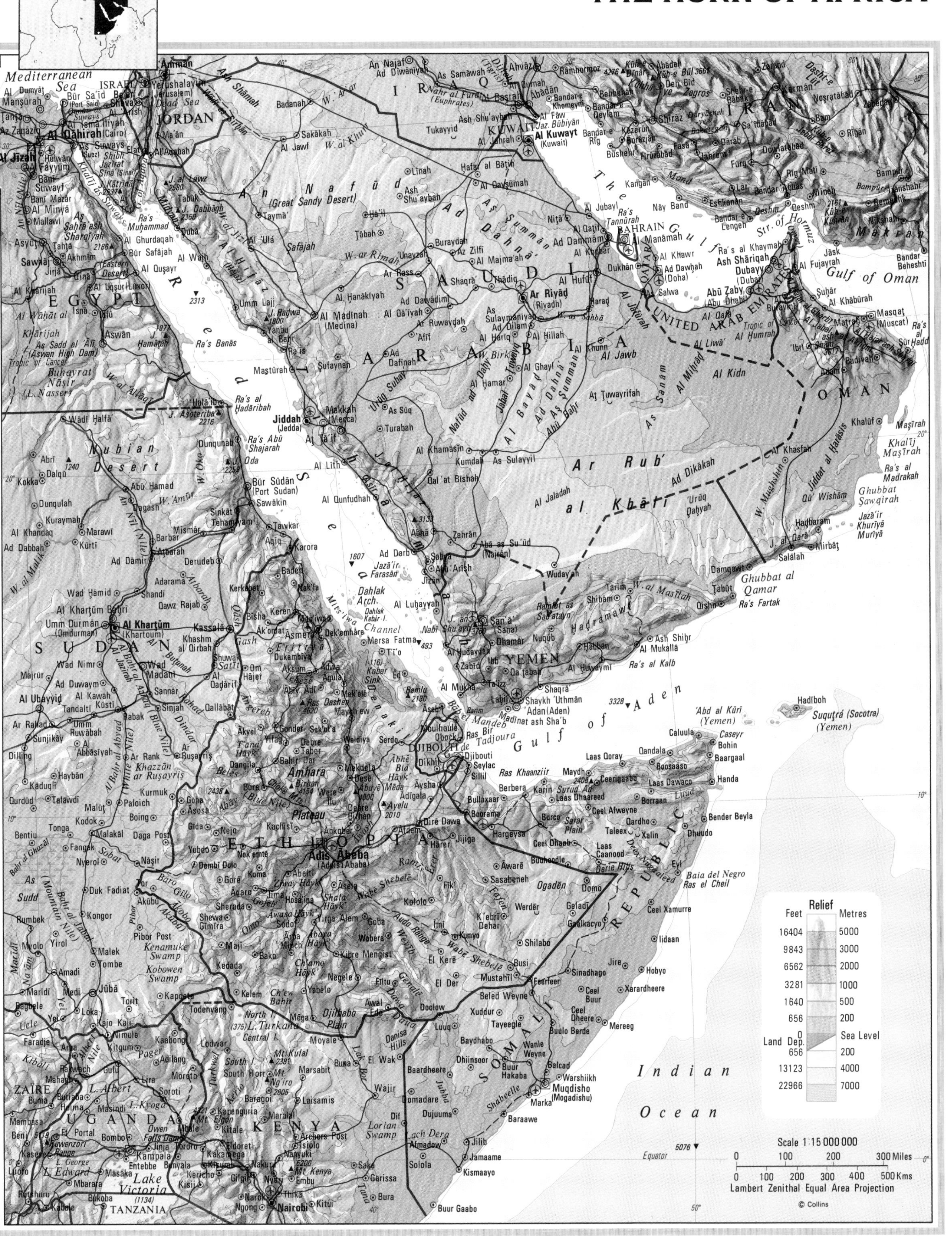

Mediterranean Sea

ISRAEL
JORDAN
EGYPT
SUDAN
SAUDI ARABIA
IRAQ
KUWAIT
BAHRAIN
QATAR
UNITED ARAB EMIRATES
OMAN
IRAN
YEMEN
Gulf of Oman
Gulf of Aden
ETHIOPIA
DJIBOUTI
SOMALI REPUBLIC
UGANDA
KENYA
TANZANIA
ZAIRE

Red Sea
Nubian Desert
An Nafūd (Great Sandy Desert)
Ar Rub' al Khālī
Ad Dahnā'

Indian Ocean

Al Qāhirah (Cairo)
Al Khartūm (Khartoum)
Adis Abeba (Addis Ababa)
Ar Riyād (Riyadh)
Al Kuwayt (Kuwait)
Jiddah (Jedda)
Makkah (Mecca)
Al Madīnah (Medina)
Masqaţ (Muscat)
Muqdisho (Mogadishu)
Nairobi

Lake Victoria
Lake Turkana

Relief		
Feet		Metres
16404		5000
9843		3000
6562		2000
3281		1000
1640		500
656		200
	Land Dep. 0	Sea Level
656		200
13123		4000
22966		7000

Scale 1:15 000 000

0   100   200   300 Miles
0 100 200 300 400 500 Kms

Lambert Zenithal Equal Area Projection

© Collins

NILE VALLEY

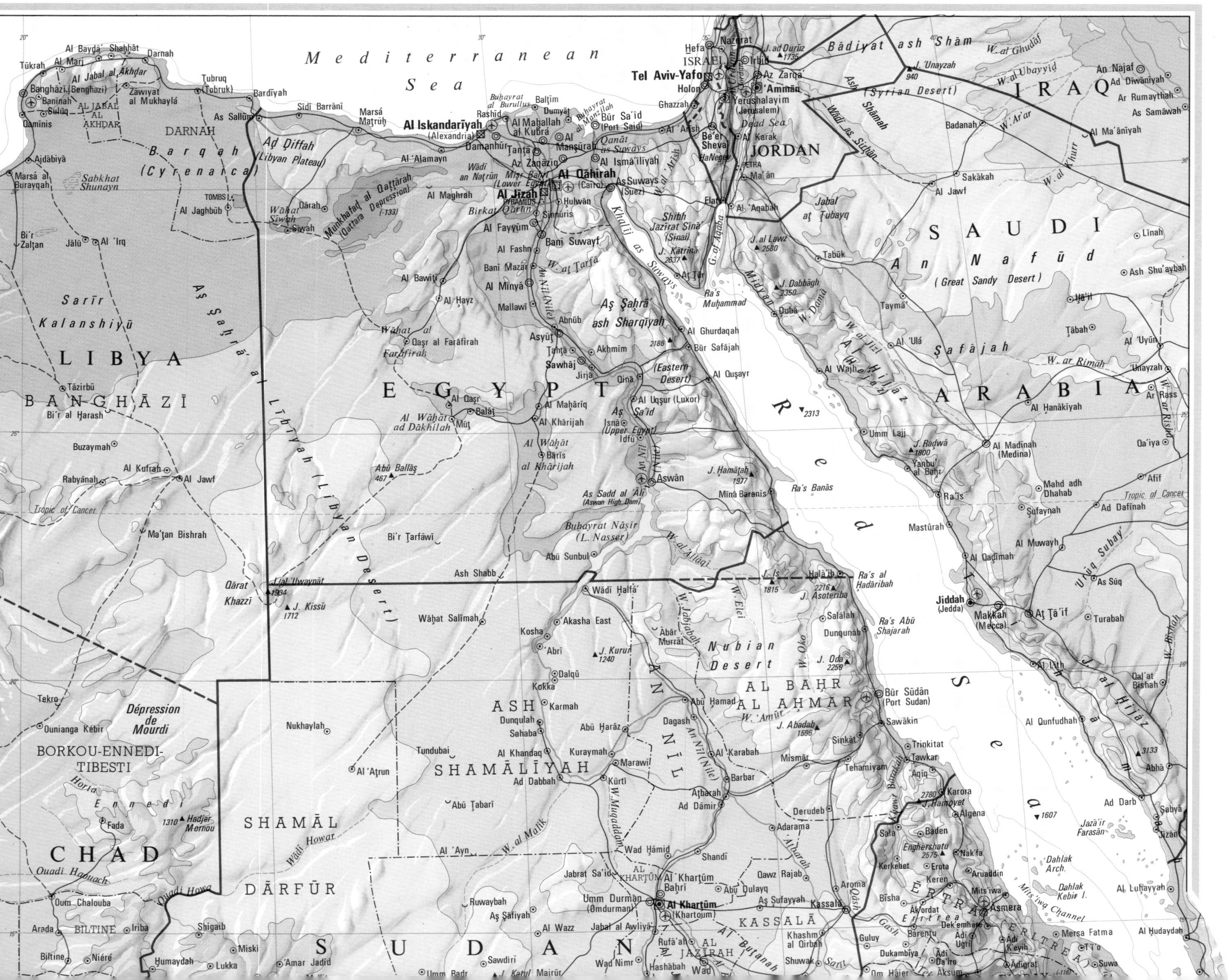

Mediterranean Sea
Red Sea
EGYPT
LIBYA
SUDAN
SAUDI ARABIA
IRAQ
JORDAN
ISRAEL
CHAD

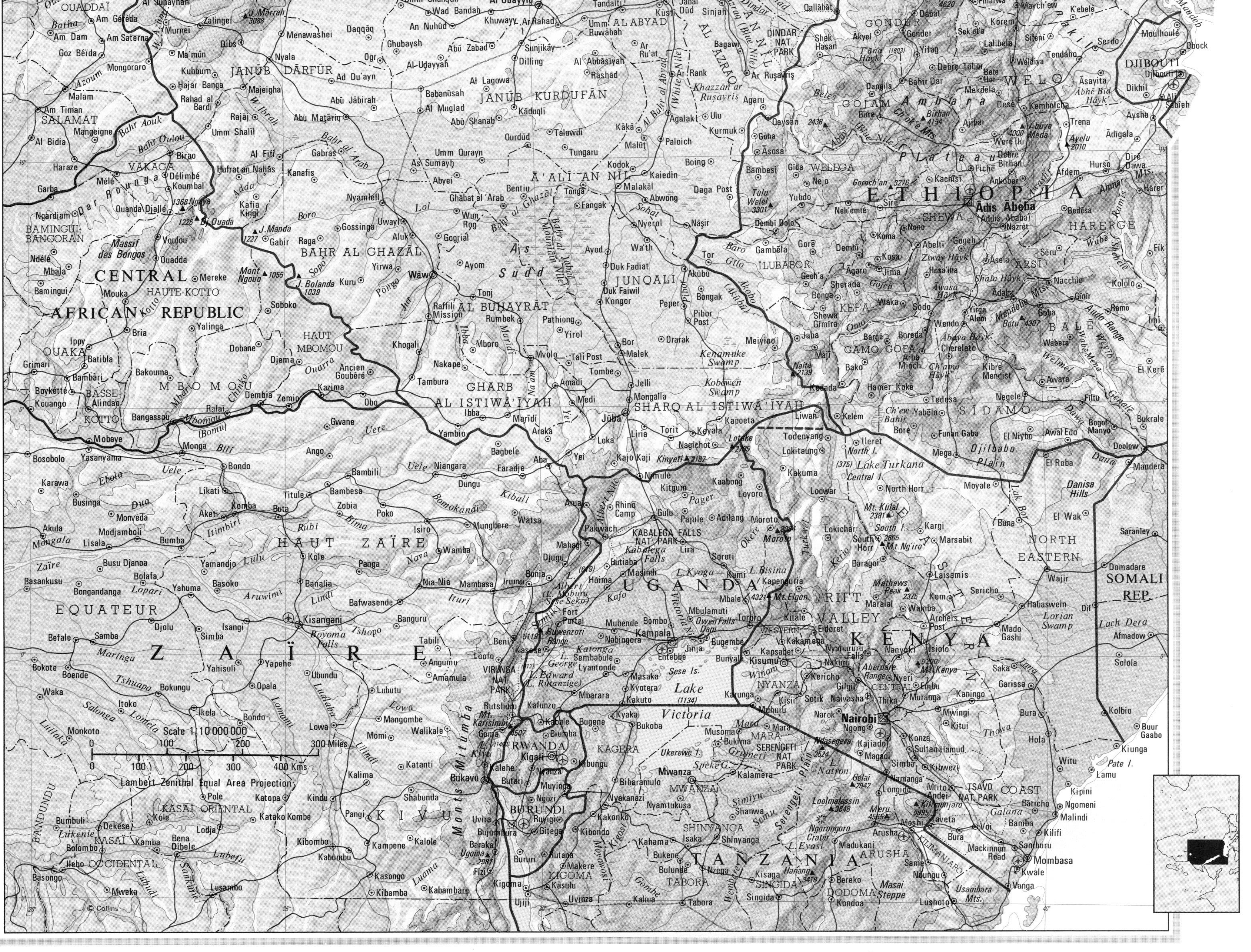
ETHIOPIA
Ādis Ābeba
(Addis Ababa)
DJIBOUTI
SOMALI REP.
KENYA
Nairobi
Mombasa
UGANDA
Kampala
Lake Victoria
Lake Turkana
RWANDA
Kigali
BURUNDI
TANZANIA
CENTRAL AFRICAN REPUBLIC
ZAÏRE
Kisangani
HAUT ZAÏRE
EQUATEUR
KIVU
Scale 1:10 000 000
0 100 200 300 Miles
0 100 200 300 400 Kms
Lambert Zenithal Equal Area Projection
© Collins

NORTHWEST AFRICA

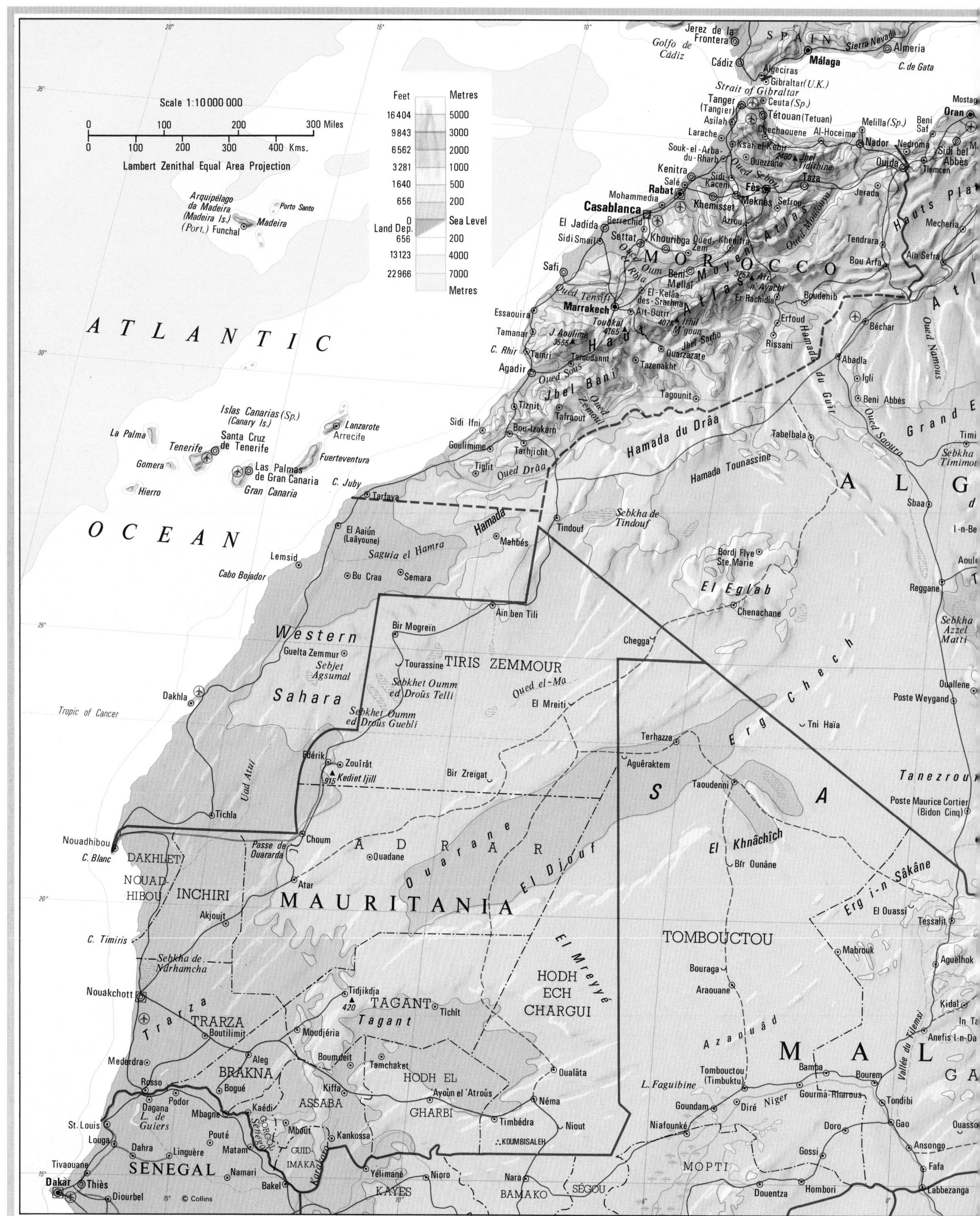

Scale 1:10 000 000

0   100   200   300 Miles
0 100 200 300 400 Kms.

Lambert Zenithal Equal Area Projection

Feet	Metres
16 404	5000
9843	3000
6562	2000
3281	1000
1640	500
656	200
0	Sea Level
Land Dep.	
656	200
13 123	4000
22 966	7000
Metres	Metres

ATLANTIC

OCEAN

Arquipélago da Madeira (Madeira Is.) (Port.)   Porto Santo
Madeira   Funchal

Islas Canarias (Sp.) (Canary Is.)
La Palma   Lanzarote
Tenerife   Arrecife
Santa Cruz de Tenerife
Gomera   Las Palmas de Gran Canaria   Fuerteventura
Hierro   Gran Canaria   C. Juby

SPAIN
Jerez de la Frontera   Sierra Nevada   Almería
Golfo de Cádiz   Málaga   C. de Gata
Cádiz   Algeciras   Gibraltar(U.K.)
Strait of Gibraltar
Tanger (Tangier)   Ceuta (Sp.)   Melilla (Sp.)   Beni Saf   Oran
Asilah   Tétouan (Tetuan)   Al-Hoceima   Nador   Nedroma   Sidi bel Abbès
Larache   Chechaouene   Tlemcen
Souk-el-Arba-du-Rharb   Ksar-el-Kébir   Jbel Tidirhine   Taza   Oujda   Hauts Pla
Kenitra   Quezzane   Jerada
Salé   Sidi Kacem   Fès   Mecheria
Rabat   Mohammedia   Meknès   Sefrou   Taza
Casablanca   Khemisset   Azrou   Bou Arfa   Ain Sefra
El Jadida   Berrechid   Oued Zem   Boudenib
Sidi Smail   Settat   Khouribga   Oued Kheniis   MOROCCO
Safi   Beni Mellal   El-Kelâa-des-Srarhna   Aït Ayachi   Er Rachidia   Abadla   Igli
Essaouira   Oum er Rbia   J. Aboulime   Toubkal 4165   Ifrane   Erfoud   Béchar   Beni Abbès
Tamanar   Marrakech   Aït-Ourir   Jbel Sarho   Rissani   Hamada du Guir   Grande
Agadir   Taroudannt   Ouarzazate   Tazenakht   Hamada du Dráa   Tabelbala
C. Rhir   Tamri   Tagounit   Hamada Tounassine
Tiznit   Tafraout   Oued Sous   Jbel Bani
Sidi Ifni   Bou-Izakarn   Hamada
Goulimime   Tarhjicht   Oued Dráa   Sebkha de Tindouf   ALG
Tiglit   Tindouf   Sbaa   n-Be
Tarfaya   Mahbés   El Eglab   Sebkha Timimo
El Aaiún (Laâyoune)   Bordj Flye Ste.Marie   Reggane   Sebkha Azzel Matti
Saguia el Hamra   Chenachane
Lemsid   Ain ben Tili   Ouallene
Cabo Bojador   Bir Mogrein   Chegga   Erg Chech   Poste Weygand
Western   Guelta Zemmur   Tourassine   TIRIS ZEMMOUR   Timi
Sebjet Agsumal   Sebkhet Oumm ed Droûs Telli   Oued el-Ma   Tni Haïa
Dakhla   Semara   El Mreiti   S   A
Sahara   Sebkhet Oumm ed Droûs Guebli   Terhazza   Taoudenni   Poste Maurice Cortier (Bidon Cinq)
Tropic of Cancer   Fdérik   Aguêraktem   Tanezrou
Zoûîrât   Bir Zreigat   El Khnâchîch
915 Kediet Ijill   Bîr Ounâne   El Ouassi   Tessalit
Tichla   Choum   A D R A R   Ouadane   Ouarane   El Djouf   Erg i-n-Sâkâne
Nouadhibou   Passe de Ouararda   TOMBOUCTOU   Mabrouk   Aguelhok
C. Blanc   DAKHLET   Atar   Kidal
NOUAD-HIBOU   INCHIRI   Akjoujt   HODH ECH CHARGUI   Bouraga   In Ta
C. Timiris   MAURITANIA   El Mreyyé   Araouane   Anefis I-n-T
Sebkha de Nkhamcha   Tidjikdja   Araouane
Nouakchott   Tichît   Azaouâd   M A L
Trarza   420 TAGANT   Oualáta   L. Faguibine   Bamba   Bourem   GA
TRARZA   Tagant   Tombouctou (Timbuktu)
Boutilimit   Moudjéria   Néma   Goundam   Diré   Niger   Gourma-Rharous   Tondibi
Mederdra   Aleg   Boumdeit   Tamchaket   Gao   Ouasso
Rosso   Bogué   HODH EL   Ayoûn el 'Atroûs   Niafounké   Doro   Gossi
Podor   BRAKNA   Kiffa   GHARBI   Diambala   Fafa
Dagana   Mbagne   Kaédi   ASSABA   Timbédra   Niout
L. de Guiers   Mbout   Kankossa   Nioura
St.Louis   Poute   Matam   GUID IMAKA   KOUMBISALEH   MOPTI   Douentza   Hombori
Louga   Dahra   Linguère   Yélimané   Nara   Ségou   Labbezanga
Tivaouane   Namari   Bakel   Nioro
SENEGAL   KAYES   BAMAKO
Dakar   Thiès   Diourbel   © Collins

74

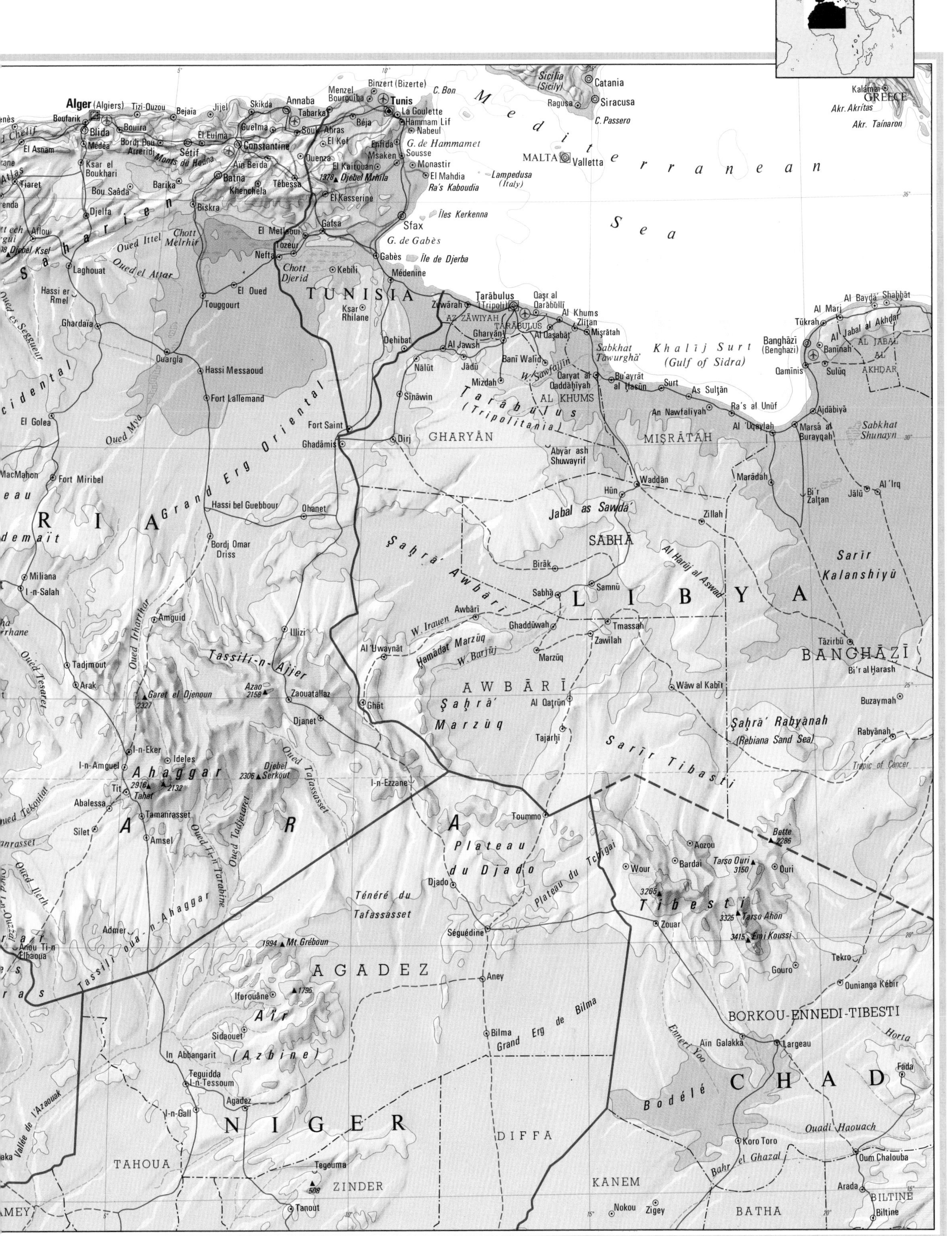
Mediterranean Sea
Alger (Algiers)
Tunis
TUNISIA
LIBYA
NIGER
CHAD
Ṭarābulus (Tripoli)
Banghāzī (Benghazi)
Khalīj Surt (Gulf of Sidra)
MALTA
Valletta
Sicilia (Sicily)
Catania
Siracusa
GREECE
Grand Erg Oriental
Ahaggar
Tassili-n-Ajjer
Tibesti
Aïr (Azbine)
AGADEZ
Ténéré du Tafassasset
Plateau du Djado
Sarīr Tibastī
Ṣaḥrā' Rabyānah (Rebiana Sand Sea)
Sarīr Kalanshiyū
Ṣaḥrā' Awbārī
Ṣaḥrā' Marzūq
Ḥamādat Marzūq
Jabal as Sawdā'
Al Harūj al Aswad
Sabhā
BORKOU-ENNEDI-TIBESTI
KANEM
BATHA
ZINDER
DIFFA
TAHOUA
Bilma
Grand Erg de Bilma
Bodélé
Tropic of Cancer

WEST AFRICA

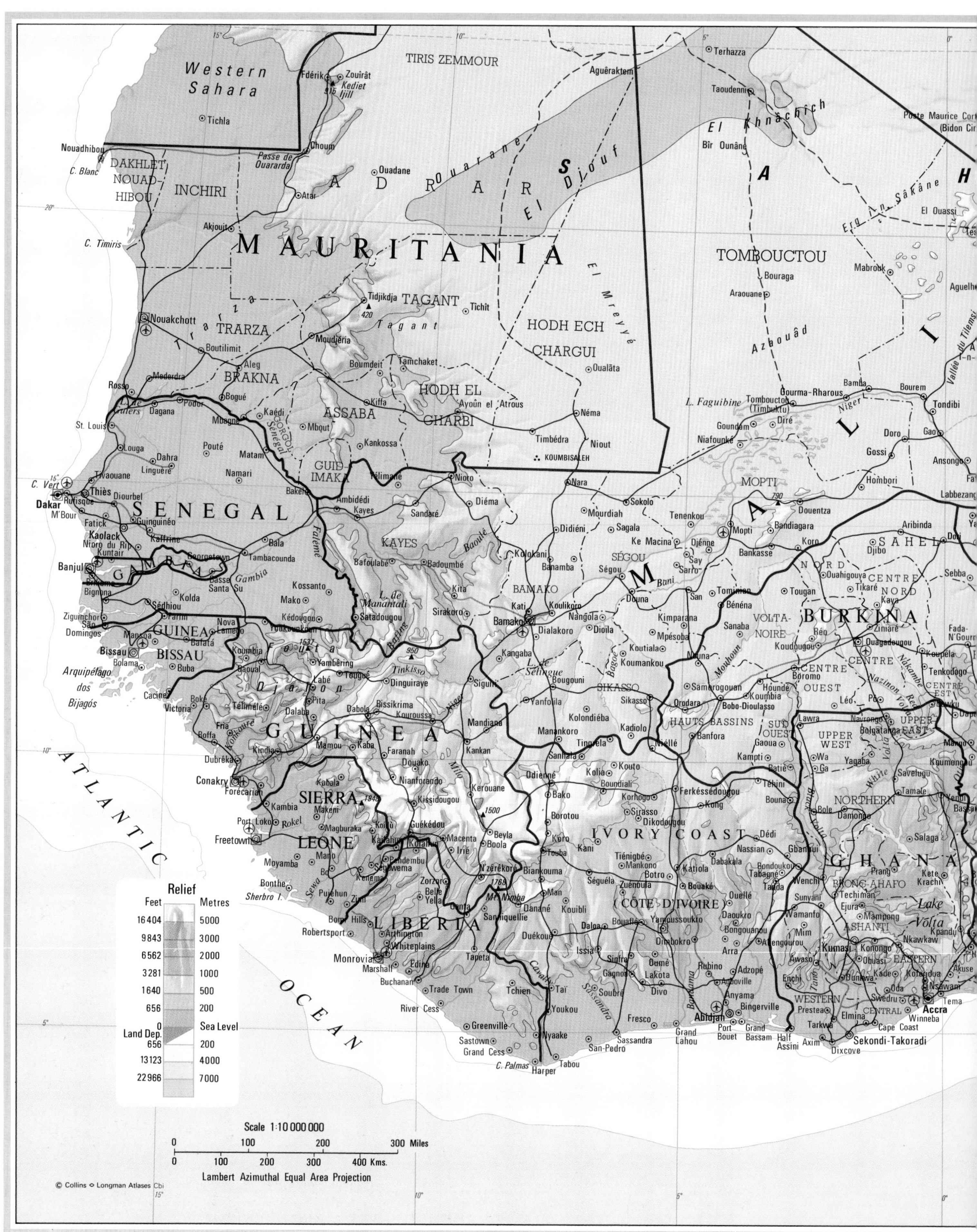

Western Sahara
MAURITANIA
SENEGAL
GAMBIA
GUINEA BISSAU
GUINEA
SIERRA LEONE
LIBERIA
IVORY COAST
(CÔTE D'IVOIRE)
GHANA
BURKINA
MALI
ATLANTIC OCEAN
Relief
Feet
Metres
16404 5000
9843 3000
6562 2000
3281 1000
1640 500
656 200
0 Sea Level
Land Dep.
656 200
13123 4000
22966 7000
Scale 1:10 000 000
0 100 200 300 Miles
0 100 200 300 400 Kms.
Lambert Azimuthal Equal Area Projection
© Collins ◇ Longman Atlases Cbi

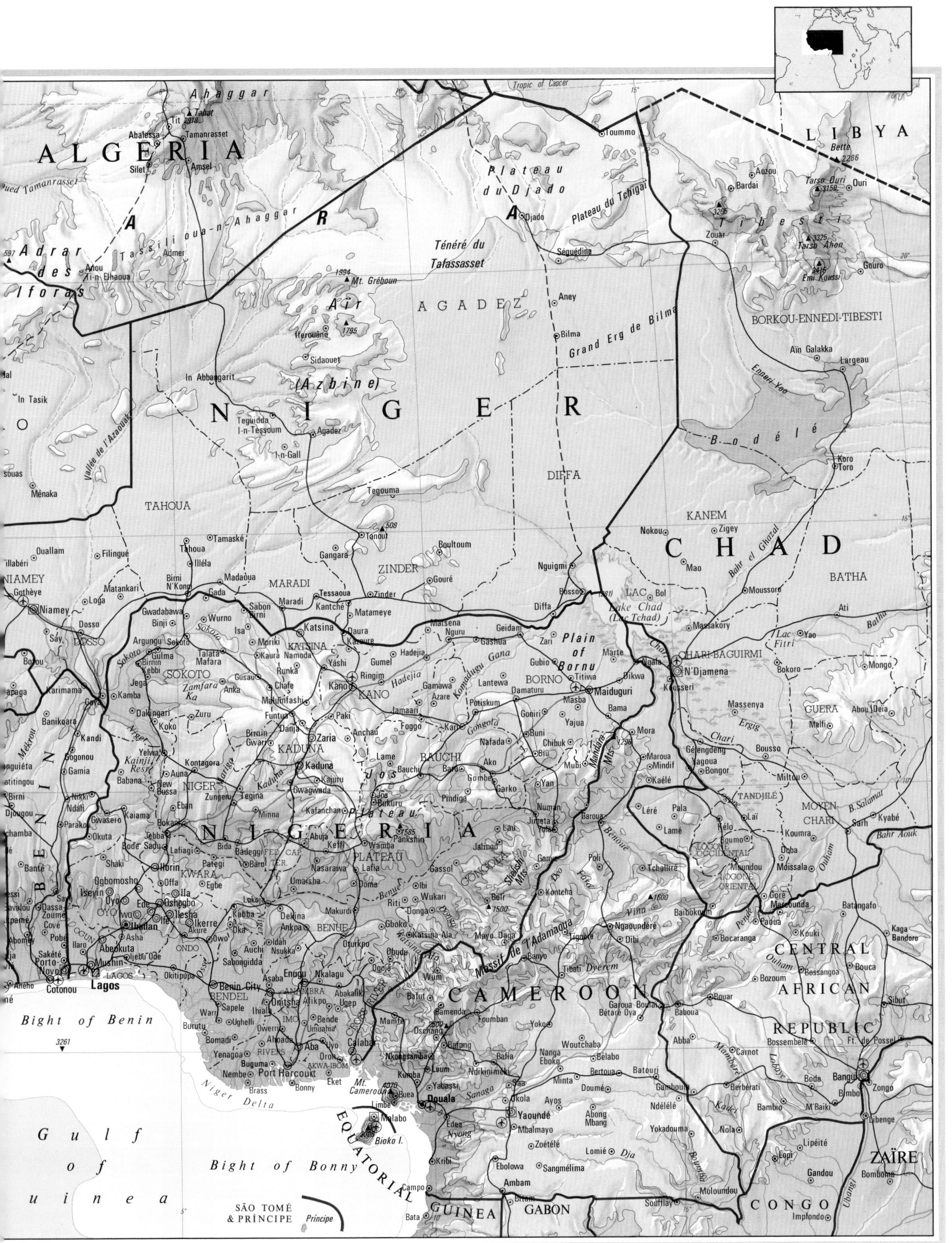

ALGERIA

Ahaggar
▲ *Tahat*
2918
Abalessa
Tamanrasset
Silet
Amsel

Oued Tamanrasset

Tassili oua-n-Ahaggar

Aïn-n-Ahaggar

Aïr

A   R   A

Plateau du Djado

Plateau du Tchigai

Toummo

LIBYA
Bette
▲ 2286

Tarso Ouri
Ouri
Bardai
▲ 3150 *Tibesti*
Zouar
▲ 3325
Tarso Ahon
Gouro
▲ 3415
Emi Koussi

Adrar des Iforas

Anou
Aïn-Elhaoua
Admer
▲ 1994 Mt Gréboun

Iferouâne
▲ 1795

Sidaouet

In Abbangarit

(Azbine)

Teguidda
I-n-Tessoum

I-n-Gall

Agadez

Ténéré du Tafassasset

AGADEZ

Aney

Bilma

Grand Erg de Bilma

BORKOU-ENNEDI-TIBESTI

Aïn Galakka

Largeau

Eppati-Yao

N I G E R

DIFFA

Séguédine

Djado

Bodélé

Koro
Toro

TAHOUA

Tegouma

▲ 508 Tanout

Boultoum

Gangara

Nguigmi

KANEM

Nokou
Zigey

Mao

CHAD

BATHA

Lac Fitri

Yao
Ati
Batha
Massory

Ouallam
Filingué
Tahoua
Illéla
Tamaské
ZINDER

Gouré
Bosso
Diffa

LAC
Bol
Lake Chad
(Lac Tchad)

Massakory

Moussoro

Niamey
Gothèye
Birni
N'Konni
Madaoua
MARADI
Tessaoua
Zinder
Kantché
Matameye

Matsena
Nguru
Gashua
Geidam
Zari

Plain of Bornu

Marte

N'Djamena
Ngala

CHARI-BAGUIRMI

Bokoro
Mongo
GUERA
Melfi
Abou Deia

Massenya

NIAMEY
Gothèye
Say
Dosso
BOSSO
Loga
Matankari
Birni N'Konni
Gada
Maradi
Sabon
Birni
Isa
Daura
Kazaure
Hadejia
Gumel

Gubio
Gana
Damaturu
BORNO
Titiwa
Maiduguri
Dikwa
Masba
Bama
Kousseri

Gelengdeng
Bousso
Ergig
Chari

Massenya

Niamey

BENIN

Kandi

Gwadabawa
Wurno
Argungu
Sokoto
Gulma
Jega
Kamba
Birnin Kebbi
SOKOTO
Zamfara
Ka
Gusau
Anka
Chafe
Runka
KATSINA
Katsina
Kaura Namoda
Yashi
Ringim
KANO
KANO
Funtua
Malumfashi
Paki
Jamaari
Azare
Potiskum
Gamawa
Lantewa
Nafada
Gombe
Ako
Biu
Chibuk
Mubi
Mandara
Mts
▲ 1290
Mora
Maroua
Mindif
Kaélé

Benoué

Léré
Pala
Lame
TANDJILÉ
Kélo
Laï

MOYEN
CHARI
Sarh
Bahr Aouk
Koumra
Doba
Moïssala
Ouham

Yelwa
Kainji
Reserve
Auna
Babana
New
Bussa
NIGER
Zungeru
Kontagora
Tegina
Minna
Bida
Baro
KWARA

KADUNA
Kaduna
Zaria
Kajuru
Gwagwada
Kafanchan
Jos
Plateau
Jos
Bukuru
Pindiga
Pankshin
FED. CAP.
TER.
Abuja
Keffi
Nasarawa
Lafia
PLATEAU
Gassol

BAUCHI
Bauchi
Bara
Garko
Yan
Numan
Yola
Jimeta
Baroua

Léré
Poli
Konteha
▲ 1600
Baibokoum
Gore
Bekoundai
LOGONE
OCCIDENTAL
Moundou
LOGONE
ORIENTAL

Bossembélé
Bossangoa
Bouca
CENTRAL
AFRICAN
REPUBLIC
Batangafo
Kaga
Bandoro

BENIN

Nikki
Ndali
Djougou
Parakou
Mékrou

N I G E R I A

Ogbomosho
Offa
Ilorin
Iseyin
Oyo
Iwo
Ede
Osogbo
Ilesha
OYO
Ife
Ikerre
Akure
ONDO
Ibadan
Abeokuta
OGUN
Ijebu Ode
Ilaro
Mushin
Lagos
Cotonou
Porto
Novo
Sakété
Pobè

Kabba
Oka
Owo
Okitipupa
Auchi
Sabongidda
Benin City
BENDEL
Warri
Sapele
Ughelli
Burutu

Lokoja
Idah
Ankpa
BENUE
Makurdi
Otukpo
Oturkpo
Obudu
Ogoja
Gboko
Katsina-Ala
Wukari
Donga
Bali
▲ 1500
Takum
Gembu
Mayo-Daga
Dyerem
Tibati
Massif de l'Adamaoua
Canyo
Banyo
Dibi
Ngaoundéré
Tignère
Viña
Baïbokoum
Koutcha
Paoua
Bocaranga
Bozoum
Bouar
Baboua

Méiganga
Garoua Boulai
Bétaré Oya
Bocaranga

ZAIRE

Asaba
Onitsha
Awka
ANAMBRA
Nnewi
Agbor
Abakaliki
Ugep
Ikom
Mamfe
Bafut
Bamenda
Foumban
Bafia
Nanga
Eboko
Belabo
Bertoua
Batouri
Gamboula
Berbérati
Boda
Bania
M'Baiki
Bimbo
Bangui
Zongo

Buguma
Port Harcourt
Nembe
Brass
Bonny
Eket
Calabar
Oron
AKWA-IBOM
RIVERS
Aba
Owerri
Umuahia
IMO
Okigwi
Bende
Enugu
ENUGU
Nkalagu
Abakaliki

Mt
Cameroon
▲ 4070
Buea
Douala
Limbe
Malabo

Bioko I.

EQUATORIAL
GUINEA

Kumba
Loum
Yabassi
Nkongsamba
Bafang
Bafoussam
Oshang
Dschang

Edéa
Nyong
Mbalmayo
Yaoundé
Okola
Ayos
Abong
Mbang
Yokadouma
Ndélélé
Nola
Lipéité
Gandou
Bomboho

Kribi
Campo
Bata
Ebolowa
Sangmélima
Zoétélé
Lomié
Dja
Moloundou
Souflay

CAMEROON

GABON

CONGO

GUINEA

Gulf
of
Guinea

Bight of Benin

▼ 3261

Niger Delta

Bight of Bonny

SÃO TOMÉ
& PRÍNCIPE *Príncipe*

Bight of Bonny

Tropic of Cancer

77

CENTRAL AND EAST AFRICA

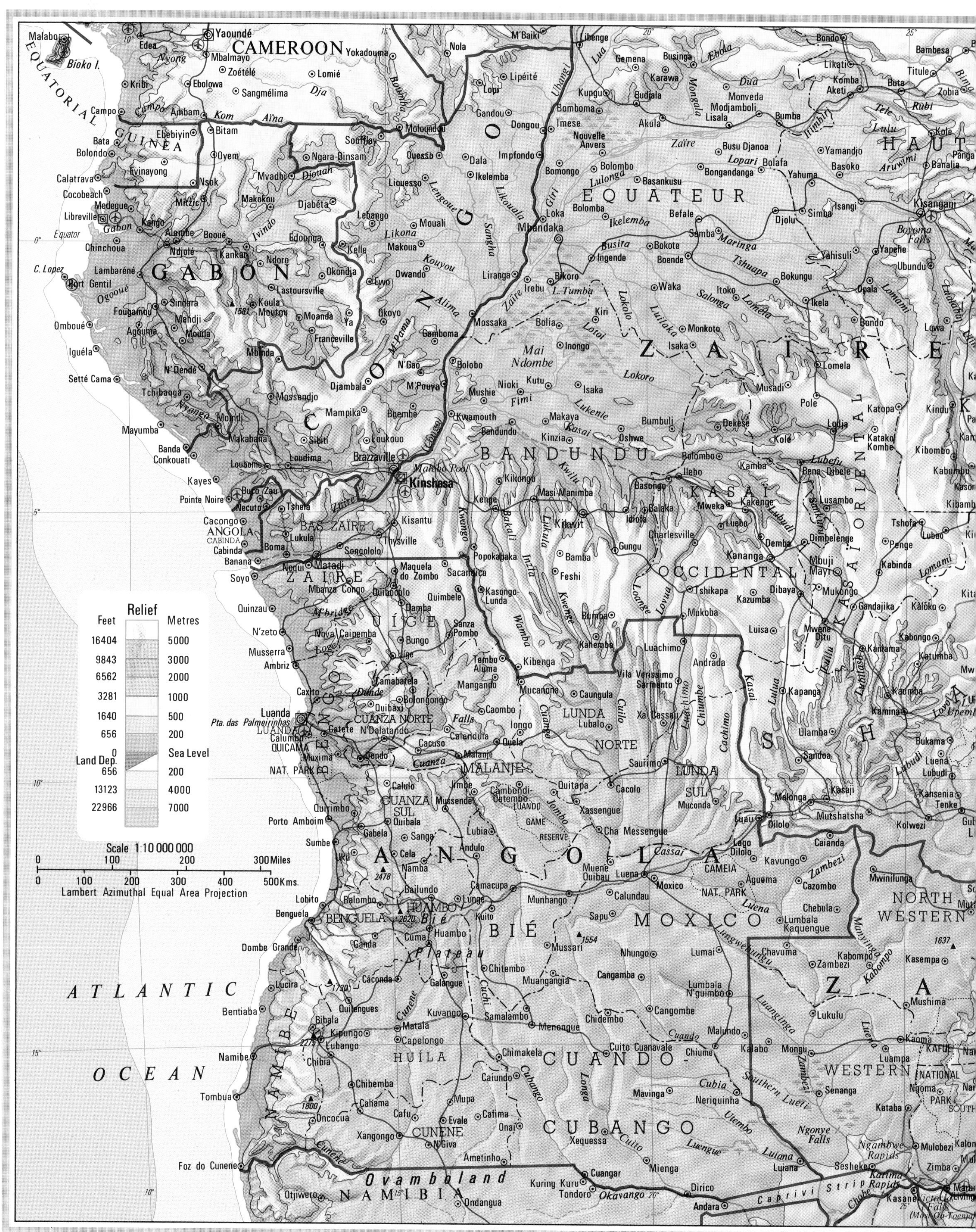

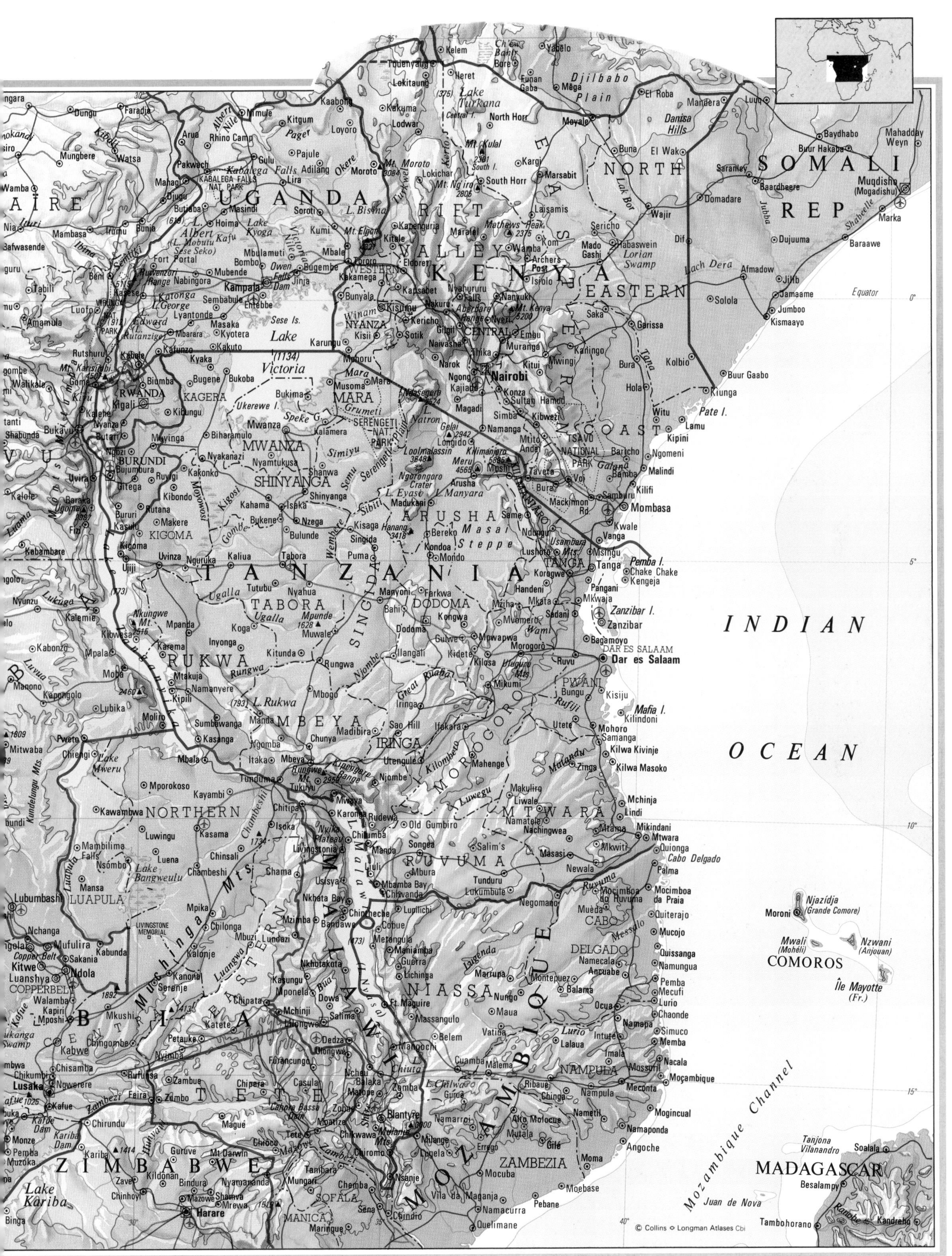
UGANDA
KENYA
TANZANIA
RWANDA
BURUNDI
SOMALI REP
MOZAMBIQUE
MALAWI
ZIMBABWE
COMOROS
MADAGASCAR
INDIAN OCEAN
Mozambique Channel
Lake Turkana
Lake Victoria
(1134)
L. Rukwa
L. Natron
L. Eyasi
L. Manyara
L. Kyoga
L. George
L. Edward
L. Albert
L. Mobutu Sese Seko
Lake Mweru
Lake Bangweulu
Lake Kariba
L. Malawi (Nyasa)
L. Chilwa
L. Chiuta
Kampala
Nairobi
Dodoma
Dar es Salaam
Mombasa
Kigali
Bujumbura
Lusaka
Harare
Muqdisho (Mogadishu)
Moroni
Lilongwe
Blantyre
Zomba
Tanga
Zanzibar
Zanzibar I.
Pemba I.
Mafia I.
Kilindoni
Arusha
Moshi
Kilimanjaro 5895
Mt. Kenya 5200
Mt. Elgon
Mt. Kulal
Ngorongoro Crater
SERENGETI NAT. PARK
TSAVO NATIONAL PARK
KABALEGA FALLS NAT. PARK
Kabalega Falls
Owen Falls Dam
RIFT VALLEY
NORTH EASTERN
EASTERN
CENTRAL
COAST
NYANZA
WESTERN
KAGERA
MWANZA
SHINYANGA
ARUSHA
KIGOMA
TABORA
SINGIDA
DODOMA
RUKWA
MBEYA
IRINGA
MOROGORO
PWANI
TANGA
MTWARA
RUVUMA
LINDI
NORTHERN
LUAPULA
COPPERBELT
CENTRAL
EASTERN
NIASSA
CABO DELGADO
NAMPULA
ZAMBEZIA
TETE
MANICA
SOFALA
Masai Steppe
Djilbabo Plain
Lorian Swamp
Danisa Hills
Kisumu
Kericho
Nakuru
Eldoret
Kitale
Malindi
Lamu
Garissa
Marsabit
Moyale
Lodwar
Mwanza
Tabora
Kigoma
Ujiji
Mbeya
Iringa
Morogoro
Mtwara
Lindi
Songea
Kisimaayo
Marka
Ndola
Kitwe
Kabwe
Tete
Quelimane
Nampula
Moçambique
Pemba
Lichinga
Zambezi
Ruvuma
Rufiji
Great Ruaha
Tana
Equator
0°
5°
10°
15°
40°
© Collins ◇ Longman Atlases Cbi

SOUTHERN AFRICA AND MADAGASCAR

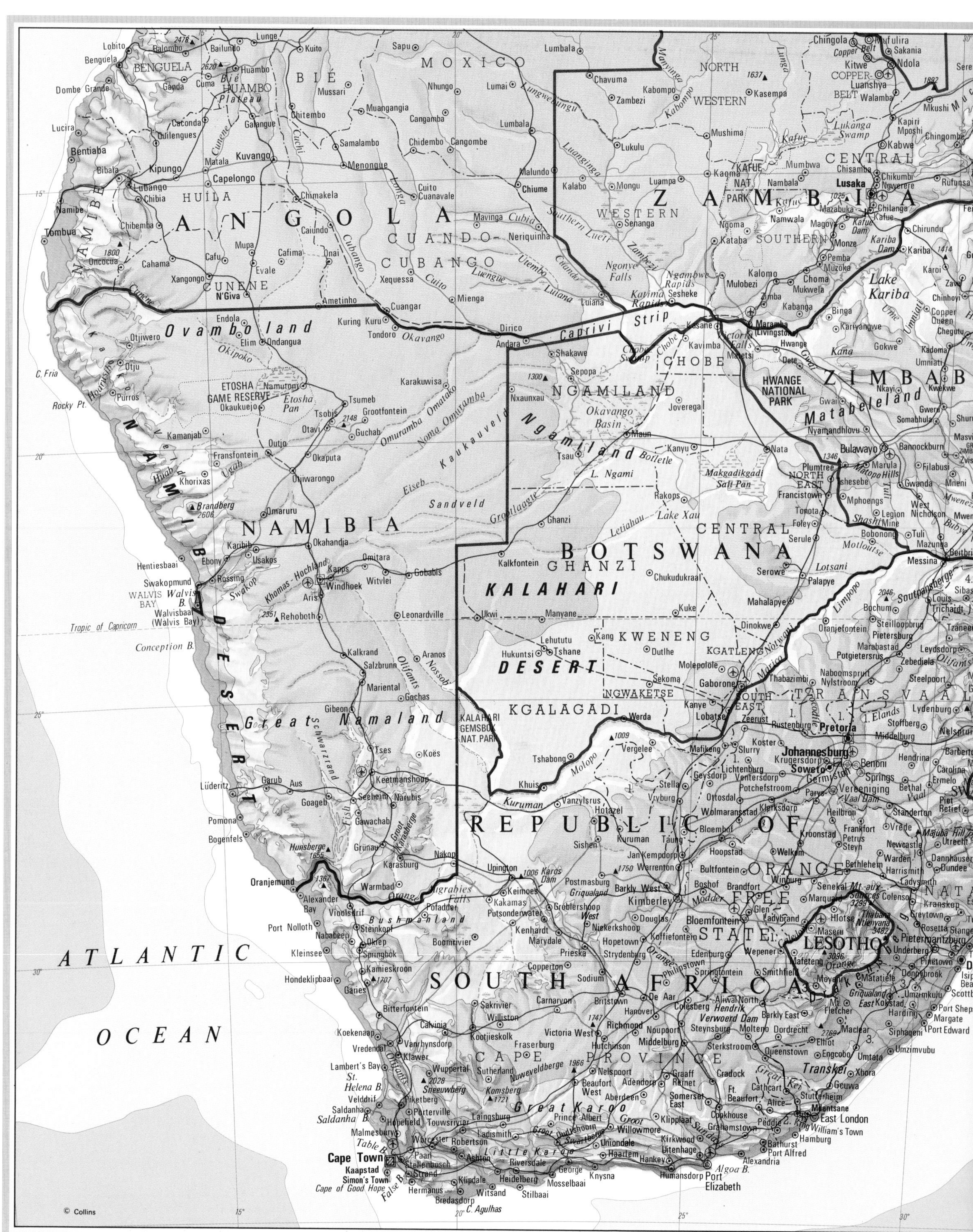

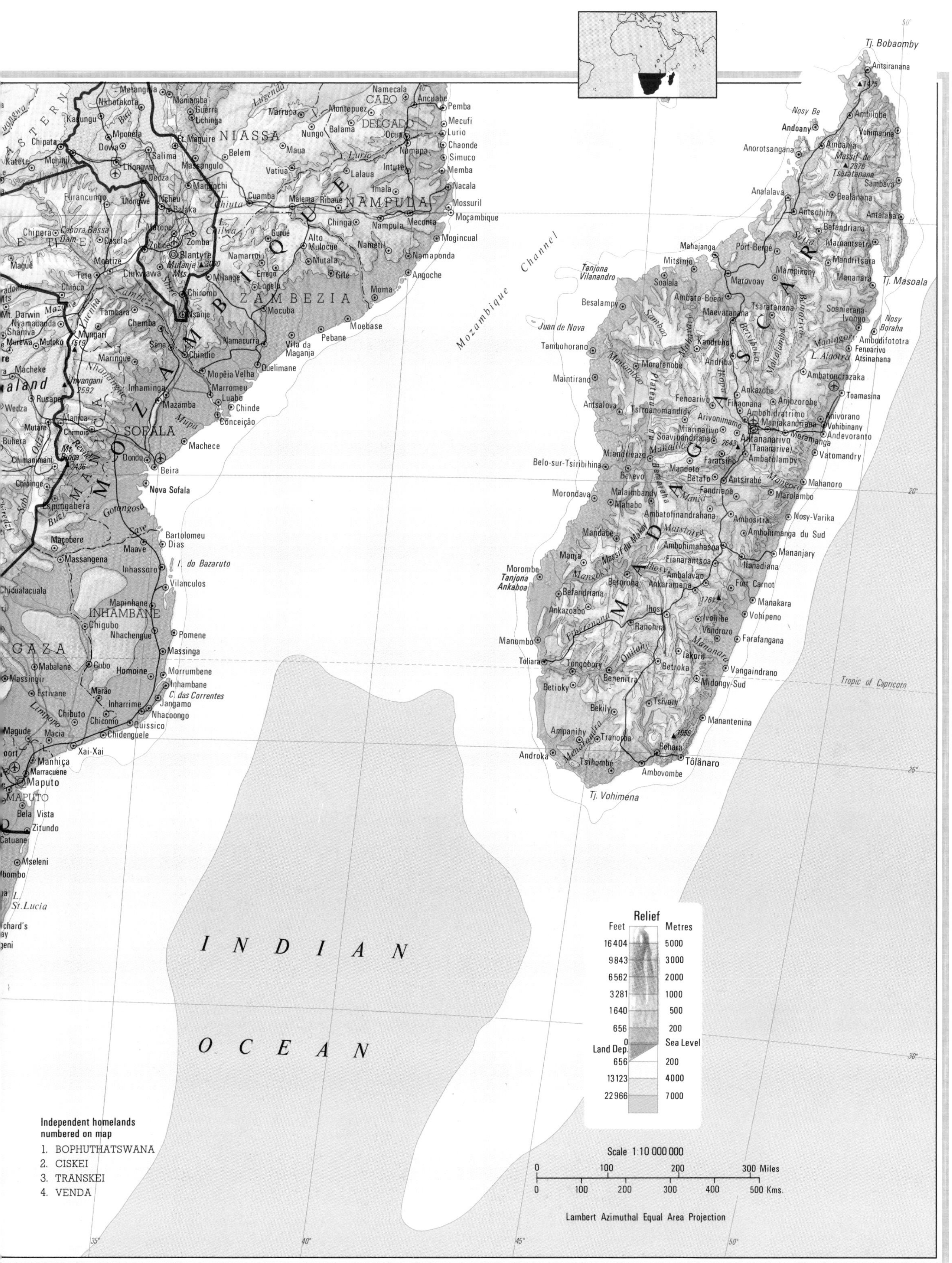

INDIAN

OCEAN

Relief

Feet		Metres
16 404		5000
9843		3000
6562		2000
3281		1000
1640		500
656		200
0		Sea Level
Land Dep.		
656		200
13123		4000
22 966		7000

Scale 1:10 000 000

0	100		200		300 Miles
0	100	200	300	400	500 Kms.

Lambert Azimuthal Equal Area Projection

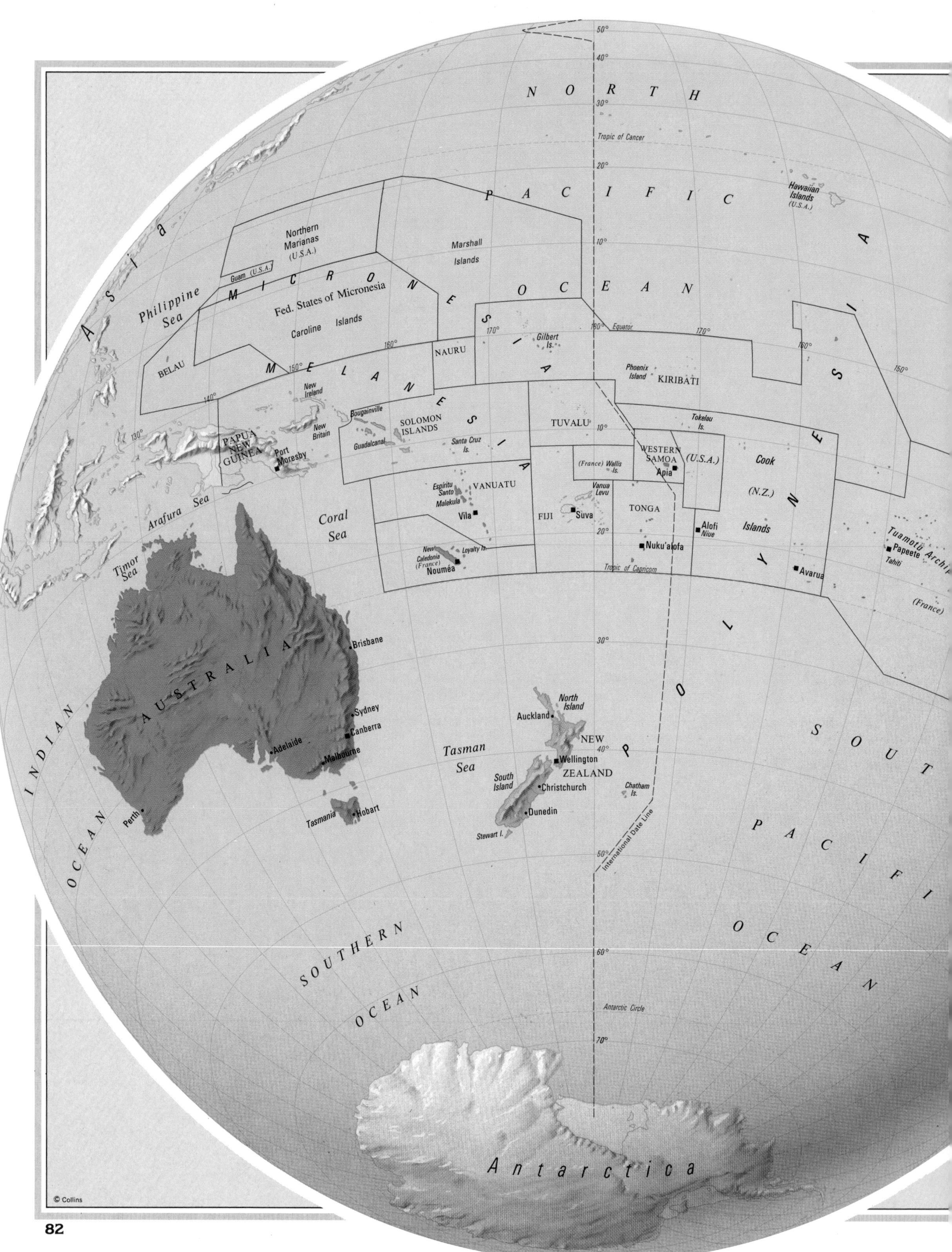

N O R T H

Tropic of Cancer

PACIFIC

Hawaiian
Islands
(U.S.A.)

A S I a

Northern
Marianas
(U.S.A.)

Marshall

Islands

OCEAN

Guam (U.S.A.)

M I C R O N E

Philippine
Sea

Fed. States of Micronesia

Caroline   Islands

BELAU

M E L A

Gilbert
Is.

Equator

NAURU

S I A

Phoenix
Island

KIRIBATI

New
Ireland

Bougainville

SOLOMON
ISLANDS

Santa Cruz
Is.

TUVALU

Tokelau
Is.

PAPUA
NEW
GUINEA

New
Britain

Guadalcanal

N E S I A

WESTERN
SAMOA   (U.S.A.)

Cook

Port
Moresby

Espíritu
Santo

VANUATU

(France) Wallis
Is.

Apia

(N.Z.)

Arafura Sea

Malekula

Vanua
Levu

Islands

Timor
Sea

Coral
Sea

Vila

FIJI

Suva

TONGA

Alofi
Niue

Tuamotu Archip.

New
Caledonia
(France)

Loyalty Is.

Nouméa

Nuku'alofa

Tropic of Capricorn

Avarua

Papeete

Tahiti

(France)

INDIAN

AUSTRALIA

Brisbane

P O L Y N E S I A

S O U T H

Sydney

Canberra

Adelaide

North
Island

Auckland

Melbourne

Perth

Tasman
Sea

NEW

Wellington

PACIFIC

OCEAN

Tasmania

Hobart

South
Island

ZEALAND

Christchurch

Chatham
Is.

O C E A N

Dunedin

Stewart I.

International Date Line

SOUTHERN

OCEAN

Antarctic Circle

Antarctica

© Collins

82

OCEANIA

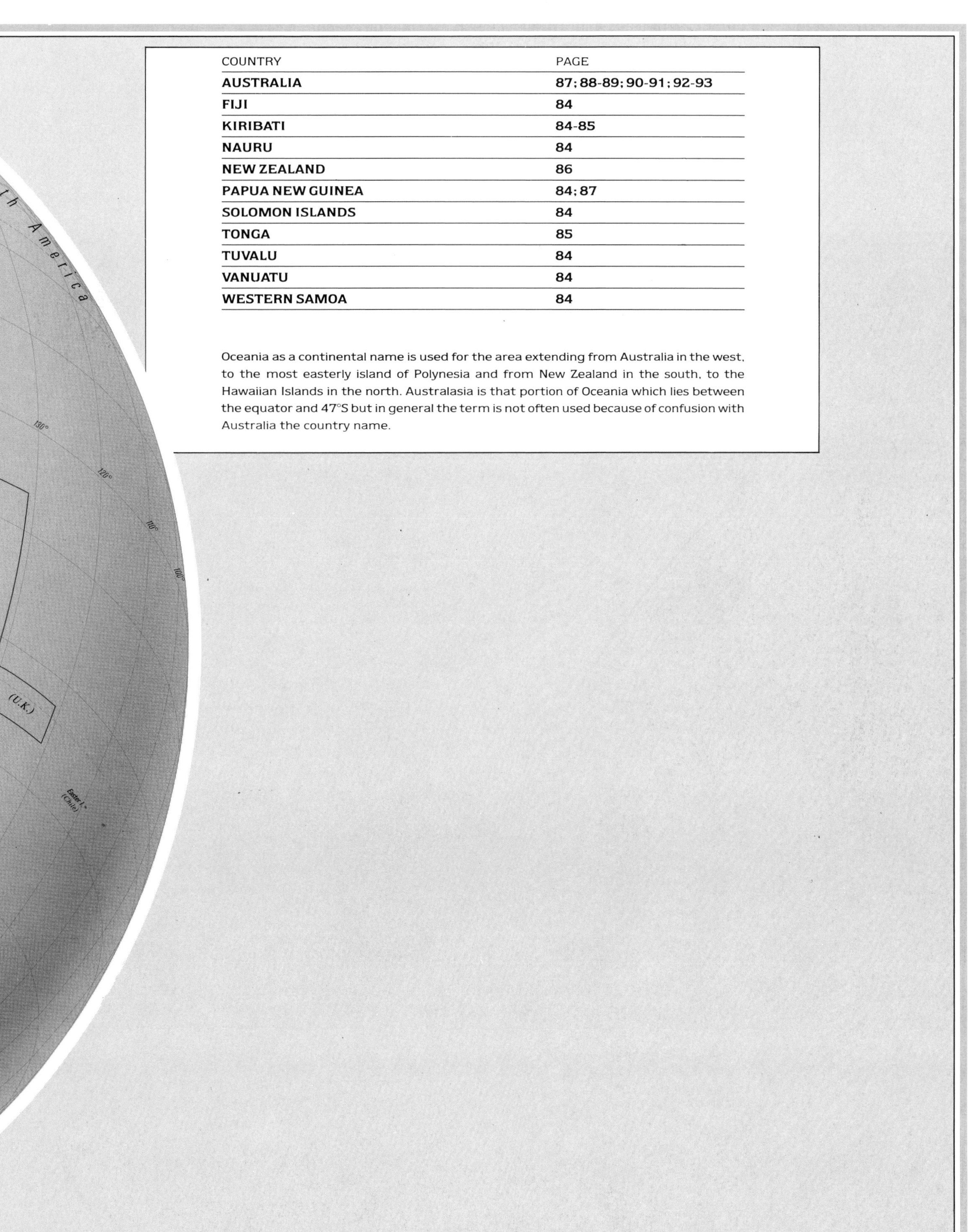

Oceania as a continental name is used for the area extending from Australia in the west, to the most easterly island of Polynesia and from New Zealand in the south, to the Hawaiian Islands in the north. Australasia is that portion of Oceania which lies between the equator and 47°S but in general the term is not often used because of confusion with Australia the country name.

PACIFIC OCEAN

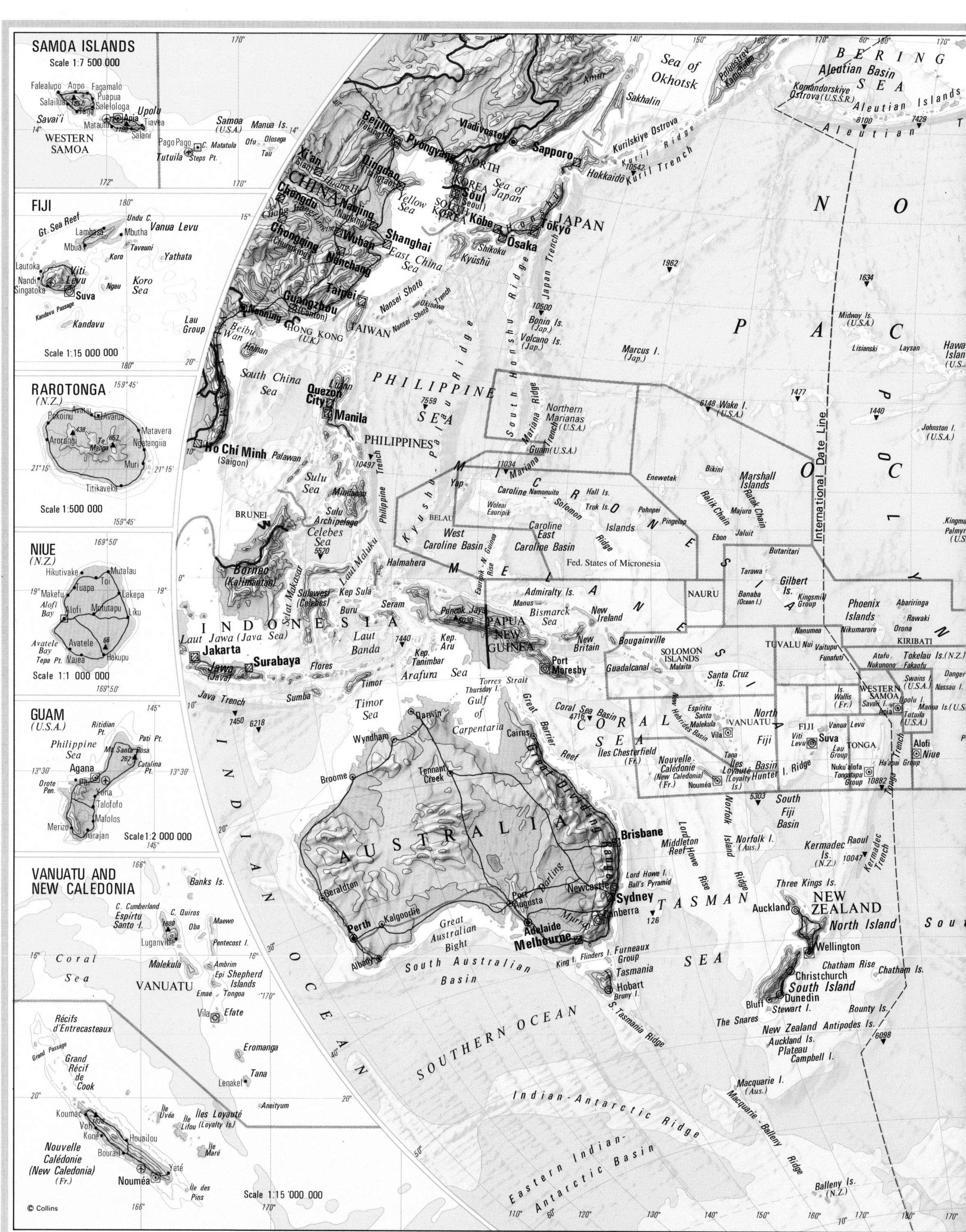

SAMOA ISLANDS
Scale 1:7 500 000

Falealupo Aopo Fagamalo
Salailua 1858 Puapua
Savai'i Safotulafai Salelologa
Matautu Upolu
WESTERN Apia Tiavea
SAMOA Salani
Samoa Manua Is.
(U.S.A.) Ofu Olosega
Pago Pago Tau
Tutuila C. Matatula
Steps Pt.

FIJI
Undu C.
Gt. Sea Reef Vanua Levu
Lambasa Mbutha
Mbua Taveuni
Lautoka Koro Yathata
Viti Ngau Lau
Levu Koro Group
Nandi Sea
Singatoka Suva
Kandavu Passage Kandavu
Scale 1:15 000 000

RAROTONGA
(N.Z.)
Pokoinu Avatiu Avarua
438 Matavera
Arorangi Te 1653 Ngatangiia
Manga
Muri
Titikaveka
Scale 1:500 000

NIUE
(N.Z.)
Hikutavake Mutalau
Makefu Tuapa Toi Lakepa
Alofi Alofi Liku
Bay Mutalapu
Avatele 86
Bay Avatele
Tepa Pt. Vaiea Hakupu
Scale 1:1 000 000

GUAM
(U.S.A.)
Ritidian Pt.
Philippine Pati Pt.
Sea Mt Santa Rosa 262
Agana Catalina Pt.
Orote Yona
Pen. Talofofo
Merizo Malolos
Inarajan
Scale 1:2 000 000

VANUATU AND NEW CALEDONIA
Banks Is.
C. Cumberland
C. Quiros
Espiritu 1890
Santo I. Oba Maewo
Luganville Pentecost I.
Malekula Ambrim
Epi Shepherd
Islands
VANUATU Emae Tongoa
Vila Efate
Récifs
d'Entrecasteaux Eromanga
Grand Passage
Grand Tana
Récif Lenakel
de Aneityum
Cook
Koumac
Voh 1628
Koné Houailou
Nouvelle Bourail
Calédonie Yaté
(New Caledonia) Ile des
(Fr.) Pins
Nouméa
© Collins Scale 1:15 000 000

84

Main map labels

BERING SEA
Aleutian Basin
Komandorskiye Ostrova (U.S.S.R.)
Aleutian Islands
8100 7429 Aleutian T.

Sea of Okhotsk
Poluostrov Kamchatka
Amur
Sakhalin

NORTH PACIFIC OCEAN

Vladivostok
Sapporo
Hokkaidō Kuril Trench
Kurilskiye Ostrova
Kuril Ridge
10542

Beijing (Peking)
Qingdao Huang He
Pyongyang NORTH KOREA
Sea of Japan
Xi'an (Sian) Seoul SOUTH KOREA
CHINA
Chengdu Nanjing (Nanking) Yellow Sea
Chang Wuhan JAPAN
Chongqing (Chungking) Shanghai Kōbe Tokyo
Nanchang East China Sea Shikoku Osaka
Guangzhou (Canton) Taipei Kyūshū
Nanning HONG KONG (U.K.) Nansei Shotō
Beibu Wan TAIWAN Nansei Shotō
Hainan Okinawa Trench
South China Sea Bonin Is. (Jap.)
Lau Group Volcano Is. (Jap.)
Marcus I. (Jap.)

Midway Is. (U.S.A.)
Lisianski Laysan
Hawaiian Islands (U.S.)

Japan Trench
1962
1634
1477
1440

PHILIPPINE SEA
Quezon City
Manila 7559
Ho Chí Minh (Saigon) Palawan
PHILIPPINES
10497 Philippine Trench
Sulu Sea Mindanao
BRUNEI Sulu Archipelago
Celebes Sea 5520
Borneo (Kalimantan) Laut Maluku
Halmahera
Selat Makasar Kep Sula
Sulawesi (Celebes) Buru Seram
INDONESIA Puncak Jaya 5030
Laut Jawa (Java Sea) Laut Banda
Jakarta 7440 Kep. Aru
Jawa (Java) Surabaya Kep. Tanimbar
Flores Arafura Sea
Java Trench Timor
7450 6218 Sumba Timor Sea

South Honshu Ridge
Japan Trench
6148 Wake I. (U.S.A.)
Northern Marianas (U.S.A.)
Guam (U.S.A.)
Mariana Trench 11034
Yap MICRONESIA
Caroline Namonuito
Woleai Eauripik Truk Is.
West Caroline Basin Caroline Hall Is.
BELAU East Pohnpei Pingelap
Caroline Basin Caroline Islands Ridge Ebon
Fed. States of Micronesia
Enewetak Bikini
Marshall Islands
Ralik Chain Ratak Chain
Majuro Jaluit
Butaritari

Kyushu-Palau Ridge
Mariana Ridge

MELANESIA
Eauripik - N. Guinea Rise
Admiralty Is. Manus
Bismarck Sea
PAPUA NEW GUINEA New Ireland
Port Moresby New Britain
Bougainville
Torres Strait SOLOMON ISLANDS Malaita
Thursday I. Guadalcanal Santa Cruz Is.
Gulf of Carpentaria
Great Barrier Reef New Hebrides Basin 4710
Cairns Coral Sea Basin
Espíritu Santo Malekula
Darwin VANUATU Vila
Wyndham CORAL SEA Îles Chesterfield (Fr.)
Tennant Creek Nouvelle Calédonie
Broome (New Caledonia) (Fr.) Nouméa
Tana Îles Loyauté (Loyalty Is.)
Geraldton AUSTRALIA 5303 Hunter I. Ridge

NAURU
Tarawa
Gilbert Is.
Banaba (Ocean I.) Kingsmill Group
Phoenix Islands
Abariringa Rawaki Orona
Nikumaroro KIRIBATI
TUVALU Nanumea Nui Vaitupu
Funafuti Atafu Tokelau Is. (N.Z.)
Nukunonu Swains I. (U.S.A.)
Wallis (Fr.) WESTERN SAMOA Danger Nassau I.
Savai'i Apia Manua Is. (U.S.)
FIJI Upolu Tutuila (U.S.A.)
Viti Levu Suva Alofi
Lau Group TONGA Niue
Iles Loyauté North Fiji Basin
Lau Basin Nuku'alofa Ha'apai Group
Tongatapu Group 10882
South Fiji Basin Tonga Trench

Lord Howe Rise
Norfolk Ridge
Brisbane
Middleton Reef Norfolk Island
Lord Howe I. Norfolk I. (Aus.)
Ball's Pyramid Kermadec Ridge
Newcastle Raoul
Sydney Kermadec Is. (N.Z.) 10047
Canberra Kermadec Trench
126 TASMAN SEA
Melbourne Three Kings Is.
Adelaide Auckland NEW ZEALAND
King I. North Island
Flinders I. Furneaux Group Wellington
Tasmania Chatham Rise Chatham Is.
Hobart South Island
Bruny I. Christchurch
S. Tasmania Ridge Dunedin
Bluff Stewart I.
The Snares Bounty Is.
New Zealand Antipodes Is.
Auckland Is. Plateau 6098
Campbell I.

Great Australian Bight
South Australian Basin
Perth
Kalgoorlie
Port Augusta
Murray
Albany
Darling

INDIAN OCEAN

SOUTHERN OCEAN

Indian-Antarctic Ridge
Macquarie I. (Aus.)
Balleny Ridge
Eastern Indian-Antarctic Basin
Balleny Is. (N.Z.)

International Date Line

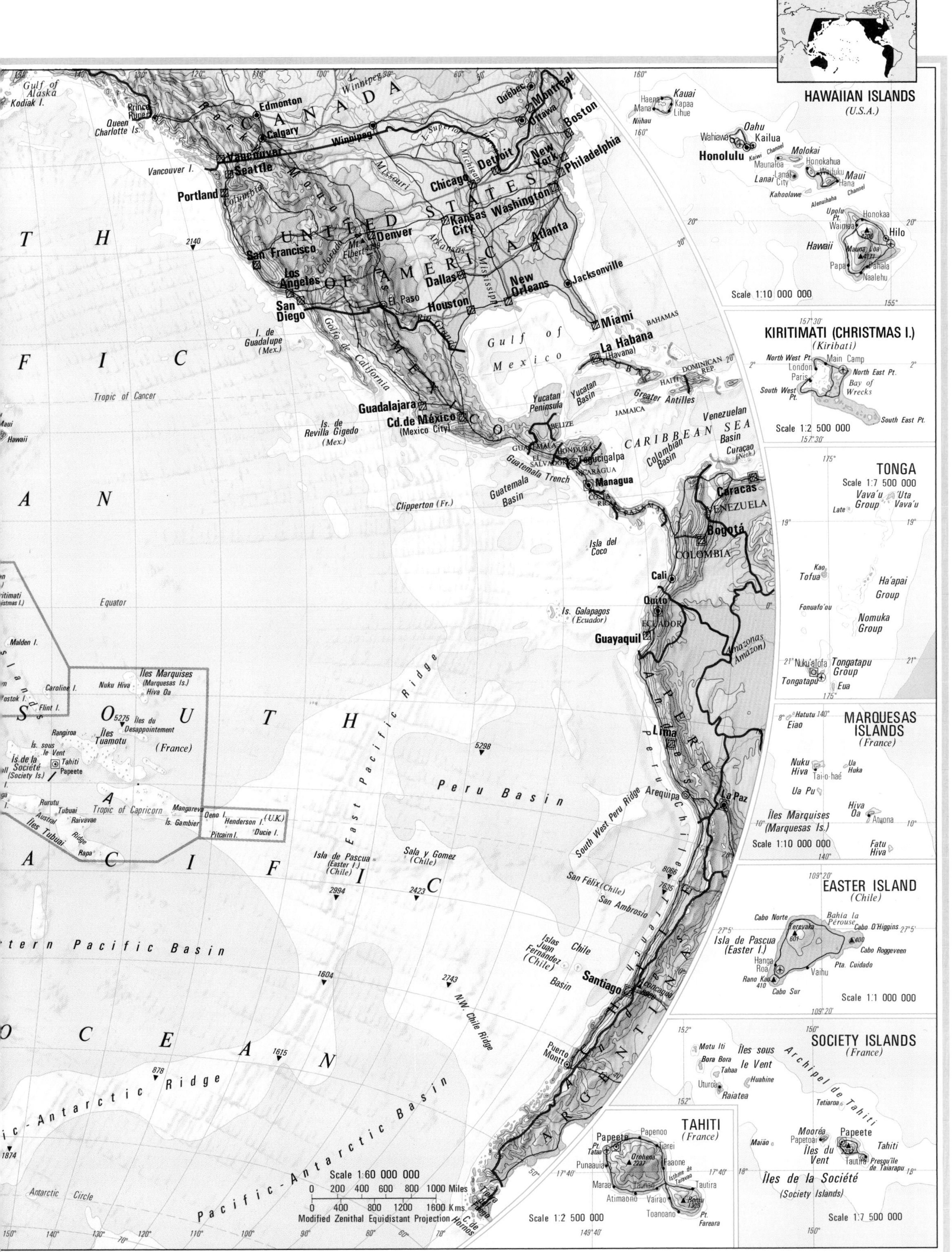

HAWAIIAN ISLANDS
(U.S.A.)

Scale 1:10 000 000

KIRITIMATI (CHRISTMAS I.)
(Kiribati)

Scale 1:2 500 000

TONGA
Scale 1:7 500 000

MARQUESAS ISLANDS
(France)

Scale 1:10 000 000

EASTER ISLAND
(Chile)

Scale 1:1 000 000

SOCIETY ISLANDS
(France)

TAHITI
(France)

Scale 1:2 500 000

Íles de la Société
(Society Islands)

Scale 1:7 500 000

Scale 1:60 000 000

0   200   400   600   800   1000 Miles

0   400   800   1200   1600 Kms.

Modified Zenithal Equidistant Projection

NEW ZEALAND

Relief

Feet		Metres
16 404		5000
9843		3000
6562		2000
3281		1000
1640		500
656		200
0		Sea Level
Land Dep.		
656		200
13 123		4000
22 966		7000

North Cape

Ninety Mile Beach

Doubtless Bay
Manganui
Kaitaia
Bay of Islands
Paihia
C. Brett
Rawene
Kaikohe
Hikurangi
NORTHLAND
Whangarei
Dargaville
Bream Bay
Waipu
Gt. Barrier I.

NORTH ISLAND

2297

Kaipara Harbour
Warkworth
Hauraki Gulf
Helensville
Coromandel
Takapuna
Coromandel Peninsula
Auckland
AUCKLAND
Manukau
Whitianga
Manukau Harbour
Thames
Mayor I.
Waiuku
Pukekohe
Waikato
Bay of Plenty
Huntly
Waihi
Tauranga
Morrinsville
Matakana I.
Ngaruawahia
Te Puke
Hamilton
Te Aroha
Whakatane
Cambridge
Matamata
Hicks Bay
Te Kaha
Te Araroa
Kawhia
Te Awamutu
Rotorua
WAIKATO
Putaruru
BAY OF PLENTY
Opotiki
East Cape
Otorohanga
Tokoroa
Rotorua
Kawerau
Hikurangi
Te Kuiti
1754
Waikato
Raglan Ra.
Tikitiki
Waipiro
North Taranaki Bight
Benneydale
Lake Taupo
Taupo
Ruatoria
Tolaga Bay
Mokau
Taumarunui
(358)
Ngauruhoe
2291
Tutangi
Huiarau Ra.
GISBORNE
New Plymouth
Waitara
Turangi
Wairoa
Gisborne
Inglewood
Ruapehu
Kaimanawa Mts
Mt. Egmont
Stratford
2792
HAWKES
Waikokopu
1518
TARANAKI
Waiouru
BAY
Opunake
Eltham
Mohakatino
Mangaweka
Hawke Bay
Hawera
Bay View
Patea
MANAWATU
Taihape
Napier
Wanganui
Marton
Hastings
WANGANUI
Mangaweka
Waipawa
112
Feilding
Dannevirke
Palmerston North
Woodville
Cape Farewell
Foxton
Collingwood
Golden Bay
Levin
D'Urville I.
Pahiatua
Takaka
Tasman Mts.
Kapiti I.
Eketahuna
Tasman Bay
Paraparaumu
WELLINGTON
Karamea Bight
Nelson
Picton
Masterton
Kumara
Porirua
Carterton
Motueka
Upper Hutt
Granity
Richmond
Havelock
Lower Hutt
Westport
Wairau
Wellington
Cape Foulwind
Buller
Murchison
Blenheim
Cook Strait
Reefton
NELSON
Seddon
C. Palliser
Greymouth
MARLBOROUGH
Cape Campbell
Mt. Travers
Kaikoura Ra.
Brunner
2338
Hanmer Springs
Clarence
Kumara
Lewis Pass
Kaikoura
Hokitika
Otira
Waiau
Ross
Arthur's Pass
Cheviot
Whataroa
Waipara
Okarito
Rangiora
Pegasus Bay
Fox Glacier
Kaiapoi
4870
SOUTHERN ALPS
Rakaia
Lincoln
Christchurch
SOUTH ISLAND
Waimakariri
Akaroa
Banks Peninsula
Mt. Cook
Springfield
3764
Darfield
Okuru
Cascade Pt.
Pukaki
Fairlie
Rakaia
Ashburton
Geraldine
Canterbury Bight
Mt. Aspiring
Tekapo
3027
L. Wanaka
Twizel
Temuka
Omarama
Timaru
Wanaka
Hawea
Milford Sound
Dunstan Mts.
Waimate
Homer Tunnel
Kurow
Arrowtown
Cromwell
Waitaki
Queenstown
Clyde
Naseby
Oamaru
Te Anau
Alexandra
Ranfurly
Pukeuri
L. Te Anau
Wakatipu
Roxburgh
Damaru
Kingston
OTAGO
Palmerston
Eyre Mts.
L. Manapouri
Lawrence
Waikouaiti
Resolution I.
Mossburn
Port Chalmers
SOUTHLAND
Clutha
Otago Peninsula
Ohai
Lumsden
Milton
Dunedin
Nightcaps
Cameron Mts.
Mataura
Winton
Gore
Balclutha
Ohai
Tapanui
Clinton
Puysegur Pt.
Otautau
Mataura
Owaka
Riverton
Edendale
Invercargill
Fortrose
Bluff
Foveaux Strait
Ruapuke I.
980
Stewart I.
Halfmoon Bay
Southwest Cape

TASMAN SEA

PACIFIC

OCEAN

Scale 1:6 000 000

| 0 | 50 | 100 | 150 Miles |

| 0 | 50 | 100 | 150 | 200 Kms. |

Conic Projection

AUSTRALIA

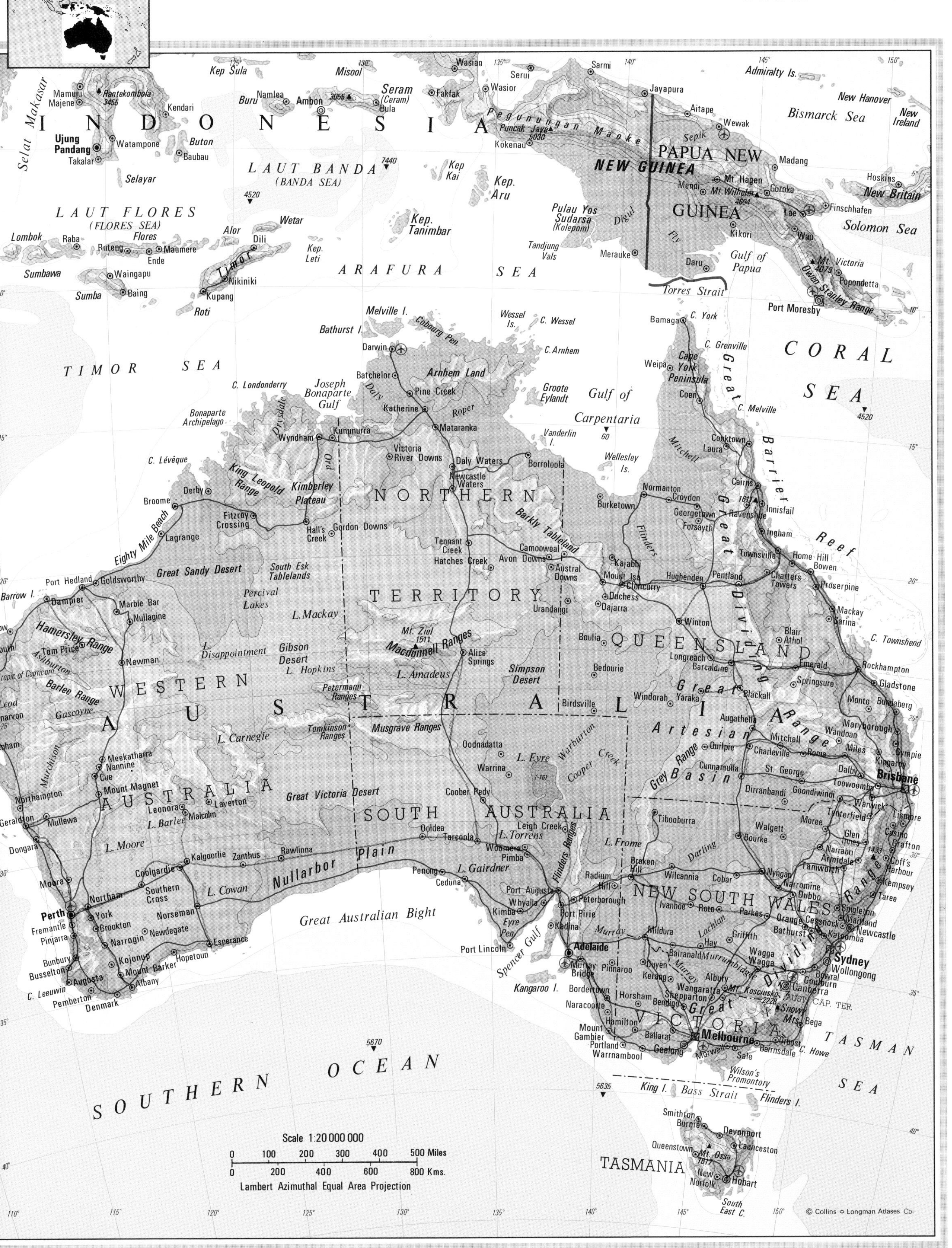

INDONESIA
LAUT BANDA
(BANDA SEA)
LAUT FLORES
(FLORES SEA)
ARAFURA SEA
TIMOR SEA
PAPUA NEW GUINEA
Bismarck Sea
Solomon Sea
CORAL SEA
Gulf of Carpentaria
Joseph Bonaparte Gulf
NORTHERN TERRITORY
WESTERN AUSTRALIA
SOUTH AUSTRALIA
QUEENSLAND
NEW SOUTH WALES
VICTORIA
TASMANIA
AUST. CAP. TER.
Great Sandy Desert
Gibson Desert
Great Victoria Desert
Simpson Desert
Nullarbor Plain
Great Artesian Basin
Great Dividing Range
Great Barrier Reef
Great Australian Bight
SOUTHERN OCEAN
TASMAN SEA
Bass Strait
Torres Strait
Perth
Adelaide
Melbourne
Sydney
Brisbane
Canberra
Hobart
Darwin
Alice Springs
Port Moresby
Scale 1:20 000 000
0 100 200 300 400 500 Miles
0 200 400 600 800 Kms.
Lambert Azimuthal Equal Area Projection
© Collins • Longman Atlases Cbi

WESTERN AUSTRALIA

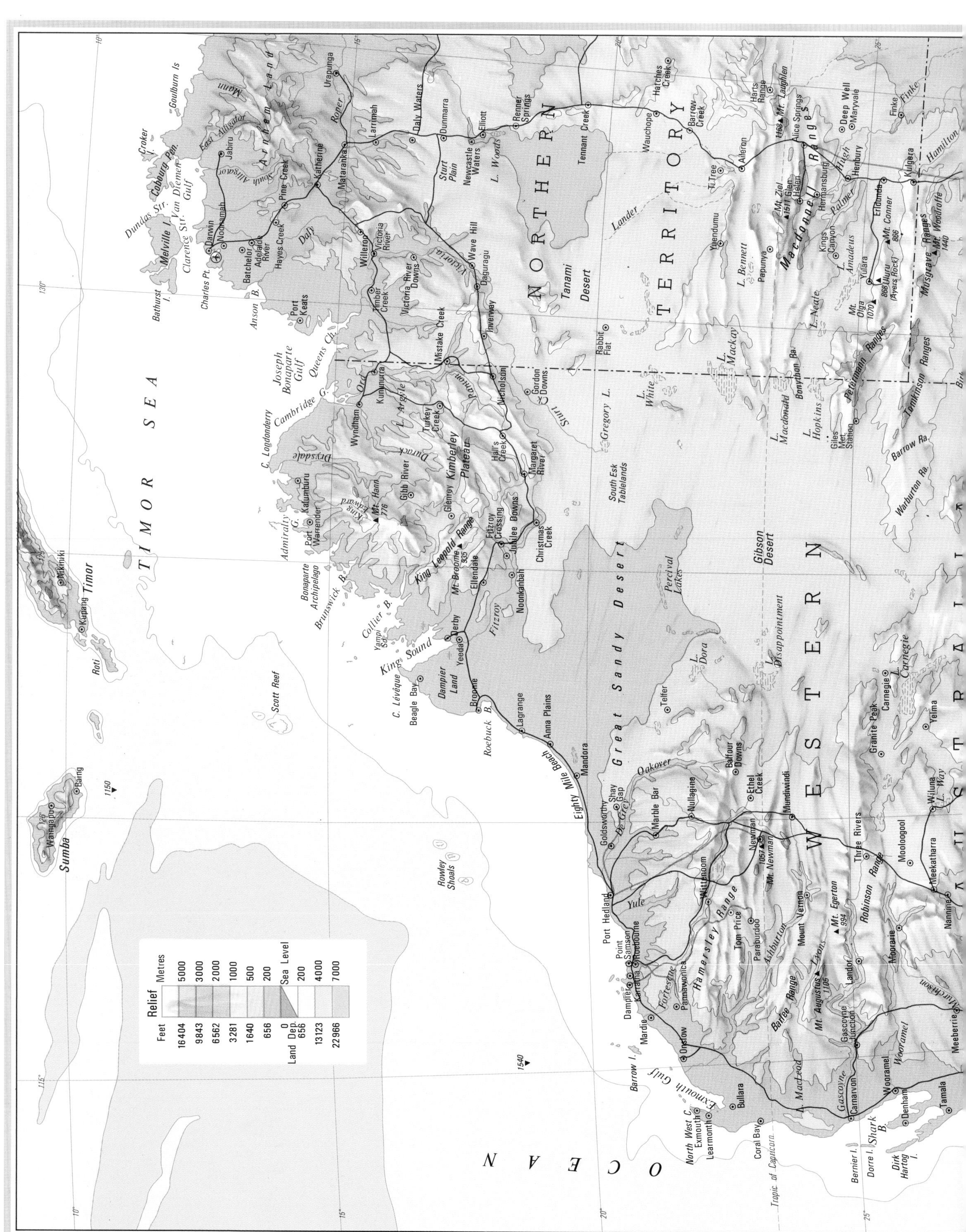

TIMOR SEA

INDIAN OCEAN

NORTHERN TERRITORY

WESTERN AUSTRALIA

Great Sandy Desert

Gibson Desert

Tanami Desert

Arnhem Land

Relief	Metres
Feet	
16404	5000
9843	3000
6562	2000
3281	1000
1640	500
656	200
	Sea Level
Land Dep.	0
13123	656
22966	4000
	7000

Tropic of Capricorn

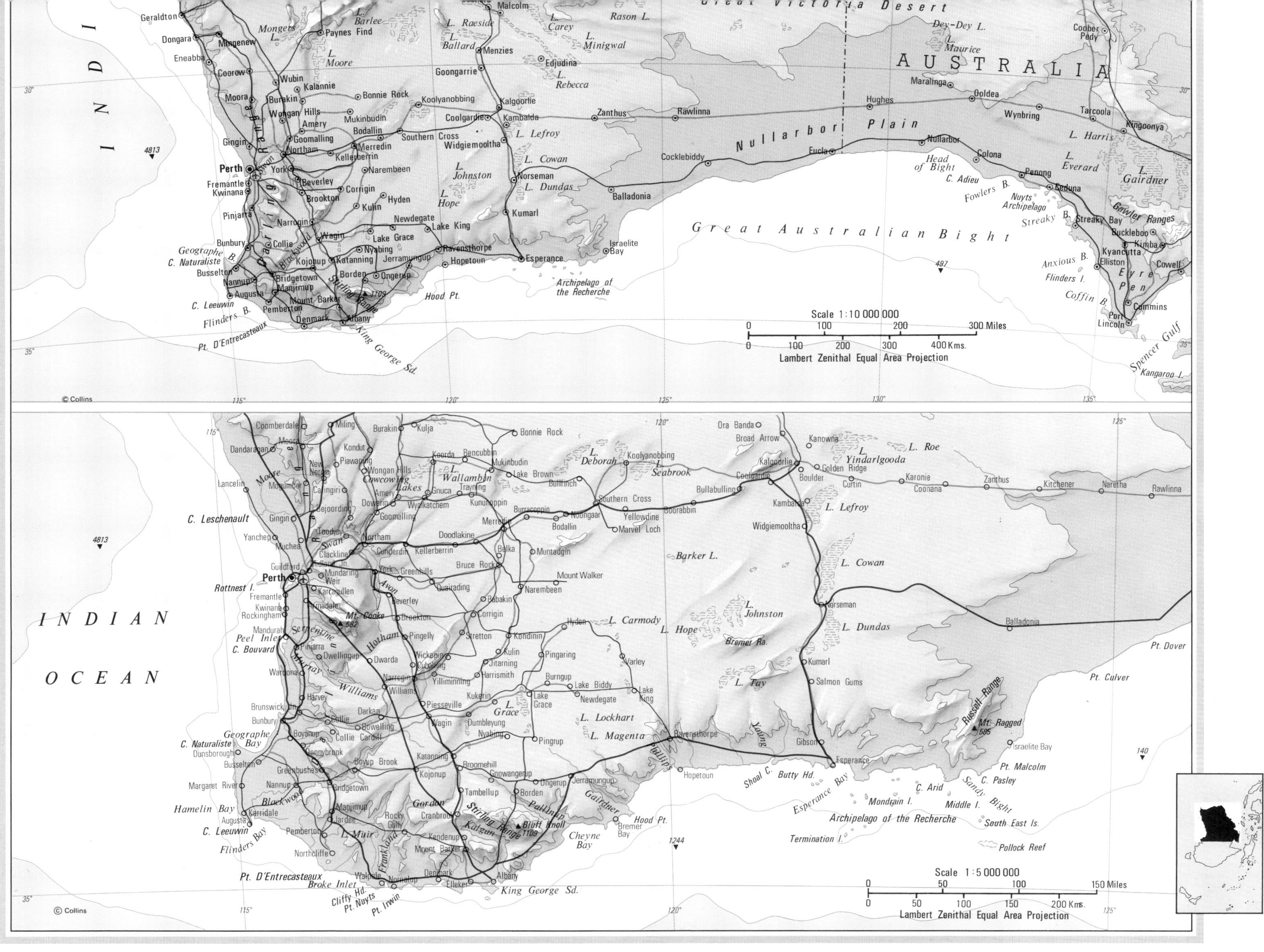

Great Victoria Desert
AUSTRALIA
Nullarbor Plain
Great Australian Bight
INDIAN OCEAN
Archipelago of the Recherche
Eyre Pen.
Spencer Gulf
Kangaroo I.
Gawler Ranges
Scale 1:10 000 000
Lambert Zenithal Equal Area Projection
Scale 1:5 000 000
Lambert Zenithal Equal Area Projection
Perth
Fremantle
Kwinana
Rockingham
Mandurah
Bunbury
Busselton
Augusta
Albany
Denmark
Esperance
Kalgoorlie
Boulder
Coolgardie
Norseman
Southern Cross
Merredin
Northam
York
Geraldton
Dongara
Eucla
Ceduna
Port Lincoln
Cowell
Kimba
Rottnest I.
C. Leeuwin
C. Naturaliste
Geographe Bay
King George Sd.
Pt. D'Entrecasteaux
Stirling Range
L. Lefroy
L. Cowan
L. Dundas
L. Johnston
L. Magenta
L. Grace
© Collins

EASTERN AUSTRALIA

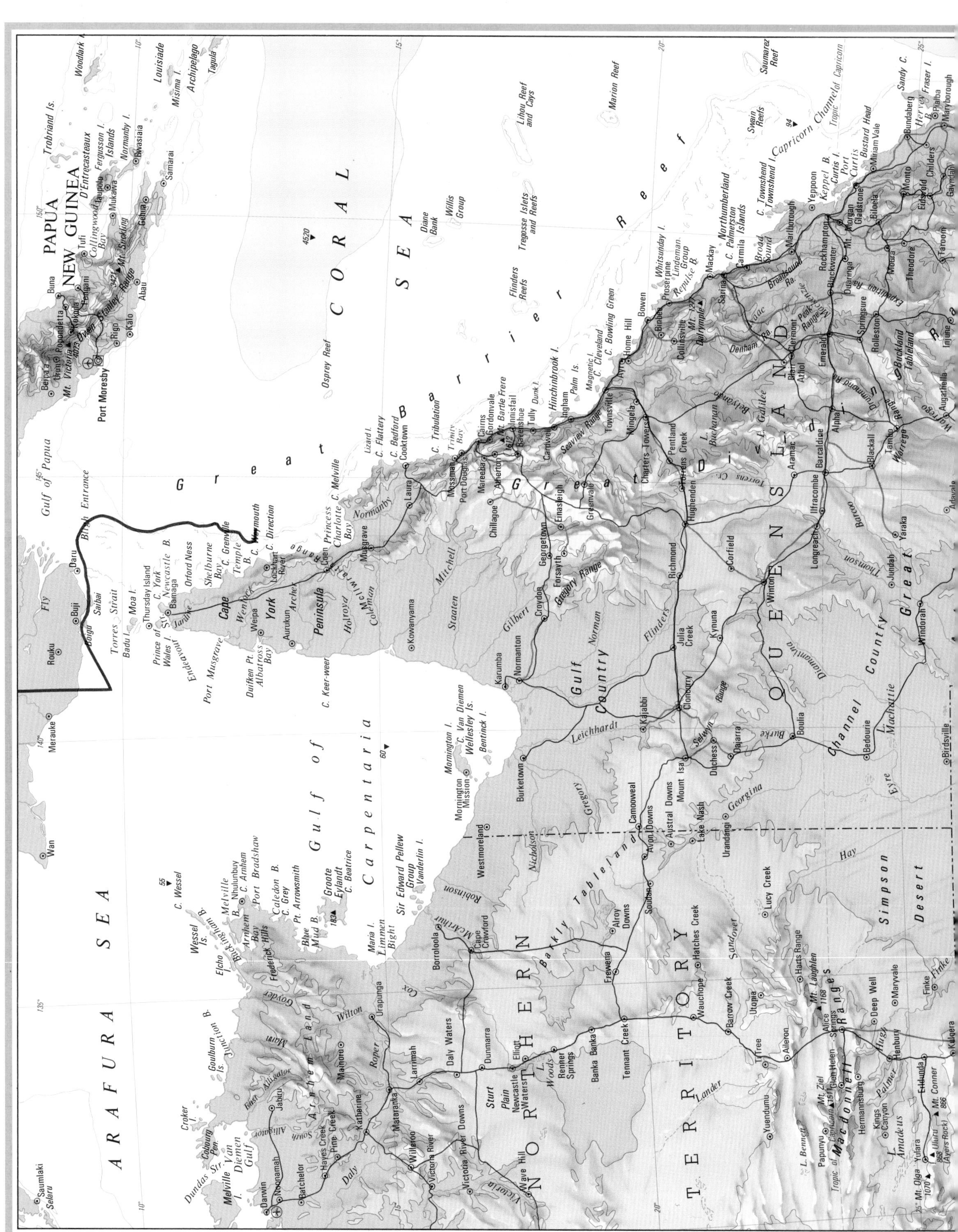

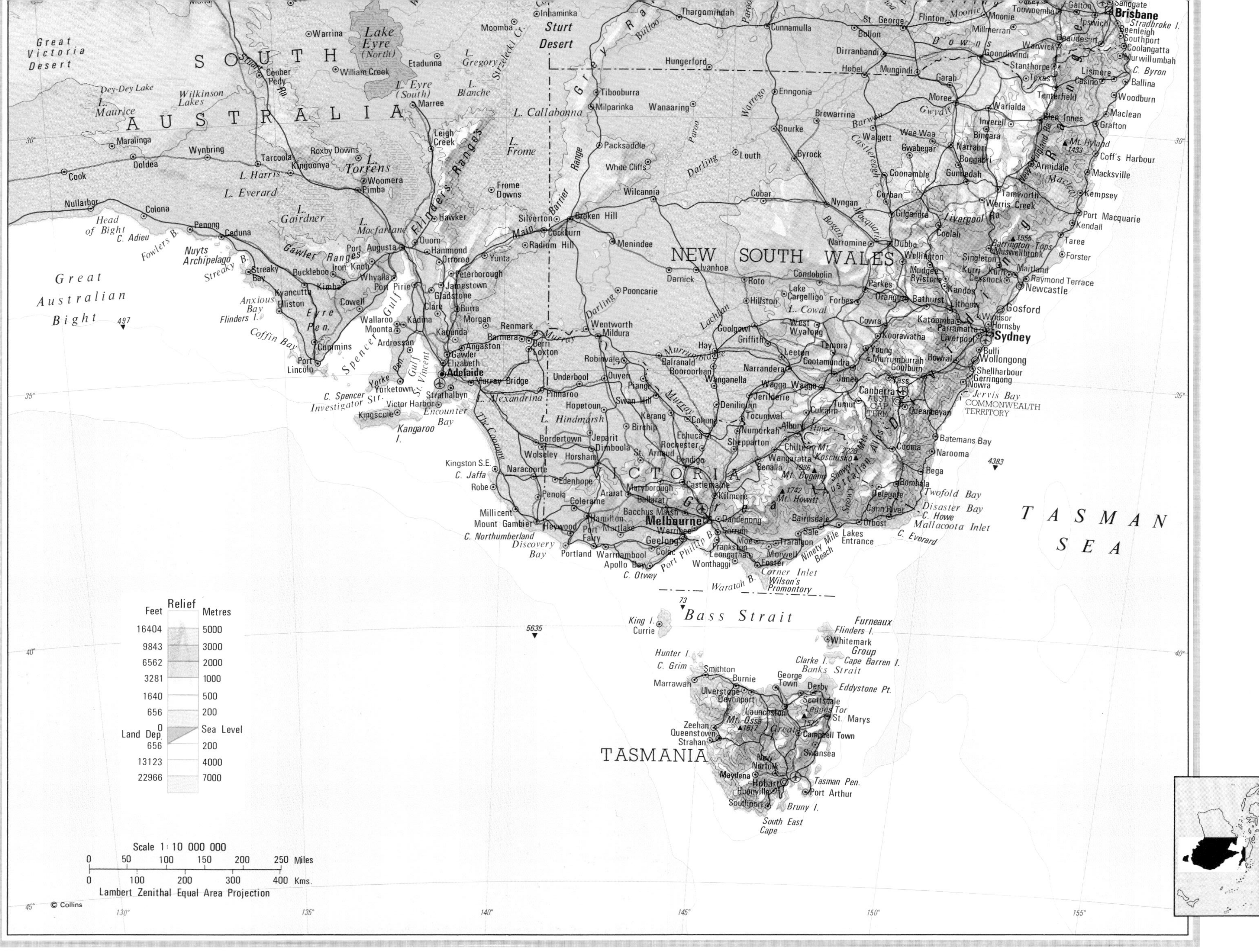
SOUTH AUSTRALIA
NEW SOUTH WALES
VICTORIA
TASMANIA
TASMAN SEA
Great Australian Bight
Bass Strait
Great Victoria Desert
Sturt Desert
Brisbane
Sydney
Canberra
Melbourne
Adelaide
Hobart
Relief
Feet
Metres
16404 5000
9843 3000
6562 2000
3281 1000
1640 500
656 200
0 Sea Level
Land Dep. 656 200
13123 4000
22966 7000
Scale 1: 10 000 000
0 50 100 150 200 250 Miles
0 100 200 300 400 Kms.
Lambert Zenithal Equal Area Projection
© Collins

SOUTHEAST AUSTRALIA

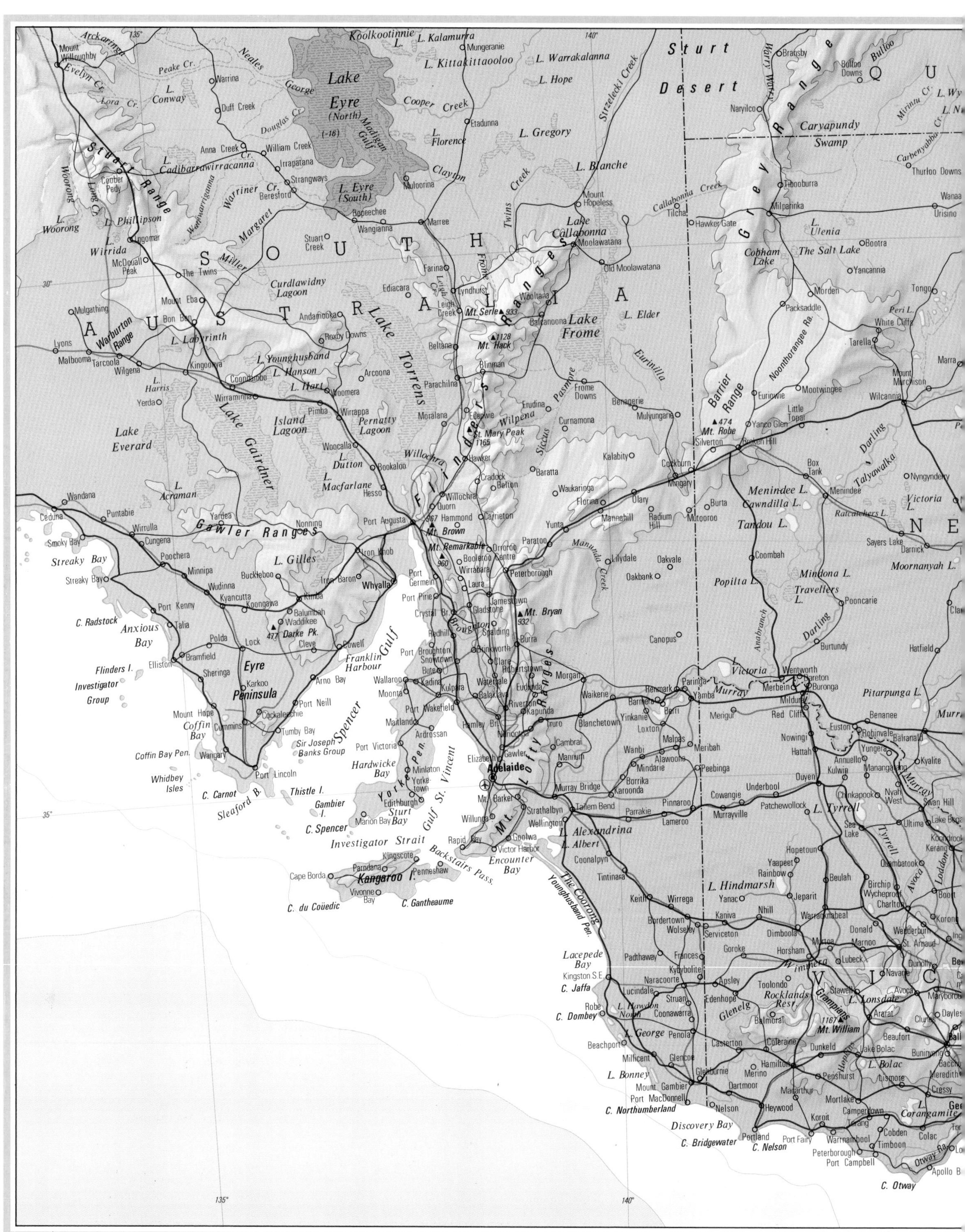

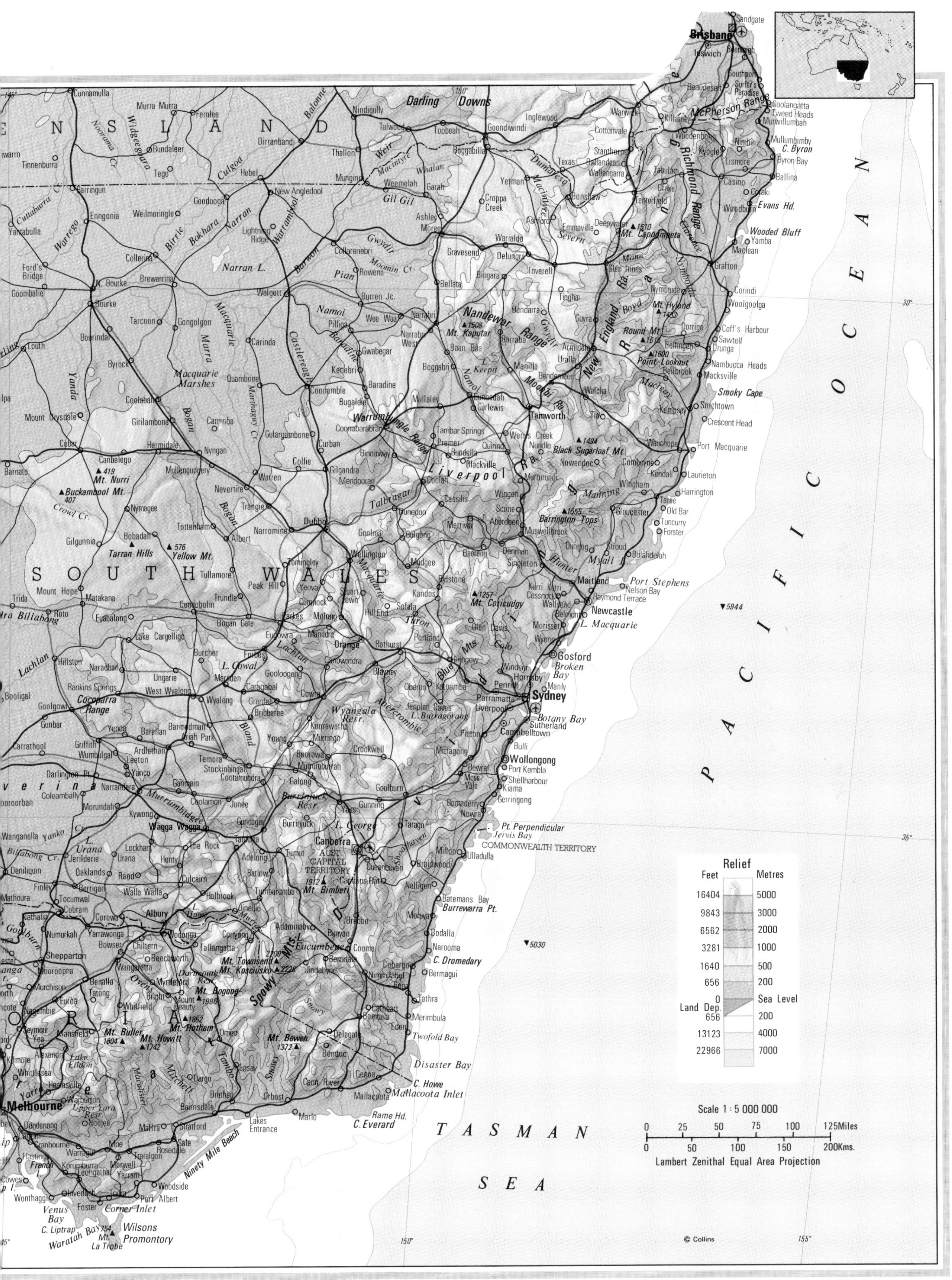

Brisbane
Ipswich
Sydney
Canberra
Melbourne
Newcastle
Wollongong
Tamworth
Dubbo
Orange
Bathurst
Wagga Wagga
Albury
Goulburn
Gosford
Maitland
Grafton
Coff's Harbour
Port Macquarie
Armidale
Lismore
Toowoomba
SOUTH WALES
AUST. CAPITAL TERRITORY
COMMONWEALTH TERRITORY
PACIFIC OCEAN
TASMAN SEA
Great Dividing Range
New England Ra.
Liverpool Ra.
Blue Mts.
Snowy Mts.
Mt. Kosciusko 2228
Mt. Townsend 2209
Darling Downs
Macquarie Marshes
Wilsons Promontory
Ninety Mile Beach
Botany Bay
Jervis Bay
C. Howe
C. Byron
Relief
Feet
Metres
16404
5000
9843
3000
6562
2000
3281
1000
1640
500
656
200
0
Sea Level
Land Dep.
656
200
13123
4000
22966
7000
Scale 1 : 5 000 000
0 25 50 75 100 125Miles
0 50 100 150 200Kms.
Lambert Zenithal Equal Area Projection
© Collins

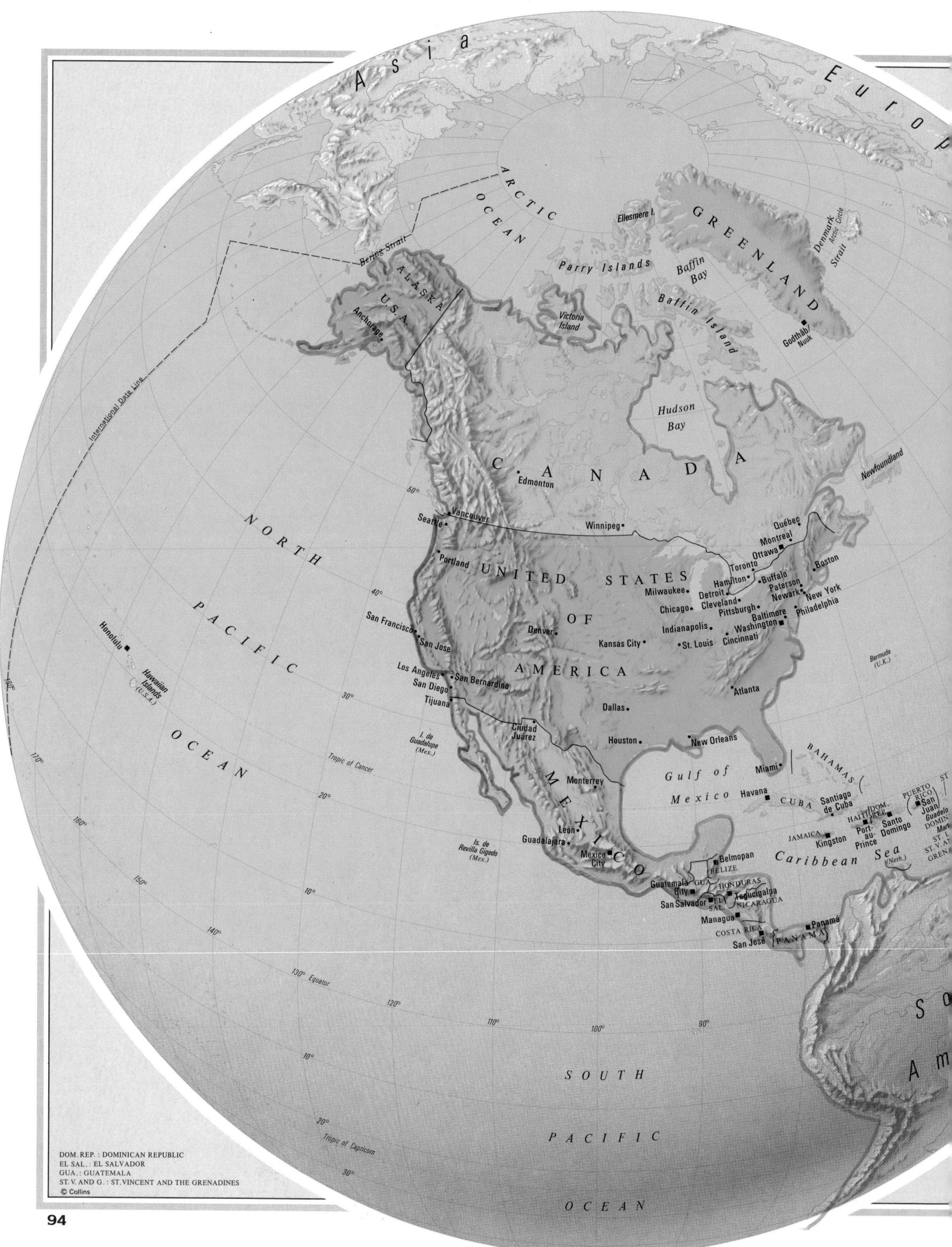

Asia

Europ

ARCTIC OCEAN

Ellesmere I.

GREENLAND

Denmark
Strait
Arctic Circle

Parry Islands

Baffin
Bay

Baffin Island

Bering Strait

ALASKA
USA

Anchorage

Victoria
Island

Godthåb/
Nuuk

International Date Line

Hudson
Bay

C A N A D A

Newfoundland

Edmonton

50°

Seattle
Vancouver

Winnipeg

Québec
Montreal
Ottawa

Portland

UNITED   STATES

Toronto
Hamilton
Buffalo
Paterson
Boston

Milwaukee
Detroit
Cleveland
Newark
New York

40°

OF

Chicago
Pittsburgh

San Francisco

Denver

AMERICA

Indianapolis
Baltimore
Philadelphia
Washington

San Jose

Kansas City
St. Louis
Cincinnati

Honolulu

N O R T H

Los Angeles
San Bernardino

Bermuda
(U.K.)

Hawaiian
Islands
(U.S.A.)

P A C I F I C

San Diego

30°

Atlanta

Tijuana

Dallas

I. de
Guadalupe
(Mex.)

Ciudad
Juárez

O C E A N

Houston

New Orleans

Tropic of Cancer

Miami

BAHAMAS

110°

Monterrey

20°

Gulf of

Mexico   Havana   CUBA

Santiago
de Cuba

PUERTO
RICO
San
Juan

ST.

160°

Is. de
Revilla Gigedo
(Mex.)

León

Guadalajara

Mexico
City

10°

MEXICO

HAITI DOM.
REP.

Guadelo
DOMIN

JAMAICA

Port-
au-
Prince

Santo
Domingo

ST. L

Kingston

ST. V. AN

150°

Belmopan

BELIZE

Caribbean Sea

(Neth.)

GRENA

Guatemala
City

GUA

HONDURAS

San Salvador

EL
SAL.

Tegucigalpa

NICARAGUA

Managua

140°

Panamá

COSTA RICA

San José

PANAMA

S o

130°   Equator

120°

S O U T H

A m

110°

100°

90°

S O U T H

10°

20°

P A C I F I C

Tropic of Capricorn

30°

O C E A N

NORTH AMERICA

NORTH AMERICA

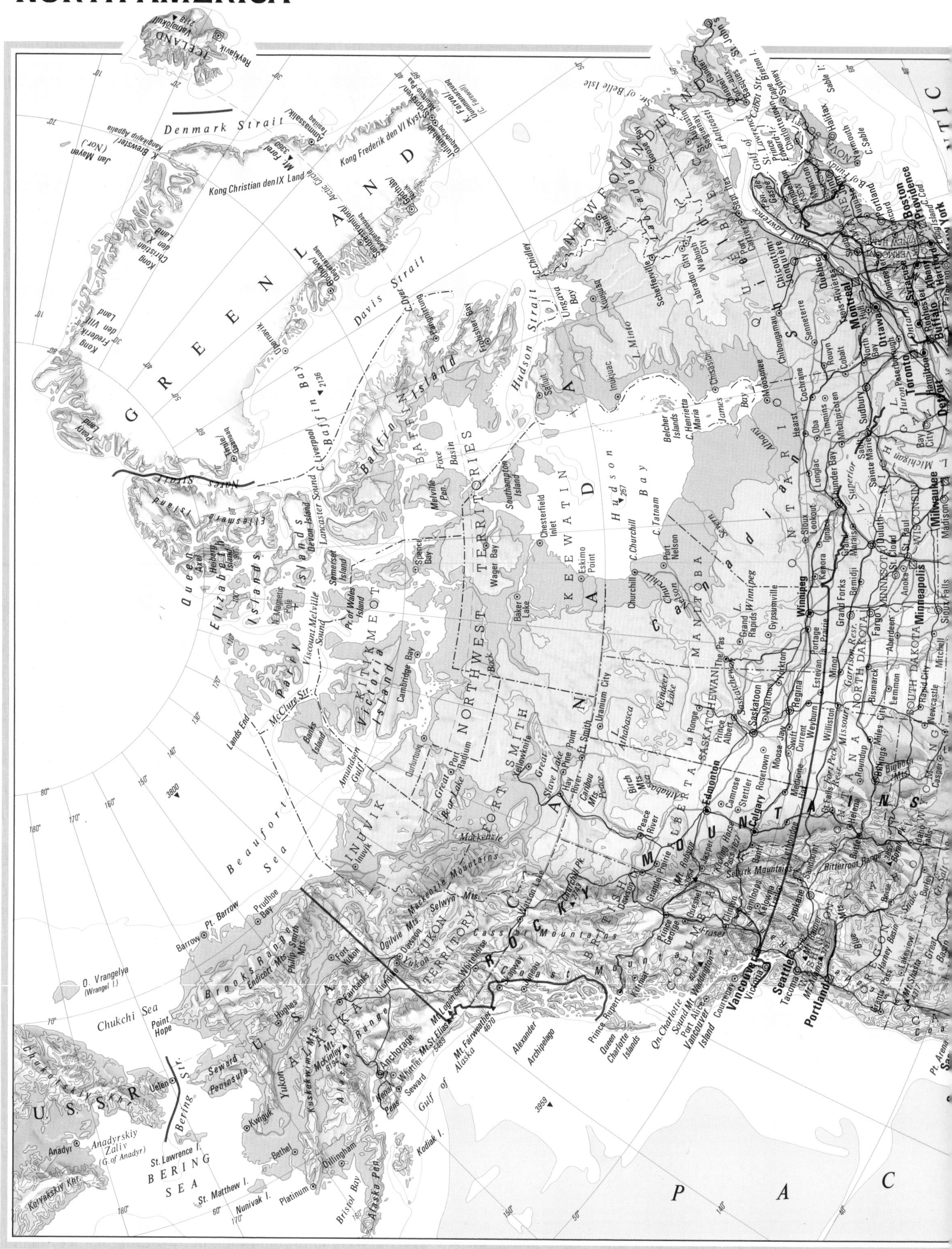

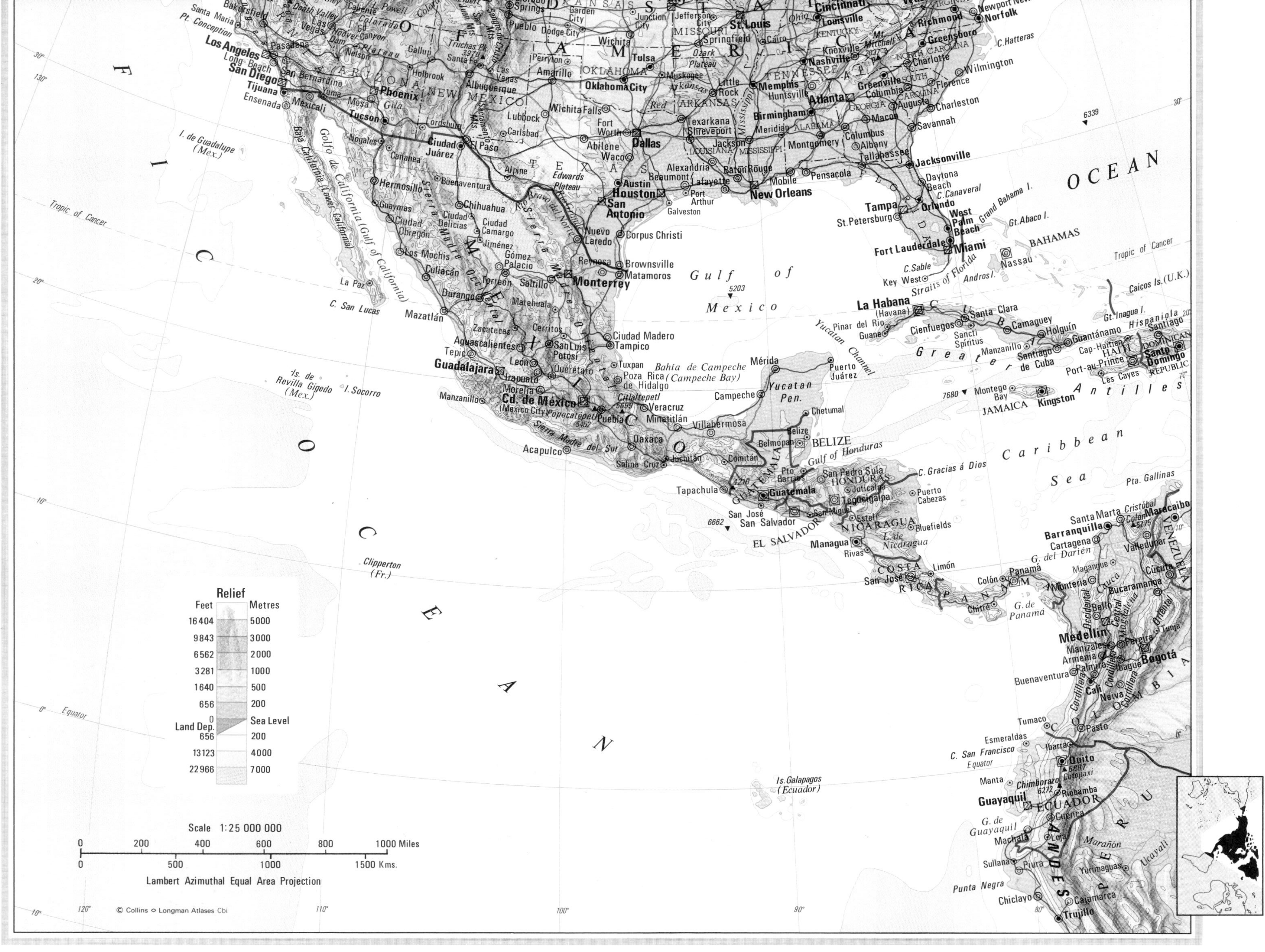

P A C I F I C   O C E A N
OCEAN
Gulf of Mexico
Caribbean Sea
Greater Antilles
Tropic of Cancer
Equator
BAHAMAS
JAMAICA
BELIZE
HONDURAS
NICARAGUA
EL SALVADOR
COSTA RICA
PANAMA
VENEZUELA
ECUADOR
ANDES
Golfo de California (Gulf of California)
Baja California (Lower California)
Yucatan Pen.
Yucatan Channel
Bahía de Campeche (Campeche Bay)
Gulf of Honduras
Clipperton (Fr.)
Is. Galapagos (Ecuador)
Is. de Revilla Gigedo (Mex.)
I. de Guadalupe (Mex.)
Relief
Feet
Metres
16404
5000
9843
3000
6562
2000
3281
1000
1640
500
656
200
0
Sea Level
Land Dep. 656
200
13123
4000
22966
7000
Scale 1:25 000 000
0 200 400 600 800 1000 Miles
0 500 1000 1500 Kms.
Lambert Azimuthal Equal Area Projection
© Collins ◇ Longman Atlases Cbi

CANADA AND ALASKA

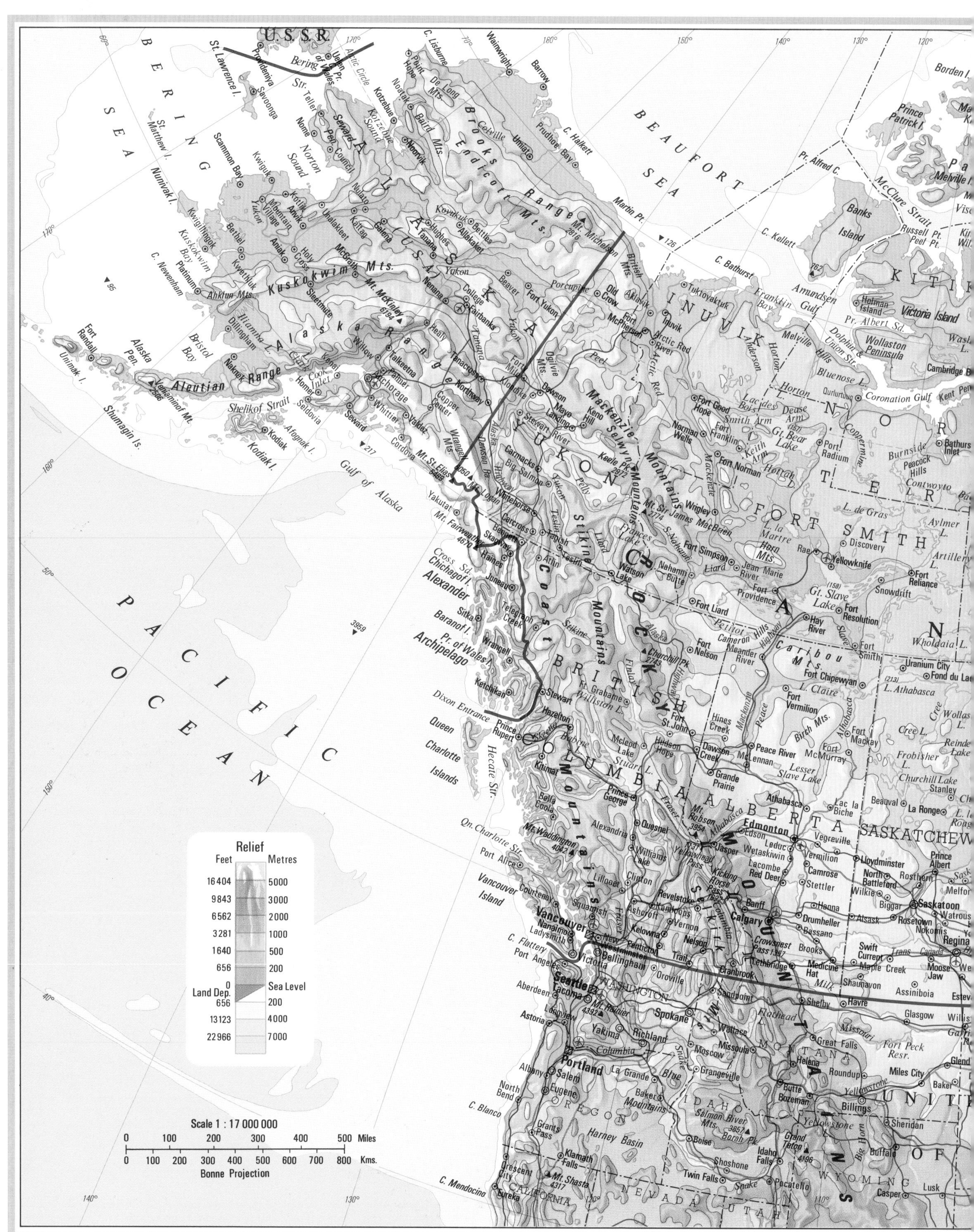

BERING SEA

U.S.S.R.

BEAUFORT SEA

PACIFIC OCEAN

ALASKA U.S.A.

Gulf of Alaska

Aleutian Range

Brooks Range

Endicott Mts.

Kuskokwim Mts.

Alaska Range

Mt. McKinley 6194

YUKON

Mackenzie Mountains

Selwyn Mountains

BRITISH COLUMBIA

Coast Mountains

ALBERTA

SASKATCHEWAN

ROCKY MOUNTAINS

COLUMBIA MOUNTAINS

N.W. TERR.

FORT SMITH

INUVIK

Gt. Slave Lake

Gt. Bear Lake

L. Athabasca

Alexander Archipelago

Queen Charlotte Islands

Vancouver Island

WASHINGTON

OREGON

IDAHO

MONTANA

WYOMING

NEVADA

CALIFORNIA

UTAH

UNITED STATES OF

Relief

Feet		Metres
16 404		5000
9 843		3000
6 562		2000
3 281		1000
1 640		500
656		200
0	Sea Level	
Land Dep.		
656		200
13 123		4000
22 966		7000

Scale 1 : 17 000 000

0	100	200	300	400	500 Miles

| 0 | 100 | 200 | 300 | 400 | 500 | 600 | 700 | 800 Kms. |

Bonne Projection

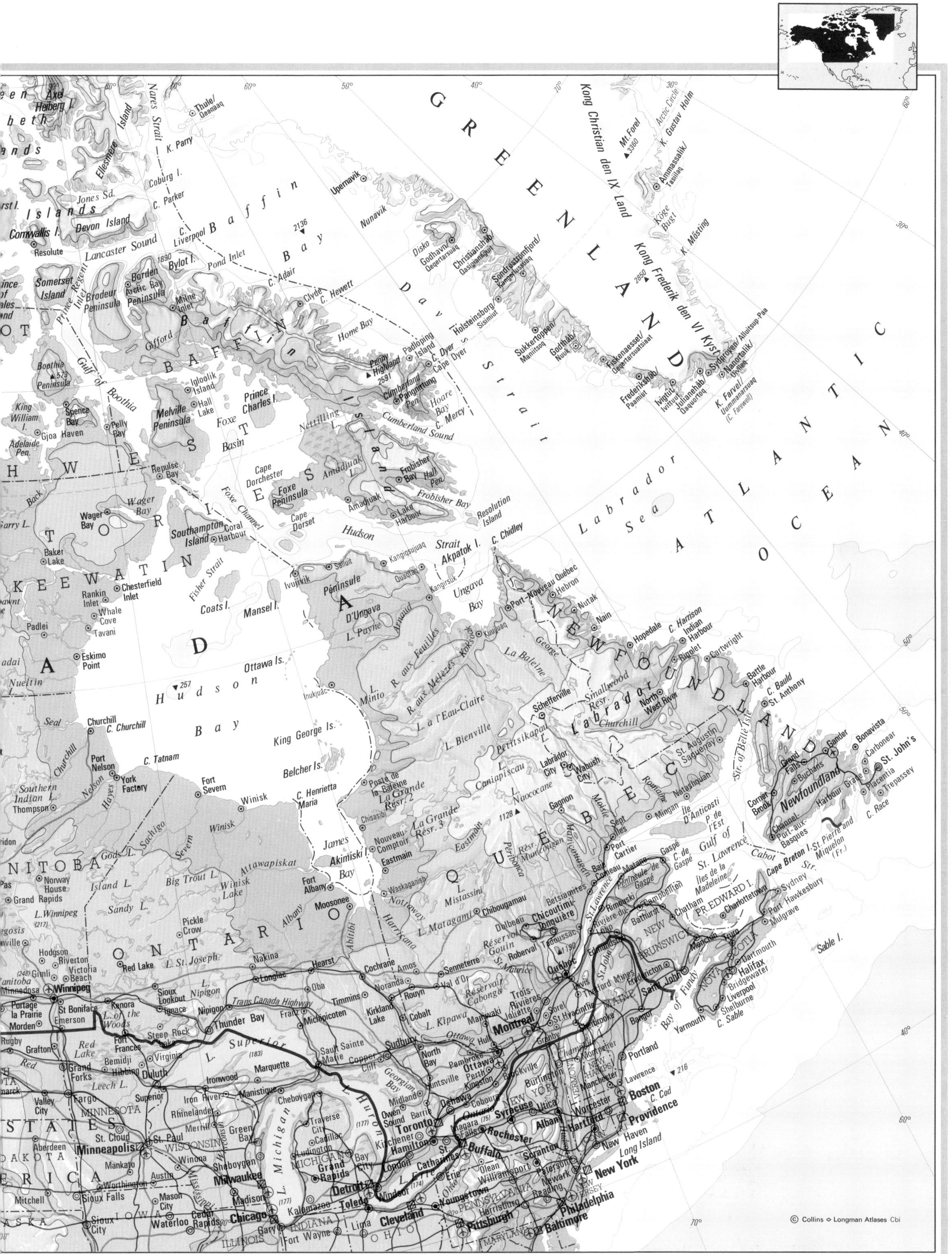
GREENLAND
Kong Christian den IX Land
Kong Frederik den VI Kyst
Davis Strait
Baffin Bay
Baffin Island
Labrador Sea
ATLANTIC OCEAN
Hudson Bay
Hudson Strait
James Bay
Ungava Bay
Foxe Basin
Foxe Channel
Foxe Peninsula
Melville Peninsula
Boothia Peninsula
Gulf of Boothia
Lancaster Sound
Devon Island
Ellesmere Island
Axel Heiberg I.
Nares Strait
Somerset Island
Cornwallis I.
Resolute
Bylot I.
Pond Inlet
Southampton Island
Coats I.
Mansel I.
Belcher Is.
Ottawa Is.
King George Is.
Akimiski I.
Akpatok I.
C. Chidley
Resolution Island
Cumberland Sound
Frobisher Bay
Prince Charles I.
NORTHWEST TERRITORIES
KEEWATIN
FRANKLIN
CANADA
MANITOBA
ONTARIO
QUEBEC
NEWFOUNDLAND
Labrador
NEW BRUNSWICK
NOVA SCOTIA
PR. EDWARD I.
Newfoundland
Gulf of St. Lawrence
Cabot Str.
Bay of Fundy
St. Pierre and Miquelon (Fr.)
Cape Breton I.
Sable I.
Île d'Anticosti
Str. of Belle Isle
Churchill
Winnipeg
Thunder Bay
L. Superior
L. Michigan
L. Huron
L. Erie
Ontario
Sault Sainte Marie
Sudbury
Ottawa
Montréal
Québec
Chicoutimi-Jonquière
Toronto
Hamilton
Windsor
Detroit
Chicago
Milwaukee
Minneapolis
St. Paul
Duluth
Buffalo
Rochester
Syracuse
Cleveland
Pittsburgh
Philadelphia
New York
Boston
Providence
Baltimore
Halifax
St. John's
Saint John
Fredericton
Charlottetown
Sydney
Gander
Corner Brook
Goose Bay
Schefferville
Labrador City
UNITED STATES
AMERICA
© Collins ◇ Longman Atlases Cbi

WESTERN CANADA

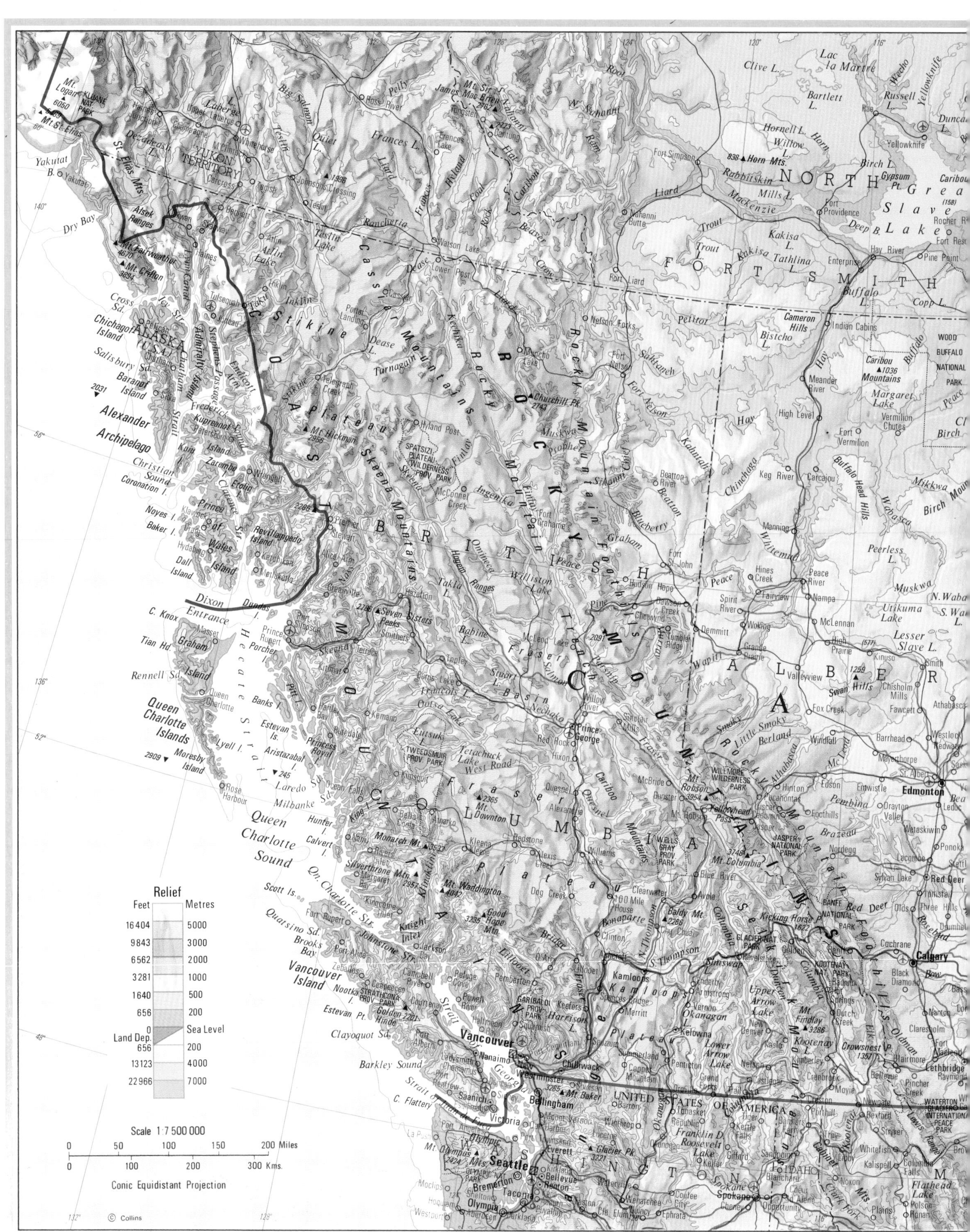

Relief

Feet	Metres
16 404	5000
9843	3000
6562	2000
3281	1000
1640	500
656	200
0	Sea Level

Land Dep.

656	200
13 123	4000
22 966	7000

Scale 1:7 500 000

0 50 100 150 200 Miles

0 100 200 300 Kms.

Conic Equidistant Projection

© Collins

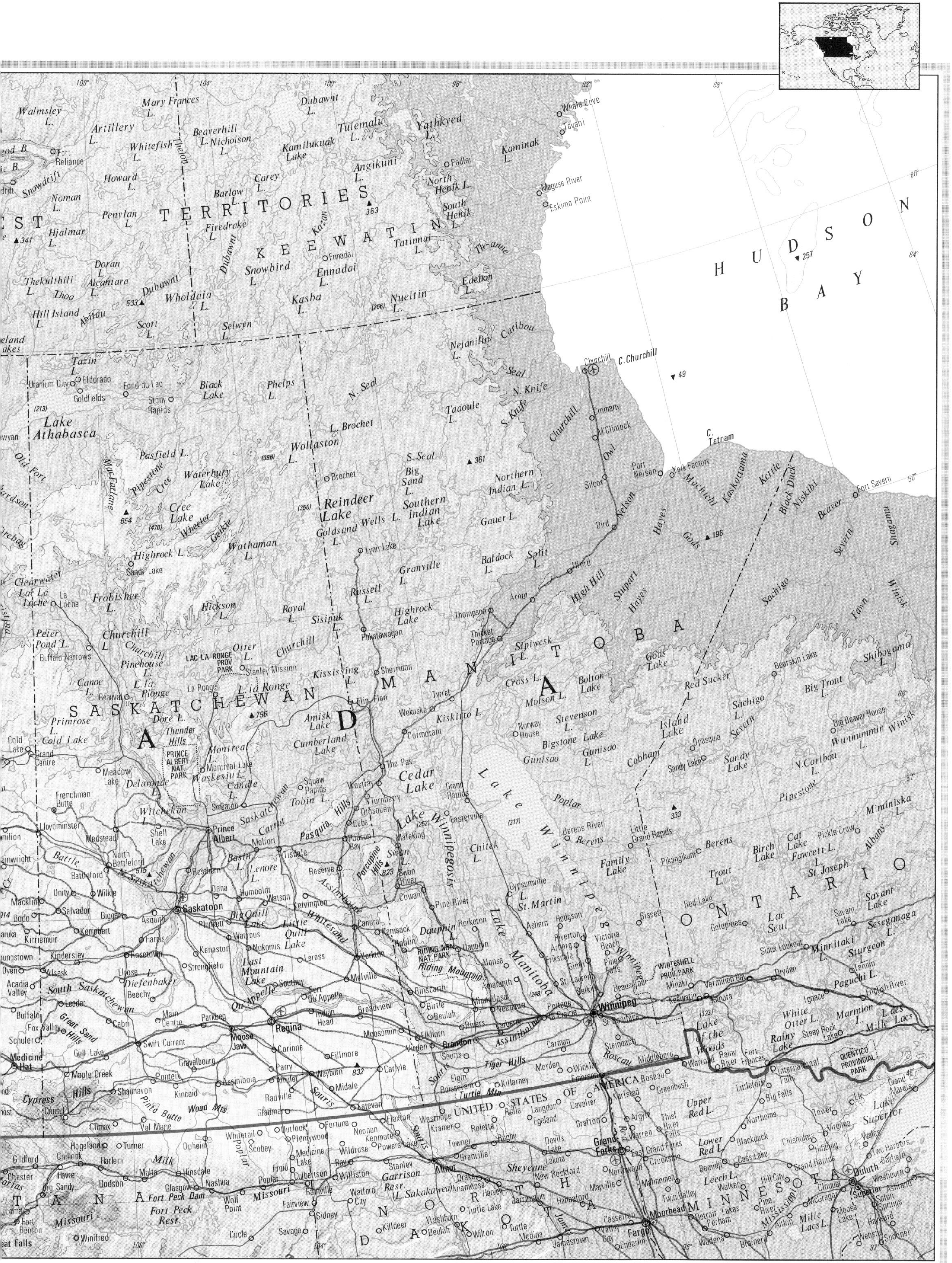

EASTERN CANADA

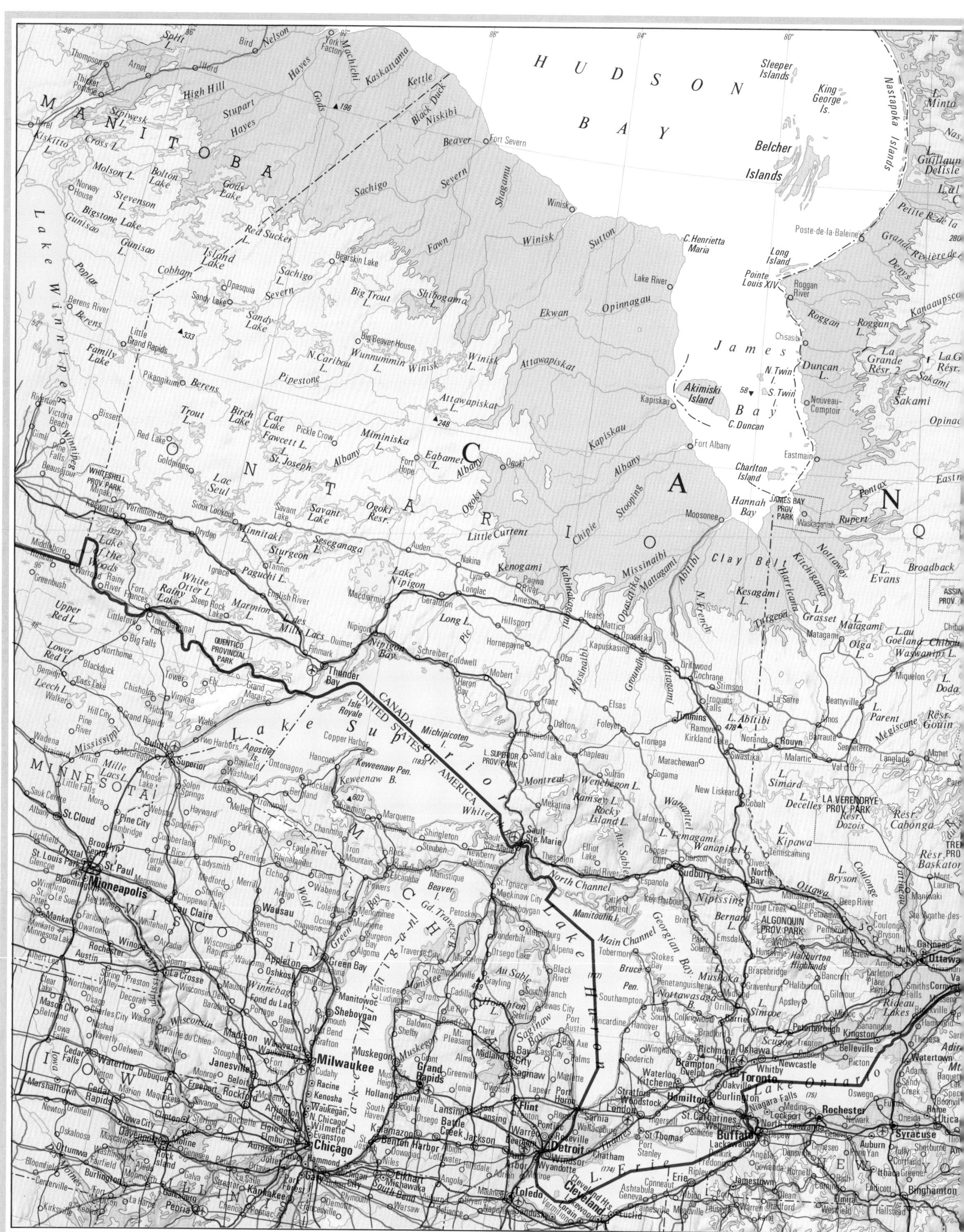

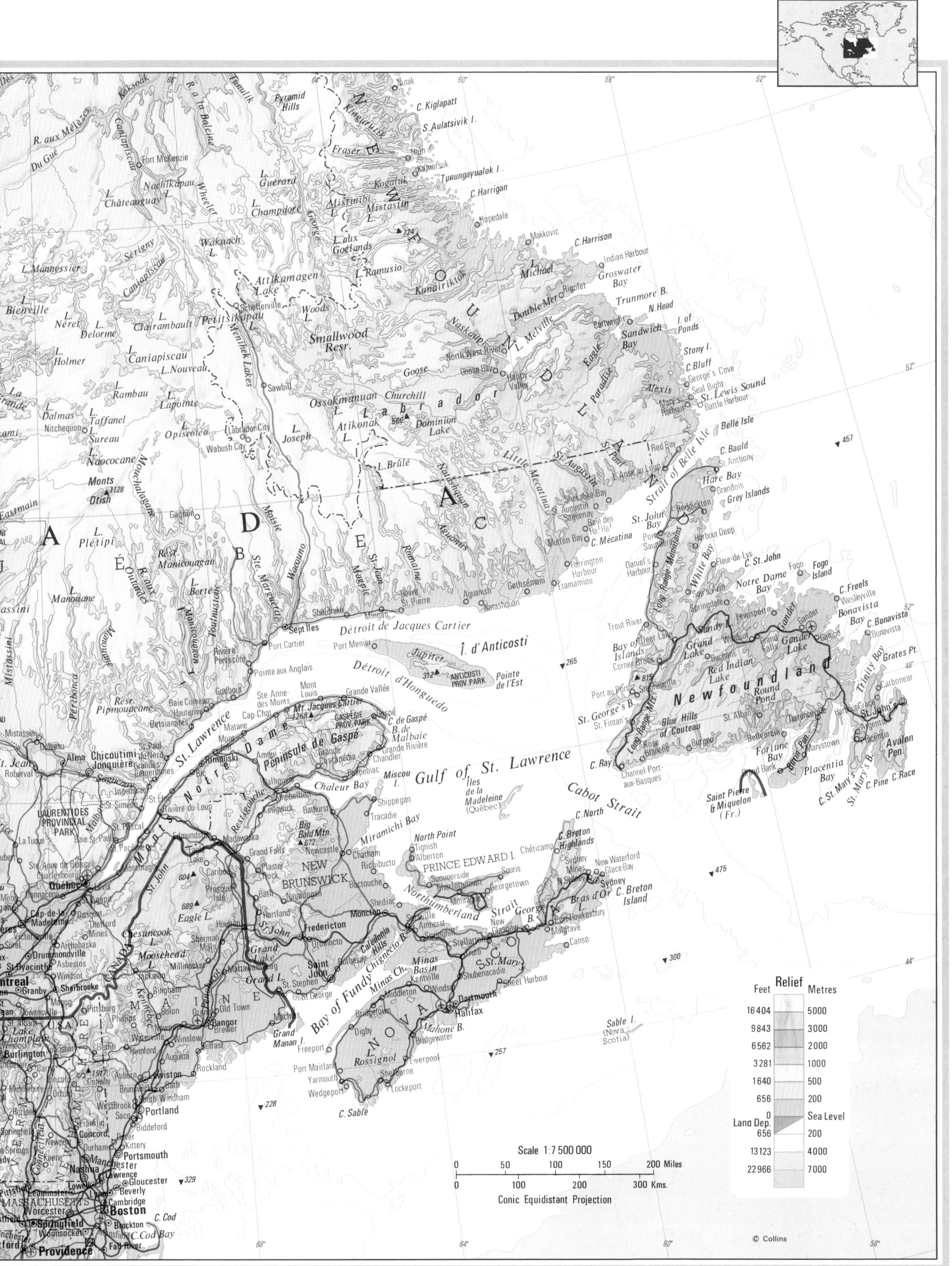

SOUTH CENTRAL CANADA

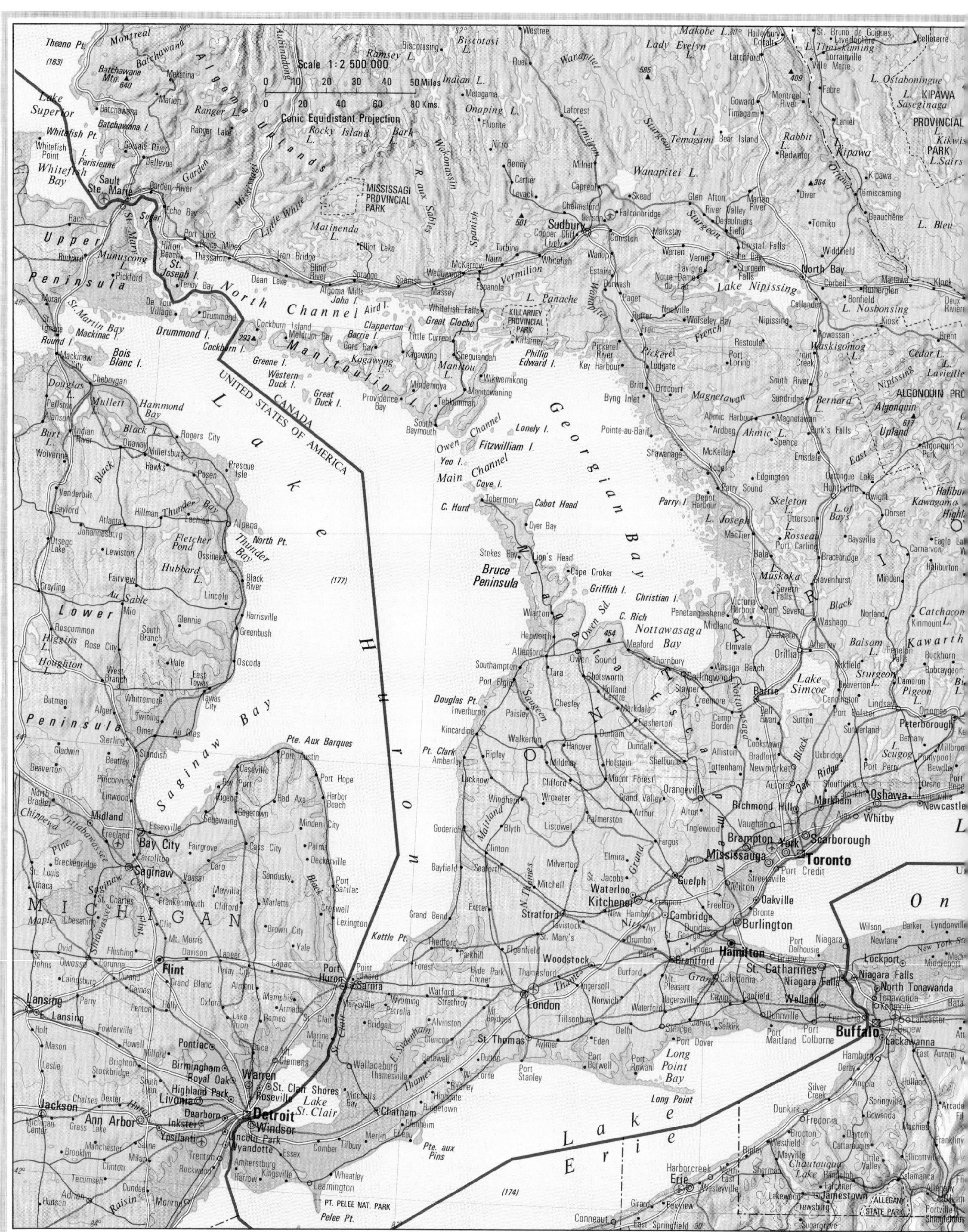

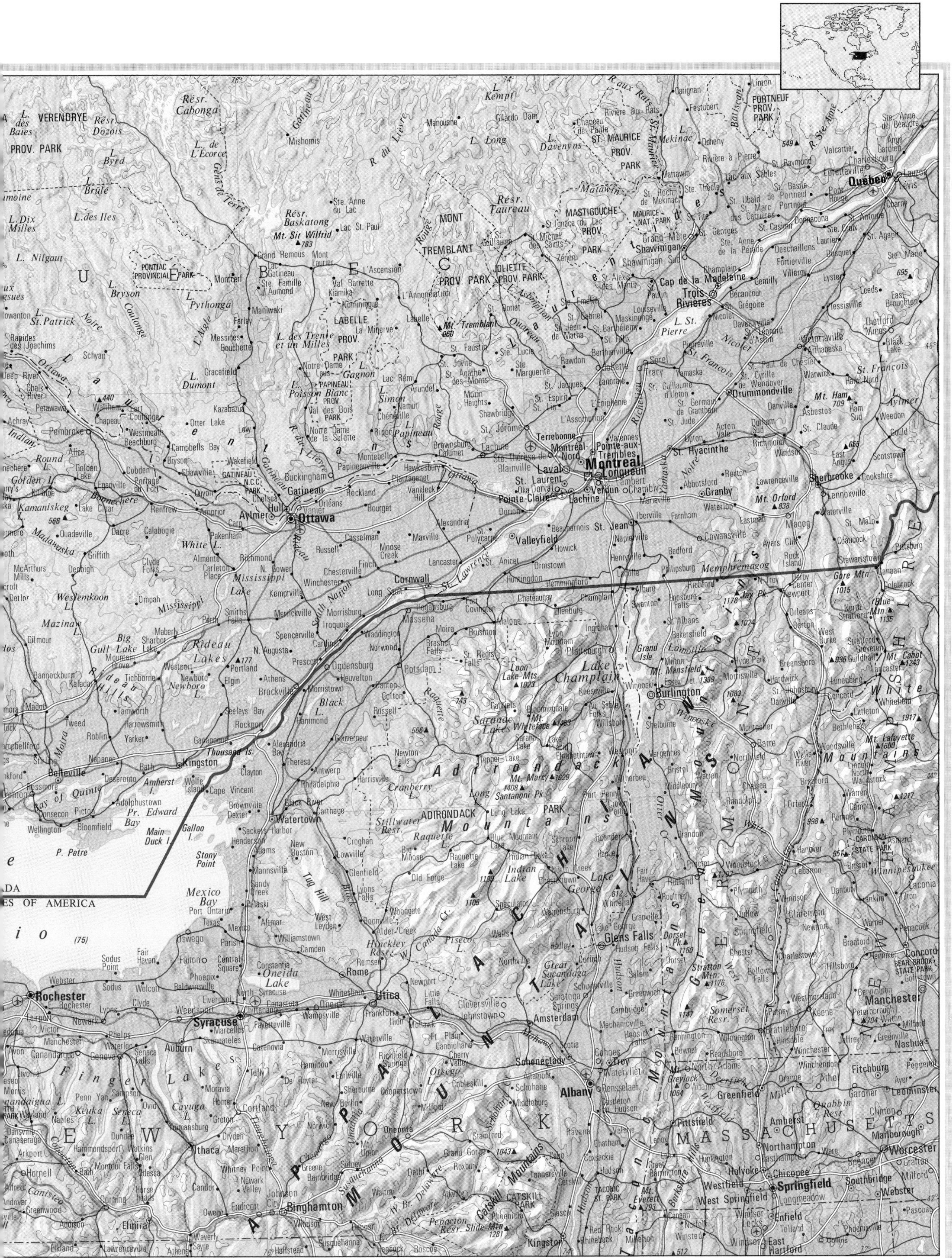
Québec
Trois Rivières
Cap de la Madeleine
Shawinigan
Montreal
Laval
Longueuil
Verdun
Lachine
Pointe-Claire
St. Laurent
Ottawa
Hull
Gatineau
Aylmer
Valleyfield
Cornwall
Drummondville
Sherbrooke
Granby
Kingston
Belleville
Watertown
Ogdensburg
Burlington
Plattsburgh
Glens Falls
Albany
Schenectady
Troy
Utica
Rome
Syracuse
Rochester
Auburn
Ithaca
Elmira
Binghamton
Kingston
Pittsfield
Springfield
West Springfield
Holyoke
Worcester
Fitchburg
Manchester
Concord
Lake Champlain
Oneida Lake
Mont Tremblant
Mt. Marcy 1629
Mt. Mansfield 1339
Adirondack Mountains
Catskill Mountains
Taconic Mountains
Green Mountains
White Mountains
Finger Lakes
Thousand Is.
St. Lawrence
Ottawa
Memphremagog
APPALACHIAN MOUNTAINS
NEW YORK
MASSACHUSETTS
VERMONT
NEW HAMPSHIRE
QUEBEC

UNITED STATES

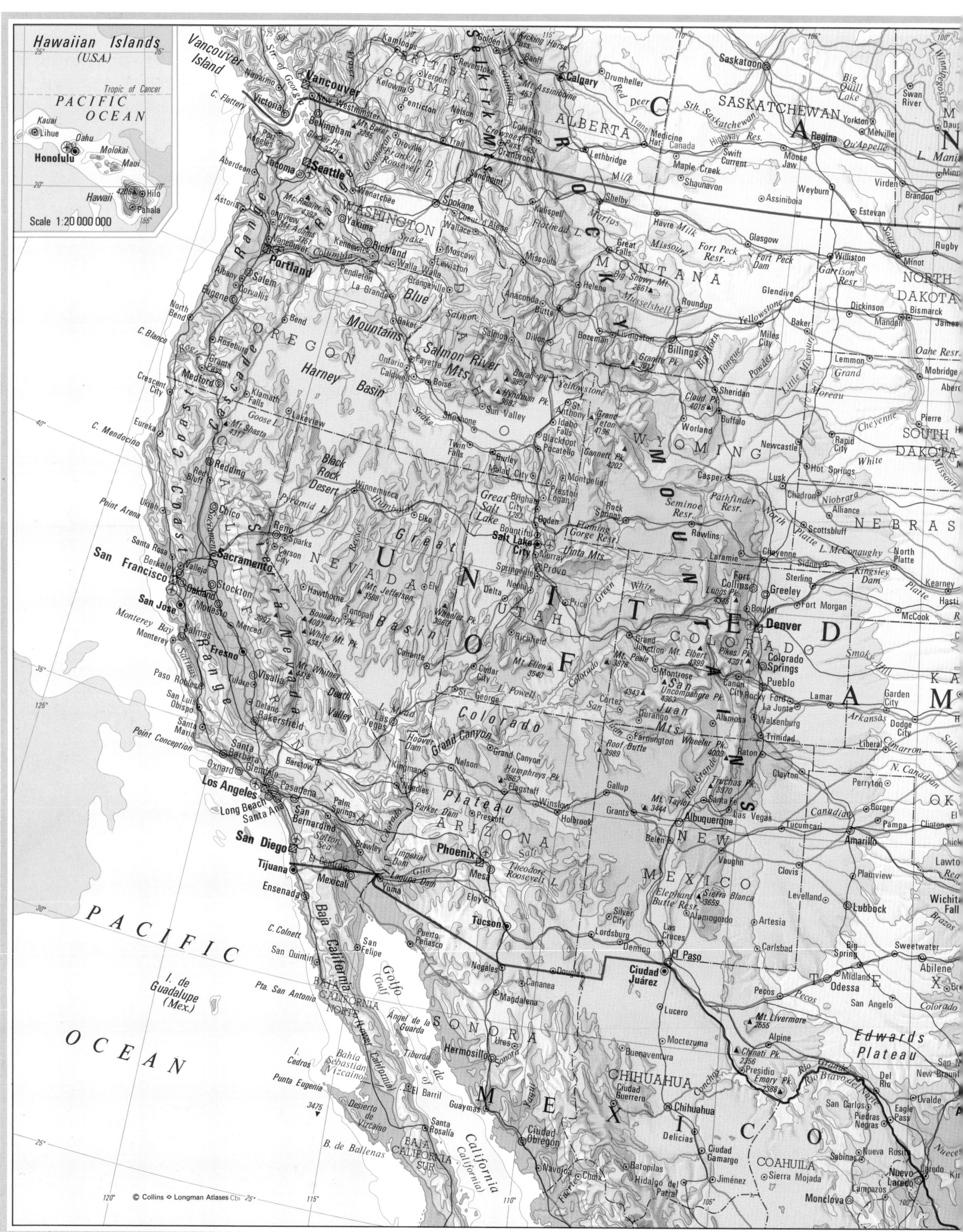

Hawaiian Islands (U.S.A.)

PACIFIC OCEAN

Scale 1:20 000 000

© Collins ◇ Longman Atlases

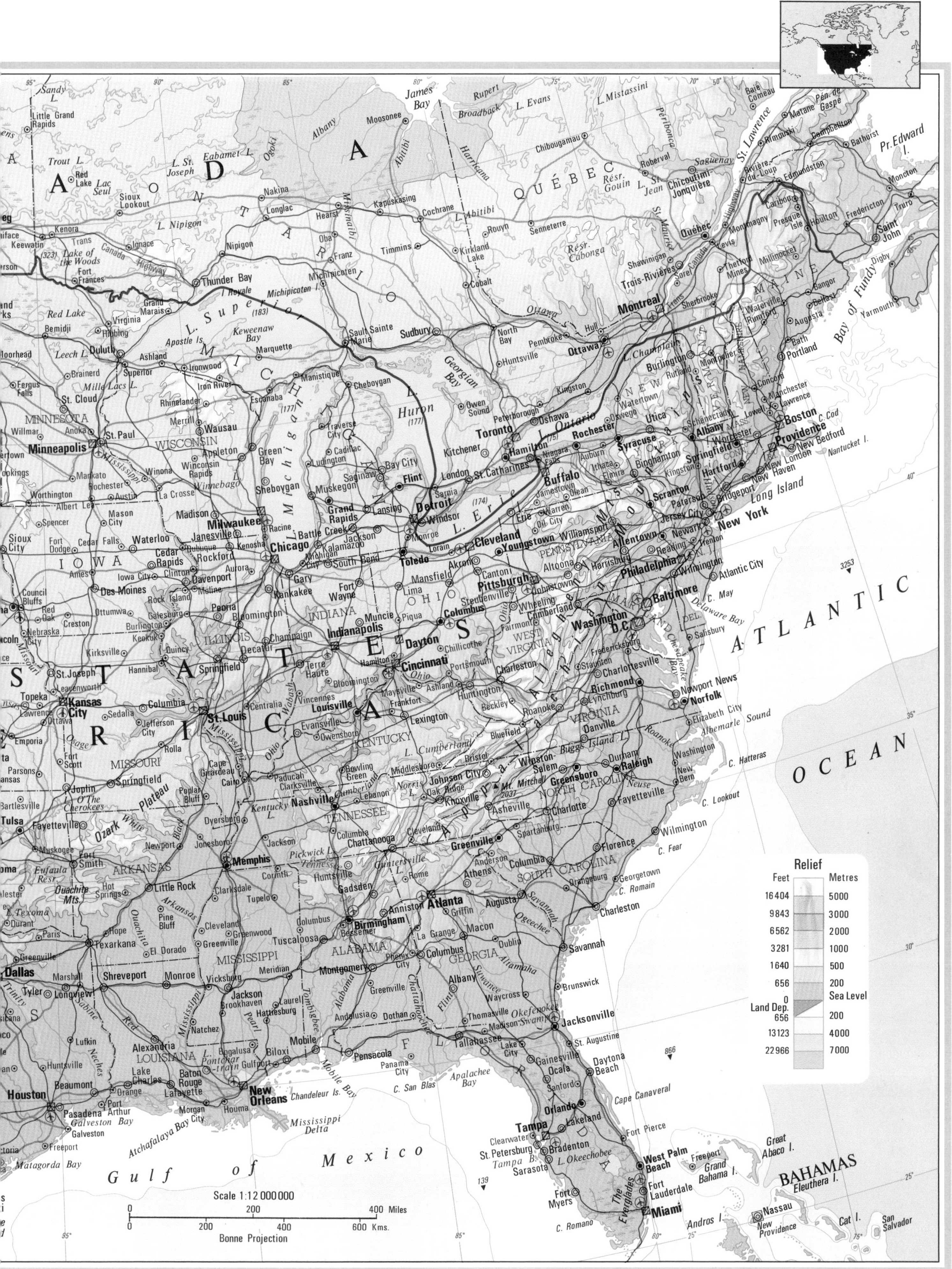

Scale 1:12 000 000

0   200   400 Miles
0   200   400   600 Kms.

Bonne Projection

Relief		
Feet		Metres
16 404		5000
9843		3000
6562		2000
3281		1000
1640		500
656		200
0		Sea Level
Land Dep.		200
656		
13123		4000
22966		7000

WESTERN UNITED STATES

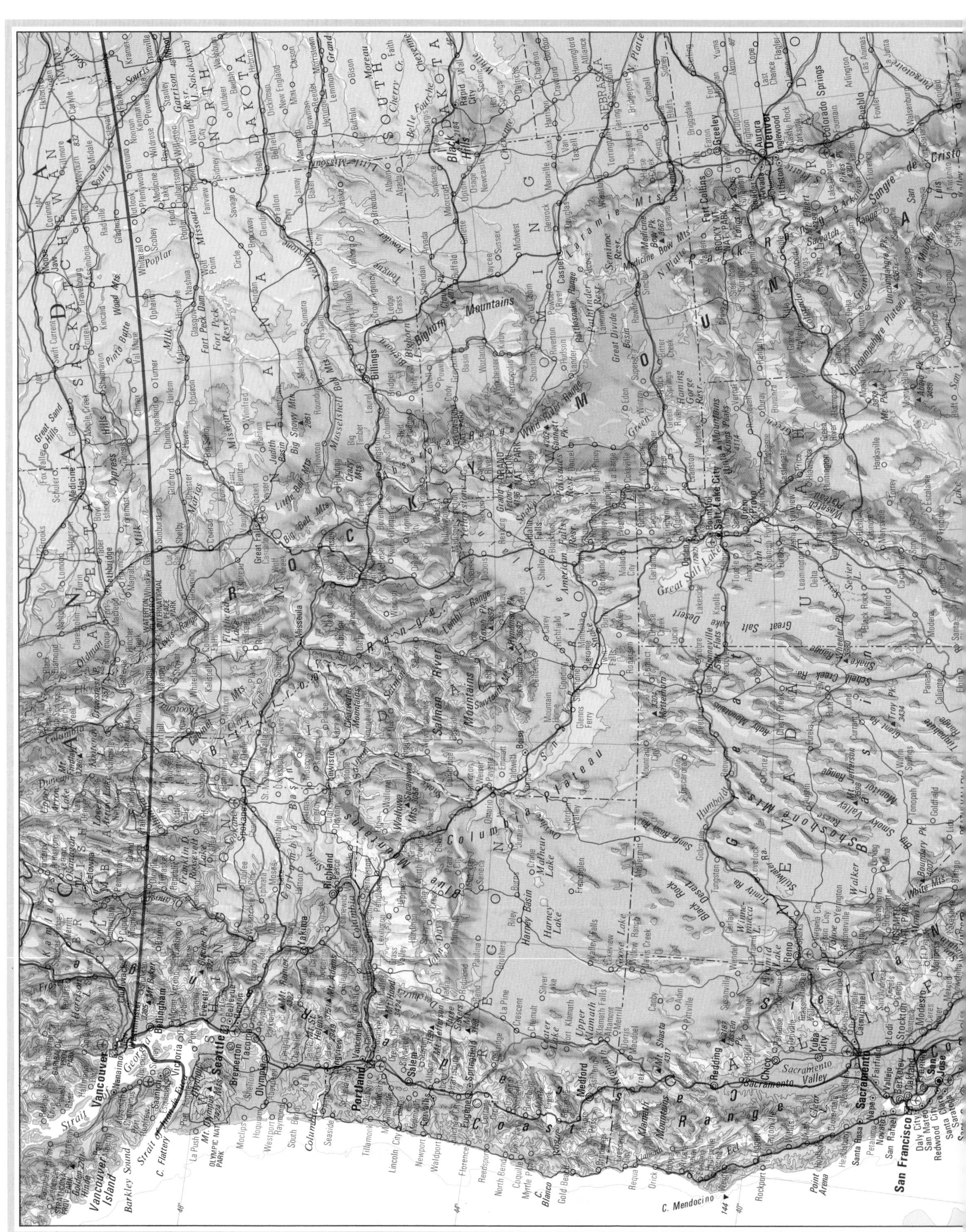

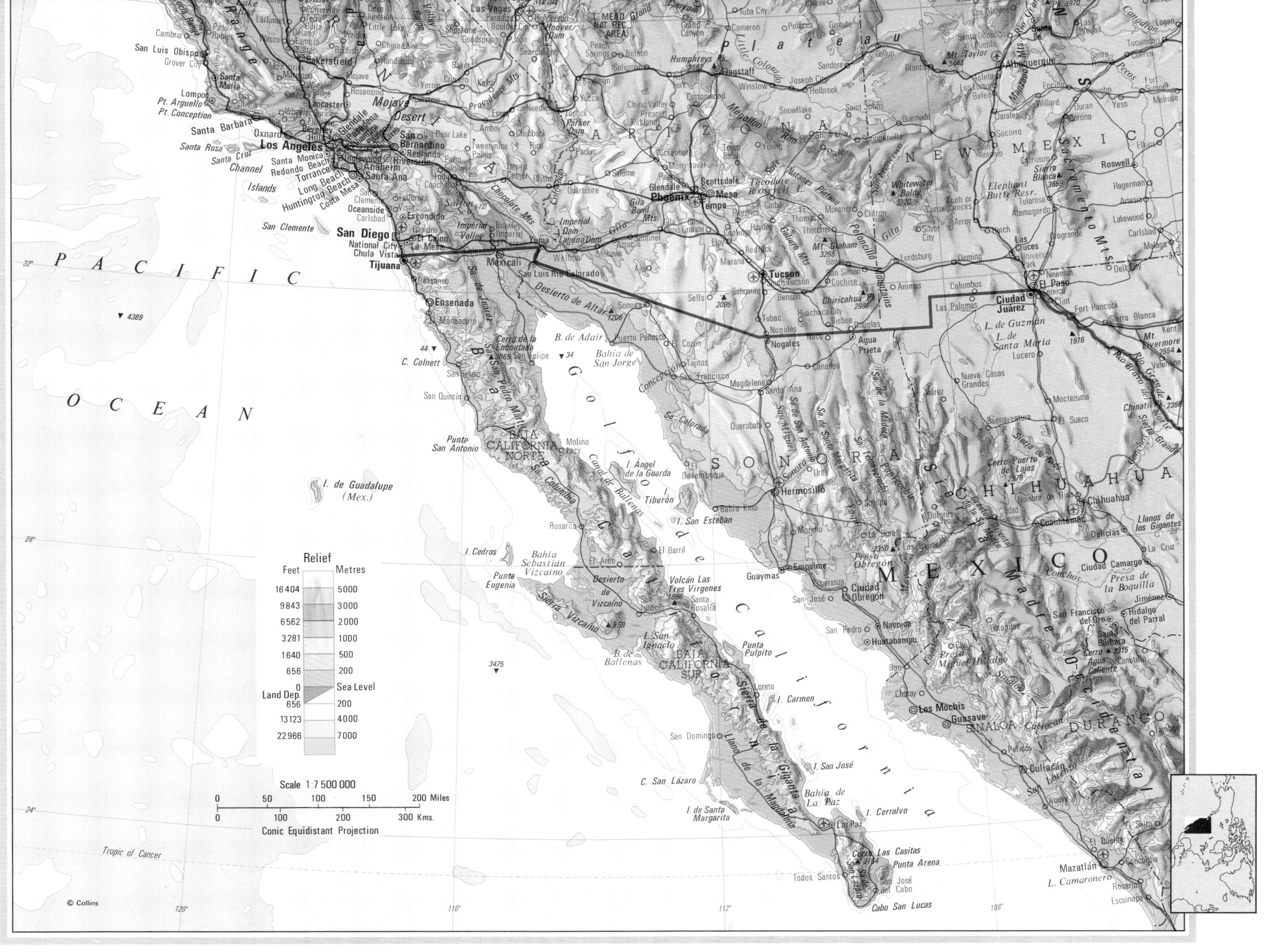
P A C I F I C
O C E A N
Golfo de California
NEW MEXICO
ARIZONA
SONORA
CHIHUAHUA
MEXICO
BAJA CALIFORNIA NORTE
BAJA CALIFORNIA SUR
SINALOA
DURANGO
Sierra Madre Occidental
Mojave Desert
Desierto de Altar
Desierto de Vizcaíno
Los Angeles
San Diego
Tijuana
Mexicali
Ensenada
Phoenix
Tucson
Nogales
Hermosillo
Guaymas
Ciudad Obregón
Los Mochis
Culiacán
Mazatlán
Chihuahua
Ciudad Juárez
El Paso
Albuquerque
Las Vegas
Bakersfield
Santa Barbara
La Paz
Cabo San Lucas
I. de Guadalupe (Mex.)
I. Cedros
I. Tiburón
I. Ángel de la Guarda
Tropic of Cancer
Relief
Feet Metres
16404 5000
9843 3000
6562 2000
3281 1000
1640 500
656 200
0 Sea Level
Land Dep. 656 200
13123 4000
22966 7000
Scale 1:7 500 000
0 50 100 150 200 Miles
0 100 200 300 Kms.
Conic Equidistant Projection
© Collins

CENTRAL UNITED STATES

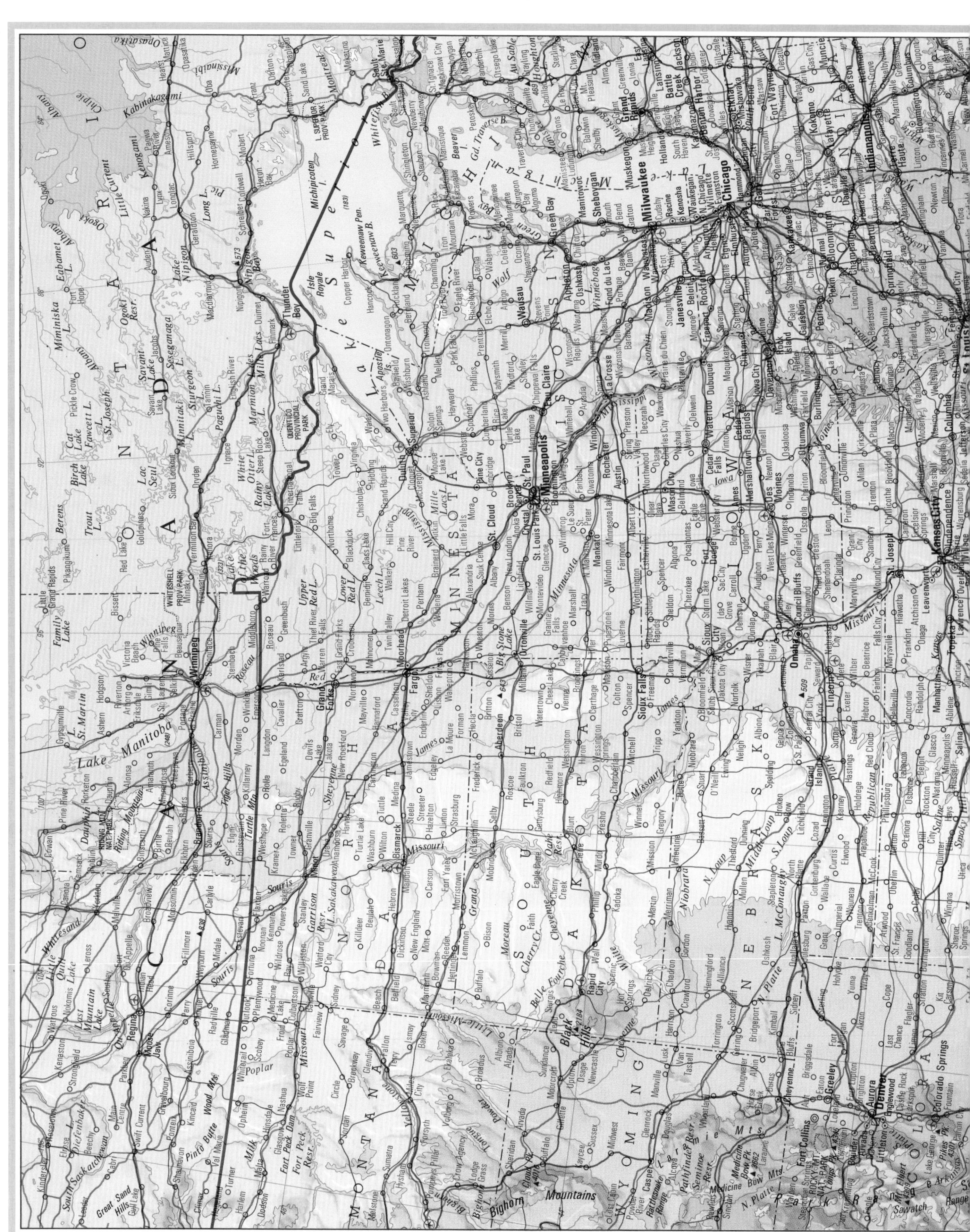

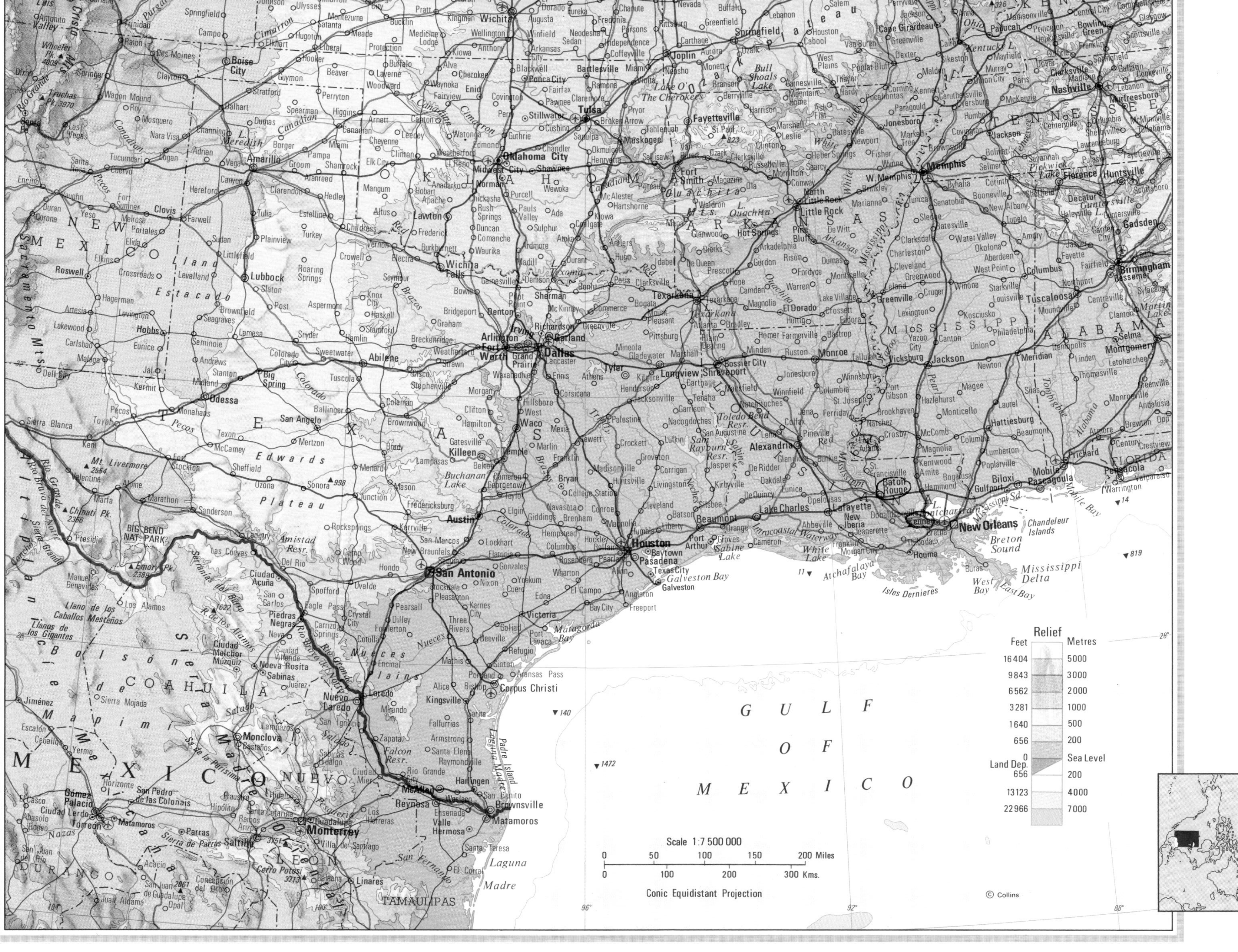

Relief

Feet	Metres
16404	5000
9843	3000
6562	2000
3281	1000
1640	500
656	200
0	Sea Level
	Land Dep.
656	200
13123	4000
22966	7000

© Collins

Scale 1:7 500 000

Conic Equidistant Projection

0   50   100   150   200 Miles

0   100   200   300 Kms.

EASTERN UNITED STATES

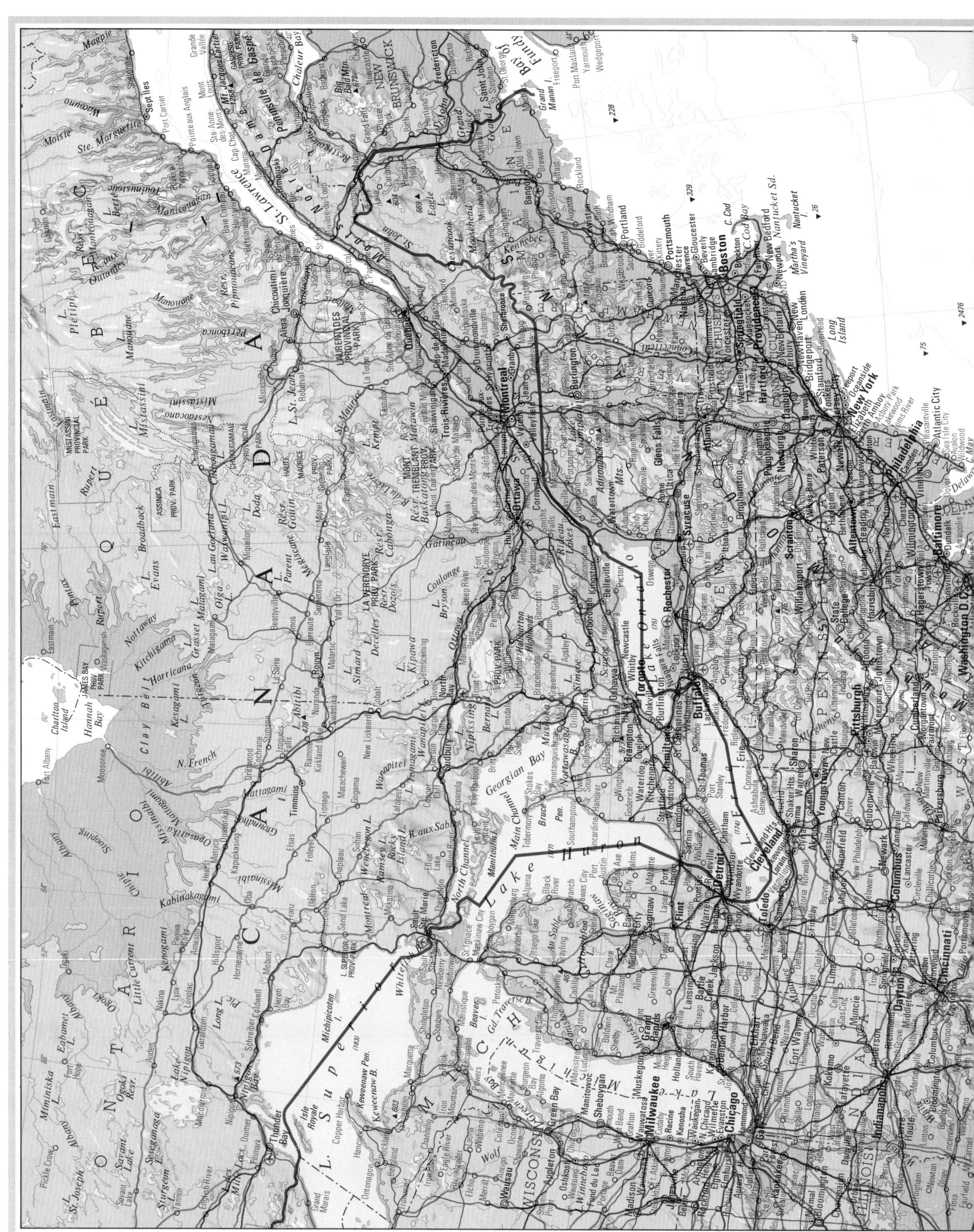

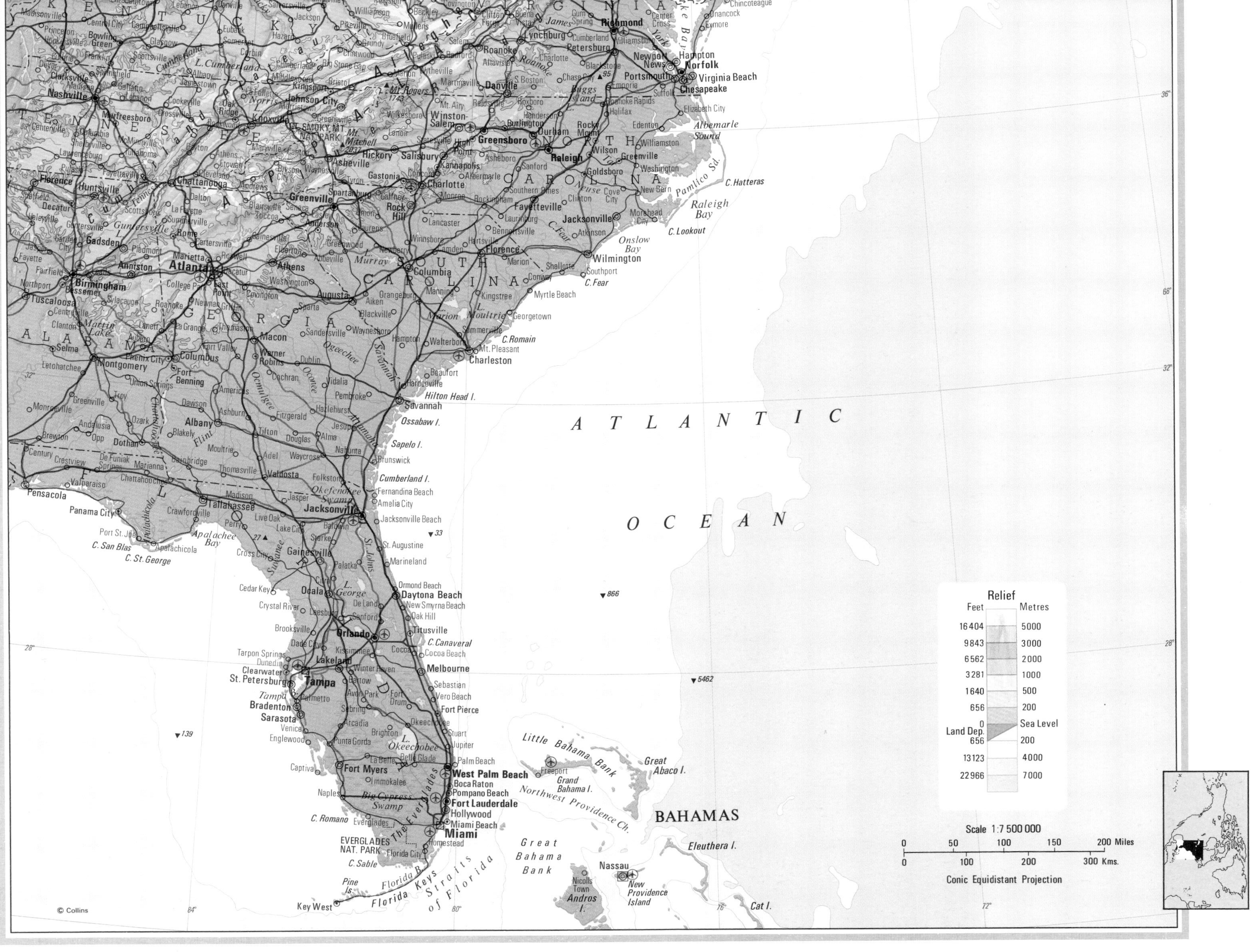

ATLANTIC
OCEAN
BAHAMAS
Relief
Feet | Metres
16404 | 5000
9843 | 3000
6562 | 2000
3281 | 1000
1640 | 500
656 | 200
0 | Sea Level
Land Dep. 656 | 200
13123 | 4000
22966 | 7000
Scale 1:7 500 000
0 50 100 150 200 Miles
0 100 200 300 Kms.
Conic Equidistant Projection
Richmond
Norfolk
Virginia Beach
Chesapeake
Portsmouth
Newport News
Hampton
Petersburg
Lynchburg
Roanoke
Danville
Durham
Raleigh
Greensboro
Winston-Salem
Charlotte
Fayetteville
Wilmington
Jacksonville
Columbia
Florence
Charleston
Savannah
Augusta
Macon
Atlanta
Athens
Columbus
Albany
Montgomery
Birmingham
Tuscaloosa
Huntsville
Nashville
Chattanooga
Knoxville
Asheville
Greenville
Tallahassee
Jacksonville
Gainesville
Ocala
Orlando
Daytona Beach
Titusville
Melbourne
Tampa
St. Petersburg
Clearwater
Lakeland
Sarasota
Bradenton
Fort Myers
West Palm Beach
Boca Raton
Pompano Beach
Fort Lauderdale
Hollywood
Miami
Miami Beach
Key West
Pensacola
Panama City
Dothan
Nassau
Freeport
C. Hatteras
C. Lookout
C. Fear
C. Romain
C. Canaveral
C. Sable
C. San Blas
C. St. George
C. Romano
Onslow Bay
Raleigh Bay
Apalachee Bay
Albemarle Sound
Pamlico Sd.
EVERGLADES NAT. PARK
L. Okeechobee
Straits of Florida
Florida Keys
Great Bahama Bank
Little Bahama Bank
Grand Bahama I.
Great Abaco I.
Eleuthera I.
Cat I.
Andros I.
New Providence Island
Northwest Providence Ch.
Hilton Head I.
Cumberland I.
Sapelo I.
Ossabaw I.
© Collins

NORTHEASTERN UNITED STATES

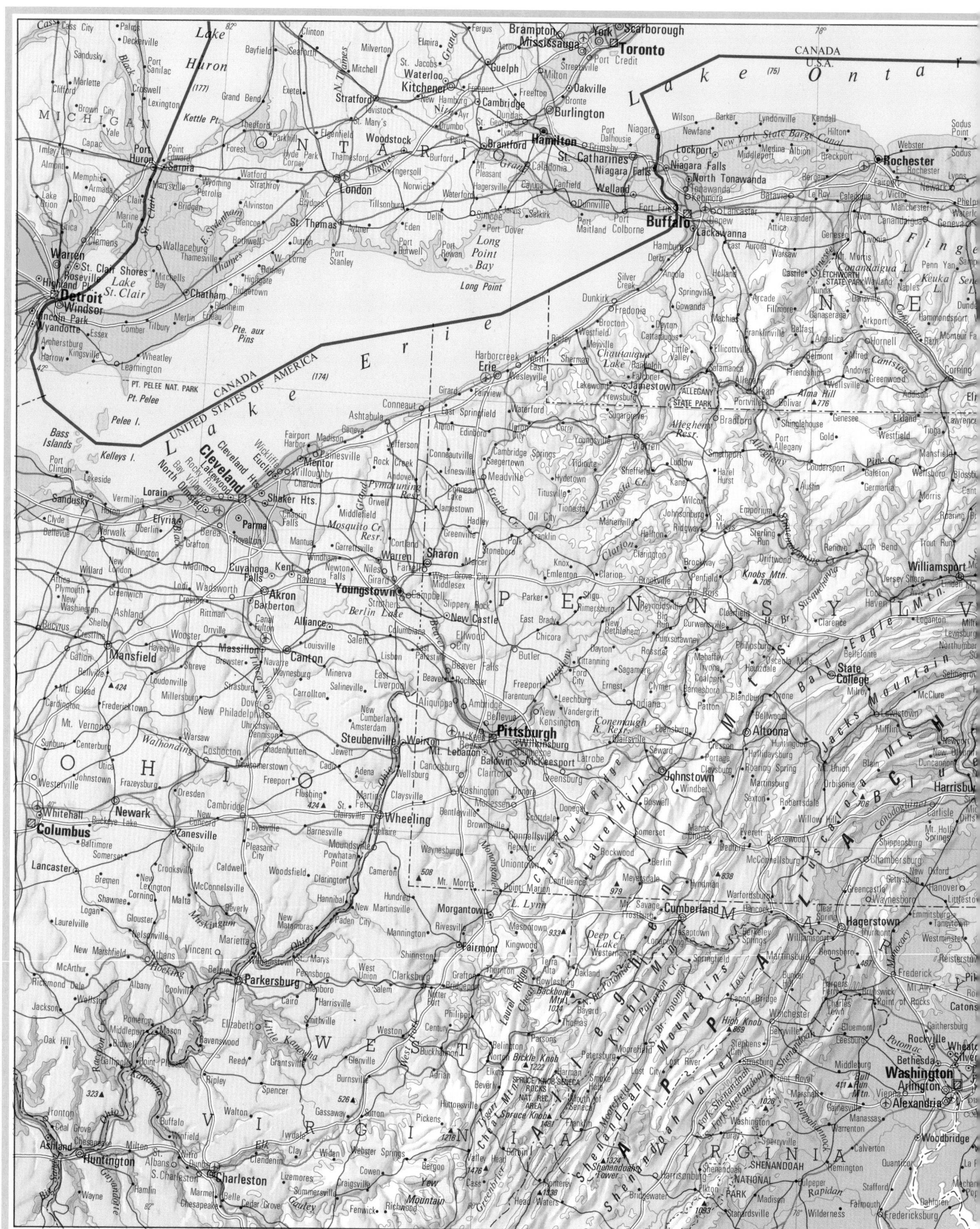

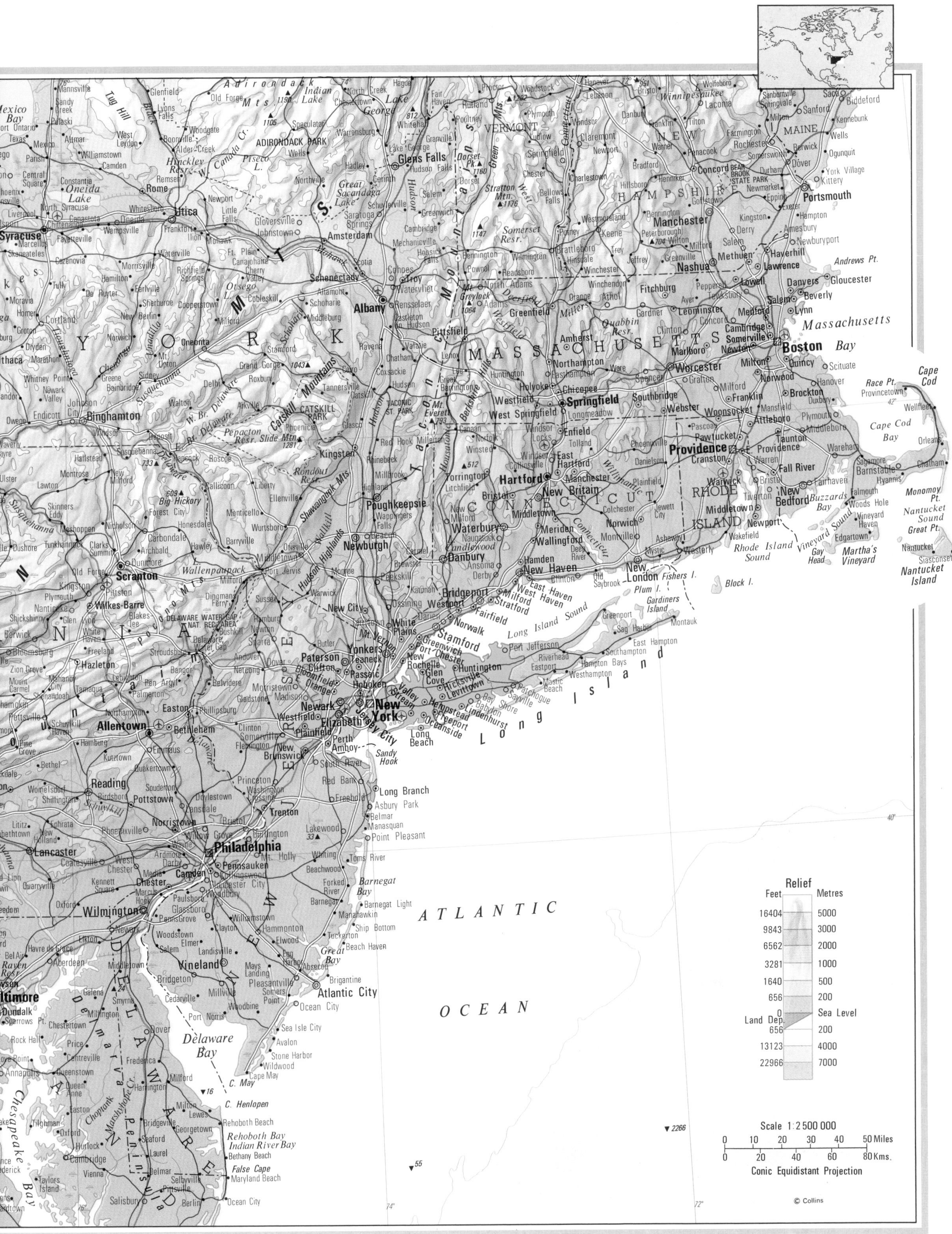
Relief
Feet
Metres
16404
5000
9843
3000
6562
2000
3281
1000
1640
500
656
200
0
Sea Level
Land Dep.
656
200
13123
4000
22966
7000
Scale 1:2 500 000
0 10 20 30 40 50 Miles
0 20 40 60 80 Kms.
Conic Equidistant Projection
© Collins
ATLANTIC
OCEAN
Long Island
Long Island Sound
Massachusetts Bay
Cape Cod Bay
Cape Cod
Nantucket Sound
Nantucket Island
Martha's Vineyard
Rhode Island Sound
Buzzards Bay
Delaware Bay
Chesapeake Bay
Adirondack Mts
Catskill Mountains
NEW YORK
PENNSYLVANIA
NEW JERSEY
DELAWARE
MASSACHUSETTS
CONNECTICUT
RHODE ISLAND
VERMONT
NEW HAMPSHIRE
MAINE
Boston
New York
Philadelphia
Providence
Hartford
Springfield
Worcester
Albany
Syracuse
Utica
Binghamton
Scranton
Wilkes-Barre
Allentown
Reading
Lancaster
Wilmington
Trenton
Atlantic City
Newark
Paterson
Yonkers
New Haven
Bridgeport
Stamford
Waterbury
New London
Poughkeepsie
Newburgh
Kingston
Schenectady
Glens Falls
Manchester
Concord
Nashua
Portsmouth
Lowell
Lawrence
Brockton
Fall River
New Bedford
Vineland
Camden
Chester
Rome
Baltimore
Dover
Cape May
C. Henlopen
Block I.
Fishers I.

CENTRAL AMERICA AND THE CARIBBEAN

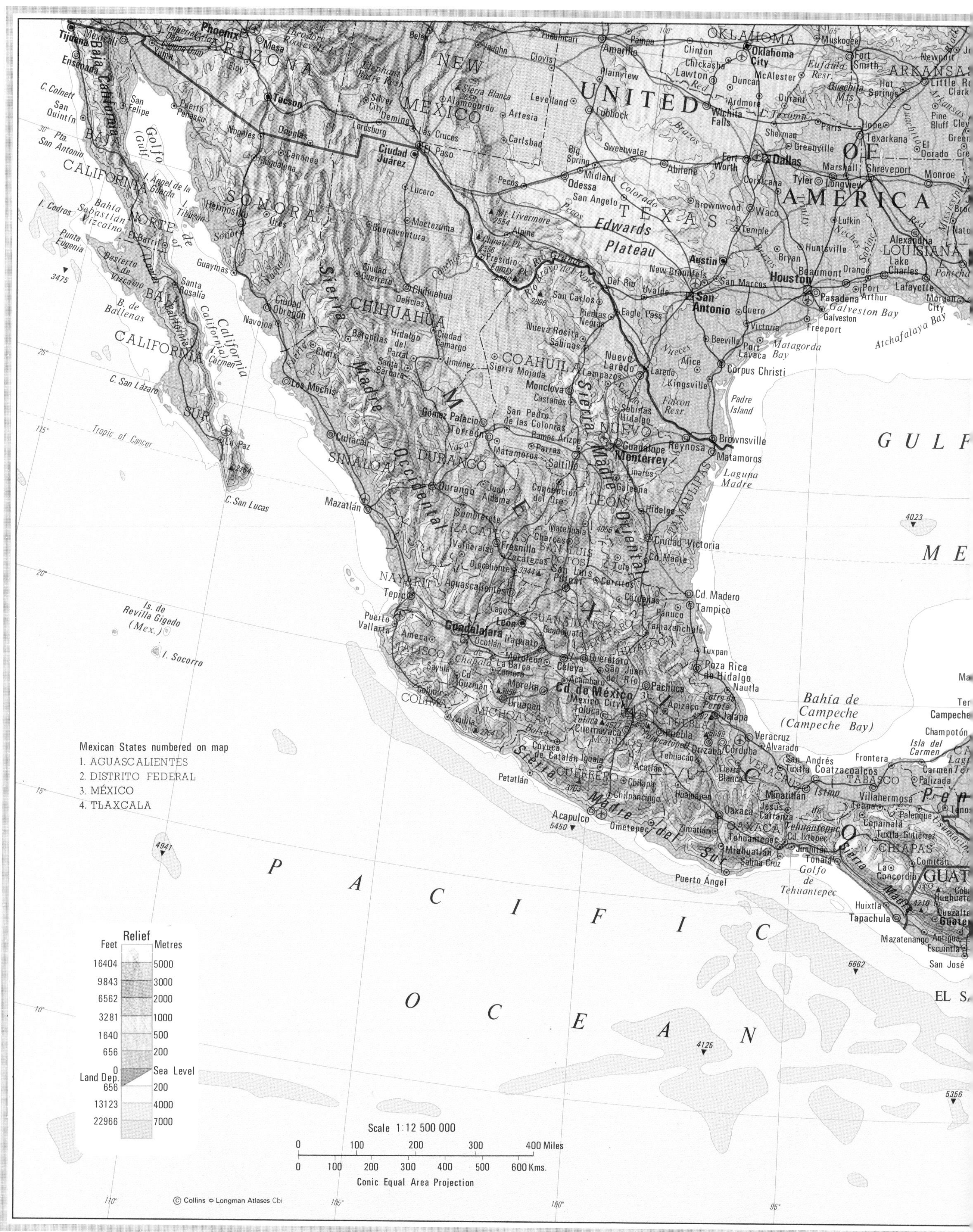

Mexican States numbered on map
1. AGUASCALIENTES
2. DISTRITO FEDERAL
3. MÉXICO
4. TLAXCALA

Relief

Feet		Metres
16404		5000
9843		3000
6562		2000
3281		1000
1640		500
656		200
0		Sea Level
Land Dep.		
656		200
13123		4000
22966		7000

Scale 1:12 500 000

0	100	200	300	400 Miles

| 0 | 100 | 200 | 300 | 400 | 500 | 600 Kms. |

Conic Equal Area Projection

© Collins ◇ Longman Atlases Cbi

116

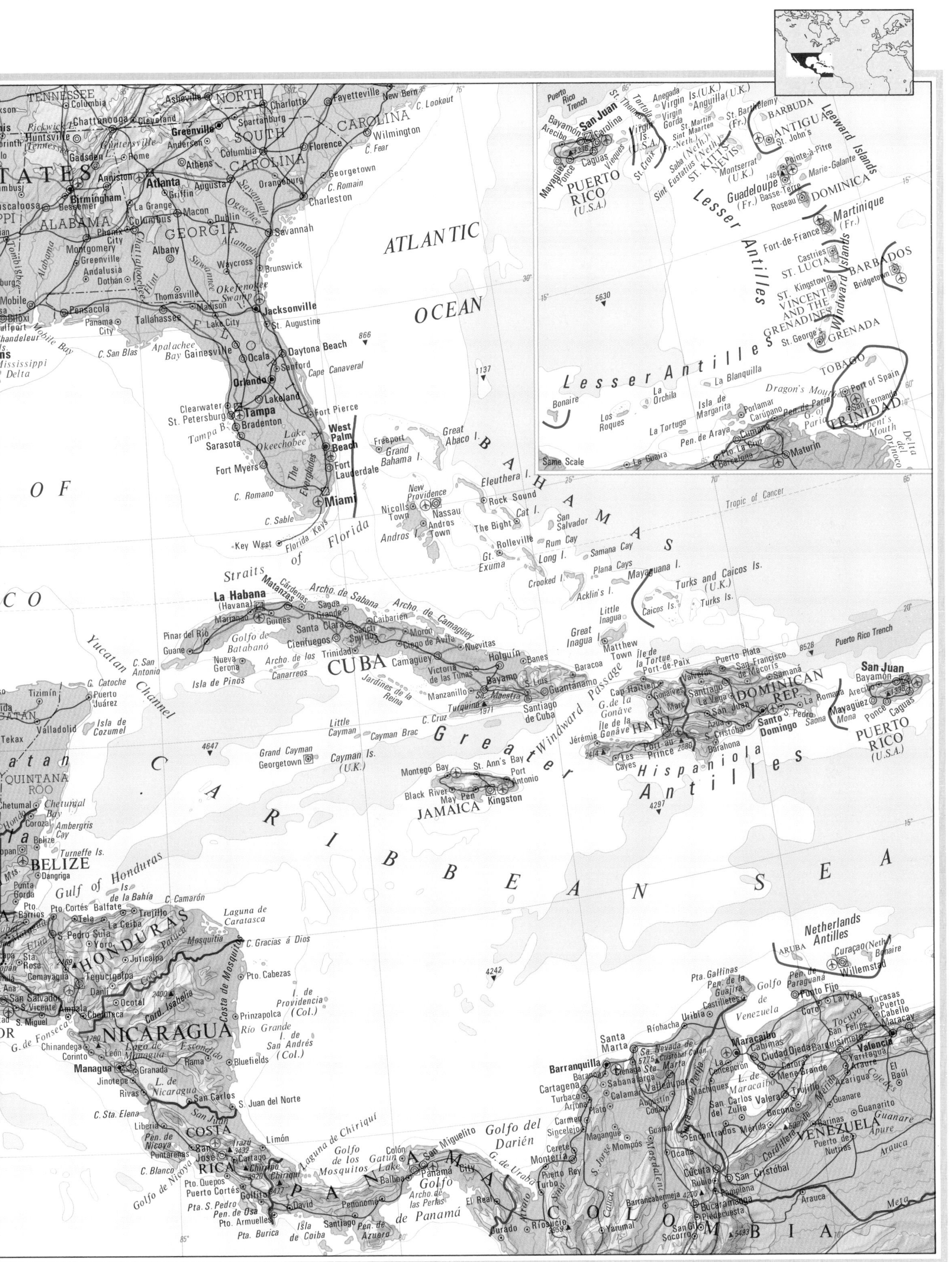

ATLANTIC

OCEAN

GULF

OF

MEXICO

TENNESSEE
Columbia
Chattanooga Cleveland
Asheville NORTH
Spartanburg Charlotte New Bern
C. Lookout
Fayetteville
Huntsville Rome SOUTH CAROLINA
Gadsden Andersen Columbia Florence
Greenville Wilmington
Anniston Athens CAROLINA C. Fear
Birmingham Atlanta Augusta Georgetown
Bessemer GEORGIA Orangeburg
Phenix La Grange Macon Savannah C. Romain
Montgomery City Columbus Griffin Charleston
Greenville Albany Dublin
Andalusia Dothan Thomasville Brunswick
Mobile Pensacola Tallahassee Waycross
Panama Madison Lake City Jacksonville
City Apalachee Okefenokee St. Augustine
Bay Gainesville Swamp
Ocala Daytona Beach
Orlando Sanford Cape Canaveral
Clearwater Lakeland Fort Pierce
St. Petersburg Tampa
Sarasota Bradenton Lake
Okeechobee West Palm Beach
Fort Myers The Fort Lauderdale
Everglades Miami
C. Romano
C. Sable Key West Florida Keys

ALABAMA
FLORIDA

Mississippi Delta
Mobile Bay
Chandeleur Is.

Tampa B.

Straits of Florida

BAHAMAS

Freeport
Grand Bahama I.
Great Abaco I.
New Providence
Nicolls Town Rock Sound Eleuthera I.
Nassau Cat I.
Andros I. Andros Town
The Bight San Salvador
Rolleville
Gt. Exuma Rum Cay
Long I. Samana Cay
Crooked I. Plana Cays
Acklin's I. Mayaguana I.
Little Inagua
Great Inagua Turks and Caicos Is. (U.K.)
Matthew Town Caicos Is. Turks Is.

Tropic of Cancer

1137
866

CUBA
La Habana (Havana)
Cárdenas Matanzas
Pinar del Río Marianao Güines Archo. de Sabana
Guane Santa Clara Sagua Caibarién
Nueva Golfo de Ciego de Ávila Archo. de Camagüey
Gerona Batabanó Cienfuegos Sancti Spíritus Morón
Isla de Pinos Trinidad Nuevitas
Archo. de los Canarreos Camagüey Holguín Banes
Victoria de las Tunas Baracoa
Jardines de la Reina Manzanillo Bayamo Sta. Luis
Sa. Maestra Guantánamo
C. Cruz Turquino 1974 Santiago
de Cuba

4647
Little Cayman
Grand Cayman Cayman Brac
Georgetown Cayman Is. (U.K.)

Montego Bay St. Ann's Bay Port
Black River Antonio
May Pen Kingston
JAMAICA

C A R I B B E A N   S E A

G r e a t e r   A n t i l l e s

Windward Passage

Cap-Haïtien
Port-de-Paix Île de la Tortue
Gonaïves Puerto Plata
G. de la Santiago San Francisco de Macorís
Gonâve Samaná
La Vega DOMINICAN REP.
Île de la Môle San Juan La Romana
Gonâve HAÏTI Santo S. Pedro Saona
Jérémie Port-au-Prince 2680 Azua Cristóbal Domingo
2414 Barahona
Les Cayes

Hispaniola

4297

C.San Antonio
Yucatán Channel

Tizimín
Puerto Juárez
Isla de Cozumel
Valladolid
Tekax
YUCATAN
QUINTANA ROO
Chetumal Chetumal Bay
Corozal Ambergris Cay
Belize
Turneffe Is.
Dangriga
BELIZE
Punta Gorda
Pto. Barrios
Pto. Cortés Balfate
S. Pedro Sula La Ceiba Trujillo
Yoro C. Camarón
Sta. Rosa Laguna de Caratasca
Comayagua **HONDURAS** Juticalpa Mosquitia
Tegucigalpa Patuca C. Gracias á Dios
Danlí
Ocotal Pto. Cabezas
S. Salvador 2400 Cord. Isabela I. de
San Vicente Prinzapolca Providencia (Col.)
S. Miguel Chinandega Río Grande
G. de Fonseca León **NICARAGUA** I. de
Corinto Lago de Managua Bluefields San Andrés
Jinotepe Managua Rama (Col.)
Granada L. de
Rivas Nicaragua
San Carlos
C. Sta. Elena S. Juan del Norte
COSTA
Liberia Pen. de San Juan
Nicoya Irazú 3432
Puntarenas San Limón
RICA José Cartago
C. Blanco Chirripó
Golfo de 3820
Pto. Quepos Nicoya Golfo Golfo de
Puerto Cortés David Penonomé los Mosquitos
Pta. S. Pedro Pen. de Osa Chiriquí Colón
Pto. Armuelles Santiago Pen. de
Pta. Burica Isla de Coiba Azuero de Panamá Gatún Lake
PANAMA
Panamá City
San Miguelito
Golfo de Darién Archo. de las Perlas
El Real

Gulf of Honduras
Is. de la Bahía
Golfo de Honduras

Costa de Mosquitos

4242

Golfo del Darién
G. de Urabá

Puerto Rico Trench
8528
San Juan Bayamón
Arecibo
Mayagüez 335 **PUERTO RICO** (U.S.A.)
Mona Ponce Caguas

Santa Marta
Barranquilla
Cartagena Sa. Nevada de 5775 Sta. Marta
Turbaco Barranca Cristóbal Colón
Arjona Calamar Maicao
Carmen Sabanalarga Valledupar
Sincelejo Magangué Plato
Montería Cereté Mompós
Puerto Rey Magdalena
Turbo San Gil
Riosucio 3659 Yarumal

Netherlands Antilles
ARUBA Curaçao (Neth.)
Bonaire
Willemstad

Pta. Gallinas
Pen. de la Guajira
Ríohacha Uribia Golfo de Paraguaná
Punto Fijo
Castilletes Coro La Vela
L. de Maracaibo Puerto Cabello Tucacas
Maracaibo Cabimas San Felipe Valencia
Ciudad Ojeda Barquisimeto Maracay
Concepción Carora Yaritagua Araure
San Carlos Trujillo Barinas El
del Zulia Valera Mérida Barinas Bául
Machiques Bocono Guanare
Ocaña Guanarito Guanare
Cúcuta Encontrados Mérida 5007
San Cristóbal Bucaramanga Pamplona Barinas 4200 Apure
Piedecuesta Cordillera Arauca Arauca
VENEZUELA
COLOMBIA
Socorro 5493 Meta

C O L O M B I A

Puerto Rico Trench
Anegada
Puerto Rico Tortola Virgin Is. (U.K.)
San Juan St. Thomas Virgin Gorda Anguilla (U.K.)
Bayamón Sint Maarten (Neth.) St. Barthélemy BARBUDA
Arecibo Virgin St. Martin (Fr.)
Is. Saba (Neth.) ST. KITTS ANTIGUA
Mayagüez (U.S.A.) St. Croix Sint Eustatius (Neth.) NEVIS St. John's
Ponce Caguas Vieques (U.S.A.) (U.K.) Pointe-à-Pitre
PUERTO RICO Montserrat 1484
(U.S.A.) (U.K.) Guadeloupe Marie-Galante
Basse-Terre (Fr.) DOMINICA
Roseau
Fort-de-France Martinique
(Fr.)
5630 Castries
ST. LUCIA BARBADOS
St. Kingstown Bridgetown
ST. VINCENT Windward Islands
AND THE
GRENADINES St. George's GRENADA

L e s s e r   A n t i l l e s

Leeward Islands

Bonaire
La Orchila
Los Roques La Tortuga La Blanquilla Dragon's Mouth TOBAGO
Isla de Margarita Porlamar Port of Spain
Pampatar San Fernando
Pen. de G. de TRINIDAD
Cumaná Araya Paria Paria
La Guaira Barcelona Pto. La Cruz Maturín Serpent's Mouth
Delta del Orinoco

Same Scale

L e s s e r   A n t i l l e s

North America

NORTH

ATLANTIC

OCEAN

Tropic of Cancer

40°

30°

20°

Caribbean Sea

Barranquilla

Maracaibo Caracas

TRINIDAD
AND TOBAGO

VENEZUELA

Georgetown
Paramaribo

Medellín

GUYANA SURINAM

Cayenne

Bogotá

COLOMBIA

GUIANA
(Fr.)

10°

Cali

Quito

ECUADOR

Belém

40°

Galapagos
Is. (Ec.)

90°

Guayaquil

30° Equator

100°

P
E
R
U

Fortaleza

BRAZIL

110°

Lima

Recife

La Paz

BOLIVIA

Brasília

10°

120°

Sucre

Salvador

SOUTH

P
A
R
A
G
U
A
Y

Belo
Horizonte

130°

Río de
Janeiro

São Paulo

Santo André

Asunción

20°

San Félix (Chile)
San Ambrosio

C
H
I
L
E

Curitiba

Tropic of Capricorn

A
R
G
E
N
T
I
N
A

Córdoba

A
T
L
A

Islas
Juan
Fernández
(Chile)

Valparaíso

Rosario

URUGUAY

Pôrto
Alegre

Santiago

Buenos
Aires

Montevideo

30°

La Plata

P
A
C
I
F
I
C

O
C
E

140°

O
C
E
A
N

40°

Falkland
Is. (U.K.)

Tierra del
Fuego

50°

South
Georgia
(U.K.)

60°

Antarctic Circle

70°

International Date Line

Antarctica

© Collins

118

SOUTH AMERICA

South America as a continental name is used for the land area extending south from the Isthmus of Panama to Cape Horn and lying between 34°W and 82°W. Latin America is a term widely used to cover those parts of the Americas where Spanish, or Portuguese as in Brazil, are the adopted national languages, and thus refers to an area that includes all of South America, Central America, Mexico and the Caribbean, except for the few English, French and Dutch speaking countries and dependencies.

SOUTH AMERICA

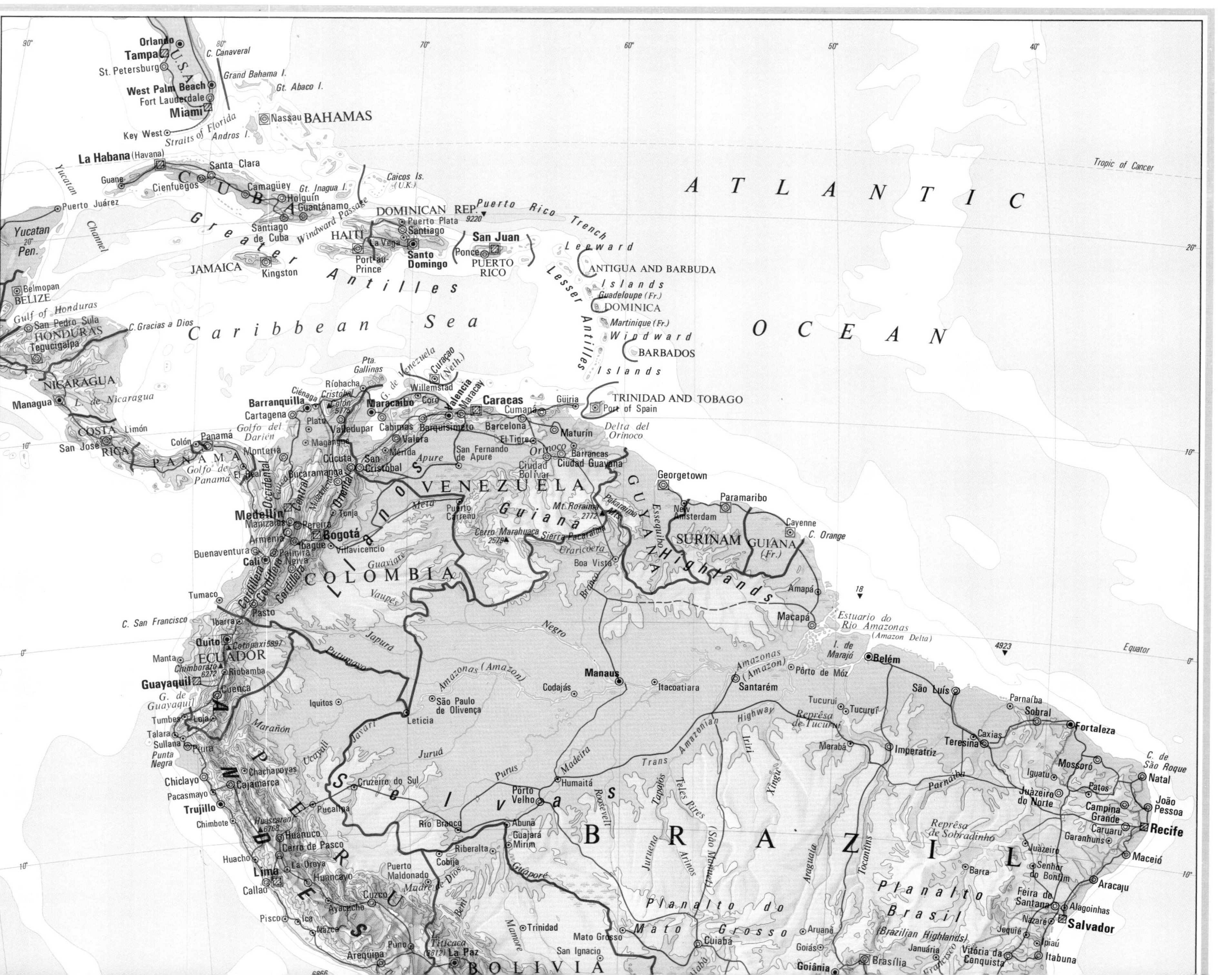

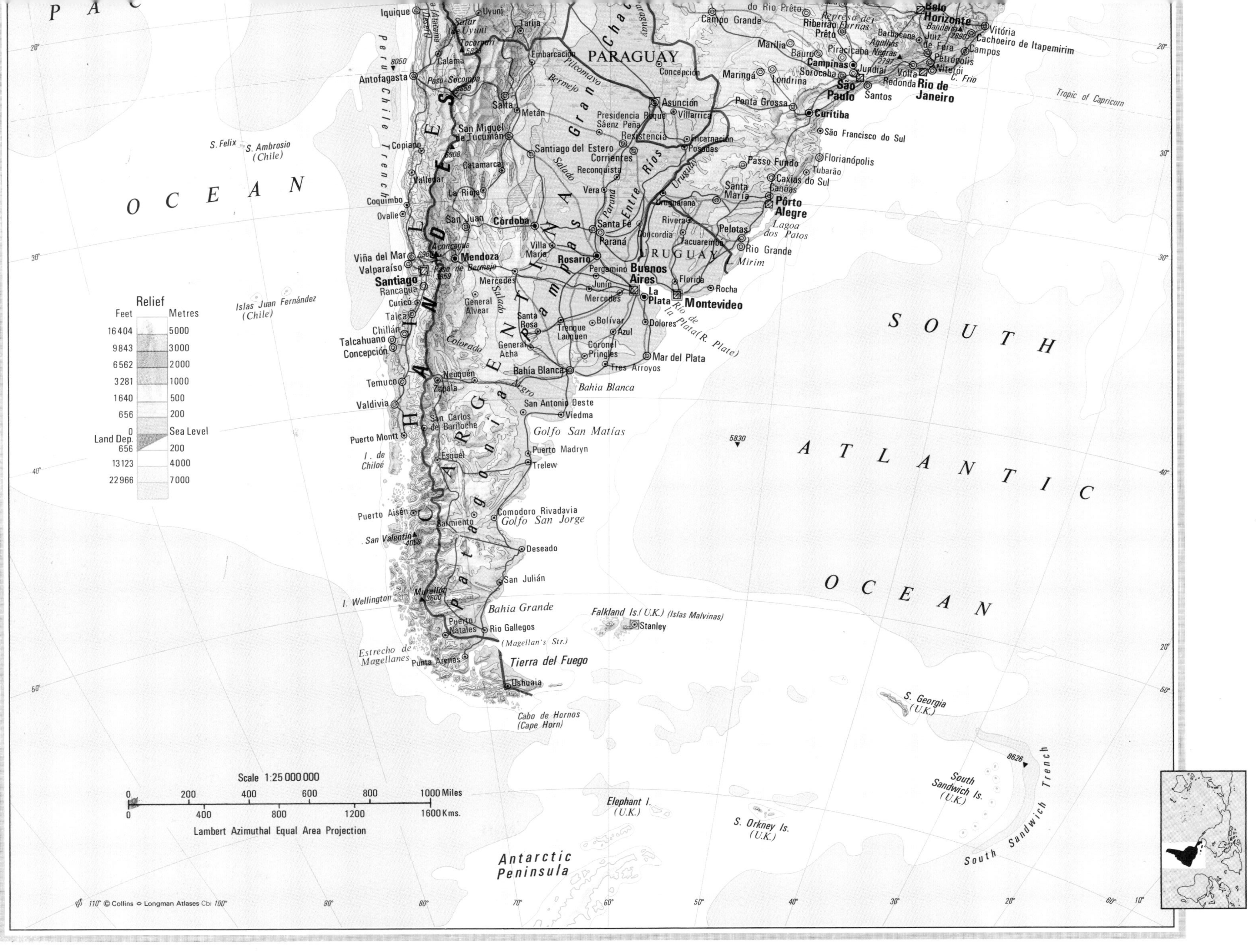

P A C I F I C   O C E A N

S O U T H   A T L A N T I C   O C E A N

Tropic of Capricorn

Belo Horizonte
Vitória
Cachoeiro de Itapemirim
Campos
C. Frio
Rio de Janeiro
Volta Redonda
Petrópolis
Niterói
Juiz de Fora
Barbacena
Bauru
Bonito
Nova Friburgo
Ribeirão Preto
Araraquara
Campinas
São Paulo
Sorocaba
Santos
Londrina
Curitiba
São Francisco do Sul
Joinville
Florianópolis
Tubarão
Campo Grande
Maringá
Ponta Grossa
Caxias do Sul
Passo Fundo
Porto Alegre
São Leopoldo
Lagoa dos Patos
Rio Grande
Santa Maria
Pelotas
Mirim

PARAGUAY
Concepción
Asunción
Villarrica
Encarnación
Posadas
URUGUAY
Rivera
Tacuarembó
Rocha
Florida
Montevideo
Rio de la Plata (R. Plate)

Gran Chaco
Presidencia Roque Sáenz Peña
Resistencia
Corrientes
Paraná
Santa Fe
Rosario
Gualeguaychú
Concordia
Mercedes
Buenos Aires
La Plata
Dolores
Mar del Plata

Embarcación
Tartagal
Salta
Santiago del Estero
Reconquista
Vera
Entre Ríos
Pergamino
Junín
Bolívar
Bahía Blanca
Tres Arroyos

Tajía
Córdoba
Villa María
Santa Rosa
Azul
Coronel Pringles

San Miguel de Tucumán
San Juan
Mendoza
General Alvear
General Acha
Neuquén
Viedma
San Antonio Oeste
Golfo San Matías

Santiago
Valparaíso
Viña del Mar
Rancagua
San Carlos de Bariloche
Esquel
Trelew
Puerto Madryn

Iquique
Antofagasta
Copiapó
Coquimbo
Ovalle
Curicó
Talca
Chillán
Talcahuano
Concepción
Temuco
Valdivia
Puerto Montt
I. de Chiloé

Comodoro Rivadavia
Golfo San Jorge
Deseado
San Julián
Bahía Grande
Río Gallegos

Puerto Aisén
San Valentín
I. Wellington

Tierra del Fuego
Ushuaia
Punta Arenas
Puerto Natales
Estrecho de Magallanes (Magellan's Str.)
Cabo de Hornos (Cape Horn)

Peru/Chile Trench

S. Félix
S. Ambrosio (Chile)

Islas Juan Fernández (Chile)

Falkland Is. (U.K.) (Islas Malvinas)
Stanley

Elephant I. (U.K.)
S. Orkney Is. (U.K.)

S. Georgia (U.K.)

South Sandwich Is. (U.K.)
South Sandwich Trench
8428

Antarctic Peninsula

Relief

Feet	Metres		Sea Level	
16404	5000		200	
9843	3000		Land Dep.	656
6562	2000			4000
3281	1000		13123	
1640	500		22966	7000
656	200			
	Sea Level	0		

Scale 1:25 000 000

0   200   400   600   800   1000 Miles
0   400   800   1200   1600 Kms.

Lambert Azimuthal Equal Area Projection

© Collins ◇ Longman Atlases

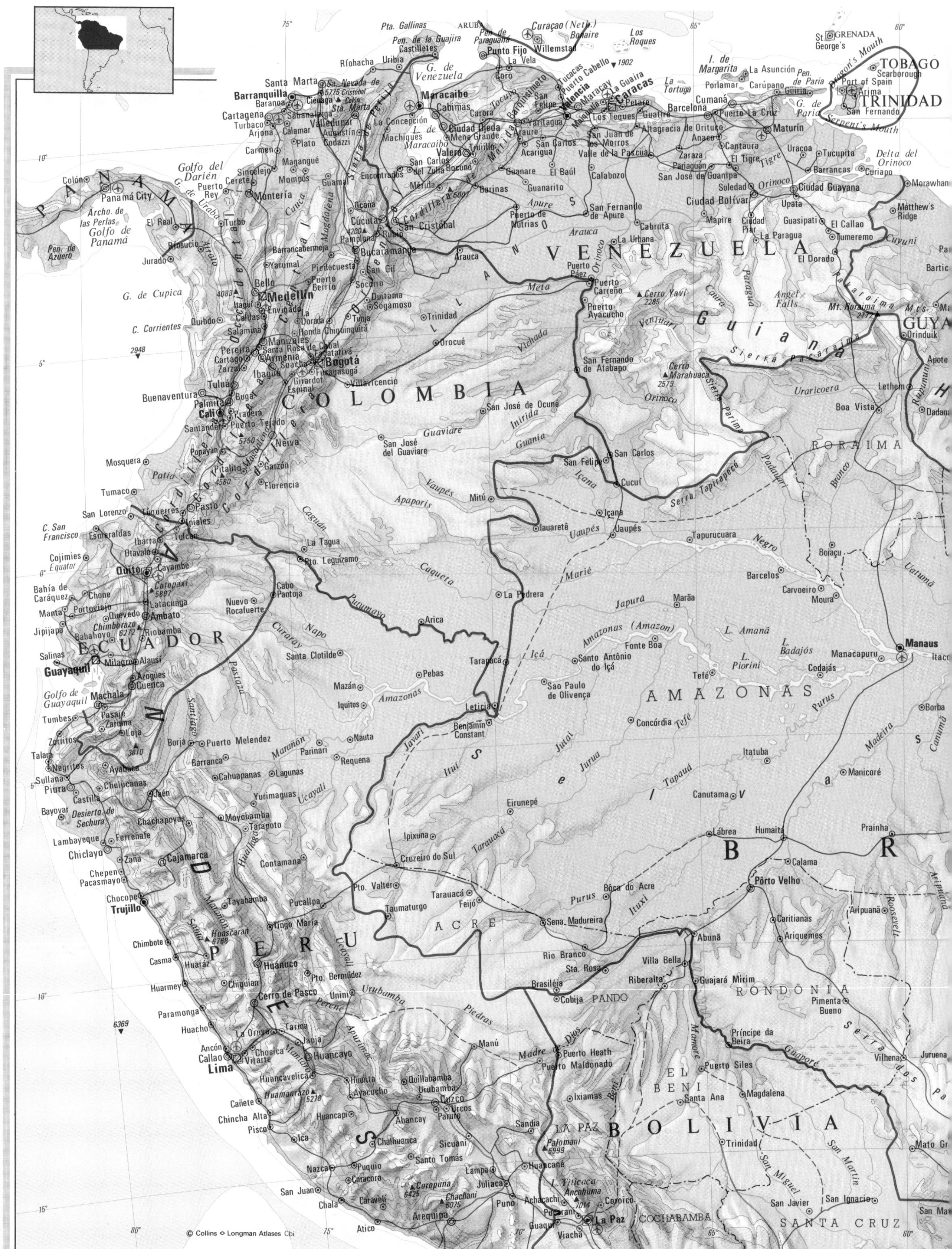

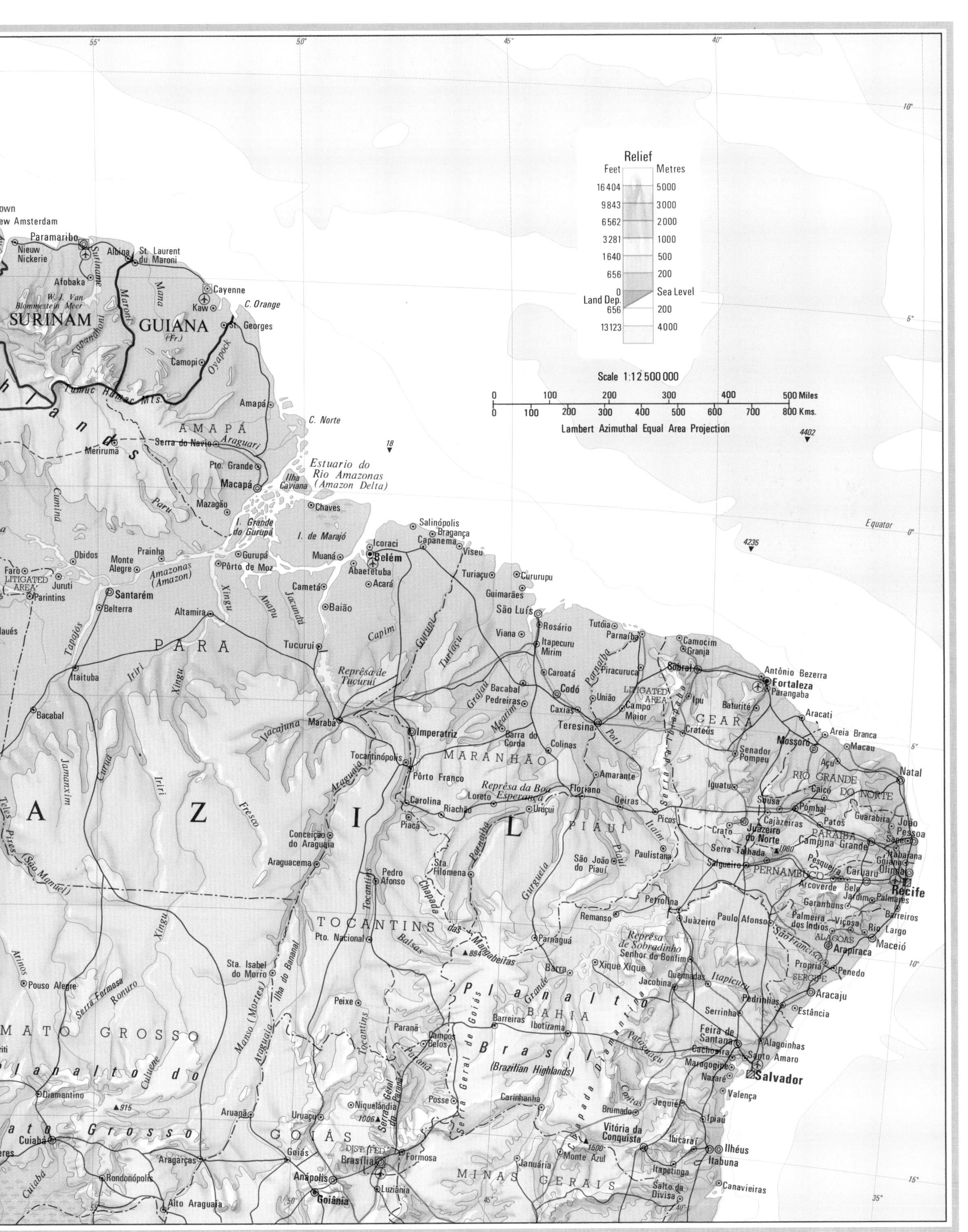

Relief

Feet		Metres
16404		5000
9843		3000
6562		2000
3281		1000
1640		500
656		200
0		Sea Level
Land Dep.		
656		200
13123		4000

Scale 1:12 500 000

| 0 | 100 | 200 | 300 | 400 | 500 Miles |

| 0 | 100 | 200 | 300 | 400 | 500 | 600 | 700 | 800 Kms. |

Lambert Azimuthal Equal Area Projection

SURINAM

GUIANA (Fr.)

AMAPÁ

PARÁ

MARANHÃO

CEARÁ

RIO GRANDE DO NORTE

PARAÍBA

PERNAMBUCO

PIAUÍ

TOCANTINS

ALAGOAS

SERGIPE

BAHIA

MATO GROSSO

GOIÁS

MINAS GERAIS

Estuario do Rio Amazonas (Amazon Delta)

Planalto do Brasil (Brazilian Highlands)

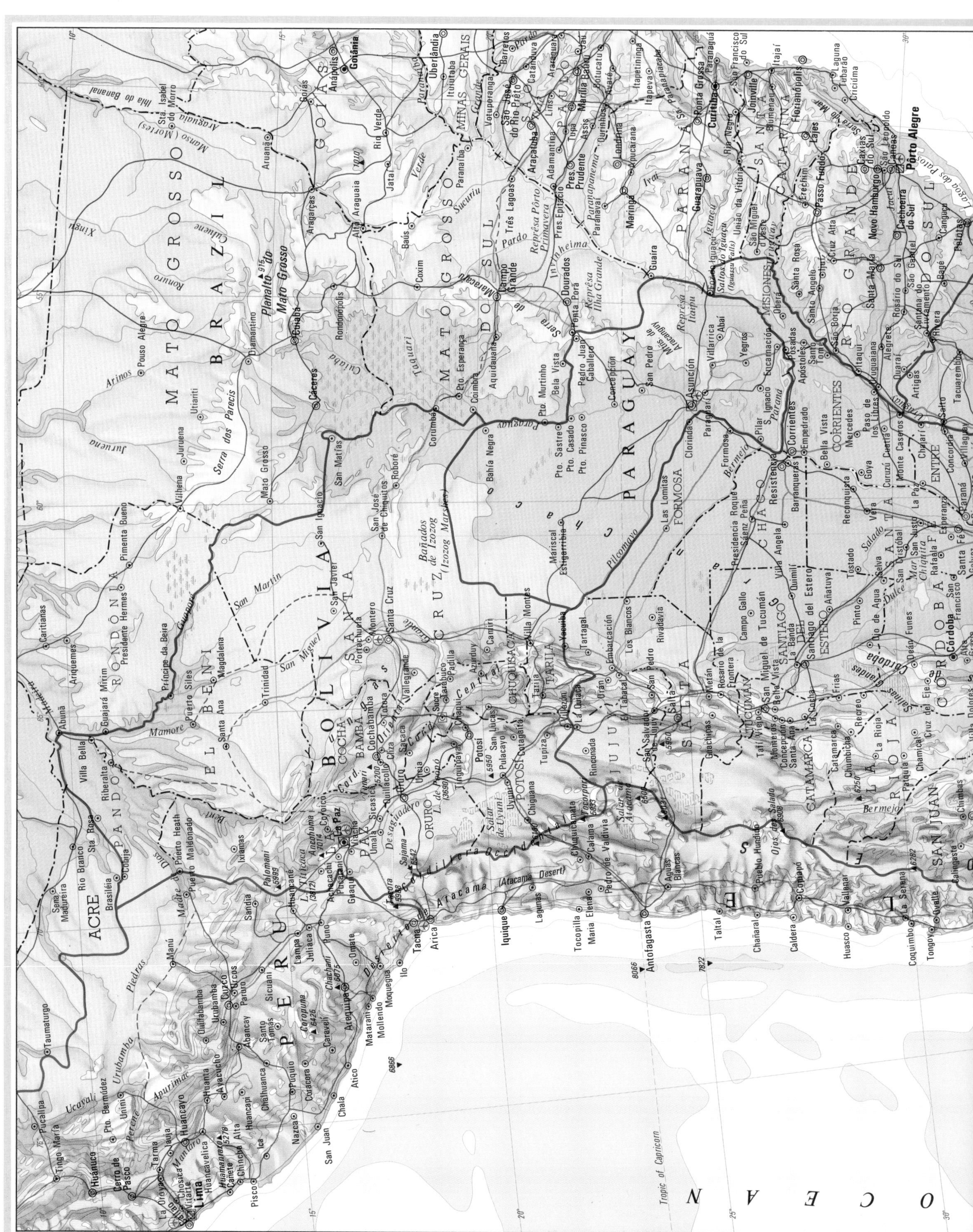

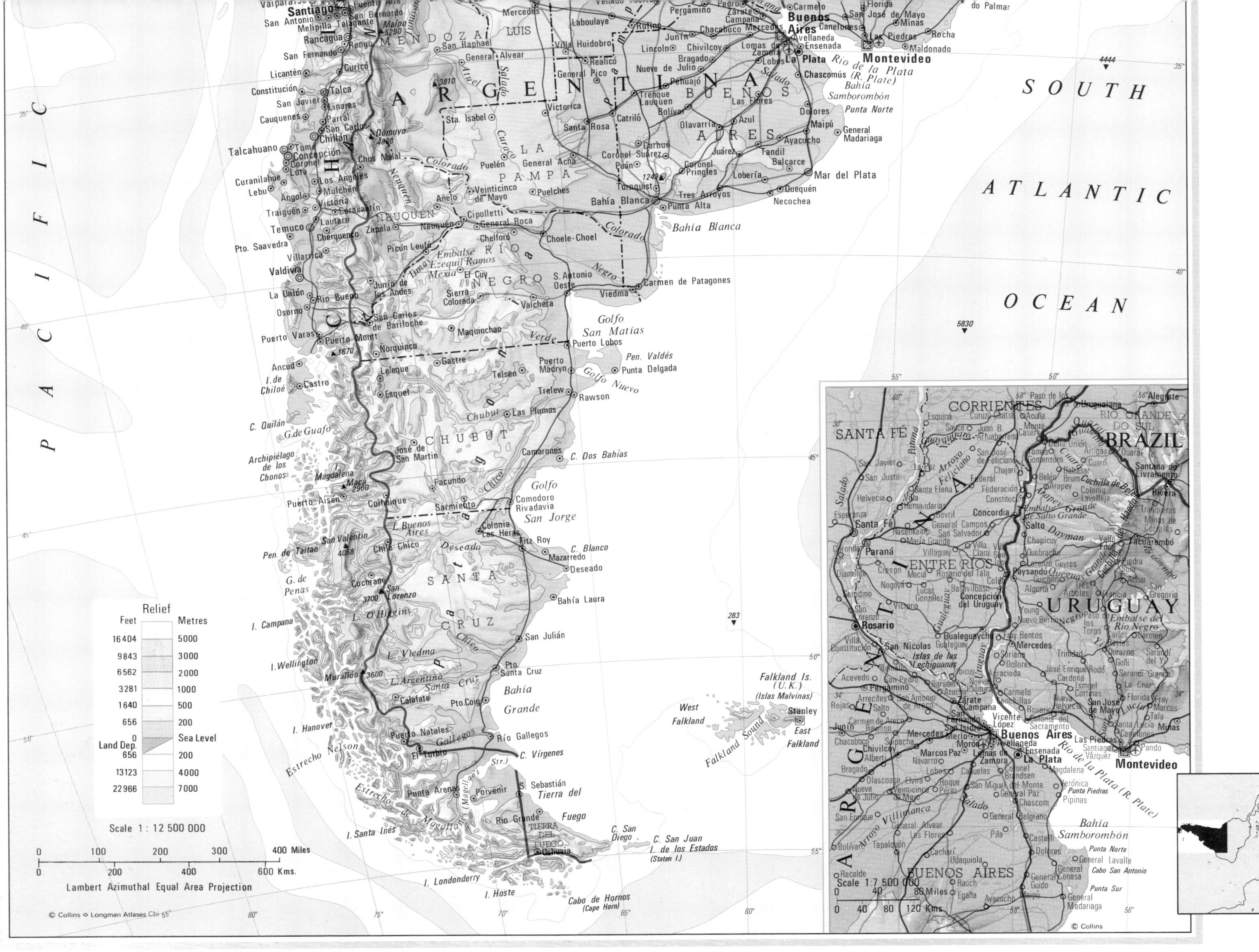

SOUTH ATLANTIC OCEAN

PACIFIC OCEAN

Relief

Feet	Metres
16 404	5000
9843	3000
6562	2000
3281	1000
1640	500
656	200
0	Sea Level
Land Dep.	656
13123	4000
22 966	7000

Scale 1 : 12 500 000

Lambert Azimuthal Equal Area Projection

© Collins © Longman Atlases Chr 185

SOUTH AMERICA — EAST

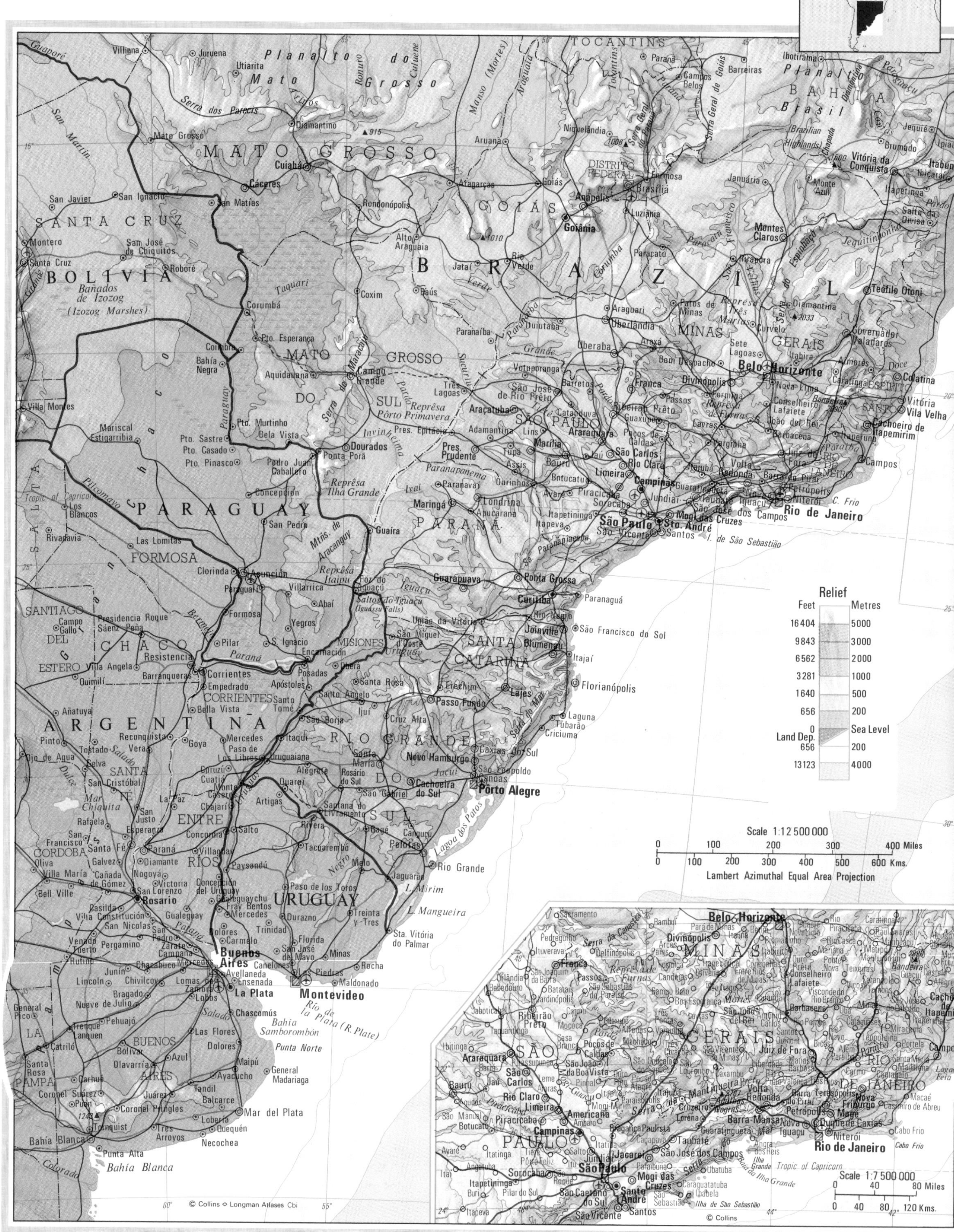

Relief

Feet	Metres
16 404	5000
9843	3000
6562	2000
3281	1000
1640	500
656	200
0	Sea Level
Land Dep.	
656	200
13 123	4000

Scale 1:12 500 000

Lambert Azimuthal Equal Area Projection

Scale 1:7 500 000

© Collins ◇ Longman Atlases Cbi

© Collins

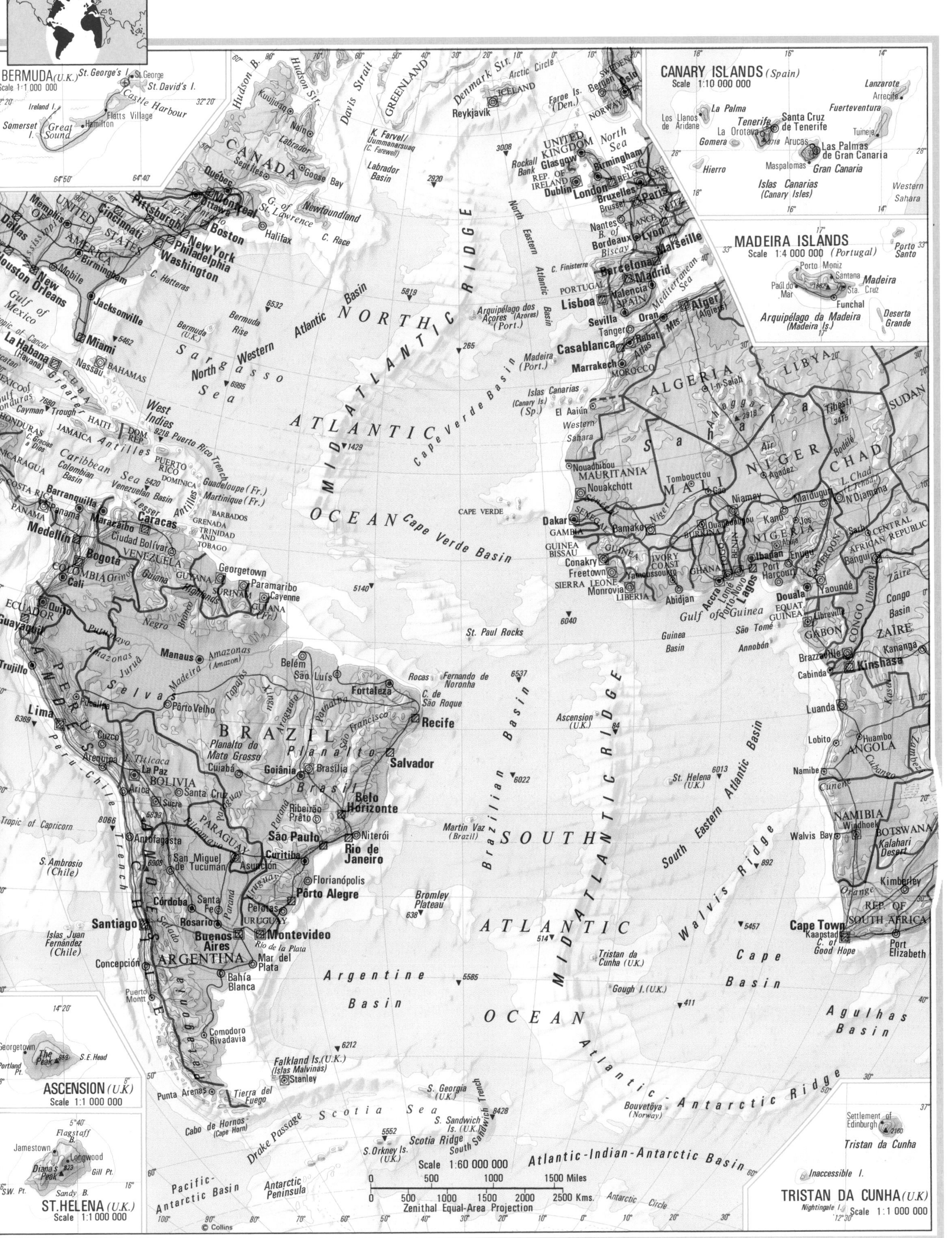

BERMUDA (U.K.)
Scale 1:1 000 000

CANARY ISLANDS (Spain)
Scale 1:10 000 000

MADEIRA ISLANDS
Scale 1:4 000 000 (Portugal)

ASCENSION (U.K.)
Scale 1:1 000 000

ST.HELENA (U.K.)
Scale 1:1 000 000

Scale 1:60 000 000

| 0 | 500 | 1000 | 1500 Miles |

| 0 | 500 | 1000 | 1500 | 2000 | 2500 Kms. |

Zenithal Equal-Area Projection

© Collins

TRISTAN DA CUNHA (U.K.)
Scale 1:1 000 000

POLAR REGIONS

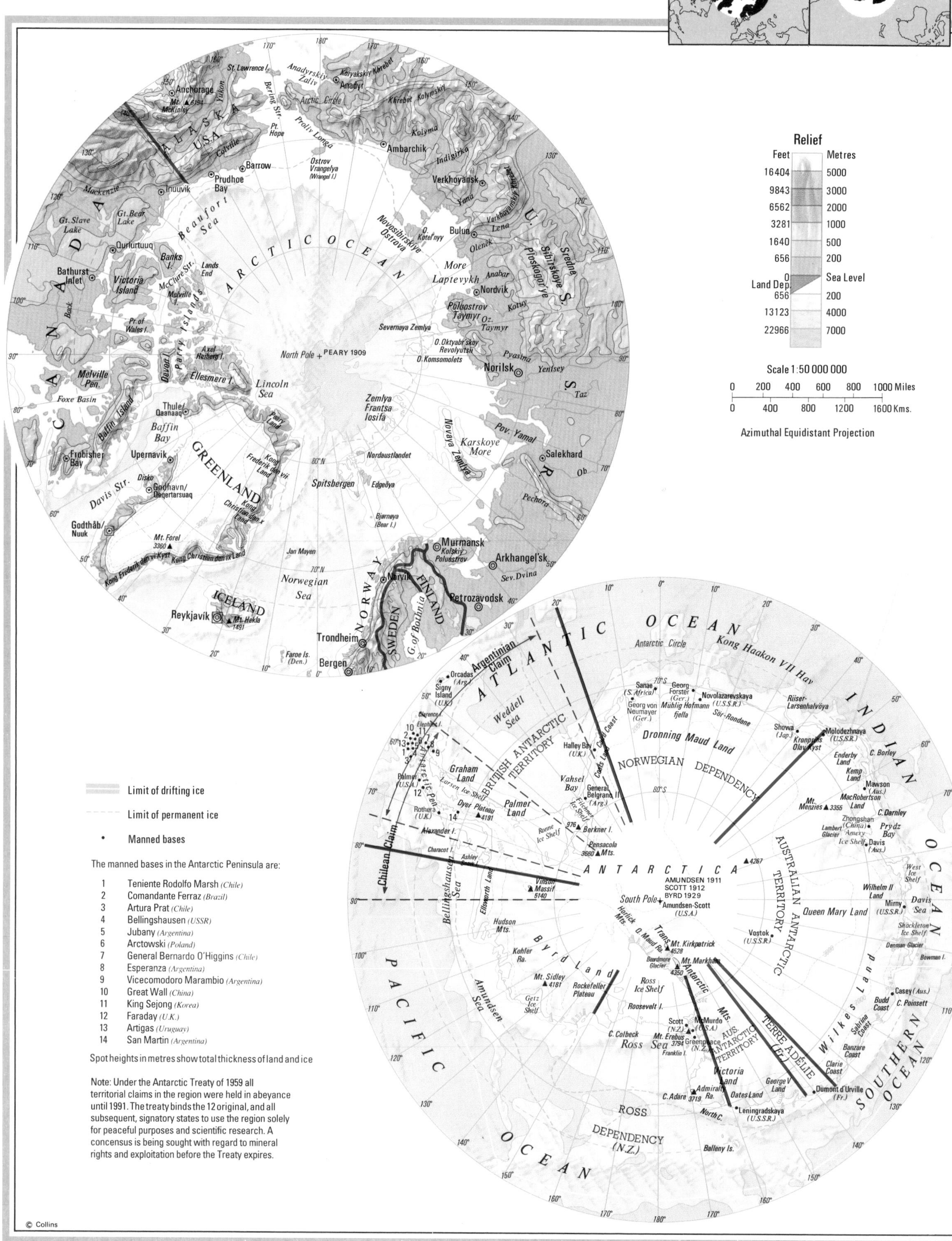

Relief

Feet		Metres
16404		5000
9843		3000
6562		2000
3281		1000
1640		500
656		200
0		Sea Level
Land Dep.		
656		200
13123		4000
22966		7000

Scale 1:50 000 000

| 0 | 200 | 400 | 600 | 800 | 1000 Miles |
| 0 | 400 | 800 | 1200 | 1600 Kms. |

Azimuthal Equidistant Projection

Limit of drifting ice

Limit of permanent ice

• Manned bases

The manned bases in the Antarctic Peninsula are:

1. Teniente Rodolfo Marsh (Chile)
2. Comandante Ferraz (Brazil)
3. Artura Prat (Chile)
4. Bellingshausen (USSR)
5. Jubany (Argentina)
6. Arctowski (Poland)
7. General Bernardo O'Higgins (Chile)
8. Esperanza (Argentina)
9. Vicecomodoro Marambio (Argentina)
10. Great Wall (China)
11. King Sejong (Korea)
12. Faraday (U.K.)
13. Artigas (Uruguay)
14. San Martin (Argentina)

Spot heights in metres show total thickness of land and ice

Note: Under the Antarctic Treaty of 1959 all territorial claims in the region were held in abeyance until 1991. The treaty binds the 12 original, and all subsequent, signatory states to use the region solely for peaceful purposes and scientific research. A consensus is being sought with regard to mineral rights and exploitation before the Treaty expires.

© Collins

GEOGRAPHICAL DATA
Part 1

WORLD
FACTS
AND
FIGURES

WORLD PHYSICAL DATA

Earth's Dimensions

Superficial area	510 066 000 km²
Land surface	148 326 000 km²
Water surface	361 740 000 km²
Equatorial circumference	40 075 km
Meridional circumference	40 007 km
Volume	1 083 230x10⁶ km³
Mass	5.976x10²¹ tonnes

The Continents

Asia	43 608 000 km²
Africa	30 355 000 km²
North America	25 349 000 km²
South America	17 611 000 km²
Antarctica	13 338 500 km²
Europe	10 498 000 km²
Oceania	8 547 000 km²

Oceans and Sea Areas

Pacific Ocean	165 384 000 km²
Atlantic Ocean	82 217 000 km²
Indian Ocean	73 481 000 km²
Arctic Ocean	14 056 000 km²
Mediterranean Sea	2 505 000 km²
South China Sea	2 318 000 km²
Bering Sea	2 269 000 km²
Caribbean Sea	1 943 000 km²
Gulf of Mexico	1 544 000 km²
Okhotskoye More (Sea of Okhotsk)	1 528 000 km²
East China Sea	1 248 000 km²
Hudson Bay	1 233 000 km²
Sea of Japan	1 008 000 km²
North Sea	575 000 km²
Black Sea	461 000 km²

Island Areas

Greenland; Arctic / Atlantic Ocean	2 175 597 km²
New Guinea; Indonesia / Papua New Guinea	808 510 km²
Borneo; Malaysia / Indonesia / Brunei	757 050 km²
Madagascar; Indian Ocean	594 180 km²
Sumatera (Sumatra) ; Indonesia	524 100 km²
Baffin Island; Canada	476 068 km²
Honshū; Japan	230 455 km²
Great Britain; United Kingdom	229 867 km²
Ellesmere Island; Canada	212 688 km²
Victoria Island; Canada	212 199 km²
Sulawesi (Celebes) ; Indonesia	189 040 km²
South Island; New Zealand	150 461 km²
Jawa (Java) ; Indonesia	134 045 km²
North Island; New Zealand	114 688 km²
Cuba; Caribbean Sea	114 525 km²

River Lengths

An Nīl (Nile) ; Africa	6695 km
Amazonas (Amazon) ; South America	6516 km
Chang Jiang (Yangtze) ; Asia	6380 km
Mississippi - Missouri; North America	6020 km
Ob-Irtysh; Asia	5570 km
Huang He (Hwang Ho) ; Asia	5464 km
Zaïre; Africa	4667 km
Mekong; Asia	4425 km
Amur; Asia	4416 km
Lena; Asia	4400 km
Mackenzie; North America	4250 km
Yenisey; Asia	4090 km
Niger; Africa	4030 km
Murray - Darling; Oceania	3750 km
Volga; Europe	3688 km

Mountain Heights (Selected)

Everest; Nepal / China	8848 m
K2; Jammu & Kashmir / China	8611 m
Kānchenjunga; Nepal / India	8586 m
Dhaulāgiri; Nepal	8167 m
Annapurna; Nepal	8091 m
Aconcagua; Argentina	6960 m
Ojos del Salado; Argentina / Chile	6908 m
McKinley; Alaska U.S.A.	6194 m
Logan; Canada	5951 m
Kilimanjaro; Tanzania	5895 m
Elbrus; U.S.S.R.	5642 m
Kenya; Kenya	5200 m
Vinson Massif; Antarctica	5139 m
Puncak Jaya; Indonesia	5030 m
Blanc; France / Italy	4807 m

Lake and Inland Sea Areas

Some areas are subject to seasonal variations.

Caspian Sea; U.S.S.R. / Iran	371 795 km²
Lake Superior; U.S.A. / Canada	83 270 km²
Lake Victoria; East Africa	69 485 km²
Lake Huron; U.S.A. / Canada	60 700 km²
Lake Michigan; U.S.A.	58 016 km²
Aralskoye More (Aral Sea) ; U.S.S.R.	36 500 km²
Lake Tanganyika; East Africa	32 893 km²
Great Bear Lake; Canada	31 792 km²
Ozero Baykal (Lake Baikal) ; U.S.S.R.	30 510 km²
Great Slave Lake; Canada	28 930 km²
Lake Erie; U.S.A. / Canada	25 667 km²
Lake Winnipeg; Canada	24 514 km²
Lake Malaŵi; Malaŵi / Mozambique	22 490 km²
Lake Ontario; U.S.A. / Canada	19 529 km²
Ladozhskoye Ozero (Lake Ladoga) ; U.S.S.R.	18 390 km²

Volcanoes (Selected)

	Last Eruption	Height
Cameroun; Cameroon	1922	4070 m
Cotopaxi; Ecuador	1975	5897 m
Elbrus; U.S.S.R.	extinct	5642 m
Erebus; Antarctica	1979	3794 m
Etna; Sicilia, Italy	1983	3340 m
Fuji san (Fujiyama) ; Japan	extinct	3776 m
Hekla; Iceland	1981	1491 m
Kilimanjaro; Tanzania	extinct	5895 m
Mauna Loa; Hawaii	1978	4171 m
Ngauruhoe; New Zealand	1975	2291 m
Popocatépetl; Mexico	1920	5452 m
St. Helens; U.S.A.	1981	2949 m
Stromboli; Italy	1975	926 m
Tristan da Cunha; Atlantic Ocean	1962	2160 m
Vesuvio (Vesuvius) ; Italy	1944	1277 m

WORLD POLITICAL DATA

National Areas

Union of Soviet Socialist Republics; Asia / Europe	22 402 000 km²
Canada; North America	9 922 385 km²
China; Asia	9 596 961 km²
United States; North America	9 363 123 km²
Brazil; South America	8 511 965 km²
Australia; Oceania	7 686 848 km²
India; Asia	3 166 830 km²
Argentina; South America	2 766 889 km²
Sudan; Africa	2 505 813 km²
Saudi Arabia; Asia	2 400 900 km²
Algeria; Africa	2 381 741 km²
Zaïre; Africa	2 345 409 km²
Greenland; North America	2 175 600 km²
Mexico; North America	1 972 547 km²
Indonesia; Asia	1 919 445 km²
Libya; Africa	1 759 540 km²
Iran; Asia	1 648 000 km²
Mongolia; Asia	1 565 000 km²
Peru; South America	1 285 216 km²
Chad; Africa	1 284 000 km²

National Populations

China; Asia	1 114 311 000
India; Asia	811 817 000
Union of Soviet Socialist Republics; Asia / Europe	286 717 000
United States; North America	249 928 000
Indonesia; Asia	179 136 000
Brazil; South America	147 404 000
Japan; Asia	123 116 000
Pakistan; Asia	108 678 000
Bangladesh; Asia	106 507 000
Nigeria; Africa	104 957 000
Mexico; North America	84 275 000
Germany; Europe	78 620 000
Vietnam; Asia	64 412 000
Philippines; Asia	60 097 000
Italy; Europe	57 557 000
United Kingdom; Europe	57 205 000
Turkey; Asia / Europe	56 741 000
France; Europe	56 160 000
Thailand; Asia	55 448 000
Egypt; Africa	53 080 000

World Cities

Ciudad de México (Mexico City) ; Mexico	19 396 000
New York; United States	17 931 000
Tōkyō; Japan	15 911 000
Cairo; Egypt	13 000 000
São Paulo; Brazil	13 000 000
Shanghai; China	12 500 000
Los Angeles; United States	10 232 000
Buenos Aires; Argentina	9 970 000
Sōul (Seoul) ; South Korea	9 646 000
Rio de Janeiro; Brazil	9 500 000
Beijing (Peking) ; China	9 470 000
Calcutta; India	9 160 000
London; United Kingdom	9 055 000
Moskva (Moscow) ; U.S.S.R.	8 967 000
Paris; France	8 706 000

Major International Organisations

United Nations - On December 1990 the United Nations had 160 members. Independent States not represented include Liechtenstein, Monaco, Nauru, North Korea, San Marino, South Korea, Switzerland, Taiwan, Tonga.

Commonwealth

Antigua	Australia	Bahamas	Bangladesh
Barbados	Belize	Botswana	Brunei
Canada	Cyprus	Dominica	Fiji
Gambia	Ghana	Grenada	Guyana
Hong Kong	India	Jamaica	Kenya
Kiribati	Lesotho	Malaŵi	Malaysia
Maldives	Malta	Mauritius	Nauru
New Zealand	Nigeria	Pakistan	Papua New Guinea
St. Kitts & Nevis	St. Lucia	St. Vincent	Seychelles
Sierra Leone	Singapore	Solomon Islands	Sri Lanka
Swaziland	Tanzania	Tonga	Trinidad & Tobago
Tuvalu	Uganda	United Kingdom	Vanuatu
Western Samoa	Zambia	Zimbabwe	

OAU - Organisation of African Unity

Algeria	Angola	Benin	Botswana
Burkina	Burundi	Cameroon	Cape Verde
Central African Rep.	Chad	Comoros	Congo
Djibouti	Egypt	Equatorial Guinea	Ethiopia
Gabon	Gambia	Ghana	Guinea
Guinea Bissau	Ivory Coast	Kenya	Lesotho
Liberia	Libya	Madagascar	Malaŵi
Mali	Mauritania	Mauritius	Mozambique
Namibia	Niger	Nigeria	Rwanda
São Tomé & Príncipe	Senegal	Seychelles	Sierra Leone
Somali Rep.	Sudan	Swaziland	Tanzania
Togo	Tunisia	Uganda	Western Sahara
Zaïre	Zambia	Zimbabwe	

OAS - Organisation of American States

Antigua	Argentina	Bahamas	Barbados
Bolivia	Brazil	Chile	Colombia
Costa Rica	Dominica	Dominican Rep.	Ecuador
El Salvador	Grenada	Guatemala	Haiti
Honduras	Jamaica	Mexico	Nicaragua
Panama	Paraguay	Peru	St. Kitts & Nevis
St. Lucia	St. Vincent	Surinam	Trinidad & Tobago
United States	Uruguay	Venezuela	

EEC - European Economic Community

Belgium	Denmark	France	Germany
Greece	Ireland	Italy	Luxembourg
Netherlands	Portugal	Spain	United Kingdom

EFTA - European Free Trade Association

Austria	Finland (assoc.)	Iceland	Norway
Sweden	Switzerland		

COMECON - Council for Mutual Economic Assistance

Bulgaria	Cuba	Czechoslovakia	Hungary
Mongolia	Poland	Romania	U.S.S.R.
Vietnam	Yugoslavia (assoc.)		

Note: as of January 1991 COMECON is to be gradually dismantled. It will be replaced by a new body called the Organisation for International Economic Co-operation (OIEC).

ASEAN - Association of Southeast Asian Nations

Brunei	Indonesia	Malaysia	Philippines
Singapore	Thailand		

ECOWAS - Economic Community of West African States

Benin	Burkina	Cape Verde	Gambia
Ghana	Guinea	Guinea Bissau	Ivory Coast
Liberia	Mali	Mauritania	Niger
Nigeria	Senegal	Sierra Leone	Togo

CARICOM - Caribbean Community and Common Market

Antigua	Bahamas	Barbados	Belize
Dominica	Grenada	Guyana	Jamaica
Montserrat	St. Kitts & Nevis	St. Lucia	St. Vincent
Trindad & Tobago			

NATIONS OF THE WORLD

COUNTRY	AREA sq. km.	POPULATION total	per sq. km.	FORM OF GOVERNMENT	CAPITAL CITY	MAIN LANGUAGES	CURRENCY
AFGHANISTAN	647,497	15,814,000	24	republic	Kābol	Pushtu, Dari (Persian)	afghani
ALBANIA	28,748	3,202,000	111	socialist republic	Tiranë	Albanian	lek
ALGERIA	2,381,741	24,597,000	10	republic	Alger (Algiers)	Arabic	dinar
ANDORRA	453	50,000	110	principality	Andorra	Catalan	French franc, Spanish peseta
ANGOLA	1,246,700	9,747,000	8	people's republic	Luanda	Portuguese	kwanza
ANTIGUA AND BARBUDA	442	85,000	192	constitutional monarchy	St John's	English	East Caribbean dollar
ARGENTINA	2,766,889	31,929,000	12	federal republic	Buenos Aires	Spanish	austral
AUSTRALIA	7,686,848	16,807,000	2	monarchy (federal)	Canberra	English	dollar
AUSTRIA	83,849	7,618,000	91	federal republic	Wien (Vienna)	German	schilling
BAHAMAS	13,935	249,000	18	constitutional monarchy	Nassau	English	dollar
BAHRAIN	622	489,000	786	emirate	Al Manāmah	Arabic	dinar
BANGLADESH	143,998	106,507,000	740	republic	Dhaka	Bengali	taka
BARBADOS	431	256,000	594	constitutional monarchy	Bridgetown	English	dollar
BELGIUM	30,513	9,883,000	324	constitutional monarchy	Bruxelles/Brussel (Brussels)	French, Dutch, German	franc
BELIZE	22,965	180,000	8	constitutional monarchy	Belmopan	English	dollar
BENIN	112,622	4,591,000	41	republic	Porto-Novo	French	CFA franc
BHUTAN	47,000	1,483,000	32	monarchy (Indian protection)	Thimbu	Dzongkha	Indian rupee, nguitrum
BOLIVIA	1,098,581	7,193,000	7	republic	La Paz/Sucre	Spanish	bolivano
BOTSWANA	600,372	1,256,000	2	republic	Gaborone	English, Tswana	pula
BRAZIL	8,511,965	147,404,000	17	federal republic	Brasília	Portuguese	cruzado
BRUNEI	5,765	249,000	43	sultanate	Bandar Seri Begawan	Malay	dollar
BULGARIA	110,912	8,981,000	81	people's republic	Sofiya (Sofia)	Bulgarian	lev
BURKINA	274,200	8,798,000	32	republic	Ouagadougou	French	CFA franc
BURMA	676,552	38,541,000	57	federal republic	Rangoon	Burmese	kyat
BURUNDI	27,834	5,302,000	190	republic	Bujumbura	French, Kirundi	franc
CAMBODIA	181,035	8,055,000	44	republic	Phnom Penh	Cambodian, Khmer	riel
CAMEROON	475,442	11,540,000	24	republic	Yaoundé	French, English	CFA franc
CANADA	9,976,139	26,248,000	3	monarchy (federal)	Ottawa	English, French	dollar
CAPE VERDE	4,033	368,000	91	republic	Praia	Portuguese, Creole	escudo
CENTRAL AFRICAN REPUBLIC	622,984	2,740,000	4	republic	Bangui	French, Sango	CFA franc
CHAD	1,284,000	5,538,000	4	republic	N'Djamena	French	CFA franc
CHILE	756,945	12,961,000	17	republic	Santiago	Spanish	peso
CHINA	9,596,961	1,114,311,000	116	people's republic	Beijing (Peking)	Mandarin	yuan
COLOMBIA	1,138,914	30,241,000	27	republic	Bogotá	Spanish	peso
COMOROS	2,171	484,000	223	federal republic	Moroni	Comoran, Arabic, French	CFA franc
CONGO	342,000	1,940,000	6	republic	Brazzaville	French	CFA franc
COSTA RICA	50,700	2,922,000	58	republic	San José	Spanish	colon
CUBA	114,524	10,594,000	93	people's republic	La Habana (Havana)	Spanish	peso
CYPRUS	9,251	694,000	75	republic	Levkosía (Nicosia)	Greek	pound
CZECHOSLOVAKIA	127,869	15,651,000	122	federal republic	Praha (Prague)	Czech, Slovak	koruna
DENMARK	43,069	5,132,000	119	constitutional monarchy	København (Copenhagen)	Danish	krone
DJIBOUTI	22,000	456,000	21	republic	Djibouti	French, Somali, Afar	franc
DOMINICA	751	81,000	108	republic	Roseau	English, French	East Caribbean dollar
DOMINICAN REPUBLIC	48,734	7,018,000	144	republic	Santo Dominigo	Spanish	peso
ECUADOR	283,561	10,490,000	37	republic	Quito	Spanish	sucre
EGYPT	1,001,449	53,080,000	53	republic	Al Qāhirah (Cairo)	Arabic	pound
EL SALVADOR	21,041	5,207,000	247	republic	San Salvador	Spanish	colón
EQUATORIAL GUINEA	28,051	341,000	12	republic	Malabo	Spanish	CFA franc
ETHIOPIA	1,221,900	50,774,000	42	people's republic	Ādīs Ābeba (Addis Ababa)	Amharic	birr
FIJI	18,274	727,000	40	republic	Suva	English, Fijian, Hindustani	dollar
FINLAND	337,032	4,962,000	15	republic	Helsinki	Finnish, Swedish	markka
FRANCE	547,026	56,160,000	103	republic	Paris	French	franc
GABON	267,667	1,206,000	5	republic	Libreville	French	CFA franc
GAMBIA	11,295	835,000	74	republic	Banjul	English	dalasi
GERMANY	356,755	78,620,000	220	federal republic	Berlin/Bonn	German	mark
GHANA	238,537	14,566,000	61	republic	Accra	English	cedi
GREECE	131,944	9,983,000	76	republic	Athínai (Athens)	Greek	drachma
GREENLAND	2,175,600	56,000	0	overseas territory (Denmark)	Godthåb/Nuuk	Danish, Greenlandic	krone

COUNTRY	AREA sq. km.	POPULATION total	per sq. km.	FORM OF GOVERNMENT	CAPITAL CITY	MAIN LANGUAGES	CURRENCY
GRENADA	344	97,000	282	constitutional monarchy	St George's	English	East Caribbean dollar
GUATEMALA	108,889	8,935,000	82	republic	Guatemala	Spanish	quetzal
GUIANA	91,000	90,000	1	overseas department (France)	Cayenne	French	franc
GUINEA	245,857	5,071,000	21	republic	Conakry	French	franc
GUINEA BISSAU	36,125	943,000	26	republic	Bissau	Portuguese	peso
GUYANA	214,969	1,023,000	5	republic	Georgetown	English	dollar
HAITI	27,750	5,609,000	202	republic	Port-au-Prince	French, Creole	goude
HONDURAS	112,088	4,951,000	44	republic	Tegucigalpa	Spanish	lempira
HONG KONG	1,045	5,681,000	5436	colony (U.K.)		English, Chinese	dollar
HUNGARY	93,030	10,563,000	114	republic	Budapest	Magyar	forint
ICELAND	103,000	250,000	2	republic	Reykjavik	Icelandic	króna
INDIA	3,287,590	811,817,000	247	republic	New Delhi	Hindi	rupee
INDONESIA	1,904,569	179,136,000	94	republic	Jakarta	Bahasa Indonesia	rupiah
IRAN	1,648,000	55,208,000	34	Islamic republic	Tehrān	Persian	rial
IRAQ	434,924	16,278,000	37	republic	Baghdād	Arabic	dinar
IRELAND, REPUBLIC OF	70,283	3,515,000	50	republic	Dublin	English, Irish	punt
ISRAEL	20,770	4,566,000	220	republic	Yerushalayim (Jerusalem)	Hebrew	shekel
ITALY	301,225	57,557,000	191	republic	Roma (Rome)	Italian	lira
IVORY COAST	322,463	12,097,000	38	republic	Yamoussoukro	French	CFA franc
JAMAICA	10,991	2,392,000	218	constitutional monarchy	Kingston	English	dollar
JAPAN	372,313	123,116,000	331	monarchy	Tōkyō	Japanese	yen
JORDAN	97,740	4,102,000	42	monarchy	'Ammān	Arabic	dinar
KENYA	582,646	24,872,000	43	republic	Nairobi	Swahili, English	shilling
KIRIBATI	886	64,000	72	republic	Tarawa	English, Gilbertese (I-Kiribati)	Australian dollar
KUWAIT	17,818	2,048,000	115	emirate	Al Kuwayt (Kuwait)	Arabic	dinar
LAOS	236,800	3,972,000	17	people's republic	Vientiane (Viangchan)	Lao	new kip
LEBANON	10,400	2,897,000	279	republic	Bayrūt (Beirut)	Arabic	pound
LESOTHO	30,355	1,700,000	56	monarchy	Maseru	English, Sesotho	maluti
LIBERIA	111,369	2,508,000	23	republic	Monrovia	English	dollar
LIBYA	1,759,540	4,385,000	2	republic (jamahiriya)	Tarābulus (Tripoli)	Arabic	dinar
LIECHTENSTEIN	157	28,000	178	constitutional monarchy	Vaduz	German	Swiss franc
LUXEMBOURG	2,586	378,000	146	constitutional monarchy	Luxembourg	Letzeburgish, French, German	franc
MADAGASCAR	587,041	9,985,000	17	republic	Antananarivo	Malagasy	Malagasy franc
MALAWI	118,484	8,022,000	68	republic	Lilongwe	English, Chichewa	kwacha
MALAYSIA	329,749	16,942,000	51	constitutional monarchy	Kuala Lumpur	Malay	ringgit
MALDIVES	298	206,000	691	republic	Malé	Divehi	rufiya
MALI	1,240,000	7,960,000	6	republic	Bamako	French, Bambara	CFA franc
MALTA	316	350,000	1108	republic	Valletta	Maltese, English	pound
MAURITANIA	1,030,700	1,969,000	2	republic	Nouakchott	French, Arabic	ouguiya
MAURITIUS	2,045	1,068,000	522	constitutional monarchy	Port-Louis	English, Creole	rupee
MEXICO	1,972,547	84,275,000	43	federal republic	Ciudad de México (Mexico City)	Spanish	peso
MONACO	2	28,000	18667	constitutional monarchy	Monaco	French	French franc
MONGOLIA	1,565,000	2,043,000	1	people's republic	Ulaanbaatar (Ulan Bator)	Mongol	tugrik
MOROCCO	446,550	24,521,000	55	monarchy	Rabat	Arabic	dirham
MOZAMBIQUE	801,590	15,326,000	19	people's republic	Maputo	Portuguese	metical
NAMIBIA	824,292	1,817,000	2	republic	Windhoek	Afrikaans, English	Namibian dollar
NAURU	21	8,000	381	republic	Nauru	Nauruan, English	Australian dollar
NEPAL	140,797	18,442,000	131	monarchy	Kātmāndu	Nepali	rupee
NETHERLANDS	40,844	14,891,000	365	constitutional monarchy	Amsterdam	Dutch	guilder
NEW ZEALAND	268,676	3,389,000	13	constitutional monarchy	Wellington	English	dollar
NICARAGUA	130,000	3,384,000	26	republic	Managua	Spanish	córdoba
NIGER	1,267,000	7,250,000	6	republic	Niamey	French	CFA franc
NIGERIA	923,768	104,957,000	114	federal republic	Abuja	English	naira
NORTH KOREA	120,538	22,418,000	186	people's republic	Pyŏngyang	Korean	won
NORWAY	324,219	4,227,000	13	constitutional monarchy	Oslo	Norwegian	krone
OMAN	212,457	1,422,000	7	sultanate	Masqaṭ (Muscat)	Arabic	rial
PAKISTAN	803,943	108,678,000	135	federal republic	Islāmābād	Urdu, Punjabi, English	rupee
PANAMA	77,082	2,370,000	31	republic	Panamá	Spanish	balboa

NATIONS OF THE WORLD

COUNTRY	AREA sq. km.	POPULATION total	POPULATION per sq. km.	FORM OF GOVERNMENT	CAPITAL CITY	MAIN LANGUAGES	CURRENCY
PAPUA NEW GUINEA	461,691	3,593,000	8	constitutional monarchy	Port Moresby	English, Pidgin, Motu	kina
PARAGUAY	406,752	4,157,000	10	republic	Asunción	Spanish, Guaraní	guaraní
PERU	1,285,216	21,792,000	17	republic	Lima	Spanish	inti
PHILIPPINES	300,000	60,097,000	200	republic	Manila	Pilipino	peso
POLAND	312,677	37,931,000	121	republic	Warszawa (Warsaw)	Polish	zloty
PORTUGAL	92,082	10,467,000	114	republic	Lisboa (Lisbon)	Portuguese	escudo
PUERTO RICO	8,897	3,293,000	370	commonwealth (U.S.A.)	San Juan	Spanish, English	dollar
QATAR	11,000	422,000	38	emirate	Ad Dawḥah (Doha)	Arabic	riyal
ROMANIA	237,500	23,152,000	97	republic	Bucureşti (Bucharest)	Romanian	leu
RWANDA	26,338	6,989,000	265	republic	Kigali	Kinyarwanda, French	franc
ST KITTS-NEVIS	266	49,000	184	constitutional monarchy	Basseterre	English	East Caribbean dollar
ST LUCIA	616	148,000	240	constitutional monarchy	Castries	English, French	East Caribbean dollar
ST VINCENT AND THE GRENADINES	389	113,000	290	constitutional monarchy	Kingstown	English	East Caribbean dollar
SAN MARINO	61	23,000	377	republic	San Marino	Italian	Italian lira
SÃO TOMÉ AND PRINCIPE	964	116,000	120	republic	São Tomé	Portuguese, Creole	dobra
SAUDI ARABIA	2,149,690	14,435,000	7	monarchy	Ar Riyāḍ (Riyadh)	Arabic	riyal
SENEGAL	196,192	7,113,000	36	republic	Dakar	French	CFA franc
SEYCHELLES	280	67,000	239	republic	Victoria	English, French	rupee
SIERRA LEONE	71,740	3,516,000	49	republic	Freetown	English	leone
SINGAPORE	602	2,704,000	4492	republic	Singapore	Malay, English, Chinese, Tamil	dollar
SOLOMON ISLANDS	28,446	299,000	11	constitutional monarchy	Honiara	English	dollar
SOMALI REPUBLIC	637,657	7,339,000	12	republic	Muqdisho	Arabic, Italian, English, Somali	shilling
SOUTH AFRICA, REPUBLIC OF	1,221,037	34,492,000	28	federal republic	Cape Town (Kaapstad)/Pretoria	Afrikaans, English	rand
SOUTH KOREA	98,484	42,380,000	430	republic	Sŏul (Seoul)	Korean	won
SPAIN	504,782	39,248,000	78	constitutional monarchy	Madrid	Spanish	peseta
SRI LANKA	65,610	16,806,000	256	republic	Colombo	Sinhala, Tamil	rupee
SUDAN	2,505,813	24,484,000	10	republic	Al Kharṭūm (Khartoum)	Arabic	pound
SURINAM	163,265	397,000	2	republic	Paramaribo	Dutch, English	guilder
SWAZILAND	17,363	681,000	39	monarchy	Mbabane	English, Siswati	lilangeni
SWEDEN	449,964	8,541,000	19	constitutional monarchy	Stockholm	Swedish	krona
SWITZERLAND	41,288	6,647,000	161	federal republic	Bern (Berne)	German, French, Italian, Romansh	franc
SYRIA	185,180	11,719,000	63	republic	Dimashq (Damascus)	Arabic	pound
TAIWAN	35,961	19,900,000	553	republic	Taipei	Mandarin	dollar
TANZANIA	945,087	24,802,000	26	republic	Dodoma	Swahili	shilling
THAILAND	514,000	54,448,000	106	monarchy	Bangkok (Krung Thep)	Thai	baht
TOGO	56,785	3,296,000	58	republic	Lomé	French	CFA franc
TONGA	699	95,000	136	monarchy	Nuku'alofa	Tongan, English	pa anga
TRINIDAD AND TOBAGO	5,130	1,212,000	236	republic	Port of Spain	English	dollar
TUNISIA	163,610	7,465,000	46	republic	Tunis	Arabic	dinar
TURKEY	780,576	56,741,000	73	republic	Ankara	Turkish	lira
TUVALU	24	7,000	292	constitutional monarchy	Funafuti	Tuvalu, English	Australian dollar
U.S.S.R.	22,402,200	286,717,000	13	federal socialist republic	Moskva (Moscow)	Russian	rouble
UGANDA	236,036	17,804,000	75	republic	Kampala	English	new shilling
UNITED ARAB EMIRATES	83,600	1,546,000	18	self-governing union		Arabic	dirham
UNITED KINGDOM	244,046	57,205,000	234	constitutional monarchy	London	English	pound
UNITED STATES OF AMERICA	9,372,614	249,928,000	27	federal republic	Washington	English	dollar
URUGUAY	176,215	3,077,000	17	republic	Montevideo	Spanish	peso
VANUATU	14,763	143,000	10	republic	Vila	English, French	vatu
VENEZUELA	912,050	19,246,000	21	federal republic	Caracas	Spanish	bolívar
VIETNAM	329,556	64,412,000	195	people's republic	Hanoi	Vietnamese	dong
WESTERN SAMOA	2,842	168,000	59	constitutional monarchy	Apia	Samoan, English	tala
YEMEN	527,968	11,619,439	22	republic	Şan'ā	Arabic	rial
YUGOSLAVIA	255,804	23,764,000	93	socialist federal republic	Beograd (Belgrade)	Serbo-Croat, Macedonian, Slovene	dinar
ZAÏRE	2,345,409	34,491,000	15	republic	Kinshasa	French, Lingala	zaïre
ZAMBIA	752,614	7,804,000	10	republic	Lusaka	English	kwacha
ZIMBABWE	390,580	9,122,000	23	republic	Harare	English	dollar

GEOGRAPHICAL DATA
Part 2

GLOSSARY
OF
GEOGRAPHICAL
TERMS

GLOSSARY

Introduction to Glossary

The Glossary of Geographical Terms lists in alphabetical order a selection of foreign language names and geographical terms, inclusive of any abbreviations, which are found in the names on the maps and in the index. The terms occur either as separate words (e.g. côte which means coast) or as parts of compound words (e.g. - oog in Langeoog which means island). A term preceded by a hyphen usually appears as an ending of a name on the map (e.g. -vesi in Puulavesi; -holm in Bornholm). Each term is followed by its language which is identified by abbreviations in brackets. A complete list of the language abbreviations used in the glossary is found below.

Language Abbreviations

Afr.	Afrikaans	Fin.	Finnish	Man.	Manchurian
Alb.	Albanian	Fr.	French	Mon.	Mongolian
Ar.	Arabic	Gae.	Gaelic	Nor.	Norwegian
Ba.	Baluchi	Ger.	German	Per.	Persian
Ber.	Berber	Gr.	Greek	Pol.	Polish
Blg.	Bulgarian	Heb.	Hebrew	Port.	Portuguese
Bur.	Burmese	Hin.	Hindi	Rom.	Romanian
Cat.	Catalan	I.-C.	Indo-Chinese	Rus.	Russian
Cbd.	Cambodian	Ice.	Icelandic	S.-C.	Serbo-Croat
Ch.	Chinese	It.	Italian	Sp.	Spanish
Cz.	Czechoslovakian	Jap.	Japanese	Swe.	Swedish
Dan.	Danish	Kor.	Korean	Th.	Thai (Siamese)
Dut.	Dutch	Lao.	Laotian	Tur.	Turkish
Est.	Estonian	Lat.	Latvian	Ur.	Urdu
Eth.	Ethiopian	Ma.	Malagasy	Viet.	Vietnamese
Fae.	Faeroese	Mal.	Malay		

Glossary of Geographical Terms

A

āb *(Per.)*	water
ada *(Tur.)*	island
adrar *(Ber., Ar.)*	mountain region
ákra, akrotírion *(Gr.)*	cape
alb *(Rom.)*	white
alin *(Man., Mon.)*	mountain range
alpes *(Fr.)*	alps
alpi *(It.)*	alps
alt/a/o *(It., Sp., Port.)*	high
-an *(Swe.)*	river
ao *(Ch., Th.)*	bay, gulf
arquipélago *(Port.)*	archipelago
-ås, -åsen *(Swe.)*	hills

B

bāb *(Ar.)*	gate
backe *(Swe.)*	hill
bādiya/t *(Ar.)*	desert
baelt *(Dan.)*	strait
b., bahía *(Sp.)*	bay
bahr *(Ar.)*	great river/lake
baía *(Port.)*	bay
b., baie *(Fr.)*	bay
ban *(Hin., Ur.)*	forest
ban *(I.-C.)*	village
bañados *(Sp.)*	marshes
bandao *(Ch.)*	peninsula
bassin *(Fr.)*	basin
batha *(Ar.)*	plain
beloyy *(Rus.)*	white
ben, beinn *(Gae.)*	mountain
bereg *(Rus.)*	shore

berg/en *(Ger., Swe.)*	mountain/s
biq'at *(Heb.)*	valley
birkat *(Ar.)*	lake
bog., boğazi *(Tur.)*	strait
bois *(Fr.)*	woods
bol., bol'shaya *(Rus.)*	big
bory *(Pol.)*	forest
bredning *(Dan.)*	bay
brú *(Ice.)*	bridge
bucht *(Ger.)*	bay
bugt *(Dan.)*	bay
buhayrat *(Ar.)*	lake
bukt/en *(Nor., Swe.)*	bay
burnu *(Tur.)*	cape
busen *(Ger.)*	bay
büyük *(Tur.)*	big

C

c., cabo *(Sp., Port.)*	cape
campo *(Sp.)*	field
c., cap *(Fr.)*	cape
capo *(It.)*	cape
causse *(Fr.)*	upland
cerro *(Sp.)*	mountain
chaco *(Sp.)*	jungle region
chaîne *(Fr.)*	chain
chapada *(Port.)*	hills
chott *(Ar.)*	salt lake
cime *(Fr.)*	summit
co *(Ch.)*	lake
co *(Viet.)*	mountain
col *(Fr.)*	pass

colline/s *(Fr.)*	hill/s
con *(Viet.)*	islands
cordillera *(Sp.)*	mountain range
costa *(Sp.)*	coast
côte *(Fr.)*	coast

D

d., daği, dağlari *(Tur.)*	mountain, mountain range
dake *(Jap.)*	peak
dal/en *(Nor., Swe.)*	valley
danau *(Mal.)*	lake
daqq *(Per.)*	salt flat
darya *(Rus.)*	river
daryācheh *(Per.)*	lake
dasht *(Per.)*	desert
denizi *(Tur.)*	sea
desierto *(Sp.)*	desert
détroit *(Fr.)*	strait
dhiórix *(Gr.)*	canal
dian *(Ch.)*	lake
-dijk *(Dut.)*	dyke
ding *(Ch.)*	mountain
do *(Kor.)*	island

E

eiland/en *(Afr., Dut.)*	island/s
embalse *(Sp.)*	reservoir
'emeq *(Heb.)*	valley
erg *(Ar.)*	sand desert
estrecho *(Sp.)*	strait
estuario *(Sp.)*	estuary

GLOSSARY

étang *(Fr.)* — pond

F

feng *(Ch.)* — peak
firth *(Gae.)* — strait
fjället *(Swe.)* — mountain
fjell *(Nor.)* — mountain
fj., fjorden *(Dan., Nor., Swe.)* — fjord
fjördhur *(Fae., Ice.)* — fjord
flói *(Ice.)* — bay
fonn *(Nor.)* — glacier

G

gau *(Ger.)* — district
gave *(Fr.)* — torrent
gebirge *(Ger.)* — mountains
ghubbat *(Ar.)* — bay
gji *(Alb.)* — bay
gobi *(Mon.)* — desert
gol *(Mon.)* — river
g., golfe *(Fr.)* — gulf
g., golfo *(Sp., It.)* — gulf
gölö *(Tur.)* — lake
golyam *(Blg.)* — great
g., gora/y *(Rus.)* — mountain/s
gorje *(S.C.)* — mountain range
gross *(Ger.)* — great
guba *(Rus.)* — bay
guntō *(Jap.)* — island group
guoyuan *(Ch.)* — plateau
gura *(Rom.)* — mouth

H

hai *(Ch.)* — sea
haixia *(Ch.)* — strait
ḥajar *(Ar.)* — mountain range
halvö *(Dan.)* — peninsula
halvöya *(Nor.)* — peninsula
hāmūn *(Per.)* — plain
hantō *(Jap.)* — peninsula
har *(Heb.)* — mountain range
hauteurs *(Fr.)* — hills
hav *(Dan., Nor., Swe.)* — sea
hawr *(Ar.)* — lake
hāyk' *(Eth.)* — lake
he *(Ch.)* — river
heiya *(Jap.)* — plain
hoch *(Ger.)* — high
hohe *(Ger.)* — height
höj *(Dan.)* — high, height
-holm *(Dan.)* — island
holt *(Nor.)* — wood
hory *(Cz.)* — mountain
hu *(Ch.)* — lake
-huk *(Swe.)* — cape

I

î., îs., île/s *(Fr.)* — island/s
ilha/s *(Port.)* — island/s
insel/n *(Ger.)* — island/s

i., is., isla/s *(Sp.)* — island/s
isola/e *(It.)* — island/s
istmo *(Sp.)* — isthmus
iztochni *(Blg.)* — eastern

J

j., jabal *(Ar., Per.)* — mountain
jarvi *(Fin.)* — lake
jaure *(Swe.)* — lake
jawb *(Ar.)* — basin, waterhole
jazā'ir *(Ar.)* — island
jezero *(S.-C., Cz.)* — lake
jezioro *(Pol.)* — lake
jiang *(Ch.)* — river
jima *(Jap.)* — island
jökulen *(Nor.)* — glacier
jökull *(Ice.)* — glacier
jūras līcis *(Lat.)* — gulf, bay

K

kaikyō *(Jap.)* — strait
kaise *(Swe.)* — mountain range
kamm *(Ger.)* — ridge
k., kanal *(Ger., Pol., Rus., S.-C., Swe.)* — canal
kap *(Ger.)* — cape
kapp *(Nor.)* — cape
kep *(Alb.)* — cape
kep., kepulauan *(Mal.)* — archipelago
khalīj *(Ar., Per.)* — gulf, bay
khazzān *(Ar.)* — dam
khr., khrebet *(Rus.)* — mountain range
kladenets *(Blg.)* — well
klong *(Th.)* — canal, creek
ko *(Jap.)* — lake, bay
ko *(Th.)* — island
-kogen *(Jap.)* — plateau
koh *(Per.)* — mountains
kólpos *(Gr.)* — gulf
kör., körfezi *(Tur.)* — gulf, bay
kou *(Ch.)* — estuary
kryazh *(Rus.)* — ridge
kūh/ha *(Per.)* — mountain/s
kul *(Rus.)* — lake
kuppe *(Ger.)* — hilltop
kyst *(Dan.)* — coast

L

lac *(Fr.)* — lake
lacul *(Rom.)* — lake
l., lago *(It. Sp.)* — lake
lagoa *(Port.)* — lagoon
laguna *(Sp.)* — lagoon, lake
laut *(Mal.)* — north, sea
liedao *(Ch.)* — islands
liehtao *(Ch.)* — islands
l., límni *(Gr.)* — lake
ling *(Ch.)* — mountain range
llanos *(Sp.)* — plains
l., loch *(Gae.)* — lake
lora *(Ba.)* — stream
l., lough *(Gae.)* — lake

lule *(Swe.)* — eastern

M

maa *(Est., Fin.)* — land
mae *(Th.)* — river
mar/e *(It., Port., Sp.)* — sea
marsch *(Ger.)* — marsh
meer *(Afr., Dut.)* — lake, sea
mer *(Fr.)* — sea
mifraż *(Heb.)* — bay
misaki *(Jap.)* — cape
mont *(Fr.)* — mountain
montagne *(Fr.)* — mountain
mont/e/i *(It., Port., Sp.)* — mountain/s
moor *(Ger.)* — swamp, moor
more *(Rus.)* — sea
mörön *(Mon.)* — river
mui *(Viet.)* — point
mull *(Gae.)* — headland
munkhafaḍ *(Ar.)* — depression
munti/i *(Rom.)* — mountain/s
m., mys *(Rus.)* — cape

N

nada *(Jap.)* — sea, bay
nafūd *(Ar.)* — sandy desert
najd *(Ar.)* — pass
nam *(I.-C., Kor.)* — southern
nes *(Ice., Nor.)* — promontory
ness *(Gae.)* — promontory
nevada *(Sp.)* — snow-capped mountains
ngoc *(Viet)* — mountain
nísoi *(Gr.)* — islands
nizh., nizhne, nizhniy *(Rus.)* — lower
nizmennost' *(Rus.)* — depression
nord *(Dan., Fr., Ger., Nor., Swe.)* — northern
nur *(Ch.)* — lake, salt lake
nusa *(Mal.)* — island
nuur *(Mon.)* — lake

O

occidental *(Sp.)* — western
odde *(Dan., Nor.)* — headland
ojo/s *(Sp.)* — spring/s
oki *(Jap.)* — bay
-oog *(Ger.)* — island
óros, óri *(Gr.)* — mountain, mountains
oriental/e *(Sp.)* — eastern
ort *(Ger.)* — settlement
o., os., ostrov/a *(Rus.)* — island/s
ost *(Ger.)* — east
oued *(Ar.)* — dry river bed
öy, öya *(Nor.)* — island
oz., ozero *(Rus.)* — lake

P

pampa/s *(Sp.)* — plain/s
parbat *(Ur.)* — mountain
passo *(It.)* — pass
peg., pegunungan *(Mal.)* — mountain range

137

GLOSSARY

pélagos (Gr.)	sea
pelleg (Alb.)	bay
peña (Sp.)	cliff
pendi (Ch.)	depression
péninsule (Fr.)	peninsula
pertuis (Fr.)	strait
peski (Rus.)	sand
phanom (I.-C., Th.)	mountain
phou (Lao.)	mountain
phu (Th.)	mountain
pic (Fr.)	peak
pico (Sp.)	peak
pik (Rus.)	peak
pingyuan (Ch.)	plain
plaine (Fr.)	plain
plana (Sp.)	plain
planalto (Port.)	plateau
pl., planina (Blg., S.-C.)	mountain range
plato (Afr., Blg., Rus.)	plateau
platosu (Tur.)	plateau
platte (Ger.)	plateau, plain
playa (Sp.)	beach
ploskogor'ye (Rus.)	plateau
pohorie (Cz.)	mountain range
pointe (Fr.)	promontory
pojezierze (Pol.)	lakeland
poleseye (Rus.)	area of marsh
polje (S.-C.)	plain, basin
pov., poluostrov (Rus.)	peninsula
porthmós (Gr.)	strait
porţi (Rom.)	entrance
portillo (Sp.)	gap
prliv (Rus.)	strait
puig (Cat.)	peak
pulau (Mal.)	island
pta., punta (It., Sp.)	point
puy (Fr.)	peak

Q

qā' (Ar.)	salt flat
qanāt (Ar., Per.)	canal
qolleh (Per.)	mountain
qu (Ch.)	canal, stream
qūr (Ar.)	buttes, ridge

R

ramlat (Ar.)	dunes
rann (Hin.)	swampy region
ras, ra's, rās (Per., Ar.)	cape
ravnina (Rus.)	plain
reprêsa (Port.)	reservoir
reshteh (Per.)	mountain range
retto (Jap.)	island group
ria, ría (Port., Sp.)	mouth of river
rijeka (S.-C.)	river
r:, rio, río (Port., Sp.)	river
riviera (It.)	coast, river
r., rivière (Fr.)	river
rocca (It.)	rock
rücken (Ger.)	ridge
rūd (Per.)	river

S

sable/s (Fr.)	sand/s
sadd (Ar.)	dam
sāgar (Hin., Ur.)	lake
ṣaḥrā (Ar.)	desert
ṣa'īd (Ar.)	highland
saki (Jap.)	cape
salar (Sp.)	salt flat
salina/s (Sp.)	salt marsh
sammyaku (Jap.)	mountain range
san (Jap., Kor.)	mountain
-sanchi (Jap.)	mountains
see (Ger.)	lake
seenplatte (Ger.)	lakeland
selat (Mal.)	strait
selatan (Mal.)	southern
selkä (Fin.)	ridge
selseleh (Per.)	mountain range
selva (Sp.)	forest
serra (Port.)	mountain range
serranía (Sp.)	ridge
sev., severo, severnyy (Rus.)	north
sha'īb (Ar.)	ravine, wadi
shamo (Ch.)	desert
shan (Ch.)	mountain
shankou (Ch.)	mountain pass
shaṭṭ (Ar.)	large river
shibh jazīrat (Ar.)	peninsula
shima (Jap.)	island
shotō (Jap.)	island group
shui (Ch.)	river
sa., sierra (Sp.)	mountain range
-sjon (Swe.)	lake
skog (Nor., Swe.)	forest
skov (Dan.)	forest
slieve (Gae.)	mountain
sor (Rus.)	salt flat
sör (Nor.)	southern
spitze (Ger.)	peak
sredne (Rus.)	central
step (Rus.)	steppe
stora (Fae.)	large
strath (Gae.)	valley
stretto (It.)	strait
suidō (Jap.)	strait
ṣummān (Ar.)	escarpment
sund (Dan., Ger., Ice., Nor., Swe.)	sound
svart (Nor., Swe.)	black

T

take (Jap.)	peak
tall (Ar.)	mountain
tanjona (Ma.)	cape
tanjung (Mal.)	cape
tau (Rus.)	mountain
teluk (Mal.)	bay
testa (It.)	head
thale (Th.)	lagoon, sea
tierra (Sp.)	land, territory
tind (Nor.)	sharp peak
tō (Jap.)	island, eastern
tônlé (Cbd.)	lake
träsk (Swe.)	marsh
tunturi (Fin.)	treeless mountain

U

'urūq (Ar.)	dunes
utara (Mal.)	northern
uul (Mon., Rus.)	mountain range

V

väin (Est.)	strait
val (Fr., It.)	valley
vand (Dan.)	water
vatn (Ice., Nor.)	lake
vatnet (Nor.)	lake
vatten (Swe.)	lake
veld (Afr.)	field
veliki (S.-C.)	large
verkh., verkhne, verkhniy (Rus.)	upper
-vesi (Fin.)	lake
vest, vester (Dan., Nor.)	west
vidda (Nor.)	plateau
-viken (Nor., Swe.)	gulf, bay
vdkhr., vodokhranilishche (Rus.)	reservoir
volcán (Sp.)	volcano
vostochno, vostochnyy (Rus.)	eastern
vozvyshennost (Rus.)	uplands
vrata (Blg.)	gate
vrh (S.-C.)	peak

W

wāhāt (Ar.)	oasis
wald (Ger.)	forest
wan (Ch., Jap.)	bay

Y

yam (Heb.)	sea
yama (Jap.)	mountain
yanchi (Ch.)	salt lake
yarimadasi (Tur.)	peninsula
yazovir (Blg.)	dam
yoma (Bur.)	mountain range
yumco (Ch.)	lake
yunhe (Ch.)	canal
yuzhnyy (Rus.)	south

Z

zaki (Jap.)	cape, peninsula
zaliv (Rus.)	bay
zan (Jap.)	mountain range
zangbo (Ch.)	stream, river
zapadno, zapadnyy (Rus.)	western
zatoka (Pol.)	bay
zemlya (Rus.)	land
zhou (Ch.)	island
zuid (Dut.)	south

GEOGRAPHICAL DATA
Part 3

WORLD
INDEX

WORLD INDEX

Introduction to World Index

The index includes an alphabetical list of all names appearing on the maps in the World Atlas section. Each entry indicates the country or region of the world in which the name is located. This is followed by a page reference and finally the name's location on the map, given by latitude and longitude co-ordinates. Most features are indexed to the largest scale map on which they appear, however when the name applies to countries or other extensive features it is generally indexed to the map on which it appears in its entirety. Areal features are generally indexed using co-ordinates which indicate

the centre of the feature. The latitude and longitude indicated for a point feature gives the location of the point on the map. In the case of rivers the mouth or confluence is always taken as the point of reference.

Names in the index are generally in the local language and where a conventional English version exists, this is cross referenced to the entry in the local language. Names of features which extend across the boundaries of more than one country are usually named in English if no single official name exists. Names in languages not

written in the Roman alphabet have been transliterated using the official system of the country if one exists, e.g. Pinyin system for China, otherwise the systems recognised by the United States Board on Geographical Names have been used.

Names abbreviated on the maps are given in full in the Index. Abbreviations are used for both geographical terms and administrative names in the Index. All abbreviations used in the Index are listed below.

Abbreviations of Geographical Terms

b., B.	bay, Bay	**f.**	physical feature e.g. valley, plain, geographic district or region	**mts., Mts.**	mountains, Mountains
c., C.	cape, Cape			**pen., Pen.**	peninsula, Peninsula
d.	internal division e.g county, region, state	**g., G.**	gulf, Gulf	Pt.	Point
des.	desert	**i., I., is., Is.**	island, Island, islands, Islands	**r.**	river
est.	estuary	**l., L.**	lake, Lake	**resr., Resr.**	reservoir, Reservoir
		mtn., Mtn.	mountain, Mountain	Sd.	Sound
				str., Str.	strait, Strait

Abbreviations of Country / Administrative Names

Afghan.	Afghanistan	Mass.	Massachusetts	R.I.	Rhode Island
A.H. Prov.	Alpes de Haut Provence	Md.	Maryland	R.S.A.	Republic of South Africa
Ala.	Alabama	Mich.	Michigan	R.S.F.S.R.	Rossiyskaya Sovetskaya
Alas.	Alaska	Minn.	Minnesota		Federativnaya
Alta.	Alberta	Miss.	Mississippi		Sotsialisticheskaya
Ariz.	Arizona	Mo.	Missouri		Respublika
Ark.	Arkansas	Mont.	Montana	S.A.	South Australia
Baja Calif. Norte	Baja California Norte	M.-Pyr.	Midi-Pyrénées	Sask.	Saskatchewan
Baja Calif. Sur	Baja California Sur	M.S.S.R.	Moldavskaya Sovetskaya	S.C.	South Carolina
Bangla.	Bangladesh		Sotsialisticheskaya	Sch.-Hol.	Schleswig-Holstein
B.C.	British Columbia		Respublika	S. Dak.	South Dakota
B.S.S.R.	Belorusskaya Sovetskaya	N.B.	New Brunswick	S. Korea	South Korea
	Sotsialisticheskaya Respublika	N.C.	North Carolina	S. Mar.	Seine Maritime
B.-Würt	Baden-Württemberg	N. Dak.	North Dakota	Sogn og Fj.	Sogn og Fjordane
Calif.	California	Nebr.	Nebraska	Somali Rep.	Somali Republic
C.A.R.	Central African Republic	Neth.	Netherlands	Switz.	Switzerland
Char. Mar.	Charente Maritime	Nev.	Nevada	Tas.	Tasmania
Colo.	Colorado	Nfld.	Newfoundland	Tenn.	Tennessee
Conn.	Connecticut	N.H.	New Hampshire	Tex.	Texas
C.P.	Cape Province	N. Ireland	Northern Ireland	T.G.	Tarn-et-Garonne
Czech.	Czechoslovakia	N.J.	New Jersey	Tk. S.S.R.	Turkmenskaya Sovetskaya
D.C.	District of Colombia	N. Korea	North Korea		Sotsialisticheskaya
Del.	Delaware	N. Mex	New Mexico		Respublika
Dom. Rep.	Dominican Republic	Nschn.	Niedersachsen	Trans.	Transvaal
Equat. Guinea	Equatorial Guinea	N.S.W.	New South Wales	U.A.E.	United Arab Emirates
Eth.	Ethiopia	N. Trönd.	North Tröndelag	U.K.	United Kingdom
Fla.	Florida	N.T.	Northern Territory	Ukr. S.S.R.	Ukrainskaya Sovetskaya
Ga.	Georgia	N.-Westfalen	Nordrhein-Westfalen		Sotsialisticheskaya
Guang. Zhuang	Guangxi Zhuangzu	N.W.T.	Northwest Territories		Respublika
H.-Gar.	Haute Garonne	N.Y.	New York State	U.S.A.	United States of America
Himachal P.	Himachal Pradesh	O.F.S.	Orange Free State	U.S.S.R.	Union of Soviet Socialist
H. Zaïre	Haut Zaïre	Okla.	Oklahoma		Republics
Ill.	Illinois	Ont.	Ontario	Uttar P.	Uttar Pradesh
Ind.	Indiana	Oreg.	Oregon	Va.	Virginia
Kans.	Kansas	P.E.I.	Prince Edward Island	Vic.	Victoria
K. Occidental	Kasai Occidental	Penn.	Pennsylvania	Vt.	Vermont
K. Oriental	Kasai Oriental	Phil.	Philippines	W.A.	Western Australia
Ky.	Kentucky	P.N.G.	Papua New Guinea	Wash.	Washington
La.	Louisiana	Poit.-Char.	Poitou-Charente	W. Bengal	West Bengal
Liech.	Liechtenstein	Pyr. Or.	Pyrénées Orientales	Wisc.	Wisconsin
Lit. S.S.R.	Litovskaya Sovetskaya	Qld.	Queensland	W. Sahara	Western Sahara
	Sotsialisticheskaya Respublika	Que.	Québec	W. Va.	West Virginia
Lux.	Luxembourg	Raj.	Rājasthān	Wyo.	Wyoming
Madhya P.	Madhya Pradesh	Rep. of Ire.	Republic of Ireland	Xin Uygur	Xinjiang Uygur
Man.	Manitoba	Rhein.-Pfalz	Rheinland-Pfalz	Yugo.	Yugoslavia

Aa to **Akhladhókambos**

A

Aa *r.* France **19** 51.01N 2.06E
Aachen Germany **38** 50.47N 6.05E
Aalen Germany **39** 48.50N 10.05E
A 'âli an Nîl *d.* Sudan **73** 9.35N 31.05E
Aalsmeer Neth. **16** 52.17N 4.46E
Aalst Belgium **16** 50.57N 4.03E
Äänekoski Finland **40** 62.36N 25.44E
Aarau Switz. **39** 47.23N 8.03E
Aarburg Switz. **39** 47.19N 7.54E
Aardenburg Neth. **16** 51.16N 3.26E
Aare *r.* Switz. **39** 47.37N 8.13E
Aargau *d.* Switz. **39** 47.25N 8.10E
Aarschot Belgium **16** 50.59N 4.50E
Aba China **61** 32.55N 101.42E
Aba Nigeria **77** 5.06N 7.21E
Aba Zaïre **73** 3.52N 30.14E
Abâ as Su'ûd Saudi Arabia **71** 17.28N 44.06E
Abadab, Jabal *mtn.* Sudan **72** 18.53N 35.59E
Âbâdân Iran **65** 30.21N 48.15E
Abadan, Jazîreh-ye *i.* Iran **65** 30.10N 48.30E
Âbâdeh Iran **65** 31.10N 52.40E
Abadla Algeria **74** 31.01N 2.44W
Abaetetuba Brazil **123** 1.45S 48.54W
Abagnar Qi China **54** 43.58N 116.02E
Abag Qi China **54** 43.53N 114.33E
Abaí Paraguay **124** 26.01S 55.57W
Abajo Peak *mtn.* U.S.A. **108** 37.51N 109.28W
Abakaliki Nigeria **77** 6.17N 8.04E
Abakan U.S.S.R. **51** 53.43N 91.25E
Abalessa Algeria **75** 22.54N 4.50E
Abancay Peru **124** 13.35S 72.55W
Abariringa *i.* Kiribati **84** 2.50S 171.40W
Âbâr Murrât *wells* Sudan **72** 21.03N 32.55E
'Abasân Egypt **67** 31.19N 34.21E
Abashiri wan *b.* Japan **57** 44.02N 144.17E
Abasolo Mexico **111** 25.18N 104.40W
Abau P.N.G. **90** 10.10S 148.40E
Abay *r.* Ethiopia *see* Azraq, Al Baḩr al *r.* Sudan **72**
Abay U.S.S.R. **50** 49.40N 72.47E
Âbaya Hâyk' Ethiopia **73** 6.20N 37.55E
Abba C.A.R. **77** 5.20N 15.11E
Abbadia San Salvatore Italy **30** 42.53N 11.41E
Abbasanta Italy **32** 40.08N 8.50E
Abbekås Sweden **43** 55.24N 13.36E
Abbeville France **19** 50.06N 1.50E
Abbeville La. U.S.A. **111** 29.58N 92.08W
Abbeville S.C. U.S.A. **113** 34.10N 82.23W
Abbiategrasso Italy **30** 45.24N 8.54E
Abbotsbury U.K. **13** 50.40N 2.36W
Abbotsford Canada **105** 45.27N 72.55W
Abbottābād Pakistan **62** 34.09N 73.13E
'Abd al Kūrī *i.* Yemen **71** 12.12N 52.13E
Abdera *site* Greece **34** 40.59N 24.58E
Abdulino U.S.S.R. **44** 53.42N 53.40E
Abéché Chad **72** 13.49N 20.49E
Abéjar Spain **26** 41.48N 2.47W
Âbeltî Ethiopia **73** 8.10N 37.37E
Abengourou Ivory Coast **76** 6.42N 3.27W
Abenójar Spain **26** 38.53N 4.21W
Åbenrå Denmark **42** 55.02N 9.26E
Abensberg Germany **39** 48.49N 11.51E
Abeokuta Nigeria **77** 7.10N 3.26E
Aberayron U.K. **13** 52.15N 4.16W
Abercrombie *r.* Australia **93** 33.50S 149.10E
Aberdare U.K. **13** 51.43N 3.27W
Aberdare Range *mts.* Kenya **79** 0.20S 36.40E
Aberdeen Australia **93** 32.10S 150.54E
Aberdeen R.S.A. **80** 32.28S 24.03E
Aberdeen U.K. **14** 57.08N 2.07W
Aberdeen Md. U.S.A. **115** 39.30N 76.14W
Aberdeen Miss. U.S.A. **111** 33.49N 88.33W
Aberdeen Ohio U.S.A. **112** 38.39N 83.46W
Aberdeen S. Dak. U.S.A. **110** 45.28N 98.29W
Aberdeen Wash. U.S.A. **108** 46.59N 123.50W
Aberdovey U.K. **13** 52.33N 4.03W
Aberfeldy U.K. **14** 56.37N 3.54W
Abergavenny U.K. **13** 51.49N 3.01W
Abersoch U.K. **12** 52.50N 4.31W
Aberystwyth U.K. **13** 52.25N 4.06W
Abetone Italy **30** 44.08N 10.40E
Abez U.S.S.R. **44** 66.33N 61.51E
Abhā Saudi Arabia **72** 18.13N 42.30E
Abhar Iran **65** 36.09N 49.13E
Âbhē bid Hâyk' *l.* Ethiopia **73** 11.06N 41.50E
Abidjan Ivory Coast **76** 5.19N 4.01W
Abilene Kans. U.S.A. **110** 38.55N 97.13W
Abilene Tex. U.S.A. **111** 32.27N 99.44W
Abingdon U.K. **13** 51.40N 1.17W
Abisko Sweden **40** 68.20N 18.51E
Abitau *r.* Canada **101** 59.53N 109.03W
Abitibi *r.* Canada **102** 51.03N 80.55W
Abitibi, L. Canada **102** 48.42N 79.45W
Âbîy Âdî Ethiopia **73** 13.36N 39.00E
Abnûb Egypt **64** 27.16N 31.09E
Åbo *see* Turku Finland **41**
Abohar India **62** 30.08N 74.12E
Abomey Benin **77** 7.14N 2.00E
Abong Mbang Cameroon **77** 3.59N 13.12E
Abou Deïa Chad **77** 11.20N 19.20E
Aboyne U.K. **14** 57.05N 2.48W
Abrantes Portugal **27** 39.28N 8.12W
'Abrī Sudan **72** 20.48N 30.20E
Abring Jammu & Kashmir **62** 33.42N 76.35E
Abrud Romania **37** 46.17N 23.04E
Abruzzi *d.* Italy **31** 42.35N 13.38E
Abruzzo, Parco Nazionale d' *Nat. Park* Italy **31** 41.45N 13.45E
Absaroka Range *mts.* U.S.A. **108** 44.45N 109.50W
Absecon U.S.A. **115** 39.26N 74.30W
Abtenau Austria **39** 47.33N 13.21E
Abū 'Arīsh Saudi Arabia **71** 16.58N 42.50E
Abū Baḩr *f.* Saudi Arabia **71** 21.30N 48.15E
Abū Ballās *hill* Egypt **72** 24.26N 27.39E
Abu Dhabi *see* Abū Ẓaby U.A.E. **65**
Abū Dharbah Egypt **66** 28.29N 33.20E
Abū Dulayq Sudan **72** 15.54N 33.49E
Abū Ḩamad Sudan **72** 19.32N 33.19E
Abū Ḩarāz Sudan **72** 19.04N 32.07E
Abuja Nigeria **77** 9.12N 7.11E
Abū Jābirah Sudan **73** 11.04N 26.51E
Abū Kabīr Egypt **66** 30.44N 31.40E
Abū Kamāl Syria **64** 34.27N 40.55E
Abū Madd, Ra's *c.* Saudi Arabia **64** 24.50N 37.07E
Abū Maṭāriq Sudan **73** 10.58N 26.17E
Abunā Brazil **122** 9.41S 65.20W
Abū Qashsh Jordan **67** 31.57N 35.11E
Abū Qurqāṣ Egypt **66** 27.56N 30.50E
Abu Road *town* India **62** 24.29N 72.47E
Abū Shajarah, Ra's *c.* Sudan **72** 21.04N 37.14E
Abū Shanab Sudan **73** 10.47N 29.32E
Abū Sulṭān Egypt **66** 30.25N 32.19E
Abū Sunbul Egypt **64** 22.18N 31.40E
Abū Ṭabarī *well* Sudan **72** 17.35N 28.31E
Abū Ṭarafah Jordan **66** 30.00N 35.56E
Abū Tīj Egypt **64** 27.06N 31.17E
Abuya Mexico **109** 24.16N 107.01W
Âbuyē Mēda *mtn.* Ethiopia **73** 10.28N 39.44E
Abū Zabad Sudan **73** 12.21N 29.15E
Abū Ẓaby U.A.E. **65** 24.27N 54.23E
Abū Zanīmah Egypt **66** 29.03N 33.06E
Abwong Sudan **73** 9.07N 32.12E
Åby Sweden **43** 58.40N 16.11E
Abyaḍ Sudan **72** 13.46N 26.28E
Abyaḍ, Al Baḩr al *r.* Sudan **72** 15.38N 32.31E
Abyār ash Shuwayrif *wells* Libya **75** 29.59N 14.16E
Åbybro Denmark **42** 57.09N 9.45E
Abyei Sudan **73** 9.36N 28.26E
Acacio Mexico **111** 24.50N 102.44W
Acadia Valley *town* Canada **101** 51.08N 110.13W
Acámbaro Mexico **116** 20.01N 101.42W
Acapulco Mexico **116** 16.51N 99.56W
Acará Brazil **123** 1.57S 48.11W
Acarigua Venezuela **122** 9.35N 69.12W
Acatlán Mexico **116** 18.12N 98.02W
Accra Ghana **76** 5.33N 0.15W
Accrington U.K. **12** 53.46N 2.22W
Aceh *d.* Indonesia **58** 4.00N 97.30E
Acerra Italy **33** 40.57N 14.22E
Acevedo Argentina **125** 33.46S 60.27W
Achacachi Bolivia **124** 16.03S 68.43W
Achalpur India **63** 21.16N 77.31E
Achar Uruguay **125** 32.25S 56.10W
Acheng China **53** 45.32N 126.59E
Achern Germany **39** 48.37N 8.04E
Achill I. Rep. of Ire. **15** 53.57N 10.00W
Āchīn Afghan. **62** 34.08N 70.42E
Achinsk U.S.S.R. **50** 56.10N 90.10E
Achray Canada **105** 45.52N 77.45W
Acireale Italy **33** 37.37N 15.10E
Acklin's I. Bahamas **117** 22.30N 74.10W
Aconcagua *mtn.* Argentina **124** 32.39S 70.00W
Açores, Arquipélago dos *is.* Atlantic Oc. **127** 38.30N 28.00W
Acquapendente Italy **30** 42.44N 11.52E
Acqui Italy **30** 44.41N 8.28E
Acraman, L. Australia **92** 32.02S 135.26E
Acre *d.* Brazil **122** 8.50S 71.30W
Acri Italy **33** 39.29N 16.23E
Acton Canada **104** 43.37N 80.02W
Acton Vale Canada **105** 45.39N 72.34W
Açu Brazil **123** 5.35S 36.57W
Acuña Argentina **125** 29.54S 57.57W
Ada U.S.A. **111** 34.46N 96.41W
Ada Yugo. **31** 45.48N 20.08E
Ādaba Ethiopia **73** 7.07N 39.20E
Adair, Bahía de *b.* Mexico **109** 31.30N 113.50W
Adair, C. Canada **99** 71.24N 71.13W
Adaja *r.* Spain **26** 41.32N 4.52W
Adam Oman **71** 22.23N 57.32E
Adamantina Brazil **126** 21.42S 51.04W
Adamaoua, Massif de l' *mts.* Cameroon/Nigeria **77** 7.05N 12.00E
Adamello *mtn.* Italy **30** 46.09N 10.30E
Adaminaby Australia **93** 36.04S 148.42E
Adamintina Brazil **124** 21.42S 51.04W
Adams Mass. U.S.A. **115** 42.37N 73.07W
Adams N.Y. U.S.A. **112** 43.49N 76.01W
Adams, Mt. U.S.A. **108** 46.12N 121.28W
'Adan Yemen **71** 12.50N 45.00E
Adana Turkey **64** 37.00N 35.19E
Adanero Spain **26** 40.56N 4.36W
Adapazari Turkey **64** 40.45N 30.23E
Adarama Sudan **72** 17.05N 34.54E
Adare, C. Antarctica **128** 71.30S 171.00E
Adavale Australia **90** 25.55S 144.36E
Adda *r.* Italy **30** 45.08N 9.53E
Ad Ḍab'ah Egypt **64** 31.02N 28.26E
Ad Dabbah Sudan **72** 18.03N 30.57E
Ad Dafīnah Saudi Arabia **64** 23.18N 41.58E
Ad Dahnā' *des.* Saudi Arabia **65** 26.00N 47.00E
Ad Dāmir Sudan **72** 17.35N 33.58E
Ad Dammām Saudi Arabia **65** 26.23N 50.08E
Ad Darb Saudi Arabia **72** 17.44N 42.15E
Ad Dawādimī Saudi Arabia **65** 24.29N 44.23E
Ad Dawḩah Qatar **65** 25.15N 51.34E
Ad Ḍiffah *f.* Africa **64** 30.45N 26.00E
Ad Dikākah *f.* Saudi Arabia **71** 19.25N 51.30E
Ad Dilam Saudi Arabia **65** 23.59N 47.10E
Ad Dīmās Syria **66** 33.35N 36.05E
Addis Ababa *see* Ādīs Ābeba Ethiopia **73**
Addison U.S.A. **114** 42.06N 77.14W
Ad Dīwānīyah Iraq **65** 31.59N 44.57E
Ad Du'ayn Sudan **73** 11.26N 26.09E
Ad Duwaym Sudan **72** 14.00N 32.19E
Adel U.S.A. **113** 31.07N 83.27W
Adelaide Australia **92** 34.56S 138.36E
Adelaide Pen. Canada **99** 68.09N 97.45W
Adelaide River *town* Australia **88** 13.14S 131.06E
Adelong Australia **93** 35.21S 148.04E
Aden *see* 'Adan Yemen **71**
Aden, G. of Indian Oc. **71** 13.00N 50.00E
Adena U.S.A. **114** 40.13N 80.53W
Adendorp R.S.A. **80** 32.18S 24.31E
Adi *i.* Indonesia **59** 4.10S 133.10E
Ādī Da'iro Ethiopia **72** 14.27N 38.16E
Adieu, C. Australia **89** 31.59S 132.09E
Ādīgala Ethiopia **73** 10.25N 42.17E
Adige *r.* Italy **30** 45.10N 12.20E
Ādīgrat Ethiopia **72** 14.18N 39.31E
Ādī K'eyih Ethiopia **72** 14.49N 39.23E
Ādilābād India **63** 19.40N 78.32E
Adilang Uganda **79** 2.44N 33.28E
Adin U.S.A. **108** 41.12N 120.57W
Adirondack Mts. U.S.A. **115** 44.00N 74.00W
Adirondack Park U.S.A. **115** 43.28N 74.23W
Ādīs Ābeba Ethiopia **73** 9.03N 38.42E
Ādī Ugrī Ethiopia **72** 14.55N 38.53E
Adiyaman Turkey **64** 37.46N 38.15E
Adjud Romania **37** 46.04N 27.11E
Admer *well* Algeria **75** 20.23N 5.27E
Admiralty G. Australia **88** 14.20S 125.50E
Admiralty I. U.S.A. **100** 57.50N 134.30W
Admiralty Is. P.N.G. **59** 2.30S 147.20E
Admiralty Range *mts.* Antarctica **128** 72.00S 164.00E
Adolphustown Canada **105** 44.04N 77.00W
Adour *r.* France **20** 43.32N 1.32W
Adra Spain **27** 36.44N 3.01W
Adrano Italy **33** 37.40N 14.50E
Adrar *d.* Mauritania **74** 21.00N 10.00W
Adrar des Iforas *mts.* Mali/Algeria **75** 20.00N 2.30E
Adraskan Afghan. **62** 33.39N 62.16E
Adria Italy **30** 45.03N 12.03E
Adrian Mich. U.S.A. **104** 41.54N 84.02W
Adrian Mo. U.S.A. **110** 38.24N 94.21W
Adrian Tex. U.S.A. **111** 35.16N 102.40W
Adrian W.Va. U.S.A. **114** 38.54N 80.17W
Adriatic Sea Med. Sea **31** 43.30N 14.30E
Ādwa Ethiopia **72** 14.12N 38.56E
Adzopé Ivory Coast **76** 6.07N 3.49W
Adzwa *r.* U.S.S.R. **44** 66.30N 59.30E
Aegean Sea Med. Sea **34** 37.00N 25.00E
Aerö *i.* Denmark **42** 54.53N 10.20E
Aëtos Greece **35** 37.15N 21.50E
Afándou Greece **35** 36.18N 28.12E
Āfdem Ethiopia **73** 9.26N 41.02E
Afghanistan Asia **62** 32.45N 65.00E
'Afīf Saudi Arabia **64** 23.53N 42.59E
Afikpo Nigeria **77** 5.53N 7.55E
Afjord Norway **40** 63.57N 10.12E
Aflou Algeria **75** 34.07N 2.06E
Afmadow Somali Rep. **79** 0.27N 42.05E
Afobaka Surinam **123** 5.00N 55.05W
Afognak I. U.S.A. **98** 58.15N 152.30W
Afonso Cláudio Brazil **126** 20.05S 41.06W
Africa **70**
Afsluitdijk *f.* Neth. **16** 53.04N 5.11E
'Afula Israel **67** 32.36N 35.17E
Afyon Turkey **64** 38.46N 30.32E
Agadez Niger **77** 17.00N 7.56E
Agadez *d.* Niger **77** 19.25N 11.00E
Agadir Morocco **74** 30.26N 9.36W
Agalak Sudan **73** 11.01N 32.42E
Agana Guam **84** 13.28N 144.45E
Agano *r.* Japan **57** 37.58N 139.02E
Agapa U.S.S.R. **51** 71.29N 86.16E
Agar India **62** 23.42N 76.01E
Āgaro Ethiopia **73** 7.50N 36.40E
Agartala India **63** 23.49N 91.16E
Agaru Sudan **73** 10.59N 34.44E
Agboville Ivory Coast **76** 5.55N 4.15W
Agde France **20** 43.19N 3.28E
Agde, Cap d' *c.* France **20** 43.16N 3.30E
Agen France **20** 44.12N 0.37E
Ageo Japan **57** 35.58N 139.36E
Agger *r.* Germany **16** 50.45N 7.06E
Aghada Rep. of Ire. **15** 51.50N 8.13W
Agia India **63** 26.05N 90.32E
Aginskoye U.S.S.R. **51** 51.10N 114.32E
Agira Italy **33** 37.39N 14.32E
Agly *r.* France **20** 42.47N 3.02E
Agnew Australia **89** 28.01S 120.30E
Agnone Italy **31** 41.48N 14.22E
Ago Japan **57** 34.17N 136.48E
Agordo Italy **30** 46.17N 12.02E
Agouma Gabon **78** 1.33S 10.08E
Agout *r.* France **20** 43.47N 1.41E
Āgra India **63** 27.11N 78.01E
Agra *r.* Spain **24** 42.12N 1.43W
Agraciada Uruguay **125** 33.48S 58.15W
Agreda Spain **25** 41.51N 1.56W
Agri *r.* Italy **33** 40.13N 16.44E
Ağrı Turkey **64** 39.44N 43.04E
Agri Bavnehöj *hill* Denmark **42** 56.14N 10.33E
Ağrı Dağı *mtn.* Turkey **65** 39.45N 44.15E
Agrigento Italy **32** 37.18N 13.35E
Agrínion Greece **35** 38.37N 21.24E
Agropoli Italy **33** 40.21N 15.00E
Agryz U.S.S.R. **44** 56.30N 53.00E
Agsumal, Sebjet *f.* W. Sahara **74** 24.21N 12.52W
Agua Caliente, Cerro *mtn.* Mexico **109** 26.27N 106.12W
Aguanish Canada **103** 50.16N 62.10W
Aguanus *r.* Canada **103** 50.12N 62.10W
Agua Prieta Mexico **109** 31.18N 109.34W
Aguas *r.* Spain **27** 37.09N 1.49W
Aguas Blancas Chile **124** 24.13S 69.50W
Aguascalientes Mexico **116** 21.51N 102.18W
Aguascalientes *d.* Mexico **116** 22.00N 102.00W
Aguasvivas *r.* Spain **25** 41.20N 0.25W
Agudos Brazil **126** 22.27S 49.03W
Águeda Portugal **26** 40.34N 8.27W
Águeda *r.* Spain **26** 41.02N 6.56W
Aguelhok Mali **74** 19.28N 0.52E
Aguema Angola **78** 12.03S 21.52E
Aguêraktem *well* Mali **74** 23.07N 6.12W
Aguilar Spain **27** 37.31N 4.39W
Aguilar de Campóo Spain **26** 42.47N 4.15W
Aguilas Spain **25** 37.24N 1.35W
Aguit China **54** 41.42N 113.20E
Āgula'i Ethiopia **72** 13.42N 39.35E
Agulhas, C. R.S.A. **80** 34.50S 20.00E
Agulhas Basin *f.* Indian Oc. **49** 45.00S 28.00E
Agulhas Negras *mtn.* Brazil **126** 22.20S 44.43W
Agung, Gunung *mtn.* Indonesia **59** 8.20S 115.28E
'Agur Israel **67** 31.41N 34.54E
Ahaggar *f.* Algeria **75** 23.36N 5.50E
Ahar Iran **65** 38.25N 47.07E
Ahaura New Zealand **86** 42.21S 171.33E
Ahaus Germany **16** 52.04N 7.01E
Ahirli Turkey **35** 38.37N 26.31E
Ahklun Mts. U.S.A. **98** 59.15N 161.00W
Ahlen Germany **38** 51.46N 7.53E
Ahlenmoor *f.* Germany **38** 53.40N 8.45E
Ahmadābād India **62** 23.02N 72.37E
Aḩmadī Iran **65** 27.56N 56.42E
Ahmadnagar India **62** 19.05N 74.44E
Ahmadpur East Pakistan **62** 29.09N 71.16E
Ahmadpur Siāl Pakistan **62** 30.41N 71.46E
Ahmad Wāl Pakistan **62** 29.25N 65.56E
Ahmar Mts. Ethiopia **73** 9.15N 41.00E
Ahmic Harbour Canada **104** 45.39N 79.42W
Ahmic L. Canada **104** 45.37N 79.42W
Ahoada Nigeria **77** 5.06N 6.39E
Ahr *r.* Germany **16** 50.34N 7.16E
Ahram Iran **65** 28.52N 51.16E
Ahraura India **63** 25.01N 83.01E
Aḩsā', Wāḩat al *oasis* Saudi Arabia **65** 25.37N 49.40E
Ähtäri Finland **40** 62.34N 24.06E
Ahun France **20** 46.05N 2.05E
Åhus Sweden **43** 55.55N 14.17E
Ahvāz Iran **65** 31.17N 48.44E
Ahvenanmaa *d.* Finland **43** 60.15N 20.00E
Ahvenanmaa *is.* Finland **41** 60.15N 20.00E
Aichach Germany **39** 48.28N 11.08E
Aichi *d.* Japan **57** 35.02N 137.15E
Aigle Switz. **39** 46.19N 6.58E
Aigre France **20** 45.54N 0.01E
Aigueperse France **20** 46.01N 3.12E
Aigues *r.* France **21** 44.07N 4.43E
Aigues-Mortes France **21** 43.34N 4.11E
Aiguilles France **21** 44.47N 6.52E
Aigurande France **19** 46.26N 1.50E
Aiken U.S.A. **113** 33.34N 81.44W
Aileron Australia **90** 22.38S 133.20E
Ailette *r.* France **16** 49.35N 3.09E
Ailsa Craig *i.* U.K. **14** 55.15N 5.07W
Aim U.S.S.R. **51** 58.50N 134.15E
Aimorés Brazil **126** 19.30S 41.04W
Ain *d.* France **21** 46.05N 5.20E
Ain *r.* France **21** 45.48N 5.10E
Aïna *r.* Gabon **78** 0.38N 12.47E
Ainaži U.S.S.R. **41** 57.52N 24.21E
Aïn Beïda Algeria **75** 35.50N 7.27E
Aïn ben Tili Mauritania **74** 26.00N 9.32W
Aïn Draham Tunisia **32** 36.47N 8.42E
Aïn Galakka Chad **75** 18.04N 18.24E
Aïn Sefra Algeria **74** 32.45N 0.35W
Aïr *mts.* Niger **77** 18.30N 8.30E
Aird I. Canada **104** 46.08N 82.25W
Airdrie U.K. **14** 55.52N 3.59W
Aire France **20** 43.42N 0.16W
Aire *r.* France **19** 49.19N 4.49E
Aire *r.* U.K. **12** 53.42N 0.54W
Airolo Switz. **39** 46.32N 8.37E
Airvault France **18** 46.50N 0.08W
Aisch *r.* Germany **39** 49.46N 11.01E
Aisne *d.* France **19** 49.30N 3.30E
Aisne *r.* France **19** 49.26N 2.50E
Aitana *mtn.* Spain **25** 38.40N 0.16W
Aitape P.N.G. **59** 3.10S 142.17E
Aitkin U.S.A. **110** 46.32N 93.43W
Aitolikón Greece **35** 38.27N 21.22E
Aït Ourir Morocco **74** 31.38N 7.42W
Aitutaki Atoll Cook Is. **85** 18.52S 159.46W
Aiud Romania **37** 46.19N 23.44E
Aix-en-Provence France **21** 43.32N 5.26E
Aix-les-Bains France **21** 45.42N 5.55E
Aíyina Greece **35** 37.44N 23.27E
Aíyina *i.* Greece **35** 37.46N 23.26E
Aiyínion Greece **34** 40.30N 22.33E
Aíyion Greece **35** 38.15N 22.05E
Aizpute U.S.S.R. **41** 56.43N 21.38E
Aizuwakamatsu Japan **57** 37.30N 139.58E
Ajaccio France **21** 41.55N 8.44E
Ajanta Range *mts.* India **62** 20.15N 75.30E
Ajax Canada **104** 43.51N 79.02W
Ajdābiyā Libya **72** 30.46N 20.14E
Ajdovščina Yugo. **31** 45.53N 13.53E
Ajībar Ethiopia **73** 10.41N 38.37E
'Ajlūn Jordan **67** 32.20N 35.45E
'Ajmah, Jabal al *f.* Egypt **66** 29.12N 33.58E
'Ajmān U.A.E. **65** 25.23N 55.26E
Ajmer India **62** 26.27N 74.38E
Ajnāla India **62** 31.51N 74.47E
Ajo U.S.A. **109** 32.22N 112.52W
Ajo, Cabo de *c.* Spain **26** 43.31N 3.35W
Akaishi sammyaku *mts.* Japan **57** 35.20N 138.10E
Akámas, Akrotírion *c.* Cyprus **66** 35.06N 32.17E
Akaroa New Zealand **86** 43.50S 172.59E
'Akasha East Sudan **72** 21.05N 30.43E
Akashi Japan **57** 34.38N 134.59E
Akbarpur India **63** 26.25N 82.33E
Akbulak U.S.S.R. **45** 51.00N 55.40E
Akelamo Indonesia **59** 1.35N 129.40E
Akershus *d.* Norway **42** 60.05N 11.25E
Aketi Zaïre **78** 2.46N 23.51E
Akhaltsikhe U.S.S.R. **64** 41.37N 42.59E
Akharnaí Greece **35** 38.05N 23.44E
Akhḍar, Al Jabal al *mts.* Libya **72** 32.30N 21.30E
Akhḍar, Al Jabal al *mts.* Oman **65** 23.10N 57.25E
Akhḍar, Wādī *r.* Egypt **66** 28.42N 33.41E
Akhḍar, Wādī al *r.* Saudi Arabia **66** 28.30N 36.48E
Akhelóös Greece **29** 38.20N 21.04E
Akhelóös *r.* Greece **35** 38.36N 21.14E
Akhisar Turkey **29** 38.54N 27.49E
Akhladhókambos Greece **35** 37.31N 22.35E

Akhmīm to Al Madīnah

Akhmīm Egypt **64** 26.34N 31.44E
Akhtyrka U.S.S.R. **45** 50.19N 34.54E
Akimiski I. Canada **102** 53.00N 81.20W
Åkirkeby Denmark **43** 55.04N 14.56E
Akita Japan **57** 39.44N140.05E
Akjoujt Mauritania **74** 19.44N 14.26W
Akkajaure *l.* Sweden **40** 67.40N 17.30E
'Akko Israel **67** 32.55N 35.05E
Akkol U.S.S.R. **52** 45.04N 75.39E
Akkoy Turkey **35** 37.29N 27.15E
Aklavik Canada **98** 68.12N135.00W
Ako Nigeria **77** 10.19N 10.48E
Åkobo *r.* Ethiopia **73** 8.30N 33.15E
Akola India **62** 20.44N 77.00E
Āk'ordat Ethiopia **72** 15.35N 37.55E
Akot India **62** 21.11N 77.04E
Akpatok I. Canada **99** 60.30N 68.30W
Åkrafjorden *est.* Norway **42** 59.46N 6.06E
Akranes Iceland **40** 64.19N 22.05W
Åkrehamn Norway **42** 59.16N 5.11E
Akrítas, Ákra *c.* Greece **35** 36.43N 21.54E
Akron Colo. U.S.A. **110** 40.10N103.13W
Akron Ohio U.S.A. **114** 41.05N 81.31W
Akrotiri Cyprus **66** 34.36N 32.57E
Aksaray Turkey **64** 38.22N 34.02E
Aksarka U.S.S.R. **50** 66.31N 67.50E
Aksay China **52** 39.28N 94.15E
Aksay U.S.S.R. **45** 51.24N 52.11E
Akşehir Turkey **64** 38.22N 31.24E
Aksu China **52** 42.10N 80.00E
Åksum Ethiopia **72** 14.08N 38.48E
Aktag *mtn.* China **52** 36.45N 84.40E
Aktogay U.S.S.R. **52** 46.59N 79.42E
Aktyubinsk U.S.S.R. **45** 50.16N 57.13E
Akūbū Sudan **73** 7.47N 33.01E
Akūbū *r. see* Åkobo *r.* Sudan **73**
Akula Zaïre **78** 2.22N 20.11E
Akure Nigeria **77** 7.14N 5.08E
Akureyri Iceland **40** 65.41N 18.04W
Akuse Ghana **76** 6.04N 0.12E
Akwa-Ibom *d.* Nigeria **77** 4.45N 7.50E
Akxokesay China **52** 36.48N 91.06E
Akyab *see* Sittwe Burma **56**
Akyel Ethiopia **73** 12.30N 37.04E
Ål Norway **41** 60.38N 8.34E
Alabama *d.* U.S.A. **113** 32.50N 87.00W
Alabama *r.* U.S.A. **111** 31.08N 87.57W
Al 'Abbāsīyah Sudan **73** 14.27N 33.31E
Alaçati Turkey **35** 38.16N 26.23E
Alādāgh, Kūh-e *mts.* Iran **65** 37.15N 57.30E
Alagoas *d.* Brazil **123** 9.30S 37.00W
Alagoinhas Brazil **123** 12.09S 38.21W
Alagón Spain **24** 41.46N 1.12W
Alakol, Ozero *l.* U.S.S.R. **52** 46.00N 81.40E
Alakurtti U.S.S.R. **44** 67.00N 30.23E
Al'Āl Syria **67** 32.48N 35.44E
Al 'Alamayn Egypt **64** 30.49N 28.57E
Al 'Amārah Iraq **65** 31.52N 47.50E
Al Āmirīyah Egypt **66** 31.01N 29.48E
Alamogordo U.S.A. **109** 32.54N105.57W
Alamos, Rio de los *r.* Mexico **111** 27.53N101.12W
Alamosa U.S.A. **108** 37.28N105.52W
Åland *is. see* Ahvenanmaa *is.* Finland **41**
Ålands Hav *sea* Finland **43** 59.50N 19.25E
Alanreed U.S.A. **111** 35.14N100.45W
Alanson U.S.A. **104** 45.27N 84.47W
Alanya Turkey **64** 36.32N 32.02E
Alaotra, Lac *l.* Madagascar **81** 17.30S 48.30E
Alapayevsk U.S.S.R. **44** 57.55N 61.42E
Alappuzha India **60** 9.30N 76.22E
Al 'Aqabah Jordan **66** 29.32N 35.00E
Al 'Aramah *f.* Saudi Arabia **65** 25.30N 46.30E
Alarcón, Embalse de *resr.* Spain **27** 39.36N 2.10W
Al 'Arīsh Egypt **66** 31.08N 33.48E
Alaşehir Turkey **29** 38.22N 28.29E
Al 'Āşimah *d.* Jordan **67** 31.45N 36.05E
Alaska *d.* U.S.A. **98** 65.00N153.00W
Alaska, G. of U.S.A. **98** 58.45N145.00W
Alaska Pen. U.S.A. **98** 56.00N160.00W
Alaska Range *mts.* U.S.A. **98** 62.10N152.00W
Alassio Italy **30** 44.00N 8.10E
Al 'Atīqah Lebanon **66** 33.42N 35.27E
Alatri Italy **30** 41.43N 13.21E
Al 'Aţrun Sudan **72** 18.11N 26.36E
Alatyr U.S.S.R. **44** 54.51N 46.35E
Alausí Ecuador **122** 2.00S 78.50W
Álava *d.* Spain **26** 42.55N 2.50W
Alavus Finland **40** 62.35N 23.37E
Alawoona Australia **92** 34.44S140.33E
Al 'Ayn *wells* Sudan **72** 16.36N 29.19E
Alayor Spain **25** 39.56N 4.08E
Al 'Ayyāţ Egypt **66** 29.37N 31.15E
Alazani *r.* U.S.S.R. **65** 41.06N 46.40E
Alba Italy **30** 44.42N 8.02E
Albacete Spain **25** 38.59N 1.51W
Albacete *d.* Spain **25** 39.05N 1.45W
Al Bad' Saudi Arabia **66** 28.29N 35.02E
Al Badārī Egypt **64** 26.59N 31.25E
Alba de Tormes Spain **26** 40.49N 5.31W
Ålbaek Denmark **42** 57.36N 10.25E
Al Bahnasā Egypt **66** 28.32N 30.39E
Al Baḩr al Aḩmar *d.* Sudan **72** 19.30N 35.30E
Al Baḩr al Mayyit *see* Dead Sea Jordan **67**
Albaida Spain **25** 38.51N 0.31W
Alba-Iulia Romania **37** 46.04N 23.33E
Al Balqā' *d.* Jordan **67** 32.00N 35.40E
Alban France **20** 43.54N 2.28E
Albania Europe **34** 41.00N 20.00E
Albano Laziale Italy **30** 41.44N 12.39E
Albany Australia **89** 34.57S117.54E
Albany *r.* Canada **102** 52.10N 82.00W
Albany Ga. U.S.A. **113** 31.37N 84.10W
Albany Ky. U.S.A. **113** 36.42N 85.08W
Albany Minn. U.S.A. **110** 45.38N 94.34W
Albany N.Y. U.S.A. **115** 42.39N 73.45W
Albany Ohio U.S.A. **114** 39.14N 82.12W
Albany Oreg. U.S.A. **108** 44.38N123.06W
Al Bāriḩah Jordan **67** 32.34N 35.50E
Albarracín Spain **25** 40.25N 1.26W
Albarracín, Sierra de *mts.* Spain **25** 40.30N 1.40W
Al Başrah Iraq **65** 30.33N 47.50E
Al Bāţinah *f.* Oman **65** 24.25N 56.50E
Albatross B. Australia **90** 12.45S141.43E
Al Batrūn Lebanon **66** 34.16N 35.40E
Al Bawīţī Egypt **64** 28.21N 25.52E
Al Bayāḑ *f.* Saudi Arabia **71** 22.00N 47.00E
Al Bayḑā' Libya **75** 32.46N 21.43E
Albegna *r.* Italy **30** 42.30N 11.11E
Albemarle Sd. U.S.A. **107** 36.10N 76.00W
Albenga Italy **30** 44.03N 8.13E
Albens France **21** 45.47N 5.57E
Alberche *r.* Spain **27** 39.58N 4.46W
Alberga Australia **91** 27.12S135.28E
Alberga *r.* Australia **91** 27.12S135.28E
Albergaria-a-Velha Portugal **26** 40.42N 8.29W
Alberique Spain **25** 39.07N 0.31W
Albermarle U.S.A. **113** 35.21N 80.12W
Albermarle Sd. U.S.A. **113** 36.03N 76.12W
Alberobello Italy **33** 40.47N 17.15E
Albert Australia **93** 32.21S147.33E
Albert France **19** 50.00N 2.39E
Albert, L. Australia **92** 35.38S139.17E
Albert, L. Uganda / Zaïre **79** 1.45N 31.00E
Alberta *d.* Canada **100** 54.00N115.00W
Alberti Argentina **125** 35.01S 60.16W
Albertirsa Hungary **37** 47.15N 19.38E
Albert Kanaal *canal* Belgium **16** 51.00N 5.15E
Albert Lea U.S.A. **110** 43.39N 93.22W
Albert Nile *r.* Uganda **79** 3.30N 32.00E
Alberton Canada **103** 46.49N 64.04W
Albertville France **21** 45.41N 6.23E
Albi France **20** 43.56N 2.08E
Al Bidia Chad **73** 10.33N 20.13E
Albin U.S.A. **108** 41.26N104.08W
Albina Surinam **123** 5.30N 54.03W
Albino Italy **30** 45.46N 9.47E
Albion Mich. U.S.A. **112** 42.14N 84.45W
Albion Mont. U.S.A. **108** 45.11N104.15W
Albion Nebr. U.S.A. **110** 41.42N 98.00W
Albion N.Y. U.S.A. **114** 43.15N 78.12W
Albion Penn. U.S.A. **114** 41.53N 80.22W
Al Bi'r Saudi Arabia **66** 28.52N 36.15E
Al Bīrah Jordan **67** 31.54N 35.13E
Albo, Monte *mtn.* Italy **32** 40.29N 9.33E
Albocácer Spain **25** 40.21N 0.02E
Alborán, Isla de *i.* Spain **27** 35.58N 3.02W
Ålborg Denmark **42** 57.03N 9.56E
Ålborg Bugt *b.* Denmark **42** 56.55N 10.30E
Alborz, Reshteh-ye Kūhhā-ye *mts.* Iran **65** 36.00N 52.30E
Albufeira Portugal **27** 37.05N 8.15W
Al Buḩayrāt *d.* Sudan **73** 6.50N 29.40E
Albuñol Spain **27** 36.47N 3.12W
Albuquerque U.S.A. **109** 35.05N106.40W
Al Buraymī U.A.E. **65** 24.15N 55.45E
Alburg U.S.A. **105** 44.59N 73.18W
Al Burj Egypt **66** 31.35N 30.59E
Alburquerque Spain **27** 39.13N 7.00W
Albury Australia **93** 36.03S146.53E
Al Buţanah *f.* Sudan **72** 14.50N 34.30E
Al Buwayḑah Jordan **67** 32.21N 36.03E
Alby Sweden **40** 62.30N 15.25E
Alcácer do Sal Portugal **27** 38.22N 8.30W
Alcains Portugal **27** 39.55N 7.27W
Alcalá de Chisvert Spain **25** 40.19N 0.13E
Alcalá de Guadaira Spain **27** 37.20N 5.50W
Alcalá de Henares Spain **26** 40.29N 3.22W
Alcalá la Real Spain **27** 37.28N 3.56W
Alcamo Italy **32** 37.59N 12.58E
Alcanadre *r.* Spain **25** 41.37N 0.12W
Alcanar Spain **25** 40.33N 0.29E
Alcañices Spain **26** 41.42N 6.21W
Alcañiz Spain **25** 41.03N 0.08W
Alcántara Spain **27** 39.43N 6.53W
Alcántara, Embalse de *resr.* Spain **27** 39.45N 6.25W
Alcantara L. Canada **101** 60.57N108.09W
Alcantarilla Spain **25** 37.58N 1.13W
Alcaraz Spain **26** 38.40N 2.29W
Alcaraz, Sierra de *mts.* Spain **27** 38.40N 2.30W
Alcarrache *r.* Portugal **27** 38.16N 7.24W
Alcaudete Spain **27** 37.36N 4.05W
Alcázar de San Juan Spain **27** 39.24N 3.12W
Alcira Spain **25** 39.09N 0.26W
Alcobaça Portugal **27** 39.33N 8.59W
Alcobendas Spain **26** 40.32N 3.38W
Alcolea del Pinar Spain **26** 41.02N 2.28W
Alconchel Portugal **27** 38.31N 7.04W
Alcova U.S.A. **108** 42.35N106.34W
Alcoy Spain **25** 38.42N 0.28W
Alcubierre Spain **25** 41.48N 0.27W
Alcubierre, Sierra de *mts.* Spain **25** 41.45N 0.21W
Alcudia Spain **25** 39.52N 3.07E
Alcudia, Bahía de *b.* Spain **25** 39.48N 3.13E
Alcudia, Sierra de la *mts.* Spain **27** 38.34N 4.30W
Aldabra Is. Seychelles **70** 9.00S 46.30E
Aldan U.S.S.R. **51** 58.44N125.22E
Aldan *r.* U.S.S.R. **51** 63.30N130.00E
Aldeburgh U.K. **13** 52.09N 1.35E
Aldeia Nova de Santo Bento Portugal **27** 37.55N 7.25W
Alder Creek *town* U.S.A. **115** 43.27N 75.17W
Alderney *i.* U.K. **13** 49.42N 2.11W
Aldershot U.K. **13** 51.15N 0.47W
Alderson Canada **101** 50.20N111.25W
Aldridge U.K. **13** 52.36N 1.55W
Aledo U.S.A. **110** 41.12N 90.45W
Aleg Mauritania **74** 17.03N 13.55W
Alegre Brazil **126** 20.44S 41.30W
Alegrete Brazil **125** 29.46S 55.46W
Aleksandrov Gay U.S.S.R. **45** 50.08N 48.34E
Aleksandrovsk Sakhalinskiy U.S.S.R. **51** 50.55N142.12E
Aleksinac Yugo. **34** 43.31N 21.42E
Alembe Gabon **78** 0.03N 10.57E
Além Paraíba Brazil **126** 21.49S 42.36W
Alençon France **18** 48.26N 0.05E
Alenuihaha Channel Hawaiian Is. **85** 20.26N156.00W
Aleppo *see* Ḩalab Syria **64**
Aléria France **21** 42.05N 9.30E
Alès France **21** 44.08N 4.05E
Alessandria Italy **30** 44.54N 8.37E
Alessano Italy **33** 39.53N 18.20E
Ålestrup Denmark **42** 56.42N 9.31E
Ålesund Norway **40** 62.28N 6.11E
Aleutian Basin Bering Sea **84** 57.00N179.00E
Aleutian Is. U.S.A. **48** 57.00N180.00
Aleutian Range *mts.* U.S.A. **98** 58.00N156.00W
Aleutian Trench Pacific Oc. **84** 50.00N176.00W
Alexander *r.* Israel **67** 32.24N 34.52E
Alexander U.S.A. **114** 42.54N 78.16W
Alexander Archipelago *is.* U.S.A. **100** 56.30N134.30W
Alexander Bay *town* R.S.A. **80** 28.36S 16.26E
Alexander I. Antarctica **128** 72.00S 70.00W
Alexandra Australia **93** 37.12S145.14E
Alexandra New Zealand **86** 45.14S169.26E
Alexandria B.C. Canada **100** 52.35N122.27W
Alexandria Ont. Canada **105** 45.19N 74.38W
Alexandria *see* Al Iskandarīyah Egypt **66**
Alexandria Romania **34** 43.58N 25.20E
Alexandria R.S.A. **80** 33.39S 26.24E
Alexandria La. U.S.A. **111** 31.18N 92.27W
Alexandria Minn. U.S.A. **110** 45.53N 95.22W
Alexandria Va. U.S.A. **114** 38.48N 77.03W
Alexandria Bay *town* U.S.A. **105** 44.20N 75.55W
Alexandrina, L. Australia **92** 35.26S139.10E
Alexandroúpolis Greece **34** 40.50N 25.52E
Alexis *r.* Canada **103** 52.32N 56.08W
Alexis Creek *town* Canada **100** 52.05N123.20W
Aleysk U.S.S.R. **50** 52.32N 82.45E
Alfambra Spain **25** 40.33N 1.02W
Al Fant Egypt **66** 28.46N 30.53E
Alfaro Spain **25** 42.11N 1.45W
Alfarrás Spain **25** 41.49N 0.35E
Al Fāshir Sudan **73** 13.38N 25.21E
Al Fashn Egypt **66** 28.49N 30.54E
Al Fāw Iraq **65** 29.57N 48.30E
Al Fayyūm Egypt **66** 29.19N 30.50E
Alfeld Germany **38** 51.59N 9.50E
Alfenas Brazil **126** 21.28S 45.48W
Al Fifi Sudan **73** 10.03N 25.01E
Alfiós *r.* Greece **35** 37.40N 21.33E
Alfonsine Italy **30** 44.30N 12.03E
Alford U.K. **14** 57.14N 2.42W
Alfred U.S.A. **114** 42.15N 77.47W
Al Fujayrah U.A.E. **65** 25.10N 56.20E
Alga U.S.S.R. **50** 49.49N 57.16E
Ålgård Norway **42** 58.46N 5.51E
Al Gebir Sudan **73** 13.43N 29.49E
Algeciras Spain **27** 36.08N 5.30W
Algemesí Spain **25** 39.11N 0.26W
Algena Ethiopia **72** 16.20N 38.34E
Alger Algeria **75** 36.50N 3.00E
Alger U.S.A. **104** 44.08N 84.08W
Algeria Africa **74** 28.00N 2.00E
Al Ghawr *f.* Jordan **67** 32.00N 35.30E
Al Ghayl Saudi Arabia **65** 22.36N 46.19E
Alghero Italy **32** 40.34N 8.19E
Al Ghurdaqah Egypt **64** 27.14N 33.50E
Algiers *see* Alger Algeria **75**
Alginet Spain **25** 39.16N 0.28W
Algoa B. R.S.A. **80** 33.50S 26.00E
Algodor *r.* Spain **27** 39.55N 3.53W
Algoma U.S.A. **110** 44.36N 87.27W
Algoma Mills Canada **104** 46.10N 82.50W
Algoma Uplands Canada **104** 47.00N 83.35W
Algona U.S.A. **110** 43.04N 94.14W
Algonquin Park *town* Canada **104** 45.34N 78.36W
Algonquin Prov. Park Canada **104** 45.27N 78.26W
Algonquin Upland Canada **104** 45.40N 78.47W
Algorta Uruguay **125** 32.25S 57.23W
Al Ḩajar al Gharbī *mts.* Oman **65** 24.00N 56.30E
Al Ḩajar ash Sharqī *mts.* Oman **65** 22.45N 58.45E
Alhama Spain **25** 37.51N 1.25W
Al Ḩamād *des.* Saudi Arabia **64** 31.45N 39.00E
Alhama de Granada Spain **27** 37.00N 3.59W
Al Ḩamar Saudi Arabia **65** 22.26N 46.12E
Alhambra U.S.A. **109** 34.06N118.08W
Al Ḩamīdīyah Syria **66** 34.43N 35.56E
Al Ḩanākīyah Saudi Arabia **64** 24.53N 40.30E
Al Ḩarāk Syria **67** 32.44N 36.18E
Al Ḩarīq Saudi Arabia **65** 23.37N 46.31E
Al Ḩārrah Syria **67** 33.03N 36.00E
Al Harūj al Aswad *hills* Libya **75** 27.00N 17.10E
Al Ḩasakah Syria **64** 36.29N 40.45E
Alhaurín el Grande Spain **27** 36.38N 4.41W
Al Ḩawāmidīyah Egypt **66** 29.54N 31.15E
Al Ḩayz Egypt **64** 28.02N 28.39E
Al Ḩijāz *f.* Saudi Arabia **64** 26.00N 37.30E
Al Ḩillah Iraq **65** 32.28N 44.29E
Al Ḩillah Saudi Arabia **65** 23.30N 46.51E
Al Hirmil Lebanon **66** 34.25N 36.23E
Al Ḩişn Jordan **67** 32.29N 35.53E
Al-Hoceima Morocco **74** 35.15N 3.55W
Al Ḩudaydah Yemen **72** 14.50N 42.58E
Al Hufūf Saudi Arabia **65** 25.20N 49.34E
Al Ḩumrah *des.* U.A.E. **65** 22.45N 55.10E
Al Ḩusaynīyah Egypt **66** 30.52N 31.55E
Al Ḩuwaymī Yemen **71** 14.05N 47.44E
Aliābād, Kūh-e *mtn.* Iran **65** 34.09N 50.48E
Aliaga Spain **25** 40.40N 0.42W
Aliákmon *r.* Greece **34** 40.30N 22.36E
Aliákmona, Límni *resr.* Greece **34** 40.15N 22.00E
Alicante Spain **25** 38.23N 0.29W
Alicante *d.* Spain **25** 38.30N 0.40W
Alice Canada **105** 45.44N 77.19W
Alice R.S.A. **80** 32.47S 26.49E
Alice U.S.A. **111** 27.45N 98.04W
Alice, Punta *c.* Italy **33** 39.24N 17.10E
Alice Arm Canada **100** 55.29N129.31W
Alice Springs *town* Australia **90** 23.42S133.52E
Alicudi, Isola *i.* Italy **33** 38.33N 14.21E
Al Ifranj Jordan **67** 31.11N 35.41E
Alīgarh India **63** 27.53N 78.05E
Alīgūdarz Iran **65** 33.25N 49.38E
'Alījūq, Kūh-e *mtn.* Iran **65** 31.27N 51.43E
Alima *r.* Congo **78** 1.36S 16.35E
Alindao C.A.R. **73** 5.02N 21.13E
Alingsås Sweden **43** 57.56N 12.31E
Alīpur Pakistan **62** 29.23N 70.55E
Alīpur Duār India **63** 26.29N 89.44E
Alīpur Janūbī Pakistan **62** 30.13N 71.18E
Aliquippa U.S.A. **114** 40.37N 80.15W
Al 'Irq Libya **75** 29.05N 15.48E
Ali Sabieh Djibouti **73** 11.09N 42.42E
Aliseda Spain **27** 39.26N 6.41W
Al Iskandarīyah Egypt **66** 31.13N 29.55E
Al Ismā'īlīyah Egypt **66** 30.36N 32.15E
Alistráti Greece **34** 41.04N 23.57E
Alivérion Greece **35** 38.24N 24.02E
Aliwal North R.S.A. **80** 30.41S 26.41E
Al Jabal al Akhḑar *d.* Libya **75** 32.00N 21.30E
Al Jafr Jordan **66** 30.16N 36.11E
Al Jāfūrah *des.* Saudi Arabia **65** 24.40N 50.20E
Al Jaghbūb Libya **72** 29.45N 24.31E
Al Jahrah Kuwait **65** 29.20N 47.41E
Al Jaladah *f.* Saudi Arabia **71** 18.30N 46.25E
Al Janūb *d.* Lebanon **67** 33.10N 35.22E
Al Jawārah Oman **60** 18.55N 57.17E
Al Jawb *f.* Saudi Arabia **65** 23.00N 50.00E
Al Jawf Libya **72** 24.12N 23.18E
Al Jawf Saudi Arabia **64** 29.49N 39.52E
Al Jawsh Libya **75** 32.00N 11.40E
Al Jazīrah *f.* Iraq **64** 35.00N 41.00E
Al Jazīrah *d.* Sudan **72** 14.35N 33.30E
Al Jazīrah *f.* Sudan **72** 14.25N 33.00E
Al Jibāb Syria **67** 33.06N 36.15E
Al Jifārah Saudi Arabia **65** 23.59N 45.11E
Al Jīzah Egypt **66** 30.01N 31.12E
Al Jīzah Jordan **67** 31.42N 35.57E
Al Jubayl Saudi Arabia **65** 27.59N 49.40E
Al Judayyidah Jordan **67** 31.15N 35.49E
Al Junaynah Sudan **73** 13.27N 22.27E
Aljustrel Portugal **27** 37.52N 8.10W
Al Karabah Sudan **72** 18.33N 33.42E
Al Karak Jordan **67** 31.11N 35.42E
Al Karak *d.* Jordan **67** 31.10N 36.00E
Al Kawah Sudan **73** 13.44N 32.30E
Al Khābūr *r.* Syria **64** 35.07N 40.30E
Al Khābūrah Oman **65** 23.58N 57.10E
Al Khalīl Jordan **67** 31.32N 35.06E
Al Khalīl *d.* Jordan **67** 31.29N 35.10E
Al Khamāsīn Saudi Arabia **71** 20.29N 44.49E
Al Khandaq Sudan **72** 18.36N 30.34E
Al Khānkah Egypt **66** 30.12N 31.21E
Al Khārijah Egypt **64** 25.26N 30.33E
Al Kharţūm Sudan **72** 15.33N 32.35E
Al Kharţūm *d.* Sudan **72** 15.45N 32.30E
Al Kharţūm Baḩrī Sudan **72** 15.39N 32.34E
Al Khasfah *well* Oman **71** 19.45N 54.19E
Al Khawr Qatar **65** 25.39N 51.32E
Al Khirbah as Samrā' Jordan **67** 32.11N 36.10E
Al Khubar Saudi Arabia **65** 26.18N 50.06E
Al Khufayfīyah Saudi Arabia **65** 24.55N 44.42E
Al Khums Libya **75** 32.39N 14.16E
Al Khums *d.* Libya **75** 31.20N 14.10E
Al Khunn Saudi Arabia **65** 23.18N 49.15E
Al Khushnīyah Syria **67** 33.00N 35.48E
Al Kidn *des.* Saudi Arabia **65** 22.20N 54.20E
Al Kiswah Syria **66** 33.21N 36.14E
Alkmaar Neth. **16** 52.37N 4.44E
Al Kufrah Libya **72** 24.14N 23.15E
Al Kuntillah Egypt **66** 30.00N 34.41E
Al Kūt Iraq **65** 32.30N 45.51E
Al Kuwayt Kuwait **65** 29.20N 48.00E
Al Labwah Lebanon **66** 34.11N 36.21E
Al Lādhiqīyah Syria **66** 35.31N 35.47E
Al Lagowa Sudan **73** 11.24N 29.08E
Allāhābād India **63** 25.27N 81.51E
Allakaket U.S.A. **98** 66.30N152.45W
'Allān *r.* Syria **67** 32.45N 35.57E
Allanche France **20** 45.14N 2.56E
'Allāqī, Wādī al *r.* Egypt **64** 22.55N 33.02E
Allariz Spain **26** 42.11N 7.48W
Allauch France **21** 43.20N 5.29E
Ålleberg *hill* Sweden **43** 58.08N 13.36E
Allegany U.S.A. **114** 42.06N 78.30W
Allegany State Park U.S.A. **114** 42.04N 78.44W
Allegheny *r.* U.S.A. **114** 40.27N 80.00W
Allegheny Mts. U.S.A. **114** 38.30N 80.00W
Allegheny Resr. U.S.A. **114** 42.00N 78.56W
Allen, Lough Rep. of Ire. **15** 54.07N 8.04W
Allenby Bridge *see* Jisr al Ḩusayn Jordan **67**
Allenford Canada **104** 44.32N 81.10W
Allentown U.S.A. **115** 40.37N 75.30W
Aller *r.* Germany **38** 52.57N 9.11E
Allevard France **21** 45.24N 6.04E
Allgäu *f.* Germany **38** 47.40N 10.15E
Allgäuer Alpen *mts.* Germany **38** 47.26N 10.15E
Alliance Nebr. U.S.A. **110** 42.06N102.52W
Alliance Ohio U.S.A. **114** 40.55N 81.06W
Allier *d.* France **20** 46.25N 3.00E
Allier *r.* France **20** 46.58N 3.30E
Allinge Denmark **43** 55.16N 14.49E
Al Lisān *pen.* Jordan **67** 31.17N 35.28E
Alliston Canada **104** 44.09N 79.52W
Al Liţānī *r.* Lebanon **66** 33.22N 35.14E
Al Lith Saudi Arabia **72** 20.09N 40.16E
Al Līwā' *f.* U.A.E. **71** 23.00N 54.00E
Alloa U.K. **14** 56.07N 3.49W
Allos France **21** 44.14N 6.38E
Al Luḩayyah Yemen **72** 15.43N 42.42E
Alluitsup-Paa *see* Sydpröven Greenland **99**
Alma Canada **103** 48.32N 71.40W
Alma Ga. U.S.A. **113** 31.33N 82.29W
Alma Mich. U.S.A. **112** 43.23N 84.40W
Al Ma'ānīyah *well* Iraq **64** 30.44N 43.00E
Alma-Ata U.S.S.R. **52** 43.19N 76.55E
Almada Portugal **27** 38.41N 9.09W
Almadén Spain **26** 38.46N 4.50W
Almadén de la Plata Spain **27** 37.52N 6.04W
Al Madīnah Saudi Arabia **64** 24.30N 39.35E

Aneityum to **Arles**

Aneityum *i.* Vanuatu **84** 20.12S169.45E
Añelo Argentina **125** 38.20S 68.45W
Aneto, Pico de *mtn.* Spain **25** 42.38N 0.40E
Aney Niger **77** 19.24N 12.56E
Angara *r.* U.S.S.R. **51** 58.00N 93.00E
Angarsk U.S.S.R. **51** 52.31N103.55E
Angaston Australia **91** 34.30S139.03E
Angathonísi *i.* Greece **35** 37.28N 27.00E
Angatuba Brazil **126** 23.27S 48.25W
Ånge Sweden **40** 62.31N 15.40E
Ángel de la Guarda, Isla *i.* Mexico **109** 29.20N113.25W
Angel Falls *f.* Venezuela **122** 5.55N 62.30W
Ängelholm Sweden **43** 56.15N 12.51E
Angelica U.S.A. **114** 42.18N 78.01W
Angels Camp U.S.A. **108** 38.04N120.32W
Ängereb *r.* Ethiopia **73** 13.45N 36.40E
Ångerman *r.* Sweden **40** 63.00N 17.43E
Angermünde Germany **38** 53.01N 14.00E
Angers France **18** 47.28N 0.33W
Angerville France **19** 48.19N 2.00E
Ångesån *r.* Sweden **40** 66.22N 22.58E
Angikuni L. Canada **101** 62.00N100.00W
Angkor *ruins* Cambodia **56** 13.30N103.50E
Anglesey *i.* U.K. **12** 53.16N 4.25W
Angleton U.S.A. **111** 29.10N 95.26W
Anglin *r.* France **18** 46.42N 0.50E
Ango Zaïre **73** 4.02N 25.52E
Angoche Mozambique **81** 16.10S 39.57E
Angol Chile **125** 37.48S 72.43W
Angola Africa **78** 11.00S 18.00E
Angola Ind. U.S.A. **112** 41.38N 85.01W
Angola N.Y. U.S.A. **114** 42.38N 79.02W
Angoram P.N.G. **59** 4.04S144.04E
Angoulême France **20** 45.39N 0.09E
Angra dos Reis Brazil **126** 22.59S 44.17W
Ang Thong Thailand **56** 14.35N100.25E
Anguilla *i.* Leeward Is. **117** 18.14N 63.05W
Angul India **63** 20.51N 85.06E
Angumu Zaïre **79** 0.10S 27.38E
Anhalt *f.* Germany **38** 52.07N 11.15E
Anholt *i.* Denmark **42** 56.42N 11.34E
Anholt Germany **16** 51.51N 6.26E
Anh Son Vietnam **56** 18.54N105.18E
Anhua China **55** 28.24N111.13E
Anhui *d.* China **55** 32.00N117.00E
Aniak U.S.A. **98** 61.32N159.40W
Anie, Pic d' *mtn.* France **20** 42.57N 0.43W
Animas U.S.A. **109** 31.57N108.48W
Anin Burma **56** 15.40N 97.46E
Anina Romania **37** 45.05N 21.51E
Anivorano Madagascar **81** 18.44S 48.58E
Anjad India **62** 22.02N 75.03E
Anjangaon India **62** 21.10N 77.18E
Anjār India **62** 23.08N 70.01E
'Anjarah Jordan **67** 32.18N 35.45E
Anjō Japan **57** 34.57N137.05E
Anjouan *see* Nzwani *i.* Comoros **79**
Anjozorobe Madagascar **81** 18.24S 47.52E
Anju N. Korea **53** 39.36N125.42E
Anka Nigeria **77** 12.06N 5.56E
Ankang China **54** 32.38N109.12E
Ankara Turkey **64** 39.55N 32.50E
Ankaramena Madagascar **81** 21.57S 46.39E
Ankarsrum Sweden **43** 57.42N 16.19E
Ankazoabo Madagascar **81** 22.18S 44.31E
Ankazobe Madagascar **81** 18.21S 47.07E
Anklam Germany **38** 53.51N 13.41E
Anklesvar India **62** 21.38N 72.59E
Ānkober Ethiopia **73** 9.30N 39.44E
Ankpa Nigeria **77** 7.26N 7.38E
Anlong China **55** 25.06N105.31E
Anlu China **55** 31.15N113.40E
Anna U.S.A. **111** 37.28N 89.15W
Annaba Algeria **75** 36.55N 7.47E
Annaberg-Buchholz Germany **38** 50.35N 13.00E
An Nabk Syria **66** 34.02N 36.43E
Anna Creek *town* Australia **92** 28.50S136.07E
An Nafūd *des.* Saudi Arabia **64** 28.40N 41.30E
An Najaf Iraq **65** 31.59N 44.19E
An Nakhl Egypt **66** 29.55N 33.45E
An Nakhl Syria **67** 33.01N 36.07E
Annam Highlands *see* Annamitique, Chaîne *mts.* Laos / Vietnam **56**
Annamitique, Chaîne *mts.* Laos / Vietnam **56** 17.00N106.00E
Annan U.K. **14** 54.59N 3.16W
Annan *r.* U.K. **14** 54.58N 3.16W
Annandale *f.* U.K. **14** 55.12N 3.25W
Anna Plains Australia **88** 19.18S121.34E
Annapolis U.S.A. **115** 38.59N 76.30W
Annapurna *mtn.* Nepal **63** 28.34N 83.50E
An Naqīrah *well* Saudi Arabia **65** 27.53N 48.15E
An Nāqūrah Lebanon **67** 33.07N 35.08E
Ann Arbor U.S.A. **104** 42.18N 83.45W
An Nāşirīyah Iraq **65** 31.04N 46.16E
An Nawfalīyah Libya **75** 30.47N 17.50E
Annecy France **21** 45.54N 6.07E
Annemasse France **21** 46.12N 6.15E
An Nīl *d.* Sudan **72** 18.30N 33.10E
An Nīl al Abyad *d.* Sudan **73** 13.10N 32.00E
An Nīl al Azraq *d.* Sudan **73** 13.00N 34.00E
Anniston U.S.A. **113** 33.38N 85.50W
Annobón *i.* Equat. Guinea **127** 1.25S 5.36E
Annonay France **21** 45.14N 4.40E
Annuello Australia **92** 34.52S142.54E
An Nuhūd Sudan **73** 12.42N 28.26E
Anoka U.S.A. **110** 45.11N 93.20W
Anorotsangana Madagascar **81** 13.56S 47.55E
Anou Ti-n Elhaoua *well* Algeria **75** 20.02N 2.55E
Anpu China **55** 21.27N110.01E
Anqing China **55** 30.40N117.03E
Ansager Denmark **42** 55.42N 8.45E
Ansbach Germany **39** 49.17N 10.34E
Anshan China **54** 41.06N122.58E
Anshun China **55** 26.11N105.50E
Anson B. Australia **88** 13.10S130.00E
Ansongo Mali **76** 15.40N 0.30E
Ansonia U.S.A. **115** 41.20N 73.05W
Anstruther U.K. **14** 56.14N 2.42W
Ansudu Indonesia **59** 2.11S139.22E
Antakya Turkey **64** 36.12N 36.10E
Antalaha Madagascar **81** 14.53S 50.16E
Antalya Turkey **64** 36.53N 30.42E
Antalya Körfezi *g.* Turkey **64** 36.38N 31.00E
Antananarivo Madagascar **81** 18.55S 47.31E
Antarctica 128
Antarctic Pen. Antarctica **121** 65.00S 64.00W
Antas Brazil **123** 10.20S 38.20W
Antela, Laguna de *l.* Spain **26** 42.07N 7.41W
Antequera Spain **27** 37.01N 4.33W
Anthony U.S.A. **111** 37.09N 89.02W
Antibes France **21** 43.35N 7.07E
Anticosti, Île d' *i.* Canada **103** 49.20N 63.00W
Anticosti Prov. Park Canada **103** 49.20N 63.00W
Antifer, Cap d' *c.* France **18** 49.41N 0.10E
Antigo U.S.A. **110** 45.09N 89.09W
Antigua Guatemala **116** 14.33N 90.42W
Antigua *i.* Leeward Is. **117** 17.09N 61.49W
Anti-Lebanon *mts. see* Sharqī, Al Jabal ash mts. *mts.* Lebanon **66**
Antipodes Is. Pacific Oc. **84** 49.42S178.50E
Antlers U.S.A. **111** 34.14N 95.47W
Antofagasta Chile **124** 23.39S 70.24W
Antônio Bezerra Brazil **123** 3.44S 38.35W
Antônio Carlos Brazil **126** 21.18S 43.48W
Antonito U.S.A. **108** 37.05N106.00W
Antrain France **18** 48.27N 1.29W
Antrim U.K. **15** 54.43N 6.14W
Antrim *d.* U.K. **15** 54.58N 6.20W
Antrim, Mts. of U.K. **15** 55.00N 6.10W
Antrodoco Italy **30** 42.25N 13.05E
Antsalova Madagascar **81** 18.40S 44.37E
Antsirabé Madagascar **81** 19.51S 47.02E
Antsiranana Madagascar **81** 12.16S 49.17E
Antsohihy Madagascar **81** 14.52S 47.59E
Anttis Sweden **40** 67.16N 22.52E
Antwerp *see* Antwerpen Belgium **16**
Antwerp U.S.A. **105** 44.12N 75.37W
Antwerpen Belgium **16** 51.13N 4.25E
Antwerpen *d.* Belgium **16** 51.16N 4.45E
Anūpgarh India **62** 29.11N 73.12E
Anvik U.S.A. **98** 62.38N160.20W
Anxi Fujian China **55** 25.03N118.13E
Anxi Gansu China **52** 40.32N 95.57E
Anxious B. Australia **92** 33.25S134.35E
Anyama Ivory Coast **76** 5.30N 4.03W
Anyang China **54** 36.05N114.20E
Anyer Lor Indonesia **59** 6.02S105.57E
Anyi China **55** 28.50N115.32E
Anyuan China **55** 25.09N115.21E
Anyue China **55** 30.09N105.18E
Anzhero-Sudzhensk U.S.S.R. **50** 56.10N 86.10E
Anzio Italy **32** 41.27N 12.37E
Ao Ban Don *b.* Thailand **56** 9.00N 99.20E
Aohan Qi China **54** 42.23N119.59E
Aoíz Spain **25** 42.47N 1.22W
Aoji N. Korea **57** 42.31N130.23E
Aomori Japan **57** 40.50N140.43E
Aóös *r.* Greece **34** 40.37N 19.20E
Aopo W. Samoa **84** 13.29S172.30W
Aosta Italy **30** 45.44N 7.20E
Aoulef Algeria **74** 26.58N 1.05E
Aoulime, Jbel *mtn.* Morocco **74** 30.48N 8.50W
Aozou Chad **77** 21.49N 17.25E
Apache U.S.A. **111** 34.54N 98.22W
Apalachee B. U.S.A. **113** 30.00N 84.13W
Apalachicola U.S.A. **113** 29.43N 85.01W
Apalachicola *r.* U.S.A. **113** 29.44N 84.59W
Apaporis *r.* Colombia **122** 1.40S 69.20W
Aparri Phil. **59** 18.22N121.40E
Apatin Yugo. **31** 45.40N 18.59E
Apatity U.S.S.R. **44** 67.32N 33.21E
Apeldoorn Neth. **16** 52.13N 5.57E
Api *mtn.* Nepal **63** 30.01N 80.56E
Apia W. Samoa **84** 13.48S171.45W
Apizaco Mexico **116** 19.25N 98.09W
Apoka Uganda **73** 3.42N 33.38E
Apolakkiá Greece **35** 36.04N 27.48E
Apolda Germany **38** 51.01N 11.31E
Apollo Bay *town* Australia **92** 38.45S143.40E
Apostle Is. U.S.A. **110** 46.50N 90.30W
Apóstoles Argentina **124** 27.55S 55.45W
Apostólou Andréa, Akrotírion *c.* Cyprus **66** 35.40N 34.35E
Apoteri Guyana **122** 4.02N 58.32W
Appalachian Mts. U.S.A. **114** 41.00N 77.00W
Appennino *mts.* Italy **30** 44.33N 9.55E
Appennino Abruzzese *mts.* Italy **30** 42.10N 13.25E
Appennino Ligure *mts.* Italy **30** 44.30N 9.00E
Appennino Lucano *mts.* Italy **33** 40.30N 15.50E
Appennino Tosco-Emiliano *mts.* Italy **30** 44.05N 11.00E
Appennino Umbro-Marchigiano *mts.* Italy **30** 43.05N 13.00E
Appenzell Switz. **39** 47.20N 9.25E
Appenzell *d.* Switz. **39** 47.00N 8.05E
Appiano Italy **30** 46.28N 11.15E
Appingedam Neth. **16** 53.18N 6.52E
Appleby U.K. **12** 54.35N 2.29W
Appleton U.S.A. **110** 44.16N 88.25W
Apsheronsk U.S.S.R. **45** 44.26N 39.45E
Apsheronskiy Poluostrov *pen.* U.S.S.R. **65** 40.28N 50.00E
Apsley Australia **92** 36.58S141.08E
Apsley Canada **104** 44.45N 78.06W
Apt France **21** 43.53N 5.24E
Apucarana Brazil **126** 23.34S 51.28W
Apure *r.* Venezuela **122** 7.40N 66.30W
Apurimac *r.* Peru **122** 10.43S 73.55W
Aqaba, G. of Asia **66** 28.45N 34.45E
Aqabat al Ḩijāzīyah Jordan **66** 29.40N 35.55E
'Aqdā Iran **65** 32.25N 33.38E
'Aqīq Sudan **72** 18.14N 38.12E
Aqqikkol Hu *l.* China **52** 35.44N 81.34E
'Aqrabā Syria **67** 33.28N 36.20E
'Aqrabah Jordan **67** 32.08N 35.21E
Aquidauana Brazil **124** 20.27S 55.45W
Aquila Mexico **116** 18.30N103.50W
Aquitaine *d.* France **20** 44.40N 0.00
'Ara Israel **67** 32.30N 35.05E
'Arab, Baḩr al *r.* Sudan **73** 9.12N 29.28E
'Arab, Wādī al Jordan **67** 32.35N 35.35E
Arabādād Iran **65** 33.02N 57.41E
'Arabah, Wādī *r.* Egypt **66** 29.07N 32.40E
Arabian Basin *f.* Indian Oc. **48** 12.00N 65.00E
Arabian Sea Asia **60** 16.00N 65.00E
Araç Turkey **64** 41.14N 33.20E
Aracaju Brazil **123** 10.54S 37.07W
Aracanguy, Montañas de *mts.* Paraguay **124** 24.00S 55.50W
Aracati Brazil **123** 4.32S 37.45W
Araçatuba Brazil **126** 21.12S 50.24W
Aracena Spain **27** 37.53N 6.33W
Aracena, Sierra de *mts.* Spain **27** 37.50N 7.00W
'Arad Israel **67** 31.15N 35.13E
Arad Romania **37** 46.12N 21.19E
Arada Chad **75** 15.01N 20.40E
Arafura Sea Austa. **90** 9.00S133.00E
Aragarças Brazil **123** 15.55S 52.12W
Aragats *mtn.* U.S.S.R. **65** 40.32N 44.11E
Aragón *d.* Spain **25** 41.30N 0.30W
Aragón *r.* Spain **25** 42.13N 1.44W
Aragona Italy **32** 37.24N 13.37E
Araguacema Brazil **123** 8.50S 49.34W
Araguaia *r.* Brazil **123** 5.20S 48.30W
Araguari Brazil **126** 18.38S 48.13W
Araguari *r.* Brazil **123** 1.15N 50.05W
Arak Algeria **75** 25.18N 3.45E
Arāk Iran **65** 34.06N 49.44E
Araka Sudan **73** 4.16N 30.21E
Arakan *d.* Burma **56** 19.00N 94.15E
Arakan Yoma *mts.* Burma **56** 19.30N 94.30E
Arákhova Greece **35** 38.28N 22.35E
Arakhthros *r.* Greece **35** 39.01N 21.03E
Araks *r.* U.S.S.R. **65** 40.00N 48.28E
Aral Sea *see* Aralskoye More *sea* U.S.S.R. **9**
Aralsk U.S.S.R. **9** 46.56N 61.43E
Aralskoye More *sea* U.S.S.R. **9** 45.00N 60.00E
Aralsor, Ozero *l.* U.S.S.R. **45** 49.00N 48.40E
Aramac Australia **90** 22.59S145.14E
Arāmbāgh India **63** 22.53N 87.47E
Aramia *r.* P.N.G. **59** 8.00S143.20E
Arana, Sierra *mts.* Spain **27** 37.20N 3.30W
Aranda de Duero Spain **26** 41.41N 3.41W
Aran I. Rep. of Ire. **15** 55.00N 8.32W
Aran Is. Rep. of Ire. **15** 53.07N 9.38W
Aranjuez Spain **27** 40.02N 3.36W
Aranos Namibia **80** 24.09S 19.09E
Aransas Pass *town* U.S.A. **111** 27.54N 97.09W
Araouane Mali **76** 18.53N 3.31W
Arapahoe U.S.A. **110** 40.18N 99.54W
Arapey Uruguay **125** 30.58S 57.30W
Arapey Grande *r.* Uruguay **125** 30.55S 57.49W
Arapiraca Brazil **123** 9.45S 36.40W
Arapkir Turkey **64** 39.03N 38.29E
Araquil *r.* Spain **25** 42.48N 1.45W
'Ar'ar, Wādī *r.* Iraq **64** 32.00N 42.30E
Araraquara Brazil **126** 21.46S 48.08W
Araras Brazil **126** 22.20S 47.23W
Ararat Australia **92** 37.20S143.00E
Ararat *mtn. see* Ağri Daği *mtn.* Turkey **65**
Aras *r.* Turkey *see* Araks *r.* U.S.S.R. **64**
Arauca Colombia **122** 7.04N 70.41W
Arauca *r.* Venezuela **122** 7.05N 70.45W
Araure Venezuela **122** 9.36N 69.15W
Arāvalli Range *mts.* India **62** 25.00N 73.45E
Araviana Spain **25** 41.41N 2.07W
Araviana *r.* Spain **26** 41.35N 2.25W
Araxá Brazil **126** 19.37S 46.50W
Araxes *r.* Iran *see* Araks *r.* U.S.S.R. **65**
Arba *r.* Spain **25** 41.52N 1.18W
Ārba Minch' Ethiopia **73** 6.02N 37.40E
Arbatax Italy **32** 39.57N 9.42E
Arboga Sweden **43** 59.24N 15.50E
Arbois France **19** 46.54N 5.46E
Arbon Switz. **39** 47.31N 9.26E
Arborea Italy **32** 39.47N 8.34E
Arborg Canada **101** 50.55N 97.15W
Arbroath U.K. **14** 56.34N 2.35W
Arc *r.* France **21** 45.34N 6.12E
Arcachon France **20** 44.37N 1.12W
Arcachon, Bassin d' *b.* France **20** 44.40N 1.10W
Arcade U.S.A. **114** 42.32N 78.25W
Arcadia Fla. U.S.A. **113** 27.12N 81.52W
Arcadia Wisc. U.S.A. **110** 44.15N 91.30W
Arcata U.S.A. **108** 40.52N124.05W
Arce Italy **32** 41.35N 13.34E
Arcevia Italy **30** 43.30N 12.56E
Archbald U.S.A. **115** 41.30N 75.32W
Archer *r.* Australia **90** 13.28S141.41E
Archers Post Kenya **79** 0.42N 37.40E
Archiac France **20** 45.31N 0.18W
Archidona Spain **27** 37.05N 4.23W
Arcidosso Italy **30** 42.52N 11.33E
Arcis-sur-Aube France **19** 48.32N 4.08E
Arckaringa *r.* Australia **92** 27.56S134.45E
Arco Italy **30** 45.55N 10.53E
Arco U.S.A. **108** 43.38N113.18W
Arco de Baúlhe Portugal **26** 41.29N 7.58W
Arcoona Australia **92** 31.06S137.19E
Arcos Brazil **126** 20.12S 45.30W
Arcos Spain **27** 36.45N 5.48W
Arcoverde Brazil **123** 8.23S 37.00W
Arctic Bay *town* Canada **99** 73.05N 85.20W
Arctic Ocean 128
Arctic Red *r.* Canada **98** 67.26N133.48W
Arctic Red River *town* Canada **98** 67.27N133.46W
Arda *r.* Greece **34** 41.39N 26.29E
Ardabīl Iran **65** 38.15N 48.18E
Ardahan Turkey **64** 41.08N 42.41E
Årdalstangen Norway **41** 61.14N 7.43E
Ardara Rep. of Ire. **15** 54.46N 8.25W
Arḑ aş Şawwān *f.* Jordan **66** 30.45N 37.15E
Ardbeg Canada **104** 45.38N 80.05W
Ardèche *d.* France **21** 44.40N 4.20E
Ardèche *r.* France **21** 44.16N 4.39E
Ardee Rep. of Ire. **11** 53.51N 6.33W
Ardennes *mts.* Belgium **16** 50.10N 5.30E
Ardennes *d.* France **19** 49.40N 4.40E
Ardennes, Canal des France **19** 49.26N 4.02E
Ardestān Iran **65** 33.22N 52.25E
Ardfert Rep. of Ire. **15** 52.20N 9.48W
Ardila *r.* Portugal **27** 38.09N 7.28W
Ardino Bulgaria **34** 41.35N 25.08E
Ardlethan Australia **93** 34.20S146.53E
Ardmore Rep. of Ire. **15** 51.58N 7.43W
Ardmore Okla. U.S.A. **111** 34.10N 97.08W
Ardmore Penn. U.S.A. **115** 40.01N 75.18W
Ardnamurchan, Pt. of U.K. **14** 56.44N 6.14W
Ardrossan Australia **92** 34.25S137.55E
Ardrossan U.K. **14** 55.38N 4.49W
Ards Pen. U.K. **15** 54.30N 5.30W
Åre Sweden **40** 63.25N 13.05E
Arecibo Puerto Rico **117** 18.29N 66.44W
Areia Branca Brazil **123** 4.56S 37.07W
Arena, Pt. U.S.A. **106** 38.58N123.44W
Arena, Punta *c.* Mexico **109** 23.32N109.30W
Arenas de San Pedro Spain **26** 40.12N 5.05W
Arendal Norway **42** 58.27N 8.48E
Arendsee Germany **38** 52.53N 11.30E
Arenys de Mar Spain **25** 41.35N 2.33E
Areópolis Greece **35** 36.40N 22.22E
Arequipa Peru **122** 16.25S 71.32W
Arès France **20** 44.46N 1.08W
Arévalo Spain **26** 41.04N 4.43W
Arezzo Italy **30** 43.25N 11.53E
Arfak *mtn.* Indonesia **59** 1.30S133.50E
Arfará Greece **35** 37.10N 23.03E
Arga Spain **25** 42.18N 1.47W
Argalastí Greece **35** 39.13N 23.13E
Argamasilla de Alba Spain **27** 39.07N 3.06W
Arganda Spain **26** 40.18N 3.26W
Argelès-Gazost France **20** 43.01N 0.06W
Argelès-sur-Mer France **20** 42.33N 3.01E
Argens *r.* France **21** 43.24N 6.44E
Argenta Italy **30** 44.37N 11.50E
Argentan France **18** 48.45N 0.01W
Argentat France **20** 45.06N 1.56E
Argentera Italy **30** 44.24N 6.57E
Argentera *mtn.* Italy **30** 44.10N 7.18E
Argenteuil France **19** 48.57N 2.15E
Argentia Canada **103** 47.18N 53.59W
Argentina S. America **125** 36.00S 63.00W
Argentine Basin *f.* Atlantic Oc. **127** 40.00S 40.00W
Argentino, L. Argentina **125** 50.15S 72.25W
Argenton France **19** 46.35N 1.31E
Argenton-Château France **18** 47.00N 0.27W
Argentré France **18** 48.05N 0.39W
Argentré du Plessis France **18** 48.03N 1.08W
Argeş *r.* Romania **29** 44.13N 26.22E
Arghandāb *r.* Afghan. **62** 31.27N 64.23E
Argolikós Kólpos *g.* Greece **35** 37.33N 22.45E
Argonne *d.* France **19** 49.30N 5.00E
Árgos Greece **35** 37.38N 22.43E
Argos Orestikón Greece **34** 40.27N 21.26E
Argostólion Greece **35** 38.10N 20.30E
Arguello, Pt. U.S.A. **109** 34.35N120.39W
Argun *r.* U.S.S.R. **53** 53.30N121.48E
Argungu Nigeria **77** 12.45N 4.35E
Argyle U.S.A. **110** 48.20N 96.49W
Ar Horqin Qi China **54** 43.45N120.00E
Århus Denmark **42** 56.09N 10.13E
Ariah Park *town* Australia **93** 34.20S147.10E
Ariana Tunisia **32** 36.52N 10.12E
Ariano Italy **33** 41.09N 15.05E
Ariano nel Polesine Italy **30** 44.56N 12.07E
Aribinda Burkina **76** 14.17N 0.52W
Arica Chile **124** 18.29S 70.20W
Arica Colombia **122** 2.07S 71.46W
Arid, C. Australia **89** 33.58S123.05E
Aridhaía Greece **34** 40.58N 22.03E
Ariège *d.* France **20** 43.00N 1.30E
Ariège *r.* France **20** 43.31N 1.25E
Arieş *r.* Romania **37** 46.26N 23.59E
Ārifwāla Pakistan **62** 30.17N 73.04E
Arīḩā Al Karak Jordan **67** 31.25N 35.47E
Arīḩā Al Quds Jordan **67** 31.51N 35.27E
Arima Trinidad **122** 10.38N 61.17W
Arinos *r.* Brazil **123** 10.20S 57.35W
Aripuanã Brazil **122** 9.10S 60.38W
Aripuanã *r.* Brazil **122** 5.05S 60.30W
Ariquemes Brazil **122** 9.56S 63.04W
Aris Namibia **80** 22.48S 17.10E
Arisaig U.K. **14** 56.55N 5.51W
'Arīsh, Wādī al *r.* Egypt **66** 31.09N 33.49E
Aristazabal I. Canada **100** 52.40N129.10W
Arivonimamo Madagascar **81** 19.01S 47.15E
Ariza Spain **25** 41.19N 2.03W
Arizgoiti Spain **26** 43.11N 2.57W
Arizona *d.* U.S.A. **106** 34.00N112.00W
Årjäng Sweden **43** 59.23N 12.08E
Arjeplog Sweden **40** 66.00N 17.58E
Arjona Colombia **122** 10.14N 75.22W
Arjona Spain **27** 37.56N 4.03W
Arkadelphia U.S.A. **111** 34.07N 93.04W
Arkaig, Loch U.K. **14** 56.58N 5.08W
Arkansas *d.* U.S.A. **111** 34.20N 92.00W
Arkansas *r.* U.S.A. **111** 33.48N 91.04W
Arkansas City U.S.A. **111** 37.04N 97.02W
Arkhangélos Greece **35** 36.13N 28.07E
Arkhangel'sk U.S.S.R. **44** 64.32N 41.10E
Árki *i.* Greece **29** 37.22N 26.45E
Arklow Rep. of Ire. **15** 52.47N 6.10W
Arkösund Sweden **43** 58.30N 16.56E
Arkport U.S.A. **114** 42.24N 77.42W
Arkville U.S.A. **115** 42.09N 74.37W
Arlanc France **20** 45.25N 3.44E
Arlanza *r.* Spain **26** 42.06N 4.09W
Arlanzón Spain **26** 42.03N 4.17W
Arlberg Pass Austria **36** 47.00N 10.05E
Arles France **21** 43.40N 4.38E

Arlington to **Ault**

Arlington Colo. U.S.A. **108** 38.20N103.19W
Arlington Oreg. U.S.A. **108** 45.16N120.13W
Arlington Tex. U.S.A. **111** 32.44N 97.07W
Arlington Va. U.S.A. **114** 38.52N 77.05W
Arlington Heights *town* U.S.A. **110** 42.06N 88.00W
Arlon Belgium **16** 49.41N 5.49E
Armada U.S.A. **114** 42.51N 82.53W
Armadale Australia **89** 32.10S115.57E
Armagh U.K. **15** 54.21N 6.41W
Armagh *d.* U.K. **15** 54.16N 6.35W
Armançon *r.* France **19** 47.57N 3.30E
Armavir U.S.S.R. **45** 44.59N 41.10E
Armenia Colombia **122** 4.32N 75.40W
Armenia *f.* Iran / Turkey / U.S.S.R. **65** 40.00N 44.30E
Armenia *see* Armyanskaya S.S.R. *d.* U.S.S.R. **65**
Armeniş Romania **37** 45.12N 22.19E
Armenistis *i.* Greece **35** 37.36N 26.08E
Armentières France **19** 50.41N 2.53E
Armidale Australia **93** 30.32S151.40E
Armori India **63** 20.28N 79.59E
Armstrong Canada **100** 50.25N119.10W
Armstrong U.S.A. **111** 26.55N 97.47W
Ārmūr India **63** 18.48N 78.17E
Armyanskaya S.S.R. *d.* U.S.S.R. **65** 40.00N 45.00E
Arnaía Greece **34** 40.29N 23.35E
Arnaud *r.* Canada **99** 60.00N 69.45W
Arnay-le-Duc France **19** 47.08N 4.29E
Arnedo Spain **26** 42.13N 2.06W
Årnes Norway **42** 60.09N 11.28E
Arnett U.S.A. **111** 36.08N 99.46W
Arnhem Neth. **16** 52.00N 5.55E
Arnhem, C. Australia **90** 12.10S137.00E
Arnhem B. Australia **90** 12.20S136.12E
Arnhem Land *f.* Australia **90** 13.10S134.30E
Árnissa Greece **34** 40.47N 21.49E
Arno *r.* Italy **30** 43.41N 10.17E
Arno Bay *town* Australia **92** 33.54S136.34E
Arnon *r.* France **19** 47.12N 2.03E
Arnot Canada **101** 55.46N 96.41W
Årnotfors Sweden **43** 59.46N 12.22E
Arnprior Canada **105** 45.26N 76.21W
Arnsberg Germany **38** 51.24N 8.03E
Arnstadt Germany **38** 50.50N 10.57E
Arolsen Germany **38** 51.23N 9.01E
Aroma Sudan **72** 15.49N 36.08E
Aron *r.* France **19** 47.15N 2.02E
Arona Italy **30** 45.46N 8.34E
Arorangi Rarotonga Cook Is. **84** 21.13S159.49W
Arosa Switz. **39** 46.47N 9.41E
Arosa, Ría de *est.* Spain **26** 42.28N 8.57W
Arpajon France **19** 48.35N 2.15E
Arpino Italy **32** 41.40N 13.35E
Arra Ivory Coast **76** 6.42N 3.57W
Ar Rabbah Jordan **67** 31.16N 35.44E
Ar Rafīd Syria **67** 32.57N 35.53E
Arrah India **63** 25.34N 84.40E
Ar Rahad Sudan **73** 12.43N 30.39E
Ar Ramādī Iraq **64** 33.27N 43.19E
Ar Ramthā Jordan **67** 32.34N 36.00E
Arran *i.* U.K. **14** 55.35N 5.14W
Ar Rank Sudan **73** 11.45N 32.48E
Ar Raqqah Syria **64** 35.57N 39.03E
Arras France **19** 50.17N 2.47E
Ar Rass Saudi Arabia **64** 25.54N 43.30E
Ar Rastān Syria **66** 34.55N 36.44E
Arrats *r.* France **20** 44.06N 0.52E
Arrecife Canary Is. **74** 28.57N 13.32W
Arrecifes Argentina **125** 34.05S 60.05W
Arrée, Monts d' *mts.* France **18** 48.26N 3.55W
Arrey U.S.A. **109** 32.51N107.19W
Ar Riyāḍ Saudi Arabia **65** 24.39N 46.44E
Arrochar U.K. **14** 56.12N 4.44W
Arromanches France **18** 49.20N 0.38W
Arronches Portugal **27** 39.07N 7.17W
Arros *r.* France **20** 43.40N 0.02W
Arroux *r.* France **19** 46.29N 3.58E
Arrow, Lough Rep.of Ire. **15** 54.03N 8.20W
Arrowsmith, Pt. Australia **90** 13.18S136.24E
Arrowtown New Zealand **86** 44.56S168.50E
Arroyo de la Luz Spain **27** 39.29N 6.35W
Arroyo Feliciano *r.* Argentina **125** 31.06S 59.53W
Arroyo Villimanca *r.* Argentina **125** 35.36S 59.05W
Ar Ru'at Sudan **73** 12.21N 32.17E
Ar Rub' al Khālī *des.* Saudi Arabia **60** 20.20N 52.30E
Ar Rubayqī Egypt **66** 30.10N 31.46E
Ar Rumaythah Iraq **65** 31.32N 45.12E
Ar Rummān Jordan **67** 32.10N 35.50E
Ar Ruşayriş Sudan **73** 11.51N 34.23E
Ar Ruṭbah Iraq **64** 33.03N 40.18E
Ar Ruwayḍah Saudi Arabia **65** 23.46N 44.46E
Års Denmark **42** 56.48N 9.32E
Ars-en-Ré France **20** 46.12N 1.31W
Ārsī *d.* Ethiopia **73** 7.50N 39.50E
Ársos Cyprus **66** 34.50N 32.46E
Árta Greece **35** 39.09N 20.59E
Artá Spain **25** 39.42N 3.21E
Artemón Greece **35** 36.59N 24.43E
Artemovsk U.S.S.R. **45** 48.35N 38.00E
Artenay France **19** 48.05N 1.53E
Artesia U.S.A. **109** 32.51N104.24W
Arthabaska Canada **105** 46.02N 71.55W
Arthal Jammu & Kashmir **62** 33.16N 76.11E
Arthington Liberia **76** 6.35N 10.45W
Arthur Canada **104** 43.50N 80.32W
Arthur's Pass New Zealand **86** 42.50S171.45E
Artigas Uruguay **125** 30.24S 56.28W
Artillery L. Canada **101** 63.09N107.52W
Artois *f.* France **16** 50.16N 2.50E
Artux China **52** 39.40N 75.49E
Artvin Turkey **64** 41.12N 41.48E
Aru, Kepulauan *is.* Indonesia **59** 6.00S134.30E
Arua Uganda **79** 3.02N 30.56E
Aruaddin Ethiopia **72** 16.16N 38.46E
Aruanã Brazil **123** 14.54S 51.05W
Aruba *i.* Neth. Ant. **117** 12.30N 70.00W
Arucas Canary Is. **127** 28.08N 15.32W
Arun *r.* U.K. **11** 50.48N 0.32W
Arunachal Pradesh *d.* India **61** 28.40N 94.60E
Arundel Canada **105** 45.58N 74.37W
Arusha Tanzania **79** 3.21S 36.40E
Arusha *d.* Tanzania **79** 4.00S 37.00E
Aruwimi *r.* Zaïre **78** 1.20N 23.36E
Arvada Colo. U.S.A. **108** 39.50N105.05W
Arvada Wyo. U.S.A. **108** 44.39N105.05W
Arvagh Rep. of Ire. **15** 53.56N 7.35W
Arve *r.* France **21** 46.12N 6.08E
Arvi India **63** 20.59N 78.14E
Arvidsjaur Sweden **40** 65.35N 19.07E
Arvika Sweden **43** 59.39N 12.35E
Arzachena Italy **32** 41.05N 9.22E
Arzamas U.S.S.R. **44** 55.24N 43.48E
Arzgir U.S.S.R. **45** 45.24N 44.04E
Arzignano Italy **30** 45.31N 11.20E
Arzúa Spain **26** 42.56N 8.09W
Ås Norway **42** 59.40N 10.48E
Asaba Nigeria **77** 6.12N 6.44E
Asadābād Afghan. **62** 34.52N 71.09E
Asahi dake *mtn.* Japan **57** 43.42N142.54E
Asahikawa Japan **57** 43.46N142.23E
Asansol India **63** 23.41N 86.59E
Åsarna Sweden **40** 62.40N 14.20E
Asarum Sweden **43** 56.12N 14.50E
Āsayita Ethiopia **73** 11.33N 41.30E
Asbest U.S.S.R. **9** 57.05N 61.30E
Asbestos Canada **105** 45.46N 71.57W
Asbury Park U.S.A. **115** 40.13N 74.01W
Ascension *i.* Atlantic Oc. **127** 7.57S 14.22W
Aschaffenburg Germany **39** 49.59N 9.09E
Aschendorf Germany **38** 53.04N 7.22E
Aschersleben Germany **38** 51.45N 11.27E
Asciano Italy **30** 43.14N 11.33E
Ascoli Piceno Italy **31** 42.51N 13.34E
Ascoli Satriano Italy **33** 41.12N 15.34E
Ascona Switz. **39** 46.09N 8.46E
Āseb Ethiopia **73** 13.01N 42.47E
Åseda Sweden **43** 57.10N 15.20E
Asedjrad Algeria **75** 24.42N 1.40E
Āsela Ethiopia **73** 7.59N 39.08E
Åsele Sweden **40** 64.10N 17.20E
Åsenbruk Sweden **43** 58.48N 12.25E
Asenovgrad Bulgaria **34** 42.01N 24.51E
Åseral Norway **42** 58.37N 7.25E
Asfeld France **19** 49.27N 4.05E
Asha Nigeria **77** 7.07N 3.43E
Ashanti *d.* Ghana **76** 6.30N 1.30W
Ashaway U.S.A. **115** 41.25N 71.47W
Ashbourne Rep. of Ire. **15** 53.31N 6.25W
Ashburn U.S.A. **113** 31.42N 83.41W
Ashburton *r.* Australia **88** 21.15S115.00E
Ashburton New Zealand **86** 43.54S171.46E
Ashby de la Zouch U.K. **13** 52.45N 1.29W
Ashcroft Canada **100** 50.40N121.20W
Ashdod Israel **67** 31.48N 34.38E
Asheboro U.S.A. **113** 35.42N 79.50W
Ashern Canada **101** 51.11N 98.21W
Asheville U.S.A. **113** 35.35N 82.35W
Ashewat Pakistan **62** 31.22N 68.32E
Ash Flat *town* U.S.A. **111** 36.12N 91.38W
Ashford Australia **93** 29.19S151.07E
Ashford Kent U.K. **13** 51.08N 0.53E
Ash Fork U.S.A. **109** 35.13N112.29W
Ashikaga Japan **57** 36.21N139.26E
Ashington U.K. **12** 55.11N 1.34W
Ashiya Japan **57** 34.43N135.17E
Ashizuri zaki *c.* Japan **57** 32.45N133.05E
Ashkhabad U.S.S.R. **65** 37.58N 58.24E
Ashland Ky. U.S.A. **114** 38.29N 82.39W
Ashland N.H. U.S.A. **105** 43.42N 71.38W
Ashland Ohio U.S.A. **114** 40.52N 82.19W
Ashland Oreg. U.S.A. **108** 42.12N122.42W
Ashland Wisc. U.S.A. **110** 46.35N 90.53W
Ashley Australia **93** 29.19S149.52E
Ashley U.S.A. **110** 38.20N 89.10W
Ashley Snow I. Antarctica **128** 72.30S 77.00W
Ashmūn Egypt **66** 30.18N 30.59E
Ashoknagar India **63** 24.34N 77.43E
Ashqelon Israel **67** 31.40N 34.35E
Ash Shabb *well* Egypt **72** 22.19N 29.46E
Ash Shāghūr Jordan **67** 31.50N 35.39E
Ash Shajarah Jordan **67** 32.39N 35.56E
Ash Shallūfah Egypt **66** 30.07N 32.34E
Ash Shāmah *des.* Saudi Arabia **64** 31.20N 38.00E
Ash Shamālīyah *d.* Sudan **72** 19.30N 29.50E
Ash Shāmīyah *des.* Iraq **65** 30.30N 45.30E
Ash Shāriqah U.A.E. **65** 25.20N 55.26E
Ash Sharmah Saudi Arabia **66** 28.01N 35.14E
Ash Shawbak Jordan **66** 30.33N 35.35E
Ash Shaykh Faḍl Egypt **66** 28.29N 30.50E
Ash Shaykh 'Ibādah Egypt **66** 27.48N 30.52E
Ash Shaykh Miskīn Syria **67** 32.49N 36.09E
Ash Shiḥr Yemen **71** 14.45N 49.36E
Ash Shu'aybah Iraq **65** 30.30N 47.40E
Ash Shu'aybah Saudi Arabia **64** 27.53N 42.43E
Ash Shumlūl Saudi Arabia **65** 26.29N 47.20E
Ashta India **62** 23.01N 76.43E
Ashtabula U.S.A. **114** 41.52N 80.48W
Ashton R.S.A. **80** 33.49S 20.04E
Ashton U.S.A. **108** 44.04N111.27W
'Āṣī *r.* Lebanon **66** 34.37N 36.30E
Asiago Italy **32** 45.52N 11.30E
Asilah Morocco **74** 35.32N 6.00W
Asinara *i.* Italy **32** 41.05N 8.18E
Asinara, Golfo dell' *g.* Italy **32** 41.00N 8.30E
'Asīr *f.* Saudi Arabia **71** 19.00N 42.00E
Aska India **63** 19.36N 84.39E
Askeaton Rep. of Ire. **15** 52.36N 9.00W
Asker Norway **42** 59.50N 10.26E
Askersund Sweden **43** 58.53N 14.54E
Askim Norway **42** 59.35N 11.10E
Askvoll Norway **41** 61.21N 5.04E
Āsmera Ethiopia **72** 15.20N 38.58E
Asnaes Denmark **42** 55.49N 11.31E
Åsnen *l.* Sweden **43** 56.38N 14.42E
Asola Italy **32** 45.13N 10.24E
Āsosa Ethiopia **73** 10.03N 34.32E
Asoteriba, Jabal *mtn.* Sudan **72** 21.51N 36.30E
Aspe Spain **25** 38.21N 0.46W
Aspe, Gave d' *r.* France **20** 43.15N 0.29W
Aspen U.S.A. **108** 39.11N106.49W
Aspermont U.S.A. **111** 33.08N100.14W
Aspiring, Mt. New Zealand **86** 44.20S168.45E
Aspres-sur-Buëch France **21** 44.31N 5.45E
Asquith Canada **101** 52.08N107.13W
Assaba *d.* Mauritania **74** 16.40N 11.40W
As Sadd al 'Ālī *dam* Egypt **72** 23.59N 32.54E
Aş Şaff Egypt **66** 29.34N 31.17E
As Saffānīyah Saudi Arabia **65** 28.00N 48.48E
Aş Şāfīyah Sudan **72** 15.31N 30.07E
Aş Şa'īd *f.* Egypt **64** 25.30N 32.00E
Aş Şāliḥīyah Egypt **66** 30.47N 31.59E
As Sallūm Egypt **64** 31.31N 25.09E
As Salṭ Jordan **67** 32.03N 35.44E
As Salwa Saudi Arabia **65** 24.44N 50.50E
Assam *d.* India **61** 26.30N 93.00E
As Samāwah Iraq **65** 31.18N 45.18E
As Sāmirah *f.* Jordan **67** 32.15N 35.15E
As Samū' Jordan **67** 31.24N 35.04E
As Sanām *f.* Saudi Arabia **71** 22.00N 51.10E
Aş Şanamayn Syria **67** 33.05N 36.10E
Aş Şarafand Lebanon **66** 33.27N 35.18E
Aş Şarīḥ Jordan **67** 32.30N 35.54E
As Sarīrīyah Egypt **66** 28.20N 30.45E
Assebroek Belgium **16** 51.11N 3.16E
Assen Neth. **16** 53.00N 6.34E
Assens Denmark **42** 55.16N 9.55E
Asseria *site* Yugo. **31** 44.02N 15.39E
As Simākīyah Jordan **67** 31.18N 35.48E
As Sinbillāwayn Egypt **66** 30.53N 31.27E
Assiniboia Canada **101** 49.38N105.59W
Assiniboine *r.* Canada **101** 49.53N 97.08W
Assinica Prov. Park Canada **102** 50.24N 75.00W
Assis Brazil **126** 22.37S 50.25W
Assisi Italy **30** 43.04N 12.37E
As Sudd Sudan **73** 7.50N 30.00E
Aş Şufayyah Sudan **72** 15.30N 34.42E
As Sukhnah Jordan **67** 32.08N 36.04E
As Sulaymānīyah Iraq **65** 35.32N 45.27E
As Sulaymānīyah Saudi Arabia **65** 24.10N 47.20E
As Sulayyil Saudi Arabia **71** 20.27N 45.34E
As Sulṭān Libya **75** 31.07N 17.09E
As Sumayḥ Sudan **73** 9.49N 27.39E
Aş Şummān *f.* Saudi Arabia **65** 27.00N 47.00E
As Sūq Saudi Arabia **72** 21.55N 42.02E
As Suwaydā' Syria **66** 32.43N 36.33E
As Suways Egypt **66** 29.59N 32.33E
Astaffort France **20** 44.04N 0.40E
Astakós Greece **35** 38.32N 21.05E
Asti Italy **30** 44.54N 8.12E
Astillero Spain **26** 43.24N 3.49W
Astipálaia Greece **35** 36.32N 26.22E
Astipálaia *i.* Greece **35** 36.35N 26.25E
Astorga Spain **26** 42.27N 6.03W
Astoria U.S.A. **108** 46.11N123.50W
Åstorp Sweden **43** 56.08N 12.57E
Astrakhan U.S.S.R. **45** 46.22N 48.00E
Åsträsk Sweden **40** 64.38N 20.00E
Astudillo Spain **26** 42.12N 4.18W
Asturias *d.* Spain **26** 43.30N 6.00W
Asturias *d.* Spain **26** 43.20N 6.10W
Asunción Paraguay **126** 25.15S 57.40W
Åsunden *l.* Sweden **43** 57.58N 15.50E
'Āşūr, Tall *mtn.* Jordan **67** 31.59N 35.17E
Aswân Egypt **64** 24.05N 32.56E
Aswan High Dam *see* As Sadd al 'Ālī Egypt **64**
Asyūṭ Egypt **64** 27.14N 31.07E
Atacama, Desierto *des.* S. America **124** 20.00S 69.00W
Atacama, Salar de *f.* Chile **124** 23.30S 68.46W
Atacama Desert *see* Atacama, Desierto *des.* S. America **124**
Atafu Pacific Oc. **84** 8.40S172.40W
Atakpamé Togo **77** 7.34N 1.14E
Atalándi Greece **35** 38.39N 22.58E
Atami Japan **57** 35.05N139.04E
Atapupu Indonesia **59** 9.00S124.51E
Atar Mauritania **74** 20.32N 13.08W
Atara U.S.S.R. **51** 63.10N129.10E
'Aṭārūt Jordan **67** 31.52N 35.13E
Atasu U.S.S.R. **50** 48.42N 71.38E
'Aṭbarah Sudan **72** 17.42N 33.59E
'Aṭbarah *r.* Sudan **72** 17.40N 33.58E
Atbasar U.S.S.R. **9** 51.49N 68.18E
Atchafalaya B. U.S.A. **111** 29.25N 91.20W
Atchison U.S.A. **110** 39.34N 95.07W
Ateca Spain **25** 41.20N 1.47W
Aterno *r.* Italy **31** 42.11N 13.51E
Ath Belgium **16** 50.38N 3.45E
Athabasca Canada **100** 54.45N113.20W
Athabasca *r.* Canada **101** 58.40N110.50W
Athabasca, L. Canada **101** 59.07N110.00W
Athea Rep. of Ire. **15** 52.28N 9.19W
Athenry Rep. of Ire. **15** 53.18N 8.45W
Athens Canada **105** 44.38N 75.57W
Athens *see* Athínai Greece **35**
Athens Ga. U.S.A. **113** 33.57N 83.24W
Athens Ohio U.S.A. **114** 39.20N 82.06W
Athens Penn. U.S.A. **115** 41.57N 76.31W
Athens Tenn. U.S.A. **113** 35.27N 84.38W
Athens Tex. U.S.A. **111** 32.12N 95.51W
Atherley Canada **104** 44.36N 79.22W
Atherton Australia **90** 17.15S145.29E
Athínai Greece **35** 38.00N 23.44E
Athlone Rep. of Ire. **15** 53.26N 7.57W
Athol U.S.A. **115** 42.36N 72.14W
Atholl, Forest of U.K. **14** 56.50N 3.55W
Áthos *mtn.* Greece **34** 40.09N 24.19E
Ath Thamad Egypt **66** 29.40N 34.18E
Ath Thanīyah Jordan **67** 31.10N 35.43E
Ati Chad **77** 13.11N 18.20E
Atico Peru **122** 16.12S 73.37W
Atienza Spain **26** 41.12N 2.52W
Atikonak L. Canada **103** 52.40N 64.30W
Atimaono Tahiti **85** 17.46S149.28W
Atkarsk U.S.S.R. **45** 51.55N 45.00E
Atkinson U.S.A. **113** 34.33N 78.12W
Atlanta Ga. U.S.A. **113** 33.45N 84.23W
Atlanta Mich. U.S.A. **104** 45.00N 84.09W
Atlanta Tex. U.S.A. **111** 33.07N 94.10W
Atlantic Iowa U.S.A. **110** 41.24N 95.01W
Atlantic-Antarctic Ridge *f.* Atlantic Oc. **127** 53.00S 0.00
Atlantic City U.S.A. **115** 39.22N 74.26W
Atlantic-Indian-Antarctic Basin *f.* Atl.Oc. / Ind.Oc. **49** 59.00S 40.00E
Atlantic Ocean **127**
Atlas Mts. Africa **22** 33.00N 2.00W
Atlas Saharien *mts.* Algeria **75** 34.00N 2.00E
Atlin Canada **100** 59.31N133.41W
Atlin L. Canada **100** 59.26N133.45W
'Atlit Israel **67** 32.41N 34.56E
'Atlit *site* Israel **67** 32.42N 34.56E
Atmore U.S.A. **111** 31.02N 87.29W
Atnarko Canada **100** 52.25N126.00W
Atnosen Norway **41** 61.44N 10.49E
Atoka U.S.A. **111** 34.23N 96.08W
Atouat *mtn.* Laos **56** 16.03N107.17E
Atouguia Portugal **27** 39.20N 9.20W
Åtrå Norway **42** 59.59N 8.45E
Atrak *r.* Iran *see* Atrek *r.* Asia **65**
Ätran *r.* Sweden **43** 56.53N 12.30E
Atrato *r.* Colombia **122** 8.15N 76.58W
Atrauli India **63** 28.02N 78.17E
Atrek *r.* Asia **65** 37.23N 54.00E
Atsugi Japan **57** 35.27N139.22E
Atsumi-hantō *pen.* Japan **57** 34.40N137.20E
Atsumi-wan *b.* Japan **57** 34.45N137.10E
Aṭ Ṭafīlah Jordan **66** 30.52N 35.36E
Aṭ Ṭā'if Saudi Arabia **72** 21.15N 40.21E
At Tall Syria **66** 33.36N 36.18E
Attapu Laos **58** 14.51N106.56E
Attar, Oued el *wadi* Algeria **75** 33.23N 5.12E
Attaviros *mtn.* Greece **35** 36.12N 27.52E
Attawapiskat *r.* Canada **102** 53.00N 82.30W
Attawapiskat L. Canada **102** 52.20N 88.00W
Aṭ Ṭayrīyah Egypt **66** 30.39N 30.46E
Aṭ Ṭayyibah Jordan **67** 31.57N 35.18E
Attendorn Germany **38** 51.07N 7.54E
Attersee *l.* Austria **39** 47.55N 13.33E
Attica N.Y. U.S.A. **114** 42.52N 78.17W
Attica Ohio U.S.A. **114** 41.04N 82.53W
Attigny France **19** 49.29N 4.35E
Attikamagen L. Canada **103** 55.00N 66.38W
'Attīl Jordan **67** 32.22N 35.04E
Attleboro U.S.A. **115** 41.56N 71.17W
Attleborough U.K. **13** 52.31N 1.01E
Attnang Austria **39** 48.01N 13.43E
Aṭ Ṭubayq *mts.* Saudi Arabia **64** 29.30N 37.15E
Aṭ Ṭunayb Jordan **67** 31.48N 35.56E
Aṭ Ṭūr Egypt **66** 28.14N 33.36E
Aṭ Ṭūr Jordan **67** 31.47N 35.15E
At Ṭuwayrifah *well* Saudi Arabia **71** 21.30N 49.35E
Atucha Argentina **125** 33.58S 59.17W
Atuel *r.* Argentina **125** 36.15S 66.55W
Atui, Uad *wadi* Mauritania **74** 20.03N 15.35W
Atui I. Cook Is. **85** 20.00S158.07W
Atuona Is. Marquises **85** 9.48S139.02W
Åtvidaberg Sweden **43** 58.12N 16.00E
Atwater U.S.A. **108** 37.21N120.36W
Atwood U.S.A. **110** 39.48N101.03W
Aubagne France **21** 43.17N 5.34E
Aube *d.* France **19** 48.15N 4.05E
Aube *r.* France **19** 48.34N 3.43E
Aubenton France **19** 49.50N 4.12E
Auberive France **19** 47.47N 5.03E
Aubigny-sur-Nère France **19** 47.29N 2.26E
Aubin France **20** 44.32N 2.14E
Aubinadong *r.* Canada **104** 46.51N 83.22W
Aubrac, Monts d' *mts.* France **20** 44.40N 3.00E
Auburn Ala. U.S.A. **113** 32.38N 85.38W
Auburn Calif. U.S.A. **108** 38.54N121.04W
Auburn Ind. U.S.A. **112** 41.22N 85.02W
Auburn Maine U.S.A. **112** 44.06N 70.14W
Auburn N.Y. U.S.A. **115** 42.56N 76.34W
Auburn Wash. U.S.A. **108** 47.18N122.13W
Aubusson France **20** 45.57N 2.11E
Auce U.S.S.R. **41** 56.28N 22.53E
Auch France **20** 43.39N 0.35E
Auchi Nigeria **77** 7.05N 6.16E
Auchterarder U.K. **14** 56.18N 3.43W
Auckland New Zealand **86** 36.55S174.45E
Auckland *d.* New Zealand **86** 36.45S174.45E
Auckland Is. Pacific Oc. **84** 50.35S166.00E
Aude *d.* France **20** 43.05N 2.30E
Aude *r.* France **20** 43.13N 3.14E
Auden Canada **102** 50.17N 87.54W
Audenge France **20** 44.41N 1.31W
Audierne France **18** 48.01N 4.32W
Audincourt France **19** 47.29N 6.50E
Audo Range *mts.* Ethiopia **73** 6.30N 41.30E
Audubon U.S.A. **110** 41.43N 94.55W
Aue Germany **38** 50.35N 12.42E
Augathella Australia **90** 25.48S146.35E
Augrabies Falls *f.* R.S.A. **80** 28.33S 20.27E
Au Gres U.S.A. **104** 44.03N 83.42W
Augsburg Germany **39** 48.23N 10.53E
Augusta Australia **89** 34.19S115.09E
Augusta Italy **33** 37.13N 15.13E
Augusta Ga. U.S.A. **113** 33.29N 82.00W
Augusta Ill. U.S.A. **110** 40.14N 90.56W
Augusta Kans. U.S.A. **111** 37.41N 96.58W
Augusta Maine U.S.A. **112** 44.19N 69.47W
Augusta, Golfo di *g.* Italy **33** 37.10N 15.20E
Augustín Codazzi Colombia **122** 10.01N 73.10W
Augustów Poland **37** 53.51N 22.59E
Augustus, Mt. Australia **88** 24.20S116.49E
Aulis *site* Greece **35** 38.27N 23.35E
Aulla Italy **30** 44.12N 9.58E
Aulnay France **20** 46.01N 0.21W
Aulne *r.* France **18** 48.17N 4.16W
Aulnoye-Aymeries France **19** 50.12N 3.50E
Ault France **18** 50.06N 1.27E
Ault U.S.A. **108** 40.35N104.44W

Aumale France **19** 49.46N 1.45E
Aumont-Aubrac France **20** 44.43N 3.17E
Auna Nigeria **77** 10.11N 4.46E
Auneau France **19** 48.27N 1.46E
Auning Denmark **42** 56.26N 10.23E
Aura Finland **41** 60.36N 22.34E
Auraiya India **63** 26.28N 79.31E
Aurangābād Bihār India **63** 24.45N 84.22E
Aurangābād Mahār India **62** 19.53N 75.20E
Auray France **18** 47.40N 2.59W
Aurdal Norway **41** 60.56N 9.24E
Aure Norway **40** 63.16N 8.34E
Aurich Germany **38** 53.28N 7.29E
Aurillac France **20** 44.56N 2.26E
Aurora Canada **104** 44.00N 79.28W
Aurora Colo. U.S.A. **108** 39.44N104.52W
Aurora Ill. U.S.A. **110** 41.45N 88.20W
Aurora Mo. U.S.A. **111** 36.58N 93.43W
Aursunden *l.* Norway **40** 62.37N 11.40E
Aurukun Australia **90** 13.20S141.42E
Aus Namibia **80** 26.41S 16.14E
Au Sable *r.* U.S.A. **104** 44.25N 83.20W
Au Sable Forks U.S.A. **105** 44.27N 73.41W
Aust-Agder *d.* Norway **42** 58.50N 7.50E
Austin Minn. U.S.A. **110** 43.40N 92.59W
Austin Nev. U.S.A. **108** 39.30N117.04W
Austin Penn. U.S.A. **114** 41.38N 78.05W
Austin Tex. U.S.A. **111** 30.16N 97.45W
Austin, L. Australia **88** 27.40S118.00E
Austral Downs *town* Australia **90** 20.28S137.55E
Australia Austa. **87**
Australian Alps *mts.* Australia **91** 36.30S148.30E
Australian Antarctic Territory Antarctica **128** 73.00S 90.00E
Australian Capital Territory *d.* Australia **93** 35.30S149.00E
Austral Ridge Pacific Oc. **85** 24.00S148.00W
Austria Europe **39** 47.20N 12.30E
Austvågöy *i.* Norway **40** 68.20N 14.40E
Authie *r.* France **19** 50.21N 1.38E
Autun France **19** 46.57N 4.18E
Auvergne *d.* France **20** 45.25N 2.30E
Auvézère *r.* France **20** 45.12N 0.51E
Aux Barques, Pointe *c.* U.S.A. **104** 44.04N 82.58W
Auxerre France **19** 47.48N 3.34E
Auxi-le-Château France **19** 50.14N 2.07E
Auxonne France **19** 47.12N 5.23E
Aux Sables *r.* Canada **104** 46.13N 82.04W
Auzances France **20** 46.02N 2.30E
Ava Burma **56** 21.49N 95.57E
Avaldsnes Norway **42** 59.21N 5.16E
Avallon France **19** 47.29N 3.54E
Avaloirs, Les *hills* France **18** 48.28N 0.07W
Avalon U.S.A. **115** 39.06N 74.43W
Avalon Pen. Canada **103** 47.00N 53.15W
Avanos Turkey **64** 38.44N 34.51E
Avaré Brazil **126** 23.06S 48.57W
Avarua Rarotonga Cook Is. **84** 21.12S159.46W
Ávas Greece **34** 40.57N 25.56E
Avatele Niue **84** 19.06S169.55W
Avatele B. Niue **84** 19.05S169.56W
Avatiu Rarotonga Cook Is. **84** 21.12S159.47W
Ave *r.* Portugal **26** 41.20N 8.45W
Aveiro Portugal **26** 40.38N 8.39W
Aveiro *d.* Portugal **26** 40.50N 8.35W
Aveiro, Ria de *est.* Portugal **26** 40.38N 8.44W
Avellaneda Argentina **125** 34.40S 58.20W
Avellino Italy **33** 40.54N 14.47E
Aversa Italy **33** 40.58N 14.12E
Avery U.S.A. **108** 47.15N115.49W
Avesnes France **19** 50.07N 3.56E
Avesta Sweden **43** 60.09N 16.12E
Aveyron *d.* France **20** 44.15N 2.40E
Aveyron *r.* France **20** 44.05N 1.16E
Avezzano Italy **31** 42.02N 13.25E
Aviemore U.K. **14** 57.12N 3.50W
Avigliano Italy **33** 40.44N 15.44E
Avignon France **21** 43.57N 4.49E
Ávila Spain **26** 40.39N 4.42W
Ávila *d.* Spain **26** 40.35N 5.00W
Ávila, Sierra de *mts.* Spain **26** 40.35N 5.00W
Avilés Spain **26** 43.33N 5.55W
Avis U.S.A. **114** 41.11N 77.19W
Aviz Portugal **27** 39.03N 7.53W
Avlum Denmark **42** 56.16N 8.48E
Avoca *r.* Australia **92** 35.56S143.44E
Avoca Vic. Australia **92** 37.04S143.29E
Avola Canada **100** 51.45N119.19W
Avola Italy **33** 36.54N 15.09E
Avon *r.* Australia **89** 31.40S116.07E
Avon *d.* U.K. **13** 51.35N 2.40W
Avon *r.*Avon U.K. **11** 51.30N 2.43W
Avon *r.* Dorset U.K. **13** 50.43N 1.45W
Avon *r.* Glos. U.K. **13** 52.00N 2.10W
Avon U.S.A. **114** 42.55N 77.45W
Avon Downs *town* Australia **90** 20.05S137.30E
Avonmouth U.K. **13** 51.30N 2.42W
Avon Park *town* U.S.A. **113** 27.36N 81.30W
Avranches France **18** 48.41N 1.22W
Avre *r.* France **19** 49.53N 2.20E
Awal Edo Ethiopia **73** 4.14N 40.39E
Awara Ethiopia **73** 5.30N 40.00E
Āwarē Ethiopia **71** 8.15N 44.10E
'Awartā Jordan **67** 32.10N 35.17E
Awasa Hāyk' *l.* Ethiopia **73** 7.05N 38.25E
Āwash *r.* Ethiopia **73** 11.45N 41.05E
Awa shima *i.* Japan **57** 38.30N139.20E
Awaso Ghana **76** 6.20N 2.22W
Awat China **52** 40.38N 80.22E
Awbārī Libya **75** 26.35N 12.46E
Awbārī *d.* Libya **75** 25.10N 12.45E
Awbārī, Şaḩrā' *des.* Libya **75** 27.30N 11.30E
Awdah, Hawr al *l.* Iraq **65** 31.36N 46.53E
Awe, Loch U.K. **14** 56.18N 5.24W
'Awjā', Wādī al Jordan **67** 31.56N 35.31E
Axarfjördhur *est.* Iceland **40** 66.10N 16.30W
Axat France **20** 42.48N 2.14E
Axel Heiberg I. Canada **99** 79.30N 90.00W
Axim Ghana **76** 4.53N 2.14W
Axiós *r.* Greece **34** 40.35N 22.50E
Ax-les-Thermes France **20** 42.43N 1.50E
Axminster U.K. **13** 50.47N 3.01W
Ayabaca Peru **122** 4.40S 79.53W
Ayachi, Ari n' *mtn.* Morocco **74** 32.29N 4.57W
Ayacucho Argentina **125** 37.10S 58.30W
Ayacucho Peru **122** 13.10S 74.15W
Ayaguz U.S.S.R. **52** 47.59N 80.27E
Ayamonte Spain **27** 37.13N 7.24W
Ayan U.S.S.R. **51** 56.29N138.00E
'Aybāl, Jabal *mtn.* Jordan **67** 32.14N 35.16E
Aydin Turkey **64** 37.52N 27.50E
Ayelu *mtn.* Ethiopia **73** 10.04N 40.46E
Ayer U.S.A. **115** 42.34N 71.35W
Ayers Cliff *town* Canada **105** 45.10N 72.03W
Ayers Rock *see* Uluru Australia **90**
Ayiá Greece **34** 39.43N 22.45E
Ayiá Ánna Greece **35** 38.52N 23.24E
Ayiá Marína Greece **35** 37.11N 26.48E
Ayía Paraskeví Greece **35** 39.14N 26.16E
Áyion Óros *f.* Greece **34** 40.15N 24.15E
Áyios Andréas Greece **35** 37.21N 22.45E
Áyios Evstrátios *i.* Greece **34** 39.34N 24.58E
Áyios Kírikos Greece **35** 37.37N 26.14E
Áyios Matthaíos Greece **34** 39.30N 19.47E
Áyios Nikólaos Greece **35** 35.11N 25.42E
Aylássos Greece **35** 39.05N 26.23E
Aylen L. Canada **105** 45.37N 77.52W
Aylesbury U.K. **13** 51.48N 0.49W
Aylmer Ont. Canada **104** 42.47N 80.58W
Aylmer Que. Canada **105** 45.23N 75.51W
Aylmer, L. Que. Canada **105** 45.50N 71.22W
Aylmer L. Canada **98** 64.05N108.30W
Aylsham U.K. **12** 52.48N 1.16E
'Ayn, Wādī al *r.* Oman **65** 22.18N 55.35E
'Ayn Dāllah *well* Egypt **64** 27.19N 27.20E
Ayod Sudan **73** 8.07N 31.26E
Ayom Sudan **73** 7.52N 28.23E
Ayon, Ostrov *i.* U.S.S.R. **51** 70.00N169.00E
Ayora Spain **25** 39.04N 1.03W
Ayos Cameroon **77** 3.55N 12.30E
'Ayoûn el' Atroûs Mauritania **74** 16.40N 9.37W
Ayr Australia **90** 19.35S147.24E
Ayr Canada **104** 43.17N 80.27W
Ayr U.K. **14** 55.28N 4.37W
Ayr *r.* U.K. **14** 55.28N 4.38W
Ayre, Pt. of U.K. **12** 54.25N 4.22W
Ayrolle, Etang de L' *l.* France **20** 43.05N 3.03E
Āysha Ethiopia **73** 10.46N 42.37E
Ayutthaya Thailand **56** 14.20N100.40E
Ayvacik Turkey **34** 39.36N 26.23E
Ayvalik Turkey **29** 39.19N 26.42E
Azaila Spain **25** 41.17N 0.29W
Azambuja Portugal **27** 39.04N 8.52W
Azamgarh India **63** 26.04N 83.11E
Azao *mtn.* Algeria **75** 25.12N 8.08E
Azaouâd *des.* Mali **76** 18.00N 3.00W
Azaouak, Vallée de l' *f.* Mali **77** 16.00N 3.40E
Azare Nigeria **77** 11.40N 10.08E
Azay-le-Rideau France **18** 47.16N 0.28E
Azbine *mts. see* Aïr *mts.* Niger **77**
Azerbaydzhanskaya S.S.R. *d.* U.S.S.R. **65** 40.10N 47.50E
Azogues Ecuador **122** 2.35S 78.00W
Azopolye U.S.S.R. **44** 65.15N 45.18E
Azor Israel **67** 32.01N 34.48E
Azores *is. see* Açores, Arquipélago dos *is.* Atlantic Oc. **127**
Azoum *r.* Chad **73** 10.53N 20.15E
Azov, Sea of *see* Azovskoye More U.S.S.R. **45**
Azovskoye More *sea* U.S.S.R. **45** 46.00N 36.30E
Azpeitia Spain **26** 43.11N 2.16W
Azraq, Al Baḩr al *r.* Sudan **72** 15.38N 32.31E
Azrou Morocco **74** 33.27N 5.14W
Aztec U.S.A. **109** 32.48N113.26W
Azua Dom. Rep. **117** 18.29N 70.44W
Azuaga Spain **26** 38.16N 5.41W
Azuer *r.* Spain **27** 39.08N 3.36W
Azuero, Península de *pen.* Panama **117** 7.30N 80.30W
Azul Argentina **125** 36.46S 59.50W
'Azūm, Wādī *r.* Sudan *see* Azoum *r.* Chad **73**
Azurduy Bolivia **124** 19.59S 64.29W
Az Zāb al Kabīr *r.* Iraq **65** 35.37N 43.20E
Az Zāb aş Şaghīr *r.* Iraq **65** 35.15N 43.27E
Az Zabdānī Syria **66** 33.43N 36.05E
Aẓ Ẓāhirīyah Jordan **67** 31.25N 34.58E
Aẓ Ẓahrān Saudi Arabia **65** 26.18N 50.08E
Az Zaqāzīq Egypt **66** 30.36N 31.30E
Az Zarqā' Jordan **67** 32.05N 36.06E
Az Zarqā' *r.* Jordan **67** 32.08N 35.32E
Az Zāwiyah *d.* Libya **75** 32.40N 12.10E
Azzel Matti, Sebkha *f.* Algeria **74** 26.00N 0.55E
Az Zilfī Saudi Arabia **65** 26.15N 44.50E
Az Zrārīyah Lebanon **66** 33.21N 35.20E

B

Baan Baa Australia **93** 30.28S149.58E
Baardheere Somali Rep. **79** 2.18N 42.18E
Baargaal Somali Rep. **71** 11.18N 51.07E
Baarle-Hertog Neth. **16** 51.26N 4.56E
Baba Burnu *c.* Turkey **34** 39.29N 26.02E
Babadag Romania **37** 44.54N 28.43E
Babahoyo Ecuador **122** 1.53S 79.31W
Babai Gaxun China **54** 40.30N104.43E
Babakin Australia **89** 32.11S117.58E
Babana Nigeria **77** 10.26N 3.51E
Babanka U.S.S.R. **37** 48.41N 30.30E
Babanūsah Sudan **73** 11.20N 27.48E
Babar, Kepulauan *is.* Indonesia **59** 8.00S129.30E
Babayevo U.S.S.R. **44** 59.24N 35.50E
B'abdā Lebanon **66** 33.50N 35.31E
Babia Gora *mtn.* Czech./Poland **37** 49.38N 19.38E
Babīna India **63** 25.15N 78.28E
Babina Greda Yugo. **31** 45.07N 18.33E
Babine L. Canada **100** 54.48N126.00W
Babo Indonesia **59** 2.33S133.25E
Bābol Iran **65** 36.32N 52.42E
Baboua C.A.R. **77** 5.49N 14.51E
Babuyan Channel Phil. **55** 18.40N121.30E
Babuyan Is. Phil. **59** 19.20N121.30E
Babylon *ruins* Iraq **65** 32.33N 44.25E
Babylon U.S.A. **115** 40.42N 73.20W
Bacabal Maranhão Brazil **123** 4.15S 44.45W
Bacabal Para Brazil **123** 5.20S 56.45W
Bacău Romania **37** 46.32N 26.59E
Baccarat France **19** 48.27N 6.45E
Bacchus Marsh *town* Australia **92** 37.41S144.27E
Bacharach Germany **39** 50.04N 7.46E
Bacheli India **61** 18.40N 81.16E
Bachelina U.S.S.R. **50** 57.45N 67.20E
Back *r.* Canada **99** 66.37N 96.00W
Bac Kan Vietnam **55** 22.06N105.57E
Bačka Palanka Yugo. **31** 45.15N 19.24E
Bačka Topola Yugo. **31** 45.49N 19.38E
Backbone Mtn. U.S.A. **114** 39.18N 79.25W
Bäckefors Sweden **43** 58.48N 12.10E
Bački Petrovac Yugo. **31** 45.22N 19.35E
Backnang Germany **39** 48.56N 9.25E
Backstairs Passage *str.* Australia **92** 35.42S138.05E
Bac Lieu Vietnam **56** 9.16N105.45E
Bac Ninh Vietnam **56** 21.10N106.04E
Bacolod Phil. **59** 10.38N122.58E
Bac Phan *f.* Vietnam **56** 22.00N105.00E
Bac Quang Vietnam **55** 22.30N104.52E
Bácsalmás Hungary **31** 46.08N 19.20E
Bács-Kiskun *d.* Hungary **31** 46.30N 19.20E
Badagara India **60** 11.36N 75.35E
Badajós, Lago *l.* Brazil **122** 3.15S 62.47W
Badajoz Spain **27** 38.53N 6.58W
Badajoz *d.* Spain **27** 38.40N 6.10W
Badal Khān Goth Pakistan **62** 26.31N 67.06E
Badalona Spain **25** 41.27N 2.15E
Badanah Saudi Arabia **64** 30.59N 41.02E
Bad Ausee Austria **39** 47.36N 13.47E
Bad Axe U.S.A. **112** 43.49N 82.59W
Bad Bergzabern Germany **39** 49.07N 8.00E
Bad Blankenburg Germany **38** 50.41N 11.16E
Bad Bramstedt Germany **38** 53.55N 9.53E
Baddo *r.* Pakistan **62** 28.15N 65.00E
Bad Doberan Germany **38** 54.06N 11.53E
Bad Dürrenberg Germany **38** 51.18N 12.04E
Badeggi Nigeria **77** 9.04N 6.09E
Bad Ems Germany **39** 50.20N 7.43E
Baden Austria **36** 48.01N 16.14E
Baden Ethiopia **72** 17.00N 38.00E
Baden Switz. **39** 47.29N 8.18E
Baden-Baden Germany **39** 48.46N 8.14E
Badenweiler Germany **39** 47.48N 7.40E
Baden-Württemberg *d.* Germany **39** 48.15N 9.00E
Bad Freienwalde Germany **38** 52.47N 14.01E
Badgastein Austria **39** 47.07N 13.08E
Bad Godesberg Germany **38** 50.41N 7.09E
Bad Hall Austria **39** 48.02N 14.13E
Bad Harzburg Germany **38** 51.53N 10.33E
Bad Hersfeld Germany **38** 50.52N 9.42E
Bad Homburg Germany **39** 50.13N 8.37E
Bad Honnef Germany **38** 50.39N 7.13E
Badīn Pakistan **62** 24.39N 68.50E
Bad Ischl Austria **39** 47.43N 13.37E
Badīyah Oman **71** 22.27N 58.48E
Bādiyat ash Shām *des.* Asia **64** 32.00N 39.00E
Bad Kissingen Germany **39** 50.12N 10.04E
Bad Kreuznach Germany **39** 49.52N 7.51E
Bad Langensalza Germany **38** 51.07N 10.40E
Bad Lauterberg Germany **38** 51.38N 10.28E
Bad Mergentheim Germany **39** 49.30N 9.46E
Bad Münstereifel Germany **38** 50.33N 6.46E
Bad Nauheim Germany **39** 50.22N 8.44E
Badnera India **63** 20.52N 77.44E
Bad Neuenahr-Ahrweiler Germany **38** 50.33N 7.08E
Bad Neustadt an der Saale Germany **39** 50.19N 10.13E
Bad Oeynhausen Germany **38** 52.12N 8.48E
Bad Oldesloe Germany **38** 53.48N 10.22E
Badong China **55** 31.02N110.20E
Bad Orb Germany **39** 50.14N 9.20E
Badou Togo **76** 7.37N 0.37E
Badoumbé Mali **76** 13.42N 10.09W
Bad Pyrmont Germany **38** 51.59N 9.15E
Bad Ragaz Switz. **39** 47.00N 9.30E
Bad Reichenhall Germany **39** 47.43N 12.52E
Badrīnāth India **63** 30.44N 79.29E
Bad Salzuflen Germany **38** 52.05N 8.44E
Bad Salzungen Germany **38** 50.48N 10.13E
Bad Sankt Leonhard im Lavanttal Austria **31** 46.58N 14.48E
Bad Schwartau Germany **38** 53.55N 10.40E
Bad Segeberg Germany **38** 53.56N 10.17E
Bad Sülze Germany **38** 54.06N 12.38E
Bad Tölz Germany **39** 47.46N 11.34E
Badu I. Australia **90** 10.07S142.08E
Bad Waldsee Germany **39** 47.55N 9.45E
Bad Wildungen Germany **38** 51.07N 9.07E
Bad Wörishofen Germany **39** 48.00N 10.36E
Baena Spain **27** 37.37N 4.19W
Baerami Australia **93** 32.23S150.30E
Baeza Spain **27** 37.59N 3.28W
Bafa Gölü *l.* Turkey **35** 37.30N 27.29E
Bafang Cameroon **77** 5.11N 10.12E
Bafatá Guinea Bissau **76** 12.09N 14.38W
Baffin *d.* Canada **99** 66.00N 72.00W
Baffin B. Canada **99** 74.00N 70.00W
Baffin I. Canada **99** 68.50N 70.00W
Bafia Cameroon **77** 4.39N 11.14E
Bafing *r.* Mali **76** 14.48N 12.10W
Bafoulabé Mali **76** 13.49N 10.50W
Bāfq Iran **65** 31.35N 55.21E
Bafra Turkey **64** 41.34N 35.56E
Bafut Cameroon **77** 6.06N 10.02E
Bafwasende Zaïre **79** 1.09N 27.12E
Bagaha India **63** 27.06N 84.05E
Bagamoyo Tanzania **79** 6.26S 38.55E
Bağarasi Turkey **35** 37.42N 27.33E
Bagasra India **62** 21.29N 70.57E
Bagawi Sudan **73** 12.19N 34.21E
Bagbele Zaïre **73** 4.21N 29.17E
Bagdarin U.S.S.R. **51** 54.28N113.38E
Bagé Brazil **126** 31.22S 54.06W
Baggy Pt. U.K. **13** 51.08N 4.15W
Baghdād Iraq **65** 33.20N 44.26E
Bāgherhāt Bangla. **63** 22.40N 89.48E
Bagheria Italy **32** 38.05N 13.30E
Baghlān Afghan. **60** 36.11N 68.44E
Baghrān Khowleh Afghan. **62** 33.01N 64.58E
Bagnara Italy **33** 38.18N 15.49E
Bagnères-de-Bigorre France **20** 43.04N 0.09E
Bagnères-de-Luchon France **20** 42.47N 0.36E
Bagni di Lucca Italy **30** 44.01N 10.35E
Bagnols-sur-Cèze France **21** 44.10N 4.37E
Bagodar India **63** 24.05N 85.52E
Bagoé *r.* Mali **76** 12.34N 6.30W
Bagolino Italy **30** 45.49N 10.28E
Bagrationovsk U.S.S.R. **37** 54.26N 20.38E
Baguio Phil. **59** 16.25N120.37E
Bāh India **63** 26.53N 78.36E
Bahamas C. America **113** 24.15N 76.00W
Bahāwalnagar Pakistan **62** 29.59N 73.16E
Bahāwalpur Pakistan **62** 29.24N 71.41E
Baheri India **63** 28.47N 79.30E
Bahi Tanzania **79** 5.59S 35.15E
Bahia *d.* Brazil **123** 12.30S 42.30W
Bahía, Islas de la *is.* Honduras **117** 16.10N 86.30W
Bahía Blanca Argentina **126** 38.45S 62.15W
Bahía de Caráquez Ecuador **122** 0.40S 80.25W
Bahía Kino Mexico **109** 28.50N111.55W
Bahía Laura Argentina **125** 48.18S 66.30W
Bahía Negra Paraguay **126** 20.15S 58.12W
Bahir Dar Ethiopia **73** 11.35N 37.28E
Bahraich India **63** 27.35N 81.36E
Bahrain Asia **65** 26.00N 50.35E
Baḩr al Ghazāl *d.* Sudan **73** 8.00N 26.30E
Baḩr al Jabal *r.* Sudan **70** 9.30N 18.10E
Bahrām Chāh Afghan. **62** 29.26N 64.03E
Bahr Aouk *r.* C.A.R. **77** 8.50N 18.50E
Bahr el Ghazal *r.* Chad **77** 12.26N 15.25E
Bahr Salamat *r.* Chad **77** 9.30N 18.10E
Bāhū Kalāt Iran **65** 25.42N 61.28E
Baia-Mare Romania **37** 47.40N 23.35E
Baião Brazil **123** 2.41S 49.41W
Baia Sprie Romania **37** 47.40N 23.42E
Baïbokoum Chad **77** 7.46N 15.43E
Baicheng China **54** 45.40N122.52E
Baie Comeau Canada **103** 49.13N 68.10W
Baie des Ha! Ha! *town* Canada **103** 50.56N 58.58W
Baiersbronn Germany **39** 48.30N 8.22E
Baies, Lac des *l.* Canada **105** 47.18N 77.40W
Baie St. Paul *town* Canada **103** 47.27N 70.30W
Baigneux-les-Juifs France **19** 47.36N 4.38E
Baihar India **63** 22.06N 80.33E
Baijnāth India **63** 29.55N 79.37E
Baikunthapur India **63** 23.15N 82.33E
Bailén Spain **26** 38.06N 3.46W
Băileşti Romania **37** 44.02N 23.21E
Bailleul France **19** 50.44N 2.44E
Bailundo Angola **78** 12.13S 15.46E
Baimuru P.N.G. **59** 7.30S144.49E
Bainang China **63** 29.10N 89.15E
Bainbridge *Ga.* U.S.A. **113** 30.54N 84.33W
Bainbridge *N.Y.* U.S.A. **115** 42.18N 75.29W
Bain-de-Bretagne France **18** 47.50N 1.41W
Baing Indonesia **88** 10.15S120.34E
Baingoin China **63** 31.45N 89.50E
Bains-les-Bains France **19** 48.00N 6.16E
Bāir Jordan **66** 30.46N 36.41E
Bā'ir, Wādī *r.* Jordan **66** 31.10N 36.55E
Baird Mts. U.S.A. **98** 67.35N161.30W
Bairin Zuoqi China **54** 43.59N119.11E
Bairnsdale Australia **93** 37.51S147.38E
Bais France **18** 48.15N 0.22W
Baïse *r.* France **20** 44.07N 0.17E
Baisha China **55** 19.13N109.26E
Baiyang Dian *l.* China **54** 38.55N116.00E
Baiyin China **54** 36.40N104.15E
Baja Hungary **31** 46.11N 18.57E
Baja California *pen.* Mexico **109** 28.40N114.40W
Baja California Norte *d.* Mexico **109** 29.45N115.30W
Baja California Sur *d.* Mexico **109** 26.00N113.00W
Bajánsenye Hungary **31** 46.48N 16.22E
Bajina Bašta Yugo. **31** 43.58N 19.34E
Bajmok Yugo. **31** 45.58N 19.25E
Bakal U.S.S.R. **44** 54.58N 58.45E
Bakali *r.* Zaïre **78** 3.58S 17.10E
Bakel Senegal **76** 14.54N 12.26W
Baker Calif. U.S.A. **109** 35.16N116.04W
Baker Mont. U.S.A. **108** 46.22N104.17W
Baker Oreg. U.S.A. **108** 44.47N117.50W
Baker, Mt. U.S.A. **108** 48.47N121.49W
Baker I. U.S.A. **100** 55.20N133.36W
Baker Lake *town* Canada **99** 64.20N 96.10W
Bakersfield *Calif.* U.S.A. **109** 35.23N119.01W
Bakersfield *Vt.* U.S.A. **105** 44.48N 72.42W
Bâ Kêv Cambodia **56** 13.42N107.12E
Bako Ethiopia **73** 5.50N 36.40E
Bako Ivory Coast **76** 9.08N 7.40W
Bakony *mts.* Hungary **31** 47.00N 17.50E
Bakouma C.A.R. **73** 5.42N 22.47E
Baku U.S.S.R. **65** 40.22N 49.53E
Bala Canada **104** 45.01N 79.37W

Bal'ā to Barryville

Bal'ā Jordan **67** 32.20N 35.07E
Bala Senegal **76** 14.01N 13.08W
Bala U.K. **12** 52.54N 3.36W
Balabac *i.* Phil. **58** 7.57N117.01E
Balabac Str. Malaysia/Phil. **58** 7.30N117.00E
Ba'labakk Lebanon **66** 34.00N 36.12E
Bālāghāt India **63** 21.48N 80.11E
Bālāghāt Range *mts.* India **62** 19.00N 76.30E
Balaguer Spain **24** 41.50N 0.50E
Balaka Malaŵi **79** 15.00S 34.56E
Balaka Zaïre **78** 4.51S 19.57E
Balaklava Australia **92** 34.08S138.24E
Balaklava U.S.S.R. **45** 44.31N 33.35E
Balakovo U.S.S.R. **44** 52.04N 47.46E
Bal'amā Jordan **67** 32.14N 36.05E
Balama Mozambique **79** 13.19S 38.35E
Bālā Morghāb Afghan. **65** 35.34N 63.20E
Balāngīr India **63** 20.43N 83.29E
Balaquer Spain **25** 41.47N 0.49E
Balarāmpur India **63** 23.07N 86.13E
Balashov U.S.S.R. **45** 51.30N 43.10E
Balasore India **63** 21.30N 86.56E
Balassagyarmat Hungary **37** 48.05N 19.18E
Balāṭ Egypt **64** 25.33N 29.16E
Balaton *l.* Hungary **31** 46.50N 17.45E
Balazote Spain **26** 38.53N 2.08W
Balboa Panama **117** 8.37N 79.33W
Balbriggan Rep. of Ire. **15** 53.36N 6.12W
Balcad Somali Rep. **71** 2.22N 45.25E
Balcarce Argentina **125** 37.52S 58.15W
Balchik Bulgaria **37** 43.24N 28.10E
Balclutha New Zealand **86** 46.16S169.46E
Bald Eagle Mtn. U.S.A. **114** 41.00N 77.45W
Baldock L. Canada **101** 56.33N 97.57W
Baldwin Fla. U.S.A. **113** 30.18N 81.59W
Baldwin Mich. U.S.A. **112** 43.54N 85.50W
Baldwin Penn. U.S.A. **114** 40.23N 79.58W
Baldwinsville U.S.A. **115** 43.09N 76.20W
Baldy Mt. Canada **100** 51.28N120.02W
Balē Ethiopia **73** 6.30N 40.45E
Bâle *see* Basel Switz. **39**
Baleanoona Australia **92** 30.33S139.22E
Baleares *d.* Spain **25** 39.00N 2.10E
Baleares, Islas *is.* Spain **25** 39.20N 2.00E
Balearic Is. *see* Baleares, Islas *is.* Spain **25**
Baleine, Grande rivière de la *r.* Canada **102** 55.20N 77.40W
Baleine, Petite rivière de la *r.* Canada **102** 56.00N 76.45W
Balfate Honduras **117** 15.48N 86.25W
Balfour Downs *town* Australia **88** 22.57S120.46E
Balfouriyya Israel **67** 32.38N 35.18E
Bali India **62** 25.50N 74.05E
Bali *d.* Indonesia **59** 8.45S115.16E
Bali *i.* Indonesia **59** 8.20S115.07E
Bali, Laut *sea* Indonesia **59** 7.30S115.15E
Bali, Selat *str.* Indonesia **59** 8.21S114.30E
Balikesir Turkey **29** 39.38N 27.51E
Balīkh *r.* Syria **64** 35.58N 39.05E
Balikpapan Indonesia **58** 1.15S116.50E
Balingen Germany **39** 48.16N 8.51E
Bali Sea *see* Bali, Laut Indonesia **59**
Balkan Mts. *see* Stara Planina *mts.* Bulgaria **34**
Balkhash U.S.S.R. **52** 46.51N 75.00E
Balkhash, Ozero *l.* U.S.S.R. **9** 46.40N 75.00E
Ballachulish U.K. **14** 56.40N 5.08W
Balladonia Australia **89** 32.27S123.51E
Ballālpur India **63** 19.50N 79.22E
Ballandean Australia **93** 28.39S151.50E
Ballantrae U.K. **14** 55.06N 5.01W
Ballarat Australia **92** 37.36S143.58E
Ballard, L. Australia **89** 29.27S120.55E
Ballater U.K. **14** 57.03N 3.03W
Ballenas, Bahía de *b.* Mexico **109** 26.45N113.25W
Ballenas, Canal de *str.* Mexico **109** 29.10N113.30W
Balleny Is. Antarctica **128** 66.30S163.00E
Balleroy France **18** 49.11N 0.50W
Ballia India **63** 25.45N 84.10E
Ballina Australia **93** 28.50S153.37E
Ballina Rep. of Ire. **15** 54.08N 9.10W
Ballinasloe Rep. of Ire. **15** 53.20N 8.15W
Ballingeary Rep. of Ire. **15** 51.50N 9.15W
Ballinger U.S.A. **111** 31.44N 99.57W
Ball's Pyramid *i.* Pacific Oc. **84** 31.45S159.15E
Ballybay Rep. of Ire. **15** 54.08N 6.56W
Ballycastle U.K. **15** 55.12N 6.15W
Ballyclare U.K. **15** 54.45N 6.00W
Ballyconnell Rep. of Ire. **15** 54.06N 7.37W
Ballydehob Rep. of Ire. **15** 51.34N 9.28W
Ballydonegan Rep. of Ire. **15** 51.38N 10.04W
Ballygar Rep. of Ire. **15** 53.32N 8.20W
Ballygawley U.K. **15** 54.28N 7.03W
Ballykelly U.K. **15** 55.03N 7.00W
Ballymena U.K. **15** 54.52N 6.17W
Ballymoney U.K. **15** 55.04N 6.31W
Ballyquintin Pt. U.K. **15** 54.40N 5.30W
Ballyragget Rep. of Ire. **15** 52.47N 7.21W
Ballyshannon Rep. of Ire. **15** 54.30N 8.11W
Ballyvaughan Rep.of Ire. **15** 53.06N 9.09W
Ballyvourney Rep. of Ire. **15** 51.57N 9.10W
Balmoral Australia **92** 37.17S141.50E
Balochistān *d.* Pakistan **62** 28.30N 65.00E
Balochistan *f.* Pakistan **60** 28.00N 66.00E
Balombo Angola **78** 12.20S 14.45E
Balonne *r.* Australia **93** 28.30S148.20E
Bālotra India **62** 25.50N 72.14E
Balrāmpur India **63** 27.26N 82.11E
Balranald Australia **92** 34.37S143.37E
Balş Romania **37** 44.21N 24.06E
Balsam L. Canada **104** 44.35N 78.50W
Balsas *r.* Brazil **123** 9.00S 48.10W
Balsas *r.* Mexico **116** 18.10N102.05W
Bålsta Sweden **43** 59.35N 17.30E
Balta U.S.S.R. **37** 47.58N 29.39E
Baltanás Spain **26** 41.56N 4.15W
Baltasar Brum Uruguay **125** 30.44S 57.19W
Baltic Sea Europe **41** 57.00N 20.00E
Balṭīm Egypt **66** 31.34N 31.05E
Baltimore Canada **104** 44.03N 78.08W
Baltimore Md. U.S.A. **115** 39.17N 76.37W
Baltimore Ohio U.S.A. **114** 39.51N 82.36W
Baltiysk U.S.S.R. **43** 54.39N 19.55E
Balumbah Australia **92** 33.16S136.14E
Bālurghāt India **63** 25.13N 88.46E
Balygychan U.S.S.R. **51** 63.55N154.12E
Balykshi U.S.S.R. **45** 47.04N 51.55E
Bām Iran **65** 29.07N 58.20E
Bama Nigeria **77** 11.35N 13.40E
Bamaga Australia **90** 10.52S142.23E
Bamako Mali **76** 12.40N 7.59W
Bamako *d.* Mali **76** 12.40N 7.55W
Bamba Kenya **79** 3.33S 39.32E
Bamba Mali **76** 17.05N 1.23W
Bamba Zaïre **78** 5.45S 18.23E
Bambari C.A.R. **73** 5.45N 20.40E
Bamberg Germany **39** 49.53N 10.53E
Bambesa Zaïre **78** 3.27N 25.43E
Bambesi Ethiopia **73** 9.45N 34.40E
Bambili Zaïre **78** 3.34N 26.07E
Bambio C.A.R. **77** 3.55N 16.57E
Bambuí Brazil **126** 20.01S 45.59W
Bam Co *l.* China **63** 31.30N 91.10E
Bamenda Cameroon **77** 5.55N 10.09E
Bāmīān Afghan. **62** 34.50N 67.50E
Bamingui C.A.R. **73** 7.34N 20.11E
Bamingui Bangoran *d.* C.A.R. **73** 8.30N 20.30E
Bampton Devon U.K. **13** 51.00N 3.29W
Bampūr Iran **65** 27.13N 60.29E
Bampūr *r.* Iran **65** 27.18N 59.02E
Bāmra Hills India **63** 21.20N 84.30E
Baña, Punta de la *c.* Spain **25** 40.34N 0.38E
Banaba *i.* Kiribati **84** 0.52S169.35E
Banagher Rep. of Ire. **15** 53.12N 8.00W
Banalia Zaïre **78** 1.33N 25.23E
Banamba Mali **76** 13.29N 7.22W
Banana Zaïre **78** 5.55S 12.27E
Bananal, Ilha do *f.* Brazil **123** 11.30S 50.15W
Ban Aranyaprathet Thailand **56** 13.43N102.31E
Banās *r.* India **62** 25.54N 76.45E
Banās, Ra's *c.* Egypt **64** 23.54N 35.48E
Ban Ban Laos **56** 19.38N103.34E
Banbridge U.K. **15** 54.21N 6.17W
Ban Bua Chum Thailand **56** 15.15N101.15E
Banbury U.K. **13** 52.04N 1.21W
Banchory U.K. **14** 57.03N 2.30W
Bancroft Canada **105** 45.03N 77.51W
Band Afghan. **62** 33.17N 68.39E
Banda Gabon **78** 3.47S 11.04E
Banda Madhya P. India **63** 24.03N 78.57E
Bānda Uttar P. India **63** 25.29N 80.20E
Banda, Laut *sea* Indonesia **59** 5.00S128.00E
Banda Aceh Indonesia **58** 5.35N 95.20E
Banda Besar *i.* Indonesia **59** 4.30S129.55E
Bānda Dāūd Shāh Pakistan **62** 33.16N 71.11E
Bandak *l.* Norway **42** 59.24N 8.15E
Bandama *r.* Ivory Coast **76** 5.10N 4.59W
Bandar 'Abbās Iran **65** 27.10N 56.15E
Bandar Beheshtī Iran **65** 25.17N 60.41E
Bandar-e Anzalī Iran **65** 37.26N 49.29E
Bandar-e Deylam Iran **65** 30.05N 50.11E
Bandar-e Khomeynī Iran **65** 30.26N 49.03E
Bandar-e-Lengeh Iran **65** 26.34N 54.53E
Bandar-e Rīg Iran **65** 29.30N 50.40E
Bandar-e Torkeman Iran **65** 36.55N 54.05E
Bandar Seri Begawan Brunei **58** 4.56N114.58E
Banda Sea *see* Banda, Laut *sea* Indonesia **59**
Bandawe Malaŵi **79** 11.57S 34.11E
Bande Spain **26** 42.02N 7.58W
Bandeira *mtn.* Brazil **126** 20.25S 41.45W
Bāndhi Pakistan **62** 26.36N 68.18E
Bandiagara Mali **76** 14.12N 3.29W
Bāndikūi India **62** 27.03N 76.34E
Bandīpur Nepal **63** 27.56N 84.25E
Bandipura Jammu & Kashmir **62** 34.25N 74.39E
Bandirma Turkey **29** 40.22N 28.00E
Bandon Rep. of Ire. **15** 51.45N 8.45W
Bandon *r.* Rep. of Ire. **15** 51.43N 8.38W
Bandundu Zaïre **78** 3.20S 17.24E
Bandundu *d.* Zaïre **78** 4.00S 18.30E
Bandung Indonesia **59** 6.57S107.34E
Banes Cuba **117** 20.59N 75.24W
Banff Canada **100** 51.10N115.34W
Banff U.K. **14** 57.40N 2.31W
Banff Nat. Park Canada **100** 51.30N116.15W
Banfora Burkina **76** 10.36N 4.45W
Bangalore India **60** 12.58N 77.35E
Bangassou C.A.R. **73** 4.50N 23.07E
Banggai, Kepulauan *is.* Indonesia **59** 1.30S123.10E
Banggi *i.* Malaysia **58** 7.17N117.12E
Banggong Co *l.* China **63** 33.45N 79.15E
Banghāzī Libya **75** 32.07N 20.05E
Banghāzī *d.* Libya **75** 25.40N 21.00E
Bangil Indonesia **59** 7.34S112.47E
Bangka *i.* Indonesia **58** 2.20S106.10E
Bangkalan Indonesia **59** 7.05S112.44E
Bangkog Co *l.* China **63** 31.45N 89.30E
Bangkok Thailand **56** 13.44N100.30E
Bangladesh Asia **63** 24.30N 90.00E
Bangor Rep. of Ire. **15** 54.09N 9.44W
Bangor *Down* U.K. **15** 54.40N 5.41W
Bangor *Gwynnedd* U.K. **12** 53.13N 4.09W
Bangor Maine U.S.A. **112** 44.49N 68.47W
Bangor Penn. U.S.A. **115** 40.52N 75.13W
Bang Saphan Thailand **56** 11.14N 99.31E
Bangui C.A.R. **77** 4.23N 18.37E
Bangui Phil. **55** 18.33N120.45E
Banguru Zaïre **79** 0.30N 27.10E
Bangweulu, L. Zambia **79** 11.15S 29.45E
Banhā Egypt **66** 30.28N 31.11E
Ban Hat Yai Thailand **56** 7.10N100.28E
Ban Houayxay Laos **56** 20.21N100.32E
Bani *r.* Mali **76** 14.30N 4.15W
Bani, Jbel *mtn.* Morocco **74** 30.00N 8.00W
Banikoara Benin **77** 11.21N 2.25E
Banī Mazār Egypt **66** 28.29N 30.48E
Baninah Libya **75** 32.05N 20.16E
Banī Na'īm Jordan **67** 31.31N 35.10E
Banī Suwayf Egypt **66** 29.05N 31.05E
Banī Walīd Libya **75** 31.46N 13.59E
Bāniyās Syria **66** 35.09N 35.58E
Bāniyās Syria **67** 33.15N 35.41E
Banja Luka Yugo. **31** 44.46N 17.11E
Banjarmasin Indonesia **58** 3.22S114.36E
Banjul Gambia **76** 13.28N 16.39W
Bānka India **63** 24.53N 86.55E
Banka Banka Australia **90** 18.48S134.01E
Ban Kan Vietnam **56** 22.08N105.49E
Ban Kantang Thailand **56** 7.25N 99.35E
Bankasse Mali **76** 14.01N 3.29W
Bankeryd Sweden **43** 57.51N 14.07E
Banks I. B.C. Canada **100** 53.25N130.10W
Banks I. N.W.T. Canada **98** 73.00N122.00W
Banks Is. Vanuatu **84** 13.50S167.30E
Banks Pen. New Zealand **86** 43.45S173.10E
Banks Str. Australia **91** 40.37S148.07E
Bānkura India **63** 23.15N 87.04E
Ban-m'drack Vietnam **56** 12.45N108.50E
Bann *r.* U.K. **15** 55.10N 6.46W
Ban Na San Thailand **56** 8.53N 99.17E
Bannockburn Canada **105** 44.38N 77.33W
Bannockburn U.K. **14** 56.06N 3.55W
Bannockburn Zimbabwe **80** 20.16S 29.51E
Bannu Pakistan **62** 32.59N 70.36E
Banon France **21** 44.02N 5.38E
Baños de Cerrato Spain **26** 41.55N 4.28W
Ban Pak Phraek Thailand **56** 8.13N100.13E
Bānsda India **62** 20.45N 73.22E
Banská Bystrica Czech. **37** 48.44N 19.07E
Bansko Bulgaria **34** 41.52N 23.28E
Bānswāra India **62** 23.33N 74.27E
Bantaeng Indonesia **58** 5.32S119.58E
Banté Benin **77** 8.26N 1.54E
Bantry Rep. of Ire. **15** 51.41N 9.27W
Bantry B. Rep. of Ire. **15** 51.40N 9.40W
Bāntva India **62** 21.29N 70.05E
Banyak, Kepulauan *is.* Indonesia **58** 2.15N 97.10E
Banyo Cameroon **77** 6.47N 11.50E
Banyoles Spain **25** 42.07N 2.46E
Banyuwangi Indonesia **59** 8.12S114.22E
Banzare Coast *f.* Antarctica **128** 66.30S125.00E
Baode China **54** 39.00N111.05E
Baoding China **54** 38.50N115.26E
Bao Ha Vietnam **55** 22.10N104.22E
Baoji China **54** 34.20N107.17E
Baojing China **55** 28.43N109.37E
Bao-Loc Vietnam **56** 11.30N107.54E
Baoshan China **61** 25.07N 99.08E
Baotou China **54** 40.35N109.59E
Baoulé *r.* Mali **76** 13.47N 10.45W
Bāp India **62** 27.23N 72.21E
Bapaume France **19** 50.06N 2.51E
Bāqa el Gharbiyya Israel **67** 32.25N 35.03E
Baqên China **63** 31.56N 94.00E
Ba'qūbah Iraq **65** 33.45N 44.38E
Bar U.S.S.R. **37** 49.05N 27.40E
Bar Yugo. **31** 42.05N 19.05E
Bara Nigeria **77** 10.24N 10.43E
Baraawe Somali Rep. **79** 1.02N 44.02E
Barabinsk U.S.S.R. **9** 55.20N 78.18E
Baraboo U.S.A. **110** 43.28N 89.50W
Baracaldo Spain **26** 43.18N 2.59W
Baracoa Cuba **117** 20.23N 74.31W
Baradero Argentina **125** 33.50S 59.30W
Baradine Australia **93** 30.56S149.05E
Baradine *r.* Australia **93** 30.17S148.27E
Baragoi Kenya **73** 1.47N 36.47E
Bārah Sudan **73** 13.42N 30.22E
Barahona Dom. Rep. **117** 18.13N 71.07W
Baraka Zaïre **79** 4.09S 29.05E
Barakaldo *see* Baracaldo Spain **26**
Barakī Barak Afghan. **62** 33.56N 68.55E
Bārākot India **63** 21.33N 85.01E
Bāramūla Jammu & Kashmir **62** 34.12N 74.21E
Bārān India **62** 25.06N 76.31E
Baranagar India **63** 22.38N 88.22E
Baranoa Colombia **122** 10.50N 74.55W
Baranof I. U.S.A. **100** 57.00N135.00W
Baranovichi U.S.S.R. **44** 53.09N 26.00E
Baranya *d.* Hungary **31** 45.55N 18.20E
Baratta Australia **92** 32.01S139.10E
Barbacena Brazil **126** 21.13S 43.47W
Barbadillo del Mercado Spain **26** 42.02N 3.21W
Barbados Lesser Antilles **117** 13.20N 59.40W
Barbar Sudan **72** 18.01N 33.59E
Barbastro Spain **25** 42.02N 0.05E
Barbate *r.* Spain **27** 36.11N 5.55W
Barbate de Franco Spain **27** 36.12N 5.55W
Barberton R.S.A. **80** 25.46S 31.02E
Barberton U.S.A. **114** 41.01N 81.36W
Barbezieux France **20** 45.28N 0.09W
Barbil India **63** 22.06N 85.20E
Barbuda *i.* Leeward Is. **117** 17.41N 61.48W
Barcaldine Australia **90** 23.31S145.15E
Barcarrota Spain **27** 38.31N 6.51W
Barcellona Italy **33** 38.09N 15.13E
Barcelona Spain **25** 41.23N 2.11E
Barcelona *d.* Spain **25** 41.45N 2.00E
Barcelona Venezuela **122** 10.08N 64.43W
Barcelos Brazil **122** 0.59S 62.58W
Barcelos Portugal **26** 41.32N 8.37W
Barcoo *r.* Australia **90** 25.30S142.50E
Barcs Hungary **31** 45.58N 17.28E
Bardai Chad **77** 21.21N 16.56E
Bardejov Czech. **37** 49.18N 21.16E
Bardi Italy **30** 44.38N 9.44E
Bardīa Nepal **63** 28.18N 81.23E
Bardīyah Libya **72** 31.46N 25.06E
Bardnovichi U.S.S.R. **37** 53.09N 26.00E
Bardoli India **62** 21.07N 73.07E
Bardonecchia Italy **30** 45.05N 6.42E
Bardsey *i.* U.K. **12** 52.45N 4.48W
Bardu Norway **40** 68.54N 18.20E
Bardufoss Norway **40** 69.00N 18.30E
Bareilly India **63** 28.21N 79.25E
Barellan Australia **93** 34.17S146.34E
Barengapāra India **63** 25.14N 90.14E
Barentsovo More *see* Barents Sea Arctic Oc. **44**
Barents Sea Arctic Oc. **44** 73.00N 40.00E
Barentu Ethiopia **72** 15.04N 37.37E
Barfleur France **18** 49.40N 1.15W
Barfleur, Pointe de *c.* France **18** 49.42N 1.16W
Barga China **63** 30.51N 81.20E
Bargarh India **63** 21.20N 83.37E
Bargas Spain **27** 39.56N 4.02W
Barge Ethiopia **73** 6.15N 37.00E
Barge Italy **30** 44.43N 7.20E
Barghanak Afghan. **62** 33.56N 62.26E
Barguzin U.S.S.R. **51** 53.40N109.35E
Barham Australia **92** 35.37S144.10E
Barharwa India **63** 24.52N 87.47E
Barhi India **63** 24.18N 85.25E
Bāri Madhya P. India **63** 23.03N 78.05E
Bāri Rāj. India **63** 26.39N 77.36E
Bari Italy **33** 41.07N 16.52E
Baricho Kenya **79** 3.07S 39.47E
Barika Algeria **75** 35.25N 5.19E
Barīm *i.* Yemen **71** 12.40N 43.24E
Barinas Venezuela **122** 8.36N 70.15W
Baripāda India **63** 21.56N 86.43E
Bariri Brazil **126** 22.04S 48.41W
Bārīs Egypt **64** 24.40N 30.36E
Bari Sādri India **62** 24.25N 74.28E
Barisāl Bangla. **63** 22.42N 90.22E
Barisan, Pegunungan *mts.* Indonesia **58** 3.30S102.30E
Barito *r.* Indonesia **58** 3.35S114.35E
Barjac France **21** 44.18N 4.21E
Barjols France **21** 43.33N 6.00E
Barjūj, Wādī Libya **75** 26.03N 12.50E
Barker U.S.A. **114** 43.20N 78.33W
Barker L. Australia **89** 31.45S120.05E
Bārkhān Pakistan **62** 29.54N 69.31E
Barking U.K. **13** 51.32N 0.05E
Bark L. Canada **104** 46.54N 82.28W
Barkley Sd. Canada **100** 48.53N125.20W
Barkly East R.S.A. **80** 30,58S 27.33E
Barkly Tableland *f.* Australia **90** 19.00S136.40E
Barkly West R.S.A. **80** 28.32S 24.29E
Bar-le-Duc France **19** 48.47N 5.10E
Barlee, L. Australia **89** 29.30S119.30E
Barlee Range *mts.* Australia **88** 23.40S116.00E
Barletta Italy **33** 41.19N 16.17E
Barlow L. Canada **101** 62.00N103.00W
Barmedman Australia **93** 34.08S147.25E
Barmer India **62** 25.45N 71.23E
Barmera Australia **92** 34.15S140.31E
Barm Fīrūz, Kūh-e *mtn.* Iran **65** 30.21N 52.00E
Barmouth U.K. **12** 52.44N 4.03W
Barnagar India **62** 23.03N 75.22E
Barnāla India **62** 30.22N 75.33E
Barnard Castle *town* U.K. **12** 54.33N 1.55W
Barnato Australia **93** 31.38S144.59E
Barnaul U.S.S.R. **9** 53.21N 83.15E
Barnegat U.S.A. **115** 39.45N 74.13W
Barnegat B. U.S.A. **115** 39.52N 74.07W
Barnegat Light U.S.A. **115** 39.46N 74.06W
Barnesboro U.S.A. **114** 40.40N 78.47W
Barnesville U.S.A. **114** 39.59N 81.11W
Barnet U.K. **13** 51.39N 0.11W
Barneveld Neth. **16** 52.10N 5.39E
Barneville France **18** 49.23N 1.45W
Barneys L. Australia **92** 33.16S144.13E
Barnsley U.K. **12** 53.33N 1.29W
Barnstable U.S.A. **115** 41.42N 70.18W
Barnstaple U.K. **13** 51.05N 4.03W
Baro *r.* Ethiopia **73** 8.26N 33.13E
Baro Nigeria **77** 8.37N 6.19E
Barpeta India **63** 26.19N 91.00E
Barqah *f.* Libya **72** 31.00N 23.00E
Barquisimeto Venezuela **122** 10.03N 69.18W
Barra Brazil **123** 11.06S 43.15W
Barra *i.* U.K. **14** 56.59N 7.28W
Barra, Sd. of U.K. **14** 57.04N 7.20W
Barraba Australia **93** 30.24S152.36E
Barra do Corda Brazil **123** 5.30S 45.15W
Barra do Piraí Brazil **126** 22.28S 43.49W
Barrafranca Italy **33** 37.23N 14.13E
Barra Head U.K. **10** 56.47N 7.36W
Barra Mansa Brazil **126** 22.35S 44.12W
Barranca Peru **122** 4.50S 76.40W
Barrancabermeja Colombia **122** 7.06N 73.54W
Barrancas Venezuela **122** 8.45N 62.13W
Barranco do Velho Portugal **27** 37.14N 7.56W
Barrancos Portugal **27** 38.08N 6.59W
Barranqueras Argentina **126** 27.30S 58.55W
Barranquilla Colombia **122** 11.10N 74.50W
Barraute Canada **102** 48.26N 77.39W
Barrax Spain **27** 39.03N 2.12W
Barre U.S.A. **105** 44.12N 72.30W
Barreiras Brazil **123** 12.09S 44.58W
Barreiro Portugal **27** 38.40N 9.04W
Barreiros Brazil **123** 8.49S 35.12W
Barrême France **21** 43.57N 6.22E
Barretos Brazil **126** 20.37S 48.38W
Barrhead Canada **100** 54.10N114.24W
Barrhead U.K. **14** 55.47N 4.24W
Barrie Canada **104** 44.24N 79.40W
Barrie I. Canada **104** 45.55N 82.40W
Barrier Range *mts.* Australia **92** 31.25S141.25E
Barrington Tops *mts.* Australia **93** 32.30S151.28E
Barringun Australia **93** 29.01S145.43E
Barron U.S.A. **108** 48.44N120.43W
Barrow *r.* Rep. of Ire. **15** 52.17N 7.00W
Barrow U.S.A. **98** 71.16N156.50W
Barrow, Pt. U.S.A. **96** 71.22N156.30W
Barrow Creek *town* Australia **90** 21.32S133.53E
Barrow I. Australia **88** 21.40S115.27E
Barrow-in-Furness U.K. **12** 54.08N 3.15W
Barrow Range *mts.* Australia **88** 26.04S127.28E
Barry U.K. **13** 51.23N 3.19W
Barry's Bay *town* Canada **105** 45.30N 77.41W
Barryville U.S.A. **115** 41.29N 74.55W

Barsinghausen to **Beloretsk**

Barsinghausen Germany **38** 52.18N 9.27E
Barstow U.S.A. **109** 34.54N117.01W
Bar-sur-Aube France **19** 48.14N 4.43E
Bar-sur-Seine France **19** 48.07N 4.22E
Barth Germany **38** 54.22N 12.43E
Bartica Guyana **122** 6.24N 58.38W
Bartin Turkey **64** 41.37N 32.20E
Bartle Frere, Mt. Australia **90** 17.23S145.49E
Bartlesville U.S.A. **111** 36.45N 95.59W
Bartlett L. Canada **100** 63.05N118.20W
Bartolomeu Dias Mozambique **81** 21.10S 35.09E
Barton U.S.A. **105** 44.45N 72.11W
Barton-upon-Humber U.K. **12** 53.41N 0.27W
Bartoszyce Poland **37** 54.16N 20.49E
Bartow U.S.A. **113** 27.54N 81.51W
Bāruni India **63** 25.29N 85.59E
Barwāh India **62** 22.16N 76.03E
Barwāni India **62** 22.02N 74.54E
Barwa Sāgar India **63** 25.23N 78.44E
Barwon *r.* Australia **93** 30.00S 148.05E
Barysh U.S.S.R. **44** 53.40N 47.09E
Basāl Pakistan **62** 33.33N 72.15E
Basankusu Zaïre **78** 1.12N 19.50E
Basavilbaso Argentina **125** 32.20S 58.52W
Basel Switz. **39** 47.33N 7.35E
Basella Spain **25** 42.01N 1.18E
Baselland *d.* Switz. **39** 47.30N 7.50E
Basento Italy **33** 40.21N 16.50E
Bashi Channel Taiwan/Phil. **55** 21.30N121.00E
Basilan Phil. **59** 6.40N121.59E
Basilan *i.* Phil. **59** 6.40N122.10E
Basildon U.K. **13** 51.34N 0.25E
Basilicata *d.* Italy **33** 40.30N 16.10E
Basin U.S.A. **108** 44.23N108.02W
Basingstoke U.K. **13** 51.15N 1.05W
Basin L. Canada **101** 52.38N105.18W
Baška Yugo. **31** 44.58N 14.46E
Baskatong, Résr. Canada **105** 46.48N 75.50W
Basmat India **62** 19.19N 77.10E
Bāsoda India **63** 23.51N 77.56E
Basoko Zaïre **73** 1.20N 23.30E
Basongo Zaïre **73** 4.23S 20.28E
Bas-Rhin *d.* France **19** 48.35N 7.40E
Bassano Canada **100** 50.48N112.20W
Bassano Italy **30** 45.46N 11.44E
Bassari Togo **76** 9.12N 0.18E
Bassein Burma **56** 16.46N 94.45E
Basse-Kotto *d.* C.A.R. **73** 5.00N 21.30E
Basse Normandie *d.* France **18** 49.00N 0.00
Basse Santa Su Gambia **76** 13.23N 14.15W
Basse-Terre Guadeloupe **117** 16.00N 61.43W
Bassett U.S.A. **110** 42.35N 99.32W
Basse-Yutz France **19** 49.21N 6.11E
Bass Is. U.S.A. **114** 41.42N 82.49W
Bass Str. Australia **91** 39.45S146.00E
Bassum Germany **38** 52.51N 8.43E
Båstad Sweden **43** 56.26N 12.51E
Bastak Iran **65** 27.15N 54.26E
Bastelica France **21** 42.00N 9.02E
Basti India **63** 26.48N 82.43E
Bastia France **21** 42.42N 9.27E
Bastogne Belgium **16** 50.00N 5.43E
Bastrop U.S.A. **111** 32.47N 91.55W
Basyūn Egypt **66** 30.57N 30.49E
Bas Zaïre *d.* Zaïre **78** 5.15S 14.00E
Bata Equat. Guinea **78** 1.51N 9.49E
Batabanó, Golfo de *g.* Cuba **117** 23.15N 82.30W
Batak Bulgaria **34** 41.57N 24.12E
Batak, Yazovir *l.* Bulgaria **34** 42.00N 24.11E
Batāla India **62** 31.48N 75.13E
Batalha Portugal **27** 39.39N 8.50W
Batang China **61** 30.02N 99.01E
Batangafo C.A.R. **77** 7.27N 18.11E
Batangas Phil. **59** 13.46N121.01E
Batan Is. Phil. **59** 20.50N121.55E
Bátaszék Hungary **31** 46.12N 18.44E
Batatais Brazil **126** 20.54S 47.37W
Batavia U.S.A. **114** 43.00N 78.11W
Bataysk U.S.S.R. **45** 47.09N 39.46E
Batchawana Canada **104** 46.54N 84.34W
Batchawana *r.* Canada **104** 46.55N 84.32W
Batchawana I. Canada **104** 46.45N 84.14W
Batchawana Mtn. Canada **104** 47.04N 84.24W
Batchelor Australia **90** 13.04S131.01E
Bătdâmbâng Cambodia **56** 13.06N103.12E
Batemans Bay *town* Australia **93** 35.55S150.09E
Batesville Ark. U.S.A. **111** 35.46N 91.39W
Batesville Miss. U.S.A. **111** 34.18N 90.00W
Bath *N.B.* Canada **103** 46.31N 67.37W
Bath *Ont.* Canada **105** 44.11N 76.47W
Bath U.K. **13** 51.22N 2.22W
Bath Maine U.S.A. **112** 43.55N 69.49W
Bath N.Y. U.S.A. **114** 42.20N 77.19W
Batha *d.* Chad **77** 14.30N 18.30E
Batha *r.* Chad **77** 12.47N 17.34E
Baṭḥā, Wādī al *r.* Oman **65** 20.01N 59.39E
Bathgate U.K. **14** 55.44N 3.38W
Bathurst Australia **93** 33.27S149.35E
Bathurst Canada **103** 47.36N 65.39W
Bathurst R.S.A. **80** 33.30S 26.48E
Bathurst, C. Canada **98** 70.30N128.00W
Bathurst I. Australia **88** 11.45S130.15E
Bathurst I. Canada **99** 76.00N100.00W
Bathurst Inlet *town* Canada **98** 66.48N108.00W
Batibla C.A.R. **73** 5.56N 21.09E
Batié Burkina **76** 9.42N 2.53W
Batina Yugo. **31** 45.51N 18.51E
Batir Jordan **67** 31.16N 35.42E
Batiscan *r.* Canada **105** 46.31N 72.15W
Batley U.K. **12** 53.43N 1.38W
Batlow Australia **93** 35.32S148.10E
Batman Turkey **64** 37.52N 41.07E
Batna Algeria **75** 35.35N 6.11E
Baton Rouge U.S.A. **111** 30.23N 91.11W
Batopilas Mexico **109** 27.00N107.45W
Batouri Cameroon **77** 4.26N 14.27E
Bat Shelomo Israel **67** 32.36N 35.00E
Batson U.S.A. **111** 30.15N 94.37W
Batticaloa Sri Lanka **61** 7.43N 81.42E
Battle *r.* Canada **101** 52.43N108.15W
Battle U.K. **13** 50.55N 0.30E
Battle Creek *town* U.S.A. **112** 42.20N 85.11W
Battleford Canada **101** 52.45N108.15W
Battle Harbour Canada **103** 52.17N 55.35W
Batu *mtn.* Ethiopia **73** 6.55N 39.46E
Batu, Kepulauan *is.* Indonesia **58** 0.30S 98.20E
Batumi U.S.S.R. **64** 41.37N 41.36E
Batu Pahat Malaysia **58** 1.50N102.48E
Baturaja Indonesia **58** 4.10S104.10E
Baturité Brazil **123** 4.20S 38.53W
Bat Yam Israel **67** 32.01N 34.45E
Baubau Indonesia **59** 5.30S122.37E
Bauchi Nigeria **77** 10.16N 9.50E
Bauchi *d.* Nigeria **77** 10.40N 10.00E
Baud France **18** 47.52N 3.01W
Baudh India **63** 20.50N 84.19E
Baugé France **18** 47.33N 0.06W
Bauld, C. Canada **103** 51.38N 55.25W
Baume-les-Dames France **19** 47.21N 6.22E
Baunei Italy **32** 40.02N 9.40E
Bauru Brazil **126** 22.19S 49.07W
Baús Brazil **126** 18.19S 53.10W
Bauska U.S.S.R. **41** 56.24N 24.14E
Bautzen Germany **38** 51.11N 14.26E
Bavay France **16** 50.18N 3.48E
Båven *l.* Sweden **43** 59.01N 16.56E
Bawean *i.* Indonesia **59** 5.50S112.39E
Bawku Ghana **76** 11.05N 0.13W
Bayamo Cuba **117** 20.23N 76.39W
Bayamón Puerto Rico **117** 18.24N 66.10W
Bāyan, Band-e *mts.* Afghan. **62** 34.20N 65.00E
Bayāna India **62** 26.54N 77.17E
Bayan Har Shan *mts.* China **52** 34.00N 97.20E
Bayan Nur China **54** 38.14N103.56E
Bayard U.S.A. **114** 39.16N 79.22W
Bayburt Turkey **64** 40.15N 40.16E
Bay City Mich. U.S.A. **104** 43.36N 83.53W
Bay City Tex. U.S.A. **111** 28.59N 95.58W
Baydaratskaya Guba *b.* U.S.S.R. **50** 70.00N 66.00E
Baydhabo Somali Rep. **79** 3.08N 43.34E
Bayerische Alpen *mts.* Germany **39** 47.38N 11.30E
Bayerischer Wald *mts.* Germany **39** 49.00N 12.50E
Bayern *d.* Germany **38** 49.06N 11.30E
Bayeux France **18** 49.17N 0.42W
Bayfield Canada **104** 43.33N 81.41W
Bayfield U.S.A. **110** 46.49N 90.49W
Baykal, Ozero *l.* U.S.S.R. **52** 53.30N100.00E
Baykit U.S.S.R. **51** 61.45N 96.22E
Baykonyr U.S.S.R. **50** 47.50N 66.03E
Bayo Spain **26** 43.09N 8.58W
Bay of Plenty *d.* New Zealand **86** 38.00S177.10E
Bayombong Phil. **59** 16.27N121.10E
Bayon France **19** 48.29N 6.19E
Bayona Spain **26** 42.07N 8.51W
Bayonne France **20** 43.29N 1.29W
Bayovar Peru **122** 5.50S 81.03W
Bay Port U.S.A. **104** 43.51N 83.23W
Bayramic Greece **34** 39.48N 26.37E
Bayreuth Germany **38** 49.57N 11.35E
Bayrischzell Germany **39** 47.40N 12.00E
Bayrūt Lebanon **66** 33.52N 35.30E
Bays, L. of Canada **104** 45.15N 79.04W
Bay Shore U.S.A. **115** 40.44N 73.15W
Baysville Canada **104** 45.09N 79.10W
Baytā al Fawqā Jordan **67** 32.09N 35.17E
Bayt Awlā Jordan **67** 31.36N 35.02E
Bayt Ḥānūn Egypt **67** 31.32N 34.32E
Baytik Shan *mts.* China **52** 45.15N 90.50E
Bayt Immar Jordan **67** 31.37N 35.06E
Bayt Jālā Jordan **67** 31.43N 35.11E
Bayt Lāhiyah Egypt **67** 31.33N 34.30E
Bayt Laḥm Jordan **67** 31.43N 35.12E
Baytown U.S.A. **111** 29.44N 94.58W
Bayt Rīmā Jordan **67** 32.02N 35.06E
Baytūniyā Jordan **67** 31.53N 35.10E
Bay View New Zealand **86** 39.26S176.52E
Bay Village U.S.A. **114** 41.29N 81.55W
Baza Spain **27** 37.29N 2.46W
Baza, Sierra de *mts.* Spain **27** 37.20N 2.45W
Bazaliya U.S.S.R. **37** 49.42N 26.29E
Bazaruto, Ilha do *i.* Mozambique **81** 21.40S 35.28E
Bazas France **20** 44.26N 0.13W
Bazdār Pakistan **62** 26.21N 65.03E
Bazhong China **55** 31.51N106.42E
Bazièģe France **20** 43.27N 1.37E
Bazmān Iran **65** 27.48N 60.12E
Bazmān, Kūh-e *mtn.* Iran **65** 28.06N 60.00E
Beach U.S.A. **110** 46.55N103.52W
Beachburg Canada **105** 45.43N 76.53W
Beach Haven U.S.A. **115** 39.34N 74.14W
Beachport Australia **92** 37.29S140.01E
Beachwood U.S.A. **115** 39.56N 74.12W
Beachy Head U.K. **13** 50.43N 0.15E
Beacon U.S.A. **115** 41.30N 73.58W
Beagle Bay *town* Australia **88** 16.58S122.40E
Bealanana Madagascar **81** 14.33S 48.44E
Bear Brook State Park U.S.A. **115** 43.05N 71.26W
Beardstown U.S.A. **110** 40.01N 90.26W
Bear I. *see* Bjørnøya *i.* Arctic Oc. **128**
Bear Island *town* Canada **104** 46.59N 80.05W
Bear L. U.S.A. **108** 42.00N111.20W
Bearskin Lake *town* Canada **102** 53.58N 91.02W
Beas *r.* India **62** 31.10N 75.00E
Beasain Spain **26** 43.03N 2.11W
Beas de Segura Spain **26** 38.15N 2.53W
Beatrice U.S.A. **110** 40.16N 96.44W
Beatrice, C. Australia **90** 14.15S136.59E
Beatton *r.* Canada **100** 56.15N120.45W
Beatton River *town* Canada **100** 57.26N121.20W
Beatty U.S.A. **108** 36.54N116.46W
Beattyville Canada **102** 48.53N 77.10W
Beaucaire France **21** 43.48N 4.38E
Beauce *f.* France **19** 48.22N 1.50E
Beauchêne Canada **104** 46.39N 78.55W
Beaudesert Australia **93** 27.58S153.01E
Beaufort Australia **92** 37.28S143.28E
Beaufort U.S.A. **113** 32.26N 80.40W
Beaufort Sea N. America **98** 72.00N141.00W
Beaufort West R.S.A. **80** 32.20S 22.34E
Beaugency France **19** 47.47N 1.38E
Beauharnois Canada **105** 45.19N 73.52W
Beaujolais, Monts du *mts.* France **21** 46.00N 4.30E
Beaulieu *r.* Canada **100** 62.03N113.11W
Beauly U.K. **14** 57.29N 4.29W
Beauly *r.* U.K. **14** 57.29N 4.25W
Beaumaris U.K. **12** 53.16N 4.07W
Beaumetz-lès-Loges France **19** 50.14N 2.39E
Beaumont Belgium **16** 50.14N 4.16E
Beaumont France **18** 49.40N 1.51W
Beaumont Miss. U.S.A. **111** 31.11N 88.55W
Beaumont Tex. U.S.A. **111** 30.05N 94.06W
Beaumont-le-Roger France **18** 49.05N 0.47E
Beaumont-sur-Sarthe France **18** 48.13N 0.08E
Beaune France **19** 47.02N 4.50E
Beaune-la-Rolande France **19** 48.04N 2.26E
Beaupréau France **18** 47.12N 1.00W
Beaurepaire France **21** 45.20N 5.03E
Beauséjour Canada **101** 50.04N 96.33W
Beauvais France **19** 49.26N 2.05E
Beauval Canada **101** 55.09N107.35W
Beauville France **20** 44.17N 0.52E
Beauvoir France **18** 46.55N 2.02W
Beauvoir-sur-Niort France **18** 46.11N 0.28W
Beaver *r.* N.W.T. Canada **100** 59.43N124.16W
Beaver *r.* Ont. Canada **102** 55.55N 87.50W
Beaver *r.* U.S.A. **114** 40.40N 80.18W
Beaver Alaska U.S.A. **98** 66.22N147.24W
Beaver Okla. U.S.A. **111** 36.49N100.31W
Beaver Penn. U.S.A. **114** 40.42N 80.18W
Beaver Dam *town* U.S.A. **110** 43.28N 88.50W
Beaver Falls *town* U.S.A. **114** 40.46N 80.19W
Beaverhill L. Alta. Canada **100** 53.27N112.32W
Beaverhill L. N.W.T. Canada **101** 63.02N104.22W
Beaver I. U.S.A. **112** 45.42N 85.28W
Beaverton Canada **104** 44.26N 79.09W
Beaverton U.S.A. **104** 43.53N 84.29W
Beāwar India **62** 26.06N 74.19E
Bebedouro Brazil **126** 20.54S 48.31W
Bebington U.K. **12** 53.23N 3.01W
Bécancour Canada **105** 46.20N 72.26W
Beccles U.K. **13** 52.27N 1.33E
Bečej Yugo. **31** 45.37N 20.03E
Béchar Algeria **74** 31.37N 2.13W
Bechater Tunisia **32** 37.18N 9.45E
Bechet Romania **34** 43.46N 23.58E
Beckley U.S.A. **113** 37.46N 81.12W
Beckum Germany **38** 51.45N 8.02E
Beclean Romania **37** 47.11N 24.10E
Bédarieux France **20** 43.37N 3.09E
Bedēsa Ethiopia **73** 8.50N 40.45E
Bedford Canada **105** 45.07N 72.59W
Bedford U.K. **13** 52.08N 0.29W
Bedford U.S.A. **114** 40.01N 78.30W
Bedford, C. Australia **90** 15.14S145.21E
Bedford Levels *f.* U.K. **13** 52.35N 0.08W
Bedfordshire *d.* U.K. **13** 52.04N 0.28W
Bedi India **62** 22.30N 70.02E
Bedlington U.K. **12** 55.08N 1.34W
Bedourie Australia **90** 24.21S139.28E
Beech Grove U.S.A. **112** 39.42N 86.06W
Beechworth Australia **93** 36.23S146.42E
Beenleigh Australia **93** 27.43S153.09E
Be'eri Israel **67** 31.25N 34.29E
Be'er Menuha Israel **66** 30.19N 35.08E
Be'erotayim Israel **67** 32.19N 34.59E
Be'er Sheva' Israel **67** 31.15N 34.47E
Be'er Sheva', Nahal *wadi* Israel **67** 31.11N 34.35E
Beerta Neth. **16** 53.12N 7.07E
Be'er Toviyya Israel **67** 31.44N 34.44E
Beeskow Germany **38** 52.10N 14.14E
Beeston U.K. **12** 52.55N 1.11W
Beeville U.S.A. **111** 28.24N 97.45W
Befale Zaïre **78** 0.27N 21.01E
Befandriana Madagascar **81** 15.16S 48.32E
Befandriana Madagascar **81** 22.06S 43.54E
Beg, Lough U.K. **15** 54.47N 6.29W
Bega Australia **93** 36.41S149.50E
Begamganj India **63** 23.36N 78.20E
Bègles France **20** 44.47N 0.34W
Begna *r.* Norway **42** 60.10N 10.18E
Begur, Cap de *c.* Spain **25** 41.57N 3.14E
Begusarai India **63** 25.25N 86.08E
Behara Madagascar **81** 25.00S 46.25E
Behbehān Iran **65** 30.35N 50.17E
Bei'an China **53** 48.17N126.33E
Beihai China **55** 21.29N109.09E
Bei Jiang *r.* China **55** 23.15N112.51E
Beijing China **54** 39.55N116.25E
Beijing *d.* China **54** 40.00N116.30E
Beijing Shi *d.* China **53** 40.15N116.30E
Beilen Neth. **16** 52.51N 6.31E
Beinn Dearg *mtn.* U.K. **14** 57.47N 4.55W
Beipa'a P.N.G. **90** 8.30S146.35E
Beipiao China **54** 41.47N120.40E
Beira Mozambique **81** 19.49S 34.52E
Beirut *see* Bayrūt Lebanon **66**
Beitang China **54** 39.06N117.43E
Beitbridge Zimbabwe **80** 22.10S 30.01E
Beit Jann Israel **67** 32.58N 35.23E
Beiuş Romania **37** 46.40N 22.21E
Beja Portugal **27** 38.01N 7.52W
Beja *d.* Portugal **27** 37.50N 7.55W
Béja Tunisia **32** 36.44N 9.11E
Bejaïa Algeria **75** 36.45N 5.05E
Béjar Spain **26** 40.23N 5.46W
Bejestān Iran **65** 34.32N 58.08E
Bejhi *r.* Pakistan **62** 29.47N 67.58E
Bejoording Australia **89** 31.22S116.30E
Békés Hungary **37** 46.46N 21.08E
Békéscsaba Hungary **37** 46.41N 21.06E
Bekily Madagascar **81** 24.13S 45.19E
Bela India **63** 25.56N 81.59E
Bela Pakistan **62** 26.14N 66.19E
Bélabo Cameroon **77** 5.00N 13.20E
Bela Crkva Yugo. **37** 44.54N 21.26E
Bel Air U.S.A. **115** 39.32N 76.21W
Belalcázar Spain **26** 38.34N 5.10W
Belampalli India **63** 19.02N 79.30E
Belang Indonesia **59** 0.58N124.56E
Bela Palanka Yugo. **34** 43.13N 22.17E
Belau Pacific Oc. **59** 7.00N134.25E
Bela Vista Brazil **124** 22.05S 56.22W
Bela Vista Mozambique **81** 26.20S 32.41E
Belaya *r.* U.S.S.R. **50** 55.40N 52.30E
Belaya Glina U.S.S.R. **45** 46.04N 40.54E
Belaya Tserkov U.S.S.R. **37** 49.49N 30.10E
Belcher Is. Canada **102** 56.00N 79.00W
Belchite Spain **25** 41.18N 0.45W
Belcoo U.K. **15** 54.18N 7.53W
Belda India **63** 22.05N 87.21E
Belebey U.S.S.R. **44** 54.05N 54.07E
Beled Weyne Somali Rep. **71** 4.47N 45.12E
Belém Brazil **123** 1.27S 48.29W
Belem Mozambique **81** 14.11S 35.59E
Belén Uruguay **125** 30.47S 57.47W
Belen U.S.A. **109** 34.40N106.46W
Belén, Cuchilla de *mts.* Uruguay **125** 30.49S 56.28W
Belene Bulgaria **34** 43.39N 25.07E
Beles *r.* Ethiopia **71** 11.10N 35.10E
Belev U.S.S.R. **44** 53.50N 36.08E
Belfast U.K. **15** 54.36N 5.57W
Belfast Maine U.S.A. **112** 44.27N 69.01W
Belfast N.Y. U.S.A. **114** 42.21N 78.07W
Belfast Lough U.K. **15** 54.42N 5.45W
Belfield U.S.A. **110** 46.53N103.12W
Belfort France **17** 47.38N 6.52E
Belfry U.S.A. **108** 45.09N109.01W
Belgaum India **60** 15.54N 74.36E
Belgium Europe **16** 51.00N 4.30E
Belgodere France **21** 42.35N 9.01E
Belgorod U.S.S.R. **45** 50.38N 36.36E
Belgorod-Dnestrovskiy U.S.S.R. **37** 46.10N 30.19E
Belgrade *see* Beograd Yugo. **37**
Beli Nigeria **77** 7.53N 10.59E
Beli Drim *r.* Yugo. **34** 42.25N 20.34E
Beli Manastir Yugo. **31** 45.46N 18.36E
Belin France **20** 44.30N 0.47W
Belington U.S.A. **114** 39.01N 79.56W
Belitung *i.* Indonesia **58** 3.00S108.00E
Belize Belize **117** 17.29N 88.20W
Belize C. America **117** 17.00N 88.30W
Belka Australia **89** 31.45S118.09E
Bellac France **20** 46.07N 1.02E
Bella Coola Canada **100** 52.25N126.40W
Bellagio Italy **30** 45.59N 9.15E
Bellaire Ohio U.S.A. **114** 40.02N 80.45W
Bellaire Tex. U.S.A. **111** 29.44N 95.03W
Bellaria Italy **30** 44.09N 12.28E
Bellary India **60** 15.11N 76.54E
Bellata Australia **93** 29.55S149.50E
Bella Unión Uruguay **125** 30.15S 57.35W
Bella Vista Corrientes Argentina **124** 28.30S 59.00W
Bella Vista Tucuman Argentina **124** 27.02S 65.19W
Bellbrook Australia **93** 30.48S152.30E
Belle U.S.A. **114** 38.14N 81.32W
Belledonne, Chaîne de *mts.* France **21** 45.18N 6.08E
Bellefontaine U.S.A. **112** 40.22N 83.45W
Bellefonte U.S.A. **114** 40.55N 77.46W
Belle Fourche *r.* U.S.A. **110** 44.26N102.19W
Bellegarde France **21** 46.06N 5.49E
Belle Glade U.S.A. **113** 26.41N 80.41W
Belle Île France **17** 47.20N 3.10W
Belle Île *i.* France **18** 47.20N 3.10W
Belle Isle Canada **103** 51.55N 55.20W
Belle Isle, Str. of Canada **103** 51.35N 56.30W
Bellême France **18** 48.22N 0.34E
Belleoram Canada **103** 47.32N 55.28W
Belleterre Canada **104** 47.25N 78.41W
Belleville Canada **105** 44.10N 77.23W
Belleville Kans. U.S.A. **110** 39.49N 97.38W
Belleville-sur-Saône France **21** 46.06N 4.45E
Bellevue Canada **100** 49.35N114.22W
Bellevue Canada **104** 46.42N 84.09W
Bellevue Idaho U.S.A. **108** 43.28N114.16W
Bellevue Ohio U.S.A. **114** 41.17N 82.50W
Bellevue Penn. U.S.A. **114** 40.30N 80.03W
Bellevue Wash. U.S.A. **108** 47.37N122.12W
Bell Ewart Canada **104** 44.16N 79.33W
Belley France **21** 45.46N 5.41E
Belle Yella Liberia **76** 7.24N 10.09W
Bellingen Australia **93** 30.28S152.43E
Bellingham U.K. **12** 55.09N 2.15W
Bellingham U.S.A. **108** 48.46N122.29W
Bellingshausen Sea Antarctica **128** 70.00S 88.00W
Bellinzona Switz. **39** 46.11N 9.02E
Bello Colombia **122** 6.20N 75.41W
Bellows Falls *town* U.S.A. **115** 43.08N 72.27W
Bellpat Pakistan **62** 28.59N 68.00E
Belluno Italy **30** 46.09N 12.13E
Bell Ville Argentina **125** 32.35S 62.41W
Bellville U.S.A. **114** 40.37N 82.31W
Bellwood U.S.A. **114** 40.36N 78.20W
Belmar U.S.A. **115** 40.11N 74.01W
Bélmez Spain **26** 38.16N 5.12W
Belmond U.S.A. **110** 42.51N 93.37W
Belmont Australia **93** 33.02S151.40E
Belmont U.S.A. **114** 42.13N 78.02W
Belmonte Portugal **26** 40.21N 7.21W
Belmonte Cuenca Spain **27** 39.34N 2.42W
Belmonte Oviedo Spain **26** 43.16N 6.13W
Belmopan Belize **117** 17.25N 88.46W
Belmullet Rep. of Ire. **15** 54.14N 10.00W
Belogradchik Bulgaria **34** 43.37N 22.40E
Belo Horizonte Brazil **126** 19.45S 43.54W
Beloit Kans. U.S.A. **110** 39.28N 98.06W
Beloit Wisc. U.S.A. **110** 42.31N 89.02W
Belo Jardim Brazil **123** 8.22S 36.22W
Belokorovichi U.S.S.R. **37** 51.04N 28.00E
Belomorsk U.S.S.R. **44** 64.34N 34.45E
Belonia India **63** 23.15N 91.27E
Belorado Spain **26** 42.25N 3.11W
Beloretsk U.S.S.R. **44** 53.59N 58.20E

Belorusskaya S.S.R. to Billingham

Belorusskaya S.S.R. *d.* U.S.S.R. **37** 53.30N 28.00E
Beloye More *sea* U.S.S.R. **44** 65.30N 38.00E
Beloye Ozero *l.* U.S.S.R. **44** 60.12N 37.45E
Belozersk U.S.S.R. **44** 60.00N 37.49E
Belpasso Italy **33** 37.35N 14.59E
Belper U.K. **12** 53.02N 1.29W
Belpre U.S.A. **114** 39.17N 81.34W
Beltana Australia **92** 30.40S138.27E
Belterra Brazil **123** 2.38S 54.57W
Belton Australia **92** 32.12S138.45E
Belton U.S.A. **111** 31.04N 97.28W
Beltsy U.S.S.R. **37** 47.45N 27.59E
Belukha, Gora *mtn.* U.S.S.R. **52** 49.48N 86.40E
Belvedere Marittimo Italy **33** 39.37N 15.52E
Belvès France **20** 44.47N 1.00E
Belvidere U.S.A. **115** 40.49N 75.05W
Belvís de la Jara Spain **27** 39.45N 4.57W
Belyando *r.* Australia **90** 21.38S146.50E
Belyayevka U.S.S.R. **37** 46.30N 30.12E
Belynichi U.S.S.R. **37** 54.00N 29.42E
Belyy, Ostrov U.S.S.R. **50** 73.10N 70.45E
Belyy Yar U.S.S.R. **50** 58.28N 85.03E
Belz France **18** 47.41N 3.10W
Bełżec Poland **37** 50.24N 23.26E
Belzig Germany **38** 52.08N 12.35E
Bemaraha, Plateau du *mts.* Madagascar **81** 20.00S 45.15E
Bemarivo *r.* Madagascar **81** 15.27S 47.40E
Bembézar Spain **26** 37.45N 5.13W
Bemidji U.S.A. **110** 47.29N 94.53W
Benaberre Spain **25** 42.07N 0.29E
Bena Dibele Zaïre **78** 4.07S 22.50E
Benagerie Australia **92** 31.30S140.21E
Benalla Australia **93** 36.35S145.58E
Benamejí Spain **27** 37.16N 4.32W
Ben 'Ammi Israel **67** 33.00N 35.07E
Benanee Australia **92** 34.32S142.56E
Benares *see* Vārānasi India **63**
Benavente Spain **26** 42.01N 5.41W
Benbecula *i.* U.K. **14** 57.26N 7.18W
Bencha China **54** 32.31N120.53E
Ben Cruachan *mtn.* U.K. **14** 56.26N 5.18W
Bencubbin Australia **89** 30.48S117.52E
Bend U.S.A. **108** 44.03N121.19W
Bende Nigeria **77** 5.34N 7.37E
Bendel *d.* Nigeria **77** 6.10N 6.00E
Bendemeer Australia **93** 30.52S151.10E
Bender Beyla Somali Rep. **71** 9.30N 50.30E
Bendery U.S.S.R. **37** 46.50N 29.29E
Bendigo Australia **92** 36.48S144.21E
Bendoc Australia **93** 37.10S148.55E
Bendorf Germany **39** 50.25N 7.34E
Bene Beraq Israel **67** 32.06N 34.51E
Bénéna Mali **76** 13.09N 4.17W
Benenitra Madagascar **81** 23.27S 45.05E
Benešov Czech. **36** 49.45N 14.22E
Bénestroff France **19** 48.55N 6.45E
Bénévent-l'Abbaye France **20** 46.07N 1.38E
Benevento Italy **33** 41.08N 14.45E
Benfeld France **19** 48.22N 7.36E
Bengal, B. of Indian Oc. **63** 20.00N 90.00E
Bengal Plateau *f.* Indian Oc. **48** 15.00N 89.00E
Bengbu China **54** 32.53N117.26E
Benghazi *see* Banghāzī Libya **75**
Bengkulu Indonesia **58** 3.46S102.16E
Bengo *d.* Angola **78** 9.00S 13.40E
Bengtsfors Sweden **43** 59.02N 12.13E
Benguela Angola **78** 12.34S 13.24E
Benguela *d.* Angola **78** 12.45S 14.00E
Ben Hope *mtn.* U.K. **14** 58.24N 4.36W
Beni *r.* Bolivia **124** 10.23S 65.24W
Beni Zaïre **79** 0.29N 29.27E
Beni Abbes Algeria **74** 30.08N 2.10W
Benicarló Spain **25** 40.25N 0.26E
Benidorm Spain **25** 38.32N 0.08W
Beni-Mellal Morocco **74** 32.22N 6.29W
Benin Africa **77** 9.00N 2.30E
Benin, Bight of Africa **77** 5.30N 3.00E
Benin City Nigeria **77** 6.19N 5.41E
Benisa Spain **25** 38.43N 0.03E
Beni Saf Algeria **74** 35.19N 1.23W
Benjamin Constant Brazil **122** 4.22S 70.02W
Benkelman U.S.A. **110** 40.03N101.32W
Benkovac Yugo. **31** 44.02N 15.37E
Ben Lawers *mtn.* U.K. **14** 56.33N 4.14W
Ben Lomond *mtn.* U.K. **14** 56.12N 4.38W
Ben Macdhui *mtn.* U.K. **14** 57.04N 3.40W
Ben More *mtn.* Central U.K. **14** 56.23N 4.31W
Ben More *mtn.* Strath. U.K. **14** 56.26N 6.02W
Ben More Assynt *mtn.* U.K. **14** 58.07N 4.52W
Bennett Canada **100** 59.49N135.01W
Bennett, L. Australia **90** 22.50S131.10E
Bennettsville U.S.A. **113** 34.36N 79.40W
Ben Nevis *mtn.* U.K. **14** 56.48N 5.00W
Benneydale New Zealand **86** 38.31S175.21E
Bennington N.H. U.S.A. **115** 43.01N 71.56W
Bennington Vt. U.S.A. **115** 42.53N 73.12W
Benny Canada **104** 46.47N 81.37W
Benoni R.S.A. **80** 26.12S 28.18E
Bénoué *r.* Cameroon *see* Benue *r.* Nigeria **77**
Bensheim Germany **39** 49.41N 8.37E
Benson Ariz. U.S.A. **109** 31.58N110.18W
Benson Minn. U.S.A. **110** 45.19N 95.36W
Bentiaba Angola **78** 14.19S 12.23E
Bentinck I. Australia **90** 17.04S139.30E
Bentiu Sudan **73** 9.14N 29.50E
Bentley U.S.A. **104** 43.57N 84.08W
Bentleyville U.S.A. **114** 40.07N 80.01W
Benton U.S.A. **110** 38.01N 88.54W
Benton Harbor U.S.A. **112** 42.07N 86.27W
Benue *d.* Nigeria **77** 7.20N 8.00E
Benue *r.* Nigeria **77** 7.52N 6.45E
Ben Wyvis *mtn.* U.K. **14** 57.40N 4.35W
Benxi China **54** 41.21N123.47E
Beograd Yugo. **37** 44.49N 20.28E
Beohāri India **63** 24.03N 81.23E
Beowawe U.S.A. **108** 40.35N116.29W
Beppu Japan **57** 33.18N131.30E
Berat Albania **34** 40.43N 19.59E
Berau, Teluk *b.* Indonesia **59** 2.20S133.00E
Berbera Somali Rep. **71** 10.28N 45.02E
Berbérati C.A.R. **77** 4.19N 15.51E
Berbería, Cabo *c.* Spain **25** 38.38N 1.23E
Berceto Italy **30** 44.31N 9.59E
Berchem Belgium **16** 50.48N 3.32E
Berchtesgaden Germany **39** 47.38N 13.01E
Berck France **19** 50.24N 1.36E
Bercu France **19** 50.31N 3.17E
Berdichev U.S.S.R. **37** 49.54N 28.39E
Berdsk U.S.S.R. **50** 54.51N 82.51E
Berdyansk U.S.S.R. **45** 46.45N 36.47E
Berea U.S.A. **114** 41.22N 81.52W
Beregovo U.S.S.R. **37** 48.13N 22.39E
Bereko Tanzania **79** 4.27S 35.43E
Berens *r.* Canada **101** 52.21N 97.02W
Berens River *town* Canada **101** 52.22N 97.02W
Beresford Australia **92** 29.14S136.40E
Berettyóújfalu Hungary **37** 47.14N 21.32E
Berevo Madagascar **81** 19.44S 44.58E
Bereza U.S.S.R. **37** 52.32N 25.00E
Berezhany U.S.S.R. **37** 49.27N 24.56E
Berezina *r.* U.S.S.R. **37** 54.10N 28.10E
Berezna U.S.S.R. **37** 51.34N 31.46E
Berezniki U.S.S.R. **44** 59.26N 56.49E
Berezno U.S.S.R. **37** 51.00N 26.41E
Berezovka U.S.S.R. **37** 47.12N 30.56E
Berezovo U.S.S.R. **9** 63.58N 65.00E
Berga Spain **25** 42.06N 1.51E
Berga Sweden **43** 57.14N 16.03E
Bergama Turkey **29** 39.08N 27.10E
Bergamo Italy **30** 45.41N 9.43E
Bergen Germany **38** 54.26N 13.27E
Bergen *Nschn.* Germany **38** 52.48N 9.58E
Bergen Neth. **16** 52.40N 4.41E
Bergen Norway **42** 60.23N 5.20E
Bergen U.S.A. **114** 43.05N 77.57W
Bergen op Zoom Neth. **16** 51.30N 4.17E
Bergerac France **20** 44.51N 0.29E
Bergheim Germany **38** 50.55N 6.38E
Berghem Neth. **16** 51.46N 5.32E
Bergisch Gladbach Germany **38** 50.59N 7.07E
Bergkamen Germany **38** 51.38N 7.38E
Bergkvara Sweden **43** 56.23N 16.05E
Bergland U.S.A. **112** 46.36N 89.33W
Bergoo U.S.A. **114** 38.29N 80.18W
Bergslagen *f.* Sweden **43** 59.55N 15.00E
Bergues France **19** 50.58N 2.26E
Bergum Neth. **16** 53.14N 5.59E
Berhampore India **63** 24.06N 88.15E
Berhampur India **63** 19.19N 84.47E
Bering Sea N. America / Asia **98** 65.00N170.00W
Bering Str. U.S.S.R. / U.S.A. **98** 65.00N170.00W
Berislav U.S.S.R. **45** 46.51N 33.26E
Berja Spain **27** 36.51N 2.57W
Berkåk Norway **40** 62.48N 10.03E
Berkel *r.* Neth. **16** 52.10N 6.12E
Berkeley U.S.A. **108** 37.57N122.18W
Berkeley Springs *town* U.S.A. **114** 39.38N 78.14W
Berkner I. Antarctica **128** 79.30S 50.00W
Berkovitsa Bulgaria **34** 43.16N 23.08E
Berkshire *d.* U.K. **13** 51.25N 1.03W
Berkshire Downs *hills* U.K. **13** 51.32N 1.36W
Berkshire Hills *mts.* U.S.A. **115** 42.20N 73.10W
Berland *r.* Canada **100** 54.00N116.50W
Berlanga de Duero Spain **26** 41.28N 2.51W
Berlin Germany **38** 52.31N 13.24E
Berlin *d.* Germany **38** 52.30N 13.20E
Berlin Md. U.S.A. **115** 38.20N 75.13W
Berlin N.H. U.S.A. **112** 44.29N 71.10W
Berlin Penn. U.S.A. **114** 39.55N 78.57W
Berlin L. U.S.A. **114** 41.00N 81.00W
Bermagui Australia **93** 36.28S150.03E
Bermeja, Sierra *mts.* Spain **27** 36.30N 5.10W
Bermejo *r.* San Juan Argentina **124** 31.40S 67.15W
Bermejo *r.* Tucumán Argentina **124** 26.47S 58.30W
Bermeo Spain **26** 43.26N 2.43W
Bermillo de Sayago Spain **26** 41.22N 6.06W
Bermo India **63** 23.47N 85.57E
Bermuda Atlantic Oc. **127** 32.18N 64.45W
Bermuda Rise *f.* Atlantic Oc. **127** 34.00N 60.00W
Bern Switz. **39** 46.57N 7.26E
Bern *d.* Switz. **39** 46.35N 7.50E
Bernalda Italy **33** 40.24N 16.41E
Bernard L. Canada **104** 45.44N 79.24W
Bernau Germany **38** 52.40N 13.35E
Bernay France **18** 49.06N 0.36E
Bernburg Germany **38** 51.48N 11.44E
Berne *see* Bern Switz. **39**
Berner Alpen *mts.* Switz. **39** 46.30N 7.37E
Bernier I. Australia **88** 24.51S113.09E
Bernina *mtn.* Italy / Switz. **30** 46.21N 9.51E
Bernkastel Germany **39** 49.55N 7.04E
Bernsdorf Germany **38** 51.22N 14.04E
Beror Hayil Israel **67** 31.33N 34.38E
Beroroha Madagascar **81** 21.41S 45.10E
Beroun Czech. **38** 49.58N 14.04E
Berounka *r.* Czech. **39** 50.00N 14.24E
Berovo Yugo. **34** 41.42N 22.51E
Berre, Étang de *b.* France **21** 43.28N 5.11E
Berrechid Morocco **74** 33.17N 7.35W
Berri Australia **92** 34.17S140.36E
Berridale Australia **93** 36.21S148.51E
Berrigan Australia **93** 35.41S145.48E
Berry Head U.K. **13** 50.24N 3.28W
Berryville Ark. U.S.A. **111** 36.22N 93.34W
Berryville Va. U.S.A. **114** 39.09N 77.59W
Bersenbrück Germany **38** 52.33N 7.56E
Bershad U.S.S.R. **37** 48.20N 29.30E
Berté, Lac *l.* Canada **103** 50.47N 68.30W
Berthierville Canada **105** 46.05N 73.10W
Bertinoro Italy **30** 44.09N 12.08E
Bertoua Cameroon **77** 4.34N 13.42E
Bertraghboy B. Rep. of Ire. **15** 53.23N 9.52W
Berwick Maine U.S.A. **115** 43.16N 70.51W
Berwick Penn. U.S.A. **115** 41.03N 76.15W
Berwick-upon-Tweed U.K. **12** 55.46N 2.00W
Besalampy Madagascar **81** 16.45S 44.30E
Besançon France **19** 47.15N 6.02E
Besor, Nahal *wadi* Egypt **67** 31.28N 34.22E
Bessarabia *f.* U.S.S.R. **37** 46.30N 28.40E
Bessemer U.S.A. **113** 33.22N 87.00W
Betafo Madagascar **81** 19.50S 46.51E
Bet Alpha Israel **67** 32.31N 35.26E
Betanzos Spain **26** 43.17N 8.12W
Betanzos, Ría de *est.* Spain **26** 43.23N 8.15W
Bétaré Oya Cameroon **77** 5.34N 14.09E
Bet Dagan Israel **67** 32.00N 34.50E
Bete Hor Ethiopia **73** 11.40N 39.00E
Bétera Spain **25** 39.35N 0.27W
Bet Guvrin *site* Israel **67** 31.36N 34.54E
Bet Ha'Emeq Israel **67** 32.58N 35.09E
Bethal R.S.A. **80** 26.26S 29.27E
Bet Hananya Israel **67** 32.32N 34.55E
Bethany Canada **104** 44.11N 78.34W
Bethany Beach *town* U.S.A. **115** 38.33N 75.00W
Bet HaShitta Israel **67** 32.33N 35.26E
Bethel Alas. U.S.A. **98** 60.48N161.46W
Bethel Penn. U.S.A. **115** 40.28N 76.18W
Bethesda U.S.A. **114** 38.59N 77.06W
Bethlehem *see* Bayt Laḩm Jordan **67**
Bethlehem R.S.A. **80** 28.13S 28.18E
Bethlehem N.H. U.S.A. **105** 44.17N 71.42W
Bethlehem Penn. U.S.A. **115** 40.37N 75.25W
Béthune France **19** 50.32N 2.38E
Béthune *r.* France **18** 49.53N 1.09E
Betim Brazil **126** 19.55S 44.07W
Betioky Madagascar **81** 23.42S 44.22E
Bet Oren Israel **67** 32.44N 35.00E
Bet Qama Israel **67** 31.27N 34.46E
Bet Qeshet Israel **67** 32.43N 35.24E
Betroka Madagascar **81** 23.16S 46.06E
Bet She'an Israel **67** 32.30N 35.30E
Bet Shemesh Israel **67** 31.45N 35.00E
Betsiamites Canada **103** 48.56N 68.38W
Betsiboka *r.* Madagascar **81** 16.03S 46.36E
Bette *mtn.* Libya **75** 22.00N 19.12E
Bettiah India **63** 26.48N 84.30E
Bettles U.S.A. **98** 66.53N151.51W
Betūl India **63** 21.55N 77.54E
Betwa *r.* India **63** 25.55N 80.12E
Betws-y-Coed U.K. **11** 53.05N 3.48W
Betzdorf Germany **16** 50.48N 7.54E
Beulah Australia **92** 35.59S142.26E
Beulah Canada **101** 50.16N101.02W
Beulah U.S.A. **110** 47.16N101.47W
Beuvron *r.* France **19** 47.29N 3.31E
Bevensen Germany **38** 53.05N 10.34E
Beverley Australia **89** 32.06S116.56E
Beverley U.K. **12** 53.52N 0.26W
Beverley Hills *town* U.S.A. **109** 34.04N118.26W
Beverly Mass. U.S.A. **115** 42.33N 70.53W
Beverly Ohio U.S.A. **114** 39.33N 81.38W
Beverly W.Va. U.S.A. **114** 38.51N 79.53W
Beverungen Germany **38** 51.39N 9.22E
Beverwijk Neth. **16** 52.29N 4.40E
Bewcastle Fells *hills* U.K. **12** 55.05N 2.50W
Bewdley Canada **104** 44.05N 78.19W
Bexhill U.K. **13** 50.51N 0.29E
Bexley U.K. **13** 51.26N 0.10E
Beyla Guinea **76** 8.42N 8.39W
Beyneu U.S.S.R. **45** 45.16N 55.04E
Beypazari Turkey **64** 40.10N 31.56E
Beyşehir Gölü *l.* Turkey **64** 37.47N 31.30E
Bezau Austria **39** 47.23N 9.54E
Bezet Israel **67** 33.05N 35.08E
Bezhanovo Bulgaria **34** 43.13N 24.26E
Bezhetsk U.S.S.R. **44** 57.49N 36.40E
Bezhitsa U.S.S.R. **44** 53.19N 34.17E
Béziers France **20** 43.21N 3.15E
Bhadohi India **63** 25.25N 82.34E
Bhādra India **62** 29.07N 75.10E
Bhadrakh India **63** 21.04N 86.30E
Bhāg Pakistan **62** 29.02N 67.49E
Bhāgalpur India **63** 25.15N 87.00E
Bhāi Pheru Pakistan **62** 31.12N 73.57E
Bhaironghāti India **63** 31.01N 78.53E
Bhaisa India **63** 19.06N 77.58E
Bhakkar Pakistan **62** 31.38N 71.04E
Bhaktapur Nepal **63** 27.42N 85.27E
Bhalwāl Pakistan **62** 32.16N 72.54E
Bhamo Burma **56** 24.10N 97.30E
Bhandāra India **63** 21.10N 79.39E
Bhānvad India **62** 21.56N 69.47E
Bharatpur India **63** 27.13N 77.29E
Bharthana India **63** 26.45N 79.14E
Bhātāpāra India **63** 21.44N 81.56E
Bhatewar India **62** 24.40N 74.05E
Bhātiāpāra Ghāt Bangla. **63** 23.12N 89.42E
Bhatinda India **62** 30.13N 74.56E
Bhatkal India **60** 13.58N 74.34E
Bhātpāra India **63** 22.52N 88.24E
Bhaunagar India **62** 21.46N 72.09E
Bhawāni Mandi India **62** 24.25N 75.50E
Bhawānipatna India **63** 19.54N 83.10E
Bhera Pakistan **62** 32.29N 72.55E
Bhikangaon India **62** 21.52N 75.57E
Bhilai India **63** 21.13N 81.26E
Bhilwāra India **62** 25.21N 74.38E
Bhima *r.* India **60** 16.30N 77.10E
Bhind India **63** 26.34N 78.48E
Bhinmāl India **62** 25.00N 72.15E
Bhiwandi India **62** 19.18N 73.04E
Bhiwāni India **62** 28.47N 76.08E
Bhognīpur India **63** 26.12N 79.48E
Bhojpur Nepal **63** 27.11N 87.02E
Bhokardan India **62** 20.16N 75.46E
Bhopāl India **63** 23.16N 77.24E
Bhor India **60** 18.12N 73.53E
Bhuban India **63** 20.53N 85.50E
Bhubaneswar India **63** 20.15N 85.50E
Bhuj India **62** 23.16N 69.40E
Bhusāwal India **62** 21.03N 75.46E
Bhutan Asia **63** 27.15N 91.00E
Bia, Phou *mtn.* Laos **56** 18.59N103.11E
Biābānak Afghan. **62** 32.11N 64.11E
Biak Indonesia **59** 1.10S136.05E
Biak *i.* Indonesia **59** 0.55S136.00E
Biała Podlaska Poland **37** 52.02N 23.06E
Białogard Poland **36** 54.00N 16.00E
Białystok Poland **37** 53.09N 23.10E
Biankouma Ivory Coast **76** 7.51N 7.34W
Biaora India **62** 23.55N 76.54E
Biarritz France **20** 43.29N 1.34W
Biasca Switz. **39** 46.22N 8.58E
Bibā Egypt **66** 28.56N 30.59E
Bibala Angola **78** 14.46S 13.21E
Biberach Germany **39** 48.20N 9.30E
Bibey *r.* Spain **26** 42.24N 7.13W
Bic Canada **103** 48.22N 68.42W
Bicas Brazil **126** 21.44S 43.04W
Bicester U.K. **13** 51.53N 1.09W
Bickle Knob *mtn.* U.S.A. **114** 38.56N 79.44W
Bida Nigeria **77** 9.06N 5.59E
Bīdar India **60** 17.54N 77.33E
Biddeford U.S.A. **115** 43.30N 70.26W
Biddiyā Jordan **67** 32.07N 35.05E
Biddū Jordan **67** 31.50N 35.09E
Bideford U.K. **13** 51.01N 4.13W
Bidon Cinq *see* Poste Maurice Cortier Algeria **74**
Bi Doup *mtn.* Vietnam **56** 12.05N108.40E
Bidwell U.S.A. **114** 38.55N 82.18W
Bié *d.* Angola **78** 12.30S 17.30E
Biedenkopf Germany **38** 50.55N 8.32E
Biel Switz. **39** 47.10N 7.12E
Bielefeld Germany **38** 52.01N 8.31E
Bielersee *l.* Switz. **39** 47.05N 7.10E
Biella Italy **30** 45.34N 8.03E
Bielsko-Biała Poland **37** 49.49N 19.02E
Bielsk Podlaski Poland **37** 52.47N 23.12E
Bien Hoa Vietnam **56** 10.58N106.50E
Bienville, Lac *l.* Canada **103** 55.05N 72.40W
Bié Plateau *f.* Angola **78** 13.00S 16.00E
Bietigheim Germany **39** 48.58N 9.07E
Biferno *r.* Italy **33** 41.59N 15.02E
Big Bald Mtn. Canada **103** 47.12N 66.25W
Big Bear Lake *town* U.S.A. **109** 34.15N116.53W
Big Beaver House *town* Canada **102** 52.59N 89.50W
Big Belt Mts. U.S.A. **108** 46.40N111.25W
Big Bend Nat. Park U.S.A. **111** 29.12N103.12W
Bigbury B. U.K. **13** 50.15N 3.56W
Big Cypress Swamp *f.* U.S.A. **113** 26.10N 81.38W
Big Falls *town* U.S.A. **110** 48.12N 93.48W
Biggar Canada **101** 52.04N107.59W
Biggar U.K. **14** 55.38N 3.31W
Big Hickory *mtn.* U.S.A. **115** 41.43N 74.22W
Bighorn *r.* U.S.A. **108** 46.09N107.28W
Bighorn L. U.S.A. **108** 45.06N108.08W
Bighorn Mts. U.S.A. **108** 44.00N107.30W
Bight, Head of *b.* Australia **91** 31.29S131.16E
Big Moose U.S.A. **105** 43.49N 74.57W
Bignasco Switz. **39** 46.20N 8.36E
Bignona Senegal **76** 12.48N 16.18W
Big Pine U.S.A. **108** 37.10N118.17W
Big Piney U.S.A. **108** 42.32N110.07W
Big Quill L. Canada **101** 51.55N104.22W
Big Run U.S.A. **114** 40.58N 78.53W
Big Salmon Canada **98** 61.53N134.55W
Big Salmon *r.* Canada **100** 61.52N134.56W
Big Sand L. Canada **101** 57.45N 99.42W
Big Sandy U.S.A. **108** 48.11N110.07W
Big Smoky Valley *f.* U.S.A. **108** 38.30N117.15W
Big Snowy Mtn. U.S.A. **108** 46.50N109.30W
Big Spring *town* U.S.A. **111** 32.15N101.28W
Big Stone Gap *town* U.S.A. **113** 36.52N 82.46W
Bigstone L. Canada **101** 53.42N 95.44W
Big Stone L. U.S.A. **110** 45.25N 96.40W
Big Sur U.S.A. **109** 36.15N121.48W
Big Timber U.S.A. **108** 45.50N109.57W
Big Trout L. Canada **102** 53.40N 90.00W
Bihać Yugo. **31** 44.49N 15.52E
Bihar India **63** 25.11N 85.31E
Bihar *d.* India **63** 24.30N 86.00E
Biharamulo Tanzania **79** 2.34S 31.20E
Bihor *mtn.* Romania **37** 46.26N 22.43E
Bihu China **55** 28.21N119.47E
Bijagós, Arquipélago dos *is.* Guinea Bissau **76** 11.30N 16.00W
Bijainagar India **62** 25.56N 74.38E
Bijaipura India **63** 24.46N 77.48E
Bijāpur India **60** 16.52N 75.47E
Bijāpur India **63** 18.48N 80.49E
Bījār Iran **65** 35.52N 47.39E
Bijāwar India **63** 24.38N 79.30E
Bijbān Chāh Pakistan **62** 26.54N 64.42E
Bijeljina Yugo. **31** 44.45N 19.13E
Bijelo Polje Yugo. **31** 43.02N 19.44E
Bijeypur India **62** 26.03N 77.22E
Bijie China **55** 27.28N105.20E
Bijnor India **63** 29.22N 78.08E
Bīkaner India **62** 28.42N 73.25E
Bikin U.S.S.R. **53** 46.52N134.15E
Bikini *i.* Pacific Oc. **84** 11.35N165.23E
Bikoro Zaïre **78** 0.45S 18.09E
Bilāra India **62** 26.10N 73.42E
Bilāspur Himachal P. India **62** 31.19N 76.45E
Bilāspur Madhya P. India **63** 22.05N 82.09E
Bilauktaung Range *mts.* Thailand **56** 13.00N 99.15E
Bilbao Spain **26** 43.15N 2.58W
Bilbays Egypt **66** 30.25N 31.34E
Bilbilis Spain **25** 41.25N 1.39W
Bilbo *see* Bilbao Spain **26**
Bileća Yugo. **31** 42.53N 18.26E
Bilecik Turkey **64** 40.10N 29.59E
Bilgrām India **63** 27.11N 80.02E
Bili *r.* Zaïre **73** 4.09N 22.29E
Bilibino U.S.S.R. **51** 68.02N166.15E
Bilimora India **62** 20.45N 72.57E
Bílina Czech. **38** 50.35N 13.45E
Billabong Creek *r.* Australia **92** 35.04S144.06E
Bill Baileys Bank *f.* Atlantic Oc. **10** 60.45N 10.30W
Billengen *f.* Sweden **43** 58.20N 13.43E
Billingham U.K. **12** 54.36N 1.18W

Billings to Bolshaya Pyssa

Billings U.S.A. **108** 45.47N108.27W
Billingsfors Sweden **43** 58.59N 12.15E
Bill of Portland *c.* U.K. **13** 50.32N 2.28W
Billom France **20** 45.44N 3.21E
Bilma Niger **75** 18.41N 12.56E
Biloela Australia **90** 24.24S150.30E
Biloxi U.S.A. **111** 30.24N 88.53W
Bilqās Qism Awwal Egypt **66** 31.14N 31.22E
Biltine Chad **75** 14.32N 20.55E
Biltine *d.* Chad **75** 15.00N 21.00E
Bilto Norway **40** 69.26N 21.35E
Bima *r.* Zaïre **78** 3.24N 25.10E
Bimberi, Mt. Australia **93** 35.40S148.47E
Bimbo C.A.R. **77** 4.15N 18.33E
Bimidji U.S.A. **96** 47.29N 94.53W
Bīna-Etāwa India **63** 24.11N 78.11E
Binaiya *mtn.* Indonesia **59** 3.10S129.30E
Bīnālūd, Kūh-e *mts.* Iran **65** 36.15N 59.00E
Binbee Australia **90** 20.20S147.55E
Binche Belgium **16** 50.25N 4.10E
Bindki India **63** 26.02N 80.36E
Bindura Zimbabwe **81** 17.18S 31.20E
Binéfar Spain **25** 41.51N 0.18E
Binga Zimbabwe **80** 17.38S 27.19E
Binga, Mt. Zimbabwe **81** 19.47S 33.03E
Bingara Australia **93** 29.51S150.38E
Bingen Germany **39** 49.58N 7.55E
Bingerville Ivory Coast **76** 5.20N 3.53W
Bingham U.K. **12** 52.57N 0.57W
Bingham U.S.A. **112** 45.03N 69.53W
Binghamton U.S.A. **115** 42.08N 75.54W
Bingkor Malaysia **58** 5.26N116.15E
Bingöl Turkey **23** 38.54N 40.29E
Bingol Dağlari *mtn.* Turkey **64** 39.21N 41.22E
Binhai China **54** 34.00N119.55E
Binh Dinh Vietnam **56** 13.53N109.07E
Binjai Indonesia **58** 3.37N 98.25E
Binji Nigeria **77** 13.12N 4.55E
Binnaway Australia **93** 31.32S149.23E
Binscarth Canada **101** 50.37N101.16W
Bintan *i.* Indonesia **58** 1.10N104.30E
Bint Jubayl Lebanon **67** 33.07N 35.26E
Bintulu Malaysia **58** 3.12N113.01E
Bin Xian China **54** 35.02N108.04E
Binyamina Israel **67** 32.31N 34.57E
Binyang China **55** 23.12N108.48E
Binzert Tunisia **32** 37.17N 9.52E
Biograd Yugo. **31** 43.56N 15.27E
Bioko I. Equat. Guinea **77** 3.25N 8.45E
Biq'at Bet Netofa *f.* Israel **67** 32.49N 35.19E
Bīr India **62** 18.59N 75.46E
Bir, Ras *c.* Djibouti **71** 11.59N 43.25E
Bi'r Abū 'Uwayqīlah *well* Egypt **66** 30.50N 34.07E
Bi'r ad Dakhal *well* Egypt **66** 28.40N 32.24E
Birāk Libya **75** 27.32N 14.17E
Birak Sulaymān *site* Jordan **67** 31.41N 35.10E
Bi'r al Ḩarash *well* Libya **75** 25.30N 22.06E
Bi'r al Jidy *well* Egypt **66** 30.13N 33.03E
Bi'r al Jufayr *well* Egypt **66** 30.49N 32.40E
Bi'r al 'Udayd *well* Egypt **66** 28.59N 34.05E
Birao C.A.R. **73** 10.17N 22.47E
Bi'r aş Şafrā' *well* Egypt **66** 28.46N 34.20E
Bi'r ath Thamadah *well* Egypt **66** 30.10N 33.28E
Birātnagar Nepal **63** 26.18N 87.17E
Bi'r Buerāt *well* Egypt **66** 28.59N 32.10E
Bi'r Bukhayt *well* Egypt **66** 29.13N 32.17E
Bîrca Romania **34** 43.59N 23.36E
Birch *r.* Canada **100** 58.30N112.15W
Birchip Australia **92** 35.59S142.59E
Birch L. N.W.T. Canada **100** 62.04N116.33W
Birch L. Ont. Canada **102** 51.24N 92.20W
Birch Mts. Canada **100** 57.30N112.30W
Bird Canada **101** 56.30N 94.13W
Birdsboro U.S.A. **115** 40.16N 75.48W
Birdsville Australia **90** 25.54S139.22E
Birecik Turkey **64** 37.03N 37.59E
Bīrganj Nepal **63** 27.01N 84.54E
Birhan *mtn.* Ethiopia **73** 11.00N 37.50E
Bi'r Ḩasanah *well* Egypt **66** 30.29N 33.47E
Bi'r Hooker *well* Egypt **66** 30.23N 30.20E
Bīrjand Iran **65** 32.54N 59.10E
Bi'r Jifjafah *well* Egypt **66** 30.28N 33.11E
Birk, Wādī *r.* Saudi Arabia **65** 24.08N 47.35E
Birkeland Norway **42** 58.20N 8.14E
Birkenfeld B.-Württ. Germany **39** 48.52N 8.38E
Birkenfeld Rhein.-Pfalz Germany **39** 49.39N 7.10E
Birkenhead U.K. **12** 53.24N 3.01W
Birkeröd Denmark **43** 55.50N 12.26E
Birksgate Range *mts.* Australia **88** 27.10S129.45E
Bi'r Kusaybah *well* Egypt **66** 22.41N 29.55E
Bîrlad Romania **37** 46.14N 27.40E
Bi'r Lahfān *well* Egypt **66** 31.01N 33.52E
Birmingham U.K. **13** 52.30N 1.55W
Birmingham Ala. U.S.A. **113** 33.30N 86.55W
Birmingham Mich. U.S.A. **104** 42.33N 83.15W
Birmitrapur India **63** 22.24N 84.46E
Bir Mogreïn Mauritania **74** 25.14N 11.35W
Birni Benin **77** 9.59N 1.34E
Birnin Gwari Nigeria **77** 11.02N 6.47E
Birnin Kebbi Nigeria **77** 12.30N 4.11E
Birni N'Konni Niger **77** 13.49N 5.19E
Birobidzhan U.S.S.R. **53** 48.49N132.54E
Bîr Ounâne *well* Mali **74** 21.02N 3.18W
Birr Rep. of Ire. **15** 53.06N 7.56W
Birrie *r.* Australia **93** 29.43S146.37E
Birsilpur India **62** 28.11N 72.15E
Birsk U.S.S.R. **44** 55.28N 55.31E
Bi'r Tābah *well* Egypt **66** 29.30N 34.53E
Bi'r Ţarfāwī *well* Egypt **72** 22.55N 28.53E
Birtle Canada **101** 50.32N101.02W
Bi'r Umm Sa'īd *well* Egypt **66** 29.40N 33.34E
Bi'r Umm 'Umayyid *well* Egypt **66** 27.53N 32.30E
Bi'r Ya'qūb *well* Jordan **67** 32.13N 35.17E
Biržai U.S.S.R. **44** 56.10N 24.48E
Bi'r Zalţan *well* Libya **75** 28.27N 19.46E
Bir Zreigat Mauritania **74** 22.27N 8.53W
Bisaccia Italy **33** 41.01N 15.22E
Bisalpur India **63** 28.18N 79.48E
Bisbee U.S.A. **109** 31.27N109.55W
Biscarosse France **20** 44.24N 1.10W
Biscarosse, Étang de *b.* France **20** 44.20N 1.10W
Biscay, B. of France **20** 44.00N 4.00W
Bisceglie Italy **33** 41.14N 16.31E
Bischheim France **19** 48.37N 7.45E
Bischofswerda Germany **38** 51.07N 14.10E
Biscotasi L. Canada **104** 47.19N 82.07W
Biscotasing Canada **104** 47.18N 82.08W
Bisha Ethiopia **72** 15.28N 37.34E
Bishnupur India **63** 23.05N 87.19E
Bishop Calif. U.S.A. **108** 37.22N118.24W
Bishop Tex. U.S.A. **111** 27.35N 97.48W
Bishop Auckland U.K. **12** 54.40N 1.40W
Bishop's Stortford U.K. **13** 51.53N 0.09E
Bisina, L. Uganda **79** 1.35N 34.08E
Biskra Algeria **75** 34.48N 5.40E
Bismarck U.S.A. **110** 46.48N100.47W
Bismarck Range *mts.* P.N.G. **59** 6.00S145.00E
Bismarck Sea Pacific Oc. **59** 4.00S146.30E
Bison U.S.A. **110** 45.31N102.28W
Bīsotūn Iran **65** 34.22N 47.29E
Bispgården Sweden **40** 63.02N 16.40E
Bissau Guinea Bissau **76** 11.52N 15.39W
Bissett Canada **101** 51.02N 95.40W
Bissikrima Guinea **76** 10.50N 10.58W
Bistcho L. Canada **100** 59.45N118.50W
Bistreţ Romania **34** 43.54N 23.23E
Bistriţa Romania **37** 47.08N 24.30E
Bistriţa *r.* Romania **37** 46.30N 26.54E
Biswān India **63** 27.30N 81.00E
Bitam Gabon **78** 2.05N 11.30E
Bitburg Germany **39** 49.58N 6.31E
Bitche France **19** 49.03N 7.26E
Bitéa, Ouadi *wadi* Chad **73** 13.11N 20.10E
Bitlis Turkey **64** 38.23N 42.04E
Bitola Yugo. **34** 41.01N 21.20E
Bitonto Italy **33** 41.06N 16.42E
Bitter Creek *town* U.S.A. **108** 41.31N109.27W
Bitterfeld Germany **38** 51.37N 12.20E
Bitterfontein R.S.A. **80** 31.02S 18.14E
Bitterroot Range *mts.* U.S.A. **108** 47.06N115.10W
Bitti Italy **32** 40.29N 9.23E
Biu Nigeria **77** 10.36N 12.11E
Biumba Rwanda **79** 1.38S 30.02E
Biwa ko *l.* Japan **57** 35.10N136.00E
Biyalā Egypt **66** 31.11N 31.13E
Biysk U.S.S.R. **9** 52.35N 85.16E
Bizerte *d.* Tunisia **32** 37.07N 9.45E
Bizerte *see* Binzert Tunisia **32**
Bizerte, Lac de *l.* Tunisia **32** 37.12N 9.52E
Bjärnum Sweden **43** 56.17N 13.42E
Bjelasica *mts.* Yugo. **31** 42.50N 19.40E
Bjelovar Yugo. **31** 45.54N 16.51E
Bjerringbro Denmark **42** 56.23N 9.40E
Björkelangen Norway **42** 59.53N 11.34E
Bjorli Norway **41** 62.16N 8.13E
Björna Sweden **40** 63.32N 18.36E
Björnafjorden *est.* Norway **42** 60.06N 5.22E
Bjørnøya *i.* Arctic Oc. **128** 74.30N 19.00E
Bjuv Sweden **43** 56.05N 12.54E
Blace Yugo. **34** 43.18N 21.17E
Black *r.* Canada **104** 44.20N 79.20W
Black *r.* Ark. U.S.A. **111** 35.38N 91.19W
Black *r.* Mich. U.S.A. **104** 45.39N 84.29W
Black *r.* Mich. U.S.A. **104** 43.00N 82.25W
Black *r.* N.Y. U.S.A. **105** 44.01N 75.59W
Black *r.* Ohio U.S.A. **114** 41.28N 82.11W
Black *r. see* Dà *r.* Vietnam **56**
Blackall Australia **90** 24.25S145.28E
Blackburn U.K. **12** 53.44N 2.30W
Black Diamond Canada **100** 50.45N114.14W
Black Duck *r.* Canada **101** 56.51N 89.02W
Blackduck U.S.A. **110** 47.44N 94.33W
Blackfoot U.S.A. **108** 43.11N112.20W
Black Hills U.S.A. **110** 44.00N104.00W
Black L. Canada **101** 59.10N105.20W
Black L. *Mich.* U.S.A. **104** 45.28N 84.15W
Black L. *N.Y.* U.S.A. **105** 44.31N 75.35W
Black Lake *town* Canada **105** 46.03N 71.21W
Black Mtn. U.K. **13** 51.52N 3.50W
Black Mts. U.K. **13** 51.52N 3.09W
Blackpool U.K. **12** 53.48N 3.03W
Black River *town* Jamaica **117** 18.02N 77.52W
Black River *town* Mich. U.S.A. **104** 44.47N 83.19W
Black River *town* N.Y. U.S.A. **105** 44.01N 75.48W
Black Rock *town* U.S.A. **108** 38.41N112.59W
Black Rock Desert U.S.A. **108** 41.10N119.00W
Black Sand Desert U.S.S.R. **65** 37.45N 60.00E
Black Sea Europe **37** 44.00N 30.00E
Blacksod B. Rep. of Ire. **15** 54.04N 10.00W
Blackstone U.S.A. **113** 37.05N 78.02W
Black Sugarloaf Mt. Australia **93** 31.24S151.34E
Blackville Australia **93** 31.34S150.10E
Blackville U.S.A. **113** 33.22N 81.17W
Black Volta *r.* Ghana **76** 8.14N 2.11W
Blackwater Australia **90** 23.34S148.53E
Blackwater *r.* Waterford Rep. of Ire. **15** 51.58N 7.52W
Blackwater *r.* U.K. **11** 54.31N 6.36W
Blackwell U.S.A. **111** 36.48N 97.17W
Blackwood *r.* Australia **89** 34.15S115.10E
Blaenau Ffestiniog U.K. **12** 53.00N 3.57W
Blagaj Yugo. **31** 43.15N 17.50E
Blagoevgrad Bulgaria **34** 42.02N 23.05E
Blagoveshchensk U.S.S.R. **53** 50.19N127.30E
Blain France **18** 47.29N 1.46W
Blain U.S.A. **114** 40.20N 77.31W
Blair U.S.A. **110** 41.33N 96.08W
Blair Athol Australia **90** 22.42S147.33E
Blair Atholl U.K. **14** 56.46N 3.51W
Blairgowrie U.K. **14** 56.36N 3.21W
Blairmore Canada **100** 49.40N114.25W
Blairsville Ga. U.S.A. **113** 34.52N 83.52W
Blairsville Penn. U.S.A. **114** 40.26N 79.16W
Blakely U.S.A. **113** 31.22N 84.58W
Blakeslee U.S.A. **115** 41.06N 75.36W
Blanc, Cap *c.* Mauritania **76** 20.44N 17.05W
Blanc, Cap *c.* Tunisia **32** 37.20N 9.50E
Blanc, Mont *mtn.* France **21** 45.50N 6.52E
Blanca, Bahía *b.* Argentina **125** 39.20S 62.00W
Blanca, Sierra *mtn.* U.S.A. **109** 33.23N105.48W
Blanchard U.S.A. **108** 48.01N116.59W
Blanche, L. Australia **92** 29.15S139.40E
Blanchetown Australia **92** 34.21S139.38E
Blanco, C. Argentina **125** 47.12S 65.20W
Blanco, C. Costa Rica **117** 9.36N 85.06W
Blanco, C. U.S.A. **108** 42.50N124.34W
Bland *r.* Australia **93** 33.42S147.30E
Blandburg U.S.A. **114** 40.41N 78.25W
Blandford Forum U.K. **13** 50.52N 2.10W
Blanes Spain **25** 41.41N 2.48E
Blangy-sur-Bresle France **19** 49.56N 1.38E
Blankenberge Belgium **16** 51.18N 3.08E
Blankenburg Germany **38** 51.48N 10.58E
Blanquefort France **20** 44.53N 0.39W
Blansko Czech. **36** 49.22N 16.39E
Blantyre Malaŵi **79** 15.46S 35.00E
Blarney Rep. of Ire. **15** 51.56N 8.34W
Blatná Czech. **38** 49.26N 13.53E
Blatnica Bulgaria **37** 43.42N 28.31E
Blaubeuren Germany **39** 48.24N 9.47E
Blaufelden Germany **39** 49.18N 9.58E
Blavet *r.* France **18** 47.43N 3.18W
Blaye France **20** 45.08N 0.39W
Blayney Australia **93** 33.32S149.19E
Bled Yugo. **31** 46.22N 14.06E
Blednaya, Gora *mtn.* U.S.S.R. **50** 76.23N 65.08E
Bleiburg Austria **31** 46.35N 14.48E
Blekinge *d.* Sweden **43** 56.15N 15.15E
Blekinge *f.* Sweden **43** 56.20N 15.20E
Blenheim Canada **104** 42.20N 82.00W
Blenheim New Zealand **86** 41.32S173.58E
Bléone *r.* France **21** 44.03N 6.00E
Bléré France **18** 47.20N 1.00E
Blerick Neth. **16** 51.22N 6.08E
Bletchley U.K. **13** 51.59N 0.45W
Bletterans France **19** 46.45N 5.27E
Bleu, Lac *l.* Canada **104** 46.35N 78.20W
Blida Algeria **75** 36.30N 2.50E
Blidö *i.* Sweden **43** 59.37N 18.54E
Bligh Entrance Australia **90** 9.18S144.10E
Blind River *town* Canada **104** 46.10N 82.58W
Blinman Australia **92** 31.05S138.11E
Blitar Indonesia **59** 8.06S112.12E
Blitta Togo **77** 8.23N 1.06E
Block I. U.S.A. **115** 41.11N 71.35W
Bloemfontein R.S.A. **80** 29.07S 26.14E
Bloemhof R.S.A. **80** 27.37S 25.34E
Blois France **18** 47.35N 1.20E
Blönduós Iceland **40** 65.39N 20.18W
Bloody Foreland *c.* Rep. of Ire. **15** 55.09N 8.17W
Bloomfield Canada **105** 43.59N 77.14W
Bloomfield Iowa U.S.A. **110** 40.45N 92.25W
Bloomfield Nebr. U.S.A. **110** 42.36N 97.39W
Bloomfield N.J. U.S.A. **115** 40.48N 74.12W
Bloomingdale U.S.A. **105** 44.25N 74.06W
Bloomington Ill. U.S.A. **110** 40.29N 89.00W
Bloomington Ind. U.S.A. **112** 39.10N 86.31W
Bloomington Minn. U.S.A. **110** 44.50N 93.17W
Bloomsburg U.S.A. **115** 41.00N 76.27W
Blora Indonesia **59** 6.55S111.29E
Blossburg U.S.A. **114** 41.41N 77.04W
Blovice Czech. **38** 49.35N 13.33E
Bludenz Austria **39** 47.09N 9.49E
Blueberry *r.* Canada **100** 56.45N120.49W
Bluefield U.S.A. **113** 37.14N 81.17W
Bluefields Nicaragua **117** 12.00N 83.49W
Blue Hills of Couteau Canada **103** 47.59N 57.43W
Bluemont U.S.A. **114** 39.06N 77.51W
Blue Mountain Lake *town* U.S.A. **105** 43.53N 74.26W
Blue Mtn. *N.H.* U.S.A. **105** 44.47N 71.28W
Blue Mts. Australia **93** 33.16S150.19E
Blue Mts. U.S.A. **108** 45.30N118.15W
Blue Mud B. Australia **90** 13.26S135.56E
Blue Nile *r. see* Azraq, Al Baḩr al *r.* Sudan **72**
Bluenose L. Canada **98** 68.30N119.35W
Blue River *town* Canada **100** 52.05N119.09W
Blue Stack Mts. Rep. of Ire. **15** 54.44N 8.09W
Bluff New Zealand **86** 46.38S168.21E
Bluff U.S.A. **108** 37.17N109.33W
Bluff, C. Canada **103** 52.48N 55.53W
Bluff Knoll *mtn.* Australia **89** 34.25S118.15E
Blumberg Germany **39** 47.50N 8.31E
Blumenau Brazil **126** 26.55S 49.07W
Blunt U.S.A. **110** 44.31N 99.59W
Blyth Canada **104** 43.44N 81.26W
Blyth Northum. U.K. **12** 55.07N 1.29W
Blythe U.S.A. **109** 33.37N114.36W
Bö Nordland Norway **40** 68.38N 14.35E
Bö Telemark Norway **42** 59.25N 9.04E
Bo Sierra Leone **76** 7.58N 11.45W
Boa Esperança Brazil **126** 21.03S 45.37W
Boa Esperança, Représa da *resr.* Brazil **123** 6.45S 44.15W
Bo'ai Henan China **54** 35.10N113.04E
Boane Mozambique **81** 26.02S 32.19E
Boa Vista Brazil **122** 2.51N 60.43W
Bobadah Australia **93** 32.18S146.42E
Bobadilla Spain **27** 37.02N 4.44W
Bobbili India **61** 18.34N 83.22E
Bobbio Italy **30** 44.46N 9.23E
Bobcaygeon Canada **104** 44.33N 78.33W
Böblingen Germany **39** 48.41N 9.01E
Bobo-Dioulasso Burkina **76** 11.11N 4.18W
Bobonong Botswana **80** 21.59S 28.29E
Bóbr *r.* Poland **36** 52.04N 15.04E
Bobr U.S.S.R. **37** 54.19N 29.18E
Bobruysk U.S.S.R. **37** 53.08N 29.10E
Bôca do Acre Brazil **122** 8.45S 67.23W
Bocaranga C.A.R. **77** 7.01N 15.35E
Boca Raton U.S.A. **113** 26.22N 80.05W
Bochnia Poland **37** 49.58N 20.26E
Bocholt Germany **38** 51.50N 6.36E
Bochum Germany **38** 51.28N 7.13E
Bochum R.S.A. **80** 23.12S 29.12E
Bockum-Hövel Germany **38** 51.42N 7.46E
Bocognano France **21** 42.05N 9.03E
Boconó Venezuela **122** 9.17N 70.17W
Boda C.A.R. **77** 4.19N 17.26E
Böda Sweden **43** 57.15N 17.03E
Boda Glasbruk Sweden **43** 56.44N 15.40E
Bodalla Australia **93** 36.05S150.03E
Bodallin Australia **89** 31.22S118.52E
Bodélé *f.* Chad **77** 16.50N 17.10E
Boden Sweden **40** 65.50N 21.42E
Bodensee *l.* Europe **39** 47.35N 9.25E
Bode Sadu Nigeria **77** 8.57N 4.49E
Bodfish U.S.A. **109** 35.36N118.30W
Bodmin U.K. **13** 50.28N 4.44W
Bodmin Moor U.K. **13** 50.53N 4.35W
Bodo Canada **101** 52.11N110.04W
Bodö Norway **40** 67.18N 14.26E
Bodrum Turkey **35** 37.02N 27.26E
Boembé Congo **78** 2.59S 15.34E
Boende Zaïre **78** 0.15S 20.49E
Boën-sur-Lignon France **20** 45.44N 3.59E
Boeo, Capo *c.* Italy **32** 37.48N 12.26E
Boffa Guinea **76** 10.12N 14.02W
Bofors Sweden **43** 59.20N 14.32E
Bogale Burma **56** 16.17N 95.24E
Bogalusa U.S.A. **111** 30.47N 89.52W
Bogan *r.* Australia **93** 30.00S146.20E
Bogan Gate *town* Australia **93** 33.08S147.50E
Bogata U.S.A. **111** 33.28N 95.13W
Bogcang Zangbo *r.* China **63** 31.50N 87.25E
Bogen Germany **39** 48.55N 12.43E
Bogenfels Namibia **80** 27.26S 15.22E
Bogense Denmark **42** 55.34N 10.06E
Boggabilla Australia **93** 28.36S150.21E
Boggabri Australia **93** 30.42S150.02E
Boggeragh Mts. Rep. of Ire. **15** 52.03N 8.53W
Bogia P.N.G. **59** 4.16S145.00E
Bognes Norway **40** 68.15N 16.00E
Bognor Regis U.K. **13** 50.47N 0.40W
Bog of Allen *f.* Rep. of Ire. **15** 53.17N 7.00W
Bogol Manyo Ethiopia **73** 4.32N 41.32E
Bogong, Mt. Australia **93** 36.45S147.21E
Bogor Indonesia **58** 6.34S106.45E
Bogotá Colombia **122** 4.38N 74.05W
Bogra Bangla. **63** 24.51N 89.22E
Bogué Mauritania **74** 16.35N 14.16W
Boguslav U.S.S.R. **37** 49.32N 30.52E
Bo Hai *b.* China **54** 38.30N119.30E
Bohain France **19** 49.59N 3.27E
Bohai Wan *b.* China **54** 38.30N117.55E
Bohemian Forest *see* Böhmerwald *mts.* Germany **39**
Bohin Somali Rep. **71** 11.42N 51.17E
Bohinjska Bistrica Yugo. **31** 46.17N 13.57E
Böhmerwald *mts.* Germany **39** 49.12N 12.55E
Bohol *i.* Phil. **59** 9.45N124.10E
Bohuslän *f.* Sweden **42** 58.15N 11.50E
Boiaçu Brazil **122** 0.27S 61.46W
Boiano Italy **33** 41.29N 14.29E
Boigu *i.* Australia **90** 9.16S142.12E
Boing Sudan **73** 9.58N 33.44E
Boiro Spain **26** 42.39N 8.54W
Bois, Lac des *l.* Canada **98** 66.40N125.15W
Bois Blanc I. U.S.A. **104** 45.45N 84.28W
Bois du Roi *mtn.* France **19** 47.00N 4.02E
Boise U.S.A. **108** 43.37N116.13W
Boise City U.S.A. **111** 36.44N102.31W
Bois-Guillaume France **18** 49.28N 1.08E
Boissevain Canada **101** 49.15N100.00W
Boizenburg Germany **38** 53.22N 10.43E
Bojador, Cabo *c.* W. Sahara **74** 26.08N 14.30W
Bojana *r.* Albania **31** 41.50N 19.25E
Bojeador, C. Phil. **55** 18.30N120.36E
Bojnūrd Iran **65** 37.28N 57.20E
Bojonegoro Indonesia **59** 7.06S111.50E
Bokani Nigeria **77** 9.27N 5.13E
Boké Guinea **76** 10.57N 14.13W
Bokhara *r.* Australia **93** 29.55S146.42E
Boknafjorden *est.* Norway **42** 59.10N 5.35E
Bokoro Chad **77** 12.17N 17.04E
Bokote Zaïre **78** 0.05S 20.08E
Bokpyin Burma **56** 11.16N 98.46E
Bokungu Zaïre **78** 0.44S 22.28E
Bol Chad **77** 13.27N 14.40E
Bol Yugo. **31** 43.16N 16.40E
Bolac Lake *town* Australia **92** 37.42S142.50E
Bolafa Zaïre **78** 1.23N 22.06E
Bolama Guinea Bissau **76** 11.35N 15.30W
Bolān *r.* Pakistan **62** 29.05N 67.45E
Bolanda, Jabal *mtn.* Sudan **73** 7.44N 25.28E
Bolaños de Calatrava Spain **26** 38.54N 3.40W
Bolān Pass Pakistan **62** 29.45N 67.35E
Bolbec France **18** 49.34N 0.29E
Bole Ghana **76** 9.03N 2.23W
Bolesławiec Poland **36** 51.16N 15.34E
Bolgatanga Ghana **76** 10.42N 0.52W
Bolgrad U.S.S.R. **37** 45.42N 28.40E
Bolia Zaïre **78** 1.36S 18.23E
Bolívar Argentina **125** 36.14S 61.07W
Bolivar N.Y. U.S.A. **114** 42.04N 78.10W
Bolivar Tenn. U.S.A. **111** 35.16N 88.59W
Bolivia S. America **124** 17.00S 65.00W
Bollène France **21** 44.17N 4.45E
Bollnäs Sweden **41** 61.21N 16.25E
Bollon Australia **91** 28.02S147.28E
Bollstabruk Sweden **40** 62.59N 17.42E
Bollullos par del Condado Spain **27** 37.20N 6.32W
Bolmen *l.* Sweden **43** 56.55N 13.40E
Bolobo Zaïre **78** 2.10S 16.17E
Bologna Italy **30** 44.29N 11.20E
Bologoye U.S.S.R. **44** 57.58N 34.00E
Bolomba Zaïre **78** 0.30N 19.13E
Bolombo Zaïre **78** 3.59S 21.22E
Bolondo Equat. Guinea **78** 1.40N 9.38E
Bolongongo Angola **78** 8.28S 15.16E
Bolovens, Plateau des *f.* Laos **56** 15.10N106.30E
Bolsena Italy **30** 42.39N 11.59E
Bolsena, Lago di *l.* Italy **30** 42.36N 11.56E
Bolshaya Glushitsa U.S.S.R. **44** 52.28N 50.30E
Bolshaya Pyssa U.S.S.R. **44** 64.11N 48.44E

Bolsherechye to **Bremer Bay**

Bolsherechye U.S.S.R. **50** 56.07N 74.40E
Bol'shevik, Ostrov *i.* U.S.S.R. **51** 78.30N 102.00E
Bolshezemelskaya Tundra *f.* U.S.S.R. **44** 67.00N 56.10E
Bolshoy Atlym U.S.S.R. **50** 62.17N 66.30E
Bol'shoy Balkhan, Khrebet *mts.* U.S.S.R. **65** 39.38N 54.30E
Bol'shoy Irgiz *r.* U.S.S.R. **44** 52.00N 47.20E
Bol'shoy Lyakhovskiy, Ostrov *i.* U.S.S.R. **51** 73.30N 142.00E
Bol'shoy Onguren U.S.S.R. **51** 53.40N 107.40E
Bolshoy Uzen *r.* U.S.S.R. **45** 49.00N 49.40E
Bolsover U.K. **12** 53.14N 1.18W
Boltaña Spain **25** 42.27N 0.04E
Bolton U.K. **12** 53.35N 2.26W
Bolton L. Canada **101** 54.16N 95.47W
Bolu Turkey **64** 40.45N 31.38E
Bolus Head Rep. of Ire. **15** 51.47N 10.20W
Bolvadin Turkey **64** 38.43N 31.02E
Boly Hungary **31** 45.58N 18.32E
Bolzano Italy **30** 46.31N 11.22E
Boma Zaïre **78** 5.50S 13.03E
Bomaderry Australia **93** 34.21S 150.34E
Bomadi Nigeria **77** 5.13N 6.01E
Bombala Australia **93** 36.55S 149.16E
Bombarral Portugal **27** 39.16N 9.09W
Bombay India **62** 18.58N 72.50E
Bombo Uganda **71** 0.35N 32.32E
Bomboma Zaïre **78** 2.25N 18.54E
Bom Despacho Brazil **126** 19.46S 45.15W
Bomi China **52** 29.50N 95.45E
Bomi Hills Liberia **76** 7.01N 10.38W
Bömitz Germany **38** 53.08N 11.13E
Bömlafjorden *est.* Norway **42** 59.39N 5.20E
Bömlo *i.* Norway **42** 59.46N 5.12E
Bomokandi *r.* Zaïre **79** 3.37N 26.09E
Bomongo Zaïre **78** 1.30N 18.21E
Bomu *r.* Zaïre *see* Mbomou *r.* C.A.R. **73**
Bon, Cap *c.* Tunisia **32** 37.05N 11.03E
Bonaigarh India **63** 21.50N 84.57E
Bonaire *i.* Neth. Antilles **122** 12.15N 68.27W
Bonanza U.S.A. **108** 40.01N 109.11W
Bonaparte *r.* Canada **100** 50.46N 121.17W
Bonaparte Archipelago *is.* Australia **88** 14.17S 125.18E
Bonar-Bridge *town* U.K. **14** 57.53N 4.21W
Bonarcado Italy **32** 40.04N 8.38E
Bonavista Canada **103** 48.39N 53.07W
Bonavista, C. Canada **103** 48.42N 53.05W
Bonavista B. Canada **103** 48.45N 53.20W
Bon Bon Australia **92** 30.26S 135.28E
Bondeno Italy **30** 44.53N 11.25E
Bondo *Equator* Zaïre **78** 1.22S 23.53E
Bondo *Haut Zaïre* Zaïre **78** 3.47N 23.45E
Bondoukou Ivory Coast **76** 8.03N 2.15W
Bondowoso Indonesia **59** 7.54S 113.50E
Bone, Teluk *b.* Indonesia **59** 4.00S 120.50E
Bo'ness U.K. **14** 56.01N 3.36W
Bonfield Canada **104** 46.14N 79.10W
Bonga Ethiopia **73** 7.17N 36.15E
Bongaigaon India **63** 26.28N 90.34E
Bongak Sudan **73** 7.27N 33.14E
Bongandanga Zaïre **78** 1.28N 21.03E
Bongor Chad **77** 10.18N 15.20E
Bongos, Massif des *mts.* C.A.R. **73** 8.20N 21.35E
Bongouanou Ivory Coast **76** 6.44N 4.10W
Bonham U.S.A. **111** 33.35N 96.11W
Bonifacio France **21** 41.23N 9.10E
Bonifacio, Str. of Italy **32** 41.20N 9.15E
Bonin Is. Japan **84** 27.00N 142.10E
Bonn Germany **38** 50.44N 7.05E
Bonnechere Canada **105** 45.39N 77.35W
Bonnechère *r.* Canada **105** 45.31N 76.33W
Bonners Ferry U.S.A. **108** 48.41N 116.18W
Bonnétable France **18** 48.11N 0.26E
Bonneval France **18** 48.11N 1.24E
Bonneville France **21** 46.05N 6.25E
Bonneville Salt Flats *f.* U.S.A. **108** 40.45N 113.52W
Bonney, L. Australia **92** 37.47S 140.23E
Bonnie Rock *town* Australia **89** 30.32S 118.21E
Bonny Nigeria **77** 4.25N 7.10E
Bonny, Bight of Africa **77** 2.58N 7.00E
Bonnyville Canada **101** 54.16N 110.44W
Bonorva Italy **32** 40.25N 8.45E
Bonshaw Australia **93** 29.08S 150.53E
Bontang Indonesia **58** 0.05N 117.31E
Bonthe Sierra Leone **76** 7.32N 12.30W
Bonyhád Hungary **31** 46.19N 18.32E
Bonython Range *mts.* Australia **88** 23.51S 129.00E
Bookaloo Australia **92** 31.56S 137.21E
Boola Guinea **76** 8.22N 8.41W
Booleroo Centre Australia **92** 32.53S 138.21E
Booligal Australia **93** 33.54S 144.54E
Boom Belgium **16** 51.07N 4.21E
Boomrivier R.S.A. **80** 29.34S 20.26E
Boone U.S.A. **110** 42.04N 93.53W
Booneville U.S.A. **111** 34.39N 88.34W
Boonsboro U.S.A. **114** 39.30N 77.39W
Boonville Mo. U.S.A. **110** 38.58N 92.44W
Boonville N.Y. U.S.A. **115** 43.29N 75.20W
Boorabbin Australia **89** 31.14S 120.21E
Boorama Somali Rep. **71** 9.58N 43.07E
Boorindal Australia **93** 30.23S 146.11E
Booroorban Australia **93** 34.56S 144.46E
Boorowa Australia **93** 34.26S 148.48E
Boort Australia **92** 36.08S 143.46E
Boosaaso Somali Rep. **71** 11.13N 49.08E
Boothia, G. of Canada **99** 70.00N 90.00W
Boothia Pen. Canada **99** 70.30N 95.00W
Bootra Australia **92** 30.00S 143.00E
Booué Gabon **78** 0.00 11.58E
Bopeechee Australia **92** 29.36S 137.23E
Bophuthatswana Africa **80** 27.00S 23.30E
Boppard Germany **39** 50.14N 7.35E
Boquilla, Presa de la *l.* Mexico **109** 27.30N 105.30W
Bor Czech. **38** 49.43N 12.47E
Bor Sudan **73** 6.12N 31.33E
Bor Yugo. **29** 44.05N 22.07E
Bora Bora *i.* Is. de la Société **85** 16.30S 151.45W
Borah Peak *mtn.* U.S.A. **108** 44.08N 113.38W
Borås Sweden **43** 57.43N 12.55E
Borāzjān Iran **65** 29.14N 51.12E
Borba Brazil **122** 4.24S 59.35W
Borba Portugal **27** 38.48N 7.27W
Borda Cape *town* Australia **92** 35.45S 136.34E
Bordeaux France **20** 44.50N 0.34W
Borden Australia **89** 34.05S 118.16E
Borden I. Canada **98** 78.30N 111.00W
Borden Pen. Canada **99** 73.00N 83.00W
Borders *d.* U.K. **14** 55.30N 2.53W
Bordertown Australia **92** 36.18S 140.49E
Bordesholm Germany **38** 54.11N 10.01E
Bordheyri Iceland **40** 65.12N 21.06W
Bordighera Italy **30** 43.46N 7.39E
Bordj Bou Arreridj Algeria **75** 36.04N 4.46E
Bordj Flye Sainte Marie Algeria **74** 27.17N 2.59W
Bordj Omar Driss Algeria **75** 28.09N 6.49E
Bordö *i.* Faroe Is. **40** 62.10N 7.13W
Bore Ethiopia **73** 4.40N 37.40E
Boreda Ethiopia **73** 6.32N 37.48E
Borensberg Sweden **43** 58.34N 15.17E
Borgå Finland **41** 60.24N 25.40E
Borga Sweden **40** 64.49N 15.05E
Börgefjell *mtn.* Norway **40** 65.20N 13.45E
Börgefjell Nat. Park Norway **40** 65.00N 13.58E
Borger Neth. **16** 52.57N 6.46E
Borger U.S.A. **111** 35.39N 101.24W
Borgholm Sweden **43** 56.53N 16.39E
Borghorst Germany **16** 52.08N 7.27E
Borgo Italy **30** 46.03N 11.27E
Borgomanero Italy **30** 45.42N 8.28E
Borgo San Dalmazzo Italy **30** 44.20N 7.30E
Borgo San Lorenzo Italy **30** 43.57N 11.23E
Borgosesia Italy **30** 45.43N 8.16E
Borgo Val di Taro Italy **30** 44.29N 9.46E
Borgund Norway **41** 61.03N 7.49E
Borislav U.S.S.R. **37** 49.18N 23.28E
Borisoglebsk U.S.S.R. **45** 51.23N 42.02E
Borisov U.S.S.R. **37** 54.09N 28.30E
Borispol U.S.S.R. **37** 50.21N 30.59E
Borja Peru **122** 4.20S 77.40W
Borja Spain **25** 41.50N 1.32W
Borken Germany **38** 51.51N 6.51E
Borkou-Ennedi-Tibesti *d.* Chad **75** 18.15N 20.00E
Borkum Germany **38** 53.35N 6.40E
Borkum *i.* Germany **38** 53.35N 6.41E
Borlänge Sweden **41** 60.29N 15.25E
Borley, C. Antarctica **128** 66.15S 55.00E
Bormes-les-Mimosas France **21** 43.09N 6.20E
Bormio Italy **30** 46.28N 10.22E
Borna Germany **38** 51.07N 12.30E
Borndiep *g.* Neth. **16** 53.28N 5.35E
Borneo *i.* Asia **58** 1.00N 114.00E
Bornheim Germany **38** 50.46N 6.59E
Bornholm *i.* Denmark **43** 55.10N 15.00E
Borno *d.* Nigeria **77** 12.20N 12.40E
Bornos, Embalse de *resr.* Spain **27** 36.50N 5.42W
Bornu, Plain of *f.* Nigeria **77** 12.30N 13.00E
Boro *r.* Sudan **73** 8.52N 26.11E
Borodyanka U.S.S.R. **37** 50.38N 29.59E
Boromo Burkina **76** 11.43N 2.53W
Borotou Ivory Coast **76** 8.46N 7.30W
Boroughbridge U.K. **12** 54.06N 1.23W
Borovan Bulgaria **34** 43.27N 23.45E
Borovichi U.S.S.R. **44** 58.22N 34.00E
Borraan Somali Rep. **71** 10.10N 48.48E
Borrby Sweden **43** 55.27N 14.10E
Borrika Australia **92** 35.00S 140.05E
Borroloola Australia **90** 16.04S 136.17E
Borşa Romania **37** 46.56N 23.40E
Borşa Romania **37** 47.39N 24.40E
Borsad India **62** 22.25N 72.54E
Borth U.K. **13** 52.29N 4.03W
Bort-les-Orgues France **20** 45.24N 2.30E
Borūjerd Iran **65** 33.54N 48.47E
Bory Tucholskie *f.* Poland **37** 53.45N 17.30E
Borzhomi U.S.S.R. **45** 41.49N 43.23E
Borzna U.S.S.R. **45** 51.15N 32.25E
Borzya U.S.S.R. **51** 50.24N 116.35E
Bosa Italy **32** 40.18N 8.30E
Bosanska Dubica Yugo. **31** 45.11N 16.49E
Bosanska Gradiška Yugo. **31** 45.09N 17.15E
Bosanska Krupa Yugo. **31** 44.53N 16.10E
Bosanski Novi Yugo. **31** 45.03N 16.23E
Bosanski Petrovac Yugo. **31** 44.33N 16.22E
Bosanski Šamac Yugo. **31** 45.03N 18.28E
Bosansko Grahovo Yugo. **31** 44.11N 16.22E
Boscastle U.K. **13** 50.42N 4.42W
Bose China **55** 23.58N 106.32E
Boshan China **54** 36.29N 117.50E
Boshof R.S.A. **80** 28.32S 25.12E
Bosilegrad Yugo. **34** 42.29N 22.28E
Bosna *r.* Yugo. **31** 45.04N 18.29E
Bosna i Hercegovina *d.* Yugo. **31** 44.20N 18.00E
Bosnik Indonesia **59** 1.09S 136.14E
Bosobolo Zaïre **73** 4.11N 19.54E
Bōsō-hantō *pen.* Japan **57** 35.08N 140.00E
Bosporus *str. see* Istanbul Boğazi *str.* Turkey **29**
Bossangoa C.A.R. **77** 6.27N 17.21E
Bossembélé C.A.R. **77** 5.10N 17.44E
Bossier City U.S.A. **111** 32.31N 93.43W
Bosso Niger **77** 13.43N 13.19E
Bostān Pakistan **62** 30.26N 67.02E
Bosten Hu *l.* China **52** 42.00N 87.00E
Boston U.K. **12** 52.59N 0.02W
Boston U.S.A. **115** 42.21N 71.04W
Bosut *r.* Yugo. **31** 44.57N 19.22E
Boswell U.S.A. **114** 40.10N 79.02W
Botād India **62** 22.10N 71.40E
Botany B. Australia **93** 34.04S 151.08E
Botev *mtn.* Bulgaria **34** 42.43N 24.55E
Botevgrad Bulgaria **34** 42.54N 23.47E
Bothnia, G. of Europe **40** 63.30N 20.30E
Bothwell Canada **104** 42.38N 81.52W
Boticas Portugal **26** 41.41N 7.40W
Botletle *r.* Botswana **80** 21.06S 24.47E
Botoşani Romania **37** 47.44N 26.41E
Botou Burkina **77** 12.47N 2.02E
Botrange *mtn.* Belgium **16** 50.30N 6.04E
Botro Ivory Coast **76** 7.51N 5.19W
Botswana Africa **80** 22.00S 24.15E
Bottrop Germany **38** 51.31N 6.55E
Botucatu Brazil **126** 22.52S 48.30W
Bouaflé Ivory Coast **76** 7.01N 5.47W
Bouaké Ivory Coast **76** 7.42N 5.00W
Bouar C.A.R. **77** 5.58N 15.35E
Bou Arfa Morocco **74** 32.30N 1.59W
Bouaye France **18** 47.09N 1.42W
Bouca C.A.R. **77** 6.30N 18.21E
Bouches-du-Rhône *d.* France **21** 43.30N 5.00E
Bouchette Canada **105** 46.11N 75.59W
Bouchoir France **19** 49.45N 2.41E
Boudenib Morocco **74** 31.57N 4.38W
Boufarik Algeria **75** 36.36N 2.54E
Bougainville *i.* Pacific Oc. **84** 6.00S 155.00E
Bougouni Mali **76** 11.25N 7.28W
Bouillon Belgium **16** 49.48N 5.03E
Bouïra Algeria **75** 36.23N 3.54E
Bou-Izakarn Morocco **74** 29.09N 9.44W
Boulay-Moselle France **19** 49.11N 6.30E
Boulder Australia **89** 30.55S 121.32E
Boulder U.S.A. **110** 40.01N 105.17W
Boulder City U.S.A. **109** 35.59N 114.50W
Boulia Australia **90** 22.54S 139.54E
Boulogne France **19** 50.43N 1.37E
Boulogne *r.* France **18** 46.50N 1.25W
Boulogne-Billancourt France **19** 48.50N 2.15E
Boulogne-sur-Gesse France **20** 43.18N 0.39E
Boultoum Niger **77** 14.45N 10.25E
Boumba *r.* Cameroon **77** 2.00N 15.10E
Boumdeit Mauritania **74** 17.26N 9.50W
Boumo Chad **77** 9.01N 16.24E
Bouna Ivory Coast **76** 9.19N 2.53W
Boundary Peak *mtn.* U.S.A. **108** 37.51N 118.21W
Boundiali Ivory Coast **76** 9.30N 6.31W
Bountiful U.S.A. **108** 40.53N 111.53W
Bounty Is. Pacific Oc. **84** 48.00S 178.30E
Bouraga *well* Mali **76** 19.00N 3.36W
Bourail N. Cal. **84** 21.34S 165.30E
Bourbon-Lancy France **19** 46.38N 3.46E
Bourbonne-les-Bains France **19** 47.57N 5.45E
Bourem Mali **76** 16.59N 0.20W
Bourg France **21** 46.12N 5.13E
Bourganeuf France **20** 45.57N 1.46E
Bourges France **19** 47.05N 2.24E
Bourget Canada **105** 45.26N 75.09W
Bourget, Lac du *l.* France **21** 45.44N 5.52E
Bourg Madame France **20** 42.26N 1.55E
Bourgneuf-en-Retz France **18** 47.02N 1.57W
Bourgogne *d.* France **19** 47.10N 4.20E
Bourgogne, Canal de France **19** 47.58N 3.30E
Bourgoin France **21** 45.36N 5.17E
Bourg-St. Andéol France **21** 44.22N 4.39E
Bourg-St. Maurice France **21** 45.37N 6.46E
Bourgueil France **18** 47.17N 0.10E
Bourke Australia **93** 30.09S 145.59E
Bournemouth U.K. **13** 50.43N 1.53W
Bou Saâda Algeria **75** 35.12N 4.11E
Bou Salem Tunisia **32** 36.36N 8.59E
Boussac France **20** 46.21N 2.13E
Bousso Chad **77** 10.32N 16.45E
Bouteldja Algeria **32** 36.47N 8.13E
Boutilimit Mauritania **74** 17.33N 14.42W
Boutonne *r.* France **20** 45.53N 0.50W
Bouvard, C. Australia **89** 32.40S 115.34E
Bouvetöya *i.* Atlantic Oc. **127** 54.26S 3.24E
Bovalino Marino Italy **33** 38.09N 16.11E
Bovec Yugo. **31** 46.20N 13.33E
Bovill U.S.A. **108** 46.51N 116.24W
Bovril Argentina **125** 31.22S 59.25W
Bow *r.* Canada **100** 51.10N 115.00W
Bowelling Australia **89** 33.25S 116.27E
Bowen Australia **90** 20.00S 148.15E
Bowen, Mt. Australia **93** 37.11S 148.34E
Bowie Ariz. U.S.A. **109** 32.19N 109.29W
Bowie Tex. U.S.A. **111** 33.34N 97.51W
Bow Island *town* Canada **101** 49.52N 111.22W
Bowling Green U.S.A. **113** 37.00N 86.29W
Bowling Green, C. Australia **90** 19.19S 146.25E
Bowman U.S.A. **110** 46.11N 103.24W
Bowman I. Antarctica **128** 65.00S 104.00E
Bowmanville Canada **104** 43.55N 78.41W
Bowral Australia **93** 34.30S 150.24E
Bowser Australia **93** 36.19S 146.23E
Boxholm Sweden **43** 58.12N 15.03E
Bo Xian China **54** 33.50N 115.46E
Boxing China **54** 37.08N 118.05E
Box Tank Australia **92** 32.13S 142.17E
Boxtel Neth. **16** 51.36N 5.20E
Boyabat Turkey **64** 41.27N 34.45E
Boyang China **55** 28.59N 116.42E
Boyanup Australia **89** 33.29S 115.40E
Boyarka U.S.S.R. **37** 50.20N 30.26E
Boyd *r.* Australia **93** 29.51S 152.25E
Boykétté C.A.R. **73** 5.28N 20.50E
Boyle Rep. of Ire. **15** 53.58N 8.19W
Boyne *r.* Rep. of Ire. **15** 53.43N 6.17W
Boyoma Falls *f.* Zaïre **78** 0.18N 25.32E
Boyup Brook Australia **89** 33.50S 116.22E
Bozburun Turkey **35** 36.43N 28.08E
Bozcaada Turkey **34** 39.49N 26.03E
Bozca Ada *i.* Turkey **34** 39.49N 26.03E
Bozel France **21** 45.27N 6.39E
Bozeman U.S.A. **108** 45.41N 111.02W
Bozen *see* Bolzano Italy **30**
Bozoum C.A.R. **77** 6.16N 16.22E
Bra Italy **30** 44.42N 7.51E
Braås Sweden **43** 57.04N 15.03E
Brabant *d.* Belgium **16** 50.47N 4.30E
Brač *i.* Yugo. **29** 43.20N 16.38E
Bracadale, Loch U.K. **14** 57.22N 6.30W
Bracciano Italy **32** 42.06N 12.10E
Bracciano, Lago di *l.* Italy **30** 42.07N 12.14E
Bracebridge Canada **104** 45.02N 79.19W
Bracieux France **19** 47.33N 1.33E
Bräcke Sweden **40** 62.44N 15.30E
Brački Kanal *str.* Yugo. **31** 43.24N 16.40E
Brad Romania **29** 46.06N 22.48E
Bradano *r.* Italy **33** 40.23N 16.51E
Bradenton U.S.A. **113** 27.29N 82.33W
Bradford Canada **104** 44.07N 79.34W
Bradford U.K. **12** 53.47N 1.45W
Bradford N.H. U.S.A. **115** 43.17N 71.59W
Bradford Penn. U.S.A. **114** 41.58N 78.39W
Bradford Vt. U.S.A. **105** 43.59N 72.09W
Bradley U.S.A. **111** 33.06N 93.39W
Bradworthy U.K. **13** 50.54N 4.22W
Brady U.S.A. **111** 31.08N 99.20W
Braemar U.K. **14** 57.01N 3.24W
Braga Portugal **26** 41.33N 8.26W
Braga *d.* Portugal **26** 41.30N 8.05W
Bragado Argentina **125** 35.10S 60.30W
Bragança Brazil **123** 1.03S 46.46W
Bragança Portugal **26** 41.49N 6.45W
Bragança *d.* Portugal **26** 41.30N 6.50W
Bragança Paulista Brazil **126** 22.59S 46.32W
Bragin U.S.S.R. **37** 51.49N 30.16E
Brāhmanbāria Bangla. **63** 23.59N 91.07E
Brāhmani *r.* India **63** 20.39N 86.46E
Brahmaputra *r.* Asia **63** 23.50N 89.45E
Braidwood Australia **93** 35.27S 149.50E
Brăila Romania **37** 45.18N 27.58E
Brainerd U.S.A. **107** 46.20N 94.10W
Braintree U.K. **13** 51.53N 0.32E
Brake Germany **38** 53.19N 8.28E
Brakna *d.* Mauritania **74** 17.00N 13.20W
Brålanda Sweden **43** 58.34N 12.22E
Bramfield Australia **92** 33.37S 134.59E
Bramming Denmark **42** 55.28N 8.42E
Brampton Canada **104** 43.41N 79.46W
Brampton U.K. **12** 54.56N 2.43W
Bramsche Germany **38** 52.24N 7.58E
Brancaleone Marina Italy **33** 37.58N 16.06E
Branco *r.* Brazil **122** 1.00S 62.00W
Brandberg *mtn.* Namibia **80** 21.08S 14.35E
Brandbu Norway **41** 60.28N 10.30E
Brande Denmark **42** 55.57N 9.07E
Brandenburg Germany **38** 52.24N 12.32E
Brandenburg *d.* Germany **38** 52.15N 13.10E
Brandenburg *f.* Germany **38** 52.40N 13.00E
Brandfort R.S.A. **80** 28.41S 26.27E
Brandon Canada **101** 49.50N 99.57W
Brandon U.S.A. **105** 43.48N 73.05W
Brandon Mtn. Rep. of Ire. **15** 52.14N 10.15W
Brandon Pt. Rep. of Ire. **15** 52.17N 10.11W
Braniewo Poland **37** 54.24N 19.50E
Bransby Australia **92** 28.40S 142.00E
Branson U.S.A. **111** 36.39N 93.13W
Brantas *r.* Indonesia **59** 7.13S 112.45E
Brantford Canada **104** 43.08N 80.16W
Brantôme France **20** 45.22N 0.39E
Bras d'Or L. Canada **103** 45.52N 60.50W
Brasher Falls U.S.A. **105** 44.48N 74.48W
Brasil, Planalto *mts.* Brazil **123** 17.02S 50.00W
Brasiléia Brazil **122** 11.00S 68.44W
Brasília Brazil **123** 15.45S 47.57W
Braşov Romania **37** 45.40N 25.35E
Brass Nigeria **77** 4.20N 6.15E
Brasschaat Belgium **16** 51.18N 4.28E
Bratislava Czech. **37** 48.10N 17.10E
Bratsk U.S.S.R. **51** 56.20N 101.15E
Bratsk Vodokhranilishche *resr.* U.S.S.R. **51** 54.40N 103.00E
Bratslav U.S.S.R. **37** 48.49N 28.51E
Brattleboro U.S.A. **115** 42.51N 72.34W
Braunau Austria **39** 48.15N 13.02E
Braunschweig Germany **38** 52.16N 10.31E
Braunton U.K. **13** 51.06N 4.09W
Bråviken *b.* Sweden **43** 58.38N 16.32E
Bravo del Norte, Rio *r.* Mexico *see* Rio Grande *r.* Mexico/U.S.A. **111**
Brawley U.S.A. **109** 32.59N 115.31W
Bray France **19** 48.25N 3.14E
Bray Rep. of Ire. **15** 53.12N 6.07W
Bray Head Kerry Rep. of Ire. **15** 51.53N 10.26W
Brazeau *r.* Canada **100** 52.55N 115.15W
Brazil S. America **120** 10.00S 52.00W
Brazilian Basin *f.* Atlantic Oc. **127** 15.00S 25.00W
Brazilian Highlands *see* Brasil, Planalto *mts.* Brazil **123**
Brazos *r.* U.S.A. **111** 28.53N 95.23W
Brazzaville Congo **78** 4.14S 15.10E
Brčko Yugo. **31** 44.53N 18.48E
Brda *r.* Poland **37** 53.07N 18.08E
Breadalbane *f.* U.K. **14** 56.30N 4.20W
Bream B. New Zealand **86** 36.00S 174.30E
Brebes Indonesia **59** 6.54S 109.00E
Brécey France **18** 48.44N 1.10W
Brechin U.K. **14** 56.44N 2.40W
Breckenridge *Mich.* U.S.A. **104** 43.24N 84.29W
Breckenridge *Tex.* U.S.A. **111** 32.45N 98.54W
Breckland *f.* U.K. **13** 52.28N 0.40E
Břeclav Czech. **36** 48.46N 16.53E
Brecon U.K. **13** 51.57N 3.23W
Brecon Beacons *mts.* U.K. **13** 51.53N 3.27W
Breda Neth. **16** 51.35N 4.46E
Bredasdorp R.S.A. **80** 34.31S 20.03E
Bredbo Australia **93** 35.57S 149.10E
Bredstedt Germany **38** 54.37N 8.59E
Breezewood U.S.A. **114** 40.01N 78.15W
Bregalnica *r.* Yugo. **34** 41.50N 22.20E
Bregenz Austria **39** 47.30N 9.46E
Bregovo Bulgaria **29** 44.08N 22.39E
Bréhal France **18** 48.54N 1.31W
Breidhafjördhur *est.* Iceland **40** 65.15N 23.00W
Breim Norway **41** 61.44N 6.25E
Breisach Germany **39** 48.01N 7.40E
Brekstad Norway **40** 63.42N 9.40E
Bremangerland *i.* Norway **41** 61.51N 5.02E
Bremen Germany **38** 53.05N 8.49E
Bremen *d.* Germany **38** 53.08N 8.46E
Bremen U.S.A. **114** 39.42N 82.26W
Bremer Bay *town* Australia **89** 34.21S 119.20E

Bremerhaven to **Burkina**

Bremerhaven Germany **38** 53.33N 8.34E
Bremer Range *mts.* Australia **89** 32.40S120.55E
Bremerton U.S.A. **108** 47.34N122.38W
Bremervörde Germany **38** 53.29N 9.08E
Brenes Spain **27** 37.33N 5.52W
Brenham U.S.A. **111** 30.10N 96.24W
Brenner Pass Austria/Italy **39** 47.00N 11.30E
Breno Italy **30** 45.57N 10.18E
Brent Canada **104** 46.02N 78.29W
Brenta *r.* Italy **30** 45.11N 12.18E
Brentwood U.K. **13** 51.38N 0.18E
Brescia Italy **30** 45.33N 10.15E
Breskens Neth. **16** 51.24N 3.34E
Bresle *r.* France **19** 50.04N 1.22E
Bressanone Italy **30** 46.43N 11.39E
Bressay *i.* U.K. **14** 60.08N 1.05W
Bresse, Plaine de *f.* France **19** 46.20N 5.10E
Bressuire France **18** 46.51N 0.30W
Brest Bulgaria **34** 43.38N 24.35E
Brest France **18** 48.24N 4.29W
Brest U.S.S.R. **37** 52.08N 23.40E
Brestanica Yugo. **31** 45.59N 15.29E
Brest-Nantes Canal France **18** 48.13N 3.26W
Bretagne *d.* France **18** 48.15N 2.30W
Breteuil France **19** 49.38N 2.18E
Breteuil-sur-Iton France **18** 48.50N 0.55E
Breton, Pertuis *str.* France **20** 46.25N 1.20W
Breton Sd. U.S.A. **111** 29.30N 89.30W
Brett, C. New Zealand **86** 35.15S174.20E
Bretten Germany **39** 49.02N 8.42E
Breuil-Cervinia Italy **30** 45.56N 7.38E
Brevik Norway **42** 59.04N 9.42E
Brewarrina Australia **93** 29.57S147.54E
Brewer U.S.A. **112** 44.48N 68.46W
Brewster N.Y. U.S.A. **115** 41.24N 73.37W
Brewster Ohio U.S.A. **114** 40.43N 81.36W
Brewster, Kap *c.* Greenland **96** 70.00N 25.00W
Brewton U.S.A. **113** 31.07N 87.04W
Brežice Yugo. **31** 45.54N 15.36E
Březniče Czech. **38** 49.33N 13.57E
Breznik Bulgaria **34** 42.44N 22.50E
Brezovo Bulgaria **34** 42.20N 25.06E
Bria C.A.R. **73** 6.32N 21.59E
Briançon France **21** 44.54N 6.39E
Briare France **19** 47.38N 2.44E
Bribbaree Australia **93** 34.07S147.51E
Brichany U.S.S.R. **37** 48.20N 27.01E
Bricquebec France **18** 49.28N 1.38W
Bride U.K. **12** 54.23N 4.24W
Bridge *r.* Canada **100** 50.50N122.40W
Bridgen Canada **104** 42.47N 82.16W
Bridgend U.K. **13** 51.30N 3.35W
Bridgeport Calif. U.S.A. **108** 38.10N119.13W
Bridgeport Conn. U.S.A. **115** 41.11N 73.11W
Bridgeport Nebr. U.S.A. **110** 41.40N103.06W
Bridgeport Tex. U.S.A. **111** 33.13N 97.45W
Bridgeport W.Va. U.S.A. **114** 39.17N 80.15W
Bridger U.S.A. **108** 45.18N108.55W
Bridgeton U.S.A. **115** 39.26N 75.14W
Bridgetown Australia **89** 33.57S116.08E
Bridgetown Barbados **117** 13.06N 59.37W
Bridgetown Canada **103** 44.51N 65.18W
Bridgetown Rep. of Ire. **15** 52.14N 6.33W
Bridgeville U.S.A. **115** 38.45N 75.36W
Bridgewater Canada **103** 44.23N 64.31W
Bridgewater U.S.A. **114** 38.18N 78.59W
Bridgewater, C. Australia **92** 38.25S141.28E
Bridgnorth U.K. **13** 52.33N 2.25W
Bridgwater U.K. **13** 51.08N 3.00W
Bridlington U.K. **12** 54.06N 0.11W
Brie *f.* France **19** 48.40N 3.20E
Briec France **18** 48.06N 4.00W
Brienne-le-Château France **19** 48.24N 4.32E
Brienz Switz. **19** 46.46N 8.03E
Briey France **19** 49.15N 5.56E
Brig Switz. **19** 46.19N 8.00E
Brigantine U.S.A. **115** 39.24N 74.22W
Brigg U.K. **12** 53.33N 0.30W
Briggsdale U.S.A. **110** 40.38N104.20W
Brigham City U.S.A. **108** 41.31N112.01W
Bright Australia **93** 36.42S146.58E
Brighton Canada **105** 44.02N 77.44W
Brighton U.K. **13** 50.50N 0.09W
Brighton Colo. U.S.A. **108** 39.59N104.49W
Brighton Fla. U.S.A. **113** 27.13N 81.06W
Brighton Mich. U.S.A. **104** 42.32N 83.47W
Brignoles France **21** 43.24N 6.04E
Brihuega Spain **26** 40.48N 2.52W
Brikama Gambia **76** 13.15N 16.39W
Brilon Germany **38** 51.24N 8.34E
Brindisi Italy **33** 40.38N 17.56E
Brinje Yugo. **31** 45.00N 15.08E
Brinkley U.S.A. **111** 34.53N 91.12W
Brinkworth Australia **92** 33.42S138.24E
Brionne France **18** 49.12N 0.43E
Brioude France **20** 45.18N 3.23E
Briouze France **18** 48.42N 0.22W
Brisbane Australia **93** 27.30S153.00E
Brisighella Italy **30** 44.13N 11.46E
Bristol U.K. **13** 51.26N 2.35W
Bristol Conn. U.S.A. **115** 41.41N 72.57W
Bristol N.H. U.S.A. **115** 43.36N 71.45W
Bristol Penn. U.S.A. **115** 40.06N 74.52W
Bristol R.I. U.S.A. **115** 41.40N 71.16W
Bristol S.Dak. U.S.A. **110** 45.21N 97.45W
Bristol Tenn. U.S.A. **113** 36.33N 82.11W
Bristol Vt. U.S.A. **105** 44.08N 73.05W
Bristol B. U.S.A. **98** 58.00N158.50W
Bristol Channel U.K. **13** 51.17N 3.20W
British Antarctic Territory Antarctica **128** 70.00S 50.00W
British Columbia *d.* Canada **100** 55.00N125.00W
British Mts. Canada **98** 69.00N140.20W
British Virgin Is. C. America **117** 18.30N 64.30W
Britstown R.S.A. **80** 30.34S 23.30E
Britt Canada **104** 45.46N 80.35W
Britton U.S.A. **110** 45.48N 97.45W
Brive France **20** 45.10N 1.32E
Briviesca Spain **26** 42.33N 3.19W
Brixham U.K. **13** 50.24N 3.31W
Brno Czech. **36** 49.11N 16.39E
Broach India **62** 21.42N 72.58E
Broad Arrow Australia **89** 30.32S121.20E
Broad B. U.K. **14** 58.15N 6.15W
Broadback *r.* Canada **102** 51.20N 78.50W
Broadford Australia **93** 37.16S145.03E
Broadmere Australia **90** 25.30S149.30E
Broad Sd. Australia **90** 22.20S149.50E
Broadsound Range *mts.* Australia **90** 22.30S149.30E
Broadus U.S.A. **108** 45.27N105.25W
Broadview Canada **101** 50.20N102.30W
Broadway U.K. **13** 52.02N 1.51W
Brochet Canada **101** 57.53N101.40W
Brochet, L. Canada **101** 58.36N101.35W
Brocken *mtn.* Germany **38** 51.50N 10.50E
Brockport U.S.A. **114** 43.13N 77.56W
Brockton U.S.A. **115** 42.05N 71.01W
Brockville Canada **105** 44.35N 75.41W
Brockway Mont. U.S.A. **108** 47.15N105.45W
Brockway Penn. U.S.A. **114** 41.15N 78.47W
Brocton U.S.A. **114** 42.23N 79.27W
Brod Hrvatska Yugo. **31** 45.10N 18.01E
Brod Makedonija Yugo. **34** 41.35N 21.17E
Brodeur Pen. Canada **99** 73.00N 88.00W
Brodick U.K. **14** 55.34N 5.09W
Brodnica Poland **37** 53.16N 19.23E
Brody U.S.S.R. **37** 50.05N 25.08E
Broglie France **18** 49.01N 0.32E
Broke Inlet Australia **89** 34.55S116.25E
Broken Arrow U.S.A. **111** 36.03N 95.48W
Broken B. Australia **93** 33.34S151.18E
Broken Bow U.S.A. **110** 41.24N 99.38W
Broken Hill *town* Australia **92** 31.57S141.30E
Bromley U.K. **13** 51.24N 0.02E
Bromley Plateau *f.* Atlantic Oc. **127** 30.00S 34.00W
Bromölla Sweden **43** 56.04N 14.28E
Bromsgrove U.K. **11** 52.20N 2.03W
Bron France **21** 45.44N 4.55E
Brönderslev Denmark **42** 57.16N 9.58E
Brong-Ahafo *d.* Ghana **76** 7.45N 1.30W
Brönnöysund Norway **40** 65.30N 12.10E
Bronte Canada **104** 43.23N 79.43W
Bronte Italy **33** 37.48N 14.50E
Brooke's Point *town* Phil. **58** 8.50N117.52E
Brookfield U.S.A. **110** 39.47N 93.04W
Brookhaven U.S.A. **111** 31.35N 90.26W
Brookings Oreg. U.S.A. **108** 42.03N124.17W
Brookings S.Dak. U.S.A. **110** 44.19N 96.48W
Brooklin Canada **104** 43.57N 78.57W
Brooklyn U.S.A. **104** 42.06N 84.15W
Brooklyn Center U.S.A. **110** 45.05N 93.20W
Brooks Canada **98** 50.35N111.53W
Brooks B. Canada **100** 50.15N127.55W
Brooks Range *mts.* U.S.A. **98** 68.50N152.00W
Brooksville U.S.A. **113** 28.34N 82.24W
Brookton Australia **89** 32.22S117.01E
Brookville U.S.A. **114** 41.09N 79.05W
Broom, Loch U.K. **14** 57.52N 5.07W
Broome Australia **88** 17.58S122.15E
Broome, Mt. Australia **88** 17.21S125.23E
Broomehill *town* Australia **89** 33.50S117.35E
Broons France **18** 48.19N 2.16W
Brora U.K. **14** 58.01N 3.52W
Brora *r.* U.K. **14** 58.00N 3.51W
Brörup Denmark **42** 55.29N 9.01E
Brosna *r.* Rep.of Ire. **15** 53.13N 7.58W
Brossac France **20** 45.20N 0.03W
Brothers U.S.A. **108** 43.49N120.36W
Broto Spain **25** 42.36N 0.06W
Brou France **18** 48.13N 1.11E
Brough England U.K. **12** 54.32N 2.19W
Brough Scotland U.K. **14** 60.29N 1.12W
Broughton *r.* Australia **92** 33.21S137.46E
Broughton in Furness U.K. **12** 54.17N 3.12W
Brouwershaven Neth. **16** 51.44N 3.53E
Brovary U.S.S.R. **37** 50.30N 30.45E
Brovst Denmark **42** 57.06N 9.32E
Brown, Mt. Australia **92** 32.33S138.02E
Brown City U.S.A. **114** 43.13N 82.59W
Brownfield U.S.A. **111** 33.11N102.16W
Browning U.S.A. **108** 48.34N113.01W
Brownsburg Canada **105** 45.41N 74.25W
Brownsville Penn. U.S.A. **114** 40.01N 79.53W
Brownsville Tenn. U.S.A. **111** 35.36N 89.15W
Brownsville Tex. U.S.A. **111** 25.54N 97.30W
Brownville U.S.A. **105** 44.01N 75.59W
Brownwood U.S.A. **111** 31.43N 98.59W
Brozas Spain **27** 39.37N 6.46W
Bruay-en-Artois France **19** 50.29N 2.33E
Bruce Mines Canada **104** 46.18N 83.48W
Bruce Pen. Canada **104** 45.00N 81.20W
Bruce Rock *town* Australia **89** 31.52S118.09E
Bruche *r.* France **19** 48.31N 7.41E
Bruchsal Germany **39** 49.07N 8.35E
Bruck Austria **39** 47.17N 12.49E
Brückenau Germany **39** 50.18N 9.47E
Bruges *see* Brugge Belgium **16**
Brugg Switz. **19** 47.29N 8.12E
Brugge Belgium **16** 51.13N 3.14E
Brühl Germany **38** 50.48N 6.54E
Brûlé, Lac *l.* *Que.* Canada **105** 46.57N 77.13W
Brûlé, Lac *l.* *Que.* Canada **103** 52.17N 63.52W
Brumadinho Brazil **126** 20.09S 44.11W
Brumado Brazil **123** 14.13S 41.40W
Brumath France **19** 48.44N 7.43E
Brunei Asia **58** 4.56N114.58E
Brünen Germany **38** 51.43N 6.39E
Brunflo Sweden **40** 63.04N 14.50E
Brunico Italy **30** 46.48N 11.56E
Brunkeberg Norway **42** 59.26N 8.29E
Brunner New Zealand **86** 42.28S171.12E
Brunsbüttel Germany **38** 53.54N 9.05E
Brunssum Neth. **16** 50.57N 5.59E
Brunswick Ga. U.S.A. **113** 31.09N 81.30W
Brunswick Maine U.S.A. **112** 43.55N 69.58W
Brunswick Md. U.S.A. **114** 39.18N 77.37W
Brunswick B. Australia **88** 15.05S125.00E
Brunswick Junction Australia **89** 33.15S115.45E
Bruny I. Australia **91** 43.15S147.16E
Brushton U.S.A. **105** 44.51N 74.30W
Brusilovka U.S.S.R. **45** 50.39N 54.59E
Brussel *see* Bruxelles Belgium **16**
Brussels *see* Bruxelles Belgium **16**
Bruthen Australia **93** 37.44S147.49E
Bruton U.K. **13** 51.06N 2.28W
Bruxelles Belgium **16** 50.50N 4.23E
Bruyères France **19** 48.12N 6.43E
Bryagovo Bulgaria **34** 41.58N 25.08E
Bryan Ohio U.S.A. **112** 41.30N 84.34W
Bryan Tex. U.S.A. **111** 30.40N 96.22W
Bryan, Mt. Australia **92** 33.26S138.27E
Bryansk U.S.S.R. **44** 53.15N 34.09E
Bryne Norway **42** 58.44N 5.39E
Bryson Canada **105** 45.40N 76.36W
Bryson, Lac *l.* Canada **105** 46.27N 77.00W
Bryson City U.S.A. **113** 35.26N 83.27W
Brzeg Poland **37** 50.52N 17.27E
Bsharrī Lebanon **66** 34.15N 36.00E
Bua *r.* Malaŵi **79** 12.42S 34.15E
Bua Yai Thailand **56** 15.34N102.24E
Bu'ayrāt al Ḩasūn Libya **75** 31.24N 15.44E
Buba Guinea Bissau **76** 11.36N 14.55W
Būbiyān, Jazīrat *i.* Kuwait **71** 29.45N 48.15E
Bubye *r.* Zimbabwe **80** 22.18S 31.00E
Bucak Turkey **64** 37.28N 30.36E
Bucaramanga Colombia **122** 7.08N 73.10W
Buccino Italy **33** 40.37N 15.23E
Buchach U.S.S.R. **37** 49.09N 25.20E
Buchanan Liberia **76** 5.57N 10.02W
Buchanan, L. Australia **90** 21.28S145.52E
Buchanan L. U.S.A. **111** 30.48N 98.25W
Buchan Ness *c.* U.K. **14** 57.28N 1.47W
Buchans Canada **103** 48.49N 56.52W
Bucharest *see* Bucureşti Romania **37**
Buchen Germany **39** 49.32N 9.12E
Buchloe Germany **39** 48.02N 10.44E
Bucholz Germany **38** 53.20N 9.52E
Buchs Switz. **39** 47.10N 9.28E
Buchy France **18** 49.35N 1.22E
Buckambool Mt. Australia **93** 31.55S145.40E
Bückeburg Germany **38** 52.16N 9.02E
Buckeye Lake *town* U.S.A. **114** 39.56N 82.29W
Buckhannon U.S.A. **114** 38.59N 80.14W
Buckhaven and Methil U.K. **12** 56.11N 3.03W
Buckhorn Canada **104** 44.33N 78.20W
Buckhorn L. Canada **104** 44.28N 78.23W
Buckie U.K. **14** 57.40N 2.58W
Buckingham Canada **105** 45.35N 75.25W
Buckingham U.K. **13** 52.00N 0.59W
Buckingham B. Australia **90** 12.10S135.46E
Buckinghamshire *d.* U.K. **13** 51.50N 0.48W
Buckland Tableland *f.* Australia **90** 25.00S148.00E
Buckleboo Australia **92** 32.55S136.12E
Buckley U.S.A. **110** 40.35N 88.04W
Bucklin U.S.A. **111** 37.33N 99.38W
Buco Zau Angola **78** 4.46S 12.34E
Bucquoy France **19** 50.08N 2.42E
Bu Craa W. Sahara **74** 26.21N 12.57W
Buctouche Canada **103** 46.28N 64.43W
Bucureşti Romania **37** 44.25N 26.06E
Bucyrus U.S.A. **114** 40.48N 82.58W
Bud Norway **40** 62.54N 6.56E
Budapest Hungary **37** 47.30N 19.03E
Budaun India **63** 28.03N 79.07E
Budda Australia **92** 31.12S144.16E
Budd Coast *f.* Antarctica **128** 67.00S112.00E
Buddh Gaya India **63** 24.42N 84.59E
Buddusò Italy **32** 40.35N 9.16E
Bude U.K. **13** 50.49N 4.33W
Bude B. U.K. **13** 50.50N 4.40W
Budennovsk U.S.S.R. **45** 44.50N 44.10E
Büdingen Germany **39** 50.17N 9.07E
Budjala Zaïre **78** 2.38N 19.48E
Buea Cameroon **77** 4.09N 9.13E
Buenaventura Colombia **122** 3.54N 77.02W
Buenaventura Mexico **109** 29.51N107.29W
Buena Vista U.S.A. **113** 37.44N 79.22W
Buendia, Embalse de *resr.* Spain **26** 40.25N 2.43W
Buenos Aires Argentina **125** 34.40S 58.25W
Buenos Aires *d.* Argentina **125** 36.30S 59.00W
Buenos Aires, L. Argentina/Chile **125** 46.35S 72.00W
Buffalo Canada **101** 50.49N110.42W
Buffalo *r.* Canada **100** 60.55N115.00W
Buffalo Mo. U.S.A. **111** 37.39N 93.06W
Buffalo N.Y. U.S.A. **114** 42.54N 78.53W
Buffalo Okla. U.S.A. **111** 36.50N 99.38W
Buffalo S.Dak. U.S.A. **110** 45.35N103.33W
Buffalo W.Va. U.S.A. **114** 38.39N 81.57W
Buffalo Wyo. U.S.A. **108** 44.21N106.42W
Buffalo Head Hills Canada **100** 57.25N115.55W
Buffalo L. Canada **100** 60.10N115.30W
Buffalo Narrows *town* Canada **101** 55.51N108.30W
Bug *r.* Poland **37** 52.29N 21.11E
Buga Colombia **122** 3.53N 76.17W
Bugaldie Australia **93** 31.02S149.08E
Bugeat France **20** 45.35N 1.59E
Bugembe Uganda **79** 0.26N 33.16E
Bugene Tanzania **79** 1.34S 31.07E
Buggs Island L. U.S.A. **113** 36.35N 78.28W
Bugojno Yugo. **31** 44.03N 17.27E
Bugrino U.S.S.R. **44** 68.45N 49.15E
Bugt China **53** 48.45N121.58E
Bugulma U.S.S.R. **44** 54.32N 52.46E
Buguma Nigeria **77** 4.43N 6.53E
Buguruslan U.S.S.R. **44** 53.36N 52.30E
Buhera Zimbabwe **81** 19.21S 31.25E
Bühl Germany **39** 48.42N 8.08E
Buhuşi Romania **37** 46.43N 26.41E
Builth Wells U.K. **13** 52.09N 3.24W
Buinsk U.S.S.R. **44** 54.58N 48.15E
Bu'in-Sofiā Iran **65** 35.51N 46.02E
Buitenpost Neth. **16** 53.15N 6.09E
Bujalance Spain **27** 37.54N 4.22W
Bujaraloz Spain **25** 41.30N 0.09W
Buje Yugo. **31** 45.24N 13.40E
Buji P.N.G. **90** 9.07S142.26E
Bujumbura Burundi **79** 3.22S 29.21E
Bukama Zaïre **78** 9.16S 25.52E
Bukavu Zaïre **79** 2.30S 28.49E
Bukene Tanzania **79** 4.13S 32.52E
Bukhara U.S.S.R. **65** 39.47N 64.26E
Buki U.S.S.R. **37** 49.02N 30.29E
Bukima Tanzania **79** 1.48S 33.25E
Bukittinggi Indonesia **58** 0.18S100.20E
Bukoba Tanzania **79** 1.20S 31.49E
Bukovica *f.* Yugo. **31** 44.10N 15.40E
Bukrale Ethiopia **73** 4.30N 42.03E
Bukuru Nigeria **77** 9.48N 8.52E
Būl, Kūh-e *mtn.* Iran **65** 30.48N 52.45E
Bula Indonesia **59** 3.07S130.27E
Bülach Switz. **39** 47.31N 8.32E
Bulahdelah Australia **93** 32.25S152.13E
Bulan Phil. **59** 12.40N123.53E
Bulandshahr India **63** 28.24N 77.51E
Bulawayo Zimbabwe **80** 20.10S 28.43E
Bulbjerg *hill* Denmark **42** 57.09N 9.02E
Buldāna India **62** 20.32N 76.11E
Buldern Germany **16** 51.52N 7.21E
Bulgan Mongolia **52** 48.34N103.12E
Bulgaria Europe **34** 42.35N 25.30E
Bullabulling Australia **89** 31.05S120.52E
Bullaque *r.* Spain **27** 38.59N 4.17W
Bullara Australia **88** 22.40S114.03E
Bullas Spain **25** 38.03N 1.40W
Bullaxaar Somali Rep. **71** 10.23N 44.27E
Bulle Switz. **39** 46.37N 7.04E
Buller *r.* New Zealand **86** 41.45S171.35E
Buller, Mt. Australia **93** 37.11S146.26E
Bullfinch Australia **89** 30.59S119.06E
Bulli Australia **93** 34.20S150.55E
Bull Mts. U.S.A. **108** 46.05N109.00W
Bulloo *r.* Australia **92** 28.43S142.27E
Bulloo Downs *town* Australia **92** 28.30S142.45E
Bull Run Mtn. U.S.A. **114** 38.52N 77.53W
Bull Shoals L. U.S.A. **111** 36.30N 92.50W
Bulolo P.N.G. **59** 7.13S146.35E
Bulsār India **62** 20.38N 72.56E
Bultfontein R.S.A. **80** 28.17S 26.09E
Bulu Indonesia **59** 4.34N126.45E
Bulu, Gunung *mtn.* Indonesia **58** 3.00N116.00E
Bulun U.S.S.R. **51** 70.50N127.20E
Bulunde Tanzania **79** 4.19S 32.57E
Bumba Bandundu Zaïre **78** 6.55S 19.16E
Bumba Equateur Zaïre **78** 2.15N 22.32E
Bumbuli Zaïre **78** 3.25S 20.30E
Buna Kenya **79** 2.49N 39.27E
Buna P.N.G. **90** 8.40S148.25E
Bunbury Australia **89** 33.20S115.34E
Buncrana Rep. of Ire. **15** 55.08N 7.27W
Bundaberg Australia **90** 24.50S152.21E
Bundaleer Australia **93** 28.39S146.31E
Bundarra Australia **93** 30.11S151.04E
Bunde Nschn. Germany **38** 53.11N 7.16E
Bünde Nschn. Germany **38** 52.12N 8.35E
Bundella Australia **93** 31.35S149.59E
Bündi India **62** 25.27N 75.39E
Bundoran Rep. of Ire. **15** 54.28N 8.17W
Bündu India **63** 23.11N 85.35E
Bungay U.K. **13** 52.27N 1.26E
Bungo Angola **78** 7.26S 15.23E
Bungo suidō *str.* Japan **57** 32.52N132.30E
Bungu Tanzania **79** 7.37S 39.07E
Buni Nigeria **77** 11.20N 11.59E
Bunia Zaïre **79** 1.30N 30.10E
Buninyong Australia **92** 37.41S143.58E
Bunker Hill *town* U.S.A. **114** 39.22N 78.04W
Bunkie U.S.A. **111** 30.57N 92.11W
Buñol Spain **25** 39.25N 0.47W
Bunyala Kenya **71** 0.07N 34.00E
Bunyan Australia **93** 36.11S149.09E
Buol Indonesia **59** 1.12N121.28E
Buqayq Saudi Arabia **65** 25.55N 49.40E
Bura Coast Kenya **79** 1.09S 39.55E
Bura Coast Kenya **79** 3.30S 38.19E
Burakin Australia **89** 30.30S117.08E
Burang China **63** 30.16N 81.11E
Buras U.S.A. **111** 29.21N 89.32W
Buraydah Saudi Arabia **65** 26.18N 43.58E
Burbach Germany **38** 50.45N 8.05E
Burcher Australia **93** 33.32S147.18E
Burco Somali Rep. **71** 9.30N 45.30E
Burdur Turkey **23** 37.44N 30.17E
Burdwān India **63** 23.15N 87.51E
Bure Ethiopia **73** 10.40N 37.04E
Büren Germany **38** 51.33N 8.33E
Burford Canada **104** 43.06N 80.26W
Burg Germany **38** 54.26N 11.12E
Burg *Sachsen-Anhalt* Germany **38** 52.16N 11.51E
Burgas Bulgaria **29** 42.30N 27.29E
Burgas *d.* Bulgaria **34** 42.30N 26.25E
Burgdorf Switz. **39** 47.04N 7.37E
Burgenland *d.* Austria **36** 47.30N 16.20E
Burgeo Canada **103** 47.36N 57.34W
Burgess Hill U.K. **13** 50.57N 0.07W
Burghausen Germany **39** 48.09N 12.49E
Burglengenfeld Germany **39** 49.13N 12.03E
Burgos Spain **26** 42.21N 3.42W
Burgos *d.* Spain **26** 42.25N 3.40W
Burgstädt Germany **38** 50.55N 12.49E
Burgsteinfurt Germany **38** 52.08N 7.20E
Burgsvik Sweden **43** 57.03N 18.16E
Burhānpur India **62** 21.18N 76.14E
Buri Brazil **126** 23.46S 48.39W
Burias *i.* Phil. **59** 12.50N123.10E
Burica, Punta *c.* Panama **117** 8.05N 82.50W
Burin Pen. Canada **103** 47.00N 55.40W
Buriram Thailand **56** 14.59N103.08E
Burjasot Spain **25** 39.31N 0.25W
Burkburnett U.S.A. **111** 34.06N 98.34W
Burke *r.* Australia **90** 23.12S139.33E
Burketown Australia **90** 17.44S139.22E
Burkina Africa **76** 12.30N 2.00W

Burk's Falls to **Canada**

Burk's Falls Canada **104** 45.37N 79.25W
Burleigh Falls Canada **104** 44.34N 78.11W
Burley U.S.A. **108** 42.32N113.48W
Burlington Canada **104** 43.19N 79.47W
Burlington Iowa U.S.A. **110** 40.49N 91.14W
Burlington Kans. U.S.A. **110** 38.12N 95.45W
Burlington N.C. U.S.A. **113** 36.05N 79.27W
Burlington N.J. U.S.A. **115** 40.04N 74.49W
Burlington Vt. U.S.A. **105** 44.29N 73.13W
Burlington Wisc. U.S.A. **110** 42.41N 88.17W
Burma Asia **56** 21.45N 97.00E
Burngup Australia **89** 33.00S118.39E
Burnham-on-Crouch U.K. **13** 51.37N 0.50E
Burnham-on-Sea U.K. **13** 51.15N 3.00W
Burnie Australia **91** 41.03S145.55E
Burnley U.K. **12** 53.47N 2.15W
Burns Oreg. U.S.A. **108** 43.35N119.03W
Burns Wyo. U.S.A. **108** 41.11N104.21W
Burnside *r.* Canada **98** 66.51N108.04W
Burns Lake *town* Canada **100** 54.20N125.45W
Burnsville U.S.A. **114** 38.51N 80.40W
Buronga Australia **92** 34.08S142.11E
Burqā Jordan **67** 32.18N 35.12E
Burqin Jordan **67** 32.27N 35.16E
Burra Australia **92** 33.40S138.57E
Burracoppin Australia **89** 31.22S118.30E
Burragorang, L. Australia **93** 33.58S150.27E
Burrel Albania **34** 41.36N 20.01E
Burren Junction Australia **93** 30.08S148.59E
Burrewarra Pt. Australia **93** 35.56S150.12E
Burriana Spain **25** 39.53N 0.05W
Burrinjuck Australia **93** 35.01S148.33E
Burrinjuck Resr. Australia **93** 35.00S148.40E
Burro, Serranías del *mts.* Mexico **111** 29.20N102.00W
Burry Port U.K. **13** 51.41N 4.17W
Bursa Turkey **29** 40.11N 29.04E
Būr Safājah Egypt **64** 26.44N 33.56E
Būr Sa'īd Egypt **66** 31.17N 32.18E
Būr Sūdān Sudan **72** 19.39N 37.01E
Burta Australia **92** 32.30S141.05E
Būr Tawfīq Egypt **66** 29.57N 32.34E
Burt L. U.S.A. **104** 45.27N 84.40W
Burton upon Trent U.K. **12** 52.58N 1.39W
Burtundy Australia **92** 33.45S142.22E
Buru *i.* Indonesia **59** 3.30S126.30E
Burullus, Buḩayrat al *l.* Egypt **66** 31.30N 30.45E
Burundi Africa **79** 3.00S 30.00E
Bururi Burundi **79** 3.58S 29.35E
Burutu Nigeria **77** 5.20N 5.31E
Burwash Canada **104** 46.19N 80.48W
Bury G.M. U.K. **12** 53.36N 2.19W
Bury St. Edmunds U.K. **13** 52.15N 0.42E
Burzil Jammu & Kashmir **62** 34.52N 75.07E
Burzil Pass Jammu & Kashmir **62** 34.54N 75.06E
Busalla Italy **30** 44.34N 8.57E
Busambra, Rocca *mtn.* Italy **32** 37.51N 13.24E
Busca Italy **30** 44.31N 7.29E
Būsh Egypt **66** 29.09N 31.07E
Būshehr Iran **65** 28.57N 50.52E
Bushkill U.S.A. **115** 41.06N 75.00W
Bushmanland *f.* R.S.A. **80** 29.25S 19.40E
Busi Ethiopia **71** 5.30N 44.30E
Busigny France **19** 50.02N 3.28E
Businga Zaïre **78** 3.16N 20.55E
Busira *r.* Zaïre **78** 0.05N 18.18E
Buskerud Norway **41** 60.20N 9.00E
Buskerud *d.* Norway **42** 60.07N 9.45E
Buşrá al Ḩarīrī Syria **67** 32.50N 36.20E
Buşrá ash Shām Syria **66** 32.30N 36.29E
Busselton Australia **89** 33.43S115.15E
Bussum Neth. **16** 52.17N 5.10E
Bustard Head *c.* Australia **90** 24.02S151.48E
Busto Arsizio Italy **30** 45.37N 8.51E
Busu Djanoa Zaïre **78** 1.42N 21.23E
Büsum Germany **38** 54.08N 8.51E
Buta Zaïre **78** 2.50N 24.50E
Butan Bulgaria **34** 43.39N 23.45E
Butari Rwanda **79** 2.38S 29.43E
Butaritari *i.* Kiribati **84** 3.07N172.48E
Buţayḩah Syria **67** 32.56N 35.53E
Bute Australia **92** 33.24S138.01E
Bute *i.* U.K. **14** 55.51N 5.07W
Bute, Sd. of U.K. **14** 55.44N 5.10W
Butedale Canada **100** 53.12N128.45W
Butera Italy **33** 37.11N 14.11E
Buthroton *site* Albania **34** 39.46N 20.00E
Butiaba Uganda **79** 1.48N 31.15E
Butler Mo. U.S.A. **111** 38.16N 94.20W
Butler N.J. U.S.A. **115** 41.00N 74.21W
Butler Penn. U.S.A. **114** 40.52N 79.54W
Butman U.S.A. **104** 44.09N 84.34W
Buton *i.* Indonesia **59** 5.00S122.50E
Butte Mont. U.S.A. **108** 46.00N112.32W
Butte Nebr. U.S.A. **110** 42.58N 98.51W
Butterworth Malaysia **58** 5.24N100.22E
Buttevant Rep. of Ire. **15** 52.14N 8.41W
Butt of Lewis *c.* U.K. **14** 58.31N 6.15W
Butty Head Australia **89** 33.52S121.35E
Butuan Phil. **59** 8.56N125.31E
Butwal Nepal **63** 27.42N 83.28E
Butzbach Germany **39** 50.26N 8.40E
Butzow Germany **38** 53.50N 11.59E
Buuhoodle Somali Rep. **71** 8.16N 46.24E
Buulo Berde Somali Rep. **71** 3.52N 45.40E
Buur Gaabo Somali Rep. **73** 1.10S 41.50E
Buur Hakaba Somali Rep. **79** 2.43N 44.10E
Buxtehude Germany **38** 53.28N 9.41E
Buxton U.K. **12** 53.16N 1.54W
Buxy France **19** 46.43N 4.41E
Buy U.S.S.R. **44** 58.23N 41.27E
Buyaga U.S.S.R. **51** 59.42N126.59E
Buynaksk U.S.S.R. **45** 42.48N 47.07E
Büyük Turkey **34** 41.02N 26.35E
Büyük Menderes *r.* Turkey **35** 37.28N 27.10E
Buzachi, Poluostrov *pen.* U.S.S.R. **45** 45.00N 51.55E
Buzançais France **18** 46.53N 1.25E
Buzancy France **19** 49.25N 4.57E
Buzău Romania **37** 45.10N 26.49E
Buzău *r.* Romania **37** 45.24N 27.48E
Buzaymah Libya **75** 24.55N 22.02E
Buzi *r.* Mozambique **81** 19.52S 34.00E
Buzuluk U.S.S.R. **44** 52.49N 52.19E
Buzzards B. U.S.A. **115** 41.33N 70.47W
Bwasiaia P.N.G. **90** 10.06S150.48E
Byala Bulgaria **34** 43.28N 25.44E
Byala Slatina Bulgaria **34** 43.26N 23.55E
Byam Martin I. Canada **98** 75.15N104.00W
Bydgoszcz Poland **37** 53.16N 17.33E
Byemoor Canada **100** 52.00N112.17W
Byesville U.S.A. **114** 39.58N 81.32W
Bygland Norway **42** 58.50N 7.49E
Byglandsfjord *town* Norway **42** 58.51N 7.48E
Byglandsfjorden *l.* Norway **42** 58.48N 7.50E
Byhalia U.S.A. **111** 34.52N 89.41W
Bykhov U.S.S.R. **37** 53.30N 30.15E
Bykle Norway **42** 59.21N 7.20E
Bylot I. Canada **99** 73.00N 78.30W
Byng Inlet Canada **104** 45.46N 80.33W
Byrd, Lac *l.* Canada **105** 47.01N 76.56W
Byrd Land *f.* Antarctica **128** 79.30S125.00W
Byrock Australia **93** 30.40S146.25E
Byron, C. Australia **93** 28.37S153.40E
Byron Bay *town* Australia **93** 28.43S153.34E
Byrranga, Gory *mts.* U.S.S.R. **51** 74.50N101.00E
Byske Sweden **40** 64.57N 21.12E
Byske *r.* Sweden **40** 64.57N 21.13E
Byten U.S.S.R. **37** 52.50N 25.28E
Bytom Poland **37** 50.22N 18.54E
Byxelkrok Sweden **43** 57.20N 17.00E
Bzipi U.S.S.R. **45** 43.15N 40.24E

C

Ca *r.* Vietnam **55** 18.47N105.40E
Caballería, Cabo de *c.* Spain **25** 40.05N 4.05E
Caballos Mesteños, Llano de los *f.* Mexico **111** 28.15N104.00W
Cabanatuan Phil. **59** 15.30N120.58E
Cabeza del Buey Spain **26** 38.43N 5.13W
Cabimas Venezuela **122** 10.26N 71.27W
Cabinda Angola **78** 5.34S 12.12E
Cabinet Mts. U.S.A. **108** 48.08N115.46W
Cabo Delgado *d.* Mozambique **79** 12.30S 39.00E
Cabo Frio *town* Brazil **126** 22.51S 42.03W
Cabonga, Résr. Canada **105** 47.20N 76.35W
Cabool U.S.A. **111** 37.07N 92.06W
Caboolture Australia **91** 27.05S152.57E
Cabo Pantoja Peru **122** 1.00S 75.10W
Cabot, Mt. U.S.A. **105** 44.31N 71.24W
Cabot Head *c.* Canada **104** 45.14N 81.17W
Cabot Str. Canada **103** 47.20N 59.30W
Cabra Spain **27** 37.28N 4.27W
Cabras Italy **32** 39.56N 8.32E
Cabrera *i.* Spain **25** 39.09N 2.56E
Cabrera *r.* Spain **26** 42.25N 6.49W
Cabrera, Sierra *mts.* Spain **26** 42.10N 6.45W
Cabri Canada **101** 50.37N108.28W
Cabriel *r.* Spain **25** 39.14N 1.03W
Cabruta Venezuela **122** 7.40N 66.16W
Čačak Yugo. **34** 43.53N 20.21E
Caçapava Brazil **126** 23.05S 45.40W
Caccamo Italy **32** 37.56N 13.40E
Caccia, Capo *c.* Italy **32** 40.34N 8.09E
Cáceres Brazil **123** 16.05S 57.40W
Cáceres Spain **27** 39.29N 6.22W
Cáceres *d.* Spain **27** 39.40N 6.20W
Cachari Argentina **125** 36.23S 59.29W
Cache Bay *town* Canada **104** 46.23N 80.00W
Cachimo *r.* Zaïre **78** 7.02S 21.13E
Cachoeira Brazil **123** 12.35S 38.59W
Cachoeira do Sul Brazil **126** 30.03S 52.52W
Cachoeiro de Itapemirim Brazil **126** 20.51S 41.07W
Cacín *r.* Spain **27** 37.13N 4.00W
Cacine Guinea **76** 11.08N 14.57W
Cacolo Angola **78** 10.09S 19.15E
Caconda Angola **78** 13.46S 15.06E
Cacongo Angola **78** 5.11S 12.10E
Cacuso Angola **78** 9.26S 15.43E
Cadaqués Spain **25** 42.17N 3.17E
Čadca Czech. **37** 49.26N 18.48E
Cader Idris *mtn.* U.K. **13** 52.40N 3.55W
Cadibarrawirracanna, L. Australia **92** 28.52S135.27E
Cadi, Serra del *mts.* Spain **25** 42.17N 1.42E
Cadillac France **20** 44.38N 0.19W
Cadillac U.S.A. **112** 44.15N 85.23W
Cadiz Phil. **59** 10.57N123.18E
Cádiz Spain **27** 36.32N 6.18W
Cádiz *d.* Spain **27** 36.40N 5.50W
Cadiz U.S.A. **114** 40.16N 81.00W
Cádiz, Golfo de *g.* Spain **27** 37.00N 7.00W
Cadomin Canada **100** 53.02N117.20W
Cadoux Australia **89** 30.47S117.05E
Caen France **18** 49.11N 0.21W
Caernarfon U.K. **12** 53.08N 4.17W
Caernarfon B. U.K. **12** 53.05N 4.25W
Caerphilly U.K. **13** 51.34N 3.13W
Caesarea *see* Horbat Qesari Israel **67**
Caeté Brazil **126** 19.54S 43.37W
Cafima Angola **78** 16.34S 16.30E
Cafu Angola **78** 16.30S 15.14E
Cagayan de Oro Phil. **59** 8.29N124.40E
Cagli Italy **30** 43.33N 12.39E
Cagliari Italy **32** 39.13N 9.06E
Cagliari, Golfo di *g.* Italy **32** 39.05N 9.10E
Cagnes France **21** 43.40N 7.09E
Caguán *r.* Colombia **122** 0.08S 74.18W
Caguas Puerto Rico **117** 18.08N 66.00W
Cahama Angola **78** 16.16S 14.23E
Caha Mts. Rep. of Ire. **15** 51.44N 9.45W
Cahelli Italy **30** 44.43N 8.17E
Caherciveen Rep. of Ire. **15** 51.51N 10.14W
Cahir Rep. of Ire. **15** 52.23N 7.56W
Cahora Bassa Dam Mozambique **79** 15.36S 32.41E
Cahore Pt. Rep. of Ire. **15** 52.34N 6.12W
Cahors France **20** 44.27N 1.26E
Cahuapanas Peru **122** 5.15S 77.00W
Caia *r.* Portugal **27** 38.50N 7.05W
Caianda Angola **78** 11.02S 23.29E
Caibarién Cuba **117** 22.31N 79.28W
Caicó Brazil **123** 6.25S 37.04W
Caicos Is. C. America **97** 21.30N 72.00W
Caicos Is. Turks & Caicos Is. **117** 21.30N 72.00W
Caird Coast *f.* Antarctica **128** 75.00S 20.00W
Cairngorms *mts.* U.K. **14** 57.04N 3.30W
Cairns Australia **90** 16.51S145.43E
Cairo *see* Al Qāhirah Egypt **66**
Cairo Ill. U.S.A. **111** 37.01N 89.09W
Cairo N.Y. U.S.A. **115** 42.18N 74.00W
Cairo W.Va. U.S.A. **114** 39.13N 81.09W
Cairo Montenotte Italy **30** 44.24N 8.16E
Caiundo Angola **78** 15.43S 17.30E
Caiwarro Australia **93** 28.38S144.45E
Caizhai China **54** 37.20N118.10E
Caizi Hu *l.* China **55** 30.50N117.06E
Cajamarca Peru **122** 7.09S 78.32W
Cajarc France **20** 44.29N 1.50E
Cajàzeiras Brazil **123** 6.52S 38.31W
Čajniče Yugo. **31** 43.33N 19.04E
Cajuru Brazil **126** 21.15S 47.18W
Čakovec Yugo. **31** 46.23N 16.26E
Cala, Embalse de *resr.* Spain **27** 37.45N 6.05W
Calabar Nigeria **77** 4.56N 8.22E
Calabogie Canada **105** 45.18N 76.43W
Calabozo Venezuela **122** 8.58N 67.28W
Calabria *d.* Italy **33** 39.25N 16.30E
Calacuccia France **21** 42.20N 9.03E
Calafat Romania **34** 43.58N 22.59E
Calafate Argentina **125** 50.20S 72.16W
Calahorra Spain **26** 42.18N 1.59W
Calais France **19** 50.57N 1.50E
Calama Brazil **122** 8.03S 62.53W
Calama Chile **121** 22.30S 68.55W
Calamar Colombia **122** 10.15N 74.55W
Calamian Group *is.* Phil. **59** 12.00N120.05E
Cala Millor Spain **25** 39.35N 3.22E
Calamocha Spain **25** 40.55N 1.18W
Calañas Spain **27** 37.39N 6.53W
Calanda Spain **25** 40.56N 0.14W
Calangianus Italy **32** 40.56N 9.12E
Calapan Phil. **59** 13.23N121.10E
Călăraşi Romania **37** 44.11N 27.21E
Calatafimi Italy **32** 37.55N 12.52E
Calatayud Spain **25** 41.21N 1.38W
Calatrava Equat. Guinea **78** 1.09N 9.24E
Calau Germany **38** 51.45N 13.56E
Calayan *i.* Phil. **55** 19.20N121.25E
Calbayog Phil. **59** 12.04N124.58E
Calbe Germany **38** 51.54N 11.46E
Calcutta India **63** 22.32N 88.22E
Caldaro Italy **30** 46.25N 11.14E
Caldas Colombia **122** 6.05N 75.36W
Caldas da Rainha Portugal **27** 39.24N 9.08W
Caldas de Reyes Spain **26** 42.36N 8.38W
Caldeirão, Serra do *mts.* Portugal **27** 37.25N 8.10W
Caldera Chile **124** 27.04S 70.50W
Caldwell Idaho U.S.A. **108** 43.40N116.41W
Caldwell Ohio U.S.A. **114** 39.45N 81.31W
Caledon *r.* R.S.A. **80** 30.27S 26.12E
Caledon B. Australia **90** 12.58S136.52E
Caledonia Canada **104** 43.04N 79.56W
Caledonia U.S.A. **114** 42.58N 77.51W
Caledonia Hills Canada **103** 45.40N 65.00W
Calella Spain **25** 41.37N 2.40E
Calexico Mexico **109** 32.40N115.30W
Calf of Man *i.* U.K. **12** 54.03N 4.49W
Calgary Canada **100** 51.00N114.10W
Cali Colombia **122** 3.24N 76.30W
Caliente U.S.A. **108** 37.37N114.31W
California *d.* U.S.A. **108** 37.29N119.58W
California, G. of *see* California, Golfo de *g.* Mexico **116**
California, Golfo de *g.* Mexico **109** 28.00N112.00W
Calingasta Argentina **124** 31.15S 69.30W
Calingiri Australia **89** 31.07S116.27E
Calitri Italy **33** 40.54N 15.27E
Callabonna, L. Australia **92** 29.47S140.07E
Callabonna Creek *r.* Australia **92** 29.37S140.08E
Callac France **18** 48.24N 3.26W
Callander Canada **104** 46.13N 79.23W
Callander U.K. **14** 56.15N 4.13W
Callao Peru **124** 12.05S 77.08W
Callicoon U.S.A. **115** 41.46N 75.03W
Callosa de Ensarriá Spain **25** 38.39N 0.07W
Callosa de Segura Spain **25** 38.08N 0.52W
Caloocan Phil. **59** 14.38N120.58E
Caloundra Australia **91** 26.47S153.08E
Caltagirone Italy **33** 37.14N 14.31E
Caltanissetta Italy **33** 37.29N 14.04E
Caluire-et-Cuire France **21** 45.48N 4.51E
Calulo Angola **78** 10.05S 14.56E
Calumbo Angola **78** 9.08S 13.24E
Calumet Canada **105** 45.39N 74.41W
Calundau Angola **78** 12.05S 19.10E
Caluula Somali Rep. **71** 11.58N 50.48E
Calvados *d.* France **18** 49.10N 0.30W
Calvert I. Canada **100** 51.30N128.00W
Calverton U.S.A. **114** 39.03N 76.56W
Calvi France **21** 42.34N 8.45E
Calvinia R.S.A. **80** 31.29S 19.44E
Calvo, Monte *mtn.* Italy **33** 41.44N 15.46E
Calw Germany **39** 48.43N 8.44E
Cam *r.* U.K. **13** 52.34N 0.21E
Camabatela Angola **78** 8.20S 15.29E
Camacupa Angola **78** 12.01S 17.22E
Camagüey Cuba **117** 21.25N 77.55W
Camagüey, Archipiélago de Cuba **117** 22.30N 78.00W
Camaiore Italy **30** 43.56N 10.18E
Camarat, Cap *c.* France **21** 43.12N 6.41E
Camarès France **20** 43.49N 2.53E
Camaret-sur-Mer France **18** 48.16N 4.37W
Camargue *d.* France **21** 43.20N 4.38E
Camariñas Spain **26** 43.08N 9.12W
Camarón, C. Honduras **117** 15.59N 85.00W
Camaronero, Laguna *l.* Mexico **109** 23.00N106.07W
Camarones Argentina **125** 44.45S 65.40W
Camas Spain **27** 37.24N 6.02W
Camas U.S.A. **108** 45.35N122.24W
Cambados Spain **26** 42.30N 8.48W
Cambay India **62** 22.18N 72.37E
Camberg Germany **39** 50.18N 8.16E
Camberley U.K. **13** 51.21N 0.45W
Cambodia Asia **56** 12.45N105.00E
Camborne U.K. **13** 50.12N 5.19W
Cambrai Australia **92** 34.39S139.17E
Cambrai France **19** 50.10N 3.14E
Cambria U.S.A. **109** 35.34N121.05W
Cambrian Mts. U.K. **13** 52.33N 3.33W
Cambridge Canada **114** 43.22N 80.19W
Cambridge New Zealand **86** 37.53S175.29E
Cambridge U.K. **13** 52.13N 0.08E
Cambridge Idaho U.S.A. **108** 44.34N116.41W
Cambridge Mass. U.S.A. **115** 42.22N 71.06W
Cambridge Md. U.S.A. **115** 38.34N 76.04W
Cambridge Minn. U.S.A. **110** 45.31N 93.14W
Cambridge N.Y. U.S.A. **115** 43.02N 73.23W
Cambridge Ohio U.S.A. **114** 40.02N 81.35W
Cambridge Bay *town* Canada **98** 69.09N105.00W
Cambridge G. Australia **88** 15.00S128.05E
Cambridgeshire *d.* U.K. **13** 52.15N 0.05E
Cambridge Springs *town* U.S.A. **114** 41.48N 80.04W
Cambrils de Mer Spain **25** 41.04N 1.03E
Cambundi-Catembo Angola **78** 10.09S 17.35E
Camden U.K. **13** 51.33N 0.10W
Camden Ark. U.S.A. **111** 33.35N 92.50W
Camden N.J. U.S.A. **115** 39.57N 75.07W
Camden N.Y. U.S.A. **115** 43.20N 75.45W
Camden S.C. U.S.A. **113** 34.16N 80.36W
Cameia Nat. Park Angola **78** 12.00S 21.30E
Camelford U.K. **13** 50.37N 4.41W
Camerino Italy **30** 43.08N 13.04E
Cameron Canada **104** 44.27N 78.46W
Cameron Ariz. U.S.A. **109** 35.51N111.25W
Cameron La. U.S.A. **111** 29.48N 93.19W
Cameron Mo. U.S.A. **110** 39.44N 94.14W
Cameron Tex. U.S.A. **111** 30.51N 96.59W
Cameron W.Va. U.S.A. **114** 39.50N 80.34W
Cameron Hills Canada **100** 59.48N118.00W
Cameron Mts. New Zealand **86** 45.50S167.00E
Cameroon Africa **77** 6.00N 12.30E
Camerota Italy **33** 40.02N 15.23E
Cameroun, Mont *mtn.* Cameroon **77** 4.20N 9.05E
Cametá Brazil **123** 2.12S 49.30W
Caminha Portugal **26** 41.52N 8.50W
Camiri Bolivia **124** 20.03S 63.31W
Camocim Brazil **123** 2.55S 40.50W
Camooweal Australia **90** 19.55S138.07E
Camopi Guiana **123** 3.12N 52.15W
Campagna Italy **33** 40.40N 15.08E
Campana Argentina **125** 34.10S 58.57W
Campana, Isla *i.* Chile **125** 48.25S 75.20W
Campanario Spain **26** 38.52N 5.37W
Campania *d.* Italy **33** 40.50N 14.50E
Campbell U.S.A. **114** 41.05N 80.36W
Campbell, C. New Zealand **86** 41.45S174.15E
Campbellford Canada **105** 44.18N 77.48W
Campbell I. Pacific Oc. **84** 52.30S169.02E
Campbellpore Pakistan **62** 33.46N 72.22E
Campbell River *town* Canada **100** 50.05N125.20W
Campbells Bay *town* Canada **105** 45.44N 76.36W
Campbellsville U.S.A. **113** 37.20N 85.21W
Campbellton Canada **103** 48.00N 66.40W
Campbelltown Australia **93** 34.04S150.49E
Campbell Town Australia **93** 41.55S147.30E
Campbeltown U.K. **14** 55.25N 5.36W
Camp Borden Canada **104** 44.18N 79.52W
Campeche Mexico **116** 19.50N 90.30W
Campeche *d.* Mexico **116** 19.00N 90.00W
Campeche, Bahía de *b.* Mexico **116** 19.30N 94.00W
Campeche B. *see* Campeche, Bahía de *b.* Mexico **116**
Camperdown Australia **92** 38.15S143.14E
Cam Pha Vietnam **56** 21.07N107.19E
Campiglia Marittima Italy **30** 43.03N 10.37E
Campillo de Llerena Spain **26** 38.30N 5.50W
Campillos Spain **27** 37.03N 4.51W
Campina Grande Brazil **123** 7.15S 35.50W
Campinas Brazil **126** 22.54S 47.06W
Campo Cameroon **77** 2.22N 9.50E
Campo *r.* Cameroon **78** 2.21N 9.51E
Campo U.S.A. **111** 37.06N102.35W
Campobasso Italy **33** 41.34N 14.39E
Campobello di Mazara Italy **32** 37.38N 12.45E
Campo Belo Brazil **126** 20.52S 45.16W
Campo de Criptana Spain **27** 39.24N 3.07W
Campo Gallo Argentina **124** 26.35S 62.50W
Campo Grande Brazil **124** 20.24S 54.35W
Campo Maior Brazil **123** 4.50S 42.12W
Campo Maior Portugal **27** 39.01N 7.04W
Campos Brazil **126** 21.45S 41.18W
Campos Belos Brazil **123** 13.09S 47.03W
Campos do Jordão Brazil **126** 23.28S 46.10W
Campo Tures Italy **30** 46.55N 11.57E
Campton U.S.A. **105** 43.53N 71.38W
Camp Wood U.S.A. **111** 29.40N100.01W
Cam Ranh Vietnam **56** 11.54N109.14E
Camrose Canada **100** 53.00N112.50W
Canaan Conn. U.S.A. **115** 42.02N 73.20W
Canaan Vt. U.S.A. **105** 45.00N 71.32W
Canada N. America **98** 60.00N105.00W

Cañada de Gómez to Catete

Cañada de Gómez Argentina **124** 32.49S 61.25W
Canadian U.S.A. **111** 35.55N100.23W
Canadian *r.* U.S.A. **111** 35.27N 95.03W
Canadian Shield *f.* Canada **96** 50.00N 82.00W
Canajohaire U.S.A. **115** 42.56N 74.38W
Çanakkale Turkey **34** 40.09N 26.24E
Çanakkale Boğazi *str.* Turkey **34** 40.15N 26.25E
Canal du Midi France **17** 43.18N 2.00E
Canal Fulton U.S.A. **114** 40.54N 81.36W
Canandaigua U.S.A. **114** 42.54N 77.17W
Canandaigua L. U.S.A. **114** 42.49N 77.16W
Cananea Mexico **109** 30.57N110.18W
Canarias, Islas *is.* Atlantic Oc. **74** 28.00N 15.00W
Canary Is. *see* Canarias, Islas *is.* Atlantic Oc. **74**
Canaseraga U.S.A. **114** 42.45N 77.50W
Canastota U.S.A. **115** 43.10N 75.45W
Canastra, Serra da *mts.* Brazil **126** 20.05S 46.30W
Canaveral, C. U.S.A. **113** 28.27N 80.32W
Cañaveras Spain **26** 40.22N 2.24W
Canavieiras Brazil **123** 15.44S 38.58W
Canbelego Australia **93** 31.33S146.19E
Canberra Australia **93** 35.18S149.08E
Canby Calif. U.S.A. **108** 41.27N120.52W
Canby Minn. U.S.A. **110** 44.43N 96.16W
Cancale France **18** 48.41N 1.51W
Canche *r.* France **19** 50.31N 1.39E
Cancon France **20** 44.32N 0.38E
Candás Spain **26** 43.35N 5.46W
Candé France **18** 47.34N 1.02W
Candeias Brazil **126** 20.44S 45.18W
Candelaro *r.* Italy **33** 41.34N 15.53E
Candeleda Spain **27** 40.09N 5.14W
Candle L. Canada **101** 53.50N105.18W
Candlewood, L. U.S.A. **115** 41.32N 73.27W
Candor U.S.A. **115** 42.14N 76.21W
Canelles, Embalse de *resr.* Spain **25** 42.10N 0.30E
Canelli Italy **30** 44.43N 8.17E
Canelones Uruguay **125** 34.32S 56.17W
Cañete Peru **122** 13.00S 76.30W
Cañete Spain **25** 40.03N 1.35W
Canfield Canada **104** 42.59N 79.43W
Canfranc Spain **25** 42.43N 0.31W
Cangamba Angola **78** 13.40S 19.50E
Cangas Spain **26** 42.16N 8.47W
Cangas de Narcea Spain **26** 43.11N 6.33W
Cangas de Onís Spain **26** 43.21N 5.07W
Cangkuang, Tanjung *c.* Indonesia **59** 6.45S105.15E
Cangombe Angola **78** 14.27S 20.00E
Canguçu Brazil **124** 31.24S 52.41W
Cangwu China **55** 23.27N111.17E
Cangzhou China **54** 38.15N116.58E
Caniapiscau *r.* Canada **103** 57.40N 69.30W
Caniapiscau, Lac *l.* Canada **103** 54.10N 69.55W
Canicattì Italy **32** 37.21N 13.51E
Canigou, Pic du *mtn.* France **20** 42.30N 2.27E
Canisteo U.S.A. **114** 42.07N 77.08W
Canisteo *r.* U.S.A. **105** 42.07N 77.08W
Canjáyar Spain **27** 37.00N 2.44W
Çankiri Turkey **64** 40.35N 33.37E
Canna *i.* U.K. **14** 57.03N 6.30W
Cannes France **21** 43.33N 7.01E
Cannich U.K. **14** 57.20N 4.45W
Cannington Canada **104** 44.21N 79.02W
Cannock U.K. **13** 52.42N 2.02W
Cann River *town* Australia **93** 37.35S149.06E
Canõas Brazil **126** 29.55S 51.10W
Canoe L. Canada **101** 55.11N108.15W
Canojoharie U.S.A. **105** 42.56N 74.38W
Canonba Australia **93** 31.19S147.22E
Canon City U.S.A. **108** 38.27N105.14W
Canonsburg U.S.A. **114** 40.16N 80.11W
Canopus Australia **92** 33.30S140.57E
Canora Canada **101** 51.37N102.26W
Canosa Italy **33** 41.13N 16.04E
Canossa *site* Italy **30** 44.35N 10.27E
Canowindra Australia **93** 33.34S148.30E
Canso Canada **103** 45.20N 61.00W
Cantabria *d.* Spain **26** 43.15N 4.00W
Cantabria, Sierra de *mts.* Spain **26** 42.35N 2.30W
Cantábrica, Cordillera *mts.* Spain **26** 43.00N 5.00W
Cantagalo Brazil **126** 21.59S 42.22W
Cantal *d.* France **20** 45.05N 2.45E
Cantalejo Spain **26** 41.15N 3.55W
Cantanhede Portugal **26** 40.21N 8.36W
Cantaura Venezuela **122** 9.22N 64.24W
Canterbury *d.* New Zealand **86** 43.30S172.00E
Canterbury U.K. **13** 51.17N 1.05E
Canterbury Bight New Zealand **86** 44.15S172.00E
Can Tho Vietnam **56** 10.03N105.40E
Canton *see* Guangzhou China **55**
Canton Miss. U.S.A. **111** 32.37N 90.02W
Canton N.C. U.S.A. **113** 35.33N 82.51W
Canton N.Y. U.S.A. **105** 44.36N 75.10W
Canton Ohio U.S.A. **114** 40.48N 81.22W
Canton Okla. U.S.A. **111** 36.03N 98.35W
Canton Penn. U.S.A. **114** 41.39N 76.51W
Cantù Italy **30** 45.44N 9.08E
Cantua Creek *town* U.S.A. **109** 36.30N120.19W
Cantung Canada **100** 62.00N128.09W
Cañuelas Argentina **125** 35.03S 58.44W
Canumã *r.* Brazil **122** 3.55S 59.10W
Canutama Brazil **122** 6.32S 64.20W
Canutillo Mexico **109** 26.21N105.25W
Cany-Barville France **18** 49.47N 0.38E
Canyon Tex. U.S.A. **111** 34.59N101.55W
Canyon Wyo. U.S.A. **108** 44.43N110.32W
Cao Bang Vietnam **55** 22.37N106.18E
Caombo Angola **78** 8.45S 16.50E
Caorle Italy **30** 45.36N 12.53E
Capac U.S.A. **114** 43.01N 82.56W
Capanema Brazil **123** 1.08S 47.07W
Cap-Chat Canada **103** 48.56N 66.53W
Cap de la Madeleine Canada **105** 46.22N 72.31W
Cape Barren I. Australia **91** 40.25S148.15E
Cape Basin *f.* Atlantic Oc. **127** 38.00S 10.00E
Cape Breton Highlands Canada **103** 46.45N 60.45W
Cape Breton I. Canada **103** 46.00N 60.30W
Cape Coast *town* Ghana **76** 5.10N 1.13W
Cape Cod B. U.S.A. **115** 41.52N 70.22W
Cape Crawford *town* Australia **90** 16.38S135.43E
Cape Croker *town* Canada **104** 44.55N 81.01W
Cape Dyer *town* Canada **99** 66.30N 61.20W
Cape Girardeau *town* U.S.A. **111** 37.19N 89.32W
Cape Johnson Depth Pacific Oc. **59** 10.20N127.20E
Capellen Lux. **16** 49.39N 5.59E
Capelongo Angola **78** 14.55S 15.03E
Cape May *town* U.S.A. **115** 38.56N 74.55W
Cape Province *d.* R.S.A. **80** 31.30S 23.30E
Cape Rise *f.* Indian Oc. **49** 38.00S 27.00E
Capernaum *see* Kefar Nahum Israel **67**
Cape Town R.S.A. **80** 33.55S 18.27E
Cape Verde Atlantic Oc. **127** 16.00N 24.00W
Cape Verde Basin *f.* Atlantic Oc. **127** 15.00N 35.00W
Cape Vincent *town* U.S.A. **105** 44.08N 76.20W
Cape York Pen. Australia **90** 12.40S142.20E
Cap-Haïtien *town* Haiti **117** 19.47N 72.17W
Capim *r.* Brazil **123** 1.40S 47.47W
Capljina Yugo. **31** 43.07N 17.42E
Capon Bridge U.S.A. **114** 39.21N 78.23W
Capoompeta, Mt. Australia **93** 29.22S151.59E
Cappoquin Rep. of Ire. **15** 52.09N 7.52W
Capraia *i.* Italy **30** 43.03N 9.50E
Caprarola Italy **30** 42.19N 12.14E
Capreol Canada **104** 46.43N 80.56W
Caprera *i.* Italy **32** 41.12N 9.28E
Capri *i.* Italy **33** 40.33N 14.13E
Caprivi Strip *f.* Namibia **80** 17.50S 23.10E
Captains Flat Australia **93** 35.34S149.28E
Captieux France **20** 44.18N 0.16W
Captiva U.S.A. **113** 26.31N 82.12W
Capua Italy **33** 41.06N 14.12E
Caqueta *r.* Colombia **122** 1.20S 70.50W
Caracal Romania **37** 44.08N 24.18E
Caracas Venezuela **122** 10.35N 66.56W
Caragabal Australia **93** 33.49S147.46E
Caraguatatuba Brazil **126** 23.39S 45.26W
Carandaí Brazil **126** 20.55S 43.46W
Carangola Brazil **126** 20.44S 42.03W
Caransebeş Romania **37** 45.25N 22.13E
Caratasca, Laguna de *b.* Honduras **117** 15.10N 84.00W
Caratinga Brazil **126** 19.50S 42.06W
Caravaca Spain **25** 38.06N 1.51W
Caravaggio Italy **30** 45.30N 9.38E
Caravelí Peru **122** 15.45S 73.25W
Carballino Spain **26** 42.26N 8.04W
Carballo Spain **26** 43.13N 8.41W
Carbenyabba Creek *r.* Australia **92** 29.02S143.28E
Carberry Canada **101** 49.52N 99.20W
Carbonara, Capo *c.* Italy **32** 39.06N 9.31E
Carbon-Blanc France **20** 44.53N 0.31W
Carbondale Ill. U.S.A. **111** 37.44N 89.13W
Carbondale Penn. U.S.A. **115** 41.35N 75.30W
Carbonear Canada **103** 47.45N 53.14W
Carboneras de Guadazaon Spain **25** 39.53N 1.48W
Carbonia Italy **32** 39.11N 8.32E
Carbonin Italy **30** 46.37N 12.13E
Carcagente Spain **25** 39.08N 0.27W
Carcajou Canada **100** 57.47N117.06W
Carcans, Étang de *b.* France **20** 45.08N 1.08W
Carcassonne France **20** 43.13N 2.21E
Carcastillo Spain **25** 42.23N 1.26W
Carcross Canada **100** 60.13N134.45W
Cárdenas Cuba **117** 23.02N 81.12W
Cárdenas Mexico **116** 22.00N 99.40W
Cardenete Spain **25** 39.46N 1.41W
Cardiff Canada **104** 44.59N 78.01W
Cardiff U.K. **13** 51.28N 3.11W
Cardigan U.K. **13** 52.06N 4.41W
Cardigan B. U.K. **13** 52.30N 4.30W
Cardigan State Park U.S.A. **105** 43.38N 71.54W
Cardinal Canada **105** 44.47N 75.23W
Cardington U.S.A. **114** 40.30N 82.53W
Cardona Spain **25** 41.56N 1.40E
Cardona Uruguay **125** 33.53S 57.23W
Cardoner *r.* Spain **25** 41.41N 1.51E
Cardwell Australia **90** 18.21S146.04E
Carei Romania **37** 47.42N 22.28E
Carentan France **18** 49.18N 1.14W
Cares *r.* Spain **26** 43.22N 4.31W
Carey U.S.A. **108** 43.18N113.56W
Carey, L. Australia **89** 29.05S122.15E
Carey L. Canada **101** 62.12N102.55W
Carhaix France **18** 48.17N 3.35W
Carhué Argentina **125** 37.11S 62.45W
Cariati Italy **33** 39.30N 16.56E
Caribbean Sea C. America **117** 15.00N 75.00W
Cariboo Mts. Canada **100** 53.00N121.00W
Caribou *r.* Man. Canada **101** 59.20N 94.44W
Caribou *r.* N.W.T. Canada **100** 61.27N125.45W
Caribou U.S.A. **112** 46.52N 68.01W
Caribou Is. Canada **100** 61.55N113.15W
Caribou Mts. Canada **100** 59.12N115.40W
Carignan Canada **105** 47.18N 72.47W
Carignan France **19** 49.38N 5.10E
Carinda Australia **93** 30.29S147.45E
Cariñena Spain **25** 41.20N 1.13W
Carinhanha Brazil **123** 14.18S 43.47W
Carini Italy **32** 38.08N 13.11E
Caritianas Brazil **122** 9.25S 63.06W
Carlentini Italy **33** 37.16N 15.02E
Carlet Spain **25** 39.14N 0.31W
Carleton Place Canada **105** 45.08N 76.09W
Carlingford Rep. of Ire. **15** 54.03N 6.12W
Carlingford Lough Rep. of Ire. **15** 54.03N 6.09W
Carlinville U.S.A. **110** 39.17N 89.52W
Carlisle U.K. **12** 54.54N 2.55W
Carlisle U.S.A. **114** 40.12N 77.12W
Carloforte Italy **32** 39.08N 8.18E
Carlos Reyles Uruguay **125** 33.03S 56.29W
Carlow Rep. of Ire. **15** 52.50N 6.46W
Carlow *d.* Rep. of Ire. **15** 52.43N 6.50W
Carlsbad Calif. U.S.A. **109** 33.10N117.21W
Carlsbad N.Mex. U.S.A. **109** 32.25N104.14W
Carlsberg Ridge *f.* Indian Oc. **49** 4.00N 65.00E
Carlyle Canada **101** 49.38N102.16W
Carmacks Canada **98** 62.04N136.21W
Carmagnola Italy **30** 44.51N 7.43E
Carman Canada **101** 49.32N 98.00W
Carmarthen U.K. **13** 51.52N 4.20W
Carmarthen B. U.K. **13** 52.30N 4.30W
Carmaux France **20** 44.03N 2.09E
Carmel U.S.A. **115** 41.26N 73.41W
Carmel, Mt. *see* Karmel, Har *mtn.* Israel **67**
Carmel Head U.K. **12** 53.24N 4.35W
Carmelo Uruguay **125** 34.00S 58.17W
Carmen Colombia **122** 9.46N 75.06W
Carmen Mexico **116** 18.38N 91.50W
Carmen Uruguay **125** 33.15S 56.01W
Carmen, Isla *i.* Mexico **109** 25.55N111.10W
Carmen, Isla del *i.* Mexico **116** 18.35N 91.40W
Carmen de Areco Argentina **125** 34.20S 59.50W
Carmen de Patagones Argentina **125** 40.48S 63.00W
Carmi U.S.A. **110** 38.05N 88.11W
Carmichael U.S.A. **108** 38.38N121.19W
Carmila Australia **90** 21.55S149.25E
Carmo Brazil **126** 21.56S 42.37W
Carmody, L. Australia **89** 32.27S119.20E
Carmona Spain **27** 37.28N 5.38W
Carnac France **18** 47.35N 3.05W
Carnarvon Australia **88** 24.53S113.40E
Carnarvon Canada **104** 45.03N 78.40W
Carnarvon R.S.A. **80** 30.58S 22.07E
Carndonagh Rep. of Ire. **15** 55.15N 7.15W
Carnegie Australia **88** 25.43S122.59E
Carnegie, L. Australia **88** 26.15S123.00E
Carnew Rep. of Ire. **15** 52.43N 6.31W
Carniche, Alpi *mts.* Italy / Austria **30** 46.35N 13.00E
Car Nicobar *i.* India **56** 9.11N 92.45E
Carnot C.A.R. **77** 4.59N 15.56E
Carnot, C. Australia **92** 34.57S135.38E
Carnoustie U.K. **14** 56.30N 2.44W
Carnsore Pt. Rep. of Ire. **15** 52.10N 6.21W
Caro U.S.A. **104** 43.29N 83.24W
Carolina Brazil **123** 7.20S 47.25W
Carolina Puerto Rico **117** 18.23N 65.57W
Carolina R.S.A. **80** 26.04S 30.07E
Caroline I. Kiribati **85** 10.00S150.30W
Caroline Is. Pacific Oc. **59** 7.50N145.00E
Caroline-Solomon Ridge Pacific Oc. **84** 8.00N150.00E
Caroní *r.* Venezuela **122** 8.20N 62.42W
Carora Venezuela **122** 10.12N 70.07W
Carp Canada **105** 45.21N 76.02W
Carpathians *mts.* Europe **37** 48.45N 23.45E
Carpaţii Meridionali *mts.* Romania **37** 45.35N 24.40E
Carpentaria, G. of Australia **90** 14.00S139.00E
Carpenter Ridge *f.* Indian Oc. **49** 3.00N 90.00E
Carpentras France **21** 44.03N 5.03E
Carpi Italy **30** 44.47N 10.53E
Carpio Spain **26** 41.13N 5.07W
Carquefou France **18** 47.18N 1.30W
Carra, Lough Rep. of Ire. **15** 53.41N 9.15W
Carrara Italy **30** 44.05N 10.06E
Carrathool Australia **93** 34.25S145.24E
Carrauntoohil *mtn.* Rep. of Ire. **15** 52.00N 9.45W
Carrickfergus U.K. **15** 54.43N 5.49W
Carrickmacross Rep. of Ire. **15** 53.58N 6.43W
Carrick-on-Shannon Rep. of Ire. **15** 53.57N 8.06W
Carrick-on-Suir Rep. of Ire. **15** 52.21N 7.26W
Carrieton Australia **92** 32.28S138.34E
Carrington U.S.A. **110** 47.27N 99.08W
Carrión *r.* Spain **26** 41.53N 4.32W
Carrión de los Condes Spain **26** 42.20N 4.36W
Carrizo Spain **26** 42.35N 5.50W
Carrizo Springs *town* U.S.A. **111** 28.31N 99.52W
Carrizozo U.S.A. **109** 33.38N105.53W
Carroll U.S.A. **110** 42.04N 94.52W
Carrollton Mich. U.S.A. **104** 43.27N 83.54W
Carrollton Mo. U.S.A. **110** 39.22N 93.30W
Carrollton Ohio U.S.A. **114** 40.34N 81.05W
Carrot *r.* Canada **101** 53.50N101.17W
Carrowmore Lough Rep. of Ire. **15** 54.11N 9.47W
Carrum Australia **93** 38.05S145.08E
Çarşamba Turkey **64** 41.13N 36.43E
Çarşamba *r.* Turkey **64** 37.52N 31.48E
Carson U.S.A. **110** 46.25N101.34W
Carson City U.S.A. **108** 39.10N119.46W
Carstairs U.K. **14** 55.42N 3.41W
Cartagena Colombia **122** 10.24N 75.33W
Cartagena Spain **25** 37.36N 0.59W
Cartago Colombia **122** 4.45N 75.55W
Cartago Costa Rica **117** 9.50N 83.52W
Cartaxo Portugal **27** 39.09N 8.47W
Cartaya Spain **27** 37.17N 7.09W
Carter U.S.A. **108** 41.27N110.25W
Carteret France **18** 49.22N 1.48W
Cartersville U.S.A. **113** 34.09N 84.49W
Carterton New Zealand **86** 41.01S175.31E
Carthage Tunisia **32** 36.51N 10.21E
Carthage *site* Tunisia **32** 36.52N 10.20E
Carthage Mo. U.S.A. **111** 37.11N 94.19W
Carthage N.Y. U.S.A. **105** 43.59N 75.37W
Carthage S.Dak. U.S.A. **110** 44.10N 97.43W
Carthage Tex. U.S.A. **111** 32.09N 94.20W
Cartier Canada **104** 46.43N 81.34W
Cartwright Canada **103** 53.50N 56.45W
Caruarú Brazil **123** 8.15S 35.55W
Carúpano Venezuela **122** 10.39N 63.14W
Caruthersville U.S.A. **111** 36.11N 89.39W
Carvin France **19** 50.29N 2.58E
Carvoeiro Brazil **122** 1.24S 61.59W
Carvoeiro, Cabo *c.* Portugal **27** 39.21N 9.24W
Caryapundy Swamp Australia **92** 29.00S142.36E
Casablanca Morocco **74** 33.39N 7.35W
Casa Branca Brazil **126** 21.45S 47.06W
Casacalenda Italy **31** 41.44N 14.51E
Casa Grande U.S.A. **109** 32.53N111.45W
Casalbordino Italy **31** 42.09N 14.35E
Casale Italy **30** 45.08N 8.27E
Casarano Italy **33** 40.00N 18.10E
Casar de Cáceres Spain **27** 39.34N 6.25W
Casas Ibáñez Spain **25** 39.17N 1.28W
Casasimarro Spain **25** 39.22N 2.02W
Casavieja Spain **26** 40.17N 4.46W
Cascade Idaho U.S.A. **108** 44.31N116.02W
Cascade Mont. U.S.A. **108** 47.16N111.42W
Cascade Pt. New Zealand **86** 44.01S168.22E
Cascade Range *mts.* U.S.A. **108** 46.15N121.00W
Cascina Italy **30** 43.41N 10.33E
Caserta Italy **33** 41.04N 14.20E
Caseville U.S.A. **104** 43.56N 83.16W
Caseyr *c.* Somali Rep. **71** 11.48N 51.22E
Cashel Tipperary Rep. of Ire. **15** 52.31N 7.54W
Casilda Argentina **125** 33.03S 61.10W
Casimiro de Abreu Brazil **126** 22.28S 42.12W
Casino Australia **93** 28.50S153.02E
Casma Peru **122** 9.30S 78.20W
Casoli Italy **31** 42.07N 14.18E
Caspe Spain **25** 41.14N 0.02W
Casper U.S.A. **108** 42.51N106.19W
Caspian Depression *see* Prikaspiyskaya Nizmennost *ost* U.S.S.R. **45**
Caspian Sea U.S.S.R. **45** 42.00N 51.00E
Cass *r.* U.S.A. **114** 43.23N 83.59W
Cassai *r.* Angola **78** 10.38S 22.15E
Cassano allo Ionio Italy **33** 39.47N 16.20E
Cass City U.S.A. **114** 43.36N 83.10W
Casselman Canada **105** 45.19N 75.05W
Casselton U.S.A. **110** 46.54N 97.13W
Cassiar Canada **100** 59.16N129.40W
Cassiar Mts. Canada **100** 59.00N129.00W
Cassilis Australia **93** 32.01S149.59E
Cassino Italy **32** 41.30N 13.49E
Cass Lake *town* U.S.A. **110** 47.22N 94.35W
Casslar Mts. Canada **96** 59.30N130.30W
Castanheira de Pêra Portugal **27** 40.00N 8.13W
Castaños Mexico **111** 26.48N101.26W
Castelbuono Italy **33** 37.56N 14.06E
Castel del Piano Italy **30** 42.53N 11.32E
Castelfiorentino Italy **30** 43.36N 10.58E
Castelfranco Veneto Italy **30** 45.40N 11.55E
Casteljaloux France **20** 44.19N 0.05E
Castellammare Italy **33** 40.42N 14.29E
Castellammare, Golfo di *g.* Italy **32** 38.10N 12.55E
Castellammare del Golfo Italy **32** 38.01N 12.53E
Castellana Grotte Italy **33** 40.53N 17.11E
Castellaneta Italy **33** 40.37N 16.57E
Castell' Arquato Italy **30** 44.51N 9.52E
Castelli Argentina **125** 36.07S 57.50W
Castellón Spain **25** 39.59N 0.02W
Castellón *d.* Spain **25** 40.20N 0.00
Castellote Spain **25** 40.48N 0.19W
Castelmassa Italy **30** 45.01N 11.18E
Castelmoron-sur-Lot France **20** 44.24N 0.30E
Castelnaudary France **20** 43.19N 1.57E
Castelnau-Montratier France **20** 44.16N 1.21E
Castelnovo ne'Monti Italy **30** 44.26N 10.24E
Castelnuovo di Garfagnana Italy **30** 44.06N 10.24E
Castelo Brazil **126** 20.33S 41.14W
Castelo Branco Portugal **27** 39.49N 7.30W
Castelo Branco *d.* Portugal **27** 40.00N 7.30W
Castel San Giovanni Italy **30** 45.04N 9.26E
Castelsardo Italy **32** 40.55N 8.42E
Castelsarrasin France **20** 44.02N 1.06E
Casteltermini Italy **32** 37.32N 13.39E
Castelvetrano Italy **32** 37.41N 12.47E
Casterton Australia **92** 37.35S141.25E
Castets France **20** 43.53N 1.09W
Castiglion Fiorentino Italy **30** 43.20N 11.55E
Castile U.S.A. **114** 42.38N 78.03W
Castilla Peru **122** 5.16S 80.36W
Castilla la Mancha *d.* Spain **27** 39.50N 3.00W
Castilla y Leon *d.* Spain **26** 41.20N 4.30W
Castilletes Colombia **122** 11.55N 71.20W
Castillon-la-Bataille France **20** 44.51N 0.03W
Castlebar Rep. of Ire. **15** 53.52N 9.19W
Castleblayney Rep. of Ire. **15** 54.08N 6.46W
Castle Douglas U.K. **14** 54.56N 3.56W
Castleford U.K. **12** 53.43N 1.21W
Castlegar Canada **100** 49.20N117.40W
Castlegate U.S.A. **108** 39.44N110.52W
Castle Harbour *b.* Bermuda **127** 32.20N 64.40W
Castleisland Rep. of Ire. **15** 52.13N 9.28W
Castlemaine Australia **92** 37.05S144.19E
Castlerea Rep. of Ire. **15** 53.45N 8.30W
Castlereagh *r.* Australia **93** 30.12S147.32E
Castle Rock *town* Colo. U.S.A. **108** 39.22N104.51W
Castle Rock *town* Wash. U.S.A. **108** 46.17N122.54W
Castleton on Hudson U.S.A. **115** 42.32N 73.45W
Castletown U.K. **12** 54.04N 4.38W
Castletownshend Rep. of Ire. **15** 51.32N 9.12W
Castres France **20** 43.36N 2.15E
Castries St. Lucia **117** 14.01N 60.59W
Castro Chile **125** 42.30S 73.46W
Castro Daire Portugal **26** 40.54N 7.56W
Castro del Río Spain **27** 37.41N 4.28W
Castrojeriz Spain **26** 42.17N 4.08W
Castro Marim Portugal **27** 37.13N 7.26W
Castronuño Spain **26** 41.23N 5.16W
Castropol Spain **26** 43.32N 7.02W
Castro Urdiales Spain **26** 43.23N 3.13W
Castro Verde Portugal **26** 37.42N 8.05W
Castrovillari Italy **33** 39.49N 16.13E
Castuera Spain **26** 38.43N 5.33W
Casula Mozambique **79** 15.26S 33.32E
Cataguases Brazil **126** 21.23S 42.39W
Çatalca Turkey **29** 41.09N 28.29E
Catalina Pt. Guam **84** 13.31N144.55E
Cataluña *d.* Spain **25** 41.30N 1.00E
Catamarca Argentina **124** 28.30S 65.45W
Catamarca *d.* Argentina **124** 27.45S 67.00W
Catanduanes *i.* Phil. **59** 13.45N124.20E
Catanduva Brazil **126** 21.03S 49.00W
Catania Italy **33** 37.30N 15.06E
Catania, Golfo di *g.* Italy **33** 37.25N 15.15E
Catanzaro Italy **33** 38.54N 16.36E
Catarman Phil. **59** 12.28N124.50E
Catarroja Spain **25** 39.24N 0.24W
Catbalogan Phil. **59** 11.46N124.55E
Catchacombe L. Canada **104** 44.45N 78.20W
Catete Angola **78** 9.09S 13.40E

Cathcart to **Chegdomyn**

Cathcart Australia **93** 36.49S149.25E
Cathcart R.S.A. **80** 32.17S 27.08E
Cat I. Bahamas **113** 24.33N 75.36W
Cat L. Canada **102** 51.40N 91.50W
Catoche, C. Mexico **117** 21.38N 87.08W
Catonsville U.S.A. **114** 39.16N 76.44W
Catriló Argentina **125** 36.23S 63.24W
Catskill U.S.A. **115** 42.13N 73.52W
Catskill Mts. U.S.A. **115** 42.10N 74.30W
Catskill Park U.S.A. **115** 42.10N 74.10W
Cattaraugus U.S.A. **114** 42.20N 78.52W
Catterick U.K. **12** 54.23N 1.38W
Cattolica Italy **30** 43.58N 12.44E
Catuane Mozambique **81** 26.49S 32.17E
Catus France **20** 44.34N 1.20E
Cauca *r.* Colombia **122** 8.57N 74.30W
Caucasus Mts. *see* Kavkazskiy Khrebet *mts.* U.S.S.R. **45**
Caudry France **19** 50.07N 3.25E
Caulonia Italy **33** 38.23N 16.25E
Caungula Angola **78** 8.26S 18.35E
Cauquenes Chile **125** 35.58S 72.21W
Caura *r.* Venezuela **122** 7.38N 64.53W
Caussade France **20** 44.10N 1.32E
Causse du Larzac *f.* France **20** 44.00N 3.15E
Causse Méjean *f.* France **20** 44.15N 3.30E
Cava Italy **33** 40.42N 14.42E
Cávado *r.* Portugal **26** 41.32N 8.48W
Cavaillon France **21** 43.50N 5.02E
Cavalaire-sur-Mer France **21** 43.10N 6.32E
Cavalese Italy **30** 46.17N 11.27E
Cavalier U.S.A. **110** 48.48N 97.37W
Cavally *r.* Ivory Coast **76** 4.25N 7.39W
Cavan Rep. of Ire. **15** 54.00N 7.22W
Cavan *d.* Rep. of Ire. **15** 53.58N 7.10W
Cavarzere Italy **30** 45.08N 12.05E
Caviana, Ilha *i.* Brazil **123** 0.02N 50.00W
Cavtat Yugo. **31** 42.35N 18.13E
Cawndilla L. Australia **92** 32.30S142.18E
Caxambu Brazil **126** 21.59S 44.54W
Caxias Brazil **123** 4.53S 43.20W
Caxias do Sul Brazil **126** 29.14S 51.10W
Caxito Angola **78** 8.32S 13.38E
Cayambe Ecuador **122** 0.03N 78.08W
Cayenne Guiana **123** 4.55N 52.18W
Caylus France **20** 44.14N 1.46E
Cayman Brac *i.* Cayman Is. **117** 19.44N 79.48W
Cayman Is. C. America **117** 19.00N 81.00W
Cayman Trough Carib. Sea **127** 18.00N 8.00W
Cayuga Canada **104** 42.56N 79.51W
Cayuga L. U.S.A. **115** 42.55N 76.44W
Cazalla de la Sierra Spain **27** 37.56N 5.45W
Cazaux, Étang de *b.* France **20** 44.30N 1.10W
Cazenovia U.S.A. **115** 42.56N 75.51W
Cazères France **20** 43.13N 1.05E
Čazma Yugo. **31** 45.45N 16.37E
Cazombo Angola **78** 11.54S 22.56E
Cazorla Spain **27** 37.55N 3.00W
Cea *r.* Spain **26** 42.00N 5.36W
Ceara *d.* Brazil **123** 4.50S 39.00W
Ceba Canada **101** 53.07N102.14W
Ceballos Mexico **111** 26.32N104.09W
Cebollera, Sierra de *mts.* Spain **26** 41.55N 2.30W
Cebreros Spain **26** 40.27N 4.28W
Cebu Phil. **59** 10.17N123.56E
Cebu *i.* Phil. **59** 10.15N123.45E
Ceccano Italy **32** 41.34N 13.20E
Cecina Italy **30** 43.19N 10.31E
Cecita, Lago di *l.* Italy **33** 39.24N 16.30E
Cedar City U.S.A. **108** 37.41N113.04W
Cedar Falls *town* U.S.A. **110** 42.32N 92.27W
Cedar Grove U.S.A. **114** 38.13N 81.26W
Cedar Key U.S.A. **113** 29.08N 83.03W
Cedar L. *Man.* Canada **101** 53.20N100.00W
Cedar L. *Ont.* Canada **104** 46.02N 78.30W
Cedar Rapids *town* U.S.A. **110** 41.59N 91.40W
Cedarville U.S.A. **115** 39.20N 75.12W
Cedeira Spain **26** 43.39N 8.03W
Cedillo, Embalse de *resr.* Spain/Portugal **27** 39.40N 7.25W
Cedrino *r.* Italy **32** 40.23N 9.44E
Cedrón *r.* Spain **27** 39.57N 3.51W
Cedros, Isla *i.* Mexico **109** 28.10N115.15W
Ceduna Australia **92** 32.07S133.42E
Ceel Afweyne Somali Rep. **71** 9.55N 47.14E
Ceel Buur Somali Rep. **71** 4.40N 46.40E
Ceel Dhaab Somali Rep. **71** 8.58N 46.38E
Ceel Dheere Somali Rep. **71** 3.55N 47.10E
Ceel Xamurre Somali Rep. **71** 7.11N 48.55E
Ceepeecee Canada **100** 49.52N126.42W
Ceerigaabo Somali Rep. **71** 10.40N 47.20E
Cefalù Italy **33** 38.02N 14.01E
Cega *r.* Spain **26** 41.33N 4.46W
Cegléd Hungary **37** 47.10N 19.48E
Ceglie Italy **33** 40.39N 17.31E
Cehegín Spain **25** 38.06N 1.48W
Cela Angola **78** 11.26S 15.05E
Celano Italy **31** 42.05N 13.33E
Celanova Spain **26** 42.09N 7.58W
Celaya Mexico **116** 20.32N100.48W
Celebes *i. see* Sulawesi *i.* Indonesia **59**
Celebes Sea Indonesia **59** 3.00N122.00E
Celina U.S.A. **112** 40.34N 84.35W
Celje Yugo. **31** 46.14N 15.16E
Celle Germany **38** 52.37N 10.05E
Celorico da Beira Portugal **26** 40.38N 7.23W
Cemaes Head U.K. **13** 52.08N 4.42W
Cenderawasih, Teluk *b.* Indonesia **59** 2.20S135.50E
Ceno *r.* Italy **30** 44.41N 10.05E
Centerburg U.S.A. **114** 40.18N 82.42W
Center Cross U.S.A. **113** 37.48N 76.48W
Centerville Iowa U.S.A. **110** 40.43N 92.52W
Centerville S.Dak. U.S.A. **110** 43.07N 96.58W
Centerville Tenn. U.S.A. **113** 35.45N 87.29W
Cento Italy **30** 44.43N 11.17E
Central *d.* Botswana **80** 21.45S 26.15E
Central *d.* Ghana **76** 5.30N 1.10W
Central *d.* Kenya **79** 0.30S 37.00E
Central *d.* U.K. **14** 56.10N 4.20W
Central *d.* Zambia **80** 14.30S 29.30E
Central, Cordillera *mts.* Bolivia **124** 18.30S 65.00W
Central, Cordillera *mts.* Colombia **120** 6.00N 75.00W
Central African Republic Africa **70** 7.00N 20.00E
Central Brāhui Range *mts.* Pakistan **62** 29.15N 67.15E
Central City Ky. U.S.A. **113** 37.17N 87.08W
Central City Nebr. U.S.A. **110** 41.07N 98.00W
Central I. Kenya **79** 3.30N 36.02E
Centralia Ill. U.S.A. **110** 38.32N 89.08W
Centralia Wash. U.S.A. **108** 46.43N122.58W
Central Makrān Range *mts.* Pakistan **62** 26.30N 65.00E
Central Siberian Plateau *see* Sredne Sibirskoye Ploskogor'ye. *f.* U.S.S.R. **51**
Central Square U.S.A. **115** 43.17N 76.09W
Centre *d.* Burkina **76** 11.50N 1.10W
Centre *d.* Ethiopia **73** 5.49N 37.35E
Centre, Canal du France **19** 46.27N 4.07E
Centre Est *d.* Burkina **76** 11.20N 0.10W
Centre Nord *d.* Burkina **76** 13.30N 1.00W
Centre Ouest *d.* Burkina **76** 12.00N 2.20W
Centreville Ala. U.S.A. **113** 32.57N 87.08W
Centreville Md. U.S.A. **115** 39.03N 76.04W
Century Fla. U.S.A. **113** 30.59N 87.18W
Century W.Va. U.S.A. **114** 39.06N 80.11W
Cepu Indonesia **59** 7.07S111.35E
Ceram *i. see* Seram *i.* Indonesia **59**
Ceram Sea *see* Seram, Laut *sea* Pacific Oc. **59**
Cère *r.* France **20** 44.55N 1.53E
Ceres U.S.A. **108** 37.35N120.57W
Ceresole Reale Italy **30** 45.26N 7.15E
Céret France **20** 42.29N 2.45E
Cereté Colombia **122** 8.54N 75.51W
Cerignola Italy **33** 41.16N 15.54E
Cérilly France **20** 46.37N 2.49E
Cerisiers France **19** 48.08N 3.29E
Cerknica Yugo. **31** 45.48N 14.22E
Cernavodă Romania **37** 44.20N 28.02E
Cernay France **19** 47.49N 7.10E
Cerralvo, Isla *i.* Mexico **109** 24.17N109.52W
Cërrik Albania **34** 41.02N 19.57E
Cerritos Mexico **116** 22.26N100.17W
Cerro de Pasco Peru **122** 10.43S 76.15W
Cervaro *r.* Italy **33** 41.30N 15.52E
Cervati, Monte *mtn.* Italy **33** 40.17N 15.29E
Cervera Lérida Spain **25** 41.40N 1.17E
Cervera Logroño Spain **26** 42.01N 1.57W
Cervera de Pisuerga Spain **26** 42.52N 4.30W
Cervia Italy **30** 44.15N 12.22E
Cervialto, Monte *mtn.* Italy **33** 40.47N 15.08E
Cervignano del Friuli Italy **30** 45.49N 13.20E
Cervione France **21** 42.20N 9.31E
Cervo Spain **26** 43.40N 7.25W
Cesena Italy **30** 44.08N 12.15E
Cesenatico Italy **30** 44.12N 12.24E
Cēsis U.S.S.R. **44** 57.18N 25.18E
Česká Kamenice Czech. **38** 50.47N 14.26E
Česká Lípa Czech. **38** 50.42N 14.32E
České Budějovice Czech. **36** 49.00N 14.30E
České Zemé *d.* Czech. **39** 49.50N 13.20E
Český Krumlov Czech. **39** 48.49N 14.19E
Çesme Turkey **35** 38.18N 26.19E
Cessnock Australia **93** 32.51S151.21E
Cetinje Yugo. **31** 42.23N 18.55E
Ceuta Spain **27** 35.53N 5.19W
Ceva Italy **30** 44.23N 8.01E
Cévennes *mts.* France **21** 44.00N 3.30E
Ceyhan Turkey **64** 37.02N 35.48E
Ceyhan *r.* Turkey **64** 36.54N 34.58E
Cèze *r.* France **21** 44.06N 4.42E
Chabanais France **20** 45.52N 0.43E
Chablis France **19** 47.49N 3.48E
Chacabuco Argentina **125** 34.38S 60.29W
Chachani *mtn.* Peru **122** 16.12S 71.32W
Chachapoyas Peru **122** 6.13S 77.54W
Chāchro Pakistan **62** 25.07N 70.15E
Chaco *d.* Argentina **124** 26.30S 60.00W
Chad Africa **70** 16.00N 18.00E
Chad, L. Africa **77** 13.30N 14.00E
Chadron U.S.A. **110** 42.50N103.02W
Chafe Nigeria **77** 11.56N 6.55E
Chāgai Pakistan **62** 29.18N 64.42E
Chāgai Hills Pakistan **62** 29.10N 63.35E
Chagda U.S.S.R. **51** 58.44N130.38E
'Chaghcharān Afghan. **62** 34.32N 65.15E
Chagny France **19** 46.55N 4.45E
Chagos Archipelago *is.* Indian Oc. **49** 7.00S 72.00E
Chagrin Falls *town* U.S.A. **114** 41.26N 81.24W
Cha'gyüngoinba China **63** 31.10N 90.42E
Chahār Borjak Afghan. **62** 30.17N 62.03E
Chāh Sandan *well* Pakistan **62** 28.59N 63.27E
Chaibāsā India **63** 22.34N 85.49E
Chaillé-les-Marais France **18** 46.24N 1.01W
Chainat Thailand **56** 15.10N100.10E
Chaiyaphum Thailand **56** 15.46N101.57E
Chajarí Argentina **125** 30.45S 57.59W
Chākāi India **63** 24.34N 86.24E
Chākdaha India **63** 23.05N 88.31E
Chake Chake Tanzania **79** 5.13S 39.46E
Chakhānsūr Afghan. **62** 31.10N 62.04E
Chakradharpur India **63** 22.42N 85.38E
Chakwāl Pakistan **62** 32.56N 72.52E
Chala Peru **122** 15.48S 74.20W
Chalais France **20** 45.16N 0.02E
Chaleur B. Canada **103** 48.00N 65.45W
Chalhuanca Peru **122** 14.20S 73.10W
Chālisgaon India **62** 20.28N 75.01E
Chalk River *town* Canada **105** 46.01N 77.27W
Challans France **18** 46.51N 1.53W
Challenger Depth Pacific Oc. **59** 11.19N142.15E
Challis U.S.A. **108** 44.30N114.14W
Chalonnes-sur-Loire France **18** 47.21N 0.46W
Châlons-sur-Marne France **19** 48.57N 4.22E
Chalon-sur-Saône France **19** 46.47N 4.51E
Chalosse *d.* France **20** 43.45N 0.30W
Châlus France **20** 45.39N 0.59E
Cham Germany **39** 49.13N 12.41E
Chama U.S.A. **108** 36.54N106.35W
Chama Zambia **79** 11.09S 33.10E
Chaman Pakistan **62** 30.55N 66.27E
Chamba India **62** 32.34N 76.08E
Chambal *r.* India **63** 26.29N 79.15E
Chamberlain U.S.A. **110** 43.49N 99.20W
Chambersburg U.S.A. **114** 39.56N 77.39W
Chambéry France **21** 45.34N 5.56E
Chambeshi Zambia **79** 10.57S 31.04E
Chambeshi *r.* Zambia **79** 11.15S 30.37E
Chambley-Bussières France **19** 49.03N 5.54E
Chambly Canada **105** 45.27N 73.17W
Chambly France **19** 49.10N 2.15E
Chambon-sur-Voueize France **20** 46.11N 2.25E
Chamburi Kalāt Pakistan **62** 26.09N 64.43E
Cha Messengue Angola **78** 11.04S 18.56E
Chamical Argentina **124** 30.22S 66.19W
Ch'amo Hāyk' *l.* Ethiopia **73** 5.49N 37.35E
Chamoli India **63** 30.24N 79.21E
Chamonix France **21** 45.55N 6.52E
Chāmpa India **63** 22.03N 82.39E
Champagne Canada **100** 60.47N136.29W
Champagne-Ardenne *d.* France **19** 49.00N 4.30E
Champagnole France **19** 46.45N 5.55E
Champaign U.S.A. **110** 40.07N 88.14W
Champdeniers France **18** 46.29N 0.24W
Champdoré, Lac *l.* Canada **103** 55.55N 65.50W
Champeix France **20** 45.36N 3.08E
Champéry Switz. **39** 46.10N 6.52E
Champlain Canada **105** 46.27N 72.21W
Champlain U.S.A. **105** 44.59N 73.27W
Champlain, L. U.S.A. **105** 44.45N 73.15W
Champlitte-et-le-Prélot France **19** 47.37N 5.31E
Champotón Mexico **116** 19.21N 90.43W
Chāmpua India **63** 22.05N 85.40E
Chamusca Portugal **27** 39.21N 8.29W
Chañaral Chile **124** 26.21S 70.37W
Chānasma India **62** 23.43N 72.07E
Chandausi India **63** 28.27N 78.46E
Chāndbāli India **63** 20.46N 86.49E
Chandeleur Is. U.S.A. **111** 29.48N 88.51W
Chandīgarh India **62** 30.44N 76.47E
Chandīgarh *d.* India **62** 30.45N 76.45E
Chāndil India **63** 22.58N 86.03E
Chandler Canada **103** 48.21N 64.41W
Chandler U.S.A. **111** 35.42N 96.53W
Chāndor Hills India **62** 20.30N 74.00E
Chandos L. Canada **105** 44.49N 78.00W
Chāndpur Bangla. **61** 22.08N 91.55E
Chāndpur Bangla. **63** 23.13N 90.39E
Chāndpur India **63** 29.09N 78.16E
Chandrapur India **63** 19.57N 79.18E
Chāndvad India **62** 20.20N 74.15E
Chānf Iran **65** 26.40N 60.31E
Chang, Ko *i.* Thailand **56** 12.04N102.23E
Changchun China **53** 43.51N125.15E
Changde China **55** 29.00N111.35E
Changfeng China **54** 32.27N117.09E
Changhua Jiang *r.* China **55** 19.20N108.38E
Chang Jiang *r.* China **55** 31.40N121.15E
Changjin N. Korea **53** 40.21N127.20E
Changle China **54** 36.42N118.49E
Changli China **54** 39.43N119.08E
Changling China **54** 44.16N123.58E
Changning China **55** 26.24N112.24E
Changping China **54** 40.12N116.12E
Changsha China **55** 28.09N112.59E
Changshan China **55** 28.57N118.31E
Changshan Qundao *is.* China **54** 39.20N123.00E
Changshou China **55** 29.50N107.02E
Changshu China **55** 31.48N120.52E
Changshun China **55** 25.59N106.25E
Changting China **55** 25.42N116.20E
Changyi China **54** 36.51N119.23E
Changzhi China **54** 36.10N113.00E
Changzhou China **55** 31.46N119.58E
Channel Is. U.K. **13** 49.28N 2.13W
Channel Is. U.S.A. **109** 34.00N120.00W
Channel-Port-aux-Basques *town* Canada **103** 47.35N 59.11W
Channing Mich. U.S.A. **112** 46.08N 88.06W
Channing Tex. U.S.A. **111** 35.41N102.20W
Chantada Spain **26** 42.37N 7.46W
Chanthaburi Thailand **56** 12.35N102.05E
Chantilly France **19** 49.12N 2.28E
Chanute U.S.A. **111** 37.41N 95.27W
Chao'an China **55** 23.40N116.32E
Chao Hu *l.* China **55** 31.32N117.30E
Chaonde Mozambique **81** 13.43S 40.31E
Chao Phraya *r.* Thailand **56** 13.34N100.35E
Chao Xian China **55** 31.36N117.52E
Chaoyang Guangdong China **55** 23.25N116.31E
Chaoyang Liaoning China **54** 41.35N120.20E
Chapada das Mangabeiras *mts.* Brazil **123** 10.00S 46.30W
Chapada Diamantina Brazil **126** 13.30S 42.30W
Chapala, Lago de *l.* Mexico **116** 20.00N103.00W
Chapayevo U.S.S.R **45** 50.12N 51.09E
Chapayevsk U.S.S.R. **44** 52.58N 49.44E
Chapeau Canada **105** 45.54N 77.05W
Chapeau de Paille Canada **105** 47.10N 73.30W
Chapelle-d'Angillon France **19** 47.22N 2.26E
Chapicuy Uruguay **125** 31.39S 57.54W
Chapleau Canada **102** 47.50N 83.24W
Chāpra India **63** 25.46N 84.45E
Chaqui Bolivia **124** 19.36S 65.32W
Characot I. Antarctica **128** 70.00S 75.00W
Charay Mexico **109** 26.01N108.50W
Charcas Mexico **116** 23.08N101.07W
Chard U.K. **13** 50.52N 2.59W
Chardon U.S.A. **114** 41.35N 81.12W
Charduār India **63** 26.52N 92.46E
Chardzhou U.S.S.R. **65** 39.09N 63.34E
Charente *d.* France **20** 45.40N 0.10E
Charente *r.* France **20** 45.57N 1.05W
Charente-Maritime *d.* France **20** 45.30N 0.45W
Charenton-du-Cher France **19** 46.44N 2.38E
Chari *r.* Chad **77** 13.00N 14.30E
Chari-Baguirmi *d.* Chad **77** 12.20N 15.30E
Chārīkār Afghan. **62** 35.01N 69.11E
Charing U.K. **13** 51.12N 0.49E
Chariton U.S.A. **110** 41.01N 93.19W
Charleroi Belgium **16** 50.25N 4.27E
Charlesbourg Canada **105** 46.51N 71.16W
Charles City U.S.A. **110** 43.04N 92.40W
Charles Pt. Australia **88** 12.23S130.37E
Charleston Miss. U.S.A. **111** 34.00N 90.04W
Charleston S.C. U.S.A. **113** 32.48N 79.58W
Charleston W.Va. U.S.A. **114** 38.21N 81.38W
Charlestown Rep. of Ire. **15** 53.57N 8.48W
Charlestown Ind. U.S.A. **112** 38.28N 85.40W
Charlestown N.H. U.S.A. **115** 43.14N 72.26W
Charles Town W.Va. U.S.A. **114** 39.17N 77.52W
Charlesville Zaïre **78** 5.27S 20.58E
Charleville Australia **90** 26.25S146.13E
Charleville-Mézières France **19** 49.46N 4.43E
Charlieu France **21** 46.10N 4.10E
Charlotte N.C. U.S.A. **113** 35.03N 80.50W
Charlotte Va. U.S.A. **113** 37.03N 78.44W
Charlottenberg Sweden **43** 59.53N 12.17E
Charlottesville U.S.A. **113** 38.02N 78.29W
Charlottetown Canada **103** 46.14N 63.08W
Charlton Australia **92** 36.18S143.27E
Charlton I. Canada **102** 52.00N 79.30W
Charly-sur-Marne France **19** 48.58N 3.17E
Charmes France **19** 48.22N 6.17E
Charny Canada **105** 46.43N 71.16W
Charolles France **19** 46.26N 4.17E
Charroux France **18** 46.09N 0.24E
Chārsadda Pakistan **62** 34.09N 71.44E
Charters Towers Australia **90** 20.05S146.16E
Chartres France **18** 48.27N 1.30E
Chascomús Argentina **125** 35.35S 58.00W
Chase City U.S.A. **113** 36.59N 78.30W
Châteaubriant France **18** 47.43N 1.23W
Château-Chinon France **19** 47.04N 3.56E
Château d'Oex Switz. **39** 46.28N 7.08E
Château-du-Loir France **18** 47.42N 0.25E
Châteaudun France **18** 48.05N 1.20E
Chateaugay U.S.A. **105** 44.56N 74.05W
Château Gontier France **18** 47.50N 0.42W
Châteauguay, Lac *l.* Canada **103** 56.27N 70.05W
Château Landon France **19** 48.09N 2.42E
Château-la-Vallière France **18** 47.33N 0.19E
Châteaulin France **18** 48.12N 4.05W
Châteaumeillant France **19** 46.34N 2.12E
Châteauneuf-de-Randon France **20** 44.39N 3.40E
Châteauneuf-en-Thymerais France **18** 48.35N 1.15E
Châteauneuf-sur-Charente France **20** 45.36N 0.03W
Châteauneuf-sur-Loire France **19** 47.52N 2.14E
Châteauneuf-sur-Sarthe France **18** 47.41N 0.30W
Château-Porcien France **19** 49.32N 4.15E
Château Renault France **18** 47.35N 0.55E
Châteauroux France **19** 46.49N 1.42E
Château-Salins France **19** 48.49N 6.30E
Château-Thierry France **19** 49.03N 3.24E
Châtelet Belgium **16** 50.24N 4.32E
Châtellerault France **18** 46.49N 0.33E
Châtel-sur-Moselle France **19** 48.18N 6.24E
Châtelus-Malvaleix France **20** 46.18N 2.01E
Chatham N.B. Canada **103** 47.02N 65.28W
Chatham Ont. Canada **104** 42.24N 82.11W
Chatham U.K. **13** 51.23N 0.32E
Chatham Alas. U.S.A. **100** 57.30N135.00W
Chatham Mass. U.S.A. **115** 41.41N 69.58W
Chatham N.Y. U.S.A. **115** 42.22N 73.36W
Chatham Is. Pacific Oc. **84** 44.00S176.35W
Chatham Rise Pacific Oc. **84** 43.30S178.00W
Chatham Str. U.S.A. **100** 57.30N134.45W
Châtillon Italy **30** 45.45N 7.37E
Châtillon-Coligny France **19** 47.50N 2.51E
Châtillon-en-Bazois France **19** 47.03N 3.49E
Châtillon-sur-Chalaronne France **21** 46.07N 4.58E
Châtillon-sur-Indre France **18** 46.59N 1.11E
Châtillon-sur-Seine France **19** 47.51N 4.33E
Chatra India **63** 24.13N 84.52E
Chatrapur India **63** 19.21N 84.59E
Chātsu India **62** 26.36N 75.57E
Chatsworth Canada **104** 44.27N 80.54W
Chattahoochee U.S.A. **113** 30.42N 84.51W
Chattahoochee *r.* U.S.A. **113** 30.52N 84.57W
Chattanooga U.S.A. **113** 35.02N 85.18W
Chatteris U.K. **13** 52.27N 0.03E
Chaudes-Aigues France **20** 44.51N 3.00E
Chauk Burma **56** 20.52N 94.50E
Chaulnes France **19** 49.49N 2.48E
Chaumont France **19** 48.07N 5.08E
Chaumont-en-Vexin France **19** 49.16N 1.53E
Chaungwabyin Burma **56** 13.41N 98.22E
Chauny France **19** 49.37N 3.13E
Chaupāran India **63** 24.23N 85.15E
Chau Phu Vietnam **56** 10.42N105.03E
Chaussin France **19** 46.58N 5.25E
Chausy U.S.S.R. **37** 53.49N 30.57E
Chautauqua L. U.S.A. **114** 42.12N 79.27W
Chauvigny France **18** 46.34N 0.39E
Chavanges France **19** 48.31N 4.34E
Chaves Brazil **123** 0.10S 49.55W
Chaves Portugal **26** 41.44N 7.28W
Chavuma Zambia **78** 13.04S 22.43E
Chawang Thailand **56** 8.25N 99.32E
Cheat *r.* U.S.A. **114** 39.06N 79.33W
Cheat Mtn. U.S.A. **114** 38.43N 79.51W
Cheb Czech. **39** 50.01N 12.25E
Cheboksary U.S.S.R. **44** 56.08N 47.12E
Cheboygan U.S.A. **104** 45.39N 84.29W
Chebsara U.S.S.R. **44** 59.14N 38.59E
Chebula Angola **78** 12.27S 23.49E
Chech, Erg *des.* Mali/Algeria **74** 24.30N 2.30W
Chechaouene Morocco **74** 35.10N 5.16W
Chechersk U.S.S.R. **37** 52.54N 30.54E
Checiny Poland **37** 50.48N 20.28E
Cheduba I. Burma **56** 18.50N 93.35E
Chef-Boutonne France **18** 46.07N 0.04W
Chegdomyn U.S.S.R. **51** 51.09N133.01E

Chegga to Ciudad Lerdo

Chegga *well* Mauritania **74** 25.30N 5.46W
Chegutu Zimbabwe **80** 18.09S 30.07E
Chehalis U.S.A. **108** 46.40N122.58W
Cheil, Ras el *c.* Somali Rep. **71** 7.45N 49.48E
Cheiron, Cime du *mtn.* France **21** 43.49N 6.58E
Cheju S. Korea **53** 33.31N126.29E
Cheju do *i.* S. Korea **53** 33.20N126.30E
Cheleken U.S.S.R. **65** 39.26N 53.11E
Chelforó Argentina **125** 39.04S 66.33W
Chelif, Oued *r.* Algeria **75** 36.15N 2.05E
Chelkar U.S.S.R. **50** 47.48N 59.39E
Chelles France **19** 48.53N 2.36E
Chełm Poland **37** 51.10N 23.28E
Chelmer *r.* U.K. **11** 51.43N 0.40E
Chelmsford Canada **104** 46.35N 81.12W
Chelmsford U.K. **13** 51.44N 0.28E
Chełmza Poland **37** 53.12N 18.37E
Chelsea Canada **105** 45.29N 75.48W
Chelsea *Mich.* U.S.A. **104** 42.19N 84.01W
Chelsea *Vt.* U.S.A. **105** 43.59N 72.27W
Cheltenham U.K. **13** 51.53N 2.07W
Chelva Spain **25** 39.45N 1.00W
Chelyabinsk U.S.S.R. **9** 55.12N 61.25E
Chelyuskin, Mys *c.* U.S.S.R. **51** 77.20N106.00E
Chemainus Canada **100** 48.55N123.48W
Chemba Mozambique **79** 17.11S 34.53E
Chemillé France **18** 47.13N 0.44W
Chemnitz Germany **38** 50.50N 12.55E
Chemult U.S.A. **108** 43.13N121.47W
Chën, Gora *mtn.* U.S.S.R. **51** 65.30N141.20E
Chenāb *r.* Pakistan **62** 29.23N 71.02E
Chenachane Algeria **74** 26.00N 4.15W
Chenango *r.* U.S.A. **115** 42.05N 75.55W
Chénéville Canada **105** 45.53N 75.03W
Cheney U.S.A. **108** 47.29N117.34W
Chengchow *see* Zhengzhou China **54**
Chengde China **54** 41.00N117.52E
Chengdu China **55** 30.41N104.05E
Chenggu China **54** 33.10N107.22E
Chenghai China **55** 23.31N116.43E
Chengkou China **55** 31.58N108.48E
Chengmai China **55** 19.44N109.59E
Cheng Xian China **54** 33.42N105.36E
Chenoa U.S.A. **110** 40.44N 88.43W
Chen Xian China **55** 25.45N113.00E
Chepelare Bulgaria **34** 41.44N 24.41E
Chepen Peru **122** 7.15S 79.20W
Chepstow U.K. **13** 51.38N 2.40W
Cher *d.* France **19** 47.05N 2.30E
Cher *r.* France **18** 47.21N 0.29E
Cherbourg France **18** 49.39N 1.39W
Cherdyn U.S.S.R. **44** 60.25N 55.22E
Cherelato Ethiopia **73** 6.00N 38.10E
Cheremkhovo U.S.S.R. **51** 53.08N103.01E
Cherepovets U.S.S.R. **44** 59.05N 37.55E
Chergui, Chott ech *f.* Algeria **75** 34.21N 0.30E
Cherikov U.S.S.R. **37** 53.35N 31.23E
Cherkassy U.S.S.R. **45** 49.27N 32.04E
Cherkessk U.S.S.R. **45** 44.14N 42.05E
Cherkovitsa Bulgaria **34** 43.41N 24.49E
Cherlak U.S.S.R. **50** 54.10N 74.52E
Chernigov U.S.S.R. **37** 51.30N 31.18E
Chernikovsk U.S.S.R. **44** 54.51N 56.06E
Chernobyl U.S.S.R. **37** 51.17N 30.15E
Chernovtsy U.S.S.R. **37** 48.19N 25.52E
Chernyakhov U.S.S.R. **37** 50.30N 28.38E
Chernyakhovsk U.S.S.R. **41** 54.38N 21.49E
Cherokee Iowa U.S.A. **110** 42.45N 95.33W
Cherokee Okla. U.S.A. **111** 36.45N 98.21W
Cherquenco Chile **125** 38.41S 72.00W
Cherrapunji India **63** 25.18N 91.42E
Cherry Creek *r.* U.S.A. **110** 44.36N101.30W
Cherry Creek *town* Nev. U.S.A. **108** 39.54N113.53W
Cherry Creek *town* S.Dak. U.S.A. **110** 44.36N101.26W
Cherry Valley *town* U.S.A. **115** 42.48N 74.45W
Cherskogo, Khrebet *mts.* U.S.S.R. **51** 65.50N143.00E
Chertkovo U.S.S.R. **45** 49.22N 40.12E
Chertsey U.K. **13** 51.23N 0.27W
Cherven-Bryag Bulgaria **34** 43.17N 24.07E
Chervonograd U.S.S.R. **37** 50.25N 24.10E
Cherwell *r.* U.K. **13** 51.44N 1.15W
Chesaning U.S.A. **104** 43.11N 84.07W
Chesapeake Ohio U.S.A. **114** 38.26N 82.28W
Chesapeake Va. U.S.A. **113** 36.43N 76.15W
Chesapeake W.Va. U.S.A. **114** 38.12N 81.33W
Chesapeake B. U.S.A. **115** 38.40N 76.25W
Chesapeake Beach *town* U.S.A. **115** 38.41N 76.32W
Chesham U.K. **13** 51.43N 0.38W
Cheshire *d.* U.K. **12** 53.14N 2.30W
Chëshskaya Guba *g.* U.S.S.R. **44** 67.20N 46.30E
Chesht-e Sharīf Afghan. **62** 34.21N 63.44E
Chesil Beach *f.* U.K. **13** 50.37N 2.33W
Chesley Canada **104** 44.17N 81.05W
Chester U.K. **12** 53.12N 2.53W
Chester Mont. U.S.A. **108** 48.31N110.58W
Chester Penn. U.S.A. **115** 39.51N 75.21W
Chester Vt. U.S.A. **115** 43.16N 72.36W
Chesterfield U.K. **12** 53.14N 1.26W
Chesterfield, Îles *is.* N. Cal. **84** 20.00S159.00E
Chesterfield Inlet *town* Canada **99** 63.00N 91.00W
Chestertown Md. U.S.A. **115** 39.13N 76.04W
Chestertown N.Y. U.S.A. **115** 43.38N 73.49W
Chesterville Canada **105** 45.06N 75.14W
Chestnut Ridge *mtn.* U.S.A. **114** 40.09N 79.24W
Chesuncook L. U.S.A. **112** 46.00N 69.20W
Chéticamp Canada **103** 46.38N 61.01W
Chetumal Mexico **117** 18.30N 88.17W
Chetumal B. Mexico **117** 18.30N 88.00W
Chetwynd Canada **100** 55.45N121.45W
Cheviot New Zealand **86** 42.49S173.16E
Cheviot U.S.A. **112** 39.10N 84.32W
Ch'ew Bahir *l.* Ethiopia **73** 4.40N 36.50E
Cheyenne *r.* U.S.A. **110** 44.40N101.15W
Cheyenne Okla. U.S.A. **111** 35.37N 99.40W
Cheyenne Wyo. U.S.A. **108** 41.08N104.49W
Cheyne B. Australia **89** 34.35S118.50E
Chhabra India **62** 24.40N 76.50E
Chhātak Bangla. **63** 25.02N 91.40E
Chhatarpur Bihār India **63** 24.23N 84.11E
Chhatarpur Madhya P. India **63** 24.54N 79.36E
Chhattīsgarh *f.* India **63** 21.00N 82.00E
Chhindwāra India **63** 22.04N 78.56E
Chhota-Chhindwāra India **63** 23.03N 79.29E
Chhota Udepur India **62** 22.19N 74.01E
Chiali Taiwan **55** 23.10N120.11E
Chiang Mai Thailand **56** 18.48N 98.59E
Chiapas *d.* Mexico **116** 16.30N 93.00W
Chiaramonte Gulfi Italy **33** 37.01N 14.43E
Chiaravalle Centrale Italy **33** 38.41N 16.25E
Chiari Italy **30** 45.32N 9.56E
Chiavari Italy **30** 44.19N 9.19E
Chiavenna Italy **30** 46.19N 9.24E
Chiba Japan **57** 35.36N140.07E
Chiba *d.* Japan **57** 35.10N140.00E
Chibemba Angola **80** 15.43S 14.07E
Chibia Angola **78** 15.10S 13.32E
Chibougamau Canada **102** 49.56N 74.24W
Chibougamau Lac *l.* Canada **102** 49.50N 74.20W
Chibougamau Prov. Park Canada **103** 49.25N 73.50W
Chibuk Nigeria **77** 10.52N 12.50E
Chibuto Mozambique **81** 24.41S 33.32E
Chicago U.S.A. **110** 41.50N 87.45W
Chichagof I. U.S.A. **100** 57.55N135.45W
Chicheng China **54** 40.52N115.50E
Chichester U.K. **13** 50.50N 0.47W
Chichibu Japan **57** 35.59N139.05E
Chickasha U.S.A. **111** 35.02N 97.58W
Chiclana Spain **27** 36.25N 6.08W
Chiclayo Peru **122** 6.47S 79.47W
Chico *r.* Chubut Argentina **125** 43.45S 66.10W
Chico *r.* Santa Cruz Argentina **125** 50.03W 68.35W
Chico U.S.A. **108** 39.44N121.50W
Chicomo Mozambique **81** 24.33S 34.11E
Chicopee U.S.A. **115** 42.10N 72.36W
Chicora U.S.A. **114** 40.57N 79.45W
Chicoutimi-Jonquière Canada **103** 48.26N 71.06W
Chicualacuala Mozambique **81** 22.06S 31.42E
Chidambarum India **61** 11.24N 79.42E
Chidembo Angola **78** 14.34S 19.17E
Chidenguele Mozambique **81** 24.54S 34.13E
Chidley, C. Canada **99** 60.30N 65.00W
Chiemsee *l.* Germany **39** 47.54N 12.29E
Chiengi Zambia **79** 8.42S 29.07E
Chieri Italy **30** 45.01N 7.49E
Chieti Italy **31** 42.21N 14.10E
Chifeng China **54** 42.13N118.56E
Chigasaki Japan **57** 35.19N139.24E
Chignecto B. Canada **103** 45.35N 64.45W
Chiguana Bolivia **124** 21.05S 67.58W
Chigubo Mozambique **81** 22.38S 33.18E
Chigu Co *l.* China **63** 28.40N 91.50E
Chihuahua Mexico **109** 28.38N106.05W
Chihuahua *d.* Mexico **109** 28.40N106.00W
Chiili U.S.S.R. **50** 44.10N 66.37E
Chikhli India **62** 20.21N 76.15E
Chikumbi Zambia **79** 15.14S 28.21E
Chikwawa Malaŵi **79** 16.00S 34.54E
Chīl *r.* Iran **65** 25.12N 61.30E
Chilanga Zambia **80** 15.33S 28.17E
Chilapa Mexico **116** 17.38N 99.11W
Chilcoot U.S.A. **108** 39.49N120.08W
Childers Australia **90** 25.14S152.17E
Childress U.S.A. **111** 34.25N100.13W
Chile S. America **124** 32.30S 71.00W
Chile Basin Pacific Oc. **85** 34.20S 80.00W
Chile Chico Chile **125** 46.33S 71.44W
Chilka L. India **63** 19.46N 85.20E
Chilko L. Canada **98** 51.20N124.05W
Chillagoe Australia **90** 17.09S144.32E
Chillán Chile **125** 36.36S 72.07W
Chillicothe Mo. U.S.A. **110** 39.48N 93.33W
Chillicothe Ohio U.S.A. **112** 39.20N 82.59W
Chilliwack Canada **100** 49.10N122.00W
Chiloé, Isla de *i.* Chile **125** 43.00S 73.00W
Chilonga Zambia **79** 12.02S 31.17E
Chilpancingo Mexico **116** 17.33N 99.30W
Chiltern Australia **93** 36.11S146.36E
Chiltern Hills U.K. **13** 51.40N 0.53W
Chilton U.S.A. **110** 44.04N 88.10W
Chilumba Malaŵi **79** 10.25S 34.18E
Chilwa, L. Malaŵi **79** 15.15S 35.45E
Chimakela Angola **78** 15.12S 16.58E
Chimanimani Zimbabwe **81** 19.48S 32.52E
Chimay Belgium **16** 50.03N 4.20E
Chimbas Argentina **124** 31.28S 68.30W
Chimborazo *mtn.* Ecuador **122** 1.29S 78.52W
Chimbote Peru **122** 9.04S 78.34W
Chimishliya U.S.S.R. **37** 46.30N 28.50E
Chimkent U.S.S.R. **52** 42.16N 69.05E
Chimoio Mozambique **81** 19.04S 33.29E
Chin *d.* Burma **56** 22.00N 93.30E
China Asia **52** 33.00N103.00E
China Lake *town* U.S.A. **109** 35.46N117.39W
Chinandega Nicaragua **117** 12.35N 87.10W
Chinati Peak U.S.A. **109** 29.57N104.29W
Chincha Alta Peru **122** 13.25S 76.07W
Chinchaga *r.* Canada **100** 58.50N118.20W
Chinchilla Australia **91** 26.44S150.39E
Chinchón Spain **27** 40.08N 3.25W
Chinchoua Gabon **78** 0.00 9.48E
Chincilla de Monte Aragón Spain **25** 38.55N 1.45W
Chincoteague U.S.A. **113** 37.55N 75.23W
Chinde Mozambique **81** 18.37S 36.24E
Chindio Mozambique **79** 17.46S 35.23E
Chindwin *r.* Burma **56** 21.30N 95.12E
Chinga Mozambique **79** 15.14S 38.40E
Chingleput India **61** 12.42N 79.59E
Chingola Zambia **79** 12.29S 27.53E
Chingombe Zambia **79** 14.25S 29.56E
Chingshui Taiwan **55** 24.15N120.35E
Chin Hills Burma **56** 22.30N 93.30E
Chinhoyi Zimbabwe **80** 17.22S 30.10E
Chīni India **63** 31.32N 78.15E
Chiniot Pakistan **62** 31.43N 72.59E
Chinjan Pakistan **62** 30.34N 67.58E
Chinkapook Australia **92** 35.11S142.57E
Chinko *r.* C.A.R. **73** 4.50N 23.53E
Chinle U.S.A. **109** 36.09N109.33W
Chinon France **18** 47.10N 0.15E
Chinook U.S.A. **108** 48.35N109.14W
Chino Valley *town* U.S.A. **109** 34.45N112.27W
Chinsali Zambia **79** 10.33S 32.05E
Chintheche Malaŵi **79** 11.50S 34.13E
Chiny Belgium **16** 49.45N 5.20E
Chiôco Mozambique **79** 16.27S 32.49E
Chioggia Italy **30** 45.13N 12.17E
Chipata Zambia **79** 13.37S 32.40E
Chipera Mozambique **79** 15.20S 32.35E
Chipie *r.* Canada **102** 51.25N 83.20W
Chipinge Zimbabwe **81** 20.12S 32.38E
Chippenham U.K. **13** 51.27N 2.07W
Chippewa *r.* U.S.A. **104** 43.35N 84.17W
Chippewa Falls *town* U.S.A. **110** 44.56N 91.24W
Chipping Norton U.K. **13** 51.56N 1.32W
Chiquian Peru **122** 10.10S 77.00W
Chiquinquirá Colombia **122** 5.37N 73.50W
Chir *r.* U.S.S.R. **45** 48.34N 42.53E
Chirāwa India **62** 28.15N 75.38E
Chirchik U.S.S.R. **9** 41.28N 69.31E
Chiredzi Zimbabwe **81** 21.03S 31.39E
Chiredzi *r.* Zimbabwe **81** 21.10S 31.50E
Chiricahua Peak *mtn.* U.S.A. **109** 31.52N109.20W
Chiriquí *mtn.* Panama **117** 8.49N 82.38W
Chiriquí, Laguna de *b.* Panama **117** 9.00N 82.00W
Chiromo Malaŵi **79** 16.28S 35.10E
Chirpan Bulgaria **34** 42.10N 25.19E
Chirripó *mtn.* Costa Rica **117** 9.31N 83.30W
Chirundu Zimbabwe **80** 16.04S 28.51E
Chisamba Zambia **80** 14.58S 28.23E
Chisasibi Canada **102** 53.50N 79.00W
Chishan Taiwan **55** 22.53N120.29E
Chisholm U.S.A. **110** 47.29N 92.53W
Chisholm Mills Canada **100** 54.55N114.09W
Chishtiān Mandi Pakistan **62** 29.48N 72.52E
Chishui China **55** 28.29N105.38E
Chisone *r.* Italy **30** 44.49N 7.25E
Chistopol U.S.S.R. **44** 55.25N 50.38E
Chita U.S.S.R. **53** 52.03N113.35E
Chitek L. Canada **101** 52.25N 99.20W
Chitembo Angola **78** 13.33S 16.47E
Chitipa Malaŵi **79** 9.41S 33.19E
Chitorgarh India **62** 24.53N 74.38E
Chitrakūt Dham India **63** 25.11N 80.52E
Chitrāl Pakistan **60** 35.52N 71.58E
Chitré Panama **97** 7.58N 80.26W
Chittagong Bangla. **63** 22.20N 91.50E
Chittenango U.S.A. **115** 43.03N 75.52W
Chittoor India **61** 13.13N 79.06E
Chiumbe *r.* Zaïre **78** 6.37S 21.04E
Chiume Angola **78** 15.08S 21.11E
Chiusi Italy **30** 43.01N 11.57E
Chiuta, L. Malaŵi / Mozambique **79** 14.45S 35.50E
Chiva Spain **25** 39.28N 0.43W
Chivasso Italy **30** 45.11N 7.53E
Chivhu Zimbabwe **80** 19.01S 30.53E
Chivilcoy Argentina **125** 34.52S 60.02W
Chiwanda Tanzania **79** 11.21S 34.55E
Chobe *d.* Botswana **80** 18.30S 25.15E
Chobe *r.* Namibia / Botswana **80** 17.48S 25.12E
Chobe Swamp *f.* Namibia **80** 18.20S 23.40E
Chocolate Mts. U.S.A. **109** 33.20N115.15W
Chocope Peru **122** 7.47S 79.12W
Choele-Choel Argentina **125** 39.15S 65.30W
Chōfu Japan **57** 35.39N139.33E
Chohtan India **62** 25.29N 71.04E
Choix Mexico **109** 26.43N108.17W
Chojnice Poland **37** 53.42N 17.32E
Chokai zan *mtn.* Japan **57** 39.08N140.04E
Ch'ok'ē Mts. Ethiopia **73** 11.00N 37.30E
Cholet France **18** 47.04N 0.53W
Cholon Vietnam **56** 10.40N106.30E
Choluteca Honduras **117** 13.16N 87.11W
Choma Zambia **79** 16.51S 27.04E
Chomu India **62** 27.10N 75.44E
Chomutov Czech. **39** 50.28N 13.26E
Chon Buri Thailand **56** 13.20N101.02E
Chone Ecuador **122** 0.44S 80.04W
Chong'an China **55** 27.46N118.01E
Ch'ŏngjin N. Korea **53** 41.55N129.50E
Ch'ŏngju S. Korea **53** 36.39N127.31E
Chŏng Kal Cambodia **56** 13.57N103.35E
Chongming *i.* China **55** 31.36N121.33E
Chongqing China **55** 29.31N106.35E
Chongren China **55** 27.44N116.02E
Chŏnju S. Korea **53** 35.50N127.05E
Chonos, Archipelago de los *is.* Chile **125** 45.00S 74.00W
Cho Oyu *mtn.* China / Nepal **63** 28.06N 86.40E
Chopda India **62** 21.15N 75.18E
Choptank *r.* U.S.A. **115** 38.38N 76.13W
Chorges France **21** 44.33N 6.17E
Chorley U.K. **12** 53.39N 2.39W
Chorokh *r.* U.S.S.R. **45** 41.36N 41.35E
Chortkov U.S.S.R. **37** 49.01N 25.42E
Chorzów Poland **37** 50.19N 18.56E
Chosica Peru **122** 11.55S 76.38W
Chos Malal Argentina **125** 37.20S 70.15W
Choszczno Poland **36** 53.10N 15.26E
Choteau U.S.A. **108** 47.49N112.11W
Chotila India **62** 22.25N 71.11E
Choum Mauritania **74** 21.10N 13.00W
Chowchilla U.S.A. **108** 37.07N120.16W
Christchurch New Zealand **86** 43.33S172.40E
Christchurch U.K. **13** 50.44N 1.47W
Christian I. Canada **104** 44.50N 80.13W
Christian Sd. U.S.A. **100** 55.56N134.40W
Christiansfeld Denmark **42** 55.21N 9.29E
Christianshåb Greenland **99** 68.50N 51.00W
Christie B. Canada **101** 62.32N111.10W
Christina *r.* Canada **101** 56.40N111.03W
Christmas Creek *town* Australia **88** 18.55S125.56E
Christmas I. Indian Oc. **58** 10.30S105.40E
Christmas I. *see* Kiritimati *i.* Kiribati **85**
Chrudim Czech. **36** 49.57N 15.48E
Chu *r.* U.S.S.R. **52** 42.30N 76.10E
Chuādānga Bangla. **63** 23.38N 88.51E
Chubbuck U.S.A. **109** 34.22N115.20W
Chūbu *d.* Japan **57** 35.25N137.40E
Chubut *d.* Argentina **125** 44.00S 68.00W
Chubut *r.* Argentina **125** 43.18S 65.06W
Chu Chua Canada **100** 51.22N120.10W
Chudleigh U.K. **13** 50.35N 3.36W
Chudnov U.S.S.R. **37** 50.05N 28.01E
Chudovo U.S.S.R. **44** 59.10N 31.41E
Chudskoye, Ozero *l.* U.S.S.R. **44** 58.30N 27.30E
Chūgoku *d.* Japan **57** 35.00N133.00E
Chūgoku sanchi *mts.* Japan **57** 35.30N133.00E
Chugwater U.S.A. **108** 41.46N104.49W
Chuiquimula Guatemala **117** 15.52N 89.50W
Chukai Malaysia **58** 4.16N103.24E
Chukchi Sea Arctic Oc. **96** 69.30N172.00W
Chukotskiy Poluostrov *pen.* U.S.S.R. **51** 66.00N174.30W
Chukudukraal Botswana **80** 22.30S 23.22E
Chula Vista U.S.A. **109** 32.39N117.05W
Chulman U.S.S.R. **51** 56.54N124.55E
Chulucanas Peru **122** 5.08S 80.00W
Chulym U.S.S.R. **50** 55.09N 80.59E
Chum U.S.S.R. **44** 67.05N 63.15E
Chumbicha Argentina **124** 28.50S 66.18W
Chumikan U.S.S.R. **51** 54.40N135.15E
Chumphon Thailand **56** 10.34N 99.15E
Chuna *r.* U.S.S.R. **51** 58.00N 94.00E
Ch'unch'ŏn S. Korea **53** 37.53N127.45E
Chungking *see* Chongqing China **55**
Chunya Tanzania **79** 8.31S 33.28E
Chuquicamata Chile **124** 22.20S 68.56W
Chuquisaca *d.* Bolivia **124** 21.00S 64.00W
Chur Switz. **39** 46.51N 9.32E
Churchill Canada **101** 58.46N 94.10W
Churchill *r.* Man. Canada **101** 58.47N 94.12W
Churchill *r.* Nfld. Canada **103** 53.20N 60.11W
Churchill, C. Canada **101** 58.46N 93.12W
Churchill L. Canada **101** 55.55N108.20W
Churchill Peak *mtn.* Canada **100** 58.10N125.10W
Church Stretton U.K. **13** 52.32N 2.49W
Churia Range *mts.* Nepal **63** 28.40N 81.30E
Churu India **62** 28.18N 74.57E
Chusovoy U.S.S.R. **44** 58.18N 57.50E
Chu Xian China **54** 32.25N118.15E
Chuxiong China **61** 25.03N101.33E
Chu Yang Sin *mtn.* Vietnam **56** 12.25N108.25E
Ciamis Indonesia **59** 7.20S108.21E
Cianjur Indonesia **59** 6.50S107.09E
Cibatu Indonesia **59** 7.10S107.59E
Ćićarija *mts.* Yugo. **31** 45.30N 14.00E
Cidacos *r.* Spain **25** 42.21N 1.38W
Ciechanów Poland **37** 52.53N 20.38E
Ciego de Avila Cuba **117** 21.51N 78.47W
Ciempozuelos Spain **26** 40.10N 3.37W
Ciénaga Colombia **122** 11.11N 74.15W
Cienfuegos Cuba **117** 22.10N 80.27W
Cíes, Islas *is.* Spain **26** 42.13N 8.54W
Cieszyn Poland **37** 49.45N 18.38E
Cieza Spain **25** 38.14N 1.25W
Cifuentes Spain **26** 40.47N 2.37W
Cigüela *r.* Spain **27** 39.08N 3.44W
Cijara, Embalse de *resr.* Spain **27** 39.18N 4.52W
Cijulang Indonesia **59** 7.44S108.30E
Cikampek Indonesia **59** 6.21S107.25E
Cilacap Indonesia **59** 7.44S109.00E
Ciledug Indonesia **59** 6.56S108.43E
Cili China **55** 29.24N111.04E
Cilleruelo de Bezana Spain **26** 43.00N 3.51W
Cimanuk *r.* Indonesia **59** 6.20S108.12E
Cimarron U.S.A. **111** 37.48N100.21W
Cimarron *r.* U.S.A. **111** 36.10N 96.17W
Cimone, Monte *mtn.* Italy **30** 44.12N 10.42E
Cîmpina Romania **29** 45.08N 25.44E
Cîmpulung Romania **29** 45.16N 25.03E
Cinca *r.* Spain **25** 41.26N 0.21E
Cincar Yugo. **31** 43.54N 17.04E
Cincinnati U.S.A. **112** 39.10N 84.30W
Ciney Belgium **16** 50.17N 5.06E
Cingoli Italy **30** 43.22N 13.13E
Cinto, Monte *mtn.* France **21** 42.23N 8.56E
Cipolletti Argentina **125** 38.56S 67.59W
Circeo, Parco Nazionale del *Nat. Park* Italy **32** 41.17N 13.05E
Circle U.S.A. **108** 47.25N105.35W
Circleville Ohio U.S.A. **112** 39.36N 82.57W
Circleville Utah U.S.A. **108** 38.10N112.16W
Cirebon Indonesia **59** 6.46S108.33E
Cirencester U.K. **13** 51.43N 1.59W
Cirey-sur-Vezouse France **19** 48.35N 6.57E
Ciriè Italy **30** 45.14N 7.36E
Cirò Marina Italy **33** 39.22N 17.08E
Cisco U.S.A. **111** 32.23N 98.59W
Ciskei Africa **80** 32.45S 27.00E
Cisterna di Latina Italy **32** 41.35N 12.49E
Cistierna Spain **26** 42.48N 5.07W
Citlaltepetl *mtn.* Mexico **97** 19.00N 97.18W
Citra U.S.A. **113** 29.24N 82.06W
Cittadella Italy **30** 45.39N 11.47E
Città di Castello Italy **30** 43.27N 12.14E
Cittanova Italy **33** 38.21N 16.05E
Ciudad Acuña Mexico **111** 29.18N100.55W
Ciudad Allende Mexico **111** 28.20N100.51W
Ciudad Bolívar Venezuela **122** 8.06N 63.36W
Ciudad Camargo Mexico **109** 27.40N105.10W
Ciudad Delicias Mexico **97** 28.13N105.28W
Ciudad de México Mexico **116** 19.25N 99.10W
Ciudadela Spain **25** 40.00N 3.50E
Ciudad Guayana Venezuela **122** 8.22N 62.40W
Ciudad Guerrero Mexico **116** 28.33N107.28W
Ciudad Guzmán Mexico **116** 19.41N103.29W
Ciudad Ixtepec Mexico **116** 16.32N 95.10W
Ciudad Jiménez Mexico **109** 27.08N104.55W
Ciudad Juárez Mexico **109** 31.44N106.29W
Ciudad Lerdo Mexico **111** 25.32N103.32W

Ciudad Madero to **Constitución**

Ciudad Madero Mexico **116** 22.19N 97.50W
Ciudad Mante Mexico **116** 22.44N 98.57W
Ciudad Melchor Múzquiz Mexico **111** 27.53N101.31W
Ciudad Mier Mexico **111** 26.26N 99.09W
Ciudad Obregón Mexico **109** 27.29N109.56W
Ciudad Ojeda Venezuela **122** 10.05N 71.17W
Ciudad Piar Venezuela **122** 7.27N 63.19W
Ciudad Real Spain **26** 38.59N 3.56W
Ciudad Real *d.* Spain **27** 38.50N 4.00W
Ciudad Rodrigo Spain **26** 40.36N 6.32W
Ciudad Victoria Mexico **116** 23.43N 99.10W
Ciurana *r.* Spain **25** 41.08N 0.39E
Civita Castellana Italy **30** 42.17N 12.25E
Civitanova Italy **31** 43.18N 13.44E
Civitavecchia Italy **30** 42.06N 11.48E
Civray France **18** 46.09N 0.18E
Çivril Turkey **64** 38.18N 29.43E
Ci Xian China **54** 36.22N114.23E
Cizre Turkey **64** 37.21N 42.11E
Clackline Australia **89** 31.43S116.31E
Clacton on Sea U.K. **13** 51.47N 1.10E
Clain *r.* France **18** 46.47N 0.32E
Clairambault, Lac *l.* Canada **103** 54.45N 69.22W
Claire, L. Canada **100** 58.30N112.00W
Clairton U.S.A. **114** 40.18N 79.53W
Clairvaux-les-Lacs France **19** 46.34N 5.45E
Claise *r.* France **18** 46.54N 0.45E
Clamecy France **19** 47.27N 3.31E
Clanton U.S.A. **113** 32.50N 86.38W
Clapperton I. Canada **104** 46.02N 82.13W
Clara Rep. of Ire. **15** 53.21N 7.37W
Clare N.S.W. Australia **92** 33.27S143.55E
Clare S.A. Australia **92** 33.50S138.38E
Clare *d.* Rep. of Ire. **15** 52.52N 8.55W
Clare *r.* Rep. of Ire. **15** 53.17N 9.04W
Clare U.S.A. **112** 43.49N 84.47W
Clare I. Rep. of Ire. **15** 53.48N 10.00W
Claremont U.S.A. **115** 43.23N 72.20W
Claremore U.S.A. **111** 36.19N 95.36W
Claremorris Rep. of Ire. **15** 53.44N 9.00W
Clarence *r.* Australia **93** 29.25S153.02E
Clarence *r.* New Zealand **86** 42.10S173.55E
Clarence U.S.A. **114** 41.03N 77.56W
Clarence I. Antarctica **128** 61.30S 53.50W
Clarence Str. Australia **88** 12.00S131.00E
Clarence Str. U.S.A. **100** 55.40N132.10W
Clarendon U.S.A. **111** 34.56N100.53W
Clarendon L. Canada **105** 44.52N 76.53W
Claresholm Canada **100** 50.00N113.45W
Clarie Coast *f.* Antarctica **128** 67.00S133.00E
Clarinda U.S.A. **110** 40.44N 95.02W
Clarington Ohio U.S.A. **114** 39.47N 80.53W
Clarington Penn. U.S.A. **114** 41.20N 79.07W
Clarion U.S.A. **114** 41.13N 79.24W
Clarion *r.* U.S.A. **114** 41.07N 79.41W
Clark, L. U.S.A. **98** 60.15N154.15W
Clark, Pt. *c.* Canada **104** 44.04N 81.45W
Clarke I. Australia **91** 40.30S148.10E
Clark Fork *r.* U.S.A. **108** 48.09N116.15W
Clarksburg U.S.A. **114** 39.17N 80.21W
Clarksdale U.S.A. **111** 34.12N 90.34W
Clarks Summit U.S.A. **115** 41.30N 75.42W
Clarkston U.S.A. **108** 46.26N117.02W
Clarksville Ark. U.S.A. **111** 35.28N 93.28W
Clarksville Tenn. U.S.A. **113** 36.31N 87.21W
Clarksville Tex. U.S.A. **111** 33.37N 95.03W
Clary France **19** 50.05N 3.24E
Clausthal-Zellerfeld Germany **38** 51.48N 10.20E
Clay U.S.A. **114** 38.28N 81.05W
Clayoquot Sd. Canada **100** 49.11N126.08W
Claysburg U.S.A. **114** 40.18N 78.27W
Claysville U.S.A. **114** 40.07N 80.25W
Clayton *r.* Australia **92** 29.06S137.59E
Clayton Idaho U.S.A. **108** 44.16N114.25W
Clayton N.J. U.S.A. **115** 39.39N 75.06W
Clayton N.Mex. U.S.A. **111** 36.27N103.11W
Clayton N.Y. U.S.A. **105** 44.14N 76.05W
Clear, C. Rep. of Ire. **11** 51.25N 9.32W
Clearfield Penn. U.S.A. **114** 41.02N 78.27W
Clearfield Utah U.S.A. **108** 41.07N112.01W
Clear I. Rep. of Ire. **15** 51.26N 9.30W
Clear L. U.S.A. **108** 39.02N122.50W
Clear Lake *town* Iowa U.S.A. **110** 43.08N 92.23W
Clear Lake *town* S.Dak. U.S.A. **110** 44.45N 96.41W
Clear Spring U.S.A. **114** 39.39N 77.55W
Clearwater Canada **100** 51.38N120.02W
Clearwater *r.* Canada **101** 56.40N109.30W
Clearwater U.S.A. **113** 27.57N 82.48W
Clearwater Mts. U.S.A. **108** 46.00N115.30W
Cle Elum U.S.A. **108** 47.12N120.56W
Cleethorpes U.K. **12** 53.33N 0.02W
Clefmont France **19** 48.06N 5.31E
Clelles France **21** 44.50N 5.37E
Clendenin U.S.A. **114** 38.29N 81.21W
Clermont Australia **90** 22.49S147.39E
Clermont France **19** 49.23N 2.24E
Clermont-en-Argonne France **19** 49.05N 5.05E
Clermont-Ferrand France **20** 45.47N 3.05E
Clervaux Lux. **16** 50.04N 6.01E
Cles Italy **30** 46.22N 11.02E
Cleve Australia **92** 33.37S136.32E
Clevedon U.K. **13** 51.26N 2.52W
Cleveland *d.* U.K. **12** 54.37N 1.08W
Cleveland Miss. U.S.A. **111** 33.45N 90.50W
Cleveland Ohio U.S.A. **114** 41.30N 81.41W
Cleveland Tenn. U.S.A. **113** 35.10N 84.51W
Cleveland Tex. U.S.A. **111** 30.21N 95.05W
Cleveland, C. Australia **90** 19.11S147.01E
Cleveland Heights *town* U.S.A. **114** 41.30N 81.34W
Cleveland Hills U.K. **12** 54.25N 1.10W
Cleveleys U.K. **12** 53.52N 3.01W
Clew B. Rep. of Ire. **15** 53.50N 9.47W
Clifden Rep. of Ire. **15** 53.29N 10.02W
Clifford Canada **104** 43.58N 80.58W
Clifford U.S.A. **114** 43.19N 83.11W
Cliffy Head Australia **89** 34.58S116.24E
Clifton Ariz. U.S.A. **109** 33.03N109.18W
Clifton N.J. U.S.A. **115** 40.53N 74.08W
Clifton Tex. U.S.A. **111** 31.47N 97.35W
Clifton Forge U.S.A. **113** 37.49N 79.49W
Climax Canada **101** 49.13N108.23W
Clint U.S.A. **109** 31.35N106.14W
Clinton B.C. Canada **100** 51.05N121.35W
Clinton Ont. Canada **104** 43.37N 81.32W
Clinton New Zealand **86** 46.13S169.23E
Clinton Ark. U.S.A. **111** 35.36N 92.38W
Clinton Conn. U.S.A. **115** 41.17N 72.32W
Clinton Ill. U.S.A. **110** 40.10N 88.59W
Clinton Iowa U.S.A. **110** 41.51N 90.12W
Clinton Mass. U.S.A. **115** 42.25N 71.41W
Clinton Mich. U.S.A. **104** 42.04N 83.58W
Clinton Mo. U.S.A. **110** 38.22N 93.46W
Clinton N.C. U.S.A. **113** 35.00N 78.20W
Clinton N.J. U.S.A. **115** 40.38N 74.55W
Clinton Okla. U.S.A. **111** 35.31N 98.59W
Clintwood U.S.A. **113** 37.09N 82.30W
Clio U.S.A. **104** 43.11N 83.44W
Clipperton *i.* Pacific Oc. **85** 10.17N109.13W
Clisham *mtn.* U.K. **14** 57.58N 6.50W
Clisson France **18** 47.05N 1.17W
Clive L. Canada **100** 63.13N118.54W
Cliza Bolivia **124** 17.36S 65.56W
Cloghan Offaly Rep. of Ire. **15** 53.13N 7.54W
Clogher Head Kerry Rep. of Ire. **15** 52.09N 10.28W
Clonakilty Rep. of Ire. **15** 51.37N 8.54W
Cloncurry Australia **90** 20.42S140.30E
Clones Rep. of Ire. **15** 54.11N 7.16W
Clonmel Rep. of Ire. **15** 52.21N 7.44W
Clonroche Rep. of Ire. **15** 52.27N 6.45W
Cloppenburg Germany **38** 52.50N 8.02E
Cloquet U.S.A. **110** 46.43N 92.28W
Clorinda Argentina **124** 25.20S 57.40W
Cloud Peak *mtn.* U.S.A. **108** 44.25N107.10W
Cloughton U.K. **12** 54.20N 0.27W
Cloverdale U.S.A. **108** 38.48N123.01W
Clovis Calif. U.S.A. **108** 36.49N119.42W
Clovis N.Mex. U.S.A. **111** 34.24N103.12W
Clowne U.K. **12** 53.18N 1.16W
Cluj-Napoca Romania **37** 46.47N 23.37E
Clunes Australia **92** 37.16S143.47E
Cluny France **19** 46.26N 4.39E
Cluses France **21** 46.04N 6.36E
Clusone Italy **30** 45.53N 9.57E
Clutha *r.* New Zealand **86** 46.18S169.05E
Clwyd *d.* U.K. **12** 53.07N 3.20W
Clwyd *r.* U.K. **12** 53.19N 3.30W
Clyde Canada **99** 70.30N 68.30W
Clyde New Zealand **86** 45.11S169.19E
Clyde *r.* U.K. **14** 55.58N 4.53W
Clyde N.Y. U.S.A. **114** 43.05N 76.52W
Clyde Ohio U.S.A. **114** 41.18N 82.59W
Clydebank U.K. **14** 55.53N 4.23W
Clyde Forks Canada **105** 45.07N 76.41W
Clymer U.S.A. **114** 40.40N 79.01W
Cõa *r.* Portugal **26** 41.05N 7.05W
Coachella U.S.A. **109** 33.41N116.10W
Coahuila *d.* Mexico **111** 27.40N102.00W
Coal *r.* Canada **100** 59.39N126.57W
Coalgate U.S.A. **111** 34.32N 96.13W
Coal Grove U.S.A. **114** 38.30N 82.39W
Coalinga U.S.A. **109** 36.09N120.21W
Coalport U.S.A. **114** 40.45N 78.32W
Coalville U.K. **13** 52.43N 1.21W
Coast *d.* Kenya **79** 3.00S 39.30E
Coast Mts. Canada **100** 55.00N129.00W
Coast Range *mts.* U.S.A. **108** 42.40N123.30W
Coatbridge U.K. **14** 55.52N 4.02W
Coatesville U.S.A. **115** 39.59N 75.49W
Coaticook Canada **105** 45.08N 71.48W
Coats I. Canada **99** 62.30N 83.00W
Coats Land *f.* Antarctica **128** 77.00S 25.00W
Coatzacoalcos Mexico **116** 18.10N 94.25W
Cobalt Canada **104** 47.24N 79.41W
Cobán Guatemala **116** 15.28N 90.20W
Cobar Australia **93** 31.32S145.51E
Cobargo Australia **93** 36.24S149.52E
Cobden Australia **92** 38.21S143.07E
Cobden Canada **105** 45.38N 76.53W
Cobh Rep. of Ire. **15** 51.50N 8.18W
Cobham L. Australia **92** 30.09S142.05E
Cobija Bolivia **124** 11.02S 68.44W
Cobleskill U.S.A. **115** 42.41N 74.29W
Cobourg Canada **104** 43.58N 78.10W
Cobourg Pen. Australia **90** 11.20S132.15E
Cobram Australia **93** 35.56S145.40E
Cobre U.S.A. **108** 41.07N114.25W
Cobue Mozambique **79** 12.10S 34.50E
Coburg Germany **39** 50.15N 10.58E
Coburg I. Canada **99** 76.00N 79.25W
Cocentaina Spain **25** 38.45N 0.26W
Cochabamba Bolivia **124** 17.24S 66.09W
Cochabamba *d.* Bolivia **124** 17.30S 65.40W
Cochem Germany **39** 50.11N 7.09E
Cochise U.S.A. **109** 32.06N109.56W
Cochran U.S.A. **113** 32.22N 83.21W
Cochrane Alta. Canada **100** 51.11N114.30W
Cochrane Ont. Canada **102** 49.00N 81.00W
Cochrane Chile **125** 47.20S 72.30W
Cockaleechie Australia **92** 34.07S135.53E
Cockburn Australia **92** 32.05S141.00E
Cockburn I. Canada **104** 45.55N 83.24W
Cockburn Island *town* Canada **104** 45.58N 83.22W
Cockburnspath U.K. **14** 55.56N 2.22W
Cockeysville U.S.A. **115** 39.29N 76.39W
Cocklebiddy Australia **89** 32.02S126.05E
Cocksackie U.S.A. **115** 42.21N 73.48W
Coco *r.* Honduras **117** 14.58N 83.15W
Coco, Isla del *i.* Pacific Oc. **85** 5.32N 87.04W
Cocoa U.S.A. **113** 28.21N 80.46W
Cocoa Beach *town* U.S.A. **113** 28.19N 80.36W
Cocobeach Gabon **78** 0.59N 9.36E
Cocoparra Range *mts.* Australia **93** 34.00S146.00E
Cocos Is. Indian Oc. **49** 13.00S 96.00E
Cod, C. U.S.A. **115** 41.42N 70.15W
Codăeşti Romania **37** 46.52N 27.46E
Codajás Brazil **122** 3.55S 62.00W
Codigoro Italy **30** 44.49N 12.08E
Codó Brazil **123** 4.28S 43.51W
Codogno Italy **30** 45.09N 9.42E
Codroipo Italy **30** 45.58N 12.59E
Cody U.S.A. **108** 44.32N109.03W
Coen Australia **90** 13.56S143.12E
Coesfeld Germany **38** 51.56N 7.10E
Coeur d'Alene U.S.A. **106** 47.40N116.46W
Coevorden Neth. **16** 52.39N 6.45E
Coffeyville U.S.A. **111** 37.02N 93.37W
Coffin B. Australia **92** 34.27S135.19E
Coffin Bay Pen. Australia **92** 34.30S135.14E
Coff's Harbour Australia **93** 30.19S153.05E
Cofre de Perote *mtn.* Mexico **116** 19.30N 97.10W
Cofrentes Spain **25** 39.14N 1.04W
Coghinas *r.* Italy **32** 40.55N 8.48E
Coghinas, Lago di *l.* Italy **32** 40.43N 9.05E
Cognac France **20** 45.42N 0.20W
Cogolludo Spain **26** 40.57N 3.05W
Cohocton U.S.A. **114** 42.09N 77.05W
Cohoes U.S.A. **115** 42.46N 73.42W
Cohuna Australia **92** 35.47S144.15E
Coiba, Isla de *i.* Panama **117** 7.23N 81.45W
Coihaique Chile **125** 45.35S 72.08W
Coimbatore India **60** 11.00N 76.57E
Coimbra Brazil **126** 19.55S 57.47W
Coimbra Portugal **26** 40.12N 8.25W
Coimbra *d.* Portugal **26** 40.10N 8.20W
Coín Spain **27** 36.40N 4.45W
Cojimies Ecuador **122** 0.20N 80.00W
Cokeville U.S.A. **108** 42.05N110.57W
Colac Australia **92** 38.22S143.38E
Colares Portugal **27** 38.48N 9.27W
Colatina Brazil **126** 19.35S 40.37W
Colbeck, C. Antarctica **128** 77.20S159.00W
Colborne Canada **105** 44.00N 77.53W
Colby U.S.A. **110** 39.24N101.03W
Colchester U.K. **13** 51.54N 0.55E
Colchester U.S.A. **115** 41.34N 72.20W
Cold L. Canada **101** 54.33N110.05W
Cold Lake *town* Canada **101** 54.27N110.10W
Coldstream U.K. **14** 55.39N 2.15W
Coldwater Canada **104** 44.44N 79.39W
Coldwater U.S.A. **112** 41.57N 85.01W
Coldwell Canada **102** 48.45N 86.30W
Coleambally Australia **93** 34.48S145.53E
Colebrook U.S.A. **105** 44.54N 71.30W
Coleman *r.* Australia **90** 15.06S141.38E
Coleman Tex. U.S.A. **111** 31.50N 99.26W
Coleman Wisc. U.S.A. **110** 45.04N 88.02W
Colenso R.S.A. **80** 28.43S 29.49E
Coleraine Australia **92** 37.36S141.42E
Coleraine U.K. **15** 55.08N 6.40W
Colesberg R.S.A. **80** 30.43S 25.05E
Colfax U.S.A. **111** 31.31N 92.42W
Colgong India **63** 25.16N 87.13E
Colico Italy **30** 46.08N 9.22E
Colima Mexico **116** 19.14N103.41W
Colima *d.* Mexico **116** 19.05N104.00W
Colinas Brazil **123** 6.02S 44.14W
Coll *i.* U.K. **14** 56.38N 6.34W
Collarenebri Australia **93** 29.33S148.36E
College U.S.A. **98** 64.54N147.55W
College Park *town* Ga. U.S.A. **113** 33.39N 84.28W
College Park *town* Md. U.S.A. **114** 39.00N 76.55W
College Station *town* U.S.A. **111** 30.37N 96.21W
Collerina Australia **93** 29.22S146.32E
Collesalvetti Italy **30** 43.35N 10.28E
Collie N.S.W. Australia **93** 31.41S148.22E
Collie W.A. Australia **89** 33.21S116.09E
Collie Cardiff Australia **89** 33.27S116.09E
Collier B. Australia **88** 16.10S124.15E
Collingswood U.S.A. **115** 39.55N 75.04W
Collingwood Canada **104** 44.29N 80.13W
Collingwood New Zealand **86** 40.41S172.41E
Collingwood B. P.N.G. **90** 9.20S149.30E
Collinsville Australia **90** 20.34S147.51E
Collinsville U.S.A. **115** 41.49N 72.55W
Collin Top *mtn.* U.K. **15** 54.58N 6.08W
Collon Rep. of Ire. **15** 53.47N 6.30W
Collooney Rep. of Ire. **15** 54.11N 8.29W
Colmar France **19** 48.05N 7.22E
Colmars France **21** 44.11N 6.38E
Colmenar Spain **27** 36.54N 4.20W
Colmenar de Oreja Spain **27** 40.06N 3.23W
Colmenar Viejo Spain **26** 40.40N 3.46W
Colne *r.* Essex U.K. **13** 51.50N 0.59E
Colnett, Cabo *c.* Mexico **109** 31.00N116.20W
Colo *r.* Australia **93** 33.26S150.53E
Cologne *see* Köln Germany **38**
Colombey-les-Belles France **19** 48.32N 5.54E
Colombia S. America **122** 4.00N 72.30W
Colombian Basin *f.* Carib. Sea **127** 14.00N 76.00W
Colombo Sri Lanka **61** 6.55N 79.52E
Colón Argentina **125** 32.15S 58.10W
Colón Panama **122** 9.21N 79.54W
Colona Australia **91** 31.38S132.05E
Colonelganj India **63** 27.08N 81.42E
Colonia del Sacramento Uruguay **125** 34.28S 57.51W
Colonia Las Heras Argentina **125** 46.33S 68.57W
Colonia Lavelleja Uruguay **125** 31.06S 57.01W
Colonna, Capo *c.* Italy **33** 39.02N 17.11E
Colonsay *i.* U.K. **14** 56.04N 6.13W
Colorado *r.* Argentina **125** 39.50S 62.02W
Colorado *d.* U.S.A. **108** 39.07N105.27W
Colorado *r.* Ariz. U.S.A. **109** 31.45N114.40W
Colorado *r.* Tex. U.S.A. **111** 28.36N 95.58W
Colorado City U.S.A. **111** 32.24N100.52W
Colorado Plateau *f.* U.S.A. **109** 36.30N108.00W
Colorado Springs *town* U.S.A. **108** 38.50N104.49W
Colton N.Y. U.S.A. **105** 44.33N 74.56W
Colton S.Dak. U.S.A. **110** 43.47N 96.56W
Columbia *r.* U.S.A. **108** 46.15N124.05W
Columbia La. U.S.A. **111** 32.06N 92.05W
Columbia Miss. U.S.A. **111** 31.15N 89.56W
Columbia Mo. U.S.A. **110** 38.57N 92.20W
Columbia S.C. U.S.A. **113** 34.00N 81.00W
Columbia Tenn. U.S.A. **113** 35.37N 87.02W
Columbia, District of U.S.A. **114** 39.13N 76.52W
Columbia, Mt. Canada **100** 52.08N117.20W
Columbia, Sierra *mts.* Mexico **109** 29.30N114.50W
Columbia Basin *f.* U.S.A. **108** 46.55N117.36W
Columbia Falls *town* U.S.A. **108** 48.23N114.11W
Columbiana U.S.A. **114** 40.53N 80.42W
Columbia Plateau *f.* U.S.A. **108** 44.00N117.30W
Columbretes, Islas *is.* Spain **25** 39.52N 0.40E
Columbus Ga. U.S.A. **113** 32.28N 84.59W
Columbus Ind. U.S.A. **112** 39.12N 85.57W
Columbus Miss. U.S.A. **111** 33.30N 88.25W
Columbus Mont. U.S.A. **108** 45.38N109.15W
Columbus Nebr. U.S.A. **110** 41.25N 97.22W
Columbus N.Mex. U.S.A. **109** 31.50N107.38W
Columbus Ohio U.S.A. **114** 39.57N 83.00W
Columbus Tex. U.S.A. **111** 29.42N 96.33W
Colville *r.* U.S.A. **98** 70.06N151.30W
Colwyn Bay *town* U.K. **12** 53.18N 3.43W
Comacchio Italy **30** 44.42N 12.11E
Comacchio, Valli di *b.* Italy **30** 44.38N 12.06E
Comai China **63** 28.28N 91.33E
Comanche U.S.A. **111** 34.22N 97.58W
Comayagua Honduras **117** 14.30N 87.39W
Combeaufontaine France **19** 47.43N 5.53E
Comber Canada **104** 42.14N 82.33W
Combermere Canada **105** 45.22N 77.37W
Comblain-au-Pont Belgium **16** 50.29N 5.32E
Combles France **19** 50.01N 2.52E
Combourg France **18** 48.25N 1.45W
Comboyne Australia **93** 31.35S152.27E
Combronde France **20** 45.59N 3.05E
Comeragh Mts. Rep. of Ire. **15** 52.17N 7.34W
Comilla Bangla. **63** 23.28N 91.10E
Comino, Capo *c.* Italy **32** 40.31N 9.50E
Comiso Italy **33** 36.56N 14.37E
Comitán Mexico **116** 16.15N 92.08W
Commentry France **20** 46.17N 2.44E
Commerce U.S.A. **111** 33.15N 95.54W
Commercy France **19** 48.45N 5.35E
Comminges *f.* France **20** 43.15N 0.45E
Commonwealth Territory *d.* Australia **93** 35.00S151.00E
Como Italy **30** 45.48N 9.04E
Como, Lago di *l.* Italy **30** 46.00N 9.20E
Comodoro Rivadavia Argentina **125** 45.50S 67.30W
Comorin, C. India **48** 8.04N 77.35E
Comoros Africa **79** 12.15S 44.00E
Compiègne France **19** 49.25N 2.50E
Cona China **63** 27.59N 91.59E
Co Nag *l.* China **63** 32.00N 91.15E
Conakry Guinea **76** 9.30N 13.43W
Concarneau France **18** 47.52N 3.55W
Conceição Mozambique **81** 18.45S 36.10E
Conceição do Araguaia Brazil **123** 8.15S 49.17W
Concepción Argentina **124** 27.20S 65.36W
Concepción Chile **125** 36.50S 73.03W
Concepción *r.* Mexico **109** 30.32N112.59W
Concepción Paraguay **124** 23.22S 57.26W
Concepción del Oro Mexico **111** 24.38N101.25W
Concepción del Uruguay Argentina **125** 32.30S 58.14W
Conception, Pt. U.S.A. **109** 34.27N120.27W
Conception B. Namibia **80** 23.53S 14.28E
Conches France **18** 48.58N 0.58E
Conchillas Uruguay **125** 34.15S 58.04W
Conchos *r.* Mexico **109** 29.32N104.25W
Concord Mass. U.S.A. **115** 42.27N 71.21W
Concord N.C. U.S.A. **113** 35.25N 80.34W
Concord N.H. U.S.A. **115** 43.12N 71.32W
Concordia Argentina **125** 31.24S 58.02W
Concórdia Brazil **122** 4.35S 66.35W
Concordia Mexico **109** 23.17N106.04W
Concordia U.S.A. **110** 39.34N 97.39W
Condé France **18** 48.51N 0.33W
Condé-sur-l'Escaut France **19** 50.27N 3.36E
Condobolin Australia **93** 33.03S147.11E
Condom France **20** 43.58N 0.22E
Conegliano Italy **30** 45.53N 12.18E
Conemaugh River Resr. U.S.A. **114** 40.28N 79.17W
Confluence U.S.A. **114** 39.49N 79.21W
Confolens France **20** 46.01N 0.41E
Conghua China **55** 23.33N113.34E
Congleton U.K. **12** 53.10N 2.12W
Congo Africa **78** 1.00S 16.00E
Congo *r. see* Zaïre *r.* Zaïre **78**
Congo Basin *f.* Zaïre **70** 1.00N 21.00E
Congonhas Brazil **126** 20.30S 43.53W
Coningsby U.K. **12** 53.07N 0.09W
Coniston Canada **104** 46.29N 80.51W
Coniston U.K. **12** 54.22N 3.06W
Conkouati Congo **78** 4.00S 11.16E
Conn, Lough Rep. of Ire. **15** 54.01N 9.15W
Connah's Quay *town* U.K. **12** 53.13N 3.03W
Conneaut U.S.A. **114** 41.57N 80.34W
Conneaut Lake *town* U.S.A. **114** 41.36N 80.19W
Conneautville U.S.A. **114** 41.36N 80.18W
Connecticut *d.* U.S.A. **115** 41.45N 72.45W
Connecticut *r.* U.S.A. **115** 41.17N 72.21W
Connellsville U.S.A. **114** 40.01N 79.35W
Connemara *f.* Rep. of Ire. **15** 53.32N 9.56W
Conner, Mt. Australia **90** 25.35S131.49E
Conodoguinet *r.* U.S.A. **114** 40.17N 76.55W
Conon *r.* U.K. **14** 57.33N 4.33W
Conrad U.S.A. **108** 48.10N111.57W
Conroe U.S.A. **111** 30.19N 95.27W
Consecon Canada **105** 44.00N 77.31W
Conselheiro Lafaiete Brazil **126** 20.40S 43.48W
Consett U.K. **12** 54.52N 1.50W
Con Son *is.* Vietnam **56** 8.45N106.38E
Constance, L. *see* Bodensee Europe **39**
Constanţa Romania **29** 44.10N 28.31E
Constantia U.S.A. **115** 43.15N 76.00W
Constantina Spain **27** 37.52N 5.37W
Constantine Algeria **75** 36.22N 6.38E
Constãnzia Portugal **27** 39.28N 8.20W
Constitución Chile **125** 35.20S 72.25W

Constitución to Cuma

Constitución Uruguay 125 31.05S 57.50W
Consuegra Spain 27 39.28N 3.36W
Consul Canada 101 49.21N109.30W
Contact U.S.A. 108 41.48N114.46W
Contai India 63 21.47N 87.45E
Contamana Peru 122 7.19S 75.00W
Contas r. Brazil 123 14.15S 39.00W
Contreras, Embalse de resr. Spain 25 39.32N 1.30W
Contres France 18 47.25N 1.26E
Contwoyto L. Canada 98 65.42N110.50W
Conty France 19 49.44N 2.09E
Conversano Italy 33 40.58N 17.08E
Conway Ark. U.S.A. 111 35.05N 92.26W
Conway N.H. U.S.A. 112 43.59N 71.07W
Conway S.C. U.S.A. 113 33.51N 79.04W
Conway, L. Australia 92 28.17S135.35E
Conwy r. U.K. 11 53.17N 3.49W
Coober Pedy Australia 92 29.01S134.43E
Cooch Behār India 63 26.19N 89.26E
Cook, C. Canada 98 50.08N127.55W
Cook, Mt. New Zealand 86 43.45S170.12E
Cooke, Mt. Australia 89 32.26S116.18E
Cookeville U.S.A. 113 36.10N 85.30W
Cookhouse R.S.A. 80 32.44S 25.47E
Cook Inlet U.S.A. 98 60.30N152.00W
Cook Is. Pacific Oc. 84 15.00S160.00W
Cookshire Canada 105 45.25N 71.38W
Cookstown Canada 104 44.11N 79.42W
Cookstown U.K. 15 54.39N 6.46W
Cook Str. New Zealand 86 41.15S174.30E
Cooktown Australia 90 15.29S145.15E
Coolabah Australia 93 31.02S146.45E
Coolah Australia 93 31.48S149.45E
Coolamara Australia 92 31.59S143.42E
Coolamon Australia 93 34.48S147.12E
Coolangatta Australia 93 28.10S153.26E
Coolgardie Australia 89 31.01S121.12E
Coolidge U.S.A. 109 32.59N111.31W
Coolville U.S.A. 114 39.13N 81.49W
Cooma Australia 93 36.15S149.07E
Coombah Australia 92 32.58S141.39E
Coomberdale Australia 89 30.29S116.03E
Coonabarabran Australia 93 31.16S149.18E
Coonalpyn Australia 92 35.41S139.52E
Coonamble Australia 93 30.55S148.26E
Coonana Australia 89 31.01S123.05E
Coonawarra Australia 92 37.16S140.50E
Coondambo Australia 92 31.07S135.20E
Cooper Creek r. Australia 92 28.33S137.46E
Cooperstown U.S.A. 115 42.42N 74.56W
Coorow Australia 89 29.53S116.01E
Coos Bay town U.S.A. 108 43.22N124.13W
Cootamundra Australia 93 34.41S148.03E
Cootehill Rep. of Ire. 15 54.05N 7.05W
Copainalá Mexico 116 17.05N 93.12W
Copán ruins Honduras 117 14.52N 89.10W
Cope U.S.A. 108 39.40N102.51W
Copenhagen see København Denmark 43
Copertino Italy 33 40.16N 18.03E
Copiapó Chile 124 27.22S 70.20W
Copparo Italy 30 44.54N 11.49E
Copperbelt d. Zambia 80 13.00S 28.00E
Copper Belt f. Zambia 79 12.40S 28.00E
Copper Center U.S.A. 98 61.58N145.19W
Copper Cliff town Canada 104 46.28N 81.04W
Copper Harbor U.S.A. 112 47.28N 87.54W
Coppermine r. Canada 98 67.54N115.10W
Coppermine see Qurlurtuuq town Canada 98
Copper Mountain town Canada 100 49.20N120.30W
Copper Queen Zimbabwe 80 17.31S 29.20E
Copperton R.S.A. 80 30.00S 22.15E
Copp L. Canada 100 60.14N114.40W
Coqên China 63 31.13N 85.12E
Coquet r. U.K. 12 55.21N 1.35W
Coquille U.S.A. 108 43.11N124.11W
Coquimbo Chile 124 29.58S 71.21W
Corabia Romania 34 43.48N 24.30E
Coracora Peru 122 15.02S 73.48W
Coraki Australia 93 23.00S153.17E
Coral Bay town Australia 88 23.02S113.48E
Coral Harbour town Canada 99 64.10N 83.15W
Coral Sea Pacific Oc. 90 14.30S149.30E
Coral Sea Basin Pacific Oc. 84 14.00S152.00E
Corangamite, L. Australia 92 38.10S143.25E
Corato Italy 33 41.09N 16.25E
Corbeil Canada 104 46.17N 79.18W
Corbeil France 19 48.36N 2.29E
Corbeny France 19 49.28N 3.49E
Corbières mts. France 20 42.55N 2.38E
Corbigny France 19 47.15N 3.40E
Corbin U.S.A. 113 36.58N 84.06W
Corby U.K. 13 52.29N 0.41W
Corcubión Spain 26 42.57N 9.11W
Cordes France 20 44.04N 1.56E
Córdoba Argentina 124 31.25S 64.10W
Córdoba d. Argentina 124 30.30S 64.30W
Córdoba Mexico 116 18.55N 96.55W
Córdoba Spain 27 37.53N 4.46W
Córdoba d. Spain 27 38.10N 4.50W
Córdoba, Sierras de mts. Argentina 124 30.30S 64.40W
Cordova U.S.A. 98 60.33N139.44W
Corentyne r. Guyana 123 5.10N 57.20W
Corfield Australia 90 21.43S143.22E
Corfu i. see Kérkira i. Greece 34
Coria Spain 27 39.59N 6.32W
Coria del Río Spain 27 37.16N 6.03W
Coricudgy, Mt. Australia 93 32.51S150.25E
Corigliano Italy 33 39.36N 16.31E
Corindi Australia 93 30.00S153.21E
Corinne Canada 101 50.04N104.40W
Corinth Miss. U.S.A. 111 34.56N 88.31W
Corinth N.Y. U.S.A. 115 43.15N 73.49W
Corinth, G. of see Korinthiakos Kólpos g. Greece 35
Corinto Nicaragua 117 12.29N 87.14W
Cork Rep. of Ire. 15 51.54N 8.28W
Cork d. Rep. of Ire. 15 52.00N 8.40W
Cork Harbour est. Rep. of Ire. 15 51.50N 8.17W
Corlay France 18 48.19N 3.03W
Corleone Italy 32 37.49N 13.18E
Corleto Italy 33 40.23N 16.03E
Cormeilles France 18 49.15N 0.23E
Cormons Italy 31 45.58N 13.28E
Cormorant Canada 101 54.14N100.35W
Corner Brook town Canada 103 48.57N 57.57W
Corner Inlet b. Australia 93 38.43S146.20E
Corning Ark. U.S.A. 111 36.24N 90.35W
Corning N.Y. U.S.A. 114 42.09N 77.04W
Corning Ohio U.S.A. 114 39.36N 82.05W
Corno, Monte mtn. Italy 31 42.28N 13.34E
Cornwall Canada 105 45.02N 74.44W
Cornwall d. U.K. 13 50.26N 4.40W
Cornwallis I. Canada 99 75.00N 95.00W
Coro Venezuela 122 11.27N 69.41W
Coroatá Brazil 123 4.08S 44.08W
Coroico Bolivia 124 16.10S 67.44W
Coromandel New Zealand 86 36.46S175.30E
Coromandel Pen. New Zealand 86 36.45S175.30E
Corona U.S.A. 109 34.15N105.36W
Coronation G. Canada 98 68.00N112.00W
Coronation I. U.S.A. 100 55.52N134.20W
Coronda Argentina 125 31.55S 60.55W
Coronel Chile 125 37.01S 73.08W
Coronel Brandsen Argentina 125 35.10S 58.15W
Coronel Pringles Argentina 125 37.56S 61.25W
Coronel Suárez Argentina 125 37.30S 61.52W
Coropuna mtn. Peru 122 15.31S 72.45W
Corowa Australia 93 36.00S146.20E
Corozal Belize 117 18.23N 88.23W
Corpus Christi U.S.A. 111 27.48N 97.24W
Corral de Amalguer Spain 27 39.46N 3.11W
Correggio Italy 30 44.46N 10.47E
Correntes, Cabo das c. Mozambique 81 24.11S 35.35E
Corrèze d. France 20 45.20N 1.50E
Corrib, Lough Rep. of Ire. 15 53.26N 9.14W
Corrientes Argentina 124 27.30S 58.48W
Corrientes d. Argentina 124 28.00S 57.00W
Corrientes, Cabo c. Colombia 122 5.30N 77.34W
Corrigan U.S.A. 111 31.00N 94.50W
Corrigin Australia 89 32.21S117.52E
Corry U.S.A. 114 41.56N 79.39W
Corryong Australia 93 36.11S147.58E
Corse d. France 21 42.00N 9.00E
Corse i. France 21 42.00N 9.10E
Corse, Cap c. France 21 43.00N 9.25E
Corse-du-Sud d. France 21 41.45N 9.00E
Corsham U.K. 13 51.25N 2.11W
Corsica i. see Corse i. France 21
Corsicana U.S.A. 111 32.06N 96.28W
Corte France 21 42.18N 9.08E
Cortegana Spain 27 37.55N 6.49W
Cortez Colo. U.S.A. 108 37.21N108.35W
Cortez Nev. U.S.A. 108 40.09N116.38W
Cortina Italy 30 46.32N 12.08E
Cortland N.Y. U.S.A. 115 42.36N 76.11W
Cortland Ohio U.S.A. 114 41.20N 80.44W
Cortona Italy 30 43.16N 11.59E
Coruche Portugal 27 38.58N 8.31W
Çoruh Nehri r. Turkey see Chorokh r. U.S.S.R. 64
Çorum Turkey 64 40.31N 34.57E
Corumbá Brazil 124 19.00S 57.27W
Corumbá r. Brazil 126 18.15S 48.55W
Corunna U.S.A. 104 42.59N 84.07W
Corvallis U.S.A. 108 44.34N123.16W
Corwen U.K. 12 52.59N 3.23W
Cosenza Italy 33 39.17N 16.15E
Coshocton U.S.A. 114 40.16N 81.51W
Cosne France 19 47.24N 2.55E
Coso Junction U.S.A. 109 36.03N117.58W
Cosson r. France 19 47.30N 1.15E
Costa Blanca f. Spain 25 38.30N 0.05E
Costa Brava f. Spain 25 41.55N 3.15E
Costa del Sol f. Spain 27 36.30N 4.30W
Costa Mesa U.S.A. 109 33.39N117.55W
Costa Rica C. America 117 10.00N 84.00W
Costeşti Romania 29 44.40N 24.53E
Coswig Sachsen Germany 38 51.07N 13.34E
Coswig Sachsen-Anhalt Germany 38 51.53N 12.26E
Cotabato Phil. 59 7.14N124.15E
Cotagaita Bolivia 124 20.50S 65.41W
Côte d'Azur f. France 21 43.30N 7.00E
Côte d'Ivoire see Ivory Coast Africa 76
Côte-d'Or d. France 19 47.30N 4.50E
Côte d'Or f. France 19 47.10N 4.50E
Côtes d'Armor d. France 18 48.26N 2.40W
Cotonou Benin 77 6.24N 2.31E
Cotopaxi mtn. Ecuador 122 0.40S 78.28W
Cotswold Hills U.K. 13 51.50N 2.00W
Cottage Grove U.S.A. 108 43.48N123.03W
Cottbus Germany 38 51.45N 14.19E
Cottiennes, Alpes mts. France 21 44.45N 7.00E
Cottonvale Australia 93 28.32S151.57E
Cottonwood U.S.A. 109 34.45N112.01W
Cotulla U.S.A. 111 28.26N 99.14W
Coubre, Pointe de la c. France 20 45.41N 1.13W
Coucy France 19 49.31N 3.19E
Coudersport U.S.A. 114 41.46N 78.01W
Couer d'Alene U.S.A. 108 47.41N117.00W
Couesnon r. France 18 48.37N 1.31W
Couhé France 18 46.18N 0.11E
Coulagh B. Rep. of Ire. 15 51.42N 10.00W
Coulee City U.S.A. 108 47.37N119.17W
Coulommiers France 19 48.49N 3.05E
Coulon r. France 21 43.51N 5.00E
Coulonge r. Canada 105 45.51N 76.45W
Council U.S.A. 98 64.55N163.44W
Council Bluffs U.S.A. 110 41.16N 95.52W
Coupar Angus U.K. 14 56.33N 3.17W
Courçon France 20 46.15N 0.49W
Courpière France 20 45.45N 3.33E
Courson-les-Carrières France 19 47.36N 3.30E
Courtalain France 18 48.05N 1.09E
Courtenay Canada 100 49.41N125.00W
Courtrai see Kortrijk Belgium 16
Coutances France 18 49.03N 1.26W
Coutras France 20 45.02N 0.08W
Couvin Belgium 16 50.03N 4.30E
Covè Benin 77 7.16N 2.20E
Cove City U.S.A. 113 35.11N 77.20W
Cove I. Canada 104 45.17N 81.44W
Coventry U.K. 13 52.25N 1.31W
Covilhã Portugal 26 40.17N 7.30W
Covington Ga. U.S.A. 113 33.35N 83.52W
Covington Ky. U.S.A. 112 39.04N 84.30W
Covington Okla. U.S.A. 111 36.18N 97.35W
Covington Tenn. U.S.A. 111 35.34N 89.38W
Covington Va. U.S.A. 113 37.48N 80.01W
Cowal, L. Australia 93 33.36S147.22E
Cowan Canada 101 52.05N100.45W
Cowan, L. Australia 89 32.00S122.00E
Cowangie Australia 92 35.14S141.28E
Cowansville Canada 105 45.12N 72.45W
Cowcowing Lakes Australia 89 31.01S117.18E
Cowdenbeath U.K. 14 56.07N 3.21W
Cowell Australia 92 33.41S136.55E
Cowen U.S.A. 114 38.25N 80.34W
Cowes Australia 93 38.27S145.15E
Cowes U.K. 13 50.45N 1.18W
Cowra Australia 93 33.50S148.45E
Cox r. Australia 90 15.19S135.25E
Coxim Brazil 124 18.28S 54.37W
Coxsackie U.S.A. 105 42.21N 73.48W
Cox's Bāzār Bangla. 63 21.26N 91.59E
Coyuca de Catalán Mexico 116 18.20N100.39W
Cozad U.S.A. 110 40.52N 99.59W
Cozes France 20 45.35N 0.50W
Cozumel, Isla de i. Mexico 117 20.30N 87.00W
Cradock Australia 92 31.59S138.34E
Cradock R.S.A. 80 32.10S 25.35E
Craig Alas. U.S.A. 100 55.29N133.09W
Craig Colo. U.S.A. 108 40.31N107.33W
Craigavon U.K. 15 54.28N 6.25W
Craignure U.K. 14 56.28N 5.42W
Craigsville U.S.A. 114 38.05N 79.23W
Crail U.K. 14 56.16N 2.38W
Crailsheim Germany 39 49.08N 10.04E
Craiova Romania 29 44.18N 23.46E
Cranberry L. U.S.A. 105 44.10N 74.50W
Cranbourne Australia 93 38.07S145.19E
Cranbrook Australia 89 34.15S117.32E
Cranbrook Canada 100 49.30N115.46W
Crane U.S.A. 108 43.25N118.34W
Cranston U.S.A. 115 41.47N 71.26W
Craon France 18 47.51N 0.57W
Craonne France 19 49.26N 3.47E
Craponne France 20 45.20N 3.51E
Craponne, Canal de France 21 43.40N 4.39E
Crater L. U.S.A. 108 42.56N122.06W
Crateús Brazil 123 5.10S 40.39W
Crati r. Italy 33 39.41N 16.30E
Crato Amazonas Brazil 122 7.25S 63.00W
Crato Ceará Brazil 123 7.10S 39.25W
Craughwell Rep. of Ire. 15 53.14N 8.44W
Crawford U.S.A. 110 42.41N103.25W
Crawfordsville U.S.A. 112 40.03N 86.54W
Crawfordville U.S.A. 113 30.12N 84.21W
Crawley U.K. 13 51.07N 0.10W
Crazy Mts. U.S.A. 108 46.08N110.20W
Crécy France 19 50.15N 1.53E
Crécy-sur-Serre France 19 49.42N 3.37E
Cree r. Canada 101 59.00N105.47W
Creede U.S.A. 108 37.51N106.56W
Cree L. Canada 101 57.30N106.30W
Creemore Canada 104 44.19N 80.06W
Creil France 19 49.16N 2.29E
Crema Italy 30 45.22N 9.41E
Cremona Italy 30 45.07N 10.02E
Crépy France 19 49.36N 3.31E
Crépy-en-Valois France 19 49.14N 2.54E
Cres i. Yugo. 31 44.50N 14.25E
Cres town Yugo. 31 44.58N 14.25E
Cresaptown U.S.A. 114 39.36N 78.50W
Crescent U.S.A. 108 43.29N121.41W
Crescent City U.S.A. 108 41.45N124.12W
Crescent Head town Australia 93 31.10S152.59E
Crespo Argentina 125 32.02S 60.20W
Cresson U.S.A. 114 40.28N 78.35W
Cressy Australia 92 38.02S143.38E
Crest France 21 44.44N 5.02E
Crestline U.S.A. 114 40.47N 82.44W
Creston Canada 100 49.10N116.31W
Creston Iowa U.S.A. 110 41.04N 94.22W
Creston Ohio U.S.A. 114 40.59N 81.54W
Creston Oriental de la Sierra Madre mts. Mexico 109 28.40N107.50W
Crestview U.S.A. 113 30.44N 86.34W
Creswick Australia 92 37.25S143.54E
Crete i. see Kríti i. Greece 35
Crete U.S.A. 110 40.38N 96.58W
Crete, Sea of see Kritikón Pélagos sea Greece 35
Crétéville Tunisia 32 36.40N 10.20E
Creus, Cabo de c. Spain 25 42.19N 3.19E
Creuse d. France 20 46.05N 2.00E
Creuse r. France 17 47.00N 0.35E
Creussen Germany 38 49.51N 11.37E
Crevillente Spain 25 38.15N 0.48W
Crewe U.K. 12 53.06N 2.28W
Crianlarich U.K. 14 56.23N 4.37W
Criccieth U.K. 12 52.55N 4.15W
Criciúma Brazil 126 28.40S 49.23W
Crieff U.K. 14 56.23N 3.52W
Crikvenica Yugo. 31 45.11N 14.42E
Crillon, Mt. U.S.A. 100 58.39N137.14W
Crimea pen. see Krym pen. U.S.S.R. 45
Crimmitschau Germany 38 50.49N 12.23E
Crinan U.K. 14 56.06N 5.34W
Cristóbal Colón mtn. Colombia 122 10.53N 73.48W
Crişu Alb r. Romania 37 46.42N 21.17E
Crivitz Germany 38 53.35N 11.38E
Crna r. Yugo. 34 41.35N 21.59E
Crna Gora d. Yugo. 31 42.55N 19.00E
Crnoljeva Planina mts. Yugo. 34 42.20N 21.00E
Črnomelj Yugo. 31 45.34N 15.11E
Croaghnameal mtn. Rep. of Ire. 15 54.40N 7.57W
Croatia d. see Hrvatska d. Yugo. 31
Crockett U.S.A. 111 31.19N 95.28W
Crocodile r. Trans. R.S.A. 80 24.11S 26.48E
Croghan U.S.A. 105 43.54N 75.24W
Croker I. Australia 90 11.12S132.32E
Cromarty Canada 101 58.03N 94.09W
Cromarty U.K. 14 57.40N 4.02W
Cromarty Firth est. U.K. 14 57.41N 4.10W
Cromer U.K. 12 52.56N 1.18E
Cromwell New Zealand 86 45.03S169.14E
Crooked I. Bahamas 117 22.45N 74.00W
Crookhaven Rep. of Ire. 15 51.29N 9.45W
Crookston U.S.A. 110 47.47N 96.37W
Crooksville U.S.A. 114 39.46N 82.06W
Crookwell Australia 93 34.27S149.28E
Croom Rep. of Ire. 15 52.31N 8.43W
Croppa Creek town Australia 93 29.08S150.20E
Crosby U.K. 12 54.11N 4.34W
Crosby U.S.A. 111 31.17N 91.04W
Cross City U.S.A. 113 29.39N 83.09W
Crossett U.S.A. 111 33.08N 91.58W
Cross Fell mtn. U.K. 12 54.43N 2.28W
Cross L. Canada 101 54.45N 97.30W
Cross River d. Nigeria 77 5.45N 8.25E
Crossroads U.S.A. 111 33.30N103.21W
Cross Sd. U.S.A. 100 58.10N136.30W
Crossville U.S.A. 113 35.57N 85.02W
Croswell U.S.A. 114 43.16N 82.37W
Crotone Italy 33 39.05N 17.07E
Crow r. Canada 100 59.41N124.20W
Crow Agency U.S.A. 108 45.36N107.27W
Crowell U.S.A. 111 33.59N 99.43W
Crowl Creek r. Australia 93 31.58S144.53E
Crown Point town U.S.A. 105 43.57N 73.25W
Crowsnest Pass Canada 100 49.40N114.40W
Croyde U.K. 13 51.07N 4.13W
Croydon Australia 90 18.12S142.14E
Croydon U.K. 13 51.23N 0.06W
Crozet, Îles is. Indian Oc. 49 46.00S 52.00E
Crozon France 18 48.15N 4.29W
Crucero U.S.A. 109 35.03N116.10W
Cruger U.S.A. 111 33.14N 90.14W
Cruz, Cabo c. Cuba 117 19.52N 77.44W
Cruz Alta Brazil 126 28.38S 53.38W
Cruz del Eje Argentina 124 30.44S 64.49W
Cruzeiro Brazil 126 22.33S 44.59W
Cruzeiro do Sul Brazil 122 7.40S 72.39W
Crvenka Yugo. 31 45.39N 19.28E
Crystal U.S.A. 110 45.00N 93.25W
Crystal Brook town Australia 92 33.21S138.13E
Crystal City U.S.A. 111 28.41N 99.50W
Crystal River town U.S.A. 113 28.54N 82.36W
Csongrád Hungary 31 46.43N 20.09E
Csongrád d. Hungary 31 46.25N 20.10E
Csorna Hungary 37 47.37N 17.16E
Csurgó Hungary 31 46.16N 17.06E
Cuamba Mozambique 79 14.48S 36.32E
Cuando r. Angola 80 18.30S 23.32E
Cuando-Cubango d. Angola 80 16.00S 20.00E
Cuangar Angola 78 17.34S 18.39E
Cuango r. see Kwango r. Zaïre 78
Cuanza r. Angola 78 9.20S 13.09E
Cuanza Norte d. Angola 78 8.45S 15.00E
Cuanza Sul d. Angola 78 11.00S 15.00E
Cua Rao Vietnam 56 19.16N104.27E
Cuaró Uruguay 125 30.37S 56.54W
Cuaró r. Uruguay 125 30.15S 57.01W
Cuauhtémoc Mexico 109 28.25N106.52W
Cuba C. America 117 22.00N 79.00W
Cuba Portugal 27 38.10N 7.53W
Cuba U.S.A. 109 36.01N107.04W
Cuballing Australia 89 32.50S117.07E
Cubango r. see Okavango r. Angola 78
Cubia r. Angola 78 16.00S 21.46E
Cubo Mozambique 81 23.48S 33.55E
Cuchi r. Angola 80 15.23S 17.12E
Cuckfield U.K. 13 51.00N 0.08W
Cucuí Brazil 122 1.12N 66.50W
Cúcuta Colombia 122 7.55N 72.31W
Cudahy U.S.A. 110 42.57N 87.52W
Cuddalore India 61 11.43N 79.46E
Cue Australia 88 27.25S117.54E
Cuéllar Spain 26 41.25N 4.19W
Cuenca Ecuador 122 2.54S 79.00W
Cuenca Spain 25 40.04N 2.08W
Cuenca d. Spain 27 40.00N 2.30W
Cuenca, Serranía de mts. Spain 25 40.00N 1.45W
Cuernavaca Mexico 116 18.57N 99.15W
Cuero U.S.A. 111 29.06N 97.18W
Cuers France 21 43.14N 6.04E
Cuervo U.S.A. 109 35.02N104.24W
Cuevas del Almanzora Spain 27 37.19N 1.52W
Cuglieri Italy 32 40.11N 8.34E
Cuiabá Brazil 123 15.32S 56.05W
Cuiabá r. Brazil 124 18.00S 57.25W
Cuidado, Punta c. I. de Pascua 85 27.08S109.19W
Cuillin Hills U.K. 14 57.12N 6.13W
Cuilo r. see Kwilu r. Zaïre 78
Cuiseaux France 19 46.30N 5.24E
Cuito r. Angola 78 18.01S 20.50E
Cuito Cuanavale Angola 80 15.11S 19.11E
Culbertson U.S.A. 108 48.09N104.31W
Culcairn Australia 93 35.40S147.03E
Culebra, Sierra de la mts. Spain 26 41.55N 6.30W
Culemborg Neth. 16 51.57N 5.14E
Culgoa r. Australia 93 29.56S146.20E
Culiacán Mexico 109 24.48N107.24W
Culiacán r. Mexico 109 24.30N107.31W
Cúllar de Baza Spain 27 37.35N 2.34W
Cullen U.K. 14 57.41N 2.50W
Cullera Spain 25 39.10N 0.15W
Cullin Sd. U.K. 14 57.03N 6.13W
Culloden Moor U.K. 14 57.29N 3.55W
Culpeper U.S.A. 114 38.28N 77.53W
Culuene r. Brazil 123 12.56S 52.51W
Culver, Pt. Australia 89 32.52S124.41E
Cuma Angola 78 12.52S 15.05E

Cumali to **Dédi**

Cumali Turkey **35** 36.42N 27.28E
Cumaná Venezuela **122** 10.29N 64.12W
Cumberland *r.* U.S.A. **113** 37.09N 88.25W
Cumberland Ky. U.S.A. **113** 36.58N 82.59W
Cumberland Md. U.S.A. **114** 39.39N 78.46W
Cumberland Va. U.S.A. **113** 37.31N 78.16W
Cumberland Wisc. U.S.A. **110** 45.32N 92.01W
Cumberland, C. Vanuatu **84** 14.39S166.37E
Cumberland, L. U.S.A. **113** 36.45N 84.51W
Cumberland I. U.S.A. **113** 30.51N 81.27W
Cumberland L. Canada **101** 54.02N102.17W
Cumberland Pen. Canada **99** 66.50N 64.00W
Cumberland Plateau *f.* U.S.A. **113** 36.00N 85.00W
Cumberland Sd. Canada **99** 65.00N 65.30W
Cumbernauld U.K. **14** 55.57N 4.00W
Cumbria *d.* U.K. **12** 54.30N 3.00W
Cumbrian Mts. U.K. **12** 54.32N 3.05W
Cuminá *r.* Brazil **123** 1.30S 56.00W
Cummins Australia **92** 34.16S135.44E
Cumnock Australia **93** 32.56S148.46E
Cumnock U.K. **14** 55.27N 4.15W
Cunderdin Australia **89** 31.39S117.15E
Cunene *d.* Angola **78** 16.00S 16.00E
Cunene *r.* Angola **78** 17.15S 11.50E
Cuneo Italy **30** 44.23N 7.32E
Cungena Australia **92** 32.33S134.40E
Cunlhat France **20** 45.38N 3.35E
Cunnamulla Australia **93** 28.04S145.40E
Cuokkaraš'ša *mtn.* Norway **40** 69.57N 24.32E
Cuorgnè Italy **30** 45.23N 7.39E
Cupar U.K. **14** 56.19N 3.01W
Cupica, Golfo de *g.* Colombia **122** 6.35N 77.25W
Cuprija Yugo. **34** 43.56N 21.23E
Curaçao *i.* Neth. Antilles **122** 12.15N 69.00W
Curacautín Chile **125** 38.26S 71.53W
Curaco *r.* Argentina **125** 38.49S 65.01W
Curanilahue Chile **125** 37.28S 73.21W
Curaray *r.* Peru **122** 2.20S 74.05W
Curban Australia **93** 31.33S148.36E
Curdlawidny L. Australia **92** 30.16S136.20E
Cure *r.* France **19** 47.40N 3.41E
Curiapo Venezuela **122** 8.33N 61.05W
Curicó Chile **125** 34.59S 71.14W
Curitiba Brazil **126** 25.24S 49.16W
Curlewis Australia **93** 31.08S150.16E
Curnamona Australia **92** 31.40S139.35E
Currane, Lough Rep. of Ire. **15** 51.50N 10.07W
Currant U.S.A. **108** 38.44N115.30W
Curranyalpa Australia **93** 30.57S144.33E
Currie Australia **91** 39.56S143.52E
Currie U.S.A. **108** 40.17N114.44W
Curtin Australia **89** 30.50S122.05E
Curtis Spain **26** 43.07N 8.03W
Curtis U.S.A. **110** 40.38N100.31W
Curtis I. Australia **90** 23.38S151.09E
Curuá *r.* Brazil **123** 5.23S 54.22W
Čurug Yugo. **31** 45.29N 20.04E
Cururupu Brazil **123** 1.50S 44.52W
Curuzú Cuatiá Argentina **125** 29.50S 58.05W
Curvelo Brazil **126** 18.45S 44.27W
Curwensville U.S.A. **114** 40.58N 78.32W
Cushendall U.K. **15** 55.06N 6.05W
Cushing U.S.A. **111** 35.59N 96.46W
Cusna, Monte *mtn.* Italy **30** 44.17N 10.23E
Cut Bank U.S.A. **108** 48.38N112.20W
Cutro Italy **33** 39.02N 16.59E
Cuttaburra Creek *r.* Australia **93** 29.18S145.00E
Cuttack India **63** 20.30N 85.50E
Cuxhaven Germany **38** 53.52N 8.42E
Cuyahoga Falls *town* U.S.A. **114** 41.08N 81.29W
Cuyuni *r.* Guyana **122** 6.24N 58.38W
Cuzco Peru **122** 13.32S 71.57W
Cuzna *r.* Spain **26** 38.04N 4.41W
Cwmbran U.K. **13** 51.39N 3.01W
Cyclades *is. see* Kikládhes *is.* Greece **35**
Cynthiana U.S.A. **112** 38.22N 84.18W
Cypress Hills Canada **101** 49.40N109.30W
Cyprus Asia **66** 35.00N 33.00E
Cyrenaica *f. see* Barqah *f.* Libya **72**
Czechoslovakia Europe **36** 49.30N 15.00E
Czeremcha Poland **37** 52.32N 23.15E
Czersk Poland **37** 53.48N 18.00E
Częstochowa Poland **37** 50.49N 19.07E

D

Dà *r.* Vietnam **56** 21.20N105.24E
Da'an China **54** 45.30N124.18E
Ḍab'ah Jordan **67** 31.36N 36.04E
Dabakala Ivory Coast **76** 8.19N 4.24W
Daba Shan *mts.* China **55** 32.00N109.00E
Dabat Ethiopia **73** 12.58N 37.48E
Dabbāgh, Jabal *mtn.* Saudi Arabia **66** 27.51N 35.43E
Dabhoi India **62** 22.11N 73.26E
Dabie Shan *mts.* China **55** 31.15N115.20E
Dabola Guinea **76** 10.48N 11.02W
Dabra India **63** 25.54N 78.20E
Dabu Jiangxi China **55** 26.47N116.04E
Dacca *see* Dhaka Bangla. **63**
Dachau Germany **39** 48.15N 11.26E
Dacre Canada **105** 45.22N 76.59W
Dadanawa Guyana **122** 2.30N 59.30W
Dade City U.S.A. **113** 28.23N 82.11W
Dādhar Pakistan **62** 29.28N 67.39E
Dādra & Nagar Haveli *d.* India **62** 20.05N 73.00E
Dādu Pakistan **62** 26.44N 67.47E
Dadu He *r.* China **61** 28.47N104.40E
Daet Phil. **59** 14.07N122.58E
Dagali Norway **41** 60.25N 8.27E
Dagana Senegal **76** 16.28N 15.35W
Daga Post Sudan **73** 9.12N 33.58E
Dagash Sudan **72** 19.22N 33.24E
Dagu China **54** 38.58N117.40E
Dagua P.N.G. **59** 3.25S143.20E
Daguan China **52** 27.44N103.53E
Dagupan Phil. **59** 16.02N120.21E
Daguragu Australia **88** 17.33S130.30E
Dagzê China **63** 29.45N105.45E
Dagzê Co *l.* China **63** 31.45N 87.50E
Dahan-e Qowmghī Afghan. **62** 34.28N 66.31E
Da Hinggan Ling *mts.* China **53** 50.00N122.10E
Dahlak Archipelago *is.* Ethiopia **72** 15.45N 40.30E
Dahlak Kebir I. Ethiopia **72** 15.38N 40.11E
Dahlem Germany **39** 50.23N 6.33E
Dahlgren U.S.A. **114** 38.20N 77.03W
Dahme Germany **38** 51.52N 13.25E
Dahra Senegal **76** 15.21N 15.29W
Dahujiang China **55** 26.06N114.58E
Dahūk Iraq **64** 36.52N 43.00E
Daḥy, Nafūd ad *f.* Saudi Arabia **71** 22.00N 45.25E
Ḍaḥyah, 'Urūq *f.* Yemen **71** 18.45N 51.15E
Dai Hai *l.* China **54** 40.31N112.43E
Dā'īl Syria **67** 32.45N 36.08E
Dailekh Nepal **63** 28.50N 81.43E
Daimiel Spain **27** 39.04N 3.37W
Daitō Japan **57** 34.42N135.38E
Daiyun Shan *mtn.* China **55** 25.41N118.11E
Dājal Pakistan **62** 29.33N 70.23E
Dajarra Australia **90** 21.42S139.31E
Dajing China **55** 28.25N121.10E
Dakar Senegal **76** 14.38N 17.27W
Dakhal, Wādī ad *r.* Egypt **66** 28.49N 32.45E
Dākhilah, Al Wāḥāt ad *oasis* Egypt **64** 25.30N 28.10E
Dakhla W. Sahara **74** 23.43N 15.57W
Dakhlet Nouadhibou *d.* Mauritania **74** 20.30N 16.00W
Dakhovskaya U.S.S.R. **23** 44.13N 40.13E
Dakingari Nigeria **77** 11.40N 4.06E
Dakota City U.S.A. **110** 42.25N 96.25W
Dakovica Yugo. **34** 42.22N 20.26E
Dakovo Yugo. **31** 45.19N 18.25E
Dal *r.* Sweden **41** 60.38N 17.27E
Dala Congo **78** 1.40N 16.39E
Dalaba Guinea **76** 10.47N 12.12W
Dalai Nur *l.* China **54** 43.27N116.25E
Dalandzadgad Mongolia **54** 43.30N104.18E
Dalane *f.* Norway **42** 58.35N 6.20E
Da Lat Vietnam **56** 11.56N108.25E
Dālbandin Pakistan **62** 28.53N 64.25E
Dalbeattie U.K. **14** 54.55N 3.49W
Dalbosjön *b.* Sweden **43** 58.45N 12.48E
Dalby Australia **91** 27.11S151.12E
Dalby Sweden **43** 55.40N 13.20E
Dale Hordaland Norway **41** 60.35N 5.49E
Dale Sogn og Fj. Norway **41** 61.22N 5.24E
Dalen Norway **42** 59.27N 8.00E
Dalhart U.S.A. **111** 36.04N102.31W
Dalhousie Canada **103** 48.04N 66.23W
Dalhousie Jammu & Kashmir **62** 32.32N 75.59E
Dali China **52** 25.42N100.11E
Dalian China **54** 38.49N121.48E
Dalías Spain **27** 36.49N 2.52W
Dāliyat el Karmel Israel **67** 32.42N 35.03E
Dalj Yugo. **31** 45.29N 18.59E
Dalkeith U.K. **14** 55.54N 3.04W
Dallas Oreg. U.S.A. **108** 44.55N123.19W
Dallas Tex. U.S.A. **111** 32.47N 96.48W
Dallastown U.S.A. **115** 39.54N 76.39W
Dall I. U.S.A. **100** 55.00N133.00W
Dalli Rajhāra India **63** 20.35N 81.04E
Dalmacija *f.* Yugo. **31** 43.33N 16.40E
Dalmally U.K. **14** 56.25N 4.58W
Dalmas, Lac *l.* Canada **103** 53.27N 71.50W
Dalmellington U.K. **14** 55.19N 4.24W
Dalnerechensk U.S.S.R. **53** 45.55N133.45E
Daloa Ivory Coast **76** 6.56N 6.28W
Dalou Shan *mts.* China **55** 28.25N107.15E
Dalqū Sudan **72** 20.07N 30.35E
Dalrymple, Mt. Australia **90** 21.02S148.38E
Dalsingh Sarai India **63** 25.40N 85.50E
Dalsland *f.* Sweden **43** 59.00N 12.10E
Dalton Canada **102** 48.10N 84.00W
Dalton U.S.A. **113** 34.46N 84.59W
Daltonganj India **63** 24.02N 84.04E
Dalupiri *i.* Phil. **55** 19.05N121.13E
Dalvik Iceland **40** 65.58N 18.28W
Dalwhinnie U.K. **14** 56.56N 4.15W
Daly *r.* Australia **88** 13.20S130.19E
Daly City U.S.A. **108** 37.42N122.29W
Daly Waters *town* Australia **90** 16.15S133.22E
Damā, Wādī *r.* Saudi Arabia **64** 27.04N 35.48E
Damān India **62** 20.25N 72.51E
Damān *d.* India **62** 20.10N 73.00E
Damanhūr Egypt **66** 31.03N 30.28E
Damar *i.* Indonesia **59** 7.10S128.30E
Damascus *see* Dimashq Syria **66**
Damaturu Nigeria **77** 11.49N 11.50E
Damāvand, Qolleh-ye *mtn.* Iran **65** 35.47N 52.04E
Damba Angola **78** 6.44S 15.17E
Damen *i.* China **55** 27.58N121.05E
Dāmghān Iran **65** 36.09N 54.22E
Damiaoshan China **55** 24.43N109.15E
Daming Shan *mts.* China **55** 23.23N108.30E
Dāmiyā Jordan **67** 32.06N 35.33E
Dammartin-en-Goële France **19** 49.03N 2.41E
Dāmodar *r.* India **63** 22.17N 88.05E
Damoh India **63** 23.50N 79.27E
Damongo Ghana **76** 9.06N 1.48W
Dampier Australia **88** 20.40S116.42E
Dampier, Selat *str.* Pacific Oc. **59** 0.30S130.50E
Dampier Land Australia **88** 17.20S123.00E
Damqawt Yemen **71** 16.34N 52.50E
Damxung China **63** 30.32N 91.06E
Dan Israel **67** 33.14N 35.39E
Dana Canada **101** 52.18N105.42W
Danané Ivory Coast **76** 7.21N 8.10W
Da Nang Vietnam **56** 16.04N108.13E
Dānāpur India **63** 25.38N 85.03E
Danba China **52** 30.57N101.55E
Danbury Conn. U.S.A. **115** 41.23N 73.27W
Danbury N.H. U.S.A. **115** 43.32N 71.54W
Dand Afghan. **62** 31.37N 65.41E
Dandaragan Australia **89** 30.40S115.42E
Dande *r.* Angola **78** 8.30S 13.23E
Dandeldhura Nepal **63** 29.17N 80.36E
Dandenong Australia **93** 37.59S145.14E
Dandong China **54** 40.10N124.25E
Danger Is. Cook Is. **84** 10.53S165.49W
Dangila Ethiopia **73** 11.18N 36.54E
Dangqên China **63** 31.41N 91.51E
Dangriga Belize **117** 16.58N 88.13W
Dangshan China **54** 34.25N116.24E
Dangyang China **55** 30.52N111.40E
Daniel U.S.A. **108** 42.52N110.04W
Daniel's Harbour Canada **103** 50.14N 57.35W
Danielson U.S.A. **115** 41.48N 71.53W
Danilov U.S.S.R. **44** 58.10N 40.12E
Daning China **54** 36.32N110.47E
Danisa Hills Kenya **79** 3.10N 39.37E
Danja Nigeria **77** 11.29N 7.30E
Danlí Honduras **117** 14.02N 86.30W
Dannenberg Germany **38** 53.06N 11.05E
Dannevirke New Zealand **86** 40.12S176.08E
Dannhauser R.S.A. **80** 28.00S 30.03E
Dansville U.S.A. **114** 42.34N 77.42W
Dantewāra India **63** 18.54N 81.21E
Danube *r.* Europe **31** 45.20N 29.40E
Danube, Mouths of the *see* Dunării, Delta *f.* Romania **37**
Danvers U.S.A. **115** 42.34N 70.56W
Danville Canada **105** 45.47N 72.01W
Danville Ill. U.S.A. **110** 40.09N 87.37W
Danville Ky. U.S.A. **113** 37.40N 84.49W
Danville Penn. U.S.A. **115** 40.57N 76.37W
Danville Va. U.S.A. **113** 36.34N 79.25W
Danville Vt. U.S.A. **105** 44.25N 72.09W
Dan Xian China **55** 19.30N109.35E
Dão *r.* Portugal **26** 40.20N 8.11W
Daordeng China **54** 40.47N119.05E
Daosa India **62** 26.53N 76.20E
Daoukro Ivory Coast **76** 7.10N 3.58W
Daoulas France **18** 48.22N 4.15W
Dao Xian China **55** 25.32N111.35E
Daozhen China **55** 28.46N107.45E
Dapango Togo **76** 10.51N 0.15E
Dapingfang China **54** 41.25N120.07E
Da Qaidam China **52** 37.44N 95.08E
Daqinggou China **54** 41.22N114.13E
Daqing Shan *mts.* China **54** 41.00N111.00E
Daqqāq Sudan **73** 12.56N 26.58E
Daqq-e Patargān *f.* Iran **65** 33.30N 60.40E
Dar'ā Syria **67** 32.37N 36.06E
Dar'ā *d.* Syria **67** 32.50N 36.10E
Dārāb Iran **65** 28.45N 54.34E
Darāban Pakistan **62** 31.44N 70.20E
Darabani Romania **37** 48.11N 26.35E
Darakht-e Yahyā Afghan. **62** 31.50N 68.08E
Dārān Iran **65** 33.00N 50.27E
Darband, Kūh-e *mtn.* Iran **65** 31.33N 57.08E
Darbhanga India **63** 26.10N 85.54E
Darby Mont. U.S.A. **108** 46.01N114.11W
Darby Penn. U.S.A. **115** 39.54N 75.15W
D'Arcy Canada **100** 50.33N122.32W
Darda Yugo. **31** 45.37N 18.41E
Dardanelles *see* Çanakkale Boğazi *str.* Turkey **34**
Dar es Salaam Tanzania **79** 6.51S 39.18E
Dar es Salaam *d.* Tanzania **79** 6.45S 39.10E
Dareton Australia **92** 34.04S142.04E
Darfield New Zealand **86** 43.29S172.07E
Dargan Ata U.S.S.R. **50** 40.30N 62.10E
Dargaville New Zealand **86** 35.57S173.53E
Dargo Australia **93** 37.30S147.16E
Darhan Mongolia **52** 49.34N106.23E
Darie Hills Somali Rep. **71** 8.15N 47.25E
Darien U.S.A. **115** 41.05N 73.28W
Darién, Golfo del *g.* Colombia **122** 9.20N 77.30W
Darjeeling India **63** 27.02N 88.16E
Darkan Australia **89** 33.19S116.42E
Darke Peak *mtn.* Australia **92** 33.28S136.12E
Darling *r.* Australia **92** 34.05S141.57E
Darling Downs *f.* Australia **91** 28.00S149.45E
Darling Range *mts.* Australia **89** 32.00S116.30E
Darlington U.K. **12** 54.33N 1.33W
Darlington Point *town* Australia **93** 34.36S146.01E
Darłowe Poland **36** 54.26N 16.23E
Darmstadt Germany **39** 49.53N 8.40E
Darnah Libya **72** 32.45N 22.39E
Darnah *d.* Libya **72** 31.30N 23.30E
Darnétal France **18** 49.27N 1.09E
Darney France **19** 48.05N 6.03E
Darnick Australia **92** 32.55S143.39E
Darnley, C. Antarctica **128** 68.00S 69.00E
Daroca Spain **25** 41.07N 1.25W
Darreh Gaz Iran **65** 37.22N 59.08E
Dar Rounga *f.* C.A.R. **73** 9.25N 21.30E
Darsser Ort *c.* Germany **38** 54.29N 12.31E
Dartmoor Australia **92** 37.58S141.19E
Dartmoor Forest *hills* U.K. **13** 50.33N 3.55W
Dartmouth Canada **103** 44.40N 63.34W
Dartmouth U.K. **13** 50.21N 3.35W
Dartmouth Resr. Australia **93** 36.36S147.38E
Dartry Mts. Rep. of Ire. **15** 54.23N 8.25W
Dartuch, Cabo *c.* Spain **25** 39.56N 3.48E
Daru P.N.G. **90** 9.04S143.12E
Daruvar Yugo. **31** 45.36N 17.13E
Darvaza U.S.S.R. **50** 40.12N 58.24E
Darvel, Teluk *b.* Malaysia **58** 4.40N118.30E
Darwen U.K. **12** 53.42N 2.29W
Dārwha India **63** 20.19N 77.46E
Darwin Australia **90** 12.23S130.44E
Daryācheh-ye Bakhtegān *l.* Iran **65** 29.20N 54.05E
Daryācheh-ye Namak *l.* Iran **65** 34.45N 51.36E
Daryācheh-ye Orūmīyeh *l.* Iran **65** 37.40N 45.28E
Daryācheh-ye Sīstān *f.* Iran **65** 31.00N 61.15E
Darya Khān Pakistan **62** 31.48N 71.06E
Daryāpur India **62** 20.56N 77.20E
Dasāda India **62** 23.19N 71.50E
Dasht *r.* Pakistan **62** 25.10N 61.40E
Dashte-e Mārgow *des.* Afghan. **65** 30.45N 63.00E
Dasht-e Kavīr *des.* Iran **65** 34.40N 55.00E
Dasht-e Lūt *des.* Iran **65** 31.30N 58.00E
Dashui Nur China **54** 42.45N116.47E
Daspalla India **63** 20.21N 84.51E
Dassa-Zoumé Benin **77** 7.50N 2.13E
Dassow Germany **38** 53.50N 10.59E
Dastgardān Iran **65** 34.19N 56.51E
Dastjerd Iran **65** 34.33N 50.15E
Datça Turkey **35** 36.46N 27.40E
Datia India **63** 25.40N 78.28E
Datong China **54** 40.10N113.15E
Datteln Germany **38** 51.40N 7.23E
Datu, Tanjung *c.* Malaysia **58** 2.00N109.30E
Datu Piang Phil. **59** 7.02N124.30E
Daua *r.* Kenya *see* Dawa *r.* Ethiopia **73**
Dāud Khel Pakistan **62** 32.53N 71.34E
Daudnagar India **63** 25.02N 84.24E
Daugavpils U.S.S.R. **44** 55.52N 26.31E
Daun Germany **39** 50.11N 6.50E
Dauphin Canada **101** 51.09N100.03W
Dauphiné, Alpes du *mts.* France **21** 44.35N 5.45E
Dauphin L. Canada **101** 51.17N 99.48W
Daura Nigeria **77** 13.05N 8.18E
Dāvangere India **60** 14.30N 75.52E
Davao Phil. **59** 7.05N125.38E
Davao G. Phil. **59** 6.30N126.00E
Daveluyville Canada **105** 46.12N 72.08W
Davenport U.S.A. **110** 41.32N 90.36W
Daventry U.K. **13** 52.16N 1.10W
Davenyns, L. Canada **105** 47.05N 73.45W
David Panama **117** 8.26N 82.26W
David-Gorodok U.S.S.R. **37** 52.04N 27.10E
Davis U.S.A. **108** 38.33N121.44W
Davis Creek *town* U.S.A. **108** 41.44N120.24W
Davison U.S.A. **104** 43.02N 83.31W
Davis Sea Antarctica **128** 66.00S 90.00E
Davis Str. N. America **99** 66.00N 58.00W
Davlekanovo U.S.S.R. **44** 54.12N 55.00E
Davos Switz. **39** 46.48N 9.50E
Davutlar Turkey **35** 37.43N 27.17E
Dawa China **54** 40.58N122.00E
Dawa *r.* Ethiopia **73** 4.11N 42.06E
Dawaxung China **63** 31.26N 85.06E
Dawlish U.K. **13** 50.34N 3.28W
Dawna Range *mts.* Burma **56** 17.00N 98.00E
Dawson Canada **98** 64.04N139.24W
Dawson U.S.A. **113** 31.47N 84.27W
Dawson Creek *town* Canada **100** 55.45N120.15W
Dawson Range *f.* Canada **98** 62.40N139.00W
Dawu China **52** 31.00N101.09E
Dax France **20** 43.43N 1.03W
Daxian China **55** 31.10N107.28E
Daxing China **54** 39.44N116.20E
Daylesford Australia **92** 37.22S144.12E
Dayman *r.* Uruguay **125** 31.25S 58.00W
Dayong Hunan China **55** 29.06N110.24E
Dayr Abū Sa'īd Jordan **67** 32.30N 35.41E
Dayr al Balaḥ Egypt **67** 31.25N 34.21E
Dayr al Ghuṣūn Jordan **67** 32.21N 35.05E
Dayr az Zawr Syria **64** 35.20N 40.08E
Dayr Dibwān Jordan **67** 31.55N 35.16E
Dayr Sharaf Jordan **67** 32.15N 35.11E
Dayton N.Y. U.S.A. **114** 42.25N 78.58W
Dayton Ohio U.S.A. **112** 39.45N 84.10W
Dayton Penn. U.S.A. **114** 40.53N 79.16W
Dayton Tenn. U.S.A. **113** 35.30N 85.01W
Dayton Wash. U.S.A. **108** 46.19N117.59W
Daytona Beach *town* U.S.A. **113** 29.11N 81.01W
Dayu China **55** 25.24N114.22E
Da Yunhe *canal* China **54** 39.10N117.12E
Dazhu China **55** 30.50N107.12E
De Aar R.S.A. **80** 30.39S 24.01E
Dead Sea Jordan **67** 31.25N 35.30E
Deal U.K. **13** 51.13N 1.25E
De'an China **55** 29.20N115.46E
Deán Funes Argentina **124** 30.25S 64.20W
Dean Lake *town* Canada **104** 46.13N 83.09W
Dearborn U.S.A. **104** 42.18N 83.10W
Dease *r.* Canada **100** 59.54N128.30W
Dease Arm *b.* Canada **98** 66.52N119.37W
Dease L. Canada **100** 58.05N130.04W
Death Valley *f.* U.S.A. **109** 36.30N117.00W
Death Valley *town* U.S.A. **109** 36.18N116.25W
Death Valley Nat. Monument U.S.A. **108** 36.30N117.00W
Deauville France **18** 49.22N 0.04E
Debar Yugo. **34** 41.31N 20.30E
Debica Poland **37** 50.04N 21.24E
Deblin Poland **37** 51.35N 21.50E
Deborah, L. Australia **89** 30.45S119.07E
Debre Birhan Ethiopia **73** 9.40N 39.33E
Debrecen Hungary **37** 47.30N 21.37E
Debre Tabor Ethiopia **73** 11.50N 38.05E
Dečani Yugo. **34** 42.30N 20.10E
Decatur Ala. U.S.A. **113** 34.36N 87.00W
Decatur Ga. U.S.A. **113** 33.45N 84.17W
Decatur Ill. U.S.A. **110** 39.51N 89.32W
Decatur Ind. U.S.A. **112** 40.50N 84.57W
Decazeville France **20** 44.34N 2.15E
Deccan *f.* India **60** 18.30N 77.30E
Decelles, Lac *l.* Canada **102** 47.40N 78.10W
Dechu India **62** 26.47N 72.20E
Decimomannu Italy **32** 39.19N 8.58E
Děčín Czech. **38** 50.48N 14.13E
Decize France **19** 46.50N 3.27E
Deckerville U.S.A. **114** 43.32N 82.44W
De Cocksdorp Neth. **16** 53.12N 4.52E
Decorah U.S.A. **110** 43.18N 91.48W
Decs Hungary **31** 46.17N 18.46E
Deda Romania **37** 46.57N 24.53E
Dédi Ivory Coast **76** 8.34N 3.33W

Dediāpada to Dnepropetrovsk

Dediāpada India **62** 21.35N 73.40E
Dedza Malaŵi **79** 14.20S 34.24E
Dee *r.* D. and G. U.K. **14** 54.50N 4.05W
Dee *r.* Grampian U.K. **14** 57.07N 2.04W
Dee *r.* Wales U.K. **12** 53.13N 3.05W
Deep B. Canada **100** 61.15N116.35W
Deep Creek L. U.S.A. **114** 39.30N 79.19W
Deep River *town* Canada **105** 46.06N 77.30W
Deep River *town* U.S.A. **115** 41.23N 72.26W
Deepwater Australia **93** 29.26S151.51E
Deep Well Australia **90** 24.25S134.05E
Deerfield *r.* U.S.A. **115** 42.35N 72.35W
Deer Lake *town* Canada **103** 49.07N 57.35W
Deer Lodge U.S.A. **108** 46.24N112.44W
Deesa India **62** 24.15N 72.10E
Deeth U.S.A. **108** 41.04N115.18W
Deex Nugaaleed *r.* Somali Rep. **71** 7.58N 49.52E
Defiance U.S.A. **112** 41.17N 84.21W
De Funiak Springs *town* U.S.A. **113** 30.41N 86.08W
Deganya Bet Israel **67** 32.42N 35.35E
Degeberga Sweden **43** 55.50N 14.05E
Degerby Finland **43** 60.02N 20.23E
Degerfors Sweden **43** 59.14N 14.26E
Degerhamn Sweden **43** 56.21N 16.24E
Deggendorf Germany **39** 48.51N 12.59E
De Grey *r.* Australia **88** 20.12S119.11E
Deh Bīd Iran **65** 30.38N 53.12E
Dehej India **62** 21.42N 72.35E
Dehibat Tunisia **75** 32.01N 10.42E
Dehra Dūn India **63** 30.19N 78.02E
Dehri India **63** 24.52N 84.11E
Deh Shū Afghan. **62** 30.28N 63.25E
Dehua China **55** 25.30N118.14E
Deinze Belgium **16** 50.59N 3.32E
Dej Romania **37** 47.08N 23.55E
Deje Sweden **43** 59.36N 13.28E
Dejiang China **55** 28.19N108.05E
Dek'emhāre Ethiopia **72** 15.05N 39.02E
Dekese Zaïre **78** 3.25S 21.24E
Dekina Nigeria **77** 7.43N 7.04E
De Land U.S.A. **113** 29.02N 81.18W
Delano U.S.A. **109** 35.41N119.15W
Delārām Afghan. **62** 32.11N 63.25E
Delaronde L. Canada **101** 54.05N107.05W
Delaware *d.* U.S.A. **115** 39.10N 75.30W
Delaware *r.* U.S.A. **115** 39.20N 75.25W
Delaware *town* U.S.A. **112** 40.18N 83.06W
Delaware, East Branch *r.* U.S.A. **115** 41.55N 75.17W
Delaware, West Branch *r.* U.S.A. **115** 41.56N 75.17W
Delaware B. U.S.A. **115** 39.05N 75.15W
Delaware Water Gap *town* U.S.A. **115** 40.59N 75.09W
Delaware Water Gap Nat. Recreation Area U.S.A. **115** 41.07N 75.06W
Delčevo Yugo. **34** 41.58N 22.46E
Delegate Australia **93** 37.03S148.58E
Delémont Switz. **39** 47.22N 7.21E
Delfinópolis Brazil **126** 20.21S 46.51W
Delft Neth. **16** 52.01N 4.23E
Delfzijl Neth. **16** 53.20N 6.56E
Delgado, C. Mozambique **79** 10.45S 40.38E
Delhi Canada **104** 42.51N 80.30W
Delhi India **62** 28.40N 77.13E
Delhi *d.* India **62** 28.37N 77.10E
Delhi U.S.A. **115** 42.17N 74.55W
Delicias Mexico **109** 28.13N105.28W
Délimbé C.A.R. **73** 9.53N 22.37E
Delingha China **52** 37.16N 97.12E
Delitzsch Germany **38** 51.31N 12.20E
Dell City U.S.A. **109** 31.56N105.12W
Delle France **19** 47.30N 7.00E
Delmar U.S.A. **115** 38.27N 75.34W
Delmarva Pen. U.S.A. **115** 38.48N 75.47W
Delmenhorst Germany **38** 53.03N 8.38E
Delnice Yugo. **31** 45.24N 14.48E
De Long Mts. U.S.A. **98** 68.20N162.00W
Delorme, Lac *l.* Canada **103** 54.40N 69.50W
Delphos U.S.A. **112** 40.50N 84.21W
Del Rio U.S.A. **111** 29.22N100.54W
Delta Colo. U.S.A. **108** 38.44N108.04W
Delta Utah U.S.A. **108** 39.21N112.35W
Delungra Australia **93** 29.38S150.50E
Delvinë Albania **34** 39.57N 20.06E
Demak Indonesia **59** 6.53S110.40E
Demanda, Sierra de la *mts.* Spain **26** 42.10N 3.00W
Demba Zaïre **78** 5.28S 22.14E
Dembī Ethiopia **73** 8.05N 36.27E
Dembia C.A.R. **73** 5.07N 24.25E
Dembī Dolo Ethiopia **73** 8.30N 34.48E
Demer *r.* Belgium **16** 50.59N 4.42E
Deming U.S.A. **109** 32.16N107.45W
Demmin Germany **36** 53.54N 13.02E
Demmitt Canada **100** 55.20N119.50W
Demonte Italy **30** 44.19N 7.17E
Demopolis U.S.A. **111** 32.31N 87.50W
Demotte U.S.A. **112** 41.07N 87.14W
Dêmqog China **63** 32.43N 79.29E
Denain France **19** 50.20N 3.23E
Denakil *f.* Ethiopia **73** 13.00N 41.00E
Denbigh Canada **105** 45.08N 77.16W
Denbigh U.K. **12** 53.11N 3.25W
Den Burg Neth. **16** 53.03N 4.47E
Dendermonde Belgium **16** 51.01N 4.07E
Dendre *r.* Belgium **16** 51.01N 4.07E
Dengkou China **54** 40.18N106.59E
Deng Xian China **54** 32.44N112.00E
Denham Australia **88** 25.54S113.35E
Denham Range *mts.* Australia **90** 21.55S147.46E
Den Helder Neth. **16** 52.58N 4.46E
Denia Spain **25** 38.51N 0.07E
Deniliquin Australia **93** 35.33S144.58E
Denison Iowa U.S.A. **110** 42.01N 95.21W
Denison Tex. U.S.A. **111** 33.45N 96.33W
Denizli Turkey **64** 37.46N 29.05E
Denman Australia **93** 32.23S150.42E
Denmark Australia **89** 34.54S117.25E
Denmark Europe **42** 56.05N 10.00E
Denmark Str. Greenland / Iceland **96** 65.00N 30.00W
Dennison U.S.A. **114** 40.24N 81.19W
Den Oever Neth. **16** 52.56N 5.01E
Denpasar Indonesia **59** 8.40S115.14E
Denton Mont. U.S.A. **108** 47.19N109.57W
Denton Tex. U.S.A. **111** 33.13N 97.08W
D'Entrecasteaux, Pt. Australia **89** 34.50S116.00E
D'Entrecasteaux, Recifs *reef* N. Cal. **84** 18.00S163.10E
D'Entrecasteaux Is. P.N.G. **90** 9.30S150.40E
Denver U.S.A. **108** 39.43N105.01W
Denys *r.* Canada **102** 55.05N 77.22W
Denzlingen Germany **39** 48.04N 7.52E
Deo *r.* Cameroon **77** 8.33N 12.45E
Deogarh *mtn.* India **63** 23.32N 82.16E
Deogarh Madhya P. India **63** 24.33N 78.15E
Deogarh Orissa India **63** 21.32N 84.44E
Deogarh Rāj. India **62** 25.32N 73.54E
Deogarh Hills India **63** 23.45N 82.30E
Deoghar India **63** 24.29N 86.42E
Deolāli India **62** 19.57N 73.50E
Deoli India **62** 25.45N 75.23E
Deori India **63** 23.08N 78.41E
Deoria India **63** 26.31N 83.47E
Deori Khās India **63** 23.24N 79.01E
Deosil India **63** 23.42N 82.15E
De Peel *f.* Belgium **16** 51.30N 5.50E
Depew U.S.A. **114** 42.54N 78.42W
Deposit U.S.A. **115** 42.04N 75.25W
Depot Harbour *town* Canada **104** 45.19N 80.06W
Dêqên China **52** 28.45N 98.58E
De Queen U.S.A. **111** 34.02N 94.21W
De Quincy U.S.A. **111** 30.27N 93.26W
Dera Bugti Pakistan **62** 29.02N 69.09E
Dera Ghāzi Khān Pakistan **62** 30.03N 70.38E
Dera Ismāil Khān Pakistan **62** 31.50N 70.54E
Derazhnya U.S.S.R. **37** 49.18N 27.28E
Derbent U.S.S.R. **65** 42.03N 48.18E
Derby Tas. Australia **91** 41.08S147.47E
Derby W.A. Australia **88** 17.19S123.38E
Derby U.K. **12** 52.55N 1.28W
Derby Conn. U.S.A. **115** 41.19N 73.05W
Derby N.Y. U.S.A. **114** 42.41N 78.58W
Derby Center U.S.A. **105** 44.58N 72.09W
Derbyshire *d.* U.K. **12** 52.55N 1.28W
Derg, Lough Donegal Rep. of Ire. **15** 54.37N 7.55W
Derg, Lough Tipperary Rep. of Ire. **15** 52.57N 8.18W
De Ridder U.S.A. **111** 30.51N 93.17W
Dernieres, Isles *is.* U.S.A. **111** 29.02N 90.47W
Déroute, Passage de la *str.* France / U.K. **13** 49.10N 1.45W
Derry U.S.A. **115** 42.53N 71.19W
Derrynasaggart Mts. Rep. of Ire. **15** 51.58N 9.15W
Derryveagh Mts. Rep. of Ire. **15** 55.00N 8.07W
Derudeb Sudan **72** 17.32N 36.06E
De Ruyter U.S.A. **115** 42.46N 75.53W
Derval France **18** 47.40N 1.40W
Dervéni Greece **35** 38.08N 22.25E
Derventa Yugo. **31** 44.58N 17.55E
Derwent *r.* Cumbria U.K. **12** 54.38N 3.34W
Derwent *r.* Derbys. U.K. **11** 52.52N 1.19W
Derwent *r.* N. Yorks. U.K. **12** 53.44N 0.57W
Desaguadero *r.* Bolivia **124** 18.24S 67.05W
Desappointement, Îles du *is.* Pacific Oc. **85** 14.02S141.24W
Desaulniers Canada **104** 46.34N 80.08W
Descanso Mexico **109** 32.14N116.58W
Descartes France **18** 46.58N 0.42E
Deschaillons Canada **105** 46.32N 72.07W
Deschutes *r.* U.S.A. **108** 45.38N120.54W
Desē Ethiopia **73** 11.05N 39.41E
Deseado Argentina **125** 47.39S 65.20W
Deseado *r.* Argentina **125** 47.45S 65.50W
Desenzano del Garda Italy **30** 45.28N 10.32E
Deseronto Canada **105** 44.12N 77.03W
Deserta Grande *is.* Madeira Is. **127** 32.32N 16.30W
Desert Center U.S.A. **109** 33.44N115.25W
Desfiladero de Despeñaperros Spain **26** 38.24N 3.30W
Deshnoke India **62** 27.48N 73.21E
Des Moines *r.* U.S.A. **110** 40.22N 91.26W
Des Moines Iowa U.S.A. **110** 41.35N 93.37W
Des Moines N.Mex. U.S.A. **108** 36.46N103.50W
Desna *r.* U.S.S.R. **37** 50.32N 30.37E
De Soto U.S.A. **111** 38.08N 90.33W
Dessau Germany **38** 51.50N 12.14E
Desvres France **19** 50.40N 1.50E
Dete Zimbabwe **80** 18.39S 26.49E
Detlor Canada **105** 45.02N 77.45W
Detmold Germany **38** 51.56N 8.52E
De Tour Village U.S.A. **104** 46.00N 83.56W
Detroit U.S.A. **114** 42.20N 83.03W
Detroit Lakes *town* U.S.A. **110** 46.49N 95.51W
Deūlgaon Rāja India **62** 20.01N 76.02E
Deurne Belgium **16** 51.13N 4.26E
Deurne Neth. **16** 51.29N 5.44E
Deutsche Bucht *b.* Germany **38** 54.10N 8.00E
Deutschlandsberg Austria **31** 46.49N 15.13E
Deux Rivières *town* Canada **104** 46.15N 78.19W
Deux-Sevres *d.* France **18** 46.30N 0.20W
Deva Romania **37** 45.54N 22.55E
Deventer Neth. **16** 52.15N 6.10E
Deveron *r.* U.K. **14** 57.40N 2.30W
Devès, Monts du *mts.* France **20** 45.00N 3.45E
Devikot India **62** 26.42N 71.12E
Devil's Bridge U.K. **13** 52.23N 3.50W
Devils Lake *town* U.S.A. **110** 48.07N 98.59W
Devin Bulgaria **34** 41.44N 24.24E
Devizes U.K. **13** 51.21N 2.00W
Devoll *r.* Albania **34** 40.57N 20.15E
Devon *d.* U.K. **13** 50.50N 3.40W
Devon I. Canada **99** 75.00N 86.00W
Devonport Australia **91** 41.09S146.16E
Devrez *r.* Turkey **64** 41.07N 34.25E
Dewās India **62** 22.58N 76.04E
De Witt U.S.A. **111** 34.18N 91.20W
Dewsbury U.K. **12** 53.42N 1.38W
Dexter Mich. U.S.A. **104** 42.20N 83.53W
Dexter Mo. U.S.A. **111** 36.48N 89.57W
Dexter N.Y. U.S.A. **105** 44.01N 76.03W
Deyang China **55** 31.05N104.18E
Dey-Dey L. Australia **91** 29.12S131.02E
Dez *r.* Iran **65** 31.38N 48.54E
Dezadeash L. Canada **100** 60.28N136.58W
Dezfūl Iran **65** 32.24N 48.27E
Dezhneva, Mys *c.* U.S.S.R. **48** 66.05N169.40W
Dezhou China **54** 37.23N116.16E
Dezh Shāhpūr Iran **65** 35.31N 46.10E
Dháfni Greece **35** 37.48N 22.01E
Dhahab Egypt **66** 28.30N 34.31E
Dhahran *see* Az̧ Z̧ahrān Saudi Arabia **65**
Dhaka Bangla. **63** 23.43N 90.25E
Dhamār Yemen **71** 14.33N 44.24E
Dhamtari India **63** 20.41N 81.34E
Dhānbād India **63** 23.48N 86.27E
Dhandhuka India **62** 22.22N 71.59E
Dhangarhi Nepal **63** 28.41N 80.38E
Dhankuta Nepal **63** 26.59N 87.21E
Dhār India **62** 22.36N 75.18E
Dharampur India **62** 20.32N 73.11E
Dharān Bāzār Nepal **63** 26.49N 87.17E
Dharangaon India **62** 21.01N 75.16E
Dhāri India **62** 21.20N 71.01E
Dharmābād India **63** 18.54N 77.51E
Dharmjaygarh India **63** 22.28N 83.13E
Dharmsāla India **62** 32.13N 76.19E
Dhārni India **62** 21.33N 76.53E
Dhaulāgiri *mtn.* Nepal **63** 28.42N 83.31E
Dhebar L. India **62** 24.16N 74.00E
Dhenkānāl India **63** 20.40N 85.36E
Dhenoúsa *i.* Greece **35** 37.08N 25.48E
Dhërmiu *site* Albania **34** 40.08N 19.42E
Dheskáti Greece **34** 39.55N 21.49E
Dhestina Greece **35** 38.25N 22.31E
Dhiavolitsion Greece **35** 37.18N 21.58E
Dhībān Jordan **67** 31.30N 35.47E
Dhidhimótikhon Greece **34** 41.22N 26.29E
Dhiinsoor Somali Rep. **71** 2.28N 43.00E
Dhíkti *mtn.* Greece **35** 35.08N 25.22E
Dhílos *site* Greece **35** 37.26N 25.16E
Dhimitsána Greece **35** 37.37N 22.03E
Dhodhekánisos *is.* Greece **35** 36.35N 27.10E
Dhodhóni *site* Greece **34** 39.34N 20.47E
Dholiana Greece **34** 39.54N 20.32E
Dholka India **62** 22.43N 72.28E
Dholpur India **63** 26.42N 77.54E
Dhomokós Greece **35** 39.10N 22.18E
Dhorāji India **62** 21.44N 70.27E
Dhoxáton Greece **34** 41.05N 24.14E
Dhrāngadhra India **62** 22.59N 71.28E
Dhrol India **62** 22.34N 70.25E
Dhubri India **63** 26.02N 89.58E
Dhule India **62** 20.54N 74.47E
Dhuliān India **63** 24.41N 87.58E
Dhuudo Somali Rep. **71** 9.20N 50.14E
Día *i.* Greece **35** 35.26N 25.13E
Dialakoro Mali **76** 12.18N 7.54W
Diamante Argentina **125** 32.05S 60.35W
Diamantina *r.* Australia **90** 26.45S139.10E
Diamantina Brazil **126** 18.17S 43.37W
Diamantina, Chapada *hills* Brazil **123** 13.00S 42.30W
Diamantino Brazil **126** 14.25S 56.29W
Diamond Harbour India **63** 22.12N 88.12E
Dianalund Denmark **42** 55.32N 11.30E
Diana's Peak *mtn.* St. Helena **127** 15.58S 5.42W
Dianbai China **55** 21.30N111.01E
Diane Bank *is.* Australia **90** 15.50S149.48E
Dianjiang China **55** 30.14N107.27E
Diapaga Burkina **77** 12.04N 1.48E
Dibai India **63** 28.13N 78.15E
Dibaya Zaïre **78** 6.31S 22.57E
Dibi Cameroon **77** 7.09N 13.43E
Dibrugarh India **61** 27.29N 94.56E
Dibs Sudan **73** 14.18N 24.23E
Dickinson U.S.A. **110** 46.53N102.47W
Dicle *r.* Turkey *see* Dijlah *r.* Asia **64**
Didcot U.K. **13** 51.36N 1.14W
Didiéni Mali **76** 14.05N 7.50W
Dīdwāna India **62** 27.24N 74.34E
Didyma *site* Turkey **35** 37.25N 27.16E
Die France **21** 44.45N 5.22E
Dieburg Germany **39** 49.54N 8.50E
Diefenbaker, L. Canada **101** 51.00N106.55W
Diekirch Lux. **16** 49.52N 6.10E
Diélette France **18** 49.33N 1.52W
Diéma Mali **76** 14.32N 9.03W
Diemen Neth. **16** 52.22N 4.58E
Diemuchuoke Jammu & Kashmir **63** 32.42N 79.29E
Dien Bien Phu Vietnam **56** 21.23N103.02E
Diepholz Germany **38** 52.35N 8.21E
Dieppe France **18** 49.56N 1.05E
Dierdorf Germany **38** 50.33N 7.39E
Dieren Neth. **16** 52.03N 6.06E
Dierks U.S.A. **111** 34.07N 94.01W
Diesdorf Germany **38** 52.45N 10.52E
Diest Belgium **16** 50.59N 5.03E
Dieulefit France **21** 44.31N 5.04E
Dieuze France **19** 48.49N 6.43E
Diez Germany **39** 50.22N 8.01E
Dif Kenya **79** 1.04N 40.57E
Diffa Niger **77** 13.19N 12.35E
Diffa *d.* Niger **77** 16.00N 13.00E
Dig India **62** 27.20N 77.25E
Digby Canada **103** 44.30N 65.47W
Dighton U.S.A. **110** 38.29N100.28W
Digne France **21** 44.06N 6.14E
Digoin France **19** 46.29N 3.59E
Digras India **63** 20.07N 77.43E
Digri Pakistan **62** 25.10N 69.07E
Digul *r.* Indonesia **59** 7.10S139.08E
Dijlah *r.* Asia **65** 31.00N 47.27E
Dijle *r.* Belgium **16** 51.02N 4.25E
Dijon France **19** 47.19N 5.01E
Dikhil Djibouti **73** 11.06N 42.22E
Dikili Turkey **29** 39.05N 26.52E
Dikirnis Egypt **66** 31.05N 31.35E
Dikodougou Ivory Coast **76** 9.00N 5.45W
Diksmuide Belgium **16** 51.01N 2.52E
Dikwa Nigeria **77** 12.01N 13.55E
Dili Indonesia **59** 8.35S125.35E
Dillenburg Germany **38** 50.44N 8.17E
Dilley U.S.A. **111** 28.40N 99.10W
Dilling Sudan **73** 12.03N 29.39E
Dillingen Germany **39** 48.34N 10.29E
Dillingham U.S.A. **98** 59.02N158.29W
Dillon U.S.A. **108** 45.13N112.38W
Dillsburg U.S.A. **114** 40.07N 77.02W
Dilolo Zaïre **78** 10.39S 22.20E
Dimashq Syria **66** 33.30N 36.19E
Dimbelenge Zaïre **78** 5.32S 23.04E
Dimbokro Ivory Coast **76** 6.43N 4.46W
Dimboola Australia **92** 36.27S142.02E
Dîmbovița *r.* Romania **37** 44.13N 26.22E
Dimitrovgrad Bulgaria **34** 42.05N 25.35E
Dimitrovo *see* Pernik Bulgaria **34**
Dimona Israel **67** 31.04N 35.01E
Dinagat *i.* Phil. **59** 10.15N125.30E
Dinājpur Bangla. **63** 25.38N 88.38E
Dinan France **18** 48.27N 2.02W
Dinant Belgium **16** 50.16N 4.55E
Dinar Turkey **64** 38.05N 30.09E
Dīnār, Kūh-e *mtn.* Iran **65** 30.45N 51.39E
Dinara Planina *mts.* Yugo. **31** 43.40N 17.00E
Dinard France **18** 48.38N 2.04W
Dinaric Alps *mts. see* Dinara Planina *mts.* Yugo. **31**
Dindar *r.* Sudan **72** 14.06N 33.40E
Dindar Nat. Park Sudan **73** 12.00N 35.00E
Dindigul India **60** 10.23N 78.00E
Dindori India **63** 22.57N 81.05E
Dinga Pakistan **62** 25.26N 67.10E
Dingbian China **54** 37.36N107.38E
Dinggyê China **63** 28.18N 88.06E
Dingle Rep. of Ire. **15** 52.09N 10.17W
Dingle B. Rep. of Ire. **15** 52.05N 10.12W
Dingmans Ferry *town* U.S.A. **115** 41.14N 74.53W
Dingolfing Germany **39** 48.38N 12.31E
Dinguiraye Guinea **76** 11.19N 10.49W
Dingwall U.K. **14** 57.35N 4.26W
Dingxi China **54** 35.33N104.32E
Ding Xian China **54** 38.30N115.00E
Dingxing China **54** 39.17N115.46E
Dinkelsbühl Germany **39** 49.04N 10.19E
Dinokwe Botswana **80** 23.24S 26.40E
Dinuba U.S.A. **109** 36.32N119.23W
Diö Sweden **43** 56.38N 14.33E
Diodār India **62** 24.06N 71.47E
Dioïla Mali **76** 12.30N 6.49W
Diourbel Senegal **76** 14.30N 16.10W
Diplo Pakistan **62** 24.28N 69.35E
Dipolog Phil. **59** 8.34N123.28E
Dirdal Norway **42** 58.47N 6.14E
Diré Mali **76** 16.16N 3.24W
Direction, C. Australia **90** 12.51S143.32E
Dirē Dawa Ethiopia **73** 9.35N 41.50E
Dirico Angola **78** 17.58S 20.40E
Dirj Libya **75** 30.09N 10.26E
Dirk Hartog I. Australia **88** 25.50S113.00E
Dirranbandi Australia **93** 28.35S148.10E
Disappointment, L. Australia **88** 23.30S122.55E
Disaster B. Australia **93** 37.20S149.58E
Discovery Canada **98** 63.10N113.58W
Discovery B. Australia **92** 38.12S141.07E
Disentis Switz. **39** 46.43N 8.51E
Disko *i.* Greenland **99** 69.45N 53.00W
Diss U.K. **13** 52.23N 1.06E
District of Columbia *d.* U.S.A. **114** 38.55N 77.00W
Distrito Federal *d.* Brazil **123** 15.45S 47.50W
Distrito Federal *d.* Mexico **116** 19.20N 99.10W
Disūq Egypt **66** 31.09N 30.39E
Dithmarschen *f.* Germany **38** 54.10N 9.15E
Diu India **62** 20.42N 70.59E
Diu *d.* India **62** 20.45N 70.59E
Diver Canada **104** 46.42N 79.30W
Dives *r.* France **18** 49.19N 0.05W
Divinópolis Brazil **126** 20.08S 44.55W
Divnoye U.S.S.R. **45** 45.55N 43.21E
Divo Ivory Coast **76** 5.48N 5.15W
Divrigi Turkey **64** 39.23N 38.06E
Dīwāl Qol Afghan. **62** 34.19N 67.54E
Dixcove Ghana **76** 4.49N 1.57W
Dixie U.S.A. **108** 45.34N115.28W
Dix Milles, Lac *l.* Canada **105** 46.46N 77.45W
Dixon Ill. U.S.A. **110** 41.50N 89.29W
Dixon N.Mex. U.S.A. **109** 36.12N105.33W
Dixon Entrance *str.* U.S.A. / Canada **100** 54.25N132.30W
Diyālā *r.* Iraq **65** 33.13N 44.33E
Diyarbakir Turkey **64** 37.55N 40.14E
Dja *r.* Cameroon **78** 1.38N 16.03E
Djabéta Gabon **78** 0.45N 14.00E
Djado Niger **77** 21.00N 12.20E
Djado, Plateau du *f.* Niger **77** 22.00N 12.30E
Djambala Congo **78** 2.33S 14.38E
Djanet Algeria **75** 24.34N 9.29E
Djebel Abiod Tunisia **32** 36.58N 9.05E
Djelfa Algeria **75** 34.40N 3.15E
Djema C.A.R. **73** 6.03N 25.19E
Djénne Mali **76** 13.55N 4.31W
Djerba, Île de *i.* Tunisia **75** 33.48N 10.54E
Djerid, Chott *f.* Tunisia **75** 33.42N 8.26E
Djibo Burkina **76** 14.09N 1.38W
Djibouti Africa **73** 12.00N 42.50E
Djibouti *town* Djibouti **73** 11.35N 43.11E
Djilbabo Plain *f.* Ethiopia **73** 4.00N 39.10E
Djolu Zaïre **78** 0.35N 22.28E
Djouah *r.* Gabon **78** 1.16N 13.12E
Djougou Benin **77** 9.40N 1.47E
Djugu Zaïre **79** 1.55N 30.31E
Djúpivogur Iceland **40** 64.41N 14.16W
Djurö *i.* Sweden **43** 58.52N 13.28E
Dmitriya Lapteva, Proliv *str.* U.S.S.R. **51** 73.00N142.00E
Dnepr *r.* U.S.S.R. **37** 50.00N 31.00E
Dneprodzerzhinsk U.S.S.R. **45** 48.30N 34.37E
Dnepropetrovsk U.S.S.R. **45** 48.29N 35.00E

Dneprovskaya Nizmennost to **Duolun**

Dneprovskaya Nizmennost *f.* U.S.S.R. **37** 52.30N 29.45E
Dneprovsko-Bugskiy Kanal U.S.S.R. **37** 52.03N 25.35E
Dnestr *r.* U.S.S.R. **37** 46.21N 30.20E
Dno U.S.S.R. **44** 57.50N 30.00E
Doba Chad **77** 8.40N 16.50E
Dobane C.A.R. **73** 6.24N 24.42E
Dobbiaco Italy **30** 46.44N 12.14E
Dobele U.S.S.R. **41** 56.37N 23.16E
Döbeln Germany **38** 51.07N 13.07E
Dobo Indonesia **59** 5.46S134.13E
Doboj Yugo. **31** 44.44N 18.06E
Dobra *r.* Yugo. **31** 45.33N 15.31E
Dobrodzień Poland **37** 50.44N 18.27E
Dobruja *f.* Romania **37** 44.30N 28.15E
Dobrush U.S.S.R. **37** 52.24N 31.19E
Dobryanka U.S.S.R. **44** 58.30N 56.26E
Dobzha China **63** 28.28N 88.13E
Doce *r.* Brazil **126** 19.32S 39.57W
Docking U.K. **12** 52.55N 0.39E
Doda Jammu & Kashmir **62** 33.08N 75.34E
Doda, Lac *l.* Canada **102** 49.24N 75.14W
Dodecanese *is. see* Dhodhekánisos *is.* Greece **35**
Dodge City U.S.A. **111** 37.45N100.01W
Dodman Pt. U.K. **13** 50.13N 4.48W
Dodoma Tanzania **79** 6.10S 35.40E
Dodoma *d.* Tanzania **79** 6.00S 36.00E
Dodson U.S.A. **108** 48.24N108.15W
Doetinchem Neth. **16** 51.57N 6.17E
Dogai Coring *l.* China **61** 34.30N 89.00E
Doğanbey Turkey **35** 37.37N 27.11E
Dog Creek *town* Canada **100** 51.35N122.14W
Dogger Bank *f.* North Sea **11** 54.45N 2.00E
Doğubayazit Turkey **65** 39.32N 44.08E
Do'gyaling China **63** 31.58N 88.24E
Doha *see* Ad Dawḩah Qatar **65**
Dohad India **62** 22.50N 74.16E
Doheny Canada **105** 47.04N 72.36W
Dohhi India **63** 24.32N 84.54E
Doilungdêqên China **63** 30.06N 90.32E
Doiran, L. Greece / Yugo. **34** 41.13N 22.44E
Dokkum Neth. **16** 53.20N 6.00E
Dokri Pakistan **62** 27.23N 68.06E
Dolbeau Canada **103** 48.53N 72.14W
Dol-de-Bretagne France **18** 48.33N 1.45W
Dole France **19** 47.06N 5.30E
Dolgellau U.K. **13** 52.44N 3.53W
Dolina U.S.S.R. **37** 49.00N 23.59E
Dolinskaya U.S.S.R. **45** 48.06N 32.46E
Dollard *b.* Germany **38** 53.17N 7.10E
Dolni Dubnik Bulgaria **34** 43.24N 24.26E
Dolni Lom Bulgaria **34** 43.31N 22.47E
Dolny Kubín Czech. **37** 49.12N 19.17E
Dolomiti *mts.* Italy **30** 46.15N 11.55E
Dolores Argentina **125** 36.19S 57.40W
Dolores Mexico **109** 28.53N108.27W
Dolores Spain **25** 38.08N 0.46W
Dolores Uruguay **125** 33.33S 58.13W
Dolores U.S.A. **108** 37.28N108.30W
Dolphin and Union Str. Canada **98** 69.20N118.00W
Doma Nigeria **77** 8.23N 8.21E
Domadare Somali Rep. **73** 1.48N 41.13E
Domažlice Czech. **38** 49.27N 12.56E
Dombås Norway **41** 62.05N 9.08E
Dombe Grande Angola **78** 13.00S 13.06E
Dombes *f.* France **21** 46.00N 5.03E
Dombey, C. Australia **92** 37.12S139.43E
Dombóvár Hungary **31** 46.23N 18.08E
Domburg Neth. **16** 51.35N 3.31E
Domfront France **18** 48.36N 0.39W
Dominica Windward Is. **117** 15.30N 61.30W
Dominican Republic C. America **117** 18.00N 70.00W
Dominion L. Canada **103** 52.40N 61.42W
Dommel *r.* Neth. **16** 51.44N 5.17E
Domo Ethiopia **71** 7.54N 46.52E
Domodossola Italy **30** 46.07N 8.17E
Dompierre-sur-Besbre France **20** 46.31N 3.41E
Domuyo *mtn.* Argentina **125** 36.37S 70.28W
Domvraina Greece **35** 38.15N 22.59E
Domžale Yugo. **31** 46.08N 14.36E
Don Mexico **109** 26.26N109.02W
Don *r.* England U.K. **12** 53.41N 0.50W
Don *r.* Scotland U.K. **14** 57.10N 2.05W
Don *r.* U.S.S.R. **45** 47.06N 39.16E
Donaghadee U.K. **15** 54.39N 5.33W
Donald Australia **92** 36.25S143.04E
Donaldsonville U.S.A. **111** 30.06N 90.59W
Donau *r.* Germany *see* Danube *r.* Europe **36**
Donaueschingen Germany **39** 47.57N 8.29E
Donauwörth Germany **39** 48.43N 10.46E
Don Benito Spain **27** 38.53N 5.51W
Doncaster U.K. **12** 53.31N 1.09W
Dondaicha India **62** 21.20N 74.34E
Dondo Angola **78** 9.40S 14.25E
Dondo Mozambique **81** 19.39S 34.39E
Donegal Rep. of Ire. **15** 54.39N 8.06W
Donegal *d.* Rep. of Ire. **15** 54.52N 8.00W
Donegal U.S.A. **114** 40.07N 79.23W
Donegal B. Rep. of Ire. **15** 54.32N 8.18W
Donegal Pt. Rep. of Ire. **15** 52.43N 9.38W
Donetsk U.S.S.R. **45** 48.00N 37.50E
Donga Nigeria **77** 7.45N 10.05E
Donga *r.* Nigeria **77** 8.20N 10.00E
Dongara Australia **89** 29.15S114.56E
Dongargarh India **63** 21.12N 80.44E
Dongbei Pingyuan *f.* China **54** 42.30N123.00E
Dongchuan China **52** 26.10N103.02E
Dongco China **63** 32.07N 84.35E
Dongfang China **55** 19.05N108.39E
Donggala Indonesia **58** 0.48S119.45E
Donggou China **54** 39.52N124.08E
Dongguang China **54** 37.53N116.32E
Donghai China **54** 34.35N118.49E
Donghai *i.* China **55** 21.02N110.25E
Dong Hoi Vietnam **56** 17.32N106.35E
Dong Jiang *r.* China **55** 23.00N113.33E
Dongkalang Indonesia **59** 0.12N120.07E
Dongling China **54** 41.44N123.32E
Dongou Congo **78** 2.05N 18.00E
Dongping Hu *l.* China **54** 35.55N116.15E
Dongqiao China **63** 31.57N 90.30E
Dongsheng China **54** 39.49N109.59E
Dongtai China **54** 32.42N120.26E
Dongting Hu *l.* China **55** 29.10N113.00E
Dongtou *i.* China **55** 27.50N121.08E
Dong Ujimqin Qi China **54** 45.33N116.50E
Dongxi China **55** 28.42N106.40E
Dongxing China **55** 21.33N107.58E
Donington U.K. **12** 52.55N 0.12W
Donja Stubica Yugo. **31** 45.59N 15.58E
Donji Vakuf Yugo. **31** 44.09N 17.25E
Dönna *i.* Norway **40** 66.05N 12.30E
Donnacona Canada **105** 46.40N 71.47W
Donnybrook Australia **89** 33.34S115.47E
Donnybrook R.S.A. **80** 29.55S 29.51E
Donora U.S.A. **114** 40.11N 79.52W
Donostia *see* San Sebastián Spain **26**
Doodlakine Australia **89** 31.41S117.23E
Doolow Somali Rep. **71** 4.13N 42.08E
Doon, Loch U.K. **14** 55.15N 4.23W
Dor Israel **67** 32.37N 34.55E
Dora, L. Australia **88** 22.05S122.55E
Dora Baltea *r.* Italy **30** 45.11N 8.05E
Doran L. Canada **101** 61.13N108.06W
Dora Riparia *r.* Italy **30** 45.05N 7.44E
Dorchester U.K. **13** 50.52N 2.28W
Dorchester, C. Canada **99** 65.29N 77.30W
Dordogne *d.* France **20** 45.10N 0.45E
Dordogne *r.* France **20** 45.02N 0.35W
Dordrecht Neth. **16** 51.48N 4.40E
Dordrecht R.S.A. **80** 31.22S 27.02E
Dore, Mont *mtn.* France **20** 45.35N 2.48E
Doré L. Canada **101** 54.46N107.17W
Dorfen Germany **39** 48.17N 12.08E
Dorgali Italy **32** 40.17N 9.35E
Dori Burkina **76** 14.03N 0.02W
Dorion Canada **105** 45.23N 74.03W
Dorking U.K. **13** 51.14N 0.20W
Dormagen Germany **38** 51.05N 6.50E
Dormans France **19** 49.04N 3.38E
Dornbirn Austria **39** 47.25N 9.44E
Dornie U.K. **14** 57.16N 5.31W
Dornoch U.K. **14** 57.52N 4.02W
Dornoch Firth *est.* U.K. **14** 57.50N 4.04W
Dornogovi *d.* Mongolia **54** 44.00N110.00E
Dornum Germany **38** 53.40N 7.28E
Doro Mali **76** 16.09N 0.51W
Dorohoi Romania **37** 47.57N 26.24E
Dörpen Germany **38** 52.57N 7.20E
Dorre I. Australia **88** 25.08S113.06E
Dorrigo Australia **93** 30.20S152.41E
Dorris U.S.A. **108** 41.58N121.55W
Dorset Canada **104** 45.14N 78.54W
Dorset *d.* U.K. **13** 50.48N 2.25W
Dorset U.S.A. **115** 43.15N 73.06W
Dorset, C. Canada **99** 64.10N 76.40W
Dorset Peak *mtn.* U.S.A. **115** 43.19N 73.02W
Dorsten Germany **38** 51.39N 6.58E
Dortmund Germany **38** 51.31N 7.28E
Dortmund-Ems Kanal Germany **38** 52.00N 7.36E
Dorval Canada **105** 45.27N 73.44W
Dos Bahías, C. Argentina **125** 44.55S 65.32W
Dos Hermanas Spain **27** 37.17N 5.55W
Dosquet Canada **105** 46.28N 71.33W
Dosse *r.* Germany **38** 53.13N 12.20E
Dosso Niger **77** 13.03N 3.10E
Dosso *d.* Niger **77** 13.00N 3.15E
Dossor U.S.S.R. **45** 47.31N 53.01E
Dothan U.S.A. **113** 31.12N 85.25W
Douai France **19** 50.22N 3.04E
Douako Guinea **76** 9.45N 10.08W
Douala Cameroon **77** 4.05N 9.43E
Douarnenez France **18** 48.06N 4.20W
Double Mer *g.* Canada **103** 54.05N 59.00W
Doubs *d.* France **19** 47.10N 6.25E
Doubs *r.* France **19** 46.54N 5.02E
Doubtless B. New Zealand **86** 35.10S173.30E
Doudeville France **18** 49.43N 0.48E
Douentza Mali **76** 14.58N 2.48W
Douglas R.S.A. **80** 29.03S 23.45E
Douglas U.K. **12** 54.09N 4.29W
Douglas Ariz. U.S.A. **109** 31.21N109.33W
Douglas Ga. U.S.A. **113** 31.30N 82.54W
Douglas Mich. U.S.A. **112** 42.38N 86.13W
Douglas Wyo. U.S.A. **108** 42.45N105.24W
Douglas Creek *r.* Australia **92** 28.35S136.50E
Douglas L. U.S.A. **113** 35.58N 83.32W
Douglas L. U.S.A. **104** 45.34N 84.39W
Douglas Pt. Canada **104** 44.20N 81.35W
Doulaincourt France **19** 48.19N 5.12E
Doulevant-le-Château France **19** 48.23N 4.55E
Doullens France **19** 50.09N 2.21E
Doumé Cameroon **77** 4.13N 13.30E
Douna Mali **76** 12.40N 6.00W
Dounreay U.K. **14** 58.35N 3.42W
Dourados Brazil **124** 22.09S 54.52W
Dourdan France **19** 48.32N 2.01E
Douro *r.* Portugal **26** 41.08N 8.40W
Douvres France **18** 49.17N 0.23W
Douze *r.* France **20** 43.54N 0.30W
Dove *r.* Derbys. U.K. **12** 52.50N 1.35W
Dover U.K. **13** 51.07N 1.19E
Dover Del. U.S.A. **115** 39.10N 75.32W
Dover N.H. U.S.A. **115** 43.12N 70.56W
Dover N.J. U.S.A. **115** 40.53N 74.34W
Dover Ohio U.S.A. **114** 40.32N 81.29W
Dover Tenn. U.S.A. **113** 36.30N 87.50W
Dover, Pt. Australia **89** 32.32S125.30E
Dover, Str. of U.K. **13** 51.00N 1.30E
Dovey *r.* U.K. **13** 52.33N 3.56W
Dovrefjell *mts.* Norway **41** 62.06N 9.25E
Dovsk U.S.S.R. **37** 53.07N 30.29E
Dowa Malaŵi **79** 13.40S 33.55E
Dowagiac U.S.A. **112** 41.58N 86.06W
Dowerin Australia **89** 31.15S117.00E
Dowlatābād Iran **65** 28.19N 56.40E
Dowlat Yār Afghan. **62** 34.33N 65.47E
Down *d.* U.K. **15** 54.20N 6.00W
Downey U.S.A. **108** 42.26N112.07W
Downham Market U.K. **13** 52.36N 0.22E
Downpatrick U.K. **15** 54.21N 5.43W
Downpatrick Head Rep. of Ire. **15** 54.20N 9.22W
Downton, Mt. Canada **100** 52.42N124.51W
Dowra Rep. of Ire. **15** 54.11N 8.02W
Doylestown U.S.A. **115** 40.19N 75.08W
Dozois, Résr. Canada **105** 47.30N 77.05W
Drâa, Hamada du *f.* Algeria **74** 29.00N 6.00W
Drâa, Oued *wadi* Morocco **74** 28.40N 11.06W
Drac *r.* France **21** 45.13N 5.41E
Drachten Neth. **16** 53.05N 6.06E
Dragaš Yugo. **34** 42.05N 20.35E
Drăgăşani Romania **37** 44.40N 24.16E
Dragoman, Pasul *pass* Bulgaria / Yugo. **29** 42.56N 22.52E
Dragonera, Isla *i.* Spain **25** 39.35N 2.19E
Dragon's Mouth *str.* Trinidad **122** 11.00N 61.35W
Dragovishtitsa Bulgaria **34** 42.22N 22.39E
Draguignan France **21** 43.32N 6.28E
Drake Australia **93** 28.55S152.24E
Drake U.S.A. **110** 47.55N100.23W
Drakensberg *mts.* R.S.A. / Lesotho **80** 30.00S 29.05E
Drake Passage *str.* Atlantic Oc. **127** 59.00S 65.00W
Dráma Greece **34** 41.09N 24.08E
Drammen Norway **42** 59.44N 10.15E
Drās Jammu & Kashmir **62** 34.27N 75.46E
Drau *r.* Austria *see* Drava *r.* Yugo. **30**
Drava *r.* Yugo. **31** 45.33N 18.55E
Dravinja *r.* Yugo. **31** 46.22N 15.57E
Drayton Valley *town* Canada **100** 53.25N114.58W
Drenovets Bulgaria **34** 43.42N 22.59E
Drenthe *d.* Neth. **16** 52.52N 6.30E
Dresden Germany **38** 51.03N 13.44E
Dresden U.S.A. **114** 40.07N 82.01W
Dreux France **18** 48.44N 1.22E
Driftwood Canada **102** 49.08N 81.23W
Driftwood U.S.A. **114** 41.20N 78.08W
Drin *r.* Albania **34** 41.37N 20.28E
Drina *r.* Yugo. **31** 44.53N 19.21E
Drniš Yugo. **31** 43.51N 16.09E
Dröbak Norway **42** 59.39N 10.39E
Drocourt Canada **104** 45.47N 80.22W
Drogheda Rep. of Ire. **15** 53.42N 6.23W
Drogobych U.S.S.R. **37** 49.10N 23.30E
Droitwich U.K. **13** 52.16N 2.10W
Drokiya U.S.S.R. **37** 48.07N 27.49E
Drôme *d.* France **21** 44.35N 5.10E
Drôme *r.* France **21** 44.46N 4.46E
Dromedary, C. Australia **93** 36.18S150.15E
Dronero Italy **30** 44.28N 7.22E
Dronfield U.K. **12** 53.18N 1.29W
Dronne *r.* France **20** 45.02N 0.09W
Dronninglund Denmark **42** 57.09N 10.18E
Dronning Maud Land *f.* Antarctica **128** 74.00S 10.00E
Drumbo Canada **104** 43.14N 80.33W
Drumheller Canada **100** 51.25N112.40W
Drum Hills Rep. of Ire. **15** 52.03N 7.42W
Drummond U.S.A. **104** 46.02N 83.42W
Drummond I. U.S.A. **104** 46.00N 83.40W
Drummond Range *mts.* Australia **90** 23.30S147.15E
Drummondville Canada **105** 45.53N 72.29W
Drummore U.K. **14** 54.41N 4.54W
Druskininkai U.S.S.R. **37** 53.48N 23.58E
Drut *r.* U.S.S.R. **37** 53.03N 30.42E
Drvar Yugo. **31** 44.22N 16.24E
Dryanovo Bulgaria **34** 42.58N 25.27E
Dry B. U.S.A. **100** 59.08N138.25W
Dryden Canada **102** 49.47N 92.50W
Dryden U.S.A. **115** 42.29N 76.18W
Drymen U.K. **14** 56.04N 4.27W
Drysdale *r.* Australia **88** 13.59S126.51E
Dschang Cameroon **77** 5.28N 10.02E
Dua *r.* Zaïre **78** 3.12N 20.55E
Du'an China **55** 24.01N108.06E
Duaringa Australia **90** 23.42S149.40E
Ḑubā Saudi Arabia **64** 27.21N 35.40E
Dubai *see* Dubayy U.A.E. **65**
Dubawnt *r.* Canada **99** 62.50N102.00W
Dubawnt L. Canada **101** 63.04N101.42W
Dubayy U.A.E. **65** 25.13N 55.17E
Dubbo Australia **93** 32.16S148.41E
Dubica Yugo. **31** 45.11N 16.48E
Dublin Rep. of Ire. **15** 53.21N 6.18W
Dublin *d.* Rep. of Ire. **15** 53.20N 6.18W
Dublin U.S.A. **113** 32.31N 82.54W
Dublin B. Rep. of Ire. **15** 53.20N 6.09W
Dubno U.S.S.R. **37** 50.28N 25.40E
Dubois Idaho U.S.A. **108** 44.10N112.14W
Du Bois Penn. U.S.A. **114** 41.07N 78.46W
Dubovka U.S.S.R. **45** 49.04N 44.48E
Dubréka Guinea **76** 9.50N 13.32W
Dubrovitsa U.S.S.R. **37** 51.38N 26.40E
Dubrovnik Yugo. **31** 42.38N 18.07E
Dubuque U.S.A. **110** 42.30N 90.41W
Duchesne U.S.A. **108** 40.10N110.24W
Duchess Australia **90** 21.22S139.52E
Ducie I. Pacific Oc. **85** 24.40S124.48W
Du Couëdic, C. Australia **92** 36.00S136.10E
Duderstadt Germany **38** 51.31N 10.16E
Dudhnai India **63** 25.59N 90.44E
Dudinka U.S.S.R. **51** 69.27N 86.13E
Dudley U.K. **13** 52.30N 2.05W
Dudna *r.* India **62** 19.07N 76.54E
Dudweiler Germany **39** 49.17N 7.02E
Duékoué Ivory Coast **76** 6.50N 7.22W
Duerna *r.* Spain **26** 42.19N 5.54W
Duero *r.* Spain *see* Douro *r.* Portugal **26**
Duff Creek *town* Australia **92** 28.28S135.51E
Dufftown U.K. **14** 57.27N 3.09W
Duga Poljana Yugo. **34** 43.15N 20.14E
Duga Resa Yugo. **31** 45.27N 15.30E
Dugi *i.* Yugo. **31** 44.00N 15.04E
Du Gué *r.* Canada **103** 57.20N 70.48W
Duifken Pt. Australia **90** 12.33S141.38E
Duisburg Germany **38** 51.25N 6.46E
Duitama Colombia **122** 5.50N 73.01W
Duiveland *i.* Neth. **16** 51.39N 4.00E
Dujuuma Somali Rep. **79** 1.14N 42.37E
Dukambīya Ethiopia **72** 14.42N 37.30E
Dukat Albania **34** 40.16N 19.32E
Duk Fadiat Sudan **73** 7.45N 31.25E
Duk Faiwil Sudan **73** 7.30N 31.29E
Dukhān Qatar **65** 25.24N 50.47E
Duki Pakistan **62** 30.09N 68.34E
Dukou China **52** 26.33N101.44E
Dukye Dzong Bhutan **63** 27.20N 89.30E
Dulce *r.* Argentina **124** 30.40S 62.00W
Duleek Rep. of Ire. **15** 53.39N 6.24W
Dülmen Germany **38** 51.51N 7.16E
Dulovo Bulgaria **37** 43.49N 27.09E
Duluth U.S.A. **110** 46.47N 92.06W
Dūmā Syria **66** 33.33N 36.24E
Dumaguete Phil. **59** 9.20N123.18E
Dumai Indonesia **58** 1.41N101.27E
Dumaran *i.* Phil. **58** 10.33N119.50E
Dumaresq *r.* Australia **93** 28.40S150.28E
Dumaring Indonesia **58** 1.36N118.12E
Dumas Ark. U.S.A. **111** 33.53N 91.29W
Dumas Tex. U.S.A. **111** 35.52N101.58W
Dumbarton U.K. **14** 55.57N 4.35W
Dumbleyung Australia **89** 33.18S117.42E
Dumbrăveni Romania **37** 46.14N 24.35E
Dum-Dum India **63** 22.35N 88.24E
Dumfries U.K. **14** 55.04N 3.37W
Dumfries and Galloway *d.* U.K. **14** 55.05N 3.40W
Dumka India **63** 24.16N 87.15E
Dumoine *r.* Canada **105** 46.13N 77.50W
Dumoine, Lac *l.* Canada **105** 46.53N 77.54W
Dumont, Lac *l.* Canada **105** 46.04N 76.28W
Dumraon India **63** 25.33N 84.09E
Dumyāţ Egypt **66** 31.26N 31.48E
Duna *r.* Hungary *see* Danube *r.* Europe **31**
Dunaföldvár Hungary **31** 46.48N 18.55E
Dunajec *r.* Poland **37** 50.15N 20.44E
Dunajská Streda Czech. **37** 48.01N 17.35E
Dunany Pt. Rep. of Ire. **15** 53.51N 6.15W
Dunărea *r.* Romania *see* Danube *r.* Europe **37**
Dunării, Delta *f.* Romania **37** 45.05N 29.45E
Dunaújváros Hungary **31** 46.58N 18.57E
Dunav *r.* Bulgaria *see* Danube *r.* Europe **37**
Dunav *r.* Yugo. *see* Danube *r.* Europe **37**
Duna-völgyi-föcsatorno *r.* Hungary **31** 46.12N 18.56E
Dunbar U.K. **14** 56.00N 2.31W
Dunbar U.S.A. **114** 38.22N 81.45W
Dunblane U.K. **14** 56.12N 3.59W
Dunboyne Rep. of Ire. **15** 53.26N 6.30W
Duncan Canada **100** 48.45N123.40W
Duncan *r.* Canada **100** 50.11N116.57W
Duncan U.S.A. **111** 34.30N 97.57W
Duncan, C. Canada **102** 52.40N 80.48W
Duncan L. N.W.T. Canada **100** 62.51N113.58W
Duncan L. Que. Canada **102** 53.35N 77.55W
Duncannon U.S.A. **114** 40.23N 77.02W
Duncansby Head U.K. **14** 58.39N 3.01W
Dundalk Canada **104** 44.10N 80.24W
Dundalk Rep. of Ire. **15** 54.01N 6.25W
Dundalk U.S.A. **115** 39.15N 76.31W
Dundalk B. Rep. of Ire. **15** 53.55N 6.17W
Dundas Canada **104** 43.16N 79.58W
Dundas, L. Australia **89** 32.35S121.50E
Dundas I. Canada **100** 54.33N130.50W
Dundas Str. Australia **90** 11.20S131.35E
Dundee R.S.A. **80** 28.09S 30.14E
Dundee U.K. **14** 56.28N 3.00W
Dundee Mich. U.S.A. **104** 41.57N 83.40W
Dundee N.Y. U.S.A. **114** 42.31N 76.59W
Dundgovĭ *d.* Mongolia **54** 45.00N106.00E
Dundrum U.K. **15** 54.16N 5.51W
Dundrum B. U.K. **15** 54.12N 5.46W
Dunedin New Zealand **86** 45.52S170.30E
Dunedin U.S.A. **113** 28.02N 82.47W
Dunedoo Australia **93** 32.00S149.25E
Dunfermline U.K. **14** 56.04N 3.29W
Dungannon U.K. **15** 54.31N 6.47W
Dūngarpur India **62** 23.50N 73.43E
Dungarvan Rep. of Ire. **15** 52.06N 7.39W
Dungeness *c.* U.K. **13** 50.55N 0.58E
Dungiven U.K. **15** 54.56N 6.56W
Dungog Australia **93** 32.24S151.46E
Dungu Zaïre **79** 3.40N 28.40E
Dunhuang China **52** 40.00N 94.40E
Dunkeld Qld. Australia **91** 26.55S148.00E
Dunkeld Vic. Australia **92** 37.40S142.23E
Dunkeld U.K. **14** 56.34N 3.36W
Dunkerque France **16** 51.02N 2.23E
Dunk I. Australia **90** 17.56S146.10E
Dunkirk *see* Dunkerque France **16**
Dunkirk U.S.A. **114** 42.29N 79.20W
Dunkwa Central Ghana **76** 5.59N 1.45W
Dun Laoghaire Rep. of Ire. **15** 53.17N 6.09W
Dunlap U.S.A. **110** 41.51N 95.36W
Dunleer Rep. of Ire. **15** 53.49N 6.24W
Dun-le-Palestel France **20** 46.17N 1.48E
Dunmahon Rep. of Ire. **15** 52.09N 7.23W
Dunmarra Australia **90** 16.37S133.22E
Dunmore U.S.A. **115** 41.25N 75.38W
Dunnet Head U.K. **14** 58.40N 3.23W
Dunning U.S.A. **110** 41.50N100.06W
Dunnville Canada **104** 42.54N 79.36W
Dunolly Australia **92** 36.50S143.45E
Dunoon U.K. **14** 55.57N 4.57W
Dunqulah Sudan **72** 19.10N 30.29E
Dunqunāb Sudan **72** 21.06N 37.05E
Duns U.K. **14** 55.47N 2.20W
Dunsborough Australia **89** 33.37S115.06E
Dunshaughlin Rep. of Ire. **15** 53.30N 6.34W
Dunstable U.K. **13** 51.53N 0.32W
Dunstan Mts. New Zealand **86** 44.45S169.45E
Dunster Canada **100** 53.08N119.50W
Dun-sur-Auron France **19** 46.53N 2.34E
Dun-sur-Meuse France **19** 49.23N 5.11E
Dunyāpur Pakistan **62** 29.48N 71.44E
Duolun China **54** 42.09N116.21E

Duong Dong to **El Maneadero**

Duong Dong Vietnam **56** 10.12N103.57E
Dupont U.S.A. **112** 38.53N 85.30W
Duque de Caxias Brazil **126** 22.47S 43.18W
Duquesne U.S.A. **114** 40.21N 79.51W
Du Quoin U.S.A. **111** 38.01N 89.14W
Dūrā Jordan **67** 31.30N 35.02E
Duran U.S.A. **109** 34.28N105.24W
Durance *r.* France **21** 43.55N 4.44E
Durand U.S.A. **104** 42.55N 83.59W
Durango Mexico **116** 24.01N104.00W
Durango *d.* Mexico **111** 24.30N104.00W
Durango Spain **26** 43.10N 2.37W
Durango U.S.A. **108** 37.16N107.53W
Durant U.S.A. **111** 34.00N 96.23W
Duras France **20** 44.41N 0.11E
Duraton *r.* Spain **26** 41.37N 4.07W
Durazno Uruguay **125** 33.22S 56.31W
Durban R.S.A. **80** 29.50S 30.59E
Durbe U.S.S.R. **41** 56.35N 21.21E
Durbin U.S.A. **114** 38.33N 79.50W
Durdevac Yugo. **31** 46.03N 17.04E
Dureji Pakistan **62** 25.53N 67.18E
Düren Germany **38** 50.48N 6.28E
Durg India **63** 21.11N 81.17E
Durgāpur India **63** 23.29N 87.20E
Durham Canada **104** 44.10N 80.49W
Durham U.K. **12** 54.47N 1.34W
Durham *d.* U.K. **12** 54.42N 1.45W
Durham N.C. U.S.A. **113** 36.00N 78.54W
Durham N.H. U.S.A. **115** 43.08N 70.56W
Durham Sud Canada **105** 45.39N 72.19W
Durlston Head *c.* U.K. **13** 50.35N 1.58W
Durmitor *mtn.* Yugo. **31** 43.08N 19.01E
Durness U.K. **14** 58.33N 4.45W
Durrës Albania **34** 41.19N 19.26E
Durrow Rep. of Ire. **15** 52.51N 7.25W
Dursey Head Rep. of Ire. **15** 51.35N 10.15W
Durūz, Jabal ad *mtn.* Syria **66** 32.42N 36.42E
D'Urville I. New Zealand **86** 40.45S173.50E
Dushak U.S.S.R. **50** 37.13N 60.01E
Dushan China **55** 25.50N107.30E
Dushanbe U.S.S.R. **52** 38.38N 68.51E
Dushore U.S.A. **115** 41.31N 76.24W
Duskotna Bulgaria **29** 42.52N 27.10E
Düsseldorf Germany **38** 51.12N 6.47E
Dutch Creek *town* Canada **100** 50.18N115.58W
Dutlhe Botswana **80** 23.55S 23.47E
Dutton Canada **104** 42.39N 81.30W
Dutton, L. Australia **92** 31.49S137.08E
Duvno Yugo. **31** 43.43N 17.14E
Duxbury U.S.A. **115** 42.02N 70.40W
Duxun China **55** 23.57N117.37E
Duyun China **55** 26.12N107.29E
Dve Mogili Bulgaria **34** 43.36N 25.52E
Dvina *r.* U.S.S.R. **9** 57.03N 24.00E
Dvinskaya Guba *b.* U.S.S.R. **44** 64.40N 39.30E
Dwarda Australia **89** 32.45S116.23E
Dwārka India **62** 22.14N 68.58E
Dwellingup Australia **89** 32.42S116.04E
Dwight Canada **104** 45.21N 78.58W
Dyatlovichi U.S.S.R. **37** 52.08N 30.49E
Dyatlovo U.S.S.R. **37** 53.28N 25.28E
Dyer, C. Canada **99** 67.45N 61.45W
Dyer Bay *town* Canada **104** 45.10N 81.18W
Dyérem *r.* Cameroon **77** 6.36N 13.10E
Dyer Plateau Antarctica **128** 70.00S 65.00W
Dyersburg U.S.A. **111** 36.03N 89.23W
Dyfed *d.* U.K. **13** 52.00N 4.17W
Dykh Tau *mtn.* U.S.S.R. **45** 43.04N 43.10E
Dymer U.S.S.R. **37** 50.50N 30.20E
Dyulevo Bulgaria **29** 42.22N 27.10E
Dyultydag *mtn.* U.S.S.R. **65** 41.55N 46.52E
Dzamīn Üüd Mongolia **54** 43.50N111.53E
Dzerzhinsk B.S.S.R. U.S.S.R. **37** 53.40N 27.01E
Dzerzhinsk R.S.F.S.R. U.S.S.R. **44** 56.15N 43.30E
Dzhambul U.S.S.R. **52** 42.50N 71.25E
Dzhankoy U.S.S.R. **23** 45.42N 34.23E
Dzhardzhan U.S.S.R. **51** 68.49N124.08E
Dzhelinde U.S.S.R. **51** 70.09N114.00E
Dzhetygara U.S.S.R. **50** 52.14N 61.10E
Dzhezkazgan U.S.S.R. **50** 47.48N 67.24E
Dzhizak U.S.S.R. **50** 40.06N 67.45E
Dzhugdzhur, Khrebet *mts.* U.S.S.R. **51** 57.30N138.00E
Dzhurin U.S.S.R. **37** 48.40N 28.16E
Działdowo Poland **37** 53.15N 20.10E
Dzierzoniów Poland **36** 50.44N 16.39E
Dzodze Ghana **76** 6.14N 1.00E

E

Eabamet L. Canada **102** 51.30N 88.00W
Eads U.S.A. **110** 38.29N102.47W
Eagle *r.* Canada **103** 53.35N 57.25W
Eagle U.S.A. **110** 39.39N106.50W
Eagle Butte *town* U.S.A. **110** 45.00N101.14W
Eagle Grove U.S.A. **110** 42.40N 93.54W
Eagle L. U.S.A. **112** 46.17N 69.20W
Eagle Lake *town* Canada **104** 45.08N 78.29W
Eagle Lake *town* U.S.A. **112** 47.02N 68.36W
Eagle Pass *town* U.S.A. **111** 28.43N100.30W
Eagle River *town* U.S.A. **110** 45.55N 89.15W
Ealing U.K. **13** 51.31N 0.20W
Earlimart U.S.A. **109** 35.53N119.16W
Earlville U.S.A. **115** 42.44N 75.33W
Earn *r.* U.K. **14** 56.21N 3.18W
Earn, Loch U.K. **14** 56.23N 4.12W
Easingwold U.K. **12** 54.08N 1.11W
Easky Rep. of Ire. **15** 54.17N 8.58W
Easley U.S.A. **113** 34.50N 82.34W
East *r.* Canada **104** 45.20N 79.17W
East Alligator *r.* Australia **90** 12.25S132.58E
East Anglian Heights *hills* U.K. **13** 52.03N 0.15E
East Angus Canada **105** 45.29N 71.40W
East Aurora U.S.A. **114** 42.46N 78.37W
East B. U.S.A. **111** 29.30N 94.35W
Eastbourne U.K. **13** 50.46N 0.18E
East Brady U.S.A. **114** 40.59N 79.37W
East Broughton Canada **105** 46.14N 71.05W
East C. New Zealand **86** 37.45S178.30E
East Caroline Basin Pacific Oc. **84** 3.00N147.00E
East China Sea Asia **53** 29.00N125.00E
East Dereham U.K. **11** 52.40N 0.57E
Easter I. *see* Pascua, Isla de *i.* Pacific Oc. **85**
Eastern *d.* Ghana **76** 6.20N 0.45W
Eastern *d.* Kenya **79** 0.00 38.00E
Eastern Desert *see* Sharqīyah, Aş Şahrā' ash *des.* Egypt **66**
Eastern Ghāts *mts.* India **61** 16.30N 80.30E
Eastern-Indian-Antarctic Basin *f.* Indian Oc. **49** 56.00S110.00E
Easterville Canada **101** 53.06N 99.53W
East Falkland *i.* Falkland Is. **125** 51.45W 58.50W
East Grand Forks U.S.A. **110** 47.56N 96.55W
East Grinstead U.K. **13** 51.08N 0.01W
Easthampton Mass. U.S.A. **115** 42.16N 72.40W
East Hampton N.Y. U.S.A. **115** 40.58N 72.11W
East Hartford U.S.A. **115** 41.46N 72.39W
East Haven U.S.A. **115** 41.17N 72.52W
East Ilsley U.K. **13** 51.33N 1.15W
East Kilbride U.K. **14** 55.46N 4.09W
East Lansing U.S.A. **104** 42.44N 84.29W
Eastleigh U.K. **13** 50.58N 1.21W
East Liverpool U.S.A. **114** 40.38N 80.35W
East London R.S.A. **80** 33.00S 27.54E
Eastmain Canada **102** 52.15N 78.30W
Eastmain *r.* Canada **102** 52.15N 78.30W
Eastman Canada **105** 45.18N 72.19W
Easton Md. U.S.A. **115** 38.46N 76.04W
Easton Penn. U.S.A. **115** 40.42N 75.12W
Easton Wash. U.S.A. **108** 47.14N121.11W
East Orange U.S.A. **115** 40.46N 74.14W
East Pacific Ridge Pacific Oc. **85** 15.00S112.00W
East Palestine U.S.A. **114** 40.50N 80.33W
East Point *town* U.S.A. **113** 33.41N 84.29W
Eastport U.S.A. **115** 40.49N 72.44W
East Providence U.S.A. **115** 41.49N 71.23W
East Retford U.K. **12** 53.19N 0.55W
East Rochester U.S.A. **114** 43.07N 77.29W
East St. Louis U.S.A. **110** 38.34N 90.04W
East Springfield U.S.A. **114** 41.57N 80.28W
East Sussex *d.* U.K. **13** 50.56N 0.12E
East Sydenham *r.* Canada **104** 42.35N 82.23W
East Tawas U.S.A. **104** 44.17N 83.29W
Eaton U.S.A. **110** 40.32N104.42W
Eau Claire U.S.A. **110** 44.50N 91.30W
Eau-Claire, Lac à l' *l.* Canada **102** 56.10N 74.30W
Eauripik *i.* Caroline Is. **59** 6.42N143.04E
Eauripik-N. Guinea Rise Pacific Oc. **84** 2.00N141.00E
Eauze France **20** 43.52N 0.06E
Eban Nigeria **77** 9.41N 4.54E
Ebbw Vale U.K. **13** 51.47N 3.12W
Ebebiyin Equat. Guinea **78** 2.09N 11.20E
Ebeltoft Denmark **42** 56.12N 10.41E
Ebensburg U.S.A. **114** 40.29N 78.44W
Ebensee Austria **39** 47.48N 13.46E
Eberbach Germany **39** 49.28N 8.59E
Ebermannstadt Germany **38** 49.23N 11.13E
Ebern Germany **39** 50.05N 10.47E
Eberndorf Austria **31** 46.35N 14.38E
Ebersbach Germany **38** 51.00N 14.35E
Ebersberg Germany **39** 48.04N 11.59E
Eberstein Austria **31** 46.48N 14.34E
Eberswalde Germany **38** 52.50N 13.49E
Ebingen Germany **39** 48.13N 9.01E
Ebinur Hu *l.* China **52** 45.00N 83.00E
Ebola *r.* Zaïre **73** 3.20N 20.57E
Eboli Italy **33** 40.37N 15.04E
Ebolowa Cameroon **78** 2.56N 11.11E
Ebon *i.* Pacific Oc. **84** 4.38N168.43E
Ebony Namibia **80** 22.05S 15.15E
Ebro *r.* Spain **25** 40.43N 0.54E
Ebro, Delta del *f.* Spain **25** 40.43N 0.54E
Ebro, Embalse del *resr.* Spain **26** 43.00N 4.00W
Ecclefechan U.K. **12** 55.03N 3.18W
Eceabat Turkey **34** 40.11N 26.21E
Echeng China **55** 30.26N114.00E
Echo Bay *town* Canada **104** 46.29N 84.02W
Echternach Lux. **16** 49.49N 6.25E
Echuca Australia **93** 36.10S144.20E
Écija Spain **27** 37.32N 5.05W
Eckernförde Germany **38** 54.28N 9.50E
Écommoy France **18** 47.50N 0.16E
Ecuador S. America **122** 1.40S 79.00W
Écueillé France **18** 47.05N 1.21E
Ēd Ethiopia **72** 13.52N 41.40E
Ed Sweden **42** 58.55N 11.55E
Edam Neth. **16** 52.30N 5.02E
Eday *i.* U.K. **10** 59.11N 2.47W
Eddrachillis B. U.K. **14** 58.17N 5.15W
Eddystone Pt. Australia **91** 40.58S148.12E
Ede Neth. **16** 52.03N 5.40E
Ede Nigeria **77** 7.45N 4.26E
Edea Cameroon **78** 3.47N 10.15E
Edehon L. Canada **101** 60.25N 97.15W
Eden Australia **93** 37.04S149.54E
Eden Canada **104** 42.47N 80.46W
Eden *r.* Cumbria U.K. **12** 54.57N 3.02W
Eden U.S.A. **108** 42.03N109.26W
Edenburg R.S.A. **80** 29.44S 25.55E
Edendale New Zealand **86** 46.19S168.47E
Edenderry Rep. of Ire. **15** 53.21N 7.05W
Edenhope Australia **92** 37.04S141.20E
Edenton U.S.A. **113** 36.04N 76.39W
Edeowie Australia **92** 31.28S138.29E
Eder *r.* Germany **38** 51.13N 9.27E
Ederny U.K. **15** 54.32N 7.40W
Edgartown U.S.A. **115** 41.23N 70.31W
Edgeley U.S.A. **110** 40.07N 98.43W
Edgeöya *i.* Arctic Oc. **128** 77.45N 22.30E
Edgeworthstown Rep. of Ire. **15** 53.42N 7.38W
Edgington Canada **104** 45.23N 79.47W
Édhessa Greece **34** 40.48N 22.05E
Ediacara Australia **92** 30.18S137.50E
Edina Liberia **76** 6.01N 10.10W
Edinboro U.S.A. **114** 41.52N 80.08W
Edinburgh U.K. **14** 55.57N 3.13W
Edirne Turkey **34** 41.40N 26.34E
Edithburgh Australia **92** 35.06S137.44E
Edjudina Australia **89** 29.48S122.23E
Edmond U.S.A. **111** 35.39N 97.29W
Edmonton Canada **100** 53.30N113.30W
Edmundston Canada **103** 47.22N 68.20W
Edna U.S.A. **111** 28.59N 96.39W
Edo *r.* Japan **57** 35.37N139.53E
Edolo Italy **30** 46.11N 10.20E
Edounga Gabon **78** 0.03S 13.43E
Edremit Turkey **29** 39.35N 27.02E
Edremit Körfezi *b.* Turkey **34** 39.30N 26.45E
Edsbruk Sweden **43** 58.02N 16.28E
Edson Canada **100** 53.35N116.26W
Edward, L. Uganda/Zaïre **79** 0.30S 29.30E
Edwards Plateau *f.* U.S.A. **111** 31.20N101.00W
Eeklo Belgium **16** 51.11N 3.34E
Eel *r.* U.S.A. **108** 40.40N124.20W
Efate *i.* Vanuatu **84** 17.40S168.25E
Eferding Austria **39** 48.18N 14.02E
Effingham U.S.A. **110** 39.07N 88.33W
Ega *r.* Spain **25** 42.19N 1.55W
Egadi, Isole *is.* Italy **32** 38.00N 12.10E
Egaña Argentina **125** 36.57S 59.06W
Eganville Canada **105** 45.32N 77.06W
Egbe Nigeria **77** 8.13N 5.31E
Egeland U.S.A. **110** 48.38N 99.10W
Eger Hungary **37** 47.54N 20.23E
Egersund Norway **42** 58.27N 6.00E
Egerton, Mt. Australia **88** 24.44S117.40E
Eggenfelden Germany **39** 48.25N 12.46E
Egg Harbor U.S.A. **115** 39.32N 74.39W
Égletons France **20** 45.24N 2.03E
Egmont, Mt. New Zealand **86** 39.20S174.05E
Eğridir Turkey **64** 37.52N 30.51E
Eğridir Gölü *l.* Turkey **64** 38.04N 30.55E
Egtved Denmark **42** 55.37N 9.18E
Egypt Africa **72** 26.00N 30.00E
Ehingen Germany **39** 48.17N 9.43E
Eiao *i.* Is. Marquises **85** 8.00S140.40W
Eibar Spain **26** 43.11N 2.28W
Eibiswald Austria **31** 46.41N 15.15E
Eichstätt Germany **38** 48.54N 11.12E
Eidsvåg Norway **40** 62.47N 8.03E
Eidsvold Australia **90** 25.23S151.08E
Eidsvoll Norway **42** 60.19N 11.14E
Eifel *f.* Germany **39** 50.10N 6.40E
Eigg *i.* U.K. **14** 56.53N 6.09W
Eighty Mile Beach *f.* Australia **88** 19.00S121.00E
Eil, Loch U.K. **14** 56.51N 5.12W
Eildon, L. Australia **93** 37.10S146.00E
Eilenburg Germany **38** 51.27N 12.37E
Einasleigh Australia **90** 18.31S144.05E
Einbeck Germany **38** 51.49N 9.52E
Eindhoven Neth. **16** 51.26N 5.30E
Einsiedeln Switz. **39** 47.08N 8.45E
Eirunepé Brazil **122** 6.40S 69.52W
Eiseb *r.* Namibia **80** 20.26S 20.05E
Eisenach Germany **38** 50.59N 10.19E
Eisenberg Germany **38** 50.58N 11.53E
Eisenerz Austria **36** 47.33N 14.53E
Eisenhut *mtn.* Austria **36** 47.00N 13.45E
Eisenhüttenstadt Germany **38** 52.10N 14.39E
Eisfeld Germany **39** 50.26N 10.54E
Eišiškes U.S.S.R. **37** 54.09N 24.55E
Eisleben Germany **38** 51.31N 11.32E
Eitorf Germany **38** 50.46N 7.26E
Ejby Denmark **42** 55.26N 9.57E
Ejde Faroe Is. **10** 62.03N 7.06W
Ejea de los Caballeros Spain **25** 42.08N 1.08W
Ejin Qi China **52** 41.50N100.50E
Ejura Ghana **76** 7.24N 1.20W
Ekalaka U.S.A. **108** 45.53N104.33W
Eket Nigeria **77** 4.39N 7.56E
Eketahuna New Zealand **86** 40.39S175.44E
Ekhinos Greece **34** 41.17N 24.59E
Ekibastuz U.S.S.R. **50** 51.45N 75.22E
Ekimchan U.S.S.R. **51** 53.09N133.00E
Eksjö Sweden **43** 57.40N 14.57E
Ekträsk Sweden **40** 64.29N 19.50E
Ekuku Zaïre **78** 0.42S 21.38E
Ekwan *r.* Canada **102** 53.30N 84.00W
El Aaiún W. Sahara **74** 27.09N 13.12W
El Alia Tunisia **32** 37.10N 10.03E
Elands *r.* Trans. R.S.A. **80** 24.52S 29.20E
El Arahal Spain **27** 37.16N 5.33W
El Arco Mexico **109** 28.00N113.25W
El Arenal Spain **25** 39.30N 2.45E
El Asnam Algeria **75** 36.10N 1.20E
Elassón Greece **34** 39.54N 22.11E
Elat Israel **66** 29.33N 34.56E
Elâzig Turkey **64** 38.41N 39.14E
Elba *i.* Italy **30** 42.46N 10.17E
El Barco de Avilla Spain **26** 40.21N 5.31W
El Barco de Valdeorras Spain **26** 42.25N 6.59W
El Barril Mexico **109** 28.22N113.00W
Elbasan Albania **34** 41.09N 20.09E
Elbasan Berat *d.* Albania **34** 40.58N 20.00E
El Baúl Venezuela **122** 8.59N 68.16W
Elbe *r.* Germany **38** 53.50N 10.00E
Elbe-Havel-Kanal Germany **38** 52.23N 12.15E
Elbe-Lübeck-Kanal Germany **38** 53.50N 10.36E
El Beni *d.* Bolivia **124** 14.00S 65.30W
Elbert, Mt. U.S.A. **110** 39.07N106.27W
Elberton U.S.A. **113** 34.05N 82.54W
Elbeuf France **18** 49.17N 1.00E
Elbistan Turkey **64** 38.14N 37.11E
Elbląg Poland **37** 54.10N 19.25E
El Bonillo Spain **26** 38.57N 2.32W
Elbrus *mtn.* U.S.S.R. **45** 43.21N 42.29E
Elburg Neth. **16** 52.27N 5.50E
El Burgo de Osma Spain **26** 41.35N 3.04W
Elburz Mts. *see* Alborz, Reshteh-ye Kūhhā-ye *ye* Iran **65**
El Cajon U.S.A. **109** 32.48N116.58W
El Callao Venezuela **122** 7.18N 61.48W
El Campo U.S.A. **111** 29.12N 96.16W
El Casco Mexico **111** 25.34N104.35W
El Cenajo, Embalse de *resr.* Spain **27** 38.25N 2.00W
El Centro U.S.A. **109** 32.48N115.34W
Elche Spain **25** 38.15N 0.42W
Elche de la Sierra Spain **25** 38.27N 2.03W
Elcho U.S.A. **110** 45.26N 89.11W
Elcho I. Australia **90** 11.55S135.45E
El Corral Mexico **111** 25.09N 97.58W
El Cozón Mexico **109** 31.18N112.29W
El Cuy Argentina **125** 39.57S 68.20W
Elda Spain **25** 38.29N 0.47W
Elde *r.* Germany **36** 53.17N 12.40E
El Der Ethiopia **71** 5.08N 43.08E
Elder, L. Australia **92** 30.39S140.13E
El Desemboque Mexico **109** 29.30N112.27W
El Djouf *des.* Mauritania **74** 20.30N 7.30W
Eldon U.S.A. **110** 38.21N 93.35W
Eldorado Canada **101** 59.35N108.30W
El Dorado Ark. U.S.A. **111** 33.13N 92.40W
El Dorado Kans. U.S.A. **111** 37.49N 96.52W
El Dorado Venezuela **122** 6.45N 61.37W
Eldoret Kenya **79** 0.31N 35.17E
Eldsdro Sweden **43** 59.53N 18.33E
Electra U.S.A. **111** 34.02N 98.55W
El Eglab *f.* Algeria **74** 26.30N 4.15W
Elei, Wādī Sudan **72** 22.04N 34.27E
Eleja U.S.S.R. **41** 56.26N 23.42E
Elektrostal U.S.S.R. **44** 55.46N 38.30E
Elena Bulgaria **34** 42.56N 25.53E
Elephant Butte Resr. U.S.A. **109** 33.19N107.10W
Elephant I. Atlantic Oc. **121** 61.00S 55.00W
El Eulma Algeria **75** 36.09N 5.41E
Eleuthera I. Bahamas **113** 25.15N 76.20W
Elevsís Greece **35** 38.02N 23.33E
Elevtheroúpolis Greece **34** 40.55N 24.16E
El Ferrol Spain **26** 43.29N 8.14W
Elgå Norway **41** 62.11N 11.07E
Elgenfield Canada **104** 43.10N 81.22W
Elgin *Man.* Canada **101** 49.26N100.15W
Elgin *Ont.* Canada **105** 44.36N 76.13W
Elgin U.K. **14** 57.39N 3.20W
Elgin Ill. U.S.A. **110** 42.03N 88.19W
Elgin Nev. U.S.A. **108** 37.21N114.30W
Elgin Oreg. U.S.A. **108** 45.34N117.55W
Elgin Tex. U.S.A. **111** 30.21N 97.22W
El Golea Algeria **75** 30.34N 2.53E
Elgon, Mt. Kenya/Uganda **79** 1.07N 34.35E
El Grove Spain **26** 42.30N 8.52W
El Haouaria Tunisia **32** 37.03N 11.02E
Elida U.S.A. **111** 33.57N103.39W
Elim Namibia **80** 17.47S 15.30E
Elin Pelin Bulgaria **34** 42.40N 23.38E
Elista U.S.S.R. **45** 46.18N 44.14E
Elizabeth Australia **92** 34.45S138.39E
Elizabeth N.J. U.S.A. **115** 40.40N 74.11W
Elizabeth W.Va. U.S.A. **114** 39.04N 81.24W
Elizabeth City U.S.A. **113** 36.18N 76.16W
Elizabethtown Ky. U.S.A. **113** 37.41N 85.51W
Elizabethtown N.Y. U.S.A. **105** 44.13N 73.36W
Elizabethtown Penn. U.S.A. **115** 40.09N 76.36W
El Jadida Morocco **74** 33.16N 8.30W
Elk *r.* Canada **100** 49.10N115.14W
Elk Poland **37** 53.50N 22.22E
Elk *r.* U.S.A. **114** 38.21N 81.38W
El Kairouan Tunisia **75** 35.41N 10.07E
El Kala Algeria **32** 36.50N 8.30E
El Kasserine Tunisia **75** 35.11N 8.48E
Elk City U.S.A. **111** 35.25N 99.25W
El Kef Tunisia **75** 36.11N 8.43E
El-Kelâa-des-Srarhna Morocco **74** 32.02N 7.23W
Ēl Kerē Ethiopia **73** 5.48N 42.10E
Elkhart Ind. U.S.A. **110** 41.52N 85.56W
Elkhart Kans. U.S.A. **111** 37.00N101.54W
El Khnâchîch *f.* Mali **76** 21.50N 3.45W
Elkhorn Canada **101** 49.58N101.14W
Elkhovo Bulgaria **34** 42.09N 26.36E
Elkins N.Mex. U.S.A. **109** 33.41N104.04W
Elkins W.Va. U.S.A. **114** 38.55N 79.51W
Elkland U.S.A. **114** 41.59N 77.21W
Elko U.S.A. **108** 40.50N115.46W
Elkton Md. U.S.A. **115** 39.36N 75.50W
Elkton Va. U.S.A. **114** 38.25N 78.38W
Elleker Australia **89** 34.55S117.40E
Ellen, Mt. U.S.A. **106** 38.06N110.50W
Ellenboro U.S.A. **114** 39.17N 81.04W
Ellenburg U.S.A. **105** 44.54N 73.51W
Ellendale Australia **88** 17.56S124.48E
Ellensburg U.S.A. **108** 47.00N120.32W
Ellenville U.S.A. **115** 41.43N 74.24W
Ellesmere I. Canada **99** 78.00N 82.00W
Ellesmere Port U.K. **12** 53.17N 2.55W
Ellicottville U.S.A. **114** 42.17N 78.40W
Elliot R.S.A. **80** 31.19S 27.49E
Elliot Lake *town* Canada **104** 46.23N 82.39W
Elliott Australia **90** 17.33S133.31E
Ellis U.S.A. **110** 38.56N 99.34W
Elliston Australia **92** 33.39S134.55E
Ellon U.K. **14** 57.22N 2.05W
Ellora India **62** 20.01N 75.10E
Ellwangen Germany **39** 48.57N 10.07E
Ellwood City U.S.A. **114** 40.50N 80.17W
Elm Switz. **39** 46.55N 9.11E
El Mahdia Tunisia **75** 35.30N 11.04E
Elmali Turkey **64** 36.43N 29.56E
El Maneadero Mexico **109** 31.45N116.35W

Elmer to Exeter

Elmer U.S.A. **115** 39.36N 75.10W
El Metlaoui Tunisia **75** 34.20N 8.24E
Elmhurst U.S.A. **110** 41.54N 87.56W
Elmina Ghana **76** 5.07N 1.21W
Elmira Canada **104** 43.36N 80.33W
Elmira U.S.A. **114** 42.06N 76.49W
El Molinillo Spain **27** 39.28N 4.13W
Elmore Australia **93** 36.30S144.40E
El Mreiti *well* Mauritania **74** 23.29N 7.52W
El Mreyyé *f.* Mauritania **74** 19.30N 7.00W
Elmshorn Germany **38** 53.45N 9.39E
Elmsta Sweden **43** 59.58N 18.45E
Elmvale Canada **104** 44.35N 79.52W
Elne France **20** 42.36N 2.58E
El Niybo Ethiopia **73** 4.32N 39.59E
El Ouassi *well* Mali **76** 20.23N 0.12E
El Oued Algeria **75** 33.20N 6.53E
Eloy U.S.A. **109** 32.45N111.33W
El Paso U.S.A. **109** 31.45N106.29W
El Portal U.S.A. **108** 37.41N119.47W
El Prat de Llobregat Spain **25** 41.20N 2.06E
El Puente del Arzobispo Spain **27** 39.48N 5.10W
El Quelite Mexico **109** 23.32N106.28W
El Real Panama **117** 8.06N 77.42W
El Reno U.S.A. **111** 35.32N 97.57W
El Roba Kenya **79** 3.57N 40.01E
Elrose Canada **101** 51.13N108.01W
El Salto Mexico **109** 23.47N105.22W
El Salvador C. America **117** 13.30N 89.00W
Elsas Canada **102** 48.32N 82.55W
Elsdorf Germany **16** 50.56N 6.35E
Elsfleth Germany **38** 53.14N 8.28E
Elsinore U.S.A. **108** 38.41N112.09W
Elspe Germany **38** 51.09N 8.04E
Elsterwerda Germany **38** 51.28N 13.31E
El Sueco Mexico **109** 29.54N106.24W
El Tabacal Argentina **124** 23.15S 64.14W
El Tarf Algeria **32** 36.45N 8.20E
El Tigre Venezuela **122** 8.44N 64.18W
Eltmann Germany **39** 49.58N 10.40E
Elton, Ozero *l.* U.S.S.R. **45** 49.10N 46.34E
El Turbio Argentina **125** 51.41S 72.05W
Elūru India **61** 16.45N 81.10E
Elvas Portugal **27** 38.53N 7.10W
Elvdal Norway **41** 61.38N 11.56E
Elven France **18** 47.44N 2.35W
El Vendrell Spain **25** 41.13N 1.32E
Elverum Norway **41** 60.53N 11.34E
Elvira Argentina **125** 35.15S 59.30W
El Wak Kenya **79** 2.45N 40.52E
Elwood Nebr. U.S.A. **110** 40.36N 99.52W
Elwood N.J. U.S.A. **115** 39.35N 74.43W
Ely U.K. **11** 52.24N 0.16E
Ely Minn. U.S.A. **110** 47.53N 91.52W
Ely Nev. U.S.A. **108** 39.15N114.53W
Elyria U.S.A. **114** 41.22N 82.06W
Elz *f.* Germany **39** 48.07N 7.45E
Emae *i.* Vanuatu **84** 17.04S168.24E
Emāmshahr Iran **65** 36.25N 55.00E
Emån *r.* Sweden **43** 57.08N 16.30E
Emba U.S.S.R. **50** 48.47N 58.05E
Emba *r.* U.S.S.R. **45** 46.38N 53.00E
Embarcación Argentina **124** 23.15S 64.10W
Embid Spain **25** 40.58N 1.43W
Embleton U.K. **12** 55.30N 1.37W
Embrun France **21** 44.34N 6.30E
Embu Kenya **79** 0.32S 37.28E
Emden Germany **38** 53.22N 7.12E
'Emeq Yizre'el *f.* Israel **67** 32.36N 35.14E
Emerald Australia **90** 23.32S148.10E
Emerson Canada **101** 49.00N 97.12W
Emi Koussi *mtn.* Chad **77** 19.58N 18.30E
Emilia-Romagna *d.* Italy **30** 44.45N 11.00E
Emlenton U.S.A. **114** 41.11N 79.43W
Emlichheim Germany **38** 52.36N 6.50E
Emmaboda Sweden **43** 56.38N 15.32E
Emmaste U.S.S.R. **41** 58.42N 22.36E
Emmaus U.S.A. **115** 40.32N 75.30W
Emmaville Australia **93** 29.25S151.39E
Emme *r.* Switz. **39** 47.13N 7.34E
Emmeloord Neth. **16** 52.43N 5.46E
Emmen Neth. **16** 52.48N 6.55E
Emmendingen Germany **39** 48.07N 7.50E
Emmerich Germany **38** 51.50N 6.15E
Emmett U.S.A. **108** 43.52N116.30W
Emmitsburg U.S.A. **114** 39.42N 77.20W
Emory Peak *mtn.* U.S.A. **111** 29.13N103.17W
Empalme Mexico **109** 27.58N110.51W
Empangeni R.S.A. **81** 28.45S 31.54E
Empedrado Argentina **124** 27.59S 58.47W
Empoli Italy **30** 43.43N 10.57E
Emporia Kans. U.S.A. **110** 38.24N 96.11W
Emporia Va. U.S.A. **113** 36.42N 77.33W
Emporium U.S.A. **114** 41.31N 78.14W
Ems *r.* Germany **38** 53.14N 7.25E
Emsdale Canada **104** 45.32N 79.19W
Emsdetten Germany **38** 52.10N 7.31E
Ems-Jade Kanal Germany **38** 53.29N 7.35E
Emyvale Rep. of Ire. **15** 54.20N 6.59W
Enard B. U.K. **14** 58.05N 5.20W
Encarnación Paraguay **126** 27.20S 55.50W
Enchi Ghana **76** 5.53N 2.48W
Encinal U.S.A. **111** 28.02N 99.21W
Encino U.S.A. **109** 34.39N105.28W
Encontada, Cerro de la *mtn.* Mexico **109** 27.03N112.31W
Encontrados Venezuela **122** 9.03N 72.14W
Encounter B. Australia **92** 35.35S138.44E
Ende Indonesia **59** 8.51S121.40E
Endeavour Str. Australia **90** 10.50S142.15E
Enderbury I. Kiribati **84** 3.08S171.05W
Enderby Canada **100** 50.35N119.10W
Enderby Land *f.* Antarctica **128** 67.00S 53.00E
Enderlin U.S.A. **110** 46.37N 97.36W
Endicott U.S.A. **115** 42.06N 76.03W
Endicott Arm *f.* U.S.A. **100** 57.38N133.22W
Endicott Mts. U.S.A. **98** 68.00N152.00W
Endola Namibia **80** 17.37S 15.50E
Eneabba Australia **89** 29.48S115.16E
Enewetak *i.* Pacific Oc. **84** 11.30N162.15E
Enez Turkey **34** 40.44N 26.04E
Enfida Tunisia **75** 36.08N 10.22E
Enfield U.K. **13** 51.40N 0.05W
Enfield U.S.A. **115** 41.58N 72.36W
Engaño, C. Phil. **59** 18.30N122.20E
Engcobo R.S.A. **80** 31.39S 28.01E
'En Gedi Israel **66** 31.28N 35.23E
Engels U.S.S.R. **45** 51.30N 46.07E
Enggano *i.* Indonesia **58** 5.20S102.15E
Enghershatu *mtn.* Ethiopia **72** 16.40N 38.20E
Enghien Belgium **16** 50.42N 4.02E
England U.K. **12** 53.00N 2.00W
Englewood Colo. U.S.A. **108** 39.39N104.59W
Englewood Fla. U.S.A. **113** 26.58N 82.21W
English Bāzār India **63** 25.00N 88.09E
English Channel U.K. **13** 50.15N 1.00W
English River *town* Canada **102** 49.20N 91.00W
Enguera Spain **25** 38.59N 0.41W
'En Harod Israel **67** 32.33N 35.23E
Enid U.S.A. **111** 36.19N 97.48W
Enkhuizen Neth. **16** 52.42N 5.17E
Enköping Sweden **43** 59.38N 17.04E
Enna Italy **33** 37.34N 14.17E
Ennadai Canada **101** 61.08N100.53W
Ennadai L. Canada **101** 61.00N101.00W
Ennedi *f.* Chad **72** 17.15N 22.00E
Enneri Yoo *wadi* Chad **77** 19.24N 16.38E
Enngonia Australia **93** 29.20S145.53E
Ennis Rep. of Ire. **15** 52.51N 9.00W
Ennis U.S.A. **111** 32.20N 96.38W
Enniscorthy Rep. of Ire. **15** 52.30N 6.35W
Enniskillen U.K. **15** 54.21N 7.40W
Ennistymon Rep. of Ire. **15** 52.56N 9.18W
Enns *r.* Austria **36** 48.14N 14.22E
Enontekiö Finland **40** 68.23N 23.38E
Enosburg Falls U.S.A. **105** 44.55N 72.48W
Enping China **55** 22.11N112.18E
Ensay Australia **93** 37.24S147.52E
Enschede Neth. **16** 52.13N 6.54E
Ensenada Argentina **125** 34.51S 57.55W
Ensenada Baja Calif. Norte Mexico **109** 31.52N116.37W
Ensenada Nuevo León Mexico **111** 25.56N 97.50W
Enshi China **55** 30.18N109.29E
Enshū-nada *sea* Japan **57** 34.30N137.30E
Entebbe Uganda **79** 0.08N 32.29E
Enterprise Canada **100** 60.47N115.45W
Entinas, Punta *c.* Spain **27** 36.41N 2.46W
Entraygues France **20** 44.39N 2.34E
Entrepeñas, Embalse de *resr.* Spain **26** 40.34N 2.42W
Entre Ríos *d.* Argentina **125** 32.10S 59.00W
Entre Rios de Minas Brazil **126** 20.39S 44.06W
Entrocamento Portugal **27** 39.28N 8.28W
Entwistle Canada **100** 53.30N115.00W
Enugu Nigeria **77** 6.20N 7.29E
Envalira, Port d' *pass* France / Andorra **20** 42.35N 1.45E
Envermeu France **18** 49.54N 1.16E
Envigado Colombia **122** 6.09N 75.35W
Enza *r.* Italy **30** 44.54N 10.31E
Enzan Japan **57** 35.42N138.44E
Eo *r.* Spain **26** 43.32N 7.03W
Eolie, Isole *is.* Italy **33** 38.50N 15.00E
Epanomi Greece **34** 40.26N 22.56E
Epe Neth. **16** 52.21N 5.59E
Epernay France **19** 49.03N 3.57E
Ephesus *site* Turkey **35** 37.55N 27.17E
Ephraim U.S.A. **108** 39.22N111.35W
Ephrata Penn. U.S.A. **115** 40.11N 76.10W
Ephrata Wash. U.S.A. **108** 47.19N119.33W
Epi *i.* Vanuatu **84** 16.43S168.15E
Épila Spain **25** 41.36N 1.17W
Épinal France **19** 48.11N 6.27E
Epitálion Greece **35** 37.37N 21.30E
Epping U.K. **13** 51.42N 0.07E
Epping U.S.A. **115** 43.02N 71.04W
Epsom U.K. **13** 51.20N 0.16W
Epte *r.* France **19** 49.04N 1.37E
Equateur *d.* Zaïre **78** 0.00 21.00E
Equatorial Guinea Africa **78** 2.00N 10.00E
Equerdreville France **18** 49.40N 1.40W
Era, Ozero *l.* U.S.S.R. **45** 47.38N 45.18E
Eraclea Italy **30** 45.35N 12.40E
Erbach Germany **39** 49.40N 8.59E
Erciyaş Dagi *mtn.* Turkey **64** 38.33N 35.25E
Erdevik Yugo. **31** 45.07N 19.25E
Erding Germany **39** 48.18N 11.54E
Erdre *r.* France **18** 47.11N 1.31W
Erebus, Mt. Antarctica **128** 77.40S167.20E
Erechim Brazil **126** 27.35S 52.15W
Eregli Konya Turkey **64** 37.30N 34.02E
Eregli Zonguldak Turkey **64** 41.17N 31.26E
Erei, Monti *mts.* Italy **33** 37.30N 14.10E
Erenhot China **54** 43.48N112.00E
Ērer *r.* Ethiopia **71** 7.35N 42.05E
Eresma *r.* Spain **26** 41.26N 4.45W
Eresós Greece **35** 39.11N 25.57E
Erétria Greece **35** 38.23N 23.50E
Erfoud Morocco **74** 31.28N 4.10W
Erft *r.* Germany **16** 51.12N 6.45E
Erfurt Germany **38** 50.58N 11.01E
Ergani Turkey **64** 38.17N 39.44E
Ergene *r.* Turkey **29** 41.02N 26.22E
Erges *r.* *see* Erjas *r.* Spain **27**
Ergig *r.* Chad **77** 11.30N 15.30E
Eria *r.* Spain **26** 42.03N 5.44W
Erica Neth. **16** 52.44N 6.56E
Erice Italy **32** 38.02N 12.36E
Ericeira Portugal **27** 38.59N 9.25W
Erie U.S.A. **114** 42.08N 80.04W
Erie, L. Canada / U.S.A. **114** 42.15N 81.00W
Erieau Canada **104** 42.16N 81.56W
Eriksdale Canada **101** 50.52N 98.06W
Erímanthos *mtn.* Greece **35** 37.59N 21.51E
Erimo misaki *c.* Japan **57** 41.55N143.13E
Eriskay *i.* U.K. **14** 57.04N 7.17W
Erithraí Greece **35** 38.13N 23.19E
Eritrea *f.* Ethiopia **72** 15.30N 38.00E
Eritrea *see* Ērtra *d.* Ethiopia **72**
Erjas *r.* Portugal **27** 39.47N 7.00W
Erkelenz Germany **38** 51.05N 6.19E
Erkner Germany **38** 52.25N 13.45E
Erlangen Germany **38** 49.36N 11.01E
Erldunda Australia **90** 25.14S133.12E
Ermelo Neth. **16** 52.19N 5.38E
Ermelo R.S.A. **80** 26.30S 29.59E
Ermidas Portugal **27** 38.00N 8.23W
Ermióni Greece **35** 37.23N 23.15E
Ermoúpolis Greece **35** 37.26N 24.56E
Erne *r.* Rep. of Ire. **11** 54.30N 8.17W
Ernée France **18** 48.18N 0.56W
Ernest U.S.A. **114** 40.41N 79.10W
Erode India **60** 11.21N 77.43E
Eromanga *i.* Vanuatu **84** 18.45S169.05E
Erota Ethiopia **72** 16.13N 37.57E
Er Rachidia Morocco **74** 31.58N 4.25W
Errego Mozambique **79** 16.02S 37.11E
Er Reina Israel **67** 32.43N 35.18E
Errenteria *see* Rentería Spain **26**
Errigal Mtn. Rep. of Ire. **15** 55.02N 8.08W
Erris Head Rep. of Ire. **15** 54.19N 10.00W
Erstein France **19** 48.26N 7.40E
Ertix He *r.* U.S.S.R. **52** 48.00N 84.20E
Ērtra *d.* Ethiopia **72** 15.30N 39.00E
Erudina Australia **92** 31.30S139.23E
Ervy-le-Châtel France **19** 48.02N 3.55E
Erzgebirge *mts.* Germany **38** 50.34N 13.00E
Erzin U.S.S.R. **52** 50.16N 95.14E
Erzincan Turkey **64** 39.44N 39.30E
Erzurum Turkey **64** 39.57N 41.17E
Esbjerg Denmark **42** 55.28N 8.27E
Esbo *see* Espoo Finland **41**
Esca *r.* Spain **25** 42.37N 1.03W
Escalante U.S.A. **108** 37.47N111.36W
Escalón Mexico **111** 26.45N104.20W
Escalona Spain **26** 40.10N 4.24W
Escanaba U.S.A. **112** 45.47N 87.04W
Escandón, Puerto de *pass* Spain **25** 40.17N 1.00W
Esch Lux. **16** 49.31N 5.59E
Eschau France **19** 48.29N 7.43E
Eschwege Germany **38** 51.11N 10.04E
Eschweiler Germany **38** 50.49N 6.16E
Escondido *r.* Nicaragua **117** 11.58N 83.45W
Escondido U.S.A. **109** 33.07N117.05W
Escuinapa Mexico **109** 22.51N105.48W
Escuintla Guatemala **116** 14.18N 90.47W
Esens Germany **38** 53.39N 7.37E
Ésera *r.* Spain **25** 42.06N 0.15E
Eşfahān Iran **65** 32.42N 51.40E
Esgueva *r.* Spain **26** 41.40N 4.43W
Eshbol Israel **67** 31.27N 34.40E
Esher U.K. **13** 51.23N 0.22W
Eshkanān Iran **65** 27.10N 53.38E
Eshowe R.S.A. **80** 28.53S 31.29E
Eshta'ol Israel **67** 31.47N 35.00E
Esk *r.* N. Yorks. U.K. **12** 54.29N 0.37W
Eskifjördhur *town* Iceland **40** 65.05N 14.00W
Eskilstrup Denmark **42** 54.51N 11.54E
Eskilstuna Sweden **43** 59.22N 16.30E
Eskimo Point *town* Canada **101** 61.10N 94.03W
Eskişehir Turkey **64** 39.46N 30.30E
Esla *r.* Spain **26** 41.29N 6.03W
Eslāmābād-e-Gharb Iran **65** 34.08N 46.35E
Eslöv Sweden **43** 55.50N 13.20E
Esmeraldas Ecuador **122** 0.56N 79.40W
Espalion France **20** 44.31N 2.46E
Espanola Canada **104** 46.15N 81.46W
Espe U.S.S.R. **50** 43.50N 74.10E
Espejo Spain **27** 37.41N 4.33W
Espelkamp Germany **38** 52.25N 8.36E
Esperance Australia **89** 33.49S121.52E
Esperance B. Australia **89** 33.51S121.53E
Esperanza Argentina **125** 31.30S 61.00W
Esperanza Mexico **109** 27.35N109.56W
Espichel, Cabo *c.* Portugal **27** 38.25N 9.13W
Espinal Colombia **122** 4.08N 75.00W
Espinhaço, Serra do *mts.* Brazil **126** 17.15S 43.10W
Espinho Portugal **26** 41.00N 8.39W
Espírito Santo *d.* Brazil **126** 20.00S 40.30W
Espíritu Santo I. Vanuatu **84** 15.50S166.50E
Espoo Finland **41** 60.13N 24.40E
Esposende Portugal **26** 41.32N 8.47W
Espuña, Sierra de *mts.* Spain **25** 37.50N 1.40E
Espungabera Mozambique **81** 20.28S 32.48E
Esquel Argentina **125** 42.55S 71.20W
Esquimalt Canada **100** 48.30N123.23W
Esquina Argentina **125** 30.00S 59.30W
Essaouira Morocco **74** 31.30N 9.47W
Essen Germany **38** 51.28N 7.01E
Essequibo *r.* Guyana **122** 6.30N 58.40W
Essex Canada **104** 42.10N 82.49W
Essex *d.* U.K. **13** 51.46N 0.30E
Essex U.S.A. **109** 34.45N115.15W
Essex Junction U.S.A. **105** 44.29N 73.07W
Essexville U.S.A. **104** 43.37N 83.50W
Esslingen Germany **39** 48.45N 9.16E
Essonne *d.* France **19** 48.36N 2.20E
Essoyes France **19** 48.04N 4.32E
Essoyla U.S.S.R. **44** 61.47N 33.11E
Es Suki Sudan **73** 13.24N 33.55E
Est *d.* Burkina **76** 12.45N 0.25E
Est, Pointe de l' *c.* Canada **103** 49.08N 61.41W
Estaca de Bares, Punta de la *c.* Spain **26** 43.46N 7.42W
Estacado, Llano *f.* U.S.A. **111** 33.30N102.40W
Estados, Isla de los *i.* Argentina **125** 54.45S 64.00W
Eşţahbānāt Iran **65** 29.05N 54.03E
Estaire Canada **104** 46.21N 80.47W
Estância Brazil **123** 11.15S 37.28W
Estand, Kūh-e *mtn.* Iran **65** 31.18N 60.03E
Estarreja Portugal **26** 40.45N 8.34W
Estats, Pic d' *mtn.* Spain **25** 42.40N 1.23E
Este Italy **30** 45.14N 11.39E
Estelí Nicaragua **97** 13.05N 86.23W
Estella Spain **26** 42.40N 2.02W
Estelline U.S.A. **111** 34.33N100.26W
Estepa Spain **27** 37.18N 4.54W
Estepona Spain **27** 36.26N 5.08W
Esternay France **19** 48.44N 3.34E
Estevan Canada **101** 49.07N103.05W
Estevan Is. Canada **100** 53.03N129.38W
Estevan Pt. Canada **100** 49.23N126.33W
Estherville U.S.A. **110** 43.24N 94.50W
Estissac France **19** 48.16N 3.49E
Estivane Mozambique **81** 24.07S 32.38E
Eston U.K. **12** 54.34N 1.07W
Estonskaya S.S.R. *d.* U.S.S.R. **41** 58.35N 24.35E
Estoril Portugal **27** 38.42N 9.23W
Estrela *mtn.* Portugal **26** 40.19N 7.37W
Estrela, Serra da *mts.* Portugal **26** 40.20N 7.40W
Estremoz Portugal **27** 38.51N 7.35W
Esztergom Hungary **37** 47.48N 18.45E
Étables France **18** 48.38N 2.50W
Etadunna Australia **92** 28.43S138.38E
Etah India **63** 27.38N 78.40E
Étain France **19** 49.13N 5.38E
Etamamiou Canada **103** 50.16N 59.58W
Étampes France **19** 48.26N 2.09E
Étaples France **19** 50.31N 1.39E
Etāwah India **63** 26.46N 79.02E
Ethel Creek *town* Australia **88** 23.05S120.14E
Ethiopia Africa **73** 9.00N 39.00E
Etive, Loch U.K. **14** 56.27N 5.15W
Etna, Monte *mtn.* Italy **33** 37.46N 15.00E
Etne Norway **42** 59.40N 5.56E
Etolin I. U.S.A. **100** 56.10N132.30W
Etosha Game Res. Namibia **80** 18.50S 15.40E
Etosha Pan *f.* Namibia **80** 18.50S 16.20E
Etowah U.S.A. **113** 35.20N 84.30W
Étretat France **18** 49.42N 0.12E
Etropole Bulgaria **34** 42.50N 24.00E
Et Taiyiba Israel **67** 32.16N 35.01E
Ettelbrück Lux. **16** 49.51N 6.06E
Et Tīra Israel **67** 32.14N 34.57E
Ettlingen Germany **39** 48.56N 8.24E
Eu France **18** 50.03N 1.25E
Eua *i.* Tonga **85** 21.23S174.55W
Euabalong Australia **93** 33.07S146.28E
Eubank U.S.A. **113** 37.16N 84.40W
Euboea *see* Évvoia *i.* Greece **35**
Eucla Australia **89** 31.40S128.51E
Euclid U.S.A. **114** 41.34N 81.32W
Eucumbene, L. Australia **93** 36.05S148.45E
Eudora U.S.A. **111** 33.07N 91.16W
Eudunda Australia **92** 34.09S139.04E
Eufaula Resr. U.S.A. **107** 35.15N 95.35W
Eugene U.S.A. **108** 44.02N123.05W
Eugenia, Punta *c.* Mexico **109** 27.50N115.03W
Eugowra Australia **93** 33.24S148.25E
Eume *r.* Spain **26** 43.25N 8.08W
Eunice La. U.S.A. **111** 30.30N 92.25W
Eunice N.Mex. U.S.A. **111** 32.26N103.09W
Eupen Belgium **16** 50.38N 6.04E
Euphrates *r.* *see* Nahr al Furāt *r.* Asia **65**
Eurdon U.S.A. **111** 33.55N 93.09W
Eure *d.* France **18** 49.10N 1.00E
Eure *r.* France **18** 49.18N 1.12E
Eure-et-Loire *d.* France **18** 48.30N 1.30E
Eureka Calif. U.S.A. **108** 40.47N124.09W
Eureka Kans. U.S.A. **111** 37.49N 96.17W
Eureka Nev. U.S.A. **108** 39.31N115.58W
Eureka Utah U.S.A. **108** 39.57N112.07W
Eurinilla *r.* Australia **92** 30.50S140.01E
Euriowie Australia **92** 31.22S141.42E
Euroa Australia **93** 36.46S145.35E
Europa, Picos de *mts.* Spain **26** 43.10N 4.50W
Europa Pt. Gibraltar **27** 36.10N 5.22W
Europe 8
Euskirchen Germany **38** 50.39N 6.47E
Euston Australia **92** 34.34S142.49E
Eutin Germany **38** 54.08N 10.37E
Eutsuk L. Canada **100** 53.20N126.45W
Evale Angola **78** 16.24S 15.50E
Evans, Lac *l.* Canada **102** 50.50N 77.00W
Evans Head *c.* Australia **93** 29.06S153.25E
Evanston Ill. U.S.A. **110** 42.02N 87.41W
Evanston Wyo. U.S.A. **108** 41.16N110.58W
Evansville U.S.A. **112** 38.00N 87.33W
Evelyn Creek *r.* Australia **92** 28.20S134.50E
Even Yehuda Israel **67** 32.16N 34.53E
Everard, C. Australia **93** 37.50S149.16E
Everard, L. Australia **92** 31.25S135.05E
Everard Range *mts.* Australia **91** 27.05S132.28E
Everest, Mt. China / Nepal **63** 27.59N 86.56E
Everett Penn. U.S.A. **114** 40.01N 78.23W
Everett Wash. U.S.A. **108** 47.59N122.13W
Everett, Mt. U.S.A. **115** 42.06N 73.25W
Everglades U.S.A. **113** 25.52N 81.23W
Everglades Nat. Park U.S.A. **113** 25.27N 80.53W
Everöd Sweden **43** 55.54N 14.06E
Evesham U.K. **13** 52.06N 1.57W
Évian-les-Bains France **21** 46.23N 6.35E
Evijärvi Finland **40** 63.22N 23.29E
Evinayong Equat. Guinea **78** 1.27N 10.34E
Evisa France **21** 42.15N 8.47E
Evje Norway **42** 58.36N 7.51E
Évora Portugal **27** 38.34N 7.54W
Évora *d.* Portugal **27** 38.40N 7.55W
Évreux France **18** 49.01N 1.09E
'Evron Israel **67** 32.59N 35.06E
Évros *r.* *see* Meriç *r.* Greece **34**
Evrótas *r.* Greece **35** 36.48N 22.40E
Évry France **19** 48.38N 2.27E
Évvoia *i.* Greece **35** 38.40N 24.00E
Ewe, Loch U.K. **14** 57.48N 5.38W
Ewing U.S.A. **110** 42.16N 98.21W
Ewo Congo **78** 0.48S 14.47E
Excelsior Springs *town* U.S.A. **110** 39.20N 94.13W
Exe *r.* U.K. **13** 50.40N 3.28W
Exeter Canada **104** 43.21N 81.29W
Exeter U.K. **13** 50.43N 3.31W

Exeter to **Flint**

Exeter Nebr. U.S.A. **110** 40.39N 97.27W
Exeter N.H. U.S.A. **115** 42.59N 70.57W
Exmoor Forest *hills* U.K. **13** 51.08N 3.45W
Exmore U.S.A. **113** 37.32N 75.49W
Exmouth Australia **88** 21.54S114.10E
Exmouth U.K. **13** 50.37N 3.24W
Exmouth G. Australia **88** 22.00S114.20E
Expedition Range *mts.* Australia **90** 24.30S149.05E
Extremadura *d.* Spain **27** 39.25N 6.00W
Exuma Is. Bahamas **117** 24.00N 76.00W
Eyasi, L. Tanzania **79** 3.40S 35.00E
Eydehavn Norway **42** 58.31N 8.53E
Eye U.K. **13** 52.19N 1.09E
Eyemouth U.K. **14** 55.52N 2.05W
Eygurande France **20** 45.40N 2.26E
Eyjafjördhur *est.* Iceland **40** 65.54N 18.15W
Eyl Somali Rep. **71** 8.00N 49.51E
Eymet France **20** 44.40N 0.24E
Eymoutiers France **20** 45.44N 1.44E
Eyrarbakki Iceland **40** 63.52N 21.09W
Eyre *r.* Australia **90** 26.40S139.00E
Eyre, L. Australia **92** 28.30S137.25E
Eyre Pen. Australia **92** 34.00S135.45E
Ezequil Ramos Mexia, Embalse *resr.* Argentina **125** 39.20S 69.00W
Ezine Turkey **34** 39.48N 26.12E

F

Faaone Tahiti **85** 17.40S149.18W
Fåberg Norway **41** 61.10N 10.22E
Fåborg Denmark **42** 55.06N 10.15E
Fabre Canada **104** 47.12N 79.23W
Fabriano Italy **30** 43.20N 12.54E
Facatativá Colombia **122** 4.48N 74.32W
Facundo Argentina **125** 45.19S 69.59W
Fada Chad **72** 17.14N 21.33E
Fada-N'Gourma Burkina **76** 12.03N 0.22E
Fadd Hungary **31** 46.28N 18.50E
Faenza Italy **30** 44.17N 11.53E
Fafa Mali **76** 15.20N 0.43E
Fafe Portugal **26** 41.27N 8.10W
Fafen *r.* Ethiopia **71** 6.07N 44.20E
Fagamalo W. Samoa **84** 13.24S172.22W
Făgăraş Romania **37** 45.51N 24.58E
Fagernes Norway **41** 60.59N 9.17E
Fagersta Sweden **43** 60.00N 15.47E
Faguibine, Lac *l.* Mali **76** 16.45N 3.54W
Fagus Egypt **66** 30.44N 31.47E
Fā'id Egypt **66** 30.19N 32.19E
Fairbanks U.S.A. **98** 64.50N147.50W
Fairborn U.S.A. **112** 39.48N 84.03W
Fairbury U.S.A. **110** 40.08N 97.11W
Fairfax U.S.A. **111** 36.34N 96.42W
Fairfield Ala. U.S.A. **113** 33.29N 86.59W
Fairfield Calif. U.S.A. **108** 38.15N122.03W
Fairfield Conn. U.S.A. **115** 41.09N 73.15W
Fairfield Ill. U.S.A. **110** 38.22N 88.23W
Fairfield Iowa U.S.A. **110** 40.56N 91.57W
Fairgrove U.S.A. **104** 43.31N 83.33W
Fairhaven Mass. U.S.A. **115** 41.39N 70.54W
Fair Haven N.Y. U.S.A. **114** 43.19N 76.42W
Fair Haven Vt. U.S.A. **115** 43.36N 73.16W
Fair Head U.K. **15** 55.13N 6.09W
Fair Isle U.K. **14** 59.32N 1.38W
Fairlie New Zealand **86** 44.06S170.50E
Fairmont Minn. U.S.A. **110** 43.39N 94.28W
Fairmont W.Va. U.S.A. **114** 39.29N 80.09W
Fairport U.S.A. **114** 43.06N 77.27W
Fairport Harbor U.S.A. **114** 41.45N 81.17W
Fairview Canada **100** 56.05N118.25W
Fairview Mich. U.S.A. **104** 44.44N 84.03W
Fairview Mont. U.S.A. **108** 47.51N104.03W
Fairview Okla. U.S.A. **111** 36.16N 98.29W
Fairview Penn. U.S.A. **114** 42.03N 80.13W
Fairview Utah U.S.A. **108** 39.38N111.26W
Fairweather, Mt. U.S.A. **100** 59.00N137.30W
Faisalābād Pakistan **62** 31.25N 73.05E
Faistós *site* Greece **35** 35.01N 24.48E
Faith U.S.A. **110** 45.02N102.02W
Faizābād India **63** 26.47N 82.08E
Fajr, Wādī *r.* Saudi Arabia **64** 30.00N 38.25E
Fakaofo Pacific Oc. **84** 9.30S171.15W
Fakenham U.K. **12** 52.50N 0.51E
Fakfak Indonesia **59** 2.55S132.17E
Fakse Denmark **43** 55.15N 12.08E
Fakse Bugte *b.* Denmark **43** 55.10N 12.15E
Falaise France **18** 48.54N 0.12W
Falakrón Óros *mts.* Greece **34** 41.15N 23.58E
Falam Burma **56** 22.58N 93.45E
Falcarragh Rep. of Ire. **15** 55.08N 8.06W
Falconara Marittima Italy **30** 43.37N 13.24E
Falconbridge Canada **104** 46.35N 80.48W
Falcone, Capo del *c.* Italy **32** 40.57N 8.12E
Falconer U.S.A. **114** 42.07N 79.12W
Falcon Resr. U.S.A. **111** 26.37N 99.11W
Falealupo W. Samoa **84** 13.29S172.47W
Falémé *r.* Senegal **76** 14.55N 12.00W
Faleshty U.S.S.R. **37** 47.30N 27.45E
Falfurrias U.S.A. **111** 27.14N 98.09W
Falkenberg Germany **38** 51.35N 13.14E
Falkenberg Sweden **43** 56.54N 12.28E
Falkenhagen Germany **38** 53.12N 12.12E
Falkensee Germany **38** 52.33N 13.04E
Falkenstein Germany **39** 49.06N 12.30E
Falkirk U.K. **14** 56.00N 3.48W
Falkland Is. Atlantic Oc. **125** 51.45W 59.00W
Falkland Sd. *str.* Falkland Is. **125** 51.45W 59.25W
Falköping Sweden **43** 58.10N 13.31E
Fallbrook U.S.A. **109** 33.23N117.15W
Fallon U.S.A. **108** 46.50N105.07W
Fall River *town* U.S.A. **115** 41.43N 71.08W
Falls City U.S.A. **110** 40.03N 95.36W
Falmouth U.K. **13** 50.09N 5.05W
Falmouth Mass. U.S.A. **115** 41.34N 70.38W
Falmouth Va. U.S.A. **114** 38.19N 77.28W
False B. R.S.A. **80** 34.10S 18.40E
False C. U.S.A. **115** 38.29N 74.59W
False Pt. India **63** 20.22N 86.52E
Falset Spain **25** 41.08N 0.49E
Falster *i.* Denmark **41** 54.48N 11.58E
Falsterbo Sweden **43** 55.24N 12.50E
Fălticeni Romania **37** 47.28N 26.18E
Falun Sweden **41** 60.36N 15.38E
Famagusta *see* Ammókhostos Cyprus **66**
Family L. Canada **101** 51.54N 95.30W
Famoso U.S.A. **109** 35.36N119.14W
Fanárion Greece **34** 39.50N 21.47E
Fandriana Madagascar **81** 20.14S 47.23E
Fangak Sudan **73** 9.04N 30.53E
Fangcheng China **54** 33.16N112.59E
Fangdou Shan *mts.* China **55** 30.36N108.45E
Fang Xian China **55** 32.04N110.47E
Fanjing Shan *mtn.* China **55** 27.57N108.50E
Fannich, Loch U.K. **14** 57.38N 5.00W
Fanning I. *see* Tabuaeran *i.* Kiribati **85**
Fanö *i.* Denmark **42** 55.25N 8.25E
Fano Italy **30** 43.50N 13.00E
Fan Xian China **54** 35.59N115.31E
Faradje Zaïre **79** 3.45N 29.43E
Faradofay Madagascar **81** 25.02S 47.00E
Farafangana Madagascar **81** 22.49S 47.50E
Farāfirah, Wāḥāt al *oasis* Egypt **64** 27.15N 28.10E
Farāh Afghan. **62** 32.22N 62.07E
Farāh *d.* Afghan. **62** 33.00N 62.00E
Farāh *r.* Afghan. **62** 31.29N 61.24E
Faranah Guinea **76** 10.01N 10.47W
Farasān, Jazā'ir *is.* Saudi Arabia **72** 16.48N 41.54E
Faratsiho Madagascar **81** 19.24S 46.57E
Faraulep *is.* Mariana Is. **59** 8.36N144.33E
Fardes *r.* Spain **27** 37.35N 3.00W
Fareara, Pt. Tahiti **85** 17.52S149.39W
Fareham U.K. **13** 50.52N 1.11W
Farewell, C. *see* Farvel, Kap *c.* Greenland **99**
Farewell, C. New Zealand **86** 40.30S172.35E
Färgelanda Sweden **42** 58.34N 11.59E
Fargo U.S.A. **110** 46.52N 96.48W
Fāri'ah *r.* Jordan **67** 32.06N 35.31E
Faribault U.S.A. **110** 44.18N 93.16W
Farīdpur Bangla. **63** 23.36N 89.50E
Farim Guinea Bissau **76** 12.30N 15.09W
Farina Australia **92** 30.05S138.20E
Färjestaden Sweden **43** 56.39N 16.27E
Farkwa Tanzania **79** 5.26S 35.15E
Farley Canada **105** 46.18N 76.00W
Farmerville U.S.A. **111** 32.47N 92.24W
Farmington Mo. U.S.A. **111** 37.47N 90.25W
Farmington N.H. U.S.A. **115** 43.24N 71.04W
Farmington N.Mex. U.S.A. **108** 36.44N108.12W
Farnborough U.K. **13** 51.17N 0.46W
Farne Is. U.K. **12** 55.38N 1.36W
Farnham Canada **105** 45.17N 72.59W
Farnham U.K. **13** 51.13N 0.49W
Faro Brazil **123** 2.11S 56.44W
Faro Portugal **27** 37.01N 7.56W
Faro *d.* Portugal **27** 37.15N 8.10W
Faroe Bank *f.* Atlantic Oc. **10** 61.00N 9.00W
Faroe Is. Europe **10** 62.00N 7.00W
Fårön *i.* Sweden **43** 57.56N 19.08E
Fårösund Sweden **43** 57.52N 19.03E
Farrell U.S.A. **114** 41.13N 80.30W
Farrukhābād India **63** 27.24N 79.34E
Fársala Greece **35** 39.18N 22.23E
Fārsī Afghan. **62** 33.47N 63.15E
Farsö Denmark **42** 56.47N 9.21E
Farsund Norway **42** 58.05N 6.48E
Fartak, Ra's *c.* Yemen **71** 15.38N 52.15E
Farvel, Kap *c.* Greenland **99** 60.00N 44.20W
Farwell U.S.A. **111** 34.23N103.02W
Fasā Iran **65** 28.55N 53.38E
Fasano Italy **33** 40.50N 17.22E
Fastov U.S.S.R. **37** 50.08N 29.59E
Fatehābād India **62** 29.31N 75.28E
Fatehjang Pakistan **62** 33.34N 72.39E
Fatehpur Rāj. India **62** 27.59N 74.57E
Fatehpur Uttar P. India **63** 25.56N 80.48E
Fatehpur Pakistan **62** 31.10N 71.13E
Fatehpur Sīkri India **63** 27.06N 77.40E
Fatick Senegal **76** 14.19N 16.27W
Fátima Portugal **27** 39.37N 8.39W
Fatu Hiva *i.* Is. Marquises **85** 10.27S138.39W
Fatwā India **63** 25.31N 85.19E
Faucilles, Monts *mts.* France **19** 48.07N 6.16E
Faulkton U.S.A. **110** 45.02N 99.08W
Faulquemont France **19** 49.03N 6.36E
Făurei Romania **37** 45.04N 27.15E
Fauske Norway **40** 67.17N 15.25E
Favara Italy **32** 37.19N 13.40E
Faverges France **21** 45.45N 6.18E
Favignana *i.* Italy **32** 37.56N 12.19E
Fawcett Canada **100** 54.34N114.06W
Fawcett L. Canada **102** 51.20N 91.46W
Fawn *r.* Canada **102** 55.20N 88.20W
Faxaflói *b.* Iceland **40** 64.30N 22.50W
Faxe *r.* Sweden **40** 63.15N 17.15E
Fayence France **21** 43.37N 6.41E
Fayette U.S.A. **113** 33.42N 87.50W
Fayetteville Ark. U.S.A. **111** 36.04N 94.10W
Fayetteville N.C. U.S.A. **113** 35.03N 78.53W
Fayetteville N.Y. U.S.A. **115** 43.02N 76.00W
Fayetteville Tenn. U.S.A. **113** 35.08N 86.33W
Fayl-Billot France **19** 47.47N 5.36E
Fāzilka India **62** 30.24N 74.02E
Fāzilpur Pakistan **62** 29.18N 70.27E
Fdérik Mauritania **74** 22.30N 12.30W
Feale *r.* Rep. of Ire. **15** 52.28N 9.37W
Fear, C. U.S.A. **113** 33.50N 77.58W
Fécamp France **18** 49.45N 0.22E
Federación Argentina **125** 31.00S 57.55W
Federal Argentina **125** 30.55S 58.45W
Federal Capital Territory *d.* Nigeria **77** 8.50N 7.00E
Federal States of Micronesia Pacific Oc. **84** 10.00N155.00E
Fedovo U.S.S.R. **44** 62.22N 39.21E
Fedulki U.S.S.R. **44** 65.00N 66.10E
Feeagh, Lough Rep. of Ire. **15** 53.56N 9.35W
Feerfeer Somali Rep. **71** 5.07N 45.07E
Fehmarn *i.* Germany **38** 54.28N 11.08E
Fehmarn Belt *str.* Germany **38** 54.33N 11.20E
Feia, Lagoa *l.* Brazil **126** 22.00S 41.20W
Feijó Brazil **122** 8.09S 70.21W
Feilding New Zealand **86** 40.10S175.25E
Feira Zambia **79** 15.30S 30.27E
Feira de Santana Brazil **123** 12.17S 38.53W
Felanitx Spain **25** 39.28N 3.08E
Feldbach Austria **31** 46.57N 15.54E
Feldberg *mtn.* Germany **39** 47.51N 8.02E
Feldkirch Austria **39** 47.14N 9.36E
Feldkirchen in Kärnten Austria **39** 46.43N 14.05E
Felixstowe U.K. **13** 51.58N 1.20E
Fellbach Germany **39** 48.48N 9.15E
Felletin France **20** 45.53N 2.10E
Feltre Italy **30** 46.01N 11.54E
Femunden *l.* Norway **41** 62.12N 11.52E
Femundsenden Norway **41** 61.55N 11.55E
Fenelon Falls Canada **104** 44.32N 78.45W
Fengcheng Jiangxi China **55** 28.10N115.45E
Fengcheng Liaoning China **54** 40.29N124.00E
Fengfeng China **54** 36.35N114.28E
Fenggang China **55** 27.58N107.47E
Fengjie China **55** 31.02N109.31E
Fengnan China **54** 39.30N117.58E
Fengpin Taiwan **55** 23.36N121.31E
Fengrun China **54** 39.51N118.08E
Fen He *r.* China **54** 35.30N110.38E
Feni Bangla. **63** 23.01N 91.20E
Feno, Capo di *c.* France **21** 41.57N 8.36E
Fenoarivo Madagascar **81** 18.26S 46.34E
Fenoarivo Atsinanana Madagascar **81** 17.22S 49.25E
Fensfjorden *est.* Norway **41** 60.51N 4.50E
Fenton U.S.A. **112** 42.48N 83.42W
Fenwick U.S.A. **114** 38.14N 80.35W
Fenyang China **54** 37.10N111.40E
Feodosiya U.S.S.R. **45** 45.03N 35.23E
Ferdows Iran **65** 34.00N 58.10E
Fère-Champenoise France **19** 48.45N 3.59E
Fère-en-Tardenois France **19** 49.12N 3.31E
Ferentino Italy **32** 41.42N 13.15E
Fergana U.S.S.R. **52** 40.23N 71.19E
Fergus Canada **104** 43.42N 80.22W
Fergus Falls *town* U.S.A. **110** 46.17N 96.04W
Ferguson U.S.A. **110** 38.46N 90.19W
Fergusson I. P.N.G. **90** 9.30S150.40E
Ferkéssédougou Ivory Coast **76** 9.30N 5.10W
Ferlach Austria **31** 46.31N 14.18E
Fermanagh *d.* U.K. **15** 54.21N 7.40W
Fermo Italy **31** 43.09N 13.43E
Fermoselle Spain **26** 41.19N 6.23W
Fermoy Rep. of Ire. **15** 52.08N 8.17W
Fernandina Beach *town* U.S.A. **113** 30.40N 81.26W
Fernando de Noronha *i* Atlantic Oc. **127** 3.50S 32.25W
Fernán-Núñez Spain **27** 37.40N 4.43W
Fernlee Australia **93** 28.12S147.05E
Férrai Greece **34** 40.53N 26.10E
Ferrandina Italy **33** 40.29N 16.28E
Ferrara Italy **30** 44.50N 11.35E
Ferrato, Capo *c.* Italy **32** 39.18N 9.38E
Ferreira do Alentejo Portugal **27** 38.03N 8.07W
Ferreñafe Peru **122** 6.42S 79.45W
Ferret, Cap *c.* France **20** 44.37N 1.15W
Ferriday U.S.A. **111** 31.38N 91.33W
Ferrières France **19** 48.05N 2.47E
Fès Morocco **74** 34.05N 4.57W
Feshi Zaïre **78** 6.08S 18.12E
Festubert Canada **105** 47.12N 72.40W
Festus U.S.A. **110** 38.13N 90.24W
Feteşti Romania **37** 44.23N 27.50E
Fethiye Turkey **64** 36.37N 29.06E
Fetlar *i.* U.K. **14** 60.37N 0.52W
Fetsund Norway **42** 59.56N 11.10E
Feucht Germany **38** 49.22N 11.13E
Feuchtwangen Germany **39** 49.10N 10.20E
Feuilles, Rivière aux *r.* Canada **99** 58.47N 70.06W
Feurs France **21** 45.45N 4.14E
Fevik Norway **42** 58.23N 8.42E
Fevzipaşa Turkey **64** 37.07N 36.38E
Fianarantsoa Madagascar **81** 21.26S 47.05E
Fichē Ethiopia **73** 9.52N 38.46E
Fichtel Gebirge *mts.* Germany **38** 50.00N 11.50E
Fidenza Italy **30** 44.52N 10.03E
Field Canada **104** 46.32N 80.03W
Fier Albania **34** 40.43N 19.33E
Fiesch Switz. **39** 46.20N 8.10E
Fife *d.* U.K. **14** 56.10N 3.10W
Fife Ness *c.* U.K. **14** 56.17N 2.36W
Figeac France **20** 44.37N 2.02E
Figeholm Sweden **43** 57.22N 16.33E
Figueira da Foz Portugal **26** 40.09N 8.52W
Figueres Spain **25** 42.16N 2.58E
Fihaonana Madagascar **81** 18.36S 47.12E
Fiherenana *r.* Madagascar **81** 23.19S 43.37E
Fiji Pacific Oc. **84** 18.00S178.00E
Fīk' Ethiopia **73** 8.10N 42.18E
Filabres, Sierra de los *mts.* Spain **27** 37.13N 2.20W
Filabusi Zimbabwe **80** 20.34S 29.20E
Filadelfia Italy **33** 38.48N 16.18E
Fildegrand *r.* Canada **105** 46.18N 77.51W
Filey U.K. **12** 54.13N 0.18W
Fili *site* Greece **35** 38.10N 23.40E
Filiaşi Romania **37** 44.33N 23.31E
Filiátes Greece **34** 39.38N 20.16E
Filiatrá Greece **35** 37.09N 21.35E
Filicudi, Isola *i.* Italy **33** 38.35N 14.34E
Filingué Niger **77** 14.21N 3.22E
Filippoi *site* Greece **34** 41.00N 24.16E
Filipstad Sweden **43** 59.43N 14.10E
Fillmore Canada **101** 49.50N103.25W
Fillmore Calif. U.S.A. **109** 34.24N118.55W
Fillmore N.Y. U.S.A. **114** 42.28N 78.07W
Filtu Ethiopia **73** 5.05N 40.42E
Fimi *r.* Zaïre **78** 3.00S 17.00E
Finale Emilia Italy **30** 44.50N 11.17E
Finale Ligure Italy **30** 44.10N 8.20E
Finarwa Ethiopia **73** 13.05N 38.58E
Finch Canada **105** 45.11N 75.07W
Findhorn *r.* U.K. **14** 57.38N 3.37W
Findlay U.S.A. **112** 41.02N 83.40W
Findlay, Mt. Canada **100** 50.04N116.10W
Finger Lakes U.S.A. **114** 42.55N 76.44W
Finistère *d.* France **18** 48.20N 4.00W
Finisterre, Cabo de *c.* Spain **26** 42.53N 9.16W
Finke Australia **90** 25.35S134.34E
Finke *r.* Australia **91** 27.00S136.10E
Finland Europe **44** 64.30N 27.00E
Finland, G. of Finland/U.S.S.R. **41** 59.30N 24.00E
Finlay *r.* Canada **100** 57.00N125.05W
Finley Australia **93** 35.40S145.34E
Finmark Canada **102** 48.36N 89.44W
Finn *r.* Rep. of Ire. **15** 54.50N 7.30W
Finnmark *d.* Norway **40** 70.10N 26.00E
Finschhafen P.N.G. **59** 6.35S147.51E
Finse Norway **41** 60.36N 7.30E
Finspång Sweden **43** 58.43N 15.47E
Finsterwalde Germany **38** 51.38N 13.42E
Fiora *r.* Italy **30** 42.20N 11.34E
Fiorenzuola d'Arda Italy **30** 44.56N 9.55E
Fīq Syria **67** 32.47N 35.42E
Firat *r.* Turkey *see* Al Furāt *r.* Asia **64**
Firebag *r.* Canada **101** 57.45N111.20W
Firedrake L. Canada **101** 61.25N104.30W
Firenze Italy **30** 43.46N 11.15E
Firenzuola Italy **30** 44.07N 11.23E
Firminy France **21** 45.23N 4.18E
Firozābād India **63** 27.09N 78.25E
Firozpur India **62** 30.55N 74.38E
Firozpur Jhirka India **62** 27.48N 76.57E
Firth of Clyde *est.* U.K. **14** 55.35N 4.53W
Firth of Forth *est.* U.K. **14** 56.05N 3.00W
Firth of Lorn *est.* U.K. **14** 56.20N 5.40W
Firth of Tay *est.* U.K. **14** 56.24N 3.08W
Firūzābād Iran **65** 28.50N 52.35E
Firyuza U.S.S.R. **50** 37.55N 58.03E
Fish *r.* Namibia **80** 28.07S 17.45E
Fisher U.S.A. **111** 35.30N 90.58W
Fishers I. U.S.A. **115** 41.16N 72.02W
Fisher Str. Canada **99** 63.00N 84.00W
Fishguard U.K. **13** 51.59N 4.59W
Fiskárdhon Greece **35** 38.27N 20.35E
Fiskebäckskil Sweden **42** 58.15N 11.27E
Fiskenaesset Greenland **99** 63.05N 50.40W
Fiskivötn *f.* Iceland **40** 64.50N 20.45W
Fismes France **19** 49.18N 3.41E
Fitchburg U.S.A. **115** 42.35N 71.48W
Fitzgerald U.S.A. **113** 31.43N 83.16W
Fitz Roy Argentina **125** 47.00S 67.15W
Fitzroy *r.* Australia **88** 17.31S123.35E
Fitzroy Crossing Australia **88** 18.13S125.33E
Fitzwilliam I. Canada **104** 45.30N 81.45W
Fiuggi Italy **32** 41.48N 13.13E
Fiumicino Italy **32** 41.46N 12.14E
Fivizzano Italy **30** 44.14N 10.08E
Fizi Zaïre **79** 4.18S 28.56E
Fjällåsen Sweden **40** 67.29N 20.10E
Fjällbacka Sweden **42** 58.36N 11.17E
Fjällsjo *r.* Sweden **40** 63.27N 17.06E
Fjerritslev Denmark **42** 57.05N 9.16E
Fjugesta Sweden **43** 59.10N 14.52E
Flå Norway **41** 60.25N 9.26E
Flagler U.S.A. **108** 39.18N103.04W
Flagstaff U.S.A. **109** 35.12N111.39W
Flagstaff B. St. Helena **127** 15.55S 5.40W
Flåm Norway **41** 60.50N 7.07E
Flamborough Head U.K. **12** 54.06N 0.05W
Fläming *f.* Germany **38** 52.00N 13.00E
Flaming Gorge Resr. U.S.A. **108** 41.15N109.30W
Flandre *f.* Belgium **16** 50.52N 3.00E
Flannan Is. U.K. **14** 58.16N 7.40W
Flåren *l.* Sweden **43** 57.02N 14.06E
Flåsjön *l.* Sweden **40** 64.06N 15.51E
Flat *r.* Canada **100** 61.51N126.00W
Flathead L. U.S.A. **108** 47.52N114.08W
Flatonia U.S.A. **111** 29.47N 97.06W
Flattery, C. Australia **90** 14.58S145.21E
Flattery, C. U.S.A. **106** 48.23N124.43W
Flatts Village Bermuda **127** 32.19N 64.44W
Flaxton U.S.A. **110** 48.54N102.24W
Fleetwood U.K. **12** 53.55N 3.01W
Flekkefjord *town* Norway **42** 58.17N 6.41E
Flemington U.S.A. **115** 40.31N 74.52W
Flen Sweden **43** 59.04N 16.35E
Flensburg Germany **38** 54.47N 9.26E
Flers France **18** 48.45N 0.34W
Flesherton Canada **104** 44.16N 80.33W
Fletcher Pond *resr.* U.S.A. **104** 44.58N 83.52W
Fleurance France **20** 43.50N 0.40E
Fleur-de-Lys Canada **103** 50.06N 56.08W
Flevoland *d.* Neth. **16** 52.25N 5.30E
Flinders *r.* Australia **90** 17.30S140.45E
Flinders B. Australia **89** 34.23S115.19E
Flinders I. S.A. Australia **92** 33.44S134.30E
Flinders I. Tas. Australia **91** 40.00S148.00E
Flinders Ranges *mts.* Australia **92** 31.25S138.45E
Flinders Reefs Australia **90** 17.37S148.31E
Flin Flon Canada **101** 54.46N101.53W
Flint U.K. **12** 53.15N 3.07W
Flint U.S.A. **104** 43.01N 83.41W
Flint *r.* Ga. U.S.A. **113** 30.52N 84.38W
Flint *r.* Mich. U.S.A. **104** 43.21N 84.03W

Fundão to **Genthin**

Fundão Portugal **27** 40.08N 7.30W
Fundy, B. of Canada **103** 45.00N 66.00W
Funing China **55** 23.37N105.36E
Funiu Shan *mts.* China **54** 33.40N112.20E
Funtua Nigeria **77** 11.34N 7.18E
Fuping China **54** 38.52N114.12E
Fuqing China **55** 25.43N119.22E
Furakawa Japan **57** 38.30N140.50E
Furancungo Mozambique **79** 14.51S 33.38E
Furculeşti Romania **34** 43.52N 25.09E
Fūrg Iran **65** 28.19N 55.10E
Furnas, Reprêsa de *resr.* Brazil **126** 20.45S 46.00W
Furneaux Group *is.* Australia **91** 40.15S148.15E
Furqlus Syria **66** 34.38N 37.08E
Fürstenau Germany **38** 52.31N 7.40E
Fürstenberg Germany **38** 52.11N 13.10E
Fürstenfeld Austria **31** 47.03N 16.05E
Fürstenfeldbruck Germany **39** 48.10N 11.15E
Fürstenwalde Germany **38** 52.21N 14.04E
Fürth Germany **39** 49.28N 10.59E
Furth im Wald Germany **39** 49.18N 12.51E
Furu-tone *r.* Japan **57** 35.58N139.51E
Fusagasugá Colombia **122** 4.22N 74.21W
Fushun China **54** 41.50N123.55E
Fusong China **53** 42.17N127.19E
Füssen Germany **38** 47.34N 10.42E
Fusui China **55** 22.35N107.57E
Fuwah Egypt **66** 31.12N 30.33E
Fu Xian Liaoning China **54** 39.35N122.07E
Fu Xian Shaanxi China **54** 36.00N109.20E
Fuxin China **54** 42.08N121.45E
Fuyang Anhui China **54** 32.52N115.52E
Fuyang Zhejiang China **55** 30.03N119.57E
Fuyang He *r.* China **54** 38.10N116.08E
Fuyu China **53** 45.12N124.49E
Fuyuan Heilongjiang China **53** 48.20N134.18E
Fuyuan Yunnan China **55** 25.40N104.14E
Fuzhou Fujian China **55** 26.09N119.21E
Fuzhou Jiangxi China **55** 28.01N116.13E
Fyn *i.* Denmark **42** 55.20N 10.30E
Fyne, Loch U.K. **14** 55.55N 5.23W
Fyresvatn *l.* Norway **42** 59.06N 8.12E

G

Ga Ghana **76** 9.48N 2.28W
Gaalkacyo Somali Rep. **71** 6.49N 47.23E
Gabare Bulgaria **34** 43.19N 23.55E
Gabas *r.* France **20** 43.46N 0.42W
Gabela Angola **78** 10.52S 14.24E
Gabès Tunisia **75** 33.53N 10.07E
Gabès, Golfe de *g.* Tunisia **75** 34.00N 10.25E
Gabir Sudan **73** 8.35N 24.40E
Gabon Africa **78** 0.00 12.00E
Gabon *r.* Gabon **78** 0.15N 10.00E
Gaborone Botswana **80** 24.45S 25.55E
Gabras Sudan **73** 10.16N 26.14E
Gabriels U.S.A. **105** 44.26N 74.13W
Gabriel y Galan, Embalse de *resr.* Spain **26** 40.15N 6.15W
Gabrovo Bulgaria **34** 42.52N 25.27E
Gacé France **18** 48.48N 0.18E
Gach Sārān Iran **65** 30.13N 50.49E
Gacko Yugo. **31** 43.10N 18.32E
Gada Nigeria **77** 13.50N 5.40E
Gādarwāra India **63** 22.55N 78.47E
Gäddede Sweden **40** 64.30N 14.15E
Gádor Spain **27** 36.57N 2.29W
Gádor, Sierra de *mts.* Spain **27** 36.54N 2.47W
Gadot Israel **67** 33.01N 35.37E
Gadra Pakistan **62** 25.40N 70.37E
Gadsden U.S.A. **113** 34.00N 86.00W
Gaeta Italy **32** 41.12N 13.35E
Gaeta, Golfo di *g.* Italy **32** 41.06N 13.30E
Gaferut *i.* Caroline Is. **59** 9.14N145.23E
Gaffney U.S.A. **113** 35.03N 81.40W
Gafsa Tunisia **75** 34.25N 8.48E
Gagarin U.S.S.R. **44** 55.38N 35.00E
Gagetown U.S.A. **104** 43.44N 83.16W
Gagliano del Capo Italy **33** 39.50N 18.22E
Gagnoa Ivory Coast **76** 6.04N 5.55W
Gagnon Canada **103** 51.53N 68.10W
Gagnon, Lac *l.* Canada **105** 46.07N 75.07W
Gaibānda Bangla. **63** 25.19N 89.33E
Gaillac France **20** 43.54N 1.55E
Gaillon France **18** 49.10N 1.20E
Gailtaler Alpen *mts.* Austria **39** 46.42N 13.15E
Gaines U.S.A. **104** 42.52N 83.55W
Gainesville Fla. U.S.A. **113** 29.37N 82.21W
Gainesville Ga. U.S.A. **113** 34.17N 83.50W
Gainesville Mo. U.S.A. **111** 36.36N 92.26W
Gainesville Tex. U.S.A. **111** 33.37N 97.08W
Gainesville Va. U.S.A. **114** 38.48N 77.34W
Gainsborough U.K. **12** 53.23N 0.46W
Gairdner *r.* Australia **89** 34.20S119.30E
Gairdner, L. Australia **92** 31.30S136.00E
Gairloch U.K. **14** 57.43N 5.40W
Gaithersburg U.S.A. **114** 39.09N 77.12W
Gai Xian China **54** 40.25N122.15E
Gaj Yugo. **31** 45.29N 17.02E
Gal, Punta de *c.* Spain **25** 39.10N 1.05E
Galana *r.* Kenya **79** 3.12S 40.09E
Galangue Angola **78** 13.40S 16.00E
Galapagos, Islas *is.* Ecuador **97** 0.20S 91.00W
Galaroza Spain **27** 37.55N 6.42W
Galashiels U.K. **14** 55.37N 2.49W
Galaţi Romania **37** 45.27N 27.59E
Galatina Italy **33** 40.10N 18.10E
Galaxídhion Greece **35** 38.22N 22.23E
Galdhöpiggen *mtn.* Norway **41** 61.37N 8.17E
Galeana Mexico **111** 24.50N100.04W
Galeh Dār Iran **65** 27.36N 52.42E
Galena Alas. U.S.A. **98** 64.43N157.00W
Galena Md. U.S.A. **115** 39.20N 75.55W
Galesburg U.S.A. **110** 40.57N 90.22W
Galeton U.S.A. **114** 41.44N 77.39W
Galich U.S.S.R. **44** 58.20N 42.12E
Galicia *d.* Spain **26** 42.45N 8.00W
Galilee *see* HaGalil *f.* Israel **67**
Galilee, L. Australia **90** 22.21S145.48E
Galilee, Sea of *see* Yam Kinneret *l.* Israel **67**
Galion U.S.A. **114** 40.44N 82.47W
Galiuro Mts. U.S.A. **109** 32.40N110.20W
Gallarate Italy **30** 45.40N 8.47E
Gallatin U.S.A. **113** 36.22N 86.28W
Galle Sri Lanka **61** 6.01N 80.13E
Gállego *r.* Spain **25** 41.39N 0.51W
Gallegos *r.* Argentina **125** 51.35S 69.00W
Galley Head Rep. of Ire. **15** 51.32N 8.57W
Galliate Italy **30** 45.29N 8.42E
Gallinas, Punta *c.* Colombia **122** 12.20N 71.30W
Gallipoli Italy **33** 40.03N 18.00E
Gallipoli *see* Gelibolu Turkey **34**
Gallipolis U.S.A. **114** 38.49N 82.12W
Gällivare Sweden **40** 67.07N 20.45E
Gällö Sweden **40** 62.56N 15.15E
Gallo, Capo *c.* Italy **32** 38.13N 13.19E
Galloo I. U.S.A. **105** 43.54N 76.25W
Galloway *f.* U.K. **14** 55.00N 4.28W
Gallup U.S.A. **109** 35.32N108.44W
Gallur Spain **25** 41.52N 1.19W
Gal'on Israel **67** 31.38N 34.51E
Galong Australia **93** 34.37S148.34E
Galston U.K. **14** 55.36N 4.23W
Galt Canada **104** 43.21N 80.19W
Galtür Austria **39** 46.58N 10.11E
Galty Mts. Rep. of Ire. **15** 52.20N 8.10W
Galva U.S.A. **110** 41.10N 90.03W
Galveston U.S.A. **111** 29.18N 94.48W
Galveston B. U.S.A. **111** 29.36N 94.57W
Galvez Argentina **124** 32.03S 61.14W
Galway Rep. of Ire. **15** 53.17N 9.04W
Galway *d.* Rep. of Ire. **15** 53.25N 9.00W
Galway B. Rep. of Ire. **15** 53.12N 9.07W
Gam *r.* Vietnam **55** 18.47N105.40E
Gamagōri Japan **57** 34.50N137.14E
Gamawa Nigeria **77** 12.10N 10.31E
Gamba China **63** 28.18N 88.32E
Gambēla Ethiopia **73** 8.18N 34.37E
Gambia Africa **76** 13.10N 16.00W
Gambia *r.* Gambia **76** 13.28N 15.55W
Gambier, Îles *is.* Pacific Oc. **85** 23.10S135.00W
Gambier I. Australia **92** 35.12S136.32E
Gambo Canada **103** 48.46N 54.14W
Gamboli Pakistan **62** 29.50N 68.26E
Gamboma Congo **78** 1.50S 15.58E
Gamboula C.A.R. **77** 4.05N 15.10E
Gamia Benin **77** 10.24N 2.45E
Gamlakarleby *see* Kokkola Finland **40**
Gamleby Sweden **43** 57.54N 16.24E
Gamo Gofa *d.* Ethiopia **73** 6.00N 37.00E
Ganado U.S.A. **109** 35.43N109.33W
Gananoque Canada **105** 44.20N 76.10W
Ganbashao China **55** 26.37N107.41E
Ganda Angola **78** 12.58S 14.39E
Gandajika Zaïre **78** 6.46S 23.58E
Gandak *r.* India **63** 25.40N 85.13E
Gāndarbal Jammu & Kashmir **62** 34.14N 74.47E
Gandāva Pakistan **62** 28.37N 67.29E
Gander Canada **103** 48.57N 54.34W
Gander *r.* Canada **103** 49.15N 54.30W
Ganderkesee Germany **38** 53.02N 8.32E
Gander L. Canada **103** 48.55N 54.40W
Gandesa Spain **25** 41.03N 0.26E
Gandevi India **62** 20.49N 73.00E
Gāndhi Sāgar *resr.* India **62** 24.18N 75.21E
Gandía Spain **25** 38.58N 0.11W
Gandou Congo **78** 2.25N 17.25E
Ganga *r.* India **63** 23.22N 90.32E
Gangāpur Rāj. India **62** 26.29N 76.43E
Gangāpur Rāj. India **62** 25.13N 74.16E
Gangara Niger **77** 14.35N 8.40E
Gāngārāmpur India **63** 25.24N 88.31E
Gangdhār India **62** 23.57N 75.37E
Gangdisê Shan *mts.* China **63** 31.15N 82.00E
Ganges France **20** 43.56N 3.42E
Ganges *r. see* Ganga *r.* India **63**
Gangi Italy **33** 37.49N 14.13E
Gangotri India **63** 30.56N 79.02E
Gangtok India **63** 27.20N 88.37E
Gangu China **54** 34.30N105.30E
Gan Jiang *r.* China **55** 29.10N116.00E
Ganmain Australia **93** 34.47S147.01E
Gannat France **20** 46.06N 3.12E
Gannett Peak *mtn.* U.S.A. **108** 43.11N109.39W
Ganquan China **54** 36.19N109.19E
Gan Shemu'el Israel **67** 32.27N 34.57E
Gansu *d.* China **52** 36.00N103.00E
Ganta Liberia **76** 7.15N 8.59W
Gantheaume, C. Australia **92** 36.05S137.27E
Gan Yavne Israel **67** 31.47N 34.43E
Ganye Nigeria **77** 8.24N 12.02E
Ganyu China **54** 34.50N119.07E
Ganzhou China **55** 25.49N114.50E
Gao Mali **76** 16.19N 0.09W
Gao *d.* Mali **77** 17.20N 1.25E
Gao'an China **55** 28.25N115.22E
Gaohe China **55** 22.46N112.57E
Gaolan China **54** 36.23N103.55E
Gaolou Ling *mtn.* China **55** 24.47N106.48E
Gaomi China **54** 36.23N119.44E
Gaoping China **54** 35.48N112.55E
Gaotai China **52** 39.20N 99.58E
Gaoua Burkina **76** 10.20N 3.09W
Gaoual Guinea **76** 11.44N 13.14W
Gaoxiong Taiwan **55** 22.40N120.18E
Gaoyou China **54** 32.40N119.30E
Gaoyou Hu *l.* China **54** 32.50N119.25E
Gaozhou China **55** 21.58N110.59E
Gap France **21** 44.34N 6.05E
Gar China **63** 32.11N 79.59E
Gara, Lough Rep. of Ire. **15** 53.57N 8.27W
Garah Australia **93** 29.04S149.38E
Garanhuns Brazil **123** 8.53S 36.28W
Garba C.A.R. **73** 9.12N 20.30E
Gārbosh, Kūh-e *mtn.* Iran **65** 32.36N 50.02E
García de Sola, Embalse de *resr.* Spain **27** 39.15N 5.05W
Gard *r.* France **21** 43.51N 4.37E
Garda Italy **30** 45.34N 10.42E
Garda, Lago di *l.* Italy **30** 45.40N 10.41E
Gardelegen Germany **38** 52.31N 11.23E
Garden *r.* Canada **104** 46.32N 84.09W
Garden City Ala. U.S.A. **113** 34.01N 86.55W
Garden City Kans. U.S.A. **111** 37.58N100.53W
Garden Reach India **63** 22.33N 88.17E
Garden River *town* Canada **104** 46.33N 84.09W
Gardermoen Norway **42** 60.13N 11.06E
Gardēz Afghan. **62** 33.37N 69.07E
Gardiner U.S.A. **108** 45.02N110.42W
Gardiners I. U.S.A. **115** 41.05N 72.07W
Gardner U.S.A. **115** 42.34N 71.59W
Gardnerville U.S.A. **108** 38.56N119.45W
Gardone Val Trompia Italy **30** 45.41N 10.11E
Gardunha, Serra de *mts.* Portugal **27** 40.06N 7.30W
Garešnica Yugo. **31** 45.35N 16.56E
Garessio Italy **30** 44.12N 8.02E
Garet el Djenoun *mtn.* Algeria **75** 25.05N 5.25E
Gargaliánoi Greece **35** 37.04N 21.38E
Gargano, Testa del *c.* Italy **33** 41.49N 16.12E
Garhākota India **63** 23.46N 79.09E
Garhi Khairo Pakistan **62** 28.04N 67.59E
Garibaldi Prov. Park Canada **100** 49.50N122.40W
Garies R.S.A. **80** 30.34S 18.00E
Garigliano *r.* Italy **28** 41.13N 13.45E
Gariglione, Monte *mtn.* Italy **33** 39.09N 16.41E
Garissa Kenya **79** 0.27S 39.49E
Garko Nigeria **77** 11.45N 8.53E
Garland Tex. U.S.A. **111** 32.54N 96.39W
Garland Utah U.S.A. **108** 41.45N112.10W
Garlasco Italy **30** 45.12N 8.55E
Garlin France **20** 43.34N 0.15W
Garm Āb Afghan. **62** 32.14N 65.01E
Garmisch Partenkirchen Germany **39** 47.29N 11.05E
Garmsār Iran **65** 35.15N 52.21E
Garnett U.S.A. **110** 38.17N 95.14W
Garo Hills India **63** 25.45N 90.30E
Garonne *r.* France **20** 45.02N 0.36W
Garoua Cameroon **77** 9.17N 13.22E
Garoua Boulaï Cameroon **77** 5.54N 14.33E
Garrel Germany **38** 52.57N 8.01E
Garrettsville U.S.A. **114** 41.17N 81.06W
Garrison U.S.A. **111** 31.49N 94.30W
Garrison Resr. U.S.A. **110** 48.00N102.30W
Garron Pt. U.K. **15** 55.03N 5.57W
Garrovillas Spain **27** 39.43N 6.33W
Garry L. Canada **99** 66.00N100.00W
Garson Canada **104** 46.34N 80.52W
Garub Namibia **80** 26.33S 16.00E
Garut Indonesia **59** 7.15S107.55E
Garvão Portugal **26** 37.42N 8.21W
Garve U.K. **14** 57.37N 4.41W
Garvie Mts. New Zealand **86** 45.15S169.00E
Garwa India **63** 24.11N 83.49E
Gary U.S.A. **112** 41.34N 87.20W
Garyarsa China **52** 31.30N 80.40E
Gar Zangbo *r.* China **63** 32.25N 79.40E
Garzón Colombia **122** 2.14N 75.376
Gas City U.S.A. **112** 40.28N 85.37W
Gascogne, Golfe de *g.* France **17** 44.00N 2.40W
Gascony, G. of *see* Gascogne, Golfe de France **17**
Gascoyne *r.* Australia **88** 25.00S113.40E
Gascoyne Junction Australia **88** 25.02S115.15E
Gash *r.* Ethiopia *see* Qāsh *r.* Sudan **72**
Gashua Nigeria **77** 12.53N 11.02E
Gaspé Canada **103** 48.50N 64.30W
Gaspé, Cap de *c.* Canada **103** 48.45N 64.09W
Gaspé, Péninsule de *pen.* Canada **103** 48.30N 65.00W
Gaspésie Prov. Park Canada **103** 48.50N 65.45W
Gassaway U.S.A. **114** 38.40N 80.47W
Gassol Nigeria **77** 8.34N 10.25E
Gasteiz *see* Vitoria Spain **26**
Gastonia U.S.A. **113** 35.14N 81.12W
Gastoúni Greece **35** 37.51N 21.16E
Gastre Argentina **125** 42.17S 69.15W
Gata, Cabo de *c.* Spain **27** 36.44N 2.10W
Gata, Sierra de *mts.* Spain **26** 40.20N 6.35W
Gátas, Akrotírion *c.* Cyprus **66** 34.33N 33.03E
Gatchina U.S.S.R. **44** 59.32N 30.05E
Gatehouse of Fleet U.K. **14** 54.53N 4.12W
Gateshead U.K. **12** 54.57N 1.35W
Gatesville U.S.A. **111** 31.26N 97.45W
Gâtine, Hauteurs de *hills* France **18** 46.40N 0.50W
Gatineau Canada **105** 45.29N 75.40W
Gatineau *r.* Canada **105** 45.27N 75.40W
Gatineau N.C.C. Park Canada **105** 45.30N 75.52W
Gattinara Italy **30** 45.37N 8.22E
Gatton Australia **91** 27.32S152.18E
Gatun L. Panama **117** 9.20N 80.00W
Gauchy France **19** 49.49N 3.13E
Gaucín Spain **27** 36.31N 5.19W
Gauer L. Canada **101** 57.00N 97.50W
Gauhāti India **63** 26.11N 91.44E
Gauley *r.* U.S.A. **114** 38.10N 81.12W
Gaurela India **63** 22.45N 81.54E
Gauri Sankar *mtn.* China / Nepal **63** 27.57N 86.21E
Gausta *mtn.* Norway **42** 59.50N 8.35E
Gauting Germany **39** 48.04N 11.23E
Gavá Spain **25** 41.18N 2.00E
Gavāter Iran **65** 25.10N 61.31E
Gávdhos *i.* Greece **35** 34.50N 24.06E
Gāv Koshī Iran **65** 28.39N 57.13E
Gävle Sweden **41** 60.40N 17.10E
Gävleborg *d.* Sweden **41** 61.30N 16.15E
Gavorrano Italy **30** 42.55N 10.54E
Gávrion Greece **35** 37.52N 24.46E
Gawachab Namibia **80** 27.03S 17.50E
Gāwīlgarh Hills India **62** 21.30N 77.00E
Gawler Australia **92** 34.38S138.44E
Gawler Ranges *mts.* Australia **92** 32.30S136.00E
Gaya India **63** 24.47N 85.00E
Gaya Niger **77** 11.53N 3.31E
Gay Head *c.* U.S.A. **115** 41.21N 70.49W
Gaylord U.S.A. **104** 45.02N 84.40W
Gayndah Australia **90** 25.37S151.36E
Gayny U.S.S.R. **44** 60.17N 54.15E
Gaysin U.S.S.R. **37** 48.50N 29.29E
Gayvoron U.S.S.R. **37** 48.20N 29.52E
Gaza *see* Ghazzah Egypt **67**
Gaza *d.* Mozambique **81** 23.20S 32.35E
Gaza Strip *f.* Egypt **67** 31.20N 34.20E
Gaziantep Turkey **64** 37.04N 37.21E
Gbanhui Ivory Coast **76** 8.12N 3.02W
Gboko Nigeria **77** 7.22N 8.58E
Gcuwa R.S.A. **80** 32.20S 28.09E
Gdańsk Poland **37** 54.22N 18.38E
Gdansk, G. of Poland **37** 54.45N 19.15E
Gdov U.S.S.R. **44** 58.48N 27.52E
Gdynia Poland **37** 54.31N 18.30E
Gebe *i.* Indonesia **59** 0.05S129.20E
Gebze Turkey **64** 40.48N 29.26E
Gech'a Ethiopia **73** 7.31N 35.22E
Gedera Israel **67** 31.48N 34.46E
Gediz *r.* Turkey **29** 38.37N 26.47E
Gedser Denmark **41** 54.35N 11.57E
Geel Belgium **16** 51.10N 5.00E
Geelong Australia **92** 38.10S144.26E
Geesthacht Germany **38** 53.26N 10.22E
Gê'gyai China **63** 32.25N 84.05E
Gehua P.N.G. **90** 10.20S150.25E
Geidam Nigeria **77** 12.55N 11.55E
Geikie *r.* Canada **101** 57.45N103.52W
Geilenkirchen Germany **16** 50.58N 6.08E
Geilo Norway **41** 60.31N 8.12E
Geisenfeld Germany **39** 48.41N 11.37E
Geisenheim Germany **39** 49.59N 7.58E
Geislingen Germany **39** 48.36N 9.50E
Gejiu China **52** 23.25N103.05E
Gela Italy **33** 37.03N 14.15E
Gela, Golfo di *g.* Italy **33** 37.00N 14.10E
Geladī Ethiopia **71** 6.58N 44.30E
Gelai *mtn.* Tanzania **79** 2.37S 36.07E
Gelderland *d.* Neth. **16** 52.05N 6.00E
Geldermalsen Neth. **16** 51.53N 5.17E
Geldern Germany **38** 51.31N 6.20E
Geldrop Neth. **16** 51.26N 5.31E
Geleen Neth. **16** 50.58N 5.51E
Gélengdeng Chad **77** 10.56N 15.32E
Gelibolu Turkey **34** 40.24N 26.40E
Gelibolu Yarimadasi *c.* Turkey **34** 40.20N 26.30E
Gélise *r.* France **20** 44.11N 0.17E
Gelligaer U.K. **13** 51.40N 3.18W
Gelsenkirchen Germany **38** 51.31N 7.07E
Gem Canada **100** 50.58N112.11W
Gemas Malaysia **58** 2.35N102.35E
Gembloux Belgium **16** 50.34N 4.42E
Gemena Zaïre **78** 3.14N 19.48E
Gemerek Turkey **64** 39.13N 36.05E
Gemla Sweden **43** 56.52N 14.38E
Gemlik Turkey **64** 40.26N 29.10E
Gemona del Friuli Italy **30** 46.16N 13.09E
Gemünden Germany **39** 50.03N 9.41E
Genalē *r.* Ethiopia **73** 4.15N 42.10E
Genappe Belgium **16** 50.37N 4.25E
Gençay France **18** 46.23N 0.24E
Gendringen Neth. **16** 51.52N 6.26E
General Acha Argentina **125** 37.20S 64.35W
General Alvear Buenos Aires Argentina **125** 36.00S 60.00W
General Alvear Mendoza Argentina **125** 34.59S 67.42W
General Belgrano Argentina **125** 35.45S 58.30W
General Campos Argentina **125** 31.30S 58.25W
General Conesa Argentina **125** 36.30S 57.19W
General Guido Argentina **125** 36.40S 57.45W
General Lavalle Argentina **125** 36.22S 56.55W
General Madariaga Argentina **125** 37.00S 57.05W
General Paz Argentina **125** 35.32S 58.18W
General Pico Argentina **125** 35.38S 63.46W
General Roca Argentina **125** 39.02S 67.33W
General Santos Phil. **59** 6.05N125.15E
Genesee U.S.A. **114** 41.59N 77.52W
Genesee *r.* U.S.A. **114** 43.16N 77.36W
Geneseo Ill. U.S.A. **110** 41.27N 90.09W
Geneseo N.Y. U.S.A. **114** 42.48N 77.49W
Geneva *see* Genève Switz. **39**
Geneva Nebr. U.S.A. **110** 40.32N 97.36W
Geneva N.Y. U.S.A. **114** 42.52N 77.00W
Geneva Ohio U.S.A. **114** 41.48N 80.57W
Geneva, L. *see* Léman, Lac *l.* Switz. **39**
Genève Switz. **39** 46.12N 6.09E
Genève *d.* Switz. **39** 46.15N 6.15E
Genichesk U.S.S.R. **45** 46.10N 34.49E
Genil *r.* Spain **27** 37.42N 5.19W
Genk Belgium **16** 50.58N 5.34E
Genlis France **19** 47.14N 5.13E
Gennargentu, Monti del *mts.* Italy **32** 39.59N 9.19E
Gennep Neth. **16** 51.43N 5.58E
Gennes France **18** 47.20N 0.14W
Genoa Australia **93** 37.29S149.35E
Genoa *see* Genova Italy **30**
Genoa U.S.A. **110** 41.27N 97.44W
Genoa, G. of *see* Genova, Golfo di *g.* Italy **30**
Genova Italy **30** 44.25N 8.57E
Genova, Golfo di *g.* Italy **30** 44.00N 9.00E
Gens de Terre *r.* Canada **105** 46.53N 76.00W
Gent Belgium **16** 51.02N 3.42E
Genthin Germany **38** 52.24N 12.09E

Gentilly to **Gordon L.**

Gentilly Canada **105** 46.24N 72.17W
Gentioux France **20** 45.47N 1.59E
Genzano di Roma Italy **32** 41.42N 12.41E
Geographe B. Australia **89** 33.35S115.15E
George *r.* Australia **92** 28.24S136.39E
George *r.* Canada **99** 58.30N 66.00W
George R.S.A. **80** 33.57S 22.27E
George, L. N.S.W. Australia **93** 35.07S149.22E
George, L. S.A. Australia **92** 37.26S140.00E
George, L. Uganda **79** 0.00 30.10E
George, L. Fla. U.S.A. **113** 29.17N 81.36W
George, L. N.Y. U.S.A. **115** 43.35N 73.35W
George B. Canada **103** 45.50N 61.45W
George's Cove Canada **103** 52.40N 55.50W
Georgetown Ascension **127** 7.56S 14.25W
Georgetown Qld. Australia **90** 18.18S143.33E
George Town Tas. Australia **91** 41.04S146.48E
Georgetown Canada **103** 46.11N 62.32W
Georgetown Cayman Is. **117** 19.20N 81.23W
Georgetown Gambia **76** 13.31N 14.50W
Georgetown Guyana **122** 6.46N 58.10W
George Town Malaysia **58** 5.30N100.16E
Georgetown Del. U.S.A. **115** 38.42N 75.23W
Georgetown S.C. U.S.A. **113** 33.23N 79.18W
Georgetown Tex. U.S.A. **111** 30.38N 97.41W
George V Land *f.* Antarctica **128** 69.00S145.00E
Georgia *d.* U.S.A. **113** 32.50N 83.15W
Georgia, Str. of Canada **100** 49.25N124.00W
Georgian B. Canada **104** 45.15N 80.50W
Georgi Dimitrov Bulgaria **34** 42.37N 23.04E
Georgina *r.* Australia **90** 23.12S139.33E
Georgiu-Dezh U.S.S.R. **45** 51.00N 39.30E
Georgiyevsk U.S.S.R. **45** 44.10N 43.30E
Gera Germany **38** 50.52N 12.04E
Geraardsbergen Belgium **16** 50.47N 3.53E
Geral de Goiás, Serra *mts.* Brazil **123** 13.00S 45.40W
Geraldine New Zealand **86** 44.05S171.15E
Geral do Paraná, Serra *mts.* Brazil **123** 14.40S 47.30W
Geraldton Australia **89** 28.49S114.36E
Geraldton Canada **102** 49.44N 86.59W
Gerar *r.* Israel **67** 31.24N 34.26E
Gérardmer France **19** 48.04N 6.53E
Gerede Turkey **64** 40.48N 32.13E
Gereshk Afghan. **62** 31.48N 64.34E
Gérgal Spain **27** 37.07N 2.33W
Gering U.S.A. **110** 41.50N103.40W
Gerlach U.S.A. **108** 40.40N119.21W
Gerlachovsky *mtn.* Czech. **37** 49.10N 20.05E
Germania U.S.A. **114** 41.39N 77.40W
Germany Europe **38** 51.05N 9.45E
Germencik Turkey **35** 37.51N 27.37E
Germersheim Germany **39** 49.13N 8.22E
Germiston R.S.A. **80** 26.14S 28.10E
Gerolstein Germany **39** 50.13N 6.40E
Gerolzhofen Germany **39** 49.54N 10.21E
Gerona *see* Girona *d.* Spain **25**
Gerona *see* Girona Spain **25**
Gerringong Australia **93** 34.45S150.50E
Gers *d.* France **20** 43.40N 0.30E
Gêrzê China **63** 32.16N 84.12E
Gescher Germany **38** 51.57N 6.59E
Geseke Germany **38** 51.38N 8.31E
Getafe Spain **26** 40.18N 3.43W
Gete *r.* Belgium **16** 50.58N 5.07E
Gethsémani Canada **103** 50.13N 60.40W
Getinge Sweden **43** 56.49N 12.44E
Gettysburg Penn. U.S.A. **114** 39.50N 77.14W
Gettysburg S.Dak. U.S.A. **110** 45.01N 99.57W
Gevān Iran **65** 26.03N 57.17E
Gevar'am Israel **67** 31.35N 34.37E
Gevelsberg Germany **38** 51.19N 7.20E
Gevgelija Yugo. **34** 41.09N 22.30E
Gévora *r.* Spain **27** 38.53N 6.57W
Gevulot Israel **67** 31.12N 34.28E
Geyikli Turkey **34** 39.50N 26.12E
Geysdorp R.S.A. **80** 26.31S 25.17E
Geyser U.S.A. **108** 47.16N110.30W
Geyve Turkey **64** 40.32N 30.18E
Gezer Israel **67** 31.52N 34.55E
Ghabāghib Syria **67** 33.10N 36.13E
Ghābat al 'Arab Sudan **73** 9.02N 29.29E
Ghadaf, Wādī al *r.* Jordan **66** 31.46N 36.50E
Ghadāmis Libya **75** 30.08N 9.30E
Ghaddūwah Libya **75** 26.26N 14.18E
Ghāghra *r.* India **63** 25.47N 84.37E
Ghana Africa **76** 8.00N 1.00W
Ghanzi Botswana **80** 21.42S 21.39E
Ghanzi *d.* Botswana **80** 21.44S 21.38E
Gharb al Istiwā'īyah *d.* Sudan **73** 5.25N 29.00E
Ghardaïa Algeria **75** 32.29N 3.40E
Gharghoda India **63** 22.10N 83.21E
Ghārib, Jabal *mtn.* Egypt **66** 28.06N 32.54E
Ghārīyat ash Sharqīyah Syria **67** 32.40N 36.16E
Gharo Pakistan **62** 24.44N 67.35E
Gharyān Libya **75** 32.10N 13.01E
Gharyān *d.* Libya **75** 30.35N 12.00E
Ghāt Libya **75** 24.58N 10.11E
Ghātsīla India **63** 22.36N 86.29E
Ghazāl, Baḩr al *r.* Sudan **73** 9.31N 30.25E
Ghāziābād India **63** 28.40N 77.26E
Ghāzīpur India **63** 25.35N 83.34E
Ghazlūna Pakistan **62** 31.24N 67.49E
Ghaznī Afghan. **62** 33.33N 68.26E
Ghaznī *d.* Afghan. **62** 32.45N 68.30E
Ghaznī *r.* Afghan. **62** 32.35N 67.58E
Ghazzah Egypt **67** 31.30N 34.28E
Ghedi Italy **30** 45.24N 10.16E
Gheorghe-Gheorghiu-Dej Romania **37** 46.14N 26.44E
Gheorgheni Romania **37** 46.43N 25.36E
Gherla Romania **37** 47.02N 23.55E
Ghisonàccia France **21** 42.00N 9.25E
Ghotki Pakistan **62** 28.01N 69.19E
Ghowr *d.* Afghan. **62** 34.00N 64.15E
Ghubaysh Sudan **73** 12.09N 27.21E
Ghudāf, Wādī al *r.* Iraq **64** 32.54N 43.33E
Ghūrīān Afghan. **62** 34.21N 61.30E
Gia Dinh Vietnam **56** 10.54N106.43E
Giarre Italy **33** 37.43N 15.11E
Gibb River *town* Australia **88** 16.29S126.20E
Gibeon Namibia **80** 25.09S 17.44E
Gibraleón Spain **27** 37.23N 6.58W
Gibraltar Europe **27** 36.09N 5.21W
Gibraltar, Str. of Africa / Europe **24** 36.00N 5.25W
Gibraltar Pt. U.K. **12** 53.05N 0.20E
Gibson Australia **89** 33.39S121.48E
Gibson Desert Australia **88** 23.10S125.35E
Gida Ethiopia **73** 9.40N 35.16E
Giddings U.S.A. **111** 30.11N 96.56W
Gien France **19** 47.42N 2.38E
Giessen Germany **38** 50.35N 8.40E
Gieten Neth. **16** 53.01N 6.45E
Gifford *r.* Canada **99** 70.21N 83.05W
Gifford U.S.A. **108** 48.20N118.08W
Gifhorn Germany **38** 52.29N 10.33E
Gifu Japan **57** 35.25N136.45E
Gifu *d.* Japan **57** 35.32N137.15E
Giganta, Sierra de la *mts.* Mexico **109** 25.30N111.15W
Gigantes, Llanos de los *f.* Mexico **109** 30.00N105.00W
Gigen Bulgaria **34** 43.40N 24.28E
Gigha *i.* U.K. **14** 55.41N 5.44W
Giglio *i.* Italy **30** 42.21N 10.54E
Gijón Spain **26** 43.32N 5.40W
Gila *r.* U.S.A. **109** 32.43N114.33W
Gila Bend U.S.A. **109** 32.57N112.43W
Gila Bend Mts. U.S.A. **109** 33.10N113.10W
Gilardo Dam Canada **105** 47.12N 73.48W
Gilat Israel **67** 31.19N 34.40E
Gilbert *r.* Australia **90** 16.35S141.15E
Gilbert Islands Kiribati **84** 2.00S175.00E
Gildford U.S.A. **108** 48.34N110.18W
Gilé Mozambique **79** 16.10S 38.17E
Gilgandra Australia **93** 31.42S148.40E
Gil Gil *r.* Australia **93** 29.10S148.50E
Gilgil Kenya **79** 0.29S 36.19E
Gilgit Jammu & Kashmir **60** 35.54N 74.20E
Gilgunnia Australia **93** 32.25S146.04E
Giljeva Planina *mts.* Yugo. **31** 43.15N 19.55E
Gill, Lough Rep. of Ire. **15** 54.15N 8.14W
Gilleleje Denmark **43** 56.07N 12.19E
Gilles, L. Australia **92** 32.50S136.45E
Gillette U.S.A. **108** 44.18N105.30W
Gillingham Kent U.K. **13** 51.24N 0.33E
Gill Pt. *c.* St. Helena **127** 15.59S 5.38W
Gilmour Canada **105** 44.48N 77.37W
Gilo *r.* Ethiopia **73** 8.10N 33.15E
Gimli Canada **101** 50.39N 97.00W
Gimo Sweden **43** 60.11N 18.11E
Gimone *r.* France **20** 44.00N 1.06E
Gimont France **20** 43.38N 0.53E
Gimzo Israel **67** 31.56N 34.57E
Gingin Australia **89** 31.21S115.42E
Gīnīr Ethiopia **73** 7.07N 40.46E
Ginnosar Israel **67** 32.51N 35.31E
Ginosa Italy **33** 40.34N 16.46E
Ginzo de Limia Spain **26** 42.03N 7.43W
Gioia del Colle Italy **33** 40.48N 16.56E
Gioia Tauro Italy **33** 38.26N 15.54E
Gióna *mtn.* Greece **35** 38.38N 22.14E
Girard Ohio U.S.A. **114** 41.10N 80.42W
Girard Penn. U.S.A. **114** 42.00N 80.19W
Girardot Colombia **122** 4.19N 74.47W
Girdle Ness U.K. **14** 57.06N 2.02W
Giresun Turkey **64** 40.55N 38.25E
Gir Hills India **62** 21.10N 71.00E
Giri *r.* Zaïre **78** 0.30N 17.58E
Giridih India **63** 24.11N 86.18E
Girilambone Australia **93** 31.14S146.55E
Girna *r.* India **62** 21.08N 75.19E
Giromagny France **19** 47.45N 6.50E
Girona Spain **25** 41.59N 2.49E
Girona *d.* Spain **25** 42.05N 2.50E
Gironde *d.* France **20** 44.45N 0.35W
Gironde *r.* France **20** 45.35N 1.00W
Girvan U.K. **14** 55.15N 4.51W
Girwa *r.* India **63** 27.20N 81.25E
Gisborne New Zealand **86** 38.41S178.02E
Gisborne *d.* New Zealand **86** 38.20S177.45E
Gislaved Sweden **43** 57.18N 13.32E
Gisors France **19** 49.17N 1.47E
Gitega Burundi **79** 3.25S 29.58E
Giugliano Italy **33** 40.56N 14.12E
Giulianova Italy **31** 42.45N 13.57E
Giurgiu Romania **34** 43.53N 25.57E
Giv'atayim Israel **67** 32.04N 34.49E
Giv'at Brenner Israel **67** 31.52N 34.48E
Give Denmark **42** 55.51N 9.15E
Givet France **17** 50.08N 4.49E
Givors France **21** 45.35N 4.46E
Givry France **19** 46.47N 4.45E
Gīzāb Afghan. **62** 33.23N 65.55E
Gizhiga U.S.S.R. **51** 62.00N160.34E
Gizhiginskaya Guba *g.* U.S.S.R. **51** 61.00N158.00E
Giżycko Poland **37** 54.03N 21.47E
Gjerstad Norway **42** 58.54N 9.00E
Gjirokastër Albania **34** 40.05N 20.10E
Gjoa Haven *town* Canada **99** 68.39N 96.08W
Gjövik Norway **41** 60.48N 10.42E
Glace Bay *town* Canada **103** 46.12N 59.57W
Glacier Nat. Park Canada **100** 51.15N117.30W
Glacier Peak *mtn.* U.S.A. **108** 48.07N121.06W
Gladewater U.S.A. **111** 32.33N 94.56W
Gladmar Canada **101** 49.12N104.31W
Gladstone Qld. Australia **90** 23.52S151.16E
Gladstone S.A. Australia **92** 33.17S138.22E
Gladstone Mich. U.S.A. **112** 45.52N 87.02W
Gladstone N.J. U.S.A. **115** 40.43N 74.40W
Gladwin U.S.A. **104** 43.59N 84.29W
Glafsfjorden *l.* Sweden **43** 59.34N 12.37E
Glåma *r.* Norway **42** 59.12N 10.57E
Glamoč Yugo. **31** 44.03N 16.51E
Glan *r.* Germany **16** 49.46N 7.43E
Glan *l.* Sweden **43** 58.37N 15.58E
Glanaman U.K. **13** 51.49N 3.54W
Glandorf Germany **38** 52.05N 7.59E
Glarner Alpen *mts.* Switz. **39** 46.55N 9.00E
Glarus Switz. **39** 47.02N 9.04E
Glarus *d.* Switz. **39** 46.59N 9.05E
Glasco Kans. U.S.A. **110** 39.22N 97.50W
Glasco N.Y. U.S.A. **115** 42.03N 73.57W
Glasgow U.K. **14** 55.52N 4.15W
Glasgow Ky. U.S.A. **113** 36.59N 85.56W
Glasgow Mont. U.S.A. **108** 48.12N106.38W
Glassboro U.S.A. **115** 39.42N 75.07W
Glastonbury U.K. **13** 51.09N 2.42W
Glauchau Germany **38** 50.49N 12.32E
Glazov U.S.S.R. **44** 58.09N 52.42E
Gleisdorf Austria **31** 47.06N 15.44E
Glen R.S.A. **80** 28.57S 26.19E
Glen Affric *f.* U.K. **14** 57.15N 5.03W
Glen Afton Canada **104** 46.39N 80.17W
Glénans, Îles de *is.* France **18** 47.43N 3.57W
Glenarm U.K. **15** 54.57N 5.58W
Glenburnie Australia **92** 37.49S140.56E
Glen Burnie U.S.A. **115** 39.10N 76.37W
Glencoe Australia **92** 37.41S140.05E
Glencoe Canada **104** 42.45N 81.43W
Glen Coe *f.* U.K. **14** 56.40N 5.03W
Glencoe U.S.A. **110** 44.45N 94.10W
Glen Cove U.S.A. **115** 40.52N 73.37W
Glendale Ariz. U.S.A. **109** 33.32N112.11W
Glendale Calif. U.S.A. **109** 34.10N118.17W
Glendale Oreg. U.S.A. **108** 42.44N123.26W
Glen Davis Australia **93** 33.07S150.22E
Glendive U.S.A. **108** 47.06N104.43W
Glenelg *r.* Australia **92** 38.03S141.00E
Glenfield U.S.A. **115** 43.43N 75.24W
Glengarriff Rep. of Ire. **15** 51.45N 9.33W
Glen Garry *f.* Highland U.K. **14** 57.03N 5.04W
Glen Head Rep. of Ire. **15** 54.44N 8.46W
Glen Helen *town* Australia **90** 23.15S132.35E
Glen Innes Australia **93** 29.42S151.45E
Glen Lyon U.S.A. **115** 41.10N 76.05W
Glen Mòr *f.* U.K. **14** 57.15N 4.30W
Glenmora U.S.A. **111** 30.59N 92.35W
Glenmorgan Australia **91** 27.19S149.40E
Glen Moriston U.K. **14** 57.09N 4.50W
Glennie U.S.A. **104** 44.33N 83.44W
Glenns Ferry U.S.A. **108** 42.57N115.18W
Glenrock U.S.A. **108** 42.52N105.52W
Glenrothes U.K. **14** 56.12N 3.10W
Glenroy Australia **88** 17.23S126.01E
Glens Falls *town* U.S.A. **115** 43.19N 73.39W
Glenshee *f.* U.K. **14** 56.45N 3.25W
Glen Spean *f.* U.K. **14** 56.53N 4.40W
Glenville U.S.A. **114** 38.56N 80.50W
Glenwood Ark. U.S.A. **111** 34.20N 93.33W
Glenwood Iowa U.S.A. **110** 41.03N 95.45W
Glenwood Oreg. U.S.A. **108** 45.39N123.16W
Glenwood Springs *town* U.S.A. **108** 39.33N107.19W
Glífa Greece **35** 38.57N 22.58E
Glimåkra Sweden **43** 56.18N 14.08E
Glimmingehus Sweden **43** 55.30N 14.13E
Glina Yugo. **31** 45.20N 16.06E
Glina *r.* Yugo. **31** 45.26N 16.07E
Glittertind *mtn.* Norway **41** 61.39N 8.33E
Gliwice Poland **37** 50.17N 18.40E
Globe U.S.A. **109** 33.24N110.47W
Głogów Poland **36** 51.40N 16.06E
Glotovo U.S.S.R. **44** 63.25N 49.28E
Gloucester Australia **93** 31.59S151.58E
Gloucester U.K. **13** 51.52N 2.15W
Gloucester U.S.A. **115** 42.41N 70.39W
Gloucester City U.S.A. **115** 39.54N 75.07W
Gloucestershire *d.* U.K. **13** 51.45N 2.00W
Glouster U.S.A. **114** 39.30N 82.05W
Gloversville U.S.A. **115** 43.03N 74.20W
Głubczyce Poland **37** 50.13N 17.49E
Glücksburg Germany **38** 54.50N 9.33E
Glückstadt Germany **38** 53.47N 9.25E
Glusha U.S.S.R. **37** 53.03N 28.55E
Glyngöre Denmark **42** 56.46N 8.52E
Gmünd Austria **31** 46.54N 13.32E
Gmunden Austria **39** 47.55N 13.48E
Gnadenhutten U.S.A. **114** 40.22N 81.26W
Gnarp Sweden **41** 62.03N 17.16E
Gnesta Sweden **43** 59.03N 17.18E
Gniewkowo Poland **37** 52.24N 18.25E
Gniezno Poland **37** 52.32N 17.32E
Gnjilane Yugo. **34** 42.28N 21.58E
Gnoien Germany **38** 53.58N 12.42E
Gnosjö Sweden **43** 57.22N 13.44E
Gnowangerup Australia **89** 33.57S117.58E
Gnuca Australia **89** 31.08S117.24E
Goa *d.* India **60** 15.30N 74.00E
Goageb Namibia **80** 26.45S 17.18E
Goālpāra India **63** 26.10N 90.37E
Goat Fell *mtn.* U.K. **14** 55.37N 5.12W
Goba Ethiopia **73** 7.02N 40.00E
Goba Mozambique **81** 26.11S 32.08E
Gobabis Namibia **80** 22.28S 18.58E
Gobi *des.* Asia **54** 45.00N108.00E
Goch Germany **38** 51.41N 6.10E
Gochas Namibia **80** 24.50S 18.48E
Godalming U.K. **13** 51.11N 0.37W
Godar Pakistan **62** 28.10N 63.14E
Godāvari *r.* India **61** 16.40N 82.15E
Godbout Canada **103** 49.19N 67.37W
Goderich Canada **104** 43.45N 81.43W
Goderville France **18** 49.39N 0.22E
Godhavn Greenland **99** 69.20N 53.30W
Godhra India **62** 22.45N 73.38E
Godoy Cruz Argentina **125** 32.55S 68.50W
Gods *r.* Canada **101** 56.22N 92.51W
Gods L. Canada **101** 54.45N 94.00W
Godthåb Greenland **99** 64.10N 51.40W
Goéland, Lac au *l.* Canada **102** 49.47N 76.41W
Goélands, Lac aux *l.* Canada **103** 55.25N 64.20W
Goes Neth. **16** 51.30N 3.54E
Goffstown U.S.A. **115** 43.01N 71.36W
Gogama Canada **102** 47.35N 81.35W
Gogeh Ethiopia **73** 8.12N 38.27E
Göggingen Germany **39** 48.20N 10.52E
Gogonou Benin **77** 10.50N 2.50E
Gogra *r. see* Ghāghra India **63**
Gogrial Sudan **73** 8.32N 28.07E
Goha Ethiopia **73** 10.25N 34.38E
Gohad India **63** 26.26N 78.27E
Goiana Brazil **123** 7.30S 35.00W
Goiânia Brazil **123** 16.43S 49.18W
Goiás Brazil **123** 15.57S 50.07W
Goiás *d.* Brazil **123** 15.00S 48.00W
Goichran India **63** 31.04N 78.07E
Góis Portugal **26** 40.09N 8.07W
Goito Italy **30** 45.15N 10.40E
Gojam *d.* Ethiopia **73** 11.10N 37.00E
Gojeb *r.* Ethiopia **73** 7.10N 37.27E
Gojō Japan **57** 34.21N135.42E
Gojra Pakistan **62** 31.09N 72.41E
Gökçe Turkey **34** 40.10N 25.57E
Gökçeada *i.* Turkey **34** 40.10N 26.00E
Göksun Turkey **64** 38.03N 36.30E
Gokteik Burma **61** 22.26N 97.00E
Gokwe Zimbabwe **80** 18.14S 28.54E
Gol Norway **41** 60.42N 8.57E
Gola Gokaran Nath India **63** 28.05N 80.28E
Golan Heights *mts.* Syria **67** 32.55N 35.42E
Golconda U.S.A. **108** 40.57N117.30W
Gold U.S.A. **114** 41.52N 77.52W
Gołdap Poland **37** 54.19N 22.19E
Gold Beach *town* U.S.A. **108** 42.25N124.25W
Golden Canada **100** 51.20N117.00W
Golden Rep. of Ire. **15** 52.30N 7.59W
Golden U.S.A. **108** 39.46N105.13W
Golden B. New Zealand **86** 40.45S172.50E
Goldendale U.S.A. **108** 45.49N120.50W
Golden Hinde *mtn.* Canada **100** 49.40N125.44W
Golden L. Canada **105** 45.35N 77.20W
Golden Lake *town* Canada **105** 45.35N 77.16W
Golden Ridge *town* Australia **89** 30.51S121.42E
Golden Vale *f.* Rep. of Ire. **15** 52.30N 8.07W
Goldfield U.S.A. **108** 37.42N117.14W
Goldfields Canada **101** 59.28N108.31W
Goldpines Canada **102** 50.45N 93.05W
Goldsand L. Canada **101** 56.58N101.02W
Goldsboro U.S.A. **113** 35.23N 78.00W
Goldsworthy Australia **88** 20.20S119.30E
Goleniów Poland **36** 53.36N 14.50E
Golets Skalisty *mtn.* U.S.S.R. **51** 56.00N130.40E
Golfito Costa Rica **117** 8.42N 83.10W
Golfo degli Aranci *town* Italy **32** 41.00N 9.38E
Goliad U.S.A. **111** 28.40N 97.23W
Goljam Perelik *mtn.* Bulgaria **34** 41.36N 24.34E
Golling Austria **39** 47.36N 13.10E
Golmud China **52** 36.22N 94.55E
Golo *r.* France **21** 42.31N 9.32E
Golovanevsk U.S.S.R. **37** 48.25N 30.30E
Golpāyegān Iran **65** 33.23N 50.18E
Golspie U.K. **14** 57.58N 3.58W
Goma Zaïre **79** 1.37S 29.10E
Gomang Co *l.* China **63** 31.10N 89.10E
Gombe Nigeria **77** 10.17N 11.20E
Gombe *r.* Tanzania **79** 4.43S 31.30E
Gomel U.S.S.R. **37** 52.25N 31.00E
Gomera *i.* Canary Is. **74** 28.08N 17.14W
Gómez Palacio Mexico **111** 25.34N103.30W
Gomīshān Iran **65** 37.04N 54.06E
Gompa Jammu & Kashmir **62** 35.02N 77.20E
Gonaïves Haiti **117** 19.29N 72.42W
Gonâve, Golfe de la *g.* Haiti **117** 19.20N 73.00W
Gonâve, Île de la *i.* Haiti **117** 18.50N 73.00W
Gonbad-e Kāvūs Iran **65** 37.15N 55.11E
Gonda India **63** 27.08N 81.56E
Gondal India **62** 21.58N 70.48E
Gonder Ethiopia **73** 12.39N 37.29E
Gonder *d.* Ethiopia **73** 12.30N 37.30E
Gondia India **63** 21.27N 80.12E
Gondomar Portugal **26** 41.09N 8.32W
Gondrecourt-le-Château France **19** 48.31N 5.30E
Gonen Israel **67** 33.08N 35.39E
Gongbo'gyamda China **63** 29.56N 93.23E
Gonggar China **63** 29.15N 90.50E
Gongga Shan *mtn.* China **52** 29.30N101.30E
Gongola *d.* Nigeria **77** 8.40N 11.30E
Gongola *r.* Nigeria **77** 9.30N 12.06E
Gongolgon Australia **93** 30.22S146.56E
Goñi Uruguay **125** 33.31S 56.24W
Goniri Nigeria **77** 11.30N 12.15E
Gonnesa Italy **32** 39.15N 8.28E
Gonzaga Italy **30** 44.57N 10.49E
Gonzales U.S.A. **111** 29.30N 97.27W
Good Hope, C. of R.S.A. **80** 34.21S 18.28E
Good Hope Mtn. Canada **100** 51.09N124.10W
Gooding U.S.A. **108** 42.56N114.43W
Goodland U.S.A. **110** 39.21N101.43W
Goodooga Australia **93** 29.08S147.30E
Goodsprings U.S.A. **109** 35.50N115.26W
Goole U.K. **12** 53.42N 0.52W
Goolgowi Australia **93** 33.59S145.42E
Goolma Australia **93** 32.21S149.20E
Gooloogong Australia **93** 33.36S148.27E
Goolwa Australia **92** 35.31S138.45E
Goomalling Australia **89** 31.19S116.49E
Goombalie Australia **93** 29.59S145.24E
Goondiwindi Australia **93** 28.30S150.17E
Goongarrie Australia **89** 30.03S121.09E
Goor Neth. **16** 52.16N 6.33E
Goose *r.* Canada **103** 53.18N 60.23W
Goose Bay *town* Canada **103** 53.19N 60.24W
Goose L. U.S.A. **108** 41.57N120.25W
Gopālganj Bangla. **63** 23.01N 89.50E
Gopālganj India **63** 26.28N 84.26E
Göppingen Germany **39** 48.42N 9.40E
Gorakhpur India **63** 26.45N 83.22E
Goras India **62** 25.32N 76.56E
Goražde Yugo. **31** 43.40N 18.58E
Gordon *r.* Australia **89** 34.12S117.00E
Gordon U.S.A. **110** 42.48N102.12W
Gordon Downs *town* Australia **88** 18.43S128.33E
Gordon L. Canada **100** 63.05N113.11W

Gordonvale to Grosseto

Gordonvale Australia **90** 17.05S145.47E
Goré Chad **77** 7.57N 16.31E
Gorē Ethiopia **73** 8.08N 35.33E
Gore New Zealand **86** 46.06S168.58E
Gore Bay *town* Canada **104** 45.55N 82.28W
Gore Mtn. U.S.A. **105** 44.55N 71.48W
Gorgān Iran **65** 36.50N 54.29E
Gorgān *r.* Iran **65** 37.00N 54.00E
Gorgol *d.* Mauritania **74** 15.45N 13.00W
Gori U.S.S.R. **65** 41.59N 44.05E
Gorinchem Neth. **16** 51.50N 4.59E
Gorizia Italy **31** 45.57N 13.38E
Gorjani Yugo. **31** 45.24N 18.21E
Gorki *see* Gor'kiy U.S.S.R. **44**
Gor'kiy U.S.S.R. **44** 56.20N 44.00E
Gorkovskoye Vodokhranilishche *resr.* U.S.S.R. **44** 56.49N 43.00E
Görlitz Germany **38** 51.09N 14.59E
Gorlovka U.S.S.R. **45** 48.17N 38.05E
Gorna Oryakhovitsa Bulgaria **34** 43.07N 25.40E
Gornja Radogna Yugo. **31** 46.41N 16.00E
Gornji Grad Yugo. **31** 46.18N 14.49E
Gornji Vakuf Yugo. **31** 43.56N 17.35E
Gorno Altaysk U.S.S.R. **50** 51.59N 85.56E
Gorno Filinskoye U.S.S.R. **50** 60.06N 69.58E
Gornyatskiy U.S.S.R. **44** 67.30N 64.03E
Goroch'an *mtn.* Ethiopia **73** 9.22N 37.04E
Gorodenka U.S.S.R. **37** 48.40N 25.30E
Gorodishche B.S.S.R. U.S.S.R. **37** 53.45N 29.45E
Gorodishche B.S.S.R. U.S.S.R. **37** 53.18N 26.00E
Gorodnitsa U.S.S.R. **37** 50.50N 27.19E
Gorodnya U.S.S.R. **37** 51.54N 31.37E
Gorodok U.S.S.R. **37** 49.48N 23.39E
Goroka P.N.G. **59** 6.02S145.22E
Goroke Australia **92** 36.43S141.30E
Gorokhov U.S.S.R. **37** 50.30N 24.46E
Gorongosa *r.* Mozambique **81** 20.29S 34.36E
Gorontalo Indonesia **59** 0.33N123.05E
Gort Rep. of Ire. **15** 53.04N 8.49W
Goryn *r.* U.S.S.R. **37** 52.08N 27.17E
Gorzów Wielkopolski Poland **36** 52.42N 15.12E
Gosford Australia **93** 33.25S151.18E
Goslar Germany **38** 51.54N 10.25E
Gospić Yugo. **31** 44.33N 15.23E
Gosport U.K. **13** 50.48N 1.08W
Gossi Mali **76** 15.49N 1.17W
Gossinga Sudan **73** 8.39N 25.59E
Gostivar Yugo. **34** 41.47N 20.24E
Gostynin Poland **37** 52.26N 19.29E
Göta *r.* Sweden **43** 57.42N 11.52E
Göta Kanal Sweden **43** 58.45N 14.05E
Göteborg Sweden **42** 57.43N 11.58E
Göteborg och Bohus *d.* Sweden **42** 58.30N 11.30E
Gotemba Japan **57** 35.18N138.56E
Götene Sweden **43** 58.32N 13.29E
Gotha Germany **38** 50.57N 10.41E
Gothem Sweden **43** 57.35N 18.43E
Gothenburg *see* Göteborg Sweden **42**
Gothenburg U.S.A. **110** 40.56N100.09W
Gothèye Niger **77** 13.51N 1.31E
Gotland *d.* Sweden **43** 57.25N 18.25E
Gotland *i.* Sweden **43** 57.30N 18.33E
Gotse Delchev Bulgaria **34** 41.34N 23.44E
Gotska Sandön *i.* Sweden **43** 58.23N 19.16E
Gōtsu Japan **57** 35.00N132.14E
Göttingen Germany **38** 51.32N 9.55E
Götzis Austria **39** 47.20N 9.38E
Gouarec France **18** 48.13N 3.11W
Gouda Neth. **16** 52.01N 4.43E
Gough I. Atlantic Oc. **127** 40.20S 10.00W
Gouin, Résr. Canada **102** 48.38N 74.54W
Goulais River *town* Canada **104** 46.43N 84.18W
Goulburn Australia **93** 34.47S149.43E
Goulburn *r.* Australia **93** 36.08S144.30E
Goulburn Is. Australia **90** 11.33S133.26E
Gould Canada **105** 45.35N 71.24W
Goulimime Morocco **74** 28.56N 10.04W
Gouménissa Greece **34** 40.56N 22.37E
Goundam Mali **76** 17.27N 3.39W
Gourdon France **20** 44.44N 1.23E
Gouré Niger **77** 13.59N 10.15E
Gourin France **18** 48.08N 3.36W
Gourma-Rharous Mali **76** 16.58N 1.50W
Gournay France **17** 49.29N 1.44E
Gouro Chad **75** 19.33N 19.33E
Gouverneur U.S.A. **105** 44.20N 75.28W
Governador Valadares Brazil **126** 18.51S 42.00W
Govind Balabh Pant Sāgar *resr.* India **63** 24.05N 82.50E
Govind Sāgar *resr.* India **62** 31.20N 76.45E
Gowanda U.S.A. **114** 42.28N 78.56W
Goward Canada **104** 47.08N 79.49W
Gowd-e Zereh *des.* Afghan. **65** 30.00N 62.00E
Gower *pen.* U.K. **13** 51.37N 4.10W
Gowmal *r.* Afghan. *see* Gumal *r.* Pakistan **62**
Gowmal Kalay Afghan. **62** 32.29N 68.55E
Goya Argentina **124** 29.10S 59.20W
Goyder *r.* Australia **90** 12.38S135.11E
Goz Béïda Chad **73** 12.13N 21.25E
Gozo *i.* Malta **28** 36.03N 14.16E
Graaff Reinet R.S.A. **80** 32.15S 24.31E
Graben Germany **39** 49.09N 8.29E
Grabow Germany **38** 53.16N 11.34E
Gračac Yugo. **31** 44.18N 15.51E
Gračanica Yugo. **31** 44.42N 18.19E
Graçay France **19** 47.08N 1.51E
Grace, L. Australia **89** 33.18S118.15E
Gracefield Canada **105** 46.06N 76.03W
Gracias á Dios, Cabo *c.* Honduras/Nicaragua **117** 15.00N 83.10W
Gradačac Yugo. **31** 44.53N 18.26E
Grado Italy **30** 45.40N 13.23E
Grado Spain **26** 43.23N 6.04W
Grafenau Germany **39** 48.52N 13.25E
Gräfenhainichen Germany **38** 51.44N 12.27E
Grafing Germany **39** 48.02N 11.59E
Gråfjell *mtn.* Norway **42** 60.16N 9.29E
Grafton Australia **93** 29.40S152.56E
Grafton Canada **104** 44.00N 78.01W
Grafton Mass. U.S.A. **115** 42.12N 71.41W
Grafton N.Dak. U.S.A. **110** 48.25N 97.25W
Grafton Ohio U.S.A. **114** 41.16N 82.04W
Grafton Wisc. U.S.A. **110** 43.20N 87.58W
Grafton W.Va. U.S.A. **114** 39.20N 80.01W
Graham *r.* Canada **100** 56.31N122.17W
Graham U.S.A. **111** 33.06N 98.35W
Graham, Mt. U.S.A. **109** 32.42N109.52W
Graham I. Canada **100** 53.40N132.30W
Graham Land *f.* Antarctica **128** 67.00S 60.00W
Grahamstown R.S.A. **80** 33.18S 26.30E
Graiguenamanagh Rep. of Ire. **15** 52.33N 6.57W
Grajaú *r.* Brazil **123** 3.41S 44.48W
Gram Denmark **42** 55.17N 9.04E
Gramada Bulgaria **34** 43.49N 22.39E
Gramat France **20** 44.47N 1.43E
Grammichele Italy **33** 37.13N 14.38E
Grámmos, Óros *mtn.* Greece **34** 40.23N 20.45E
Grampian *d.* U.K. **14** 57.22N 2.35W
Grampian Mts. U.K. **14** 56.55N 4.00W
Grampians *mts.* Australia **92** 37.12S142.34E
Gramsh Albania **34** 40.52N 20.12E
Granada Nicaragua **117** 11.58N 85.59W
Granada Spain **27** 37.13N 3.41W
Granada *d.* Spain **27** 37.30N 3.00W
Granby Canada **105** 45.24N 72.44W
Gran Canaria *i.* Canary Is. **74** 28.00N 15.30W
Gran Chaco *f.* S. America **124** 22.00S 60.00W
Grand *r.* Canada **104** 42.51N 79.34W
Grand *r.* Ohio U.S.A. **114** 41.46N 81.17W
Grand *r.* S.Dak. U.S.A. **110** 45.40N100.32W
Grandas Spain **26** 43.13N 6.52W
Grandas de Salime, Embalse de *resr.* Spain **26** 43.10N 6.45W
Grand Bahama I. Bahamas **113** 26.40N 78.20W
Grand Ballon *mtn.* France **19** 47.55N 7.08E
Grand Bank *town* Canada **103** 47.06N 55.47W
Grand Bassam Ivory Coast **76** 5.14N 3.45W
Grand Bend Canada **104** 43.15N 81.45W
Grand Blanc U.S.A. **104** 42.56N 83.38W
Grand Canal *see* Da Yunhe *canal* China **54**
Grand Canyon *f.* U.S.A. **109** 36.10N112.45W
Grand Canyon *town* U.S.A. **109** 36.03N112.09W
Grand Canyon Nat. Park U.S.A. **109** 36.15N112.58W
Grand Cayman *i.* Cayman Is. **117** 19.20N 81.30W
Grand Centre Canada **101** 54.25N110.13W
Grand Cess Liberia **76** 4.40N 8.12W
Grand Couronne France **18** 49.21N 1.00E
Grande *r.* Bolivia **124** 15.10S 64.55W
Grande *r.* Bahia Brazil **123** 11.05S 43.09W
Grande *r.* Minas Gerais Brazil **124** 20.00S 51.00W
Grande *r.* Spain **25** 39.07N 0.44W
Grande, Bahía *b.* Argentina **125** 51.30S 67.30W
Grande, Ilha *i.* Brazil **126** 23.07S 44.16W
Grande, Sierra *mts.* Mexico **109** 29.35N104.55W
Grande Cascapédia Canada **103** 48.19N 65.54W
Grande Comore *see* Njazídja *i.* Comoros **79**
Grande do Gurupá, Ilha *i.* Brazil **123** 1.00S 51.30W
Grande Prairie Canada **100** 55.15N118.50W
Grand Erg de Bilma *des.* Niger **77** 18.30N 14.00E
Grand Erg Occidental *des.* Algeria **74** 30.10N 0.20E
Grand Erg Oriental *des.* Algeria **75** 30.00N 7.00E
Grande Rivière *town* Canada **103** 48.24N 64.30W
Grandes, Salinas *f.* Argentina **124** 29.37S 64.56W
Grandes Bergeronnes Canada **103** 48.15N 69.33W
Grande Vallée Canada **103** 49.14N 65.08W
Grand Falls *town* N.B. Canada **103** 46.55N 67.45W
Grand Falls *town* Nfld. Canada **103** 48.56N 55.40W
Grand Forks Canada **100** 49.00N118.30W
Grand Forks U.S.A. **110** 47.55N 97.03W
Grand Fougeray France **18** 47.44N 1.44W
Grand Gorge U.S.A. **115** 42.22N 74.30W
Grand Hers *r.* France **20** 43.47N 1.20E
Grand Island *town* U.S.A. **110** 40.55N 98.21W
Grand Isle U.S.A. **105** 44.44N 72.18W
Grand Junction U.S.A. **108** 39.05N108.33W
Grand L. N.B. Canada **103** 45.38N 67.38W
Grand L. Nfld. Canada **103** 49.00N 57.25W
Grand L. U.S.A. **112** 45.15N 67.50W
Grand Lahou Ivory Coast **76** 5.09N 5.01W
Grand Lieu, Lac de *l.* France **18** 47.06N 1.40W
Grand Manan I. Canada **103** 44.40N 66.50W
Grand Marais U.S.A. **110** 47.45N 90.20W
Grand' Mère Canada **105** 46.37N 72.41W
Grandois Canada **103** 51.07N 55.46W
Grândola Portugal **27** 38.10N 8.34W
Grand Passage N. Cal. **84** 18.45S163.10E
Grand Prairie *town* U.S.A. **111** 32.45N 96.59W
Grand Rapids *town* Canada **101** 53.08N 99.20W
Grand Rapids *town* Mich. U.S.A. **112** 42.57N 85.40W
Grand Rapids *town* Minn. U.S.A. **110** 47.14N 93.31W
Grand Récif de Cook *reef* N. Cal. **84** 19.25S163.50E
Grand Remous Canada **105** 46.37N 75.53W
Grandrieu France **20** 44.47N 3.38E
Grand St. Bernard, Col du *pass* Italy/Switz. **30** 45.52N 7.11E
Grand Teton *mtn.* U.S.A. **108** 43.44N110.48W
Grand Teton Nat. Park U.S.A. **108** 43.30N110.37W
Grand Traverse B. U.S.A. **112** 45.02N 85.30W
Grand Valley Canada **104** 43.54N 80.19W
Grand Valley *town* U.S.A. **108** 39.27N108.03W
Grandville U.S.A. **112** 42.54N 85.48W
Grañén Spain **25** 41.56N 0.22W
Grangärde Sweden **43** 60.16N 14.59E
Grangemouth U.K. **14** 56.01N 3.44W
Granger U.S.A. **108** 41.35N109.58W
Grängesberg Sweden **43** 60.05N 14.59E
Grangeville U.S.A. **108** 45.56N116.07W
Granite City U.S.A. **110** 38.43N 90.04W
Granite Falls *town* U.S.A. **110** 44.49N 95.31W
Granite Peak *town* Australia **88** 25.38S121.21E
Granite Peak *mtn.* U.S.A. **106** 45.10N109.50W
Granitola, Capo *c.* Italy **32** 37.33N 12.40E
Granity New Zealand **86** 41.38S171.51E
Granja Brazil **123** 3.06S 40.50W
Gränna Sweden **43** 58.01N 14.28E
Granollers Spain **25** 41.37N 2.18E
Granön Sweden **40** 64.15N 19.19E
Gran Paradiso *mtn.* Italy **30** 45.32N 7.16E
Gran Sasso d'Italia *mts.* Italy **31** 42.26N 13.35E
Gransee Germany **38** 53.00N 13.09E
Grant Mich. U.S.A. **112** 43.20N 85.49W
Grant Nebr. U.S.A. **110** 40.50N101.56W
Grant City U.S.A. **110** 40.29N 94.25W
Grantham U.K. **12** 52.55N 0.39W
Grantown-on-Spey U.K. **14** 57.20N 3.38W
Grant Range *mts.* U.S.A. **108** 38.25N115.30W
Grants U.S.A. **109** 35.09N107.52W
Grants Pass *town* U.S.A. **108** 42.26N123.19W
Grantsville U.S.A. **114** 38.55N 81.06W
Granville France **18** 48.50N 1.36W
Granville N.Dak. U.S.A. **110** 48.16N100.47W
Granville N.Y. U.S.A. **115** 43.24N 73.16W
Granville L. Canada **101** 56.18N100.30W
Gras, Lac de *l.* Canada **98** 64.30N110.30W
Graskop R.S.A. **80** 24.55S 30.50E
Grassano Italy **33** 40.38N 16.18E
Grasse France **21** 43.40N 6.55E
Grasset, L. Canada **102** 49.55N 78.00W
Grass Lake *town* U.S.A. **104** 42.15N 84.13W
Grass Valley *town* Calif. U.S.A. **108** 39.13N121.04W
Grass Valley *town* Oreg. U.S.A. **108** 45.22N120.47W
Gråsten Denmark **42** 54.55N 9.36E
Grates Pt. Canada **103** 48.09N 52.57W
Graubünden *d.* Switz. **39** 46.42N 9.25E
Grave Neth. **16** 51.45N 5.45E
Grave, Pointe de *c.* France **20** 45.34N 1.04W
Gravelbourg Canada **101** 49.53N106.34W
Gravenhurst Canada **104** 44.55N 79.22W
Gravesend Australia **93** 29.35S150.20E
Gravesend U.K. **13** 51.27N 0.24E
Gravina in Puglia Italy **33** 40.49N 16.25E
Gray France **19** 47.27N 5.35E
Grayling U.S.A. **104** 44.40N 84.43W
Grays U.K. **13** 51.29N 0.20E
Graz Austria **31** 47.05N 15.27E
Grazalema Spain **27** 36.46N 5.22W
Grdelica Yugo. **34** 42.54N 22.04E
Great Abaco I. Bahamas **113** 26.25N 77.10W
Great Artesian Basin *f.* Australia **90** 26.30S143.02E
Great Australian Bight Australia **89** 33.10S129.30E
Great B. U.S.A. **115** 39.30N 74.23W
Great Bahama Bank *f.* Bahamas **113** 23.15N 78.00W
Great Barrier I. New Zealand **86** 36.15S175.30E
Great Barrier Reef *f.* Australia **90** 16.30S146.30E
Great Barrington U.S.A. **115** 42.12N 73.22W
Great Basin *f.* U.S.A. **108** 40.35N116.00W
Great Bear L. Canada **98** 66.00N120.00W
Great Bend *town* U.S.A. **110** 38.22N 98.46W
Great Bitter L. *see* Murrah al Kubrá, Al Buḩayrah al *h5ayrah al* Egypt **66**
Great Blasket I. Rep. of Ire. **15** 52.05N 10.32W
Great Cloche I. Canada **104** 46.01N 81.54W
Great Coco *i.* Burma **56** 14.06N 93.21E
Great Divide Basin *f.* U.S.A. **108** 42.00N108.10W
Great Dividing Range *mts.* Australia **93** 29.00S152.00E
Great Driffield U.K. **12** 54.01N 0.26W
Great Duck I. Canada **104** 45.40N 82.58W
Greater Antilles *is.* C. America **117** 17.00N 70.00W
Greater London *d.* U.K. **13** 51.31N 0.06W
Greater Manchester *d.* U.K. **12** 53.30N 2.18W
Great Exuma *i.* Bahamas **117** 23.00N 76.00W
Great Falls *town* U.S.A. **108** 47.30N111.17W
Great Inagua I. Bahamas **117** 21.00N 73.20W
Great Indian Desert *see* Thar Desert India/Pakistan **62**
Great Karoo *f.* R.S.A. **80** 32.40S 22.20E
Great Kei *r.* R.S.A. **80** 32.39S 28.23E
Great L. Australia **91** 41.50S146.43E
Great Malvern U.K. **13** 52.07N 2.19W
Great Namaland *f.* Namibia **80** 25.30S 17.20E
Great Nicobar *i.* India **56** 7.00N 93.45E
Great Ouse *r.* U.K. **12** 52.47N 0.23E
Great Pt. U.S.A. **115** 41.23N 70.03W
Great Rift Valley *f.* Africa **70** 8.00S 31.30E
Great Ruaha *r.* Tanzania **79** 7.55S 37.52E
Great Sacandaga L. U.S.A. **115** 43.08N 74.10W
Great Salt L. U.S.A. **108** 41.10N112.30W
Great Salt Lake Desert U.S.A. **108** 40.40N113.30W
Great Sand Hills Canada **101** 50.35N109.05W
Great Sandy Desert Australia **88** 20.30S123.35E
Great Sandy Desert *see* An Nafūd *des.* Saudi Arabia **64**
Great Sea Reef Fiji **84** 16.25S179.20E
Great Slave L. Canada **100** 61.23N115.38W
Great Smoky Mountain Nat. Park U.S.A. **113** 35.56N 82.48W
Great Sound *b.* Bermuda **127** 32.18N 64.60W
Great Victoria Desert Australia **89** 29.00S127.30E
Great Whernside *mtn.* U.K. **12** 54.09N 1.59W
Great Yarmouth U.K. **13** 52.40N 1.45E
Great Zimbabwe *ruins* Zimbabwe **80** 20.30S 30.30E
Grebbestad Sweden **42** 58.42N 11.15E
Gréboun, Mont *mtn.* Niger **75** 20.01N 8.35E
Gredos, Sierra de *mts.* Spain **26** 40.15N 5.20W
Greece Europe **34** 40.00N 23.00E
Greeley U.S.A. **108** 40.25N104.42W
Green *r.* U.S.A. **108** 38.11N109.53W
Green B. U.S.A. **110** 45.00N 87.30W
Green Bay *town* U.S.A. **110** 44.30N 88.01W
Greenbush Mich. U.S.A. **104** 44.34N 83.19W
Greenbush Minn. U.S.A. **110** 48.42N 96.11W
Greenbushes Australia **89** 33.50S116.00E
Greencastle Ind. U.S.A. **112** 39.39N 86.51W
Greencastle Penn. U.S.A. **114** 39.47N 77.44W
Greene U.S.A. **115** 42.20N 75.46W
Greene I. Canada **104** 45.51N 83.08W
Greeneville U.S.A. **113** 36.10N 82.50W
Greenfield Ill. U.S.A. **110** 39.21N 90.21W
Greenfield Iowa U.S.A. **110** 41.18N 94.28W
Greenfield Mass. U.S.A. **115** 42.36N 72.36W
Greenfield Mo. U.S.A. **111** 37.25N 93.51W
Greenhills Australia **89** 31.58S117.01E
Greening Canada **102** 48.08N 74.55W
Greenland N. America **99** 68.00N 45.00W
Greenlaw U.K. **14** 55.43N 2.28W
Green Mts. U.S.A. **115** 43.45N 72.45W
Greenock U.K. **14** 55.57N 4.45W
Greenore Pt. Rep. of Ire. **15** 52.14N 6.19W
Greenough *r.* Australia **89** 29.22S114.34E
Greenport U.S.A. **115** 41.06N 72.22W
Green River *town* Utah U.S.A. **108** 38.59N110.10W
Green River *town* Wyo. U.S.A. **108** 41.32N109.28W
Greensboro N.C. U.S.A. **113** 36.04N 79.47W
Greensboro Vt. U.S.A. **105** 44.32N 72.17W
Greensburg Ind. U.S.A. **112** 39.20N 85.29W
Greensburg Penn. U.S.A. **114** 40.18N 79.33W
Greenvale Australia **90** 18.57S144.53E
Greenville Canada **100** 55.03N129.33W
Greenville Liberia **76** 5.01N 9.03W
Greenville Ala. U.S.A. **113** 31.50N 86.40W
Greenville Mich. U.S.A. **112** 43.11N 85.13W
Greenville Miss. U.S.A. **111** 33.25N 91.05W
Greenville Mo. U.S.A. **111** 37.08N 90.27W
Greenville N.C. U.S.A. **113** 35.36N 77.23W
Greenville N.H. U.S.A. **115** 42.46N 71.49W
Greenville Penn. U.S.A. **114** 41.24N 80.23W
Greenville S.C. U.S.A. **113** 34.52N 82.25W
Greenville Tex. U.S.A. **111** 33.08N 96.07W
Greenwich Conn U.S.A. **115** 41.01N 73.38W
Greenwich N.Y. U.S.A. **115** 41.05N 73.30W
Greenwich Ohio U.S.A. **114** 41.02N 82.31W
Greenwood Miss. U.S.A. **111** 33.31N 90.11W
Greenwood N.Y. U.S.A. **114** 42.08N 77.39W
Greenwood S.C. U.S.A. **113** 34.11N 82.10W
Gregory *r.* Australia **90** 17.53S139.17E
Gregory U.S.A. **110** 43.14N 99.26W
Gregory, L. S.A. Australia **92** 28.55S139.00E
Gregory L. W.A. Australia **88** 20.10S127.20E
Gregory Range *mts.* Australia **90** 19.00S143.05E
Greifswald Germany **38** 54.05N 13.23E
Greifswalder Bodden *c.* Germany **38** 54.15N 13.35E
Greiz Germany **38** 50.39N 12.12E
Gremikha U.S.S.R. **44** 68.03N 39.38E
Grenå Denmark **42** 56.25N 10.53E
Grenada C. America **117** 12.07N 61.40W
Grenade France **20** 43.47N 1.10E
Grenchen Switz. **39** 47.11N 7.24E
Grenen *c.* Denmark **42** 57.45N 10.40E
Grenfell Australia **93** 33.53S148.11E
Grenoble France **21** 45.10N 5.43E
Grenville, C. Australia **90** 12.00S143.13E
Gréoux-les-Bains France **21** 43.45N 5.53E
Gresik Indonesia **59** 7.12S112.38E
Gretna U.K. **14** 55.00N 3.04W
Gretna U.S.A. **111** 29.55N 90.03W
Greven Germany **38** 52.05N 7.36E
Grevená Greece **34** 40.04N 21.25E
Grevenbroich Germany **16** 51.07N 6.33E
Grevesmühlen Germany **38** 53.51N 11.10E
Grey *r.* New Zealand **86** 42.28S171.13E
Grey, C. Australia **90** 13.00S136.40E
Greybull U.S.A. **108** 44.30N108.03W
Grey Is. Canada **103** 50.50N 55.37W
Greylock, Mt. U.S.A. **115** 42.38N 73.10W
Greymouth New Zealand **86** 42.28S171.12E
Grey Range *mts.* Australia **91** 27.30S143.59E
Greystones Rep. of Ire. **15** 53.09N 6.04W
Greytown R.S.A. **80** 29.04S 30.36E
Griesbach Germany **39** 48.28N 13.11E
Griesheim Germany **39** 49.50N 8.34E
Griffin U.S.A. **107** 33.15N 84.17W
Griffith Australia **93** 34.18S146.04E
Griffith Canada **105** 45.14N 77.12W
Griffith I. Canada **104** 44.51N 80.54W
Griggsville U.S.A. **110** 39.42N 90.43W
Grignan France **21** 44.25N 4.54E
Grignols France **20** 44.23N 0.03W
Grigoriopol U.S.S.R. **37** 47.08N 29.18E
Grim, C. Australia **91** 40.45S144.45E
Grimari C.A.R. **73** 5.44N 20.03E
Grimma Germany **38** 51.14N 12.43E
Grimmen Germany **38** 54.07N 13.02E
Grimsby Canada **104** 43.12N 79.34W
Grimsby U.K. **12** 53.35N 0.05W
Grimsel Pass Switz. **39** 46.34N 8.21E
Grimstad Norway **42** 58.20N 8.36E
Grímsvötn *mtn.* Iceland **40** 64.30N 17.10W
Grindavik Iceland **40** 63.50N 22.27W
Grindelwald Switz. **39** 46.37N 8.02E
Grindsted Denmark **42** 55.45N 8.56E
Grinnell U.S.A. **110** 41.45N 92.43W
Grintavec *mtn.* Yugo. **31** 46.21N 14.32E
Griqualand East *f.* R.S.A. **80** 30.40S 29.10E
Griqualand West *f.* R.S.A. **80** 28.50S 23.30E
Gris-Nez, Cap *c.* France **18** 50.52N 1.35E
Grisslehamn Sweden **43** 60.06N 18.50E
Griva U.S.S.R. **44** 60.35N 50.58E
Grmeč *mts.* Yugo. **31** 44.40N 16.15E
Grobina U.S.S.R. **41** 56.33N 21.10E
Groblershoop R.S.A. **80** 28.55S 20.59E
Grodno U.S.S.R. **37** 53.40N 23.50E
Grodzisk Poland **36** 52.14N 16.22E
Grodzyanka U.S.S.R. **37** 53.30N 28.41E
Groenlo Neth. **16** 52.02N 6.36E
Groix, Île de *i.* France **18** 47.38N 3.27W
Gronau Germany **38** 52.13N 7.00E
Grong Norway **40** 64.27N 12.19E
Groningen Neth. **16** 53.13N 6.35E
Groningen *d.* Neth. **16** 53.15N 6.45E
Groom U.S.A. **111** 35.12N101.06W
Groot *r.* C.P. *r.* R.S.A. **80** 33.58S 25.03E
Groote Eylandt *i.* Australia **90** 14.00S136.40E
Grootfontein Namibia **80** 19.32S 18.07E
Groot Karasberge *mts.* Namibia **80** 27.20S 18.50E
Grootlaagte *r.* Botswana **80** 20.58S 21.42E
Groot Swartberge *mts.* R.S.A. **80** 33.20S 22.00E
Grossenbrode Germany **38** 54.22N 11.05E
Grossenhain Germany **38** 51.17N 13.31E
Grosser Arber *mtn.* Germany **39** 49.07N 13.07E
Grosser Priel *mtn.* Austria **39** 47.43N 14.04E
Grosseto Italy **30** 42.46N 11.08E

Gross-Gerau to **Hälleforsnäs**

Gross-Gerau Germany **39** 49.55N 8.29E
Gross Glockner *mtn.* Austria **30** 47.04N 12.42E
Grossräschen Germany **38** 51.35N 14.00E
Gross Venediger *mtn.* Austria **30** 47.06N 12.21E
Groswater B. Canada **103** 54.20N 57.30W
Grote Nete *r.* Belgium **16** 51.07N 4.20E
Groton U.S.A. **115** 42.35N 76.22W
Grottaglie Italy **33** 40.32N 17.26E
Grottaminarda Italy **33** 41.04N 15.02E
Grottammare Italy **31** 42.59N 13.52E
Groundhog *r.* Canada **102** 49.40N 82.06W
Grouse Creek *town* U.S.A. **108** 41.22N113.53W
Grove City U.S.A. **114** 41.10N 80.05W
Grover City U.S.A. **109** 35.07N120.37W
Groves U.S.A. **111** 29.57N 93.55W
Groveton N.H. U.S.A. **105** 44.36N 71.31W
Groveton Tex. U.S.A. **111** 31.03N 95.08W
Groznyy U.S.S.R. **45** 43.21N 45.42E
Grubišno Polje Yugo. **31** 45.42N 17.10E
Grudziądz Poland **37** 53.29N 18.45E
Grumeti *r.* Tanzania **79** 2.05S 33.45E
Grumo Appula Italy **33** 41.01N 16.43E
Grums Sweden **43** 59.21N 13.06E
Grünau Austria **39** 47.51N 13.57E
Grünau Namibia **80** 27.44S 18.18E
Grundarfjördhur *town* Iceland **40** 64.55N 23.20W
Grundy U.S.A. **113** 37.13N 82.08W
Grungedal Norway **42** 59.44N 7.43E
Grünstadt Germany **39** 49.34N 8.10E
Gruzinskaya S.S.R. *d.* U.S.S.R. **45** 42.00N 43.30E
Gryazovets U.S.S.R. **44** 58.52N 40.12E
Gryfice Poland **36** 53.56N 15.12E
Grythyttan Sweden **43** 59.42N 14.32E
Gstaad Switz. **39** 46.28N 7.17E
Guachipas Argentina **124** 25.31S 65.31W
Guacuí Brazil **126** 20.44S 41.40W
Guadajoz *r.* Spain **27** 37.50N 4.51W
Guadalajara Mexico **116** 20.30N103.20W
Guadalajara Spain **26** 40.38N 3.10W
Guadalajara *d.* Spain **26** 40.50N 2.50W
Guadalamar *r.* Spain **26** 38.05N 3.36W
Guadalaviar *r.* Spain **25** 40.21N 1.08W
Guadalcanal *i.* Solomon Is. **84** 9.32S160.12E
Guadalcanal Spain **26** 38.06N 5.49W
Guadalén Spain **26** 38.05N 3.32W
Guadalén, Embalse de *resr.* Spain **26** 38.25N 3.15W
Guadalete *r.* Spain **27** 36.35N 6.13W
Guadalmena *r.* Spain **26** 38.19N 2.56W
Guadalmez *r.* Spain **26** 38.46N 5.04W
Guadalope *r.* Spain **25** 41.15N 0.03W
Guadalquivir *r.* Spain **27** 36.47N 6.22W
Guadalupe Mexico **111** 25.41N100.15W
Guadalupe, Isla de *i.* Mexico **109** 29.00N118.16W
Guadalupe, Sierra de *mts.* Spain **27** 39.35N 5.25W
Guadarrama *r.* Spain **27** 39.53N 4.10W
Guadarrama, Puerto de *pass* Spain **26** 40.43N 4.10W
Guadarrama, Sierra de *mts.* Spain **26** 41.00N 3.50W
Guadazaón Spain **25** 39.42N 1.36W
Guadeloupe *i.* Leeward Is. **117** 16.20N 61.40W
Guadiana *r.* Portugal **27** 37.11N 7.24W
Guadiana Menor *r.* Spain **27** 37.56N 3.15W
Guadiaro *r.* Spain **27** 36.17N 5.17W
Guadix Spain **27** 37.18N 3.08W
Guafo, Golfo de *g.* Chile **125** 43.35S 74.15W
Guainía *r.* Colombia **122** 2.01N 67.07W
Guaíra Brazil **124** 24.04S 54.15W
Guajará Mirim Brazil **122** 10.48S 65.22W
Guajira, Península de la *pen.* Colombia **122** 12.00N 72.00W
Gualdo Tadino Italy **30** 43.14N 12.47E
Gualeguay Argentina **125** 33.10S 59.20W
Gualeguay *r.* Argentina **125** 33.18S 59.38W
Gualeguaychu Argentina **125** 33.00S 58.30W
Guam *i.* Mariana Is. **84** 13.30N144.40E
Guamal Colombia **122** 9.10N 74.15W
Guanajuato Mexico **116** 21.00N101.16W
Guanajuato *d.* Mexico **116** 21.00N101.00W
Guanare Venezuela **122** 9.04N 69.45W
Guanarito Venezuela **122** 8.43N 69.12W
Guane Cuba **117** 22.13N 84.07W
Guang'an China **55** 30.30N106.35E
Guangchang China **55** 26.50N116.16E
Guangdong *d.* China **55** 23.00N113.00E
Guanghan China **55** 30.59N104.15E
Guanghua China **54** 32.26N111.41E
Guangji China **55** 29.42N115.39E
Guangming Ding *mtn.* China **55** 30.09N118.11E
Guangnan China **55** 24.03N105.03E
Guangrao China **54** 37.04N118.22E
Guangxi Zhuangzu *d.* China **55** 23.30N109.00E
Guangyuan China **54** 32.29N105.55E
Guangze China **55** 27.27N117.23E
Guangzhou China **55** 23.08N113.20E
Guanling China **55** 25.57N105.38E
Guantánamo Cuba **117** 20.09N 75.14W
Guan Xian Shandong China **54** 36.29N115.25E
Guan Xian Sichuan China **61** 30.59N103.40E
Guanyun China **54** 34.17N119.15E
Guaporé *r.* Bolivia/Brazil **124** 12.00S 65.15W
Guaqui Bolivia **124** 16.35S 68.51W
Guara, Sierra de *mts.* Spain **25** 42.20N 0.20W
Guarabira Brazil **123** 6.46S 35.25W
Guarapuava Brazil **126** 25.22S 51.28W
Guaratinguetá Brazil **126** 22.49S 45.09W
Guarda Portugal **26** 40.32N 7.16W
Guarda *d.* Portugal **26** 40.40N 7.15W
Guardavalle Italy **33** 38.30N 16.30E
Guardiagrele Italy **31** 42.11N 14.13E
Guardo Spain **26** 42.47N 4.50W
Guareim *r.* Uruguay *see* Quarí *r.* Brazil **125**
Guareña Spain **27** 38.51N 6.06W
Guareña *r.* Spain **26** 41.29N 5.23W
Guasave Mexico **109** 25.34N108.27W
Guasipati Venezuela **122** 7.28N 61.54W
Guastalla Italy **30** 44.55N 10.39E
Guatemala C. America **117** 15.40N 90.00W
Guatemala *town* Guatemala **116** 14.38N 90.22W
Guatemala Basin Pacific Oc. **85** 12.00N 95.00W
Guatemala Trench Pacific Oc. **85** 15.00N 93.00W
Guatire Venezuela **122** 10.28N 66.32W
Guaviare *r.* Colombia **122** 4.00N 67.35W
Guaxupé Brazil **126** 21.17S 46.44W
Guayaquil Ecuador **122** 2.13S 79.54W
Guayaquil, Golfo de *g.* Ecuador **122** 3.00S 80.35W
Guaymallén Argentina **125** 32.54S 68.47W
Guaymas Mexico **109** 27.56N110.54W
Guayquiraró *r.* Argentina **125** 30.25S 59.36W
Guba Zaïre **78** 10.40S 26.26E
Gubakha U.S.S.R. **44** 58.55N 57.30E
Gubbio Italy **30** 43.21N 12.35E
Gubeikou China **54** 40.41N117.09E
Gubin Poland **36** 51.59N 14.42E
Gubio Nigeria **77** 12.31N 12.44E
Guchab Namibia **80** 19.40S 17.47E
Gucheng China **54** 37.20N115.57E
Gúdar, Sierra de *mts.* Spain **25** 40.30N 0.40W
Gudbrandsdalen *f.* Norway **41** 61.30N 10.00E
Gudhjem Denmark **43** 55.13N 14.59E
Gudvangen Norway **41** 60.52N 6.50E
Guebwiller France **19** 47.55N 7.12E
Guecho Spain **26** 43.22N 3.00W
Guékédou Guinea **76** 8.35N 10.11W
Guelma Algeria **75** 36.28N 7.26E
Guelph Canada **104** 43.33N 80.15W
Guelta Zemmur W. Sahara **74** 25.15N 12.20W
Guéméné-sur-Scorff France **18** 48.04N 3.12W
Guera *d.* Chad **77** 11.22N 18.00E
Guerande France **18** 47.20N 2.26W
Guérard, Lac *l.* Canada **103** 56.20N 65.35W
Guéret France **20** 46.10N 1.52E
Guernica Spain **26** 43.19N 2.40W
Guernsey *i.* U.K. **13** 49.27N 2.35W
Guerra Mozambique **79** 13.05S 35.12E
Guerrero *d.* Mexico **116** 18.00N100.00W
Guiana S. America **123** 3.40N 53.00W
Guiana Highlands S. America **122** 4.00N 59.00W
Guichen France **18** 47.58N 1.48W
Guichón Uruguay **125** 32.21S 57.12W
Guidimaka *d.* Mauritania **74** 15.20N 12.00W
Guiding China **55** 26.32N107.15E
Guidong China **55** 26.12N114.00E
Guiers, Lac de *l.* Senegal **76** 16.12N 15.50W
Gui Jiang *r.* China **55** 23.25N111.20E
Guijuelo Spain **26** 40.33N 5.40W
Guildford Australia **89** 31.55S115.55E
Guildford U.K. **13** 51.14N 0.35W
Guildhall U.S.A. **105** 44.34N 71.34W
Guilin China **55** 25.20N110.10E
Guillaume-Delisle, Lac *l.* Canada **102** 56.20N 75.50W
Guillaumes France **21** 44.05N 6.51E
Guillestre France **21** 44.40N 6.39E
Guilvinec France **18** 47.47N 4.17W
Guimarães Brazil **123** 2.08S 44.36W
Guimarães Portugal **26** 41.27N 8.18W
Guimeng Ding *mtn.* China **54** 35.34N117.50E
Guinan China **52** 35.20N100.50E
Guinea Africa **76** 10.30N 11.30W
Guinea, G. of Africa **77** 3.00N 3.00E
Guinea Basin *f.* Atlantic Oc. **127** 0.00 5.00W
Guinea Bissau Africa **76** 11.30N 15.00W
Güines Cuba **117** 22.50N 82.02W
Guînes France **19** 50.52N 1.52E
Guingamp France **18** 48.33N 3.11W
Guinguinéo Senegal **76** 14.20N 15.57W
Guiping China **55** 23.20N110.02E
Guipúzcoa *d.* Spain **26** 43.00N 2.20W
Guir, Hammada du *f.* Morocco/Algeria **74** 31.00N 3.20W
Güiria Venezuela **122** 10.37N 62.21W
Guiscard France **19** 49.39N 3.03E
Guise France **19** 49.54N 3.38E
Guitiriz Spain **26** 43.11N 7.54W
Guitres France **20** 45.03N 0.11W
Guiuan Phil. **59** 11.02N125.44E
Guixi China **55** 28.12N117.10E
Gui Xian China **55** 23.02N109.40E
Guiyang China **55** 26.31N106.39E
Guizhou *d.* China **55** 27.00N107.00E
Gujarat *d.* India **62** 22.20N 70.30E
Gūjar Khān Pakistan **62** 33.16N 73.19E
Gujrānwāla Pakistan **62** 32.26N 74.33E
Gujrāt Pakistan **62** 32.34N 74.05E
Gulang Gansu China **54** 37.30N102.54E
Gulargambone Australia **93** 31.21S148.32E
Gulbarga India **60** 17.22N 76.47E
Gulfport U.S.A. **111** 30.22N 89.06W
Gulgong Australia **93** 32.20S149.49E
Gulin China **55** 28.07N105.51E
Gulistān Pakistan **62** 30.36N 66.35E
Gullholmen Sweden **42** 58.11N 11.24E
Gull Lake *town* Canada **101** 50.08N108.27W
Gullspång Sweden **43** 58.59N 14.06E
Güllük Turkey **35** 37.14N 27.36E
Gulma Nigeria **77** 12.41N 4.24E
Gülpinar Turkey **34** 39.32N 26.10E
Gulshad U.S.S.R. **52** 46.37N 74.22E
Gulu Uganda **79** 2.46N 32.21E
Guluy Ethiopia **72** 14.43N 36.45E
Gulwe Tanzania **79** 6.27S 36.27E
Gulyantsi Bulgaria **34** 43.38N 24.42E
Gumal *r.* Pakistan **62** 32.08N 69.50E
Gumel Nigeria **77** 12.39N 9.23E
Gumla India **63** 23.03N 84.33E
Gummersbach Germany **38** 51.02N 7.34E
Gum Spring *town* U.S.A. **113** 37.47N 77.54W
Gümüşhane Turkey **64** 40.26N 39.26E
Guna India **62** 24.39N 77.19E
Gunbar Australia **93** 34.04S145.25E
Gundagai Australia **93** 35.07S148.05E
Gundlupet India **60** 11.48N 76.41E
Gungu Zaïre **78** 5.43S 19.20E
Gunisao *r.* Canada **101** 53.54N 97.58W
Gunisao L. Canada **101** 53.33N 96.15W
Gunnebo Sweden **43** 57.43N 16.32E
Gunnedah Australia **93** 30.59S150.15E
Gunning Australia **93** 34.46S149.17E
Gunnison *r.* U.S.A. **108** 39.03N108.35W
Gunnison Colo. U.S.A. **108** 38.33N106.56W
Gunnison Utah U.S.A. **108** 39.09N111.49W
Guntersville U.S.A. **113** 34.20N 86.18W
Guntersville L. U.S.A. **113** 34.45N 86.03W
Guntūr India **61** 16.20N 80.27E
Gunungsitoli Indonesia **58** 1.17N 97.37E
Gunupur India **63** 19.05N 83.49E
Günz *r.* Germany **39** 48.27N 10.16E
Günzburg Germany **39** 48.27N 10.16E
Gunzenhausen Germany **39** 49.07N 10.45E
Guochengyi China **54** 36.14N104.52E
Gurais Jammu & Kashmir **62** 34.38N 74.50E
Gura Portiţei *f.* Romania **37** 44.40N 29.00E
Gurban Obo China **54** 43.05N112.27E
Gurdāspur Jammu & Kashmir **62** 32.02N 75.31E
Gurgaon India **62** 28.28N 77.02E
Gurgueia *r.* Brazil **123** 6.45S 43.35W
Gūrha India **62** 25.14N 71.45E
Gurk *r.* Austria **31** 46.36N 14.31E
Gursköy *i.* Norway **40** 62.16N 5.42E
Gurué Mozambique **81** 15.30S 36.58E
Gürün Turkey **64** 38.44N 37.15E
Gurupá Brazil **123** 1.25S 51.39W
Gurupi *r.* Brazil **123** 1.13S 46.06W
Guru Sikhar *mtn.* India **62** 24.39N 72.46E
Guruve Zimbabwe **80** 16.42S 30.40E
Gurvan Sayhan Uul *mts.* Mongolia **54** 43.45N103.30E
Guryev U.S.S.R. **45** 47.08N 51.59E
Gusau Nigeria **77** 12.12N 6.40E
Gusev U.S.S.R. **37** 54.32N 22.12E
Gusong China **55** 28.25N105.12E
Guspini Italy **32** 39.32N 8.38E
Güssing Austria **31** 47.04N 16.20E
Gustav Holm, Kap *c.* Greenland **99** 67.00N 34.00W
Güstrow Germany **38** 53.48N 12.10E
Gusum Sweden **43** 58.16N 16.29E
Gütersloh Germany **38** 51.54N 8.23E
Guthrie Ky. U.S.A. **113** 36.40N 87.10W
Guthrie Okla. U.S.A. **111** 35.53N 97.25W
Guvrin, Nahal *wadi* Israel **67** 31.43N 34.42E
Guyana S. America **122** 4.40N 59.00W
Guyang China **54** 41.03N110.03E
Guymon U.S.A. **111** 36.41N101.29W
Guyra Australia **93** 30.14S151.40E
Guyuan Hebei China **54** 41.40N115.41E
Guyuan Ningxia Huizu China **54** 36.00N106.25E
Guzhen Anhui China **54** 33.19N117.19E
Guzman, Laguna de *l.* Mexico **109** 31.25N107.25W
Gwa Burma **61** 17.36N 94.35E
Gwabegar Australia **93** 30.34S149.00E
Gwadabawa Nigeria **77** 13.23N 5.15E
Gwādar Pakistan **62** 25.07N 62.19E
Gwagwada Nigeria **77** 10.15N 7.15E
Gwai Zimbabwe **80** 19.15S 27.42E
Gwai *r.* Zimbabwe **80** 17.59S 26.55E
Gwalior India **63** 26.13N 78.10E
Gwanda Zimbabwe **80** 20.59S 29.00E
Gwane Zaïre **73** 4.43N 25.50E
Gwasero Nigeria **77** 9.30N 8.30E
Gweebarra B. Rep. of Ire. **15** 54.52N 8.28W
Gwent *d.* U.K. **13** 51.44N 3.00W
Gweru Zimbabwe **80** 19.25S 29.50E
Gwydir *r.* Australia **93** 29.35S148.45E
Gwynedd *d.* U.K. **12** 53.00N 4.00W
Gy France **19** 47.24N 5.49E
Gyaca China **63** 29.05N 92.55E
Gyandzha U.S.S.R. **65** 40.39N 46.20E
Gyangrang China **63** 30.47N 85.09E
Gyangzê China **63** 28.57N 89.38E
Gyaring Co *l.* China **63** 31.05N 88.00E
Gydanskiy Poluostrov *pen.* U.S.S.R. **50** 70.00N 78.30E
Gyimda China **63** 31.03N 97.18E
Gyirong China **63** 29.00N 85.15E
Gympie Australia **90** 26.11S152.40E
Gyōda Japan **57** 36.08N139.28E
Gyöngyös Hungary **37** 47.47N 19.56E
Györ Hungary **37** 47.41N 17.40E
Gypsum Pt. Canada **100** 61.53N114.35W
Gypsumville Canada **101** 51.45N 98.35W
Gyueshovo Bulgaria **34** 42.14N 22.28E

H

Haag Germany **39** 48.10N 12.11E
Haan Germany **16** 51.10N 7.02E
Ha'apai Group *is.* Tonga **85** 19.50S174.30W
Haapajärvi Finland **40** 63.45N 25.20E
Haapamäki Finland **40** 62.15N 24.28E
Haapavesi Finland **40** 64.08N 25.22E
Haapsalu U.S.S.R. **41** 58.56N 23.33E
Haar Germany **39** 48.06N 11.44E
Hā Arava *r.* Israel/Jordan **66** 30.30N 35.10E
Haarlem Neth. **16** 52.22N 4.38E
Haarlem R.S.A. **80** 33.46S 23.28E
Hab *r.* Pakistan **62** 24.53N 66.41E
Habahe China **52** 47.53N 86.12E
Ḥabarūt Yemen **60** 17.18N 52.44E
Habaswein Kenya **79** 1.06N 39.26E
Habay-la-Neuve Belgium **16** 49.45N 5.38E
Ḥabbān Yemen **71** 14.21N 47.05E
Hab Chauki Pakistan **62** 25.01N 66.53E
Habiganj Bangla. **63** 24.23N 91.25E
Habikino Japan **57** 34.33N135.37E
Habo Sweden **43** 57.55N 14.04E
Hachinohe Japan **57** 40.30N141.30E
Hachiōji Japan **57** 35.39N139.20E
Hack, Mt. Australia **92** 30.44S138.45E
Hadāli Pakistan **62** 32.18N 72.12E
Hadano Japan **57** 35.22N139.14E
Ḥadāribah, Ra's al *c.* Sudan **72** 22.04N 36.54E
Hadarom *d.* Israel **67** 31.15N 34.50E
Ḥaḍbaram Oman **71** 17.27N 55.15E
Ḥadd, Ra's al *c.* Oman **65** 22.32N 59.49E
Haddington U.K. **14** 55.57N 2.47W
Hadejia Nigeria **77** 12.30N 10.03E
Hadejia *r.* Nigeria **77** 12.47N 10.44E
Hadera Israel **67** 32.26N 34.55E
Hadera *r.* Israel **67** 32.27N 35.53E
Haderslev Denmark **42** 55.15N 9.30E
Hadībоh Yemen **71** 12.39N 54.02E
Hadjer Mornou *mtn.* Chad **72** 17.12N 23.08E
Hadley N.Y. U.S.A. **115** 43.19N 73.51W
Hadley Penn. U.S.A. **114** 41.25N 80.14W
Ha Dong Vietnam **55** 20.40N105.58E
Ḥaḍramawt *f.* Yemen **71** 16.30N 49.30E
Hadsten Denmark **42** 56.20N 10.03E
Hadsund Denmark **42** 56.43N 10.07E
Haedo, Cuchilla de *mts.* Uruguay **125** 31.50S 56.10W
Haegeland Norway **42** 58.15N 7.47E
Haeju N. Korea **53** 38.04N125.40E
Haena Hawaiian Is. **85** 22.14N159.34W
Ḥafar al Bāṭin Saudi Arabia **65** 28.28N 46.00E
Ḥafīrah, Qā'al *f.* Jordan **67** 31.06N 36.14E
Hāfizābād Pakistan **62** 32.04N 73.41E
Hafnarfjördhur *town* Iceland **40** 64.04N 21.58W
Haft Gel Iran **65** 31.28N 49.35E
HaGalil *f.* Israel **67** 32.54N 35.20E
Hagen Germany **38** 51.22N 7.28E
Hagenow Germany **38** 53.26N 11.11E
Hagerman U.S.A. **109** 33.07N104.20W
Hagerstown U.S.A. **114** 39.39N 77.43W
Hagersville Canada **104** 42.58N 80.03W
Hagetmau France **20** 43.40N 0.35W
Hagfors Sweden **43** 60.02N 13.42E
Hagi Japan **57** 34.25N131.22E
Ha Giang Vietnam **55** 22.50N105.00E
Hagondange France **19** 49.15N 6.10E
Hags Head Rep. of Ire. **15** 52.56N 9.29W
Hague U.S.A. **115** 43.45N 73.31W
Hague, Cap de la *c.* France **18** 49.44N 1.56W
Haguenau France **19** 48.49N 7.47E
Hahn Germany **38** 50.31N 7.53E
Hai'an Shan *mts.* China **55** 23.00N115.30E
Haicheng China **54** 40.52N122.48E
Hai Duong Vietnam **56** 20.56N106.21E
Haifa *see* Hefa Israel **67**
Haifa, B. of *see* Mifraz Hefa Israel **67**
Haifeng China **55** 22.58N115.20E
Haikang China **55** 20.55N110.04E
Haikou China **55** 20.03N110.27E
Ḥā'il Saudi Arabia **64** 27.31N 41.45E
Hailākāndi India **63** 24.41N 92.34E
Hailar China **53** 49.15N119.41E
Haileybury Canada **104** 47.27N 79.38W
Hailong China **54** 42.39N125.49E
Hailsham U.K. **13** 50.52N 0.17E
Hailun China **53** 47.29N126.58E
Hailuoto *i.* Finland **40** 65.02N 24.42E
Haimen China **55** 28.41N121.30E
Hainan *d.* China **55** 19.00N109.30E
Hainaut *d.* Belgium **16** 50.30N 3.45E
Haines Alas. U.S.A. **100** 59.11N135.23W
Haines Oreg. U.S.A. **108** 44.55N117.56W
Haines Junction Canada **100** 60.45N137.30W
Haining China **55** 30.30N120.35E
Haiphong Vietnam **55** 20.48N106.40E
Haiti C. America **117** 19.00N 73.00W
Haiyang China **54** 36.46N121.09E
Haiyuan China **54** 36.35N105.40E
Ḥajar Banga Sudan **73** 11.30N 23.00E
Hajdúböszörmény Hungary **37** 47.41N 21.30E
Hajdúszoboszló Hungary **37** 47.27N 21.24E
Hajiki saki *c.* Japan **57** 38.25N138.32E
Hājīpur India **63** 25.41N 85.13E
Hakkâri Turkey **65** 37.36N 43.45E
Hakodate Japan **57** 41.46N140.44E
Hakupu Niue **84** 19.07S169.51W
Hala Pakistan **62** 25.49N 68.25E
Ḥalab Syria **64** 36.14N 37.10E
Ḥalabjah Iraq **65** 35.10N 45.59E
Ḥalā'ib Sudan **72** 22.13N 36.38E
Hålaveden *hills* Sweden **43** 58.05N 14.45E
Ḥalbā Lebanon **66** 34.34N 36.05E
Halberstadt Germany **38** 51.54N 11.02E
Halden Norway **42** 59.09N 11.23E
Haldensleben Germany **38** 52.18N 11.26E
Haldia India **63** 22.05N 88.03E
Haldwāni India **63** 29.13N 79.31E
Hale U.S.A. **104** 44.23N 83.48W
Haleyville U.S.A. **113** 34.12N 87.38W
Half Assini Ghana **76** 5.04N 2.53W
Halfmoon Bay *town* Canada **100** 49.31N123.54W
Halfmoon Bay *town* New Zealand **86** 46.45S168.08E
Ḥalḥūl Jordan **67** 31.35N 35.07E
Haliburton Canada **104** 45.03N 78.30W
Haliburton Highlands Canada **104** 45.16N 78.19W
Halicarnassus *site* Turkey **35** 37.03N 27.28E
Halifax Canada **103** 44.39N 63.36W
Halifax U.K. **12** 53.43N 1.51W
Halifax U.S.A. **113** 36.46N 78.57W
Halīl *r.* Iran **60** 27.35N 58.44E
Halkett, C. U.S.A. **98** 71.00N152.00W
Halkirk U.K. **14** 58.30N 3.30W
Halladale *r.* U.K. **14** 58.34N 3.54W
Halland *d.* Sweden **43** 56.48N 12.50E
Halland *f.* Sweden **43** 57.03N 12.45E
Hallands Väderö *i.* Sweden **43** 56.26N 12.33E
Halle Belgium **16** 50.45N 4.14E
Halle Germany **38** 51.29N 11.58E
Hällefors Sweden **43** 59.47N 14.30E
Hälleforsnäs Sweden **43** 59.10N 16.30E

Hallein to Helgoland

Hallein Austria 39 47.41N 13.06E
Halligen is. Germany 38 54.35N 8.35E
Hallingdal f. Norway 41 60.30N 9.00E
Hall Is. Pacific Oc. 84 8.37N152.00E
Hall Lake town Canada 99 68.40N 81.30W
Hällnäs Sweden 40 64.19N 19.38E
Hall Pen. Canada 99 63.30N 66.00W
Hallsberg Sweden 43 59.04N 15.07E
Hall's Creek town Australia 88 18.13S127.39E
Hallstahammar Sweden 43 59.37N 16.13E
Hallstatt Austria 39 47.33N 13.39E
Hallstavik Sweden 43 60.03N 18.36E
Hallstead U.S.A. 115 41.58N 75.45W
Hallton U.S.A. 114 41.26N 78.56W
Halmahera i. Indonesia 59 0.45N128.00E
Halmstad Sweden 43 56.39N 12.50E
Halsa Norway 40 63.03N 8.14E
Hälsingborg Sweden 43 56.03N 12.42E
Haltern Germany 38 51.46N 7.10E
Haltia Tunturi mtn. Finland 40 69.17N 21.21E
Haltwhistle U.K. 12 54.58N 2.27W
Ham France 19 49.45N 3.04E
Ham, Mt. Canada 105 45.47N 71.37W
Ḩamaḑ, Wādī al r. Saudi Arabia 64 25.49N 36.37E
Hamada f. see Drâa, Hamada du f. W. Sahara 74
Hamadān Iran 65 34.47N 48.33E
Ḩamādat Marzūq f. Libya 75 26.00N 12.30E
Ḩamāh Syria 66 35.09N 36.44E
Hamakita Japan 57 34.48N137.47E
Hamamatsu Japan 57 34.42N137.44E
Hamar Norway 41 60.48N 11.06E
Hamaröy Norway 40 68.05N 15.40E
Ḩamāţah, Jabal mtn. Egypt 64 24.11N 35.01E
Hamborn Germany 16 51.29N 6.46E
Hamburg Germany 38 53.33N 9.59E
Hamburg d. Germany 38 53.35N 10.00E
Hamburg R.S.A. 80 33.17S 27.27E
Hamburg N.J. U.S.A. 115 41.09N 74.35W
Hamburg N.Y. U.S.A. 114 42.43N 78.50W
Hamburg Penn. U.S.A. 115 40.34N 75.59W
Hamburgsund Sweden 42 58.33N 11.16E
Hamden U.S.A. 115 41.21N 72.56W
Häme d. Finland 41 61.20N 24.30E
Hämeenlinna Finland 41 61.00N 24.27E
Hamelin B. Australia 89 34.10S115.00E
Hameln Germany 38 52.06N 9.21E
HaMerkaz d. Israel 67 32.05N 34.55E
Hamer Koke Ethiopia 73 5.12N 36.45E
Hamersley Range mts. Australia 88 22.00S118.00E
Hamhŭng N. Korea 53 39.54N127.35E
Hami China 52 42.40N 93.30E
Hamidiye Turkey 34 41.09N 26.40E
Hamilton Australia 92 37.45S142.04E
Hamilton r. Australia 91 27.12S135.28E
Hamilton Bermuda 127 32.18N 64.48W
Hamilton Canada 104 43.15N 79.51W
Hamilton New Zealand 86 37.46S175.18E
Hamilton U.K. 14 55.46N 4.10W
Hamilton Mont. U.S.A. 108 46.15N114.09W
Hamilton N.Y. U.S.A. 115 42.50N 75.33W
Hamilton Ohio U.S.A. 112 39.23N 84.33W
Hamilton Tex. U.S.A. 111 31.42N 98.07W
Hamley Bridge town Australia 92 34.21S138.41E
Hamlin Tex. U.S.A. 111 32.53N100.08W
Hamlin W.Va. U.S.A. 114 38.17N 82.06W
Hamm Germany 38 51.41N 7.49E
Hammamet, Golfe de g. Tunisia 75 36.05N 10.40E
Hammam Lif Tunisia 32 36.44N 10.20E
Hammān, Wādī al Jordan 67 31.38N 36.00E
Ḩammār, Hawr al l. Iraq 65 30.50N 47.00E
Hammel Denmark 42 56.15N 9.52E
Hammelburg Germany 39 50.07N 9.53E
Hammerdal Sweden 40 63.35N 15.20E
Hammerfest Norway 40 70.40N 23.42E
Hammond Australia 92 32.33S138.20E
Hammond La. U.S.A. 111 30.30N 90.28W
Hammond N.Y. U.S.A. 105 44.27N 75.42W
Hammond B. U.S.A. 104 45.33N 84.00W
Hammondsport U.S.A. 114 42.25N 77.13W
Hammonton U.S.A. 115 39.38N 74.48W
Ham Nord Canada 105 45.54N 71.39W
Hamoir Belgium 16 50.25N 5.32E
Hamoyet, Jabal mtn. Sudan 72 17.33N 38.00E
Hampshire d. U.K. 13 51.03N 1.20W
Hampton N.H. U.S.A. 115 42.56N 70.50W
Hampton S.C. U.S.A. 113 32.52N 81.06W
Hampton Va. U.S.A. 113 37.02N 76.23W
Hampton Bays town U.S.A. 115 40.53N 72.31W
Hamra, Saguia el wadi W. Sahara 74 27.15N 13.21W
Ḩamrīn, Jabal mts. Iraq 65 34.40N 44.10E
Ham Sud Canada 105 45.46N 71.36W
Hāmūn-e Jaz Mūrīān l. Iran 60 27.20N 58.55E
Hana Hawaiian Is. 85 20.45N155.59W
Hanamaki Japan 57 39.23N141.07E
Hanang mtn. Tanzania 79 4.30S 35.21E
Hanau Germany 39 50.08N 8.55E
Hancheng China 54 35.29N110.30E
Hancock Md. U.S.A. 114 39.42N 78.13W
Hancock Mich. U.S.A. 112 47.08N 88.34W
Hancock N.Y. U.S.A. 115 41.57N 75.17W
Handa Japan 57 34.53N136.56E
Handa Somali Rep. 71 10.39N 51.08E
Handan China 54 36.37N114.26E
Handen Sweden 43 59.10N 18.08E
Handeni Tanzania 79 5.25S 38.04E
HaNegev des. Israel 66 30.42N 34.55E
Hanford U.S.A. 109 36.20N119.39W
Hanga Roa I. de Pascua 85 27.09S109.26W
Hanggin Houqi China 54 40.50N107.06E
Hanggin Qi China 54 39.56N108.54E
Hangö Finland 41 59.50N 22.57E
Hangu China 54 39.11N117.45E
Hangu Pakistan 62 33.32N 71.04E
Hangzhou China 55 30.14N120.08E
Hangzhou Wan b. China 55 30.25N121.00E
Hanita Israel 67 33.05N 35.10E
Hanjiang China 55 25.30N119.14E
Hankey R.S.A. 80 33.50S 24.52E
Hankinson U.S.A. 110 46.04N 96.55W
Hanksville U.S.A. 108 38.21N110.44W
Hānle Jammu & Kashmir 63 32.48N 79.00E
Hanmer Springs town New Zealand 86 42.31S172.50E
Hann, Mt. Australia 88 15.55S125.57E
Hanna Canada 101 51.38N111.54W
Hannaford U.S.A. 110 47.19N 98.11W
Hannah B. Canada 102 51.20N 80.00W
Hannibal Mo. U.S.A. 107 39.41N 91.25W
Hannibal Ohio U.S.A. 114 39.39N 80.51W
Hannover Germany 38 52.24N 9.44E
Hannut Belgium 16 50.40N 5.05E
Hanöbukten b. Sweden 43 55.47N 15.00E
Hanoi Vietnam 55 21.01N105.53E
Hanover Canada 104 44.09N 81.02W
Hanover R.S.A. 80 31.04S 24.25E
Hanover Mass. U.S.A. 115 42.07N 70.49W
Hanover N.H. U.S.A. 115 43.42N 72.18W
Hanover Penn. U.S.A. 114 39.48N 76.59W
Hanover, Isla i. Chile 125 50.57S 74.40W
Han Pijesak Yugo. 31 44.04N 18.59E
Hānsdiha India 63 24.36N 87.05E
Hanshou China 55 28.55N111.58E
Han Shui r. China 55 30.32N114.20E
Hānsi Haryana India 62 29.06N 75.58E
Hansi Himachal P. India 63 32.27N 77.50E
Hanson, L. Australia 92 31.02S136.13E
Hanstholm Denmark 42 57.07N 8.38E
Hantengri Feng mtn. China 52 42.09N 80.12E
Han Ul China 54 45.10N119.48E
Hanyang China 55 30.42N113.50E
Hanyin China 54 32.53N108.37E
Hanzhong China 54 33.08N107.04E
Haouach, Ouadi wadi Chad 75 16.45N 19.35E
Haparanda Sweden 40 65.50N 24.10E
Happy Valley town Canada 103 53.16N 60.14W
Hapsu N. Korea 53 41.12N128.48E
Hāpur India 63 28.43N 77.47E
Ḩaql Saudi Arabia 66 29.14N 34.56E
Ḩaraḑ Saudi Arabia 65 24.12N 49.08E
Harare Zimbabwe 81 17.49S 31.04E
Har-Ayrag Mongolia 54 45.42N109.14E
Haraze Chad 73 9.55N 20.48E
Harbin China 53 45.45N126.41E
Harboör Denmark 42 56.37N 8.12E
Harbor Beach U.S.A. 104 43.51N 82.39W
Harborcreek U.S.A. 114 42.10N 79.57W
Harbour Deep town Canada 103 50.22N 56.27W
Harbour Grace town Canada 103 47.42N 53.13W
Harburg Germany 36 53.27N 9.58E
Hårby Denmark 42 55.13N 10.07E
Harda India 62 22.20N 77.06E
Hardangerfjorden est. Norway 41 60.10N 6.00E
Hardangerjökulen mtn. Norway 41 60.33N 7.26E
Hardanger Vidda f. Norway 42 60.15N 7.20E
Hardeeville U.S.A. 113 32.18N 81.05W
Hardenberg Neth. 16 52.36N 6.40E
Harderwijk Neth. 16 52.21N 5.37E
Harding R.S.A. 80 30.34S 29.52E
Hardman U.S.A. 108 45.10N119.40W
Hardoi India 63 27.25N 80.07E
Hardwār India 63 29.58N 78.10E
Hardwick U.S.A. 105 44.30N 72.22W
Hardwicke B. Australia 92 34.52S137.10E
Hardy U.S.A. 111 36.19N 91.29W
Hare B. Canada 103 51.18N 55.50W
Haren Germany 38 52.47N 7.14E
Hārer Ethiopia 73 9.20N 42.10E
Hārergē d. Ethiopia 73 8.00N 41.00E
Harfleur France 18 49.30N 0.12E
Hargeysa Somali Rep. 71 9.31N 44.02E
Har Hu l. China 52 38.20N 97.40E
Hari r. Indonesia 58 1.00S104.15E
Harima nada str. Japan 57 34.30N134.30E
Harīpur Pakistan 62 33.59N 72.56E
Ḩarīr r. Syria 67 32.45N 35.55E
Harīrūd r. Afghan. 60 35.42N 61.12E
Harlan U.S.A. 110 41.39N 95.19W
Harlech U.K. 12 52.52N 4.08W
Harlem U.S.A. 108 48.32N108.47W
Harlingen Neth. 16 53.10N 5.25E
Harlingen U.S.A. 111 26.11N 97.42W
Harlow U.K. 13 51.47N 0.08E
Harlowton U.S.A. 108 46.26N109.50W
Harman U.S.A. 114 38.55N 79.32W
Harnai Pakistan 62 30.06N 67.56E
Harnātānr India 63 27.19N 84.01E
Harney Basin f. U.S.A. 108 43.15N120.40W
Harney L. U.S.A. 108 43.14N119.07W
Härnösand Sweden 40 62.37N 17.55E
Har Nuur l. Mongolia 52 48.00N 93.25E
Haro Spain 26 42.35N 2.51W
Haroldswick U.K. 10 60.47N 0.50W
Harper Liberia 76 4.25N 7.43W
Harpers Ferry town U.S.A. 114 39.13N 77.45W
Harrai India 63 22.37N 79.13E
Harricana r. Canada 102 51.10N 79.45W
Harrigan, C. Canada 103 55.50N 60.21W
Harrington Australia 93 31.50S152.43E
Harrington U.S.A. 115 38.56N 75.35W
Harrington Harbour Canada 103 50.31N 59.30W
Harris Canada 101 51.44N107.35W
Harris i. U.K. 14 57.50N 6.55W
Harris, L. Australia 92 31.08S135.14E
Harris, Sd. of U.K. 14 57.43N 7.05W
Harrisburg Ill. U.S.A. 111 37.44N 88.33W
Harrisburg Oreg. U.S.A. 108 44.16N123.10W
Harrisburg Penn. U.S.A. 114 40.16N 76.52W
Harrismith Australia 89 32.55S117.50E
Harrismith R.S.A. 80 28.15S 29.07E
Harrison Ark. U.S.A. 111 36.14N 93.07W
Harrison Nebr. U.S.A. 110 42.41N103.53W
Harrison, C. Canada 103 54.55N 57.55W
Harrisonburg U.S.A. 114 38.27N 78.54W
Harrison L. Canada 100 49.33N121.50W
Harrisonville U.S.A. 110 38.39N 94.21W
Harrisville W.Va. U.S.A. 114 39.13N 81.03W
Harrisville Mich. U.S.A. 104 44.39N 83.17W
Harrisville N.Y. U.S.A. 105 44.09N 75.19W
Harrodsburg U.S.A. 113 37.46N 84.51W
Harrogate U.K. 12 53.59N 1.32W
Harrow Canada 104 42.02N 82.55W
Harrow U.K. 13 51.35N 0.21W
Harrowsmith Canada 105 44.24N 76.40W
Harstad Norway 40 68.48N 16.30E
Harsūd India 62 22.06N 76.44E
Hart, L. Australia 92 31.08S136.24E
Ḩartā Jordan 67 32.48N 36.34E
Hartford U.S.A. 115 41.46N 72.41W
Hartland Canada 103 46.18N 67.32W
Hartland U.K. 13 50.59N 4.29W
Hartland Pt. U.K. 13 51.01N 4.32W
Hartlepool U.K. 12 54.42N 1.11W
Hartley Bay town Canada 100 53.27N129.18W
Hartola Finland 41 61.35N 26.01E
Hartshorne U.S.A. 111 34.51N 95.33W
Harts Range town Australia 90 23.06S134.55E
Hartsville U.S.A. 113 34.23N 80.05W
Hārūnābād Pakistan 62 29.37N 73.08E
Har Us Nuur l. Mongolia 52 48.10N 92.10E
Hārūt r. Afghan. 62 31.35N 61.18E
Harvey Australia 89 33.06S115.50E
Harvey Ill. U.S.A. 110 41.37N 87.39W
Harvey N.Dak. U.S.A. 110 47.47N 99.56W
Harwich U.K. 13 51.56N 1.18E
Haryana d. India 62 29.15N 76.30E
Harz mts. Germany 38 51.43N 10.40E
Ḩasā, Wādī al r. Jordan 66 31.01N 35.29E
Hasa Oasis see Aḩsā', Wāḩat al oasis Saudi Arabia 65
Hasdo r. India 63 21.44N 82.44E
Hase r. Germany 38 52.41N 7.18E
Haselünne Germany 38 52.40N 7.29E
Hasenkamp Argentina 125 31.30S 59.50W
Hashābah Sudan 72 14.19N 32.19E
Ḩasharūd Iran 65 37.29N 47.05E
Hashefela f. Israel 67 31.40N 34.55E
Hashimoto Japan 57 34.19N135.37E
Haskell U.S.A. 111 33.10N 99.44W
Hasle Denmark 43 55.11N 14.43E
Haslemere U.K. 13 51.05N 0.41W
Haslev Denmark 42 55.20N 11.58E
Hasselt Belgium 16 50.56N 5.20E
Hassfurt Germany 39 50.02N 10.31E
Hassi bel Guebbour Algeria 75 28.30N 6.41E
Hassi er Rmel well Algeria 75 32.57N 3.11E
Hassi Messaoud Algeria 75 31.43N 6.03E
Hassi Tagsist well Algeria 74 25.20N 1.35E
Hässleholm Sweden 43 56.09N 13.46E
Hassloch Germany 39 49.22N 8.16E
Hastings Australia 93 38.18S145.12E
Hastings Canada 105 44.18N 77.57W
Hastings New Zealand 86 39.39S176.52E
Hastings U.K. 13 50.51N 0.36E
Hastings Nebr. U.S.A. 110 40.35N 98.23W
Hatanbulag Mongolia 54 43.08N109.05E
Hatch U.S.A. 109 32.40N107.09W
Hatches Creek town Australia 90 20.56S135.12E
Hatfield Australia 92 33.53S143.47E
Hatfield U.K. 13 51.46N 0.13W
Hāthras India 63 27.36N 78.03E
Hātia I. Bangla. 63 22.40N 90.55E
Ha Tinh Vietnam 56 18.21N105.55E
Hatta India 63 24.07N 79.36E
Hattah Australia 92 34.52S142.23E
Hattem Neth. 16 52.29N 6.06E
Hatteras, C. U.S.A. 113 35.13N 75.32W
Hattiesburg U.S.A. 111 31.19N 89.16W
Hattingen Germany 16 51.24N 7.09E
Hatton U.S.A. 108 46.46N118.49W
Hatutu i. Is. Marquises 85 7.56S140.38W
Hatvan Hungary 37 47.40N 19.41E
Hauge Norway 42 58.18N 6.15E
Haugesund Norway 42 59.25N 5.18E
Haugsdorf Austria 36 48.42N 16.05E
Hauraki G. New Zealand 86 36.30S175.00E
Hausach Germany 39 48.17N 8.10E
Haut Atlas mts. Morocco 74 31.30N 7.00W
Haute-Corse d. France 21 42.30N 9.20E
Haute-Garonne d. France 20 43.25N 1.30E
Haute Kotto d. C.A.R. 73 7.15N 23.30E
Haute-Loire d. France 20 45.05N 3.50E
Haute-Marne d. France 19 48.05N 5.10E
Haute Maurice Prov. Park Canada 102 48.38N 74.30W
Haute-Normandie d. France 18 49.30N 1.00E
Haute-Pyrénées d. France 20 43.00N 0.10E
Hauterive Canada 103 49.11N 68.16W
Hautes-Alpes d. France 21 44.40N 6.30E
Haute-Saône d. France 19 47.40N 6.10E
Haute-Savoie d. France 21 46.00N 6.20E
Haute-Vienne d. France 20 45.50N 1.15E
Haut Mbomou d. C.A.R. 73 6.25N 26.10E
Hautmont France 19 50.15N 3.56E
Haut-Rhin d. France 19 47.53N 7.13E
Hauts Bassins d. Burkina 76 10.45N 4.30W
Hauts Plateau f. Morocco/Algeria 74 34.00N 0.10W
Haut Zaïre d. Zaïre 79 2.00N 27.00E
Havana see La Habana Cuba 117
Havant U.K. 13 50.51N 0.59W
Havel r. Germany 38 52.53N 11.58E
Havelange Belgium 16 50.23N 5.14E
Havelberg Germany 38 52.50N 12.04E
Havelland f. Germany 38 52.30N 12.35E
Havelock Canada 105 44.26N 77.53W
Havelock New Zealand 86 41.17S173.46E
Haverfordwest U.K. 13 51.48N 4.59W
Haverhill U.K. 13 52.06N 0.27E
Haverhill U.S.A. 115 42.47N 71.05W
Havlíčkuv Brod Czech. 36 49.38N 15.35E
Havre U.S.A. 108 48.33N109.41W
Havre de Grace U.S.A. 115 39.33N 76.06W
Havre St. Pierre Canada 103 50.15N 63.36W
Hawaii d. U.S.A. 106 21.00N156.00W
Hawaii i. Hawaii U.S.A. 106 19.30N155.30W
Hawaiian Is. U.S.A. 106 21.00N157.00W
Hawdon North, L. Australia 92 37.09S139.54E
Hawea, L. New Zealand 86 44.30S169.15E
Hawera New Zealand 86 39.35S174.19E
Hawick U.K. 14 55.25N 2.47W
Hawke B. New Zealand 86 39.18S177.15E
Hawker Australia 92 31.53S138.25E
Hawker Gate Australia 92 29.46S141.00E
Hawke's Bay d. New Zealand 86 39.00S176.35E
Hawkesbury Canada 105 45.36N 74.37W
Hawks U.S.A. 104 45.16N 83.53W
Hawley U.S.A. 115 41.28N 75.11W
Ḩawrān, Wādī r. Iraq 64 33.57N 42.35E
Ḩawsh 'Īsá Egypt 66 30.55N 30.17E
Hawthorne U.S.A. 108 38.32N118.38W
Hay Australia 93 34.31S144.31E
Hay r. Australia 90 25.00S138.00E
Hay r. Canada 100 60.49N115.52W
Haya r. Japan 57 35.30N138.26E
Hayange France 19 49.20N 6.03E
Haybān Sudan 71 11.13N 30.31E
Haydān, Wādī al Jordan 67 31.27N 35.36E
Hayden U.S.A. 109 33.00N110.47W
Hayes r. Canada 101 57.03N 92.09W
Hayes Creek town Australia 88 13.27S131.25E
Hayesville U.S.A. 114 40.46N 82.16W
Hay-on-Wye U.K. 13 52.04N 3.09W
Hay River town Canada 100 60.51N115.44W
Hays U.S.A. 110 38.53N 99.20W
Hayward U.S.A. 110 46.02N 91.26W
Haywards Heath f. U.K. 13 51.00N 0.05E
HaZafon d. Israel 67 32.50N 35.20E
Hazārān, Kūh-e mtn. Iran 65 29.30N 57.18E
Hazard U.S.A. 113 37.14N 83.11W
Hazārībāgh India 63 23.59N 85.21E
Hazel Hurst U.S.A. 114 41.42N 78.35W
Hazelton Canada 100 55.20N127.42W
Hazelton U.S.A. 110 46.29N100.17W
Hazen U.S.A. 108 39.34N119.03W
Hazerim Israel 67 31.14N 34.43E
Hazlehurst Ga. U.S.A. 113 31.53N 82.34W
Hazlehurst Miss. U.S.A. 111 31.52N 90.24W
Hazleton U.S.A. 115 40.58N 75.59W
Hazor Israel 67 32.59N 35.33E
Hazor Ashdod Israel 67 31.46N 34.43E
Head Waters U.S.A. 114 38.20N 79.21W
Healdsburg U.S.A. 108 38.37N122.52W
Healesville Australia 93 37.40S145.31E
Healy U.S.A. 98 63.52N148.58W
Heanor U.K. 12 53.01N 1.20W
Heard I. Indian Oc. 49 53.07S 73.20E
Hearne L. Canada 100 62.20N113.10W
Hearst Canada 102 49.40N 83.41W
Heathcote Australia 93 36.54S144.42E
Hebei d. China 54 39.00N116.00E
Hebel Australia 93 28.55S147.49E
Heber Springs town U.S.A. 111 35.30N 92.02W
Hebi China 54 35.57N114.05E
Hebrides is. U.K. 8 57.45N 7.00W
Hebrides, Sea of the U.K. 10 57.00N 7.20W
Hebron Canada 99 58.05N 62.30W
Hebron see Al Khalīl Jordan 67
Hebron N.Dak. U.S.A. 110 46.54N102.03W
Hebron Nebr. U.S.A. 110 40.10N 97.35W
Heby Sweden 43 59.56N 16.53E
Hecate Str. Canada 100 53.00N131.00W
Hechi China 55 24.42N108.02E
Hechingen Germany 39 48.21N 8.58E
Hechtel Belgium 16 51.07N 5.22E
Hechuan China 55 30.05N106.14E
Hecla U.S.A. 110 45.53N 98.09W
Hede Sweden 41 62.25N 13.30E
Hedemora Sweden 43 60.17N 15.59E
Hedensted Denmark 42 55.46N 9.42E
Hedi Shuiku resr. China 55 21.50N110.19E
Hedley U.S.A. 111 34.52N100.39W
Hedmark d. Norway 41 61.20N 11.30E
Heemstede Neth. 16 52.21N 4.38E
Heerde Neth. 16 52.23N 6.02E
Heerenveen Neth. 16 52.57N 5.55E
Heerlen Neth. 16 50.53N 5.59E
Hefa Israel 67 32.49N 34.59E
Hefa d. Israel 67 32.50N 35.00E
Hefei China 55 31.50N117.16E
Hegang China 53 47.36N130.30E
Heide Germany 38 54.12N 9.06E
Heide f. Germany 38 52.50N 10.30E
Heidelberg Germany 39 49.25N 8.43E
Heidelberg C.P. R.S.A. 80 34.05S 20.58E
Heidenheim Germany 39 48.40N 10.08E
Heilbron R.S.A. 80 27.16S 27.57E
Heilbronn Germany 39 49.08N 9.13E
Heiligenblut Austria 39 47.02N 12.50E
Heiligenhafen Germany 38 54.22N 10.58E
Heiligenstadt Germany 38 51.23N 10.09E
Heilongjiang d. China 53 47.15N128.50E
Heiloo Neth. 16 52.37N 4.43E
Heinola Finland 41 61.13N 26.02E
Heinsberg Germany 38 51.03N 6.05E
Heishan China 54 41.40N122.03E
Heishui China 54 42.03N119.21E
Heishuisi China 54 36.01N108.56E
Hejaz f. see Al Ḩijāz f. Saudi Arabia 64
Hejian China 54 38.26N116.05E
Hejiang China 55 28.48N105.47E
Hekinan Japan 57 34.51N136.58E
Hekla, Mt. Iceland 40 64.00N 19.45W
Hekou China 61 22.39N103.57E
Hekura jima i. Japan 57 37.52N136.56E
Helagsfjället mtn. Sweden 40 62.58N 12.25E
Helan China 54 38.35N106.16E
Helan Shan mts. China 54 38.40N106.00E
Helbra Germany 38 51.33N 11.29E
Helena U.S.A. 108 46.36N112.01W
Helen Reef i. Caroline Is. 59 2.43N131.46E
Helensburgh U.K. 14 56.01N 4.44W
Helensville New Zealand 86 36.40S174.27E
Helez Israel 67 31.35N 34.40E
Helgoland i. Germany 38 54.12N 7.53E

Helgoländer Bucht to **Hose, Pegunungan**

Helgoländer Bucht *b.* Germany **38** 54.05N 8.15E
Hellendoorn Neth. **16** 52.24N 6.29E
Hellenthal Germany **38** 50.29N 6.26E
Hellesylt Norway **41** 62.05N 6.54E
Hellevoetsluis Neth. **16** 51.49N 4.08E
Hellín Spain **25** 38.31N 1.41W
Helmand *d.* Afghan. **62** 31.15N 64.00E
Helmand *r.* Asia **62** 31.12N 61.34E
Helmond Neth. **16** 51.28N 5.40E
Helmsdale U.K. **14** 58.07N 3.40W
Helmsdale *r.* U.K. **14** 58.05N 3.39W
Helmstedt Germany **38** 52.13N 11.00E
Helsingfors *see* Helsinki Finland **41**
Helsingör Denmark **43** 56.02N 12.37E
Helsinki Finland **41** 60.08N 25.00E
Helston U.K. **13** 50.07N 5.17W
Helvecia Argentina **125** 31.06S 60.05W
Hemaruka Canada **101** 51.48N111.10W
Hemau Germany **38** 49.03N 11.47E
Hemel Hempstead U.K. **13** 51.46N 0.28W
Hemingford U.S.A. **110** 42.19N103.04W
Hemmingford Canada **105** 45.03N 73.36W
Hempstead N.Y. U.S.A. **115** 40.42N 73.37W
Hempstead Tex. U.S.A. **111** 30.06N 96.05W
Hemse Sweden **43** 57.14N 18.22E
Hemsedal Norway **41** 60.52N 8.34E
Henan *d.* China **54** 34.00N114.00E
Henares *r.* Spain **26** 40.24N 3.30W
Henbury Australia **90** 24.35S133.15E
Hendaye France **20** 43.22N 1.46W
Henderson Ky. U.S.A. **113** 37.50N 87.35W
Henderson N.C. U.S.A. **113** 36.20N 78.26W
Henderson Nev. U.S.A. **109** 36.02N114.59W
Henderson N.Y. U.S.A. **105** 43.51N 76.11W
Henderson Tex. U.S.A. **111** 32.09N 94.48W
Henderson I. Pacific Oc. **85** 24.20S128.20W
Hendrik Verwoerd Dam R.S.A. **80** 30.37S 25.29E
Hendrina R.S.A. **80** 26.09S 29.42E
Hengelo Neth. **16** 52.16N 6.46E
Hengshan Hunan China **55** 27.14N112.52E
Hengshan Shaanxi China **54** 37.57N109.11E
Hengshui China **54** 37.40N115.48E
Heng Xian China **55** 22.35N109.26E
Hengyang China **55** 26.52N112.35E
Hénin-Beaumont France **19** 50.25N 2.56E
Henlopen, C. U.S.A. **115** 38.48N 75.05W
Hennebont France **18** 47.48N 3.17W
Hennigsdorf Germany **38** 52.38N 13.12E
Henniker U.S.A. **115** 43.11N 71.49W
Henrietta Maria, C. Canada **102** 55.00N 82.15W
Henryetta U.S.A. **111** 35.27N 95.59W
Henryville Canada **105** 45.08N 73.11W
Hentiesbaai Namibia **80** 22.10S 14.19E
Henty Australia **93** 35.30S147.03E
Henzada Burma **56** 17.36N 95.26E
Heppenheim Germany **39** 49.39N 8.38E
Heppner U.S.A. **108** 45.21N119.33W
Hepu China **55** 21.31N109.10E
Hepworth Canada **104** 44.37N 81.09W
Heqing China **61** 26.34N100.12E
Herāt Afghan. **62** 34.20N 62.12E
Herāt *d.* Afghan. **62** 34.10N 62.30E
Herault *r.* France **20** 43.17N 3.26E
Herbignac France **18** 47.27N 2.19W
Herborn Germany **38** 50.40N 8.17E
Herceg-Novi Yugo. **31** 42.27N 18.32E
Hereford U.K. **13** 52.04N 2.43W
Hereford Md. U.S.A. **115** 39.35N 76.40W
Hereford Tex. U.S.A. **111** 34.49N102.24W
Hereford and Worcester *d.* U.K. **13** 52.08N 2.30W
Herencia Spain **27** 39.21N 3.22W
Herentals Belgium **16** 51.12N 4.42E
Herford Germany **38** 52.06N 8.40E
Herington U.S.A. **110** 38.40N 96.57W
Herisau Switz. **39** 47.23N 9.17E
Herleshausen Germany **38** 51.00N 10.09E
Hermagor Austria **39** 46.37N 13.22E
Hermannsburg Australia **90** 23.56S132.46E
Hermanus R.S.A. **80** 34.24S 19.16E
Hermidale Australia **93** 31.33S146.44E
Hermiston U.S.A. **108** 45.51N119.17W
Hermosillo Mexico **109** 29.04N110.58W
Herndon U.S.A. **114** 40.43N 76.50W
Herne Germany **38** 51.32N 7.13E
Herne Bay *town* U.K. **13** 51.23N 1.10E
Herning Denmark **42** 56.08N 8.59E
Heron Bay *town* Canada **102** 48.40N 86.25W
Herrera del Duque Spain **27** 39.10N 5.03W
Herrera de Pisuerga Spain **26** 42.36N 4.20W
Herrljunga Sweden **43** 58.05N 13.02E
Hershey U.S.A. **115** 40.17N 76.39W
Herstal Belgium **16** 50.14N 5.38E
Herten Germany **38** 51.35N 7.07E
Hertford U.K. **13** 51.48N 0.05W
Hertfordshire *d.* U.K. **13** 51.51N 0.05W
Hervás Spain **26** 40.16N 5.51W
Hervey B. Australia **90** 25.00S153.00E
Herzberg *Brandenburg* Germany **38** 51.41N 13.14E
Herzberg *Nschn.* Germany **38** 51.39N 10.20E
Herzliyya Israel **67** 32.10N 34.50E
Hesbaye *f.* Belgium **16** 50.32N 5.07E
Hesdin France **19** 50.22N 2.02E
Hesel Germany **38** 53.18N 7.35E
Heshui China **54** 35.43N108.07E
Heshun China **54** 37.19N113.34E
Hesselö *i.* Denmark **42** 56.12N 11.43E
Hessen *d.* Germany **38** 50.44N 9.00E
Hesso Australia **92** 32.08S137.58E
Hetou China **55** 21.05N109.44E
Hettinger U.S.A. **110** 46.00N102.39W
Hettstedt Germany **38** 51.38N 11.30E
Hetzerath Germany **39** 49.52N 6.49E
Heuvelton U.S.A. **105** 44.37N 75.25W
Hevron, Nahal *wadi* Israel **67** 31.15N 34.50E
Hewett, C. Canada **99** 70.20N 68.00W
Hexham U.K. **12** 54.58N 2.06W
Hexi China **55** 24.51N117.13E
He Xian China **55** 24.25N111.31E
Hexigten Qi China **54** 43.17N117.24E
Heyrieux France **21** 45.38N 5.03E
Heysham U.K. **12** 54.03N 2.53W
Heyuan China **55** 23.42N114.48E
Heywood Australia **92** 38.08S141.38E
Heywood U.K. **12** 53.36N 2.13W
Heze China **54** 35.12N115.15E
Hezhang China **55** 27.08N104.43E
Hiawatha Kans. U.S.A. **110** 39.51N 95.32W
Hiawatha Utah U.S.A. **108** 39.29N111.01W
Hibbing U.S.A. **110** 47.25N 92.55W
Hickman, Mt. Canada **100** 57.11N131.10W
Hickory U.S.A. **113** 35.44N 81.23W
Hicks Bay *town* New Zealand **86** 37.35S178.18E
Hickson L. Canada **101** 56.17N104.25W
Hicksville U.S.A. **115** 40.46N 73.32W
Hidaka Sammyaku *mts.* Japan **57** 42.50N143.00E
Hidalgo *d.* Mexico **116** 20.50N 98.30W
Hidalgo Nuevo León Mexico **111** 25.59N100.27W
Hidalgo Tamaulipas Mexico **116** 24.15N 99.26W
Hidalgo del Parral Mexico **109** 26.56N105.40W
Hieradhsvotn *r.* Iceland **40** 65.45N 18.50W
Hierro *i.* Canary Is. **74** 27.45N 18.00W
Higashimatsuyama Japan **57** 36.02N139.24E
Higashimurayama Japan **57** 35.46N139.29E
Higashiōsaka Japan **57** 34.39N135.35E
Higgins U.S.A. **111** 36.07N100.02W
Higgins L. U.S.A. **104** 44.30N 84.45W
Higginsville Australia **89** 31.46S121.43E
Highgate Canada **104** 42.30N 81.49W
High Hill *r.* Canada **101** 55.52N 94.42W
High Knob *mtn.* U.S.A. **114** 39.08N 78.26W
Highland *d.* U.K. **14** 57.42N 5.00W
Highland *town* U.S.A. **115** 41.43N 73.58W
Highland Park *town* U.S.A. **114** 42.24N 83.06W
High Level Canada **100** 58.31N117.08W
Highmore U.S.A. **110** 44.31N 99.27W
High Peak *mtn.* U.K. **12** 53.22N 1.48W
High Point *town* U.S.A. **113** 35.58N 80.00W
High Prairie Canada **100** 55.30N116.30W
Highrock L. Man. Canada **101** 55.45N100.30W
Highrock L. Sask. Canada **101** 57.04N105.30W
High Willhays *mtn.* U.K. **13** 50.41N 4.00W
High Wycombe U.K. **13** 51.38N 0.46W
Hiiumaa *i.* U.S.S.R. **41** 58.52N 22.40E
Híjar Spain **25** 41.10N 0.27W
Ḩijāz, Jabal al *mts.* Saudi Arabia **72** 19.45N 41.55E
Hikone Japan **57** 35.15N136.15E
Hikurangi New Zealand **86** 35.36S174.17E
Hikurangi *mtn.* New Zealand **86** 37.50S178.10E
Hikutavake Niue **84** 18.57S169.53W
Hildburghausen Germany **39** 50.25N 10.44E
Hilden Germany **38** 51.10N 6.56E
Hildesheim Germany **38** 52.09N 9.57E
Hill City Kans. U.S.A. **110** 39.22N 99.51W
Hill City Minn. U.S.A. **110** 46.59N 93.44W
Hillegom Neth. **16** 52.19N 4.35E
Hill End Australia **93** 33.01S149.26E
Hilleröd Denmark **43** 55.56N 12.19E
Hill Island L. Canada **101** 60.30N109.50W
Hillman U.S.A. **104** 45.04N 83.54W
Hillsboro N.H. U.S.A. **115** 43.07N 71.54W
Hillsboro Oreg. U.S.A. **108** 45.31N122.59W
Hillsboro Tex. U.S.A. **111** 32.01N 97.08W
Hillsdale U.S.A. **112** 41.56N 84.37W
Hillsport Canada **102** 49.27N 85.34W
Hillston Australia **93** 33.30S145.33E
Hilo Hawaii U.S.A. **106** 19.42N155.04W
Hilton U.S.A. **114** 43.17N 77.48W
Hilton Beach Canada **104** 46.16N 83.56W
Hilton Head I. U.S.A. **113** 32.12N 80.45W
Hiltrup Germany **38** 51.54N 7.38E
Hilversum Neth. **16** 52.14N 5.12E
Himachal Pradesh *d.* India **62** 32.05N 77.15E
Himalaya *mts.* Asia **63** 29.00N 84.30E
Himanka Finland **40** 64.04N 23.39E
Himarë Albania **34** 40.08N 19.43E
Himatnagar India **62** 23.36N 72.57E
Himeji Japan **57** 34.50N134.40E
Himi Japan **57** 36.51N136.59E
Himmerland *f.* Denmark **42** 56.52N 9.30E
Ḩimş Syria **66** 34.44N 36.43E
Hinchinbrook I. Australia **90** 18.23S146.17E
Hinckley U.K. **13** 52.33N 1.21W
Hinckley Resr. U.S.A. **115** 43.20N 75.05W
Hindaun India **62** 26.43N 77.01E
Hindmarsh, L. Australia **92** 36.03S141.53E
Hindubāgh Pakistan **62** 30.49N 67.45E
Hindu Kush *mts.* Asia **60** 36.40N 70.00E
Hindupur India **60** 13.49N 77.29E
Hines Creek *town* Canada **100** 56.20N118.40W
Hinganghāt India **63** 20.34N 78.50E
Hingol *r.* Pakistan **62** 25.23N 65.28E
Hingoli India **62** 19.43N 77.09E
Hinnöy *i.* Norway **40** 68.35N 15.50E
Hinojosa Spain **26** 38.30N 5.09W
Hinsdale Mont. U.S.A. **108** 48.24N107.05W
Hinsdale N.H. U.S.A. **115** 42.47N 72.29W
Hinterrhein *r.* Switz. **39** 46.49N 9.25E
Hinton Canada **100** 53.25N117.34W
Hipólito Mexico **111** 25.41N101.26W
Hippolytushoef Neth. **16** 52.57N 4.58E
Hirakata Japan **57** 34.48N135.38E
Hirākud India **63** 21.31N 83.57E
Hirākud *resr.* India **63** 21.31N 83.52E
Hirāpur India **63** 24.22N 79.13E
Hiratsuka Japan **57** 35.19N139.21E
Hirmand *r. see* Helmand *r.* Iran **62**
Hirok Sāmi Pakistan **62** 26.02N 63.25E
Hirosaki Japan **57** 40.34N140.28E
Hiroshima Japan **57** 34.30N132.27E
Hirson France **19** 49.55N 4.05E
Hîrşova Romania **37** 44.41N 27.57E
Hirtshals Denmark **42** 57.35N 9.58E
Hisai Japan **57** 34.40N136.28E
Hisār India **62** 29.10N 75.43E
Ḩisbān Jordan **67** 31.48N 35.48E
Ḩismá *f.* Saudi Arabia **66** 28.45N 35.56E
Hispaniola *i.* C. America **117** 19.00N 71.00W
Hisua India **63** 24.50N 85.25E
Ḩisyah Syria **66** 34.24N 36.45E
Hīt Iraq **64** 33.38N 42.50E
Hitachi Japan **57** 36.35N140.40E
Hitchin U.K. **13** 51.57N 0.16W
Hitra *i.* Norway **40** 63.37N 8.46E
Hiva Oa *i.* Is. Marquises **85** 9.45S139.00W
Hixon Canada **100** 53.27N122.36W
Hjälmaren *l.* Sweden **43** 59.15N 15.45E
Hjalmar L. Canada **101** 61.33N109.25W
Hjelmelandsvågen Norway **42** 59.14N 6.11E
Hjo Sweden **43** 58.18N 14.17E
Hjörring Denmark **42** 57.28N 9.59E
Hlotse Lesotho **80** 28.52S 28.02E
Ho Ghana **76** 6.38N 0.38E
Hòa Binh Vietnam **55** 20.40N105.17E
Hoare B. Canada **99** 65.20N 62.30W
Hoarusib *r.* Namibia **80** 19.04S 12.33E
Hobart Australia **91** 42.54S147.18E
Hobart Ind. U.S.A. **112** 41.32N 87.14W
Hobart Okla. U.S.A. **111** 35.01N 99.06W
Hobbs U.S.A. **111** 32.42N103.08W
Hoboken Belgium **16** 51.11N 4.21E
Hoboken U.S.A. **115** 40.45N 74.03W
Hobq Shamo *des.* China **54** 40.00N109.00E
Hobro Denmark **42** 56.38N 9.48E
Hoburgen *c.* Sweden **43** 56.55N 18.07E
Hobyo Somali Rep. **71** 5.20N 48.30E
Hochgolling *mtn.* Austria **39** 47.16N 13.45E
Ho Chi Minh Vietnam **56** 10.46N106.43E
Höchstadt an der Aisch Germany **39** 49.42N 10.44E
Hockenheim Germany **39** 49.19N 8.33E
Hocking *r.* U.S.A. **114** 39.12N 81.45W
Hockley U.S.A. **111** 30.02N 95.51W
Hodal India **62** 27.54N 77.22E
Hodgson Canada **101** 51.13N 97.34W
Hod HaSharon Israel **67** 32.15N 34.55E
Hodh ech Chargui *d.* Mauritania **76** 19.00N 7.15W
Hodh el Gharbi *d.* Mauritania **76** 16.30N 10.00W
Hodiyya Israel **67** 31.41N 34.38E
Hódmezövásárhely Hungary **31** 46.25N 20.20E
Hodna, Monts du *mts.* Algeria **75** 35.50N 4.50E
Hoek van Holland Neth. **16** 51.59N 4.08E
Hoeryŏng N. Korea **57** 42.27N129.44E
Hof Germany **38** 50.18N 11.55E
Hofgeismar Germany **38** 51.30N 9.22E
Hofheim Bayern Germany **39** 50.08N 10.31E
Hofheim Hessen Germany **39** 50.07N 8.26E
Höfn Iceland **40** 64.16N 15.10W
Hofors Sweden **41** 60.33N 16.17E
Hofsjökull *mtn.* Iceland **40** 64.50N 19.00W
Hofsos Iceland **40** 65.53N 19.26W
Höganäs Sweden **43** 56.12N 12.33E
Hogansburg U.S.A. **105** 44.59N 74.40W
Hogeland U.S.A. **108** 48.51N108.39W
Hogem Ranges *f.* Canada **100** 55.40N126.00W
Högsby Sweden **43** 57.10N 16.02E
Hohe Acht *mtn.* Germany **39** 50.23N 7.00E
Hohenthurn Austria **39** 46.33N 13.40E
Hoher Dachstein *mtn.* Austria **39** 47.28N 13.35E
Hohhot China **54** 40.42N111.38E
Hoh Tolgoin Sum China **54** 44.27N112.41E
Hohultslätt Sweden **43** 56.58N 15.39E
Hoi An Vietnam **56** 15.54N108.19E
Hoima Uganda **79** 1.25N 31.22E
Hojāi India **63** 26.00N 92.51E
Höjer Denmark **42** 54.58N 8.43E
Hökensås *hills* Sweden **43** 58.11N 14.08E
Hokitika New Zealand **86** 42.42S170.59E
Hokkaidō *d.* Japan **57** 43.00N143.00E
Hokkaidō *i.* Japan **57** 43.00N144.00E
Hokksund Norway **42** 59.47N 9.59E
Hola Kenya **79** 1.29S 40.02E
Holbaek Denmark **42** 55.43N 11.43E
Holbrook Australia **93** 35.46S147.20E
Holbrook U.S.A. **109** 34.54N110.10W
Holdrege U.S.A. **110** 40.26N 99.22W
Holguín Cuba **117** 20.54N 76.15W
Höljes Sweden **41** 60.54N 12.36E
Hollabrunn Austria **36** 48.34N 16.05E
Holland Mich. U.S.A. **112** 42.46N 86.06W
Holland N.Y. U.S.A. **114** 42.38N 78.33W
Holland Centre Canada **104** 44.24N 80.48W
Hollidaysburg U.S.A. **114** 40.26N 78.23W
Holly Kans. U.S.A. **111** 38.03N102.07W
Holly Mich. U.S.A. **104** 42.48N 83.38W
Hollywood U.S.A. **113** 26.01N 80.09W
Holman Island *town* Canada **98** 70.43N117.43W
Holmavik Iceland **40** 65.43N 21.39W
Holmenkollen Norway **42** 59.58N 10.40E
Holmer, Lac *l.* Canada **103** 54.10N 71.44W
Holmestrand Norway **42** 59.29N 10.18E
Holmön *i.* Sweden **40** 63.47N 20.53E
Holmsund Sweden **40** 63.41N 20.20E
Holon Israel **67** 32.01N 34.46E
Holroyd *r.* Australia **90** 14.10S141.36E
Holstebro Denmark **42** 56.21N 8.38E
Holstein Canada **104** 44.03N 80.45W
Holsteinsborg Greenland **99** 66.55N 53.30W
Holsworthy U.K. **13** 50.48N 4.21W
Holt U.K. **12** 52.55N 1.04E
Holten Neth. **16** 52.18N 6.26E
Holwerd Neth. **16** 53.22N 5.54E
Holy Cross U.S.A. **98** 62.12N159.47W
Holyhead U.K. **12** 53.18N 4.38W
Holyhead B. U.K. **12** 53.22N 4.40W
Holy I. England U.K. **12** 55.41N 1.47W
Holy I. Wales U.K. **12** 53.15N 4.38W
Holyoke Colo. U.S.A. **110** 40.35N102.18W
Holyoke Mass. U.S.A. **115** 42.12N 72.37W
Holýšov Czech. **38** 49.36N 13.05E
Holywood U.K. **15** 54.38N 5.50W
Holzkirchen Germany **39** 47.52N 11.42E
Holzminden Germany **38** 51.50N 9.27E
Homberg Germany **38** 51.02N 9.24E
Hombori Mali **76** 15.20N 1.38W
Homburg Germany **39** 49.19N 7.20E
Home B. Canada **99** 69.00N 66.00W
Home Hill *town* Australia **90** 19.40S147.25E
Homer Alas. U.S.A. **98** 59.40N151.37W
Homer La. U.S.A. **111** 32.48N 93.04W
Homer N.Y. U.S.A. **115** 42.38N 76.11W
Homer Tunnel New Zealand **86** 44.40S168.15E
Homestead U.S.A. **113** 25.29N 80.29W
Hommersåk Norway **42** 58.58N 5.42E
Homoine Mozambique **81** 23.45S 35.09E
Homoljske Planina *f.* Yugo. **37** 44.20N 21.45E
Honda Colombia **122** 5.15N 74.50W
Hondeklipbaai R.S.A. **80** 30.19S 17.12E
Hondo *r.* Mexico **117** 18.33N 88.22W
Hondo U.S.A. **111** 29.21N 99.09W
Honduras C. America **117** 14.30N 87.00W
Honduras, G. of Carib. Sea **117** 16.20N 87.30W
Honesdale U.S.A. **115** 41.34N 75.16W
Honfleur France **18** 49.25N 0.14E
Höng Denmark **42** 55.31N 11.18E
Hong'an China **55** 31.18N114.33E
Hòn Gay Vietnam **55** 21.01N107.02E
Hong Hà *r.* Vietnam **56** 20.15N106.36E
Honghu China **55** 29.42N113.26E
Hong Hu *l.* China **55** 29.50N113.15E
Hongjiang China **55** 27.08N109.54E
Hongjian Nur *l.* China **54** 39.09N109.56E
Hong Kong Asia **55** 22.15N114.15E
Hongor Mongolia **54** 45.45N112.56E
Hongshui He *r.* China **55** 23.20N110.04E
Hongtong China **54** 36.15N111.37E
Honguedo, Détroit d' *str.* Canada **103** 49.25N 64.00W
Hongze China **54** 33.18N118.51E
Hongze Hu *l.* China **54** 33.15N118.40E
Honiton U.K. **13** 50.48N 3.13W
Honjō Japan **57** 39.23N140.03E
Honkajoki Finland **41** 62.00N 22.15E
Hönö Sweden **42** 57.42N 11.39E
Honokaa Hawaiian Is. **85** 20.05N155.28W
Honokahua Hawaiian Is. **85** 21.00N156.39W
Honolulu Hawaii U.S.A. **106** 21.19N157.50W
Honshū *i.* Japan **57** 36.00N138.00E
Hood, Mt. U.S.A. **108** 45.23N121.41W
Hood Pt. Australia **89** 34.23S119.34E
Hood Range *mts.* Australia **93** 28.35S144.30E
Hoogeveen Neth. **16** 52.44N 6.29E
Hoogezand Neth. **16** 53.10N 6.47E
Hooghly *r.* India **63** 21.55N 88.05E
Hoogstade Belgium **16** 50.59N 2.42E
Hooker U.S.A. **111** 36.52N101.13W
Hook Head Rep. of Ire. **15** 52.07N 6.55W
Hoopa U.S.A. **108** 41.03N123.40W
Hoopeston U.S.A. **110** 40.28N 87.41W
Hoopstad R.S.A. **80** 27.48S 25.52E
Höör Sweden **43** 55.56N 13.32E
Hoorn Neth. **16** 52.38N 5.03E
Hoosick Falls *town* U.S.A. **115** 42.54N 73.21W
Hoover Dam U.S.A. **109** 36.00N114.27W
Hope U.S.A. **111** 33.40N 93.36W
Hope, L. *S.A.* Australia **92** 28.23S139.19E
Hope, L. *W.A.* Australia **89** 32.31S120.25E
Hope, Pt. U.S.A. **96** 68.20N166.49W
Hopedale Canada **103** 55.50N 60.10W
Hopefield R.S.A. **80** 33.04S 18.19E
Hopetoun Vic. Australia **92** 35.43S142.20E
Hopetoun W.A. Australia **89** 33.57S120.05E
Hopetown R.S.A. **80** 29.37S 24.04E
Hopkins *r.* Australia **92** 38.25S142.00E
Hopkins, L. Australia **88** 24.15S128.50E
Hopkinsville U.S.A. **113** 36.50N 87.30W
Hopland U.S.A. **108** 38.58N123.07W
Hoquiam U.S.A. **108** 46.59N123.53W
Horaždovice Czech. **38** 49.20N 13.43E
Horb Germany **39** 48.26N 8.41E
Horbat Qesari *site* Israel **67** 32.30N 34.53E
Hörby Sweden **43** 55.51N 13.39E
Hordaland *d.* Norway **42** 60.00N 6.00E
Horde Germany **16** 51.29N 7.30E
Horgen Switz. **39** 47.15N 8.36E
Hörh Uul *mts.* Mongolia **54** 42.20N105.30E
Horinger China **54** 40.23N111.53E
Horizonte Mexico **111** 25.50N103.48W
Horlick Mts. Antarctica **128** 86.00S102.00W
Hormuz, Str. of Asia **65** 26.35N 56.20E
Horn Austria **36** 48.40N 15.40E
Horn *r.* Canada **100** 61.30N118.01W
Horn, C. *see* Hornos, Cabo de *c.* S. America **125**
Hornavan *l.* Sweden **40** 66.10N 17.30E
Horncastle U.K. **12** 53.13N 0.08W
Horndal Sweden **43** 60.18N 16.25E
Hornell U.S.A. **114** 42.19N 77.40W
Hornell L. Canada **100** 62.20N119.25W
Hornepayne Canada **102** 49.14N 84.48W
Hornindal Norway **41** 61.58N 6.31E
Horn Mts. Canada **100** 62.15N119.15W
Hornos, Cabo de *c.* S. America **125** 55.47S 67.00W
Hornsby Australia **93** 33.11S151.06E
Hornsea U.K. **12** 53.55N 0.10W
Hornslet Denmark **42** 56.19N 10.20E
Hořovice Czech. **36** 49.50N 13.54E
Horqin Zuoyi Houqi China **54** 42.57N122.21E
Horqin Zuoyi Zhongqi China **54** 44.08N123.18E
Horru China **63** 30.30N 91.32E
Horse Creek *town* U.S.A. **108** 41.25N105.11W
Horseheads U.S.A. **114** 42.10N 76.50W
Horsens Denmark **42** 55.52N 9.52E
Horsham Australia **92** 36.45S142.15E
Horsham U.K. **13** 51.04N 0.20W
Hörsholm Denmark **43** 55.53N 12.30E
Horšovský Týn Czech. **38** 49.32N 12.56E
Horta *wadi* Chad **72** 17.15N 21.52E
Horten Norway **42** 59.25N 10.30E
Horton *r.* Canada **98** 70.00N127.00W
Horton L. Canada **98** 67.30N122.28W
Horvot Mezada *site* Israel **67** 31.19N 35.21E
Hosa'ina Ethiopia **73** 7.38N 37.52E
Hösbach Germany **39** 50.00N 9.12E
Hose, Pegunungan *mts.* Malaysia **58** 1.30N114.10E

Hoshāb to Ille-et-Vilaine

Hoshāb Pakistan **62** 26.01N 63.56E
Hoshangābād India **63** 22.45N 77.43E
Hoshiārpur India **62** 31.32N 75.54E
Hôsh 'Isa Egypt **66** 30.55N 30.17E
Hoskins P.N.G. **87** 5.30S 150.27E
Hospital de Orbigo Spain **26** 42.28N 5.53W
Hospitalet de Llobregat Spain **25** 41.22N 2.08E
Hossegor France **20** 43.40N 1.27W
Hoste, Isla *i.* Chile **125** 55.10S 69.00W
Hotan China **52** 37.07N 79.57E
Hotazel R.S.A. **80** 27.16S 22.57E
Hotham *r.* Australia **89** 32.58S 116.22E
Hotham, Mt. Australia **93** 36.58S 147.11E
Hoting Sweden **40** 64.07N 16.10E
Hotin Gol China **54** 38.58N 104.14E
Hot Springs *town* Ark. U.S.A. **111** 34.30N 93.02W
Hot Springs *town* S.Dak. U.S.A. **110** 43.26N 103.29W
Hottah L. Canada **98** 65.04N 118.29W
Houailou N. Cal. **84** 21.17S 165.38E
Houdan France **19** 48.47N 1.36E
Houeillès France **20** 44.12N 0.02E
Houffalize Belgium **16** 50.08N 5.50E
Houghton L. U.S.A. **112** 44.16N 84.48W
Houghton-le-Spring U.K. **12** 54.51N 1.28W
Houlton U.S.A. **112** 46.08N 67.51W
Houma China **54** 35.36N 111.21E
Houma U.S.A. **111** 29.36N 90.43W
Houndé Burkina **76** 11.34N 3.31W
Hourn, Loch U.K. **14** 57.06N 5.33W
Housatonic *r.* U.S.A. **115** 41.10N 73.07W
Houston Mo. U.S.A. **111** 37.22N 91.58W
Houston Tex. U.S.A. **111** 29.46N 95.22W
Houtzdale U.S.A. **114** 40.49N 78.21W
Hova Sweden **43** 58.52N 14.13E
Hovd Mongolia **52** 46.40N 90.45E
Hove U.K. **13** 50.50N 0.10W
Hovlya U.S.S.R. **45** 49.19N 44.01E
Hövsgöl Mongolia **54** 43.36N 109.40E
Hövsgöl Nuur *l.* Mongolia **52** 51.00N 100.30E
Howa, Ouadi *see* Howar, Wādī Chad **72**
Howar, Wādī Sudan **72** 17.30N 27.08E
Howard L. Canada **101** 62.15N 105.57W
Howe, C. Australia **93** 37.30S 149.59E
Howell U.S.A. **104** 42.36N 83.55W
Howick Canada **105** 45.11N 73.51W
Howitt, Mt. Australia **93** 37.15S 146.40E
Howrah India **63** 22.35N 88.20E
Howth Head Rep. of Ire. **15** 53.22N 6.03W
Höxter Germany **38** 51.46N 9.23E
Hoy *i.* U.K. **14** 58.51N 3.17W
Höyanger Norway **41** 61.13N 6.05E
Hoyerswerda Germany **38** 51.26N 14.14E
Hoyos Spain **27** 40.10N 6.43W
Hradec Králové Czech. **36** 50.13N 15.50E
Hron *r.* Czech. **37** 47.49N 18.45E
Hrubieszów Poland **37** 50.49N 23.55E
Hrvatska *d.* Yugo. **31** 45.35N 16.10E
Hsenwi Burma **56** 23.18N 97.58E
Hsipaw Burma **56** 22.42N 97.21E
Hsuphāng Burma **56** 20.18N 98.42E
Huab *r.* Namibia **80** 20.55S 13.28E
Huabei Pingyuan *f.* China **54** 35.00N 115.30E
Huachi China **54** 36.32N 108.14E
Huacho Peru **122** 11.05S 77.36W
Huachuca City U.S.A. **109** 31.34N 110.21W
Huade China **54** 41.57N 114.04E
Hua Hin Thailand **56** 12.34N 99.58E
Huahine *i.* Îs. de la Société **85** 16.45S 151.00W
Huai'an Hebei China **54** 40.40N 114.18E
Huai'an Jiangsu China **54** 33.29N 119.15E
Huaibei China **54** 33.58N 116.50E
Huai He *r.* China **54** 32.58N 118.18E
Huaiji China **55** 23.58N 112.10E
Huailai China **54** 40.25N 115.27E
Huainan China **54** 32.39N 117.01E
Huaining China **55** 30.21N 116.42E
Huairen China **54** 39.50N 113.07E
Huairou China **54** 40.20N 116.37E
Huaiyang China **54** 33.47N 114.59E
Huaiyuan China **54** 32.57N 117.12E
Huajuápan Mexico **116** 17.50N 97.48W
Hualian Taiwan **55** 24.00N 121.39E
Huallaga *r.* Peru **122** 5.02S 75.30W
Huamanrazo *mtn.* Peru **122** 12.54S 75.04W
Huambo Angola **78** 12.47S 15.44E
Huambo *d.* Angola **78** 12.30S 15.45E
Huanan China **53** 46.13N 130.31E
Huancané Peru **122** 15.10S 69.44W
Huancapi Peru **122** 13.35S 74.05W
Huancavelica Peru **122** 12.45S 75.03W
Huancayo Peru **122** 12.05S 75.12W
Huangchuan China **55** 32.07N 115.02E
Huanggang China **55** 30.33N 114.59E
Huanggang Shan *mtn.* China **55** 27.50N 117.47E
Huang Hai *b.* N. Korea **54** 39.30N 123.40E
Huang He *r.* China **54** 38.00N 118.40E
Huanghe Kou *est.* China **54** 37.54N 118.48E
Huanghua China **54** 38.22N 117.20E
Huangling China **54** 35.36N 109.17E
Huangpi China **55** 30.52N 114.22E
Huangping China **55** 26.54N 107.53E
Huangshi China **55** 30.10N 115.04E
Huang Xian China **54** 37.38N 120.30E
Huangyan China **55** 28.42N 121.25E
Huan Jiang *r.* China **54** 35.13N 108.00E
Huanren China **54** 41.16N 125.21E
Huanta Peru **122** 12.54S 74.13W
Huánuco Peru **122** 9.55S 76.11W
Huaráz Peru **122** 9.33S 77.31W
Huarmey Peru **122** 10.05S 78.05W
Huascaran *mtn.* Peru **122** 9.08S 77.36W
Huasco Chile **124** 28.28S 71.14W
Huatabampo Mexico **109** 26.50N 109.38W
Huatong China **54** 40.03N 121.56E
Hua Xian Guangdong China **55** 23.22N 113.12E
Hua Xian Shaanxi China **54** 34.31N 109.46E
Huayuan China **55** 28.37N 109.28E
Hubbard L. U.S.A. **104** 44.49N 83.34W
Hubei *d.* China **55** 31.00N 112.00E
Hubli India **60** 15.20N 75.14E
Hückelhoven Germany **38** 51.03N 6.13E
Hucknall U.K. **12** 53.03N 1.12W
Huddersfield U.K. **12** 53.38N 1.49W
Huddinge Sweden **43** 59.14N 17.59E
Hudiksvall Sweden **41** 61.44N 17.07E
Hudson *r.* U.S.A. **115** 40.42N 74.02W
Hudson Mich. U.S.A. **104** 41.51N 84.21W
Hudson N.Y. U.S.A. **115** 42.15N 73.47W
Hudson Wyo. U.S.A. **108** 42.54N 108.35W
Hudson B. Canada **99** 58.00N 86.00W
Hudson Bay *town* Canada **101** 52.52N 102.25W
Hudson Falls *town* U.S.A. **115** 43.18N 73.35W
Hudson Highlands U.S.A. **115** 41.24N 74.15W
Hudson Hope Canada **100** 56.03N 121.59W
Hudson Mts. Antarctica **128** 76.00S 99.00W
Hudson Str. Canada **99** 62.00N 70.00W
Hue Vietnam **56** 16.28N 107.40E
Huebra *r.* Spain **26** 41.02N 6.48W
Huedin Romania **37** 46.52N 23.02E
Huehuetenango Guatemala **116** 15.19N 91.26W
Huelgoat France **18** 48.22N 3.45W
Huelma Spain **27** 37.39N 3.27W
Huelva Spain **27** 37.16N 6.57W
Huelva *d.* Spain **27** 37.35N 7.10W
Huelva *r.* Spain **27** 37.27N 6.00W
Huércal-Overa Spain **25** 37.23N 1.57W
Huerva *r.* Spain **25** 41.39N 0.52W
Huesca Spain **25** 42.08N 0.25W
Huesca *d.* Spain **25** 42.20N 0.00
Huéscar Spain **27** 37.49N 2.32W
Huete Spain **26** 40.08N 2.41W
Ḥufrat an Naḥās Sudan **73** 9.45N 24.19E
Hugh *r.* Australia **90** 25.01S 134.01E
Hughenden Australia **90** 20.51S 144.12E
Hughes Australia **91** 30.40S 129.32E
Hughes U.S.A. **98** 66.03N 154.16W
Hugo U.S.A. **111** 34.01N 95.31W
Hugoton U.S.A. **111** 37.11N 101.21W
Hugou China **54** 33.22N 117.07E
Hui'an China **55** 25.02N 118.48E
Huiarau Range *mts.* New Zealand **86** 38.20S 177.15E
Huikou China **55** 29.49N 116.15E
Huila *d.* Angola **78** 15.10S 15.30E
Huilai China **55** 23.03N 116.17E
Huimin China **54** 37.30N 117.29E
Huining China **54** 35.42N 105.06E
Huisne *r.* France **18** 47.59N 0.11E
Huixtla Mexico **116** 15.09N 92.30W
Huizen Neth. **16** 52.18N 5.12E
Huizhou China **55** 23.05N 114.29E
Hukuntsi Botswana **80** 24.02S 21.48E
Ḥulayfā' Saudi Arabia **64** 26.00N 40.47E
Hulda Israel **67** 31.50N 34.53E
Hulín Czech. **37** 49.19N 17.28E
Hull Canada **105** 45.26N 75.43W
Hüls Germany **38** 51.22N 6.30E
Hulst Neth. **16** 51.18N 4.01E
Hultsfred Sweden **43** 57.29N 15.50E
Hulun Nur *l.* China **53** 49.00N 117.27E
Ḥulwān Egypt **66** 29.51N 31.20E
Humaitá Brazil **122** 7.31S 63.02W
Humansdorp R.S.A. **80** 34.02S 24.45E
Ḥumaydah Sudan **72** 14.22N 22.31E
Humber *r.* U.K. **12** 53.40N 0.12W
Humberside *d.* U.K. **12** 53.48N 0.35W
Humble U.S.A. **111** 30.00N 95.16W
Humboldt Canada **101** 52.12N 105.07W
Humboldt U.S.A. **111** 35.49N 88.55W
Humboldt *r.* U.S.A. **108** 40.02N 118.31W
Hume, L. Australia **93** 36.06S 147.05E
Hūmedān Iran **65** 25.24N 59.39E
Humenné Czech. **37** 48.56N 21.55E
Humphreys Peak *mtn.* U.S.A. **109** 35.20N 111.40W
Hūn Libya **75** 29.07N 15.56E
Húnaflói *b.* Iceland **40** 65.45N 20.50W
Hunan *d.* China **55** 27.30N 111.30E
Hundested Denmark **42** 55.58N 11.52E
Hundred U.S.A. **114** 39.41N 80.28W
Hundred Mile House *town* Canada **100** 51.38N 121.18W
Hunedoara Romania **37** 45.45N 22.54E
Hünfeld Germany **38** 50.40N 9.46E
Hungary Europe **37** 47.30N 19.00E
Hungerford Australia **92** 29.00S 144.26E
Hungerford U.K. **13** 51.25N 1.30W
Hungfou Hsü *i.* Taiwan **55** 22.03N 121.33E
Hŭngnam N. Korea **53** 39.49N 127.40E
Hung Yen Vietnam **55** 20.38N 106.05E
Huningue France **19** 47.36N 7.35E
Hunnebostrand Sweden **42** 58.27N 11.18E
Hunsberge *mts.* Namibia **80** 27.40S 17.12E
Hunse *r.* Neth. **16** 53.20N 6.18E
Hunsrück *mts.* Germany **39** 49.45N 7.00E
Hunstanton U.K. **12** 52.57N 0.30E
Hunte *r.* Germany **38** 53.14N 8.18E
Hunter *r.* Australia **93** 32.50S 151.42E
Hunter I. Australia **91** 40.30S 144.46E
Hunter I. Canada **100** 51.55N 128.00W
Hunter Island Ridge Pacific Oc. **84** 21.30S 175.00E
Huntingdon Canada **105** 45.05N 74.10W
Huntingdon U.K. **13** 52.20N 0.11W
Huntingdon Penn. U.S.A. **114** 40.29N 78.01W
Huntington Ind. U.S.A. **112** 40.54N 85.30W
Huntington Mass. U.S.A. **115** 42.14N 72.53W
Huntington N.Y. U.S.A. **115** 40.51N 73.25W
Huntington Oreg. U.S.A. **108** 44.21N 117.16W
Huntington Utah U.S.A. **108** 39.20N 110.58W
Huntington W.Va. U.S.A. **114** 38.25N 82.26W
Huntington Beach *town* U.S.A. **109** 33.39N 118.01W
Huntly New Zealand **86** 37.35S 175.10E
Huntly U.K. **14** 57.27N 2.47W
Huntsville Canada **104** 45.20N 79.14W
Huntsville Ala. U.S.A. **113** 34.44N 86.35W
Huntsville Tex. U.S.A. **111** 30.43N 95.33W
Hunyani *r.* Mozambique **81** 15.41S 30.38E
Hunyuan China **54** 39.45N 113.35E
Huon Pen. P.N.G. **59** 6.00S 147.00E
Huonville Australia **91** 43.01S 147.01E
Huoshan China **55** 31.24N 116.20E
Huqoq Israel **67** 32.53N 35.29E
Hurd, C. Canada **104** 45.13N 81.44W
Hure Qi China **54** 42.44N 121.44E
Huretin Sum China **54** 40.19N 103.02E
Huriel France **20** 46.23N 2.29E
Hurlock U.S.A. **115** 38.38N 75.52W
Hurmāgai Pakistan **62** 28.18N 64.26E
Huron *r.* U.S.A. **104** 42.03N 83.14W
Huron Ohio U.S.A. **114** 41.24N 82.33W
Huron S.Dak. U.S.A. **110** 44.22N 98.13W
Huron, L. Canada / U.S.A. **114** 44.30N 82.15W
Hurso Ethiopia **73** 9.38N 41.38E
Hurup Denmark **42** 56.45N 8.25E
Húsavík Iceland **40** 66.03N 17.21W
Husevig Faroe Is. **10** 61.49N 6.41W
Huşi Romania **37** 46.40N 28.04E
Huskvarna Sweden **43** 57.48N 14.16E
Husum Germany **38** 54.28N 9.03E
Hutchinson R.S.A. **80** 31.30S 23.10E
Hutchinson U.S.A. **111** 38.05N 97.56W
Hüttental Germany **38** 50.54N 8.02E
Huttig U.S.A. **111** 33.02N 92.11W
Huttonsville U.S.A. **114** 38.43N 80.00W
Hutuo He *r.* China **54** 39.10N 117.12E
Hut Yanchi *l.* China **54** 39.24N 105.01E
Ḥuwwārah Jordan **67** 32.09N 35.15E
Huy Belgium **16** 50.31N 5.14E
Hvar *i.* Yugo. **31** 43.09N 16.45E
Hvar *town* Yugo. **31** 43.10N 16.27E
Hvarski Kanal *str.* Yugo. **31** 43.20N 16.45E
Hvide Sande Denmark **42** 55.59N 8.08E
Hvita *r.* Iceland **40** 64.33N 21.45W
Hvittingfoss Norway **42** 59.29N 10.01E
Hwange Zimbabwe **80** 18.20S 26.29E
Hwange Nat. Park Zimbabwe **80** 19.00S 26.30E
Hwang Ho *r. see* Huang He *r.* China **54**
Hyannis Mass. U.S.A. **115** 41.39N 70.17W
Hyannis Nebr. U.S.A. **110** 41.59N 101.44W
Hyargas Nuur *l.* Mongolia **52** 49.30N 93.35E
Hydaburg U.S.A. **100** 55.15N 132.50W
Hyde U.K. **12** 53.26N 2.06W
Hyden Australia **89** 32.27S 118.53E
Hyde Park U.S.A. **105** 44.36N 72.37W
Hyde Park Corner *town* Canada **104** 43.00N 81.28W
Hyderābād India **61** 17.22N 78.26E
Hyderābād Pakistan **62** 25.22N 68.22E
Hydesville U.S.A. **108** 40.31N 124.00W
Hydetown U.S.A. **114** 41.40N 79.44W
Hyères France **21** 43.07N 6.07E
Hyères, Îles d' *is.* France **21** 43.00N 6.20E
Hyland *r.* Canada **100** 59.50N 128.10W
Hyland, Mt. Australia **93** 30.09S 152.25E
Hyland Post Canada **100** 57.40N 128.10W
Hylestad Norway **42** 59.05N 7.32E
Hyllestad Norway **41** 61.10N 5.18E
Hyltebruk Sweden **43** 57.00N 13.14E
Hyndman U.S.A. **114** 39.49N 78.44W
Hyndman Peak U.S.A. **108** 43.50N 114.10W
Hysham U.S.A. **108** 46.18N 107.14W
Hythe Kent U.K. **13** 51.04N 1.05E
Hyvinkää Finland **41** 60.38N 24.52E

I

Iakoro Madagascar **81** 23.06S 46.40E
Ialomiţa *r.* Romania **37** 44.41N 27.52E
Iar Connacht *f.* Rep. of Ire. **15** 53.21N 9.22W
Iaşi Romania **37** 47.09N 27.38E
Iasmos Greece **34** 41.07N 25.12E
Iauaretê Brazil **122** 0.36N 69.12W
Iaupolo P.N.G. **90** 9.34S 150.30E
Ibadan Nigeria **77** 7.23N 3.56E
Ibagué Colombia **122** 4.25N 75.20W
Ibar *r.* Yugo. **34** 43.15N 20.40E
Ibaraki Japan **57** 34.49N 135.34E
Ibarra Ecuador **122** 0.23N 78.05W
Ibb Yemen **71** 13.58N 44.11E
Ibba Sudan **73** 4.48N 29.06E
Ibba *wadi* Sudan **73** 7.09N 28.41E
Ibbenbüren Germany **38** 52.16N 7.43E
Iberville Canada **105** 45.18N 73.14W
Ibi *r.* Japan **57** 35.03N 136.42E
Ibi Nigeria **77** 8.11N 9.44E
Ibiapaba, Serra da *mts.* Brazil **123** 5.30S 41.00W
Ibicaraí Brazil **123** 14.52S 39.37W
Ibicuy Argentina **125** 33.45S 59.13W
Ibina *r.* Zaïre **79** 1.00N 28.40E
Ibitinga Brazil **126** 21.43S 48.47W
Ibiza *i.* Spain **25** 39.00N 1.25E
Ibiza *town* Spain **25** 38.54N 1.26E
Iblei, Monti *mts.* Italy **33** 37.07N 14.40E
Ibor *r.* Spain **27** 39.49N 5.33W
Ibotirama Brazil **123** 12.13S 43.12W
Ibrah, Wadi Sudan **73** 10.36N 25.05E
'Ibrī Oman **71** 23.14N 56.30E
İbriktepe Turkey **34** 41.00N 26.30E
Ibshawāy Egypt **66** 29.21N 30.40E
Ibta' Syria **67** 32.47N 36.09E
Ibusuki Japan **57** 31.16N 130.39E
Içá *r.* Brazil **122** 3.07S 67.58W
Ica Peru **122** 14.02S 75.48W
Içana Brazil **122** 0.21N 67.19W
Içana *r.* Brazil **122** 0.00 67.10W
Iceland Europe **40** 64.45N 18.00W
Ichchāpuram India **63** 19.07N 84.42E
Ichihara Japan **57** 35.31N 140.05E
Ichikawa Japan **57** 35.44N 139.55E
Ichinomiya Japan **57** 35.18N 136.48E
Icoraci Brazil **123** 1.16S 48.28W
Icy Str. U.S.A. **100** 58.20N 135.30W
Idabel U.S.A. **111** 33.54N 94.50W
Ida Grove U.S.A. **110** 42.21N 95.28W
Idah Nigeria **77** 7.05N 6.45E
Idaho *d.* U.S.A. **108** 44.58N 115.56W
Idaho Falls *town* U.S.A. **108** 43.30N 112.02W
Idanha-a-Nova Portugal **27** 39.55N 7.14W
Idar India **62** 23.50N 73.00E
Idar-Oberstein Germany **39** 49.42N 7.19E
Ideles Algeria **75** 23.49N 5.55E
Idfū Egypt **64** 24.58N 32.50E
Ídhi Óros *mtn.* Greece **35** 35.18N 24.43E
Ídhra *i.* Greece **35** 37.20N 23.32E
Ídhra *town* Greece **35** 37.20N 23.29E
Idiofa Zaïre **78** 4.58S 19.38E
Idmū Egypt **66** 28.09N 30.41E
Idnah Jordan **67** 31.34N 34.59E
Idre Sweden **41** 61.52N 12.43E
Idrija Yugo. **31** 46.00N 14.01E
Idstein Germany **39** 50.13N 8.16E
Ieper Belgium **16** 50.51N 2.53E
Ierápetra Greece **35** 35.00N 25.44E
Ierissós Greece **34** 40.24N 23.52E
Ierzu Italy **32** 39.48N 9.32E
Iesi Italy **30** 43.31N 13.14E
Iesolo Italy **30** 45.32N 12.38E
Ifakara Tanzania **79** 8.09S 36.41E
Ifalik *is.* Caroline Is. **59** 7.15N 144.27E
Ifanadiana Madagascar **81** 21.19S 47.39E
Ife Oyo Nigeria **77** 7.33N 4.34E
Iferouâne Niger **77** 19.04N 8.24E
Iga *r.* Japan **57** 34.45N 136.01E
Igatpuri India **62** 19.42N 73.33E
Iggesund Sweden **41** 61.38N 17.04E
Iglesias Italy **32** 39.19N 8.32E
Igli Algeria **74** 30.27N 2.18W
Igloolik Island *town* Canada **99** 69.05N 81.25W
Ignace Canada **102** 49.30N 91.40W
İğneada Burnu *c.* Turkey **29** 41.50N 28.05E
Igoumenítsa Greece **34** 39.30N 20.16E
Igra U.S.S.R. **44** 57.31N 53.09E
Iguaçu *r.* Brazil **126** 25.33S 54.35W
Iguaçu, Saltos do *f.* Brazil / Argentina **126** 25.35S 54.22W
Iguala Mexico **116** 18.21N 99.31W
Igualada Spain **25** 41.35N 1.38E
Iguassu Falls *see* Iguaçu, Saltos do *f.* Brazil / Argentina **126**
Iguatu Brazil **123** 6.22S 39.20W
Iguéla Gabon **78** 1.57S 9.22E
Ihiala Nigeria **77** 5.51N 6.52E
Ihosy Madagascar **81** 22.24S 46.08E
Ihosy *r.* Madagascar **81** 21.58S 43.38E
Ii *r.* Finland **40** 65.19N 25.20E
Iida Japan **57** 35.31N 137.50E
Iidaan Somali Rep. **71** 6.03N 49.01E
Iide yama *mtn.* Japan **57** 37.50N 139.42E
Iisalmi Finland **40** 63.34N 27.11E
Ijebu Ode Nigeria **77** 6.47N 3.54E
Ijill, Kediet *mtn.* Mauritania **74** 22.38N 12.33W
IJmuiden Neth. **16** 52.28N 4.37E
IJssel *r.* Overijssel Neth. **16** 52.34N 5.50E
IJssel *r.* Zuid Holland Neth. **16** 51.54N 4.32E
IJsselmeer *l.* Neth. **16** 52.45N 5.20E
Ijuí Brazil **126** 28.23S 53.55W
Ijzendijke Neth. **16** 51.19N 3.37E
Ijzer *r.* Belgium **16** 51.09N 2.44E
Ikaría *i.* Greece **35** 37.41N 26.20E
Ikdū Egypt **66** 31.18N 30.18E
Ikela Zaïre **78** 1.06S 23.04E
Ikelemba Congo **78** 1.15N 16.38E
Ikelemba *r.* Zaïre **78** 0.08N 18.19E
Ikerre Nigeria **77** 7.30N 5.14E
Ikhast Denmark **42** 56.09N 9.08E
Ikhtiman Bulgaria **34** 42.27N 23.48E
Iki shima *i.* Japan **57** 33.47N 129.43E
Ikopa *r.* Madagascar **81** 16.29S 46.43E
Ila Nigeria **77** 8.01N 4.55E
Ilagan Phil. **59** 17.07N 121.53E
Īlām Iran **65** 33.27N 46.27E
Ilām Nepal **63** 26.55N 87.56E
Ilan Taiwan **55** 24.45N 121.44E
Ilangali Tanzania **79** 6.50S 35.06E
Ilanz Switz. **39** 46.46N 9.12E
Ilaro Nigeria **77** 6.53N 3.03E
Iława Poland **37** 53.37N 19.33E
Ilebo Zaïre **78** 4.20S 20.35E
Ilek *r.* U.S.S.R. **45** 51.30N 54.00E
Ileret Kenya **79** 4.22N 36.13E
Ilerh, Oued *wadi* Algeria **75** 20.59N 2.14E
Îles, Lac des *l.* Canada **105** 46.50N 77.10W
Ilesha Oyo Nigeria **77** 7.39N 4.45E
Ilford Canada **101** 56.04N 95.35W
Ilfracombe Australia **90** 23.30S 144.30E
Ilfracombe U.K. **13** 51.13N 4.08W
Ilhabela Brazil **126** 23.47S 45.20W
Ilha Grande, Baía da *b.* Brazil **126** 23.09S 44.30W
Ilha Grande, Represa *resr.* Brazil **126** 23.10S 53.40W
Ilhavo Portugal **26** 40.36N 8.40W
Ilhéus Brazil **123** 14.50S 39.06W
Ili *r.* U.S.S.R. **52** 45.00N 74.20E
Ilia Romania **37** 45.56N 22.39E
Iliamna L. U.S.A. **98** 59.30N 155.00W
Ilich U.S.S.R. **52** 40.50N 68.29E
Iligan Phil. **59** 8.12N 124.13E
Ilintsy U.S.S.R. **37** 49.08N 29.11E
Ilion U.S.A. **115** 43.01N 75.02W
Ilirska Bistrica Yugo. **31** 45.34N 14.15E
Ilkley U.K. **12** 53.56N 1.49W
Illapel Chile **124** 31.38S 71.10W
Ille-et-Vilaine *d.* France **18** 48.10N 1.30W

Illéla to **Izyum**

Illéla Niger **77** 14.30N 5.09E
Iller *r.* Germany **39** 48.23N 9.58E
Illeret Kenya **73** 4.19N 36.13E
Illertissen Germany **39** 48.13N 10.06E
Illescas Spain **27** 40.07N 3.50W
Illiers France **18** 48.18N 1.15E
Illinois *d.* U.S.A. **110** 40.30N 89.30W
Illinois *r.* U.S.A. **110** 38.58N 90.27W
Illizi Algeria **75** 26.29N 8.28E
Ilmajoki Finland **40** 62.44N 22.34E
Ilmenau *r.* Germany **38** 53.23N 10.10E
Ilminster U.K. **13** 50.55N 2.56W
Ilo Peru **124** 17.38S 71.20W
Iloilo Phil. **59** 10.45N122.33E
Ilorin Nigeria **77** 8.32N 4.34E
Ilubabor *d.* Ethiopia **73** 7.50N 34.55E
Imabari Japan **57** 34.04N132.59E
Imala Mozambique **79** 14.39S 39.34E
Imandra U.S.S.R. **44** 67.53N 33.30E
Imandra, Ozero *l.* U.S.S.R. **44** 67.30N 32.45E
Imbâbah Egypt **66** 30.05N 31.12E
Imese Zaïre **78** 2.07N 18.06E
Imī Ethiopia **73** 6.28N 42.18E
Imlay City U.S.A. **114** 43.02N 83.05W
Immenstadt Germany **38** 47.33N 10.13E
Immingham U.K. **12** 53.37N 0.12W
Immokalee U.S.A. **113** 26.25N 81.26W
Imo *d.* Nigeria **77** 5.30N 7.20E
Imola Italy **30** 44.21N 11.42E
Imotski Yugo. **31** 43.27N 17.13E
Imperatriz Brazil **123** 5.32S 47.28W
Imperia Italy **30** 43.53N 8.03E
Imperial Calif. U.S.A. **109** 32.51N115.34W
Imperial Nebr. U.S.A. **110** 40.31N101.39W
Imperial Dam U.S.A. **109** 32.55N114.30W
Imperial de Aragón, Canal Spain **25** 41.37N 1.00W
Imperial Valley *f.* U.S.A. **109** 32.50N115.30W
Impfondo Congo **78** 1.36N 17.58E
Imphāl India **61** 24.47N 93.55E
Imroz *i. see* Gökçeada *i.* Turkey **34**
Imst Austria **39** 47.14N 10.44E
Ina Japan **57** 35.50N137.57E
Ina *r.* Japan **57** 34.43N135.28E
In Abbangarit *well* Niger **77** 17.49N 6.15E
Inaccessible I. Tristan da Cunha **127** 37.19S 12.44W
I-n-Amguel Algeria **75** 23.40N 5.08E
Inangahua Junction New Zealand **86** 41.53S171.58E
Inanwatan Indonesia **59** 2.08S132.10E
Inarajan Guam **84** 13.16N144.45E
Inari *l.* Finland **40** 69.00N 28.00E
Inari *town* Finland **40** 68.54N 27.01E
Inazawa Japan **57** 35.15N136.47E
I-n-Belbel Algeria **74** 27.54N 1.10E
Inca Spain **25** 39.43N 2.54E
Incesu Turkey **64** 38.39N 35.12E
Inchiri *d.* Mauritania **74** 20.10N 15.00W
Inch'on S. Korea **53** 37.30N126.38E
Incudine, L' *mtn.* France **21** 41.51N 9.12E
Indals *r.* Sweden **40** 62.30N 17.20E
Indaw Burma **56** 23.40N 94.46E
Independence Calif. U.S.A. **108** 36.48N118.12W
Independence Kans. U.S.A. **111** 37.13N 95.42W
Independence Mo. U.S.A. **110** 39.05N 94.24W
Inderborskiy U.S.S.R. **45** 48.32N 51.44E
India Asia **61** 23.00N 78.30E
Indian *r.* Canada **105** 45.16N 76.14W
Indiana *d.* U.S.A. **112** 40.00N 86.15W
Indiana *town* U.S.A. **114** 40.37N 79.09W
Indian-Antarctic Ridge *f.* Indian Oc. **49** 49.00S125.00E
Indianapolis U.S.A. **112** 39.45N 86.10W
Indian Cabins Canada **100** 59.52N117.02W
Indian Harbour Canada **103** 54.25N 57.20W
Indian Head Canada **101** 50.32N103.40W
Indian L. Canada **104** 47.08N 82.08W
Indian L. U.S.A. **115** 43.47N 74.16W
Indian Lake *town* U.S.A. **105** 43.47N 74.16W
Indian Ocean 49
Indianola U.S.A. **110** 41.22N 93.34W
Indian River *town* U.S.A. **104** 45.25N 84.37W
Indian River B. U.S.A. **115** 38.36N 75.05W
Indiga U.S.S.R. **44** 67.40N 49.00E
Indigirka *r.* U.S.S.R. **51** 71.00N148.45E
Indija Yugo. **31** 45.03N 20.05E
Indio U.S.A. **109** 33.43N116.13W
Indonesia Asia **58** 6.00S118.00E
Indore India **62** 22.43N 75.50E
Indragiri *r.* Indonesia **58** 0.30S103.08E
Indramayu Indonesia **59** 6.22S108.20E
Indrāvati *r.* India **63** 18.44N 80.16E
Indre *d.* France **19** 46.45N 1.30E
Indre *r.* France **18** 47.16N 0.19E
Indre-et-Loire *d.* France **18** 47.15N 0.45E
Indus *r.* Pakistan **62** 24.20N 67.47E
Inebolu Turkey **64** 41.57N 33.45E
Inegöl Turkey **64** 40.06N 29.31E
I-n-Eker Algeria **75** 24.01N 5.05E
I-n-Ezzane *well* Algeria **75** 23.29N 11.15E
Infiesto Spain **26** 43.21N 5.22W
I-n-Gall Niger **77** 16.47N 6.56E
Ingatestone U.K. **13** 51.41N 0.22E
Ingelstad Sweden **43** 56.45N 14.55E
Ingende Zaïre **78** 0.17S 18.58E
Ingenika *r.* Canada **100** 56.43N125.07W
Ingersoll Canada **104** 43.02N 80.53W
Inggen China **54** 41.35N104.47E
Ingham Australia **90** 18.35S146.12E
Ingleborough *mtn.* U.K. **12** 54.10N 2.23W
Inglewood *Qld.* Australia **93** 28.25S151.02E
Inglewood Vic. Australia **92** 36.33S143.53E
Inglewood Canada **104** 43.47N 79.56W
Inglewood New Zealand **86** 39.09S174.12E
Inglewood U.S.A. **109** 33.58N118.21W
Ingolstadt Germany **39** 48.46N 11.27E
Ingomar Australia **92** 29.38S134.48E
Ingraham U.S.A. **105** 44.47N 73.30W
Ingulets U.S.S.R. **45** 47.43N 33.16E
Ingwiller France **19** 48.52N 7.29E
Inhambane Mozambique **81** 23.51S 35.29E
Inhambane *d.* Mozambique **81** 22.20S 34.00E
Inhaminga Mozambique **81** 18.24S 35.00E
Inharrime Mozambique **81** 24.29S 35.01E
Inhassoro Mozambique **81** 21.32S 35.10E
Iniesta Spain **25** 39.26N 1.45W
Inirida *r.* Colombia **122** 3.59N 67.45W
Inishbofin *i.* Galway Rep. of Ire. **15** 53.38N 10.14W
Inisheer *i.* Rep. of Ire. **15** 53.04N 9.32W
Inishmaan *i.* Rep. of Ire. **15** 53.06N 9.36W
Inishmore *i.* Rep. of Ire. **15** 53.08N 9.43W
Inishowen Pen. Rep. of Ire. **15** 55.08N 7.20W
Inishturk *i.* Rep. of Ire. **15** 53.43N 10.08W
Injune Australia **90** 25.51S148.34E
Inklin Canada **100** 58.56N133.05W
Inklin *r.* Canada **100** 58.50N133.10W
Inkster U.S.A. **104** 42.17N 83.17W
Inn *r.* Europe **39** 48.35N 13.28E
Innaminka Australia **91** 27.43S140.46E
Inner Hebrides *is.* U.K. **14** 56.50N 6.45W
Inner Mongolia *d. see* Nei Monggol *d.* China **54**
Inner Sd. U.K. **14** 57.30N 5.55W
Innisfail Australia **90** 17.32S146.02E
Innisfail Canada **100** 52.00N113.57W
Innsbruck Austria **39** 47.16N 11.24E
Innset Norway **40** 68.41N 18.50E
Innviertel *f.* Austria **39** 48.05N 13.08E
Inongo Zaïre **78** 1.55S 18.20E
Inowrocław Poland **37** 52.49N 18.12E
I-n-Salah Algeria **75** 27.13N 2.28E
Insein Burma **56** 16.54N 96.08E
In Tasik *well* Mali **77** 18.03N 2.00E
Intepe Turkey **34** 40.01N 26.19E
Interlaken Switz. **39** 46.41N 7.51E
International Falls *town* U.S.A. **110** 48.38N 93.26W
Intracoastal Waterway *canal* U.S.A. **111** 28.45N 95.40W
Intute Mozambique **79** 14.08S 39.55E
Inubō saki *c.* Japan **57** 35.41N140.52E
Inukjuac Canada **99** 58.25N 78.18W
Inuvik Canada **98** 68.16N133.40W
Inuvik *d.* Canada **98** 68.00N130.00W
Inuyama Japan **57** 35.23N136.56E
Inveraray U.K. **14** 56.24N 5.05W
Inverbervie U.K. **14** 56.51N 2.17W
Invercargill New Zealand **86** 46.26S168.21E
Inverell Australia **93** 29.46S151.10E
Invergordon U.K. **14** 57.42N 4.10W
Inverhuron Canada **104** 44.17N 81.34W
Inverness U.K. **14** 57.27N 4.15W
Inverurie U.K. **14** 57.17N 2.23W
Inverway Australia **88** 17.49S129.40E
Investigator Group *is.* Australia **92** 33.45S134.30E
Investigator Str. Australia **92** 35.25S137.10E
Invinheima *r.* Brazil **124** 22.52S 53.20W
Inya U.S.S.R. **50** 50.24N 86.47E
Inyangani *mtn.* Zimbabwe **81** 18.18S 32.50E
Inyonga Tanzania **79** 6.43S 32.02E
Inzia *r.* Zaïre **78** 3.47S 17.57E
Ioánnina Greece **34** 39.39N 20.57E
Iola U.S.A. **111** 37.55N 95.24W
Iona *i.* U.K. **14** 56.20N 6.25W
Iongo Angola **78** 9.11S 17.45E
Ionia U.S.A. **112** 42.58N 85.06W
Ionian Is. *see* Iónioi Nísoi *is.* Greece **35**
Ionian Sea Med. Sea **35** 38.30N 18.45E
Iónioi Nísoi *is.* Greece **35** 38.40N 20.08E
Íos *i.* Greece **35** 36.44N 25.16E
Íos *town* Greece **35** 36.44N 25.16E
Iowa *d.* U.S.A. **110** 42.00N 93.30W
Iowa *r.* U.S.A. **110** 41.10N 91.02W
Iowa City U.S.A. **110** 41.40N 91.32W
Iowa Falls *town* U.S.A. **110** 42.31N 93.16W
Ipati Greece **35** 38.52N 22.14E
Ipatovo U.S.S.R. **45** 45.44N 42.56E
Ipeiros *f.* Greece **34** 39.30N 20.30E
Ipiales Colombia **122** 0.52N 77.38W
Ipiaú Brazil **123** 14.07S 39.43W
Ipixuna Brazil **122** 7.00S 71.30W
Ipoh Malaysia **58** 4.36N101.02E
Ippa *r.* U.S.S.R. **37** 52.13N 29.08E
Ippy C.A.R. **73** 6.15N 21.12E
Ipsala Turkey **34** 40.55N 26.23E
Ipswich Australia **93** 27.38S152.40E
Ipswich U.K. **13** 52.04N 1.09E
Ipu Brazil **123** 4.23S 40.44W
Ipuh Indonesia **58** 2.58S101.28E
Iquique Chile **124** 20.13S 70.10W
Iquitos Peru **122** 3.51S 73.13W
Irago-suidō *str.* Japan **57** 34.35N137.00E
Iráklia *i.* Greece **35** 36.50N 25.28E
Iráklion Greece **35** 35.20N 25.09E
Iran Asia **65** 32.00N 54.30E
Iran, Pegunungan *mts.* Indonesia / Malaysia **58** 3.20N115.00E
Īrānshahr Iran **65** 27.14N 60.42E
Irapuato Mexico **116** 20.40N101.40W
Iraq Asia **64** 33.00N 44.00E
Irauen, Wādī Libya **75** 26.28N 12.00E
Irayel U.S.S.R. **44** 64.23N 55.25E
Irazú *mtn.* Costa Rica **117** 9.59N 83.52W
Irbid Jordan **67** 32.33N 35.51E
Irbid *d.* Jordan **67** 32.27N 35.51E
Irbil Iraq **65** 36.12N 44.01E
Irdning Austria **39** 47.33N 14.01E
Irebu Zaïre **78** 0.37S 17.45E
Iregua *r.* Spain **26** 42.27N 2.24W
Ireland I. Bermuda **127** 32.19N 64.51W
Irgiz U.S.S.R. **9** 48.36N 61.14E
Irgiz *r.* U.S.S.R. **9** 48.00N 62.30E
Irharhar, Oued *wadi* Algeria **75** 23.45N 5.55E
Irian Jaya *d.* Indonesia **59** 4.00S138.00E
Iriba Chad **72** 15.07N 22.15E
Irié Guinea **76** 8.15N 9.10W
Iringa Tanzania **79** 7.49S 35.39E
Iringa *d.* Tanzania **79** 8.30S 35.00E
Iriomote jima *i.* Japan **53** 24.30N124.00E
Iriri *r.* Brazil **123** 3.50S 52.40W
Irish Sea U.K. / Rep. of Ire. **15** 53.30N 5.40W
Irkutsk U.S.S.R. **52** 52.18N104.15E
Iroise *b.* France **18** 48.15N 4.55W
Iron Baron Australia **92** 32.59S137.09E
Iron Bridge *town* Canada **104** 46.17N 83.14W
Iron Gate *f.* Romania / Yugo. **37** 44.40N 22.30E
Iron Knob Australia **92** 32.44S137.08E
Iron Mountain *town* U.S.A. **112** 45.51N 88.03W
Iron Mts. Rep. of Ire. **15** 54.10N 7.56W
Iron River *town* U.S.A. **110** 46.05N 88.38W
Irons U.S.A. **112** 44.08N 85.55W
Ironton U.S.A. **114** 38.31N 82.40W
Ironwood U.S.A. **112** 46.25N 90.08W
Iroquois Canada **105** 44.51N 75.19W
Iroquois Falls *town* Canada **102** 48.40N 80.40W
Irosin Phil. **59** 12.45N124.02E
Irō-zaki *c.* Japan **57** 34.36N138.51E
Irpen U.S.S.R. **37** 50.31N 30.29E
Irrapatana Australia **92** 29.03S136.28E
Irrawaddy *d.* Burma **56** 17.00N 95.00E
Irrawaddy *r.* Burma **56** 15.50N 95.00E
Irrawaddy Delta Burma **56** 16.45N 95.00E
Irsha *r.* U.S.S.R. **37** 50.45N 29.30E
Irsina Italy **33** 40.45N 16.15E
Irthing *r.* U.K. **11** 54.55N 2.50W
Irtysh *r.* U.S.S.R. **9** 61.00N 69.00E
Iruma *r.* Japan **57** 35.57N139.30E
Irumu Zaïre **79** 1.29N 29.48E
Irún Spain **26** 43.20N 1.48W
Iruñea *see* Pamplona Spain **25**
Irurzun Spain **25** 42.55N 1.50W
Irvine U.K. **14** 55.37N 4.40W
Irvinestown U.K. **15** 54.29N 7.40W
Irving U.S.A. **111** 32.49N 96.56W
Irvona U.S.A. **114** 40.46N 78.33W
Irwin, Pt. Australia **89** 35.03S116.20E
Is, Jabal *mtn.* Sudan **72** 22.03N 35.28E
Isa Nigeria **77** 13.14N 6.24E
Isaac *r.* Australia **90** 22.52S149.20E
Isaba Spain **25** 42.52N 0.55W
Isabelia, Cordillera *mts.* Nicaragua **117** 13.30N 85.00W
Isábena *r.* Spain **25** 42.11N 0.21E
Ísafjördhur *town* Iceland **40** 66.05N 23.06W
Isaka Tanzania **79** 3.52S 32.54E
Isaka Bandundu Zaïre **78** 2.35S 18.48E
Isaka Equateur Zaïre **78** 1.49S 20.50E
Īsa Khel Pakistan **62** 32.41N 71.17E
Isakogorka U.S.S.R. **44** 64.23N 40.31E
Isangi Zaïre **78** 0.48N 24.03E
Isar *r.* Germany **39** 48.49N 12.58E
Isbergues France **16** 50.38N 2.24E
Ischia Italy **32** 40.43N 13.57E
Ischia *i.* Italy **32** 40.43N 13.54E
Ise Japan **57** 34.29N136.42E
Isefjord *b.* Denmark **42** 55.52N 11.49E
Iseo, Lago d' *l.* Italy **30** 45.43N 10.04E
Isère *d.* France **21** 45.10N 5.50E
Isère *r.* France **21** 44.59N 4.51E
Iserlohn Germany **38** 51.22N 7.41E
Isernia Italy **33** 41.36N 14.14E
Ise-wan *b.* Japan **57** 34.45N136.40E
Iseyin Nigeria **77** 7.59N 3.36E
Isfahan *see* Eşfahān Iran **60**
Ishikari *r.* Japan **57** 43.15N141.21E
Ishikari wan *b.* Japan **57** 43.15N141.20E
Ishim U.S.S.R. **50** 56.10N 69.30E
Ishim *r.* U.S.S.R. **9** 57.50N 71.00E
Ishinomaki Japan **57** 38.25N141.18E
Ishpeming U.S.A. **112** 46.29N 87.40W
Ishurdi Bangla. **63** 24.09N 89.03E
Isigny France **18** 49.18N 1.06W
Isiolo Kenya **79** 0.20N 37.36E
Isipingo Beach *town* R.S.A. **80** 30.00S 30.57E
Isiro Zaïre **79** 2.50N 27.40E
Iskår *r.* Bulgaria **34** 43.44N 24.27E
Iskenderun Turkey **64** 36.37N 36.08E
Iskenderun Körfezi *g.* Turkey **64** 36.40N 35.50E
Iskilip Turkey **64** 40.45N 34.28E
Iskŭr *r.* Bulgaria **34** 43.35N 24.20E
Iskŭr, Yazovir *l.* Bulgaria **34** 42.27N 23.38E
Isla *r.* U.K. **14** 56.32N 3.22W
Isla Cristina *town* Spain **27** 37.12N 7.19W
Islāmābād Pakistan **62** 33.40N 73.10E
Islāmkot Pakistan **62** 24.42N 70.11E
Islāmpur Bihār India **63** 25.09N 85.12E
Islāmpur W. Bengal India **63** 26.16N 88.12E
Island L. Australia **92** 31.30S136.40E
Island L. Canada **101** 53.47N 94.25W
Island Magee *pen.* U.K. **15** 54.48N 5.44W
Islands, B. of Canada **103** 49.10N 58.15W
Islands, B. of New Zealand **86** 35.15S174.15E
Islay *i.* U.K. **14** 55.45N 6.20W
Isle *r.* France **20** 44.55N 0.15W
Isle of Portland *f.* U.K. **13** 50.32N 2.25W
Isle of Wight *d.* U.K. **13** 50.40N 1.17W
Isleta U.S.A. **109** 34.55N106.42W
Ismael Cortinas Uruguay **125** 33.58S 57.06W
Ismay U.S.A. **108** 46.30N104.48W
Isnā Egypt **64** 25.16N 32.30E
Isny Germany **38** 47.41N 10.02E
Isoka Zambia **79** 10.06S 32.39E
Isola della Scala Italy **32** 45.16N 11.00E
Isola del Liri *town* Italy **31** 41.41N 13.34E
Isola di Capo Rizzuto *town* Italy **33** 38.58N 17.06E
Isparta Turkey **64** 37.46N 30.32E
Isperikh Bulgaria **34** 43.43N 26.50E
Ispica Italy **33** 36.46N 14.55E
Ispikān Pakistan **62** 26.14N 62.12E
Israel Asia **67** 32.00N 34.50E
Israelite B. Australia **89** 33.40S123.55E
Israelite Bay *town* Australia **89** 33.37S123.48E
Issia Ivory Coast **76** 6.33N 6.33W
Issigeac France **20** 44.44N 0.36E
Issoire France **20** 45.33N 3.15E
Issoudun France **19** 46.57N 2.00E
Is-sur-Tille France **19** 47.31N 5.06E
Issyk Kul *l.* U.S.S.R. **52** 43.30N 77.20E
Istanbul Turkey **29** 41.02N 28.58E
Istanbul Boğazi *str.* Turkey **29** 41.07N 29.04E
Isthmus of Kra Thailand **56** 10.20N 99.10E
Istiaía Greece **35** 38.57N 23.10E
Istok Yugo. **34** 42.45N 20.24E
Istra *pen.* Yugo. **31** 45.10N 13.55E
Itabaiana Brazil **123** 7.20S 35.20W
Itabira Brazil **126** 19.39S 43.14W
Itabirito Brazil **126** 20.21S 43.45W
Itabuna Brazil **123** 14.48S 39.18W
Itacajuna *r.* Brazil **123** 5.20S 49.08W
Itacoatiara Brazil **122** 3.06S 58.22W
Itagüí Colombia **122** 6.10N 75.36W
Itaí Brazil **126** 23.23S 49.05W
Itaim *r.* Brazil **123** 6.43S 42.48W
Itaipu, Reprêsa *resr.* Brazil / Paraguay **126** 24.30S 54.20W
Itaituba Brazil **123** 4.17S 55.59W
Itajaí Brazil **126** 26.50S 48.39W
Itajubá Brazil **126** 22.24S 45.25W
Itaka Tanzania **79** 8.51S 32.48E
Itálica *site* Spain **27** 37.30N 6.05W
Italy Europe **28** 43.00N 12.00E
Itami Japan **57** 34.46N135.25E
Itapecerica Brazil **126** 20.28S 45.09W
Itapecuru Mirim Brazil **123** 3.24S 44.20W
Itaperuna Brazil **126** 21.14S 41.51W
Itapetinga Brazil **123** 15.17S 40.16W
Itapetininga Brazil **126** 23.36S 48.07W
Itapeva Brazil **126** 23.59S 48.59W
Itapicuru *r.* Brazil **123** 11.50S 37.30W
Itapira Brazil **126** 22.24S 46.56W
Itaqui Brazil **126** 29.07S 56.33W
Itārsi India **63** 22.37N 77.45E
Itatiba Brazil **126** 22.59S 46.51W
Itatinga Brazil **126** 23.06S 48.36W
Itatuba Brazil **122** 5.40S 63.20W
Itaúna Brazil **126** 20.04S 44.14W
Itboyat *i.* Phil. **55** 20.45N121.50E
Itéa Greece **35** 38.25N 22.25E
Ithaca U.S.A. **115** 42.27N 76.30W
Itháki Greece **35** 38.23N 20.42E
Itháki *i.* Greece **35** 38.24N 20.42E
Itimbiri *r.* Zaïre **78** 2.02N 22.47E
Itmurinkol, Ozero *l.* U.S.S.R. **45** 49.30N 52.17E
Itō Japan **57** 34.58N139.05E
Itoko Zaïre **78** 1.00S 21.45E
Iton *r.* France **18** 49.09N 1.12E
Itsa Egypt **66** 29.14N 30.47E
Ittel, Oued *wadi* Algeria **75** 34.18N 6.02E
Ittiri Italy **32** 40.36N 8.33E
Itu Brazil **126** 23.17S 47.18W
Ituí *r.* Brazil **122** 4.38S 70.19W
Ituiutaba Brazil **126** 19.00S 49.25W
Ituri *r.* Zaïre **79** 1.45N 27.06E
Iturup *i.* U.S.S.R. **53** 44.00N147.30E
Ituverava Brazil **126** 20.22S 47.48W
Ituxi *r.* Brazil **122** 7.20S 64.50W
Ityāy al Bārūd Egypt **66** 30.53N 30.40E
Itzehoe Germany **38** 53.55N 9.31E
Ivaí *r.* Brazil **126** 23.20S 53.23W
Ivalo Finland **40** 68.42N 27.30E
Ivalo *r.* Finland **40** 68.43N 27.36E
Ivanec Yugo. **31** 46.13N 16.08E
Ivangrad Yugo. **31** 42.50N 19.52E
Ivanhoe Australia **92** 32.56S144.22E
Ivanhoe U.S.A. **110** 44.28N 96.12W
Ivanić Grad Yugo. **31** 45.42N 16.24E
Ivanjica Yugo. **34** 43.35N 20.14E
Ivano-Frankovsk U.S.S.R. **37** 48.55N 24.42E
Ivanovo B.S.S.R. U.S.S.R. **37** 52.10N 25.13E
Ivanovo R.S.F.S.R. U.S.S.R. **44** 57.00N 41.00E
Ivdel U.S.S.R. **44** 60.45N 60.30E
Ivenets U.S.S.R. **37** 53.50N 26.40E
Ivigtût Greenland **99** 61.10N 48.00W
Ivindo Gabon **78** 0.02S 12.13E
Ivittuut *see* Ivigtût Greenland **99**
Iviza *i. see* Ibiza *i.* Spain **25**
Ivohibe Madagascar **81** 22.29S 45.52E
Ivory Coast Africa **76** 8.00N 5.30W
Ivösjön *l.* Sweden **43** 56.06N 14.27E
Ivrea Italy **30** 45.28N 7.52E
Ivujivik Canada **99** 62.24N 77.55W
Ivybridge U.K. **13** 50.24N 3.56W
Ivydale U.S.A. **114** 38.32N 81.03W
Iwaki Japan **57** 36.58N140.58E
Iwaki *r.* Japan **57** 41.20N140.00E
Iwakuni Japan **57** 34.10N132.09E
Iwata Japan **57** 34.42N137.48E
Iwo Nigeria **77** 7.38N 4.11E
Ixiamas Bolivia **124** 13.45S 68.09W
Iyo nada *str.* Japan **57** 33.40N132.20E
Izabal, Lago de *l.* Guatemala **117** 15.30N 89.00W
Izberbash U.S.S.R. **45** 42.31N 47.52E
Izhevsk U.S.S.R. **44** 56.49N 53.11E
Izhma U.S.S.R. **44** 65.03N 53.48E
Izhma *r.* U.S.S.R. **44** 65.16N 53.18E
Izmail U.S.S.R. **37** 45.20N 28.50E
Izmir Turkey **29** 38.24N 27.09E
Izmir Körfezi *g.* Turkey **29** 38.30N 26.45E
Izmit Turkey **64** 40.48N 29.55E
Iznajar, Embalse de *resr.* Spain **27** 37.15N 4.20W
Iznalloz Spain **27** 37.23N 3.31W
Izozog, Bañados de *f.* Bolivia **124** 18.30S 62.05W
Izozog Marshes *f. see* Izozog, Bañados de *f.* Bolivia **124**
Izra' Syria **67** 32.51N 36.15E
Izsák Hungary **31** 46.48N 19.22E
Iztochni Rodopi *mts.* Bulgaria **34** 41.44N 25.28E
Izu-hantō *pen.* Japan **57** 34.53N138.55E
Izuhara Japan **57** 34.12N129.17E
Izumi Japan **57** 34.29N135.26E
Izumi-ōtsu Japan **57** 34.30N135.24E
Izumi-sano Japan **57** 34.25N135.19E
Izumo Japan **57** 35.33N132.50E
Izumo *r.* Japan **57** 34.38N136.33E
Izyaslav U.S.S.R. **37** 50.10N 26.46E
Izyum U.S.S.R. **45** 49.12N 37.19E

J

Jaba Ethiopia 73 6.17N 35.12E
Jaba' Jordan 67 32.19N 35.13E
Jabā Syria 67 33.10N 35.56E
Jabal, Baḩr al r. Sudan 73 9.30N 30.30E
Jabal al Awliyā' Sudan 72 15.14N 32.30E
Jabal Dūd Sudan 73 13.22N 33.09E
Jabalón r. Spain 26 38.53N 4.05W
Jabalpur India 63 23.10N 79.57E
Jabālyah Egypt 67 31.32N 34.29E
Jabbān, Arḑ al f. Jordan 66 32.08N 36.35E
Jabiru Australia 90 12.39S132.55E
Jabjabah, Wādī Egypt 72 22.37N 33.17E
Jablah Syria 66 35.22N 35.56E
Jablanac Yugo. 31 44.42N 14.54E
Jablanica Yugo. 31 43.39N 17.45E
Jablaničko Jezero resr. Yugo. 31 43.40N 17.50E
Jablonec nad Nisou Czech. 36 50.44N 15.10E
Jabori Pakistan 62 34.36N 73.16E
Jaboticabal Brazil 126 21.15S 48.17W
Jabrat Sa'īd wells Sudan 72 16.06N 31.50E
Jaca Spain 25 42.34N 0.33W
Jacareí Brazil 126 23.17S 45.57W
Jackman U.S.A. 112 45.38N 70.16W
Jacks Mtn. U.S.A. 114 40.45N 77.30W
Jackson Ky. U.S.A. 113 37.32N 83.24W
Jackson Mich. U.S.A. 104 42.15N 84.24W
Jackson Miss. U.S.A. 111 32.18N 90.12W
Jackson Mo. U.S.A. 111 37.23N 89.40W
Jackson Ohio U.S.A. 114 39.03N 82.39W
Jackson Tenn. U.S.A. 111 35.37N 88.49W
Jackson Wyo. U.S.A. 108 43.29N110.38W
Jackson Bay town Canada 100 50.32N125.57W
Jacksonville Fla. U.S.A. 113 30.20N 81.40W
Jacksonville Ill. U.S.A. 110 39.44N 90.14W
Jacksonville N.C. U.S.A. 113 34.45N 77.26W
Jacksonville Tex. U.S.A. 111 31.58N 95.17W
Jacksonville Beach town U.S.A. 113 30.18N 81.24W
Jacobābād Pakistan 62 28.17N 68.26E
Jacobina Brazil 123 11.13S 40.30W
Jacob Lake town U.S.A. 109 36.41N112.14W
Jacob's Well see Bi'r Yaqūb Jordan 67
Jacques Cartier, Détroit de str. Canada 103 50.00N 63.30W
Jacques Cartier, Mt. Canada 103 48.59N 65.57W
Jacuí r. Brazil 126 29.56S 51.13W
Jacundá r. Brazil 123 1.57S 50.26W
Jaddi, Rās c. Pakistan 62 25.14N 63.31E
Jade Germany 38 53.20N 8.14E
Jadebusen b. Germany 38 53.30N 8.10E
Jadraque Spain 26 40.55N 2.55W
Jādū Libya 75 31.57N 12.01E
Jaén Peru 122 5.21S 78.28W
Jaén Spain 27 37.46N 3.47W
Jaén d. Spain 27 37.55N 3.30W
Jaeren f. Norway 42 58.40N 5.45E
Jāfarābād India 62 20.52N 71.22E
Jaffa see Tel Aviv-Yafo Israel 67
Jaffa, C. Australia 92 36.58S139.39E
Jaffna Sri Lanka 61 9.38N 80.02E
Jaffrey U.S.A. 115 42.50N 72.04W
Jagādhri India 62 30.10N 77.18E
Jāgan Pakistan 62 28.05N 68.30E
Jagatsingpur India 63 20.16N 86.10E
Jagdalpur India 63 19.04N 82.02E
Jaggang China 63 32.52N 79.45E
Jagst r. Germany 39 49.14N 9.11E
Jagtiāl India 63 18.48N 78.56E
Jaguarão Brazil 126 32.30S 53.25W
Jahānābād India 63 25.13N 84.59E
Jahrom Iran 65 28.30N 53.30E
Jailolo Indonesia 59 1.05N127.29E
Jainti India 63 26.42N 89.36E
Jaintiāpur Bangla. 63 25.08N 92.07E
Jaipur India 62 26.53N 75.50E
Jāis India 63 26.15N 81.32E
Jaisalmer India 62 26.55N 70.54E
Jājarkot Nepal 63 28.42N 82.14E
Jajawijaya Mts. Asia 59 4.20S139.10E
Jajce Yugo. 31 44.21N 17.16E
Jajjha Pakistan 62 28.45N 70.34E
Jājpur India 63 20.51N 86.20E
Jakarta Indonesia 59 6.08S106.45E
Jakarta d. Indonesia 59 6.10S106.48E
Jakhāu India 62 23.13N 68.43E
Jäkkvik Sweden 40 66.23N 17.00E
Jakobstad see Pietarsaari Finland 40
Jakupica mts. Yugo. 34 41.45N 21.22E
Jal U.S.A. 111 32.07N103.12W
Jalālābād Afghan. 62 34.26N 70.28E
Jalālah al Baḩrīyah, Jabal mts. Egypt 66 29.20N 32.12E
Jalālat al Qiblīyah, Jabal al mts. Egypt 66 28.42N 32.23E
Jalālpur India 63 26.19N 82.44E
Jalapa Mexico 116 19.45N 96.48W
Jālaun India 63 26.09N 79.21E
Jaldak Afghan. 62 31.58N 66.44E
Jalesar India 63 27.29N 78.19E
Jaleswar India 63 21.49N 87.13E
Jālgaon Mahār. India 62 21.01N 75.34E
Jālgaon Mahār. India 62 21.03N 76.32E
Jalingo Nigeria 77 8.54N 11.21E
Jalisco d. Mexico 116 21.00N103.00W
Jallas r. Spain 26 42.54N 9.08W
Jālna India 62 19.50N 75.53E
Jalón r. Spain 25 41.47N 1.04W
Jālor India 62 25.21N 72.37E
Jalpaiguri India 63 26.31N 88.44E
Jālū Libya 75 29.02N 21.33E
Jaluit i. Pacific Oc. 84 6.00N169.35E
Jalūlā Iraq 65 34.16N 45.10E
Jamaame Somali Rep. 79 0.04N 42.46E
Jamaari Nigeria 77 11.44N 9.53E
Jamaica C. America 117 18.00N 77.00W
Jamālpur Bangla. 63 24.55N 89.56E
Jamālpur India 63 25.18N 86.30E
Jamanxim r. Brazil 123 4.43S 56.18W
Jambes Belgium 16 50.28N 4.52E
Jambi Indonesia 58 1.36S103.39E
Jambi d. Indonesia 58 2.00S102.30E
Jambusar India 62 22.03N 72.48E
James r. S.Dak. U.S.A. 110 42.55N 97.28W
James r. Va. U.S.A. 113 36.57N 76.26W
James B. Canada 102 53.30N 80.00W
James Bay Prov. Park Canada 102 51.30N 79.00W
Jamestown Australia 92 33.12S138.38E
Jamestown St. Helena 127 15.56S 5.44W
Jamestown N.Dak. U.S.A. 110 46.54N 98.42W
Jamestown N.Y. U.S.A. 114 42.06N 79.14W
Jamestown Penn. U.S.A. 114 41.29N 80.27W
Jamestown Tenn. U.S.A. 113 36.24N 84.58W
Jamjodhpur India 62 21.54N 70.01E
Jammerbught b. Denmark 42 57.20N 9.30E
Jammu Jammu & Kashmir 62 32.42N 74.52E
Jammu & Kashmir Asia 62 34.45N 76.00E
Jāmnagar India 62 22.28N 70.04E
Jamnotri India 63 31.01N 78.27E
Jampang Kulon Indonesia 59 7.18S106.33E
Jāmpur Pakistan 62 28.45N 70.36E
Jamsah Egypt 66 27.39N 33.35E
Jämsänkoski Finland 41 61.55N 25.11E
Jamshedpur India 63 22.48N 86.11E
Jämtland d. Sweden 40 63.00N 14.30E
Jamūi India 63 24.55N 86.13E
Jamuna r. Bangla. 63 23.51N 89.45E
Jand Pakistan 62 33.26N 72.01E
Janda, Laguna de la l. Spain 27 36.15N 5.51W
Jandiāla India 62 31.33N 75.02E
Jándula Spain 26 38.03N 4.06W
Jándula, Embalse de resr. Spain 26 38.30N 4.00W
Janesville U.S.A. 110 42.42N 89.02W
Jangamo Mozambique 81 24.06S 35.21E
Jangipur India 63 24.28N 88.04E
Janīn Jordan 67 32.28N 35.18E
Janja Yugo. 31 44.40N 19.15E
Janjevo Yugo. 34 42.35N 21.19E
Janjina Yugo. 31 42.56N 17.26E
Jan Kempdorp R.S.A. 80 27.55S 24.48E
Jan Mayen i. Arctic Oc. 96 68.00N 8.00W
Jánoshalma Hungary 31 46.18N 19.20E
Januária Brazil 126 15.28S 44.23W
Janūb Dārfūr d. Sudan 73 11.45N 25.00E
Janūb Kurdufān d. Sudan 73 11.10N 30.00E
Janzé France 18 47.58N 1.30W
Jaora India 62 23.38N 75.08E
Japan Asia 57 36.00N138.00E
Japan, Sea of Asia 57 40.00N135.00E
Japan Trench Pacific Oc. 84 33.00N142.00E
Japla India 63 24.33N 84.01E
Japurá r. Brazil 122 3.00S 64.50W
Jaraicejo Spain 27 39.40N 5.49W
Jaraiz de la Vera Spain 27 40.04N 5.45W
Jarales U.S.A. 109 34.37N106.46W
Jarama r. Spain 26 40.02N 3.39W
Jarandilla Spain 27 40.08N 5.39W
Jarānwāla Pakistan 62 31.20N 73.26E
Jarash Jordan 67 32.17N 35.54E
Jardee Australia 89 34.18S116.04E
Jardine r. Australia 90 11.07S142.30E
Jardines de la Reina is. Cuba 117 20.30N 79.00W
Jardinópolis Brazil 126 20.59S 47.48W
Jargeau France 19 47.52N 2.07E
Jāria Jhānjail Bangla. 63 25.02N 90.39E
Jaridih India 63 23.38N 86.04E
Järna Sweden 43 59.06N 17.34E
Jarnac France 20 45.41N 0.10W
Jarocin Poland 37 51.59N 17.31E
Jarosław Poland 37 50.02N 22.42E
Jarrāḩī r. Iran 65 30.40N 48.23E
Jartai China 54 39.45N105.46E
Jartai Yanchi l. China 54 39.43N105.41E
Jarud Qi China 54 44.30N120.35E
Järvenpää Finland 41 60.28N 25.06E
Jarvis Canada 104 42.53N 80.06W
Jarvis I. Pacific Oc. 84 0.23S160.02W
Jasdan India 62 22.02N 71.12E
Jāsk Iran 65 25.40N 57.45E
Jasło Poland 37 49.45N 21.29E
Jasper Canada 100 52.55N118.05W
Jasper Ala. U.S.A. 113 33.48N 87.18W
Jasper Fla. U.S.A. 113 30.31N 82.58W
Jasper Tex. U.S.A. 111 30.55N 94.01W
Jasper Nat. Park Canada 100 52.50N118.08W
Jasra India 63 25.17N 81.48E
Jastrebarsko Yugo. 31 45.40N 15.39E
Jastrowie Poland 36 53.26N 16.49E
Jászberény Hungary 37 47.30N 19.55E
Jataí Brazil 126 17.58S 51.45W
Jāti Pakistan 62 24.21N 68.16E
Jatibarang Indonesia 59 6.26S108.18E
Jatinegara Indonesia 59 6.12S106.51E
Játiva Spain 25 38.59N 0.31W
Jatni India 63 20.10N 85.42E
Jatt Israel 67 32.24N 35.02E
Jaú Brazil 126 22.11S 48.35W
Jauja Peru 122 11.50S 75.15W
Jaunjelgava U.S.S.R. 44 56.34N 25.02E
Jaunpur India 63 25.44N 82.41E
Java i. see Jawa i. Indonesia 59
Javalambre mtn. Spain 25 40.06N 1.03W
Javari r. Peru 122 4.30S 71.20W
Java Sea see Jawa, Laut sea Indonesia 58
Java Trench f. Indonesia 58 10.00S110.00E
Jávea Spain 25 38.47N 0.10E
Jawa i. Indonesia 59 7.25S110.00E
Jawa, Laut sea Indonesia 58 5.00S111.00E
Jawa Barat d. Indonesia 59 7.10S107.00E
Jawa Tengah d. Indonesia 59 7.49S110.35E
Jawa Timur d. Indonesia 59 8.42S113.10E
Jayah, Wādī al see Hā 'Arava Jordan/Israel 66
Jayapura Indonesia 59 2.28S140.38E
Jaynagar India 63 26.32N 86.07E
Jay Peak mtn. U.S.A. 105 44.55N 72.32W
Jazirah Doberai f. Indonesia 59 1.10S132.30E
Jazzīn Lebanon 66 33.32N 35.34E
Jean U.S.A. 109 35.46N115.20W
Jeanerette U.S.A. 111 29.55N 91.40W
Jean Marie River town Canada 98 61.32N120.40W
Jebāl Bārez, Kūh-e mts. Iran 65 28.40N 58.10E
Jebba Nigeria 77 9.11N 4.49E
Jebri Pakistan 62 27.18N 65.44E
Jedburgh U.K. 14 55.29N 2.33W
Jedda see Jiddah Saudi Arabia 72
Jedrzejów Poland 37 50.39N 20.18E
Jefferson U.S.A. 114 41.44N 80.46W
Jefferson, Mt. Nev. U.S.A. 108 38.46N116.55W
Jefferson, Mt. Oreg. U.S.A. 108 44.40N121.47W
Jefferson City U.S.A. 110 38.34N 92.10W
Jeffersonville U.S.A. 112 38.16N 85.45W
Jega Nigeria 77 12.12N 4.23E
Jēkabpils U.S.S.R. 44 56.28N 25.58E
Jelenia Góra Poland 36 50.55N 15.45E
Jelgava U.S.S.R. 41 56.39N 23.42E
Jelli Sudan 73 5.22N 31.48E
Jelling Denmark 42 55.45N 9.26E
Jember Indonesia 59 8.07S113.45E
Jena Germany 38 50.56N 11.35E
Jena U.S.A. 111 31.41N 92.08W
Jenbach Austria 39 47.24N 11.47E
Jendouba d. Tunisia 32 36.45N 8.45E
Jennersdorf Austria 31 46.57N 16.08E
Jenolan Caves town Australia 93 33.53S150.03E
Jepara Indonesia 59 6.32S110.40E
Jeparit Australia 92 36.09S141.59E
Jeppo Finland 40 63.24N 22.37E
Jequié Brazil 123 13.52S 40.06W
Jequitinhonha r. Brazil 126 16.46S 39.45W
Jerada Morocco 74 34.17N 2.13W
Jerantut Malaysia 58 3.56N102.22E
Jérémie Haiti 117 18.40N 74.09W
Jerez Spain 27 38.19N 6.46W
Jerez de la Frontera Spain 27 36.41N 6.08W
Jericho see Arīḩā Jordan 67
Jerilderie Australia 93 35.23S145.41E
Jerome U.S.A. 108 42.43N114.31W
Jerramungup Australia 89 33.57S118.53E
Jersey i. U.K. 13 49.13N 2.08W
Jersey City U.S.A. 115 40.44N 74.02W
Jersey Shore U.S.A. 114 41.12N 77.16W
Jerseyville U.S.A. 110 39.07N 90.20W
Jerusalem see Yerushalayim Israel/Jordan 67
Jervis B. Australia 93 35.05S150.44E
Jesenice Czech. 39 50.04N 13.29E
Jesenice Yugo. 31 46.27N 14.04E
Jessen Germany 38 51.47N 12.58E
Jessore Bangla. 63 23.10N 89.13E
Jesup U.S.A. 113 31.36N 81.54W
Jesús Carranza Mexico 116 17.26N 95.02W
Jetmore U.S.A. 111 38.03N 99.54W
Jetpur India 62 21.44N 70.37E
Jever Germany 38 53.34N 7.54E
Jevnaker Norway 42 60.15N 10.28E
Jewett Ohio U.S.A. 114 40.22N 81.00W
Jewett Tex. U.S.A. 111 31.22N 96.09W
Jewett City U.S.A. 115 41.36N 71.59W
Jeypore India 63 18.51N 82.35E
Jezerce mtn. Albania 34 42.26N 19.49E
Jeziorak, Jezioro l. Poland 37 53.40N 19.04E
Jhābua India 62 22.46N 74.36E
Jhajha India 63 24.46N 86.22E
Jhal Pakistan 62 28.17N 67.27E
Jhālakāti Bangla. 63 22.39N 90.12E
Jhālawār India 62 24.36N 76.09E
Jhal Jhao Pakistan 62 26.18N 65.35E
Jhālod India 62 23.06N 74.09E
Jhang Sadar Pakistan 62 31.16N 72.20E
Jhānsi India 63 25.26N 78.35E
Jharia India 63 23.45N 86.24E
Jhārsuguda India 63 21.51N 84.02E
Jhawāni Nepal 63 27.35N 84.38E
Jhelum Pakistan 62 32.56N 73.44E
Jhelum r. Pakistan 62 31.12N 72.08E
Jhinkpāni India 63 22.25N 85.47E
Jhok Rind Pakistan 62 31.27N 70.26E
Jhūnjhunu India 62 28.08N 75.24E
Jiaganj India 63 24.14N 88.16E
Jialing Jiang r. China 55 29.30N106.35E
Jiamusi China 53 46.50N130.21E
Ji'an China 55 27.03N115.00E
Jianchang China 54 40.50N119.50E
Jiange China 54 32.04N105.26E
Jiangling China 55 30.20N112.14E
Jiangmen China 55 22.31N113.08E
Jiangshan China 55 28.43N118.39E
Jiangsu d. China 54 33.00N119.30E
Jiangxi d. China 55 27.00N115.30E
Jiangyou China 55 31.47N104.45E
Jianhe China 55 26.39N108.35E
Jian'ou China 55 27.04N118.17E
Jianping China 54 41.23N119.40E
Jianshi China 55 30.42N109.20E
Jianyang Fujian China 55 27.19N118.01E
Jianyang Sichuan China 55 30.25N104.32E
Jiaochangba Sichuan China 54 32.05N103.43E
Jiaohe China 53 43.42N127.19E
Jiaolai He r. China 54 43.48N123.00E
Jiaoling China 55 24.40N116.10E
Jiaonan China 54 35.53N119.58E
Jiao Xian China 54 36.16N120.00E
Jiaozou China 54 35.11N113.27E
Jiashan China 54 32.49N118.01E
Jiawang China 54 34.27N117.27E
Jiaxian China 54 38.02N110.29E
Jiaxing China 55 30.52N120.45E
Jiayi Taiwan 55 23.30N120.24E
Jiazi China 55 22.57N116.01E
Jiblava Czech. 23 49.24N 15.36E
Jiddah Saudi Arabia 72 21.30N 39.10E
Jiddat al Ḩarāsīs f. Oman 71 19.45N 56.30E
Jiepai China 55 31.11N113.42E
Jiexi China 55 23.26N115.52E
Jiexiu China 54 37.00N111.55E
Jieyang China 55 23.29N116.19E
Jifnā Jordan 67 31.58N 35.13E
Jihlava Czech. 36 49.24N 15.35E
Jijel Algeria 75 36.48N 5.46E
Jijiga Ethiopia 71 9.22N 42.47E
Jijona Spain 25 38.32N 0.30W
Jilib Somali Rep. 79 0.28N 42.50E
Jilin China 53 43.53N126.35E
Jilin d. China 53 44.50N125.00E
Jiloca r. Spain 25 41.21N 1.39W
Jilong Taiwan 55 25.09N121.45E
Jīma Ethiopia 73 7.36N 36.50E
Jimbe Angola 78 10.20S 16.40E
Jimena de la Frontera Spain 27 36.26N 5.27W
Jiménez Mexico 116 27.08N104.55W
Jimeta Nigeria 77 9.19N 12.25E
Jimo China 54 36.23N120.27E
Jinan China 54 36.40N117.01E
Jīnd India 62 29.19N 76.19E
Jindabyne Australia 93 36.24S148.37E
Jing'an China 55 28.52N115.22E
Jingbian China 54 37.33N108.36E
Jingchuan China 54 35.15N107.22E
Jingde China 55 30.19N118.31E
Jingdezhen China 55 29.14N117.14E
Jingellic Australia 93 35.54S147.44E
Jinggu Gansu China 54 35.05N103.41E
Jinggu Yunnan China 61 23.29N100.19E
Jinghai China 55 23.02N116.31E
Jing He r. China 54 34.26N109.00E
Jinghong China 52 21.59N100.49E
Jingmen China 55 31.02N112.06E
Jingning China 54 35.30N105.45E
Jingou China 54 41.37N120.33E
Jingtai China 54 37.10N104.08E
Jingxi China 55 23.03N106.36E
Jing Xian China 55 26.35N109.41E
Jingyuan Gansu China 54 36.40N104.40E
Jingyuan Ningxia Huizu China 54 35.29N106.20E
Jinhua China 55 29.05N119.40E
Jining Nei Monggol China 53 40.56N113.00E
Jining Shantung China 54 35.22N116.45E
Jinja Uganda 79 0.27N 33.10E
Jinotepe Nicaragua 117 11.50N 86.10W
Jinsha Jiang r. China 61 26.30N101.40E
Jinshi China 55 29.35N111.56E
Jintang China 55 30.51N104.27E
Jinxi Fujian China 55 26.12N117.34E
Jinxi Liaoning China 54 40.48N120.46E
Jinxian China 55 28.13N116.34E
Jin Xian Liaoning China 54 39.06N121.49E
Jin Xian Liaoning China 54 41.10N121.20E
Jinxiang China 54 35.08N116.20E
Jinzhou China 54 41.06N121.05E
Jipijapa Ecuador 122 1.23S 80.35W
Jire Somali Rep. 71 5.22N 48.05E
Jirjā Egypt 72 26.20N 31.53E
Jishui China 55 27.13N115.07E
Jisr al Ḩusayn Jordan 67 31.52N 35.32E
Jitarning Australia 89 32.48S117.57E
Jiu r. Romania 29 43.44N 23.52E
Jiuding Shan mtn. China 55 31.36N103.54E
Jiudongshan China 55 23.44N117.32E
Jiujiang China 55 29.39N116.02E
Jiulian Shan mts. China 55 24.40N115.00E
Jiuling Shan mts. China 55 28.40N114.45E
Jiulong Jiang r. China 55 24.30N117.47E
Jiuzhou Jiang r. China 55 21.25N109.58E
Jixi China 57 45.17N130.59E
Ji Xian Henan China 54 35.25N114.05E
Ji Xian Tianjin China 54 40.03N117.24E
Jīzān Saudi Arabia 72 16.54N 42.32E
Jizl, Wādī al r. Saudi Arabia 64 25.37N 38.20E
João Pessoa Brazil 123 7.06S 34.53W
Jódar Spain 27 37.50N 3.21W
Jodhpur India 62 26.17N 73.02E
Jodiya India 62 22.42N 70.18E
Jodoigne Belgium 16 50.45N 4.52E
Joensuu Finland 44 62.35N 29.46E
Joetsu Japan 57 37.07N138.15E
Jogdor China 54 42.30N115.52E
Johannesburg R.S.A. 80 26.11S 28.04E
Johannesburg U.S.A. 104 44.59N 84.29W
Johi Pakistan 62 26.41N 67.37E
John Day U.S.A. 108 44.25N118.57W
John Day r. U.S.A. 108 45.44N120.39W
John I. Canada 104 46.09N 82.32W
John O'Groats U.K. 14 58.39N 3.02W
Johnson U.S.A. 111 37.34N101.45W
Johnsonburg U.S.A. 114 41.29N 78.41W
Johnson City N.Y. U.S.A. 115 42.07N 75.57W
Johnson City Tenn. U.S.A. 113 36.20N 82.23W
Johnsons Crossing Canada 100 60.29N133.18W
Johnston, L. Australia 89 32.25S120.30E
Johnstone Str. Canada 100 50.28N126.00W
Johnston I. Pacific Oc. 84 16.45N169.32W
Johnstown N.Y. U.S.A. 115 43.00N 74.22W
Johnstown Ohio U.S.A. 114 40.09N 82.41W
Johnstown Penn. U.S.A. 114 40.20N 78.55W
Johor Baharu Malaysia 58 1.29N103.40E
Joigny France 19 47.59N 3.24E
Joinville Brazil 126 26.20S 48.49W
Joinville France 19 48.27N 5.08E
Jokkmokk Sweden 40 66.37N 19.50E
Jökulsá á Brú r. Iceland 40 65.33N 14.23W
Jökulsá á Fjöllum r. Iceland 40 66.05N 16.32W
Jolfa Iran 65 32.40N 51.39E
Joliet U.S.A. 110 41.32N 88.05W
Joliette Canada 105 46.01N 73.27W
Joliette Prov. Park Canada 105 46.30N 74.00W
Jolo i. Phil. 59 5.55N121.20E
Jolo town Phil. 59 6.03N121.00E
Jombang Indonesia 59 7.30S112.21E
Jombo r. Angola 78 10.20S 16.37E

Jomda to **Kandavu Passage**

Jomda China **61** 31.30N 98.16E
Jonava U.S.S.R. **41** 55.05N 24.17E
Jonê China **54** 34.35N103.32E
Jonesboro Ark. U.S.A. **111** 35.50N 90.42W
Jonesboro La. U.S.A. **111** 32.15N 92.43W
Jones Sd. Canada **99** 76.00N 85.00W
Jönköping Sweden **43** 57.47N 14.11E
Jönköping *d.* Sweden **43** 57.34N 14.40E
Jonzac France **20** 45.27N 0.26W
Joplin U.S.A. **111** 37.06N 94.31W
Jora India **63** 26.20N 77.49E
Jordan Asia **64** 31.00N 36.00E
Jordan *r. see* Al Urdunn *r.* Asia **67**
Jordan Mont. U.S.A. **108** 47.19N106.55W
Jordan N.Y. U.S.A. **105** 43.04N 76.30W
Jordan Valley *town* U.S.A. **108** 42.58N117.03W
Jorhāt India **61** 26.45N 94.13E
Jörn Sweden **40** 65.04N 20.02E
Jörpeland Norway **42** 59.01N 6.03E
Jos Nigeria **77** 9.54N 8.53E
José de San Martin Argentina **125** 44.04S 70.26W
José Enrique Rodó Uruguay **125** 33.41S 57.34W
Joseph, L. Canada **104** 45.14N 79.45W
Joseph, Lac *l.* Canada **103** 52.45N 65.15W
Joseph Bonaparte G. Australia **88** 14.00S128.30E
Joseph City U.S.A. **109** 34.57N110.20W
Joshīmath India **63** 30.34N 79.34E
Jos Plateau *f.* Nigeria **77** 10.00N 9.00E
Josselin France **18** 47.57N 2.33W
Jotunheimen *mts.* Norway **41** 61.38N 8.18E
Joué-lès-Tours France **18** 47.21N 0.40E
Joure Neth. **16** 52.59N 5.49E
Joverega Botswana **80** 19.08S 24.15E
Jowai India **63** 25.27N 92.12E
Juan Aldama Mexico **111** 24.19N103.21W
Juan B. Arruabarrena Argentina **125** 30.25S 58.15W
Juan de Fuca, Str. of Canada/U.S.A. **100** 48.15N124.00W
Juan de Nova *i.* Madagascar **81** 17.03S 42.45E
Juan Fernández, Islas *is.* Chile **121** 34.20S 80.00W
Juárez Argentina **125** 37.40S 59.48W
Juárez Chihuahua Mexico **109** 30.20N108.03W
Juárez Coahuila Mexico **111** 27.37N100.44W
Juárez, Sierra de *mts.* Mexico **109** 32.00N115.45W
Juàzeiro Brazil **123** 9.25S 40.30W
Juàzeiro do Norte Brazil **123** 7.10S 39.18W
Jūbā Sudan **73** 4.51N 31.37E
Jūbāl, Maḍīq *str.* Egypt **66** 27.40N 33.55E
Jubal, Str. of *see* Jūbāl, Maḍīq *str.* Egypt **66**
Jubba *r.* Somali Rep. **79** 0.20S 42.40E
Jubbātā al Khashab Syria **67** 33.13N 35.49E
Jubilee Downs *town* Australia **88** 18.22S125.17E
Juby, Cap *c.* Morocco **74** 27.58N 12.55W
Júcar *r.* Spain **25** 39.09N 0.14W
Juchitán Mexico **116** 16.27N 95.05W
Judaea *f.* Israel/Jordan **67** 31.10N 35.00E
Judenburg Austria **36** 47.10N 14.40E
Judith Basin *f.* U.S.A. **108** 47.10N109.58W
Juelsminde Denmark **42** 55.43N 10.01E
Jugon France **18** 48.25N 2.20W
Juillac France **20** 45.19N 1.19E
Juist Germany **38** 53.40N 6.59E
Juist *i.* Germany **38** 53.40N 7.00E
Juiz de Fora Brazil **126** 21.47S 43.23W
Jujuy *d.* Argentina **124** 23.00S 66.00W
Juklegga *mtn.* Norway **41** 61.03N 8.13E
Juliaca Peru **122** 15.29S 70.09W
Julia Creek *town* Australia **90** 20.39S141.45E
Juliana Kanaal *canal* Neth. **16** 51.00N 5.48E
Julian Alps *mts.* Yugo. **31** 46.20N 13.50E
Julianehåb Greenland **99** 60.45N 46.00W
Jülich Germany **38** 50.55N 6.21E
Jullundur India **62** 31.20N 75.35E
Jumboo Somali Rep. **79** 0.12S 42.38E
Jumet Belgium **16** 50.27N 4.27E
Jumilla Spain **25** 38.29N 1.17W
Jumla Nepal **63** 29.17N 82.13E
Jumna *r. see* Yamuna India **63**
Junāgadh India **62** 21.31N 70.28E
Junan China **54** 35.11N118.50E
Junction U.S.A. **111** 30.29N 99.46W
Junction B. Australia **90** 11.50S134.15E
Junction City Kans. U.S.A. **110** 39.02N 96.50W
Junction City Oreg. U.S.A. **108** 44.13N123.12W
Jundah Australia **90** 24.50S143.02E
Jundiaí Brazil **126** 23.10S 46.54W
Juneau U.S.A. **100** 58.26N134.30W
Junee Australia **93** 34.51S147.40E
Jungfrau *mtn.* Switz. **39** 46.32N 7.58E
Junggar Pendi *f.* Asia **52** 44.20N 86.30E
Junglinster Lux. **16** 49.41N 6.13E
Jungshāhi Pakistan **62** 24.51N 67.46E
Junín Argentina **125** 34.35S 60.58W
Junín de los Andes Argentina **125** 39.57S 71.05W
Juniville France **19** 49.24N 4.23E
Jūniyah Lebanon **66** 33.59N 35.38E
Junlian China **55** 28.08N104.29E
Junnah, Jabal *mts.* Egypt **66** 28.52N 34.15E
Junnar India **62** 19.12N 73.53E
Junqali *d.* Sudan **73** 7.30N 32.30E
Junsele Sweden **40** 63.40N 16.55E
Juntura U.S.A. **108** 43.46N118.05W
Jun Xian China **54** 32.40N111.18E
Jupiter *r.* Canada **103** 49.29N 63.32W
Jupiter U.S.A. **113** 26.57N 80.08W
Jur *r.* Sudan **73** 7.45N 28.00E
Jura *mts.* Europe **39** 46.48N 6.30E
Jura *d.* France **19** 46.50N 5.50E
Jura *d.* Switz. **39** 47.20N 7.10E
Jura *i.* U.K. **14** 55.58N 5.55W
Jura, Sd. of U.K. **14** 56.00N 5.45W
Jurado Colombia **122** 7.07N 77.46W
Jura Krakowska *mts.* Poland **37** 50.30N 19.30E
Jurhen Ul Shan *mts.* China **63** 34.00N 91.00E
Jūrmala U.S.S.R. **41** 56.58N 23.42E
Juruá *r.* Brazil **122** 2.33S 65.50W
Juruena Brazil **124** 12.50S 58.58W
Juruena *r.* Brazil **123** 7.20S 57.30W
Juruti Brazil **123** 2.09S 56.04W
Jussey France **19** 47.49N 5.54E
Jutaí *r.* Brazil **122** 2.35S 67.00W
Jüterbog Germany **38** 51.59N 13.04E
Juticalpa Honduras **117** 14.45N 86.12W
Jutland *pen. see* Jylland *pen.* Denmark **42**
Juye China **54** 35.23N116.06E
Jūyom Iran **65** 28.10N 53.52E
Južna *r.* Yugo. **34** 43.40N 21.22E
Jwayyā Lebanon **67** 33.14N 35.20E
Jyderup Denmark **42** 55.40N 11.26E
Jylland *pen.* Denmark **42** 56.12N 9.20E
Jyväskylä Finland **40** 62.14N 25.44E

K

K2 *mtn.* Asia **52** 35.53N 76.32E
Ka *r.* Nigeria **77** 11.35N 4.10E
Kaabong Uganda **79** 3.28N 34.08E
Kaapstad *see* Cape Town R.S.A. **80**
Kaba Guinea **76** 10.08N 11.49W
Kabaena *i.* Indonesia **59** 5.25S122.00E
Kabala Sierra Leone **76** 9.40N 11.36W
Kabale Uganda **79** 1.13S 30.00E
Kabalega Falls *f.* Uganda **79** 2.17N 31.46E
Kabalega Falls Nat. Park Uganda **79** 2.15N 31.45E
Kabalo Zaïre **79** 6.02S 27.00E
Kabambare Zaïre **79** 4.40S 27.41E
Kabanga Zambia **80** 17.36S 26.45E
Kabba Nigeria **77** 7.50N 6.07E
Kabberi Israel **67** 33.01N 35.09E
Kabinakagami *r.* Canada **112** 50.20N 84.20W
Kabinda Zaïre **78** 6.10S 24.29E
Kabīr Kūh *mts.* Iran **65** 33.00N 47.00E
Kabkābīyah Sudan **73** 13.39N 24.05E
Kābol Afghan. **62** 34.31N 69.12E
Kābol *d.* Afghan. **62** 34.45N 69.15E
Kabompo Zambia **78** 13.35S 24.10E
Kabompo *r.* Zambia **78** 14.17S 23.15E
Kabongo Zaïre **78** 7.22S 25.34E
Kabonzo Zaïre **79** 6.41S 27.49E
Kaboudia, Ra's *c.* Tunisia **75** 35.14N 11.10E
Kabūd Gonbad Iran **65** 37.02N 59.46E
Kabul *see* Kābol Afghan. **62**
Kabumbu Zaïre **78** 4.07S 26.17E
Kabunda Zaïre **79** 12.27S 29.15E
Kabundi Zaïre **79** 10.07S 27.13E
Kabwe Zambia **79** 14.27S 28.25E
Kačanik Yugo. **34** 42.13N 21.12E
Kāchā Kūh *mts.* Iran **65** 29.30N 61.20E
Kachchh, G. of India **62** 22.40N 69.30E
Kachin *d.* Burma **56** 26.00N 97.30E
Kachiry U.S.S.R. **9** 53.07N 76.08E
Kachīsī Ethiopia **73** 9.39N 37.50E
Kadaň Czech. **39** 50.20N 13.15E
Kadaney *r.* Afghan. **62** 31.20N 65.47E
Kade Ghana **76** 6.08N 0.51W
Kadei *r.* C.A.R. **77** 3.28N 16.05E
Kadi India **62** 23.18N 72.20E
Kadina Australia **92** 33.58S137.14E
Kadioli Mali **76** 10.38N 5.45W
Kadoka U.S.A. **110** 43.50N101.31W
Kadoma Zimbabwe **80** 18.23S 29.52E
Kaduna Nigeria **77** 10.28N 7.25E
Kaduna *d.* Nigeria **77** 11.00N 7.35E
Kaduna *r.* Nigeria **77** 8.45N 5.45E
Kāduqlī Sudan **73** 11.01N 29.43E
Kadusam *mtn.* China **61** 28.30N 96.45E
Kadzherom U.S.S.R. **44** 64.42N 55.59E
Kaédi Mauritania **74** 16.09N 13.30W
Kaélé Cameroon **77** 10.05N 14.28E
Kaesŏng N. Korea **53** 37.59N126.30E
Kafanchan Nigeria **77** 9.38N 8.20E
Kaffrine Senegal **76** 14.08N 15.34W
Kafia Kingi Sudan **73** 9.16N 24.25E
Kafirévs, Ákra *c.* Greece **35** 38.10N 24.35E
Kafr ad Dawwār Egypt **66** 31.08N 30.08E
Kafr al Baṭṭīkh Egypt **66** 31.24N 31.44E
Kafr ash Shaykh Egypt **66** 31.07N 30.56E
Kafrayn, Wādī al Jordan **67** 31.50N 35.35E
Kafr az Zayyāt Egypt **66** 30.50N 30.49E
Kafr Kammā Israel **67** 32.43N 35.26E
Kafr Kannā Israel **67** 32.45N 35.20E
Kafr Mandā Israel **67** 32.49N 35.15E
Kafr Naffākh Syria **67** 33.04N 35.44E
Kafr Qaddūm Jordan **67** 32.13N 35.09E
Kafr Qūd Jordan **67** 32.27N 35.14E
Kafr Salīm Egypt **66** 31.09N 30.07E
Kafr Yāsīf Israel **67** 32.57N 35.10E
Kafu *r.* Uganda **79** 1.40N 32.07E
Kafue Zambia **79** 15.40S 28.13E
Kafue *r.* Zambia **79** 15.53S 28.55E
Kafue Dam Zambia **79** 15.40S 27.10E
Kafue Nat. Park Zambia **78** 15.30S 25.35E
Kafunzo Uganda **79** 1.05S 30.26E
Kaga Bandoro C.A.R. **77** 7.00N 19.10E
Kāgān Pakistan **62** 34.47N 73.32E
Kagan U.S.S.R. **50** 39.45N 64.32E
Kagarlyk U.S.S.R. **37** 49.50N 30.50E
Kagawong Canada **104** 45.54N 82.17W
Kagawong L. Canada **104** 45.49N 82.18W
Kagaznagar India **63** 19.18N 79.50E
Kagera *d.* Tanzania **79** 2.00S 31.20E
Kağizman Turkey **64** 40.08N 43.07E
Kagoshima Japan **57** 31.37N130.32E
Kagoshima wan *b.* Japan **57** 31.00N131.00E
Kagul U.S.S.R. **29** 45.54N 28.11E
Kahama Tanzania **79** 3.48S 32.38E
Kahayan *r.* Indonesia **58** 3.20S114.04E
Kahemba Zaïre **78** 7.20S 19.00E
Kahler Asten *mtn.* Germany **38** 51.11N 8.29E
Kahntah *r.* Canada **100** 58.15N120.55W
Kahnūj Iran **65** 27.55N 57.45E
Kahoolawe *i.* Hawaiian Is. **85** 20.33N156.37W
Kahraman Maraş Turkey **64** 37.34N 36.54E
Kai, Kepulauan *is.* Indonesia **59** 5.45S132.55E
Kaiama Nigeria **77** 9.37N 4.03E
Kaiapoi New Zealand **86** 43.23S172.39E
Kaiedin Sudan **73** 9.45N 32.11E
Kaifeng China **54** 34.46N114.22E
Kaikohe New Zealand **86** 35.25S173.49E
Kaikoura New Zealand **86** 42.24S173.41E
Kaikoura Range *mts.* New Zealand **86** 42.00S173.40E
Kailahun Sierra Leone **76** 8.21N 10.21W
Kaili China **55** 26.35N107.55E
Kailu China **54** 43.35N121.12E
Kailua Hawaiian Is. **85** 21.24N157.44W
Kaïmakchalán *mtn.* Greece **34** 40.55N 21.48E
Kaimana Indonesia **59** 3.39S133.44E
Kaimanawa Mts. New Zealand **86** 39.10S176.15E
Kainantu P.N.G. **59** 6.16S145.50E
Kainji Resr. Nigeria **77** 10.00N 4.35E
Kaintragarh India **63** 20.47N 84.40E
Kaipara Harbour New Zealand **86** 36.30S174.00E
Kaiserslautern Germany **39** 49.26N 7.46E
Kaitaia New Zealand **86** 35.08S173.18E
Kaithal India **62** 29.48N 76.23E
Kaitum *r.* Sweden **40** 67.30N 21.05E
Kaiwi Channel Hawaiian Is. **85** 21.15N157.30W
Kaiyuan China **54** 42.45N123.50E
Kaizuka Japan **57** 34.27N135.21E
Kajaani Finland **40** 64.14N 27.41E
Kajabbi Australia **90** 20.02S140.02E
Kajiado Kenya **79** 1.50S 36.48E
Kajo Kaji Sudan **73** 3.53N 31.40E
Kajuru Nigeria **77** 10.19N 7.40E
Kākā Sudan **73** 10.36N 32.11E
Kakamas R.S.A. **80** 28.44S 20.35E
Kakamega Kenya **79** 0.21N 34.47E
Kakamigahara Japan **57** 35.28N136.48E
Kākdwīp India **63** 21.53N 88.11E
Kakegawa Japan **57** 34.46N138.01E
Kakenge Zaïre **78** 4.51S 21.55E
Kakhovskoye Vodokhranilishche *resr.* U.S.S.R. **45** 47.33N 34.40E
Kākī Iran **65** 28.19N 51.34E
Kākināda India **61** 16.59N 82.20E
Kakisa *r.* Canada **100** 61.03N117.10W
Kakisa L. Canada **100** 60.55N117.40W
Kakonko Tanzania **79** 3.19S 30.54E
Kakuma Kenya **79** 3.38N 34.48E
Kakuto Uganda **79** 0.54S 31.26E
Kala *r.* Finland **40** 64.17N 23.55E
Kālābāgh Pakistan **62** 32.58N 71.34E
Kalabahi Indonesia **59** 8.13S124.31E
Kalabáka Greece **34** 39.42N 21.43E
Kalabity Australia **92** 31.53S140.18E
Kalabo Zambia **78** 14.58S 22.33E
Kalach-na-Donu U.S.S.R. **45** 48.43N 43.31E
Kaladan *r.* Burma **56** 20.09N 92.55E
Kaladar Canada **105** 44.39N 77.07W
Kalahari Desert Botswana **80** 23.30S 22.00E
Kalahari Gemsbok Nat. Park R.S.A. **80** 25.45S 20.25E
Kalajoki Finland **40** 64.15N 23.57E
Kalakan U.S.S.R. **51** 55.10N116.45E
Kalámai Greece **35** 37.04N 22.07E
Kalamariá Greece **34** 40.33N 22.55E
Kalamazoo U.S.A. **112** 42.17N 85.36W
Kalamb India **62** 18.56N 73.55E
Kalamera Tanzania **79** 2.07S 33.43E
Kalamurra, L. Australia **92** 28.00S138.00E
Kalandula Angola **78** 9.06S 16.11E
Kalannie Australia **89** 30.21S117.04E
Kalanshiyū, Sarīr *des.* Libya **75** 27.00N 21.30E
Kalarash U.S.S.R. **37** 47.18N 28.16E
Kalāt Pakistan **62** 29.02N 66.35E
Kalavárdha Greece **35** 36.20N 27.57E
Kalávrita Greece **35** 38.03N 22.08E
Kalb, Ra's al *c.* Yemen **71** 14.02N 48.41E
Kalbarri Australia **89** 27.40S114.12E
Kalchās Pakistan **62** 29.21N 69.42E
Kalecik Turkey **64** 40.06N 33.22E
Kalehe Zaïre **79** 2.05S 28.53E
Kalemie Zaïre **79** 5.57S 29.10E
Kalgan *r.* Australia **89** 34.55S117.58E
Kalgoorlie Australia **89** 30.49S121.29E
Kaliakra, Nos *c.* Bulgaria **29** 43.23N 28.29E
Kalianda Indonesia **58** 5.50S105.45E
Kalima Zaïre **78** 2.35S 26.34E
Kalimantan *d.* Indonesia **58** 1.00S113.00E
Kalimantan *f.* Indonesia **58** 0.05N112.30E
Kalimantan Barat *d.* Indonesia **58** 0.30N110.00E
Kalimantan Selatan *d.* Indonesia **58** 2.30S115.30E
Kalimantan Tengah *d.* Indonesia **58** 2.00S113.30E
Kalimantan Timur *d.* Indonesia **58** 2.20N116.30E
Kálimnos Greece **35** 36.57N 26.59E
Kálimnos *i.* Greece **35** 37.00N 27.00E
Kālimpong India **63** 27.04N 88.29E
Kaliningrad U.S.S.R. **41** 54.43N 20.30E
Kalinkovichi U.S.S.R. **37** 52.10N 29.13E
Kalinovik Yugo. **31** 43.31N 18.26E
Kalinovka U.S.S.R. **37** 49.29N 28.30E
Kalisat Indonesia **59** 8.02S113.50E
Kāli Sindh *r.* India **62** 25.32N 76.17E
Kalispell U.S.A. **108** 48.12N114.19W
Kalisz Poland **37** 51.46N 18.02E
Kaliua Tanzania **79** 5.08S 31.50E
Kalix *r.* Sweden **40** 65.50N 23.11E
Kalkar Germany **38** 51.46N 6.17E
Kalkfontein Botswana **80** 22.08S 20.54E
Kalkrand Namibia **80** 24.05S 17.34E
Källandsö *i.* Sweden **43** 58.40N 13.09E
Kallinge Sweden **43** 56.14N 15.17E
Kallithea Greece **35** 37.05N 23.41E
Kallsjön *l.* Sweden **40** 63.35N 13.00E
Kalmar Sweden **43** 56.40N 16.22E
Kalmar *d.* Sweden **43** 57.15N 16.00E
Kalmarsund *str.* Sweden **43** 56.40N 16.25E
Kalmthout Belgium **16** 51.23N 4.28E
Kalmykovo U.S.S.R. **45** 49.02N 51.55E
Kālna India **63** 23.13N 88.22E
Kalnička Gorje *mts.* Yugo. **31** 46.10N 16.30E
Kalo P.N.G. **90** 10.05S147.45E
Kalocsa Hungary **31** 46.32N 18.59E
Kalofer Bulgaria **34** 42.37N 24.59E
Kaloko Zaïre **78** 6.47S 25.47E
Kālol Gujarat India **62** 23.15N 72.29E
Kālol Gujarat India **62** 22.36N 73.27E
Kalole Zaïre **79** 3.40S 27.22E
Kalomo Zambia **78** 16.55S 26.29E
Kalonje Zambia **79** 12.21S 31.06E
Kālpi India **63** 26.07N 79.44E
Kāl Qal 'eh Afghan. **62** 32.38N 62.32E
Kalsö *i.* Faroe Is. **10** 62.19N 6.42W
Kalsūbai *mtn.* India **62** 19.36N 73.43E
Kaltag U.S.A. **98** 64.20N158.44W
Kaluga U.S.S.R. **44** 54.31N 36.16E
Kālu Khuhar Pakistan **62** 25.08N 67.46E
Kalumburu Australia **88** 14.14S126.38E
Kalundborg Denmark **42** 55.41N 11.06E
Kalush U.S.S.R. **37** 49.02N 24.20E
Kalutara Sri Lanka **61** 6.35N 79.58E
Kalyān India **62** 19.15N 73.09E
Kama *r.* U.S.S.R. **44** 55.30N 52.00E
Kamaishi Japan **57** 39.16N141.53E
Kamakura Japan **57** 35.19N139.33E
Kamālia Pakistan **62** 30.44N 72.39E
Kaman Turkey **23** 39.22N 33.44E
Kamanashi *r.* Japan **57** 35.33N138.28E
Kamaniskeg L. Canada **105** 45.25N 77.42W
Kamanjab Namibia **80** 19.39S 14.50E
Kamarsuk Canada **103** 56.18N 61.38W
Kamba Nigeria **77** 11.52N 3.42E
Kamba Zaïre **78** 4.00S 22.22E
Kambalda Australia **89** 31.12S121.40E
Kambar Pakistan **62** 27.36N 68.00E
Kambarka U.S.S.R. **44** 56.18N 54.13E
Kambia Sierra Leone **76** 9.09N 12.53W
Kamchatka, Poluostrov *pen.* U.S.S.R. **51** 56.00N160.00E
Kameda Japan **57** 41.48N140.36E
Kamen *mtn.* U.S.S.R. **51** 68.40N 94.20E
Kamenets Podolskiy U.S.S.R. **37** 48.40N 26.36E
Kamenka R.S.F.S.R. U.S.S.R. **44** 65.55N 44.02E
Kamenka R.S.F.S.R. U.S.S.R. **44** 53.10N 44.05E
Kamenka Bugskaya U.S.S.R. **37** 50.07N 24.30E
Kamen Kashirskiy U.S.S.R. **37** 51.32N 24.59E
Kamen-na-Obi U.S.S.R. **50** 53.46N 81.18E
Kamenskoye U.S.S.R. **51** 62.31N165.15E
Kamensk-Shakhtinskiy U.S.S.R. **45** 48.20N 40.16E
Kamensk-Ural'skiy U.S.S.R. **50** 56.29N 61.49E
Kamenz Germany **38** 51.16N 14.06E
Kāmet *mtn.* India/China **63** 30.54N 79.37E
Kameyama Japan **57** 34.51N136.27E
Kamiah U.S.A. **108** 46.14N116.02W
Kamieskroon R.S.A. **80** 30.12S 17.53E
Kamilukuak L. Canada **101** 62.22N101.40W
Kamina Zaïre **78** 8.46S 24.58E
Kaminak L. Canada **101** 62.10N 95.00W
Kámiros *site* Greece **35** 36.19N 27.57E
Kamloops Canada **100** 50.40N120.20W
Kamloops Plateau *f.* Canada **100** 50.00N120.20W
Kamnik Yugo. **31** 46.13N 14.37E
Kamo *r.* Japan **57** 35.00N139.52E
Kāmoke Pakistan **62** 31.58N 74.13E
Kamp Germany **39** 50.14N 7.37E
Kampa Indonesia **58** 1.46S105.26E
Kampala Uganda **79** 0.19N 32.35E
Kampar *r.* Indonesia **58** 0.20N102.55E
Kampen Neth. **16** 52.33N 5.55E
Kampene Zaïre **78** 3.36S 26.40E
Kamphaeng Phet Thailand **56** 16.28N 99.31E
Kamp-Lintfort Germany **16** 51.34N 6.38E
Kamp 'O S. Korea **57** 35.48N129.29E
Kâmpóng Cham Cambodia **56** 11.59N105.26E
Kâmpóng Chhnăng Cambodia **56** 12.16N104.39E
Kâmpóng Saôm Cambodia **58** 10.38N103.30E
Kâmpóng Thum Cambodia **56** 12.42N104.52E
Kâmpôt Cambodia **56** 10.37N104.11E
Kampti Burkina **76** 10.07N 3.22W
Kampuchea *see* Cambodia Asia **56**
Kamsack Canada **101** 51.34N101.54W
Kamskoye Vodokhranilishche *resr.* U.S.S.R. **44** 58.55N 56.20E
Kāmthi India **63** 21.14N 79.12E
Kamui misaki *c.* Japan **57** 43.30N140.15E
Kamyshin U.S.S.R. **45** 50.05N 45.24E
Kana *r.* Zimbabwe **80** 18.30S 26.50E
Kanaaupscow *r.* Canada **102** 53.40N 77.10W
Kanafis Sudan **73** 9.48N 25.40E
Kanagawa *d.* Japan **57** 35.25N139.10E
Kanairiktok *r.* Canada **103** 55.05N 60.20W
Kanākir Syria **67** 33.15N 36.05E
Kanália Greece **34** 39.30N 22.53E
Kananga Zaïre **78** 5.53S 22.26E
Kanash U.S.S.R. **44** 55.30N 47.27E
Kanastraion, Ákra *c.* Greece **34** 39.56N 23.47E
Kanaudi India **63** 23.36N 81.23E
Kanawha *r.* U.S.A. **114** 38.50N 82.08W
Kanazawa Japan **57** 36.35N136.40E
Kanchanaburi Thailand **56** 14.02N 99.28E
Kānchenjunga *mtn.* Nepal/India **63** 27.44N 88.11E
Kānchipuram India **61** 12.50N 79.44E
Kandāhu Pakistan **62** 27.33N 69.24E
Kandalaksha U.S.S.R. **44** 67.09N 32.31E
Kandalakshskaya Guba *g.* U.S.S.R. **44** 66.30N 34.00E
Kandangan Indonesia **58** 2.50S115.15E
Kandavu *i.* Fiji **84** 19.05S178.15E
Kandavu Passage Fiji **84** 18.45S178.00E

Kandel to Kellerberrin

Kandel Germany 39 49.05N 8.11E
Kandhkot Pakistan 62 28.14N 69.11E
Kandi Benin 77 11.05N 2.59E
Kāndi India 63 23.57N 88.02E
Kandiāro Pakistan 62 27.04N 68.13E
Kandira Turkey 64 41.05N 30.08E
Kandla India 62 23.00N 70.10E
Kandos Australia 93 32.53S149.59E
Kandrāch Pakistan 62 25.29N 65.29E
Kandreho Madagascar 81 17.29S 46.06E
Kandy Sri Lanka 61 7.18N 80.43E
Kane U.S.A. 114 41.40N 78.49W
Kanem *d.* Chad 77 15.10N 15.30E
Kanevka U.S.S.R. 44 67.08N 39.50E
Kang Botswana 80 23.43S 22.51E
Kangaba Mali 76 11.56N 8.25W
Kangān Iran 65 27.50N 52.07E
Kangar Malaysia 58 6.28N100.10E
Kangaroo I. Australia 92 35.50S137.06E
Kangding China 52 30.05N102.04E
Kangean, Kepulauan *is.* Indonesia 59 7.00S115.30E
Kangerlussuaq *see* Söndreströmfjord Greenland 99
Kangikajiip Agpalia *see* Brewster, K. *c.* Greenland 96
Kangiqsujuaq Canada 99 61.30N 72.00W
Kangirsuk Canada 99 60.01N 70.01W
Kangle China 54 35.16N103.39E
Kangmar Xizang China 63 30.45N 85.43E
Kangmar Xizang China 63 28.30N 89.45E
Kango Gabon 78 0.15N 10.14E
Kangping China 54 42.45N123.20E
Kangrinboqê Feng *mtn.* China 63 31.05N 81.21E
Kangto *mtn.* China 63 27.54N 92.32E
Kanhar *r.* India 63 24.28N 83.08E
Kani Ivory Coast 76 8.34N 6.35W
Kaniama Zaïre 78 7.32S 24.11E
Kanin, Poluostrov *pen.* U.S.S.R. 44 68.00N 45.00E
Kaningo Kenya 79 0.52S 38.31E
Kanin Nos, Mys *c.* U.S.S.R. 44 68.38N 43.20E
Kaniva Australia 92 36.33S141.17E
Kanjiža Yugo. 31 46.04N 20.04E
Kankakee U.S.A. 110 41.08N 87.52W
Kankan Gabon 78 0.03S 12.14E
Kankan Guinea 76 10.22N 9.11W
Kānker India 63 20.17N 81.29E
Kankossa Mauritania 74 15.58N 11.31W
Kannack Vietnam 56 14.07N108.36E
Kannapolis U.S.A. 113 35.30N 80.36W
Kannauj India 63 27.04N 79.55E
Kannod India 62 22.40N 76.44E
Kano *r.* Japan 57 35.05N138.52E
Kano Nigeria 77 12.00N 8.31E
Kano *d.* Nigeria 77 12.00N 9.00E
Kanona Zambia 79 13.03S 30.37E
Kanowna Australia 89 30.36S121.36E
Kanoya Japan 57 31.22N130.50E
Kānpur India 63 26.28N 80.21E
Kansas *d.* U.S.A. 110 38.30N 99.00W
Kansas *r.* U.S.A. 110 39.07N 94.36W
Kansas City Kans. U.S.A. 110 39.07N 94.39W
Kansas City Mo. U.S.A. 110 39.05N 94.35W
Kansenia Zaïre 78 10.19S 26.02E
Kansk U.S.S.R. 51 56.11N 95.20E
Kansŏng S. Korea 53 38.20N128.28E
Kantābānji India 63 20.29N 82.55E
Kantché Niger 77 13.31N 8.30E
Kantemirovka U.S.S.R. 45 49.40N 39.52E
Kantō *d.* Japan 57 35.35N139.30E
Kantōheiya *f.* Japan 57 36.02N140.10E
Kantō-sanchi *mts.* Japan 57 36.00N138.35E
Kanye Botswana 80 24.58S 25.17E
Kanyu Botswana 80 20.05S 24.39E
Kao *i.* Tonga 85 19.40S175.01W
Kaohsiung Taiwan 48 22.36N120.17E
Kaoko Veld *f.* Namibia 80 18.30S 13.30E
Kaolack Senegal 76 14.09N 16.08W
Kaoma Zambia 78 14.55S 24.58E
Kapaa Hawaiian Is. 85 22.05N159.19W
Kapadvanj India 62 23.01N 73.04E
Kapanga Zaïre 78 8.22S 22.37E
Kapaonik *mts.* Yugo. 34 43.10N 21.00E
Kap Arkona *c.* Germany 38 54.41N 13.26E
Kapchagay U.S.S.R. 52 43.51N 77.14E
Kapenguria Kenya 79 1.13N 35.07E
Kapfenberg Austria 36 47.27N 15.18E
Kapiri Mposhi Zambia 79 13.59S 28.40E
Kapiskau Canada 102 52.20N 82.01W
Kapiskau *r.* Canada 102 52.20N 83.40W
Kapit Malaysia 58 2.01N112.56E
Kapiti I. New Zealand 86 40.50S174.50E
Kapoeta Sudan 73 4.47N 33.35E
Kapongolo Zaïre 79 7.51S 28.12E
Kapos *r.* Hungary 31 46.44N 18.30E
Kaposvár Hungary 31 46.22N 17.47E
Kappar Pakistan 62 25.19N 62.42E
Kappeln Germany 38 54.40N 9.56E
Kappelshamn Sweden 43 57.52N 18.50E
Kapps Namibia 80 22.22S 17.52E
Kapsabet Kenya 79 0.12N 35.05E
Kaptai Bangla. 63 22.21N 92.17E
Kaptol Yugo. 31 45.26N 17.44E
Kapuas *r.* Indonesia 58 0.13S109.12E
Kapunda Australia 92 34.21S138.54E
Kapūrthala India 62 31.23N 75.23E
Kapuskasing Canada 102 49.25N 82.30W
Kaputar, Mt. Australia 93 30.20S150.10E
Kapuvár Hungary 37 47.36N 17.02E
Kara U.S.S.R. 50 69.12N 65.00E
Kara-Bogaz Gol, Zaliv *b.* U.S.S.R. 65 41.20N 53.40E
Karabük Turkey 64 41.12N 32.36E
Karabutak U.S.S.R. 50 49.55N 60.05E
Karāchi Pakistan 62 24.52N 67.03E
Karād India 60 17.17N 74.12E
Karaganda U.S.S.R. 9 49.53N 73.07E
Karaginskiy, Ostrov *i.* U.S.S.R. 51 59.00N165.00E
Karakas U.S.S.R. 52 48.20N 83.30E
Karakelong *i.* Indonesia 59 4.20N126.50E
Karakoram Pass Asia 61 35.33N 77.51E
Karakoram Range *mts.* Jammu & Kashmir 60 35.30N 76.30E
Karakoro *r.* Mauritania 74 14.43N 12.03W
Karaköse *see* Ağri Turkey 45
Karakumskiy Kanal *canal* U.S.S.R. 65 37.30N 65.48E
Karakumy, Peski *f.* U.S.S.R. 65 37.45N 60.00E
Karakuwisa Namibia 80 18.56S 19.43E
Karaman Turkey 64 37.11N 33.13E
Karamay China 52 45.48N 84.30E
Karamea New Zealand 86 41.15S172.07E
Karamea Bight *b.* New Zealand 86 41.15S171.30E
Karamürsel Turkey 64 40.42N 29.37E
Karand Iran 65 34.16N 46.15E
Kāranja India 63 20.29N 77.29E
Karanjia India 63 21.47N 85.58E
Karasburg Namibia 80 28.00S 18.46E
Karasjok Norway 40 69.27N 25.30E
Karasuk U.S.S.R. 50 53.45N 78.01E
Karatau, Khrebet *mts.* U.S.S.R. 45 44.15N 52.10E
Karatobe U.S.S.R. 45 49.44N 53.30E
Karaton U.S.S.R. 45 46.26N 53.32E
Karauli India 62 26.30N 77.01E
Karawa Zaïre 78 3.12N 20.20E
Karawanken *mts.* Austria 31 46.30N 14.10E
Karazhal U.S.S.R. 50 48.00N 70.55E
Karbalā' Iraq 65 32.37N 44.03E
Karcag Hungary 37 47.19N 20.56E
Kardhámaina Greece 35 36.47N 27.09E
Kardhamíla Greece 35 38.33N 22.14E
Kardhámilia Greece 35 38.34N 26.05E
Kardhítsa Greece 35 39.21N 21.55E
Kärdla U.S.S.R. 41 59.00N 22.42E
Kareli India 63 22.55N 79.04E
Karema Tanzania 79 6.50S 30.25E
Karen *d.* Burma 56 17.30N 97.45E
Karen India 61 12.50N 92.55E
Karepino U.S.S.R. 44 61.05N 58.02E
Karesuando Finland 40 68.25N 22.30E
Kargasok U.S.S.R. 50 59.07N 80.58E
Kargi Kenya 79 2.31N 37.34E
Kargil Jammu & Kashmir 62 34.34N 76.06E
Kargopol U.S.S.R. 44 61.32N 38.59E
Kari Nigeria 77 11.17N 10.35E
Kariaí Greece 34 40.16N 24.15E
Kariba Zimbabwe 80 16.32S 28.50E
Kariba, L. Zimbabwe / Zambia 80 16.50S 28.00E
Kariba Dam Zimbabwe / Zambia 80 16.15S 28.55E
Karibib Namibia 80 21.56S 15.52E
Kārikāl India 61 10.58N 79.50E
Karimama Benin 77 12.02N 3.15E
Karīmganj India 63 24.52N 92.20E
Karin Somali Rep. 71 10.51N 45.45E
Karis Finland 41 60.05N 23.40E
Karisimbi, Mt. Zaïre / Rwanda 79 1.31S 29.25E
Káristos Greece 35 38.01N 24.25E
Kariya Japan 57 34.59N136.59E
Kariyangwe Zimbabwe 80 17.57S 27.30E
Karkaralinsk U.S.S.R. 9 49.21N 75.27E
Karkar I. P.N.G. 59 4.40S146.00E
Karkas, Kūh-e *mtn.* Iran 65 33.25N 51.40E
Karkheh *r.* Iran 65 31.45N 47.52E
Karkinitskiy Zaliv *g.* U.S.S.R. 45 45.50N 32.45E
Karkoo Australia 92 34.02S135.44E
Karkur Israel 67 32.28N 35.00E
Karlino Poland 36 54.03N 15.51E
Karl-Marx-Stadt *see* Chemnitz Germany 38
Karlobag Yugo. 31 44.32N 15.05E
Karlovac Yugo. 31 45.29N 15.34E
Karlovo Bulgaria 34 42.38N 24.48E
Karlovy Vary Czech. 39 50.11N 12.52E
Karlsborg Sweden 43 58.32N 14.31E
Karlshamn Sweden 43 56.10N 14.51E
Karlskoga Sweden 43 59.20N 14.31E
Karlskrona Sweden 43 56.10N 15.35E
Karlsruhe Germany 39 49.03N 8.24E
Karlstad Sweden 43 59.22N 13.30E
Karlstad U.S.A. 110 48.35N 96.31W
Karlstadt Germany 39 49.57N 9.45E
Karmah Sudan 72 19.38N 30.25E
Karmel, Har *mtn.* Israel 67 32.44N 35.02E
Karmi'el Israel 67 32.55N 35.18E
Karmöy *i.* Norway 42 59.15N 5.15E
Karnafuli Resr. Bangla. 61 22.40N 92.05E
Karnāl India 62 29.41N 76.59E
Karnāli *r.* Nepal 63 28.45N 81.16E
Karnaphuli Resr. Bangla. 63 22.30N 92.20E
Karnataka *d.* India 60 14.45N 76.00E
Karnes City U.S.A. 111 28.53N 97.54W
Karnobat Bulgaria 29 42.40N 27.00E
Kärnten *d.* Austria 39 46.50N 13.30E
Karoi Zimbabwe 80 16.51S 29.39E
Karokh Afghan. 62 34.28N 62.35E
Karonga Malaŵi 79 9.54S 33.55E
Karonie Australia 89 30.58S122.32E
Karoonda Australia 92 35.09S139.54E
Karor Pakistan 62 31.13N 70.57E
Karora Sudan 72 17.42N 38.22E
Káros *i.* Greece 35 36.54N 25.40E
Karos Dam R.S.A. 80 28.27S 21.39E
Karousádhes Greece 34 39.47N 19.45E
Karpach U.S.S.R. 37 48.00N 27.10E
Kárpathos Greece 35 35.40N 27.10E
Kárpathos *i.* Greece 35 35.40N 27.10E
Karpenísion Greece 35 38.55N 21.40E
Karpineny U.S.S.R. 37 46.46N 28.18E
Karpinsk U.S.S.R. 44 59.48N 59.59E
Karpogory U.S.S.R. 44 64.01N 44.30E
Karragullen Australia 89 32.05S116.03E
Karratha Australia 88 20.44S116.50E
Karridale Australia 89 34.12S115.04E
Kars Turkey 64 40.35N 43.05E
Karsakpay U.S.S.R. 9 47.47N 66.43E
Kärsämäki Finland 40 63.58N 25.46E
Kārsava U.S.S.R. 44 56.45N 27.40E
Karskoye More *sea* U.S.S.R. 50 73.00N 65.00E
Karstädt Germany 38 53.09N 11.44E
Kartaly U.S.S.R. 50 53.06N 60.37E
Karufa Indonesia 59 3.50S133.27E
Karumba Australia 90 17.28S140.50E
Kārūn *r.* Iran 65 30.25N 48.12E
Karunga Kenya 73 1.09S 36.49E
Karungi Sweden 40 66.03N 23.55E
Karungu Kenya 79 0.50S 34.09E
Karup Denmark 42 56.18N 9.10E
Karviná Czech. 37 49.50N 18.30E
Kasai *r.* Zaïre 78 3.10S 16.13E
Kasai Occidental *d.* Zaïre 78 5.00S 21.30E
Kasai Oriental *d.* Zaïre 78 5.00S 24.00E
Kasaji Zaïre 78 10.22S 23.27E
Kasama Zambia 79 10.10S 31.11E
Kasane Botswana 80 17.48S 25.09E
Kasanga Tanzania 79 8.27S 31.10E
Kāsaragod India 60 12.30N 75.00E
Kasba India 63 25.51N 87.33E
Kasba L. Canada 101 60.20N102.10W
Kasba-Tadla Morocco 22 32.34N 6.18W
Kåseberga Sweden 43 55.23N 14.04E
Kasempa Zambia 78 13.28S 25.48E
Kasese Uganda 79 0.07N 30.06E
Kāsganj India 63 27.49N 78.39E
Kāshān Iran 65 33.59N 51.31E
Kashi China 52 39.29N 76.02E
Kashin U.S.S.R. 44 57.22N 37.39E
Kashīpur India 63 29.13N 78.57E
Kashiwa Japan 57 35.52N139.59E
Kāshmar Iran 65 35.12N 58.26E
Kashmor Pakistan 62 28.26N 69.35E
Kasia India 63 26.45N 83.55E
Kasimov U.S.S.R. 44 54.55N 41.25E
Kaskaskia *r.* U.S.A. 111 37.59N 89.56W
Kaskattama *r.* Canada 101 57.03N 90.07W
Kaskinen Finland 40 62.23N 21.13E
Kaskö *see* Kaskinen Finland 40
Kaslo Canada 100 49.55N117.00W
Kasongo Zaïre 78 4.32S 26.33E
Kasongo-Lunda Zaïre 78 6.30S 16.47E
Kásos *i.* Greece 35 35.22N 26.56E
Kassalā Sudan 72 15.28N 36.24E
Kassalā *d.* Sudan 72 15.30N 35.00E
Kassándra *pen.* Greece 34 40.00N 23.30E
Kassel Germany 38 51.19N 9.29E
Kastamonu Turkey 64 41.22N 33.47E
Kastanéai Greece 34 41.38N 26.28E
Kastl Germany 38 49.22N 11.42E
Kastoría Greece 34 40.30N 21.19E
Kastorías, Límni *l.* Greece 34 40.30N 21.20E
Kastrávion, Tekhnití Límni *l.* Greece 35 38.45N 21.20E
Kastrosikiá Greece 35 39.09N 20.36E
Kasugai Japan 57 35.14N136.58E
Kasukabe Japan 57 35.58N139.45E
Kasulu Tanzania 79 4.34S 30.06E
Kasumi Japan 57 35.38N134.38E
Kasungu Malaŵi 79 13.04S 33.29E
Kasūr Pakistan 62 31.07N 74.27E
Kataba Zambia 78 16.12S 25.05E
Katako Kombe Zaïre 78 3.27S 24.21E
Katákolon Greece 35 37.38N 21.19E
Katangi India 63 23.27N 79.47E
Katanning Australia 89 33.42S117.33E
Katanti Zaïre 79 2.19S 27.08E
Katarniān Ghāt India 63 28.20N 81.09E
Katchall *i.* India 61 7.57N 93.22E
Kateríni Greece 34 40.16N 22.30E
Katete Zambia 79 14.08S 31.50E
Katha Burma 56 24.11N 95.20E
Katherine Australia 90 14.29S132.20E
Kāthgodām India 63 29.16N 79.32E
Kathla India 62 32.00N 76.47E
Kathmandu Nepal 63 27.42N 85.20E
Kathor India 62 21.18N 72.57E
Kathrabbā Jordan 67 31.08N 35.37E
Kathua Jammu & Kashmir 62 32.22N 75.31E
Kati Mali 76 12.41N 8.04W
Katihār India 63 25.32N 87.35E
Katima Rapids *f.* Zambia 78 17.15S 24.20E
Katiola Ivory Coast 76 8.10N 5.10W
Kātlang Pakistan 62 34.22N 72.05E
Katlanovo Yugo. 34 41.52N 21.40E
Káto Akhaía Greece 35 38.09N 21.32E
Kātol India 63 21.16N 78.35E
Katonah U.S.A. 115 41.16N 73.41W
Katonga *r.* Uganda 79 0.03N 30.15E
Katoomba Australia 93 33.42S150.23E
Katopa Zaïre 78 2.45S 25.06E
Káto Stavrós Greece 34 40.39N 23.43E
Katoúna Greece 35 38.47N 21.07E
Katowice Poland 37 50.15N 18.59E
Kātrīnā, Jabal *mtn.* Egypt 66 28.30N 33.57E
Katrine, Loch U.K. 14 56.15N 4.30W
Katrineholm Sweden 43 59.00N 16.12E
Katsina Nigeria 77 13.00N 7.32E
Katsina *d.* Nigeria 77 12.25N 7.55E
Katsina Ala Nigeria 77 7.10N 9.30E
Katsina Ala *r.* Nigeria 77 7.50N 8.58E
Katsura *r.* Japan 57 34.53N135.42E
Katsuura Japan 57 35.08N140.18E
Kattaviá Greece 35 35.57N 27.46E
Kattegat *str.* Denmark / Sweden 42 57.25N 11.30E
Katthammarsvik Sweden 43 57.26N 18.50E
Katul, Jabal *mtn.* Sudan 72 14.16N 29.23E
Katumba Zaïre 78 7.45S 25.18E
Kātwa India 63 23.39N 88.08E
Katwijk aan Zee Neth. 16 52.13N 4.27E
Katzenbuckel *mtn.* Germany 39 49.28N 9.02E
Katzenfurt Germany 38 50.37N 8.21E
Kauai *i.* Hawaii U.S.A. 106 22.05N159.30W
Kaub Germany 39 50.05N 7.46E
Kaufbeuren Germany 39 47.53N 10.37E
Kauhajoki Finland 40 62.26N 22.11E
Kauhava Finland 40 63.06N 23.05E
Kaukauna U.S.A. 110 44.20N 88.16W
Kaukauveld *mts.* Namibia 80 20.00S 20.15E
Kauliranta Finland 40 66.26N 23.40E
Kaumba Zaïre 78 8.26S 24.40E
Kaunas U.S.S.R. 41 54.54N 23.54E
Kaura Namoda Nigeria 77 12.39N 6.38E
Kautokeino Norway 40 69.00N 23.02E
Kavadarci Yugo. 34 41.26N 22.03E
Kavajë Albania 34 41.11N 19.33E
Kavála Greece 34 40.56N 24.25E
Kāvali India 61 14.55N 80.01E
Kavarna Bulgaria 29 43.26N 28.22E
Kavimba Botswana 80 18.05S 24.34E
Kavkaz U.S.S.R. 45 45.20N 36.39E
Kavkazskiy Khrebet *mts.* U.S.S.R. 45 43.00N 44.00E
Kävlinge Sweden 43 55.48N 13.06E
Kavungo Angola 78 11.28S 23.01E
Kaw Guiana 123 4.29N 52.02W
Kawachi-nagano Japan 57 34.25N135.32E
Kawagama L. Canada 104 45.18N 78.45W
Kawagoe Japan 57 35.55N139.29E
Kawaguchi Japan 57 35.48N139.43E
Kawambwa Zambia 79 9.47S 29.10E
Kawardha India 63 22.01N 81.15E
Kawartha L. Canada 104 44.40N 78.10W
Kawasaki Japan 57 35.32N139.43E
Kawerau New Zealand 86 38.05S176.42E
Kawhia New Zealand 86 38.04S174.49E
Kawm Sudan 73 13.31N 22.50E
Kawthaung Burma 56 10.09N 98.33E
Kaya Burkina 76 13.04N 1.04W
Kayah *d.* Burma 56 19.15N 97.30E
Kayambi Zambia 79 9.26S 32.01E
Kayan *r.* Indonesia 58 2.47N117.46E
Kaycee U.S.A. 108 43.43N106.38W
Kayenta U.S.A. 108 36.44N110.17W
Kayes Congo 78 4.25S 11.41E
Kayes Mali 76 14.26N 11.28W
Kayes *d.* Mali 76 14.00N 10.55W
Kayonza Rwanda 73 1.53S 30.31E
Kayseri Turkey 64 38.42N 35.28E
Kaysville U.S.A. 108 41.02N111.56W
Kazabazua Canada 105 45.56N 76.01W
Kazachye U.S.S.R. 51 70.46N136.15E
Kazakhskaya S.S.R. *d.* U.S.S.R. 45 48.00N 52.30E
Kazakhskiy Zaliv *b.* U.S.S.R. 45 42.43N 52.30E
Kazan U.S.S.R. 44 55.45N 49.10E
Kazanlŭk Bulgaria 34 42.38N 25.35E
Kazatin U.S.S.R. 37 49.41N 28.49E
Kazaure Nigeria 77 12.40N 8.25E
Kazbek *mtn.* U.S.S.R. 45 42.42N 44.30E
Kāzerūn Iran 65 29.35N 51.39E
Kazhim U.S.S.R. 44 60.18N 51.34E
Kazima C.A.R. 73 5.16N 26.11E
Kazincbarcika Hungary 37 48.16N 20.37E
Kazo Japan 57 36.07N139.36E
Kazumba Zaïre 78 6.30S 22.02E
Kbal Dâmrei Cambodia 56 14.03N105.20E
Kdyně Czech. 38 49.23N 13.02E
Kéa Greece 35 37.38N 24.21E
Kéa *i.* Greece 35 37.34N 24.22E
Kearney U.S.A. 110 40.42N 99.05W
Keban Turkey 64 38.48N 38.45E
K'ebelē Ethiopia 73 12.52N 40.40E
Kebili Tunisia 75 33.42N 8.58E
Kebnekaise *mtn.* Sweden 40 67.53N 18.33E
K'ebrī Dehar Ethiopia 71 6.47N 44.17E
Kebumen Indonesia 59 7.40S109.41E
Kecel Hungary 31 46.32N 19.16E
Kech *r.* Pakistan 62 26.00N 62.44E
Kechika *r.* Canada 100 59.36N127.05W
Kecskemét Hungary 37 46.54N 19.42E
Kedada Ethiopia 73 5.20N 36.00E
Kedainiai U.S.S.R. 41 55.17N 24.00E
Kedgwick Canada 103 47.39N 67.21W
Kédhros Greece 35 39.13N 22.03E
Kediri Indonesia 59 7.45S112.01E
Kédougou Senegal 76 12.35N 12.09W
Keefers Canada 100 50.00N121.40W
Keele Peak *mtn.* Canada 98 63.15N129.50W
Keene Canada 104 44.15N 78.10W
Keene U.S.A. 115 42.56N 72.17W
Keepit, L. Australia 93 30.52S150.30E
Keer-Weer, C. Australia 90 13.58S141.30E
Keeseville U.S.A. 105 44.30N 73.29W
Keetmanshoop Namibia 80 26.34S 18.07E
Keewatin Canada 102 49.46N 94.34W
Keewatin *d.* Canada 99 65.00N 90.00W
Kefa *d.* Ethiopia 73 7.00N 36.30E
Kefallinía *i.* Greece 35 38.15N 20.35E
Kefalos Greece 35 36.46N 27.00E
Kefar 'Eqron Israel 67 31.51N 34.49E
Kefar Gil'adi Israel 67 33.15N 35.34E
Kefar Nahum *site* Israel 67 32.53N 35.34E
Kefar Sava Israel 67 32.11N 34.54E
Kefar Szold Israel 67 33.11N 35.39E
Kefar Tavor Israel 67 32.41N 35.25E
Kefar Vitkin Israel 67 32.23N 34.53E
Kefar Yona Israel 67 32.19N 34.56E
Kefar Zekharya Israel 67 31.42N 34.57E
Kefar Zetim Israel 67 32.49N 35.28E
Keffi Nigeria 77 8.52N 7.53E
Keflavík Iceland 40 64.01N 22.35W
K'eftya Ethiopia 72 13.56N 37.13E
Keg River *town* Canada 100 57.54N117.07W
Kehsi Mānsām Burma 56 21.56N 97.51E
Keighley U.K. 12 53.52N 1.54W
Keila U.S.S.R. 41 59.18N 24.29E
Keimoes R.S.A. 80 28.41S 20.58E
Keitele *l.* Finland 40 62.55N 26.00E
Keith Australia 92 36.06S140.22E
Keith U.K. 14 57.32N 2.57W
Keith Arm *b.* Canada 98 65.20N122.15W
Kekri India 62 25.58N 75.09E
Kelang Malaysia 58 2.57N101.24E
Kelberg Germany 39 50.17N 6.55E
Kelem Ethiopia 73 4.48N 36.06E
Kelheim Germany 39 48.55N 11.54E
Kelibia Tunisia 32 36.51N 11.06E
Kelkit *r.* Turkey 64 40.46N 36.32E
Kelle Congo 78 0.05S 14.33E
Keller U.S.A. 108 48.03N118.40W
Kellerberrin Australia 89 31.38S117.43E

Kellett, C. to **Kinross**

Kellett, C. Canada 98 71.59N125.34W
Kelleys I. U.S.A. 114 41.36N 82.42W
Kelloselkä Finland 44 66.55N 28.50E
Kells Meath Rep. of Ire. 15 53.44N 6.53W
Kelme U.S.S.R. 41 55.38N 22.56E
Kélo Chad 77 9.21N 15.50E
Kelowna Canada 100 49.50N119.25W
Kelso U.K. 14 55.36N 2.26W
Kelso Calif. U.S.A. 109 35.01N115.39W
Kelso Wash. U.S.A. 108 46.09N122.54W
Keluang Malaysia 58 2.01N103.18E
Kelvedon U.K. 13 51.50N 0.43E
Kelvington Canada 101 52.10N103.30W
Kem U.S.S.R. 44 64.58N 34.39E
Kema Indonesia 59 1.22N125.08E
Ke Macina Mali 76 14.05N 5.20W
Kemah Turkey 64 39.35N 39.02E
Kemaliye Turkey 64 39.16N 38.29E
Kemano Canada 100 53.35N128.00W
Kembolcha Ethiopia 73 11.02N 39.43E
Kemerovo U.S.S.R. 50 55.25N 86.10E
Kemi Finland 40 65.49N 24.32E
Kemi r. Finland 40 65.47N 24.30E
Kemijärvi Finland 40 66.36N 27.24E
Kemmerer U.S.A. 108 41.48N110.32W
Kemnath Germany 38 49.52N 11.54E
Kempen f. Belgium 16 51.05N 5.00E
Kemp Land f. Antarctica 128 69.00S 57.00E
Kempsey Australia 93 31.05S152.50E
Kempt, Lac l. Canada 105 47.25N 74.22W
Kempten Germany 39 47.43N 10.19E
Kemptville Canada 105 45.01N 75.38W
Ken r. India 63 25.46N 80.31E
Kenai U.S.A. 98 60.33N151.15W
Kenai Pen. U.S.A. 96 64.40N150.18W
Kenamuke Swamp Sudan 73 5.55N 33.48E
Kenaston Canada 101 51.30N106.18W
Kendai India 63 22.45N 82.37E
Kendal Indonesia 59 6.56S110.14E
Kendal U.K. 12 54.19N 2.44W
Kendall Australia 93 31.28S152.40E
Kendall U.S.A. 114 43.20N 78.02W
Kendari Indonesia 59 3.57S122.36E
Kendenup Australia 89 34.28S117.35E
Kendrāpāra India 63 20.30N 86.25E
Kendrick U.S.A. 108 46.37N116.39W
Kenebri Australia 93 30.45S149.02E
Kenema Sierra Leone 76 7.57N 11.11W
Kenge Zaïre 78 4.56S 17.04E
Kengeja Tanzania 79 5.24S 39.45E
Keng Tung Burma 56 21.16N 99.39E
Kenhardt R.S.A. 80 29.21S 21.08E
Kenilworth U.K. 13 52.22N 1.35W
Kenitra Morocco 74 34.20N 6.34W
Kenli China 54 37.35N118.34E
Kenmare Rep. of Ire. 15 51.53N 9.36W
Kenmare U.S.A. 108 48.40N102.05W
Kenmore U.S.A. 114 42.58N 78.53W
Kennebec r. U.S.A. 112 44.00N 69.50W
Kennebunk U.S.A. 115 43.23N 70.33W
Kenner U.S.A. 111 29.59N 90.15W
Kennet r. U.K. 13 51.28N 0.57W
Kennett Square U.S.A. 115 39.51N 75.43W
Kennewick U.S.A. 108 46.12N119.07W
Kenogami r. Canada 102 50.24N 84.20W
Keno Hill town Canada 98 63.58N135.22W
Kenora Canada 102 49.47N 94.29W
Kenosha U.S.A. 110 42.35N 87.49W
Kenozero, Ozero l. U.S.S.R. 44 62.20N 37.00E
Kent d. U.K. 13 51.12N 0.40E
Kent Ohio U.S.A. 114 41.09N 81.22W
Kent Tex. U.S.A. 109 31.04N104.13W
Kent Wash. U.S.A. 108 47.23N122.14W
Kentau U.S.S.R. 9 43.28N 68.36E
Kentland U.S.A. 112 40.46N 87.26W
Kenton U.S.A. 112 40.38N 83.38W
Kent Pen. Canada 98 68.30N107.00W
Kentucky d. U.S.A. 113 37.30N 85.15W
Kentucky r. U.S.A. 113 38.40N 85.09W
Kentucky L. U.S.A. 111 36.25N 88.05W
Kentville Canada 103 45.05N 64.30W
Kenya Africa 79 1.00N 38.00E
Kenya, Mt. Kenya 79 0.10S 37.19E
Keokuk U.S.A. 110 40.24N 91.24W
Keonjhargarh India 63 21.38N 85.35E
Kepi Indonesia 59 6.32S139.19E
Kepno Poland 37 51.17N 17.59E
Keppel B. Australia 90 23.21S150.55E
Kerala d. India 60 10.30N 76.30E
Kerang Australia 92 35.42S143.59E
Keratéa Greece 35 37.48N 23.59E
Kerch U.S.S.R. 45 45.22N 36.27E
Kerchenskiy Proliv str. U.S.S.R. 45 45.15N 36.35E
Kerema P.N.G. 59 7.59S145.46E
Kerem Ben Zimra Israel 67 33.02N 35.28E
Kerem Maharal Israel 67 32.39N 34.59E
Keren Ethiopia 72 15.46N 38.28E
Kerguelen, Îles de is. Indian Oc. 49 49.15S 69.10E
Kerguelen Basin f. Indian Oc. 49 35.00S 65.00E
Kerguelen-Gaussberg Ridge f. Indian Oc. 49 55.00S 75.00E
Kericho Kenya 79 0.22S 35.19E
Kerinci, Gunung mtn. Indonesia 58 1.45S101.20E
Kerio r. Kenya 79 3.00N 36.14E
Keríon Greece 35 37.40N 20.48E
Kerkebet Ethiopia 72 16.13N 37.30E
Kerkenna, Îles is. Tunisia 75 34.44N 11.12E
Kerki R.S.F.S.R. U.S.S.R. 44 63.40N 54.00E
Kerki Tk.S.S.R. U.S.S.R. 50 37.53N 65.10E
Kerkinitis, Límni l. Greece 34 41.10N 23.08E
Kérkira Greece 34 39.36N 19.56E
Kérkira i. Greece 34 39.40N 19.42E
Kerkrade Neth. 16 50.52N 6.02E
Kermadec Is. Pacific Oc. 84 30.00S178.30W
Kermadec Trench Pacific Oc. 84 33.30S176.00W
Kermān Iran 65 30.18N 57.05E
Kermānshāh Iran 65 34.19N 47.04E
Kerme Körfezi g. Turkey 35 36.50N 28.00E
Kermit U.S.A. 111 31.51N103.06W
Kerouane Guinea 76 9.16N 9.00W
Kerpen Germany 16 50.52N 6.42E
Kerrobert Canada 101 51.55N109.08W
Kerrville U.S.A. 111 30.03N 99.08W
Kerry d. Rep. of Ire. 15 52.07N 9.35W
Kerry Head Rep. of Ire. 15 52.24N 9.56W
Kerteminde Denmark 42 55.27N 10.40E
Kerulen r. Mongolia 53 48.45N117.00E
Kesagami L. Canada 102 50.23N 80.15W
Keşan Turkey 34 40.51N 26.37E
Keshod India 62 21.18N 70.15E
Keskal India 63 20.03N 81.34E
Keski-Suomi d. Finland 40 62.30N 25.30E
Keswick U.K. 12 54.35N 3.09W
Keszthely Hungary 31 46.46N 17.15E
Ketapang Jawa Indonesia 59 6.56S113.14E
Ketapang Kalimantan Indonesia 58 1.50S110.02E
Ketchikan U.S.A. 100 55.25N131.40W
Ketchum U.S.A. 108 43.41N114.22W
Kete Krachi Ghana 76 7.50N 0.03W
Keti Bandar Pakistan 62 24.08N 67.27E
Kętrzyn Poland 37 54.06N 21.23E
Kettering U.K. 13 52.24N 0.44W
Kettering U.S.A. 112 39.41N 84.10W
Kettle r. Canada 101 56.55N 89.25W
Kettle Falls town U.S.A. 108 48.36N118.03W
Kettle Pt. Canada 104 43.11N 82.01W
Keuka L. U.S.A. 114 42.27N 77.10W
Keweenaw B. U.S.A. 112 46.46N 88.26W
Keweenaw Pen. U.S.A. 112 47.10N 88.30W
Key, Lough Rep. of Ire. 15 54.00N 8.15W
Keyala Sudan 73 4.27N 32.52E
Key Harbour Canada 104 45.53N 80.44W
Keynsham U.K. 13 51.25N 2.30W
Key West U.S.A. 113 24.33N 81.48W
Kezhma U.S.S.R. 51 58.58N101.08E
Kežmarok Czech. 37 49.08N 20.25E
Kgalagadi d. Botswana 80 25.00S 21.30E
Kgatleng d. Botswana 80 24.20S 26.20E
Khaanziir, Ras c. Somali Rep. 71 10.55N 45.47E
Khabab Syria 67 33.01N 36.16E
Khabarovsk U.S.S.R. 53 48.32N135.08E
Khairāgarh India 63 21.25N 80.58E
Khairpur Punjab Pakistan 62 29.35N 72.14E
Khairpur Sind Pakistan 62 27.32N 68.46E
Khajrāho India 63 24.50N 79.58E
Khalatse Jammu & Kashmir 62 34.20N 76.49E
Khalkhāl Iran 65 37.36N 48.36E
Khálki Greece 34 39.36N 22.30E
Khálki i. Greece 35 36.17N 27.35E
Khalkidhikí f. Greece 23 40.25N 23.27E
Khalkís Greece 35 38.28N 23.36E
Khalmer Yu U.S.S.R. 44 67.58N 64.48E
Khālsar Jammu & Kashmir 63 34.31N 77.41E
Khalturin U.S.S.R. 44 58.38N 48.50E
Khalūf Oman 60 20.31N 58.04E
Khambhāliya India 62 22.12N 69.39E
Khambhāt, G. of India 62 20.30N 71.45E
Khāmgaon India 62 20.41N 76.34E
Khamkeut Laos 56 18.14N104.44E
Khānaqīn Iraq 65 34.22N 45.22E
Khān az Zabīb Jordan 67 31.28N 36.06E
Khandela India 62 27.36N 75.30E
Khandwa India 62 21.50N 76.20E
Khāneh Khvodī Iran 65 36.05N 56.04E
Khānewāl Pakistan 62 30.18N 71.56E
Khāngarh Punjab Pakistan 62 29.55N 71.10E
Khāngarh Punjab Pakistan 62 28.22N 71.43E
Khanh Hung Vietnam 56 9.36N105.55E
Khaniá Greece 35 35.31N 24.02E
Khaníon, Kólpos g. Greece 35 35.34N 23.48E
Khanka, Ozero l. U.S.S.R. 53 45.00N132.30E
Khanna India 62 30.42N 76.14E
Khannā, Qā' f. Jordan 67 32.04N 36.26E
Khānozai Pakistan 62 30.37N 67.19E
Khānpur Pakistan 62 28.39N 70.39E
Khanty-Mansiysk U.S.S.R. 50 61.00N 69.00E
Khān Yūnus Egypt 67 31.21N 34.18E
Khapalu Jammu & Kashmir 62 35.10N 76.20E
Khapcheranga U.S.S.R. 53 49.46N112.20E
Kharagpur India 63 22.20N 87.20E
Khārān r. Iran 65 27.37N 58.48E
Khārān Pakistan 62 28.35N 65.25E
Kharbatā Jordan 67 31.57N 35.04E
Khargon India 62 21.49N 75.36E
Khāriān Pakistan 62 32.49N 73.52E
Khariār Road town India 63 20.54N 82.31E
Khārijah, Al Wāḥāt al oasis Egypt 64 24.55N 30.35E
Kharkov U.S.S.R. 45 50.00N 36.15E
Khār Kūh mtn. Iran 65 31.37N 53.47E
Kharmanli Bulgaria 34 41.56N 25.54E
Kharovsk U.S.S.R. 44 59.67N 40.07E
Khartoum see Al Kharṭūm Sudan 72
Kharutayuvam U.S.S.R. 44 66.51N 59.31E
Khasavyurt U.S.S.R. 45 43.16N 46.36E
Khāsh Afghan. 62 31.31N 62.52E
Khāsh r. Afghan. 62 31.11N 61.50E
Khāsh Iran 65 28.14N 61.15E
Khāsh, Dasht-e des. Afghan. 62 31.50N 62.30E
Khashgort U.S.S.R. 44 65.25N 65.40E
Khashm al Qirbah Sudan 72 14.58N 35.55E
Khaskovo Bulgaria 34 41.56N 25.33E
Khaskovo d. Bulgaria 34 41.57N 25.32E
Khatanga U.S.S.R. 51 71.50N102.31E
Khatangskiy Zaliv g. U.S.S.R. 51 75.00N112.10E
Khāvda India 62 23.51N 69.43E
Khawr Barakah r. Sudan 72 18.13N 37.35E
Khemisset Morocco 74 33.50N 6.03W
Khemmarat Thailand 56 16.00N105.10E
Khenchela Algeria 75 35.26N 7.08E
Khenifra Morocco 74 33.00N 5.40W
Khersān r. Iran 65 31.29N 48.53E
Kherson U.S.S.R. 45 46.39N 32.38E
Kherwāra India 62 23.59N 73.35E
Khetia India 62 21.40N 74.35E
Khewāri Pakistan 62 26.36N 68.52E
Khiliomódhion Greece 35 37.48N 22.51E
Khíos Greece 35 38.22N 26.08E
Khíos i. Greece 35 38.22N 26.00E
Khipro Pakistan 62 25.50N 69.22E
Khirbat al Ghazālah Syria 67 32.44N 36.12E
Khisfīn Syria 67 32.51N 35.49E
Khiva U.S.S.R. 65 41.25N 60.49E
Khmelnik U.S.S.R. 37 49.36N 27.59E
Khmelnitskiy U.S.S.R. 37 49.25N 26.49E
Khodorov U.S.S.R. 37 49.20N 24.19E
Khogali Sudan 73 6.08N 27.47E
Khok Kloi Thailand 56 8.19N 98.18E
Kholm U.S.S.R. 44 57.10N 31.11E
Kholmogory U.S.S.R. 44 63.51N 41.46E
Khomas-Hochland mts. Namibia 80 22.50S 16.25E
Khondmāl Hills India 63 20.15N 84.00E
Khonu U.S.S.R. 51 66.29N143.12E
Khoper r. U.S.S.R. 45 49.35N 42.17E
Khóra Greece 35 37.03N 21.42E
Khorāl India 62 26.30N 71.14E
Khóra Sfakíon Greece 35 35.12N 24.09E
Khorixas Namibia 80 20.24S 14.58E
Khorog U.S.S.R. 52 37.32N 71.32E
Khorramābād Iran 65 33.29N 48.21E
Khorramshahr Iran 65 30.26N 48.09E
Khotimsk U.S.S.R. 37 53.24N 32.36E
Khotin U.S.S.R. 37 48.30N 26.31E
Khouribga Morocco 74 32.54N 6.57W
Khowai India 63 24.06N 91.38E
Khowrnag, Kūh-e mtn. Iran 65 32.10N 54.38E
Khowst Afghan. 62 33.22N 69.57E
Khoyniki U.S.S.R. 37 51.54N 30.00E
Khrisoúpolis Greece 34 40.58N 24.42E
Khudzhand U.S.S.R. 52 40.14N 69.40E
Khugīānī Afghan. 62 31.33N 66.15E
Khūgīānī Šānī Afghan. 62 31.31N 66.12E
Khūiāla India 62 27.15N 70.25E
Khuis Botswana 80 26.37S 21.45E
Khulga r. U.S.S.R. 44 63.33N 61.53E
Khulna Bangla. 63 22.48N 89.33E
Khumbur Khule Ghar mtn. Afghan. 62 33.05N 69.00E
Khunti India 63 23.05N 85.17E
Khurai India 63 24.03N 78.19E
Khurda India 63 20.11N 85.37E
Khurīyā Murīyā, Jazā'ir is. Oman 60 17.30N 56.00E
Khurja India 63 28.15N 77.51E
Khurli Pakistan 62 28.59N 65.52E
Khurr, Wādī al r. Iraq 71 31.02N 42.00E
Khurra Bārīk r. Iraq 64 32.00N 44.15E
Khushāb Pakistan 62 32.18N 72.21E
Khust U.S.S.R. 37 48.11N 23.19E
Khuwayy Sudan 73 13.05N 29.14E
Khuzdār Pakistan 62 27.48N 66.37E
Khvājeh Ra'ūf Afghan. 62 33.19N 64.43E
Khvor Iran 65 33.47N 55.06E
Khvormuj Iran 65 28.40N 51.20E
Khvoy Iran 65 38.32N 45.02E
Khyber Pass Afghan./Pakistan 62 34.06N 71.05E
Kiama Australia 93 34.41S150.49E
Kiamika Canada 105 46.25N 75.23W
Kiáton Greece 35 38.01N 22.45E
Kibaek Denmark 42 56.02N 8.51E
Kibali r. Zaïre 79 3.37N 28.38E
Kibamba Zaïre 78 4.53S 26.33E
Kibar India 63 32.20N 78.01E
Kibenga Zaïre 78 7.55S 17.35E
Kibombo Zaïre 78 3.58S 25.57E
Kibondo Tanzania 79 3.35S 30.41E
Kibre Mengist Ethiopia 73 5.52N 39.00E
Kibungu Rwanda 79 2.10S 30.31E
Kibwesa Tanzania 79 6.30S 29.57E
Kibwezi Kenya 79 2.28S 37.57E
Kičevo Yugo. 34 41.34N 20.59E
Kichiga U.S.S.R. 51 59.50N163.27E
Kicking Horse Pass Canada 100 51.27N116.25W
Kidal Mali 77 18.27N 1.25E
Kidderminster U.K. 13 52.24N 2.13W
Kidete Morogoro Tanzania 79 6.39S 36.42E
Kidsgrove U.K. 12 53.06N 2.15W
Kiefersfelden Austria 39 47.37N 12.11E
Kiel Germany 38 54.20N 10.08E
Kiel Canal see Nord-Ostsee-Kanal Germany 38
Kielce Poland 37 50.52N 20.37E
Kielder resr. U.K. 12 55.12N 2.30W
Kieler Bucht b. Germany 38 54.35N 10.35E
Kiev see Kiyev U.S.S.R. 37
Kiffa Mauritania 74 16.38N 11.28W
Kifisiá Greece 35 38.04N 23.49E
Kifissós r. Greece 35 38.30N 23.00E
Kigali Rwanda 79 1.59S 30.05E
Kiglapatt, C. Canada 103 57.05N 61.05W
Kigoma Tanzania 79 4.52S 29.36E
Kigoma d. Tanzania 79 4.45S 30.00E
Kigosi r. Tanzania 79 4.37S 31.29E
Kiiminkin r. Finland 40 65.12N 25.18E
Kii sanchi mts. Japan 57 34.00N135.20E
Kii suidō str. Japan 57 34.00N135.00E
Kikinda Yugo. 37 45.51N 20.30E
Kikládhes is. Greece 35 37.30N 25.00E
Kikongo Zaïre 78 4.16S 17.11E
Kikori P.N.G. 59 7.25S144.13E
Kikori r. P.N.G. 59 7.10S144.05E
Kikwissi, L. Canada 104 47.00N 78.30W
Kikwit Zaïre 78 5.02S 18.51E
Kil Sweden 43 59.30N 13.19E
Kilafors Sweden 41 61.14N 16.34E
Kila Kila P.N.G. 59 9.31S147.10E
Kilchu N. Korea 53 40.55N129.21E
Kilcoy Australia 91 26.57S152.33E
Kilcullen Rep. of Ire. 15 53.08N 6.46W
Kildare Rep. of Ire. 15 53.10N 6.55W
Kildare d. Rep. of Ire. 15 53.10N 6.50W
Kildonan Zimbabwe 80 17.22S 30.33E
Kilfinan U.K. 14 55.58N 5.18W
Kilgore U.S.A. 111 32.23N 94.53W
Kilifi Kenya 79 3.30S 39.50E
Kilimanjaro d. Tanzania 79 3.45S 37.40E
Kilimanjaro mtn. Tanzania 79 3.02S 37.20E
Kilindoni Tanzania 79 7.55S 39.39E
Kilingi-Nõmme U.S.S.R. 41 58.09N 24.58E
Kilis Turkey 64 36.43N 37.07E
Kiliya U.S.S.R. 37 45.30N 29.16E
Kilkee Rep. of Ire. 15 52.41N 9.40W
Kilkenny Rep. of Ire. 15 52.39N 7.16W
Kilkenny d. Rep. of Ire. 15 52.35N 7.15W
Kilkieran B. Rep. of Ire. 15 53.20N 9.42W
Kilkís Greece 34 41.00N 22.53E
Killala B. Rep. of Ire. 15 54.15N 9.10W
Killaloe Canada 105 45.33N 77.25W
Killard Pt. U.K. 15 54.19N 5.31W
Killarney Australia 93 28.18S152.15E
Killarney Man. Canada 101 49.12N 99.42W
Killarney Ont. Canada 104 45.58N 81.31W
Killarney Rep. of Ire. 15 52.04N 9.32W
Killarney Prov. Park Canada 104 46.05N 81.30W
Killary Harbour est. Rep. of Ire. 15 53.38N 9.56W
Killdeer U.S.A. 108 47.22N102.45W
Killeen U.S.A. 111 31.08N 97.44W
Killin U.K. 14 56.29N 4.19W
Killíni Greece 35 37.55N 21.09E
Killíni mtn. Greece 35 37.57N 22.23E
Killorglin Rep. of Ire. 15 52.07N 9.45W
Killybegs Rep. of Ire. 15 54.38N 8.27W
Killyleagh U.K. 15 54.24N 5.39W
Kilmarnock U.K. 14 55.37N 4.30W
Kilmichael Pt. Rep. of Ire. 15 52.44N 6.09W
Kilmore Australia 93 37.18S144.58E
Kilninver U.K. 14 56.21N 5.30W
Kilombero r. Tanzania 79 8.30S 37.28E
Kilosa Tanzania 79 6.49S 37.00E
Kilronan Rep. of Ire. 15 53.08N 9.41W
Kilrush Rep. of Ire. 15 52.39N 9.30W
Kilsyth U.K. 14 55.59N 4.04W
Kilvo Sweden 40 66.50N 21.04E
Kilwa Kivinje Tanzania 79 8.45S 39.21E
Kilwa Masoko Tanzania 79 8.55S 39.31E
Kimaan Indonesia 59 7.54S138.51E
Kimba Australia 92 33.09S136.25E
Kimball U.S.A. 110 41.14N103.40W
Kimberley Canada 100 49.40N115.59W
Kimberley R.S.A. 80 28.44S 24.44E
Kimberley Plateau Australia 88 17.20S127.20E
Kimch'aek N. Korea 57 40.41N129.12E
Kími Greece 35 38.38N 24.06E
Kimito i. Finland 41 60.10N 22.30E
Kímolos i. Greece 35 36.47N 24.35E
Kimparana Mali 76 12.52N 4.59W
Kimry U.S.S.R. 44 56.51N 37.20E
Kimsquit Canada 100 52.45N126.57W
Kinabalu mtn. Malaysia 58 6.10N116.40E
Kincaid Canada 101 49.39N107.00W
Kincardine Canada 104 44.11N 81.38W
Kindersley Canada 101 51.27N109.10W
Kindia Guinea 76 10.03N 12.49W
Kindu Zaïre 78 3.00S 25.56E
Kinel U.S.S.R. 44 53.17N 50.42E
Kineshma U.S.S.R. 44 57.28N 42.08E
Kingaroy Australia 90 26.33S151.50E
King City U.S.A. 109 36.13N121.08W
Kingcome Inlet town Canada 100 50.58N125.15W
King Edward r. Australia 88 14.12S126.34E
King George Is. Canada 102 57.20N 78.25W
King George Sd. Australia 89 35.03S117.57E
King I. Australia 91 39.50S144.00E
King I. Canada 100 52.10N127.40W
King Leopold Range mts. Australia 88 17.00S125.30E
Kingman Ariz. U.S.A. 109 35.12N114.04W
Kingman Kans. U.S.A. 111 37.39N 98.07W
Kingman Reef Pacific Oc. 84 6.24N162.22W
Kingoonya Australia 92 30.54S135.18E
Kingri Pakistan 62 30.27N 69.49E
Kings r. U.S.A. 109 36.03N119.49W
Kingsbridge U.K. 13 50.17N 3.46W
Kings Canyon Australia 90 24.15S131.33E
Kings Canyon Nat. Park U.S.A. 108 36.48N118.30W
Kingsclere U.K. 13 51.20N 1.14W
Kingscote Australia 92 35.40S137.38E
King Sd. Australia 88 17.00S123.30E
Kingsdown Kent U.K. 13 51.21N 0.17E
Kingsley Dam U.S.A. 106 41.15N101.30W
King's Lynn U.K. 12 52.45N 0.25E
Kingsmill Group is. Kiribati 84 1.00S175.00E
Kings Peaks mts. U.S.A. 108 40.46N110.23W
Kingsport U.S.A. 113 36.33N 82.34W
Kingston Canada 105 44.14N 76.30W
Kingston Jamaica 117 17.58N 76.48W
Kingston New Zealand 86 45.20S168.43E
Kingston N.H. U.S.A. 115 42.55N 71.02W
Kingston N.Y. U.S.A. 115 41.56N 74.00W
Kingston Penn. U.S.A. 115 41.16N 75.54W
Kingston W.Va. U.S.A. 113 37.58N 81.19W
Kingston S.E. Australia 92 36.50S139.50E
Kingston upon Hull U.K. 12 53.45N 0.20W
Kingstown St. Vincent 117 13.12N 61.14W
Kingstree U.S.A. 113 33.40N 79.50W
Kingsville Canada 104 42.02N 82.45W
Kingsville U.S.A. 111 27.31N 97.52W
Kingswood Avon U.K. 13 51.27N 2.29W
Kings Worthy U.K. 13 51.06N 1.18W
Kington U.K. 13 52.12N 3.02W
Kingurutik r. Canada 103 56.49N 62.00W
Kingussie U.K. 14 57.05N 4.04W
King William I. Canada 99 69.00N 97.30W
King William's Town R.S.A. 80 32.52S 27.23E
Kingwood U.S.A. 114 39.28N 79.41W
Kinki d. Japan 57 35.10N135.00E
Kinloch Rannoch U.K. 14 56.42N 4.11W
Kinmount Canada 104 44.47N 78.39W
Kinna Sweden 43 57.30N 12.41E
Kinnairds Head U.K. 14 57.42N 2.00W
Kinnegad Rep. of Ire. 15 53.28N 7.08W
Kinnekulle hill Sweden 43 58.35N 13.23E
Kinneret Israel 67 32.44N 35.34E
Kinneret-Negev Conduit canal Israel 67 32.52N 35.32E
Kino r. Japan 57 34.13N135.09E
Kinross U.K. 14 56.13N 3.27W

Korsze to Kzyl Orda

Korsze Poland **37** 54.10N 21.09E
Kortrijk Belgium **16** 50.49N 3.17E
Koryakskiy Khrebet *mts.* U.S.S.R. **51** 62.20N171.00E
Koryazhma U.S.S.R. **44** 61.19N 47.12E
Kos Greece **35** 36.53N 27.18E
Kos *i.* Greece **35** 36.50N 27.10E
Kosa Ethiopia **73** 7.51N 36.51E
Kościan Poland **36** 52.06N 16.38E
Kościerzyna Poland **37** 54.08N 18.00E
Kosciusko U.S.A. **111** 32.58N 89.35W
Kosciusko, Mt. Australia **93** 36.28S148.17E
Kosha Sudan **72** 20.49N 30.32E
Koshikijima rettō *is.* Japan **57** 31.45N129.49E
Koshk-e Kohneh Afghan **65** 34.52N 62.29E
Košice Czech. **37** 48.44N 21.15E
Koski Finland **41** 60.39N 23.09E
Koslan U.S.S.R. **44** 63.29N 48.59E
Kosovska-Mitrovica Yugo. **34** 42.54N 20.52E
Kossanto Senegal **76** 13.12N 11.56W
Kossovo U.S.S.R. **37** 52.40N 25.18E
Kosta Sweden **43** 56.51N 15.23E
Kostajnica Yugo. **31** 45.14N 16.33E
Koster R.S.A. **80** 25.51S 26.52E
Kostopol U.S.S.R. **37** 50.51N 26.22E
Kostroma U.S.S.R. **44** 57.46N 40.59E
Kostrzyn Poland **36** 52.24N 17.11E
Kostyukovichi U.S.S.R. **37** 53.20N 32.01E
Kosyu U.S.S.R. **44** 65.36N 59.00E
Koszalin Poland **36** 54.12N 16.09E
Kota Madhya P. India **63** 22.18N 82.02E
Kota Rāj. India **62** 25.11N 75.50E
Kota Baharu Malaysia **58** 6.07N102.15E
Kota Belud Malaysia **58** 6.00N116.00E
Kotabumi Indonesia **58** 4.52S104.59E
Kot Addu Pakistan **62** 30.28N 70.58E
Kota Kinabalu Malaysia **58** 5.59N116.04E
Kotari *mts.* Yugo. **31** 44.05N 15.17E
Kotelnich U.S.S.R. **44** 58.20N 48.10E
Kotelnikovo U.S.S.R. **45** 47.39N 43.08E
Kotel'nyy, Ostrov *i.* U.S.S.R. **51** 75.30N141.00E
Köthen Germany **38** 51.45N 11.58E
Kotka Finland **44** 60.26N 26.55E
Kot Kapūra India **62** 30.35N 74.49E
Kotlas U.S.S.R. **44** 61.15N 46.28E
Kotli Jammu & Kashmir **62** 33.31N 73.55E
Kotlik U.S.A. **98** 63.02N163.33W
Kotor Yugo. **31** 42.25N 18.46E
Kotoriba Yugo. **31** 46.21N 16.49E
Kotor Varoš Yugo. **31** 44.37N 17.23E
Kotovsk M.S.S.R. U.S.S.R. **37** 46.50N 28.31E
Kotovsk Ukr.S.S.R. U.S.S.R. **37** 47.42N 29.30E
Kot Pūtli India **62** 27.43N 76.12E
Kotra India **62** 24.22N 73.10E
Kotri Pakistan **62** 25.22N 68.18E
Kotri Allāhrakhio Pakistan **62** 24.24N 67.50E
Kötschach Austria **39** 46.40N 13.00E
Kottagūdem India **61** 17.32N 80.39E
Kotto *r.* C.A.R. **73** 4.14N 22.02E
Kotuy *r.* U.S.S.R. **51** 71.40N103.00E
Kotzebue U.S.A. **98** 66.51N162.40W
Kotzebue Sd. U.S.A. **98** 66.20N163.00W
Kötzting Germany **39** 49.11N 12.52E
Kouango C.A.R. **73** 4.58N 20.00E
Koudougou Burkina **76** 12.15N 2.21W
Kouibli Ivory Coast **76** 7.09N 7.16W
Kouki C.A.R. **77** 7.09N 17.13E
Koúklia Cyprus **66** 34.42N 32.34E
Koula Moutou Gabon **78** 1.12S 12.29E
Koulikoro Mali **76** 12.55N 7.31W
Koumac N. Cal. **84** 20.33S164.17E
Koumankou Mali **76** 11.58N 6.06W
Koumbal C.A.R. **73** 9.26N 22.39E
Koumbia Burkina **76** 11.18N 3.38W
Koumbia Guinea **76** 11.54N 13.40W
Koumbisaleh *site* Mauritania **74** 15.55N 8.05W
Koumongou Togo **76** 10.10N 0.29E
Koumra Chad **77** 8.56N 17.32E
Koupéla Burkina **76** 12.09N 0.22W
Kouroussa Guinea **76** 10.40N 9.50W
Kousseri Chad **77** 12.05N 14.56E
Koutiala Mali **76** 12.20N 5.23W
Kouto Ivory Coast **76** 9.53N 6.25W
Kouvola Finland **44** 60.54N 26.45E
Kouyou *r.* Congo **78** 0.40S 16.37E
Kovdor U.S.S.R. **44** 67.33N 30.30E
Kovel U.S.S.R. **37** 51.12N 24.48E
Kovpyta U.S.S.R. **37** 51.22N 30.51E
Kovrov U.S.S.R. **44** 56.23N 41.21E
Kovzha *r.* U.S.S.R. **44** 61.05N 36.27E
Kowanyama Australia **90** 15.29S141.44E
Kowloon Hong Kong **55** 22.19N114.12E
Kowt-e 'Ashrow Afghan. **62** 34.27N 68.48E
Koyukuk *r.* U.S.A. **98** 64.50N157.30W
Kozan Turkey **64** 37.27N 35.47E
Kozáni Greece **34** 40.19N 21.47E
Kozara *mts.* Yugo. **31** 45.05N 16.50E
Kozarac Yugo. **31** 44.58N 16.51E
Kozelets U.S.S.R. **37** 50.54N 31.09E
Kozhikode India **60** 11.15N 75.45E
Kozhim U.S.S.R. **44** 65.45N 59.30E
Kozhposelok U.S.S.R. **44** 63.10N 38.10E
Kpandu Ghana **76** 7.02N 0.17E
Kpessi Togo **77** 8.07N 1.17E
Krabi Thailand **56** 8.08N 98.52E
Krâchéh Cambodia **56** 12.30N106.00E
Kragan Indonesia **59** 6.40S111.33E
Kragerö Norway **42** 58.52N 9.25E
Kragujevac Yugo. **29** 44.01N 20.55E
Kraków Poland **37** 50.03N 19.55E
Kraljevica Yugo. **31** 45.16N 14.34E
Kraljevo Yugo. **34** 43.43N 20.41E
Kralovice Czech. **38** 49.59N 13.29E
Kralupy nad Vltavou Czech. **38** 50.11N 14.18E
Kramatorsk U.S.S.R. **45** 48.43N 37.33E
Kramer U.S.A. **110** 48.20N100.42W
Kramfors Sweden **40** 62.55N 17.50E
Kranídhion Greece **35** 37.22N 23.10E
Kranj Yugo. **31** 46.15N 14.21E
Kranskop R.S.A. **80** 28.58S 30.52E
Krapina Yugo. **31** 46.10N 15.52E
Krapkowice Poland **37** 50.29N 17.56E
Krasavino U.S.S.R. **44** 60.58N 46.25E
Krasilov U.S.S.R. **37** 49.39N 26.59E
Kraskino U.S.S.R. **53** 42.42N130.48E
Krasnaya Gora U.S.S.R. **37** 53.00N 31.36E
Kraśnik Poland **37** 50.56N 22.13E
Krasnodar U.S.S.R. **45** 45.02N 39.00E
Krasnograd U.S.S.R. **45** 49.22N 35.28E
Krasnokamsk U.S.S.R. **44** 58.05N 55.49E
Krasnoperekopsk U.S.S.R. **45** 45.56N 33.47E
Krasnoselkup U.S.S.R. **50** 65.45N 82.31E
Krasnoturinsk U.S.S.R. **44** 59.46N 60.10E
Krasnoufimsk U.S.S.R. **44** 56.40N 57.49E
Krasnouralsk U.S.S.R. **50** 58.25N 60.00E
Krasnovishersk U.S.S.R. **44** 60.25N 57.02E
Krasnovodsk U.S.S.R. **65** 40.01N 53.00E
Krasnovodskiy Poluostrov *pen.* U.S.S.R. **65** 40.30N 53.10E
Krasnovodskiy Zaliv *g.* U.S.S.R. **65** 39.50N 53.15E
Krasnoyarsk U.S.S.R. **51** 56.05N 92.46E
Krasnyy Yar U.S.S.R. **45** 46.32N 48.21E
Kratovo Yugo. **34** 42.06N 22.10E
Krawang Indonesia **59** 6.15S107.15E
Krefeld Germany **38** 51.20N 6.34E
Kremastón, Tekhnití Limni *l.* Greece **35** 38.52N 21.30E
Kremenchug U.S.S.R. **45** 49.03N 33.25E
Kremenchugskoye Vodokhranilishche *resr.* U.S.S.R. **45** 49.20N 32.30E
Kremenets U.S.S.R. **37** 50.05N 25.48E
Kremmling U.S.A. **108** 40.03N106.24W
Krems Austria **36** 48.25N 15.36E
Krestovka U.S.S.R. **44** 66.24N 52.31E
Kretinga U.S.S.R. **41** 55.53N 21.13E
Kría Vrísi Greece **34** 40.41N 22.18E
Kribi Cameroon **77** 2.56N 9.56E
Krichev U.S.S.R. **37** 53.40N 31.44E
Krichim Bulgaria **34** 42.08N 24.32E
Kriens Switz. **39** 47.02N 8.17E
Krimml Austria **39** 47.13N 12.11E
Krionéri Greece **35** 38.20N 21.35E
Krishna *r.* India **61** 16.00N 81.00E
Krishnanagar India **63** 23.24N 88.30E
Kristdala Sweden **43** 57.24N 16.11E
Kristianopel Sweden **43** 56.15N 16.02E
Kristiansand Norway **42** 58.10N 8.00E
Kristianstad Sweden **43** 56.02N 14.08E
Kristianstad *d.* Sweden **43** 56.10N 13.40E
Kristiansund Norway **40** 63.07N 7.45E
Kristiinankaupunki Finland **41** 62.17N 21.23E
Kristinehamn Sweden **43** 59.20N 14.07E
Kristinestad *see* Kristiinankaupunki Finland **41**
Kristinovka U.S.S.R. **37** 48.50N 29.58E
Kríti *i.* Greece **35** 35.29N 24.42E
Kritikón Pélagos *sea* Greece **35** 35.46N 23.54E
Kriva *r.* Yugo. **34** 42.12N 22.18E
Krivaja *r.* Yugo. **31** 44.27N 18.09E
Kriva Palanka Yugo. **34** 42.12N 22.20E
Krivodol Bulgaria **34** 43.23N 23.29E
Krivoy Rog U.S.S.R. **45** 47.55N 33.24E
Križevci Yugo. **31** 46.02N 16.33E
Krk *i.* Yugo. **31** 45.05N 14.35E
Krnov Czech. **37** 50.05N 17.41E
Kröderen *l.* Norway **42** 60.15N 9.38E
Krokek Sweden **43** 58.40N 16.24E
Kroken Norway **40** 65.23N 14.15E
Krokom Sweden **40** 63.20N 14.30E
Krokowa Poland **43** 54.48N 18.11E
Kronach Germany **38** 50.14N 11.20E
Krŏng Kaôh Kŏng Cambodia **56** 11.37N102.59E
Kronoberg *d.* Sweden **43** 56.40N 14.35E
Kronprins Olav Kyst *f.* Antarctica **128** 69.00S 42.00E
Kronshtadt U.S.S.R. **44** 60.00N 29.40E
Kroonstad R.S.A. **80** 27.38S 27.12E
Kropotkin U.S.S.R. **45** 45.25N 40.35E
Kropperfjäll *hill* Sweden **43** 58.40N 12.13E
Krosno Poland **37** 49.42N 21.46E
Krotoszyn Poland **37** 51.42N 17.26E
Kroya Indonesia **59** 7.37S109.13E
Krško Yugo. **31** 45.58N 15.29E
Kruger Nat. Park R.S.A. **81** 24.10S 31.36E
Krugersdorp R.S.A. **80** 26.06S 27.46E
Krujë Albania **34** 41.30N 19.48E
Krumbach Germany **39** 48.14N 10.22E
Krumovgrad Bulgaria **34** 41.29N 25.38E
Krung Thep *see* Bangkok Thailand **56**
Krupki U.S.S.R. **37** 54.19N 29.05E
Kruševac Yugo. **34** 43.35N 21.20E
Kruševo Yugo. **34** 41.23N 21.19E
Krušnéhory *mts. see* Erzgebirge *mts.* Czech. **38**
Krylbo Sweden **43** 60.08N 16.13E
Krym *pen.* U.S.S.R. **45** 45.30N 34.00E
Krymsk U.S.S.R. **45** 44.56N 38.00E
Krzyz Poland **36** 52.54N 16.01E
Ksar el Boukhari Algeria **75** 35.53N 2.45E
Ksar-el-Kebir Morocco **74** 35.01N 5.54W
Ksar Rhilane Tunisia **75** 33.00N 9.38E
Ksel, Djebel *mtn.* Algeria **75** 33.44N 1.10E
Kuala Dungun Malaysia **58** 4.47N103.26E
Kualakapuas Indonesia **58** 3.01S114.21E
Kuala Lipis Malaysia **58** 4.11N102.00E
Kuala Lumpur Malaysia **58** 3.08N101.42E
Kuala Trengganu Malaysia **58** 5.10N103.10E
Kuancheng China **54** 40.36N118.27E
Kuandang Indonesia **59** 0.53N122.58E
Kuandian China **54** 40.47N124.43E
Kuantan Malaysia **58** 3.50N103.19E
Kuba U.S.S.R. **65** 41.23N 48.33E
Kuban *r.* U.S.S.R. **45** 45.20N 37.17E
Kubbum Sudan **73** 11.47N 23.47E
Kubrat Bulgaria **34** 43.49N 26.31E
Kuchaiburi India **63** 22.16N 86.10E
Kuchāman India **62** 27.09N 74.52E
Kuching Malaysia **58** 1.32N110.20E
Kuchinoerabu jima *i.* Japan **57** 30.30N130.20E
Küchnay Darvīshān Afghan. **62** 30.59N 64.11E
Küçükbahce Turkey **35** 38.33N 26.24E
Kūd Jammu & Kashmir **62** 33.05N 75.17E
Kudat Malaysia **58** 6.45N116.47E
Kudus Indonesia **59** 6.46S110.48E
Kufrinjah Jordan **67** 32.18N 35.42E
Kufrinjah, Wādī Jordan **67** 32.16N 35.33E
Kufsfein Austria **39** 47.35N 12.10E
Kūhpāyeh Iran **65** 32.42N 52.25E
Kūhrān, Kūh-e *mtn.* Iran **65** 26.46N 58.15E
Kuito Angola **78** 12.25S 16.58E
Kuiu I. U.S.A. **100** 56.40N134.00W
Kuivaniemi Finland **40** 65.35N 25.11E
Kujū san *mtn.* Japan **57** 33.08N131.10E
Kuke Botswana **80** 23.19S 24.29E
Kukerin Australia **89** 33.11S118.03E
Kukës Albania **34** 42.05N 20.20E
Kukshi India **62** 22.12N 74.45E
Kūl *r.* Iran **65** 28.00N 55.45E
Kula Bulgaria **34** 43.52N 22.36E
Kula Turkey **64** 38.33N 28.38E
Kula Yugo. **31** 45.36N 19.32E
Kulāchi Pakistan **62** 31.56N 70.27E
Kulakshi U.S.S.R. **45** 47.09N 55.22E
Kulal, Mt. Kenya **79** 2.44N 36.56E
Kulaura Bangla. **63** 24.30N 92.03E
Kuldīga U.S.S.R. **41** 56.58N 21.59E
Kulen Vakuf Yugo. **31** 44.34N 16.06E
Kulgera Australia **90** 25.50S133.18E
Kulin Australia **89** 32.40S118.10E
Kulja Australia **89** 30.28S117.17E
Kulkyne *r.* Australia **93** 30.16S144.12E
Kulmbach Germany **38** 50.06N 11.27E
Kulpara Australia **92** 34.07S137.59E
Kulsary U.S.S.R. **45** 46.59N 54.02E
Kulu India **62** 31.58N 77.07E
Kulu Turkey **45** 39.06N 33.02E
Kulunda U.S.S.R. **50** 52.34N 78.58E
Kulwin Australia **92** 35.02S142.40E
Kulyab U.S.S.R. **52** 37.55N 69.47E
Kuma *r.* U.S.S.R. **45** 44.40N 46.55E
Kumagaya Japan **57** 36.08N139.23E
Kumai Indonesia **58** 2.45S111.44E
Kumamoto Japan **57** 32.50N130.42E
Kumanovo Yugo. **34** 42.08N 21.43E
Kumara New Zealand **86** 42.38S171.11E
Kumarl Australia **89** 32.47S121.33E
Kumasi Ghana **76** 6.45N 1.35W
Kumba Cameroon **77** 4.39N 9.26E
Kumbakonam India **61** 10.59N 79.24E
Kum Dag U.S.S.R. **65** 39.14N 54.33E
Kumdah Saudi Arabia **71** 20.23N 45.05E
Kumertau U.S.S.R. **44** 52.48N 55.46E
Kumi Uganda **79** 1.26N 33.54E
Kumla Sweden **43** 59.08N 15.08E
Kummerower See *l.* Germany **38** 53.49N 12.52E
Kumon Range *mts.* Burma **56** 26.30N 97.15E
Kunashir *i.* U.S.S.R. **53** 44.25N146.00E
Kunchha Nepal **63** 28.08N 84.22E
Kundam India **63** 23.13N 80.21E
Kundelungu Mts. Zaïre **79** 9.30S 27.50E
Kundiān Pakistan **62** 32.27N 71.28E
Kundip Australia **89** 33.44S120.11E
Kundla India **62** 21.20N 71.18E
Kungälv Sweden **42** 57.52N 11.58E
Kungsbacka Sweden **43** 57.29N 12.04E
Kungshamn Sweden **42** 58.22N 11.15E
Kungsör Sweden **43** 59.25N 16.05E
Kungu Zaïre **78** 2.47N 19.12E
Kungur U.S.S.R. **44** 57.27N 56.50E
Kuningan Indonesia **59** 7.02S108.30E
Kunkuri India **63** 22.45N 83.57E
Kunlong Burma **56** 23.25N 98.39E
Kunlun Shan *mts.* China **52** 36.40N 88.00E
Kunming China **52** 25.04N102.41E
Kunö *i.* Faroe Is. **10** 62.20N 6.39W
Kunsan S. Korea **53** 35.57N126.42E
Kunshan China **55** 31.24N121.08E
Kunszentmárton Hungary **31** 46.51N 20.18E
Kuntair Gambia **76** 13.36N 16.20W
Kununoppin Australia **89** 31.09S117.53E
Kununurra Australia **87** 15.42S128.50E
Kunyo Ethiopia **71** 6.20N 42.32E
Künzelsau Germany **39** 49.16N 9.41E
Kuolayarvi U.S.S.R. **40** 66.58N 29.12E
Kuopio Finland **44** 62.51N 27.30E
Kupa *r.* Yugo. **31** 45.28N 16.24E
Kupang Indonesia **59** 10.13S123.38E
Küplü Turkey **34** 41.07N 26.21E
Kupreanof I. U.S.A. **100** 56.50N133.30W
Kupres Yugo. **31** 44.00N 17.17E
Kupyansk U.S.S.R. **45** 49.41N 37.37E
Kuqa China **52** 41.43N 82.58E
Kura *r.* U.S.S.R. **65** 39.18N 49.22E
Kurashiki Japan **57** 34.36N133.43E
Kuraymah Sudan **72** 18.33N 31.51E
Kurayyimah Jordan **67** 32.16N 35.36E
Kurchum U.S.S.R. **52** 48.35N 83.39E
Kurdistan *f.* Asia **65** 37.00N 43.30E
Kŭrdzhali Bulgaria **34** 41.39N 25.22E
Kure Japan **57** 34.20N132.40E
Kuressaare U.S.S.R. **41** 58.12N 22.30E
Kurgaldzhino U.S.S.R. **50** 50.35N 70.03E
Kurgan U.S.S.R. **9** 55.30N 65.20E
Kurīgrām Bangla. **63** 25.49N 89.39E
Kurikka Finland **40** 62.37N 22.25E
Kuril Ridge Pacific Oc. **84** 46.10N152.30E
Kurilskiye Ostrova *is.* U.S.S.R. **53** 46.00N150.30E
Kuril Trench Pacific Oc. **84** 46.00N155.00E
Kuring Kuru Namibia **80** 17.36S 18.36E
Kurlovski U.S.S.R. **44** 55.26N 40.40E
Kurmuk Sudan **73** 10.33N 34.17E
Kurnool India **61** 15.51N 78.01E
Kurow New Zealand **86** 44.44S170.28E
Kurram Pakistan **62** 30.06N 66.31E
Kurri Kurri Australia **93** 32.49S151.29E
Kurseong India **63** 26.53N 88.17E
Kursk U.S.S.R. **45** 51.45N 36.14E
Kurškiy Zaliv *b.* U.S.S.R. **41** 55.00N 21.00E
Kuršumlija Yugo. **34** 43.09N 21.19E
Kūrtī Sudan **72** 18.07N 31.33E
Kuru Finland **41** 61.52N 23.44E
Kuru Sudan **73** 7.43N 26.31E
Kuruman R.S.A. **80** 27.28S 23.25E
Kuruman *r.* R.S.A. **80** 26.53S 20.38E
Kurume Japan **57** 33.20N130.29E
Kurur, Jabal *mtn.* Sudan **72** 20.31N 31.32E
Kuşadasi Turkey **35** 37.51N 27.15E
Kusadasi Körfezi *b.* Greece **35** 37.50N 27.08E
Kusatsu Japan **57** 35.02N135.57E
Kusel Germany **39** 49.32N 7.24E
Kushālgarh India **62** 23.10N 74.27E
Kushchevskaya U.S.S.R. **45** 46.34N 39.39E
Kushida *r.* Japan **57** 34.36N136.34E
Kushiro Japan **57** 42.58N144.24E
Kushka U.S.S.R. **65** 35.14N 62.15E
Kushtia Bangla. **63** 23.55N 89.07E
Kusiyāra *r.* Bangla. **63** 24.36N 91.44E
Kuskokwim B. U.S.A. **98** 59.45N162.25W
Kuskokwim Mts. U.S.A. **98** 62.50N156.00W
Kusma Nepal **63** 28.13N 83.41E
Kussharo ko *l.* Japan **57** 43.40N144.20E
Küssnacht Switz. **39** 47.05N 8.27E
Kustanay U.S.S.R. **48** 53.15N 63.40E
Küstenkanal Germany **38** 53.08N 8.00E
Kūstī Sudan **73** 13.10N 32.40E
Kütahya Turkey **64** 39.25N 29.56E
Kutaisi U.S.S.R. **45** 42.15N 42.44E
Kutina Yugo. **31** 45.29N 16.46E
Kutiyāna India **62** 21.38N 69.59E
Kutná Hora Czech. **36** 49.57N 15.16E
Kutno Poland **37** 52.15N 19.23E
Kutu Zaïre **78** 2.42S 18.09E
Kutubdia I. Bangla. **63** 21.50N 91.52E
Kutum Sudan **72** 14.12N 24.40E
Kutztown U.S.A. **115** 40.31N 75.47W
Kuujjuaq Canada **99** 58.10N 68.15W
Kuusamo Finland **44** 65.57N 29.15E
Kuvango Angola **78** 14.28S 16.25E
Kuwait Asia **65** 29.20N 47.40E
Kuwait *town see* Al Kuwayt Kuwait **65**
Kuwana Japan **57** 35.04N136.42E
Kuybyshev U.S.S.R. **44** 53.10N 50.15E
Kuybyshevskoye Vodokhranilishche *resr.* U.S.S.R. **44** 55.00N 49.00E
Kuyeda U.S.S.R. **44** 56.25N 55.33E
Kuzey Anadolu Dağlari *mts.* Turkey **64** 40.32N 38.00E
Kuznetsk U.S.S.R. **44** 53.08N 46.36E
Kuzomen U.S.S.R. **44** 66.15N 36.51E
Kuzreka U.S.S.R. **44** 66.35N 34.48E
Kvaenangen *est.* Norway **40** 69.50N 21.30E
Kvarner *g.* Yugo. **31** 45.00N 14.10E
Kvarnerić *str.* Yugo. **31** 44.45N 14.35E
Kvenna *r.* Norway **42** 60.01N 7.56E
Kvina *r.* Norway **42** 58.17N 6.56E
Kwale Kenya **79** 4.20S 39.25E
Kwamouth Zaïre **78** 3.11S 16.16E
Kwangju S. Korea **53** 35.07N126.52E
Kwango *r.* Zaïre **78** 3.20S 17.23E
Kwara *d.* Nigeria **77** 8.20N 5.35E
Kwatisore Indonesia **59** 3.18S134.50E
Kwa Zulu *f.* R.S.A. **80** 27.30S 32.00E
Kwekwe Zimbabwe **80** 18.59S 29.46E
Kweneng *d.* Botswana **80** 24.30S 25.40E
Kwenge *r.* Zaïre **78** 4.53S 18.47E
Kwethluk U.S.A. **98** 60.49N161.27W
Kwidzyn Poland **37** 53.45N 18.56E
Kwigillingok U.S.A. **98** 59.51N163.08W
Kwiguk U.S.A. **98** 62.45N164.28W
Kwilu *r.* Zaïre **78** 3.18S 17.22E
Kwinana Australia **89** 32.15S115.48E
Kwoka *mtn.* Indonesia **59** 1.30S132.30E
Kyabé Chad **77** 9.28N 18.54E
Kyabram Australia **93** 36.18S145.05E
Kyaiklat Burma **56** 16.25N 95.42E
Kyaikto Burma **56** 17.16N 97.01E
Kyaka Tanzania **79** 1.16S 31.27E
Kyakhta U.S.S.R. **52** 50.22N106.30E
Kyalite Australia **92** 34.57S143.31E
Kyancutta Australia **92** 33.08S135.34E
Kyaukpadaung Burma **56** 20.50N 95.08E
Kyaukpyu Burma **56** 19.20N 93.33E
Kybybolite Australia **92** 36.54S140.58E
Kychema U.S.S.R. **44** 65.32N 42.42E
Kyle of Lochalsh *town* U.K. **14** 57.17N 5.43W
Kyll *r.* Germany **16** 49.48N 6.42E
Kyllburg Germany **39** 50.02N 6.35E
Kyluchevskaya *mtn.* U.S.S.R. **51** 56.00N160.30E
Kyneton Australia **92** 37.14S144.28E
Kynnefjäll *hill* Sweden **42** 58.42N 11.41E
Kynuna Australia **90** 21.35S141.55E
Kyoga, L. Uganda **79** 1.30N 33.00E
Kyogle Australia **93** 28.36S152.59E
Kyong Burma **56** 20.49N 96.40E
Kyonpyaw Burma **56** 17.18N 95.12E
Kyotera Uganda **79** 0.40S 31.31E
Kyōto Japan **57** 35.00N135.45E
Kyōto *d.* Japan **57** 34.55N135.35E
Kyritz Germany **38** 52.56N 12.23E
Kyrkheden Sweden **43** 60.10N 13.29E
Kyrön *r.* Finland **40** 63.14N 21.45E
Kyrta U.S.S.R. **44** 64.02N 57.40E
Kyshtym U.S.S.R. **9** 55.43N 60.32E
Kyūshū *d.* Japan **57** 32.00N130.00E
Kyūshū *i.* Japan **57** 32.00N130.00E
Kyushu Palau Ridge Pacific Oc. **84** 15.00N135.00E
Kyūshū sanchi *mts.* Japan **57** 32.20N131.20E
Kyustendil Bulgaria **34** 42.25N 22.41E
Kywong Australia **93** 35.01S146.45E
Kyyjärvi Finland **40** 63.02N 24.34E
Kyzyl U.S.S.R. **52** 51.42N 94.28E
Kyzyl Kum, Peski *f.* U.S.S.R. **9** 42.00N 64.30E
Kzyl Orda U.S.S.R. **9** 44.52N 65.28E

La Alagaba to **Laptevykh, More**

L

La Alagaba Spain **27** 37.28N 6.01W
La Albuera Spain **27** 38.43N 6.49W
La Albufera *l.* Spain **25** 39.20N 0.22W
La Almarcha Spain **27** 39.41N 2.22W
La Almunia de Doña Godina Spain **25** 41.29N 1.22W
Laas Caanood Somali Rep. **71** 8.26N 47.24E
Laas Dawaco Somali Rep. **71** 10.22N 49.03E
Laas Dhaareed Somali Rep. **71** 10.10N 46.01E
Laas Qoray Somali Rep. **71** 11.10N 48.16E
La Asunción Venezuela **122** 11.06N 63.53W
Laâyoune *see* El Aaiún W. Sahara **74**
La Baleine *r.* Canada **99** 58.00N 57.50W
La Banda Argentina **124** 27.44S 64.15W
La Bañeza Spain **26** 42.18N 5.54W
Labao Indonesia **59** 8.12S122.49E
La Barca Mexico **116** 20.20N102.33W
La Barge U.S.A. **108** 42.16N110.12W
La Bassée France **19** 50.32N 2.48E
Labastide-Murat France **20** 44.39N 1.34E
La Baule France **18** 47.17N 2.24W
Labbezanga Mali **76** 14.57N 0.42E
Labe *r.* Czech. *see* Elbe *r.* Germany **38**
Labé Guinea **76** 11.17N 12.11W
Labelle Canada **105** 46.16N 74.44W
La Belle U.S.A. **113** 26.43N 81.27W
Labelle Prov. Park Canada **105** 46.13N 75.19W
Laberge, L. Canada **100** 61.11N135.12W
Labin Yugo. **31** 45.05N 14.07E
Labinsk U.S.S.R. **45** 44.39N 40.44E
La Bisbal Spain **25** 41.57N 3.03E
La Blanquilla *i.* Venezuela **117** 11.53N 64.38W
Laboe Germany **38** 54.24N 10.15E
Labouheyre France **20** 44.13N 0.55W
Laboulaye Argentina **125** 34.05S 63.25W
Labrador *f.* Canada **103** 53.00N 62.00W
Labrador Basin *f.* Atlantic Oc. **127** 55.00N 45.00W
Labrador City Canada **103** 52.57N 66.54W
Labrador Sea Canada / Greenland **99** 57.00N 53.00W
Lábrea Brazil **122** 7.16S 64.47W
Labrède France **20** 44.41N 0.31W
Labrit France **20** 44.07N 0.33W
Labuan Indonesia **59** 6.25S105.49E
Labuan *i.* Malaysia **58** 5.20N115.15E
Labuha Indonesia **59** 0.37S127.29E
Labutta Burma **56** 16.09N 94.46E
Labyrinth, L. Australia **92** 30.43S135.07E
Laç Albania **34** 41.38N 19.40E
Lac *d.* Chad **77** 13.30N 14.35E
La Calera Chile **125** 32.47S 71.12W
La Campana Spain **27** 37.34N 5.26W
Lacanau France **20** 44.59N 1.05W
Lacanau, Étang de *b.* France **20** 44.58N 1.07W
La Cañiza Spain **26** 42.13N 8.16W
La Canourgue France **20** 44.26N 3.13E
La Capelle France **19** 49.58N 3.55E
Lacapelle-Marival France **20** 44.44N 1.54E
La Carlota Argentina **125** 33.25S 63.18W
La Carolina Spain **26** 38.15N 3.37W
Lacaune France **20** 43.43N 2.42E
Lacaune, Monts de *mts.* France **20** 43.43N 2.50E
Lac aux Sables *town* Canada **105** 46.52N 72.24W
Lacedonia Italy **33** 41.03N 15.25E
La Ceiba Honduras **117** 15.45N 86.45W
Lacepede B. Australia **92** 36.47S139.45E
Lac Gatineau *town* Canada **105** 46.34N 75.44W
Lac Giao Vietnam **56** 12.41N108.02E
Lacha, Ozero *l.* U.S.S.R. **44** 61.25N 39.00E
La Chaise-Dieu France **20** 45.19N 3.42E
La Chambre France **21** 45.22N 6.18E
La Charité France **19** 47.11N 3.01E
La Chartre France **18** 47.44N 0.35E
La Châtaigneraie France **18** 46.39N 0.44W
La Châtre France **19** 46.35N 1.59E
La Chaux-de-Fonds Switz. **39** 47.06N 6.50E
Lach Dera *r.* Somali Rep. **79** 0.01S 42.45E
Lachhmangarh India **62** 27.49N 75.02E
Lachine Canada **105** 45.26N 73.40W
Lachine U.S.A. **104** 45.26N 83.40W
Lachlan *r.* Australia **92** 34.21S143.58E
Lachute Canada **105** 45.38N 74.20W
La Ciotat France **21** 43.10N 5.36E
Lackan Resr. Rep. of Ire. **15** 53.09N 6.31W
Lackawanna U.S.A. **114** 42.49N 78.50W
Läckö Sweden **43** 58.41N 13.13E
Lac la Biche *town* Canada **101** 54.46N111.58W
Lac la Ronge Prov. Park Canada **101** 55.14N104.45W
La Clayette France **19** 46.18N 4.19E
La Cocha Argentina **124** 27.45S 65.35W
Lacolle Canada **105** 45.05N 73.22W
Lacombe Canada **100** 52.30N113.44W
La Concepción Venezuela **122** 10.25N 71.41W
La Concordia Mexico **116** 16.05N 92.38W
Laconia U.S.A. **115** 43.31N 71.29W
La Coruña Spain **26** 43.22N 8.23W
La Coruña *d.* Spain **26** 43.10N 8.30W
La Courtine le-Trucq France **20** 45.42N 2.16E
Lac Rémi *town* Canada **105** 46.01N 74.47W
La Crosse Kans. U.S.A. **110** 38.32N 99.18W
La Crosse Wisc. U.S.A. **110** 43.48N 91.15W
La Cruz Mexico **109** 27.50N105.11W
La Cruz Uruguay **125** 33.56S 56.15W
Lac St. Paul *town* Canada **105** 46.44N 75.18W
Ladākh Range *mts.* Jammu & Kashmir **63** 34.15N 78.00E
La Demanda, Sierra de *mts.* Spain **24** 42.10N 3.20W
Ládhi Greece **34** 41.28N 26.15E
Ladhón *r.* Greece **35** 37.40N 21.50E
Ladismith R.S.A. **80** 33.29S 21.15E
Ladispoli Italy **32** 41.56N 12.05E
Lādīz Iran **65** 28.57N 61.18E
Lādnun India **62** 27.39N 74.23E
Ladoga *l. see* Ladozhskoye Ozero *l.* U.S.S.R. **44**
La Dorada Colombia **122** 5.27N 74.40W
Ladozhskoye Ozero *l.* U.S.S.R. **44** 61.00N 32.00E
La Dura Mexico **109** 28.22N109.33W
Ladushkin U.S.S.R. **37** 54.30N 20.05E
Ladva Vetka U.S.S.R. **44** 61.16N 34.23E
Ladybrand R.S.A. **80** 29.11S 27.26E
Lady Evelyn L. Canada **104** 47.20N 80.10W
Ladysmith Canada **100** 49.58N123.49W
Ladysmith R.S.A. **80** 28.32S 29.47E
Ladysmith U.S.A. **110** 45.27N 91.07W
Lae P.N.G. **59** 6.45S146.30E
Lae Thailand **56** 19.25N101.00E
Laesö *i.* Denmark **42** 57.16N 11.01E
La Estrada Spain **26** 42.41N 8.29W
La Fayette Ga. U.S.A. **113** 34.42N 85.18W
Lafayette Ind. U.S.A. **112** 40.25N 86.54W
Lafayette La. U.S.A. **111** 30.14N 92.01W
Lafayette, Mt. U.S.A. **105** 44.10N 71.38W
La Fère France **19** 49.40N 3.22E
La Ferté-Bernard France **18** 48.11N 0.40E
La Ferté-Gaucher France **19** 48.47N 3.18E
La Ferté-Macé France **18** 48.36N 0.22W
La Ferté-St. Aubin France **19** 47.43N 1.56E
Lafia Nigeria **77** 8.35N 8.34E
Lafiagi Nigeria **77** 8.50N 5.23E
La Flèche France **18** 47.42N 0.05W
Lafollette U.S.A. **113** 36.23N 84.09W
Laforest Canada **104** 47.02N 81.13W
La Fregeneda Spain **26** 40.59N 6.52W
La Fuente de San Esteban Spain **26** 40.48N 6.15W
La Galite *i.* Tunisia **32** 37.32N 8.56E
La Galite, Canal de *str.* Tunisia **32** 37.20N 9.15E
La Gallega Spain **26** 41.54N 3.16W
Lagan Sweden **43** 56.55N 13.59E
Lagan *r.* Sweden **43** 56.33N 12.56E
Lagan *r.* U.K. **15** 54.37N 5.44W
La Garde, Lac *l.* Canada **104** 46.46N 78.14W
Lage Spain **26** 43.13N 9.00W
Lågen *r.* Akershus Norway **41** 60.10N 11.28E
Lågen *r.* Vestfold Norway **42** 59.03N 10.05E
Laghouat Algeria **75** 33.49N 2.55E
Lago Dilolo *town* Angola **78** 11.27S 22.03E
Lagonegro Italy **33** 40.07N 15.46E
Lagos Mexico **116** 21.21N101.55W
Lagos Nigeria **77** 6.27N 3.28E
Lagos *d.* Nigeria **77** 6.32N 3.30E
Lagos Portugal **27** 37.06N 8.40W
La Goulette Tunisia **32** 36.49N 10.18E
La Granadella Spain **25** 41.21N 0.40E
La Grand'Combe France **20** 44.13N 4.02E
La Grande *r.* Canada **102** 53.50N 79.00W
La Grande U.S.A. **108** 45.20N118.05W
La Grande Résr. 2 Canada **102** 53.35N 77.10W
La Grande Résr. 3 Canada **102** 53.35N 74.55W
La Grande Résr. 4 Canada **102** 53.50N 73.30W
Lagrange Australia **88** 18.46S121.49E
La Grange U.S.A. **113** 33.02N 85.02W
La Grave France **21** 45.03N 6.18E
La Guaira Venezuela **122** 10.38N 66.55W
La Guardia Pontevedra Spain **26** 41.54N 8.51W
Laguardia Vascongadas Spain **26** 42.33N 2.35W
La Gudiña Spain **26** 42.04N 7.08W
La Guerche-de-Bretagne France **18** 47.56N 1.14W
La Guerche-sur-l'Aubois France **19** 46.57N 2.57E
Laguiole France **20** 44.41N 2.51E
Laguna Brazil **124** 28.29S 48.47W
Laguna Dam U.S.A. **109** 32.55N114.25W
Lagunas Chile **124** 20.59S 69.37W
Lagunas Peru **122** 5.10S 73.35W
La Habana Cuba **117** 23.07N 82.25W
Lahad Datu Malaysia **58** 5.05N118.20E
La Harpe U.S.A. **110** 40.35N 90.57W
Lahat Indonesia **58** 3.46S103.32E
La Haye-du-Puits France **18** 49.18N 1.33W
Laḥij Yemen **71** 13.04N 44.53E
Lāhījān Iran **65** 37.12N 50.00E
Lahn *r.* Germany **16** 50.18N 7.36E
Lahnstein Germany **39** 50.18N 7.37E
Laholm Sweden **43** 56.31N 13.02E
Laholmsbukten *b.* Sweden **43** 56.35N 12.50E
Lahore Pakistan **62** 31.35N 74.18E
Lahr Germany **39** 48.20N 7.52E
Lahri Pakistan **62** 29.11N 68.13E
Lahti Finland **41** 60.58N 25.40E
Laï Chad **77** 9.22N 16.14E
Laiagam P.N.G. **59** 5.31S143.39E
Laibin China **55** 23.42N109.16E
Lai Chau Vietnam **56** 22.04N103.12E
L'Aigle *r.* Canada **105** 46.28N 76.01W
L'Aigle France **18** 48.45N 0.38E
Laignes France **19** 47.50N 4.22E
Laihia Finland **40** 62.58N 22.01E
Lainá Greece **34** 41.03N 26.19E
Laingsburg R.S.A. **80** 33.11S 20.49E
Laingsburg U.S.A. **104** 42.54N 84.21W
Lainio *r.* Sweden **40** 67.28N 22.50E
Lairg U.K. **14** 58.01N 4.25W
Laisamis Kenya **79** 1.38N 37.47E
Laissac France **20** 44.23N 2.49E
Laitila Finland **41** 60.53N 21.41E
Laiyuan China **54** 39.19N114.41E
Laizhou Wan *b.* China **54** 37.30N119.30E
La Jarrie France **20** 46.08N 1.00W
La Javie France **21** 44.10N 6.21E
Lajes Brazil **126** 27.48S 50.20W
La Junta U.S.A. **108** 37.59N103.33W
Lakaband Pakistan **62** 31.00N 69.30E
Lak Bor *r.* Kenya **73** 1.18N 40.40E
Lak Bor *r.* Somali Rep. **79** 0.32N 42.05E
Lake Biddy *town* Australia **89** 33.01S118.51E
Lake Boga *town* Australia **92** 35.27S143.39E
Lake Brown *town* Australia **89** 30.57S118.19E
Lake Cargelligo *town* Australia **93** 33.19S146.23E
Lake Charles *town* U.S.A. **111** 30.13N 93.12W
Lake City U.S.A. **113** 30.12N 82.39W
Lake Clear *town* Canada **105** 45.27N 77.17W
Lake District *f.* U.K. **12** 54.30N 3.10W
Lakefield Canada **104** 44.26N 78.16W
Lake George *town* Colo. U.S.A. **108** 38.58N105.23W
Lake George *town* N.Y. U.S.A. **115** 43.26N 73.43W
Lake Grace *town* Australia **89** 33.06S118.28E
Lake Harbour *town* Canada **99** 62.50N 69.50W
Lake King *town* Australia **89** 33.05S119.40E
Lakeland *town* U.S.A. **113** 28.02N 81.59W
Lake Mead Nat. Recreation Area U.S.A. **109** 36.00N114.30W
Lake Nash *town* Australia **90** 21.00S137.55E
Lake Orion *town* U.S.A. **114** 42.47N 83.14W
Lakepa Niue **84** 19.01S169.49W
Lake Placid *town* U.S.A. **112** 44.17N 73.59W
Lake River *town* Canada **102** 54.30N 82.30W
Lakes Entrance *town* Australia **93** 37.53S147.59E
Lakeshore U.S.A. **108** 37.15N119.12W
Lakeside Ohio U.S.A. **114** 41.32N 82.45W
Lakeside Utah U.S.A. **108** 41.13N112.54W
Lake Superior Prov. Park Canada **102** 47.30N 84.50W
Lakeview U.S.A. **108** 42.11N120.21W
Lake Village U.S.A. **111** 33.20N 91.17W
Lakewood N.J. U.S.A. **115** 40.06N 74.13W
Lakewood N.Mex. U.S.A. **109** 32.39N104.39W
Lakewood N.Y. U.S.A. **114** 42.06N 79.20W
Lakewood Ohio U.S.A. **114** 41.29N 81.48W
Lākheri India **62** 25.40N 76.10E
Lakhīmpur India **63** 27.57N 80.46E
Lakhish, Nahal *wadi* Israel **67** 31.37N 34.46E
Lakhnādon India **63** 22.36N 79.36E
Lakhpat India **62** 23.49N 68.47E
Lakonikós Kólpos *g.* Greece **35** 36.25N 22.37E
Lakota Ivory Coast **76** 5.50N 5.30W
Lakota U.S.A. **110** 48.02N 98.21W
Laksefjorden *est.* Norway **40** 70.58N 27.00E
Lakselv Norway **40** 70.03N 24.55E
Lakshadweep Is. Indian Oc. **60** 11.00N 72.00E
Lala India **63** 24.25N 92.40E
Lāla Mūsa Pakistan **62** 32.42N 73.58E
Lalaua Mozambique **79** 14.20S 38.30E
Lalbenque France **20** 44.20N 1.33E
Lālehzār, Kūh-e *mtn.* Iran **65** 29.26N 56.48E
Lālganj India **63** 25.52N 85.11E
Lalībela Ethiopia **73** 12.02N 39.02E
La Libertad El Salvador **117** 13.28N 89.20W
Lalín Spain **26** 42.39N 8.07W
Lalinde France **20** 44.51N 0.44E
La Línea Spain **27** 36.10N 5.19W
Lalitpur India **63** 24.41N 78.25E
Lalitpur Nepal **63** 27.41N 85.20E
Lālmanir Hāt Bangla. **63** 25.54N 89.27E
La Loche Canada **101** 56.29N109.27W
La Loche, Lac *l.* Canada **101** 56.25N109.30W
La Loupe France **18** 48.28N 1.01E
La Louvière Belgium **16** 50.29N 4.11E
Lālpur India **62** 22.12N 69.58E
Lālsot India **62** 26.34N 76.20E
La Maddalena Italy **32** 41.13N 9.24E
Lamar U.S.A. **110** 38.05N102.37W
Lamarche France **19** 48.04N 5.47E
La Marsa Tunisia **32** 36.53N 10.20E
Lamastre France **21** 44.59N 4.35E
Lamballe France **18** 48.28N 2.31W
Lambaréné Gabon **78** 0.40S 10.15E
Lambasa Fiji **84** 16.25S179.24E
Lambayeque Peru **122** 6.36S 79.50W
Lambay I. Rep. of Ire. **15** 53.29N 6.01W
Lambert's Bay *town* R.S.A. **80** 32.06S 18.16E
Lámbia Greece **35** 37.52N 21.53E
Lamé Chad **77** 9.14N 14.33E
Lame Nigeria **77** 10.27N 9.12E
Lamego Portugal **26** 41.06N 7.49W
Lameroo Australia **92** 35.20S140.33E
La Mesa Calif. U.S.A. **109** 32.46N117.01W
Lamesa Tex. U.S.A. **111** 32.44N101.57W
Lamía Greece **35** 38.54N 22.26E
La Minerve Canada **105** 46.15N 74.56W
Lammermuir Hills U.K. **14** 55.51N 2.40W
Lammhult Sweden **43** 57.10N 14.35E
Lamoille *r.* U.S.A. **105** 44.35N 73.10W
Lamongan Indonesia **59** 7.05S112.26E
Lamont U.S.A. **108** 42.12N107.28W
La Mothe-Achard France **18** 46.37N 1.40W
Lamotrek *i.* Caroline Is. **59** 7.28N146.23E
Lamotte-Beuvron France **19** 47.36N 2.01E
La Motte-Chalençon France **21** 44.29N 5.23E
La Motte du-Claire France **21** 44.21N 6.02E
La Moure U.S.A. **110** 46.21N 98.18W
Lampa Peru **122** 15.10S 70.30W
Lampasas U.S.A. **111** 31.04N 98.12W
Lampazos Mexico **111** 27.00N100.30W
Lampedusa *i.* Italy **28** 35.30N 12.35E
Lampertheim Germany **39** 49.35N 8.28E
Lampeter U.K. **13** 52.06N 4.06W
Lampinoú Greece **34** 39.22N 23.10E
Lampione *i.* Italy **28** 35.33N 12.18E
Lamu Kenya **79** 2.20S 40.54E
La Mure France **21** 44.54N 5.47E
Lana Italy **30** 46.37N 11.09E
Lanai *i.* Hawaiian Is. **85** 20.50N156.55W
Lanai City Hawaiian Is. **85** 20.50N156.55W
La Nao, Cabo de Spain **24** 38.42N 0.15E
Lanark U.K. **14** 55.41N 3.47W
La Nava de Ricomalillo Spain **27** 39.39N 4.59W
Lancang Jiang *r.* China *see* Mekong *r.* Asia **56**
Lancashire *d.* U.K. **12** 53.53N 2.30W
Lancaster Canada **105** 45.08N 74.30W
Lancaster U.K. **12** 54.03N 2.48W
Lancaster Calif. U.S.A. **109** 34.42N118.08W
Lancaster N.H. U.S.A. **105** 44.29N 71.34W
Lancaster N.Y. U.S.A. **114** 42.54N 78.40W
Lancaster Ohio U.S.A. **114** 39.43N 82.36W
Lancaster Penn. U.S.A. **115** 40.02N 76.19W
Lancaster S.C. U.S.A. **113** 34.43N 80.47W
Lancaster Tex. U.S.A. **111** 32.36N 96.46W
Lancaster Sd. Canada **99** 74.00N 85.00W
Lancelin Australia **89** 31.01S115.19E
Lanchow *see* Lanzhou China **54**
Lanciano Italy **31** 42.14N 14.23E
Lancun China **54** 36.24N120.10E
Landau Bayern Germany **39** 48.40N 12.43E
Landau Rhein.-Pfalz. Germany **39** 49.12N 8.07E
Landay Afghan. **62** 30.31N 63.47E
Landeck Austria **39** 47.08N 10.34E
Landen Belgium **16** 50.46N 5.04E
Lander *r.* Australia **90** 20.25S132.00E
Lander U.S.A. **108** 42.50N108.44W
Landerneau France **18** 48.27N 4.15W
Landes *d.* France **20** 44.20N 1.00W
Landes *f.* France **20** 44.00N 1.00W
Landete Spain **25** 39.56N 1.25W
Landisville U.S.A. **115** 39.31N 74.55W
Landivisiau France **18** 48.31N 4.04W
Landor Australia **88** 25.06S116.50E
Landquart Switz. **39** 46.58N 9.33E
Landrecies France **19** 50.08N 3.42E
Landsberg Germany **39** 48.05N 10.55E
Landsbro Sweden **43** 57.22N 14.54E
Lands End *c.* Canada **96** 76.10N123.00W
Land's End *c.* U.K. **13** 50.03N 5.45W
Landshut Germany **39** 48.33N 12.09E
Landskrona Sweden **43** 55.52N 12.50E
Lanett U.S.A. **113** 32.52N 85.12W
Langå Denmark **42** 56.23N 9.55E
La'nga Co *l.* China **63** 30.45N 81.15E
Langadhás Greece **34** 40.45N 23.04E
Langádhia Greece **35** 37.41N 22.02E
Langanes *c.* Iceland **40** 66.30N 14.30W
Langao China **54** 33.22N109.04E
Långban Sweden **43** 59.51N 14.15E
Langdon U.S.A. **110** 48.46N 98.22W
Langeac France **20** 45.06N 3.30E
Langeais France **18** 47.20N 0.24E
L'Ange Gardien Canada **105** 46.55N 71.07W
Langeland *i.* Denmark **42** 55.00N 10.50E
Längelmävesi *l.* Finland **41** 61.32N 24.22E
Langen Germany **39** 49.59N 8.41E
Längenfeld Austria **39** 47.04N 10.58E
Langenhagen Germany **38** 52.27N 9.44E
Langenthal Switz. **39** 47.13N 7.47E
Langeoog *i.* Germany **38** 53.46N 7.32E
Langesund Norway **42** 59.00N 9.45E
Langholm U.K. **14** 55.09N 3.00W
Langjökull *ice cap* Iceland **40** 63.43N 20.03W
Langkawi *i.* Malaysia **58** 6.20N 99.30E
Langlade Canada **102** 48.14N 76.00W
Langnau Switz. **39** 46.57N 7.47E
Langogne France **20** 44.43N 3.51E
Langon France **20** 44.33N 0.15W
Langöy *i.* Norway **40** 68.45N 15.00E
Langres France **19** 47.52N 5.20E
Langres, Plateau de *f.* France **19** 47.41N 5.03E
Langsa Indonesia **58** 4.28N 97.59E
Langshan China **54** 41.02N107.27E
Lang Shan *mts.* China **54** 41.30N107.10E
Lang Son Vietnam **55** 21.49N106.45E
Langtry U.S.A. **111** 29.48N101.34W
Languedoc-Roussillon *d.* France **20** 43.50N 3.30E
Langxi China **55** 31.08N119.10E
Laniel Canada **104** 47.04N 79.18W
Lannemezan France **20** 43.08N 0.23E
Lannilis France **18** 48.34N 4.31W
Lannion France **18** 48.44N 3.28W
L'Annonciation Canada **105** 46.25N 74.52W
Lanoraie Canada **105** 45.58N 73.13W
Lansdale U.S.A. **115** 40.15N 75.17W
Lansdowne India **63** 29.50N 78.41E
L'Anse au Loup Canada **103** 51.34N 56.48W
Lansing U.S.A. **112** 42.44N 84.34W
Lanslebourg France **21** 45.17N 6.52E
Lantewa Nigeria **77** 12.15N 11.45E
Lanusei Italy **32** 39.52N 9.34E
Lanxi China **55** 29.17N119.31E
Lanzarote *i.* Canary Is. **74** 29.00N 13.40W
Lanzhou China **54** 36.01N103.46E
Lanzo Torinese Italy **30** 45.16N 7.28E
Laoag Phil. **59** 18.14N120.36E
Lào Cai Vietnam **56** 22.30N104.00E
Laochang China **55** 25.12N104.35E
Laoha He *r.* China **54** 43.30N120.42E
Laois *d.* Rep. of Ire. **15** 53.00N 7.20W
Laojun Shan *mtn.* China **54** 33.45N111.38E
Laon France **19** 49.34N 3.40E
Laona U.S.A. **102** 45.35N 88.40W
La Orotava Canary Is. **127** 28.26N 16.30W
La Oroya Peru **122** 11.36S 75.54W
Laos Asia **56** 18.30N104.00E
Lapalisse France **20** 46.15N 3.38E
La Palma *i.* Canary Is. **74** 28.50N 18.00W
La Palma Spain **27** 37.23N 6.33W
La Pampa *d.* Argentina **125** 37.00S 66.00W
La Paragua Venezuela **122** 6.53N 63.22W
La Paz Entre Ríos Argentina **125** 30.45S 59.38W
La Paz Mendoza Argentina **125** 33.28S 67.34W
La Paz Bolivia **124** 16.30S 68.09W
La Paz *d.* Bolivia **124** 16.00S 68.10W
La Paz Mexico **109** 24.10N110.18W
La Paz, Bahía de *b.* Mexico **109** 24.15N110.30W
La Pedrera Colombia **122** 1.18S 69.43W
Lapeer U.S.A. **104** 43.03N 83.19W
La Peña, Sierra de *mts.* Spain **24** 42.30N 0.50W
La Perouse Str. U.S.S.R. **51** 45.50N142.30E
La Pine U.S.A. **108** 43.40N121.30W
Lapinjärvi Finland **41** 60.38N 26.13E
Lapland *f.* Sweden / Finland **40** 68.10N 24.10E
La Plata Argentina **125** 34.55S 57.57W
La Plata Md. U.S.A. **114** 38.32N 76.59W
La Plata Mo. U.S.A. **110** 40.02N 92.29W
La Plata, Río de *est.* Argentina / Uruguay **125** 35.15S 56.45W
Lapointe, Lac *l.* Canada **103** 53.32N 68.56W
Laporte U.S.A. **115** 41.25N 76.30W
Lappajärvi *l.* Finland **40** 63.08N 23.40E
Lappeenranta Finland **44** 61.04N 28.05E
Lappi *d.* Finland **40** 67.20N 26.00E
Laptevykh, More *sea* U.S.S.R. **51** 74.30N125.00E

Lapua to **Leuven**

Lapua Finland **40** 62.57N 23.00E
La Puebla Spain **25** 39.46N 3.01E
La Puebla de Cazalla Spain **27** 37.14N 5.19W
La Puebla de Montalbán Spain **27** 39.52N 4.21W
La Push U.S.A. **108** 47.55N124.38W
La Quiaca Argentina **124** 22.05S 65.36W
L'Aquila Italy **30** 42.22N 13.22E
Lār Iran **65** 27.37N 54.16E
Lara Australia **92** 38.01S144.26E
Laracha Spain **26** 43.15N 8.35W
Larache Morocco **74** 35.12N 6.10W
Laragne-Montéglin France **21** 44.19N 5.49E
La Rambla Spain **27** 37.36N 4.44W
Laramie U.S.A. **108** 41.19N105.35W
Laramie Mts. U.S.A. **108** 42.00N105.40W
L'Arbresle France **21** 45.50N 4.37E
Lärbro Sweden **43** 57.47N 18.47E
Larche, Col de *pass* France / Italy **21** 44.25N 6.53E
Laredo Spain **26** 43.24N 3.25W
Laredo U.S.A. **111** 27.31N 99.30W
Laredo Sd. Canada **100** 52.30N128.53W
La Réole France **20** 44.35N 0.02E
Largeau Chad **77** 17.55N 19.07E
L'Argentière-la-Bessée France **21** 44.47N 6.33E
Largs U.K. **14** 55.48N 4.52W
Lariang Indonesia **58** 1.35S119.25E
Lárimna Greece **35** 38.34N 23.17E
Larino Italy **33** 41.48N 14.54E
La Rioja Argentina **124** 29.25S 66.50W
La Rioja *d.* Argentina **124** 29.00S 66.00W
La Rioja *d.* Spain **26** 42.25N 2.30W
Lárisa Greece **34** 39.38N 22.28E
Lark *r.* U.K. **13** 52.26N 0.20E
Lārkāna Pakistan **62** 27.33N 68.13E
Larkspur U.S.A. **108** 39.13N104.54W
Larnaca *see* Lárnax Cyprus **66**
Lárnax Cyprus **66** 34.54N 33.39E
Larne U.K. **15** 54.51N 5.49W
La Robla Spain **26** 42.48N 5.37W
La Roca de la Sierra Spain **27** 39.07N 6.41W
La Roche Belgium **16** 50.11N 5.35E
La Roche-Bernard France **18** 47.31N 2.18W
La Rochelle France **20** 46.10N 1.10W
La Roche-sur-Yon France **18** 46.40N 1.26W
La Roda Spain **27** 39.13N 2.09W
La Romana Dom. Rep. **117** 18.27N 68.57W
La Ronge Canada **101** 55.06N105.17W
La Ronge, Lac *l.* Canada **98** 55.07N105.15W
Laroquebrou France **20** 44.58N 2.11E
Larrimah Australia **90** 15.35S133.12E
Larvik Norway **42** 59.04N 10.00E
La Sagra *mtn.* Spain **27** 37.57N 2.34W
La Salle U.S.A. **110** 41.20N 89.06W
Las Animas U.S.A. **108** 38.04N103.13W
La Sarre Canada **102** 48.45N 79.15W
Las Cabezas de San Juan Spain **27** 36.59N 5.56W
Las Casitas, Cerro *mtn.* Mexico **109** 23.32N109.59W
L'Ascension Canada **105** 46.33N 74.50W
Las Cruces U.S.A. **109** 32.23N106.29W
Las Cuevas Mexico **111** 29.38N101.19W
La Seine, Baie de France **17** 49.40N 0.30W
La Serena Chile **124** 29.54S 71.16W
La Seu d'Urgell Spain **25** 42.22N 1.23E
La Seyne France **21** 43.06N 5.53E
Las Flores Argentina **125** 36.02S 59.07W
Lāsh-e Joveyn Afghan. **62** 31.43N 61.37E
Las Heras Argentina **125** 32.50S 68.50W
Lashio Burma **56** 22.58N 96.51E
Lashkar Gāh Afghan. **62** 31.30N 64.21E
Laško Yugo. **31** 46.09N 15.14E
Las Lomitas Argentina **124** 24.43S 60.35W
Las Marismas *f.* Spain **27** 37.05N 6.20W
La Solana Spain **26** 38.56N 3.14W
L'Asomption *r.* Canada **105** 45.43N 73.29W
Las Palmas de Gran Canaria Canary Is. **74** 28.08N 15.27W
Las Palomas Mexico **109** 31.44N107.37W
Las Perlas, Archipelago de Panama **117** 8.45N 79.30W
La Spezia Italy **30** 44.07N 9.50E
Las Piedras Uruguay **125** 34.44S 56.13W
Las Plumas Argentina **125** 43.40S 67.15W
Lassay France **18** 48.26N 0.30W
Lassen Peak *mtn.* U.S.A. **108** 40.29N121.31W
L'Assomption Canada **105** 45.50N 73.25W
Last Chance U.S.A. **108** 39.45N103.36W
Last Mountain L. Canada **101** 51.05N105.10W
Lastoursville Gabon **78** 0.50S 12.47E
Lastovo *i.* Yugo. **31** 42.45N 16.53E
Lastovski Kanal *str.* Yugo. **31** 42.50N 16.59E
Las Tres Vírgenes, Volcán *mtn.* Mexico **109** 27.27N112.37W
Lastrup Germany **38** 52.48N 7.52E
La Suze France **18** 47.54N 0.02E
Las Vegas Nev. U.S.A. **109** 36.11N115.08W
Las Vegas N.Mex. U.S.A. **109** 35.36N105.13W
Latacunga Ecuador **122** 0.58S 78.36W
La Tagua Colombia **122** 0.03S 74.40W
Latakia *see* Al Lādhiqīyah Syria **66**
Latambar Pakistan **62** 33.07N 70.52E
Latchford Canada **104** 47.20N 79.48W
Late *i.* Tonga **85** 18.49S174.40W
Lātēhar India **63** 23.45N 84.30E
La Teste-de-Buch France **20** 44.38N 1.09W
Lathen Germany **38** 52.52N 7.19E
Lāthi India **62** 21.43N 71.23E
Latina Italy **32** 41.28N 12.52E
Latisana Italy **30** 45.47N 13.00E
La Tortuga *i.* Venezuela **122** 11.00N 65.20W
La Tour-d'Auvergne France **20** 45.32N 2.41E
La Tour-du-Pin France **21** 45.34N 5.27E
La Tremblade France **20** 45.46N 1.08W
La Trimouille France **18** 46.28N 1.02E
Latrobe U.S.A. **114** 40.19N 79.23W
La Trobe, Mt. Australia **93** 39.03S146.25E
La Truite, Lac à *l.* Canada **104** 47.16N 78.17W
Laṭrūn Jordan **67** 31.50N 34.59E
La Tuque Canada **103** 47.27N 72.47W
Latviyskaya S.S.R. *d.* U.S.S.R. **41** 56.45N 23.00E
Lau Nigeria **77** 9.14N 11.15E
Lauchhammer Germany **38** 51.30N 13.47E
Lauenburg Germany **38** 53.22N 10.33E
Lauf an der Pegnitz Germany **38** 49.30N 11.17E
Laughlen, Mt. Australia **90** 23.23S134.23E
Lau Group *is.* Fiji **84** 19.00S178.30W
Launceston Australia **91** 41.25S147.07E
Launceston U.K. **13** 50.38N 4.21W
La Unión Chile **125** 40.15S 73.02W
La Unión Spain **25** 37.37N 0.52W
Laupheim Germany **39** 48.14N 9.52E
Laura Australia **92** 33.08S138.19E
La Urbana Venezuela **122** 7.08N 66.56W
Laureana di Borrello Italy **33** 38.30N 16.05E
Laurel Del. U.S.A. **115** 38.33N 75.34W
Laurel Miss. U.S.A. **111** 31.42N 89.08W
Laurel Mont. U.S.A. **108** 45.40N108.46W
Laurel Hill *mtn.* U.S.A. **114** 40.02N 79.17W
Laurel Ridge *mtn.* U.S.A. **114** 39.20N 79.53W
Laurelville U.S.A. **114** 39.28N 82.44W
Laurencekirk U.K. **14** 56.50N 2.29W
Laurens U.S.A. **113** 34.29N 82.01W
Laurentians *mts.* Canada **105** 45.43N 75.52W
Laurentides *mts.* Canada **105** 46.25N 73.28W
Laurentides Prov. Park Canada **103** 47.30N 71.30W
Lauria Italy **33** 40.02N 15.50E
Laurier Canada **105** 46.32N 71.38W
Laurière France **20** 46.05N 1.28E
Laurieton Australia **93** 31.38S152.46E
Laurinburg U.S.A. **113** 34.46N 79.29W
Lauro, Monte *mtn.* Italy **33** 37.08N 14.47E
Lausanne Switz. **39** 46.31N 6.38E
Laut *i.* Indonesia **58** 3.45S116.20E
Lauta Germany **38** 51.27N 14.04E
Lautaro Chile **125** 38.31S 72.27W
Lauterbach Germany **38** 50.38N 9.24E
Lauterbrunnen Switz. **39** 46.36N 7.55E
Lauterecken Germany **39** 49.39N 7.35E
Lautoka Fiji **84** 17.37S177.27E
Lauzerte France **20** 44.15N 1.08E
Lauzon Canada **105** 46.50N 71.10W
Lauzun France **20** 44.38N 0.28E
Lavagh More *mtn.* Rep. of Ire. **15** 54.45N 8.07W
Lava Hot Springs *town* U.S.A. **108** 42.37N112.01W
Laval Canada **105** 45.35N 73.45W
Laval France **18** 48.04N 0.46W
Lávara Greece **34** 41.19N 26.22E
Lavardac France **20** 44.11N 0.18E
La Vecilla de Curueño Spain **26** 42.51N 5.24W
La Vega Dom. Rep. **117** 19.15N 70.33W
La Vela Venezuela **122** 11.27N 69.34W
Lavelanet France **20** 42.56N 1.51E
Lavello Italy **33** 41.03N 15.48E
La Verendrye Prov. Park Canada **105** 47.30N 77.30W
Laverlochère Canada **104** 47.26N 79.19W
Laverne U.S.A. **111** 36.43N 99.54W
Laverton Australia **89** 28.49S122.25E
Lavi Israel **67** 32.47N 35.26E
Lavia Finland **41** 61.36N 22.36E
Lavielle, L. Canada **104** 45.51N 78.14W
Lavigne Canada **104** 46.20N 80.05W
Lavik Norway **41** 61.06N 5.30E
La Voulte-sur-Rhône France **21** 44.48N 4.47E
Lavras Brazil **126** 21.15S 44.59W
Lávrion Greece **35** 37.44N 24.04E
Lawra Ghana **76** 10.40N 2.49W
Lawrence New Zealand **86** 45.55S169.42E
Lawrence Kans. U.S.A. **110** 38.58N 95.14W
Lawrence Mass. U.S.A. **115** 42.42N 71.09W
Lawrenceburg U.S.A. **113** 35.16N 87.20W
Lawrenceville Canada **105** 45.25N 72.19W
Lawrenceville Penn. U.S.A. **114** 42.00N 77.08W
Lawton Okla. U.S.A. **111** 34.37N 98.25W
Lawton Penn. U.S.A. **115** 41.46N 76.05W
Lawz, Jabal al *mtn.* Saudi Arabia **66** 28.40N 35.20E
Laxå Sweden **43** 58.59N 14.37E
Lay *r.* France **18** 46.20N 1.18W
Laysan *i.* Hawaiian Is. **84** 25.46N171.44W
Laytonville U.S.A. **108** 39.41N123.29W
Lazio *d.* Italy **30** 42.05N 12.20E
Lead U.S.A. **110** 44.21N103.46W
Leader Canada **101** 50.53N109.31W
Leadhills U.K. **14** 55.25N 3.46W
Leamington Canada **104** 42.03N 82.36W
Leamington U.S.A. **108** 39.31N112.17W
Learmonth Australia **88** 22.13S114.04E
Leavenworth U.S.A. **110** 39.19N 94.55W
Lebak Phil. **59** 6.32N124.03E
Lebane Yugo. **34** 42.56N 21.44E
Lebango Congo **78** 0.24N 14.44E
Lebanon Asia **66** 34.00N 36.00E
Lebanon Ind. U.S.A. **112** 40.02N 87.28W
Lebanon Kans. U.S.A. **110** 39.49N 98.33W
Lebanon Ky. U.S.A. **113** 37.33N 85.15W
Lebanon Mo. U.S.A. **111** 37.41N 92.40W
Lebanon N.H. U.S.A. **115** 43.38N 72.15W
Lebanon Oreg. U.S.A. **108** 44.32N122.54W
Lebanon Penn. U.S.A. **115** 40.20N 76.25W
Lebanon Tenn. U.S.A. **113** 36.11N 86.19W
Lebec U.S.A. **109** 34.50N118.52W
Lebesby Norway **40** 70.34N 27.00E
Le Blanc France **18** 46.38N 1.04E
Lebork Poland **37** 54.33N 17.44E
Le Bourg-d'Oisans France **21** 45.03N 6.02E
Lebrija Spain **27** 36.55N 6.04W
Lebu Chile **125** 37.37S 73.39W
Le Bugue France **20** 44.55N 0.56E
Le Cannet France **21** 43.34N 7.01E
Le Cateau France **19** 50.06N 3.33E
Le Catelet France **19** 50.00N 3.15E
Lecce Italy **33** 40.23N 18.11E
Lecco Italy **30** 45.51N 9.23E
Lech *r.* Germany **39** 48.44N 10.56E
Lechang China **55** 25.08N113.20E
Le Château d'Oléron France **20** 45.53N 1.11W
Le Châtelet France **19** 46.39N 2.17E
Le Chesne France **19** 49.31N 4.46E
Le Cheylard France **21** 44.54N 4.25E
Lechiguanas, Islas de las *is.* Argentina **125** 33.26S 59.42W
Lechtaler Alpen *mts.* Austria **39** 47.15N 10.33E
Le Conquet France **18** 48.22N 4.46W
L'Écorce, Lac de *l.* Canada **105** 47.05N 76.24W
Le Creusot France **19** 46.48N 4.26E
Le Croisic France **18** 47.18N 2.31W
Lectoure France **20** 43.56N 0.38E
Ledbury U.K. **13** 52.03N 2.25W
Ledesma Spain **26** 41.05N 6.00W
Le Donjon France **20** 46.21N 3.48E
Le Dorat France **20** 46.13N 1.05E
Leduc Canada **100** 53.20N113.30W
Lee *r.* Rep. of Ire. **15** 51.53N 8.25W
Lee U.S.A. **115** 42.19N 73.15W
Leechburg U.S.A. **114** 40.38N 79.36W
Leech L. U.S.A. **110** 47.09N 94.23W
Leedey U.S.A. **111** 35.52N 99.21W
Leeds Canada **105** 46.16N 71.22W
Leeds U.K. **12** 53.48N 1.34W
Leeds U.S.A. **113** 33.32N 86.31W
Leek U.K. **12** 53.07N 2.02W
Leer Germany **38** 53.14N 7.26E
Leesburg Fla. U.S.A. **113** 28.49N 81.54W
Leesburg Va. U.S.A. **114** 39.07N 77.34W
Leeston New Zealand **86** 43.46S172.18E
Leeton Australia **93** 34.33S146.24E
Leeuwarden Neth. **16** 53.12N 5.48E
Leeuwin, C. Australia **89** 34.22S115.08E
Leeward Is. C. America **117** 18.00N 61.00W
Lefroy, L. Australia **89** 31.15S121.40E
Legazpi Phil. **59** 13.10N123.45E
Legges Tor *mtn.* Australia **91** 41.32S147.40E
Legget U.S.A. **108** 39.52N123.34W
Leghorn *see* Livorno Italy **30**
Legion Mine Zimbabwe **80** 21.23S 28.33E
Legionowo Poland **37** 52.25N 20.56E
Legnago Italy **30** 45.11N 11.18E
Legnano Italy **30** 45.36N 8.54E
Legnica Poland **36** 51.12N 16.10E
Le Grand-Lucé France **18** 47.52N 0.28E
Le Grand-Quevilly France **18** 49.25N 1.02E
Le Grau-du-Roi France **21** 43.32N 4.08E
Leh Jammu & Kashmir **63** 34.10N 77.35E
Le Havre France **18** 49.30N 0.08E
Lehighton U.S.A. **115** 40.49N 75.45W
Lehrte Germany **38** 52.22N 9.59E
Lehututu Botswana **80** 23.54S 21.52E
Leiah Pakistan **62** 30.58N 70.56E
Leibnitz Austria **31** 46.48N 15.32E
Leicester U.K. **13** 52.39N 1.09W
Leicestershire *d.* U.K. **13** 52.29N 1.10W
Leichardt *r.* Australia **90** 17.35S139.48E
Leiden Neth. **16** 52.10N 4.30E
Leie *r.* Belgium **16** 51.03N 3.44E
Leifeng China **55** 25.35N118.17E
Leigh Creek *r.* Australia **92** 29.49S138.10E
Leigh Creek *town* Australia **92** 30.31S138.25E
Leighton Buzzard U.K. **13** 51.55N 0.39W
Leikanger Norway **41** 61.10N 6.52E
Leine Germany **38** 52.41N 9.36E
Leinster Australia **89** 27.59S120.30E
Leipzig Germany **38** 51.19N 12.20E
Leiria Portugal **27** 39.45N 8.48W
Leiria *d.* Portugal **27** 39.50N 8.50W
Leirvik Norway **42** 59.45N 5.30E
Lei Shui *r.* China **55** 26.57N112.33E
Leithbridge Canada **100** 49.40N112.45W
Leitrim *d.* Rep. of Ire. **15** 54.08N 8.00W
Leiyang China **55** 26.30N112.42E
Leizhou Bandao *pen.* China **55** 21.00N110.00E
Lek *r.* Neth. **16** 51.55N 4.29E
Lekhainá Greece **35** 37.56N 21.17E
Leksvik Norway **40** 63.40N 10.40E
Leland U.S.A. **111** 33.24N 90.54W
Leland Lakes Canada **101** 60.00N110.59W
Lelång *l.* Sweden **43** 59.08N 12.10E
Lelchitsy U.S.S.R. **37** 51.48N 28.20E
Leleque Argentina **125** 42.24S 71.04W
Leling China **54** 37.45N117.13E
Le Lion-d'Angers France **18** 47.38N 0.43W
Le Locle Switz. **39** 47.03N 6.45E
Le Lude France **18** 47.39N 0.09E
Lelystad Neth. **16** 52.32N 5.29E
Le Madonie Italy **33** 37.55N 14.00E
Léman, Lac *l.* Switz. **39** 46.25N 6.30E
Le Mans France **18** 48.00N 0.12E
Le Mars U.S.A. **110** 42.47N 96.10W
Le Mayet-de-Montagne France **20** 46.05N 3.40E
Leme Brazil **126** 22.10S 47.23W
Le Merlerault France **18** 48.42N 0.18E
Lemesós Cyprus **66** 34.40N 33.03E
Lemgo Germany **38** 52.02N 8.54E
Lemhi Range *mts.* U.S.A. **108** 44.30N113.25W
Lemland *i.* Finland **43** 60.03N 20.10E
Lemmer Neth. **16** 52.50N 5.43E
Lemmon U.S.A. **110** 45.56N102.10W
Le Monastier France **20** 44.56N 4.00E
Le Montet France **20** 46.25N 3.03E
Lemsid W. Sahara **74** 26.32N 13.49W
Lemvig Denmark **42** 56.32N 8.18E
Lena U.S.A. **111** 31.47N 92.48W
Lena *r.* U.S.S.R. **51** 72.00N127.10E
Lenakel Vanuatu **84** 19.32S169.16E
Lenart Yugo. **31** 46.35N 15.50E
Lencloître France **18** 46.49N 0.20E
Lendery U.S.S.R. **44** 63.24N 31.04E
Lendinara Italy **30** 45.05N 11.36E
Lengerich Germany **38** 52.11N 7.50E
Lengoue *r.* Congo **78** 1.15S 16.42E
Lenhovda Sweden **43** 57.00N 15.17E
Lenina, Kanal *canal* U.S.S.R. **45** 43.46N 45.00E
Lenina, Pik *mtn.* U.S.S.R. **52** 40.14N 69.40E
Leninakan U.S.S.R. **65** 40.47N 43.49E
Leningrad U.S.S.R. **44** 59.55N 30.25E
Leninogorsk U.S.S.R. **50** 50.23N 83.32E
Leninsk U.S.S.R. **45** 48.42N 45.14E
Leninsk Kuznetskiy U.S.S.R. **50** 54.44N 86.13E
Lenk Switz. **39** 46.28N 7.27E
Lenkoran U.S.S.R. **65** 38.45N 48.50E
Lenmalu Indonesia **59** 1.58S130.00E
Lenne *r.* Germany **38** 51.25N 7.30E
Lennoxville Canada **105** 45.22N 71.51W
Lenoir U.S.A. **113** 35.56N 81.31W
Lenora Czech. **38** 48.56N 13.48E
Lenora U.S.A. **110** 39.38N100.03W
Lenore L. Canada **101** 52.30N105.00W
Lenox U.S.A. **115** 42.22N 73.17W
Lens France **19** 50.26N 2.50E
Lenti Hungary **31** 46.37N 16.33E
Lentini Italy **33** 37.17N 15.00E
Lenvik Norway **40** 69.22N 18.10E
Léo Burkina **76** 11.05N 2.06W
Leoben Austria **36** 47.23N 15.06E
Leominster U.K. **13** 52.15N 2.43W
Leominster U.S.A. **115** 42.32N 71.45W
Léon France **20** 43.53N 1.18W
León Mexico **116** 21.10N101.42W
León *d.* Mexico **111** 25.00N100.20W
León Nicaragua **117** 12.24N 86.52W
León Spain **26** 42.36N 5.34W
Leon U.S.A. **110** 40.44N 93.45W
León, Montes de *mts.* Spain **26** 42.30N 6.15W
Leonardtown U.S.A. **115** 38.17N 76.38W
Leonardville Namibia **80** 23.21S 18.47E
Leonárisson Cyprus **66** 35.28N 34.08E
Leonberg Germany **39** 48.48N 9.01E
Leondári Greece **35** 39.11N 22.08E
Leonforte Italy **33** 37.39N 14.24E
Leongatha Australia **93** 38.29S145.57E
Leonídhion Greece **35** 37.10N 22.52E
Leonora Australia **89** 28.54S121.20E
Leopoldina Brazil **126** 21.30S 42.38W
Leopoldsburg Belgium **16** 51.08N 5.13E
Leovo U.S.S.R. **37** 46.29N 28.12E
Le Palais France **18** 47.21N 3.09W
Lepe Spain **27** 37.15N 7.12W
Lepel U.S.S.R. **44** 54.48N 28.40E
Le Pellerin France **18** 47.12N 1.45W
Leping China **55** 28.58N117.08E
L'Epiphanie Canada **105** 45.51N 73.30W
Le Pont-de-Beauvoisin France **21** 45.32N 5.40E
Lepontine, Alpi *mts.* Switz. **39** 46.20N 8.37E
Le Puy France **20** 45.02N 3.53E
Lequeitio Spain **26** 43.22N 2.30W
Le Quesnoy France **19** 50.15N 3.38E
Lerbäck Sweden **43** 58.56N 15.02E
Lercara Friddi Italy **32** 37.45N 13.36E
Léré Chad **77** 9.41N 14.17E
Lerici Italy **30** 44.04N 9.55E
Lérida *see* Lleida Spain **25**
Lérida *see* Lleida *d.* Spain **25**
Lerma Spain **26** 42.02N 3.45W
Le Rochefoucauld France **20** 45.45N 0.23E
Léros Greece **35** 37.10N 26.50E
Leross Canada **101** 51.17N103.53W
Le Roy Kans. U.S.A. **111** 38.05N 95.38W
Le Roy Mich. U.S.A. **112** 44.03N 85.29W
Le Roy N.Y. U.S.A. **114** 42.59N 77.59W
Lerwick U.K. **14** 60.09N 1.09W
Les Aix-d'Angillon France **19** 47.12N 2.34E
Les Andelys France **18** 49.15N 1.25E
Les Borges Blanques Spain **25** 41.31N 0.52E
Les Cayes Haiti **117** 18.15N 73.46W
Leschenault, C. Australia **89** 31.50S115.23E
Les Échelles France **21** 45.26N 5.45E
Les Ecrins *mtn.* France **21** 44.50N 6.20E
Les Essarts France **18** 46.46N 1.14W
Lesh Albania **34** 41.46N 19.39E
Leshan China **55** 29.30N103.45E
Les Herbiers France **18** 46.52N 1.01W
Leshukonskoye U.S.S.R. **44** 64.55N 45.50E
Lesina, Lago di *l.* Italy **31** 41.53N 15.26E
Lesjaskog Norway **41** 62.15N 8.22E
Lesjöfors Sweden **43** 59.59N 14.11E
Leskovac Yugo. **34** 42.59N 21.57E
Leslie Ark. U.S.A. **111** 35.50N 92.34W
Leslie Mich. U.S.A. **104** 42.27N 84.26W
Lešnica Yugo. **31** 44.39N 19.19E
Lesotho Africa **80** 29.00S 28.00E
Lesozavodsk U.S.S.R. **53** 45.30N133.29E
Les Pieux France **18** 49.31N 1.48W
Les Riceys France **19** 47.59N 4.22E
Les Sables d'Olonne France **18** 46.30N 1.47W
Lessay France **18** 49.13N 1.32W
Lessebo Sweden **43** 56.45N 15.16E
Lesser Antilles *is.* C. America **117** 13.00N 65.00W
Lesser Slave L. Canada **100** 55.30N115.25W
Lesser Sunda Is. *see* Nusa Tenggara *is.* Indonesia **58**
Lessines Belgium **16** 50.43N 3.50E
Lesti *r.* Finland **40** 64.04N 23.38E
Le Sueur U.S.A. **110** 44.27N 93.54W
Les Vans France **21** 44.24N 4.08E
Lésvos *i.* Greece **35** 39.10N 25.50E
Leszno Poland **36** 51.51N 16.35E
Letchworth U.K. **13** 51.58N 0.13W
Letchworth State Park U.S.A. **114** 42.42N 77.56W
Letenye Hungary **31** 46.26N 16.43E
Lethbridge Canada **98** 49.43N112.48W
Lethem Guyana **122** 3.18N 59.46W
Le Thillot France **19** 47.53N 6.46E
Leti, Kepulauan *is.* Indonesia **59** 8.20S128.00E
Letiahau *r.* Botswana **80** 21.16S 24.00E
Leticia Colombia **122** 4.09S 69.57W
Leting China **54** 39.26N118.56E
Letohatchee U.S.A. **113** 32.08N 86.30W
Le Trayas France **21** 43.28N 6.55E
Le Tréport France **18** 50.04N 1.22E
Letterkenny Rep. of Ire. **15** 54.56N 7.45W
Leucate, Étang de *b.* France **20** 42.51N 3.00E
Leuk Switz. **39** 46.19N 7.38E
Leuser *mtn.* Indonesia **58** 3.50N 97.10E
Leutkirch Germany **39** 47.49N 10.01E
Leuven Belgium **16** 50.53N 4.45E

Leuze to **Lockerbie**

Leuze Hainaut Belgium **16** 50.36N 3.37E
Leuze Namur Belgium **16** 50.34N 4.53E
Levack Canada **104** 46.38N 81.23W
Levádhia Greece **35** 38.27N 22.54E
Levanger Norway **40** 63.45N 11.19E
Levanto Italy **30** 44.10N 9.38E
Levanzo, Isola di *i.* Italy **32** 38.00N 12.20E
Levelland U.S.A. **111** 33.35N102.23W
Lévêque, C. Australia **88** 16.25S123.00E
Le Verdon France **20** 45.33N 1.04W
Leverkusen Germany **38** 51.03N 6.59E
Levice Czech. **37** 48.13N 18.37E
Levier France **19** 46.57N 6.08E
Levin New Zealand **86** 40.37S175.18E
Lévis Canada **105** 46.48N 71.11W
Levittown U.S.A. **115** 40.41N 73.31W
Lévka Cyprus **66** 35.06N 32.51E
Lévka Óri *mtn.* Greece **35** 35.18N 24.01E
Levkás Greece **35** 38.48N 20.43E
Levkás *i.* Greece **35** 38.39N 20.27E
Levkimni Greece **34** 39.25N 20.04E
Levkosía Cyprus **66** 35.11N 33.23E
Levroux France **19** 46.59N 1.37E
Levski Bulgaria **34** 43.21N 25.10E
Lewes U.K. **13** 50.53N 0.02E
Lewes U.S.A. **115** 38.47N 75.08W
Lewis *i.* U.K. **14** 58.10N 6.40W
Lewisburg U.S.A. **114** 40.58N 76.53W
Lewis Pass *f.* New Zealand **86** 42.30S172.15E
Lewisporte Canada **103** 49.15N 55.04W
Lewis Range *mts.* U.S.A. **108** 48.30N113.15W
Lewiston Idaho U.S.A. **108** 46.25N117.01W
Lewiston Maine U.S.A. **112** 44.06N 70.13W
Lewiston Mich. U.S.A. **104** 44.53N 84.18W
Lewistown Mont. U.S.A. **108** 47.04N109.26W
Lewistown Penn. U.S.A. **114** 40.36N 77.31W
Lexington Ky. U.S.A. **113** 38.03N 84.30W
Lexington Mich. U.S.A. **114** 43.16N 82.32W
Lexington Miss. U.S.A. **111** 33.07N 90.03W
Lexington Nebr. U.S.A. **110** 40.47N 99.45W
Lexington Oreg. U.S.A. **108** 45.27N119.41W
Leyburn U.K. **12** 54.19N 1.50W
Leydsdorp R.S.A. **80** 23.59S 30.32E
Leyre *r.* France **20** 44.39N 1.01W
Leyte *i.* Phil. **59** 10.40N124.50E
Lezignan France **20** 43.12N 2.46E
Lhari China **63** 30.47N 93.24E
Lhasa China **63** 29.39N 91.06E
Lhasa He *r.* China **63** 29.21N 90.45E
Lhazê China **63** 29.10N 87.45E
Lhazhong China **63** 32.02N 86.34E
Lhokseumawe Indonesia **58** 5.09N 97.09E
Lhozhag China **63** 28.23N 90.49E
Lhuntsi Dzong Bhutan **63** 27.39N 91.09E
Lhünzê China **63** 28.26N 92.27E
Lhünzhub China **63** 30.00N 91.12E
Li Thailand **56** 17.50N 98.55E
Liancheng China **55** 25.47N116.48E
Liangcheng China **54** 40.31N112.29E
Liangdang China **54** 33.59N106.23E
Lianjiang Fujian China **55** 26.10N119.33E
Lianjiang Guangdong China **55** 21.33N110.19E
Lianshan China **55** 24.37N112.02E
Lianshui China **54** 33.46N119.18E
Lian Xian China **55** 24.52N112.27E
Lianyungang China **54** 34.36N119.10E
Liaocheng China **54** 36.25N115.58E
Liaodong Bandao *pen.* China **54** 40.00N122.20E
Liaodong Wan *b.* China **54** 40.00N121.00E
Liao He *r.* China **54** 40.40N122.20E
Liaoning *d.* China **54** 41.40N121.20E
Liaoyang China **54** 41.17N123.13E
Liaoyuan China **54** 42.50N125.08E
Liapádhes Greece **34** 39.40N 19.44E
Liard *r.* Canada **100** 61.51N121.18W
Liāri Pakistan **62** 25.41N 66.29E
Liart France **19** 49.46N 4.20E
Libby U.S.A. **108** 48.23N115.33W
Libenge Zaïre **78** 3.39N 18.39E
Liberal U.S.A. **111** 37.02N100.55W
Liberdade Brazil **126** 22.01S 44.22W
Liberec Czech. **36** 50.48N 15.05E
Liberia Africa **76** 6.30N 9.30W
Liberia Costa Rica **117** 10.39N 85.28W
Liberty N.Y. U.S.A. **115** 41.48N 74.45W
Liberty Tex. U.S.A. **111** 30.03N 94.47W
Lībīyah, Aş Şaḩrā' al *des.* Africa **64** 24.00N 25.30E
Libo China **55** 25.25N107.53E
Libourne France **20** 44.55N 0.14W
Libramont Belgium **16** 49.56N 5.22E
Librazhd Albania **34** 41.12N 20.22E
Libreville Gabon **78** 0.25N 9.30E
Libya Africa **75** 26.30N 17.00E
Libyan Desert *see* Lībīyah, Aş Şaḩrā' al *a-' al* Africa **64**
Libyan Plateau *see* Aḑ Diffah *f.* Africa **64**
Licantén Chile **125** 34.59S 72.00W
Licata Italy **32** 37.05N 13.56E
Lich Germany **38** 50.33N 8.50E
Lichfield U.K. **13** 52.40N 1.50W
Lichinga Mozambique **79** 13.09S 35.17E
Lichtenburg R.S.A. **80** 26.08S 26.09E
Lichtenfels Germany **38** 50.09N 11.04E
Lichtenvoorde Neth. **16** 51.59N 6.32E
Lichuan Hubei China **55** 30.18N108.51E
Lichuan Jiangxi China **55** 27.22N116.59E
Lickdale U.S.A. **115** 40.28N 76.31W
Lickershamn Sweden **43** 57.50N 18.31E
Licko Polje *f.* Yugo. **31** 44.35N 15.25E
Lida U.S.A. **108** 37.29N117.29W
Lida U.S.S.R. **37** 53.50N 25.19E
Lidan *r.* Sweden **43** 58.31N 13.09E
Lidhorikion Greece **35** 38.28N 22.12E
Lidingö Sweden **43** 59.22N 18.08E
Lidköping Sweden **43** 58.30N 13.10E
Liechtenstein Europe **39** 47.09N 9.32E
Liège Belgium **16** 50.38N 5.35E
Liège *d.* Belgium **16** 50.32N 5.35E
Lien-Huong Vietnam **56** 11.13N108.48E
Lienz Austria **30** 46.50N 12.47E
Liepāja U.S.S.R. **41** 56.31N 21.01E
Lier Belgium **16** 51.08N 4.35E
Lierneux Belgium **16** 50.18N 5.50E
Liestal Switz. **39** 47.29N 7.44E
Lieşti Romania **37** 45.38N 27.32E
Lietariegos, Puerto de *pass* Spain **26** 43.00N 6.25W
Liévin France **19** 50.25N 2.46E
Lièvre, Rivière du *r.* Canada **105** 45.31N 75.26W
Liffey *r.* Rep. of Ire. **15** 53.21N 6.14W
Liffré France **18** 48.13N 1.30W
Lifjell *mtn.* Norway **42** 59.30N 8.52E
Lifou, Île *i.* N. Cal. **84** 20.53S167.13E
Lightning Ridge *town* Australia **93** 29.27S148.00E
Lignières France **19** 46.45N 2.11E
Ligny-en-Barrois France **19** 48.41N 5.20E
Ligoúrion Greece **35** 37.37N 23.02E
Ligueil France **18** 47.03N 0.49E
Liguria *d.* Italy **30** 44.30N 8.50E
Ligurian Sea Med. Sea **30** 43.40N 9.00E
Lihou Reef and Cays Australia **90** 17.25S151.40E
Lihue Hawaiian Is. **85** 21.59N159.23W
Lihula U.S.S.R. **41** 58.41N 23.50E
Lijiang China **61** 26.50N100.15E
Lijin China **54** 37.29N118.16E
Likasi Zaïre **78** 10.58S 26.50E
Likati Zaïre **78** 3.21N 23.53E
Liknes Norway **42** 58.19N 6.59E
Likona *r.* Congo **78** 0.11N 16.25E
Likouala *r.* Congo **78** 0.51S 17.17E
Liku Niue **84** 19.03S169.48W
L'Ile Bouchard France **18** 47.07N 0.25E
L'Ile Rousse France **21** 42.38N 8.56E
Lilla Edet Sweden **43** 58.08N 12.08E
Lille France **19** 50.38N 3.04E
Lille Baelt *str.* Denmark **42** 55.20N 9.45E
Lillebonne France **18** 49.31N 0.33E
Lillehammer Norway **41** 61.08N 10.30E
Lillers France **19** 50.34N 2.29E
Lillesand Norway **42** 58.15N 8.24E
Lilleström Norway **42** 59.57N 11.05E
Lillhärdal Sweden **41** 61.51N 14.04E
Lillo Spain **27** 39.43N 3.18W
Lillooet Canada **100** 50.42N121.56W
Lillooet *r.* Canada **100** 49.15N121.57W
Lilongwe Malaŵi **79** 13.58S 33.49E
Liloy Phil. **59** 8.08N122.40E
Lilydale Australia **92** 32.58S139.59E
Lim *r.* Yugo. **31** 43.45N 19.13E
Lima Peru **122** 12.06S 77.03W
Lima *r.* Portugal **26** 41.41N 8.50W
Lima Sweden **41** 60.56N 13.26E
Lima Mont. U.S.A. **108** 44.38N112.36W
Lima Ohio U.S.A. **112** 40.43N 84.06W
Limassol *see* Lemesós Cyprus **66**
Limavady U.K. **15** 55.03N 6.57W
Limay *r.* Argentina **125** 39.02S 68.07W
Limbang Malaysia **58** 4.50N115.00E
Limbara, Monte *mtn.* Italy **32** 40.51N 9.11E
Limbdi India **62** 22.34N 71.48E
Limbe Cameroon **77** 4.01N 9.12E
Limbourg Belgium **16** 50.36N 5.57E
Limburg *d.* Belgium **16** 50.36N 5.57E
Limburg *d.* Neth. **16** 51.15N 5.45E
Limburg an der Lahn Germany **39** 50.23N 8.04E
Limeira Brazil **126** 22.34S 47.25W
Limerick Rep. of Ire. **15** 52.40N 8.37W
Limerick *d.* Rep. of Ire. **15** 52.40N 8.37W
Limfjorden *str.* Denmark **42** 56.55N 9.10E
Liminka Finland **40** 64.49N 25.24E
Limmared Sweden **43** 57.32N 13.21E
Limmen Bight Australia **90** 14.45S135.40E
Límni Greece **35** 38.43N 23.18E
Límnos *i.* Greece **34** 39.54N 25.21E
Limoges France **20** 45.50N 1.16E
Limogne France **20** 44.24N 1.46E
Limón Costa Rica **117** 10.00N 83.01W
Limon U.S.A. **108** 39.16N103.41W
Limone Piemonte Italy **30** 44.12N 7.34E
Limousin *d.* France **20** 45.45N 1.30E
Limousin, Plateaux du *f.* France **20** 45.30N 1.15E
Limoux France **20** 43.04N 2.14E
Limpopo *r.* Mozambique **81** 25.14S 33.33E
Līnah Saudi Arabia **65** 28.48N 43.45E
Linakhamari U.S.S.R. **44** 69.39N 31.21E
Linares Chile **125** 35.51S 71.36W
Linares Mexico **111** 24.52N 99.34W
Linares Spain **26** 38.05N 3.38W
Linariá Greece **35** 38.50N 24.32E
Lincang China **52** 24.00N100.10E
Lincheng China **54** 37.26N114.34E
Lincoln Argentina **125** 34.55S 61.30W
Lincoln New Zealand **86** 43.38S172.29E
Lincoln U.K. **12** 53.14N 0.32W
Lincoln Ill. U.S.A. **110** 40.10N 89.21W
Lincoln Mich. U.S.A. **104** 44.41N 83.25W
Lincoln Nebr. U.S.A. **110** 40.48N 96.42W
Lincoln N.H. U.S.A. **105** 44.03N 71.40W
Lincoln City U.S.A. **108** 44.59N124.00W
Lincoln Park *town* U.S.A. **114** 42.14N 83.09W
Lincoln Sea Greenland **128** 82.00N 55.00W
Lincolnshire *d.* U.K. **12** 53.14N 0.32W
Lincoln Wolds *hills* U.K. **12** 53.22N 0.08W
Lindau Germany **39** 47.33N 9.41E
Lindeman Group *is.* Australia **90** 20.28S149.05E
Linden Ala. U.S.A. **111** 32.18N 87.47W
Linden Penn. U.S.A. **114** 41.14N 77.08W
Lindenhurst U.S.A. **115** 40.41N 73.22W
Linderödsåsen *hills* Sweden **43** 55.44N 13.06E
Lindesberg Sweden **43** 59.35N 15.15E
Lindesnes *c.* Norway **42** 58.00N 7.02E
Líndhos Greece **35** 36.06N 28.04E
Líndhos *site* Greece **35** 36.06N 28.05E
Lindi Tanzania **79** 10.00S 39.41E
Lindi *r.* Zaïre **78** 0.30N 25.06E
Lindome Sweden **43** 57.34N 12.05E
Lindsay Canada **104** 44.21N 78.44W
Lindsay U.S.A. **109** 36.12N119.05W
Line Is. Pacific Oc. **85** 3.00S155.00W
Linesville U.S.A. **114** 41.39N 80.26W
Linfen China **54** 36.07N111.34E
Lingao China **55** 19.54N109.40E
Lingayen Phil. **59** 16.02N120.14E
Lingbo Sweden **41** 61.03N 16.41E
Lingchuan China **55** 25.25N110.20E
Lingen Germany **38** 52.31N 7.19E
Lingga *i.* Indonesia **58** 0.20S104.30E
Lingling China **55** 26.12N111.30E
Lingshan China **55** 22.17N109.27E
Lingshui China **55** 18.31N110.00E
Linguère Senegal **76** 15.22N 15.11W
Linhai China **55** 28.49N121.08E
Linhe China **54** 40.50N107.30E
Linköping Sweden **43** 58.25N 15.37E
Linnhe, Loch U.K. **14** 56.35N 5.25W
Linosa *i.* Italy **28** 35.52N 12.50E
Linquan China **54** 33.03N115.17E
Linru China **54** 34.12N112.45E
Lins Brazil **126** 21.40S 49.44W
Linshui China **55** 30.18N106.55E
Lintan China **54** 34.33N103.40E
Lintao China **54** 35.20N104.00E
Linthal Switz. **39** 46.55N 9.00E
Linton Canada **105** 47.16N 72.15W
Linton Ind. U.S.A. **112** 39.01N 87.10W
Linton N.Dak. U.S.A. **110** 46.16N100.14W
Lintong China **54** 34.24N109.13E
Lintorf Germany **38** 51.20N 6.49E
Linwood U.S.A. **104** 43.44N 83.59W
Linxe France **20** 43.56N 1.10W
Linxi China **54** 43.31N118.02E
Linxia China **54** 35.30N103.10E
Lin Xian China **54** 37.57N110.57E
Linyi Shandong China **54** 35.08N118.20E
Linyi Shanxi China **54** 35.12N110.45E
Linz Austria **39** 48.18N 14.18E
Linz Germany **38** 50.34N 7.17E
Linzgau *f.* Germany **39** 47.50N 9.20E
Lion, Golfe du *g.* France **20** 43.00N 4.00E
Lions, G. of *see* Lion, Golfe du *g.* France **20**
Lion's Head *town* Canada **104** 44.59N 81.15W
Liouesso Congo **78** 1.12N 15.47E
Lipari, Isola *i.* Italy **33** 38.30N 14.57E
Lipéité Congo **78** 3.09N 17.22E
Lipetsk U.S.S.R. **44** 52.37N 39.36E
Liphook U.K. **13** 51.05N 0.49W
Liping China **55** 26.16N109.08E
Lipkany U.S.S.R. **37** 48.18N 26.48E
Lipova Romania **37** 46.05N 21.40E
Lipovets U.S.S.R. **37** 49.11N 29.01E
Lippe *r.* Germany **38** 51.39N 6.38E
Lippstadt Germany **38** 51.40N 8.19E
Lipsoí *i.* Greece **35** 37.19N 26.50E
Liptovský Mikuláš Czech. **37** 49.06N 19.37E
Liptrap, C. Australia **93** 38.53S145.55E
Lipu China **55** 24.28N110.12E
Lira Uganda **79** 2.15N 32.55E
Liranga Congo **78** 0.43S 17.32E
Liri *r.* Italy **32** 41.25N 13.52E
Liria Spain **25** 39.38N 0.36W
Liria Sudan **73** 4.38N 32.05E
Lisala Zaïre **78** 2.13N 21.37E
Lisboa Portugal **27** 38.43N 9.08W
Lisboa *d.* Portugal **27** 39.05N 9.00W
Lisbon *see* Lisboa Portugal **27**
Lisbon N.Dak. U.S.A. **110** 46.27N 97.41W
Lisbon Ohio U.S.A. **114** 40.47N 80.46W
Lisburn U.K. **15** 54.30N 6.03W
Lisburne, C. U.S.A. **98** 69.00N165.50W
Liscannor B. Rep. of Ire. **15** 52.55N 9.24W
Liscia *r.* Italy **32** 41.05N 9.17E
Lishi China **54** 37.30N111.07E
Lishui China **55** 28.28N119.59E
Lisianski *i.* Hawaiian Is. **84** 26.04N173.58W
Lisichansk U.S.S.R. **45** 48.53N 38.25E
Lisieux France **18** 49.09N 0.14E
Liskeard U.K. **13** 50.27N 4.29W
L'Isle Jourdain H.-Gar. France **20** 43.37N 1.05E
L'Isle Jourdain Poit.-Char. France **18** 46.14N 0.41E
L'Isle-sur-le-Doubs France **19** 47.27N 6.35E
Lismore N.S.W. Australia **93** 28.48S153.17E
Lismore Vic. Australia **92** 37.58S143.22E
Lismore Rep. of Ire. **15** 52.08N 7.57W
Liss U.K. **13** 51.03N 0.53W
Lisse Neth. **16** 52.18N 4.33E
Lista *f.* Norway **42** 58.07N 6.40E
Lištica Yugo. **31** 43.23N 17.36E
Listowel Canada **104** 43.44N 80.57W
Listowel Rep. of Ire. **15** 52.27N 9.30W
Litang China **55** 23.09N109.09E
Litang Qu *r.* China **61** 28.09N101.30E
Litchfield Conn. U.S.A. **115** 41.45N 73.11W
Litchfield Ill. U.S.A. **110** 39.11N 89.40W
Litchfield Minn. U.S.A. **110** 45.08N 94.31W
Litchfield Nebr. U.S.A. **110** 41.09N 99.09W
Lithgow Australia **93** 33.30S150.09E
Líthinon, Ákra *c.* Greece **35** 34.55N 24.44E
Lititz U.S.A. **115** 40.09N 76.18W
Litókhoron Greece **34** 40.06N 22.30E
Litoměřice Czech. **38** 50.35N 14.09E
Litovskaya S.S.R. *d.* U.S.S.R. **37** 54.30N 24.00E
Little Andaman *i.* India **56** 10.40N 92.24E
Little Bahama Bank *f.* Bahamas **113** 26.40N 78.00W
Little Belt Mts. U.S.A. **108** 46.45N110.35W
Little Cayman *i.* Cayman Is. **117** 19.40N 80.00W
Little Coco *i.* Burma **56** 13.59N 93.12E
Little Colorado *r.* U.S.A. **109** 36.11N111.48W
Little Current *r.* Canada **102** 50.00N 84.35W
Little Current *town* Canada **104** 45.58N 81.56W
Little Falls *town* Minn. U.S.A. **110** 45.59N 94.21W
Little Falls *town* N.Y. U.S.A. **115** 43.03N 74.52W
Littlefield U.S.A. **111** 33.55N102.20W
Little Grand Rapids *town* Canada **101** 52.05N 95.29W
Littlehampton U.K. **13** 50.48N 0.32W
Little Inagua *i.* Bahamas **117** 21.30N 73.00W
Little Kanawha *r.* U.S.A. **114** 39.16N 81.34W
Little Karoo *f.* R.S.A. **80** 33.40S 21.40E
Little Lake *town* U.S.A. **109** 35.58N117.53W
Little Mecatina *r.* Canada **103** 50.28N 59.35W
Little Missouri *r.* U.S.A. **110** 47.30N102.25W
Little Nicobar *i.* India **61** 7.20N 93.40E
Little Ouse *r.* U.K. **13** 52.34N 0.20E
Little Quill L. Canada **101** 51.55N104.05W
Little Rann of Kachchh *f.* India **62** 23.25N 71.30E
Little Rock *town* U.S.A. **111** 34.44N 92.15W
Little Smoky *r.* Canada **100** 55.42N117.38W
Littlestown U.S.A. **114** 39.45N 77.05W
Littleton Colo. U.S.A. **108** 39.37N105.01W
Littleton N.H. U.S.A. **105** 44.18N 71.46W
Little Topar Australia **92** 31.44S142.14E
Little Valley *town* U.S.A. **114** 42.15N 78.48W
Little White *r.* Canada **104** 46.21N 83.20W
Litvínov Czech. **38** 50.37N 13.36E
Liuba China **54** 33.37N106.55E
Liucheng China **55** 24.39N109.14E
Liuchong He *r.* China **55** 26.50N106.04E
Liuli Tanzania **79** 11.07S 34.34E
Liulin China **54** 37.26N110.52E
Liuzhou China **55** 24.19N109.12E
Livadherón Greece **34** 40.02N 21.57E
Livanátai Greece **35** 38.42N 23.03E
Livanjsko Polje *f.* Yugo. **31** 44.00N 16.40E
Livarot France **18** 49.01N 0.09E
Lively Canada **104** 46.26N 81.09W
Live Oak U.S.A. **113** 30.19N 82.59W
Livermore, Mt. U.S.A. **109** 30.39N104.11W
Liverpool Australia **93** 33.57S150.52E
Liverpool Canada **103** 44.02N 64.43W
Liverpool U.K. **12** 53.25N 3.00W
Liverpool U.S.A. **115** 43.06N 76.13W
Liverpool, C. Canada **99** 73.38N 78.06W
Liverpool B. U.K. **12** 53.30N 3.10W
Liverpool Range *mts.* Australia **93** 31.45S150.45E
Livigno Italy **30** 46.32N 10.04E
Livingston U.K. **14** 55.54N 3.31W
Livingston Mont. U.S.A. **108** 45.40N110.34W
Livingston Tex. U.S.A. **111** 30.43N 94.56W
Livingstone *see* Maramba Zambia **80**
Livingstonia Malaŵi **79** 10.35S 34.10E
Livno Yugo. **31** 43.50N 17.01E
Livo *r.* Finland **40** 65.24N 26.48E
Livonia Mich. U.S.A. **104** 42.25N 83.23W
Livonia N.Y. U.S.A. **114** 42.49N 77.40W
Livorno Italy **30** 43.33N 10.19E
Liwale Tanzania **79** 9.47S 38.00E
Liwan Sudan **73** 4.55N 35.41E
Li Xian Gansu China **54** 34.11N105.02E
Li Xian Hunan China **55** 29.38N111.45E
Lixoúrion Greece **35** 38.14N 20.24E
Liyujiang China **55** 25.59N113.12E
Lizard U.K. **13** 49.58N 5.12W
Lizard I. Australia **90** 14.39S145.28E
Lizard Pt. U.K. **13** 49.57N 5.15W
Lizarra *see* Estella Spain **26**
Lizemores U.S.A. **114** 38.20N 81.12W
Ljan Norway **42** 59.51N 10.48E
Ljubija Yugo. **31** 44.56N 16.37E
Ljubinje Yugo. **31** 42.57N 18.05E
Ljubljana Yugo. **31** 46.03N 14.31E
Ljubovija Yugo. **31** 44.11N 19.22E
Ljubški Yugo. **31** 43.12N 17.33E
Ljugarn Sweden **43** 57.19N 18.42E
Ljungan *r.* Sweden **41** 62.19N 17.23E
Ljungby Sweden **43** 56.50N 13.56E
Ljungbyholm Sweden **43** 56.38N 16.10E
Ljungdalen Sweden **40** 62.54N 12.45E
Ljungsbro Sweden **43** 58.31N 15.30E
Ljusdal Sweden **41** 61.50N 16.05E
Ljusnan *r.* Sweden **41** 61.12N 17.08E
Ljusne Sweden **41** 61.13N 17.08E
Ljusterö *i.* Sweden **43** 59.31N 18.37E
Ljutomer Yugo. **31** 46.31N 16.12E
Llança Spain **25** 42.22N 3.09E
Llandeilo U.K. **13** 51.54N 4.00W
Llandovery U.K. **13** 51.59N 3.49W
Llandrindod Wells U.K. **13** 52.15N 3.23W
Llandudno U.K. **12** 53.19N 3.49W
Llanelli U.K. **13** 51.41N 4.11W
Llanes Spain **26** 43.25N 4.45W
Llangadfan U.K. **13** 52.41N 3.28W
Llangollen U.K. **12** 52.58N 3.10W
Llanidloes U.K. **13** 52.28N 3.31W
Llanos *f.* S. America **122** 7.30N 70.00W
Llanwrtyd Wells U.K. **13** 52.06N 3.39W
Lleida Spain **25** 41.37N 0.37E
Lleida *d.* Spain **25** 42.00N 1.10E
Llentrisca, Cabo de *c.* Spain **25** 38.51N 1.14E
Llerena Spain **26** 38.14N 6.01W
Llobregat *r.* Spain **25** 41.19N 2.09E
Lloret de Mar Spain **25** 41.42N 2.53E
Lloydminster Canada **101** 53.17N110.00W
Lluchmayor Spain **25** 39.29N 2.54E
Loange *r.* Zaïre **78** 4.18S 20.05E
Lobatse Botswana **80** 25.12S 25.39E
Löbau Germany **38** 51.05N 14.40E
Lobaye *r.* C.A.R. **77** 3.40N 18.35E
Lobería Argentina **125** 38.08S 58.48W
Lobito Angola **78** 12.20S 13.34E
Lobonäs Sweden **41** 61.33N 15.20E
Lobos Argentina **125** 35.10S 59.05W
Locarno Switz. **39** 46.10N 8.48E
Lochboisdale *town* U.K. **14** 57.09N 7.19W
Lochem Neth. **16** 52.10N 6.25E
Loches France **18** 47.08N 1.00E
Lochgilphead U.K. **14** 56.02N 5.26W
Lochinver U.K. **14** 58.09N 5.15W
Lochmaddy *town* U.K. **14** 57.36N 7.10W
Lochnagar *mtn.* U.K. **14** 56.57N 3.15W
Lochranza U.K. **14** 55.42N 5.18W
Loch Raven Resr. U.S.A. **115** 39.27N 76.36W
Lochy, Loch U.K. **14** 56.58N 4.55W
Lock Australia **92** 33.34S135.46E
Lockeport Canada **103** 43.42N 65.07W
Lockerbie U.K. **14** 55.07N 3.21W

Lockhart to **Luleå**

Lockhart Australia **93** 35.16S146.42E
Lockhart U.S.A. **111** 29.53N 97.41W
Lockhart, L. Australia **89** 33.27S119.00E
Lockhart River *town* Australia **90** 12.58S143.29E
Lock Haven U.S.A. **114** 41.08N 77.27W
Löcknitz Germany **38** 53.27N 14.12E
Lockport U.S.A. **114** 43.10N 78.42W
Loc Ninh Vietnam **56** 11.51N106.35E
Locri Italy **33** 38.14N 16.16E
Lod Israel **67** 31.57N 34.54E
Lodalskåpa *mtn.* Norway **41** 61.47N 7.13E
Loddon *r.* Australia **92** 35.40S143.59E
Lodève France **20** 43.43N 3.19E
Lodeynoye Pole U.S.S.R. **44** 60.43N 33.30E
Lodge Grass U.S.A. **108** 45.19N107.22W
Lodhrān Pakistan **62** 29.32N 71.38E
Lodi Italy **30** 45.19N 9.30E
Lodi Calif. U.S.A. **108** 38.08N121.16W
Lodi Ohio U.S.A. **114** 41.03N 82.01W
Lodja Zaïre **78** 3.29S 23.33E
Lodosa Spain **25** 42.25N 2.05W
Lodwar Kenya **79** 3.06N 35.38E
Łódź Poland **37** 51.49N 19.28E
Loei Thailand **56** 17.32N101.34E
Lofer Austria **39** 47.35N 12.41E
Lofoten *is.* Norway **8** 68.15N 13.50E
Lofoten Vesterålen *is.* Norway **40** 68.15N 13.50E
Log U.S.S.R. **45** 49.28N 43.51E
Loga Niger **77** 13.40N 3.15E
Logan N.Mex. U.S.A. **109** 35.22N103.25W
Logan Ohio U.S.A. **114** 39.32N 82.25W
Logan Utah U.S.A. **108** 41.44N111.50W
Logan, Mt. Canada **100** 60.34N140.24W
Logansport U.S.A. **112** 40.45N 86.25W
Loganton U.S.A. **114** 41.02N 77.18W
Loge *r.* Angola **78** 7.52S 13.08E
Logone *r.* Cameroon/Chad **77** 12.10N 15.00E
Logone Occidental *d.* Chad **77** 8.40N 15.50E
Logone Oriental *d.* Chad **77** 8.10N 16.00E
Logoysk U.S.S.R. **37** 54.08N 27.42E
Logroño Spain **25** 42.28N 2.27W
Logrosán Spain **27** 39.20N 5.29W
Løgstør Denmark **42** 56.58N 9.15E
Løgumkloster Denmark **42** 55.03N 8.57E
Lohārdaga India **63** 23.26N 84.41E
Lohāru India **62** 28.27N 75.49E
Lohja Finland **41** 60.15N 24.05E
Lohjanjärvi *l.* Finland **41** 60.15N 23.55E
Lohne Germany **38** 52.42N 8.12E
Lohr Germany **39** 50.00N 9.34E
Loikaw Burma **56** 19.40N 97.17E
Loimaa Finland **41** 60.51N 23.03E
Loir *r.* France **18** 47.33N 0.32W
Loire *d.* France **21** 45.30N 4.00E
Loire *r.* France **18** 47.16N 2.11W
Loire-Atlantique *d.* France **18** 47.20N 1.35W
Loiret *d.* France **19** 47.55N 2.20E
Loir-et-Cher *d.* France **18** 47.30N 1.30E
Loja Ecuador **122** 3.59S 79.16W
Loja Spain **27** 37.10N 4.09W
Loka Sudan **73** 4.16N 31.01E
Loka Zaïre **78** 0.20N 17.57E
Løken Norway **42** 59.48N 11.29E
Loken tekojärvi *resr.* Finland **40** 67.55N 27.40E
Lokeren Belgium **16** 51.06N 3.59E
Loket Czech. **39** 50.09N 12.43E
Lokichar Kenya **79** 2.23N 35.39E
Lokitaung Kenya **79** 4.15N 35.45E
Lokka Finland **40** 67.49N 27.44E
Løkken Denmark **42** 57.22N 9.43E
Løkken Norway **40** 63.06N 9.43E
Loknya U.S.S.R. **44** 56.49N 30.00E
Lokoja Nigeria **77** 7.49N 6.44E
Lokolo *r.* Zaïre **78** 0.45S 19.36E
Lokoro *r.* Zaïre **78** 1.40S 18.29E
Lol *r.* Sudan **73** 9.11N 29.12E
Lolland *i.* Denmark **41** 54.46N 11.30E
Lom Bulgaria **34** 43.49N 23.14E
Lom Norway **41** 61.50N 8.33E
Loma U.S.A. **108** 47.57N110.30W
Lomami *r.* Zaïre **78** 0.45N 24.10E
Lomas de Zamora Argentina **125** 34.46S 58.24W
Lombardia *d.* Italy **30** 45.45N 9.00E
Lombok *i.* Indonesia **58** 8.30S116.20E
Lombok, Selat *str.* Indonesia **59** 8.38S115.40E
Lomé Togo **77** 6.10N 1.21E
Lomela Zaïre **78** 2.15S 23.15E
Lomela *r.* Zaïre **78** 0.14S 20.45E
Lomié Cameroon **77** 3.09N 13.35E
Lomme France **19** 50.39N 2.59E
Lommel Belgium **16** 51.15N 5.18E
Lomond Canada **100** 50.21N112.39W
Lomond, Loch U.K. **14** 56.07N 4.36W
Lompoc U.S.A. **109** 34.38N120.27W
Łomża Poland **37** 53.11N 22.04E
Lonaconing U.S.A. **114** 39.34N 78.59W
Londinières France **18** 49.50N 1.24E
London Canada **104** 42.59N 81.14W
London Kiribati **85** 1.58N157.28W
London U.K. **13** 51.32N 0.06W
Londonderry U.K. **15** 55.00N 7.21W
Londonderry *d.* U.K. **15** 55.00N 7.00W
Londonderry, C. Australia **88** 13.58S126.55E
Londonderry, Isla *i.* Chile **125** 55.03S 70.40W
Londrina Brazil **124** 23.30S 51.13W
Lonely I. Canada **104** 45.34N 81.29W
Lone Pine U.S.A. **109** 36.36N118.04W
Long, L. Canada **105** 47.05N 74.06W
Longa *r.* Angola **78** 16.15S 19.07E
Longá Greece **35** 36.53N 21.55E
Longa, Proliv *str.* U.S.S.R. **51** 70.00N178.00E
Long'an China **55** 23.11N107.41E
Longarone Italy **30** 46.16N 12.18E
Long Beach *town* Calif. U.S.A. **109** 33.46N118.11W
Long Beach *town* N.Y. U.S.A. **115** 40.35N 73.41W
Long Branch U.S.A. **115** 40.18N 74.00W
Longchamps Belgium **16** 50.05N 5.42E
Longchang China **55** 29.18N105.20E
Longchuan China **55** 24.12N115.25E
Long Creek *town* U.S.A. **108** 44.43N119.06W
Long Eaton U.K. **12** 52.54N 1.16W
Longeau France **19** 47.46N 5.18E
Longford Rep. of Ire. **15** 53.44N 7.48W
Longford *d.* Rep. of Ire. **15** 53.42N 7.45W
Longhua Hebei China **54** 41.17N117.37E
Long I. Bahamas **117** 23.00N 75.00W
Long I. Canada **102** 54.55N 79.30W
Long I. U.S.A. **115** 40.50N 73.00W
Longido Tanzania **79** 2.43S 36.41E
Longiram Indonesia **58** 0.05S115.45E
Long Island Sd. U.S.A. **115** 41.05N 72.58W
Long Jiang *r.* China **55** 24.12N109.30E
Long L. Canada **102** 49.30N 86.50W
Long L. U.S.A. **105** 44.04N 74.20W
Longlac *town* Canada **102** 49.45N 86.25W
Long Lake *town* U.S.A. **105** 43.58N 74.25W
Longli China **55** 26.29N107.59E
Longlin China **55** 24.43N105.26E
Longmeadow U.S.A. **115** 42.03N 72.34W
Longmont U.S.A. **108** 40.10N105.06W
Longnan China **55** 24.54N114.47E
Longnawan Indonesia **58** 1.54N114.53E
Longniddry U.K. **14** 55.58N 2.53W
Long Point B. Canada **104** 42.40N 80.14W
Long Pt. Canada **104** 42.33N 80.04W
Longquan China **55** 28.05N119.07E
Long Range Mts. Nfld. Canada **103** 48.00N 58.30W
Long Range Mts. Nfld. Canada **103** 50.00N 57.00W
Longreach Australia **90** 23.26S144.15E
Long Sault Canada **105** 45.00N 74.55W
Longsheng China **55** 25.59N110.01E
Longs Peak U.S.A. **108** 40.15N105.37W
Longtown U.K. **12** 55.01N 2.58W
Longué France **18** 47.23N 0.06W
Longueuil Canada **105** 45.32N 73.30W
Longuyon France **19** 49.26N 5.36E
Longview Tex. U.S.A. **111** 32.30N 94.44W
Longview Wash. U.S.A. **108** 46.08N122.57W
Longwood St. Helena **127** 15.57S 5.42W
Longwy France **19** 49.31N 5.46E
Longxi China **54** 34.59N104.45E
Long Xian China **54** 34.52N106.50E
Long Xuyen Vietnam **56** 10.23N105.23E
Longyan China **55** 25.10N117.02E
Longzhou China **55** 22.24N106.50E
Lonigo Italy **30** 45.23N 11.23E
Löningen Germany **38** 52.44N 7.46E
Lonja *r.* Yugo. **31** 45.30N 16.40E
Lönsboda Sweden **43** 56.24N 14.19E
Lönsdal Norway **40** 66.46N 15.26E
Lonsdale, L. Australia **92** 37.05S142.15E
Lons-le-Saunier France **19** 46.40N 5.33E
Looc Phil. **59** 12.20N122.05E
Looe U.K. **13** 50.51N 4.26W
Lookout, C. U.S.A. **113** 34.35N 76.32W
Loolmalassin *mtn.* Tanzania **79** 3.00S 35.45E
Loon Lake Mts. U.S.A. **105** 44.35N 74.08W
Loop Head Rep. of Ire. **15** 52.33N 9.56W
Lopari Zaïre **73** 1.15N 19.59E
Lopari *r.* Zaïre **78** 1.20N 20.22E
Lop Buri Thailand **56** 14.49N100.37E
Lopez, C. Gabon **78** 0.36S 8.40E
Lopi Congo **78** 2.57N 16.47E
Lop Nur *l.* China **52** 40.30N 90.30E
Lopphavet *est.* Norway **40** 70.30N 20.00E
Lopydino U.S.S.R. **44** 61.10N 52.02E
Lora, Hāmūn-i- *l.* Pakistan **62** 29.20N 64.50E
Lora Creek *r.* Australia **92** 28.10S135.22E
Lora del Río Spain **27** 37.39N 5.32W
Lorain U.S.A. **114** 41.28N 82.10W
Loralai Pakistan **62** 30.22N 68.36E
Lorca Spain **25** 37.40N 1.42W
Lord Howe I. Pacific Oc. **84** 31.28S159.09E
Lord Howe Rise Pacific Oc. **84** 29.00S162.30E
Lordsburg U.S.A. **109** 32.21N108.43W
Lorena Brazil **126** 22.44S 45.07W
Lorengau P.N.G. **59** 2.01S147.15E
Lorenzo Geyres Uruguay **125** 32.05S 57.55W
Loreto Brazil **123** 7.05S 45.09W
Loreto Italy **31** 43.26N 13.36E
Loreto Mexico **109** 26.01N111.21W
Loretteville Canada **105** 46.51N 71.21W
Lorian Swamp Kenya **79** 0.35N 39.40E
Lorient France **18** 47.45N 3.22W
Loriol France **21** 44.45N 4.49E
Lormes France **19** 47.17N 3.49E
Lorne Australia **92** 38.34S144.01E
Lörrach Germany **39** 47.37N 7.40E
Lorraine *d.* France **19** 49.00N 6.00E
Lorrainville Canada **104** 47.20N 79.21W
Lorris France **19** 47.53N 2.31E
Lorsch Germany **39** 49.39N 8.34E
Lorup Germany **38** 52.55N 7.38E
Los Alamos Mexico **111** 28.40N103.30W
Los Alamos U.S.A. **109** 35.53N106.19W
Los Andes Chile **125** 32.50S 70.37W
Los Angeles Chile **125** 37.28S 72.21W
Los Angeles U.S.A. **106** 34.00N118.17W
Los Bajíos Mexico **109** 28.31N108.25W
Los Banos U.S.A. **108** 37.04N120.51W
Los Blancos Argentina **124** 23.40S 62.35W
Los Blancos Spain **25** 37.38N 0.49W
Los Canarreos, Archipiélago de Cuba **117** 21.40N 82.30W
Los Herreras Mexico **111** 25.55N 99.24W
Lošinj *i.* Yugo. **31** 44.36N 14.24E
Losinovka U.S.S.R. **37** 50.50N 31.57E
Los Llanos de Aridane Canary Is. **127** 28.39N 17.54W
Los Lunas U.S.A. **109** 34.48N106.44W
Los Mochis Mexico **116** 25.45N108.57W
Los Navalmorales Spain **27** 39.43N 4.38W
Los Olivos U.S.A. **109** 34.40N120.06W
Los Palacios y Villafranca Spain **27** 37.10N 5.56W
Los Roques *is.* Venezuela **122** 12.00N 67.00W
Los Santos de Maimona Spain **27** 38.27N 6.23W
Lossiemouth U.K. **14** 57.43N 3.18W
Lost *r.* U.S.A. **114** 39.05N 78.36W
Lost Cabin U.S.A. **108** 43.19N107.36W
Lost City U.S.A. **114** 38.55N 78.51W
Los Teques Venezuela **122** 10.25N 67.01W
Lost River *town* U.S.A. **114** 38.57N 78.50W
Los Vilos Chile **124** 31.55S 71.31W
Los Yébenes Spain **27** 39.34N 3.53W
Lot *d.* France **20** 44.35N 1.40E
Lot *r.* France **20** 44.18N 0.20E
Lota Chile **125** 37.05S 73.10W
Lot-et-Garonne *d.* France **20** 44.20N 0.20E
Lothian *d.* U.K. **14** 55.50N 3.00W
Lotoi *r.* Zaïre **78** 1.30S 18.30E
Lotsani *r.* Botswana **80** 22.42S 28.11E
Lötschberg Tunnel Switz. **38** 46.25N 7.53E
Lotuke *mtn.* Sudan **73** 4.07N 33.48E
Louang Namtha Laos **56** 20.57N101.25E
Louangphrabang Laos **56** 19.53N102.10E
Loubomo Congo **78** 4.09S 12.40E
Loudéac France **18** 48.10N 2.45W
Loudima Congo **78** 4.06S 13.05E
Loudonville U.S.A. **114** 40.38N 82.14W
Loudun France **18** 47.01N 0.05E
Loué France **18** 48.00N 0.09W
Loue *r.* France **19** 47.04N 6.10E
Louga Senegal **76** 15.37N 16.13W
Loughborough U.K. **12** 52.47N 1.11W
Loughrea Rep. of Ire. **15** 53.12N 8.35W
Loughros More B. Rep. of Ire. **15** 54.48N 8.32W
Louhans France **19** 46.38N 5.13E
Louisburgh Rep. of Ire. **15** 53.46N 9.49W
Louiseville Canada **105** 46.14N 72.56W
Louisiade Archipelago *is.* P.N.G. **90** 11.00S153.00E
Louisiana *d.* U.S.A. **111** 30.60N 92.30W
Louis Trichardt R.S.A. **80** 23.03S 29.54E
Louisville Ky. U.S.A. **112** 38.13N 85.48W
Louisville Miss. U.S.A. **111** 33.07N 89.03W
Louisville Ohio U.S.A. **114** 40.50N 81.16W
Louis XIV, Pointe *c.* Canada **102** 54.35N 79.50W
Loukhi U.S.S.R. **44** 66.05N 33.04E
Loukouo Congo **78** 3.38S 14.39E
Loulé Portugal **27** 37.08N 8.00W
Loum Cameroon **77** 4.46N 9.45E
Louny Czech. **39** 50.19N 13.46E
Lourches France **19** 50.19N 3.21E
Lourdes France **20** 43.06N 0.03W
Loures Portugal **27** 38.50N 9.10W
Lourinhã Portugal **27** 39.14N 9.19W
Lourosa Portugal **26** 40.19N 7.56W
Lousã Portugal **27** 40.07N 8.15W
Louth Australia **93** 30.34S145.09E
Louth *d.* Rep. of Ire. **15** 53.55N 6.30W
Louth U.K. **12** 53.23N 0.00
Loutra Greece **35** 37.51N 21.06E
Loutrá Aidhipsoú Greece **35** 38.54N 23.02E
Louviers France **18** 49.13N 1.10E
Louvigné-du-Désert France **18** 48.29N 1.08W
Lövånger Sweden **40** 64.22N 21.18E
Lovat *r.* U.S.S.R. **44** 58.06N 31.37E
Lovech Bulgaria **34** 43.08N 24.43E
Lovech *d.* Bulgaria **34** 43.10N 25.00E
Loveland U.S.A. **108** 40.24N105.05W
Lovell U.S.A. **108** 44.50N108.24W
Lovelock U.S.A. **108** 40.11N118.28W
Love Point *town* U.S.A. **115** 39.02N 76.18W
Lovere Italy **30** 45.49N 10.04E
Lovington U.S.A. **111** 32.57N103.21W
Lovoi *r.* Zaïre **79** 8.14S 26.40E
Lovosice Czech. **38** 50.31N 14.03E
Lovozero U.S.S.R. **44** 68.01N 35.08E
Lovrin Romania **37** 45.58N 20.48E
Lovua *r.* Zaïre **78** 6.08S 20.35E
Low Canada **105** 45.48N 75.57W
Lowa Zaïre **78** 1.24S 25.51E
Lowa *r.* Kivu Zaïre **78** 1.25S 25.55E
Lowell U.S.A. **115** 42.39N 71.18W
Löwenberg Germany **38** 52.54N 13.08E
Lower Arrow L. Canada **100** 49.40N118.05W
Lower California *pen.* *see* Baja California *pen.* Mexico **116**
Lower Egypt *see* Mişr Bahrī *f.* Egypt **66**
Lower Hutt New Zealand **86** 41.13S174.55E
Lower Lough Erne U.K. **15** 54.28N 7.48W
Lower Pen. *f.* U.S.A. **104** 44.34N 84.28W
Lower Post Canada **100** 59.55N128.30W
Lower Red L. U.S.A. **110** 48.00N 94.50W
Lowestoft U.K. **13** 52.29N 1.44E
Lowgar *d.* Afghan. **62** 34.10N 69.20E
Łowicz Poland **37** 52.06N 19.55E
Lowrah *r.* Afghan. *see* Pishīn Lora *r.* Pakistan **62**
Lowville U.S.A. **105** 43.47N 75.29W
Loxton Australia **92** 34.38S140.38E
Loyalsock *r.* U.S.A. **114** 41.14N 76.56W
Loyalty Is. *see* Loyauté, Îles *is.* N. Cal. **84**
Loyauté, Îles *is.* N. Cal. **84** 21.00S167.00E
Loyoro Uganda **79** 3.22N 34.16E
Lozère *d.* France **20** 44.30N 3.30E
Loznica Yugo. **31** 44.32N 19.13E
Lozoyuela Spain **26** 40.55N 3.37W
Lua *r.* Zaïre **78** 2.45N 18.28E
Luabo Mozambique **81** 18.30S 36.10E
Luachimo Angola **78** 7.25S 20.43E
Lualaba *r.* Zaïre **78** 0.18N 25.32E
Luama *r.* Zaïre **79** 4.45S 26.55E
Luampa Zambia **78** 15.04S 24.20E
Lu'an China **55** 31.47N116.30E
Luancheng Guang. Zhuang. China **55** 22.48N108.55E
Luancheng Hebei China **54** 37.53N114.39E
Luanda Angola **78** 8.50S 13.20E
Luanda *d.* Angola **78** 9.00S 13.20E
Luando Game Res. Angola **78** 11.00S 17.45E
Luanginga *r.* Zambia **78** 15.11S 23.05E
Luangwa *r.* Central Zambia **79** 15.32S 30.28E
Luan He *r.* China **54** 39.25N119.10E
Luanping China **54** 40.55N117.17E
Luanshya Zambia **79** 13.09S 28.24E
Luan Xian China **54** 39.45N118.44E
Luapula *r.* Zambia **79** 9.25S 28.36E
Luarca Spain **26** 43.32N 6.32W
Luau Angola **78** 10.41S 22.09E
Lubalo Angola **78** 9.13S 19.21E
Lubango Angola **78** 14.52S 13.30E
Lubao Zaïre **78** 5.19S 25.43E
Lübben Germany **38** 51.56N 13.53E
Lübbenau Germany **38** 51.52N 13.57E
Lubbock U.S.A. **111** 33.35N101.51W
Lubeck Australia **92** 36.47S142.38E
Lübeck Germany **38** 53.52N 10.40E
Lübecker Bucht *b.* Germany **38** 54.10N 11.20E
Lubefu *r.* Zaïre **78** 4.05S 23.00E
Lubenka U.S.S.R. **45** 50.22N 54.13E
Lubersac France **20** 45.27N 1.24E
Lubia Angola **78** 11.01S 17.06E
Lubika Zaïre **79** 7.50S 29.12E
Lubilash *r.* Zaïre **78** 4.59S 23.25E
Lubin Poland **36** 51.24N 16.13E
Lublin Poland **37** 51.18N 22.31E
Lubliniec Poland **37** 50.40N 18.41E
Lubny U.S.S.R. **45** 50.01N 33.00E
Lübtheen Germany **38** 53.18N 11.04E
Lubudi Zaïre **78** 9.57S 25.59E
Lubudi *r.* K.Occidental Zaïre **78** 4.00S 21.23E
Lubudi *r.* Shaba Zaïre **78** 9.13S 25.40E
Lubumbashi Zaïre **79** 11.44S 27.29E
Lubutu Zaïre **78** 0.48S 26.19E
Lübz Germany **38** 53.27N 12.01E
Lucas González Argentina **125** 32.25S 59.33W
Lucca Italy **30** 43.50N 10.29E
Luce B. U.K. **14** 54.45N 4.47W
Lucena Phil. **59** 13.56N121.37E
Lucena Spain **27** 37.24N 4.29W
Lucena del Cid Spain **25** 40.08N 0.17W
Lucenay-l'Évêque France **19** 47.05N 4.15E
Luc-en-Diois France **21** 44.37N 5.27E
Lučenec Czech. **37** 48.20N 19.40E
Lucera Italy **33** 41.30N 15.20E
Lucerne U.S.A. **108** 48.12N120.36W
Lucero Mexico **109** 30.49N106.30W
Luchena *r.* Spain **25** 37.44N 1.50W
Lüchow Germany **38** 52.58N 11.10E
Lucin U.S.A. **108** 41.22N113.55W
Lucindale Australia **92** 36.59S140.25E
Lucira Angola **78** 13.51S 12.31E
Luckau Germany **38** 51.51N 13.43E
Luckeesarai India **63** 25.11N 86.05E
Luckenwalde Germany **38** 52.05N 13.10E
Lucknow Canada **104** 43.57N 81.31W
Lucknow India **63** 26.51N 80.55E
Luçon France **18** 46.27N 1.10W
Lucy Creek *town* Australia **90** 22.25S136.20E
Lüda *see* Dalian China **54**
Luda Kamchiya *r.* Bulgaria **34** 42.50N 27.00E
Ludbreg Yugo. **31** 46.15N 16.37E
Lüdenscheid Germany **38** 51.13N 7.38E
Lüderitz Namibia **80** 26.37S 15.09E
Ludgate Canada **104** 45.54N 80.32W
Ludhiāna India **62** 30.55N 75.51E
Lüdinghausen Germany **16** 51.46N 7.27E
Ludington U.S.A. **112** 43.58N 86.27W
Ludlow U.K. **13** 52.23N 2.42W
Ludlow Penn. U.S.A. **114** 41.44N 78.57W
Ludlow Vt. U.S.A. **115** 43.24N 72.42W
Ludogorie *mts.* Bulgaria **37** 43.45N 27.00E
Luduş Romania **37** 46.29N 24.05E
Ludvika Sweden **43** 60.09N 15.11E
Ludwigsburg Germany **39** 48.53N 9.11E
Ludwigsfelde Germany **38** 52.17N 13.16E
Ludwigshafen Germany **39** 49.29N 8.26E
Ludwigslust Germany **38** 53.19N 11.30E
Luebo Zaïre **78** 5.16S 21.27E
Luena Angola **78** 11.46S 19.55E
Luena *r.* Angola **78** 12.30S 22.37E
Luena Zaïre **78** 9.27S 25.47E
Luena Zambia **79** 10.40S 30.21E
Luena *r.* Western Zambia **78** 14.47S 23.05E
Luengue *r.* Angola **78** 16.58S 21.15E
Luenha *r.* Mozambique **81** 16.29S 33.40E
Lüeyang China **54** 33.20N106.03E
Lufeng China **55** 23.01N115.35E
Lufira *r.* Zaïre **78** 8.15S 26.30E
Lufkin U.S.A. **107** 31.21N 94.47W
Luga U.S.S.R. **44** 58.42N 29.49E
Lugano Switz. **39** 46.01N 8.58E
Lugano, Lago di *l.* Switz./Italy **39** 46.00N 9.00E
Lugansk U.S.S.R. **45** 48.35N 39.20E
Luganville Vanuatu **84** 15.32S167.08E
Lugela Mozambique **81** 16.25S 36.42E
Lugenda *r.* Mozambique **79** 11.23S 38.30E
Luginy U.S.S.R. **37** 51.05N 28.21E
Lugnaquilla Mtn. Rep. of Ire. **15** 52.58N 6.28W
Lugo Italy **30** 44.25N 11.54E
Lugo Spain **26** 43.02N 7.34W
Lugo *d.* Spain **26** 42.55N 7.30W
Lugoj Romania **37** 45.42N 21.56E
Luiana Angola **78** 17.08S 22.59E
Luiana *r.* Angola **78** 17.28S 23.02E
Luilaka *r.* Zaïre **78** 0.15S 19.00E
Luilu *r.* Zaïre **78** 6.22S 23.53E
Luino Italy **30** 46.00N 8.44E
Luiro *r.* Finland **40** 67.18N 27.28E
Luisa Zaïre **78** 7.15S 22.27E
Lujiang China **55** 31.14N117.17E
Lukala Zaïre **78** 5.23S 13.02E
Lukanga Swamp *f.* Zambia **79** 14.15S 27.30E
Lukenie *r.* Zaïre **78** 2.43S 18.12E
Lukka Sudan **72** 14.33N 23.42E
Lukovit Bulgaria **34** 43.12N 24.10E
Łuków Poland **37** 51.56N 22.23E
Lukoyanov U.S.S.R. **44** 55.03N 44.29E
Lukuga *r.* Zaïre **79** 5.37S 26.58E
Lukula *r.* Zaïre **78** 4.15S 17.59E
Lukulu Zambia **78** 14.35S 23.25E
Lukumbule Tanzania **79** 11.34S 37.24E
Lule *r.* Sweden **40** 65.35N 22.03E
Luleå Sweden **40** 65.34N 22.10E

Lüleburgaz to **Maizuru**

Lüleburgaz Turkey **29** 41.25N 27.23E
Lüliang Shan *mts.* China **54** 37.00N111.20E
Lulonga *r.* Zaïre **78** 0.42N 18.26E
Lulu *r.* Zaïre **78** 1.18N 23.42E
Lulua *r.* Zaïre **78** 5.03S 21.07E
Lumai Angola **78** 13.13S 21.13E
Lumajangdong Co *l.* China **63** 34.02N 81.40E
Lumbala Kaquengue Angola **78** 12.37S 22.33E
Lumbala N'guimbo Angola **78** 14.02S 21.35E
Lumberton Miss. U.S.A. **111** 31.00N 89.27W
Lumberton N.Mex. U.S.A. **108** 36.55N106.56W
Lumbrales Spain **26** 40.56N 6.43W
Lumbres France **19** 50.42N 2.08E
Lumsden New Zealand **86** 45.44S168.26E
Lūnāvāda India **62** 23.08N 73.37E
Lund Sweden **43** 55.42N 13.11E
Lund Nev. U.S.A. **108** 38.52N115.00W
Lund Utah U.S.A. **108** 38.01N113.28W
Lunda Norte *d.* Angola **78** 8.30S 19.00E
Lunda Sul *d.* Angola **78** 11.00S 20.00E
Lundazi Zambia **79** 12.19S 33.11E
Lundevatn *l.* Norway **42** 58.22N 6.36E
Lundi *r.* Zimbabwe **81** 21.20S 32.23E
Lundy *i.* U.K. **13** 51.10N 4.41W
Lune *r.* U.K. **12** 54.03N 2.49W
Lüneburg Germany **38** 53.15N 10.23E
Lüneburger *f.* Germany **38** 53.06N 10.30E
Lunel France **21** 43.41N 4.08E
Lünen Germany **16** 51.37N 7.31E
Lunenburg U.S.A. **105** 44.28N 71.39W
Lunéville France **19** 48.36N 6.30E
Lunga *r.* Zambia **78** 14.28S 26.27E
Lunge Angola **78** 12.13S 16.07E
Lunggar China **63** 31.10N 84.01E
Lungwebungu *r.* Zambia **78** 14.20S 23.15E
Lūni India **62** 26.00N 73.00E
Lūni *r.* India **62** 24.41N 71.15E
Luninets U.S.S.R. **37** 52.18N 26.50E
Luning U.S.A. **108** 38.30N118.10W
Lūnkaransar India **62** 28.32N 73.50E
Luocheng China **55** 24.47N108.54E
Luodian China **55** 25.29N106.39E
Luoding China **55** 22.44N111.32E
Luofo Zaïre **79** 0.12S 29.15E
Luogosanto Italy **32** 41.04N 9.12E
Luohe China **54** 33.30N114.04E
Luo He *r.* China **54** 34.40N110.15E
Luonan China **54** 34.06N110.10E
Luoyang China **54** 34.48N112.25E
Lupilichi Mozambique **79** 11.45S 35.15E
Luquan China **61** 25.35N102.30E
Luque Spain **27** 37.33N 4.16W
Lūrah *r.* Afghan. **62** 31.20N 65.45E
Luray U.S.A. **114** 38.40N 78.28W
Lure France **19** 47.41N 6.30E
Lurgan U.K. **15** 54.28N 6.21W
Lurio Mozambique **79** 13.30S 40.30E
Lurio *r.* Mozambique **79** 13.32S 40.31E
Lusaka Zambia **79** 15.20S 28.14E
Lusambo Zaïre **78** 4.59S 23.26E
Luscar Canada **100** 53.05N117.26W
Lu Shan *mtn.* China **54** 36.18N118.03E
Lüshi China **54** 34.04N111.02E
Lushnje Albania **34** 40.55N 19.41E
Lushoto Tanzania **79** 4.48S 38.20E
Lüshun China **54** 38.42N121.15E
Lusignan France **18** 46.26N 0.07E
Lusk U.S.A. **108** 42.46N104.27W
Lussac-les-Châteaux France **18** 46.24N 0.44E
Lüta *see* Lüda China **54**
Luton U.K. **13** 51.53N 0.25W
Lutsk U.S.S.R. **37** 50.42N 25.15E
Lutterworth U.K. **13** 52.28N 1.12W
Lützow Germany **38** 53.40N 11.11E
Luud *r.* Somali Rep. **71** 10.25N 51.05E
Luuq Somali Rep. **79** 3.56N 42.32E
Luverne U.S.A. **110** 43.39N 96.13W
Luvua *r.* Zaïre **79** 6.45S 27.00E
Luwegu *r.* Tanzania **79** 8.30S 37.28E
Luwingu Zambia **79** 10.13S 30.05E
Luxembourg *d.* Belgium **16** 49.58N 5.30E
Luxembourg Europe **16** 49.50N 6.15E
Luxembourg *town* Lux. **16** 49.37N 6.08E
Luxeuil-les-Bains France **19** 47.49N 6.23E
Luxi China **55** 28.17N110.10E
Luxor *see* Al Uqşur Egypt **64**
Luy de Béarn *r.* France **20** 43.36N 0.44W
Luy de France *r.* France **20** 43.38N 0.47W
Luza U.S.S.R. **44** 60.41N 47.12E
Luza *r.* U.S.S.R. **44** 60.45N 46.25E
Luzarches France **19** 49.07N 2.25E
Luzern Switz. **39** 47.03N 8.18E
Luzern *d.* Switz. **39** 47.12N 8.05E
Luzhai China **55** 24.29N109.29E
Luzhou China **55** 28.48N105.23E
Luziânia Brazil **123** 16.18S 47.57W
Luzon *i.* Phil. **59** 17.50N121.00E
Luzon Str. Pacific Oc. **59** 20.20N122.00E
Luzy France **19** 46.48N 3.58E
Lvov U.S.S.R. **37** 49.50N 24.00E
Lyantonde Uganda **79** 0.26S 31.08E
Lybster U.K. **14** 58.18N 3.18W
Lyckeby Sweden **43** 56.12N 15.39E
Lycksele Sweden **40** 64.36N 18.40E
Lydenburg R.S.A. **80** 25.06S 30.27E
Lyell I. Canada **100** 52.40N131.35W
Lygnern *l.* Sweden **43** 57.29N 12.20E
Lykens U.S.A. **114** 40.34N 76.43W
Lyme B. U.K. **13** 50.40N 2.55W
Lyme Regis U.K. **13** 50.44N 2.57W
Lymington U.K. **13** 50.46N 1.32W
Łyna *r.* Poland **37** 54.37N 21.14E
Lynchburg U.S.A. **113** 37.24N 79.10W
Lynden Canada **104** 43.14N 80.09W
Lyndhurst Australia **92** 30.19S138.24E
Lyndonville U.S.A. **114** 43.19N 78.23W
Lyngdal Norway **42** 58.08N 7.05E
Lyngen Norway **40** 69.36N 20.10E
Lyngen *est.* Norway **40** 69.35N 20.20E
Lynn U.S.A. **115** 42.28N 70.57W
Lynn, L. U.S.A. **114** 39.41N 79.55W
Lynn Canal U.S.A. **100** 58.38N135.08W
Lynn Lake *town* Canada **101** 56.51N101.03W
Lynton U.K. **13** 51.14N 3.50W
Lynx Canada **102** 50.08N 85.55W
Lyon France **21** 45.45N 4.51E
Lyon Mountain *town* U.S.A. **105** 44.43N 73.55W
Lyonnais, Monts du *mts.* France **21** 45.40N 4.30E
Lyons Australia **92** 30.34S133.50E
Lyons *r.* Australia **88** 25.02S115.09E
Lyons U.S.A. **114** 43.04N 77.00W
Lyons Falls U.S.A. **115** 43.37N 75.22W
Lysefjorden *est.* Norway **42** 59.00N 6.14E
Lysekil Sweden **42** 58.16N 11.26E
Lyster Canada **105** 46.22N 71.38W
Lysva U.S.S.R. **44** 58.07N 57.49E
Lysyanka U.S.S.R. **37** 49.16N 30.49E
Lysyye Gory U.S.S.R. **45** 51.32N 44.48E
Lytham St. Anne's U.K. **12** 53.45N 3.01W
Lyubar U.S.S.R. **37** 49.58N 27.41E
Lyubech U.S.S.R. **37** 51.42N 30.41E
Lyubertsy U.S.S.R. **44** 55.38N 37.58E
Lyubeshov U.S.S.R. **37** 51.42N 25.32E
Lyubimets Bulgaria **34** 41.50N 26.05E
Lyushcha U.S.S.R. **37** 52.28N 26.41E

M

Ma *r.* Vietnam **55** 19.48N105.55E
Ma, Oued el- *wadi* Mauritania **74** 24.30N 9.10W
Ma'ād Jordan **67** 32.36N 35.37E
Maamakeogh *mtn.* Rep. of Ire. **15** 54.17N 9.29W
Maamturk Mts. Rep. of Ire. **15** 53.32N 9.42W
Ma'ān Jordan **66** 30.11N 35.43E
Ma'anshan China **55** 31.47N118.33E
Maarianhamina Finland **43** 60.06N 19.57E
Maas *r.* Neth. **16** 51.44N 4.42E
Maaseik Belgium **16** 51.08N 5.48E
Maassluis Neth. **16** 51.58N 4.12E
Maastricht Neth. **16** 50.51N 5.42E
Maave Mozambique **81** 21.06S 34.48E
Maaza Plateau Egypt **66** 27.39N 31.45E
Mabalane Mozambique **81** 23.49S 32.36E
Ma'barot Israel **67** 32.22N 34.54E
Maberly Canada **105** 44.50N 76.36W
Mablethorpe U.K. **12** 53.21N 0.14E
Mabrouk Mali **76** 19.29N 1.15W
Macá *mtn.* Chile **125** 45.06S 73.12W
Macaé Brazil **126** 22.21S 41.48W
Macalister *r.* Australia **93** 37.55S146.50E
Macão Portugal **27** 39.33N 8.00W
Macapá Brazil **123** 0.04N 51.04W
Macarthur Australia **92** 38.01S142.01E
Macau Asia **55** 22.11N113.33E
Macau Brazil **123** 5.05S 36.37W
Macclesfield U.K. **12** 53.16N 2.09W
Macdiarmid Canada **102** 49.27N 88.08W
Macdoel U.S.A. **108** 41.50N122.00W
Macdonald, L. Australia **88** 23.30S129.00E
Macdonnell Ranges *mts.* Australia **90** 23.45S133.20E
Macduff U.K. **14** 57.40N 2.29W
Macedo de Cavaleiros Portugal **26** 41.32N 6.58W
Macedon, Mt. Australia **93** 37.27S144.34E
Macedonia *see* Makedonija *d.* Yugo. **34**
Maceió Brazil **123** 9.40S 35.44W
Macenta Guinea **76** 8.31N 9.32W
Macerata Italy **31** 43.18N 13.27E
MacFarlane *r.* Canada **101** 59.12N107.58W
Macfarlane, L. Australia **92** 31.55S136.42E
Macgillycuddy's Reeks *mts.* Rep. of Ire. **15** 52.00N 9.43W
Machado Brazil **126** 21.39S 45.33W
Machala Ecuador **122** 3.20S 79.57W
Machattie, L. Australia **90** 24.50S139.48E
Machece Mozambique **81** 19.17S 35.33E
Machecoul France **18** 47.00N 1.50W
Macheke Zimbabwe **81** 18.08S 31.49E
Macheng China **55** 31.11N115.02E
Machevna U.S.S.R. **51** 60.46N171.40E
Machias Maine U.S.A. **112** 44.43N 67.28W
Machias N.Y. U.S.A. **114** 42.25N 78.30W
Machichaco, Cabo *c.* Spain **26** 43.27N 2.45W
Machichi *r.* Canada **101** 57.03N 92.06W
Machida Japan **57** 35.32N139.27E
Machilipatnam India **61** 16.13N 81.12E
Machiques Venezuela **122** 10.04N 72.37W
Machiya *r.* Japan **57** 35.01N136.42E
Machrihanish U.K. **14** 55.25N 5.44W
Machynlleth U.K. **13** 52.35N 3.51W
Maciá Argentina **125** 32.11S 59.25W
Macia Mozambique **81** 25.03S 33.10E
Macintyre *r.* Australia **93** 28.50S150.50E
Mackay Australia **90** 21.09S149.11E
MacKay U.S.A. **108** 43.55N113.37W
Mackay, L. Australia **88** 22.30S149.10E
Mackenzie *r.* Australia **90** 22.48S149.15E
Mackenzie *r.* Canada **98** 69.20N134.00W
Mackenzie King I. Canada **98** 77.30N112.00W
Mackenzie Mts. Canada **98** 64.00N130.00W
Mackinac I. U.S.A. **104** 45.51N 84.38W
Mackinaw City U.S.A. **104** 45.47N 84.44W
Mackinnon Road *town* Kenya **79** 3.50S 39.03E
Macklin Canada **101** 52.20N109.56W
Macksville Australia **93** 30.43S152.55E
Maclean Australia **91** 29.27S153.14E
Maclear R.S.A. **80** 31.04S 28.21E
Macleay *r.* Australia **93** 30.52S153.01E
MacLeod, L. Australia **88** 24.10S113.35E
Maçobere Mozambique **81** 21.14S 32.50E
Macomer Italy **32** 40.16N 8.46E
Mâcon France **21** 46.18N 4.50E
Macon Ga. U.S.A. **113** 32.49N 83.37W
Macon Mo. U.S.A. **110** 39.44N 92.28W
Mâconnais, Monts du *mts.* France **19** 46.18N 4.45E
Macquarie *r.* Australia **93** 30.07S147.24E
Macquarie, L. Australia **93** 33.05S151.35E
Macquarie-Balleny Ridge Pacific Oc. **84** 58.00S160.00E
Macquarie I. Pacific Oc. **84** 54.29S158.58E
Macquarie Marshes Australia **93** 30.50S147.32E
MacRobertson Land *f.* Antarctica **128** 69.30S 64.00E
Macroom Rep. of Ire. **15** 51.54N 8.58W
Mac Tier Canada **104** 45.08N 79.47W
Macumba *r.* Australia **91** 27.55S137.15E
Ma'dabā Jordan **67** 31.44N 35.48E
Madagascar Africa **81** 17.00S 46.00E
Madan Bulgaria **34** 41.30N 24.57E
Madang P.N.G. **59** 5.14S145.45E
Madaoua Niger **77** 14.05N 6.27E
Mādārīpur Bangla. **63** 23.10N 90.12E
Madawaska Canada **105** 45.30N 77.59W
Madawaska *r.* Canada **105** 45.27N 76.21W
Madawaska U.S.A. **112** 47.21N 68.20W
Maddalena *i.* Italy **32** 41.13N 9.24E
Maddaloni Italy **33** 41.02N 14.23E
Madeira *r.* Brazil **122** 3.20S 59.00W
Madeira *i.* Madeira Is. **127** 32.45N 17.00W
Madeira, Arquipélago da *is.* Atlantic Oc. **127** 32.45N 17.00W
Madeira Is. *see* Madeira, Arquipélago da *is.* Atlantic Oc. **127**
Mädelegabel *mtn.* Austria **39** 47.18N 10.18E
Madeleine, Îles de la *is.* Canada **103** 47.20N 61.50W
Madera U.S.A. **108** 36.57N120.03W
Madera, Sierra de la *mts.* Mexico **109** 30.20N109.00W
Madgaon India **60** 15.26N 73.50E
Madhubani India **63** 26.22N 86.05E
Madhupur India **63** 24.16N 86.39E
Madhya Pradesh *d.* India **63** 23.30N 78.30E
Madibira Tanzania **79** 8.13S 34.47E
Madigan G. Australia **92** 28.55S137.48E
Madill U.S.A. **111** 34.06N 96.46W
Madinat ash Sha'b Yemen **71** 12.50N 44.56E
Madingley Rise *f.* Indian Oc. **49** 5.00S 62.00E
Madison Fla. U.S.A. **107** 30.29N 83.39W
Madison Ind. U.S.A. **112** 38.46N 85.22W
Madison N.J. U.S.A. **115** 40.46N 74.25W
Madison Ohio U.S.A. **114** 41.47N 81.04W
Madison S.Dak. U.S.A. **110** 44.00N 97.07W
Madison Tenn. U.S.A. **113** 36.16N 86.44W
Madison Va. U.S.A. **114** 38.23N 78.15W
Madison Wisc. U.S.A. **110** 43.05N 89.22W
Madison W.Va. U.S.A. **113** 38.03N 81.50W
Madison Junction U.S.A. **108** 44.39N110.51W
Madisonville Ky. U.S.A. **113** 37.20N 87.30W
Madisonville Tex. U.S.A. **111** 30.57N 95.55W
Madiun Indonesia **59** 7.37S111.33E
Madoc Canada **105** 44.30N 77.28W
Mado Gashi Kenya **79** 0.40N 39.11E
Madoi China **52** 34.28N 98.56E
Madonna di Campiglio Italy **30** 46.14N 10.49E
Madrakah, Ra's al *c.* Oman **60** 19.00N 57.50E
Madras India **61** 13.05N 80.18E
Madras U.S.A. **108** 44.38N121.08W
Madre, Laguna *b.* Mexico **111** 25.00N 97.40W
Madre, Laguna *b.* U.S.A. **111** 27.00N 97.35W
Madre, Sierra *mts.* Mexico/Guatemala **116** 15.20N 92.20W
Madre de Dios *r.* Bolivia **122** 10.24S 65.30W
Madre del Sur, Sierra *mts.* Mexico **116** 17.00N100.00W
Madre Occidental, Sierra *mts.* Mexico **109** 25.00N105.00W
Madre Oriental, Sierra *mts.* Mexico **111** 28.10N102.10W
Madrid Spain **26** 40.24N 3.41W
Madrid *d.* Spain **26** 40.15N 3.30W
Madridejos Spain **27** 39.28N 3.32W
Madrigalejo Spain **27** 39.09N 5.37W
Madrona, Sierra *mts.* Spain **26** 38.30N 3.00W
Madroñera Spain **27** 39.26N 5.46W
Madukani Tanzania **79** 3.57S 35.49E
Madura *i.* Indonesia **59** 7.02S113.22E
Madurai India **48** 9.55N 78.07E
Maebashi Japan **57** 36.30N139.04E
Mae Klong *r.* Thailand **56** 13.21N100.00E
Mae Sot Thailand **56** 16.40N 98.35E
Maestra, Sierra *mts.* Cuba **117** 20.10N 76.30W
Maestu Spain **26** 42.44N 2.27W
Maevatanana Madagascar **81** 16.56S 46.49E
Maewo *i.* Vanuatu **84** 15.10S168.10E
Mafeking Canada **101** 52.43N100.59W
Mafeteng Lesotho **80** 29.51S 27.13E
Maffra Australia **93** 37.58S146.59E
Mafia I. Tanzania **79** 7.50S 39.50E
Mafikeng R.S.A. **80** 25.52S 25.36E
Mafra Portugal **27** 38.56N 9.20W
Magadan U.S.S.R. **51** 59.38N150.50E
Magadi Kenya **79** 1.53S 36.18E
Magallanes, Estrecho de *str.* Chile **125** 53.00S 71.00W
Magallan's Str. *see* Magellanes, Estrecho destr. *str.* Chile **125**
Magalluf Spain **25** 39.30N 2.30E
Magangué Colombia **122** 9.14N 74.46W
Magazine U.S.A. **111** 35.10N 93.40W
Magburaka Sierra Leone **76** 8.44N 11.57W
Magdalena Argentina **125** 35.04S 57.32W
Magdalena Bolivia **124** 13.50S 64.08W
Magdalena *r.* Colombia **122** 10.56N 74.58W
Magdalena Mexico **109** 30.38N110.59W
Magdalena, Isla *i.* Chile **125** 44.42S 73.10W
Magdalena, Llano de la *f.* Mexico **109** 24.55N111.40W
Magdalene *mtn.* Malaysia **58** 4.25N117.55E
Magdeburg Germany **38** 52.08N 11.38E
Magé Brazil **126** 22.37S 43.03W
Magee U.S.A. **111** 31.52N 89.44W
Magelang Indonesia **59** 7.28S110.11E
Magen Israel **67** 31.18N 34.26E
Magenta Italy **30** 45.28N 8.53E
Magenta, L. Australia **89** 33.26S119.10E
Mageröya *i.* Norway **40** 71.03N 25.45E
Maggiorasca, Monte *mtn.* Italy **30** 44.33N 9.29E
Maggiore, Lago *l.* Italy **30** 46.00N 8.40E
Maghāghah Egypt **66** 28.39N 30.50E
Maghār Israel **67** 32.53N 35.24E
Magherafelt U.K. **15** 54.45N 6.38W
Magina *mtn.* Spain **27** 37.44N 3.28W
Magione Italy **30** 43.08N 12.12E
Maglaj Yugo. **31** 44.33N 18.06E
Magna U.S.A. **108** 40.42N112.06W
Magnetawan Canada **104** 45.40N 79.38W
Magnetawan *r.* Canada **104** 45.46N 80.37W
Magnetic I. Australia **90** 19.08S146.50E
Magnitogorsk U.S.S.R. **44** 53.28N 59.06E
Magnolia Ark. U.S.A. **111** 33.16N 93.14W
Magnolia Miss. U.S.A. **111** 31.09N 90.28W
Magnolia Tex. U.S.A. **111** 30.13N 95.45W
Magny-en-Vexin France **19** 49.09N 1.47E
Magog Canada **105** 45.16N 72.09W
Magoye Zambia **79** 16.00S 27.38E
Magpie *r.* Canada **103** 50.18N 64.28W
Magrath Canada **100** 49.25N112.50W
Magro *r.* Spain **25** 39.11N 0.25W
Magude Mozambique **81** 25.01S 32.39E
Magué Mozambique **79** 15.46S 31.42E
Maguse River *town* Canada **101** 61.20N 94.25W
Magwe Burma **56** 20.08N 95.00E
Magwe *d.* Burma **56** 23.00N 95.00E
Mahābād Iran **65** 36.44N 45.44E
Mahābhārat Range *mts.* Nepal **63** 28.00N 84.30E
Mahabo Madagascar **81** 20.23S 44.40E
Mahadday Weyne Somali Rep. **79** 2.58N 45.32E
Mahādeo Hills India **63** 22.15N 78.30E
Mahaffey U.S.A. **114** 40.53N 78.44W
Mahagi Zaïre **79** 2.16N 30.59E
Mahajamba *r.* Madagascar **81** 15.33S 47.08E
Mahājan India **62** 28.47N 73.50E
Mahajanga Madagascar **81** 15.43S 46.19E
Mahajilo *r.* Madagascar **81** 19.42S 45.22E
Maḩajjah Syria **67** 32.57N 36.14E
Mahalapye Botswana **80** 23.04S 26.47E
Mahalás Greece **35** 38.41N 21.11E
Maḩallāt Iran **65** 33.54N 50.28E
Mahānadi India **63** 20.19N 86.45E
Mahānadi *r.* India **61** 20.17N 86.43E
Mahanoro Madagascar **81** 19.54S 48.48E
Mahanoy City U.S.A. **115** 40.49N 76.08W
Mahārājpur India **63** 25.01N 79.44E
Mahārāshtra *d.* India **62** 19.40N 76.00E
Mahāsamund India **63** 21.06N 82.06E
Maha Sarakham Thailand **56** 15.50N103.47E
Mahavavy *r.* Madagascar **81** 15.57S 45.54E
Mahbés W. Sahara **74** 27.13N 9.44W
Mahd adh Dhahab Saudi Arabia **64** 23.30N 40.52E
Mahdia Guyana **122** 5.10N 59.12W
Mahendraganj India **63** 25.20N 89.45E
Mahenge Tanzania **79** 8.46S 36.38E
Mahi *r.* India **62** 22.30N 72.58E
Mahia Pen. New Zealand **86** 39.10S177.50E
Mahmūdābād India **63** 27.18N 81.07E
Mahmūd-e 'Erāqī Afghan. **62** 35.01N 69.20E
Mahnomen U.S.A. **110** 47.19N 96.01W
Maho Sri Lanka **61** 7.49N 80.17E
Mahoba India **63** 25.17N 79.52E
Mahón Spain **25** 39.53N 4.15E
Mahone B. Canada **103** 44.30N 64.15W
Mahora Spain **25** 39.13N 1.44W
Mahroni India **63** 24.35N 78.43E
Mahuva India **62** 21.05N 71.48E
Maia Portugal **26** 41.14N 8.37W
Maiäo *i.* Îs. de la Société **85** 17.23S150.37W
Maîche France **19** 47.15N 6.48E
Maidenhead U.K. **13** 51.32N 0.44W
Maidstone U.K. **13** 51.17N 0.32E
Maiduguri Nigeria **77** 11.53N 13.16E
Maignelay France **19** 49.33N 2.31E
Maihar India **63** 24.16N 80.45E
Maikala Range *mts.* India **63** 21.45N 81.00E
Maiko *r.* Zaïre **78** 0.15N 25.35E
Maillezais France **18** 46.22N 0.44W
Main *r.* Germany **39** 50.00N 8.18E
Mā'īn Jordan **67** 31.41N 35.44E
Mainburg Germany **39** 48.38N 11.47E
Main Camp Kiribati **85** 2.01N157.25W
Main Centre Canada **101** 50.38N107.20W
Main Channel *str.* Canada **104** 45.22N 81.50W
Mai Ndombe *l.* Zaïre **78** 2.00S 18.20E
Main Duck I. Canada **105** 43.56N 76.37W
Maine *d.* U.S.A. **112** 45.15N 69.15W
Maine-et-Loire *d.* France **18** 47.25N 0.30W
Mainhardt Germany **39** 49.04N 9.33E
Mainland *i.* Orkney Is. U.K. **14** 59.00N 3.10W
Mainoru Australia **90** 14.02S134.05E
Mainpuri India **63** 27.14N 79.01E
Maintenon France **19** 48.35N 1.35E
Maintirano Madagascar **81** 18.03S 44.01E
Mainz Germany **39** 50.01N 8.16E
Maipo *mtn.* Argentina **125** 34.10S 69.50W
Maipú Argentina **125** 36.52S 57.54W
Maiquetía Venezuela **122** 10.03N 66.57W
Maiskhāl I. Bangla. **63** 21.36N 91.56E
Maitland N.S.W. Australia **93** 32.33S151.33E
Maitland S.A. Australia **92** 34.21S137.42E
Maitland *r.* Canada **104** 43.45N 81.43W
Maizhokunggar China **63** 29.50N 91.44E
Maizuru Japan **57** 35.30N135.20E

Majd el Kurūm to **Marans**

Majd el Kurūm Israel **67** 32.55N 35.15E
Majeigha Sudan **73** 11.33N 24.40E
Majene Indonesia **58** 3.33S118.59E
Maji Ethiopia **73** 6.11N 35.38E
Majiahewan China **54** 37.12N105.48E
Majiang China **55** 26.30N107.35E
Majorca *i.* *see* Mallorca *i.* Spain **25**
Majrūr Sudan **72** 14.01N 30.27E
Majuba Hill R.S.A. **80** 27.26S 29.48E
Majuro *i.* Pacific Oc. **84** 7.09N171.12E
Makabana Congo **78** 3.25S 12.41E
Makale Indonesia **58** 3.06S119.53E
Makalu *mtn.* China / Nepal **63** 27.54N 87.06E
Makarikha U.S.S.R. **44** 66.17N 58.28E
Makarska Yugo. **31** 43.18N 17.02E
Makaryev U.S.S.R. **44** 57.52N 43.40E
Makasar, Selat *str.* Indonesia **58** 3.00S118.00E
Makassar Str. *see* Makasar, Selat *str.* Indonesia **58**
Makat U.S.S.R. **45** 47.38N 53.16E
Makaw Burma **56** 26.27N 96.42E
Makay, Massif du *mts.* Madagascar **81** 21.15S 45.15E
Makaya Zaïre **78** 3.22S 18.02E
Makedonija *d.* Yugo. **34** 41.53N 21.40E
Makefu Niue **84** 19.01S169.55W
Makeni Sierra Leone **76** 8.57N 12.02W
Makere Tanzania **79** 4.15S 30.26E
Makeyevka U.S.S.R. **45** 48.01N 38.00E
Makgadikgadi Salt Pan *f.* Botswana **80** 20.50S 25.45E
Makhachkala U.S.S.R. **45** 42.59N 47.30E
Makham Thailand **56** 12.40N102.12E
Makhfar al Quwayrah Jordan **66** 29.49N 35.18E
Makhrūq, Wādī al *r.* Jordan **66** 31.30N 37.10E
Makinsk U.S.S.R. **9** 52.37N 70.26E
Makkah Saudi Arabia **72** 21.26N 39.49E
Makkovik Canada **103** 55.00N 59.10W
Makó Hungary **37** 46.13N 20.30E
Mako Senegal **76** 13.00N 12.26W
Makobe L. Canada **104** 47.27N 80.25W
Makokou Gabon **78** 0.38N 12.47E
Makoua Congo **78** 0.01S 15.40E
Makrai India **62** 22.04N 77.06E
Makran *f.* Asia **65** 26.30N 61.20E
Makrāna India **62** 27.03N 74.43E
Makrān Coast Range *mts.* Pakistan **62** 25.30N 64.30E
Maksamaa Finland **40** 63.14N 22.05E
Makuliro Tanzania **79** 9.34S 37.26E
Makurdi Nigeria **77** 7.44N 8.35E
Māl India **63** 26.52N 88.44E
Malabo Equat. Guinea **77** 3.45N 8.48E
Malacca *see* Melaka Malaysia **58**
Malacca, Str. of Indian Oc. **58** 3.00N100.30E
Malad City U.S.A. **108** 42.12N112.15W
Málaga Spain **27** 36.43N 4.25W
Málaga *d.* Spain **27** 36.45N 4.40W
Malaga U.S.A. **109** 32.14N104.04W
Malagón Spain **27** 39.35N 3.51W
Malagón *r.* Spain **27** 37.35N 7.29W
Malaimbandy Madagascar **81** 20.20S 45.36E
Malaita Solomon Is. **84** 9.00S161.00E
Malakāl Sudan **73** 9.31N 31.39E
Malakand Pakistan **62** 34.34N 71.56E
Mala Kapela *mts.* Yugo. **31** 45.00N 15.20E
Malam Chad **73** 11.27N 20.59E
Malang Indonesia **59** 7.59S112.45E
Malangwa Nepal **63** 26.52N 85.34E
Malanje Angola **78** 9.36S 16.21E
Malanje *d.* Angola **78** 8.40S 16.50E
Mälaren *l.* Sweden **43** 59.30N 17.12E
Malartic Canada **102** 48.09N 78.09W
Malatya Turkey **64** 38.22N 38.18E
Malaucène France **21** 44.10N 5.08E
Malaut India **62** 30.11N 74.30E
Malaŵi Africa **79** 12.00S 34.00E
Malaŵi, L. Africa **79** 12.00S 34.30E
Malaya Vishera U.S.S.R. **44** 58.53N 32.08E
Malāyer Iran **65** 34.19N 48.51E
Malaysia Asia **58** 5.00N110.00E
Malazgirt Turkey **64** 39.09N 42.31E
Malbaie *r.* Canada **103** 47.40N 70.05W
Malbaie, Baie de *b.* Canada **103** 48.35N 64.16W
Malbooma Australia **92** 30.41S134.11E
Malbork Poland **37** 54.02N 19.01E
Malchin Germany **38** 53.44N 12.46E
Malchow Germany **38** 53.28N 12.25E
Malcolm Australia **89** 28.56S121.30E
Malcolm, Pt. Australia **89** 33.47S123.44E
Malden Mo. U.S.A. **111** 36.34N 89.57W
Malden I. Kiribati **85** 4.03S154.49W
Maldive Ridge *f.* Indian Oc. **49** 0.00 73.00E
Maldives Indian Oc. **60** 6.20N 73.00E
Maldon U.K. **13** 51.43N 0.41E
Maldonado Uruguay **126** 34.57S 54.59W
Male Italy **30** 46.21N 10.55E
Maléa, Ákra *c.* Greece **35** 36.26N 23.12E
Malebo Pool *f.* Zaïre **78** 4.15S 15.25E
Mālegaon India **62** 20.33N 74.32E
Malek Sudan **73** 6.04N 31.36E
Malek Dīn Afghan. **62** 32.25N 68.04E
Malekula *i.* Vanuatu **84** 16.15S167.30E
Malema Mozambique **79** 14.55S 37.09E
Malenga U.S.S.R. **44** 63.50N 36.50E
Malente Germany **38** 54.10N 10.33E
Māler Kotla India **62** 30.32N 75.53E
Malesherbes France **19** 48.18N 2.25E
Malesína Greece **35** 38.37N 23.15E
Malestroit France **18** 47.49N 2.23W
Malgomaj *l.* Sweden **40** 64.47N 16.12E
Malheur L. U.S.A. **108** 43.20N118.45W
Mali Africa **76** 17.30N 2.30E
Mali *r.* Burma **56** 25.43N 97.29E
Malik, Wādī al Sudan **72** 18.02N 30.58E
Malili Indonesia **59** 2.38S121.06E
Målilla Sweden **43** 57.23N 15.48E
Malin U.S.S.R. **37** 50.48N 29.08E
Malinau Indonesia **58** 3.35N116.38E
Malindi Kenya **79** 3.14S 40.08E
Malingping Indonesia **59** 6.45S106.01E
Malin Head Rep. of Ire. **15** 55.23N 7.24W
Malin More Rep. of Ire. **15** 54.42N 8.48W
Malipo China **55** 23.11N104.41E
Maliquit Albania **34** 40.45N 20.48E
Mali Rajinac Yugo. **31** 44.48N 15.02E
Malita Phil. **59** 6.19N125.39E
Māliya India **62** 23.05N 70.46E
Malkāpur India **62** 20.53N 76.12E
Mallacoota Australia **93** 37.34S149.43E
Mallacoota Inlet *b.* Australia **93** 37.34S149.43E
Mallaig U.K. **14** 57.00N 5.50W
Mallawī Egypt **66** 27.44N 30.50E
Mallersdorf Germany **39** 48.47N 12.16E
Mallnitz Austria **30** 46.59N 13.10E
Mallorca *i.* Spain **25** 39.30N 3.00E
Mallow Rep. of Ire. **15** 52.08N 8.39W
Malm Norway **40** 64.04N 11.12E
Malmbäck Sweden **43** 57.35N 14.28E
Malmberget Sweden **40** 67.10N 20.40E
Malmédy Belgium **16** 50.25N 6.02E
Malmesbury R.S.A. **80** 33.28S 18.43E
Malmö Sweden **43** 55.36N 13.00E
Malmöhus *d.* Sweden **43** 55.45N 13.30E
Malmslätt Sweden **43** 58.25N 15.30E
Malmyzh U.S.S.R. **44** 56.34N 50.41E
Maloja Switz. **39** 46.24N 9.41E
Malolos Guam **84** 13.18N144.46E
Malone U.S.A. **105** 44.51N 74.17W
Malonga Zaïre **78** 10.26S 23.10E
Malorita U.S.S.R. **37** 51.50N 24.08E
Målöy Norway **41** 61.56N 5.07E
Malozemelskaya Tundra *f.* U.S.S.R. **44** 67.40N 50.10E
Malpartida de Plasencia Spain **27** 39.59N 6.02W
Malpas Australia **92** 34.44S140.43E
Malta Europe **28** 35.55N 14.25E
Malta Mont. U.S.A. **108** 48.21N107.52W
Malta Ohio U.S.A. **114** 39.39N 81.52W
Malta Channel Med. Sea **28** 36.20N 14.45E
Maltby U.K. **12** 53.25N 1.12W
Malton U.K. **12** 54.09N 0.48W
Maluku *d.* Indonesia **59** 4.00S129.00E
Maluku, Laut *sea* Pacific Oc. **59**
Malumfashi Nigeria **77** 11.48N 7.36E
Malundo Angola **78** 14.51S 22.00E
Malung Sweden **41** 60.40N 13.44E
Malūt Sudan **73** 10.26N 32.12E
Malvinas, Islas *see* Falkland Is. Atlantic Ocean **125**
Mama U.S.S.R. **51** 58.20N112.55E
Mamadysh U.S.S.R. **44** 55.43N 51.20E
Mamaia Romania **37** 44.15N 28.37E
Mambasa Zaïre **79** 1.20N 29.05E
Mamberamo *r.* Indonesia **59** 1.45S137.25E
Mambéré *r.* C.A.R. **77** 3.30N 16.08E
Mambilima Falls *town* Zambia **79** 10.32S 28.45E
Mamers France **18** 48.21N 0.23E
Mamfe Cameroon **77** 5.46N 9.18E
Mamonovo U.S.S.R. **37** 54.30N 19.59E
Mamore *r.* Bolivia **124** 12.00S 65.15W
Mamou Guinea **76** 10.24N 12.05W
Mampika Congo **78** 2.58S 14.38E
Mampikony Madagascar **81** 16.06S 47.38E
Mampong Ghana **76** 7.06N 1.24W
Mamry, Jezioro *l.* Poland **37** 54.08N 21.42E
Mamuju Indonesia **58** 2.41S118.55E
Ma'mūn Sudan **73** 12.15N 22.41E
Man Ivory Coast **76** 7.31N 7.37W
Man Jammu & Kashmir **63** 33.51N 78.32E
Man, Isle of U.K. **12** 54.15N 4.30W
Mana *r.* Guiana **123** 5.35N 53.55W
Mana Hawaiian Is. **85** 22.02N156.46W
Manacapuru Brazil **122** 3.16S 60.37W
Manacor Spain **25** 39.34N 3.12E
Manado Indonesia **59** 1.30N124.58E
Managua Nicaragua **117** 12.06N 86.18W
Managua, Lago de *l.* Nicaragua **117** 12.10N 86.30W
Manahawkin U.S.A. **115** 39.42N 74.16W
Manakara Madagascar **81** 22.08S 48.01E
Manāli India **62** 32.16N 77.10E
Manambao *r.* Madagascar **81** 17.43S 43.57E
Mananara Madagascar **81** 16.10S 49.46E
Mananara *r.* Madagascar **81** 23.21S 47.42E
Manangatang Australia **92** 35.02S142.54E
Mananjary Madagascar **81** 21.13S 48.20E
Manankoro Mali **76** 10.25N 7.26W
Manantali, Lac de *l.* Mali **76** 13.00N 10.20W
Manantenina Madagascar **81** 24.17S 47.19E
Manapouri, L. New Zealand **86** 45.30S167.00E
Manār *r.* India **62** 18.39N 77.44E
Manāslu *mtn.* Nepal **63** 28.33N 84.35E
Manasquan U.S.A. **115** 40.07N 74.03W
Manassas U.S.A. **114** 38.45N 77.28W
Manau P.N.G. **59** 8.02S148.00E
Manaus Brazil **122** 3.06S 60.00W
Manāwar India **62** 22.14N 75.05E
Manawatu-Wanganui *d.* New Zealand **86** 39.00S175.25E
Mancelona U.S.A. **112** 44.54N 85.03W
Mancha Real Spain **27** 37.47N 3.37W
Manche *d.* France **18** 49.00N 1.10W
Mancherāl India **63** 18.52N 79.26E
Manchester U.K. **12** 53.30N 2.15W
Manchester Conn. U.S.A. **115** 41.47N 72.31W
Manchester Mich. U.S.A. **104** 42.09N 84.02W
Manchester N.H. U.S.A. **115** 42.59N 71.28W
Manchester N.Y. U.S.A. **114** 42.58N 77.14W
Manchurian Plain *f.* *see* Dongbei Pingyuan *f.* China **53**
Manciano Italy **30** 42.35N 11.31E
Mand *r.* Iran **65** 28.09N 51.16E
Manda Iringa Tanzania **79** 10.30S 34.37E
Manda Mbeya Tanzania **79** 7.59S 32.27E
Manda, Jabal *mtn.* Sudan **73** 8.39N 24.27E
Mandabe Madagascar **81** 21.03S 44.55E
Mandal Norway **42** 58.02N 7.27E
Mandala Peak Indonesia **59** 4.45S140.15E
Mandalay Burma **56** 21.58N 96.04E
Mandalay *d.* Burma **56** 22.00N 96.00E
Mandalgovi Mongolia **54** 45.40N106.10E
Mandals *r.* Norway **42** 58.02N 7.28E
Mandalya Körfezi *b.* Turkey **35** 37.12N 27.20E
Mandan U.S.A. **110** 46.50N100.54W
Mandara Mts. Nigeria / Cameroon **77** 10.30N 13.30E
Mandas Italy **32** 39.39N 9.08E
Mandasor India **62** 24.04N 75.04E
Mandeb, Bāb el *str.* Asia **73** 13.00N 43.10E
Mandel Afghan. **62** 33.17N 61.52E
Mandera Kenya **79** 3.55N 41.50E
Mandi India **62** 31.42N 76.55E
Mandiana Guinea **76** 10.37N 8.39W
Mandi Būrewāla Pakistan **62** 30.09N 72.41E
Mandi Dabwāli India **62** 29.58N 74.42E
Mandji Gabon **78** 1.37S 10.53E
Mandla India **63** 22.36N 80.23E
Mandora Australia **88** 19.45S120.50E
Mandoto Madagascar **81** 19.34S 46.17E
Mandoúdhion Greece **35** 38.48N 23.29E
Mandra Pakistan **62** 33.22N 73.14E
Mandritsara Madagascar **81** 15.50S 48.49E
Māndu India **62** 22.22N 75.23E
Mandurah Australia **89** 32.31S115.41E
Manduria Italy **33** 40.24N 17.38E
Māndvi India **62** 22.50N 69.22E
Mandya India **60** 12.33N 76.54E
Måne *r.* Norway **42** 59.00N 9.40E
Manendragarh India **63** 23.13N 82.13E
Manerbio Italy **32** 45.21N 10.08E
Manevichi U.S.S.R. **37** 51.19N 25.35E
Manfredonia Italy **33** 41.38N 15.55E
Manfredonia, Golfo di *g.* Italy **33** 41.35N 16.05E
Mangaia I. Cook Is. **85** 21.56S157.56W
Mangaldai India **63** 26.26N 92.02E
Mangalia Romania **37** 43.50N 28.35E
Mangalore India **60** 12.54N 74.51E
Mangando Angola **78** 8.02S 17.08E
Mangareva *i.* Pacific Oc. **85** 23.07S134.57W
Mangawān India **63** 24.41N 81.33E
Mangaweka New Zealand **86** 38.49S175.48E
Mangeigne Chad **73** 10.31N 21.19E
Mangnai China **52** 37.52N 91.26E
Mango Togo **76** 10.23N 0.30E
Mangochi Malaŵi **79** 14.29S 35.15E
Mangoky *r.* Madagascar **81** 21.29S 43.41E
Mangombe Zaïre **79** 1.23S 26.50E
Mangonui New Zealand **86** 35.00S173.34E
Mangoro *r.* Madagascar **81** 20.00S 48.45E
Māngrol India **62** 21.07N 70.07E
Mangualde Portugal **26** 40.36N 7.46W
Mangueira, L. Brazil **126** 33.06S 52.48W
Mangum U.S.A. **111** 34.53N 99.30W
Mangyshlak, Poluostrov *pen.* U.S.S.R. **45** 44.00N 52.30E
Manhattan U.S.A. **110** 39.11N 96.35W
Manhiça Mozambique **81** 25.24S 32.49E
Manhuaçu Brazil **126** 20.16S 42.01W
Manhumirim Brazil **126** 20.22S 41.57W
Mania *r.* Madagascar **81** 19.42S 45.22E
Maniago Italy **30** 46.10N 12.43E
Maniamba Mozambique **79** 12.30S 35.05E
Manica Mozambique **81** 19.00S 33.00E
Manica *d.* Mozambique **81** 20.00S 34.00E
Manicoré Brazil **122** 5.49S 61.17W
Manicouagan *r.* Canada **103** 49.15N 68.20W
Manicouagan, Résr. Canada **103** 51.20N 68.48W
Maniitsoq *see* Sukkertoppen Greenland **99**
Mānikganj Bangla. **63** 23.19N 87.03E
Mānikpur India **63** 25.04N 81.07E
Manila Phil. **59** 14.36N120.59E
Manila U.S.A. **108** 40.59N109.43W
Manildra Australia **93** 33.12S148.41E
Manilla Australia **93** 30.45S150.45E
Maningory *r.* Madagascar **81** 17.13S 49.28E
Manipur *d.* India **61** 25.00N 93.40E
Manisa Turkey **29** 38.37N 27.28E
Manistee U.S.A. **112** 44.14N 86.20W
Manistee *r.* U.S.A. **112** 44.14N 86.20W
Manistique U.S.A. **112** 45.58N 86.17W
Manitoba *d.* Canada **101** 55.00N 96.00W
Manitoba, L. Canada **101** 51.00N 98.45W
Manitou L. Canada **104** 45.48N 82.00W
Manitoulin I. Canada **104** 45.45N 82.30W
Manitowaning Canada **104** 45.45N 81.49W
Manitowoc U.S.A. **110** 44.06N 87.40W
Maniwaki Canada **105** 46.23N 75.58W
Manizales Colombia **122** 5.03N 75.32W
Manjā Jordan **67** 31.45N 35.51E
Manja Madagascar **81** 21.26S 44.20E
Manjakandriana Madagascar **81** 18.55S 47.47E
Mānjhand Pakistan **62** 25.55N 68.14E
Manjil Iran **65** 36.44N 49.29E
Manjimup Australia **89** 34.14S116.06E
Mankato U.S.A. **110** 44.10N 94.01W
Mankera Pakistan **62** 31.23N 71.26E
Mankono Ivory Coast **76** 8.01N 6.09W
Manlléu Spain **25** 42.00N 2.17E
Manly Australia **93** 33.47S151.17E
Manmād India **62** 20.15N 74.27E
Mann *r.* Australia **90** 12.20S134.07E
Mann *r.* N.S.W. Australia **93** 29.38S152.21E
Mān Na Burma **56** 23.27N 97.14E
Manna Indonesia **58** 4.27S102.55E
Mannahill Australia **92** 32.26S139.59E
Mannar Sri Lanka **61** 8.59N 79.54E
Mannar, G. of India / Sri Lanka **61** 8.20N 79.00E
Mannessier, Lac *l.* Canada **103** 55.28N 70.38W
Mannheim Germany **39** 49.29N 8.29E
Mannin B. Rep. of Ire. **15** 53.28N 10.06W
Manning Canada **100** 56.53N117.39W
Manning U.S.A. **113** 33.42N 80.12W
Mannington U.S.A. **114** 39.32N 80.20W
Manns Choice U.S.A. **114** 40.01N 78.39W
Mannsville U.S.A. **115** 43.43N 76.04W
Mannu *r.* Sardegna Italy **32** 40.50N 8.23E
Mannu *r.* Sardegna Italy **32** 39.16N 9.00E
Mannum Australia **92** 34.50S139.20E
Mano Sierra Leone **76** 8.04N 12.02W
Manoharpur India **63** 22.23N 85.12E
Manokwari Indonesia **59** 0.53S134.05E
Manolás Greece **35** 38.04N 21.21E
Manombo Madagascar **81** 22.57S 43.28E
Manono Zaïre **79** 7.18S 27.24E
Manorhamilton Rep. of Ire. **15** 54.18N 8.10W
Manosque France **21** 43.50N 5.47E
Manouane Canada **105** 47.14N 74.25W
Manouane *r.* Canada **103** 49.29N 71.13W
Manouane, Lac *l.* Canada **103** 50.40N 70.45W
Manouba Tunisia **32** 36.50N 10.06E
Mānpur India **63** 20.22N 80.43E
Manresa Spain **25** 41.44N 1.50E
Mānsa Gujarat India **62** 23.26N 72.40E
Mānsa Punjab India **62** 29.59N 75.23E
Mansa Zambia **79** 11.10S 28.52E
Mānsehra Pakistan **62** 34.20N 73.12E
Mansel I. Canada **99** 62.00N 80.00W
Mansfield U.K. **12** 53.08N 1.12W
Mansfield La. U.S.A. **111** 32.02N 93.43W
Mansfield Mass. U.S.A. **115** 42.02N 71.13W
Mansfield Ohio U.S.A. **114** 40.46N 82.31W
Mansfield Penn. U.S.A. **114** 41.48N 77.05W
Mansfield, Mt. U.S.A. **105** 44.33N 72.49W
Mansle France **20** 45.53N 0.11E
Manso *r.* Brazil **124** 11.59S 50.25W
Mansôa Guinea Bissau **76** 12.08N 15.18W
Mansūrah Syria **67** 33.08N 35.48E
Manta Ecuador **122** 0.59S 80.44W
Mantaro *r.* Peru **122** 12.00S 74.00W
Manteca U.S.A. **108** 37.48N121.13W
Mantes France **19** 48.59N 1.43E
Mantiqueira, Serra da *mts.* Brazil **126** 22.25S 45.00W
Mantova Italy **30** 45.09N 10.48E
Mänttä Finland **41** 62.02N 24.38E
Mantua U.S.A. **114** 41.17N 81.14W
Manturovo U.S.S.R. **44** 58.20N 44.42E
Mäntyluoto Finland **41** 61.35N 21.29E
Manú Peru **122** 12.14S 70.51W
Manua Is. Samoa **84** 14.13S169.35W
Manuel Benavides Mexico **111** 29.05N103.55W
Manui *i.* Indonesia **59** 3.35S123.08E
Manukau New Zealand **86** 36.59S174.53E
Manukau Harbour *est.* New Zealand **86** 37.10S174.00E
Manunda Creek *r.* Australia **92** 32.50S138.58E
Manus *i.* P.N.G. **59** 2.00S147.00E
Manville U.S.A. **108** 42.47N104.37W
Manyane Botswana **80** 23.23S 21.44E
Manyara, L. Tanzania **79** 3.40S 35.50E
Manych *r.* U.S.S.R. **45** 47.14N 40.20E
Manych Gudilo, Ozero *l.* U.S.S.R. **45** 46.20N 42.45E
Manyinga *r.* Zambia **80** 13.28S 24.25E
Manyoni Tanzania **79** 5.46S 34.50E
Mānzai Pakistan **62** 30.07N 68.52E
Manzanares Spain **27** 39.00N 3.22W
Manzanillo Cuba **117** 20.21N 77.21W
Manzanillo Mexico **97** 19.00N104.20W
Manzano Mts. U.S.A. **109** 34.48N106.12W
Manzhouli China **53** 49.36N117.28E
Manzil Pakistan **62** 29.15N 63.05E
Manzilah, Buḩayrat al *l.* Egypt **66** 31.20N 32.00E
Manzini Swaziland **80** 26.29S 31.24E
Mao Chad **77** 14.06N 15.11E
Maobitou *c.* Taiwan **55** 22.00N120.45E
Maoke, Pegunungan *mts.* Indonesia **59** 4.00S137.30E
Maokui Shan *mtn.* China **54** 33.55N111.33E
Maoming China **55** 21.50N110.58E
Maoniu Shan *mtn.* China **54** 33.00N103.56E
Mapai Mozambique **81** 22.51S 32.00E
Mapam Yumco *l.* China **63** 30.40N 81.20E
Mapi Indonesia **59** 7.06S139.23E
Mapia, Kepulauan *is.* Indonesia **59** 1.00N134.15E
Mapimí, Bolsón de *des.* Mexico **111** 27.30N103.15W
Mapinhane Mozambique **81** 22.19S 35.03E
Mapire Venezuela **122** 7.46N 64.41W
Maple Creek *town* Canada **101** 49.55N109.27W
Maprik P.N.G. **59** 3.38S143.02E
Mapuera *r.* Brazil **123** 2.00S 55.40W
Maputo Mozambique **81** 25.58S 32.35E
Maputo *d.* Mozambique **81** 26.00S 32.30E
Maqnā Saudi Arabia **66** 28.26N 34.44E
Maqu China **61** 34.05N102.15E
Maquan He *r.* China **63** 29.35N 84.10E
Maqueda Spain **27** 40.04N 4.22W
Maquela do Zombo Angola **78** 6.06S 15.12E
Maquinchao Argentina **125** 41.15S 68.44W
Maquoketa U.S.A. **110** 42.04N 90.40W
Mar, Serra do *mts.* Brazil **126** 23.00S 44.40W
Mara Tanzania **79** 1.30S 34.31E
Mara *d.* Tanzania **79** 1.45S 34.30E
Mara *r.* Tanzania **79** 1.30S 33.52E
Maraã Brazil **122** 1.50S 65.22W
Maraa Tahiti **85** 17.46S149.34W
Marabá Brazil **123** 5.23S 49.10W
Marabastad R.S.A. **80** 23.58S 29.21E
Maracaibo Venezuela **122** 10.44N 71.37W
Maracaibo, Lago de *l.* Venezuela **122** 9.50N 71.30W
Maracaju, Serra de *mts.* Brazil **126** 21.38S 55.10W
Maracay Venezuela **122** 10.20N 67.28W
Marādah Libya **75** 29.14N 19.13E
Maradi Niger **77** 13.29N 7.10E
Maradi *d.* Niger **77** 14.00N 8.10E
Marāgheh Iran **65** 37.25N 46.13E
Maragogipe Brazil **123** 12.48S 38.59W
Marahuaca, Cerro *mtn.* Venezuela **122** 3.37N 65.25W
Marajó, Ilha de *i.* Brazil **123** 1.00S 49.40W
Maralal Kenya **79** 1.15N 36.48E
Maralinga Australia **89** 30.13S131.32E
Maramba Zambia **78** 17.40S 25.50E
Maramsilli Resr. India **63** 20.32N 81.41E
Mārān, Koh-i- *mtn.* Pakistan **62** 29.33N 66.53E
Marana U.S.A. **109** 32.27N111.13W
Maranchón Spain **26** 41.03N 2.12W
Marand Iran **65** 38.25N 45.50E
Maranhão *d.* Brazil **123** 6.00S 45.30W
Maranoa *r.* Australia **91** 27.55S148.30E
Marañón *r.* Peru **122** 4.40S 73.20W
Marans France **20** 46.19N 1.00W

Marão to Mayenne

Marão Mozambique **81** 24.21S 34.07E
Marapi *mtn.* Indonesia **58** 0.20S100.45E
Mărășești Romania **37** 45.52N 27.14E
Maratea Italy **33** 39.59N 15.45E
Marathón Greece **35** 38.09N 23.57E
Marathon N.Y. U.S.A. **115** 42.26N 76.02W
Marathon Tex. U.S.A. **111** 30.12N103.15W
Maratua *i.* Indonesia **58** 2.10N118.35E
Marāveh Tappeh Iran **65** 37.55N 55.57E
Marav L. Pakistan **62** 29.04N 69.18E
Marawī Sudan **72** 18.29N 31.49E
Marbella Spain **27** 36.31N 4.53W
Marble Bar Australia **88** 21.16S119.45E
Marburg Germany **38** 50.49N 8.46E
Marcali Hungary **31** 46.35N 17.25E
Marcaria Italy **32** 45.07N 10.32E
Marcellus U.S.A. **115** 42.59N 76.20W
March U.K. **13** 52.33N 0.05E
Marche Belgium **16** 50.13N 5.21E
Marche *d.* Italy **30** 43.35N 13.00E
Marchena Spain **27** 37.20N 5.24W
Mar Chiquita *l.* Argentina **124** 30.42S 62.36W
Marcigny France **19** 46.17N 4.02E
Marcos Paz Argentina **125** 34.49S 58.51W
Marcounda C.A.R. **77** 7.37N 16.59E
Marcq-en-Baroeul France **16** 50.40N 3.01E
Marcus Hook U.S.A. **115** 39.49N 75.25W
Marcus I. Pacific Oc. **84** 24.18N153.58E
Marcy, Mt. U.S.A. **105** 44.07N 73.56W
Mardān Pakistan **62** 34.12N 72.02E
Mar del Plata Argentina **125** 38.00S 57.32W
Marden U.K. **13** 51.11N 0.30E
Mardie Australia **88** 21.14S115.57E
Mardin Turkey **64** 37.19N 40.43E
Maré, Île *i.* N. Cal. **84** 21.30S168.00E
Maree, Loch U.K. **14** 57.41N 5.28W
Mareeba Australia **90** 17.00S145.26E
Marennes France **20** 45.50N 1.06W
Marettimo *i.* Italy **32** 37.58N 12.04E
Mareuil-sur-Belle France **20** 45.28N 0.28E
Marfa U.S.A. **111** 30.18N104.01W
Margai Caka *l.* China **61** 35.11N 86.57E
Margaret *r.* Australia **92** 29.26S137.00E
Margaret Bay *town* Canada **100** 51.20N127.20W
Margaret L. Canada **100** 58.56N115.25W
Margaret River *town* W. Aust. Australia **88** 18.38S126.52E
Margaret River *town* W. Aust. Australia **89** 33.57S115.04E
Margarita, Isla de *i.* Venezuela **122** 11.00N 64.00W
Margarítion Greece **34** 39.22N 20.26E
Margate R.S.A. **80** 30.51S 30.22E
Margate U.K. **13** 51.23N 1.24E
Margeride, Monts de la *mts.* France **20** 44.50N 3.30E
Margherita di Savoia Italy **33** 41.23N 16.09E
Māgow, Dasht-e *des.* Afghan. **62** 30.45N 63.10E
Maria Elena Chile **124** 22.21S 69.40W
Maria Gail Austria **39** 46.36N 13.52E
Mariager Denmark **42** 56.39N 10.00E
María Grande Argentina **125** 31.40S 59.55W
Maria I. Australia **90** 14.52S135.40E
Mariana Brazil **126** 20.23S 43.23W
Marianao Cuba **117** 23.03N 82.29W
Mariana Ridge Pacific Oc. **84** 17.00N146.00E
Mariana Trench Pacific Oc. **84** 16.00N148.00E
Marianna Ark. U.S.A. **111** 34.46N 90.46W
Marianna Fla. U.S.A. **113** 30.45N 85.15W
Mariannelund Sweden **43** 57.37N 15.34E
Mariánské Lázně Czech. **39** 49.59N 12.43E
Marias *r.* U.S.A. **108** 47.56N110.30W
Maribo Denmark **41** 54.46N 11.31E
Maribor Yugo. **31** 46.33N 15.39E
Marico *r.* R.S.A. **80** 24.12S 26.57E
Maricopa U.S.A. **109** 35.03N119.24W
Marīdī Sudan **73** 4.55N 29.28E
Marīdī *r.* Sudan **73** 6.55N 29.00E
Marié *r.* Brazil **122** 0.27S 66.26W
Marieburg Belgium **16** 50.07N 4.30E
Mariefred Sweden **43** 59.18N 17.15E
Marie-Galante *i.* Guadeloupe **117** 15.54N 61.11W
Mariehamn *see* Maarianhamina Finland **43**
Mariemberg Neth. **16** 52.32N 6.35E
Mariental Namibia **80** 24.38S 17.58E
Marienville U.S.A. **114** 41.28N 79.07W
Mariestad Sweden **43** 58.43N 13.51E
Marietta Ga. U.S.A. **113** 33.57N 84.34W
Marietta Ohio U.S.A. **114** 39.25N 81.27W
Marieville Canada **105** 45.26N 73.10W
Mariga *r.* Nigeria **77** 9.37N 5.55E
Marignane France **21** 43.25N 5.13E
Marijampolė U.S.S.R. **41** 54.33N 23.21E
Marília Brazil **126** 22.13S 50.20W
Marín Spain **26** 42.23N 8.42W
Marina di Gioiosa Ionica Italy **33** 38.18N 16.20E
Marina di Ravenna Italy **30** 44.29N 12.17E
Marine City U.S.A. **114** 42.43N 82.30W
Marineland U.S.A. **113** 29.39N 81.13W
Marinette U.S.A. **110** 45.06N 87.38W
Maringá Brazil **126** 23.36S 52.02W
Maringa Zaïre **73** 1.14N 20.00E
Maringa *r.* Zaïre **78** 1.13N 19.50E
Maringue Mozambique **81** 17.55S 34.24E
Marinha Grande Portugal **27** 39.45N 8.56W
Marion Canada **104** 47.00N 84.10W
Marion Ill. U.S.A. **111** 37.44N 88.56W
Marion Ind. U.S.A. **112** 40.33N 85.40W
Marion Iowa U.S.A. **110** 42.02N 91.36W
Marion Ohio U.S.A. **112** 40.35N 83.08W
Marion S.C. U.S.A. **113** 34.11N 79.23W
Marion Va. U.S.A. **113** 36.51N 81.30W
Marion, L. U.S.A. **113** 33.30N 80.25W
Marion Bay *town* Australia **92** 35.13S137.00E
Marion Reef Australia **90** 19.10S152.17E
Mariposa U.S.A. **108** 37.29N119.58W
Mariscal Estigarribia Paraguay **126** 22.03S 60.35W
Maritimes, Alpes *mts.* France **21** 44.15N 7.10E
Maritsa Bulgaria **34** 42.02N 25.50E
Maritsa *r.* Bulgaria **34** 42.15N 24.00E
Maritsa *r.* Turkey **29** 41.00N 26.15E
Mariupol' U.S.S.R. **45** 47.05N 37.34E
Mārkā Jordan **67** 31.59N 35.59E
Marka Somali Rep. **79** 1.42N 44.47E
Markaryd Sweden **43** 56.26N 13.36E
Markdale Canada **104** 44.19N 80.39W
Marked Tree U.S.A. **111** 35.32N 90.25W
Marken *i.* Neth. **16** 52.28N 5.03E
Markerwaard *f.* Neth. **16** 52.30N 5.15E
Market Drayton U.K. **12** 52.55N 2.30W
Market Harborough U.K. **13** 52.29N 0.55W
Market Rasen U.K. **12** 53.24N 0.20W
Market Weighton U.K. **12** 53.52N 0.04W
Markha *r.* U.S.S.R. **51** 63.37N119.00E
Markham Canada **104** 43.52N 79.16W
Markham, Mt. Antarctica **128** 83.00S164.00E
Markoupolon Greece **35** 37.53N 23.57E
Marks U.S.S.R. **45** 51.43N 46.45E
Markstay Canada **104** 46.29N 80.33W
Marktheidenfeld Germany **39** 49.50N 9.36E
Marktoberdorf Germany **39** 47.47N 10.37E
Marktredwitz Germany **39** 50.00N 12.06E
Marl Germany **38** 51.38N 7.05E
Marla Australia **90** 27.22S133.48E
Marlboro U.S.A. **115** 42.21N 71.33W
Marlborough Australia **90** 22.51S149.50E
Marlborough U.K. **13** 51.26N 1.44W
Marlborough U.S.A. **105** 42.21N 71.33W
Marle France **19** 49.44N 3.46E
Marlette U.S.A. **114** 43.20N 83.05W
Marlin U.S.A. **111** 31.18N 96.53W
Marlo Australia **93** 37.50S148.35E
Marmande France **20** 44.30N 0.10E
Marmara *i.* Turkey **29** 40.38N 27.37E
Marmara, Sea of *see* Marmara Denizi *sea* Turkey **29**
Marmara Denizi *sea* Turkey **29** 40.45N 28.15E
Marmaris Turkey **35** 36.50N 28.14E
Marmarth U.S.A. **110** 46.18N103.54W
Marmet U.S.A. **114** 38.15N 81.04W
Marmion L. Canada **102** 48.55N 91.25W
Marmolada *mtn.* Italy **30** 46.26N 11.51E
Marmora Canada **105** 44.29N 77.41W
Marnay France **19** 47.17N 5.46E
Marne *d.* France **19** 48.55N 4.10E
Marne *r.* France **19** 48.49N 2.24E
Marne Germany **38** 53.57N 9.00E
Marne à la Saône, Canal de la France **19** 49.44N 4.36E
Marne au Rhin, Canal de la France **19** 48.35N 7.47E
Marnoo Australia **92** 36.40S142.55E
Maroantsetra Madagascar **81** 15.26S 49.44E
Marobi Pakistan **62** 32.36N 69.52E
Marolambo Madagascar **81** 20.02S 48.07E
Maromme France **18** 49.28N 1.02E
Marondera Zimbabwe **81** 18.11S 31.31E
Maroni *r.* Guiana **123** 5.30N 54.00W
Maronne *r.* France **20** 45.07N 1.57E
Maroochydore Australia **91** 26.40S153.07E
Maros *r.* Hungary **31** 46.15N 20.13E
Maroua Cameroon **77** 10.35N 14.20E
Marovoay Madagascar **81** 16.06S 46.39E
Marquard R.S.A. **80** 28.39S 27.25E
Marquesas Is. *see* Marquises, Îles *is.* Pacific Oc. **85**
Marquette U.S.A. **112** 46.33N 87.23W
Marquina-Jemein Spain **26** 43.16N 2.30W
Marquise France **19** 50.49N 1.42E
Marquises, Îles *is.* Pacific Oc. **85** 9.00S139.30W
Marra Australia **92** 31.11S144.03E
Marra *r.* Australia **93** 30.05S147.05E
Marracuene Mozambique **81** 25.44S 32.41E
Marradi Italy **30** 44.04N 11.37E
Marrah, Jabal *mtn.* Sudan **73** 13.10N 24.22E
Marrakech Morocco **74** 31.49N 8.00W
Marrawah Australia **91** 40.55S144.42E
Marree Australia **92** 29.40S138.04E
Marromeu Mozambique **81** 18.20S 35.56E
Marrupa Mozambique **79** 13.10S 37.30E
Marsá al Burayqah Libya **72** 30.25N 19.35E
Marsabit Kenya **79** 2.20N 37.59E
Marsala Italy **32** 37.48N 12.26E
Marsá Maṭrūḥ Egypt **64** 31.21N 27.14E
Marsciano Italy **30** 42.54N 12.20E
Marsden Australia **93** 33.46S147.35E
Marseille France **21** 43.18N 5.24E
Marseille-en-Beauvaisis France **19** 49.35N 1.57E
Marsfjället *mtn.* Sweden **40** 65.05N 15.28E
Marshall Liberia **76** 6.10N 10.23W
Marshall Ark. U.S.A. **111** 35.55N 92.38W
Marshall Minn. U.S.A. **110** 44.27N 95.47W
Marshall Mo. U.S.A. **110** 39.07N 93.12W
Marshall Tex. U.S.A. **111** 32.33N 94.23W
Marshall Va. U.S.A. **114** 38.52N 77.52W
Marshall Is. Pacific Oc. **84** 10.00N172.00E
Marshalltown U.S.A. **110** 42.03N 92.55W
Marshyhope Creek *r.* U.S.A. **115** 38.32N 75.45W
Märsta Sweden **43** 59.37N 17.51E
Marstrand Sweden **42** 57.53N 11.35E
Martaban Burma **56** 16.32N 97.35E
Martaban, G. of Burma **56** 15.10N 96.30E
Martapura Indonesia **58** 3.22S114.56E
Marte Nigeria **77** 12.23N 13.46E
Martelange Belgium **16** 49.50N 5.44E
Marten River *town* Canada **104** 46.42N 79.41W
Martés, Sierra *mts.* Spain **25** 39.20N 1.10W
Marthaguy Creek *r.* Australia **93** 30.16S147.35E
Martha's Vineyard *i.* U.S.A. **115** 41.25N 70.40W
Martigny Switz. **39** 46.06N 7.04E
Martigues France **21** 43.24N 5.03E
Martin Czech. **37** 49.05N 18.55E
Martín *r.* Spain **25** 41.18N 0.19W
Martin U.S.A. **110** 43.10N101.44W
Martina Franca Italy **33** 40.42N 17.21E
Martinique *i.* Windward Is. **117** 14.40N 61.00W
Martin L. U.S.A. **113** 32.50N 85.55W
Martin Pt. U.S.A. **98** 70.10N143.50W
Martinsburg Penn. U.S.A. **114** 40.19N 78.20W
Martinsburg W.Va. U.S.A. **114** 39.27N 77.58W
Martins Ferry *town* U.S.A. **114** 40.06N 80.44W
Martinsville Ind. U.S.A. **112** 39.25N 86.25W
Martinsville Va. U.S.A. **113** 36.43N 79.53W
Martin Vaz *is.* Atlantic Oc. **127** 20.30S 28.51W
Marton New Zealand **86** 40.04S175.25E
Martos Spain **27** 37.43N 3.58W
Martre, Lac la *l.* Canada **100** 63.15N116.55W
Martti Finland **40** 67.28N 28.28E
Marudi Malaysia **58** 4.15N114.19E
Ma'rūf Afghan. **62** 31.34N 67.03E
Marula Zimbabwe **80** 20.26S 28.06E
Marum Neth. **16** 53.06N 6.16E
Marvejols France **20** 44.33N 3.18E
Marvel Loch *town* Australia **89** 31.31S119.30E
Marviken Sweden **43** 58.34N 16.51E
Mārwār India **62** 25.44N 73.36E
Mary U.S.S.R. **50** 37.42N 61.54E
Maryborough Qld. Australia **90** 25.32S152.36E
Maryborough Vic. Australia **92** 37.05S143.47E
Marydale R.S.A. **80** 29.24S 22.06E
Mary Frances L. Canada **101** 63.19N106.13W
Maryland *d.* U.S.A. **114** 39.00N 76.45W
Maryland Beach *town* U.S.A. **115** 38.26N 74.59W
Maryport U.K. **12** 54.43N 3.30W
Mary's Harbour Canada **103** 52.18N 55.51W
Marystown Canada **103** 47.11N 55.10W
Marysvale U.S.A. **108** 38.27N112.11W
Marysville Kans. U.S.A. **110** 39.51N 96.39W
Marysville Mich. U.S.A. **114** 42.54N 82.29W
Marysville Penn. U.S.A. **114** 40.20N 76.56W
Maryvale Australia **90** 24.41S134.04E
Maryville Mo. U.S.A. **110** 40.21N 94.52W
Maryville Tenn. U.S.A. **113** 35.45N 83.59W
Marzūq Libya **75** 25.55N 13.55E
Marzūq, Ṣaḥrā' *des.* Libya **75** 24.30N 13.00E
Mas'adah Syria **67** 33.14N 35.45E
Masāhim, Kūh-e *mtn.* Iran **65** 30.26N 55.08E
Masai Steppe *f.* Tanzania **79** 4.30S 37.00E
Masaka Uganda **79** 0.20S 31.46E
Masan S. Korea **53** 35.10N128.35E
Masasi Tanzania **79** 10.43S 38.48E
Masba Nigeria **77** 10.35N 13.01E
Masbate *i.* Phil. **59** 12.00N123.30E
Mascara Algeria **74** 35.24N 0.08E
Mascarene Basin *f.* Indian Oc. **49** 17.00S 55.00E
Mascarene Is. Indian Oc. **49** 21.00S 56.00E
Mascarene Ridge *f.* Indian Oc. **49** 10.00S 60.00E
Maseru Lesotho **80** 29.18S 27.28E
Mashhad Iran **65** 36.16N 59.34E
Mashkai *r.* Pakistan **62** 26.02N 65.19E
Māshkel *r.* Pakistan **62** 28.02N 63.25E
Māshkel, Hāmūn-i- *l.* Pakistan **62** 28.15N 63.00E
Mashki Chāh Pakistan **62** 29.01N 62.27E
Mashonaland *f.* Zimbabwe **81** 18.20S 32.00E
Mashūray Afghan. **62** 32.12N 68.21E
Masi Norway **40** 69.26N 23.40E
Masīlah, Wādī al *f.* Yemen **71** 15.10N 51.08E
Masi-Manimba Zaïre **78** 4.47S 17.54E
Masindi Uganda **79** 1.41N 31.45E
Maṣīrah *i.* Oman **60** 20.30N 58.50E
Maṣīrah, Khalīj *b.* Oman **71** 20.10N 58.10E
Masjed Soleymān Iran **65** 31.59N 49.18E
Mask, Lough Rep. of Ire. **15** 53.38N 9.22W
Maskinongé Canada **105** 46.35N 73.30W
Mason Mich. U.S.A. **104** 42.35N 84.26W
Mason Tex. U.S.A. **111** 30.45N 99.14W
Mason W.Va. U.S.A. **114** 39.00N 82.02W
Mason City U.S.A. **110** 43.09N 93.12W
Masontown U.S.A. **114** 39.51N 79.54W
Maspalomas Canary Is. **127** 27.42N 15.34W
Masqaṭ Oman **65** 23.36N 58.37E
Massa Italy **30** 44.01N 10.09E
Massachusetts *d.* U.S.A. **115** 42.15N 71.50W
Massachusetts B. U.S.A. **115** 42.20N 70.50W
Massafra Italy **33** 40.35N 17.07E
Massakory Chad **77** 13.02N 15.43E
Massa Marittima Italy **30** 43.03N 10.53E
Massangena Mozambique **81** 21.31S 33.03E
Massangulo Mozambique **81** 13.54S 35.24E
Massarosa Italy **30** 43.52N 10.20E
Massena U.S.A. **105** 44.56N 74.54W
Massenya Chad **77** 11.21N 16.09E
Masset Canada **100** 54.00N132.09W
Masseube France **20** 43.26N 0.35E
Massey Canada **104** 46.12N 82.05W
Massiac France **20** 45.15N 3.12E
Massif Central *mts.* France **20** 45.00N 3.10E
Massillon U.S.A. **114** 40.48N 81.32W
Massinga Mozambique **81** 23.20S 35.25E
Massingir Mozambique **81** 23.49S 32.04E
Masterton New Zealand **86** 40.57S175.39E
Mastic Beach *town* U.S.A. **115** 40.45N 72.50W
Mastigouche Prov. Park Canada **105** 46.39N 73.24W
Mastung Pakistan **62** 29.48N 66.51E
Mastūrah Saudi Arabia **64** 23.06N 38.50E
Masuda Japan **57** 34.40N131.51E
Masvingo Zimbabwe **80** 20.10S 30.49E
Maṣyāf Syria **66** 35.03N 36.21E
Mat *r.* Albania **34** 41.40N 20.00E
Matabeleland *f.* Zimbabwe **80** 19.50S 28.15E
Matabuena Spain **26** 41.06N 3.48W
Matachel *r.* Spain **26** 38.50N 6.17W
Matachewan Canada **102** 47.56N 80.39W
Matadi Zaïre **78** 5.50S 13.36E
Matagami Canada **102** 49.45N 77.34W
Matagami, L. Canada **102** 49.50N 77.40W
Matagorda B. U.S.A. **111** 28.35N 96.20W
Matakana Australia **93** 32.59S145.53E
Matakana I. New Zealand **86** 37.35S176.15E
Matala Angola **78** 14.45S 15.02E
Matam Senegal **74** 15.40N 13.15W
Matamata New Zealand **86** 37.49S175.46E
Matameye Niger **77** 13.26N 8.28E
Matamoros Coahuila Mexico **111** 25.32N103.15W
Matamoros Tamaulipas Mexico **111** 25.53N 97.30W
Ma'ṭan Bishrah *well* Libya **72** 22.58N 22.39E
Matandu *r.* Tanzania **79** 8.44S 39.22E
Matane Canada **103** 48.51N 67.32W
Matang China **55** 29.30N113.08E
Matankari Niger **77** 13.47N 4.00E
Matanzas Cuba **117** 23.04N 81.35W
Mataram Indonesia **59** 8.36S116.07E
Matarani Peru **124** 16.58S 72.07W
Mataranka Australia **88** 14.56S133.07E
Mataró Spain **25** 41.32N 2.27E
Matarraña *r.* Spain **25** 41.14N 0.22E
Matatiele R.S.A. **80** 30.19S 28.48E
Matatula, C. Samoa **84** 14.15S170.35W
Mataura *r.* New Zealand **86** 46.34S168.45E
Matautu W. Samoa **84** 13.57S171.56W
Matavera Rarotonga Cook Is. **84** 21.13S159.44W
Matawai New Zealand **86** 38.21S177.32E
Matawin *r.* Canada **105** 46.50N 72.45W
Maṭāy Egypt **66** 28.25N 30.46E
Matehuala Mexico **116** 23.40N100.40W
Mateke Hills Zimbabwe **80** 21.48S 31.00E
Matelica Italy **30** 43.15N 13.00E
Matera Italy **33** 40.40N 16.37E
Matetsi Zimbabwe **80** 18.17S 25.57E
Mateur Tunisia **32** 37.03N 9.40E
Matfors Sweden **41** 62.21N 17.02E
Matha France **20** 45.52N 0.19W
Mathews Peak *mtn.* Kenya **79** 1.18N 37.20E
Mathis U.S.A. **111** 28.06N 97.50W
Mathoura Australia **93** 35.49S144.54E
Mathura India **63** 27.30N 77.41E
Mati Phil. **59** 6.55N126.15E
Matias Barbosa Brazil **126** 21.52S 43.21W
Matignon France **18** 48.36N 2.18W
Matinenda L. Canada **104** 46.22N 82.57W
Matipó Brazil **126** 20.16S 42.17W
Mātli Pakistan **62** 25.02N 68.39E
Matlock U.K. **12** 53.09N 1.32W
Matochkin Shar U.S.S.R. **50** 73.15N 56.35E
Mato Grosso *d.* Brazil **124** 13.00S 55.00W
Mato Grosso *town* Brazil **124** 15.05S 59.57W
Mato Grosso, Planalto do *f.* Brazil **124** 16.00S 54.00W
Mato Grosso do Sul *d.* Brazil **124** 20.00S 54.30W
Matope Malaŵi **79** 15.20S 34.57E
Matopo Hills Zimbabwe **80** 20.45S 28.30E
Matosinhos Portugal **26** 41.11N 8.42W
Maṭraḥ Oman **65** 23.37N 58.33E
Matrei in Osttirol Austria **39** 47.00N 12.32E
Matsena Nigeria **77** 13.13N 10.04E
Matsiatra *r.* Madagascar **81** 21.25S 45.33E
Matsubara Japan **57** 34.34N135.33E
Matsudo Japan **57** 35.47N139.54E
Matsue Japan **57** 35.29N133.00E
Matsumae Japan **57** 41.26N140.07E
Matsumoto Japan **57** 36.18N137.58E
Matsusaka Japan **57** 34.34N136.32E
Matsuyama Japan **57** 33.50N132.47E
Mattagami *r.* Canada **102** 50.43N 81.29W
Mattawa Canada **104** 46.19N 78.42W
Mattawamkeag U.S.A. **112** 45.31N 68.21W
Mattawin Canada **105** 46.55N 72.55W
Matterhorn *mtn.* Switz./Italy **39** 45.59N 7.43E
Matterhorn *mtn.* U.S.A. **108** 41.49N115.23W
Matthews Ridge *town* Guyana **122** 7.30N 60.10W
Matthew Town Bahamas **117** 20.57N 73.40W
Mattice Canada **102** 49.39N 83.20W
Mattighofen Austria **39** 48.06N 13.09E
Mattmar Sweden **40** 63.19N 13.45E
Mattoon U.S.A. **110** 39.29N 88.21W
Matua Indonesia **58** 2.58S110.52E
Maturín Venezuela **122** 9.45N 63.10W
Maua Mozambique **81** 13.53S 37.10E
Mau Aimma India **63** 25.42N 81.55E
Maubeuge France **19** 50.17N 3.58E
Maudaha India **63** 25.41N 80.07E
Maude Australia **92** 34.27S144.21E
Maués Brazil **123** 3.24S 57.42W
Mauganj India **63** 24.41N 81.53E
Maui *i.* Hawaii U.S.A. **106** 20.45N156.15W
Mauléon France **18** 46.56N 0.45W
Mauléon-Licharre France **20** 43.14N 0.54W
Maulvi Bāzār Bangla. **63** 24.29N 91.42E
Maumee U.S.A. **112** 41.34N 83.41W
Maumee *r.* U.S.A. **112** 41.40N 83.35W
Maumere Indonesia **59** 8.35S122.13E
Maun Botswana **80** 19.52S 23.40E
Maunaloa Hawaiian Is. **85** 21.08N157.13W
Mauna Loa *mtn.* Hawaiian Is. **85** 19.29N155.36W
Maunath Bhanjan India **63** 25.57N 83.33E
Mau Rānīpur India **63** 25.15N 79.08E
Maure-de-Bretagne France **18** 47.54N 1.59W
Maures *mts.* France **21** 43.16N 6.23E
Mauriac France **20** 45.13N 2.20E
Maurice, L. Australia **91** 29.28S130.58E
Maurice Nat. Park Canada **105** 46.42N 73.00W
Mauritania Africa **74** 20.00N 10.00W
Mauritius Indian Oc. **49** 20.10S 58.00E
Mauritius Basin *f.* Indian Oc. **49** 26.00S 55.00E
Mauron France **18** 48.05N 2.18W
Maurs France **20** 44.43N 2.11E
Mauston U.S.A. **110** 43.48N 90.05W
Mauvezin France **20** 43.44N 0.55E
Mavinga Angola **78** 15.47S 20.21E
Mavqi'im Israel **67** 31.37N 34.35E
Mavuradonha Mts. Zimbabwe **81** 16.30S 31.20E
Mawjib, Wādī al Jordan **67** 31.28N 35.34E
Mawlaik Burma **56** 23.50N 94.30E
Maxcanú Mexico **116** 20.35N 89.59W
Maxville Canada **105** 45.17N 74.51W
May, C. U.S.A. **115** 38.56N 74.55W
Maya Spain **26** 43.12N 1.29W
Mayaguana I. Bahamas **117** 22.30N 73.00W
Mayagüez Puerto Rico **117** 18.13N 67.09W
Mayāmey Iran **65** 36.27N 55.40E
Maya Mts. Belize **117** 16.30N 89.00W
Maybole U.K. **14** 55.21N 4.41W
Maych'ew Ethiopia **71** 13.02N 39.34E
Maydena Australia **91** 42.45S146.38E
Maydh Somali Rep. **71** 10.57N 47.06E
Mayen Germany **39** 50.19N 7.13E
Mayenne France **18** 48.18N 0.37W

Mayenne to **Meymac**

Mayenne *d.* France **18** 48.05N 0.40W
Mayenne *r.* France **18** 47.30N 0.33W
Mayerthorpe Canada **100** 53.57N115.08W
Mayfield U.S.A. **111** 36.44N 88.38W
Maykop U.S.S.R. **45** 44.37N 40.48E
Maymyo Burma **56** 22.05N 96.28E
Maynooth Canada **105** 45.13N 77.57W
Maynooth Rep. of Ire. **15** 53.23N 6.37W
Mayo *r.* Mexico **109** 26.45N109.47W
Mayo *d.* Rep. of Ire. **15** 53.47N 9.07W
Mayo, Plains of *f.* Rep. of Ire. **15** 53.46N 9.05W
Mayo Daga Nigeria **77** 6.59N 11.25E
Mayo Landing Canada **98** 63.45N135.45W
Mayor I. New Zealand **86** 37.15S176.15E
Mayotte, Île *i.* Comoros **79** 12.50S 45.10E
May Pen Jamaica **117** 17.58N 77.14W
Maysah, Tall al *mtn.* Jordan **67** 31.08N 35.40E
Mays Landing U.S.A. **115** 39.27N 74.44W
Maysville U.S.A. **112** 38.38N 83.46W
Maythalūn Jordan **67** 32.21N 35.16E
Mayumba Gabon **78** 3.23S 10.38E
Mayville Mich. U.S.A. **104** 43.20N 83.21W
Mayville N.Dak. U.S.A. **110** 47.30N 97.19W
Mayville N.Y. U.S.A. **114** 42.15N 79.30W
Mazabuka Zambia **79** 15.50S 27.47E
Mazagão Brazil **123** 0.07S 51.17W
Mazamba Mozambique **81** 18.32S 34.50E
Mazamet France **20** 43.30N 2.24E
Mazán Peru **122** 3.15S 73.00W
Mazara del Vallo Italy **32** 37.39N 12.36E
Mazarredo Argentina **125** 47.00S 66.45W
Mazarrón Spain **25** 37.36N 1.19W
Mazarrón, Golfo de *g.* Spain **25** 37.30N 1.18W
Mazatenango Guatemala **116** 14.31N 91.30W
Mazatlán Mexico **109** 23.13N106.25W
Mažeikiai U.S.S.R. **41** 56.19N 22.20E
Mazinaw L. Canada **105** 44.55N 77.12W
Mazirbe U.S.S.R. **41** 57.41N 22.21E
Mazowe *r.* Mozambique **81** 16.32S 33.25E
Mazowe Zimbabwe **81** 17.30S 30.58E
Mazu Liedao *is.* China **53** 26.12N120.00E
Mazunga Zimbabwe **80** 21.45S 29.52E
Mazurski, Pojezierze *lakes* Poland **37** 53.50N 21.00E
Mbabane Swaziland **80** 26.19S 31.08E
Mbagne Mauritania **74** 16.06N 14.47W
M'Baiki C.A.R. **77** 3.53N 18.01E
Mbala C.A.R. **73** 7.48N 20.51E
Mbala Zambia **79** 8.50S 31.24E
Mbale Uganda **79** 1.04N 34.12E
Mbalmayo Cameroon **77** 3.35N 11.31E
Mbamba Bay *town* Tanzania **79** 11.18S 34.50E
Mbandaka Zaïre **78** 0.03N 18.21E
Mbanza Congo Angola **78** 6.18S 14.16E
Mbarara Uganda **79** 0.36S 30.40E
Mbari *r.* C.A.R. **73** 4.34N 22.43E
Mbeya Tanzania **79** 8.54S 33.29E
Mbeya *d.* Tanzania **79** 8.30S 32.30E
Mbinda Congo **78** 2.11S 12.55E
Mbogo Tanzania **79** 7.26S 33.26E
Mbomou *d.* C.A.R. **73** 5.10N 23.00E
Mbomou *r.* C.A.R. **73** 4.08N 22.26E
Mboro Sudan **73** 6.18N 28.45E
M'Bour Senegal **76** 14.22N 16.54W
Mbout Mauritania **74** 16.02N 12.35W
M'bridge *r.* Angola **78** 7.12S 12.55E
Mbua Fiji **84** 16.48S178.37E
Mbuji Mayi Zaïre **78** 6.08S 23.39E
Mbulamuti Uganda **79** 0.50N 33.05E
Mbura Tanzania **79** 11.14S 35.25E
Mbutha Fiji **84** 16.39S179.50E
Mbuzi Zambia **79** 12.20S 32.17E
McAlester U.S.A. **111** 34.56N 95.46W
McAllen U.S.A. **111** 26.12N 98.15W
McArthur *r.* Australia **90** 15.54S136.40E
McArthur U.S.A. **114** 39.15N 82.29W
McArthurs Mills Canada **105** 45.06N 77.38W
McBride Canada **100** 53.20N120.10W
McCamey U.S.A. **111** 31.08N102.13W
McClintock Canada **101** 57.50N 94.10W
McClintock Channel Canada **99** 71.20N102.00W
McClure U.S.A. **114** 40.42N 77.19W
McClure Str. Canada **98** 74.30N116.00W
McComb U.S.A. **111** 31.14N 90.27W
McConaughy, L. U.S.A. **110** 41.15N102.00W
McConnel Creek *town* Canada **100** 56.53N126.30W
McConnellsburg U.S.A. **114** 39.57N 78.01W
McConnelsville U.S.A. **114** 39.39N 81.51W
McCook U.S.A. **110** 40.12N100.38W
McDermitt U.S.A. **108** 41.59N117.36W
McDouall Peak Australia **92** 29.51S134.55E
McGrath U.S.A. **98** 62.58N155.40W
McGregor U.S.A. **110** 46.36N 93.19W
McHenry U.S.A. **110** 42.21N 88.16W
Mchinja Tanzania **79** 9.44S 39.45E
Mchinji Malaŵi **79** 13.48S 32.55E
McIlwraith Range *mts.* Australia **90** 14.00S143.10E
McKeesport U.S.A. **114** 40.21N 79.52W
McKees Rocks *town* U.S.A. **114** 40.28N 80.10W
Mckellar Canada **104** 45.30N 79.55W
McKenzie U.S.A. **111** 36.08N 88.31W
McKerrow Canada **104** 46.18N 81.44W
McKinley, Mt. U.S.A. **98** 63.00N151.00W
McKinney U.S.A. **111** 33.12N 96.37W
McKittrick U.S.A. **109** 35.18N119.37W
McLaughlin U.S.A. **110** 45.49N100.49W
McLennan Canada **100** 55.42N116.50W
McLeod *r.* Canada **100** 54.08N115.42W
McLeod B. Canada **101** 62.53N110.00W
Mcleod Lake *town* Canada **100** 54.58N123.00W
M'Clintock Canada **100** 60.35N134.25W
McMinnville Oreg. U.S.A. **108** 45.13N123.12W
McMinnville Tenn. U.S.A. **113** 35.40N 85.49W
McNary U.S.A. **109** 34.04N109.51W
McPherson U.S.A. **110** 38.22N 97.40W
McPherson Range *mts.* Australia **93** 28.15S153.00E
Mdantsane R.S.A. **80** 32.54S 27.24E
Mead, L. U.S.A. **109** 36.05N114.25W
Meade U.S.A. **111** 37.17N100.20W
Meadow Lake *town* Canada **101** 54.07N108.20W
Meadville U.S.A. **114** 41.38N 80.09W
Meaford Canada **104** 44.36N 80.35W
Mealhada Portugal **26** 40.22N 8.27W
Meander River *town* Canada **100** 59.02N117.42W
Mearim *r.* Brazil **123** 3.20S 44.20W
Meath *d.* Rep. of Ire. **15** 53.32N 6.40W
Meaux France **19** 48.57N 2.52E
Mécatina, Cap *c.* Canada **103** 50.45N 59.01W
Mecca *see* Makkah Saudi Arabia **72**
Mecca U.S.A. **109** 33.35N116.03W
Mechanicsville U.S.A. **114** 38.26N 76.44W
Mechanicville U.S.A. **115** 42.54N 73.42W
Mechelen Belgium **16** 51.01N 4.28E
Mecheria Algeria **74** 33.33N 0.17W
Mecidiye Turkey **34** 40.38N 26.32E
Mecklenburger Bucht *b.* Germany **38** 54.20N 11.50E
Mecklenburg-Vorpommern *d.* Germany **38** 53.36N 12.45E
Meconta Mozambique **79** 15.00S 39.50E
Mecsek *mts.* Hungary **31** 46.15N 18.05E
Mecufi Mozambique **79** 13.20S 40.32E
Meda Portugal **26** 40.58N 7.16W
Medan Indonesia **58** 3.35N 98.39E
Mede Italy **30** 45.06N 8.44E
Médéa Algeria **75** 36.15N 2.48E
Mededsiz *mtn.* Turkey **64** 37.33N 34.38E
Medegue Gabon **78** 0.37N 10.08E
Medellín Colombia **122** 6.15N 75.36W
Medemblik Neth. **16** 52.48N 5.06E
Médenine Tunisia **75** 33.21N 10.30E
Mederdra Mauritania **76** 17.02N 15.41W
Medevi Sweden **43** 58.40N 14.57E
Medford Mass. U.S.A. **115** 42.25N 71.07W
Medford Oreg. U.S.A. **108** 42.19N122.52W
Medford Wisc. U.S.A. **110** 45.09N 90.20W
Medgidia Romania **37** 44.15N 28.16E
Medi Sudan **73** 5.04N 30.44E
Media U.S.A. **115** 39.54N 75.23W
Mediaş Romania **37** 46.10N 24.21E
Medicina Italy **30** 44.28N 11.38E
Medicine Bow Mts. U.S.A. **108** 41.10N106.10W
Medicine Bow Peak *mtn.* U.S.A. **108** 41.21N106.19W
Medicine Hat Canada **101** 50.03N110.40W
Medicine Lake *town* U.S.A. **108** 48.30N104.30W
Medicine Lodge U.S.A. **111** 37.17N 98.35W
Medina *see* Al Madīnah Saudi Arabia **64**
Medina N.Dak. U.S.A. **110** 46.54N 99.18W
Medina N.Y. U.S.A. **114** 43.13N 78.23W
Medina Ohio U.S.A. **114** 41.08N 81.52W
Medinaceli Spain **26** 41.10N 2.26W
Medina del Campo Spain **26** 41.18N 4.55W
Medina de Rioseco Spain **26** 41.53N 5.02W
Medina-Sidonia Spain **27** 36.27N 5.55W
Mediterranean Sea 23 36.00N 16.00E
Medjerda, Monts de la *mts.* Tunisia **32** 36.40N 8.40E
Medjerda, Oued *r.* Tunisia **32** 37.07N 10.13E
Medjez el Bab Tunisia **32** 36.39N 9.37E
Medoc *d.* France **20** 45.20N 1.00W
Mêdog China **52** 29.19N 95.19E
Medstead Canada **101** 53.19N108.02W
Medveda Yugo. **34** 42.50N 21.32E
Medveditsa *r.* U.S.S.R. **45** 49.35N 42.45E
Medvezhyegorsk U.S.S.R. **44** 62.56N 34.28E
Medvin U.S.S.R. **37** 49.25N 30.48E
Medway *r.* U.K. **13** 51.24N 0.31E
Medzhibozh U.S.S.R. **37** 49.29N 27.28E
Meeberrie Australia **88** 26.58S115.51E
Meekatharra Australia **88** 26.35S118.30E
Meeker U.S.A. **108** 40.02N107.55W
Meer Belgium **16** 51.27N 4.46E
Meerane Germany **38** 50.51N 12.28E
Meerhusener Moor *f.* Germany **38** 53.35N 7.30E
Meersburg Germany **39** 47.41N 9.16E
Meerut India **63** 28.59N 77.42E
Mefallesim Israel **67** 31.30N 34.34E
Mēga Ethiopia **73** 4.07N 38.16E
Megalon Khorion Greece **35** 36.27N 27.24E
Megalópolis Greece **35** 37.24N 22.08E
Mégara Greece **35** 38.00N 23.20E
Megasini *mtn.* India **63** 21.38N 86.21E
Meghalaya *d.* India **63** 25.30N 91.00E
Meghna *r.* Bangla. **63** 22.50N 90.50E
Mégiscane *r.* Canada **102** 48.36N 76.00W
Mehadia Romania **37** 44.55N 22.22E
Mehar Pakistan **62** 27.11N 67.49E
Mehekar India **62** 20.09N 76.34E
Mehidpur India **62** 23.49N 75.40E
Mehndāwal India **63** 26.59N 83.07E
Mehsāna India **62** 23.36N 72.24E
Mehtar Lām Afghan. **62** 34.39N 70.10E
Mehun-sur-Yèvre France **19** 47.09N 2.13E
Meiktila Burma **56** 20.53N 95.50E
Meiningen Germany **38** 50.34N 10.25E
Meira, Sierra de *mts.* Spain **26** 43.15N 7.15W
Meiringen Switz. **39** 46.43N 8.12E
Me'ir Shefeya Israel **67** 32.35N 34.57E
Meishan China **55** 30.02N103.50E
Meissen Germany **38** 51.10N 13.28E
Mei Xian China **55** 24.20N116.15E
Meiyino Sudan **73** 6.12N 34.40E
Mekatina Canada **104** 47.05N 84.07W
Mekdela Ethiopia **73** 11.28N 39.23E
Mek'elē Ethiopia **73** 13.33N 39.30E
Mekerrhane, Sebkha *f.* Algeria **74** 26.22N 1.20E
Mekhtar Pakistan **62** 30.28N 69.22E
Mekinac, L. Canada **105** 47.05N 73.39W
Meknès Morocco **74** 33.53N 5.37W
Mekong *r.* Asia **56** 10.00N106.40E
Mekong Delta Vietnam **56** 10.00N105.40E
Mekongga *mtn.* Indonesia **59** 3.39S121.15E
Mékôngk *r.* Cambodia *see* Mekong *r.* Asia **56**
Mékrou *r.* Benin **77** 12.20N 2.47E
Melaka Malaysia **58** 2.11N102.16E
Melanesia *is.* Pacific Oc. **84** 5.00N165.00E
Melbourne Australia **93** 37.45S144.58E
Melbourne U.S.A. **113** 28.04N 80.38W
Meldorf Germany **38** 54.05N 9.05E
Meldrum Bay *town* Canada **104** 45.56N 83.07W
Mélé C.A.R. **73** 9.46N 21.33E
Melegnano Italy **30** 45.21N 9.19E
Meleuz U.S.S.R. **44** 52.58N 55.56E
Mélèzes, Rivière aux *r.* Canada **103** 57.40N 69.29W
Melfi Chad **77** 11.04N 18.03E
Melfi Italy **33** 40.59N 15.40E
Melfort Canada **101** 52.52N104.36W
Melgaço Portugal **26** 42.07N 8.16W
Melilla Spain **24** 35.17N 2.57W
Melilot Israel **67** 31.23N 34.36E
Melipilla Chile **125** 33.42S 71.13W
Melito di Porto Salvo Italy **33** 37.56N 15.47E
Melitopol U.S.S.R. **45** 46.51N 35.22E
Melk Austria **36** 48.14N 15.20E
Melle France **18** 46.13N 0.09W
Mellen U.S.A. **110** 46.20N 90.40W
Mellerud Sweden **43** 58.42N 12.28E
Mellid Spain **26** 42.55N 8.00W
Mellit Sudan **72** 14.08N 25.33E
Melmore Pt. Rep. of Ire. **15** 55.15N 7.49W
Melnik Bulgaria **34** 41.58N 23.25E
Mělník Czech. **36** 50.20N 14.29E
Melo Uruguay **126** 32.22S 54.10W
Melrhir, Chott *f.* Algeria **75** 34.20N 6.20E
Melrose U.K. **14** 55.36N 2.43W
Melrose Mont. U.S.A. **108** 45.37N112.41W
Melrose N.Mex U.S.A. **109** 34.26N103.38W
Melstone U.S.A. **108** 46.36N107.52W
Melsungen Germany **38** 51.08N 9.32E
Meltaus Finland **40** 66.54N 25.22E
Melton Australia **93** 37.41S144.36E
Melton Mowbray U.K. **12** 52.46N 0.53W
Melun France **19** 48.32N 2.40E
Melvich U.K. **14** 58.33N 3.55W
Melville Canada **101** 50.55N102.48W
Melville, C. Australia **90** 14.11S144.30E
Melville, L. Canada **103** 53.45N 59.30W
Melville B. Australia **90** 12.10S136.32E
Melville Hills Canada **98** 69.20N122.00W
Melville I. Australia **90** 11.30S131.00E
Melville I. Canada **98** 75.30N110.00W
Melville Pen. Canada **99** 68.00N 84.00W
Melvin, Lough Rep. of Ire./U.K. **15** 54.26N 8.12W
Mélykút Hungary **31** 46.13N 19.24E
Melzo Italy **30** 45.30N 9.25E
Mêmar Co *l.* China **63** 34.10N 82.15E
Memba Mozambique **81** 14.16S 40.30E
Memboro Indonesia **58** 9.22S119.32E
Memmingen Germany **39** 47.59N 10.11E
Memphis *ruins* Egypt **66** 29.52N 31.12E
Memphis Mich. U.S.A. **114** 42.54N 82.46W
Memphis Tenn. U.S.A. **111** 35.08N 90.03W
Memphremagog, L. Canada **105** 45.05N 72.15W
Mena U.S.A. **111** 34.35N 94.15W
Mena U.S.S.R. **37** 51.30N 32.15E
Menai Str. U.K. **12** 53.17N 4.20W
Ménaka Mali **75** 15.55N 2.24E
Mènam Khong *r.* Laos *see* Mekong *r.* Asia **56**
Menarandra *r.* Madagascar **81** 25.17S 44.30E
Menard U.S.A. **111** 30.55N 99.47W
Menawashei Sudan **73** 12.40N 24.59E
Mendawai *r.* Indonesia **58** 3.17S113.20E
Mende France **20** 44.30N 3.30E
Mendebo Mts. Ethiopia **73** 7.00N 39.30E
Mendi P.N.G. **59** 6.13S143.39E
Mendip Hills U.K. **13** 51.15N 2.40W
Mendocino, C. U.S.A. **108** 40.25N124.25W
Mendooran Australia **93** 31.48S149.08E
Mendoza Argentina **125** 32.54S 68.50W
Mendoza *d.* Argentina **125** 34.30S 68.00W
Mendung Indonesia **58** 0.31N103.12E
Ménéac France **18** 48.09N 2.28W
Mene Grande Venezuela **122** 9.51N 70.57W
Menemen Turkey **64** 38.34N 27.03E
Menen Belgium **16** 50.48N 3.07E
Menfi Italy **32** 37.36N 12.59E
Mengcheng China **54** 33.16N116.33E
Mengzi China **61** 23.20N103.21E
Menihek Lakes Canada **103** 54.00N 66.35W
Menindee Australia **92** 32.23S142.30E
Menindee L. Australia **92** 32.21S142.20E
Menominee U.S.A. **110** 45.07N 87.37W
Menomonie U.S.A. **110** 44.53N 91.55W
Menongue Angola **78** 14.40S 17.41E
Menor, Mar *b.* Spain **25** 37.43N 0.48W
Menorca *i.* Spain **25** 40.00N 4.00E
Mens France **21** 44.49N 5.45E
Mentawai, Kepulauan *is.* Indonesia **58** 2.50S 99.00E
Mentekab Malaysia **58** 3.29N102.21E
Mentok Indonesia **58** 2.04S105.12E
Menton France **21** 43.47N 7.30E
Mentor U.S.A. **114** 41.40N 81.20W
Menyapa, Gunung *mtn.* Indonesia **58** 1.00N116.20E
Menzel Bourguiba Tunisia **32** 37.10N 9.48E
Menzel Bou Zelfa Tunisia **32** 36.41N 10.36E
Menzel Djemil Tunisia **32** 37.14N 9.55E
Menzel Temime Tunisia **32** 36.47N 10.59E
Menzies Australia **89** 29.41S121.02E
Menzies, Mt. Antarctica **128** 71.50S 61.00E
Me'ona Israel **67** 33.01N 35.16E
Meppel Neth. **16** 52.42N 6.12E
Meppen Germany **38** 52.41N 7.17E
Mer France **18** 47.42N 1.30E
Merambéllou, Kólpos *g.* Greece **35** 35.14N 25.47E
Merano Italy **30** 46.40N 11.09E
Merauke Indonesia **90** 8.30S140.22E
Merbein Australia **92** 34.11S142.04E
Mercato Saraceno Italy **30** 43.57N 12.12E
Merced U.S.A. **108** 37.18N120.29W
Mercedes Buenos Aires Argentina **125** 34.40S 59.25W
Mercedes Corrientes Argentina **124** 29.15S 58.05W
Mercedes San Luis Argentina **125** 33.40S 65.30W
Mercedes Uruguay **125** 33.16S 58.01W
Mercer U.S.A. **114** 41.14N 80.15W
Mercy, C. Canada **99** 65.00N 63.30W
Mere U.K. **13** 51.05N 2.16W
Meredith Australia **92** 37.50S144.05E
Meredith, L. U.S.A. **111** 35.36N101.42W
Mereeg Somali Rep. **71** 3.47N 47.18E
Merefa U.S.S.R. **45** 49.49N 36.05E
Mereke C.A.R. **73** 7.34N 23.09E
Mergenevo U.S.S.R. **45** 49.59N 51.19E
Mergui Burma **56** 12.26N 98.38E
Mergui Archipelago *is.* Burma **56** 11.15N 98.00E
Meribah Australia **92** 34.42S140.53E
Meriç *r.* Turkey **34** 40.52N 26.12E
Mérida Mexico **117** 20.59N 89.39W
Mérida Spain **27** 38.55N 6.20W
Mérida Venezuela **122** 8.24N 71.08W
Mérida, Cordillera de *mts.* Venezuela **122** 8.30N 71.00W
Meriden U.S.A. **115** 41.32N 72.48W
Meridian U.S.A. **111** 32.22N 88.42W
Mérignac France **20** 44.50N 0.42W
Merigur Australia **92** 34.21S141.23E
Merikarvia Finland **41** 61.51N 21.30E
Merimbula Australia **93** 36.52S149.55E
Merino Australia **92** 37.45S141.35E
Merir *i.* Caroline Is. **59** 4.19N132.18E
Merirumã Brazil **123** 1.15N 54.50W
Merizo Guam **84** 13.16N144.40E
Merkendorf Germany **39** 49.12N 10.42E
Merksem Belgium **16** 51.14N 4.25E
Merlin Canada **104** 42.14N 82.14W
Merlo Argentina **125** 34.40S 58.45W
Meron, Har *mtn.* Israel **67** 33.00N 35.25E
Merredin Australia **89** 31.29S118.16E
Merrick *mtn.* U.K. **14** 55.08N 4.29W
Merrickville Canada **105** 44.55N 75.50W
Merrill Oreg. U.S.A. **108** 42.01N121.36W
Merrill Wisc. U.S.A. **110** 45.11N 89.41W
Merriman U.S.A. **110** 42.55N101.42W
Merritt Canada **100** 50.10N120.45W
Merriwa Australia **93** 32.08S150.20E
Mersa Fatma Ethiopia **72** 14.55N 40.20E
Mersch Lux. **16** 49.44N 6.05E
Mersea I. U.K. **13** 51.47N 0.58E
Merseburg Germany **38** 51.21N 11.59E
Mersey *r.* U.K. **12** 53.22N 2.37W
Merseyside *d.* U.K. **12** 53.28N 3.00W
Mersin Turkey **64** 36.47N 34.37E
Mersing Malaysia **58** 2.25N103.50E
Merta India **62** 26.39N 74.02E
Merta Road *town* India **62** 26.43N 73.55E
Merthyr Tydfil U.K. **13** 51.45N 3.23W
Mértola Portugal **27** 37.38N 7.40W
Merton U.K. **13** 51.25N 0.12W
Mertzon U.S.A. **111** 31.16N100.49W
Méru France **19** 49.14N 2.08E
Meru *mtn.* Tanzania **79** 3.15S 36.44E
Méry France **19** 48.30N 3.53E
Merzifon Turkey **64** 40.52N 35.28E
Merzig Germany **39** 49.27N 6.36E
Mesa *r.* Spain **25** 41.15N 1.48W
Mesa U.S.A. **109** 33.25N111.50W
Mesagne Italy **33** 40.33N 17.49E
Mesarás, Kólpos *g.* Greece **35** 34.58N 24.36E
Meschede Germany **38** 51.20N 8.17E
Meshoppen U.S.A. **115** 41.34N 76.03W
Meslay-du-Maine France **18** 47.57N 0.33W
Mesocco Switz. **39** 46.23N 9.14E
Mesolóngion Greece **35** 38.21N 21.17E
Mesopotamia *f.* Iraq **65** 33.30N 44.30E
Messalo *r.* Mozambique **79** 11.38S 40.27E
Messina Italy **33** 38.11N 15.33E
Messina R.S.A. **80** 22.20S 30.03E
Messina, Stretto di *str.* Italy **33** 38.10N 15.35E
Messines Canada **105** 46.14N 76.01W
Messíni Greece **35** 37.03N 22.00E
Messíni *site* Greece **35** 37.11N 21.57E
Messiniakós, Kólpos *g.* Greece **35** 36.58N 22.00E
Messkirch Germany **39** 47.59N 9.07E
Mestá Greece **35** 38.16N 25.53E
Mesta *r.* Bulgaria *see* Nestos *r.* Greece **34**
Mestre Italy **30** 45.29N 12.15E
Meta *r.* Venezuela **122** 6.10N 67.30W
Metagama Canada **104** 47.05N 81.57W
Metallifere, Colline *mts.* Italy **30** 43.15N 11.00E
Metán Argentina **124** 25.30S 65.00W
Metangula Mozambique **79** 12.41S 34.51E
Metapontum *site* Italy **33** 40.24N 16.49E
Metéora *site* Greece **34** 39.46N 21.36E
Methóni Greece **35** 36.50N 21.43E
Methuen U.S.A. **115** 42.44N 71.11W
Metkovets Bulgaria **34** 43.37N 23.10E
Metković Yugo. **31** 43.03N 17.39E
Metlakatla U.S.A. **100** 55.09N131.35W
Metlika Yugo. **31** 45.39N 15.19E
Métsovon Greece **34** 39.46N 21.11E
Metulla Israel **67** 33.16N 35.35E
Metz France **19** 49.08N 6.10E
Metzingen Germany **39** 48.32N 9.17E
Meu *r.* France **18** 48.02N 1.47W
Meulaboh Indonesia **58** 4.10N 96.09E
Meulan France **19** 49.01N 1.54E
Meurthe *r.* France **19** 48.47N 6.09E
Meurthe-et-Moselle *d.* France **19** 48.35N 6.10E
Meuse *d.* France **19** 49.00N 5.30E
Meuse *r.* Belgium *see* Maas *r.* Neth. **16**
Meuselwitz Germany **38** 51.02N 12.17E
Mexia U.S.A. **111** 31.41N 96.29W
Mexicali Mexico **109** 32.40N115.29W
Mexico C. America **116** 20.00N100.00W
México *d.* Mexico **116** 19.45N 99.30W
Mexico Mo. U.S.A. **110** 39.10N 91.53W
Mexico N.Y. U.S.A. **115** 43.28N 76.14W
Mexico, G. of N. America **116** 25.00N 90.00W
Mexico B. U.S.A. **115** 43.31N 76.17W
Mexico City *see* Ciudad de México Mexico **116**
Meximieux France **21** 45.54N 5.12E
Meydān Kalay Afghan. **62** 32.25N 66.44E
Meydān Khvolah Afghan. **62** 33.36N 69.51E
Meyenburg Germany **38** 53.18N 12.14E
Meyersdale U.S.A. **114** 39.45N 79.05W
Meymac France **20** 45.32N 2.09E

Meymaneh to Moebase

Meymaneh Afghan. 60 35.54N 64.43E
Meyrueis France 20 44.10N 3.26E
Mezdra Bulgaria 34 43.12N 23.35E
Mèze France 20 43.25N 3.36E
Mézel France 21 43.59N 6.12E
Mezen U.S.S.R. 44 65.50N 44.20E
Mezen r. U.S.S.R. 44 65.50N 44.18E
Mézenc, Mont mtn. France 21 44.55N 4.11E
Mezenskaya Guba g. U.S.S.R. 44 66.30N 44.00E
Mezer Israel 67 32.26N 35.03E
Mézières-en-Brenne France 18 46.49N 1.13E
Mézin France 20 44.03N 0.16E
Mezőkövesd Hungary 37 47.50N 20.34E
Mezzolombardo Italy 30 46.13N 11.05E
M'goun, Irhil mtn. Morocco 22 31.31N 6.25W
Mhow India 62 22.33N 75.46E
Miahuatlán Mexico 116 16.20N 96.36W
Miajadas Spain 27 39.09N 5.54W
Miājlar India 62 26.15N 70.23E
Miami Fla. U.S.A. 113 25.45N 80.15W
Miami Okla. U.S.A. 111 36.53N 94.53W
Miami Tex. U.S.A. 111 35.42N 100.38W
Miami Beach town U.S.A. 113 25.47N 80.07W
Miāndow Āb Iran 65 36.57N 46.06E
Miandrivazo Madagascar 81 19.31S 45.28E
Miāneh Iran 65 37.23N 47.45E
Miang, Phukao mtn. Thailand 56 16.55N 101.00E
Miāni India 62 21.51N 69.23E
Miāni Hōr b. Pakistan 62 25.34N 66.19E
Miānwāli Pakistan 62 32.35N 71.33E
Mianyang Hubei China 55 30.25N 113.30E
Mianyang Sichuan China 55 31.26N 104.45E
Miao'er Shan mtn. China 55 25.50N 110.22E
Miaoli Taiwan 55 24.34N 120.48E
Miarinarivo Madagascar 81 18.57S 46.55E
Miass U.S.S.R. 50 55.00N 60.00E
Mibu r. Japan 57 35.49N 137.57E
Mica R.S.A. 80 24.09S 30.49E
Micang Shan mts. China 54 32.40N 107.28E
Michael, L. Canada 103 54.32N 58.15W
Michalovce Czech. 37 48.45N 21.55E
Michelson, Mt. U.S.A. 98 69.19N 144.17W
Michigan d. U.S.A. 112 44.00N 85.00W
Michigan, L. U.S.A. 112 44.00N 87.00W
Michigan Center U.S.A. 104 42.14N 84.20W
Michigan City U.S.A. 112 41.43N 86.54W
Michipicoten Canada 102 47.59N 84.55W
Michipicoten I. Canada 102 47.40N 85.50W
Michoacán d. Mexico 116 19.20N 101.00W
Michurin Bulgaria 29 42.09N 27.51E
Michurinsk U.S.S.R. 44 52.54N 40.30E
Micronesia is. Pacific Oc. 84 8.00N 160.00E
Midale Canada 101 49.22N 103.27W
Mid Atlantic Ridge f. Atlantic Oc. 127 20.00N 45.00W
Middelburg Neth. 16 51.30N 3.36E
Middelburg C.P. R.S.A. 80 31.29S 25.00E
Middelburg Trans. R.S.A. 80 25.45S 29.27E
Middelfart Denmark 42 55.30N 9.45E
Middelharnis Neth. 16 51.46N 4.09E
Middenmeer Neth. 16 52.51N 4.59E
Middleboro Canada 101 49.01N 95.21W
Middleboro U.S.A. 115 41.49N 70.55W
Middleburg N.Y. U.S.A. 115 42.36N 74.20W
Middleburg Va. U.S.A. 114 38.58N 77.44W
Middlebury U.S.A. 105 44.01N 73.10W
Middlefield U.S.A. 114 41.28N 81.05W
Middle I. Australia 89 34.07S 123.12E
Middle Loup r. U.S.A. 110 41.17N 98.23W
Middleport N.Y. U.S.A. 114 43.13N 78.29W
Middleport Ohio U.S.A. 114 39.00N 82.03W
Middlesboro U.S.A. 113 36.37N 83.43W
Middlesbrough U.K. 12 54.34N 1.13W
Middleton Canada 103 44.57N 65.04W
Middleton Reef Pacific Oc. 84 29.28S 159.06E
Middletown Conn. U.S.A. 115 41.33N 72.39W
Middletown Del. U.S.A. 115 39.25N 75.47W
Middletown Ind. U.S.A. 112 39.31N 84.13W
Middletown N.Y. U.S.A. 115 41.27N 74.25W
Middletown Penn. U.S.A. 114 40.12N 76.44W
Middletown R.I. U.S.A. 115 41.32N 71.17W
Mid Glamorgan d. U.K. 13 51.38N 3.25W
Midi, Canal du France 20 43.26N 1.58E
Midi de Bigorre, Pic du mtn. France 20 42.56N 0.08E
Mid-Indian Basin f. Indian Oc. 49 15.00S 80.00E
Mid-Indian Ridge f. Indian Oc. 49 30.00S 75.00E
Midi-Pyrénées d. France 20 44.10N 2.00E
Midland Canada 104 44.45N 79.53W
Midland Mich. U.S.A. 104 43.37N 84.14W
Midland Tex. U.S.A. 111 32.00N 102.05W
Midland Junction Australia 89 31.54S 115.57E
Midleton Rep. of Ire. 15 51.55N 8.10W
Midnapore India 63 22.26N 87.20E
Midongy-Sud Madagascar 81 23.35S 47.01E
Midou r. France 20 43.54N 0.30W
Midway Is. Hawaiian Is. 84 28.15N 177.25W
Midwest U.S.A. 108 43.25N 106.16W
Midwest City U.S.A. 111 35.27N 97.24W
Midyan f. Saudi Arabia 66 27.50N 35.30E
Midye Turkey 29 41.37N 28.07E
Midžor mtn. Bulgaria 34 43.24N 22.40E
Mie d. Japan 57 34.42N 136.08E
Miechów Poland 37 50.23N 20.01E
Miedzychód Poland 36 52.36N 15.55E
Miélan France 20 43.26N 0.19E
Mielec Poland 37 50.18N 21.25E
Mien l. Sweden 43 56.25N 14.51E
Mienga Angola 78 17.16S 19.50E
Mieres Spain 26 43.15N 5.46W
Miesbach Germany 39 47.47N 11.50E
Mifflin U.S.A. 114 40.34N 77.24W
Mifraz Hefa b. Israel 67 32.52N 35.03E
Migang Shan mtn. China 54 35.32N 106.13E
Migdal Israel 67 32.50N 35.30E
Migdal Ha'Emeq Israel 67 32.41N 35.15E
Miguel Hidalgo, Presa resr. Mexico 109 26.41N 108.19W
Migyaunglaung Burma 56 14.40N 98.09E
Mijares r. Spain 25 39.55N 0.01W
Mijet i. Yugo. 31 42.45N 17.30E
Mikhaylov U.S.S.R. 44 54.14N 39.00E
Mikhaylovgrad Bulgaria 34 43.27N 23.16E
Mikhaylovka U.S.S.R. 45 50.05N 43.15E
Miki Japan 57 34.48N 134.59E
Mikínai Greece 35 37.43N 22.46E
Mikindani Tanzania 79 10.16S 40.05E
Mikjaylovgrad d. Bulgaria 34 43.25N 23.11E
Mikkeli Finland 44 61.44N 27.15E
Mikkwa r. Canada 100 58.25N 114.46W
Míkonos Greece 35 37.30N 25.25E
Míkonos i. Greece 35 37.29N 25.25E
Mikre Bulgaria 34 43.02N 24.31E
Mikumi Tanzania 79 7.22S 37.00E
Mikun U.S.S.R. 44 62.20N 50.01E
Mikuni sanmyaku mts. Japan 57 37.00N 139.20E
Milagro Ecuador 122 2.11S 79.36W
Milan see Milano Italy 30
Milan Mich. U.S.A. 104 42.05N 83.40W
Milan Mo. U.S.A. 110 40.12N 93.07W
Milange Mozambique 79 16.09S 35.44E
Milano Italy 30 45.28N 9.12E
Milâs Turkey 35 37.19N 27.47E
Milazzo Italy 33 38.14N 15.15E
Milbank U.S.A. 110 45.14N 96.38W
Milbanke Sd. Canada 100 52.18N 128.33W
Mildenhall U.K. 13 52.20N 0.30E
Mildmay Canada 104 44.03N 81.07W
Mildura Australia 92 34.14S 142.13E
Miléai Greece 35 39.20N 23.09E
Miles Australia 90 26.40S 150.11E
Miles City U.S.A. 108 46.25N 105.51W
Miletto, Monte mtn. Italy 33 41.27N 14.22E
Miletus site Turkey 35 37.30N 27.18E
Milevsko Czech. 39 49.27N 14.22E
Milford Conn. U.S.A. 115 41.13N 73.04W
Milford Del. U.S.A. 115 38.55N 75.25W
Milford Mass. U.S.A. 115 42.08N 71.32W
Milford Mich. U.S.A. 104 42.35N 83.36W
Milford N.H. U.S.A. 115 42.50N 71.39W
Milford N.Y. U.S.A. 115 42.35N 74.57W
Milford Penn. U.S.A. 115 41.19N 74.48W
Milford Utah U.S.A. 108 38.24N 113.01W
Milford Haven town U.K. 13 51.43N 5.02W
Milford Sound town New Zealand 86 44.41S 167.56E
Miliana Algeria 75 27.21N 2.28E
Miling Australia 89 30.27S 116.20E
Milk r. U.S.A. 108 48.05N 106.15W
Millau France 20 44.06N 3.05E
Millbrook Canada 104 44.09N 78.27W
Millbrook U.S.A. 115 41.47N 73.42W
Mille Lacs, Lac des l. Canada 102 48.45N 90.35W
Mille Lacs L. U.S.A. 110 46.10N 93.45W
Miller r. Australia 92 30.05S 136.07E
Millerovo U.S.S.R. 45 48.55N 40.25E
Millers r. U.S.A. 115 42.35N 72.30W
Millersburg Mich. U.S.A. 104 45.20N 84.04W
Millersburg Ohio U.S.A. 114 40.33N 81.55W
Millersburg Penn. U.S.A. 114 40.33N 76.58W
Millerton U.S.A. 115 41.57N 73.31W
Milleur Pt. U.K. 14 55.01N 5.07W
Millicent Australia 92 37.36S 140.22E
Millington U.S.A. 115 39.16N 75.50W
Millinocket U.S.A. 112 45.39N 68.43W
Millmerran Australia 91 27.51S 151.17E
Millom U.K. 12 54.13N 3.16W
Mills L. Canada 100 61.30N 118.10W
Millstatt Austria 31 46.48N 13.35E
Millville U.S.A. 115 39.24N 75.02W
Milne Inlet town Canada 99 72.30N 80.59W
Milnet Canada 104 46.49N 80.59W
Milo r. Guinea 76 11.05N 9.05W
Mílos Greece 35 36.45N 24.27E
Mílos i. Greece 35 36.41N 24.15E
Milparinka Australia 92 29.45S 141.55E
Milroy U.S.A. 114 40.43N 77.35W
Miltenberg Germany 39 49.42N 9.15E
Milton Australia 93 35.19S 150.24E
Milton Canada 104 43.31N 79.53W
Milton Del. U.S.A. 115 38.47N 75.19W
Milton Mass. U.S.A. 115 42.15N 71.05W
Milton N.H. U.S.A. 115 43.23N 70.59W
Milton Penn. U.S.A. 114 41.01N 76.51W
Milton Vt. U.S.A. 105 44.38N 73.07W
Milton W.Va. U.S.A. 114 38.26N 82.08W
Milton Keynes U.K. 13 52.03N 0.42W
Miltou Chad 77 10.10N 17.30E
Miluo China 55 28.50N 113.05E
Milverton Canada 104 43.34N 80.55W
Milwaukee U.S.A. 110 43.02N 87.55W
Milwaukie U.S.A. 108 45.27N 122.38W
Milyatino U.S.S.R. 44 54.30N 34.20E
Mim Ghana 76 6.55N 2.34W
Miminiska L. Canada 102 51.32N 88.33W
Mimizan France 20 44.12N 1.14W
Mina U.S.A. 108 38.24N 118.07W
Mīnā 'al Aḥmadī Kuwait 60 29.04N 48.08E
Mīnāb Iran 65 27.07N 57.05E
Mīnā Baranīs Egypt 72 23.55N 35.28E
Minaki Canada 102 50.00N 94.48W
Minamata Japan 57 32.13N 130.24E
Minas Uruguay 125 34.23S 55.14W
Minas Basin b. Canada 103 45.20N 64.00W
Minas Channel str. Canada 103 45.15N 64.45W
Minas de Corrales Uruguay 125 31.35S 55.28W
Minas de Ríotinto Spain 27 37.42N 6.22W
Minas Gerais d. Brazil 126 18.00S 45.00W
Minatitlán Mexico 116 17.59N 94.32W
Minbu Burma 56 20.09N 94.52E
Mindanao i. Phil. 59 7.30N 125.00E
Mindanao Sea Phil. 59 9.10N 124.25E
Mindarie Australia 92 34.51S 140.12E
Mindemoya Canada 104 45.44N 82.10W
Minden Canada 104 44.55N 78.43W
Minden Germany 38 52.17N 8.55E
Minden U.S.A. 111 32.37N 93.17W
Minden City U.S.A. 104 43.40N 82.47W
Mindif Cameroon 77 10.25N 14.23E
Mindiptana Indonesia 59 5.45S 140.22E
Mindona L. Australia 92 33.09S 142.09E
Mindoro i. Phil. 59 13.00N 121.00E
Mindoro Str. Pacific Oc. 59 12.30N 120.10E
Mindra mtn. Romania 37 45.20N 23.32E
Minehead U.K. 13 51.12N 3.29W
Mineola U.S.A. 111 32.40N 95.29W
Minerva Australia 90 24.00S 148.05E
Minerva U.S.A. 114 40.44N 81.06W
Minervino Murge Italy 33 41.05N 16.05E
Mingan Canada 103 50.18N 64.02W
Mingary Australia 92 32.09S 140.46E
Mingela Australia 90 19.53S 146.40E
Mingenew Australia 89 29.11S 115.26E
Mingin Burma 56 22.52N 94.39E
Mingin Range mts. Burma 56 24.00N 95.45E
Minglanilla Spain 25 39.32N 1.36W
Mingorría Spain 26 40.45N 4.40W
Minhe China 54 36.12N 102.59E
Minho r. see Miño r. Portugal 26
Minićevo Yugo. 34 43.42N 22.18E
Minidoka U.S.A. 108 42.46N 113.30W
Minigwal, L. Australia 89 29.35S 123.12E
Min Jiang r. China 55 26.06N 119.15E
Minlaton Australia 92 34.46S 137.37E
Minna Nigeria 77 9.39N 6.32E
Minneapolis Kans. U.S.A. 110 39.08N 97.42W
Minneapolis Minn. U.S.A. 110 44.59N 93.13W
Minnedosa Canada 101 50.14N 99.51W
Minnesota d. U.S.A. 110 46.00N 94.00W
Minnesota r. U.S.A. 110 44.54N 93.10W
Minnesota Lake town U.S.A. 110 43.51N 93.50W
Minnipa Australia 92 32.51S 135.09E
Minnitaki L. Canada 102 50.00N 91.50W
Mino Japan 57 35.34N 136.56E
Miño r. Spain 26 41.52N 8.51W
Minobu-sanchi mts. Japan 57 35.05N 138.15E
Mino-kamo Japan 57 35.26N 137.01E
Mino-mikawa-kōgen mts. Japan 57 35.16N 137.10E
Minorca i. see Menorca i. Spain 25
Minot U.S.A. 110 48.16N 101.19W
Minqin China 54 38.42N 103.11E
Minsen Germany 38 53.42N 7.58E
Min Shan mts. China 54 32.40N 104.40E
Minsk U.S.S.R. 37 53.51N 27.30E
Minta Cameroon 77 4.37N 12.47E
Minto, Lac l. Canada 102 57.15N 74.50W
Minturno Italy 32 41.15N 13.45E
Minūf Egypt 66 30.28N 30.56E
Min Xian China 54 34.26N 104.02E
Minyā al Qamḥ Egypt 66 30.31N 31.21E
Minyar U.S.S.R. 44 55.06N 57.29E
Mio U.S.A. 104 44.39N 84.08W
Mionica Yugo. 31 44.15N 20.05E
Miquelon Canada 102 49.25N 76.32W
Mira Italy 30 45.26N 12.08E
Mira Portugal 26 40.26N 8.44W
Mira r. Portugal 27 37.43N 8.47W
Mīrābād Afghan. 62 30.25N 61.50E
Miracema Brazil 126 21.22S 42.09W
Mīrah, Wādī al r. Iraq 64 32.27N 41.21E
Miraj India 60 16.51N 74.42E
Miramas France 21 43.35N 5.00E
Mirambeau France 20 45.23N 0.34W
Miramichi B. Canada 103 47.08N 65.08W
Mīram Shāh Pakistan 62 33.01N 70.04E
Mīrān Pakistan 62 31.24N 70.43E
Miranda de Ebro Spain 26 42.41N 2.57W
Miranda do Douro Portugal 26 41.30N 6.16W
Mirande France 20 43.31N 0.25E
Mirandela Portugal 26 41.29N 7.11W
Mirando City U.S.A. 111 27.26N 99.00W
Mirandola Italy 30 44.53N 11.04E
Miravete, Puerto de pass Spain 27 39.43N 5.43W
Mīr Bachcheh Kūt Afghan. 62 34.45N 69.08E
Mirbāṭ Oman 60 17.00N 54.45E
Mirebeau-sur-Bèze France 19 47.24N 5.19E
Mirecourt France 19 48.18N 6.08E
Miri Malaysia 58 4.28N 114.00E
Mirim, L. Brazil 126 33.10S 53.30W
Mirína Greece 34 39.52N 25.04E
Mirintu Creek r. Australia 92 28.58S 143.18E
Mironovka U.S.S.R. 37 49.40N 30.59E
Miroşi Romania 37 44.25N 24.58E
Mirow Germany 38 53.16N 12.49E
Mīrpur Jammu & Kashmir 62 33.15N 73.55E
Mīrpur Batoro Pakistan 62 24.44N 68.16E
Mīrpur Khās Pakistan 60 25.33N 69.05E
Mīrpur Sakro Pakistan 62 24.33N 67.37E
Mirtóön Pélagos sea Greece 35 36.51N 23.18E
Miryeny U.S.S.R. 37 47.00N 29.06E
Mirzāpur India 63 25.09N 82.35E
Mi saki c. Japan 57 40.09N 141.52E
Misawa Japan 57 40.41N 141.24E
Miscou I. Canada 103 47.57N 64.33W
Mishawaka U.S.A. 112 41.38N 86.10W
Mishima Japan 57 35.07N 138.55E
Mishkino U.S.S.R. 44 55.34N 56.00E
Mishmar Ayyalon Israel 67 31.52N 34.57E
Mishmar Ha'Emeq Israel 67 32.36N 35.09E
Mishmar HaNegev Israel 67 31.21N 34.43E
Mishmar Hayarden Israel 67 33.00N 35.36E
Mishomis Canada 105 47.11N 75.40W
Misilmeri Italy 32 38.01N 13.27E
Misima I. P.N.G. 90 10.40S 152.45E
Misiones d. Argentina 124 27.00S 54.40W
Miskī Sudan 72 14.51N 24.13E
Miskolc Hungary 37 48.07N 20.47E
Mismār Sudan 72 18.13N 35.38E
Misool i. Indonesia 59 1.50S 130.10E
Miṣr al Jadīdah Egypt 66 30.06N 31.20E
Miṣrātah Libya 75 32.23N 15.06E
Miṣrātah d. Libya 75 30.30N 17.00E
Miṣr Baḥrī f. Egypt 66 30.30N 31.00E
Missinaibi r. Canada 102 50.44N 81.29W
Mission U.S.A. 110 43.18N 100.40W
Mississagi r. Canada 104 46.10N 83.01W
Mississagi Prov. Park Canada 104 46.35N 82.30W
Mississauga Canada 104 43.35N 79.37W
Mississippi r. Canada 105 45.26N 76.16W
Mississippi d. U.S.A. 111 32.40N 90.00W
Mississippi r. U.S.A. 111 29.00N 89.15W
Mississippi Delta U.S.A. 111 29.10N 89.15W
Mississippi L. Canada 105 45.05N 76.12W
Mississippi Sd. U.S.A. 111 30.15N 88.40W
Missoula U.S.A. 108 46.52N 114.01W
Missouri d. U.S.A. 110 38.30N 92.00W
Missouri r. U.S.A. 110 38.50N 90.08W
Missouri Valley town U.S.A. 110 41.33N 95.53W
Mistake Creek town Australia 88 17.06S 129.04E
Mistassini Canada 103 48.54N 72.13W
Mistassini r. Canada 103 48.53N 72.14W
Mistassini, Lac l. Canada 103 51.15N 73.10W
Mistassini Prov. Park Canada 103 51.30N 73.20W
Mistastin Canada 103 55.55N 63.30W
Misterbianco Italy 33 37.31N 15.01E
Mistinibi, L. Canada 103 55.55N 64.10W
Mistretta Italy 33 37.56N 14.22E
Mitchell Australia 90 26.29S 147.58E
Mitchell r. Qld. Australia 90 15.12S 141.35E
Mitchell r. Vic. Australia 93 37.53S 147.41E
Mitchell Canada 104 43.28N 81.12W
Mitchell Oreg. U.S.A. 108 44.34N 120.09W
Mitchell S.Dak. U.S.A. 110 43.40N 98.00W
Mitchell, Mt. U.S.A. 113 35.47N 82.16W
Mitchells Bay town Canada 104 42.28N 82.26W
Mitchelstown Rep. of Ire. 15 52.16N 8.17W
Mīt Ghamr Egypt 66 30.43N 31.16E
Mithapur India 62 22.25N 69.00E
Mithi Pakistan 62 24.44N 69.48E
Mitilíni Greece 35 39.00N 26.20E
Mitla, Mamarr pass Egypt 66 30.00N 32.53E
Mitla Pass see Mitla, Mamarr pass Egypt 66
Mito Japan 57 36.30N 140.29E
Mitri Prespa, Límni l. Greece 34 40.55N 21.00E
Mitsinjo Madagascar 81 16.01S 45.52E
Mits'iwa Ethiopia 72 15.36N 39.29E
Mits'iwa Channel Ethiopia 72 15.30N 40.00E
Mittagong Australia 93 34.27S 150.25E
Mittelandkanal Germany 38 52.23N 8.00E
Mittenwald Germany 39 47.27N 11.15E
Mittersill Austria 39 47.16N 12.29E
Mittweida Germany 38 50.59N 12.59E
Mitú Colombia 122 1.08N 70.03W
Mitumba, Monts mts. Zaïre 79 3.00S 28.30E
Mitwaba Zaïre 79 8.32S 27.20E
Mitzic Gabon 78 0.48N 11.30E
Miura Japan 57 35.08N 139.37E
Mivtahim Israel 67 31.14N 34.23E
Miya r. Japan 57 34.32N 136.44E
Miyako Japan 57 39.40N 141.59E
Miyako jima i. Japan 53 24.45N 125.25E
Miyakonojō Japan 57 31.43N 131.02E
Miyazaki Japan 57 31.58N 131.50E
Mizdah Libya 75 31.26N 12.59E
Mizen Head Rep. of Ire. 15 51.27N 9.50W
Mizil Romania 37 45.00N 26.26E
Mizoch U.S.S.R. 37 50.30N 25.50E
Mizoram d. India 61 23.40N 92.40E
Mizpa Israel 67 32.47N 35.31E
Mizpe Ramon Israel 66 30.36N 34.48E
Mizra' Israel 67 32.39N 35.17E
Mizukaidō Japan 57 36.01N 139.59E
Mizunami Japan 57 35.22N 137.15E
Mizusawa Japan 57 39.08N 141.08E
Mjölby Sweden 43 58.19N 15.08E
Mjøndalen Norway 42 59.45N 10.01E
Mjörn l. Sweden 43 57.54N 12.25E
Mjøsa l. Norway 41 60.40N 11.00E
Mkata Tanga Tanzania 79 5.47S 38.18E
Mkushi Zambia 79 13.40S 29.26E
Mkuze R.S.A. 81 27.10S 32.00E
Mkwaja Tanzania 79 5.46S 38.51E
Mkwiti Tanzania 79 10.27S 39.18E
Mladá Boleslav Czech. 36 50.26N 14.55E
Mława Poland 37 53.06N 20.23E
Mljet i. Yugo. 29 42.45N 17.30E
Mljetski Kanal str. Yugo. 31 42.48N 17.35E
Mneni Zimbabwe 80 20.38S 30.03E
Moab U.S.A. 108 38.35N 109.33W
Moa I. Australia 90 10.12S 142.16E
Moama Australia 93 36.05S 144.50E
Moamba Mozambique 81 25.35S 32.13E
Moanda Gabon 78 1.25S 13.18E
Moapa U.S.A. 109 36.40N 114.39W
Moatize Mozambique 81 16.10S 33.40E
Moba Zaïre 79 7.03S 29.42E
Mobara Japan 57 35.25N 140.18E
Mobaye C.A.R. 73 4.19N 21.11E
Moberly U.S.A. 110 39.25N 92.26W
Mobert Canada 102 48.41N 85.40W
Mobile U.S.A. 111 30.42N 88.05W
Mobile B. U.S.A. 111 30.25N 88.00W
Mobridge U.S.A. 110 45.32N 100.26W
Mobutu Sese Seko, L. see Albert, L. Uganda / Zaïre 79
Moçambique town Mozambique 79 15.00S 40.47E
Mocimboa da Praia Mozambique 79 11.19S 40.19E
Mocimboa do Ruvuma Mozambique 79 11.05S 39.15E
Möckeln l. Sweden 43 56.40N 14.10E
Moclips U.S.A. 108 47.14N 124.13W
Mococa Brazil 126 21.28S 47.00W
Moctezuma Mexico 109 30.10N 106.28W
Mocuba Mozambique 79 16.52S 37.02E
Močurica r. Bulgaria 34 42.31N 26.32E
Modane France 21 45.12N 6.40E
Modāsa India 62 23.28N 73.18E
Modder r. R.S.A. 80 29.03S 23.56E
Modena Italy 30 44.40N 10.54E
Modena U.S.A. 108 37.48N 113.57W
Modesto U.S.A. 108 37.39N 121.00W
Modica Italy 33 36.51N 14.47E
Modjamboli Zaïre 78 2.28N 22.06E
Modriča Yugo. 31 44.57N 18.18E
Moe Australia 93 38.10S 146.15E
Moebase Mozambique 81 17.04S 38.41E

Moelv to **Mosby**

Moelv Norway **41** 60.56N 10.42E
Moffat U.K. **14** 55.20N 3.27W
Moga India **62** 30.48N 75.10E
Mogadishu *see* Muqdisho Somali Rep. **79**
Mogadouro Portugal **26** 41.20N 6.39W
Mogaung Burma **56** 25.15N 96.54E
Mogi das Cruzes Brazil **126** 23.33S 46.14W
Mogi-Guaçu Brazil **126** 20.55S 48.06W
Mogilev U.S.S.R. **37** 53.54N 30.20E
Mogilev Podolskiy U.S.S.R. **37** 48.29N 27.49E
Mogilno Poland **37** 52.40N 17.58E
Mogi-Mirim Brazil **126** 22.29S 46.55W
Mogincual Mozambique **79** 15.33S 40.29E
Mogliano Veneto Italy **30** 45.33N 12.14E
Mogok Burma **56** 23.00N 96.30E
Mogollon Rim *f.* U.S.A. **109** 32.30N111.00W
Moguer Spain **27** 37.16N 6.50W
Mogumber Australia **89** 31.01S116.02E
Mohács Hungary **31** 45.59N 18.42E
Mohammedia Morocco **74** 33.44N 7.24W
Mohana India **63** 25.54N 77.45E
Mohawk *r.* U.S.A. **115** 42.47N 73.42W
Mohawk Ariz. U.S.A. **109** 32.41N113.47W
Mohawk N.Y. U.S.A. **115** 43.00N 75.00W
Moheda Sweden **43** 57.00N 14.34E
Mohéli *see* Mwali *i.* Comoros **79**
Mohon France **19** 49.45N 4.44E
Mohoro Tanzania **79** 8.09S 39.07E
Mohoru Kenya **79** 1.01S 34.07E
Moi Norway **42** 58.28N 6.32E
Moincêr China **63** 31.10N 80.52E
Moindi Gabon **78** 3.24S 11.43E
Mointy U.S.S.R. **9** 47.10N 73.18E
Moira *r.* Canada **105** 44.09N 77.23W
Moira U.S.A. **105** 44.50N 74.34W
Mo-i-Rana Norway **40** 66.19N 14.10E
Mõisaküla U.S.S.R. **41** 58.06N 25.11E
Moisdon France **18** 47.37N 1.22W
Moisie *r.* Canada **103** 50.13N 66.02W
Moissac France **20** 44.06N 1.05E
Moïssala Chad **77** 8.20N 17.40E
Moita Portugal **27** 38.39N 8.59W
Mojácar Spain **27** 37.09N 1.50W
Mojave U.S.A. **109** 35.03N118.10W
Mojave Desert U.S.A. **109** 35.00N117.00W
Mojokerto Indonesia **59** 7.25S112.31E
Mokameh India **63** 25.24N 85.55E
Mokau New Zealand **86** 38.41S174.37E
Mokmer Indonesia **59** 1.13S136.13E
Mokpo S. Korea **53** 34.50N126.25E
Mokra Gora *mts.* Yugo. **34** 42.50N 20.30E
Mokren Bulgaria **34** 42.45N 26.39E
Mol Belgium **16** 51.11N 5.09E
Mola di Bari Italy **33** 41.04N 17.05E
Moláoi Greece **35** 36.48N 22.52E
Molat *i.* Yugo. **31** 44.15N 14.49E
Molchanovo U.S.S.R. **50** 57.39N 83.45E
Mold U.K. **12** 53.10N 3.08W
Moldavskaya S.S.R. *d.* U.S.S.R. **37** 47.30N 28.30E
Molde Norway **40** 62.44N 7.08E
Molepolole Botswana **80** 24.26S 25.34E
Molfetta Italy **33** 41.12N 16.36E
Molihong Shan *mtn.* China **54** 42.11N124.43E
Molina de Aragón Spain **25** 40.51N 1.53W
Molina de Segura Spain **25** 38.04N 1.12W
Moline U.S.A. **110** 41.30N 90.30W
Molinella Italy **30** 44.37N 11.40E
Molino Lacy Mexico **109** 30.05N114.24W
Molins Spain **25** 41.25N 2.01E
Moliro Zaïre **79** 8.11S 30.29E
Molise *d.* Italy **33** 41.40N 14.30E
Molkom Sweden **43** 59.36N 13.43E
Mölle Sweden **43** 56.17N 12.29E
Mollendo Peru **124** 17.02S 72.01W
Mölln Germany **38** 53.37N 10.41E
Mollösund Sweden **42** 58.04N 11.28E
Mölndal Sweden **43** 57.39N 12.01E
Molodechno U.S.S.R. **37** 54.16N 26.50E
Molokai *i.* Hawaii U.S.A. **106** 21.20N157.00W
Molong Australia **93** 33.08S148.53E
Molopo *r.* R.S.A. **80** 28.30S 20.22E
Mólos Greece **35** 38.47N 22.37E
Moloundou Cameroon **78** 2.55N 12.01E
Molsheim France **19** 48.32N 7.29E
Molson L. Canada **101** 54.12N 96.45W
Molt U.S.A. **110** 46.22N102.20W
Molteno R.S.A. **80** 31.23S 26.21E
Moluccas *is.* Indonesia **59** 4.00S128.00E
Molucca Sea *see* Maluku, Laut *sea* Pacific Oc. **59**
Moma Mozambique **79** 16.40S 39.10E
Mombasa Kenya **79** 4.04S 39.40E
Mombuey Spain **26** 42.02N 6.20W
Momchilgrad Bulgaria **34** 41.32N 25.25E
Momi Zaïre **79** 1.42S 27.03E
Mommark Denmark **36** 54.55N 10.03E
Mompós Colombia **122** 9.15N 74.29W
Mon *d.* Burma **56** 16.45N 97.25E
Møn *i.* Denmark **43** 55.00N 12.20E
Mona *i.* Puerto Rico **117** 18.06N 67.54W
Monaco Europe **21** 43.40N 7.25E
Monadhliath Mts. U.K. **14** 57.09N 4.08W
Monaghan Rep. of Ire. **15** 54.15N 6.58W
Monaghan *d.* Rep. of Ire. **15** 54.10N 7.00W
Monahans U.S.A. **111** 31.36N102.54W
Monarch Mt. Canada **100** 51.55N125.57W
Monastir Tunisia **75** 35.35N 10.50E
Moncalieri Italy **30** 45.00N 7.40E
Moncão Portugal **26** 42.05N 8.29W
Moncayo, Sierra del *mts.* Spain **25** 41.48N 1.50W
Monchegorsk U.S.S.R. **44** 67.55N 33.01E
Mönchen Gladbach Germany **38** 51.12N 6.28E
Monchique Portugal **27** 37.19N 8.33W
Monclova Mexico **111** 26.54N101.25W
Moncontour France **18** 48.21N 2.39W
Moncton Canada **103** 46.06N 64.47W
Mondego *r.* Portugal **26** 40.09N 8.52W
Mondego, Cabo *c.* Portugal **26** 40.11N 8.55W
Mondo Tanzania **79** 5.00S 35.54E
Mondoñedo Spain **26** 43.26N 7.22W
Mondoubleau France **18** 47.59N 0.54E
Mondovì Italy **30** 44.23N 7.49E
Mondragone Italy **32** 41.07N 13.53E
Mondrain I. Australia **89** 34.08S122.15E
Monemvasía Greece **35** 36.41N 23.03E
Monessen U.S.A. **114** 40.09N 79.53W
Monesterio Spain **26** 38.05N 6.16W
Monet Canada **102** 48.10N 75.40W
Monett U.S.A. **111** 36.55N 93.55W
Monfalcone Italy **31** 45.49N 13.32E
Monflanquin France **20** 44.32N 0.46E
Monforte Portugal **27** 39.03N 7.26W
Monforte Spain **26** 42.31N 7.33W
Monga Zaïre **73** 4.12N 22.49E
Mongala *r.* Zaïre **78** 1.58N 19.55E
Mongalla Sudan **73** 5.12N 31.46E
Mong Cai Vietnam **55** 21.36N107.55E
Mongers L. Australia **89** 29.15S117.05E
Monghyr India **63** 25.23N 86.28E
Mongo Chad **77** 12.14N 18.45E
Mongolia Asia **52** 46.30N104.00E
Mongororo Chad **73** 12.01N 22.28E
Mongu Zambia **78** 15.10S 23.09E
Monheim Germany **39** 48.50N 10.51E
Monifieth U.K. **14** 56.29N 2.50W
Monistrol-sur-Loire France **21** 45.17N 4.10E
Monitor Range *mts.* U.S.A. **108** 38.45N116.30W
Monkoto Zaïre **73** 1.38S 20.39E
Monmouth U.K. **13** 51.48N 2.43W
Monmouth Ill. U.S.A. **110** 40.54N 90.39W
Monmouth Oreg. U.S.A. **108** 44.51N123.14W
Monocacy *r.* U.S.A. **114** 39.13N 77.27W
Mono L. U.S.A. **108** 38.00N119.00W
Monomoy Pt. U.S.A. **115** 41.33N 70.02W
Monongahela *r.* U.S.A. **114** 40.27N 80.00W
Monopoli Italy **33** 40.57N 17.19E
Monor Hungary **37** 47.21N 19.27E
Monóvar Spain **25** 38.25N 0.47W
Monreal Spain **25** 42.42N 1.30W
Monreal del Campo Spain **25** 40.47N 1.21W
Monreale Italy **32** 38.05N 13.17E
Monroe La. U.S.A. **111** 32.33N 92.07W
Monroe Mich. U.S.A. **104** 41.55N 83.24W
Monroe N.C. U.S.A. **113** 35.00N 80.35W
Monroe N.Y. U.S.A. **115** 41.20N 74.11W
Monroe Wisc. U.S.A. **110** 42.36N 89.38W
Monroe City U.S.A. **110** 39.39N 91.44W
Monroeville U.S.A. **113** 31.32N 87.21W
Monrovia Liberia **76** 6.20N 10.46W
Mons Belgium **16** 50.27N 3.57E
Monselice Italy **30** 45.14N 11.45E
Mönsterås Sweden **43** 57.02N 16.26E
Montabaur Germany **39** 50.26N 7.50E
Montagnana Italy **30** 45.14N 11.28E
Montague Canada **103** 46.10N 62.39W
Montaigu France **18** 46.59N 1.19W
Montaigut-en-Combraille France **20** 46.11N 2.38E
Montalbán Spain **25** 40.50N 0.48W
Montalbano di Elicona Italy **33** 38.02N 15.02E
Montalbano Ionico Italy **33** 40.17N 16.34E
Montalcino Italy **30** 43.03N 11.29E
Montalegre Portugal **26** 41.49N 7.48W
Montalto *mtn.* Italy **33** 38.10N 15.55E
Montalto di Castro Italy **30** 42.21N 11.37E
Montalto Uffugo Italy **33** 39.25N 16.09E
Montana Switz. **39** 46.18N 7.29E
Montana *d.* U.S.A. **108** 47.14N109.26W
Montánchez Spain **27** 39.13N 6.09W
Montargil Portugal **27** 39.05N 8.10W
Montargis France **19** 48.00N 2.45E
Montauban France **20** 44.01N 1.21E
Montauk U.S.A. **115** 41.03N 71.57W
Montbard France **19** 47.37N 4.20E
Montbarrey France **19** 47.01N 5.39E
Montbéliard France **19** 47.31N 6.48E
Montblanch Spain **25** 41.22N 1.10E
Montbrison France **21** 45.36N 4.03E
Montbron France **20** 45.40N 0.30E
Montceau-les-Mines France **19** 46.40N 4.22E
Mont Cenis, Col du *pass* France **21** 45.15N 6.54E
Montcerf Canada **105** 46.32N 76.02W
Montchannin France **19** 46.45N 4.27E
Montcornet France **19** 49.41N 4.01E
Mont de Marsan *town* France **20** 43.53N 0.30W
Montdidier France **19** 49.39N 2.34E
Monte Alegre *town* Brazil **123** 2.01S 54.04W
Monte Azul *town* Brazil **126** 15.53S 42.53W
Montebello Canada **105** 45.39N 74.56W
Montebello Iónico Italy **33** 37.59N 15.45E
Monte Carlo Monaco **21** 43.44N 7.25E
Monte Caseros Argentina **125** 30.15S 57.38W
Montecatini Terme Italy **30** 43.53N 10.46E
Montecristo *i.* Italy **30** 42.20N 10.19E
Montefalco Italy **30** 42.54N 12.39E
Montefrío Spain **27** 37.19N 4.01W
Montego Bay *town* Jamaica **117** 18.27N 77.56W
Montejicar Spain **27** 37.34N 3.30W
Montélimar France **21** 44.34N 4.45E
Montellano Spain **27** 37.00N 5.34W
Montemor-o-Novo Portugal **27** 38.39N 8.13W
Montemor-o-Velho Portugal **26** 40.10N 8.41W
Montemura *mtn.* Portugal **26** 40.59N 7.59W
Montendre France **20** 45.17N 0.24W
Montenegro *see* Crna Gora *d.* Yugo. **31**
Montenero di Bisaccia Italy **33** 41.57N 14.47E
Montepuez Mozambique **81** 13.09S 39.33E
Montepulciano Italy **30** 43.05N 11.47E
Montereau France **19** 48.23N 2.57E
Monterey Calif. U.S.A. **108** 36.37N121.55W
Monterey Va. U.S.A. **114** 38.25N 79.35W
Monterey B. U.S.A. **108** 36.45N121.55W
Montería Colombia **122** 8.45N 75.54W
Montero Bolivia **124** 17.20S 63.15W
Monteros Argentina **124** 27.10S 65.30W
Monterotondo Italy **30** 42.03N 12.37E
Monterrey Mexico **111** 25.40N100.19W
Montesano Italy **33** 40.16N 15.43E
Monte Sant 'Angelo Italy **33** 41.42N 15.59E
Monte Santu, Capo di *c.* Italy **32** 40.05N 9.44E
Montesarchio Italy **33** 41.04N 14.38E
Montes Claros Brazil **126** 16.45S 43.52W
Montevarchi Italy **30** 43.31N 11.34E
Montevideo Uruguay **125** 34.53S 56.11W
Montevideo U.S.A. **110** 44.57N 95.43W
Montezuma U.S.A. **111** 37.36N100.26W
Montfaucon France **21** 45.10N 4.18E
Montfort-sur-Meu France **18** 48.08N 1.58W
Montgomery U.K. **13** 52.34N 3.09W
Montgomery Ala. U.S.A. **113** 32.22N 86.20W
Montgomery Penn. U.S.A. **114** 41.10N 76.52W
Montguyon France **20** 45.13N 0.11W
Monthey Switz. **39** 46.15N 6.57E
Monthois France **19** 49.19N 4.43E
Monticello Ark. U.S.A. **111** 33.38N 91.47W
Monticello Miss. U.S.A. **111** 31.33N 90.07W
Monticello N.Y. U.S.A. **115** 41.39N 74.42W
Monticello Utah U.S.A. **108** 37.52N109.21W
Montichiari Italy **30** 45.25N 10.23E
Montiel, Campo de *f.* Spain **26** 38.46N 2.45W
Montignac France **20** 45.04N 1.10E
Montigny-le-Roi France **19** 48.00N 5.30E
Montijo Portugal **27** 38.42N 8.58W
Montijo Spain **27** 38.55N 6.37W
Montijo Dam Spain **24** 38.52N 6.20W
Montilla Spain **27** 37.35N 4.38W
Montivilliers France **18** 49.33N 0.12E
Mont Joli *town* Canada **103** 48.35N 68.14W
Mont Laurier *town* Canada **105** 46.33N 75.30W
Mont Louis *town* Canada **103** 49.15N 65.46W
Mont-Louis France **20** 42.31N 2.07E
Montluçon France **20** 46.21N 2.36E
Montmagny Canada **103** 46.59N 70.33W
Montmédy France **19** 49.31N 5.22E
Montmirail France **19** 48.52N 3.32E
Montmoreau St. Cybard France **20** 45.24N 0.08E
Montmorillon France **18** 46.26N 0.52E
Montmort France **19** 48.55N 3.49E
Monto Australia **90** 24.52S151.07E
Montorio al Vomano Italy **31** 42.35N 13.38E
Montoro Spain **26** 38.01N 4.23W
Montour Falls *town* U.S.A. **114** 42.21N 76.51W
Montoursville U.S.A. **114** 41.15N 76.55W
Montpelier Idaho U.S.A. **108** 42.20N111.20W
Montpelier Vt. U.S.A. **105** 44.16N 72.35W
Montpellier France **20** 43.36N 3.53E
Montpon-sur-l'Isle France **20** 45.00N 0.10E
Montreal Canada **105** 45.31N 73.34W
Montreal *r.* Canada **104** 47.14N 84.39W
Montreal L. Canada **101** 54.20N105.40W
Montreal Lake *town* Canada **101** 54.03N105.46W
Montréal-Nord Canada **105** 45.36N 73.38W
Montreal River *town* Canada **104** 46.41N 79.50W
Montrejeau France **20** 43.05N 0.33E
Montrésor France **18** 47.09N 1.12E
Montreuil France **19** 50.28N 1.46E
Montreuil-Bellay France **18** 47.08N 0.09W
Montreux Switz. **39** 46.26N 6.55E
Montrevel France **21** 46.20N 5.08E
Montrichard France **18** 47.21N 1.11E
Montrose U.K. **14** 56.43N 2.29W
Montrose Colo. U.S.A. **108** 38.29N107.53W
Montrose Penn. U.S.A. **115** 41.50N 75.56W
Montserrat *i.* Leeward Is. **117** 16.45N 62.14W
Montserrat, Serra de *mts.* Spain **25** 41.15N 0.55E
Mont Tremblant Prov. Park Canada **105** 46.42N 74.20W
Montuenga Spain **26** 41.03N 4.37W
Montville U.S.A. **115** 41.27N 72.08W
Monument Valley *f.* U.S.A. **108** 36.50N110.20W
Monveda Zaïre **78** 2.57N 21.27E
Monywa Burma **56** 22.05N 95.15E
Monza Italy **30** 45.35N 9.16E
Monze Zambia **79** 16.16S 27.28E
Monzón Spain **25** 41.55N 0.12E
Moolawatana Australia **92** 29.55S139.43E
Mooloogool Australia **88** 26.06S119.05E
Moomba Australia **91** 28.08S140.16E
Moomin Creek *r.* Australia **93** 29.35S148.45E
Moonbi Range *mts.* Australia **93** 31.00S151.10E
Moonie Australia **91** 27.40S150.19E
Moonie *r.* Australia **91** 29.30S148.40E
Moonta Australia **92** 34.04S137.37E
Moora Australia **89** 30.40S116.01E
Moorarie Australia **88** 25.56S117.35E
Moorcroft U.S.A. **108** 44.16N104.57W
Moore *r.* Australia **89** 31.22S115.29E
Moore, L. Australia **89** 29.30S117.30E
Mooréa *i.* Îs. de la Société **85** 17.32S149.50W
Moorefield U.S.A. **114** 39.04N 78.58W
Moorefield *r.* U.S.A. **114** 39.04N 78.58W
Moorfoot Hills U.K. **14** 55.43N 3.03W
Moorhead U.S.A. **110** 46.53N 96.45W
Moor Lake *town* Canada **105** 46.09N 77.42W
Moornanyah L. Australia **92** 33.02S143.58E
Mooroopna Australia **93** 36.24S145.22E
Moosburg Germany **39** 48.29N 11.57E
Moose Creek *town* Canada **105** 45.15N 74.58W
Moosehead L. U.S.A. **112** 45.40N 69.40W
Moose Jaw Canada **101** 50.23N105.32W
Moose Lake *town* U.S.A. **110** 46.26N 92.45W
Moosomin Canada **101** 50.07N101.40W
Moosonee Canada **102** 51.17N 80.39W
Mootwingee Australia **92** 31.52S141.14E
Mopanzhang China **54** 33.07N117.22E
Mopêia Velha Mozambique **81** 17.58S 35.40E
Mopti Mali **76** 14.29N 4.10W
Mopti *d.* Mali **74** 15.30N 3.40W
Moqor Afghan. **62** 32.55N 67.40E
Moquegua Peru **124** 17.20S 70.55W
Mora Cameroon **77** 11.02N 14.07E
Mora Portugal **27** 38.56N 8.10W
Mora Spain **27** 39.41N 3.46W
Mora Sweden **41** 61.00N 14.33E
Mora U.S.A. **110** 45.53N 93.18W
Morādābād India **63** 28.50N 78.47E
Mora de Rubielos Spain **25** 40.15N 0.45W
Morafenobe Madagascar **81** 17.49S 44.45E
Mórahalom Hungary **31** 46.13N 19.54E
Moralana Australia **92** 31.42S138.12E
Moral de Calatrava Spain **26** 38.50N 3.35W
Moramanga Madagascar **81** 18.56S 48.12E
Moran U.S.A. **104** 46.00N 84.50W
Morar, Loch U.K. **14** 56.56N 4.00W
Morasverdes Spain **26** 40.36N 6.16W
Moratalla Spain **25** 38.12N 1.53W
Morava *r.* Czech. **37** 48.10N 16.59E
Morava *r.* Yugo. **37** 44.43N 21.02E
Moravia U.S.A. **115** 42.43N 76.25W
Moravské Budějovice Czech. **36** 49.03N 15.49E
Morawhanna Guyana **122** 8.17N 59.44W
Moray Firth *est.* U.K. **14** 57.35N 5.15W
Morbach Germany **39** 49.48N 7.07E
Morbegno Italy **30** 46.08N 9.34E
Morbihan *d.* France **18** 47.55N 2.50W
Mörbylånga Sweden **43** 56.31N 16.23E
Morcenx France **20** 44.02N 0.55W
Morden Australia **92** 30.30S142.23E
Morden Canada **101** 49.11N 98.05W
Mordovo U.S.S.R. **45** 52.06N 40.45E
Moreau *r.* U.S.A. **110** 45.18N100.43W
Morecambe U.K. **12** 54.03N 2.52W
Morecambe B. U.K. **12** 54.05N 3.00W
Moree Australia **93** 29.29S149.53E
Morée France **18** 47.54N 1.14E
Morehead U.S.A. **113** 38.11N 83.27W
Morehead City U.S.A. **113** 34.43N 76.44W
Morelia Mexico **116** 19.40N101.11W
Morella Spain **25** 40.37N 0.06W
Morelos *d.* Mexico **116** 18.40N 99.00W
Morena India **63** 26.30N 78.09E
Morena, Sierra *mts.* Spain **27** 38.20N 4.25W
Morenci U.S.A. **109** 33.05N109.22W
Moreno Mexico **109** 28.29N110.41W
Möre og Romsdal *d.* Norway **40** 63.00N 9.00E
Moresby I. Canada **100** 52.30N131.40W
Moreton I. Australia **91** 27.10S153.25E
Morez France **19** 46.31N 6.02E
Mórfou Cyprus **66** 35.12N 33.00E
Mórfou, Kólpos *b.* Cyprus **66** 35.15N 32.50E
Morgan Australia **92** 34.02S139.40E
Morgan U.S.A. **111** 32.01N 97.37W
Morgan City U.S.A. **111** 29.42N 91.12W
Morganfield U.S.A. **113** 37.41N 87.55W
Morgantown U.S.A. **114** 39.38N 79.57W
Morghāb *r.* Afghan. **60** 36.50N 63.00E
Morgongåva Sweden **43** 59.56N 16.57E
Moriki Nigeria **77** 12.55N 6.30E
Moringen Germany **38** 51.42N 9.52E
Morin Heights Canada **105** 45.54N 74.21W
Morioka Japan **57** 39.43N141.10E
Morisset Australia **93** 33.06S151.29E
Moriyama Japan **57** 35.04N135.59E
Morlaix France **18** 48.35N 3.50W
Mörlunda Sweden **43** 57.19N 15.51E
Mormanno Italy **33** 39.53N 16.00E
Mormon Range *mts.* U.S.A. **108** 37.08N114.20W
Mornington I. Australia **90** 16.33S139.24E
Mornington Mission Australia **90** 16.40S139.10E
Morobe P.N.G. **59** 7.45S147.35E
Morocco Africa **74** 32.30N 5.00W
Moro G. Phil. **59** 6.30N123.20E
Morogoro Tanzania **79** 6.47S 37.40E
Morogoro *d.* Tanzania **79** 8.30S 37.00E
Moroleón Mexico **116** 20.08N101.12W
Morombe Madagascar **81** 21.45S 43.22E
Morón Argentina **125** 34.39S 58.37W
Morón Cuba **117** 22.08N 78.39W
Mörön Mongolia **52** 49.36N100.08E
Morón Spain **27** 37.08N 5.27W
Morondava Madagascar **81** 20.17S 44.17E
Morón de Almazán Spain **25** 41.25N 2.25W
Moroni Comoros **79** 11.40S 43.19E
Morotai *i.* Indonesia **59** 2.10N128.30E
Moroto Uganda **79** 2.32N 34.41E
Moroto, Mt. Uganda **79** 2.30N 34.46E
Morpeth U.K. **12** 55.10N 1.40W
Morrilton U.S.A. **111** 35.09N 92.45W
Morrinsville New Zealand **86** 37.39S175.32E
Morris Minn. U.S.A. **110** 45.35N 95.55W
Morris Penn. U.S.A. **114** 41.36N 77.18W
Morrisburg Canada **105** 44.54N 75.11W
Morristown Ariz. U.S.A. **109** 33.51N112.37W
Morristown N.J. U.S.A. **115** 40.48N 74.29W
Morristown N.Y. U.S.A. **105** 44.35N 75.39W
Morristown S.Dak. U.S.A. **110** 45.56N101.43W
Morristown Tenn. U.S.A. **113** 36.13N 83.18W
Morrisville N.Y. U.S.A. **115** 42.54N 75.39W
Morrisville Vt. U.S.A. **105** 44.34N 72.44W
Mörrum Sweden **43** 56.11N 14.45E
Morrumbene Mozambique **81** 23.41S 35.25E
Mörrumsån *r.* Sweden **43** 56.09N 14.44E
Mors *i.* Denmark **42** 56.50N 8.45E
Morsbach Germany **38** 50.52N 7.43E
Morsi India **63** 21.21N 78.00E
Mortagne France **18** 48.31N 0.33E
Mortagne *r.* France **19** 48.33N 6.27E
Mortagne-sur-Sèvre France **18** 47.00N 0.57W
Mortain France **18** 48.39N 0.56W
Mortara Italy **30** 45.15N 8.44E
Morteau France **19** 47.04N 6.37E
Mortes *r.* Brazil **126** 21.09S 45.06W
Mortes *r. see* Manso *r.* Brazil **124**
Mortlake *town* Australia **92** 38.05S142.48E
Morundah Australia **93** 34.56S146.18E
Moruya Australia **93** 35.56S150.06E
Morvan, Monts du *mts.* France **19** 47.05N 4.00E
Morven Australia **90** 26.25S147.05E
Morvern *f.* U.K. **14** 56.37N 5.45W
Morvi India **62** 22.49N 70.50E
Morwell Australia **93** 38.14S146.25E
Morzhovets *i.* U.S.S.R. **44** 66.45N 42.30E
Mosbach Germany **39** 49.21N 9.08E
Mosby Norway **42** 58.14N 7.54E

Moscow to Mutoko

Moscow U.S.A. **108** 46.44N117.00W
Moscow *see* Moskva U.S.S.R. **44**
Mosel *r.* Germany **39** 50.22N 7.36E
Moselle *d.* France **19** 49.00N 6.30E
Moselle *r. see* Mosel *r.* France **19**
Moses Lake *town* U.S.A. **108** 47.08N119.17W
Mosgiel New Zealand **86** 45.53S170.22E
Moshi Tanzania **79** 3.20S 37.21E
Mosjöen Norway **40** 65.50N 13.10E
Moskenes Norway **40** 67.55N 13.00E
Moskenesöy *i.* Norway **40** 67.55N 13.00E
Moskva U.S.S.R. **44** 55.45N 37.42E
Moskva *r.* U.S.S.R. **44** 55.08N 38.50E
Mosquera Colombia **122** 2.30N 78.29W
Mosquero U.S.A. **109** 35.47N103.58W
Mosquitia Plain Honduras **117** 15.00N 84.00W
Mosquito Creek Resr. U.S.A. **114** 41.10N 80.45W
Mosquitos, Costa de *f.* Nicaragua **117** 13.00N 84.00W
Mosquitos, Golfo de los *g.* Panama **117** 9.00N 81.00W
Moss Norway **42** 59.26N 10.42E
Mossaka Congo **78** 1.20S 16.44E
Mossburn New Zealand **86** 45.41S168.15E
Mosselbaai R.S.A. **80** 34.11S 22.08E
Mossendjo Congo **78** 2.52S 12.46E
Mossgiel Australia **93** 33.18S144.05E
Mossman Australia **90** 16.28S145.22E
Mossoró Brazil **123** 5.10S 37.18W
Mossuril Mozambique **81** 14.58S 40.42E
Moss Vale *town* Australia **93** 34.33S150.24E
Most Czech. **38** 50.32N 13.39E
Mostaganem Algeria **74** 35.56N 0.05E
Mostar Yugo. **31** 43.20N 17.49E
Mösting, Kap *c.* Greenland **99** 64.00N 41.00W
Mostiska U.S.S.R. **37** 49.48N 23.05E
Mosul *see* Al Mawşil Iraq **64**
Mösvatnet *l.* Norway **42** 59.52N 8.05E
Mota del Cuervo Spain **27** 39.30N 2.52W
Mota del Marqués Spain **26** 41.38N 5.10W
Motagua *r.* Guatemala **117** 15.56N 87.45W
Motala Sweden **43** 58.33N 15.03E
Moth India **63** 25.43N 78.57E
Motherwell U.K. **14** 55.48N 4.00W
Motihāri India **63** 26.39N 84.55E
Motilla del Palancar Spain **25** 39.34N 1.53W
Motloutse *r.* Botswana **80** 22.15S 29.00E
Motol U.S.S.R. **37** 52.25N 25.05E
Motou China **54** 32.17N120.35E
Motril Spain **27** 36.45N 3.31W
Mott U.S.A. **108** 46.22N102.20W
Mottola Italy **33** 40.38N 17.03E
Motueka New Zealand **86** 41.08S173.01E
Motu Iti *i.* Îs. de la Société **85** 16.15S151.50W
Motutapu Niue **84** 19.02S169.52W
Mouali Congo **78** 0.10N 15.33E
Mouchalagane *r.* Canada **103** 53.32N 69.00W
Moúdhros Greece **34** 39.52N 25.16E
Moudjéria Mauritania **74** 17.53N 12.20W
Moudon Switz. **39** 46.40N 6.48E
Mouhoun *r.* Burkina *see* Black Volta *r.* Ghana **76**
Mouila Gabon **78** 1.50S 11.02E
Mouka C.A.R. **73** 7.16N 21.52E
Moulamein Australia **92** 35.03S144.05E
Moulhoulé Djibouti **73** 12.36N 43.12E
Moulins France **20** 46.34N 3.20E
Moulins-la-Marche France **18** 48.39N 0.29E
Moulmein Burma **56** 16.55N 97.49E
Moulouya, Oued *r.* Morocco **74** 35.05N 2.25W
Moultrie U.S.A. **113** 31.11N 83.47W
Moultrie, L. U.S.A. **113** 33.20N 80.05W
Mound City U.S.A. **110** 40.07N 95.14W
Moundou Chad **77** 8.36N 16.02E
Moundsville U.S.A. **114** 39.55N 80.44W
Moundville U.S.A. **111** 32.59N 87.38W
Mountain Ash U.K. **13** 51.42N 3.22W
Mountain City U.S.A. **108** 41.50N115.58W
Mountain Grove Canada **105** 44.44N 76.51W
Mountain Home Ark. U.S.A. **111** 36.20N 92.23W
Mountain Home Idaho U.S.A. **108** 43.08N115.41W
Mountain Nile *r. see* Jabal, Baḩr al *r.* Sudan **73**
Mountain Village U.S.A. **98** 62.05N163.44W
Mount Airy *town* Md. U.S.A. **114** 39.23N 77.09W
Mount Airy *town* N.C. U.S.A. **113** 36.31N 80.38W
Mount Barker *town* S.A. Australia **92** 35.06S138.52E
Mount Barker *town* W.A. Australia **89** 34.36S117.37E
Mount Beauty *town* Australia **93** 36.43S147.11E
Mount Bellew *town* Rep. of Ire. **15** 53.28N 8.30W
Mount Brydges *town* Canada **104** 42.54N 81.29W
Mount Carmel *town* Ill. U.S.A. **110** 38.25N 87.46W
Mount Carmel *town* Penn. U.S.A. **115** 40.48N 76.25W
Mount Clemens *town* U.S.A. **114** 42.36N 82.53W
Mount Darwin *town* Zimbabwe **81** 16.46S 31.36E
Mount Drysdale *town* Australia **93** 31.11S145.51E
Mount Eba *town* Australia **92** 30.12S135.33E
Mount Fletcher *town* R.S.A. **80** 30.41S 28.30E
Mount Forest *town* Canada **104** 43.59N 80.44W
Mount Gambier *town* Australia **92** 37.51S140.50E
Mount Gilead *town* U.S.A. **114** 40.33N 82.50W
Mount Hagen *town* P.N.G. **59** 5.54S144.13E
Mount Holly *town* U.S.A. **115** 39.59N 74.47W
Mount Holly Springs *town* U.S.A. **114** 40.07N 77.11W
Mount Hope *town* N.S.W. Australia **93** 32.49S145.48E
Mount Hope *town* S.A. Australia **92** 34.07S135.23E
Mount Hopeless *town* Australia **92** 29.42S139.41E
Mount Isa *town* Australia **90** 20.50S139.29E
Mount Lebanon *town* U.S.A. **114** 40.23N 80.03W
Mount Lofty Range *mts.* Australia **92** 34.40S139.03E
Mount Magnet *town* Australia **89** 28.06S117.50E
Mount Manara *town* Australia **92** 32.28S143.59E
Mountmellick Rep. of Ire. **15** 53.08N 7.21W
Mount Morgan *town* Australia **90** 23.39S150.23E
Mount Morris *town* Mich. U.S.A. **104** 43.07N 83.42W
Mount Morris *town* N.Y. U.S.A. **114** 42.44N 77.53W
Mount Morris *town* Penn. U.S.A. **114** 39.44N 80.02W
Mount Murchison *town* Australia **92** 31.23S143.42E
Mount Pleasant *town* Canada **104** 43.05N 80.19W
Mount Pleasant *town* Mich. U.S.A. **112** 43.36N 84.46W
Mount Pleasant *town* S.C. U.S.A. **113** 32.48N 79.54W
Mount Pleasant *town* Tex. U.S.A. **111** 33.09N 94.58W
Mount Robson *town* Canada **100** 52.56N119.15W
Mount Savage *town* U.S.A. **114** 39.42N 78.53W
Mount's B. U.K. **13** 50.05N 5.25W
Mount Sterling *town* U.S.A. **113** 38.03N 83.56W
Mount Union *town* U.S.A. **114** 40.23N 77.53W
Mount Upton *town* U.S.A. **115** 42.26N 75.23W
Mount Vernon *town* Australia **88** 24.09S118.10E
Mount Vernon *town* Ill. U.S.A. **110** 38.19N 88.52W
Mount Vernon *town* N.Y. U.S.A. **115** 40.54N 73.50W
Mount Vernon *town* Ohio U.S.A. **114** 40.23N 82.29W
Mount Vernon *town* Wash. U.S.A. **108** 48.25N122.20W
Mount Walker *town* Australia **89** 27.47S152.32E
Mount Willoughby Australia **92** 27.58S134.08E
Moura Australia **90** 24.33S149.58E
Moura Brazil **122** 1.27S 61.38W
Moura Chad **72** 13.47N 21.13E
Moura Portugal **27** 38.08N 7.27W
Mourdi, Dépression de *f.* Chad **72** 18.10N 23.00E
Mourdiah Mali **76** 14.35N 7.25W
Mourne *r.* U.K. **11** 54.50N 7.29W
Mourne Mts. U.K. **15** 54.10N 6.02W
Mouscron Belgium **16** 50.46N 3.10E
Moussoro Chad **77** 13.41N 16.31E
Mouth of Seneca U.S.A. **114** 38.52N 79.21W
Moutier Switz. **39** 47.17N 7.23E
Moûtiers France **21** 45.29N 6.32E
Mouzákion Greece **34** 39.26N 21.40E
Moxico Angola **78** 11.50S 20.05E
Moxico *d.* Angola **78** 13.00S 21.00E
Moy *r.* Rep. of Ire. **15** 54.10N 9.09W
Moyale Kenya **79** 3.31N 39.04E
Moyamba Sierra Leone **76** 8.04N 12.03W
Moyen Atlas *mts.* Morocco **74** 33.30N 5.00W
Moyen-Chari *d.* Chad **77** 9.20N 17.35E
Moyeni Lesotho **80** 30.24S 27.41E
Moyeuvre-Grande France **19** 49.15N 6.02E
Moyie Canada **100** 49.17N115.50W
Moyobamba Peru **122** 6.04S 76.56W
Moyowosi *r.* Tanzania **79** 4.59S 30.58E
Moza Israel **67** 31.47N 35.09E
Mozambique Africa **81** 17.30S 35.45E
Mozambique Channel Indian Oc. **81** 16.00S 42.30E
Mozdok U.S.S.R. **45** 43.45N 44.43E
Mozyr U.S.S.R. **37** 52.02N 29.10E
Mpala Zaïre **79** 6.45S 29.31E
M'Pama *r.* Congo **78** 0.59S 15.40E
Mpanda Tanzania **79** 6.21S 31.01E
Mpésoba Mali **76** 12.31N 5.39W
Mphoengs Zimbabwe **80** 21.10S 27.51E
Mpika Zambia **79** 11.52S 31.30E
Mponela Malaŵi **79** 13.32S 33.43E
Mporokoso Zambia **79** 9.22S 30.06E
M'Pouya Congo **78** 2.38S 16.08E
Mpunde *mtn.* Tanzania **79** 6.12S 33.48E
Mpwapwa Tanzania **79** 6.23S 36.38E
M'qoun, Irhil *mtn.* Morocco **74** 31.31N 6.25W
Mrhila, Djebel *mtn.* Tunisia **75** 35.25N 9.14E
Mrkonjić Grad Yugo. **31** 44.25N 17.05E
Mrkopalj Yugo. **31** 45.19N 14.51E
Msaken Tunisia **22** 35.42N 10.33E
Mseleni R.S.A. **81** 27.21S 32.33E
Msingu Tanzania **79** 4.52S 39.08E
Msta *r.* U.S.S.R. **44** 58.28N 31.20E
Mtakuja Tanzania **79** 7.21S 30.37E
Mtama Tanzania **79** 10.20S 39.19E
Mtito Andei Kenya **79** 2.32S 38.10E
Mtsensk U.S.S.R. **44** 53.18N 36.35E
Mtwara Tanzania **79** 10.17S 40.11E
Mtwara *d.* Tanzania **79** 10.00S 38.30E
Mu *r.* Japan **57** 42.30N142.20E
Muaná Brazil **123** 1.32S 49.13W
Muangangia Angola **78** 13.33S 18.04E
Muang Chiang Rai Thailand **56** 19.56N 99.51E
Muang Khammouan Laos **56** 17.22N104.50E
Muang Khon Kaen Thailand **56** 16.25N102.52E
Muang Lampang Thailand **56** 18.16N 99.30E
Muang Lamphun Thailand **56** 18.36N 99.02E
Muang Nakhon Phanom Thailand **56** 17.22N104.45E
Muang Nakhon Sawan Thailand **56** 15.42N100.04E
Muang Nan Thailand **56** 18.47N100.50E
Muang Ngoy Laos **56** 20.43N102.41E
Muang Pak Lay Laos **56** 18.12N101.25E
Muang Phaya Thailand **56** 19.10N 99.55E
Muang Phetchabun Thailand **56** 16.25N101.08E
Muang Phichit Thailand **56** 16.29N100.21E
Muang Phitsanulok Thailand **56** 16.45N100.18E
Muang Phrae Thailand **56** 18.07N100.09E
Muang Sakon Nakhon Thailand **56** 17.10N104.08E
Muang Sing Laos **56** 21.11N101.09E
Muang Soum Laos **56** 18.46N102.36E
Muang Ubon Thailand **56** 15.15N104.50E
Muar Malaysia **58** 2.01N102.35E
Muara Brunei **58** 5.01N115.01E
Muara Indonesia **58** 0.32S101.20E
Muarakaman Indonesia **58** 0.02S116.45E
Muaratewe Indonesia **58** 0.57S114.53E
Muāri, Rās *c.* Pakistan **62** 24.49N 66.40E
Mubende Uganda **79** 0.30N 31.24E
Mubi Nigeria **77** 10.16N 13.17E
Mucanona Angola **78** 8.13S 16.39E
Muchea Australia **89** 31.36S115.57E
Mücheln Germany **38** 51.18N 11.48E
Muchinga Mts. Zambia **79** 12.15S 31.00E
Muck *i.* U.K. **14** 56.50N 6.14W
Mucojo Mozambique **79** 12.05S 40.26E
Muconda Angola **78** 10.31S 21.20E
Mudanjiang China **53** 44.36N129.42E
Mudaysīsāt, Jabal al *mtn.* Jordan **67** 31.39N 36.14E
Mudgee Australia **93** 32.37S149.36E
Mudon Burma **56** 16.15N 97.44E
Mudyuga U.S.S.R. **44** 63.45N 39.29E
Muèda Mozambique **79** 11.40S 39.31E
Muene Quibau Angola **78** 11.27S 19.14E
Mufulira Zambia **79** 12.30S 28.12E
Mufu Shan *mts.* China **55** 29.30N114.45E
Muganskaya Ravnina *f.* U.S.S.R. **65** 39.40N 48.30E
Mughr Syria **67** 33.05N 35.43E
Mughshin, Wādī Oman **71** 19.44N 55.15E
Mugi Japan **57** 33.40N134.25E
Mugía Spain **26** 43.06N 9.10W
Muğla Turkey **29** 37.12N 28.22E
Muhamdi India **63** 27.57N 80.13E
Muḩammad, Ra's *c.* Egypt **66** 27.42N 34.13E
Mühlacker Germany **39** 48.57N 8.50E
Mühldorf Germany **39** 48.15N 12.32E
Mühlhausen Germany **38** 51.12N 10.27E
Mühlig Hofmann fjella *mts.* Antarctica **128** 72.30S 5.00E
Muhola Finland **40** 63.20N 25.05E
Muhos Finland **40** 64.48N 25.59E
Muhu *i.* U.S.S.R. **41** 58.32N 23.20E
Muhuru Kenya **73** 1.01S 34.07E
Muhu Väin *str.* U.S.S.R. **41** 58.45N 23.30E
Mui Ca Mau *c.* Vietnam **56** 8.30N104.35E
Muine Bheag *town* Rep. of Ire. **15** 52.42N 6.58W
Muir, L. Australia **89** 34.30S116.30E
Mukachevo U.S.S.R. **37** 48.26N 22.45E
Mukah Malaysia **58** 2.56N112.02E
Mukallik, Wādī al Jordan **67** 31.46N 35.29E
Mukandwara India **62** 24.49N 75.59E
Mukawa P.N.G. **90** 9.48S150.00E
Mukāwir *site* Jordan **67** 31.34N 35.38E
Mukeriān India **62** 31.57N 75.37E
Mukinbudin Australia **89** 30.52S118.08E
Muko *r.* Japan **57** 34.41N135.23E
Mukoba Zaïre **78** 6.50S 20.50E
Mukongo Zaïre **78** 6.32S 23.30E
Muktsar India **62** 30.28N 74.52E
Mukwela Zambia **78** 17.00S 26.40E
Mūl India **63** 20.04N 79.40E
Mula *r.* India **62** 19.35N 74.50E
Mūla *r.* Pakistan **62** 27.57N 67.37E
Mula Spain **25** 38.03N 1.30W
Mulanje Mts. Malaŵi **79** 15.57S 35.33E
Mulchén Chile **125** 37.43S 72.14W
Mulde *r.* Germany **38** 51.10N 12.48E
Mulgathing Australia **92** 30.15S134.00E
Mulgrave Canada **103** 45.37N 61.23W
Mulhacén *mtn.* Spain **27** 37.03N 3.19W
Mülheim N.-Westfalen Germany **38** 51.24N 6.54E
Mülheim N.-Westfalen Germany **38** 50.58N 7.00E
Mulhouse France **19** 47.45N 7.20E
Mull *i.* U.K. **14** 56.28N 5.56W
Mull, Sd. of *str.* U.K. **14** 56.32N 5.55W
Mullaghanattin *mtn.* Rep. of Ire. **15** 51.56N 9.51W
Mullaghareirk Mts. Rep. of Ire. **15** 52.19N 9.06W
Mullaghmore *mtn.* U.K. **15** 54.51N 6.51W
Mullaley Australia **93** 31.06S149.55E
Mullen U.S.A. **110** 42.03N101.01W
Mullengudgery Australia **93** 31.40S147.23E
Mullens U.S.A. **113** 37.35N 81.25W
Mullet Pen. Rep. of Ire. **15** 54.12N 10.04W
Mullett L. U.S.A. **104** 45.30N 84.30W
Mullewa Australia **89** 28.33S115.31E
Müllheim Germany **39** 47.48N 7.38E
Mullingar Rep. of Ire. **15** 53.31N 7.21W
Mull of Galloway *c.* U.K. **14** 54.39N 4.52W
Mull of Kintyre *c.* U.K. **14** 55.17N 5.45W
Mullovka U.S.S.R. **44** 54.12N 49.26E
Mullsjö Sweden **43** 57.55N 13.53E
Mullumbimby Australia **93** 28.32S153.30E
Mulobezi Zambia **80** 16.49S 25.09E
Muloorina Australia **92** 29.10S137.51E
Multai India **63** 21.46N 78.15E
Multān Pakistan **62** 30.11N 71.29E
Multyfarnham Rep. of Ire. **15** 53.37N 7.25W
Mulyungarie Australia **92** 31.30S140.45E
Mumbwa Zambia **79** 14.57S 27.01E
Mumcular Turkey **35** 37.05N 27.40E
Mun *r.* Thailand **56** 15.15N104.50E
Mun, Jabal *mtn.* Sudan **72** 14.08N 22.42E
Muna *i.* Indonesia **59** 5.00S122.30E
Munābāo India **62** 25.45N 70.17E
Munan Pass China / Vietnam **55** 22.06N106.46E
Münchberg Germany **38** 50.11N 11.47E
München Germany **39** 48.08N 11.34E
Muncho Lake *town* Canada **100** 59.00N125.50W
Muncie U.S.A. **112** 40.11N 85.23W
Mundaring Weir Australia **89** 31.59S116.13E
Münden Germany **38** 51.25N 9.39E
Mundiwindi Australia **88** 23.50S120.07E
Mundo *r.* Spain **25** 38.19N 1.40W
Mundra India **62** 22.51N 69.44E
Munera Spain **27** 39.02N 2.28W
Mungari Mozambique **81** 17.12S 33.31E
Mungbere Zaïre **79** 2.40N 28.25E
Mungeli India **63** 22.04N 81.41E
Mungeranie Australia **92** 28.00S138.36E
Mungindi Australia **93** 28.58S148.56E
Munhango Angola **78** 12.10S 18.36E
Munich *see* München Germany **39**
Muniesa Spain **25** 41.02N 0.48W
Muniz Freire Brazil **126** 20.25S 41.23W
Munkedal Sweden **42** 58.29N 11.41E
Munkfors Sweden **43** 59.50N 13.32E
Munning *r.* Australia **93** 31.50S152.30E
Münsingen Germany **39** 48.25N 9.29E
Münsingen Switz. **39** 46.53N 7.34E
Munster France **19** 48.03N 7.08E
Munster Nschn. Germany **38** 52.59N 10.05E
Münster N.-Westfalen Germany **38** 51.57N 7.37E
Muntadgin Australia **89** 31.41S118.32E
Munuscong L. U.S.A. **104** 46.10N 84.08W
Muong Hinh Vietnam **55** 19.49N105.03E
Muonio Finland **40** 67.57N 23.42E
Muonio *r.* Finland / Sweden **40** 67.10N 23.40E
Mupa Angola **80** 16.07S 15.45E
Mupa *r.* Mozambique **81** 19.07S 35.50E
Muping China **54** 37.23N121.35E
Muqaddam, Wādī Sudan **72** 18.04N 31.30E
Muqdisho Somali Rep. **79** 2.02N 45.21E
Mur *r.* Austria *see* Mura *r.* Yugo. **31**
Mura *r.* Yugo. **31** 46.18N 16.53E
Murallón *mtn.* Argentina / Chile **125** 49.48S 73.25W
Muranga Kenya **79** 0.43S 37.10E
Murashi U.S.S.R. **44** 59.20N 48.59E
Murat France **20** 45.07N 2.52E
Murau Austria **39** 47.07N 14.10E
Muravera Italy **32** 39.25N 9.35E
Murça Portugal **26** 41.24N 7.27W
Murchison Australia **93** 36.36S145.14E
Murchison *r.* Australia **88** 27.30S114.10E
Murchison New Zealand **86** 41.48S172.20E
Murcia Spain **25** 37.59N 1.07W
Murcia *d.* Spain **25** 37.55N 1.40W
Mur-de-Barrez France **20** 44.51N 2.39E
Murdo U.S.A. **110** 43.53N100.43W
Mureş *r.* Romania **37** 46.16N 20.10E
Muret France **20** 43.28N 1.21E
Murewa Zimbabwe **81** 17.40S 31.47E
Murfreesboro U.S.A. **113** 35.50N 86.25W
Murg *r.* Germany **39** 48.55N 8.10E
Murgha Faqirzai Pakistan **62** 31.03N 67.48E
Murgha Kibzai Pakistan **62** 30.44N 69.25E
Murgon Australia **90** 26.15S151.57E
Murguía Spain **26** 42.57N 2.49W
Muri Cook Is. **84** 21.14S159.43W
Muria, Gunung *mtn.* Indonesia **59** 6.39S110.51E
Muriaé Brazil **126** 21.08S 42.33W
Murias de Paredes Spain **26** 42.51N 6.11W
Müritzsee *l.* Germany **38** 53.25N 12.43E
Murjek Sweden **40** 66.29N 20.50E
Murliganj India **63** 25.54N 86.59E
Murmansk U.S.S.R. **44** 68.59N 33.08E
Murnau Germany **39** 47.40N 11.12E
Murnei Sudan **73** 12.57N 22.52E
Muro, Capo di *c.* France **21** 41.44N 8.40E
Muro Lucano Italy **33** 40.45N 15.30E
Murom U.S.S.R. **44** 55.04N 42.04E
Muroran Japan **57** 42.21N140.59E
Muros Spain **26** 42.47N 9.04W
Muros y Noya, Ría de *est.* Spain **26** 42.45N 9.00W
Murrah al Kubrá, Al Buḩayrah al *l.* Egypt **66** 30.20N 32.20E
Murra Murra Australia **93** 28.18S146.48E
Murray *r.*S.A. Australia **92** 35.23S139.20E
Murray *r.*W.A. Australia **89** 32.35S115.46E
Murray *r.* Canada **100** 56.11N120.45W
Murray Ky. U.S.A. **111** 36.37N 88.19W
Murray Utah U.S.A. **108** 40.40N111.53W
Murray, L. P.N.G. **59** 7.00S141.30E
Murray, L. U.S.A. **113** 34.04N 81.23W
Murray Bridge *town* Australia **92** 35.10S139.17E
Murrayville Australia **92** 35.16S141.14E
Murree Pakistan **62** 33.54N 73.24E
Murrhardt Germany **39** 48.59N 9.34E
Murringo Australia **93** 34.19S148.36E
Murrumbidgee *r.* Australia **92** 34.38S143.10E
Murrumburrah Australia **93** 34.33S148.21E
Murrurundi Australia **93** 31.47S150.51E
Murshidābād India **63** 24.11N 88.16E
Murska Sobota Yugo. **31** 46.40N 16.10E
Murten Switz. **39** 46.56N 7.07E
Murtoa Australia **92** 36.40S142.31E
Murtosa Portugal **26** 40.44N 8.38W
Murud *mtn.* Malaysia **58** 3.45N115.30E
Murwāra India **63** 23.51N 80.24E
Murwillumbah Australia **93** 28.20S153.24E
Muş Turkey **64** 38.45N 41.30E
Mūsá, Jabal *mtn.* Egypt **66** 28.31N 33.59E
Musadi Zaïre **78** 2.31S 22.50E
Mūsa Khel Pakistan **62** 32.38N 71.44E
Mūsa Khel Bāzār Pakistan **62** 30.52N 69.49E
Musala *mtn.* Bulgaria **34** 42.13N 23.37E
Musan N. Korea **57** 42.14N129.13E
Mūsā Qal 'eh Afghan. **62** 32.05N 64.51E
Mūsā Qal 'eh *r.* Afghan. **62** 32.22N 64.46E
Musay'īd Qatar **65** 24.47N 51.36E
Mūsāzai Pakistan **62** 30.23N 66.32E
Muscat *see* Masqaţ Oman **65**
Muscatine U.S.A. **110** 41.25N 91.03W
Müsgebi Turkey **35** 37.02N 27.21E
Musgrave Australia **90** 14.47S143.30E
Musgrave Ranges *mts.* Australia **88** 26.10S131.50E
Mushāsh, Wādī al Jordan **67** 31.35N 35.22E
Mushie Zaïre **78** 2.59S 16.55E
Mushima Zambia **80** 14.13S 25.05E
Mushin Nigeria **77** 6.33N 3.22E
Musi *r.* Indonesia **58** 2.20S104.57E
Muskegon U.S.A. **112** 43.13N 86.15W
Muskegon *r.* U.S.A. **112** 43.13N 86.16W
Muskegon Heights *town* U.S.A. **112** 43.03N 86.16W
Muskingum *r.* U.S.A. **114** 40.03N 81.59W
Muskö *i.* Sweden **43** 59.00N 18.06E
Muskogee U.S.A. **111** 35.45N 95.22W
Muskoka, L. Canada **104** 45.00N 79.25W
Muskwa *r.* Alta. Canada **100** 56.16N114.06W
Muskwa *r.* B.C. Canada **100** 58.47N122.48W
Musoma Tanzania **79** 1.31S 33.48E
Mussari Angola **80** 13.07S 17.56E
Musselburgh U.K. **14** 55.57N 3.04W
Musselkanaal Neth. **16** 52.57N 7.01E
Musselshell *r.* U.S.A. **108** 47.21N107.58W
Mussende Angola **78** 10.33S 16.02E
Musserra Angola **78** 7.31S 13.02E
Mussidan France **20** 45.02N 0.22E
Mussomeli Italy **32** 37.35N 13.46E
Mustahīl Ethiopia **71** 5.12N 44.17E
Mustāng Nepal **63** 29.11N 83.57E
Mustjala U.S.S.R. **41** 58.28N 22.14E
Muswellbrook Australia **93** 32.17S150.55E
Mūţ Egypt **72** 25.29N 28.59E
Mut Turkey **64** 36.38N 33.27E
Mutala Mozambique **81** 15.54S 37.51E
Mutalau Niue **84** 18.58S169.50W
Mutanda Zambia **78** 12.23S 26.16E
Mutare Zimbabwe **81** 18.59S 32.40E
Mutbīn Syria **67** 33.09N 36.15E
Mutoko Zimbabwe **81** 17.23S 32.13E

Mutooroo to **Nawá**

Mutooroo Australia **92** 32.30S140.58E
Mutoray U.S.S.R. **51** 61.20N100.32E
Mutshatsha Zaïre **78** 10.39S 24.27E
Mutsu Japan **57** 41.17N141.10E
Mutsu wan *b.* Japan **57** 41.10N141.05E
Mutton Bay *town* Canada **103** 50.47N 59.02W
Muwale Tanzania **79** 6.22S 33.46E
Muxima Angola **78** 9.33S 13.58E
Muya U.S.S.R. **51** 56.28N115.50E
Muyinga Burundi **79** 2.48S 30.21E
Muynak U.S.S.R. **50** 43.46N 59.00E
Muzaffarābād Jammu & Kashmir **62** 34.22N 73.28E
Muzaffargarh Pakistan **62** 30.04N 71.12E
Muzaffarnagar India **63** 29.28N 77.41E
Muzaffarpur India **63** 26.07N 85.24E
Muzhi U.S.S.R. **44** 65.25N 64.40E
Muzillac France **18** 47.33N 2.29W
Muzoka Zambia **80** 16.43S 27.18E
Muztag *mtn.* China **52** 36.25N 87.25E
Mvadhi Gabon **78** 1.13N 13.10E
Mvolo Sudan **73** 6.03N 29.56E
Mvomero Tanzania **79** 6.18S 37.26E
Mvuma Zimbabwe **80** 19.16S 30.30E
Mvurwi Range *mts.* Zimbabwe **80** 17.10S 30.45E
Mwali *i.* Comoros **79** 12.22S 43.45E
Mwanza Tanzania **79** 2.30S 32.54E
Mwanza *d.* Tanzania **79** 3.00S 32.30E
Mwanza Zaïre **78** 7.51S 26.43E
Mwaya Mbeya Tanzania **79** 9.33S 33.56E
Mweka Zaïre **78** 4.51S 21.34E
Mwene Ditu Zaïre **78** 7.04S 23.27E
Mwenezi *r.* Mozambique **81** 22.42S 31.45E
Mwenezi Zimbabwe **80** 21.22S 30.45E
Mweru, L. Zaïre / Zambia **79** 9.00S 28.40E
Mwingi Kenya **79** 1.00S 38.04E
Mwinilunga Zambia **78** 11.44S 24.24E
Mya, Oued *wadi* Algeria **75** 31.40N 5.15E
Myanaung Burma **61** 18.25N 95.10E
Myanma *see* Burma Asia **56**
Myaungmya Burma **56** 16.33N 94.55E
Myingyan Burma **56** 21.22N 95.28E
Myinkyado Burma **56** 20.56N 96.42E
Myinmu Burma **56** 21.58N 95.43E
Myitkyinā Burma **56** 25.24N 97.25E
Mymensingh Bangla. **63** 24.45N 90.24E
Myrdal Norway **41** 60.44N 7.08E
Myrdalsjökull *ice cap* Iceland **40** 63.40N 19.06W
Myrtle Beach *town* U.S.A. **113** 33.42N 78.54W
Myrtle Creek *town* U.S.A. **108** 43.01N123.17W
Myrtleford Australia **93** 36.35S146.44E
Myrtle Point *town* U.S.A. **108** 43.04N124.08W
Mysen Norway **42** 59.33N 11.20E
Myślenice Poland **37** 49.51N 19.56E
Mysore India **60** 12.18N 76.37E
Mystic U.S.A. **115** 41.21N 71.58W
My Tho Vietnam **56** 10.27N106.20E
Mytishchi U.S.S.R. **44** 55.54N 37.47E
Mziha Tanzania **79** 5.53S 37.48E
Mzimba Malaŵi **79** 12.00S 33.39E

N

Naab *r.* Germany **39** 49.01N 12.02E
Naalehu Hawaiian Is. **85** 19.04N155.35W
Na'ām *r.* Sudan **73** 6.48N 29.57E
Na'an Israel **67** 31.53N 34.51E
Naantali Finland **41** 60.27N 22.02E
Naas Rep. of Ire. **15** 53.13N 6.41W
Näätämö *r.* Norway **40** 69.40N 29.30E
Nabā, Jabal *mtn.* Jordan **67** 31.46N 35.45E
Nababeep R.S.A. **80** 29.36S 17.44E
Nabadwip India **63** 23.25N 88.22E
Nabari *r.* Japan **57** 34.45N136.01E
Naberezhnyye Chelny U.S.S.R. **44** 55.42N 52.20E
Nabeul Tunisia **75** 36.28N 10.44E
Nabeul *d.* Tunisia **32** 36.45N 10.45E
Nābha India **62** 30.22N 76.09E
Nabingora Uganda **79** 0.31N 31.11E
Nabī Shu'ayb, Jabal an *mtn.* Yemen **71** 15.17N 43.59E
Naboomspruit R.S.A. **80** 24.31S 28.24E
Nabq Egypt **66** 28.04N 34.26E
Nābulus Jordan **67** 32.13N 35.16E
Nābulus *d.* Jordan **67** 32.15N 35.17E
Nacala Mozambique **81** 14.34S 40.41E
Nacchio Ethiopia **73** 7.30N 40.15E
Nachikapau L. Canada **103** 56.44N 68.00W
Nachingwea Tanzania **79** 10.21S 38.46E
Nāchna India **62** 27.30N 71.43E
Nacka Sweden **43** 59.18N 18.10E
Naco Mexico **109** 31.20N109.56W
Nacogdoches U.S.A. **111** 31.36N 94.39W
Nadela Spain **26** 42.58N 7.30W
Nadiād India **62** 22.42N 72.52E
Nador Morocco **74** 35.12N 2.55W
Nadūshan Iran **65** 32.03N 53.33E
Nadvoitsy U.S.S.R. **44** 63.56N 34.20E
Nadvornaya U.S.S.R. **37** 48.37N 24.30E
Nadym U.S.S.R. **50** 65.25N 72.40E
Naenwa India **62** 25.46N 75.51E
Naerbö Norway **42** 58.40N 5.39E
Naeröy Norway **40** 64.48N 11.17E
Naestved Denmark **42** 55.14N 11.46E
Nafada Nigeria **77** 11.08N 11.20E
Nafishah Egypt **66** 30.34N 32.15E
Naft-e Safīd Iran **65** 31.38N 49.20E
Nāg Pakistan **62** 27.24N 65.08E
Naga Phil. **59** 13.36N123.12E
Nāgāland *d.* India **61** 26.10N 94.30E
Nagambie Australia **93** 36.48S145.12E
Nagano Japan **57** 36.39N138.10E
Nagano *d.* Japan **57** 35.33N137.50E
Nagaoka Japan **57** 37.30N138.50E
Nāgappattinam India **61** 10.45N 79.50E
Nagara *r.* Japan **57** 35.01N136.43E
Nagar Pārkar Pakistan **62** 24.22N 70.45E
Nagarzê China **63** 28.58N 90.24E
Nagasaki Japan **57** 32.45N129.52E
Nāgaur India **62** 27.12N 73.44E
Nāgāvali *r.* India **63** 18.13N 83.56E
Nāgda India **62** 23.27N 75.25E
Nagele Neth. **16** 52.39N 5.43E
Nāgercoil India **60** 8.11N 77.30E
Nagichot Sudan **73** 4.16N 33.34E
Nagīna India **63** 29.27N 78.27E
Nagles Mts. Rep. of Ire. **15** 52.06N 8.26W
Nagold Germany **39** 48.33N 8.43E
Nagorskoye U.S.S.R. **44** 58.18N 50.50E
Nagoya Japan **57** 35.10N136.55E
Nāgpur India **63** 21.09N 79.06E
Nagqên China **61** 32.15N 96.13E
Nagqu China **63** 31.30N 92.00E
Nagyatád Hungary **31** 46.14N 17.22E
Nagybajom Hungary **31** 46.23N 17.31E
Nagykanizsa Hungary **31** 46.27N 16.59E
Naha Japan **53** 26.10N127.40E
Nahalal Israel **67** 32.41N 35.12E
Nāhan India **63** 30.33N 77.18E
Nahanni Butte *town* Canada **98** 61.03N123.31W
Nahariyya Israel **67** 33.01N 35.05E
Nahāvand Iran **65** 34.13N 48.23E
Nahe *r.* Germany **39** 49.58N 7.57E
Nahf Israel **67** 32.56N 35.19E
Nahr al Furāt *r.* Asia **65** 31.00N 47.27E
Nahunta U.S.A. **113** 31.12N 82.00W
Nai Ga Burma **56** 27.48N 97.30E
Naila Germany **38** 50.19N 11.42E
Naiman Qi China **54** 42.53N120.40E
Nain Canada **103** 57.00N 61.40W
Nā'īn Iran **65** 32.52N 53.05E
Naini Tāl India **63** 29.23N 79.27E
Nainpur India **63** 22.26N 80.07E
Nairn Canada **104** 46.21N 81.36W
Nairn U.K. **14** 57.35N 3.52W
Nairobi Kenya **79** 1.17S 36.50E
Naita *mtn.* Ethiopia **73** 5.31N 35.18E
Naivasha Kenya **79** 0.44S 36.26E
Najac France **20** 44.17N 2.00E
Najd *f.* Saudi Arabia **64** 25.00N 45.00E
Nájera Spain **26** 42.25N 2.44W
Naj 'Hammādī Egypt **64** 26.04N 32.13E
Najrān *see* Abā as Su'ūd Saudi Arabia **71**
Nāka Khārari Pakistan **62** 25.15N 66.44E
Nakambe *r.* Burkina *see* White Volta *r.* Ghana **76**
Nakaminato Japan **57** 36.21N140.36E
Nakano shima *i.* Japan **57** 29.55N129.55E
Nakape Sudan **73** 5.47N 28.38E
Nakatsu Japan **57** 33.37N131.11E
Nakatsugawa Japan **57** 35.29N137.30E
Nak'fa Ethiopia **72** 16.43N 38.32E
Nakhichevan U.S.S.R. **65** 39.12N 45.24E
Nakhodka U.S.S.R. **53** 42.53N132.54E
Nakhola India **63** 26.07N 92.11E
Nakhon Pathom Thailand **56** 13.50N100.01E
Nakhon Ratchasima Thailand **56** 14.58N102.06E
Nakhon Si Thammarat Thailand **56** 8.24N 99.58E
Nakhtarana India **62** 23.20N 69.15E
Nakina Canada **102** 50.10N 86.40W
Nakło Poland **37** 53.08N 17.35E
Naknek U.S.A. **98** 58.45N157.00W
Nakop Namibia **80** 28.05S 19.57E
Nakskov Denmark **41** 54.50N 11.09E
Näkten *l.* Sweden **40** 65.50N 14.35E
Nakuru Kenya **79** 0.16S 36.04E
Nāl *r.* Pakistan **62** 26.02N 65.19E
Nalbāri India **63** 26.26N 91.30E
Nalchik U.S.S.R. **45** 43.31N 43.38E
Nalón *r.* Spain **26** 43.32N 6.04W
Nālūt Libya **75** 31.52N 10.59E
Namacurra Mozambique **79** 17.35S 37.00E
Namakī *r.* Iran **65** 31.02N 55.20E
Namanga Kenya **79** 2.33S 36.48E
Namangan U.S.S.R. **52** 40.59N 71.41E
Namanyere Tanzania **79** 7.34S 31.00E
Namapa Mozambique **81** 13.48S 39.44E
Namaponda Mozambique **81** 15.51S 39.52E
Namari Senegal **74** 15.05N 13.39W
Namarroi Mozambique **81** 15.58S 36.55E
Namatele Tanzania **79** 10.01S 38.26E
Namba Angola **78** 11.32S 15.33E
Nambala Zambia **80** 15.07S 27.02E
Nambour Australia **91** 26.36S152.59E
Nambucca Heads *town* Australia **93** 30.38S152.59E
Namco China **63** 30.53N 91.06E
Nam Co *l.* China **63** 30.45N 90.30E
Nam Dinh Vietnam **55** 20.21N106.09E
Namecala Mozambique **81** 12.50S 39.38E
Nametil Mozambique **81** 15.41S 39.30E
Namib Desert Namibia **80** 23.00S 15.20E
Namibe Angola **78** 15.10S 12.10E
Namibe *d.* Angola **80** 15.30S 12.30E
Namibia Africa **80** 21.30S 16.45E
Namīn Iran **65** 38.25N 48.30E
Namlea Indonesia **59** 3.15S127.07E
Namling China **63** 29.40N 89.03E
Namoi *r.* Australia **93** 30.14S148.28E
Namonuito *i.* Pacific Oc. **84** 8.46N150.02E
Namous, Oued *wadi* Algeria **74** 30.28N 0.14W
Nampa Canada **100** 56.02N117.07W
Nampa U.S.A. **108** 43.44N116.34W
Nam Phan *f.* Vietnam **56** 10.40N106.00E
Nam Phong Thailand **56** 16.45N102.52E
Namp'o N. Korea **53** 38.40N125.30E
Nampula Mozambique **81** 15.09S 39.14E
Nampula *d.* Mozambique **81** 15.00S 39.00E
Namsen *r.* Norway **40** 64.27N 12.19E
Namsos Norway **40** 64.28N 11.30E
Namtu Burma **56** 23.04N 97.26E
Namu Canada **100** 51.52N127.41W
Namuchabawashan *mtn.* China **61** 29.30N 95.10E
Namungua Mozambique **79** 13.11S 40.30E
Namur Belgium **16** 50.28N 4.52E
Namur *d.* Belgium **16** 50.20N 4.45E
Namur Canada **105** 45.54N 74.56W
Namutoni Namibia **80** 18.48S 16.58E
Namwala Zambia **78** 15.44S 26.25E
Nanaimo Canada **100** 49.10N124.00W
Nanam N. Korea **57** 41.43N129.41E
Nanango Australia **91** 26.42S151.58E
Nanao Japan **57** 37.03N136.58E
Nanchang China **55** 28.37N115.57E
Nancheng China **55** 27.35N116.33E
Nanchong China **55** 30.53N106.05E
Nanchuan China **55** 29.12N107.30E
Nancy France **19** 48.41N 6.12E
Nanda Devi *mtn.* India **63** 30.23N 79.59E
Nandan China **55** 24.59N107.32E
Nānded India **62** 19.09N 77.20E
Nandewar Range *mts.* Australia **93** 30.20S150.45E
Nāndgaon India **62** 20.19N 74.39E
Nandi Fiji **84** 17.48S177.25E
Nandu Jiang *r.* China **55** 20.04N110.20E
Nandurbār India **62** 21.22N 74.15E
Nandyāl India **61** 15.29N 78.29E
Nanfeng China **55** 27.10N116.24E
Nanga Eboko Cameroon **77** 4.41N 12.21E
Nānga Parbat *mtn.* Jammu & Kashmir **60** 35.10N 74.35E
Nangapinoh Indonesia **58** 0.20S111.44E
Nangola Mali **76** 12.41N 6.35W
Nangqên China **52** 32.15N 96.13E
Nangrūl Pīr India **62** 20.19N 77.21E
Nang Xian China **63** 29.03N 93.12E
Nanhui China **55** 31.03N121.46E
Nanjiang China **54** 32.21N106.50E
Nanjing China **55** 32.02N118.52E
Nanking *see* Nanjing China **55**
Nanling China **55** 30.56N118.19E
Nan Ling *mts.* China **55** 25.10N110.00E
Nannine Australia **88** 26.53S118.20E
Nanning China **55** 22.48N108.18E
Nannup Australia **89** 33.57S115.42E
Nanortalik Greenland **99** 60.09N 45.15W
Nānpāra India **63** 27.52N 81.30E
Nanpi China **54** 38.02N116.42E
Nanping Fujian China **55** 26.38N118.10E
Nanpu Xi *r.* China **55** 26.38N118.10E
Nanri *i.* China **55** 25.13N119.30E
Nansa *r.* Spain **26** 43.22N 4.29W
Nansei shotō *is.* Japan **53** 26.30N125.00E
Nansei-Shotō Trench Pacific Oc. **84** 25.00N129.00E
Nanshan *is.* S. China Sea **58** 10.30N116.00E
Nant France **20** 44.01N 3.18E
Nantes France **18** 47.13N 1.33W
Nanteuil-le-Haudouin France **19** 49.08N 2.48E
Nanticoke U.S.A. **115** 41.12N 76.00W
Nanton Canada **100** 50.21N113.46W
Nantong China **54** 32.02N120.55E
Nantou Taiwan **55** 23.54N120.41E
Nantua France **21** 46.09N 5.37E
Nantucket U.S.A. **115** 41.17N 70.06W
Nantucket I. U.S.A. **115** 41.16N 70.03W
Nantucket Sd. U.S.A. **115** 41.30N 70.15W
Nantwich U.K. **12** 53.05N 2.31W
Nanumea *i.* Tuvalu **84** 5.40S176.10E
Nanwan Shuiku *resr.* China **55** 32.05N113.55E
Nanxi China **55** 28.52N104.59E
Nan Xian China **55** 29.22N112.25E
Nanxiong China **55** 25.10N114.16E
Nanyang China **54** 33.07N112.30E
Nanyō Japan **57** 38.03N140.10E
Nanzhang China **55** 31.47N111.42E
Nao, Cabo de la *c.* Spain **25** 38.44N 0.14E
Naococane, Lac *l.* Canada **103** 52.50N 70.40W
Naogaon Bangla. **63** 24.47N 88.56E
Naokot Pakistan **62** 24.51N 69.27E
Náousa Greece **34** 40.37N 22.05E
Napa U.S.A. **108** 38.18N122.17W
Napadogan Canada **103** 46.24N 67.01W
Napanee Canada **105** 44.15N 76.57W
Napè Laos **56** 18.18N105.07E
Napier New Zealand **86** 39.29S176.58E
Napierville Canada **105** 45.11N 73.25W
Naples *see* Napoli Italy **33**
Naples Fla. U.S.A. **113** 26.09N 81.48W
Naples N.Y. U.S.A. **114** 42.37N 77.25W
Napo China **55** 23.23N105.48E
Napo *r.* Peru **122** 3.30S 73.10W
Napoleon U.S.A. **112** 41.24N 84.09W
Napoli Italy **33** 40.51N 14.17E
Napoli, Golfo di *g.* Italy **33** 40.45N 14.15E
Naqb Ishtar Jordan **66** 30.00N 35.30E
Nār, Wādī an Jordan **67** 31.40N 35.27E
Nara Japan **57** 34.41N135.50E
Nara *d.* Japan **57** 34.27N135.55E
Nara Mali **74** 15.13N 7.20W
Nāra Pakistan **62** 24.07N 69.07E
Naracoorte Australia **92** 36.58S140.46E
Naradhan Australia **93** 33.39S146.20E
Naraini India **63** 25.11N 80.29E
Naran Mongolia **54** 45.20N113.41E
Narathiwat Thailand **56** 6.25N101.48E
Nara Visa U.S.A. **111** 35.37N103.06W
Nārāyanganj Bangla. **63** 23.37N 90.30E
Narbada *r. see* Narmada *r.* India **62**
Narbonne France **20** 43.11N 3.00E
Narcea Spain **26** 43.28N 6.06W
Nardò Italy **33** 40.11N 18.02E
Narembeen Australia **89** 32.04S118.23E
Nares Str. Canada **99** 78.30N 75.00W
Naretha Australia **89** 31.01S124.50E
Nāri *r.* Pakistan **62** 29.10N 67.50E
Naria U.S.A. **63** 23.18N 90.25E
Narita Japan **57** 35.47N140.19E
Närke *f.* Sweden **43** 59.03N 14.55E
Narmada *r.* India **62** 21.40N 73.00E
Nārnaul India **62** 28.03N 76.06E
Narni Italy **30** 42.31N 12.31E
Naro Italy **32** 37.17N 13.48E
Nāro, Koh-i- *mtn.* Pakistan **62** 29.15N 63.30E
Narodichi U.S.S.R. **37** 51.11N 29.01E
Narodnaya *mtn.* U.S.S.R. **44** 65.00N 61.00E
Narok Kenya **79** 1.04S 35.54E
Narón Spain **26** 43.32N 8.10W
Narooma Australia **93** 36.15S150.06E
Narrabri Australia **93** 30.20S149.49E
Narrabri West Australia **93** 30.22S149.47E
Narran *r.* Australia **93** 29.45S147.20E
Narrandera Australia **93** 34.36S146.34E
Narran L. Australia **93** 29.40S147.25E
Narrogin Australia **89** 32.58S117.10E
Narromine Australia **93** 32.17S148.20E
Narsimhapur India **63** 22.57N 79.12E
Narsingdi Bangla. **63** 23.55N 90.43E
Narsinghgarh India **62** 23.42N 77.06E
Narubis Namibia **80** 26.56S 18.36E
Narva U.S.S.R. **44** 59.22N 28.17E
Narvik Norway **40** 68.26N 17.25E
Narwāna India **62** 29.37N 76.07E
Naryan Mar U.S.S.R. **44** 67.37N 53.02E
Narylico Australia **92** 28.41S141.50E
Naryn U.S.S.R. **50** 41.24N 76.00E
Nasa *mtn.* Norway **40** 66.29N 15.23E
Nasarawa Nigeria **77** 8.35N 7.44E
Nasbinals France **20** 44.40N 3.03E
Naseby New Zealand **86** 45.01S170.09E
Nashua Iowa U.S.A. **110** 42.57N 92.32W
Nashua Mont. U.S.A. **108** 48.08N106.22W
Nashua N.H. U.S.A. **115** 42.46N 71.27W
Nashville U.S.A. **113** 36.10N 86.50W
Naşīb Syria **67** 32.33N 36.11E
Našice Yugo. **31** 45.29N 18.06E
Näsijärvi *l.* Finland **41** 61.37N 23.42E
Nāsik India **62** 19.59N 73.48E
Nāşir Sudan **73** 8.36N 33.04E
Nāşir, Buḩayrat *l.* Egypt **72** 22.40N 32.00E
Nasīrābād India **62** 26.18N 74.44E
Nasīrābād Pakistan **62** 28.23N 68.24E
Naskaupi *r.* Canada **103** 53.45N 60.50W
Naşr Egypt **66** 30.36N 30.23E
Nass *r.* Canada **100** 55.00N129.50W
Nassau Bahamas **113** 25.05N 77.21W
Nassau I. Cook Is. **84** 11.33S165.25W
Nasser, L. *see* Nāşir, Buḩayrat *l.* Egypt **72**
Nassereith Austria **39** 47.19N 10.50E
Nassian Ivory Coast **76** 8.33N 3.18W
Nässjö Sweden **43** 57.39N 14.41E
Nastapoca *r.* Canada **102** 56.55N 76.33W
Nastapoka Is. Canada **102** 57.00N 77.00W
Nata Botswana **80** 20.12S 26.12E
Natal Brazil **123** 5.46S 35.15W
Natal Indonesia **58** 0.35N 99.07E
Natal *d.* R.S.A. **80** 28.30S 30.30E
Natal Basin *f.* Indian Oc. **49** 35.00S 39.00E
Natanes Plateau *f.* U.S.A. **109** 33.35N110.15W
Naţanz Iran **65** 33.30N 51.57E
Natashquan Canada **103** 50.11N 61.49W
Natashquan *r.* Canada **103** 50.06N 61.49W
Natchez U.S.A. **111** 31.34N 91.23W
Natchitoches U.S.A. **111** 31.46N 93.05W
Nathalia Australia **93** 36.02S145.14E
Nāthdwāra India **62** 24.56N 73.49E
National City U.S.A. **109** 32.40N117.06W
Natitingou Benin **77** 10.17N 1.19E
Natl Jordan **67** 31.39N 35.52E
Natoma U.S.A. **110** 39.11N 99.01W
Natron, L. Tanzania **79** 2.18S 36.05E
Naţrūn, Wādī an *f.* Egypt **66** 30.25N 30.18E
Natuna Besar *i.* Indonesia **58** 4.00N108.20E
Naturaliste, C. Australia **89** 33.32S115.01E
Naubinway U.S.A. **112** 46.05N 85.27W
Naucelle France **20** 44.12N 2.20E
Nauders Austria **39** 46.53N 10.30E
Nauen Germany **38** 52.36N 12.52E
Naugatuck U.S.A. **115** 41.30N 73.04W
Naumburg Germany **38** 51.09N 11.48E
Nā'ūr Jordan **67** 31.53N 35.50E
Nauroz Kalāt Pakistan **62** 28.47N 65.38E
Nauru Pacific Oc. **84** 0.32S166.55E
Naushahro Fīroz Pakistan **62** 26.50N 68.07E
Naustdal Norway **41** 61.31N 5.43E
Nauta Peru **122** 4.30S 73.40W
Nautanwa India **63** 27.26N 83.25E
Nautla Mexico **116** 20.13N 96.47W
Nava Mexico **111** 28.25N100.46W
Nava *r.* Zaïre **79** 1.45N 27.06E
Nava del Rey Spain **26** 41.20N 5.05W
Navahermosa Spain **27** 39.38N 4.28W
Navalcarnero Spain **26** 40.18N 4.00W
Navalmoral de la Mata Spain **27** 39.54N 5.32W
Navalvillar de Pela Spain **27** 39.06N 5.28W
Navan Rep. of Ire. **15** 53.39N 6.42W
Navāpur India **62** 21.15N 73.55E
Navarra *d.* Spain **25** 42.45N 1.30W
Navarre Australia **92** 36.54S143.09E
Navarre U.S.A. **114** 40.43N 81.32W
Navarro Argentina **125** 35.00S 59.10W
Navasota U.S.A. **111** 30.23N 96.05W
Naver *r.* U.K. **14** 58.32N 4.14W
Navia Spain **26** 43.32N 6.43W
Navia *r.* Spain **26** 43.33N 6.44W
Navlya U.S.S.R. **44** 52.51N 34.30E
Navoi U.S.S.R. **9** 40.04N 65.20E
Navojoa Mexico **109** 27.06N109.26W
Návpaktos Greece **35** 38.23N 21.50E
Návplion Greece **35** 37.34N 22.48E
Navrongo Ghana **76** 10.51N 1.03W
Navsāri India **62** 20.57N 72.59E
Nawá Syria **67** 32.53N 36.03E

Nawābganj to **Nicholson**

Nawābganj Bangla. **63** 24.36N 88.17E
Nawābganj India **63** 26.56N 81.13E
Nawābshāh Pakistan **62** 26.15N 68.25E
Nawāda India **63** 24.53N 85.32E
Nāwah Afghan. **62** 32.19N 67.53E
Nawākot Nepal **63** 27.55N 85.10E
Nawa Kot Pakistan **62** 28.20N 71.22E
Nawalgarh India **62** 27.51N 75.16E
Nawāpāra India **63** 20.58N 81.51E
Naxi China **55** 28.44N105.27E
Náxos Greece **35** 37.06N 25.23E
Náxos *i.* Greece **35** 37.02N 25.35E
Nayāgarh India **63** 20.08N 85.06E
Nayak Afghan. **62** 34.44N 66.57E
Nayarit *d.* Mexico **116** 21.30N104.00W
Nāy Band Iran **65** 32.20N 57.34E
Nāy Band Iran **65** 27.23N 52.38E
Nāy Band, Kūh-e *mtn.* Iran **65** 32.25N 57.30E
Nayoro Japan **57** 44.21N142.28E
Nazaré Brazil **123** 13.00S 39.00W
Nazaré Portugal **27** 39.36N 9.04W
Nazareth *see* Nazerat Israel **67**
Nazareth Trough *f.* Indian Oc. **49** 15.00S 64.00E
Nazarovka U.S.S.R. **44** 54.19N 41.20E
Nazas *r.* Mexico **116** 25.34N103.25W
Nazca Peru **122** 14.53S 74.54W
Nazerat Israel **67** 32.41N 35.16E
Nazilli Turkey **64** 37.55N 28.20E
Nazinon *r.* Burkina *see* Red Volta *r.* Ghana **76**
Nāzir Hāt Bangla. **63** 22.38N 91.47E
Nazrēt Ethiopia **73** 8.32N 39.22E
Nazuo China **55** 24.06N105.19E
Nchanga Zambia **79** 12.30S 27.55E
Ncheu Malaŵi **79** 14.50S 34.45E
N'dalatando Angola **78** 9.12S 14.54E
Ndali Benin **77** 9.53N 2.45E
Ndasegera *mtn.* Tanzania **79** 1.58S 35.41E
Ndélé C.A.R. **73** 8.24N 20.39E
Ndélélé Cameroon **77** 4.03N 14.55E
N'Dendé Gabon **78** 2.20S 11.23E
Ndikiniméki Cameroon **77** 4.46N 10.49E
N'Djamena Chad **77** 12.10N 14.59E
Ndjolé Gabon **78** 0.07S 10.45E
Ndola Zambia **80** 12.58S 28.39E
Ndoro Gabon **78** 0.24S 12.34E
Ndrhamcha, Sebkha de *f.* Mauritania **74** 18.45N 15.48W
Ndungu Tanzania **79** 4.25S 38.04E
Nea *r.* Norway **40** 63.15N 11.00E
Neagh, Lough U.K. **15** 54.36N 6.25W
Néa Kallikrátia Greece **34** 40.21N 23.01E
Neale, L. Australia **90** 24.21S130.04E
Néa Páfos Cyprus **66** 34.45N 32.25E
Neápolis Greece **34** 40.20N 21.24E
Neápolis Greece **35** 36.31N 23.03E
Neápolis *Kríti* Greece **35** 35.15N 25.37E
Neath U.K. **13** 51.39N 3.49W
Nebit-Dag U.S.S.R. **65** 39.31N 54.24E
Nebraska *d.* U.S.A. **110** 41.50N100.06W
Nebraska City U.S.A. **110** 40.41N 95.52W
Nebrodi, Monti *mts.* Italy **33** 37.55N 14.35E
Nechako *r.* Canada **100** 53.30N122.44W
Neches *r.* U.S.A. **111** 29.55N 93.50W
Neckar *r.* Germany **39** 49.31N 8.26E
Neckarsulm Germany **39** 49.12N 9.13E
Necochea Argentina **125** 38.31S 58.46W
Necuto Angola **78** 4.55S 12.38E
Nêdong China **63** 29.14N 91.48E
Nedroma Algeria **74** 35.00N 1.44W
Nedstrand Norway **42** 59.21N 5.51E
Needles U.S.A. **109** 34.51N114.37W
Neepawa Canada **101** 50.13N 99.29W
Neerpelt Belgium **16** 51.13N 5.28E
Nefta Tunisia **75** 33.52N 7.33E
Neftegorsk U.S.S.R. **45** 44.21N 39.44E
Nefyn U.K. **12** 52.55N 4.31W
Negara Indonesia **59** 8.21S114.35E
Negaunee U.S.A. **112** 46.31N 87.37W
Negba Israel **67** 31.40N 34.41E
Negele Ethiopia **73** 5.20N 39.36E
Negev *des. see* HaNegev *des.* Israel **66**
Negoiu *mtn.* Romania **37** 45.36N 24.32E
Negomano Mozambique **79** 11.26S 38.30E
Negombo Sri Lanka **61** 7.13N 79.50E
Negotin Yugo. **37** 44.14N 22.33E
Negra, Punta *c.* Peru **120** 6.06S 81.09W
Negrais, C. Burma **56** 16.00N 94.12E
Negreira Spain **26** 42.54N 8.44W
Negritos Peru **122** 4.42S 81.18W
Negro *r.* Argentina **125** 40.50S 63.00W
Negro *r.* Brazil **122** 3.00S 59.55W
Negro *r.* Uruguay **125** 33.27S 58.20W
Negro, Baia del *b.* Somali Rep. **71** 7.52N 49.50E
Negros *i.* Phil. **59** 10.00N123.00E
Negru-Vodă Romania **37** 43.50N 28.12E
Neheim-Hüsten Germany **38** 51.27N 7.57E
Neijiang China **55** 29.29N105.03E
Nei Monggol *d.* China **54** 41.50N112.30E
Neisse *r.* Germany **38** 52.04N 14.46E
Neiva Colombia **122** 2.58N 75.15W
Nejanilini L. Canada **101** 59.33N 97.48W
Nejdek Czech. **39** 50.17N 12.42E
Nejo Ethiopia **73** 9.30N 35.30E
Nek'emtē Ethiopia **73** 9.02N 36.31E
Neksö Denmark **43** 55.04N 15.09E
Nelidovo U.S.S.R. **44** 56.13N 32.46E
Neligh U.S.A. **110** 42.08N 98.02W
Nelkan U.S.S.R. **51** 57.40N136.04E
Nelligen Australia **93** 35.39S150.06E
Nellore India **61** 14.29N 80.00E
Nelson Australia **92** 38.04S141.05E
Nelson Canada **100** 49.30N117.20W
Nelson *r.* Canada **101** 57.04N 92.30W
Nelson New Zealand **86** 41.18S173.17E
Nelson U.K. **12** 53.50N 2.14W
Nelson U.S.A. **109** 35.30N113.16W
Nelson, C. Australia **92** 38.27S141.35E
Nelson, Estrecho *str.* Chile **125** 51.33S 74.40W
Nelson Bay *town* Australia **93** 32.43S152.08E
Nelson Forks Canada **100** 59.30N124.00W
Nelson-Marlborough *d.* New Zealand **86** 41.40S173.40E
Nelsonville U.S.A. **114** 39.27N 82.14W
Nelspoort R.S.A. **80** 32.07S 23.00E
Nelspruit R.S.A. **80** 25.27S 30.58E
Néma Mauritania **74** 16.40N 7.15W
Neman *r.* U.S.S.R. **41** 55.18N 21.23E
Nembe Nigeria **77** 4.32N 6.25E
Neméa Greece **35** 37.49N 22.40E
Nemours France **19** 48.16N 2.42E
Nemuro Japan **57** 43.22N145.36E
Nemuro kaikyō *str.* Japan **57** 44.00N145.50E
Nenagh Rep. of Ire. **15** 52.52N 8.13W
Nenana U.S.A. **98** 64.35N149.20W
Nene *r.* U.K. **12** 52.49N 0.12E
Nenjiang China **53** 49.10N125.15E
Neodesha U.S.A. **111** 37.25N 95.41W
Néon Karlovásion Greece **35** 37.47N 26.40E
Néon Petrítsi Greece **34** 41.16N 23.15E
Neosho U.S.A. **111** 36.52N 94.22W
Neosho *r.* U.S.A. **110** 35.48N 95.18W
Nepal Asia **63** 28.00N 84.00E
Nepālganj Nepal **63** 28.03N 81.38E
Nepa Nagar India **62** 21.28N 76.23E
Nephi U.S.A. **108** 39.43N111.50W
Nephin Beg *mtn.* Rep. of Ire. **15** 54.02N 9.38W
Nephin Beg Range *mts.* Rep. of Ire. **15** 54.00N 9.37W
Nepomuk Czech. **38** 49.29N 13.36E
Nera Italy **30** 42.26N 12.24E
Nera *r.* Italy **28** 42.33N 12.43E
Nérac France **20** 44.08N 0.20E
Nerekhta U.S.S.R. **44** 57.30N 40.40E
Néret, Lac *l.* Canada **103** 54.45N 70.50W
Neretva *r.* Yugo. **31** 43.01N 17.27E
Neriquinha Angola **80** 15.50S 21.40E
Nerja Spain **27** 36.44N 3.52W
Nero Deep Pacific Oc. **59** 12.40N145.50E
Néronde France **17** 45.50N 4.14E
Nérondes France **19** 47.00N 2.49E
Nerva Spain **27** 37.42N 6.32W
Nes Neth. **16** 53.27N 5.46E
Nesbyen Norway **41** 60.34N 9.09E
Nesher Israel **67** 32.46N 35.03E
Nesle France **19** 49.46N 2.55E
Nesna Norway **40** 66.13N 13.04E
Nesöy *i.* Norway **40** 66.35N 12.40E
Ness, Loch U.K. **14** 57.16N 4.30W
Nesselwang Germany **38** 47.37N 10.30E
Nestaocano *r.* Canada **103** 48.40N 73.25W
Nesterov U.S.S.R. **37** 50.04N 24.00E
Nestórion Greece **34** 40.24N 21.02E
Néstos *r.* Greece **34** 40.41N 24.44E
Nesttun Norway **42** 60.19N 5.23E
Nesvizh U.S.S.R. **37** 53.16N 26.40E
Nes Ziyyona Israel **67** 31.55N 34.48E
Netanya Israel **67** 32.20N 34.51E
Netcong U.S.A. **115** 40.54N 74.42W
Netherlands Europe **16** 52.00N 5.30E
Netherlands Antilles S. America **117** 12.30N 69.00W
Neto *r.* Italy **33** 39.13N 17.08E
Netolice Czech. **39** 49.03N 14.12E
Netrakona Bangla. **63** 24.53N 90.43E
Nettilling L. Canada **99** 66.30N 70.40W
Nettuno Italy **32** 41.27N 12.39E
Neubrandenburg Germany **38** 53.33N 13.15E
Neuburg an der Donau Germany **39** 48.44N 11.11E
Neuchâtel Switz. **39** 46.59N 6.56E
Neuchâtel *d.* Switz. **39** 47.02N 6.50E
Neuchâtel, Lac de *l.* Switz. **39** 46.52N 6.50E
Neuenhagen Germany **38** 52.32N 13.41E
Neuenhaus Germany **38** 52.30N 6.59E
Neuf-Brisach France **19** 48.01N 7.32E
Neufchâteau Belgium **16** 49.51N 5.26E
Neufchâteau France **19** 48.21N 5.42E
Neufchâtel France **18** 49.44N 1.27E
Neuhausen Switz. **39** 47.41N 8.37E
Neuillé-Pont-Pierre France **18** 47.33N 0.33E
Neu-Isenberg Germany **39** 50.03N 8.41E
Neumarkt Austria **39** 48.16N 13.45E
Neumarkt Germany **38** 49.16N 11.28E
Neumarkt in Steiermark Austria **31** 47.05N 14.26E
Neumarkt-Sankt-Veit Germany **39** 48.22N 12.30E
Neumünster Germany **38** 54.04N 9.59E
Neunkirchen Germany **39** 49.30N 7.29E
Neuquén Argentina **125** 39.00S 68.05W
Neuquén *d.* Argentina **125** 38.30S 70.00W
Neuquén *r.* Argentina **125** 39.02S 68.07W
Neuruppin Germany **38** 52.55N 12.48E
Neuse *r.* U.S.A. **113** 35.06N 76.30W
Neusiedler See *l.* Austria **36** 47.52N 16.45E
Neuss Germany **38** 51.12N 6.41E
Neustadt *Thüingen* Germany **38** 50.44N 11.44E
Neustadt Bayern Germany **39** 49.34N 10.37E
Neustadt Bayern Germany **39** 49.44N 12.11E
Neustadt B.-Würt. Germany **39** 47.54N 8.13E
Neustadt Sch.-Hol. Germany **38** 54.06N 10.48E
Neustadt an der Weinstrasse Germany **39** 49.21N 8.08E
Neustadt bei Coburg Germany **38** 50.19N 11.07E
Neustrelitz Germany **38** 53.21N 13.04E
Neu-Ulm Germany **39** 48.23N 10.01E
Neuvic France **20** 45.23N 2.16E
Neuville-de-Poitou France **18** 46.41N 0.15E
Neuville-sur-Saône France **21** 45.52N 4.51E
Neuwied Germany **39** 50.25N 7.27E
Nevada U.S.A. **111** 37.51N 94.22W
Nevada *d.* U.S.A. **108** 39.50N116.10W
Nevada, Sierra *mts.* Spain **27** 37.05N 3.10W
Nevada, Sierra *mts.* U.S.A. **106** 37.30N119.00W
Nevanka U.S.S.R. **51** 56.31N 98.57E
Nevatim Israel **67** 31.13N 34.54E
Nevel U.S.S.R. **44** 56.00N 29.59E
Nevers France **19** 47.00N 3.09E
Nevertire Australia **93** 31.52S147.47E
Nevesinje Yugo. **31** 43.15N 18.07E
Nevinnomyssk U.S.S.R. **45** 44.38N 41.59E
Nevlunghamn Norway **42** 58.58N 9.52E
Nevşehir Turkey **64** 38.38N 34.43E
Newala Tanzania **79** 10.56S 39.15E
New Albany Ind. U.S.A. **112** 38.17N 85.50W
New Albany Miss. U.S.A. **111** 34.29N 89.00W
New Amsterdam Guyana **123** 6.18N 57.30W
New Angledool Australia **93** 29.06S147.57E
Newark Del. U.S.A. **115** 39.41N 75.45W
Newark N.J. U.S.A. **115** 40.44N 74.10W
Newark N.Y. U.S.A. **114** 43.03N 77.06W
Newark Ohio U.S.A. **114** 40.04N 82.24W
Newark-on-Trent U.K. **12** 53.06N 0.48E
Newark Valley *town* U.S.A. **115** 42.14N 76.11W
New Athens U.S.A. **110** 38.19N 89.53W
New Bedford U.S.A. **115** 41.38N 70.56W
Newberg U.S.A. **108** 45.18N122.58W
New Berlin U.S.A. **115** 42.38N 75.20W
New Bern U.S.A. **113** 35.05N 77.04W
Newberry Mich. U.S.A. **112** 46.22N 85.30W
Newberry S.C. U.S.A. **113** 34.17N 81.39W
New Bethlehem U.S.A. **114** 41.00N 79.20W
Newbiggin-by-the-Sea U.K. **12** 55.11N 1.30W
New Bloomfield U.S.A. **114** 40.25N 77.11W
Newboro Canada **105** 44.39N 76.19W
Newboro L. Canada **105** 44.38N 76.20W
New Boston U.S.A. **105** 43.47N 75.45W
New Braunfels U.S.A. **111** 29.42N 98.08W
New Britain *i.* P.N.G. **87** 6.00S150.00E
New Britain U.S.A. **115** 41.40N 72.47W
New Brunswick *d.* Canada **103** 46.50N 66.00W
New Brunswick U.S.A. **115** 40.29N 74.27W
Newburgh U.S.A. **115** 41.30N 74.01W
Newbury U.K. **13** 51.24N 1.19W
Newburyport U.S.A. **115** 42.49N 70.53W
New Bussa Nigeria **77** 9.53N 4.29E
New Caledonia *is. see* Nouvelle Calédonie *is.* Pacific Oc. **84**
Newcastle Australia **93** 32.55S151.46E
Newcastle N.B. Canada **103** 47.00N 65.34W
Newcastle Ont. Canada **104** 43.55N 78.35W
Newcastle R.S.A. **80** 27.44S 29.55E
Newcastle U.K. **15** 54.13N 5.53W
New Castle Penn. U.S.A. **114** 41.00N 80.20W
Newcastle Wyo. U.S.A. **108** 43.50N104.11W
Newcastle B. Australia **90** 10.50S142.37E
Newcastle Emlyn U.K. **13** 52.02N 4.29W
Newcastle-under-Lyme U.K. **12** 53.02N 2.15W
Newcastle upon Tyne U.K. **12** 54.58N 1.36W
Newcastle Waters *town* Australia **90** 17.24S133.24E
Newcastle West Rep. of Ire. **15** 52.26N 9.04W
New City U.S.A. **115** 41.09N 73.59W
Newcomerstown U.S.A. **114** 40.16N 81.36W
New Concord U.S.A. **114** 40.00N 81.44W
New Cumberland U.S.A. **114** 40.30N 80.36W
Newdegate Australia **89** 33.06S119.01E
New Delhi India **62** 28.36N 77.12E
New Denver Canada **100** 50.00N117.25W
New England U.S.A. **110** 46.32N102.52W
New England Range *mts.* Australia **93** 30.30S151.50E
Newenham, C. U.S.A. **98** 58.37N162.12W
Newent U.K. **13** 51.56N 2.24W
Newfane U.S.A. **114** 43.17N 78.43W
New Forest *f.* U.K. **13** 50.50N 1.35W
Newfoundland *d.* Canada **103** 54.00N 60.10W
Newfoundland *i.* Canada **103** 48.30N 56.00W
New Freedom U.S.A. **115** 39.44N 76.42W
New Galloway U.K. **14** 55.05N 4.09W
Newgate Canada **100** 49.01N115.08W
New Glasgow Canada **103** 45.35N 62.39W
New Guinea *i.* Austa. **59** 5.00S140.00E
New Hamburg Canada **104** 43.23N 80.42W
New Hampshire *d.* U.S.A. **112** 43.35N 71.40W
New Hanover *i.* Pacific Oc. **87** 2.00S150.00E
Newhaven U.K. **13** 50.47N 0.04E
New Haven U.S.A. **115** 41.18N 72.56W
New Hebrides Basin Pacific Oc. **84** 16.00S162.00E
New Holland U.S.A. **115** 40.06N 76.05W
New Iberia U.S.A. **111** 30.00N 91.49W
New Ireland *i.* P.N.G. **87** 2.30S151.30E
New Jersey *d.* U.S.A. **115** 40.15N 74.30W
New Kensington U.S.A. **114** 40.34N 79.46W
New Lexington U.S.A. **114** 39.43N 82.31W
New Liskeard Canada **102** 47.31N 79.41W
New London Conn. U.S.A. **115** 41.21N 72.07W
New London Minn. U.S.A. **110** 45.18N 94.56W
New London Ohio U.S.A. **114** 41.05N 82.24W
Newman Australia **88** 23.22S119.43E
Newman U.S.A. **109** 31.55N106.20W
Newman, Mt. Australia **88** 23.15S119.33E
Newmarket Canada **104** 44.03N 79.28W
Newmarket Rep. of Ire. **15** 52.13N 9.00W
Newmarket U.K. **13** 52.15N 0.23E
Newmarket U.S.A. **115** 43.05N 70.56W
Newmarket on Fergus Rep. of Ire. **15** 52.46N 8.55W
New Marshfield U.S.A. **114** 39.20N 82.15W
New Martinsville U.S.A. **114** 39.39N 80.52W
New Matamoras U.S.A. **114** 39.31N 81.06W
New Meadows U.S.A. **108** 44.58N116.32W
New Mexico *d.* U.S.A. **108** 33.30N106.00W
New Milford Conn. U.S.A. **115** 41.35N 73.25W
New Milford Penn. U.S.A. **115** 41.52N 75.44W
Newnan U.S.A. **113** 33.23N 84.48W
New Norcia Australia **89** 30.58S116.15E
New Norfolk Australia **91** 42.46S147.02E
New Orleans U.S.A. **111** 29.58N 90.07W
New Oxford U.S.A. **114** 39.52N 77.04W
New Philadelphia U.S.A. **114** 40.30N 81.27W
New Plymouth New Zealand **86** 39.03S174.04E
Newport Mayo Rep. of Ire. **15** 53.53N 9.34W
Newport Tipperary Rep. of Ire. **15** 52.42N 8.25W
Newport Dyfed U.K. **13** 52.01N 4.51W
Newport Essex U.K. **13** 51.58N 0.13E
Newport Gwent U.K. **13** 51.34N 2.59W
Newport Hants. U.K. **13** 50.43N 1.18W
Newport Ark. U.S.A. **111** 35.35N 91.16W
Newport Maine U.S.A. **112** 44.50N 69.17W
Newport N.H. U.S.A. **115** 43.21N 72.09W
Newport N.Y. U.S.A. **115** 43.11N 75.01W
Newport Oreg. U.S.A. **108** 44.38N124.03W
Newport Penn. U.S.A. **114** 40.29N 77.08W
Newport R.I. U.S.A. **115** 41.13N 71.18W
Newport Vt. U.S.A. **105** 44.57N 72.12W
Newport News U.S.A. **113** 36.59N 76.26W
New Providence I. Bahamas **113** 25.25N 78.35W
Newquay U.K. **13** 50.24N 5.06W
New Quay U.K. **13** 52.13N 4.22W
New Radnor U.K. **13** 52.15N 3.10W
New Rochelle U.S.A. **115** 40.55N 73.47W
New Rockford U.S.A. **110** 47.41N 99.15W
New Romney U.K. **13** 50.59N 0.58E
New Ross Rep. of Ire. **15** 52.24N 6.57W
Newry U.K. **15** 54.11N 6.21W
New Scone U.K. **14** 56.25N 3.25W
New Smyrna Beach *town* U.S.A. **113** 29.01N 80.56W
New South Wales *d.* Australia **93** 32.40S147.40E
Newton Ill. U.S.A. **110** 38.59N 88.10W
Newton Iowa U.S.A. **110** 41.42N 93.03W
Newton Kans. U.S.A. **111** 38.03N 97.21W
Newton Mass. U.S.A. **115** 42.21N 71.11W
Newton Miss. U.S.A. **111** 32.19N 89.10W
Newton N.J. U.S.A. **115** 41.03N 74.45W
Newton Abbot U.K. **13** 50.32N 3.37W
Newton Aycliffe U.K. **12** 54.36N 1.34W
Newton Falls *town* N.Y. U.S.A. **105** 44.13N 74.59W
Newton Falls *town* Ohio U.S.A. **114** 41.11N 80.59W
Newtonmore U.K. **14** 57.04N 4.08W
Newton Stewart U.K. **14** 54.57N 4.29W
Newtown U.K. **13** 52.31N 3.19W
Newtownabbey U.K. **15** 54.39N 5.57W
Newtownards U.K. **15** 54.35N 5.41W
Newtown Butler U.K. **15** 54.12N 7.22W
Newtown St. Boswells U.K. **14** 55.35N 2.40W
Newtownstewart U.K. **15** 54.43N 7.25W
New Washington U.S.A. **114** 40.58N 82.51W
New Waterford Canada **103** 46.15N 60.05W
New Westminster Canada **100** 49.10N122.52W
New York U.S.A. **115** 40.43N 74.01W
New York *d.* U.S.A. **115** 40.43N 74.01W
New York State Barge Canal U.S.A. **114** 43.05N 78.43W
New Zealand Austa. **86** 41.00S175.00E
New Zealand Plateau Pacific Oc. **84** 50.00S170.00E
Nexon France **20** 45.41N 1.11E
Neya U.S.S.R. **44** 58.18N 43.40E
Neyagawa Japan **57** 34.46N135.38E
Neyrīz Iran **65** 29.12N 54.17E
Neyshābūr Iran **65** 36.13N 58.49E
Nezhin U.S.S.R. **37** 51.03N 31.54E
Ngala Nigeria **77** 12.21N 14.10E
Ngambwe Rapids *f.* Zambia **78** 17.08S 24.10E
Ngami, L. Botswana **80** 20.32S 22.38E
Ngamiland *d.* Botswana **80** 19.40S 22.00E
Ngamiland *f.* Botswana **80** 20.00S 22.30E
Ngamring China **63** 29.14N 87.10E
Ngangla Ringco *l.* China **63** 31.40N 83.00E
Nganglong Kangri *mtn.* China **63** 32.40N 81.00E
Nganglong Kangri *mts.* China **63** 32.15N 82.00E
Ngangzê Co *l.* China **63** 31.00N 87.00E
Nganjuk Indonesia **59** 7.36S111.56E
N'Gao Congo **78** 2.28S 15.40E
Ngaoundéré Cameroon **77** 7.20N 13.35E
Ngara-Binsam Congo **78** 1.36N 13.30E
Ngardiam C.A.R. **73** 9.00N 20.58E
Ngaruawahia New Zealand **86** 37.40S175.09E
Ngaruroro *r.* New Zealand **86** 39.34S176.54E
Ngatangiia Rarotonga Cook Is. **84** 21.14S159.44W
Ngau *i.* Fiji **84** 18.02S179.18E
Ngauruhoe *mtn.* New Zealand **86** 39.10S175.35E
Ngawi Indonesia **59** 7.23S111.22E
Ngaya *mtn.* C.A.R. **73** 9.18N 23.28E
Ng'iro, Mt. Kenya **79** 2.06N 36.44E
N'Giva Angola **80** 17.03S 15.47E
Ngoc Linh *mtn.* Vietnam **56** 15.04N107.59E
Ngoma Zambia **78** 16.04S 26.06E
Ngomba Tanzania **79** 8.16S 32.51E
Ngomeni Kenya **79** 3.00S 40.11E
Ngong Kenya **79** 1.22S 36.40E
Ngonye Falls *f.* Zambia **78** 16.35S 23.39E
Ngorongoro Crater *f.* Tanzania **79** 3.13S 35.32E
Ngouo, Mont *mtn.* C.A.R. **73** 7.55N 24.38E
Ngozi Burundi **79** 2.52S 29.50E
Nguigmi Niger **77** 14.00N 13.11E
Nguru Nigeria **77** 12.53N 10.30E
Nguruka Tanzania **79** 5.08S 30.58E
Ngwaketse *d.* Botswana **80** 25.10S 25.00E
Ngwerere Zambia **79** 15.18S 28.20E
Nhaccongo Mozambique **81** 24.18S 35.14E
Nhachengue Mozambique **81** 22.52S 35.10E
Nhandugue *r.* Mozambique **81** 18.47S 34.30E
Nha Trang Vietnam **56** 12.15N109.10E
Nhill Australia **92** 36.20S141.40E
Nhulunbuy Australia **90** 12.11S136.46E
Nhungo Angola **80** 13.17S 20.06E
Niafounké Mali **74** 15.56N 4.00W
Niagara Canada **104** 43.05N 79.20W
Niagara Escarpment *f.* Canada **104** 44.25N 80.30W
Niagara Falls *town* Canada **104** 43.06N 79.04W
Niagara Falls *town* U.S.A. **114** 43.06N 79.02W
Niah Malaysia **58** 3.52N113.44E
Niamey Niger **77** 13.32N 2.05E
Niamey *d.* Niger **77** 14.00N 1.40E
Nianforando Guinea **76** 9.37N 10.36W
Niangara Zaïre **79** 3.47N 27.54E
Nia-Nia Zaïre **79** 1.30N 27.41E
Niapa, Gunung *mtn.* Indonesia **58** 1.45N117.30E
Nias *i.* Indonesia **58** 1.05N 97.30E
Niassa *d.* Mozambique **79** 13.00S 36.30E
Nibe Denmark **42** 56.59N 9.38E
Nicaragua C. America **117** 13.00N 85.00W
Nicaragua, Lago de *l.* Nicaragua **117** 11.30N 85.30W
Nicastro Italy **33** 38.59N 16.20E
Nice France **21** 43.42N 7.16E
Nichelino Italy **30** 44.59N 7.38E
Nicholson Australia **88** 18.02S128.54E
Nicholson *r.* Australia **90** 17.31S139.36E
Nicholson U.S.A. **115** 41.38N 75.47W

Nicholson L. to **Notre Dame B.**

Nicholson L. Canada 101 62.40N 102.35W
Nicobar Is. India 56 8.00N 93.30E
Nicolet Canada 105 46.13N 72.37W
Nicolet *r.* Canada 105 46.14N 72.39W
Nicolls Town Bahamas 117 25.08N 78.00W
Nicosia *see* Levkosía Cyprus 66
Nicosia Italy 33 37.45N 14.24E
Nicotera Italy 33 38.34N 15.57E
Nicoya, Golfo de *g.* Costa Rica 117 9.30N 85.00W
Nicoya, Península de *pen.* Costa Rica 117 10.30N 85.30W
Nid *r.* Norway 42 58.24N 8.48E
Nida *r.* Poland 37 50.18N 20.52E
Nido, Sierra de *mts.* Mexico 109 29.30N 107.00W
Nidzica Poland 37 53.22N 20.26E
Niebüll Germany 38 54.48N 8.50E
Niederbronn-les-Bains France 19 48.57N 7.38E
Niederösterreich *d.* Austria 36 48.20N 15.50E
Niedersachsen *d.* Germany 38 52.53N 9.30E
Niekerkshoop R.S.A. 80 29.19S 22.48E
Niéllé Ivory Coast 76 10.05N 5.28W
Nienburg Germany 38 52.38N 9.13E
Niéré Chad 72 14.30N 21.09E
Niers *r.* Neth. 16 51.43N 5.56E
Niesky Germany 38 51.17N 14.49E
Nieuw Nickerie Surinam 123 5.57N 56.59W
Nieuwpoort Belgium 16 51.08N 2.45E
Nièvre *d.* France 19 47.05N 3.30E
Nifi Ya'qūb Jordan 67 31.50N 35.14E
Niğde Turkey 64 37.58N 34.42E
Niger Africa 70 17.00N 10.00E
Niger *d.* Nigeria 77 9.50N 6.00E
Niger *r.* Nigeria 77 4.15N 6.05E
Niger Delta Nigeria 77 4.00N 6.10E
Nigeria Africa 77 9.00N 9.00E
Nightcaps New Zealand 86 45.58S 168.02E
Nightingale I. Tristan da Cunha 127 37.28S 12.32W
Nigrita Greece 34 40.55N 23.30E
Nihing *r.* Pakistan 62 26.00N 62.44E
Nihoa *i.* Hawaiian Is. 84 23.03N 161.55W
Niigata Japan 57 37.58N 139.02E
Niihama Japan 57 33.57N 133.15E
Niihau *i.* Hawaiian Is. 85 21.55N 160.10W
Niiza Japan 57 35.48N 139.34E
Níjar Spain 27 36.58N 2.11W
Nijmegen Neth. 16 51.50N 5.52E
Nikel U.S.S.R. 40 69.20N 30.00E
Nikiniki Indonesia 88 9.49S 124.29E
Nikki Benin 77 9.55N 3.18E
Nikolayev U.S.S.R. 45 46.57N 32.00E
Nikolayevskiy U.S.S.R. 45 50.05N 45.32E
Nikolayevsk-na-Amure U.S.S.R. 51 53.20N 140.44E
Nikolsk U.S.S.R. 44 59.33N 45.30E
Nikopol Bulgaria 34 43.43N 24.54E
Nikopol U.S.S.R. 45 47.34N 34.25E
Niksar Turkey 64 40.35N 36.59E
Nikshahr Iran 65 26.14N 60.15E
Nikšić Yugo. 31 42.46N 18.56E
Nikumaroro *i.* Kiribati 84 4.40S 174.32W
Nil, An *r.* Egypt 66 31.30N 30.25E
Nila *i.* Indonesia 59 6.45S 129.30E
Nile *r. see* Nil, An *r.* Egypt 66
Nile Delta Egypt 66 31.00N 31.00E
Niles Mich. U.S.A. 112 41.51N 86.15W
Niles Ohio U.S.A. 114 41.11N 80.45W
Nilgaut, Lac *l.* Canada 105 46.36N 77.15W
Nilgiri India 63 21.28N 86.46E
Nilgiri Hills India 60 11.30N 77.30E
Nimach India 62 24.28N 74.52E
Nimai *r.* Burma 56 25.44N 97.30E
Nimba, Mt. Guinea 76 7.35N 8.28W
Nimbin Australia 93 28.35S 153.12E
Nîmes France 21 43.50N 4.21E
Nimfaíon, Ákra *c.* Greece 34 40.05N 24.20E
Nim Ka Thāna India 62 27.44N 75.48E
Nimrūz *d.* Afghan. 62 30.40N 62.15E
Nimule Sudan 73 3.36N 32.03E
Nindigully Australia 93 28.20S 148.47E
Ninety-East Ridge *f.* Indian Oc. 49 21.00S 89.00E
Ninety Mile Beach *f.* Australia 93 38.07S 147.30E
Ninety Mile Beach *f.* New Zealand 86 34.45S 173.00E
Nineveh *ruins* Iraq 64 36.24N 43.08E
Ningan China 57 44.22N 129.25E
Ningbo China 55 29.56N 121.32E
Ningde China 55 26.41N 119.32E
Ningdu China 55 26.29N 115.46E
Ninggang China 55 26.45N 113.58E
Ningguo China 55 30.38N 118.58E
Ningming China 55 22.04N 107.02E
Ningnan China 52 27.03N 102.46E
Ningqiang China 54 32.49N 106.13E
Ningwu China 54 38.59N 112.12E
Ningxia Huizu *d.* China 54 37.00N 105.00E
Ning Xian China 54 35.27N 107.50E
Ningxiang China 55 28.15N 112.33E
Ninh Binh Vietnam 56 20.14N 106.00E
Ninove Belgium 16 50.50N 4.02E
Niobrara U.S.A. 110 42.45N 98.02W
Niobrara *r.* U.S.A. 110 42.45N 98.00W
Nioki Zaïre 78 2.43S 17.41E
Nioro Mali 74 15.12N 9.35W
Nioro du Rip Senegal 76 13.40N 15.50W
Niort France 18 46.19N 0.27W
Niout *well* Mauritania 74 16.03N 6.52W
Nipāni India 60 16.24N 74.23E
Nipigon Canada 102 49.00N 88.17W
Nipigon, L. Canada 102 49.50N 88.30W
Nipigon B. Canada 102 48.55N 88.00W
Nipissing Canada 104 46.06N 79.30W
Nipissing *r.* Canada 104 46.00N 78.30W
Nipissing, L. Canada 104 46.17N 80.00W
Niquelândia Brazil 126 14.27S 48.27W
Nirasaki Japan 57 35.42N 138.27E
Nirim Israel 67 31.20N 34.24E
Nirmal India 63 19.06N 78.21E
Nirmali India 63 26.19N 86.35E
Nirwāno Pakistan 62 26.22N 62.43E
Nir Yisra'el Israel 67 31.41N 34.38E
Niš Yugo. 34 43.19N 21.58E
Nisa Portugal 27 39.31N 7.39W
Nisava *r.* Yugo. 34 43.20N 22.10E
Niscemi Italy 33 37.08N 14.24E
Nishi China 55 29.54N 110.38E
Nishinomiya Japan 57 34.43N 135.20E
Nísiros *i.* Greece 35 36.35N 27.10E
Niška Banja Yugo. 34 43.17N 22.02E
Niskibi *r.* Canada 102 56.28N 88.10W
Nisko Poland 37 50.35N 22.07E
Nissan *r.* Sweden 43 56.40N 12.51E
Nissedal Norway 42 59.15N 8.30E
Nisser *l.* Norway 42 59.10N 8.30E
Nissum Bredning *b.* Denmark 42 56.38N 8.22E
Nissum Fjord *est.* Denmark 42 56.21N 8.14E
Niṭā' Saudi Arabia 65 27.13N 48.25E
Nitchequon Canada 103 53.12N 70.47W
Niterói Brazil 126 22.54S 43.06W
Nith *r.* Canada 104 43.12N 80.22W
Nith *r.* U.K. 14 55.00N 3.35W
Nitra Czech. 37 48.20N 18.05E
Nitro Canada 104 46.51N 81.42W
Nitro U.S.A. 114 38.25N 81.50W
Nittedal Norway 42 60.04N 10.53E
Niue *i.* Cook Is. 84 19.02S 169.52W
Niut, Gunung *mtn.* Indonesia 58 1.00N 110.00E
Nivala Finland 40 63.55N 24.58E
Nivelles Belgium 16 50.36N 4.20E
Nixon U.S.A. 111 29.16N 97.46W
Nizāmābād India 61 18.40N 78.05E
Nizgān *r.* Afghan. 62 33.05N 63.20E
Nizhneangarsk U.S.S.R. 51 55.48N 109.35E
Nizhnekamskoye Vodokhranilishche U.S.S.R. 44 55.45N 53.50E
Nizhne Kolymsk U.S.S.R. 51 68.34N 160.58E
Nizhneudinsk U.S.S.R. 51 54.55N 99.00E
Nizhnevartovsk U.S.S.R. 50 60.57N 76.40E
Nizhniy Tagil U.S.S.R. 44 58.00N 60.00E
Nizhnyaya Tunguska *r.* U.S.S.R. 51 65.50N 88.00E
Nizhnyaya Tura U.S.S.R. 44 58.40N 59.48E
Nizke Tatry *mts.* Czech. 37 48.54N 19.40E
Nizza Monferrato Italy 30 44.46N 8.21E
Nizzanim Israel 67 31.43N 34.38E
Njazídja *i.* Comoros 79 11.35S 43.20E
Njombe Tanzania 79 9.20S 34.47E
Njombe *r.* Tanzania 79 7.02S 35.55E
Njoro Tanzania 79 5.16S 36.30E
Nkalagu Nigeria 77 6.28N 7.46E
Nkawkaw Ghana 76 6.35N 0.47W
Nkayi Zimbabwe 80 19.00S 28.54E
Nkhata Bay *town* Malaŵi 79 11.37S 34.20E
Nkhotakota Malaŵi 79 12.55S 34.19E
Nkongsamba Cameroon 77 4.59N 9.53E
Nkungwe Mt. Tanzania 79 6.15S 29.54E
Noākhāli Bangla. 63 22.51N 91.06E
Noatak U.S.A. 98 67.34N 162.59W
Nobel Canada 104 45.25N 80.06W
Nobeoka Japan 57 32.36N 131.40E
Noboribetsu Japan 57 42.27N 141.11E
Noce *r.* Italy 30 46.09N 11.04E
Nocera Italy 33 40.44N 14.39E
Noci Italy 33 40.48N 17.08E
Noelville Canada 104 46.09N 80.26W
Nogales Mexico 109 31.20N 110.56W
Nogara Italy 32 45.11N 11.04E
Nogaro France 20 43.46N 0.02W
Nogayskiye Step *f.* U.S.S.R. 45 44.25N 45.30E
Nogent-le-Rotrou France 18 48.19N 0.50E
Nogent-sur-Seine France 19 48.29N 3.30E
Nogoyá Argentina 125 32.22S 59.49W
Noguera Pallarese *r.* Spain 25 42.15N 0.54E
Noguera Ribagorçana *r.* Spain 25 41.40N 0.43E
Nohar India 62 29.11N 74.46E
Nohta India 63 23.40N 79.34E
Noire *r.* Que. Canada 105 45.33N 72.58W
Noire *r.* Que. Canada 105 45.55N 76.56W
Noire, Montagne *mtn.* France 18 48.11N 3.40W
Noire, Montagne *mts.* France 20 43.26N 2.12E
Noirétable France 20 45.49N 3.46E
Noirmoutier France 18 47.00N 2.14W
Noirmoutier, Île de *i.* France 18 47.00N 2.15W
Nojima-zaki *c.* Japan 57 34.56N 139.53E
Nokha India 62 27.35N 73.29E
Nokia Finland 41 61.28N 23.30E
Nok Kundi Pakistan 62 28.46N 62.46E
Nokomis Canada 101 51.30N 105.00W
Nokou Chad 77 14.35N 14.47E
Nola C.A.R. 77 3.28N 16.08E
Nola Italy 33 40.55N 14.33E
Nolinsk U.S.S.R. 44 57.38N 49.52E
Noman L. Canada 101 62.15N 108.55W
Noma Omuramba *r.* Botswana 80 19.14S 22.15E
Nombre de Dios Mexico 109 28.41N 106.05W
Nome U.S.A. 98 64.30N 165.30W
Nomgon Mongolia 54 42.50N 105.13E
Nominingue Canada 105 46.24N 75.02W
Nomuka Group *is.* Tonga 85 20.15S 174.46W
Nonancourt France 18 48.46N 1.12E
Nonburg U.S.S.R. 44 65.32N 50.37E
Nong Khai Thailand 56 17.50N 102.46E
Nongoma R.S.A. 81 27.58S 31.35E
Nongpoh India 63 25.54N 91.53E
Nongstoin India 63 25.31N 91.16E
Nonning Australia 92 32.30S 136.30E
Nono Ethiopia 73 8.31N 37.30E
Nonthaburi Thailand 56 13.48N 100.11E
Nontron France 20 45.32N 0.40E
Noojee Australia 93 37.57S 146.00E
Noonamah Australia 88 12.35S 131.03E
Noonan U.S.A. 110 48.54N 103.01W
Noongaar Australia 89 31.21S 118.55E
Noonkanbah Australia 88 18.30S 124.50E
Noonthorangee Range *mts.* Australia 92 31.00S 142.20E
Noorama Creek *r.* Australia 93 28.05S 145.55E
Noord Beveland *f.* Neth. 16 51.35N 3.45E
Noord Brabant *d.* Neth. 16 51.37N 5.00E
Noord Holland *d.* Neth. 16 52.37N 4.50E
Noordoost-Polder *f.* Neth. 16 52.45N 5.45E
Noordwijk Neth. 16 52.16N 4.29E
Noorvik U.S.A. 98 66.50N 161.14W
Noosa Heads *town* Australia 90 26.23S 153.07E
Nootka I. Canada 100 49.32N 126.42W
Noqui Angola 78 5.51S 13.25E
Nora Sweden 43 59.31N 15.02E
Noranda Canada 102 48.20N 79.00W
Norberg Sweden 43 60.04N 15.56E
Norcia Italy 30 42.48N 13.05E
Nord *d.* Burkina 76 13.50N 2.20W
Nord *d.* France 19 50.20N 3.40E
Nordaustlandet *i.* Arctic Oc. 128 79.55N 23.00E
Nordborg Denmark 42 55.03N 9.45E
Norddeich Germany 38 53.37N 7.10E
Nordegg Canada 100 52.29N 116.05W
Norden Germany 38 53.36N 7.12E
Nordenham Germany 38 53.29N 8.28E
Norderney Germany 38 53.42N 7.08E
Norderney *i.* Germany 38 53.42N 7.10E
Norderstedt Germany 38 53.43N 9.59E
Nordfjord *est.* Norway 41 61.54N 5.12E
Nordfjordeid Norway 41 61.54N 6.00E
Nordfold Norway 40 67.48N 15.20E
Nordfriesische Inseln *is.* Germany 38 54.35N 8.30E
Nordhausen Germany 38 51.30N 10.47E
Nordhorn Germany 38 52.27N 7.05E
Nordkapp *c.* Norway 40 71.11N 25.48E
Nordkinnhalvöya *pen.* Norway 40 70.55N 27.45E
Nordland *d.* Norway 40 66.50N 14.50E
Nördlingen Germany 39 48.51N 10.30E
Nord-Ostsee-Kanal Germany 38 54.10N 9.25E
Nordreisa Norway 40 69.46N 21.00E
Nordrhein-Westfalen *d.* Germany 38 52.04N 7.20E
Nordstrand *i.* Germany 38 54.30N 8.53E
Nord Tröndelag *d.* Norway 40 64.20N 12.00E
Nordvik U.S.S.R. 51 73.40N 110.50E
Nore Norway 42 60.10N 9.01E
Nore *r.* Rep. of Ire. 15 52.25N 6.58W
Norfolk *d.* U.K. 13 52.39N 1.00E
Norfolk Conn. U.S.A. 115 41.59N 73.12W
Norfolk Nebr. U.S.A. 110 42.02N 97.25W
Norfolk Va. U.S.A. 113 36.54N 76.18W
Norfolk Broads *f.* U.K. 12 52.43N 1.35E
Norfolk I. Pacific Oc. 84 29.02S 167.57E
Norfolk Island Ridge Pacific Oc. 84 29.00S 167.00E
Norheimsund Norway 41 60.22N 6.08E
Norilsk U.S.S.R. 51 69.21N 88.02E
Norland Canada 104 44.43N 78.49W
Normal U.S.A. 110 40.31N 89.00W
Norman *r.* Australia 90 17.28S 140.49E
Norman U.S.A. 111 35.13N 97.26W
Normanby *r.* Australia 90 14.25S 144.08E
Normanby New Zealand 86 39.32S 174.16E
Normanby I. P.N.G. 90 10.05S 151.05E
Normandie, Collines de *hills* France 18 48.55N 0.45W
Normanton Australia 90 17.40S 141.05E
Norman Wells Canada 98 65.19N 126.46W
Nornalup Australia 89 34.58S 116.49E
Norquinco Argentina 125 41.50S 70.55W
Norrahammar Sweden 43 57.42N 14.06E
Norra Kvarken *str.* Sweden / Finland 40 63.36N 20.43E
Norra Storfjället *mtn.* Sweden 40 65.52N 15.18E
Norrbotten *d.* Sweden 40 67.00N 19.50E
Nörresundby Denmark 42 57.04N 9.55E
Norris L. U.S.A. 113 36.18N 83.58W
Norristown U.S.A. 115 40.07N 75.21W
Norrköping Sweden 43 58.36N 16.11E
Norrsundet Sweden 41 60.56N 17.08E
Norrtälje Sweden 43 59.46N 18.42E
Norseman Australia 89 32.15S 121.47E
Norsjå *l.* Norway 42 59.18N 9.20E
Norsk U.S.S.R. 51 52.22N 129.57E
Norte *d.* W. Sahara 74 26.50N 11.15W
Norte, C. Brazil 123 1.40N 49.55W
Norte, Cabo *c.* I. de Pascua 85 27.03S 109.24W
Norte, Punta *c.* Argentina 125 36.17S 56.46W
Norte Interior *d.* Portugal 26 41.30N 7.00W
Norte Litoral *d.* Portugal 26 41.00N 8.25W
North, C. Canada 103 47.01N 60.28W
North Adams U.S.A. 115 42.42N 73.07W
Northallerton U.K. 12 54.20N 1.26W
Northam Australia 89 31.41S 116.40E
North America 96
Northampton Australia 89 28.21S 114.37E
Northampton U.K. 13 52.14N 0.54W
Northampton Mass. U.S.A. 115 42.19N 72.38W
Northampton Penn. U.S.A. 115 40.41N 75.30W
Northamptonshire *d.* U.K. 13 52.18N 0.55W
North Augusta Canada 105 44.44N 75.45W
North Battleford Canada 101 52.47N 108.17W
North Bay *town* Canada 104 46.19N 79.28W
North Bend Penn. U.S.A. 114 41.21N 77.42W
North Berwick U.K. 14 56.04N 2.43W
North Bourke Australia 93 30.01S 145.59E
North Bradley U.S.A. 104 43.44N 84.31W
North C. Antarctica 128 71.00S 166.00E
North C. New Zealand 86 34.28S 173.00E
North Canadian *r.* U.S.A. 111 35.17N 95.31W
North Caribou L. Canada 102 52.50N 90.50W
North Carolina *d.* U.S.A. 113 35.30N 80.00W
North Channel *str.* Canada 104 46.02N 82.50W
North Channel U.K. 15 55.15N 5.52W
North Chicago U.S.A. 110 42.20N 87.51W
North China Plain *f. see* Huabei Pingyuan *f.* China 54
Northcliffe Australia 89 34.36S 116.04E
North Creek *town* U.S.A. 115 43.42N 73.59W
North Dakota *d.* U.S.A. 110 47.00N 100.00W
North Dorset Downs *hills* U.K. 13 50.46N 2.25W
North Downs *hills* U.K. 13 51.18N 0.40E
North East *d.* Botswana 80 20.45S 27.05E
North East U.S.A. 114 42.13N 79.50W
North Eastern *d.* Kenya 79 1.00N 40.00E
North Eastern Atlantic Basin *f.* Atlantic Oc. 127 45.00N 17.00W
North East Pt. Kiribati 85 1.57N 157.16W
Northeim Germany 38 51.42N 10.00E
Northern *d.* Ghana 76 9.00N 1.30W
Northern Indian L. Canada 101 57.20N 97.20W
Northern Ireland *d.* U.K. 15 54.40N 6.45W
Northern Marianas *is.* Pacific Oc. 84 15.00N 145.00E
Northern Territory *d.* Australia 90 20.00S 133.00E
North Esk *r.* U.K. 14 56.45N 2.25W
Northfield U.S.A. 105 44.09N 72.40W
North Fiji Basin Pacific Oc. 84 17.00S 173.00E
North Foreland *c.* U.K. 13 51.23N 1.26E
North French *r.* Canada 102 51.04N 80.46W
North Frisian Is. *see* Nordfriesische Inseln *is.* Germany 36
North Gower Canada 105 45.08N 75.43W
North Head *c.* Canada 103 53.42N 56.24W
North Henik L. Canada 101 61.45N 97.40W
North Horr Kenya 79 3.19N 37.00E
North I. Kenya 73 4.04N 36.03E
North I. New Zealand 86 39.00S 175.00E
Northiam U.K. 13 50.59N 0.39E
North Knife *r.* Canada 101 58.53N 94.45W
North Korea Asia 53 40.00N 128.00E
Northland *d.* New Zealand 86 35.25S 174.00E
North Las Vegas U.S.A. 109 36.12N 115.07W
North Little Rock U.S.A. 111 34.46N 92.14W
North Loup *r.* U.S.A. 110 41.17N 98.23W
North Mankato U.S.A. 110 44.15N 94.06W
North Nahanni *r.* Canada 100 62.15N 123.20W
North Ogden U.S.A. 108 41.18N 112.00W
North Olmsted U.S.A. 114 41.25N 81.56W
Northome U.S.A. 110 47.52N 94.17W
North Platte U.S.A. 110 41.08N 100.46W
North Platte *r.* U.S.A. 110 41.15N 100.45W
Northport U.S.A. 113 33.14N 87.33W
North Powder U.S.A. 108 45.13N 117.55W
North Pt. Canada 103 47.05N 64.00W
North Pt. U.S.A. 104 45.02N 83.16W
North Rona *i.* U.K. 10 59.09N 5.43W
North Ronaldsay *i.* U.K. 14 59.23N 2.26W
North Saskatchewan *r.* Canada 101 53.15N 105.06W
North Sea Europe 36 54.00N 4.00E
North Seal *r.* Canada 101 58.50N 98.10W
North Sporades *see* Vorіai Sporádhes *is.* Greece 35
North Stratford U.S.A. 105 44.46N 71.36W
North Sydney Canada 103 46.13N 60.15W
North Syracuse U.S.A. 115 43.08N 76.08W
North Taranaki Bight *b.* New Zealand 86 38.45S 174.15E
North Tawton U.K. 13 50.48N 3.55W
North Thames *r.* Canada 104 42.59N 81.16W
North Thompson *r.* Canada 100 50.40N 120.20W
North Tonawanda U.S.A. 114 43.02N 78.53W
North Troy U.S.A. 105 45.00N 72.24W
North Twin I. Canada 102 53.20N 80.00W
North Uist *i.* U.K. 14 57.35N 7.20W
Northumberland *d.* U.K. 12 55.12N 2.00W
Northumberland U.S.A. 114 40.49N 76.39W
Northumberland, C. Australia 92 38.04S 140.40E
Northumberland Is. Australia 90 21.40S 150.00E
Northumberland Str. Canada 103 46.00N 63.30W
Northville U.S.A. 115 43.13N 74.11W
North Wabasca L. Canada 100 56.00N 113.55W
North Walsham U.K. 12 52.49N 1.22E
Northway U.S.A. 98 62.58N 142.00W
North West C. Australia 88 21.48S 114.10E
North West Chile Ridge Pacific Oc. 85 42.00S 90.00W
North Western *d.* Zambia 80 13.00S 25.00E
North Western Atlantic Basin *f.* Atlantic Oc. 127 33.00N 55.00W
Northwest Frontier *d.* Pakistan 62 33.45N 71.00E
North West Highlands U.K. 14 57.30N 5.15W
Northwest Providence Channel Bahamas 113 26.10N 78.20W
North West Pt. Kiribati 85 2.02N 157.29W
North West River *town* Canada 103 53.32N 60.09W
Northwest Territories *d.* Canada 99 66.00N 95.00W
Northwich U.K. 12 53.16N 2.30W
Northwood Iowa U.S.A. 110 43.27N 93.13W
Northwood N.Dak. U.S.A. 110 47.44N 97.34W
North Woodstock U.S.A. 105 44.02N 71.41W
North York Moors *hills* U.K. 12 54.21N 0.50W
North Yorkshire *d.* U.K. 12 54.14N 1.14W
Norton Kans. U.S.A. 110 39.50N 99.53W
Norton W.Va. U.S.A. 114 38.58N 79.55W
Norton Sound *b.* U.S.A. 98 63.50N 164.00W
Nortorf Germany 38 54.10N 9.50E
Nort-sur-Erdre France 18 47.26N 1.30W
Norwalk Conn. U.S.A. 115 41.07N 73.27W
Norwalk Ohio U.S.A. 114 41.15N 82.37W
Norway Europe 40 65.00N 13.00E
Norway House *town* Canada 101 53.59N 97.50W
Norwegian Dependency Antarctica 128 77.00S 10.00E
Norwegian Sea Europe 128 65.00N 5.00E
Norwich Canada 104 42.59N 80.36W
Norwich U.K. 13 52.38N 1.17E
Norwich Conn. U.S.A. 115 41.32N 72.05W
Norwich N.Y. U.S.A. 115 42.32N 75.31W
Norwood Canada 105 44.23N 77.59W
Norwood Mass. U.S.A. 115 42.11N 71.12W
Norwood N.Y. U.S.A. 105 44.45N 75.00W
Norwood Ohio U.S.A. 112 39.12N 84.21W
Nosbonsing, L. Canada 104 46.12N 79.13W
Noshiro Japan 57 40.12N 140.02E
Noshul U.S.S.R. 44 60.04N 49.30E
Nosovka U.S.S.R. 37 50.55N 31.37E
Noṣratābād Iran 65 29.54N 59.58E
Nossebro Sweden 43 58.11N 12.43E
Noss Head U.K. 14 58.28N 3.03W
Nosy Be *i.* Madagascar 81 13.20S 48.15E
Nosy Boraha *i.* Madagascar 81 16.50S 49.55E
Nosy Varika Madagascar 81 20.35S 48.32E
Noteć *r.* Poland 36 52.44N 15.26E
Notera Israel 67 33.06N 35.38E
Noto Italy 33 36.53N 15.05E
Noto, Golfo di *g.* Italy 33 36.50N 15.15E
Notodden Norway 42 59.34N 9.17E
Notre Dame, Monts *mts.* Canada 103 48.00N 69.00W
Notre Dame B. Canada 103 49.45N 55.15W

Notre Dame de la Salette to **Okinawa jima**

Notre Dame de la Salette Canada **105** 45.46N 75.35W
Notre Dame du Lac *town* Canada **104** 46.19N 80.10W
Notre Dame du Laus Canada **105** 46.05N 75.37W
Nottawasaga *r.* Canada **104** 44.32N 80.01W
Nottawasaga B. Canada **104** 44.40N 80.30W
Nottaway *r.* Canada **102** 51.25N 78.50W
Nottingham U.K. **12** 52.57N 1.10W
Nottinghamshire *d.* U.K. **12** 53.10N 1.00W
Notwani *r.* Botswana **80** 23.46S 26.57E
Nouadhibou Mauritania **74** 20.54N 17.01W
Nouakchott Mauritania **74** 18.09N 15.58W
Nouméa N.Cal. **84** 22.16S166.27E
Nouna Burkina **76** 12.44N 3.54W
Noupoort R.S.A. **80** 31.11S 24.56E
Nouveau, Lac *l.* Canada **103** 51.59N 68.58W
Nouveau-Comptoir Canada **102** 53.02N 78.55W
Nouvelle Anvers Zaïre **78** 1.38N 19.10E
Nouvelle Calédonie *is.* Pacific Oc. **84** 21.30S165.30E
Nouzonville France **19** 49.49N 4.45E
Nova Caipemba Angola **78** 7.25S 14.36E
Novafeltria Bagnodi Romagna Italy **30** 43.53N 12.17E
Nova Friburgo Brazil **126** 22.16S 42.32W
Nova Gradiška Yugo. **31** 45.16N 17.23E
Nova Iguaçu Brazil **126** 22.45S 43.27W
Nova Lamego Guinea Bissau **76** 12.19N 14.11W
Nova Lima Brazil **126** 19.59S 43.51W
Novara Italy **30** 45.28N 8.38E
Nova Scotia *d.* Canada **103** 45.00N 63.30W
Nova Sofala Mozambique **81** 20.09S 34.24E
Novato U.S.A. **108** 38.06N122.34W
Nova Varoš Yugo. **31** 43.28N 19.48E
Novaya Ladoga U.S.S.R. **44** 60.09N 32.15E
Novaya Lyalya U.S.S.R. **50** 59.02N 60.38E
Novaya Sibir, Ostrov *i.* U.S.S.R. **51** 75.20N148.00E
Novaya Ushitsa U.S.S.R. **37** 48.50N 27.12E
Novaya Zemlya *i.* U.S.S.R. **50** 74.00N 56.00E
Nova Zagora Bulgaria **34** 42.29N 26.01E
Novelda Spain **25** 38.23N 0.46W
Nové Zámky Czech. **37** 47.59N 18.11E
Novgorod U.S.S.R. **44** 58.30N 31.20E
Novgorod Severskiy U.S.S.R. **44** 52.00N 33.15E
Novi Bečej Yugo. **31** 45.36N 20.08E
Novi di Modena Italy **30** 44.54N 10.54E
Novigrad Yugo. **31** 45.19N 13.34E
Novi Ligure Italy **30** 44.46N 8.47E
Novi Pazar Yugo. **34** 43.08N 20.31E
Novi Sad Yugo. **31** 45.15N 19.50E
Novi Vinodolski Yugo. **31** 45.08N 14.48E
Novoanninskiy U.S.S.R. **45** 50.32N 42.42E
Novo Arkhangel'sk U.S.S.R. **37** 48.34N 30.50E
Novocherkassk U.S.S.R. **45** 47.25N 40.05E
Novofedorovka U.S.S.R. **45** 47.04N 35.18E
Novograd Volynskiy U.S.S.R. **37** 50.34N 27.32E
Novogrudok U.S.S.R. **37** 53.35N 25.50E
Novo Hamburgo Brazil **126** 29.37S 51.07W
Novokazalinsk U.S.S.R. **9** 45.48N 62.06E
Novokuznetsk U.S.S.R. **48** 53.45N 87.12E
Novo Mesto Yugo. **31** 45.48N 15.10E
Novomoskovsk R.S.F.S.R. U.S.S.R. **44** 54.06N 38.15E
Novomoskovsk Ukr.S.S.R. U.S.S.R. **45** 48.38N 35.15E
Novorossiysk U.S.S.R. **45** 44.44N 37.46E
Novoshakhtinsk U.S.S.R. **45** 47.46N 39.55E
Novosibirsk U.S.S.R. **9** 55.04N 83.05E
Novosibirskiye Ostrova *is.* U.S.S.R. **51** 76.00N144.00E
Novouzensk U.S.S.R. **45** 50.29N 48.08E
Novo-Vyatsk U.S.S.R. **44** 58.30N 49.40E
Novozybkov U.S.S.R. **37** 52.31N 31.58E
Novska Yugo. **31** 45.21N 16.59E
Nový Bor Czech. **38** 50.40N 14.33E
Nový Jičín Czech. **37** 49.36N 18.00E
Novyy Bykhov U.S.S.R. **37** 53.20N 30.21E
Novyy Port U.S.S.R. **50** 67.38N 72.33E
Nowa Ruda Poland **36** 50.34N 16.30E
Nowa Sól Poland **36** 51.49N 15.41E
Nowendoc Australia **93** 31.35S151.45E
Nowgong Assam India **63** 26.21N 92.40E
Nowgong Madhya P. India **63** 25.04N 79.27E
Nowingi Australia **92** 34.36S142.15E
Nowra Australia **93** 35.54S150.36E
Nowrangapur India **63** 19.14N 82.33E
Nowshera Pakistan **62** 34.01N 71.59E
Nowy Dwór Mazowiecki Poland **37** 52.26N 20.43E
Nowy Korczyn Poland **37** 50.19N 20.48E
Nowy Sącz Poland **37** 49.39N 20.40E
Nowy Targ Poland **37** 49.29N 20.02E
Nowy Tomśyl Poland **36** 52.20N 16.07E
Now Zād Afghan. **62** 32.24N 64.28E
Noxon U.S.A. **108** 48.01N115.47W
Noya Spain **26** 42.47N 8.53W
Noya *r.* Spain **25** 41.28N 1.56E
Noyant France **18** 47.31N 0.08E
Noyes I. U.S.A. **100** 55.30N133.40W
Noyon France **19** 49.35N 3.00E
Nozay France **18** 47.34N 1.38W
Nsanje Malaŵi **79** 16.55S 35.12E
Nsawam Ghana **76** 5.49N 0.20W
Nsok Equat. Guinea **78** 1.10N 11.19E
Nsombo Zambia **79** 10.50S 29.56E
Nsukka Nigeria **77** 6.51N 7.29E
Nuatja Togo **77** 6.59N 1.11E
Nubian Desert Sudan **72** 20.30N 34.00E
Nueces *r.* U.S.A. **111** 27.50N 97.30W
Nueces Plains *f.* U.S.A. **111** 28.30N 99.15W
Nueltin L. Canada **101** 60.30N 99.30W
Nueva Casas Grandes Mexico **109** 30.25N107.55W
Nueva Gerona Cuba **117** 21.53N 82.49W
Nueva Helvecia Uruguay **125** 34.19S 57.13W
Nueva Palmira Uruguay **125** 33.53S 58.25W
Nueva Rosita Mexico **111** 27.57N101.13W
Nueve de Julio Argentina **125** 35.30S 60.50W
Nuevitas Cuba **117** 21.34N 77.18W
Nuevo *d.* Mexico **111** 26.00N100.00W
Nuevo, Golfo *g.* Argentina **125** 42.42S 64.35W
Nuevo Berlín Uruguay **125** 32.59S 58.03W
Nuevo Laredo Mexico **111** 27.30N 99.31W
Nuevo León *d.* Mexico **116** 26.00N 99.00W
Nuevo Rocafuerte Ecuador **122** 0.56S 75.24W
Nūh, Rās *c.* Pakistan **62** 25.05N 62.24E
Nui *i.* Tuvalu **84** 7.12S177.10E
Nuits-St. Georges France **19** 47.08N 4.57E
Nu Jiang *r.* China *see* Salween *r.* Burma **61**
Nukha U.S.S.R. **65** 41.12N 47.10E
Nukhaylah Sudan **72** 19.03N 26.19E
Nuku'alofa Tonga **85** 21.07S175.12W
Nuku Hiva *i.* Is. Marquises **85** 8.56S140.00W
Nukunonu Pacific Oc. **84** 9.10S171.55W
Nulato U.S.A. **98** 64.43N158.06W
Nules Spain **25** 39.51N 0.09W
Nullagine Australia **88** 21.56S120.06E
Nullarbor Australia **89** 31.26S130.55E
Nullarbor Plain *f.* Australia **89** 31.30S128.00E
Numalla, L. Australia **92** 28.45S144.21E
Numan Nigeria **77** 9.30N 12.01E
Numancia *site* Spain **25** 41.48N 2.25W
Numazu Japan **57** 35.06N138.52E
Numedal *f.* Norway **42** 60.06N 9.06E
Numurkah Australia **93** 36.05S145.26E
Nunavik *c.* Greenland **99** 71.55N 55.00W
Nunda U.S.A. **114** 42.35N 77.57W
Nundle Australia **93** 31.28S151.08E
Nuneaton U.K. **13** 52.32N 1.29W
Nungo Mozambique **81** 13.25S 37.45E
Nunivak I. U.S.A. **98** 60.00N166.30W
Nunkun *mtn.* Jammu & Kashmir **62** 33.59N 76.01E
Nuoro Italy **32** 40.19N 9.20E
Nuqūb Yemen **71** 14.59N 45.48E
Nurallao Italy **32** 39.46N 9.05E
Nürburg Germany **39** 50.21N 6.57E
Nure *r.* Italy **30** 45.03N 9.49E
Nuriootpa Australia **92** 34.27S139.02E
Nürnberg Germany **38** 49.27N 11.04E
Nurri Italy **32** 39.42N 9.14E
Nurri, Mt. Australia **93** 31.44S146.04E
Nürtingen Germany **39** 48.38N 9.20E
Nusa Tenggara *is.* Indonesia **58** 8.30S118.00E
Nusa Tenggara Barat *d.* Indonesia **58** 8.50S117.30E
Nusa Tenggara Timur *d.* Indonesia **59** 9.30S122.00E
Nusaybin Turkey **64** 37.05N 41.11E
Nushki Pakistan **62** 29.33N 66.01E
Nutak Canada **103** 57.39N 61.50W
Nutter Fort U.S.A. **114** 39.20N 80.19W
Nuuk *see* Godthåb Greenland **99**
Nuwākot Nepal **63** 28.08N 83.53E
Nuwaybi'al Muzayyinah Egypt **66** 28.58N 34.38E
Nuweveldberge *mts.* R.S.A. **80** 32.15S 21.50E
Nuyts, Pt. Australia **89** 35.02S116.32E
Nuyts Archipelago *is.* Australia **91** 32.35S133.17E
Nxaunxau Botswana **80** 18.19S 21.04E
Nyaake Liberia **76** 4.52N 7.37W
Nyabing Australia **89** 33.32S118.09E
Nyahua Tanzania **79** 5.25S 33.16E
Nyahururu Falls *town* Kenya **79** 0.04N 36.22E
Nyah West Australia **92** 35.11S143.21E
Nyainqêntanglha Feng *mtn.* China **63** 30.27N 90.33E
Nyainqêntanglha Shan *mts.* China **63** 30.00N 90.00E
Nyainrong China **63** 32.02N 92.15E
Nyakanazi Tanzania **79** 3.05S 31.16E
Nyaksimvol U.S.S.R. **44** 62.30N 60.52E
Nyala Sudan **73** 12.03N 24.53E
Nyalam China **63** 28.12N 85.58E
Nyamandhlovu Zimbabwe **80** 19.50S 28.15E
Nyamapanda Zimbabwe **81** 16.59S 32.50E
Nyamlell Sudan **73** 9.07N 26.58E
Nyamtukusa Tanzania **79** 3.03S 32.44E
Nyandoma U.S.S.R. **44** 61.33N 40.05E
Nyanga *r.* Gabon **78** 3.00S 10.17E
Nyang Qu *r.* China **63** 29.19N 88.52E
Nyanza *d.* Kenya **79** 0.30S 34.30E
Nyanza Rwanda **79** 2.20S 29.42E
Nyashabozh U.S.S.R. **44** 65.28N 53.42E
Nyaunglebin Burma **56** 17.57N 96.44E
Nyaungu Burma **56** 21.12N 94.55E
Nyborg Denmark **42** 55.19N 10.48E
Nybro Sweden **43** 56.45N 15.54E
Nyda U.S.S.R. **50** 66.35N 72.58E
Nyêmo China **63** 29.25N 90.15E
Nyeri Kenya **79** 0.22S 36.56E
Nyerol Sudan **73** 8.41N 32.02E
Nyhammar Sweden **43** 60.17N 14.58E
Nyika Plateau *f.* Malaŵi **79** 10.25S 33.50E
Nyima China **63** 31.50N 87.48E
Nyimba Zambia **79** 14.33S 30.49E
Nyíregyháza Hungary **37** 47.59N 21.43E
Nyköbing Falster Denmark **41** 54.46N 11.53E
Nyköbing Jylland Denmark **42** 56.48N 8.52E
Nyköbing Sjaelland Denmark **42** 55.55N 11.41E
Nyköping Sweden **43** 58.45N 17.00E
Nykroppa Sweden **43** 59.38N 14.18E
Nylstroom R.S.A. **80** 24.42S 28.24E
Nymagee Australia **93** 32.05S146.20E
Nymboida Australia **93** 29.57S152.32E
Nymboida *r.* Australia **93** 29.39S152.30E
Nymburk Czech. **36** 50.11N 15.03E
Nynäshamn Sweden **43** 58.54N 17.57E
Nyngan Australia **93** 31.34S147.14E
Nyngynderry Australia **92** 32.16S143.22E
Nyoma Jammu & Kashmir **63** 33.11N 78.38E
Nyon Switz. **39** 46.23N 6.14E
Nyong *r.* Cameroon **77** 3.15N 9.55E
Nyons France **21** 44.22N 5.08E
Nýřany Czech. **38** 49.43N 13.13E
Nýrsko Czech. **38** 49.18N 13.09E
Nysa Poland **37** 50.29N 17.20E
Nysa Kłodzka *r.* Poland **37** 50.49N 17.50E
Nyssa U.S.A. **108** 43.53N117.00W
Nyuksenitsa U.S.S.R. **44** 60.24N 44.08E
Nyunzu Zaïre **79** 5.55S 28.00E
Nyurba U.S.S.R. **51** 63.18N118.28E
Nyuri India **63** 27.42N 92.13E
Nzega Tanzania **79** 4.13S 33.09E
N'zérékoré Guinea **76** 7.49N 8.48W
N'zeto Angola **78** 7.13S 12.56E
Nzwani *i.* Comoros **79** 12.12S 44.28E

O

Oahe Resr. U.S.A. **110** 45.30N100.25W
Oahu *i.* Hawaiian Is. **85** 21.30N158.00W
Oakbank Australia **92** 33.07S140.33E
Oakdale U.S.A. **111** 30.49N 92.40W
Oakesdale U.S.A. **108** 47.08N117.15W
Oakey Australia **91** 27.26S151.43E
Oak Harbour U.S.A. **108** 48.18N122.39W
Oak Hill *town* Fla. U.S.A. **113** 28.52N 80.52W
Oak Hill *town* Ohio U.S.A. **114** 38.54N 82.34W
Oakland Calif. U.S.A. **108** 37.47N122.13W
Oakland Md. U.S.A. **114** 39.25N 79.24W
Oakland Oreg. U.S.A. **108** 43.25N123.18W
Oaklands Australia **93** 35.25S146.15E
Oakley U.S.A. **108** 42.15N113.53W
Oakover *r.* Australia **88** 20.49S120.40E
Oak Ridge *f.* Canada **104** 44.01N 79.19W
Oakridge U.S.A. **108** 43.45N122.28W
Oak Ridge *town* U.S.A. **113** 36.02N 84.12W
Oakvale Australia **92** 33.01S140.41E
Oakville Canada **104** 43.27N 79.41W
Oamaru New Zealand **86** 45.07S170.58E
Oates Land *f.* Antarctica **128** 70.00S155.00E
Oaxaca Mexico **116** 17.05N 96.41W
Oaxaca *d.* Mexico **116** 17.30N 97.00W
Ob *r.* U.S.S.R. **44** 66.50N 69.00E
Oba Canada **102** 49.04N 84.07W
Oba *i.* Vanuatu **84** 15.25S167.50E
Oban U.K. **14** 56.26N 5.28W
Oberá Argentina **124** 27.30S 55.07W
Oberammergau Germany **39** 47.35N 11.04E
Oberdrauburg Austria **39** 46.45N 12.58E
Obergurgl Austria **39** 46.52N 11.01E
Oberhausen Germany **38** 51.28N 6.50E
Oberkirch Germany **39** 48.31N 8.05E
Oberlin Kans. U.S.A. **110** 39.49N100.32W
Oberlin Ohio U.S.A. **114** 41.18N 82.13W
Obernai France **19** 48.28N 7.29E
Oberon Australia **93** 33.41S149.52E
Oberösterreich *d.* Austria **39** 48.05N 13.40E
Oberpfälzer Wald *mts.* Germany **39** 49.35N 12.15E
Oberursel Germany **39** 50.11N 8.35E
Obervellach Austria **39** 46.56N 13.12E
Obi *i.* Indonesia **59** 1.45S127.30E
Obidos Brazil **123** 1.55S 55.31W
Obihiro Japan **57** 42.55N143.00E
Obing Germany **39** 48.00N 12.24E
Obitsu *r.* Japan **57** 35.24N139.54E
Obnova Bulgaria **34** 43.26N 24.59E
Obo C.A.R. **73** 5.24N 26.30E
Obock Djibouti **73** 11.59N 43.16E
Obodovka U.S.S.R. **37** 48.28N 29.10E
Oboyan U.S.S.R. **45** 51.13N 36.17E
Obozerskiy U.S.S.R. **44** 63.28N 40.29E
Obregón, Presa *resr.* Mexico **109** 28.00N109.50W
Obrenovac Yugo. **31** 44.39N 20.12E
Obrovac Yugo. **31** 44.12N 15.41E
Obruk Platosu *f.* Turkey **64** 38.00N 33.30E
Obskaya Guba *g.* U.S.S.R. **50** 68.30N 74.00E
Ōbu Japan **57** 35.00N136.58E
Obuasi Ghana **76** 6.15N 1.36W
Obudu Nigeria **77** 6.42N 9.07E
Ocala U.S.A. **113** 29.11N 82.09W
Ocaña Colombia **122** 8.16N 73.21W
Ocaña Spain **27** 39.56N 3.31W
Occidental, Cordillera *mts.* Colombia **122** 5.00N 76.15W
Occidental, Cordillera *mts.* S. America **124** 17.00S 69.00W
Ocean City Md. U.S.A. **115** 38.20N 75.05W
Ocean City N.J. U.S.A. **115** 39.16N 74.36W
Ocean Falls *town* Canada **100** 52.25N127.40W
Ocean I. *see* Banaba *i.* Kiribati **84**
Oceanside Calif. U.S.A. **109** 33.12N117.23W
Oceanside N.Y. U.S.A. **115** 40.38N 73.38W
Ochamchire U.S.S.R. **45** 42.44N 41.30E
Ochil Hills U.K. **14** 56.16N 3.25W
Ochsenfurt Germany **39** 49.40N 10.03E
Ockelbo Sweden **41** 60.53N 16.43E
Öckerö Sweden **42** 57.43N 11.39E
Ocmulgee *r.* U.S.A. **113** 31.58N 82.32W
Oconee *r.* U.S.A. **113** 31.58N 82.32W
Oconto U.S.A. **110** 44.55N 87.52W
Ocotal Nicaragua **117** 13.37N 86.31W
Ocotlán Mexico **116** 20.21N102.42W
Ocreza, Ribeira da *r.* Portugal **27** 39.32N 7.50W
Octeville France **18** 49.37N 1.39W
Ocua Mozambique **81** 13.40S 39.46E
Oda Ghana **76** 5.55N 0.56W
Oda, Jabal *mtn.* Sudan **72** 20.21N 36.39E
Odádhahraun *mts.* Iceland **40** 65.00N 17.30W
Ōdate Japan **57** 40.16N140.34E
Odawara Japan **57** 35.15N139.10E
Odda Norway **42** 60.04N 6.33E
Odder Denmark **42** 55.58N 10.10E
Ödeborg Sweden **43** 58.30N 12.01E
Odeleite *r.* Portugal **27** 37.21N 7.27W
Odemira Portugal **27** 37.36N 8.38W
Ödemiş Turkey **29** 38.12N 28.00E
Odense Denmark **42** 55.24N 10.23E
Odenwald *mts.* Germany **39** 49.35N 9.05E
Oder *r.* Germany *see* Odra *r.* Poland **36**
Oderberg Germany **38** 52.52N 14.02E
Oderhaff *b.* Germany **38** 53.46N 14.14E
Oder-Havel-Kanal Germany **38** 52.51N 13.30E
Oder-Spree-Kanal Germany **38** 52.16N 14.30E
Oderzo Italy **30** 45.47N 12.29E
Ödeshög Sweden **43** 58.14N 14.39E
Odessa N.Y. U.S.A. **114** 42.20N 76.48W
Odessa Tex. U.S.A. **111** 31.51N102.22W
Odessa U.S.S.R. **37** 46.30N 30.46E
Odiel *r.* Spain **27** 37.10N 6.55W
Odienné Ivory Coast **76** 9.36N 7.32W
Odorhei Romania **37** 46.18N 25.18E
Odra *r.* Poland **36** 53.30N 14.36E
Odžaci Yugo. **31** 45.30N 19.16E
Odžak Yugo. **31** 45.03N 18.18E
Odzi *r.* Zimbabwe **81** 19.46S 32.22E
Oebisfelde Germany **38** 52.25N 10.59E
Oegstgeest Neth. **16** 52.12N 4.31E
Oeiras Brazil **123** 7.00S 42.07W
Oelde Germany **38** 51.59N 8.08E
Oelrichs U.S.A. **110** 43.10N103.13W
Oelsnitz Germany **39** 50.24N 12.10E
Oelwein U.S.A. **110** 42.41N 91.55W
Oeno I. Pacific Oc. **85** 23.55S130.45W
Oettingen in Bayern Germany **39** 48.57N 10.36E
Oetz Austria **39** 47.12N 10.54E
Ofanto *r.* Italy **33** 41.22N 16.13E
Ofaqim Israel **67** 31.19N 34.37E
Offa Nigeria **77** 8.09N 4.44E
Offaly *d.* Rep. of Ire. **15** 53.15N 7.30W
Offenbach Germany **39** 50.08N 8.47E
Offenburg Germany **39** 48.28N 7.57E
Offerdal Sweden **40** 63.28N 14.03E
Offida Italy **31** 42.56N 13.41E
Offranville France **18** 49.52N 1.03E
Ofir Portugal **26** 41.31N 8.47W
Ofotfjorden *est.* Norway **40** 68.25N 17.00E
Ofu *i.* Samoa **84** 14.11S169.40W
Ōfunato Japan **57** 39.04N141.43E
Oga Japan **57** 39.53N139.51E
Ogadēn *f.* Ethiopia **71** 7.50N 45.40E
Ōgaki Japan **57** 35.21N136.37E
Ogallala U.S.A. **110** 41.08N101.43W
Ogbomosho Nigeria **77** 8.05N 4.11E
Ogden Iowa U.S.A. **110** 42.02N 94.02W
Ogden Utah U.S.A. **108** 41.14N111.58W
Ogdensburg U.S.A. **105** 44.42N 75.29W
Ogeechee *r.* U.S.A. **113** 31.51N 81.06W
Ogilvie Mts. Canada **98** 65.00N139.30W
Oginskiy, Kanal *canal* U.S.S.R. **37** 52.25N 25.55E
Oglio *r.* Italy **30** 45.02N 10.39E
Ognon *r.* France **19** 47.20N 5.29E
Ogoja Nigeria **77** 6.40N 8.45E
Ogoki Canada **102** 51.35N 86.00W
Ogoki *r.* Canada **102** 51.35N 86.00W
Ogoki Resr. Canada **102** 51.00N 88.15W
Ogooué *r.* Gabon **78** 1.00S 9.05E
Ogosta *r.* Bulgaria **34** 43.35N 23.35E
Ogr Sudan **73** 12.02N 27.06E
Ograżden *mts.* Yugo. **34** 41.30N 22.50E
Ogulin Yugo. **31** 45.16N 15.14E
Ogun *d.* Nigeria **77** 6.50N 3.20E
Ogunquit U.S.A. **115** 43.15N 70.36W
Ohai New Zealand **86** 45.56S167.57E
Ohanet Algeria **75** 28.40N 8.50E
Ohey Belgium **16** 50.26N 5.06E
O'Higgins, Cabo *c.* I. de Pascua **85** 27.05S109.15W
O'Higgins, L. Chile **125** 48.03S 73.10W
Ohio *d.* U.S.A. **112** 40.15N 82.45W
Ohio *r.* U.S.A. **112** 36.59N 89.08W
Ōhito Japan **57** 34.59N138.56E
Ohne Germany **38** 52.42N 8.12E
Ohře *r.* Czech. **39** 50.32N 14.08E
Ohrid Yugo. **34** 41.07N 20.47E
Ohrid, L. Albania/Yugo. **34** 41.08N 20.52E
Öhringen Germany **39** 49.12N 9.29E
Ōi *r.* Japan **57** 34.45N138.18E
Oil City U.S.A. **114** 41.26N 79.42W
Oise *d.* France **19** 49.30N 2.30E
Oise *r.* France **19** 49.00N 2.04E
Oisterwijk Neth. **16** 51.34N 5.10E
Oita Japan **57** 33.15N131.40E
Ojai U.S.A. **109** 34.27N119.15W
Ojika zan *pen.* Japan **57** 38.20N141.32E
Ojocaliente Mexico **116** 22.35N102.18W
Ojo de Agua Argentina **124** 29.30S 63.44W
Ojos del Salado *mtn.* Argentina/Chile **124** 27.05S 68.05W
Oka Canada **105** 45.29N 74.06W
Oka Nigeria **77** 7.28N 5.48E
Oka *r.* U.S.S.R. **44** 56.09N 43.00E
Okaba Indonesia **59** 8.06S139.46E
Okahandja Namibia **80** 21.58S 16.44E
Okanagan L. Canada **100** 50.00N119.30W
Okanogan U.S.A. **108** 48.39N120.41W
Okanogan *r.* U.S.A. **108** 48.22N119.35W
Okaputa Namibia **80** 20.08S 16.58E
Okāra Pakistan **62** 30.49N 73.27E
Okarito New Zealand **86** 43.14S.170.07
Okaukuejo Namibia **80** 19.12S 15.56E
Okavango *r.* Botswana **80** 18.30S 22.04E
Okavango Basin *f.* Botswana **80** 19.30S 22.30E
Okayama Japan **57** 34.40N133.54E
Okeechobee U.S.A. **113** 27.14N 80.50W
Okeechobee, L. U.S.A. **113** 26.55N 80.45W
Okefenokee Swamp *f.* U.S.A. **113** 30.42N 82.20W
Okehampton U.K. **13** 50.44N 4.01W
Okere *r.* Uganda **79** 1.37N 33.53E
Okha U.S.S.R. **51** 53.35N142.50E
Okhaldhunga Nepal **63** 27.19N 86.31E
Okhansk U.S.S.R. **44** 57.42N 55.20E
Okhotsk U.S.S.R. **51** 59.20N143.15E
Okhotsk, Sea of U.S.S.R. **51** 55.00N150.00E
Okhotskiy Perevoz U.S.S.R. **51** 61.55N135.40E
Okiep R.S.A. **80** 29.36S 17.49E
Oki guntō *is.* Japan **57** 36.10N133.10E
Okinawa jima *i.* Japan **53** 26.30N128.00E

Okino Torishima to **Otaru**

Okino Torishima *i.* Pacific Oc. **59** 20.24N136.02E
Okipoko *r.* Namibia **80** 18.40S 16.03E
Okitipupa Nigeria **77** 6.31N 4.50E
Oklahoma *d.* U.S.A. **111** 35.20N 98.00W
Oklahoma City U.S.A. **111** 35.28N 97.32W
Okmulgee U.S.A. **111** 35.37N 95.58W
Oknitsa U.S.S.R. **37** 48.22N 27.30E
Oko, Wādi Sudan **72** 21.15N 35.56E
Okola Cameroon **77** 4.03N 11.23E
Okolona U.S.A. **111** 34.00N 88.45W
Okondja Gabon **78** 0.03S 13.45E
Okoyo Congo **78** 1.28S 15.00E
Oksböl Denmark **42** 55.38N 8.17E
Oksskolten *mtn.* Norway **40** 65.59N 14.15E
Oktyabr'sk U.S.S.R. **45** 49.30N 57.22E
Oktyabrskiy B.S.S.R. U.S.S.R. **37** 52.35N 28.45E
Oktyabrskiy R.S.F.S.R. U.S.S.R. **44** 54.30N 53.30E
Oktyabr'skoy Revolyutsii, Ostrov *i.* U.S.S.R. **51** 79.30N 96.00E
Okučani Yugo. **31** 45.16N 17.12E
Okuru New Zealand **86** 43.56S168.55E
Okushiri tō *i.* Japan **57** 42.00N139.50E
Okuta Nigeria **77** 9.13N 3.12E
Ola U.S.A. **111** 35.02N 93.13W
Ólafsvík Iceland **40** 64.53N 23.44W
Olancha U.S.A. **109** 36.17N118.01W
Öland *i.* Sweden **43** 56.45N 16.38E
Olary Australia **92** 32.18S140.19E
Olascoaga Argentina **125** 35.14S 60.37W
Olavarría Argentina **125** 36.57S 60.20W
Oława Poland **37** 50.57N 17.17E
Olbia Italy **32** 40.55N 9.29E
Old Bar Australia **93** 31.59S152.35E
Old Crow Canada **98** 67.34N139.43W
Oldenburg *f.* Germany **38** 53.06N 8.25E
Oldenburg Nschn. Germany **38** 53.08N 8.13E
Oldenburg Sch.-Hol. Germany **38** 54.17N 10.52E
Oldenzaal Neth. **16** 52.19N 6.55E
Old Forge N.Y. U.S.A. **115** 43.43N 74.58W
Old Forge Penn. U.S.A. **115** 41.22N 75.44W
Old Fort *r.* Canada **101** 58.30N110.30W
Old Gumbiro Tanzania **79** 10.00S 35.24E
Oldham U.K. **12** 53.33N 2.08W
Old Head of Kinsale *c.* Rep. of Ire. **15** 51.37N 8.33W
Oldman *r.* Canada **101** 49.56N111.42W
Old Moolawatana Australia **92** 30.04S140.02E
Olds Canada **100** 51.50N114.10W
Old Saybrook U.S.A. **115** 41.18N 72.23W
Old Town U.S.A. **112** 44.56N 68.39W
Olean U.S.A. **114** 42.05N 78.26W
Olecko Poland **37** 54.03N 22.30E
Olekma *r.* U.S.S.R. **51** 60.20N120.30E
Olekminsk U.S.S.R. **51** 60.25N120.00E
Olema U.S.S.R. **44** 64.25N 40.15E
Ølen Norway **42** 59.36N 5.48E
Olenëk U.S.S.R. **51** 68.38N112.15E
Olenëk *r.* U.S.S.R. **51** 73.00N120.00E
Olenëkskiy Zaliv *g.* U.S.S.R. **51** 74.00N120.00E
Oléron, Île d' *i.* France **20** 45.56N 1.15W
Oleśnica Poland **37** 51.13N 17.23E
Olevsk U.S.S.R. **37** 51.12N 27.35E
Olga U.S.S.R. **53** 43.46N135.14E
Olga, Mt. Australia **90** 25.18S130.44E
Olga L. Canada **102** 49.44N 77.18W
Ölgiy Mongolia **52** 48.54N 90.00E
Ølgod Denmark **42** 55.49N 8.37E
Olgopol U.S.S.R. **37** 48.10N 29.30E
Olhão Portugal **27** 37.02N 8.50W
Olib *i.* Yugo. **31** 44.22N 14.48E
Oliena Italy **32** 40.16N 9.24E
Olifants *r.* Namibia **80** 25.28S 19.23E
Olifants *r.* C.P. R.S.A. **80** 31.42S 18.10E
Olifants *r.* Trans. R.S.A. **80** 24.08S 32.39E
Olimbía *site* Greece **35** 37.38N 21.41E
Ólimbos *mtn.* Cyprus **66** 34.55N 32.52E
Ólimbos Greece **35** 35.44N 27.11E
Ólimbos *mtn.* Greece **34** 40.05N 22.21E
Olinda Brazil **123** 8.00S 34.51W
Olite Spain **25** 42.29N 1.39W
Oliva Argentina **124** 32.05S 63.35W
Oliva Spain **25** 38.55N 0.07W
Oliva de la Frontera Spain **27** 38.16N 6.55W
Olivares Spain **27** 39.46N 2.20W
Oliveira Brazil **126** 20.39S 44.47W
Olivenza Spain **27** 38.41N 7.06W
Olmedillo de Roa Spain **26** 41.47N 3.56W
Olmedo Spain **26** 41.23N 4.41W
Olney U.K. **13** 52.09N 0.42W
Olney U.S.A. **110** 38.45N 88.05W
Olofström Sweden **43** 56.16N 14.30E
Olomouc Czech. **37** 49.36N 17.16E
Olonets U.S.S.R. **44** 61.00N 32.59E
Oloron France **20** 43.12N 0.36W
Oloron, Gave d' *r.* France **20** 43.33N 1.05W
Olosega *i.* Samoa **84** 14.12S169.38W
Olot Spain **25** 42.11N 2.29E
Olovyannaya U.S.S.R. **53** 50.58N115.35E
Olshammar Sweden **43** 58.45N 14.48E
Olsztyn Poland **37** 53.48N 20.29E
Olsztynek Poland **37** 53.36N 20.17E
Olt *r.* Romania **34** 43.43N 24.51E
Olten Switz. **39** 47.21N 7.54E
Oltenița Romania **37** 44.05N 26.31E
Olteț *r.* Romania **37** 44.13N 24.28E
Olvera Spain **27** 36.56N 5.16W
Olympia U.S.A. **108** 47.03N122.53W
Olympic Mts. U.S.A. **108** 47.50N123.45W
Olympic Nat. Park U.S.A. **108** 47.48N123.30W
Olympus *mtn. see* Ólimbos *mtn.* Greece **34**
Olympus, Mt. U.S.A. **108** 47.48N123.43W
Oma China **63** 32.30N 83.14E
Omae-zaki *c.* Japan **57** 34.36N138.14E
Omagh U.K. **15** 54.36N 7.20W
Omaha U.S.A. **110** 41.16N 95.57W
Oman Asia **60** 22.30N 57.30E
Oman, G. of Asia **65** 25.00N 58.00E
Omarama New Zealand **86** 44.29S169.58E
Omaruru Namibia **80** 21.25S 15.57E
Omate Peru **124** 16.40S 70.58W
Omberg *hill* Sweden **43** 58.20N 14.39E
Omboué Gabon **78** 1.38S 9.20E
Ombrone *r.* Italy **30** 42.39N 11.00E
Ombu China **63** 31.20N 86.34E
Omdurman *see* Umm Durmān Sudan **72**
Omegna Italy **30** 45.53N 8.24E
Omeo Australia **93** 37.05S147.37E
'Omer Israel **67** 31.17N 34.51E
Omer U.S.A. **104** 44.03N 83.50W
Ometepec Mexico **116** 16.41N 98.25W
Om Hājer Ethiopia **72** 14.24N 36.46E
Ōmi-hachiman Japan **57** 35.08N136.06E
Omineca *r.* Canada **100** 56.05N124.30W
Omišalj Yugo. **31** 45.13N 14.34E
Omitara Namibia **80** 22.18S 18.01E
Ōmiya Japan **57** 35.54N139.38E
Ommen Neth. **16** 52.32N 6.25E
Ömnögovi *d.* Mongolia **54** 43.00N105.00E
Omo *r.* Ethiopia **73** 4.51N 36.55E
Omolon *r.* U.S.S.R. **51** 68.50N158.30E
Omomee Canada **104** 44.19N 78.31W
Omono *r.* Japan **57** 39.44N140.05E
Ompah Canada **105** 45.00N 76.49W
Omsk U.S.S.R. **9** 55.00N 73.22E
Omulew *r.* Poland **37** 53.05N 21.32E
Omuramba Omatako *r.* Namibia **80** 18.19S 19.52E
Omurtag Bulgaria **34** 43.08N 26.26E
Ōmuta Japan **57** 33.02N130.26E
Oña Spain **26** 42.43N 3.25W
Onaga U.S.A. **110** 39.29N 96.10W
Onai Angola **80** 16.43S 17.33E
Onancock U.S.A. **113** 37.43N 75.46W
Onaping L. Canada **104** 46.57N 81.30W
Onaway U.S.A. **104** 45.21N 84.14W
Oncocua Angola **80** 16.40S 13.25E
Onda Spain **25** 39.58N 0.15W
Ondangua Namibia **80** 17.59S 16.02E
Ondo *d.* Nigeria **77** 7.10N 5.20E
Onega U.S.S.R. **44** 63.57N 38.11E
Onega *r.* U.S.S.R. **44** 63.59N 38.11E
Oneida U.S.A. **115** 43.06N 75.39W
Oneida L. U.S.A. **115** 43.13N 76.00W
O'Neill U.S.A. **110** 42.27N 98.39W
Oneonta U.S.A. **115** 42.27N 75.04W
Onezhskaya Guba *b.* U.S.S.R. **44** 63.55N 37.30E
Onezhskoye Ozero *l.* U.S.S.R. **44** 62.00N 35.30E
Ongerup Australia **89** 33.58S118.29E
Ongiyn Gol *r.* Mongolia **54** 43.40N103.45E
Ongniud Qi China **54** 43.00N118.43E
Ongole India **61** 15.31N 80.04E
Onilahy *r.* Madagascar **81** 23.34S 43.45E
Onitsha Nigeria **77** 6.10N 6.47E
Ons, Isla de *i.* Spain **26** 42.23N 8.56W
Onslow Australia **88** 21.41S115.12E
Onslow B. U.S.A. **113** 34.20N 77.20W
Onstwedde Neth. **16** 53.04N 7.02E
Ontake san *mtn.* Japan **57** 35.55N137.29E
Ontario *d.* Canada **102** 51.00N 88.00W
Ontario Calif. U.S.A. **109** 34.04N117.39W
Ontario Oreg. U.S.A. **108** 44.02N116.58W
Ontario, L. Canada / U.S.A. **114** 43.45N 78.00W
Onteniente Spain **25** 38.49N 0.37W
Ontonagon U.S.A. **112** 46.52N 89.18W
Oodnadatta Australia **91** 27.30S135.27E
Ooldea Australia **91** 30.27S131.50E
Oostelijk-Flevoland *f.* Neth. **16** 52.30N 5.40E
Oostende Belgium **16** 51.13N 2.55E
Oosterhout Neth. **16** 51.38N 4.50E
Oosterschelde *est.* Neth. **16** 51.35N 3.57E
Oosthuizen Neth. **16** 52.33N 5.00E
Oostmalle Belgium **16** 51.18N 4.45E
Oost Vlaanderen *d.* Belgium **16** 51.00N 3.45E
Oost Vlieland Neth. **16** 53.18N 5.04E
Ootsa L. Canada **100** 53.50N126.20W
Opaka Bulgaria **34** 43.28N 26.10E
Opal Mexico **111** 24.18N102.22W
Opala U.S.S.R. **51** 51.58N156.30E
Opala Zaïre **78** 0.42S 24.15E
Oparino U.S.S.R. **44** 59.53N 48.10E
Opasatika Canada **102** 49.30N 82.50W
Opasatika *r.* Canada **102** 50.24N 82.26W
Opasquia Canada **102** 53.16N 93.34W
Opatija Yugo. **31** 45.21N 14.19E
Opava Czech. **37** 49.56N 17.54E
Opelousas U.S.A. **111** 30.32N 92.05W
Opeongo L. Canada **104** 45.42N 78.23W
Opheim U.S.A. **108** 48.51N106.24W
Opinaca *r.* Canada **102** 52.20N 78.00W
Opinnagau *r.* Canada **102** 54.12N 82.21W
Opiscotéo, Lac *l.* Canada **103** 53.10N 68.10W
Opochka U.S.S.R. **44** 56.41N 28.42E
Opole Poland **37** 50.40N 17.56E
Oporto *see* Porto Portugal **26**
Opotiki New Zealand **86** 38.00S177.18E
Opp U.S.A. **113** 31.16N 86.18W
Oppdal Norway **40** 62.36N 9.41E
Oppida Mamertina Italy **33** 38.16N 16.00E
Oppland *d.* Norway **41** 61.30N 9.00E
Opportunity U.S.A. **108** 47.39N117.15W
Opunake New Zealand **86** 39.27S173.51E
Ora Italy **30** 46.21N 11.18E
Ora Banda Australia **89** 30.27S121.04E
Oradea Romania **37** 47.03N 21.55E
Öraefajökull *mtn.* Iceland **40** 64.02N 16.39W
Orahovica Yugo. **31** 45.31N 17.53E
Orai India **63** 25.59N 79.28E
Oran Algeria **74** 35.42N 0.38W
Orán Argentina **124** 23.07S 64.16W
Orange Australia **93** 33.19S149.10E
Orange France **21** 44.08N 4.48E
Orange *r.* R.S.A. **80** 28.38S 16.38E
Orange Mass. U.S.A. **115** 42.35N 72.19W
Orange N.J. U.S.A. **115** 40.46N 74.14W
Orange Tex. U.S.A. **111** 30.01N 93.44W
Orange, C. Brazil **123** 4.25N 51.32W
Orangeburg U.S.A. **113** 33.28N 80.53W
Orange Free State *d.* R.S.A. **80** 28.00S 28.00E
Orangevale U.S.A. **108** 38.41N121.13W
Orangeville Canada **104** 43.55N 80.06W
Oranienburg Germany **38** 52.45N 13.14E
Oranjefontein R.S.A. **80** 23.27S 27.40E
Oranjemund Namibia **80** 28.35S 16.26E
Or 'Aqiva Israel **67** 32.30N 34.55E
Orarak Sudan **73** 6.15N 32.23E
Oras Phil. **59** 12.09N125.22E
Orbe Switz. **39** 46.43N 6.32E
Orbetello Italy **30** 42.27N 11.13E
Orbieu *r.* France **20** 43.14N 2.54E
Orbigo *r.* Spain **26** 41.58N 5.40W
Orbisonia U.S.A. **114** 40.15N 77.54W
Orbost Australia **93** 37.42S148.30E
Örbyhus Sweden **41** 60.14N 17.42E
Orcera Spain **26** 38.19N 2.39W
Orchies France **19** 50.28N 3.14E
Orchila *i.* Venezuela **117** 11.52N 66.10W
Orco *r.* Italy **30** 45.10N 7.52E
Ord *r.* Australia **88** 15.30S128.30E
Ordenes Spain **26** 43.04N 8.24W
Ordu Turkey **64** 41.00N 37.52E
Orduña Spain **26** 42.58N 2.58W
Örebro Sweden **43** 59.17N 15.13E
Örebro *d.* Sweden **43** 59.30N 15.00E
Oregon *d.* U.S.A. **108** 43.49N120.36W
Oregon City U.S.A. **108** 45.21N122.36W
Öregrund Sweden **41** 60.20N 18.26E
Orekhovo-Zuyevo U.S.S.R. **44** 55.47N 39.00E
Orel U.S.S.R. **44** 52.58N 36.04E
Orellana, Embalse de *resr.* Spain **27** 39.00N 5.25W
Orem U.S.A. **108** 40.19N111.42W
Orenburg U.S.S.R. **44** 51.50N 55.00E
Orense Spain **26** 42.20N 7.51W
Orense *d.* Spain **26** 42.15N 7.40W
Oressa *r.* U.S.S.R. **37** 52.33N 28.45E
Orestiás Greece **34** 41.30N 26.31E
Orfanoú, Kólpos *g.* Greece **34** 40.33N 24.00E
Orford U.S.A. **105** 43.54N 72.10W
Orford, Mt. Canada **105** 45.18N 72.08W
Orford Ness *c.* Australia **90** 11.22S142.50E
Orford Ness *c.* U.K. **13** 52.05N 1.36E
Orgaz Spain **27** 39.39N 3.54W
Orgelet France **19** 46.31N 5.37E
Orgeyev U.S.S.R. **37** 47.24N 28.50E
Orgūn Afghan. **62** 32.55N 69.10E
Orick U.S.A. **108** 41.17N124.04W
Oriental, Cordillera *mts.* Bolivia **124** 17.00S 65.00W
Oriental, Cordillera *mts.* Colombia **122** 5.00N 74.30W
Origny France **19** 49.54N 3.30E
Orihuela Spain **25** 38.05N 0.57W
Orillia Canada **104** 44.37N 79.25W
Orimattila Finland **41** 60.48N 25.45E
Orinduik Guyana **122** 4.42N 60.01W
Orinoco *r.* Venezuela **122** 9.00N 61.30W
Orinoco, Delta del *f.* Venezuela **122** 9.00N 61.00W
Orissa *d.* India **63** 20.20N 84.00E
Oristano Italy **32** 39.54N 8.35E
Oristano, Golfo di *g.* Italy **32** 39.50N 8.30E
Orizaba Mexico **116** 18.51N 97.08W
Ørje Norway **42** 59.29N 11.39E
Orjen *mtn.* Yugo. **31** 42.30N 18.38E
Orjiva Spain **27** 36.53N 3.24W
Orkanger Norway **40** 63.17N 9.52E
Orkney Is. *d.* U.K. **14** 59.00N 3.00W
Orlândia Brazil **126** 20.55S 47.54W
Orlando U.S.A. **113** 28.33N 81.21W
Orléans Canada **105** 45.28N 75.31W
Orléans France **19** 47.55N 1.54E
Orleans Mass. U.S.A. **115** 41.47N 70.00W
Orleans N.H. U.S.A. **105** 44.49N 72.12W
Orléans, Canal d' France **19** 47.54N 1.55E
Ormāra Pakistan **62** 25.12N 64.38E
Ormāra, Rās *c.* Pakistan **62** 25.09N 64.35E
Ormilia Greece **34** 40.16N 23.33E
Ormoc Phil. **59** 11.00N124.37E
Ormond New Zealand **86** 38.35S177.58E
Ormond Beach *town* U.S.A. **113** 29.26N 81.03W
Ormož Yugo. **31** 46.25N 16.09E
Ormskirk U.K. **12** 53.35N 2.53W
Ormstown Canada **105** 45.08N 74.00W
Ornans France **19** 47.06N 6.09E
Orne *d.* France **18** 48.40N 0.05E
Orne *r.* France **18** 49.17N 0.11W
Ornö *i.* Sweden **43** 59.04N 18.24E
Örnsköldsvik Sweden **40** 63.17N 18.50E
Orobie, Alpi *mts.* Italy **30** 46.03N 10.00E
Orocué Colombia **122** 4.48N 71.20W
Orodara Burkina **76** 11.00N 4.54W
Orogrande U.S.A. **109** 32.23N106.28W
Orohena *mtn.* Tahiti **85** 17.37S149.28W
Oromocto Canada **103** 45.51N 66.29W
Oron Israel **66** 30.55N 35.01E
Oron Nigeria **77** 4.49N 8.15E
Orona *i.* Kiribati **84** 4.29S172.10W
Orono Canada **104** 43.59N 78.37W
Orono U.S.A. **112** 44.53N 68.40W
Orosei Italy **32** 40.23N 9.42E
Orosei, Golfo di *g.* Italy **32** 40.10N 9.50E
Orosháza Hungary **37** 46.34N 20.40E
Orote Pen. Guam **84** 13.26N144.38E
Orotukan U.S.S.R. **51** 62.16N151.43E
Oroville Calif. U.S.A. **108** 39.31N121.33W
Oroville Wash. U.S.A. **108** 48.56N119.26W
Orrefors Sweden **43** 56.50N 15.45E
Orroroo Australia **92** 32.46S138.39E
Orrville U.S.A. **114** 40.50N 81.46W
Orsa Sweden **41** 61.07N 14.37E
Orsha U.S.S.R. **44** 54.30N 30.23E
Orsières Switz. **39** 46.02N 7.09E
Orsk U.S.S.R. **44** 51.13N 58.35E
Orșova Romania **37** 44.42N 22.22E
Ortaklar Turkey **35** 37.53N 27.30E
Orta Nova Italy **33** 41.19N 15.42E
Ortegal, Cabo *c.* Spain **26** 43.45N 7.53W
Orthez France **20** 43.29N 0.46W
Ortigueira Spain **26** 43.41N 7.51W
Ortigueira, Ría de *est.* Spain **26** 43.45N 7.50W
Ortisei Italy **30** 46.34N 11.40E
Ortona Italy **31** 42.21N 14.24E
Ortonville U.S.A. **110** 45.18N 96.28W
Orūmīyeh Iran **65** 37.32N 45.02E
Oruro Bolivia **124** 17.59S 67.09W
Oruro *d.* Bolivia **124** 18.00S 72.30W
Orust *i.* Sweden **42** 58.10N 11.38E
Orūzgān Afghan. **62** 32.56N 66.38E
Orūzgān *d.* Afghan. **62** 33.40N 66.00E
Orvieto Italy **30** 42.43N 12.07E
Orwell U.S.A. **114** 41.32N 80.52W
Oryakhovo Bulgaria **34** 43.40N 23.57E
Or Yehuda Israel **67** 32.01N 34.51E
Orzinuovi Italy **30** 45.24N 9.55E
Os Norway **40** 62.31N 11.11E
Osa, Península de *pen.* Costa Rica **117** 8.20N 83.30W
Osage *r.* U.S.A. **107** 38.35N 91.57W
Osage Iowa U.S.A. **110** 43.17N 92.49W
Osage Wyo. U.S.A. **108** 43.59N104.25W
Ōsaka Japan **57** 34.40N135.30E
Ōsaka *d.* Japan **57** 34.24N135.25E
Ōsaka-wan *b.* Japan **57** 34.30N135.18E
Osborne U.S.A. **110** 39.26N 98.42W
Osby Sweden **43** 56.22N 13.59E
Osceola Iowa U.S.A. **110** 41.02N 93.46W
Osceola Mo. U.S.A. **111** 38.03N 93.42W
Osceola Mills U.S.A. **114** 40.51N 78.16W
Oschatz Germany **38** 51.18N 13.07E
Oschersleben Germany **38** 52.01N 11.13E
Oscoda U.S.A. **104** 44.26N 83.20W
Osečina Yugo. **31** 44.23N 19.36E
Osen Norway **40** 64.18N 10.32E
Osh U.S.S.R. **50** 40.37N 72.49E
Oshawa Canada **104** 43.54N 78.51W
Ō shima *i.* Hokkaido Japan **57** 41.40N139.40E
Ō shima *i.* Tosan Japan **57** 34.43N139.24E
Oshkosh Nebr. U.S.A. **110** 41.24N102.21W
Oshmyany U.S.S.R. **37** 54.22N 25.52E
Oshnovīyeh Iran **65** 37.03N 45.05E
Oshogbo Nigeria **77** 7.50N 4.35E
Oshtorān, Kūh *mtn.* Iran **65** 33.18N 49.15E
Oshvor U.S.S.R. **44** 66.59N 62.59E
Oshwe Zaïre **78** 3.27S 19.32E
Osiān India **62** 26.43N 72.55E
Osijek Yugo. **31** 45.33N 18.41E
Osilo Italy **32** 40.44N 8.39E
Osimo Italy **31** 43.29N 13.29E
Osipovichi U.S.S.R. **37** 53.19N 28.36E
Oskaloosa U.S.A. **110** 41.18N 92.39W
Oskarshamn Sweden **43** 57.16N 16.26E
Oskarström Sweden **43** 56.48N 12.58E
Oskol *r.* U.S.S.R. **45** 49.08N 37.10E
Oslo Norway **42** 59.55N 10.45E
Oslofjorden *est.* Norway **42** 59.20N 10.35E
Osmancık Turkey **64** 40.58N 34.50E
Osmaniye Turkey **64** 37.04N 36.15E
Ösmo Sweden **43** 58.59N 17.54E
Osnabrück Germany **38** 52.16N 8.02E
Osogovska Planina *mts.* Yugo. **34** 42.08N 22.18E
Osorno Chile **125** 40.35S 73.14W
Osorno Spain **26** 42.24N 4.22W
Osöyra Norway **42** 60.11N 5.28E
Osprey Reef Australia **90** 13.55S146.38E
Oss Neth. **16** 51.46N 5.31E
Ossa *mtn.* Greece **34** 39.47N 22.42E
Ossa, Mt. Australia **91** 41.52S146.04E
Ossabaw I. U.S.A. **113** 31.47N 81.06W
Osse *r.* France **20** 44.07N 0.17E
Osse *r.* Nigeria **77** 5.55N 5.15E
Ossineke U.S.A. **104** 44.54N 83.27W
Ossining U.S.A. **115** 41.10N 73.52W
Ossokmanuan L. Canada **103** 53.25N 65.00W
Ostaboningue, L. Canada **104** 47.09N 78.53W
Ostashkov U.S.S.R. **44** 57.09N 33.10E
Oste *r.* Germany **38** 53.33N 9.10E
Ostend *see* Oostende Belgium **16**
Oster U.S.S.R. **37** 50.55N 30.53E
Oster *r.* U.S.S.R. **37** 53.47N 31.46E
Osterburg Germany **38** 52.47N 11.44E
Österbybruk Sweden **43** 60.12N 17.54E
Österbymo Sweden **43** 57.50N 15.16E
Österdal *r.* Sweden **41** 61.03N 14.30E
Østerdalen *f.* Norway **41** 61.15N 11.10E
Östergötland *d.* Sweden **43** 58.20N 16.00E
Östergötland *f.* Sweden **43** 58.17N 15.40E
Osterholz-Scharmbeck Germany **38** 53.14N 8.47E
Österö *i.* Faroe Is. **10** 62.16N 6.54W
Osterode Germany **38** 51.43N 10.14E
Osteröy *i.* Norway **41** 60.33N 5.35E
Östersund Sweden **40** 63.10N 14.40E
Östervåla Sweden **43** 60.11N 17.11E
Osterwieck Germany **38** 51.58N 10.42E
Østfold *d.* Norway **42** 59.20N 11.25E
Ostfriesische Inseln *is.* Germany **38** 53.44N 7.25E
Östhammar Sweden **41** 60.16N 18.22E
Ostia Italy **32** 41.44N 12.14E
Östmark Sweden **43** 60.17N 12.45E
Ostrava Czech. **37** 49.50N 18.15E
Ostróda Poland **37** 53.43N 19.59E
Ostrog U.S.S.R. **37** 50.20N 26.29E
Ostrołeka Poland **37** 53.06N 21.34E
Ostrov Czech. **39** 50.17N 12.57E
Ostrov U.S.S.R. **44** 57.22N 28.22E
Ostrowiec-Świetokrzyski Poland **37** 50.57N 21.23E
Ostrów Mazowiecka Poland **37** 52.50N 21.51E
Ostrów Wielkopolski Poland **37** 51.39N 17.49E
Ostuni Italy **33** 40.44N 17.35E
Osum *r.* Albania **34** 40.40N 20.10E
Osūm *r.* Bulgaria **29** 43.41N 24.51E
Ōsumi kaikyō *str.* Japan **57** 31.30N131.00E
Ōsumi shotō *is.* Japan **53** 30.30N131.00E
Osuna Spain **27** 37.14N 5.07W
Oswego U.S.A. **115** 43.27N 76.31W
Oswestry U.K. **12** 52.52N 3.03W
Otago *d.* New Zealand **86** 45.10S169.20E
Otago Pen. New Zealand **86** 45.48S170.45E
Otaki New Zealand **86** 40.45S175.08E
Otaru Japan **57** 43.14N140.59E

Otavalo to **Parachilna**

Otavalo Ecuador **122** 0.14N 78.16W
Otavi Namibia **80** 19.37S 17.21E
Ōtawara Japan **57** 36.52N140.02E
Otelec Romania **37** 45.36N 20.50E
Otematata New Zealand **86** 44.37S170.11E
Othonoí *i.* Greece **33** 39.50N 19.26E
Óthris, Óros *mtn.* Greece **35** 39.04N 22.42E
Oti *r.* Ghana **76** 8.43N 0.10E
Otira New Zealand **86** 42.51S171.33E
Otish, Monts *mts.* Canada **103** 52.22N 70.30W
Otisville U.S.A. **115** 41.28N 74.32W
Otiwarongo Namibia **80** 20.30S 16.39E
Otjiwero Namibia **80** 17.59S 13.22E
Otju Namibia **80** 18.15S 13.18E
Otočac Yugo. **31** 44.52N 15.14E
Otog Qi China **54** 39.05N107.59E
Otosquen Canada **101** 53.17N102.01W
Otra *r.* Norway **42** 58.09N 8.00E
Otradnyy U.S.S.R. **44** 53.26N 51.30E
Otranto Italy **33** 40.09N 18.30E
Otranto, Str. of Med. Sea **33** 40.00N 19.00E
Otrokovice Czech. **37** 49.13N 17.31E
Otsego U.S.A. **112** 42.26N 85.42W
Otsego L. U.S.A. **115** 42.45N 74.52W
Otsego Lake *town* U.S.A. **104** 44.55N 84.41W
Ōtsu Japan **57** 35.02N135.52E
Ōtsuki Japan **57** 35.36N138.57E
Otta Norway **41** 61.46N 9.32E
Ottawa Canada **105** 45.25N 75.42W
Ottawa *r.* Canada **105** 45.20N 73.58W
Ottawa Ill. U.S.A. **110** 41.21N 88.51W
Ottawa Kans. U.S.A. **110** 38.37N 95.16W
Ottawa Is. Canada **99** 59.50N 80.00W
Ottenby Sweden **43** 56.14N 16.25E
Otter *r.* U.K. **13** 50.38N 3.19W
Otterbäcken Sweden **43** 58.57N 14.02E
Otterburn U.K. **12** 55.14N 2.10W
Otter Creek *r.* U.S.A. **105** 44.13N 73.17W
Otter L. Canada **101** 55.35N104.39W
Otter Lake *town* Canada **105** 45.51N 76.26W
Otterndorf Germany **38** 53.48N 8.53E
Otteröy *i.* Norway **40** 62.45N 6.50E
Otterup Denmark **42** 55.31N 10.24E
Ottosdal R.S.A. **80** 26.48S 26.00E
Ottumwa U.S.A. **110** 41.01N 92.25W
Oturkpo Nigeria **77** 7.13N 8.10E
Otway, C. Australia **92** 38.51S143.34E
Ötztaler Alpen *mts.* Austria / Italy **30** 46.52N 10.50E
Ou *r.* Laos **56** 20.03N102.19E
Ouachita *r.* U.S.A. **111** 31.38N 91.49W
Ouachita, L. U.S.A. **111** 34.40N 93.25W
Ouachita Mts. U.S.A. **111** 34.40N 94.25W
Ouada, Djebel *mtn.* C.A.R. **73** 8.56N 23.26E
Ouadane Mauritania **74** 20.56N 11.37W
Ouadda C.A.R. **73** 8.04N 22.24E
Ouaddaï *d.* Chad **73** 13.00N 21.00E
Ouagadougou Burkina **76** 12.20N 1.40W
Ouahigouya Burkina **76** 13.31N 2.21W
Ouaka *d.* C.A.R. **73** 6.00N 21.00E
Oualâta Mauritania **74** 17.18N 7.02W
Ouallam Niger **77** 14.23N 2.09E
Ouallene Algeria **74** 24.35N 1.17E
Ouanda Djallé C.A.R. **73** 8.54N 22.48E
Ouarane *f.* Mauritania **74** 21.00N 9.30W
Ouararda, Passe de *pass* Mauritania **74** 21.01N 13.03W
Ouareau *r.* Canada **105** 45.56N 73.25W
Ouargla Algeria **75** 31.57N 5.20E
Ouarra *r.* C.A.R. **73** 5.05N 24.26E
Ouarzazate Morocco **74** 30.57N 6.50W
Ouassouas *well* Mali **74** 16.01N 1.26E
Ouche *r.* France **19** 47.06N 5.16E
Ouddorp Neth. **16** 51.49N 3.57E
Oudenaarde Belgium **16** 50.50N 3.37E
Oudenbosch Neth. **16** 51.35N 4.30E
Oude Rijn *r.* Neth. **16** 52.14N 4.26E
Oudon *r.* France **18** 47.47N 1.02W
Oudtshoorn R.S.A. **80** 33.35S 22.11E
Oued Zarga Tunisia **32** 36.40N 9.25E
Oued-Zem Morocco **74** 32.55N 6.30W
Ouellé Ivory Coast **76** 7.26N 4.01W
Ouenza Algeria **75** 35.57N 8.07E
Ouessant, Île d' *i.* France **18** 48.28N 5.05W
Ouesso Congo **78** 1.38N 16.03E
Ouezzane Morocco **74** 34.52N 5.35W
Oughter, Lough Rep. of Ire. **15** 54.01N 7.28W
Ouham *r.* Chad **77** 9.15N 18.13E
Ouimet Canada **102** 48.43N 88.35W
Ouistreham France **18** 49.17N 0.15W
Oujda Morocco **74** 34.41N 1.45W
Oulu Finland **40** 65.01N 25.28E
Oulu *d.* Finland **40** 65.00N 27.00E
Oulu *r.* Finland **40** 65.01N 25.25E
Oulujärvi *l.* Finland **40** 64.20N 27.15E
Oum Chalouba Chad **75** 15.48N 20.46E
Oumé Ivory Coast **76** 6.25N 5.23W
Oum er Rbia, Oued *r.* Morocco **74** 33.19N 8.21W
Oumm ed Droûs Guebli, Sebkhet *f.* Mauritania **74** 24.03N 11.45W
Oumm ed Droûs Telli, Sebkhet *f.* Mauritania **74** 24.20N 11.30W
Ounas *r.* Finland **40** 66.30N 25.45E
Oundle U.K. **13** 52.28N 0.28W
Ounianga Kébir Chad **75** 19.04N 20.29E
Our *r.* Lux. **16** 49.53N 6.16E
Ouray U.S.A. **108** 40.06N109.40W
Ourcq *r.* France **19** 49.01N 3.01E
Ouri Chad **75** 21.34N 19.13E
Ourinhos Brazil **126** 23.00S 49.54W
Ourique Portugal **26** 37.39N 8.13W
Ouro Fino Brazil **126** 22.16S 46.25W
Ouro Prêto Brazil **126** 20.54S 43.30W
Ourthe *r.* Belgium **16** 50.38N 5.36E
Ouse *r.* Humber. U.K. **12** 53.41N 0.42W
Oust *r.* France **18** 47.39N 2.06W
Outardes, Rivière aux *r.* Canada **103** 49.04N 68.25W
Outer Hebrides *is.* U.K. **14** 57.40N 7.35W
Outjo Namibia **80** 20.07S 16.10E
Outlook U.S.A. **108** 48.53N104.47W
Ouvèze *r.* France **21** 43.59N 4.51E
Ouyen Australia **92** 35.06S142.22E
Ouzouer-le-Marché France **19** 47.55N 1.32E
Ouzzal, Oued I-n- *wadi* Algeria **75** 20.54N 2.28E
Ovalle Chile **124** 30.36S 71.12W
Ovamboland *f.* Namibia **80** 17.45S 16.00E
Ovar Portugal **26** 40.52N 8.38W
Ovens *r.* Australia **93** 36.20S146.18E
Overath Germany **16** 50.56N 7.18E
Overflakkee *i.* Neth. **16** 51.45N 4.08E
Overijssel *d.* Neth. **16** 52.25N 6.30E
Överkalix Sweden **40** 66.21N 22.56E
Overland Park *town* U.S.A. **110** 38.59N 94.40W
Overton U.S.A. **109** 36.33N114.27W
Övertorneå Sweden **40** 66.23N 23.40E
Överum Sweden **43** 57.59N 16.19E
Ovid Mich. U.S.A. **104** 43.01N 84.22W
Ovid N.Y. U.S.A. **114** 42.41N 76.49W
Ovidiopol U.S.S.R. **37** 46.18N 30.28E
Oviedo Spain **26** 43.22N 5.50W
Ovinishche U.S.S.R. **44** 58.20N 37.00E
Övörhangay *d.* Mongolia **54** 45.00N103.00E
Ovruch U.S.S.R. **37** 51.20N 28.50E
Owaka New Zealand **86** 46.27S169.40E
Owando Congo **78** 0.30S 15.48E
Owase Japan **57** 34.04N136.12E
Owatonna U.S.A. **110** 44.06N 93.10W
Owbeh Afghan. **62** 34.22N 63.10E
Owego U.S.A. **115** 42.06N 76.16W
Owel, Lough Rep. of Ire. **15** 53.34N 7.24W
Owen Channel Canada **104** 45.31N 81.48W
Owen Falls Dam Uganda **79** 0.30N 33.07E
Owensboro U.S.A. **113** 37.46N 87.07W
Owen Sd. *b.* Canada **104** 44.40N 80.55W
Owens L. U.S.A. **109** 36.25N117.56W
Owen Sound *town* Canada **104** 44.34N 80.56W
Owen Stanley Range *mts.* P.N.G. **90** 9.30S148.00E
Owerri Nigeria **77** 5.29N 7.02E
Owl *r.* Canada **101** 57.51N 92.44W
Owo Nigeria **77** 7.10N 5.39E
Owosso U.S.A. **104** 43.00N 84.10W
Owyhee *r.* U.S.A. **108** 43.46N117.02W
Oxelösund Sweden **43** 58.40N 17.06E
Oxford U.K. **13** 51.45N 1.15W
Oxford Md. U.S.A. **115** 38.42N 76.10W
Oxford Mich. U.S.A. **104** 42.49N 83.16W
Oxford Penn. U.S.A. **115** 39.47N 75.59W
Oxfordshire *d.* U.K. **13** 51.46N 1.10W
Oxley Australia **92** 34.11S144.10E
Oxnard U.S.A. **109** 34.12N119.11W
Oxtongue Lake *town* Canada **104** 45.22N 78.55W
Oyapock *r.* Guiana **123** 4.10N 51.40W
Oyem Gabon **78** 1.34N 11.31E
Oyen Canada **101** 51.22N110.28W
Øyer Norway **41** 61.12N 10.22E
Øyeren *l.* Norway **42** 59.48N 11.14E
Oykel *r.* U.K. **14** 57.53N 4.21W
Oymyakon U.S.S.R. **51** 63.30N142.44E
Oyo Nigeria **77** 7.50N 3.55E
Oyo *d.* Nigeria **77** 8.10N 3.40E
Oyonnax France **21** 46.15N 5.40E
Ozamiz Phil. **59** 8.09N123.59E
Ozarichi U.S.S.R. **37** 52.28N 29.12E
Ozark Ala. U.S.A. **113** 31.27N 85.40W
Ozark Ark. U.S.A. **111** 35.29N 93.50W
Ozark Mo. U.S.A. **111** 37.01N 93.12W
Ozark Plateau U.S.A. **111** 37.00N 93.00W
Ózd Hungary **37** 48.14N 20.18E
Ozernoye U.S.S.R. **44** 51.45N 51.29E
Ozersk U.S.S.R. **37** 54.26N 22.00E
Ozieri Italy **32** 40.35N 9.00E
Ozinki U.S.S.R. **45** 51.11N 49.43E
Ozona U.S.A. **111** 30.43N101.12W

P

Paamiut *see* Frederikshåb Greenland **99**
Pa-an Burma **56** 16.51N 97.37E
Paarl R.S.A. **80** 33.44S 18.58E
Pabianice Poland **37** 51.40N 19.22E
Pābna Bangla. **63** 24.00N 89.15E
Pacaraima, Sierra *mts.* Venezuela **122** 4.00N 62.30W
Pacasmayo Peru **122** 7.27S 79.33W
Pachino Italy **33** 36.42N 15.06E
Pachmarhi India **63** 22.28N 78.26E
Pāchora India **62** 20.40N 75.21E
Pachuca Mexico **116** 20.10N 98.44W
Pacific-Antarctic Basin Pacific Oc. **85** 58.00S 98.00W
Pacific-Antarctic Ridge Pacific Oc. **85** 57.00S145.00W
Pacific Ocean 85
Pacitan Indonesia **59** 8.12S111.05E
Packsaddle Australia **92** 30.28S141.28E
Packwood U.S.A. **108** 46.36N121.40W
Pacy-sur-Eure France **18** 49.01N 1.23E
Padam Jammu & Kashmir **62** 33.28N 76.53E
Padampur India **63** 20.59N 83.04E
Padang Indonesia **58** 0.55S100.21E
Padangpanjang Indonesia **58** 0.30S100.26E
Padangsidempuan Indonesia **58** 1.20N 99.11E
Padany U.S.S.R. **44** 63.12N 33.20E
Padauari *r.* Brazil **122** 0.15S 64.05W
Paden City U.S.A. **114** 39.36N 80.56W
Paderborn Germany **38** 51.43N 8.45E
Padilla Bolivia **124** 19.19S 64.20W
Padlei Canada **101** 62.10N 97.05W
Padloping Island *town* Canada **99** 67.00N 62.50W
Padova Italy **32** 45.25N 11.53E
Pādra India **62** 22.14N 73.05E
Padrauna India **63** 26.55N 83.59E
Padre I. U.S.A. **111** 27.00N 97.15W
Padrón Spain **26** 42.44N 8.40W
Padstow U.K. **13** 50.33N 4.57W
Padthaway Australia **92** 36.37S140.28E
Padua *see* Padova Italy **32**
Paducah U.S.A. **111** 37.05N 88.36W
Paeroa New Zealand **86** 37.23S175.41E
Paestum *site* Italy **33** 40.25N 15.00E
Pafúri Mozambique **81** 22.27S 31.21E
Pag Yugo. **31** 44.27N 15.04E
Pag *i.* Yugo. **31** 44.30N 15.00E
Pagadian Phil. **59** 7.50N123.30E
Pagai Selatan *i.* Indonesia **58** 3.00S100.18E
Pagai Utara *i.* Indonesia **58** 2.42S100.05E
Pagan Burma **56** 21.07N 94.53E
Pagasitikós Kólpos *b.* Greece **35** 39.15N 23.12E
Page U.S.A. **108** 36.57N111.27W
Pager *r.* Uganda **79** 3.05N 32.28E
Paget Canada **104** 46.18N 80.48W
Paghmān Afghan. **62** 34.36N 68.57E
Pago Pago Samoa **84** 14.16S170.42W
Pagosa Springs *town* U.S.A. **108** 37.16N107.01W
Pagri China **63** 27.45N 89.10E
Paguchi L. Canada **102** 49.38N 91.40W
Pagwa River *town* Canada **102** 50.02N 85.14W
Pahala Hawaii U.S.A. **106** 19.12N155.28W
Pahiatua New Zealand **86** 40.26S175.49E
Paible U.K. **14** 57.35N 7.27W
Paide U.S.S.R. **41** 58.54N 25.33E
Paihia New Zealand **86** 35.16S174.05E
Päijänne *l.* Finland **41** 61.35N 25.30E
Paikü Co *l.* China **63** 28.48N 85.36E
Paimboeuf France **18** 47.17N 2.02W
Paimpol France **18** 48.46N 3.03W
Painan Indonesia **58** 1.21S100.34E
Painesville U.S.A. **114** 41.43N 81.15W
Pains Brazil **126** 20.23S 45.38W
Paintsville U.S.A. **113** 37.49N 82.48W
Paisley Canada **104** 44.18N 81.16W
Paisley U.K. **14** 55.50N 4.26W
País Vasco *d.* Spain **26** 43.00N 2.25W
Paiton Indonesia **59** 7.42S113.30E
Pajala Sweden **40** 67.11N 23.22E
Pajares, Puerto de *pass* Spain **26** 43.00N 5.46W
Pajule Uganda **79** 2.58N 32.53E
Pakaraima Mts. Guyana **122** 5.00N 60.00W
Pakaur India **63** 24.38N 87.51E
Pakenham Canada **105** 45.20N 76.17W
Paki Nigeria **77** 11.33N 8.08E
Pakistan Asia **62** 29.00N 67.00E
Pakokku Burma **56** 21.20N 95.10E
Pākpattan Pakistan **62** 30.21N 73.24E
Paks Hungary **31** 46.39N 18.53E
Paktīā *d.* Afghan. **62** 33.25N 69.30E
Pakwach Uganda **79** 2.27N 31.18E
Pakxé Laos **56** 15.07N105.47E
Pala Chad **77** 9.25N 15.05E
Palagonia Italy **33** 37.19N 14.45E
Palaiá Epídhavros Greece **35** 37.38N 23.09E
Palaia Kórinthos *site* Greece **35** 37.54N 22.56E
Palaiá Psará Greece **35** 38.46N 25.36E
Palaiokhóra Greece **35** 35.14N 23.41E
Páliros Greece **35** 38.45N 20.51E
Palaiseau France **19** 48.43N 2.15E
Palamás Greece **34** 39.26N 22.04E
Palamós Spain **25** 41.51N 3.08E
Palana U.S.S.R. **51** 59.05N159.59E
Palangkaraya Indonesia **58** 2.16S113.56E
Palanguinos Spain **24** 42.27N 5.31W
Pālanpur India **62** 24.10N 72.26E
Palanquinos Spain **26** 42.27N 5.30W
Palapye Botswana **80** 22.33S 27.07E
Palas del Rey Spain **26** 42.52N 7.52W
Palatka U.S.A. **113** 29.38N 81.40W
Palaw Burma **56** 12.58N 98.39E
Palawan *i.* Phil. **58** 9.30N118.30E
Palazzolo Acreide Italy **33** 37.03N 14.54E
Palazzo San Gervasio Italy **33** 40.56N 16.00E
Paldiski U.S.S.R. **41** 59.20N 24.06E
Paleleh Indonesia **59** 1.04N121.57E
Palembang Indonesia **58** 2.59S104.50E
Palena Italy **33** 41.59N 14.08E
Palencia Spain **26** 42.01N 4.32W
Palencia *d.* Spain **26** 42.30N 4.40W
Palenque Mexico **116** 17.32N 91.59W
Palermo Italy **32** 38.07N 13.21E
Palermo, Golfo di *g.* Italy **32** 38.10N 13.30E
Palestine U.S.A. **111** 31.46N 95.38W
Palestrina Italy **32** 41.50N 12.53E
Paletwa Burma **56** 21.25N 92.49E
Pāli India **62** 25.46N 73.20E
Palimé Togo **76** 6.55N 0.38E
Palinges France **19** 46.33N 4.13E
Palisades Resr. U.S.A. **108** 43.15N111.05W
Pālitāna India **62** 21.31N 71.50E
Palizada Mexico **116** 18.15N 92.05W
Palk Str. India / Sri Lanka **61** 10.00N 79.40E
Pallës, Bishti i *c.* Albania **34** 41.24N 19.24E
Pallinup *r.* Australia **89** 34.29S118.54E
Palliser, C. New Zealand **86** 41.35S175.15E
Pallu India **62** 28.56N 74.13E
Palma Mozambique **79** 10.48S 40.25E
Palma Spain **25** 39.34N 2.39E
Palma, Bahía de *b.* Spain **25** 39.27N 2.35E
Palma del Río Spain **27** 37.42N 5.17W
Palma di Montechiaro Italy **32** 37.11N 13.46E
Palmahim Israel **67** 31.56N 34.42E
Palmanova Italy **30** 45.54N 13.19E
Palmares Brazil **123** 8.41S 35.36W
Palmas, C. Liberia **76** 4.30N 7.55W
Palmas, Golfo di *g.* Italy **32** 39.00N 8.30E
Palm Beach *town* U.S.A. **113** 26.41N 80.02W
Palmeira dos Indios Brazil **123** 9.25S 36.38W
Palmeirinhas, Punta das Angola **78** 9.09S 12.58E
Palmer *r.* Australia **88** 24.46S133.25E
Palmer U.S.A. **98** 61.36N149.07W
Palmer Land Antarctica **128** 74.00S 61.00W
Palmerston Canada **104** 43.50N 80.51W
Palmerston New Zealand **86** 45.29S170.43E
Palmerston, C. Australia **90** 21.32S149.29E
Palmerston Atoll Cook Is. **84** 18.04S163.10W
Palmerston North New Zealand **86** 40.20S175.39E
Palmerton U.S.A. **115** 40.48N 75.37W
Palmetto U.S.A. **113** 27.31N 82.32W
Palmi Italy **33** 38.21N 15.51E
Palmira Colombia **122** 3.33N 76.17W
Palm Is. Australia **90** 18.48S146.37E
Palms U.S.A. **114** 43.37N 82.46W
Palm Springs *town* U.S.A. **109** 33.50N116.33W
Palmyra I. Pacific Oc. **84** 5.52N162.05W
Palmyras Pt. India **63** 20.46N 87.02E
Paloh Indonesia **58** 1.46N109.17E
Paloich Sudan **73** 10.28N 32.32E
Palojoensuu Finland **40** 68.17N 23.05E
Palomani *mtn.* Bolivia **124** 14.38S 69.14W
Palopo Indonesia **59** 3.01S120.12E
Palos, Cabo de *c.* Spain **25** 37.38N 0.41W
Pålsboda Sweden **43** 59.04N 15.20E
Palu Turkey **64** 38.43N 39.56E
Palwal India **62** 28.09N 77.20E
Pama Burkina **76** 11.15N 0.44E
Pamanukan Indonesia **59** 6.16S107.46E
Pamekasan Indonesia **59** 7.11S113.30E
Pameungpeuk Indonesia **59** 7.39S107.40E
Pamiers France **20** 43.07N 1.36E
Pamir *mts.* U.S.S.R. **52** 37.50N 73.30E
Pamlico Sd. U.S.A. **113** 35.20N 75.55W
Pampa U.S.A. **111** 35.32N100.58W
Pampas *f.* Argentina **125** 34.00S 64.00W
Pamplona Colombia **122** 7.24N 72.38W
Pamplona Spain **25** 42.49N 1.38W
Pana U.S.A. **110** 39.23N 89.05W
Panaca U.S.A. **108** 37.47N114.23W
Panache, L. Canada **104** 46.15N 81.20W
Panagyurishte Bulgaria **34** 42.39N 24.15E
Panaji India **60** 15.29N 73.50E
Panama C. America **117** 9.00N 80.00W
Panamá *town* Panama **117** 8.57N 79.30W
Panama Sri Lanka **61** 6.46N 81.47E
Panamá, Golfo de *g.* Panama **117** 8.30N 79.00W
Panama City U.S.A. **113** 30.10N 85.41W
Panamint Range *mts.* U.S.A. **109** 36.30N117.20W
Panarea, Isola *i.* Italy **33** 38.38N 15.05E
Panaro *r.* Italy **30** 44.55N 11.25E
Panay *i.* Phil. **59** 11.10N122.30E
Panayía Greece **34** 39.56N 25.20E
Pandan Phil. **59** 11.45N122.10E
Pandaria India **63** 22.14N 81.25E
Pandeglang Indonesia **59** 6.19S106.05E
Pāndharkawada India **63** 20.01N 78.32E
Pāndhurna India **63** 21.36N 78.31E
Pando *d.* Bolivia **124** 11.20S 67.40W
Pando Uruguay **125** 34.43S 55.57W
Panevežys U.S.S.R. **41** 55.44N 24.21E
Panfilov U.S.S.R. **52** 44.10N 80.01E
Panga Zaïre **78** 1.51N 26.25E
Pangaíon Óros *mts.* Greece **34** 40.50N 24.00E
Pangandaran Indonesia **59** 7.41S108.40E
Pangani Tanga Tanzania **79** 5.21S 39.00E
Pangi Zaïre **78** 3.10S 26.38E
Pangkalpinang Indonesia **58** 2.05S106.09E
Pang Long Burma **61** 23.11N 98.45E
Pangnirtung Canada **99** 66.05N 65.45W
Pānīpat India **62** 29.23N 76.58E
Panjāb Afghan. **62** 34.22N 67.01E
Panjgūr Pakistan **62** 26.58N 64.06E
Panjpāi Pakistan **62** 29.55N 66.30E
Pankshin Nigeria **77** 9.22N 9.25E
Panna India **63** 24.43N 80.12E
Pannawonica Australia **88** 21.42S116.22E
Páno Lévkara Cyprus **66** 34.55N 33.10E
Páno Plátres Cyprus **66** 34.53N 32.52E
Pánormos Greece **35** 37.38N 25.02E
Panshan China **54** 41.10N122.01E
Pantano del Esla *l.* Spain **24** 41.40N 5.50W
Pantelleria Italy **32** 36.49N 11.57E
Pantelleria *i.* Italy **32** 36.47N 12.00E
Panton *r.* Australia **88** 17.05S128.46E
Pánuco Mexico **116** 22.03N 98.10W
Panvel India **62** 18.59N 73.06E
Pan Xian China **55** 25.46N104.39E
Panyu China **55** 23.00N113.30E
Paola Italy **33** 39.22N 16.03E
Paola U.S.A. **110** 38.35N 94.53W
Paoua C.A.R. **77** 7.09N 16.20E
Paôy Pêt Thailand **56** 13.41N102.34E
Papa Hawaiian Is. **85** 19.12N155.53W
Pápa Hungary **37** 47.19N 17.28E
Papa Stour *i.* U.K. **10** 60.20N 1.42W
Papa Westray *i.* U.K. **10** 59.22N 2.54W
Papeete Tahiti **85** 17.32S149.34W
Papenburg Germany **38** 53.05N 7.23E
Papenoo Tahiti **85** 17.30S149.25W
Papetoai Ïs. de la Société **85** 17.29S149.52W
Paphos *see* Néa Páfos Cyprus **66**
Papigochic *r.* Mexico **109** 29.09N109.40W
Papillion U.S.A. **110** 41.09N 96.04W
Papineau, Lac *l.* Canada **105** 45.48N 74.46W
Papineau Prov. Park Canada **105** 45.55N 75.20W
Papineauville Canada **105** 45.37N 75.01W
Papua, G. of P.N.G. **90** 8.30S145.00E
Papua New Guinea Austa. **87** 6.00S144.00E
Papun Burma **56** 18.05N 97.26E
Papunya Australia **90** 23.15S131.53E
Para *d.* Brazil **123** 4.00S 53.00W
Paraburdoo Australia **88** 23.12S117.40E
Paracatu Brazil **126** 17.14S 46.52W
Paracatu *r.* Brazil **126** 16.30S 45.10W
Paracel Is. S. China Sea **58** 16.20N112.00E
Parachilna Australia **92** 31.09S138.24E

Pārachinār to **Perryville**

Pārachinār Pakistan **62** 33.54N 70.06E
Paraćin Yugo. **34** 43.52N 21.24E
Pará de Minas Brazil **126** 19.53S 44.35W
Paradip India **63** 20.15N 86.35E
Paradise *r.* Canada **103** 53.23N 57.18W
Paradise Calif. U.S.A. **108** 39.46N121.37W
Paradise Nev. U.S.A. **109** 36.09N115.10W
Paragonah U.S.A. **108** 37.53N112.46W
Paragould U.S.A. **111** 36.03N 90.29W
Paragua *r.* Venezuela **122** 6.55N 62.55W
Paraguaçu *r.* Brazil **123** 12.35S 38.59W
Paraguaná, Península de *pen.* Venezuela **122** 11.50N 69.59W
Paraguarí Paraguay **126** 25.36S 57.06W
Paraguay *r.* Argentina **126** 27.30S 58.50W
Paraguay S. America **126** 23.00S 57.00W
Paraíba *d.* Brazil **123** 7.30S 36.30W
Paraíba *r.* Brazil **126** 21.45S 41.10W
Paraibuna Brazil **126** 23.29S 45.32W
Paraisópolis Brazil **126** 22.33S 45.48W
Parakou Benin **77** 9.23N 2.40E
Parálion Astrous Greece **35** 37.25N 22.45E
Paramagudi India **61** 9.33N 78.36E
Paramaribo Surinam **123** 5.52N 55.14W
Paramithiá Greece **34** 39.30N 20.35E
Paramonga Peru **122** 10.42S 77.50W
Paraná Argentina **125** 31.45S 60.30W
Paraná *r.* Argentina **125** 34.00S 58.30W
Paranã Brazil **123** 12.33S 47.48W
Paraná *d.* Brazil **126** 24.30S 52.00W
Paranã *r.* Brazil **123** 12.30S 48.10W
Paranaguá Brazil **126** 25.32S 48.36W
Paranaíba Brazil **126** 19.44S 51.12W
Paranaíba *r.* Brazil **126** 20.00S 51.00W
Paranapanema *r.* Brazil **126** 22.30S 53.03W
Paranapiacaba, Serra *mts.* Brazil **126** 24.30S 49.15W
Paranavaí Brazil **126** 23.02S 52.36W
Paranéstion Greece **34** 41.16N 24.32E
Parangaba Brazil **123** 3.45S 38.33W
Paraparaumu New Zealand **86** 40.55S175.00E
Paratoo Australia **92** 32.46S139.40E
Paray-le-Monial France **19** 46.27N 4.07E
Pārbati *r.* India **62** 25.51N 76.36E
Pārbatipur Bangla. **63** 25.39N 88.55E
Parbhani India **62** 19.16N 76.47E
Parchim Germany **38** 53.25N 11.51E
Parczew Poland **37** 51.39N 22.54E
Pardes Hanna Israel **67** 32.28N 34.58E
Pārdi India **62** 20.31N 72.57E
Pardo *r.* Bahia Brazil **126** 15.40S 39.38W
Pardo *r.* Mato Grosso Brazil **126** 21.56S 52.07W
Pardo *r.* São Paulo Brazil **126** 20.10S 48.36W
Pardubice Czech. **36** 50.03N 15.45E
Parecis, Serra dos *mts.* Brazil **122** 13.30S 58.30W
Paredes de Nava Spain **26** 42.09N 4.41W
Pareloup, Lac de *l.* France **20** 44.15N 2.45E
Parent Canada **102** 47.55N 74.35W
Parent, Lac *l.* Canada **102** 48.40N 77.03W
Parentis-en-Born France **20** 44.21N 1.05W
Parepare Indonesia **58** 4.03S119.40E
Párga Greece **35** 39.17N 20.23E
Pargas Finland **41** 60.18N 22.18E
Paria, Golfo de *g.* Venezuela **122** 10.30S 62.00W
Paria, Península de *pen.* Venezuela **122** 10.45N 62.30W
Pariaguán Venezuela **122** 8.51N 64.43W
Pariaman Indonesia **58** 0.36S100.09E
Parichi U.S.S.R. **37** 52.48N 29.25E
Parigi Indonesia **59** 0.49S120.10E
Parika Guyana **122** 6.51N 58.25W
Parima, Sierra *mts.* Venezuela **122** 2.30N 64.00W
Parinari Peru **122** 4.35S 74.25W
Paringa Australia **92** 34.10S140.49E
Parintins Brazil **123** 2.36S 56.44W
Paris Canada **104** 43.12N 80.23W
Paris France **19** 48.52N 2.20E
Paris Kiribati **85** 1.56N157.29W
Paris Ill. U.S.A. **110** 39.35N 87.41W
Paris Ky. U.S.A. **112** 38.13N 84.15W
Paris Tenn. U.S.A. **111** 36.19N 88.20W
Paris Tex. U.S.A. **111** 33.40N 95.33W
Parish U.S.A. **115** 43.24N 76.08W
Parisienne *d.* France **19** 48.30N 2.30E
Parisienne, Île *i.* Canada **104** 46.40N 84.44W
Parkano Finland **41** 62.01N 23.01E
Parkbeg Canada **101** 50.28N106.18W
Parker Ariz. U.S.A. **109** 34.09N114.17W
Parker Penn. U.S.A. **114** 41.06N 79.41W
Parker, C. Canada **99** 75.04N 79.40W
Parker Dam U.S.A. **109** 34.18N114.10W
Parkersburg U.S.A. **114** 39.17N 81.32W
Parkes Australia **93** 33.10S148.13E
Park Falls *town* U.S.A. **110** 45.56N 90.32W
Park Forest *town* U.S.A. **110** 41.35N 87.41W
Parkhill Canada **104** 43.09N 81.41W
Parkland U.S.A. **108** 47.09N122.26W
Park Range *mts.* U.S.A. **108** 40.00N106.30W
Parkton U.S.A. **115** 39.38N 76.40W
Parlākimidi India **63** 18.46N 84.05E
Parma Italy **30** 44.48N 10.20E
Parma *r.* Italy **30** 44.56N 10.26E
Parma U.S.A. **114** 41.22N 81.43W
Parnaguá Brazil **123** 10.17S 44.39W
Parnaíba Brazil **123** 2.58S 41.46W
Parnaíba *r.* Brazil **123** 2.58S 41.47W
Parnassós *mtn.* Greece **35** 38.17N 21.30E
Parndana Australia **92** 35.44S137.14E
Párnis *mtn.* Greece **35** 38.11N 23.42E
Párnon Óros *mts.* Greece **35** 37.18N 22.35E
Pärnu U.S.S.R. **41** 58.24N 24.32E
Pärnu *r.* U.S.S.R. **41** 58.23N 24.29E
Pārola India **62** 20.53N 75.07E
Paroo *r.* Australia **92** 31.30S143.34E
Páros Greece **35** 37.04N 25.06E
Páros *i.* Greece **35** 37.08N 25.12E
Parrakie Australia **92** 35.18S140.12E
Parral Chile **125** 36.09S 71.50W
Parramatta Australia **93** 33.50S150.57E
Parras Mexico **111** 25.30N102.11W
Parras, Sierra de *mts.* Mexico **111** 25.20N102.10W
Parrett *r.* U.K. **13** 51.10N 3.00W
Parry Canada **101** 49.47N104.41W
Parry, C. Greenland **99** 76.50N 71.00W
Parry I. Canada **104** 45.18N 80.10W
Parry Is. Canada **99** 76.00N102.00W
Parry Sound *town* Canada **104** 45.21N 80.02W
Parsad India **62** 24.11N 73.42E
Parsęta *r.* Poland **36** 54.12N 15.33E
Parsnip *r.* Canada **100** 55.10N123.02W
Parsons Kans. U.S.A. **111** 37.20N 95.16W
Parsons W.Va. U.S.A. **114** 39.06N 79.41W
Partanna Italy **32** 37.43N 12.53E
Parthenay France **18** 46.39N 0.15W
Partille Sweden **43** 57.44N 12.07E
Partinico Italy **32** 38.03N 13.07E
Partry Mts. Rep. of Ire. **15** 53.40N 9.30W
Paru *r.* Brazil **123** 1.33S 52.38W
Pārvatīpuram India **63** 18.47N 83.26E
Paryang China **63** 30.04N 83.28E
Parys R.S.A. **80** 26.54S 27.26E
Pasadena Calif. U.S.A. **109** 34.09N118.09W
Pasadena Tex. U.S.A. **111** 29.42N 95.13W
Pasaje Ecuador **122** 3.23S 79.50W
Pasawng Burma **56** 18.52N 97.18E
Pasay Phil. **59** 14.33N121.00E
Pascagoula U.S.A. **111** 30.23N 88.31W
Paşcani Romania **37** 47.15N 26.44E
Pasco U.S.A. **108** 46.14N119.06W
Pascoag U.S.A. **115** 41.57N 71.42W
Pascua, Isla de *i.* Pacific Oc. **85** 27.08S109.23W
Pas-de-Calais *d.* France **19** 50.30N 2.20E
Pasewalk Germany **38** 53.30N 14.00E
Pasfield L. Canada **101** 58.25N105.20W
Pasinler Turkey **64** 39.59N 41.41E
Pasir Puteh Malaysia **58** 5.50N102.24E
Påskallavik Sweden **43** 57.10N 16.27E
Pasley, C. Australia **89** 33.55S123.30E
Pašman *i.* Yugo. **31** 43.58N 15.21E
Pasmore *r.* Australia **92** 31.07S139.48E
Pasni Pakistan **62** 25.16N 63.28E
Paso de Bermejo *f.* Argentina **121** 32.50S 70.00W
Paso de los Libres *town* Argentina **125** 29.45S 57.05W
Paso de los Toros *town* Uruguay **125** 32.49S 56.31W
Paso Robles U.S.A. **109** 35.38N120.41W
Paso Socompa *f.* Chile **121** 24.27S 68.18W
Paspébiac Canada **103** 48.01N 65.20W
Pasquia Hills Canada **101** 53.13N102.37W
Pasrūr Pakistan **62** 32.16N 74.40E
Passaic U.S.A. **115** 40.51N 74.08W
Passau Germany **39** 48.35N 13.28E
Passero, Capo *c.* Italy **33** 36.40N 15.09E
Passo Fundo Brazil **126** 28.16S 52.20W
Passos Brazil **126** 20.45S 46.38W
Pastaza *r.* Peru **122** 4.50S 76.25W
Pasto Colombia **122** 1.12N 77.17W
Pastrana Spain **26** 40.25N 2.55W
Pasuquin Phil. **55** 18.25N120.37E
Pasuruan Indonesia **59** 7.38S112.54E
Patagonia *f.* Argentina **125** 42.20S 67.00W
Pātan India **62** 23.50N 72.07E
Patchewollock Australia **92** 35.25S142.14E
Patchogue U.S.A. **115** 40.46N 73.00W
Patea New Zealand **86** 39.46S174.29E
Pategi Nigeria **77** 8.44N 5.47E
Pate I. Kenya **79** 2.08S 41.02E
Paterna Spain **25** 39.30N 0.26W
Paternion Austria **39** 46.43N 13.38E
Paternò Italy **33** 37.34N 14.54E
Paterson U.S.A. **115** 40.55N 74.10W
Pathānkot India **62** 32.17N 75.39E
Pathfinder Resr. U.S.A. **108** 42.30N106.50W
Pathiong Sudan **73** 6.46N 30.54E
Pati Indonesia **59** 6.45S111.00E
Patía *r.* Colombia **122** 1.54N 78.30W
Patiāla India **62** 30.19N 76.23E
Pati Pt. Guam **84** 13.36N144.57E
Patkai Hills Burma **56** 26.30N 95.30E
Pátmos *i.* Greece **35** 37.20N 26.33E
Patna India **63** 25.36N 85.07E
Patnāgarh India **63** 20.43N 83.09E
Patos Brazil **123** 6.55S 37.15W
Patos, Lagoa dos *l.* Brazil **126** 31.00S 51.10W
Patos de Minas Brazil **126** 18.35S 46.32W
Patquía Argentina **124** 30.02S 66.55W
Pátrai Greece **35** 38.15N 21.44E
Patraïkós Kólpos *g.* Greece **35** 38.14N 21.15E
Patrasuy U.S.S.R. **44** 63.35N 61.50E
Patrickswell Rep. of Ire. **15** 52.36N 8.43W
Pattada Italy **32** 40.35N 9.07E
Pattani Thailand **56** 6.51N101.16E
Pattaya Thailand **56** 12.57N100.53E
Patterson Creek *r.* U.S.A. **114** 39.34N 78.23W
Patti Italy **33** 38.09N 14.58E
Patti, Golfo di *g.* Italy **33** 38.12N 15.05E
Pattoki Pakistan **62** 31.01N 73.51E
Patton U.S.A. **114** 40.38N 78.39W
Patuākhāli Bangla. **63** 22.21N 90.21E
Patuca *r.* Honduras **117** 15.50N 84.18W
Pātūr India **62** 20.27N 76.56E
Patuxent *r.* U.S.A. **115** 38.18N 76.25W
Pau France **20** 43.18N 0.22W
Pau, Gave de *r.* France **20** 43.33N 1.12W
Pauillac France **20** 45.12N 0.44W
Paúl do Mar Madeira Is. **127** 32.45N 17.14W
Paulhan France **20** 43.32N 3.27E
Paulina U.S.A. **108** 44.09N119.58W
Paulistana Brazil **123** 8.09S 41.09W
Paulo Afonso Brazil **123** 9.25S 38.15W
Paulsboro U.S.A. **115** 39.50N 75.15W
Pauls Valley *town* U.S.A. **111** 34.44N 97.13W
Paungde Burma **56** 18.30N 95.30E
Pauni India **63** 20.47N 79.38E
Pauri Madhya P. India **62** 25.32N 77.21E
Pauri Uttar P. India **63** 30.09N 78.47E
Pavia Italy **30** 45.10N 9.10E
Pavilly France **18** 49.34N 0.58E
Pavlikeni Bulgaria **34** 43.14N 25.20E
Pavlodar U.S.S.R. **9** 52.21N 76.59E
Pavlograd U.S.S.R. **45** 48.34N 35.50E
Pavlovo U.S.S.R. **44** 55.58N 43.05E
Pavlovsk U.S.S.R. **45** 50.28N 40.07E
Pavlovskaya U.S.S.R. **45** 46.18N 39.48E
Pavullo nel Frignano Italy **30** 44.20N 10.50E
Pawnee U.S.A. **111** 36.20N 96.48W
Pawtucket U.S.A. **115** 41.53N 71.23W
Paxoí *i.* Greece **35** 39.14N 20.12E
Paxton U.S.A. **110** 41.07N101.21W
Payerne Switz. **39** 46.49N 6.56E
Payette U.S.A. **108** 44.05N116.56W
Payne, L. Canada **99** 59.25N 74.00W
Paynes Find Australia **89** 29.15S117.41E
Paysandú Uruguay **125** 32.19S 58.05W
Pays de Caux *f.* France **18** 49.40N 0.40E
Pays de la Loire *d.* France **18** 47.30N 1.00W
Pazardzhik Bulgaria **34** 42.12N 24.20E
Pazin Yugo. **31** 45.14N 13.56E
Pčinja *r.* Yugo. **34** 42.00N 21.45E
Peace *r.* Canada **100** 59.00N111.25W
Peace River *town* Canada **100** 56.15N117.18W
Peach Springs *town* U.S.A. **109** 35.32N113.25W
Peacock Hills Canada **98** 66.05N110.45W
Peak, The *mtn.* Ascension **127** 7.57S 14.21W
Peake Creek *r.* Australia **92** 28.05S136.07E
Peak Hill *town* N.S.W. Australia **93** 32.47S148.13E
Peak Range *mts.* Australia **90** 23.18S148.30E
Peale, Mt. U.S.A. **108** 38.26N109.14W
Pearl *r.* U.S.A. **111** 30.11N 89.32W
Pearland U.S.A. **111** 29.34N 95.17W
Pearsall U.S.A. **111** 28.53N 99.06W
Peary Land *f.* Greenland **96** 83.00N 35.00W
Pebane Mozambique **81** 17.14S 38.10E
Pebas Peru **122** 3.17S 71.55W
Peć Yugo. **34** 42.40N 20.17E
Pechenga U.S.S.R. **40** 69.28N 31.04E
Pechora U.S.S.R. **44** 65.14N 57.18E
Pechora *r.* U.S.S.R. **44** 68.10N 54.00E
Pechorskaya Guba *g.* U.S.S.R. **44** 69.00N 56.00E
Pechorskoye More *sea* U.S.S.R. **44** 69.00N 55.00E
Pecoraro, Monte *mtn.* Italy **33** 38.32N 16.20E
Pecos U.S.A. **111** 31.25N103.30W
Pecos *r.* U.S.A. **111** 29.42N101.22W
Pécs Hungary **31** 46.05N 18.13E
Pécs *d.* Hungary **31** 46.05N 18.10E
Peddie R.S.A. **80** 33.12S 27.07E
Pedras Salgadas Portugal **26** 41.32N 7.36W
Pedregulho Brazil **126** 20.15S 47.29W
Pedreiras Brazil **123** 4.32S 44.40W
Pedrinhas Brazil **123** 11.12S 37.41W
Pedro Afonso Brazil **123** 8.59S 48.11W
Pedro de Valdivia Chile **124** 22.36S 69.40W
Pedrógão Grande Portugal **27** 39.55N 8.09W
Pedro Juan Caballero Paraguay **126** 22.30S 55.44W
Pedro Muñoz Spain **27** 39.24N 2.58W
Peduyim Israel **67** 31.20N 34.37E
Peebinga Australia **92** 34.55S140.57E
Peebles U.K. **14** 55.39N 3.12W
Peebles U.S.A. **112** 38.57N 83.14W
Peekskill U.S.A. **115** 41.17N 73.55W
Peel *r.* Canada **98** 68.13N135.00W
Peel U.K. **12** 54.14N 4.42W
Peel Inlet Australia **89** 32.35S115.44E
Peel Pt. Canada **98** 73.22N114.35W
Peene *r.* Germany **38** 54.09N 13.46E
Peera Peera Poolanna L. Australia **90** 26.43S137.42E
Peerless L. Canada **100** 56.37N114.35W
Pegasus B. New Zealand **86** 43.15S173.00E
Pegin Albania **34** 41.04N 19.44E
Pegnitz Germany **38** 49.45N 11.33E
Pegnitz *r.* Germany **38** 49.29N 11.00E
Pego Spain **25** 38.51N 0.07W
Pegu Burma **56** 17.20N 96.36E
Pegu *d.* Burma **56** 17.30N 96.30E
Pegunungan Van Rees *mts.* Indonesia **59** 2.35S138.15E
Pegu Yoma *mts.* Burma **56** 18.30N 96.00E
Pehčevo Yugo. **34** 41.41N 23.03E
Pehuajó Argentina **125** 35.50S 61.50W
Peikang Taiwan **55** 23.35N120.19E
Peine Germany **38** 52.19N 10.13E
Peissenberg Germany **39** 47.48N 11.04E
Peixe Brazil **123** 12.03S 48.32W
Pei Xian China **54** 34.44N116.55E
Pekalongan Indonesia **59** 6.54S109.37E
Pekanbaru Indonesia **58** 0.33N101.20E
Pekin U.S.A. **110** 40.34N 89.40W
Peking *see* Beijing China **54**
Pelabuanratu Indonesia **59** 7.00S106.32E
Pelat, Mont *mtn.* France **21** 44.16N 6.42E
Peleaga *mtn.* Romania **37** 45.22N 22.54E
Pelee, Pt. Canada **114** 41.54N 82.30W
Pelee I. Canada **114** 41.46N 82.39W
Peleng *i.* Indonesia **59** 1.30S123.10E
Peleniya U.S.S.R. **37** 47.58N 27.48E
Pelican U.S.A. **100** 57.55N136.10W
Pelister *mtn.* Yugo. **34** 41.00N 21.12E
Pelješac, Poluotok *pen.* Yugo. **31** 42.58N 17.20E
Pelkum Germany **38** 51.39N 7.45E
Pélla *site* Greece **34** 40.45N 22.33E
Pelleg i Drinit *b.* Albania **34** 41.45N 19.28E
Pellegrino, Cozzo *mtn.* Italy **33** 39.45N 16.03E
Pello Finland **40** 66.47N 24.00E
Pellston U.S.A. **104** 45.33N 84.47W
Pellworm *i.* Germany **38** 54.31N 8.38E
Pelly *r.* Canada **98** 62.50N137.35W
Pelly Bay *town* Canada **99** 68.38N 89.45W
Pelly L. Canada **99** 65.59N101.12W
Peloncillo Mts. U.S.A. **109** 32.16N109.00W
Pelopónnisos *f.* Greece **35** 37.30N 22.00E
Peloritani, Monti *mts.* Italy **33** 38.00N 15.25E
Pelotas Brazil **126** 31.45S 52.20W
Pelvoux, Massif du *f.* France **21** 44.55N 6.20E
Pemalang Indonesia **59** 6.53S109.21E
Pematangsiantar Indonesia **58** 2.59N 99.01E
Pemba Mozambique **81** 13.02S 40.30E
Pemba Zambia **79** 16.33S 27.20E
Pemba I. Tanzania **79** 5.10S 39.45E
Pemberton Australia **89** 34.28S116.01E
Pemberton Canada **100** 50.20N122.48W
Pembina *r.* Canada **100** 54.45N114.15W
Pembroke Canada **105** 45.49N 77.07W
Pembroke U.K. **13** 51.41N 4.57W
Pembroke U.S.A. **113** 32.09N 81.39W
Peña, Sierra de la *mts.* Spain **25** 42.30N 0.50W
Penacook U.S.A. **115** 43.17N 71.37W
Penafiel Portugal **26** 41.12N 8.17W
Peñafiel Spain **26** 41.36N 4.07W
Peñagolosa *mtn.* Spain **25** 40.13N 0.21W
Peñalara *mtn.* Spain **26** 40.51N 3.57W
Penang *see* Pinang, Pulau *i.* Malaysia **58**
Peñaranda de Bracamonte Spain **26** 40.54N 5.12W
Pen Argyl U.S.A. **115** 40.52N 75.16W
Peñarroya *mtn.* Spain **25** 40.24N 0.40W
Peñarroya-Pueblonuevo Spain **26** 38.18N 5.16W
Penarth U.K. **13** 51.26N 3.11W
Peñas, Cabo de *c.* Spain **26** 43.39N 5.51W
Penas, Golfo de *g.* Chile **125** 47.20S 75.00W
Pendálofon Greece **34** 40.14N 21.12E
Pende *r.* Chad **77** 7.30N 16.20E
Pendembu Eastern Sierra Leone **76** 8.09N 10.42W
Pendine U.K. **13** 51.44N 4.33W
Pendleton U.S.A. **108** 45.40N118.47W
Penedo Brazil **123** 10.16S 36.33W
Penedono Portugal **26** 40.59N 7.24W
Penela Portugal **27** 40.02N 8.23W
Penetanguishene Canada **104** 44.47N 79.55W
Penfield U.S.A. **114** 41.13N 78.34W
Penganga *r.* India **63** 19.53N 79.09E
Penge Zaïre **78** 5.31S 24.37E
Penghu Liedao *is.* Taiwan **55** 23.35N119.32E
Pengshui China **55** 29.17N108.13E
Peniche Portugal **27** 39.21N 9.23W
Penicuik U.K. **14** 55.49N 3.13W
Peninsular Malaysia *d.* Malaysia **58** 5.00N102.00E
Peñíscola Spain **25** 40.21N 0.25E
Penmarc'h, Pointe de *c.* France **18** 47.48N 4.22W
Penne Italy **31** 42.27N 13.55E
Penne-d'Agenais France **20** 44.23N 0.49E
Penneshaw Australia **92** 35.42S137.55E
Pennsauken U.S.A. **115** 39.58N 75.04W
Pennsboro U.S.A. **114** 39.17N 80.58W
Penns Grove U.S.A. **115** 39.43N 75.28W
Pennsylvania *d.* U.S.A. **114** 40.45N 77.30W
Penn Yan U.S.A. **114** 42.40N 77.03W
Penny Highland *mtn.* Canada **99** 67.10N 66.50W
Penobscot *r.* U.S.A. **112** 44.30N 68.50W
Penola Australia **92** 37.23S140.21E
Penong Australia **89** 31.55S133.01E
Penonomé Panama **117** 8.30N 80.20W
Penrhyn Atoll Cook Is. **85** 9.00S158.00W
Penrith Australia **93** 33.47S150.44E
Penrith U.K. **12** 54.40N 2.45W
Penryn U.K. **13** 50.10N 5.07W
Pensacola U.S.A. **113** 30.26N 87.12W
Pensacola Mts. Antarctica **128** 84.00S 45.00W
Penshurst Australia **92** 37.52S142.20E
Pentecost I. Vanuatu **84** 15.42S168.10E
Penticton Canada **100** 49.30N119.30W
Pentland Australia **90** 20.32S145.24E
Pentland Firth *str.* U.K. **14** 58.40N 3.00W
Pentland Hills U.K. **14** 55.50N 3.20W
Penylan L. Canada **101** 61.50N106.20W
Penza U.S.S.R. **44** 53.11N 45.00E
Penzance U.K. **13** 50.07N 5.32W
Penzberg Germany **39** 47.45N 11.23E
Penzhinskaya Guba *g.* U.S.S.R. **51** 61.00N163.00E
Peoria Ariz. U.S.A. **109** 33.35N112.14W
Peoria Ill. U.S.A. **110** 40.43N 89.38W
Pepacton Resr. U.S.A. **115** 42.06N 74.54W
Peper Sudan **73** 7.04N 33.00E
Pepperell U.S.A. **115** 42.40N 71.35W
Perabumulih Indonesia **58** 3.29S104.14E
Perales de Alfambra Spain **25** 40.38N 1.00W
Perche, Collines du *hills* France **18** 48.25N 0.40E
Percival Lakes Australia **88** 21.25S125.00E
Perdido, Monte *mtn.* Spain **25** 42.40N 0.05E
Pereira Colombia **122** 4.47N 75.46W
Perekop U.S.S.R. **45** 46.10N 33.42E
Perené *r.* Peru **124** 11.02S 74.19W
Perevolotskiy U.S.S.R. **44** 51.10N 54.15E
Pereyaslav-Khmelnitskiy U.S.S.R. **37** 50.05N 31.28E
Pergamino Argentina **125** 33.53S 60.35W
Pergine Valsugana Italy **30** 46.04N 11.14E
Pergola Italy **30** 43.34N 12.50E
Perham U.S.A. **110** 46.36N 95.34W
Péribonca *r.* Canada **103** 48.45N 72.05W
Pericos Mexico **109** 25.03N107.42W
Périers France **18** 49.11N 1.25W
Périgueux France **20** 45.11N 0.43E
Perija, Sierra de *mts.* Venezuela **122** 10.30N 72.30W
Peri L. Australia **92** 30.44S143.34E
Perleberg Germany **38** 53.04N 11.51E
Perm U.S.S.R. **44** 58.01N 56.10E
Përmet Albania **34** 40.15N 20.21E
Pernambuco *d.* Brazil **123** 8.00S 39.00W
Pernatty L. Australia **92** 31.31S137.14E
Pernik Bulgaria **34** 42.36N 23.02E
Perniö Finland **41** 60.12N 23.08E
Péronne France **19** 49.56N 2.56E
Perosa Argentina Italy **30** 44.58N 7.10E
Pérouse, Bahía la *b.* I. de Pascua **85** 27.04S109.20W
Perpendicular, Pt. Australia **93** 35.03S150.50E
Perpignan France **20** 42.41N 2.53E
Perranporth U.K. **13** 50.21N 5.09W
Perro, Punta del *c.* Spain **27** 36.45N 6.26W
Perros-Guirec France **18** 48.49N 3.27W
Perry Fla. U.S.A. **113** 30.08N 83.36W
Perry Iowa U.S.A. **110** 41.50N 94.06W
Perry Mich. U.S.A. **104** 42.50N 84.13W
Perry Okla. U.S.A. **111** 36.17N 97.17W
Perryton U.S.A. **111** 36.24N100.48W
Perryville U.S.A. **111** 37.43N 89.52W

Plymouth to **Poûthĭsăt**

Plymouth Vt. U.S.A. **115** 43.32N 72.45W
Plymouth Wisc. U.S.A. **110** 43.44N 87.58W
Plzeň Czech. **39** 49.45N 13.23E
Pô Burkina **76** 11.11N 1.10W
Po *r.* Italy **30** 44.57N 12.04E
Pobé Benin **77** 7.00N 2.56E
Pobeda, Gora *mtn.* U.S.S.R. **51** 65.20N145.50E
Pobla de Segur Spain **25** 42.15N 0.58E
Pocahontas Canada **100** 53.15N118.00W
Pocahontas Ark. U.S.A. **111** 36.16N 90.58W
Pocahontas Iowa U.S.A. **110** 42.44N 94.40W
Pocatello U.S.A. **108** 42.52N112.27W
Pocklington U.K. **12** 53.56N 0.48W
Pocono Mts. U.S.A. **115** 41.10N 75.20W
Poços de Caldas Brazil **126** 21.48S 46.33W
Poděbrady Czech. **36** 50.08N 15.07E
Podensac France **20** 44.39N 0.22W
Podgaytsy U.S.S.R. **37** 49.19N 25.10E
Podkamennaya Tunguska U.S.S.R. **51** 61.45N 90.13E
Podkamennaya Tunguska *r.* U.S.S.R. **51** 61.40N 90.00E
Podolsk U.S.S.R. **44** 55.23N 37.32E
Podor Senegal **76** 16.35N 15.02W
Podporozhye U.S.S.R. **44** 60.55N 34.02E
Podravska Slatina Yugo. **31** 45.42N 17.42E
Podujevó Yugo. **34** 42.54N 21.10E
Poel *i.* Germany **38** 54.00N 11.26E
Pofadder R.S.A. **80** 29.08S 19.22E
Poggibonsi Italy **30** 43.28N 11.09E
Pogoniani Greece **34** 40.00N 20.25E
Pogradec Albania **34** 40.57N 20.48E
Pogrebishche U.S.S.R. **37** 49.30N 29.15E
Poh Indonesia **59** 1.00S122.50E
P'ohang S. Korea **53** 36.00N129.26E
Pohorje Yugo. **31** 46.30N 15.20E
Poiana Mare Romania **34** 43.57N 23.05E
Poinsett, C. Antarctica **128** 65.35S113.00E
Point Arena *f.* U.S.A. **108** 38.55N123.41W
Pointe-à-Pitre Guadeloupe **117** 16.14N 61.32W
Pointe-au-Baril *town* Canada **104** 45.35N 80.30W
Pointe-au-Baril Station *town* Canada **104** 45.36N 80.23W
Pointe aux Anglais *town* Canada **103** 49.34N 67.10W
Pointe-aux-Trembles *town* Canada **105** 45.39N 73.30W
Pointe-Claire Canada **105** 45.26N 73.50W
Point Edward *town* Canada **104** 43.00N 82.24W
Pointe Noire *town* Congo **78** 4.46S 11.53E
Point Hope *town* U.S.A. **98** 68.21N166.41W
Point Lookout *town* Australia **93** 30.33S152.20E
Point Marion *town* U.S.A. **114** 39.44N 79.53W
Point of Rocks *town* U.S.A. **114** 39.17N 77.32W
Point Pelee Nat. Park Canada **104** 41.57N 82.30W
Point Pleasant *town* N.J. U.S.A. **115** 40.05N 74.04W
Point Pleasant *town* W.Va. U.S.A. **114** 38.52N 82.08W
Point Samson *town* Australia **88** 20.46S117.10E
Poisson Blanc, Lac *l.* Canada **105** 46.00N 75.45W
Poissy France **19** 48.56N 2.03E
Poitiers France **18** 46.35N 0.20E
Poitou-Charentes *d.* France **20** 46.00N 0.00
Poix France **19** 49.47N 1.59E
Poix-Terron France **19** 49.39N 4.39E
Pokaran India **62** 26.55N 71.55E
Pokhara Nepal **63** 28.12N 83.59E
Poko Zaïre **78** 3.08N 26.51E
Pokoinu Rarotonga Cook Is. **84** 21.12S159.50W
Polacca U.S.A. **109** 35.50N110.23W
Pola de Laviana Spain **26** 43.15N 5.34W
Pola de Lena Spain **26** 43.10N 5.49W
Pola de Siero Spain **26** 43.23N 5.40W
Polān Iran **65** 25.29N 61.15E
Poland Europe **37** 52.30N 19.00E
Polatli Turkey **64** 39.34N 32.08E
Polch Germany **39** 50.18N 7.18E
Polda Australia **92** 33.30S135.10E
Pole Zaïre **78** 2.51S 23.12E
Polesye *f.* U.S.S.R. **37** 52.15N 28.00E
Poli Cameroon **77** 8.30N 13.15E
Políaigos *i.* Greece **35** 36.45N 24.38E
Policastro, Golfo di *g.* Italy **33** 40.00N 15.30E
Poligny France **19** 46.50N 5.43E
Polikastron Greece **34** 41.00N 22.34E
Políkhnitos Greece **35** 39.04N 26.10E
Pólis Cyprus **66** 35.02N 32.26E
Polistena Italy **33** 38.25N 16.05E
Políyiros Greece **34** 40.23N 23.27E
Polk U.S.A. **114** 41.22N 79.56W
Polla Italy **33** 40.30N 15.30E
Pollino, Monte *mtn.* Italy **33** 39.55N 16.11E
Pollock Reef Australia **89** 34.28S123.40E
Polnovat U.S.S.R. **50** 63.47N 65.54E
Polonnoye U.S.S.R. **37** 50.10N 27.30E
Polotsk U.S.S.R. **44** 55.30N 28.43E
Polperro U.K. **13** 50.19N 4.31W
Polski Trŭmbesh Bulgaria **34** 43.20N 25.38E
Polson U.S.A. **108** 47.41N114.09W
Poltava U.S.S.R. **45** 49.35N 34.35E
Polunochnoye U.S.S.R. **44** 60.52N 60.28E
Polyarnyy U.S.S.R. **44** 69.14N 33.30E
Polynesia *is.* Pacific Oc. **84** 4.00S165.00W
Pomarkku Finland **41** 61.42N 22.00E
Pombal Brazil **123** 6.45S 37.45W
Pombal Portugal **27** 39.55N 8.38W
Pomene Mozambique **81** 22.53S 35.33E
Pomeranian Bay Germany **38** 54.06N 14.25E
Pomeroy Ohio U.S.A. **114** 39.02N 82.02W
Pomeroy Wash. U.S.A. **108** 46.28N117.36W
Pomona Namibia **80** 27.09S 15.18E
Pomona U.S.A. **109** 34.04N117.45W
Pompano Beach *town* U.S.A. **113** 26.14N 80.07W
Pompei *site* Italy **33** 40.45N 14.30E
Pompey's Pillar *town* U.S.A. **108** 45.59N107.56W
Ponape *i.* Pacific Oc. **84** 6.55N158.15E
Ponca City U.S.A. **111** 36.42N 97.05W
Ponce Puerto Rico **117** 18.00N 66.40W
Pondicherry India **61** 11.59N 79.50E
Pond Inlet *str.* Canada **99** 72.30N 75.00W
Ponds, I. of Canada **103** 53.24N 55.55W
Ponferrada Spain **26** 42.33N 6.35W
Pongani P.N.G. **90** 9.05S148.35E
Pongo *r.* Sudan **73** 8.52N 27.40E
Pongola *r.* Mozambique **81** 26.13S 32.38E
Ponnāni India **60** 10.46N 75.54E
Ponnyadaung Range *mts.* Burma **56** 22.30N 94.20E
Ponoka Canada **100** 52.42N113.40W
Ponorogo Indonesia **59** 7.51S111.30E
Ponoy U.S.S.R. **44** 67.02N 41.03E
Ponoy *r.* U.S.S.R. **44** 67.00N 41.10E
Pons France **20** 45.35N 0.33W
Ponsul *r.* Portugal **27** 39.40N 7.31W
Ponta Grossa Brazil **126** 25.00S 50.09W
Pont-à-Mousson France **19** 48.54N 6.04E
Pontão Portugal **27** 39.55N 8.22W
Ponta Porã Brazil **126** 22.27S 55.39W
Pontarlier France **19** 46.54N 6.22E
Pontassieve Italy **30** 43.46N 11.26E
Pont-Audemer France **18** 49.21N 0.31E
Pontaumur France **20** 45.52N 2.40E
Pont-Aven France **18** 47.51N 3.45W
Pontax *r.* Canada **102** 51.30N 78.48W
Pont Canavese Italy **30** 45.25N 7.36E
Pontchartrain, L. U.S.A. **111** 30.10N 90.10W
Pontchâteau France **18** 47.26N 2.05W
Pont-Croix France **18** 48.02N 4.29W
Pont d'Ain France **21** 46.03N 5.20E
Pont-de-Salars France **20** 44.17N 2.44E
Pont de Suert Spain **25** 42.24N 0.45E
Pont-de-Vaux France **21** 46.26N 4.56E
Pontecorvo Italy **32** 41.27N 13.40E
Ponte da Barca Portugal **26** 41.48N 8.25W
Pontedera Italy **30** 43.40N 10.38E
Ponte de Sor Portugal **27** 39.15N 8.01W
Ponte do Lima Portugal **26** 41.46N 8.35W
Pontefract U.K. **12** 53.42N 1.19W
Ponteix Canada **101** 49.49N107.30W
Ponte Nova Brazil **126** 20.25S 42.54W
Pontevedra Spain **26** 42.26N 8.38W
Pontevedra *d.* Spain **26** 42.35N 8.35W
Pontevedra, Ría de *est.* Spain **26** 42.22N 8.45W
Pontgibaud France **20** 45.50N 2.51E
Pontiac Ill. U.S.A. **110** 40.54N 88.36W
Pontiac Mich. U.S.A. **104** 42.37N 83.18W
Pontiac Prov. Park Canada **105** 46.36N 76.32W
Pontianak Indonesia **58** 0.05S109.16E
Pontivy France **18** 48.04N 2.59W
Pont-l'Abbé France **18** 47.52N 4.13W
Pont l'Évêque France **18** 49.18N 0.11E
Pontoise France **19** 49.03N 2.06E
Pontorson France **18** 48.33N 1.31W
Pontremoli Italy **30** 44.22N 9.53E
Pontresina Switz. **39** 46.28N 9.53E
Pontrilas U.K. **13** 51.56N 2.53W
Pont Rouge Canada **105** 46.45N 71.42W
Ponts Spain **25** 41.55N 1.12E
Pont-sur-Yonne France **19** 48.17N 3.12E
Pontypool Canada **104** 44.06N 78.38W
Pontypool U.K. **13** 51.42N 3.01W
Pontypridd U.K. **13** 51.36N 3.21W
Ponziane, Isole *is.* Italy **32** 40.55N 12.57E
Poochera Australia **92** 32.42S134.52E
Poole U.K. **13** 50.42N 2.02W
Pooncarie Australia **92** 33.23S142.34E
Poopelloe L. Australia **92** 31.39S144.00E
Poopó, Lago de *l.* Bolivia **124** 19.00S 67.00W
Popayán Colombia **122** 2.27N 76.32W
Poperinge Belgium **16** 50.51N 2.44E
Popes Creek *town* U.S.A. **114** 38.09N 76.58W
Popilta L. Australia **92** 33.09S141.45E
Popintsi Bulgaria **34** 42.25N 24.17E
Poplar *r.* Canada **101** 53.00N 97.18W
Poplar U.S.A. **108** 48.07N105.12W
Poplar Bluff *town* U.S.A. **111** 36.45N 90.24W
Poplarville U.S.A. **111** 30.51N 89.32W
Popocatépetl *mtn.* Mexico **116** 19.02N 98.38W
Popokabaka Zaïre **78** 5.41S 16.40E
Popoli Italy **31** 42.10N 13.50E
Popondetta P.N.G. **90** 8.45S148.15E
Popovo Bulgaria **34** 43.21N 26.18E
Poppi Italy **30** 43.43N 11.46E
Poprad Czech. **37** 49.03N 20.18E
Popricani Romania **37** 47.18N 27.31E
Porāli *r.* Pakistan **62** 25.30N 66.25E
Porbandar India **62** 21.38N 69.36E
Por Chaman Afghan. **62** 33.08N 63.51E
Porcher I. Canada **100** 54.00N130.30W
Porcuna Spain **27** 37.52N 4.11W
Porcupine *r.* U.S.A. **98** 66.25N145.20W
Porcupine Hills Canada **101** 52.30N101.45W
Pordenone Italy **32** 45.57N 12.39E
Pordim Bulgaria **34** 43.23N 24.51E
Poreč Yugo. **31** 45.13N 13.37E
Pori Finland **41** 61.29N 21.47E
Porirua New Zealand **86** 41.08S174.50E
Porjus Sweden **40** 66.57N 19.50E
Porkhov U.S.S.R. **44** 57.43N 29.31E
Porkkala Finland **41** 59.59N 24.26E
Porlamar Venezuela **122** 11.01N 63.54W
Porma *r.* Spain **26** 42.29N 5.28W
Pornic France **18** 47.07N 2.06W
Porog U.S.S.R. **44** 63.50N 38.32E
Poronaysk U.S.S.R. **51** 49.13N142.55E
Póros Greece **35** 37.30N 23.30E
Porosozero U.S.S.R. **44** 62.45N 32.48E
Porrentruy Switz. **39** 47.25N 7.05E
Porretta Terme Italy **30** 44.09N 10.59E
Porsangen *est.* Norway **40** 70.58N 25.30E
Porsangerhalvöya *pen.* Norway **40** 70.50N 25.00E
Porsgrunn Norway **42** 59.09N 9.40E
Porsuk *r.* Turkey **64** 39.41N 31.56E
Portachuela Bolivia **124** 17.21S 63.24W
Portadown U.K. **15** 54.25N 6.27W
Portaferry U.K. **15** 54.23N 5.33W
Portage Penn. U.S.A. **114** 40.23N 78.41W
Portage Wisc. U.S.A. **110** 43.33N 89.28W
Portage du Fort Canada **105** 45.36N 76.38W
Portage la Prairie *town* Canada **101** 49.57N 98.25W
Port Alberni Canada **100** 49.14N124.48W
Port Albert Australia **93** 38.09S146.40E
Portalegre Portugal **27** 39.17N 7.26W
Portalegre *d.* Portugal **27** 39.10N 7.40W
Portales U.S.A. **111** 34.11N103.20W
Port Alfred R.S.A. **80** 33.36S 26.52E
Port Alice Canada **100** 50.25N127.25W
Port Allegany U.S.A. **114** 41.49N 78.17W
Port Angeles U.S.A. **108** 48.07N123.27W
Port Antonio Jamaica **117** 18.10N 76.27W
Port Arthur Australia **91** 43.08S147.50E
Port Arthur U.S.A. **111** 29.55N 93.55W
Port Augusta Australia **92** 32.30S137.46E
Port au Port Canada **103** 48.33N 58.45W
Port-au-Prince Haiti **117** 18.33N 72.20W
Port Austin U.S.A. **104** 44.03N 83.01W
Port Bergé Madagascar **81** 15.33S 47.40E
Port Blair India **56** 11.40N 92.40E
Port Bolster Canada **104** 44.20N 79.10W
Portbou Spain **25** 42.25N 3.09E
Port Bouet Ivory Coast **76** 5.14N 3.58W
Port Bradshaw *b.* Australia **90** 12.30S136.42E
Port Broughton Australia **92** 33.36S137.56E
Port Burwell Canada **104** 42.39N 80.49W
Port Campbell Australia **92** 38.37S143.04E
Port Canning India **63** 22.18N 88.40E
Port Carling Canada **104** 45.07N 79.35W
Port Cartier Canada **103** 50.01N 66.53W
Port Chalmers New Zealand **86** 45.49S170.37E
Port Chester U.S.A. **115** 41.00N 73.40W
Port Clinton U.S.A. **114** 41.31N 82.56W
Port Colborne Canada **104** 42.53N 79.14W
Port Coquitlam Canada **100** 49.20N122.45W
Port Credit Canada **104** 43.33N 79.35W
Port Curtis Australia **90** 23.50S151.13E
Port Dalhousie Canada **104** 43.12N 79.16W
Port-de-Paix Haiti **117** 19.57N 72.50W
Port Dover Canada **104** 42.47N 80.12W
Port Edward R.S.A. **80** 31.03S 30.13E
Portel Portugal **27** 38.18N 7.42W
Portela Brazil **126** 21.38S 41.59W
Port Elgin Canada **104** 44.26N 81.24W
Port Elizabeth R.S.A. **80** 33.57S 25.34E
Port Ellen U.K. **14** 55.38N 6.12W
Port-en-Bessin France **18** 49.21N 0.45W
Port Erin U.K. **12** 54.05N 4.45W
Porter Landing Canada **100** 58.46N130.05W
Porterville R.S.A. **80** 33.01S 19.00E
Porterville U.S.A. **109** 36.04N119.01W
Porte-Vecchio France **22** 41.35N 9.16E
Port Fairy Australia **92** 38.23S142.17E
Port Gentil Gabon **78** 0.40S 8.46E
Port Germein Australia **92** 33.01S138.00E
Port Gibson U.S.A. **111** 31.58N 90.58W
Portglenone U.K. **15** 54.52N 6.30W
Port Harcourt Nigeria **77** 4.43N 7.05E
Port Harrison *see* Inoucdjouac Canada **99**
Port Hawkesbury Canada **103** 45.37N 61.21W
Porthcawl U.K. **13** 51.28N 3.42W
Port Hedland Australia **88** 20.24S118.36E
Port Henry U.S.A. **105** 44.03N 73.28W
Porthill U.S.A. **108** 49.00N116.30W
Porthmadog U.K. **12** 52.55N 4.08W
Port Hope Canada **104** 43.57N 78.18W
Port Hope U.S.A. **104** 43.57N 82.43W
Port Huron U.S.A. **114** 42.58N 82.27W
Portimão Portugal **27** 37.08N 8.32W
Port Isaac B. U.K. **13** 50.36N 4.50W
Portiţei, Gura *f.* Romania **29** 44.40N 29.00E
Port Jefferson U.S.A. **115** 40.57N 73.04W
Port Jervis U.S.A. **115** 41.22N 74.41W
Port Keats Australia **88** 14.15S129.35E
Port Kembla Australia **93** 34.28S150.54E
Port Kenny Australia **92** 33.09S134.42E
Portland N.S.W. Australia **93** 33.20S150.00E
Portland Vic. Australia **92** 38.21S141.38E
Portland Canada **105** 44.41N 76.13W
Portland Maine U.S.A. **112** 43.39N 70.17W
Portland Oreg. U.S.A. **108** 45.33N122.36W
Portland Tex. U.S.A. **111** 27.53N 97.20W
Portland Pt. Ascension **127** 7.58S 14.26W
Port-La-Nouvelle France **20** 43.01N 3.03E
Port Laoise Rep. of Ire. **15** 53.03N 7.20W
Port Lavaca U.S.A. **111** 28.37N 96.38W
Port Lincoln Australia **92** 34.43S135.49E
Port Loko Sierra Leone **76** 8.50N 12.50W
Port Loring Canada **104** 45.56N 79.58W
Port Louis France **18** 47.43N 3.21W
Port Luck Canada **104** 46.20N 83.52W
Port MacDonnell Australia **92** 38.03S140.46E
Port Macquarie Australia **93** 31.28S152.25E
Port Maitland N.S. Canada **103** 43.59N 66.09W
Port Maitland Ont. Canada **104** 42.52N 79.34W
Portmarnock Rep. of Ire. **15** 53.25N 6.09W
Port Menier Canada **103** 49.49N 64.20W
Port Moresby P.N.G. **90** 9.30S147.07E
Port Musgrave *b.* Australia **90** 11.59S142.00E
Portnaguiran U.K. **14** 58.15N 6.10W
Port Neill Australia **92** 34.07S136.20E
Port Nelson Canada **101** 57.03N 92.36W
Portneuf Canada **105** 46.42N 71.53W
Portneuf Prov. Park Canada **105** 47.12N 72.05W
Port Nolloth R.S.A. **80** 29.16S 16.54E
Port Norris U.S.A. **115** 39.15N 75.02W
Port-Nouveau Québec Canada **99** 58.35N 65.59W
Porto Portugal **26** 41.11N 8.36W
Porto *d.* Portugal **26** 41.15N 8.15W
Pôrto Alegre Brazil **126** 30.03S 51.10W
Porto Amboim Angola **78** 10.45S 13.43E
Pôrto de Mós Portugal **27** 39.36N 8.39W
Pôrto de Moz Brazil **123** 1.45S 52.13W
Porto Empedocle Italy **32** 37.17N 13.32E
Porto Esperança Brazil **126** 19.36S 57.24W
Porto Farina Tunisia **32** 37.10N 10.12E
Pôrto Feliz Brazil **126** 23.11S 47.32W
Portoferraio Italy **30** 42.49N 10.19E
Port of Ness U.K. **14** 58.30N 6.13W
Pôrto Franco Brazil **123** 6.21S 47.25W
Port of Spain Trinidad **117** 10.38N 61.31W
Porto Grande Brazil **123** 0.42N 51.24W
Portogruaro Italy **30** 45.47N 12.50E
Pórto Lágo Greece **34** 41.01N 25.06E
Pörtom Finland **40** 62.42N 21.37E
Portomaggiore Italy **30** 44.42N 11.48E
Porto Moniz Madeira Is. **127** 32.52N 17.12W
Pôrto Murtinho Brazil **126** 21.42S 57.52W
Porton U.K. **13** 51.08N 1.44W
Pôrto Nacional Brazil **123** 10.42S 48.25W
Porto-Novo Benin **77** 6.30N 2.47E
Port Ontario U.S.A. **115** 43.32N 76.11W
Pôrto Primavera, Reprêsa *resr.* Brazil **126** 21.50S 52.00W
Porto Recanati Italy **31** 43.26N 13.40E
Porto San Giorgio Italy **31** 43.11N 13.48E
Porto Santo *i.* Madeira Is. **74** 33.04N 16.20W
Porto Santo Stefano Italy **30** 42.26N 11.07E
Porto Tolle Italy **30** 44.56N 12.22E
Porto Torres Italy **32** 40.50N 8.23E
Pôrto Valter Brazil **122** 8.15S 72.45W
Porto-Vecchio France **21** 41.35N 9.16E
Pôrto Velho Brazil **122** 8.45S 63.54W
Portoviejo Ecuador **122** 1.07S 80.28W
Portpatrick U.K. **14** 54.51N 5.07W
Port Perry Canada **104** 44.06N 78.57W
Port Phillip B. Australia **93** 38.05S144.50E
Port Pirie Australia **92** 33.11S138.01E
Port Radium Canada **98** 66.05N118.02W
Portree U.K. **14** 57.24N 6.12W
Port Renfrew Canada **100** 48.30N124.20W
Port Rowan Canada **104** 42.37N 80.28W
Portrush U.K. **15** 55.12N 6.40W
Port Said *see* Būr Sa'īd Egypt **66**
Port-Sainte-Marie France **20** 44.15N 0.24E
Port St. Joe U.S.A. **113** 29.49N 85.19W
Port St. Louis France **21** 43.23N 4.48E
Port Sanilac U.S.A. **114** 43.26N 82.33W
Port Saunders Canada **103** 50.39N 57.18W
Portsea Australia **93** 38.19S144.43E
Port Severn Canada **104** 44.47N 79.42W
Port Shepstone R.S.A. **80** 30.44S 30.27E
Port Simpson Canada **100** 54.32N130.25W
Portsmouth U.K. **13** 50.48N 1.06W
Portsmouth N.H. U.S.A. **115** 43.04N 70.46W
Portsmouth Ohio U.S.A. **112** 38.45N 82.59W
Portsmouth Va. U.S.A. **113** 36.50N 76.20W
Portsoy U.K. **14** 57.41N 2.41W
Port Stanley Canada **104** 42.40N 81.13W
Portstewart U.K. **15** 55.11N 6.43W
Port Sudan *see* Būr Sūdān Sudan **72**
Port Talbot U.K. **13** 51.35N 3.48W
Porttipahdan tekojärvi *resr.* Finland **40** 68.08N 26.40E
Port Townsend U.S.A. **108** 48.07N122.46W
Portugal Europe **24** 39.30N 8.05W
Portugalete Spain **26** 43.19N 3.01W
Portumna Rep. of Ire. **11** 53.06N 8.14W
Port Vendres France **20** 42.31N 3.07E
Port Victoria Australia **92** 34.30S137.30E
Portville U.S.A. **114** 42.02N 78.20W
Port Wakefield Australia **92** 34.12S138.11E
Port Warrender Australia **88** 14.30S125.50E
Porvenir Chile **125** 53.18S 70.22W
Porz Germany **38** 50.53N 7.03E
Porzuna Spain **27** 39.09N 4.09W
Posada Italy **32** 40.38N 9.43E
Posada *r.* Italy **32** 40.39N 9.45E
Posadas Argentina **124** 27.25S 55.48W
Posavina *f.* Yugo. **31** 45.20N 17.00E
Poschiavo Switz. **39** 46.18N 10.04E
Posen U.S.A. **104** 45.16N 83.42W
Posets, Pico de *mtn.* Spain **25** 42.39N 0.25E
Posht *r.* Iran **65** 29.09N 58.09E
Positano Italy **33** 40.38N 14.29E
Poso Indonesia **59** 1.23S120.45E
Posse Brazil **126** 14.05S 46.22W
Possidhonia *site* Greece **35** 37.40N 24.00E
Pössneck Germany **38** 50.42N 11.37E
Post U.S.A. **111** 33.12N101.23W
Postavy U.S.S.R. **44** 55.07N 26.50E
Poste-de-la-Baleine *town* Canada **102** 55.20N 77.40W
Poste Maurice Cortier Algeria **74** 22.18N 1.05E
Poste Weygand Algeria **74** 24.29N 0.40E
Postmasburg R.S.A. **80** 28.19S 23.03E
Postojna Yugo. **31** 45.47N 14.13E
Postoli U.S.S.R. **37** 52.30N 28.00E
Potamós Greece **35** 36.38N 22.59E
Potchefstroom R.S.A. **80** 26.42S 27.05E
Poteau U.S.A. **111** 35.03N 94.37W
Potelu, Lacul *l.* Romania **34** 43.44N 24.20E
Potenza Italy **33** 40.38N 15.49E
Potes Spain **26** 43.09N 4.37W
Potgietersrus R.S.A. **80** 24.11S 29.00E
Poti *r.* Brazil **123** 5.01S 42.48W
Poti U.S.S.R. **45** 42.11N 41.41E
Potiskum Nigeria **77** 11.40N 11.03E
Potomac *r.* U.S.A. **114** 38.00N 76.18W
Potomac, North Branch *r.* U.S.A. **114** 39.15N 79.21W
Potomac, South Branch *r.* U.S.A. **114** 39.04N 78.59W
Potosí Bolivia **124** 19.35S 65.45W
Potosí *d.* Bolivia **124** 21.00S 67.00W
Potosi Cerro *mtn.* Mexico **111** 24.50N100.15W
Pototan Phil. **59** 10.54N122.38E
Potsdam Germany **38** 52.24N 13.04E
Potsdam U.S.A. **105** 44.40N 74.59W
Pottstown U.S.A. **115** 40.15N 75.38W
Pottsville U.S.A. **115** 40.41N 76.12W
Pouancé France **18** 47.44N 1.11W
Poughkeepsie U.S.A. **115** 41.42N 73.56W
Poultney U.S.A. **115** 43.31N 73.14W
Pournári, Tekhnití Límni *l.* Greece **35** 39.15N 21.00E
Pouso Alegre Brazil **126** 22.13S 45.49W
Pouté Senegal **74** 15.42N 1.11W
Poûthĭsăt Cambodia **56** 12.27N103.50E

Qatar to **Rashīd**

Qatar Asia **65** 25.20N 51.10E
Qaţrānī, Jabal *mts.* Egypt **66** 29.40N 30.36E
Qattara Depression *see* Qaţţārah, Munkhafaḑ al *f.* Egypt **64**
Qaţţārah, Munkhafaḑ al *f.* Egypt **64** 29.40N 27.30E
Qawz Rajab Sudan **72** 16.04N 35.34E
Qāyen Iran **65** 33.44N 59.07E
Qaysān Sudan **73** 10.45N 34.48E
Qāzigund Jammu & Kashmir **62** 33.38N 75.09E
Qazvīn Iran **65** 36.16N 50.00E
Qeqertarsuaq *see* Godhavn Greenland **99**
Qeqertarsuatsiaat *see* Fiskenaesset Greenland **99**
Qeshm Iran **65** 26.58N 57.17E
Qeshm *i.* Iran **65** 26.48N 55.48E
Qezel Owzan *r.* Iran **65** 36.44N 49.27E
Qezi'ot Israel **66** 30.52N 34.28E
Qian'an China **54** 45.00N124.00E
Qianjiang China **55** 29.28N108.43E
Qianxi China **54** 40.10N118.19E
Qianyang China **55** 27.22N110.14E
Qiaotou China **54** 42.56N118.54E
Qibyā Jordan **67** 31.59N 35.01E
Qidong Hunan China **55** 26.47N112.07E
Qidong Jiangsu China **55** 31.49N121.40E
Qiemo China **52** 38.08N 85.33E
Qijiang China **55** 29.00N106.40E
Qila Abdullāh Pakistan **62** 30.43N 66.38E
Qila Lādgasht Pakistan **62** 27.54N 62.57E
Qila Saifullāh Pakistan **62** 30.43N 68.21E
Qilian Shan *mts.* China **52** 38.30N 99.20E
Qimantag *mts.* China **52** 37.45N 89.40E
Qimen China **55** 29.50N117.38E
Qinā Egypt **64** 26.10N 32.43E
Qinā, Wādī *r.* Egypt **64** 26.07N 32.42E
Qingdao China **54** 36.02N120.25E
Qinghai *d.* China **63** 34.20N 91.00E
Qinghai Hu *l.* China **52** 36.40N100.00E
Qingjian China **54** 37.02N110.06E
Qingjiang China **55** 28.01N115.30E
Qing Jiang Shuiku *resr.* China **55** 30.00N112.12E
Qinglong Guizhou China **55** 25.47N105.12E
Qinglong Hebei China **54** 40.24N118.53E
Qingshui Jiang *r.* China **55** 28.08N110.06E
Qing Xian China **54** 38.35N116.48E
Qingxu China **54** 37.36N112.21E
Qingyang China **54** 36.03N107.52E
Qingyuan Guangdong China **55** 23.42N113.00E
Qingyuan Jilin China **54** 42.05N125.01E
Qingyuan Zhejiang China **55** 27.37N119.03E
Qing Zang Gaoyuan *f.* China **52** 33.40N 86.00E
Qinhuangdao China **54** 39.52N119.42E
Qin Ling *mts.* China **54** 33.30N109.00E
Qin Xian China **54** 36.45N112.41E
Qinyang China **54** 35.06N112.57E
Qinzhou China **55** 21.58N108.34E
Qionghai China **55** 19.12N110.31E
Qiongshan China **55** 19.59N110.30E
Qiongzhou Haixia *str.* China **55** 20.09N110.20E
Qipanshan China **54** 42.05N117.37E
Qiqihar China **53** 47.23N124.00E
Qira China **52** 37.02N 80.53E
Qiryat Ata Israel **67** 32.48N 35.06E
Qiryat Bialik Israel **67** 32.50N 35.05E
Qiryat Gat Israel **67** 31.37N 34.47E
Qiryat Motzkin Israel **67** 32.50N 35.04E
Qiryat Shemona Israel **67** 33.13N 35.35E
Qiryat Tiv'on Israel **67** 32.43N 35.08E
Qiryat Yam Israel **67** 32.51N 35.04E
Qishn Yemen **60** 15.25N 51.40E
Qishon *r.* Israel **67** 32.49N 35.02E
Qiuxizhen China **55** 29.54N104.40E
Qi Xian Henan China **54** 35.35N114.08E
Qi Xian Henan China **54** 34.30N114.50E
Qom Iran **65** 34.40N 50.57E
Qonggyai China **63** 29.03N 91.41E
Qornet'es Sauda *mtn.* Lebanon **66** 34.17N 36.04E
Qoţūr Iran **65** 38.28N 44.25E
Quabbin Resr. U.S.A. **115** 42.22N 72.18W
Quadeville Canada **105** 45.18N 77.24W
Quairading Australia **89** 32.00S117.22E
Quakenbrück Germany **38** 52.40N 7.57E
Quakertown U.S.A. **115** 40.26N 75.21W
Qu'ali China **55** 29.46N117.15E
Quambatook Australia **92** 35.52S143.36E
Quambone Australia **93** 30.54S147.55E
Quang Ngai Vietnam **56** 15.09N108.50E
Quang Tri Vietnam **56** 16.44N107.10E
Quang Yen Vietnam **56** 20.56N106.49E
Quan Long Vietnam **56** 9.11N105.09E
Quannan China **55** 24.45N114.32E
Quantico U.S.A. **114** 38.31N 77.17W
Quanzhou Fujian China **55** 24.57N118.36E
Quanzhou Guang. Zhuang. China **55** 26.00N111.00E
Qu'Appelle *r.* Canada **101** 50.33N101.20W
Quaqtaq Canada **99** 61.05N 69.36W
Quaraí Brazil **125** 30.23S 56.27W
Quaraí *r.* Brazil **125** 30.12S 57.36W
Quarryville U.S.A. **115** 39.54N 76.10W
Quartu Sant'Elena Italy **32** 39.14N 9.11E
Quartzsite U.S.A. **109** 33.40N114.13W
Quatsino Sd. Canada **100** 50.42N127.58W
Qūchān Iran **65** 37.04N 58.29E
Queanbeyan Australia **93** 35.24S149.17E
Québec Canada **105** 46.50N 71.20W
Québec *d.* Canada **103** 51.20N 68.45W
Quebracho Uruguay **125** 31.57S 57.53W
Quedlinburg Germany **38** 51.48N 11.09E
Queen Anne U.S.A. **115** 38.55N 75.57W
Queen Charlotte Canada **100** 53.18N132:04W
Queen Charlotte Is. Canada **100** 53.00N132.00W
Queen Charlotte Sd. Canada **100** 51.30N129.30W
Queen Charlotte Str. Canada **100** 51.00N128.00W
Queen Elizabeth Is. Canada **99** 78.30N 99.00W
Queen Maud G. Canada **99** 68.30N 99.00W
Queen Maud Range *mts.* Antarctica **128** 86.20S165.00W
Queens Channel Australia **88** 14.46S129.24E
Queenscliff Australia **93** 38.17S144.42E
Queensland *d.* Australia **90** 23.30S144.00E
Queenstown Australia **91** 42.07S145.33E
Queenstown New Zealand **86** 45.03S168.41E
Queenstown R.S.A. **80** 31.52S 26.51E
Queenstown U.S.A. **115** 38.59N 76.09W
Queguay Grande *r.* Uruguay **125** 32.09S 58.09W
Queimadas Brazil **123** 10.58S 39.38W
Quela Angola **78** 9.18S 17.05E
Quelimane Mozambique **79** 17.53S 36.57E
Quemado U.S.A. **109** 34.20N108.30W
Quemoy *i.* China **55** 24.30N118.20E
Quentico Prov. Park Canada **102** 48.20N 91.30W
Quequén Argentina **125** 38.34S 58.42W
Querétaro Mexico **116** 20.38N100.23W
Querétaro *d.* Mexico **116** 21.03N100.00W
Querobabi Mexico **109** 30.03N111.01W
Quesada Spain **27** 37.51N 3.04W
Queshan China **54** 32.48N114.01E
Quesnel Canada **100** 53.05N122.30W
Quesnel *r.* Canada **100** 52.58N122.29W
Questembert France **18** 47.40N 2.27W
Quetta Pakistan **62** 30.12N 67.00E
Quettehou France **18** 49.36N 1.18W
Quevedo Ecuador **122** 0.59S 79.27W
Quezaltenango Guatemala **116** 14.50N 91.30W
Quezon City Phil. **59** 14.39N121.01E
Quibala Angola **78** 10.48S 14.56E
Quibaxi Angola **78** 8.34S 14.37E
Quibdo Colombia **122** 5.40N 76.38W
Quiberon France **18** 47.29N 3.07W
Quibocolo Angola **78** 6.20S 15.05E
Quicama Nat. Park Angola **78** 9.40S 13.30E
Quiet L. Canada **100** 61.05N133.05W
Quilán, C. Chile **125** 43.16S 74.27W
Quilengues Angola **78** 14.09S 14.04E
Quillabamba Peru **122** 12.50S 72.50W
Quillacollo Bolivia **124** 17.26S 66.17W
Quillan France **20** 42.52N 2.11E
Quillota Chile **125** 32.53S 71.16W
Quilpie Australia **90** 26.37S144.15E
Quilpué Chile **125** 33.03S 71.27W
Quimbele Angola **78** 6.29S 16.25E
Quimilí Argentina **124** 27.35S 62.25W
Quimper France **18** 48.00N 4.06W
Quimperlé France **18** 47.52N 3.33W
Quincy Ill. U.S.A. **110** 39.56N 91.23W
Quincy Mass. U.S.A. **115** 42.15N 71.01W
Quincy Wash. U.S.A. **108** 47.14N119.51W
Qui Nhon Vietnam **56** 13.47N109.11E
Quintanar de la Orden Spain **27** 39.34N 3.03W
Quintana Roo *d.* Mexico **117** 19.00N 88.00W
Quinte, B. of Canada **105** 44.07N 77.15W
Quinter U.S.A. **110** 39.04N100.14W
Quintin France **18** 48.24N 2.55W
Quinto Spain **25** 41.25N 0.29W
Quinzau Angola **78** 6.51S 12.46E
Quionga Mozambique **79** 10.37S 40.31E
Quipar *r.* Spain **25** 38.14N 1.36W
Quirigua *ruins* Guatemala **117** 15.20N 89.25W
Quirimbo Angola **78** 10.41S 14.16E
Quirindi Australia **93** 31.30S150.42E
Quiroga Spain **26** 42.29N 7.16W
Quiros, C. Vanuatu **84** 14.55S167.01E
Quissanga Mozambique **79** 12.24S 40.33E
Quissico Mozambique **81** 24.42S 34.44E
Quitapa Angola **78** 10.10S 18.16E
Quiterajo Mozambique **79** 11.46S 40.25E
Quito Ecuador **122** 0.14S 78.30W
Qu Jiang *r.* China **55** 30.02N106.20E
Qumigxung China **63** 30.53N 86.38E
Qumrān *site* Jordan **67** 31.44N 35.27E
Quorn Australia **92** 32.20S138.02E
Qurayyah, Wādī *r.* Egypt **66** 30.26N 34.01E
Qurdūd Sudan **73** 10.17N 29.56E
Qurlurtuuq Canada **98** 67.49N115.12W
Quşrah Jordan **67** 32.05N 35.20E
Qū' Wishām *f.* Oman **71** 18.55N 55.55E
Quxian China **55** 30.50N106.54E
Qu Xian China **55** 28.59N118.56E
Quyon Canada **105** 45.31N 76.14W
Qüzü China **63** 29.21N 90.39E

R

Raab *r. see* Rába *r.* Austria **31**
Raahe Finland **40** 64.41N 24.29E
Raalte Neth. **16** 52.22N 6.17E
Ra'ananna Israel **67** 32.11N 34.53E
Raasay *i.* U.K. **14** 57.25N 6.05W
Rab Yugo. **31** 44.46N 14.46E
Rab *i.* Yugo. **31** 44.45N 14.45E
Rába *r.* Hungary **31** 47.42N 17.38E
Raba Indonesia **58** 8.27S118.45E
Rabaçal *r.* Portugal **26** 41.30N 7.12W
Rábade Spain **26** 43.07N 7.37W
Rabak Sudan **73** 13.09N 32.44E
Rabang China **63** 33.03N 80.29E
Rabat Morocco **74** 34.02N 6.51W
Rabbit Flat *town* Australia **88** 20.10S129.53E
Rabbit L. Canada **104** 47.00N 79.37W
Rabbitskin *r.* Canada **100** 61.47N120.42W
Rābor Iran **65** 29.18N 56.56E
Rabyānah Libya **72** 24.14N 21.59E
Rabyānah, Şaḩrā' *f.* Libya **75** 24.30N 21.00E
Racconigi Italy **30** 44.46N 7.46E
Raccoon Creek U.S.A. **114** 40.02N 82.24W
Race, C. Canada **103** 46.40N 53.10W
Race Pt. U.S.A. **115** 42.04N 70.14W
Rach Gia Vietnam **56** 10.02N105.05E
Racibórz Poland **37** 50.06N 18.13E
Racine U.S.A. **110** 42.42N 87.50W
Raco U.S.A. **104** 46.24N 84.31W
Rădăuţi Romania **37** 47.51N 25.55E
Råde Norway **42** 59.21N 10.51E
Radeberg Germany **38** 51.13N 13.43E
Radebeul Germany **38** 51.06N 13.40E
Radeče Yugo. **31** 46.04N 15.11E
Radekhov U.S.S.R. **37** 50.18N 24.35E
Radford U.S.A. **113** 37.07N 80.34W
Rādhanpur India **62** 23.50N 71.36E
Radium Hill *town* Australia **92** 32.30S140.32E
Radium Hot Springs *town* Canada **100** 50.48N116.12W
Radnevo Bulgaria **34** 42.18N 25.56E
Radnice Czech. **38** 49.51N 13.37E
Radom Poland **37** 51.26N 21.10E
Radomir Bulgaria **34** 42.37N 23.04E
Radomsko Poland **37** 51.05N 19.25E
Radomyshl U.S.S.R. **37** 50.30N 29.14E
Radotin Czech. **38** 50.00N 14.22E
Radoviš Yugo. **34** 41.38N 22.28E
Radovljica Yugo. **31** 46.21N 14.11E
Radöy *i.* Norway **41** 60.38N 5.05E
Radstadt Austria **39** 47.23N 13.27E
Radstock U.K. **13** 51.17N 2.25W
Radstock, C. Australia **92** 33.11S134.21E
Radville Canada **101** 49.27N104.17W
Raḑwá, Jabal *mtn.* Saudi Arabia **64** 24.36N 38.18E
Rae Canada **100** 62.50N116.03W
Rāe Bareli India **63** 26.13N 81.14E
Raeren Germany **38** 50.41N 6.07E
Raeside, L. Australia **89** 29.30S122.00E
Rafaela Argentina **124** 31.16S 61.44W
Rafaḩ Egypt **67** 31.18N 34.15E
Rafaï C.A.R. **73** 4.58N 23.56E
Raffadali Italy **32** 37.24N 13.33E
Raffili Mission Sudan **73** 6.53N 27.58E
Rafḩā Saudi Arabia **64** 29.38N 43.30E
Rafsanjān Iran **65** 30.24N 56.00E
Raga Sudan **73** 8.28N 25.41E
Ragged, Mt. Australia **89** 33.27S123.27E
Ragunda Sweden **40** 63.06N 16.23E
Ragusa Italy **33** 36.55N 14.44E
Raha Indonesia **59** 4.50S122.43E
Raḩá, Ḩarrat ar *f.* Saudi Arabia **66** 28.00N 36.35E
Rahad *r.* Sudan **72** 14.28N 33.31E
Rahad al Bardī Sudan **73** 11.18N 23.53E
Rahīm Ki Bāzār Pakistan **62** 24.19N 69.09E
Rahīmyār Khān Pakistan **62** 28.25N 70.18E
Raiatea *i.* Îs. de la Société **85** 16.50S151.25W
Rāichūr India **60** 16.15N 77.20E
Raiganj India **63** 25.37N 88.07E
Raigarh India **63** 21.54N 83.24E
Rainbow Australia **92** 35.56S142.01E
Rainelle U.S.A. **113** 37.58N 80.47W
Rainier, Mt. U.S.A. **108** 46.52N121.46W
Rainy L. Canada/U.S.A. **102** 48.42N 93.10W
Rainy River *town* Canada **102** 48.43N 94.29W
Raipur India **63** 21.14N 81.38E
Raipur Uplands *mts.* India **63** 20.45N 82.30E
Rairākhol India **63** 21.03N 84.23E
Ra'īs Saudi Arabia **64** 23.35N 38.36E
Raisen India **63** 23.20N 77.48E
Raisin *r.* U.S.A. **104** 41.53N 83.20W
Raivavae *i.* Pacific Oc. **85** 23.52S147.40W
Rājahmundry India **61** 17.01N 81.52E
Rajāj Sudan **73** 10.55N 24.43E
Rajang *r.* Malaysia **58** 2.10N112.45E
Rājanpur Pakistan **62** 29.06N 70.19E
Rājapālaiyam India **60** 9.26N 77.36E
Rājasthān *d.* India **62** 26.15N 74.00E
Rājasthān Canal India **62** 31.10N 75.00E
Rājbāri Bangla. **63** 23.46N 89.39E
Rāj Gāngpur India **63** 22.11N 84.36E
Rājgarh Madhya P. India **62** 23.56N 76.58E
Rājgarh Rāj. India **62** 28.38N 75.23E
Rājgarh Rāj. India **62** 27.14N 76.38E
Rājkot India **62** 22.18N 70.47E
Rāj-Nāndgaon India **63** 21.06N 81.02E
Rājpīpla India **62** 21.47N 73.34E
Rājpur India **62** 21.56N 75.08E
Rājshāhi Bangla. **63** 24.22N 88.36E
Rājula India **62** 21.01N 71.34E
Rakahanga Atoll Cook Is. **84** 10.03S161.06W
Rakaia New Zealand **86** 43.45S172.01E
Rakaia *r.* New Zealand **86** 43.52S172.13E
Raka Zangbo *r.* China **63** 29.24N 87.58E
Rakhni Pakistan **62** 30.03N 69.55E
Rakhov U.S.S.R. **37** 48.02N 24.10E
Rakhshān *r.* Pakistan **62** 27.10N 63.25E
Rākīn Jordan **67** 31.14N 35.42E
Rakitnoye U.S.S.R. **37** 51.18N 27.10E
Rakkestad Norway **42** 59.26N 11.21E
Rakops Botswana **80** 21.00S 24.32E
Rakov U.S.S.R. **37** 53.58N 26.59E
Rakovník Czech. **39** 50.05N 13.43E
Rakovski Bulgaria **34** 42.18N 24.58E
Rakulka U.S.S.R. **44** 62.19N 46.52E
Råkvåg Norway **40** 63.47N 10.10E
Rakvere U.S.S.R. **44** 59.22N 26.28E
Raleigh U.S.A. **113** 35.46N 78.39W
Raleigh B. U.S.A. **113** 35.47N 76.09W
Ralik Chain *is.* Pacific Oc. **84** 8.00N168.00E
Ram *r.* Canada **100** 62.01N123.41W
Rama Israel **67** 32.56N 35.22E
Rama Nicaragua **117** 12.09N 84.15W
Ramacca Italy **33** 37.23N 14.42E
Rāmah Saudi Arabia **65** 25.33N 47.08E
Ramales de la Victoria Spain **26** 43.15N 3.27W
Rām Allāh Jordan **67** 31.55N 35.12E
Ramallo Argentina **125** 33.28S 60.02W
Rāmānuj Ganj India **63** 23.48N 83.42E
Ramat Dawid Israel **67** 32.40N 35.12E
Ramat Gan Israel **67** 32.05N 34.48E
Ramat HaSharon Israel **67** 32.09N 34.50E
Ramat HaShofet Israel **67** 32.37N 35.06E
Ramat Yishay Israel **67** 32.42N 35.10E
Ramat Yohanan Israel **67** 32.47N 35.07E
Rambau, Lac *l.* Canada **103** 53.40N 70.10W
Rambervillers France **19** 48.21N 6.38E
Rambla del Judío *r.* Spain **25** 38.15N 1.27W
Rambouillet France **19** 48.39N 1.50E
Rām Dās India **62** 31.58N 74.55E
Rame Head Australia **93** 37.50S149.25E
Rame Head U.K. **13** 50.18N 4.13W
Ramelton Rep. of Ire. **15** 55.02N 7.40W
Rāmgarh Bangla. **63** 22.59N 91.43E
Rāmgarh Bihār India **63** 23.38N 85.31E
Rāmgarh Rāj. India **62** 27.15N 75.11E
Rāmgarh Rāj. India **62** 27.22N 70.30E
Rāmhormoz Iran **65** 31.14N 49.37E
Ramillies Belgium **16** 50.39N 4.56E
Ramingstein Austria **39** 47.04N 13.50E
Ramīs *r.* Ethiopia **73** 7.59N 41.34E
Ramla Israel **67** 31.56N 34.52E
Ramlu *mtn.* Ethiopia **73** 13.20N 41.45E
Rāmnagar India **63** 25.17N 83.02E
Ramnäs Sweden **43** 59.46N 16.12E
Ramo Ethiopia **73** 6.50N 41.15E
Ramona Calif. U.S.A. **109** 33.08N116.52W
Ramona Okla. U.S.A. **111** 36.32N 95.55W
Ramore Canada **102** 48.30N 80.25W
Ramos Arizpe Mexico **111** 25.33N100.58W
Ramot Naftali Israel **67** 33.06N 35.33E
Rāmpur Himachal P. India **63** 31.27N 77.38E
Rāmpur Uttar P. India **63** 28.49N 79.02E
Rampura India **62** 24.28N 75.26E
Ramree I. Burma **56** 19.06N 93.48E
Ramsey England U.K. **13** 52.27N 0.06W
Ramsey I.o.M. U.K. **12** 54.19N 4.23W
Ramsey L. Canada **104** 47.15N 82.16W
Ramsgate U.K. **13** 51.20N 1.25E
Rāmshīr Iran **65** 30.54N 49.24E
Ramsjö Sweden **41** 62.11N 15.39E
Rāmtek India **63** 21.24N 79.20E
Ramu *r.* P.N.G. **59** 4.00S144.40E
Ramusio, Lac *l.* Canada **103** 55.04N 63.40W
Ranau Malaysia **58** 5.58N116.41E
Rancagua Chile **125** 34.10S 70.45W
Rance *r.* France **18** 48.31N 1.59W
Rancheria *r.* Canada **100** 60.13N129.07W
Rānchī India **63** 23.21N 85.20E
Rand Australia **93** 35.34S146.35E
Randalstown U.K. **15** 54.45N 6.20W
Randan France **20** 46.01N 3.21E
Randazzo Italy **33** 37.53N 14.57E
Rānder India **62** 21.14N 72.47E
Randers Denmark **42** 56.28N 10.03E
Randolph Kans. U.S.A. **110** 39.27N 96.44W
Randolph N.Y. U.S.A. **114** 42.10N 78.59W
Randolph Vt. U.S.A. **105** 43.55N 72.40W
Randsburg U.S.A. **109** 35.22N117.39W
Randsfjorden *l.* Norway **41** 60.25N 10.24E
Råne *r.* Sweden **40** 65.52N 22.19E
Råneå Sweden **40** 65.52N 22.18E
Rāner India **62** 28.53N 73.17E
Ranfurly New Zealand **86** 45.08S170.08E
Rangdong China **54** 32.51N112.18E
Rangely U.S.A. **108** 40.05N108.48W
Ranger U.S.A. **113** 38.07N 82.10W
Ranger L. Canada **104** 46.54N 83.35W
Ranger Lake *town* Canada **104** 46.52N 83.36W
Rangia India **63** 26.28N 91.38E
Rangiora New Zealand **86** 43.18S172.38E
Rangiroa *i.* Pacific Oc. **85** 15.00S147.40W
Rangitaiki *r.* New Zealand **86** 37.55S176.50E
Rangkasbitung Indonesia **59** 6.21S106.12E
Rangoon Burma **56** 16.47N 96.10E
Rangpur Bangla. **63** 25.45N 89.15E
Rānīganj India **63** 23.37N 87.08E
Rānīkhet India **63** 29.39N 79.25E
Rāniwāra India **62** 24.45N 72.13E
Rankin Inlet *town* Canada **99** 62.52N 92.00W
Rankins Springs *town* Australia **93** 33.52S146.18E
Rannoch, Loch U.K. **14** 56.41N 4.20W
Rann of Kachchh *f.* India **62** 23.50N 69.50E
Ranohira Madagascar **81** 22.29S 45.24E
Rano Kao *mtn.* I. de Pascua **85** 27.11S109.27W
Ranong Thailand **56** 9.59N 98.40E
Ransäter Sweden **43** 59.46N 13.26E
Rantauprapat Indonesia **58** 2.05N 99.46E
Rantekombola *mtn.* Indonesia **58** 3.30S119.58E
Råö Sweden **42** 57.24N 11.56E
Rao Co *mtn.* Laos **56** 18.10N105.25E
Raoping China **55** 23.45N117.05E
Raoul *i.* Pacific Oc. **84** 29.15S177.55W
Rapa *i.* Pacific Oc. **85** 27.35S144.20W
Rapallo Italy **30** 44.21N 9.14E
Rāpar India **62** 23.34N 70.38E
Rapidan *r.* U.S.A. **114** 38.22N 77.37W
Rapid Bay *town* Australia **92** 35.33S138.09E
Rapid City U.S.A. **110** 44.05N103.14W
Rapides des Joachims *town* Canada **105** 46.13N 77.43W
Rappahannock *r.* U.S.A. **114** 37.34N 76.18W
Rapperswil Switz. **39** 47.14N 8.50E
Rapsáni Greece **34** 39.54N 22.33E
Raquette *r.* U.S.A. **105** 45.00N 74.42W
Raquette L. U.S.A. **105** 43.52N 74.38W
Raquette Lake *town* U.S.A. **105** 43.49N 74.41W
Rarotonga *i.* Cook Is. **84** 21.14S159.46W
Ra's al Ḩadd *c.* Oman **60** 22.32N 59.49E
Ra's al Khaymah U.A.E. **65** 25.48N 55.56E
Ra's al Unūf Libya **75** 30.31N 18.34E
Ra's an Nabq *town* Egypt **66** 29.36N 34.51E
Ra's an Naqb *town* Jordan **66** 30.30N 35.29E
Ras Dashen *mtn.* Ethiopia **73** 13.20N 38.10E
Ras Djebel Tunisia **32** 37.13N 10.09E
Râs Ghârib Egypt **66** 28.22N 33.04E
Rashād Sudan **73** 11.51N 31.04E
Rashīd Egypt **66** 31.25N 30.25E

Rashīd Qal 'eh to Rittman

Rashīd Qal 'eh Afghan. **62** 31.31N 67.31E
Rasht Iran **65** 37.18N 49.38E
Rasina *r.* Yugo. **34** 43.38N 21.21E
Raška Yugo. **34** 43.17N 20.37E
Rās Koh *mtn.* Pakistan **62** 28.50N 65.12E
Rason L. Australia **89** 28.46S124.20E
Rasra India **63** 25.51N 83.51E
Rastatt Germany **39** 48.51N 8.12E
Rastede Germany **38** 53.15N 8.11E
Rasu, Monte *mtn.* Italy **32** 40.25N 9.00E
Ratak Chain *is.* Pacific Oc. **84** 8.00N172.00E
Ratangarh India **62** 28.05N 74.36E
Rat Buri Thailand **56** 13.30N 99.50E
Ratcatchers L. Australia **92** 32.40S143.13E
Rāth India **63** 25.35N 79.34E
Rathcormack Rep. of Ire. **15** 52.05N 8.18W
Rathdrum Rep. of Ire. **15** 52.56N 6.15W
Rathenow Germany **38** 52.36N 12.20E
Rathlin I. U.K. **15** 55.17N 6.15W
Rath Luirc Rep. of Ire. **15** 52.21N 8.41W
Rathmullen Rep. of Ire. **15** 55.06N 7.32W
Ratlām India **62** 23.19N 75.04E
Ratnāgiri India **60** 16.59N 73.18E
Ratno U.S.S.R. **37** 51.40N 24.32E
Ratodero Pakistan **62** 27.48N 68.18E
Raton U.S.A. **108** 36.54N104.24W
Rats, Rivière aux *r.* Canada **105** 47.12N 72.52W
Rattlesnake Range *mts.* U.S.A. **108** 42.45N107.10W
Rattray Head U.K. **14** 57.37N 1.50W
Rättvik Sweden **41** 60.53N 15.06E
Ratzeburg Germany **38** 53.42N 10.46E
Ratzeburger See *l.* Germany **38** 53.45N 10.47E
Rauch Argentina **125** 36.47S 59.05W
Raufoss Norway **41** 60.43N 10.37E
Raul Soares Brazil **126** 20.04S 42.27W
Rauma Finland **41** 61.08N 21.30E
Rauma *r.* Norway **40** 62.32N 7.43E
Raung, Gunung *mtn.* Indonesia **59** 8.07S114.03E
Raurkela India **63** 22.13N 84.53E
Rautas Sweden **40** 68.00N 19.55E
Ravalgaon India **62** 20.38N 74.25E
Ravanusa Italy **32** 37.16N 13.58E
Rāvar Iran **65** 31.14N 56.51E
Rava-Russkaya U.S.S.R. **37** 50.15N 23.36E
Ravena U.S.A. **115** 42.29N 73.49W
Ravenna Italy **30** 44.25N 12.12E
Ravenna U.S.A. **114** 41.09N 81.15W
Ravensburg Germany **39** 47.47N 9.37E
Ravenshoe Australia **90** 17.37S145.29E
Ravensthorpe Australia **89** 33.35S120.02E
Ravenswood U.S.A. **114** 38.57N 81.46W
Rāver India **62** 21.15N 76.05E
Ravi *r.* Pakistan **60** 30.30N 72.13E
Ravna Gora Yugo. **31** 45.23N 14.57E
Rawaki *i.* Kiribati **84** 3.43S170.43W
Rāwalpindi Pakistan **62** 33.36N 73.04E
Rawāndūz Iraq **65** 36.38N 44.32E
Rawdon Canada **105** 46.03N 73.44W
Rawene New Zealand **86** 35.24S173.30E
Rawicz Poland **36** 51.37N 16.52E
Rawlinna Australia **89** 31.00S125.21E
Rawlins U.S.A. **108** 41.47N107.14W
Rawson Argentina **125** 34.40S 60.02W
Raxaul India **63** 26.59N 84.51E
Ray U.S.A. **110** 48.21N103.10W
Ray, C. Canada **103** 47.40N 59.18W
Raya *mtn.* Indonesia **58** 0.45S112.45E
Rāyagada India **63** 19.10N 83.25E
Rāyen Iran **65** 29.34N 57.26E
Raymond Canada **100** 49.30N112.35W
Raymond U.S.A. **108** 46.41N123.44W
Raymond Terrace Australia **93** 32.47S151.45E
Raymondville U.S.A. **111** 26.29N 97.47W
Rayong Thailand **56** 12.43N101.20E
Raz, Pointe du *c.* France **18** 48.02N 4.44W
Razan Iran **65** 35.22N 49.02E
Razanj Yugo. **34** 43.40N 21.31E
Razdelnaya U.S.S.R. **37** 46.50N 30.02E
Razgrad Bulgaria **34** 43.33N 26.34E
Razgrad *d.* Bulgaria **34** 43.32N 26.10E
Razlog Bulgaria **34** 41.53N 23.28E
Ré, Île de *i.* France **20** 46.10N 1.26W
Reading U.K. **13** 51.27N 0.57W
Reading U.S.A. **115** 40.20N 75.56W
Readsboro U.S.A. **115** 42.46N 72.57W
Realicó Argentina **125** 35.02S 64.14W
Réalmont France **20** 43.47N 2.12E
Reay Forest *f.* U.K. **14** 58.17N 4.48W
Rebecca, L. Australia **89** 30.07S122.32E
Rebi Indonesia **59** 6.24S134.07E
Rebiana Sand Sea *see* Rabyānah, Ṣaḥrā'. *f.* Libya **75**
Reboly U.S.S.R. **44** 63.50N 30.49E
Rebun jima *i.* Japan **57** 45.25N141.04E
Recalde Argentina **125** 36.39S 61.05W
Recanati Italy **31** 43.24N 13.32E
Rechāh Lām Afghan. **62** 34.58N 70.51E
Recherche, Archipelago of the *is.* Australia **89** 34.05S122.45E
Rechitsa U.S.S.R. **37** 52.21N 30.24E
Recife Brazil **123** 8.06S 34.53W
Recklinghausen Germany **38** 51.36N 7.13E
Recknitz *r.* Germany **38** 54.14N 12.28E
Reconquista Argentina **124** 29.08S 59.38W
Recreo Argentina **124** 29.20S 65.04W
Red *r.* Canada **101** 50.20N 96.50W
Red *r.* U.S.A. **111** 31.00N 91.40W
Red *r. see* Hong Hà *r.* Vietnam **56**
Red Bank U.S.A. **115** 40.21N 74.03W
Red Basin *f. see* Sichuan Pendi *f.* China **55**
Red Bay *town* Canada **103** 51.44N 56.45W
Red Bluff U.S.A. **108** 40.11N122.15W
Redcar U.K. **12** 54.37N 1.04W
Red Cliffs *town* Australia **92** 34.22S142.13E
Red Cloud U.S.A. **110** 40.04N 98.31W
Red Deer Canada **100** 52.20N113.50W
Red Deer *r.* Canada **101** 50.56N109.54W
Redding U.S.A. **108** 40.35N122.24W
Redditch U.K. **13** 52.18N 1.57W
Rede *r.* U.K. **12** 55.08N 2.13W
Redfield U.S.A. **110** 44.53N 98.31W
Redhill *town* Australia **92** 33.34S138.12E
Red Hook U.S.A. **115** 41.55N 73.53W
Red Indian L. Canada **103** 48.40N 56.50W
Red L. U.S.A. **107** 48.00N 95.00W
Red Lake *town* Canada **102** 51.03N 93.49W
Redlands U.S.A. **109** 34.03N117.11W
Red Lion U.S.A. **115** 39.54N 76.36W
Red Lodge U.S.A. **108** 45.11N109.15W
Redmond U.S.A. **108** 44.17N121.11W
Rednitz *r.* Germany **38** 49.28N 10.59E
Red Oak U.S.A. **110** 41.01N 95.14W
Redon France **18** 47.39N 2.05W
Redondela Spain **26** 42.17N 8.36W
Redondo Portugal **27** 38.39N 7.33W
Redondo Beach *town* U.S.A. **109** 33.51N118.23W
Red Rock Canada **100** 53.39N122.41W
Redrock U.S.A. **109** 32.35N111.19W
Redruth U.K. **13** 50.14N 5.14W
Red Sea Africa / Asia **71** 20.00N 39.00E
Redstone Canada **100** 52.13N123.50W
Red Sucker L. Canada **101** 54.09N 93.40W
Red Volta *r.* Ghana **76** 10.32N 0.31W
Redwater Alta. Canada **100** 53.55N113.06W
Redwater Ont. Canada **104** 46.54N 79.34W
Red Wing U.S.A. **110** 44.33N 92.31W
Redwood City U.S.A. **108** 37.29N122.13W
Ree, Lough Rep. of Ire. **15** 53.31N 7.58W
Reed City U.S.A. **112** 43.54N 85.31W
Reeder U.S.A. **110** 46.06N102.57W
Reedsport U.S.A. **108** 43.42N124.06W
Reedy U.S.A. **114** 38.54N 81.26W
Reefton New Zealand **86** 42.07S171.52E
Reese *r.* U.S.A. **108** 40.39N116.54W
Reftele Sweden **43** 57.11N 13.35E
Refuge Cove *town* Canada **100** 50.07N124.50W
Refugio U.S.A. **111** 28.18N 97.17W
Rega *r.* Poland **36** 54.10N 15.18E
Regavim Israel **67** 32.32N 35.02E
Regen Germany **39** 48.59N 13.07E
Regen *r.* Germany **39** 49.01N 12.06E
Regensburg Germany **39** 49.01N 12.06E
Reggane Algeria **74** 26.42N 0.10E
Reggello Italy **30** 43.41N 11.32E
Reggio Calabria Italy **33** 38.07N 15.39E
Reggio Emilia-Romagna Italy **30** 44.43N 10.36E
Reghin Romania **37** 46.47N 24.42E
Regina Canada **101** 50.25N104.39W
Regiwar Pakistan **62** 25.57N 65.44E
Regnéville France **18** 49.01N 1.33W
Reguengos de Monsaraz Portugal **27** 38.25N 7.32W
Rehau Germany **39** 50.15N 12.02E
Rehoboth Namibia **80** 23.19S 17.10E
Rehoboth B. U.S.A. **115** 38.40N 75.06W
Rehoboth Beach *town* U.S.A. **115** 38.43N 75.05W
Rehovot Israel **67** 31.54N 34.46E
Reichenbach Germany **38** 50.37N 12.18E
Reidsville U.S.A. **113** 36.21N 79.40W
Reigate U.K. **13** 51.14N 0.13W
Reims France **19** 49.15N 4.02E
Reinach Switz. **39** 47.30N 7.35E
Reindeer L. Canada **101** 57.15N102.40W
Reinosa Spain **26** 43.00N 4.08W
Reisterstown U.S.A. **114** 39.28N 76.50W
Rejmyra Sweden **43** 58.50N 15.55E
Rekovac Yugo. **34** 43.51N 21.03E
Relizane Algeria **75** 35.45N 0.33E
Remanso Brazil **123** 9.41S 42.04W
Remarkable, Mt. Australia **92** 32.48S138.10E
Rembang Indonesia **59** 6.45S111.22E
Remeshk Iran **65** 26.52N 58.46E
Remich Lux. **16** 49.34N 6.23E
Remington U.S.A. **114** 38.32N 77.49W
Remiremont France **19** 48.01N 6.35E
Remoulins France **21** 43.56N 4.34E
Remscheid Germany **38** 51.11N 7.11E
Remsen U.S.A. **115** 43.19N 75.11W
Rena Norway **41** 61.08N 11.22E
Rende Italy **33** 39.19N 16.11E
Rendina Greece **35** 39.04N 21.58E
Rendsburg Germany **38** 54.18N 9.40E
Renfrew Canada **105** 45.28N 76.41W
Rengat Indonesia **58** 0.26S102.35E
Rengo Chile **125** 34.25S 70.52W
Renheji China **55** 31.56N115.07E
Reni India **62** 28.41N 75.02E
Reni U.S.S.R. **37** 45.28N 28.17E
Renkum Neth. **16** 51.59N 5.46E
Renmark Australia **92** 34.10S140.45E
Rennell Sd. Canada **100** 53.23N132.35W
Renner Springs *town* Australia **90** 18.20S133.48E
Rennes France **18** 48.05N 1.41W
Reno *r.* Italy **30** 44.37N 12.17E
Reno U.S.A. **108** 39.31N119.48W
Renovo U.S.A. **114** 41.20N 77.38W
Rensselaer U.S.A. **115** 42.39N 73.44W
Rentería Spain **26** 43.19N 1.54W
Renton U.S.A. **108** 47.30N122.11W
Ren Xian China **54** 37.07N114.41E
Réo Burkina **76** 12.20N 2.27W
Repki U.S.S.R. **37** 51.47N 31.06E
Republic Penn. U.S.A. **114** 39.56N 79.55W
Republic Wash. U.S.A. **108** 48.39N118.44W
Republican *r.* U.S.A. **110** 39.03N 96.48W
Republic of Ireland Europe **15** 53.00N 8.00W
Republic of South Africa Africa **80** 28.30S 24.50E
Repulse B. Australia **90** 20.36S148.43E
Repulse Bay *town* Canada **99** 66.35N 86.20W
Requa U.S.A. **108** 41.34N124.05W
Requena Peru **122** 5.05S 73.52W
Requena Spain **25** 39.29N 1.06W
Réquista France **20** 44.02N 2.31E
Resadiye Karimadasi *pen.* Turkey **35** 36.45N 27.40E
Reschenpass Italy / Austria **39** 46.50N 10.30E
Resen Yugo. **34** 41.05N 21.00E
Reserve Canada **101** 52.28N102.39W
Resistencia Argentina **124** 27.28S 59.00W
Reşiţa Romania **37** 45.17N 21.53E
Resolute Canada **99** 74.40N 95.00W
Resolution I. Canada **99** 61.30N 65.00W
Resolution I. New Zealand **86** 45.40S166.30E
Restigouche *r.* Canada **103** 48.04N 66.20W
Restoule Canada **104** 46.03N 79.47W
Rethel France **19** 49.31N 4.22E
Réthimnon Greece **35** 35.22N 24.29E
Réunion *i.* Indian Oc. **49** 22.00S 55.00E
Reus Spain **25** 41.09N 1.07E
Reusel Neth. **16** 51.21N 5.09E
Reuterstadt Stavenhagen Germany **38** 53.40N 12.54E
Reutlingen Germany **39** 48.29N 9.11E
Reutte Austria **39** 47.29N 10.43E
Revda U.S.S.R. **44** 56.49N 59.58E
Revelstoke Canada **100** 51.00N118.00W
Revigny-sur-Ornain France **19** 48.50N 4.59E
Revilla del Campo Spain **26** 42.13N 3.32W
Revilla Gigedo, Islas de *is.* Mexico **116** 19.00N111.00W
Revillagigedo I. U.S.A. **100** 55.50N131.20W
Revin France **19** 49.56N 4.38E
Revue *r.* Mozambique **81** 19.58S 34.40E
Rewa India **63** 24.32N 81.18E
Rewāri India **62** 28.11N 76.37E
Rexburg U.S.A. **108** 43.49N111.47W
Rexford U.S.A. **108** 48.53N115.13W
Rey Iran **65** 35.35N 51.27E
Reykjavík Iceland **40** 64.09N 21.58W
Reynoldsville U.S.A. **114** 41.06N 78.53W
Reynosa Mexico **111** 26.07N 98.18W
Rezé France **18** 47.12N 1.34W
Rēzekne U.S.S.R. **44** 56.30N 27.22E
Rhaetian Alps *mts.* Switz. **39** 46.45N 9.55E
Rhayader U.K. **13** 52.19N 3.30W
Rheda-Wiedenbrück Schloss Germany **38** 51.51N 8.17E
Rheden Neth. **16** 52.01N 6.02E
Rhein *r.* Europe **16** 51.53N 6.03E
Rheinbach Germany **38** 50.37N 6.57E
Rheine Germany **38** 52.17N 7.26E
Rheinfelden Germany **39** 47.33N 7.47E
Rheinland-Pfalz *d.* Germany **39** 49.50N 7.30E
Rheinsberg Germany **38** 53.06N 12.53E
Rhenen Neth. **16** 51.58N 5.34E
Rheydt Germany **38** 51.10N 6.25E
Rhine *see* Rhein *r.* Europe **16**
Rhinebeck U.S.A. **115** 41.56N 73.55W
Rhinelander U.S.A. **110** 45.39N 89.23W
Rhino Camp *town* Uganda **79** 2.58N 31.20E
Rhir, Cap *c.* Morocco **74** 30.38N 9.55W
Rho Italy **30** 45.32N 9.02E
Rhode Island *d.* U.S.A. **115** 41.40N 71.30W
Rhode Island Sd. U.S.A. **115** 41.25N 71.15W
Rhodes *i. see* Ródhos *i.* Greece **35**
Rhodope Mts. *see* Rhodopi Planina *mts.* Bulgaria **34**
Rhodopi Planina *mts.* Bulgaria **34** 41.40N 24.20E
Rhondda U.K. **13** 51.39N 3.30W
Rhône *d.* France **21** 45.54N 4.35E
Rhône *r.* France **21** 43.20N 4.50E
Rhône-Alpes *d.* France **21** 45.20N 5.45E
Rhône au Rhin, Canal du France **19** 47.06N 5.19E
Rhosneigr U.K. **12** 53.14N 4.31W
Rhue *r.* France **20** 45.23N 2.29E
Rhum *i.* U.K. **14** 57.00N 6.20W
Rhyl U.K. **12** 53.19N 3.29W
Riachão Brazil **123** 7.22S 46.37W
Riāng India **63** 27.32N 92.56E
Riánsares *r.* Spain **27** 39.32N 3.18W
Riāsi Jammu & Kashmir **62** 33.05N 74.50E
Riau *d.* Indonesia **58** 0.00 102.35E
Riau, Kepulauan *is.* Indonesia **58** 0.50N104.00E
Riaza Spain **26** 41.17N 3.28W
Riaza *r.* Spain **26** 41.42N 3.55W
Ribadeo Spain **26** 43.33N 7.02W
Ribadesella Spain **26** 43.28N 5.04W
Ribarroja, Embalse de *resr.* Spain **25** 41.12N 0.20E
Ribauè Mozambique **79** 14.57S 38.27E
Ribble *r.* U.K. **12** 53.45N 2.44W
Ribe Denmark **42** 55.21N 8.46E
Ribeauvillé France **19** 48.12N 7.19E
Ribécourt France **19** 49.31N 2.55E
Ribeirão Prêto Brazil **126** 21.09S 47.48W
Ribera Italy **32** 37.30N 13.16E
Ribérac France **20** 45.14N 0.22E
Riberalta Bolivia **124** 10.59S 66.06W
Ribnica Yugo. **31** 45.44N 14.44E
Ribnitz-Damgarten Germany **38** 54.15N 12.28E
Ribstone Creek *r.* Canada **101** 52.51N110.05W
Riccia Italy **33** 41.29N 14.50E
Riccione Italy **30** 43.59N 12.39E
Rice U.S.A. **109** 34.06N114.50W
Rice L. Canada **104** 44.08N 78.13W
Rice Lake *town* U.S.A. **110** 45.30N 91.43W
Rich, C. Canada **104** 44.43N 80.38W
Richard's Bay *town* R.S.A. **81** 28.47S 32.06E
Richardson *r.* Canada **101** 58.30N111.30W
Richardson U.S.A. **111** 32.57N 96.44W
Richelieu *r.* Canada **105** 46.03N 73.07W
Richelieu France **18** 47.01N 0.19E
Richfield Idaho U.S.A. **108** 43.03N114.09W
Richfield Utah U.S.A. **108** 38.46N112.05W
Richfield Springs U.S.A. **115** 42.51N 74.59W
Richford U.S.A. **105** 45.00N 72.40W
Rich Hill *town* U.S.A. **111** 38.06N 94.22W
Richibucto Canada **103** 46.41N 64.52W
Richland U.S.A. **108** 46.17N119.18W
Richmond Qld. Australia **90** 20.44S143.08E
Richmond Ont. Canada **105** 45.11N 75.50W
Richmond Que. Canada **105** 45.40N 72.09W
Richmond New Zealand **86** 41.20S173.10E
Richmond C.P. R.S.A. **80** 31.24S 23.56E
Richmond U.K. **12** 54.24N 1.43W
Richmond Ind. U.S.A. **112** 39.50N 84.51W
Richmond Utah U.S.A. **108** 41.55N111.48W
Richmond Va. U.S.A. **113** 37.34N 77.27W
Richmond Dale U.S.A. **114** 39.13N 82.54W
Richmond Hill Canada **104** 43.52N 79.27W
Richmond Range *mts.* Australia **93** 29.00S152.48E
Richwood U.S.A. **114** 38.14N 80.32W
Ricobayo, Embalse de *resr.* Spain **26** 41.30N 5.55W
Ridderkerk Neth. **16** 51.53N 4.39E
Rideau *r.* Canada **105** 45.27N 75.42W
Rideau Hills Canada **105** 44.37N 77.00W
Rideau Lakes Canada **105** 44.45N 76.17W
Ridgetown Canada **104** 42.26N 81.54W
Ridgway U.S.A. **114** 41.26N 78.44W
Riding Mtn. Canada **101** 50.37N 99.50W
Riding Mtn. Nat. Park Canada **101** 50.55N100.25W
Ried Austria **39** 48.13N 13.30E
Riemst Belgium **16** 50.49N 5.38E
Riesa Germany **38** 51.18N 13.17E
Riesi Italy **33** 37.17N 14.05E
Rieti Italy **30** 42.24N 12.51E
Rifle U.S.A. **108** 39.32N107.47W
Rift Valley *d.* Kenya **79** 1.00N 36.00E
Riga U.S.S.R. **41** 56.53N 24.08E
Riga, G. of *see* Rīgas Jūras Līcis *g.* U.S.S.R. **41**
Rīgān Iran **65** 28.40N 58.58E
Rīgas Jūras Līcis *g.* U.S.S.R. **41** 57.30N 23.35E
Rīgestān *f.* Afghan. **62** 30.35N 65.00E
Riggins U.S.A. **108** 45.25N116.19W
Rīg Matī Iran **65** 27.40N 58.11E
Rigo P.N.G. **90** 9.50S147.35E
Rigolet Canada **103** 54.20N 58.35W
Riihimäki Finland **41** 60.45N 24.46E
Riiser-Larsenhalvöya *pen.* Antarctica **128** 68.00S 35.00E
Riječki Zaljev *b.* Yugo. **31** 45.15N 14.25E
Rijeka Yugo. **31** 45.20N 14.27E
Rijssen Neth. **16** 52.19N 6.31E
Rijswijk Neth. **16** 52.03N 4.22E
Rila Planina *mts.* Bulgaria **34** 42.10N 23.30E
Riley U.S.A. **108** 43.31N119.28W
Rimah, Wādī ar *r.* Saudi Arabia **64** 26.10N 44.00E
Rimavská Sobota Czech. **37** 48.23N 20.02E
Rimbo Sweden **43** 59.45N 18.22E
Rimersburg U.S.A. **114** 41.02N 79.30W
Rimforsa Sweden **43** 58.08N 15.40E
Rimini Italy **30** 44.04N 12.34E
Rîmnicu-Sărat Romania **37** 45.24N 27.06E
Rîmnicu-Vîlcea Romania **37** 45.06N 24.22E
Rimouski Canada **103** 48.27N 68.32W
Rinbung China **63** 29.16N 89.54E
Rinconada Argentina **124** 22.26S 66.10W
Rindal Norway **40** 63.04N 9.13E
Ringe Denmark **42** 55.14N 10.29E
Ringebu Norway **41** 61.31N 10.10E
Ringerike Norway **42** 60.10N 10.18E
Ringim Nigeria **77** 12.09N 9.08E
Ringköbing Denmark **42** 56.05N 8.15E
Ringköbing Fjord *est.* Denmark **42** 56.00N 8.15E
Ringling U.S.A. **108** 46.16N110.49W
Ringsted Denmark **42** 55.27N 11.49E
Ringus India **62** 27.21N 75.34E
Ringvassöy *i.* Norway **40** 69.55N 19.10E
Ringwood U.K. **13** 50.50N 1.48W
Rintein Germany **38** 52.11N 9.04E
Riobamba Ecuador **122** 1.44S 78.40W
Rio Branco Brazil **122** 9.59S 67.49W
Río Bueno Chile **125** 40.20S 72.55W
Rio Casca Brazil **126** 20.13S 42.38W
Rio Claro Brazil **126** 22.19S 47.35W
Río Cuarto Argentina **125** 33.08S 64.20W
Rio de Janeiro Brazil **126** 22.53S 43.17W
Rio de Janeiro *d.* Brazil **126** 22.00S 42.30W
Río Gallegos Argentina **125** 51.37S 69.10W
Río Grande *town* Argentina **125** 53.50S 67.40W
Rio Grande *town* Brazil **126** 32.03S 52.08W
Río Grande *r.* Mexico / U.S.A. **111** 25.57N 97.09W
Río Grande *r.* Nicaragua **117** 12.48N 83.30W
Rio Grande City U.S.A. **111** 26.23N 98.49W
Rio Grande do Norte *d.* Brazil **123** 6.00S 36.30W
Rio Grande do Sul *d.* Brazil **126** 30.15S 53.30W
Ríohacha Colombia **122** 11.34N 72.58W
Rio Largo Brazil **123** 9.28S 35.50W
Riom France **20** 45.54N 3.07E
Río Negro *d.* Argentina **125** 40.00S 67.00W
Rio Negro Brazil **126** 26.06S 49.48W
Río Negro, Embalse del *resr.* Uruguay **125** 32.45S 56.00W
Rionero in Vulture Italy **33** 40.56N 15.41E
Rio Novo Brazil **126** 21.15S 43.09W
Riópar Spain **26** 38.30N 2.27W
Rio Piracicaba Brazil **126** 19.54S 43.10W
Rio Pomba Brazil **126** 21.15S 43.12W
Rio Prêto Brazil **126** 22.06S 43.52W
Ríosucio Colombia **122** 7.27N 77.07W
Río Tercero Argentina **124** 32.10S 64.05W
Rio Verde *town* Brazil **124** 17.50S 50.55W
Rioz France **19** 47.25N 6.04E
Ripatransone Italy **31** 43.00N 13.46E
Ripley Canada **104** 44.04N 81.34W
Ripley N.Y. U.S.A. **114** 42.16N 79.43W
Ripley W.Va. U.S.A. **114** 38.49N 81.43W
Ripoll Spain **25** 42.12N 2.12E
Ripon Canada **105** 45.47N 75.06W
Ripon U.K. **12** 54.08N 1.31W
Riposto Italy **33** 37.45N 15.12E
Rirapora Brazil **126** 17.20S 45.02W
Risbäck Sweden **40** 64.42N 15.32E
Riscle France **20** 43.40N 0.05W
Rishā, Wādī ar *r.* Saudi Arabia **65** 25.40N 44.08E
Rishikesh India **63** 30.07N 78.42E
Rishiri tō *i.* Japan **57** 45.11N141.15E
Rishon LeZiyyon Israel **67** 31.57N 34.48E
Rishpon Israel **67** 32.12N 34.49E
Risle *r.* France **18** 49.26N 0.23E
Risnjak *mtn.* Yugo. **31** 45.26N 14.37E
Rison U.S.A. **111** 33.58N 92.11W
Risör Norway **42** 58.43N 9.14E
Rissani Morocco **74** 31.23N 4.09W
Riti Nigeria **77** 7.57N 9.41E
Ritidian Pt. Guam **84** 13.39N144.51E
Rittman U.S.A. **114** 40.58N 81.47W

Runka to **St. Magnus B.**

Runka Nigeria **77** 12.28N 7.20E
Ruoqiang China **52** 39.00N 88.00E
Ruo Shui *r.* China **52** 42.15N101.03E
Rūpar India **62** 30.58N 76.32E
Rupert *r.* Canada **102** 51.30N 78.45W
Rupununi *r.* Guyana **122** 4.00N 58.30W
Ruqqad *r.* Syria **67** 32.44N 35.46E
Rur *r.* Neth. **16** 51.12N 5.58E
Rurutu *i.* Pacific Oc. **85** 22.25S151.20W
Rusape Zimbabwe **81** 18.30S 32.08E
Ruşayriş, Khazzān ar *resr.* Sudan **73** 11.40N 34.20E
Ruse Bulgaria **34** 43.48N 25.59E
Rusera India **63** 25.45N 86.02E
Rushan China **54** 36.54N121.30E
Rushden U.K. **13** 52.17N 0.37W
Rush Springs *town* U.S.A. **111** 34.47N 97.58W
Rushworth Australia **93** 36.38S145.02E
Rusken *l.* Sweden **43** 57.17N 14.20E
Russell Canada **105** 45.17N 75.17W
Russell U.S.A. **105** 44.26N 75.11W
Russellkonda India **63** 19.56N 84.35E
Russell L. Man. Canada **101** 56.15N101.30W
Russell L. N.W.T. Canada **100** 63.05N115.44W
Russell Pt. Canada **98** 73.30N115.00W
Russell Range *mts.* Australia **89** 33.15S123.30E
Russellville U.S.A. **111** 35.17N 93.08W
Rüsselsheim Germany **39** 50.00N 8.25E
Russkaya Polyana U.S.S.R. **50** 53.48N 73.54E
Rustavi U.S.S.R. **45** 41.34N 45.03E
Rustenburg R.S.A. **80** 25.39S 27.13E
Ruston U.S.A. **111** 32.32N 92.38W
Rutana Burundi **79** 3.58S 30.00E
Rutanzige, L. *see* Edward, L. Uganda / Zaïre **79**
Rütenbrock Germany **38** 52.50N 7.10E
Ruteng Indonesia **59** 8.35S120.28E
Rutenga Zimbabwe **80** 21.15S 30.46E
Ruth U.S.A. **108** 39.17N114.59W
Rutherglen Canada **104** 46.16N 79.04W
Ruthin U.K. **12** 53.07N 3.18W
Rutland U.S.A. **115** 43.36N 72.59W
Rutledge *r.* Canada **101** 61.04N112.00W
Rutledge L. Canada **101** 61.33N110.47W
Rutog China **63** 33.27N 79.43E
Rutshuru Zaïre **79** 1.10S 29.26E
Rutter Canada **104** 46.06N 80.40W
Ruvu Coast Tanzania **79** 6.50S 38.42E
Ruvuma *r.* Mozambique / Tanzania **79** 10.30S 40.30E
Ruvuma *d.* Tanzania **79** 10.45S 36.15E
Ruwaybah *wells* Sudan **72** 15.39N 28.45E
Ruwayfi, Jabal ar *mtn.* Jordan **67** 31.12N 36.00E
Ruwenzori Range *mts.* Uganda / Zaïre **79** 0.30N 30.00E
Ruyigi Burundi **79** 3.26S 30.14E
Ruzayevka U.S.S.R. **44** 54.04N 44.55E
Ruzitgort U.S.S.R. **44** 62.51N 64.52E
Ružomberok Czech. **37** 49.06N 19.18E
Rwanda Africa **79** 2.00S 30.00E
Ryan, Loch U.K. **14** 54.56N 5.02W
Ryasna U.S.S.R. **37** 54.00N 31.14E
Ryazan U.S.S.R. **44** 54.37N 39.43E
Ryazhsk U.S.S.R. **44** 53.40N 40.07E
Rybachiy, Poluostrov *pen.* U.S.S.R. **44** 69.45N 32.30E
Rybachye U.S.S.R. **52** 46.27N 81.30E
Rybinskoye Vodokhranilishche *resr.* U.S.S.R. **44** 58.30N 38.25E
Rybnik Poland **37** 50.06N 18.32E
Rybnitsa U.S.S.R. **37** 47.42N 29.00E
Ryd Sweden **43** 56.28N 14.41E
Rydaholm Sweden **43** 56.59N 14.16E
Rye U.K. **13** 50.57N 0.46E
Rye *r.* U.K. **12** 54.10N 0.44W
Ryfylke *f.* Norway **42** 59.30N 5.30E
Rygnestad Norway **42** 59.16N 7.29E
Ryki Poland **37** 51.39N 21.56E
Rylstone Australia **93** 32.48S149.58E
Ryōtsu Japan **57** 38.05N138.26E
Ryūgasaki Japan **57** 35.54N140.11E
Ryukyu Is. *see* Nansei shotō *is.* Japan **53**
Rzeszów Poland **37** 50.04N 22.00E
Rzhev U.S.S.R. **44** 56.15N 34.18E

S

Saa Cameroon **77** 4.24N 11.25E
Sa'ad Israel **67** 31.28N 34.32E
Saale *r.* Germany **38** 51.57N 11.55E
Saales France **19** 48.21N 7.07E
Saalfeld Germany **38** 50.39N 11.22E
Saanich Canada **100** 48.28N123.22W
Saar *r.* Germany **39** 49.42N 6.34E
Saarbrücken Germany **39** 49.14N 6.59E
Saarburg Germany **39** 49.36N 6.33E
Saaremaa *i.* U.S.S.R. **41** 58.25N 22.30E
Saarijärvi Finland **40** 62.43N 25.16E
Saariselkä *mts.* Finland **40** 68.15N 28.30E
Saarland *d.* Germany **39** 49.25N 6.45E
Saarlouis Germany **39** 49.21N 6.45E
Saba *i.* Leeward Is. **117** 17.42N 63.26W
Šabac Yugo. **31** 44.45N 19.42E
Sabadell Spain **25** 41.33N 2.06E
Sabah *d.* Malaysia **58** 5.30N117.00E
Sabalān, Kūhhā-ye *mts.* Iran **65** 38.15N 47.50E
Sabana, Archipiélago de Cuba **117** 23.30N 80.00W
Sabanalarga Colombia **122** 10.38N 75.00W
Sabasţīyah Jordan **67** 32.17N 35.12E
Sab'atayn, Ramlat as *f.* Yemen **71** 15.30N 46.10E
Sabatini, Monti *mts.* Italy **30** 42.10N 12.15E
Sabaudia Italy **32** 41.18N 13.01E
Sabbioneta Italy **32** 45.00N 10.39E
Sabhā Libya **75** 27.02N 14.26E
Sabhā *d.* Libya **75** 27.02N 15.30E
Sabi *r.* Zimbabwe **81** 21.16S 32.20E
Sabiñánigo Spain **25** 42.31N 0.22W
Sabinas Mexico **111** 27.51N101.07W
Sabinas Hidalgo Mexico **111** 26.30N100.10W
Sabine *r.* U.S.A. **111** 30.00N 93.45W
Sabine L. U.S.A. **111** 29.50N 93.50W
Sabini, Monti *mts.* Italy **30** 42.13N 12.50E
Sabkhat al Bardawīl *l.* Egypt **66** 31.10N 33.15E
Sablayan Phil. **59** 12.50N120.50E
Sable, C. Canada **103** 43.25N 65.35W
Sable, C. U.S.A. **113** 25.05N 65.50W
Sable I. Canada **103** 43.55N 59.50W
Sablé-sur-Sarthe France **18** 47.50N 0.20W
Sabon Birni Nigeria **77** 13.37N 6.15E
Sabongidda Nigeria **77** 6.54N 5.56E
Sabor *r.* Portugal **26** 41.10N 7.07W
Sabres France **20** 44.09N 0.44W
Sabrina Coast *f.* Antarctica **128** 67.00S120.00E
Sabugal Portugal **26** 40.21N 7.05W
Şabyā Saudi Arabia **72** 17.09N 42.37E
Sabzevār Iran **65** 36.13N 57.38E
Sacaca Bolivia **124** 18.05S 66.25W
Sacajawea *mtn.* U.S.A. **108** 45.15N117.17W
Sacandica Angola **78** 5.58S 15.56E
Sac City U.S.A. **110** 42.25N 95.00W
Sacedón Spain **26** 40.29N 2.43W
Sachigo *r.* Canada **102** 55.00N 89.00W
Sachigo L. Canada **102** 53.50N 92.00W
Sachsen *d.* Germany **38** 50.59N 13.15E
Sachsen *f.* Germany **38** 52.20N 11.20E
Sachsen-Anhalt *d.* Germany **38** 51.58N 11.30E
Sachsenburg Austria **39** 46.50N 13.21E
Sackets Harbor U.S.A. **105** 43.57N 76.07W
Säckingen Germany **39** 47.43N 7.56E
Sackville Canada **103** 45.54N 64.22W
Saco U.S.A. **115** 43.29N 70.28W
Sacramento Brazil **126** 19.51S 26.47W
Sacramento U.S.A. **108** 38.35N121.30W
Sacramento *r.* U.S.A. **108** 38.03N121.56W
Sacramento Mts. U.S.A. **109** 33.10N105.50W
Sacramento Valley *f.* U.S.A. **108** 39.15N122.00W
Sada Spain **26** 43.21N 8.15W
Sádaba Spain **25** 42.17N 1.16W
Sadani Tanzania **79** 6.00S 38.40E
Sadda Pakistan **62** 33.42N 70.20E
Sa Dec Vietnam **56** 10.19N105.45E
Sādiqābād Pakistan **62** 28.18N 70.08E
Sadiya India **61** 27.49N 95.38E
Sado *i.* Japan **57** 38.00N138.20E
Sado *r.* Portugal **27** 38.29N 8.55W
Sādri India **62** 25.11N 73.26E
Sadulgarh India **62** 29.35N 74.19E
Saeby Denmark **42** 57.20N 10.32E
Saegertown U.S.A. **114** 41.43N 80.09W
Şafājah *des.* Saudi Arabia **64** 26.30N 39.30E
Şafānīyah Egypt **66** 28.49N 30.48E
Şafarābād Iran **65** 38.59N 47.25E
Säffle Sweden **43** 59.08N 12.56E
Saffron Walden U.K. **13** 52.02N 0.15E
Safi Morocco **74** 32.20N 9.17W
Safīd *r.* Iran **65** 37.23N 50.11E
Safonovo R.S.F.S.R. U.S.S.R. **44** 65.40N 48.10E
Safonovo R.S.F.S.R. U.S.S.R. **44** 55.08N 33.16E
Saga China **63** 29.30N 85.09E
Saga Japan **57** 33.08N130.30E
Sagaing Burma **56** 22.00N 96.00E
Sagaing *d.* Burma **56** 24.00N 95.00E
Sagala Mali **76** 14.09N 6.38W
Sagami *r.* Japan **57** 35.14N139.23E
Sagamihara Japan **57** 35.32N139.23E
Sagami-nada *b.* Japan **57** 34.55N139.30E
Sagamore Mass. U.S.A. **115** 41.45N 70.33W
Sagamore Penn. U.S.A. **114** 40.47N 79.14W
Sāgar India **63** 23.50N 78.43E
Sagara Japan **57** 34.41N138.12E
Sage U.S.A. **108** 41.49N110.59W
Sag Harbor U.S.A. **115** 41.00N 72.18W
Saginaw U.S.A. **104** 43.25N 83.58W
Saginaw *r.* U.S.A. **104** 43.39N 83.51W
Saginaw B. U.S.A. **104** 43.50N 83.40W
Sagiz U.S.S.R. **45** 47.31N 54.55E
Sagres Portugal **27** 37.00N 8.56W
Saguache U.S.A. **108** 38.05N106.08W
Sagua la Grande Cuba **117** 22.55N 80.05W
Saguenay *r.* Canada **103** 48.10N 69.43W
Sagunto Spain **25** 39.41N 0.16W
Sāgwāra India **62** 23.41N 74.01E
Sa'gya China **63** 28.55N 88.03E
Saḩāb Jordan **67** 31.53N 36.00E
Sahaba Sudan **72** 18.55N 30.28E
Sahagún Spain **26** 42.22N 5.02W
Saḩam Jordan **67** 32.42N 35.47E
Saḩam al Jawlān Syria **67** 32.46N 35.56E
Sahand, Kūh-e *mtn.* Iran **65** 37.37N 46.27E
Sahara *des.* Africa **75** 22.30N 3.00E
Sahāranpur India **63** 29.58N 77.33E
Saharsa India **63** 25.53N 86.36E
Sahaswān India **63** 28.05N 78.45E
Sahbā, Wādī as *r.* Saudi Arabia **65** 23.48N 49.50E
Sahel *d.* Burkina **76** 14.00N 0.50W
Sāhibganj India **63** 25.15N 87.39E
Sāhīwāl Punjab Pakistan **62** 30.40N 73.06E
Sāhīwāl Punjab Pakistan **62** 31.58N 72.20E
Sahtaneh *r.* Canada **100** 59.02N122.28W
Sahuarita U.S.A. **109** 31.57N110.58W
Sahwat al Qamḩ Syria **67** 32.36N 36.23E
Saibai *i.* Australia **90** 9.24S142.40E
Sa'idābād Iran **65** 29.28N 55.43E
Saidpur Bangla. **63** 25.47N 88.54E
Saidu Pakistan **62** 34.45N 72.21E
Saigon *see* Ho Chi Minh Vietnam **56**
Saillans France **21** 44.42N 5.11E
Saimaa *l.* Finland **44** 61.20N 28.00E
Saimbeyli Turkey **64** 38.07N 36.08E
Saindak Pakistan **62** 29.17N 61.34E
St. Abb's Head U.K. **14** 55.54N 2.07W
St. Afrique France **20** 43.57N 2.53E
St. Agapit Canada **105** 46.34N 71.27W
St. Agathe des Monts Canada **105** 46.03N 74.17W
St. Agrève France **21** 45.01N 4.24E
St. Alban's Canada **103** 47.52N 55.51W
St. Albans U.K. **13** 51.46N 0.21W
St. Albans Vt. U.S.A. **105** 44.49N 73.05W
St. Albans W.Va. U.S.A. **114** 38.23N 81.49W
St. Albert Canada **100** 53.37N113.40W
St. Alexis des Monts Canada **105** 46.28N 73.08W
St. Amand France **19** 50.26N 3.26E
St. Amand-Mont-Rond France **19** 46.44N 2.30E
St. Ambroix France **21** 44.15N 4.11E
St. Amour France **19** 46.26N 5.21E
St. André-les-Alpes France **21** 43.58N 6.30E
St. Andrews U.K. **14** 56.20N 2.48W
St. Andries Belgium **16** 51.12N 3.10E
St. Anicet Canada **105** 45.07N 74.20W
St. Ann's Bay *town* Jamaica **117** 18.26N 77.12W
St. Anthony Canada **103** 51.22N 55.35W
St. Anthony U.S.A. **106** 43.59N111.40W
St. Antoine Canada **105** 46.39N 71.34W
St. Antonin France **20** 44.09N 1.45E
St. Arnaud Australia **92** 36.40S143.20E
St. Astier France **20** 45.09N 0.32E
St. Auban France **21** 43.51N 6.44E
St. Augustin *r.* Canada **103** 51.14N 58.41W
St. Augustine U.S.A. **113** 29.54N 81.19W
St. Augustin Saguenay Canada **103** 51.14N 58.39W
St. Aulaye France **20** 45.12N 0.08E
St. Austell U.K. **13** 50.20N 4.48W
St. Avold France **19** 49.06N 6.42E
St. Barthélemy Canada **105** 46.12N 73.08W
St. Barthélemy *i.* Leeward Is. **117** 17.55N 62.50W
St. Basile de Portneuf Canada **105** 46.45N 71.49W
St. Béat France **20** 42.55N 0.42E
St. Bees Head U.K. **12** 54.31N 3.39W
St. Benoît-du-Sault France **18** 46.27N 1.23E
St. Boniface Canada **101** 49.55N 97.06W
St. Bonnet-de-Joux France **19** 46.29N 4.27E
St. Brides B. U.K. **13** 51.48N 5.03W
St. Brieuc France **18** 48.31N 2.47W
St. Bruno de Guigues Canada **104** 47.27N 79.26W
St. Calais France **18** 47.55N 0.45E
St. Casimir Canada **105** 46.40N 72.08W
St. Catharines Canada **104** 43.10N 79.15W
St. Catherine's Pt. U.K. **13** 50.34N 1.18W
St. Céré France **20** 44.52N 1.53E
St. Chamond France **21** 45.28N 4.30E
St. Charles Mich. U.S.A. **104** 43.18N 84.09W
St. Charles Mo. U.S.A. **110** 38.47N 90.29W
St. Chély d'Apcher France **20** 44.48N 3.17E
St. Ciers-sur-Gironde France **20** 45.18N 0.37W
St. Clair *r.* Canada **104** 42.37N 82.31W
St. Clair U.S.A. **114** 42.49N 82.30W
St. Clair, L. Canada **104** 42.25N 82.41W
St. Clair Shores *town* U.S.A. **114** 42.30N 82.54W
St. Clairsville U.S.A. **114** 40.05N 80.54W
St. Claud France **20** 45.53N 0.23E
St. Claude Canada **105** 45.40N 72.00W
St. Claude France **19** 46.23N 5.52E
St. Cloud U.S.A. **110** 45.33N 94.10W
St. Croix *i.* U.S.V.Is. **117** 17.45N 64.35W
St. Cyprien France **20** 44.52N 1.02E
St. Cyrille de Wendover Canada **105** 45.56N 72.26W
St. David's U.K. **13** 51.54N 5.16W
St. David's I. Bermuda **127** 32.23N 64.42W
St. Denis France **19** 48.56N 2.22E
St. Dié France **19** 48.17N 6.57E
St. Dizier France **19** 48.38N 4.57E
St. Donat Canada **105** 46.19N 74.13W
Sainte-Agathe-des-Monts Canada **102** 46.03N 74.17W
Sainte Anne, Rivière *r.* Canada **105** 46.52N 71.49W
Sainte Anne de Beaupré Canada **105** 47.02N 70.56W
Sainte Anne de la Pérade Canada **105** 46.35N 72.12W
Sainte-Anne-des-Monts Canada **103** 49.07N 66.29W
Sainte Anne du Lac Canada **105** 46.52N 75.21W
Sainte Croix Canada **105** 46.38N 71.44W
Sainte-Croix Switz. **39** 46.49N 6.31E
Sainte Emelie Canada **105** 46.19N 73.39W
Sainte Famille d'Aumond Canada **105** 46.27N 75.52W
Sainte Foy la Grande France **20** 44.50N 0.13E
Sainte Hermine France **18** 46.33N 1.04W
St. Elias, Mt. U.S.A. **100** 60.18N140.55W
St. Elias Mts. Canada **100** 60.30N139.30W
St. Éloi Canada **103** 48.02N 69.13W
Sainte-Lucia France **21** 41.42N 9.22E
Sainte Lucie Canada **105** 46.07N 74.13W
Sainte Marguerite Canada **105** 46.03N 74.05W
Sainte Marguerite *r.* Canada **103** 50.10N 66.40W
Sainte-Marie-aux-Mines France **19** 48.15N 7.11E
Sainte-Mathieu, Pointe de *c.* France **18** 48.20N 4.46W
Sainte Maure de Touraine France **18** 47.07N 0.37E
Sainte-Maxime France **21** 43.18N 6.38E
Sainte Menehould France **19** 49.05N 4.54E
Sainte Mère-Église France **18** 49.24N 1.19W
St. Enimie France **20** 44.22N 3.26E
Saintes France **20** 45.44N 0.38W
Saintes-Maries-de-la-Mer France **21** 43.27N 4.26E
St. Espirit Canada **105** 45.56N 73.40W
Sainte Thècle Canada **105** 46.49N 72.31W
Sainte-Thérèse-de-Blainville Canada **105** 45.38N 73.51W
St. Étienne France **21** 45.26N 4.24E
St. Fargeau France **19** 47.38N 3.04E
St. Faustin Canada **105** 46.07N 74.30W
St. Félix Canada **105** 46.10N 73.26W
Saintfield U.K. **15** 54.28N 5.50W
St. Fintan's Canada **103** 48.10N 58.50W
St. Florent France **21** 42.41N 9.18E
St. Florentin France **19** 48.00N 3.44E
St. Florent-sur-Cher France **19** 46.59N 2.15E
St. Flour France **20** 45.02N 3.05E
St. Francis U.S.A. **110** 39.47N101.47W
St. Francisville U.S.A. **111** 30.47N 91.23W
St. Francois *r.* Canada **105** 46.07N 72.55W
St. François, Lac *l.* Canada **105** 45.55N 71.10W
St. Gabriel Canada **105** 46.17N 73.23W
St. Gallen Switz. **39** 47.25N 9.23E
St. Gallen *d.* Switz. **39** 47.00N 9.15E
St. Gaudens France **20** 43.07N 0.44E
St. Gaultier France **18** 46.38N 1.25E
St. Genis-de-Saintonge France **20** 45.29N 0.34W
St. George Australia **91** 28.03S148.30E
St. George Bermuda **127** 32.24N 64.42W
St. George N.B. Canada **103** 45.11N 66.57W
St. George Ont. Canada **104** 43.15N 80.15W
St. George U.S.A. **108** 37.06N113.35W
St. George, C. U.S.A. **113** 29.35N 85.04W
St. Georges Belgium **16** 50.37N 5.20E
St. Georges Canada **105** 46.37N 72.40W
St. George's Grenada **117** 12.04N 61.44W
St. Georges Guiana **123** 3.54N 51.48W
St. George's B. Canada **103** 48.20N 59.00W
St. George's Channel Rep. of Ire. / U.K. **15** 51.30N 6.20W
St. George's I. Bermuda **127** 32.24N 64.42W
St. Germain France **19** 48.54N 2.05E
St. Germain de Grantham Canada **105** 45.50N 72.34W
St. Germain-du-Bois France **19** 46.45N 5.15E
St. Germain-Lembron France **20** 45.28N 3.14E
St. Germain-l'Herm France **20** 45.28N 3.33E
St. Gervais d'Auvergne France **20** 46.02N 2.49E
St. Géry France **20** 44.29N 1.35E
St. Gheorghe's Mouth *est.* Romania **29** 44.51N 29.37E
St. Gilles-Croix-de-Vie France **18** 46.42N 1.57W
St. Girons France **20** 42.59N 1.09E
St. Gotthard Pass Switz. **17** 46.30N 8.55E
St. Govan's Head U.K. **13** 51.36N 4.55W
St. Grégoire Canada **105** 46.16N 72.30W
St. Guénolé France **18** 47.49N 4.20W
St. Guillaume d'Upton Canada **105** 45.53N 72.46W
St. Helena *i.* Atlantic Oc. **127** 15.58S 5.43W
St. Helena B. R.S.A. **80** 32.35S 18.05E
St. Helens U.K. **12** 53.28N 2.43W
St. Helens U.S.A. **108** 45.52N122.48W
St. Helens, Mt. U.S.A. **108** 46.12N122.11W
St. Helier U.K. **13** 49.12N 2.07W
St. Hilaire-du-Harcouët France **18** 48.35N 1.06W
St. Hippolyte France **19** 47.19N 6.49E
St. Hubert Belgium **16** 50.02N 5.22E
St. Hyacinthe Canada **105** 45.37N 72.57W
St. Ignace U.S.A. **104** 45.52N 84.43W
St. Ignace du Lac Canada **105** 46.43N 73.49W
St. Ives U.K. **13** 50.13N 5.29W
St. Jacobs Canada **104** 43.32N 80.33W
St. Jacques Canada **105** 45.57N 73.34W
St. Jean Canada **105** 45.19N 73.16W
St. Jean *r.* Canada **103** 50.17N 64.20W
St. Jean France **21** 45.17N 6.21E
St. Jean, Lac *l.* Canada **103** 48.35N 72.00W
St. Jean-d'Angély France **20** 45.57N 0.31W
St. Jean-de-Bournay France **21** 45.29N 5.08E
St. Jean-de-Losne France **19** 47.06N 5.15E
St. Jean-de-Luz France **20** 43.23N 1.40W
St. Jean de Matha Canada **105** 46.14N 73.33W
St. Jean-de-Monts France **18** 46.48N 2.03W
St. Jean-du-Gard France **20** 44.06N 3.53E
St. Jean Pied-de-Port France **20** 43.10N 1.14W
St. Jérôme Canada **105** 45.47N 74.00W
St. John Canada **103** 45.16N 66.03W
St. John *r.* Canada **103** 45.16N 66.04W
St. John U.S.A. **111** 38.00N 98.46W
St. John, C. Canada **103** 50.00N 55.32W
St. John B. Canada **103** 50.40N 57.08W
St. John's Antigua **117** 17.07N 61.51W
St. John's Canada **103** 47.34N 52.43W
St. Johns U.S.A. **109** 34.30N109.22W
St. Johns *r.* U.S.A. **113** 30.24N 81.24W
St. Johnsbury U.S.A. **105** 44.25N 72.01W
St. John's Pt. U.K. **15** 54.14N 5.39W
St. Jordi, Golf de *g.* Spain **25** 40.53N 1.00E
St. Joseph La. U.S.A. **111** 31.55N 91.14W
St. Joseph Mich. U.S.A. **112** 42.05N 86.30W
St. Joseph Mo. U.S.A. **110** 39.46N 94.51W
St. Joseph, L. Canada **102** 51.05N 90.35W
St. Joseph I. Canada **104** 46.13N 83.57W
St. Jovite Canada **105** 46.07N 74.36W
St. Jude Canada **105** 45.46N 72.59W
St. Julien-en-Born France **20** 44.04N 1.14W
St. Julien-en-Genevois France **21** 46.08N 6.05E
St. Junien France **20** 45.53N 0.54E
St. Just-en-Chaussée France **19** 49.30N 2.26E
St. Just-en-Chevalet France **20** 45.55N 3.50E
St. Kilda *i.* U.K. **10** 57.55N 8.20W
St. Kitts-Nevis Leeward Is. **117** 17.20N 62.45W
St. Lambert Canada **105** 45.30N 73.30W
St. Laurent Man. Canada **101** 50.24N 97.56W
St. Laurent Que. Canada **105** 45.30N 73.40W
St. Laurent du Maroni Guiana **123** 5.30N 54.02W
St. Laurent-et-Benon France **20** 45.09N 0.49W
St. Lawrence *r.* Canada **105** 44.15N 76.10W
St. Lawrence, G. of Canada **103** 48.00N 62.00W
St. Lawrence I. U.S.A. **98** 63.00N170.00W
St. Léonard d'Aston Canada **105** 46.06N 72.22W
St. Lewis Sd. Canada **103** 52.20N 55.40W
St. Lin Canada **105** 45.51N 73.45W
St. Lô France **18** 49.07N 1.05W
St. Louis Senegal **76** 16.01N 16.30W
St. Louis U.S.A. **110** 38.38N 90.11W
St. Louis Park *town* U.S.A. **110** 44.56N 93.22W
St. Loup-sur-Semouse France **19** 47.53N 6.16E
St. Lucia Windward Is. **117** 14.05N 61.00W
St. Lucia, L. R.S.A. **81** 28.05S 32.26E
St. Magnus B. U.K. **10** 60.25N 1.35W

St. Maixent to **San Francisco**

St. Maixent France 18 46.25N 0.12W
St. Malo Canada 105 45.12N 71.30W
St. Malo France 18 48.39N 2.01W
St. Malo, Golfe de *g.* France 18 48.45N 2.00W
St. Mamert France 21 43.53N 4.12E
St.-Marc Haiti 117 19.08N 72.41W
St. Marc des Carrières Canada 105 46.41N 72.03W
St. Marcellin France 21 45.09N 5.19E
St. Margaret's Hope U.K. 14 58.49N 2.57W
St. Maries U.S.A. 108 47.19N116.35W
St. Martin *i.* Leeward Is. 117 18.05N 63.05W
St. Martin U.K. 13 49.27N 2.34W
St. Martin, L. Canada 101 51.37N 98.29W
St. Martin B. U.S.A. 104 45.57N 84.35W
St. Martin-de-Londres France 20 43.47N 3.44E
St. Martin d'Hères France 21 45.10N 5.46E
St. Martin's *i.* U.K. 13 49.57N 6.16W
St. Mary U.K. 13 49.14N 2.10W
St. Mary *r.* U.S.A. 104 46.30N 84.36W
St. Mary Peak Australia 92 31.30S138.35E
St. Marys Australia 91 41.33S148.12E
St. Mary's Canada 104 43.16N 81.08W
St. Mary's *r.* Canada 103 45.02N 61.54W
St. Mary's *i.* U.K. 13 49.55N 6.16W
St. Marys Penn. U.S.A. 114 41.26N 78.34W
St. Marys W.Va. U.S.A. 114 39.23N 81.12W
St. Mary's, C. Canada 103 46.49N 54.12W
St. Mary's B. Canada 103 46.50N 53.47W
St. Mathieu France 20 45.42N 0.46E
St. Matthew I. U.S.A. 98 60.30N172.45W
St. Maur France 19 48.48N 2.30E
St. Maurice *r.* Canada 105 46.21N 72.31W
St. Maurice Prov. Park Canada 105 46.52N 73.10W
St. Méen-le-Grand France 18 48.11N 2.12W
St. Michel des Saints Canada 105 46.41N 73.55W
St. Mihiel France 19 48.54N 5.33E
St. Moritz Switz. 39 46.30N 9.50E
St. Nazaire France 18 47.17N 2.12W
St. Neots U.K. 13 52.14N 0.16W
St. Niklaas Belgium 16 51.10N 4.09E
St. Omer France 19 50.45N 2.15E
St. Pacôme Canada 103 47.24N 69.57W
St. Pascal Canada 103 47.32N 69.48W
St. Patrick, Lac *l.* Canada 105 46.21N 77.18W
St. Paul *r.* Canada 103 51.26N 57.40W
St. Paul A.H.Prov. France 21 44.31N 6.45E
St. Paul Pyr. Or. France 20 42.49N 2.29E
St. Paul Ark. U.S.A. 111 35.50N 93.48W
St. Paul Minn. U.S.A. 110 45.00N 93.10W
St. Paul Nebr. U.S.A. 110 41.13N 98.27W
St. Paul, Île *i.* Indian Oc. 49 38.43S 77.29E
St. Paul de Chester Canada 105 45.57N 71.49W
St. Paul du Nord Canada 103 48.27N 69.15W
St. Paulien France 20 45.08N 3.49E
St. Paulin Canada 105 46.25N 73.01W
St. Paul Rocks *is.* Atlantic Oc. 127 1.00N 29.23W
St. Peter U.S.A. 110 44.17N 93.57W
St. Peter Port U.K. 13 49.27N 2.32W
St. Petersburg U.S.A. 113 27.45N 82.40W
St. Pierre Char. Mar. France 20 45.59N 1.14W
St. Pierre S.Mar. France 18 49.48N 0.29E
St. Pierre, Lac *l.* Canada 105 46.12N 72.52W
St. Pierre and Miquelon *is.* N. America 103 46.55N 56.10W
St. Pierre-Église France 18 49.40N 1.24W
St. Pierre le Moûtier France 19 46.48N 3.07E
St. Pierreville France 21 44.49N 4.29E
St. Pol-de-Leon France 18 48.41N 3.59W
St. Pol-sur-Ternoise France 19 50.23N 2.20E
St. Pölten Austria 36 48.13N 15.37E
St. Polycarpe Canada 105 45.18N 74.18W
St. Pons France 20 43.29N 2.46E
St. Pourçain France 20 46.19N 3.17E
St. Priest France 21 45.42N 4.57E
St. Quentin France 19 49.51N 3.17E
St. Raphaël France 21 43.25N 6.46E
St. Raymond Canada 105 46.54N 71.50W
St. Regis Falls U.S.A. 105 44.40N 74.33W
St. Rémy France 21 43.47N 4.50E
St. Renan France 18 48.26N 4.37W
St. Roch de Mekinac Canada 105 46.48N 72.44W
St. Savin France 18 46.34N 0.52E
St. Savinien France 20 45.53N 0.50W
St. Seine-l'Abbaye France 19 47.26N 4.47E
St. Siméon Canada 103 47.55N 69.58W
St. Stephen Canada 103 45.12N 67.17W
St. Sulpice les Feuilles France 20 46.19N 1.22E
St. Symphorien France 20 44.26N 0.30W
St. Thomas Canada 104 42.47N 81.12W
St. Thomas *i.* U.S.V.Is. 117 18.22N 64.57W
St. Tite Canada 105 46.44N 72.34W
St. Tropez France 21 43.16N 6.38E
St. Truiden Belgium 16 50.49N 5.11E
St. Ubald Canada 105 46.45N 72.16W
St. Valéry France 18 49.52N 0.44E
St. Valéry-sur-Somme France 19 50.11N 1.38E
St. Vallier France 21 45.10N 4.49E
St. Vallier-de-Thiey France 21 43.42N 6.51E
St. Varent France 18 46.53N 0.14W
St. Vincent, G. Australia 92 35.00S138.05E
St. Vincent and the Grenadines Windward Is. 117 13.00N 61.15W
St. Vincent-de-Tyrosse France 20 43.40N 1.18W
St. Vith Belgium 16 50.15N 6.08E
St. Vivien-de-Médoc France 20 45.26N 1.02W
St. Wendel Germany 39 49.28N 7.10E
St. Yrieix France 20 45.31N 1.12E
St. Zénon Canada 105 46.33N 73.49W
Sairs, L. Canada 104 46.51N 78.12W
Saitama *d.* Japan 57 35.55N139.00E
Sajama *mtn.* Bolivia 124 18.06S 69.00W
Saka Kenya 79 0.09S 39.18E
Sakai Japan 57 34.35N135.28E
Sakākah Saudi Arabia 64 29.59N 40.12E
Sakakawea, L. *see* Garrison Resr. U.S.A. 110
Sakami *r.* Canada 102 53.40N 76.40W
Sakami, Lac *l.* Canada 102 53.10N 77.00W
Sâkâne, Erg i-n *f.* Mali 74 21.00N 1.00W
Sakania Zaïre 79 12.44S 28.34E
Sakarya *r.* Turkey 64 41.08N 30.36E
Sakata Japan 57 38.55N139.51E
Sakété Benin 77 6.45N 2.45E
Sakhalin *i.* U.S.S.R. 53 50.00N143.00E
Sākhar Afghan. 62 32.57N 65.32E
Sakhi Sarwar Pakistan 62 29.59N 70.18E
Sakhnīn Israel 67 32.52N 35.17E
Sakht-Sar Iran 65 36.54N 50.41E
Sākib Jordan 67 32.17N 35.49E
Sākoli India 63 21.05N 79.59E
Sakrand Pakistan 62 26.08N 68.16E
Sakri India 62 21.02N 74.40E
Sakrivier R.S.A. 80 30.53S 20.24E
Sakti India 63 22.02N 82.58E
Sakuma Japan 57 35.05N137.48E
Sal *r.* U.S.S.R. 45 47.33N 40.40E
Sala Ethiopia 72 16.58N 37.27E
Sala Sweden 43 59.55N 16.36E
Salaca *r.* U.S.S.R. 41 57.45N 24.21E
Salacgriva U.S.S.R. 41 57.45N 24.21E
Sala Consilina Italy 33 40.24N 15.36E
Salado *r.* Buenos Aires Argentina 125 35.44S 57.22W
Salado *r.* Santa Fé Argentina 125 31.40S 60.41W
Salado *r.* La Pampa Argentina 125 36.15S 66.55W
Salado *r.* Mexico 111 26.50N 99.17W
Salaga Ghana 76 8.36N 0.32W
Salailua W. Samoa 84 13.42S172.35W
Salālah Oman 60 17.00N 54.04E
Salālah Sudan 72 21.19N 36.13E
Salamanca Spain 26 40.58N 5.39W
Salamanca *d.* Spain 26 40.45N 6.00W
Salamanca U.S.A. 114 42.09N 78.43W
Salamat *d.* Chad 73 11.00N 20.40E
Salāmbek Pakistan 62 28.18N 65.09E
Salamina Colombia 122 5.24N 75.31W
Salamís *i.* Greece 35 37.54N 23.26E
Salamís *town* Greece 35 37.59N 23.28E
Salām Khān Afghan. 62 31.47N 66.45E
Salani W. Samoa 84 14.02S171.35W
Salar de Uyuni *l.* Bolivia 121 20.30S 67.45W
Salas de los Infantes Spain 26 42.01N 3.17W
Salatiga Indonesia 59 7.15S110.34E
Salāya India 62 22.19N 69.35E
Sala y Gomez *i.* Pacific Oc. 85 26.28S105.28W
Salbris France 19 47.26N 2.03E
Salcia Romania 34 43.57N 24.56E
Salcombe U.K. 13 50.14N 3.47W
Saldaña Spain 26 42.31N 4.44W
Saldanha R.S.A. 80 33.00S 17.56E
Saldanha B. R.S.A. 80 33.05S 17.50E
Saldus U.S.S.R. 41 56.40N 22.30E
Sale Australia 93 38.06S147.06E
Salé Morocco 74 34.04N 6.50W
Salekhard U.S.S.R. 44 66.33N 66.35E
Salelologa W. Samoa 84 13.43S172.13W
Salem India 61 11.38N 78.08E
Salem Ind. U.S.A. 112 38.38N 86.06W
Salem Mass. U.S.A. 115 42.31N 70.55W
Salem Mo. U.S.A. 111 37.39N 91.32W
Salem N.H. U.S.A. 115 42.47N 71.12W
Salem N.J. U.S.A. 115 39.34N 75.28W
Salem N.Y. U.S.A. 115 43.10N 73.20W
Salem Ohio U.S.A. 114 40.54N 80.52W
Salem Oreg. U.S.A. 108 44.57N123.01W
Salem Va. U.S.A. 113 37.17N 80.04W
Salem W.Va. U.S.A. 114 39.17N 80.34W
Salemi Italy 32 37.49N 12.49E
Sälen Sweden 41 61.10N 13.16E
Salerno Italy 33 40.41N 14.47E
Salerno, Golfo di *g.* Italy 33 40.32N 14.42E
Salers France 20 45.08N 2.30E
Salfīt Jordan 67 32.05N 35.11E
Salford U.K. 12 53.30N 2.17W
Salgótarján Hungary 37 48.07N 19.48E
Salgueiro Brazil 123 8.04S 39.05W
Sali Yugo. 31 43.56N 15.10E
Salies-de-Béarn France 20 43.29N 0.55W
Salignac Eyvignes France 20 44.59N 1.19E
Salima Malaŵi 79 13.45S 34.29E
Salim's Tanzania 79 10.37S 36.33E
Salina U.S.A. 110 38.50N 97.37W
Salina, Isola *i.* Italy 33 38.34N 14.51E
Salina Cruz Mexico 116 16.11N 95.12W
Salinas Ecuador 122 2.13S 80.58W
Salinas U.S.A. 108 36.40N121.38W
Salinas *r.* U.S.A. 106 36.45N121.48W
Salinas, Cabo de *c.* Spain 25 39.16N 3.03E
Saline U.S.A. 104 42.10N 83.47W
Saline *r.* U.S.A. 110 38.51N 97.30W
Salineville U.S.A. 114 40.37N 80.51W
Salinópolis Brazil 123 0.37S 47.20W
Salins France 19 46.57N 5.53E
Salisbury U.K. 13 51.04N 1.48W
Salisbury Md. U.S.A. 115 38.22N 75.36W
Salisbury N.C. U.S.A. 113 35.20N 80.30W
Salisbury Plain *f.* U.K. 13 51.15N 1.55W
Salisbury Sd. U.S.A. 100 57.30N135.56W
Şalkhad Syria 66 32.29N 36.42E
Sallanches France 21 45.56N 6.38E
Salles-Curan France 20 44.11N 2.47E
Salling *f.* Denmark 42 56.40N 9.00E
Sallisaw U.S.A. 111 35.28N 94.47W
Salluit Canada 99 62.10N 75.40W
Sallyāna Nepal 63 28.22N 82.12E
Salmās Iran 65 38.13N 44.50E
Salmi U.S.S.R. 44 61.19N 31.46E
Salmon *r.* Canada 100 54.03N122.40W
Salmon U.S.A. 108 45.11N113.55W
Salmon *r.* U.S.A. 108 45.51N116.46W
Salmon Gums Australia 89 32.59S121.39E
Salmon River Mts. U.S.A. 108 44.45N115.30W
Salo Finland 41 60.23N 23.08E
Salò Italy 30 45.36N 10.31E
Salobreña Spain 27 36.44N 3.35W
Salome U.S.A. 109 33.47N113.37W
Salon France 21 43.38N 5.06E
Salonga *r.* Zaïre 78 0.09S 19.52E
Salonika *see* Thessaloníki Greece 34
Salonta Romania 37 46.48N 21.40E
Salor *r.* Spain 27 39.39N 7.03W
Salsk U.S.S.R. 45 46.30N 41.33E
Salso *r.* Italy 32 37.05N 13.57E
Salsomaggiore Terme Italy 30 44.49N 9.59E
Salt *r.* U.S.A. 109 33.23N112.18W
Salta Argentina 124 24.47S 65.24W
Salta *d.* Argentina 124 25.00S 65.00W
Saltdal Norway 40 67.06N 15.25E
Saltee Is. Rep. of Ire. 15 52.08N 6.36W
Saltfjorden *est.* Norway 40 67.15N 14.10E
Saltfleet U.K. 12 53.25N 0.11E
Salt Fork *r.* U.S.A. 107 36.41N 97.05W
Saltillo Mexico 111 25.25N101.00W
Salt Lake City U.S.A. 108 40.46N111.53W
Salto Argentina 125 34.17S 60.15W
Salto Brazil 126 23.10S 47.16W
Salto *r.* Italy 30 42.23N 12.54E
Salto Uruguay 125 31.23S 57.58W
Salto da Divisa Brazil 123 16.04S 40.00W
Salto Grande, Embalse de *resr.* Argentina/Uruguay 125 31.00S 57.50W
Salton Sea *l.* U.S.A. 109 33.19N115.50W
Salūmbar India 62 24.08N 74.03E
Saluzzo Italy 30 44.39N 7.29E
Salvador Brazil 123 12.58S 38.29W
Salvador Canada 101 52.12N109.32W
Salvaterra de Magos Portugal 27 39.01N 8.48W
Salversville U.S.A. 113 37.43N 83.06W
Salviac France 20 44.41N 1.16E
Salween *r.* Burma 56 16.32N 97.35E
Salyany U.S.S.R. 65 39.36N 48.59E
Salzach *r.* Austria 39 48.12N 12.56E
Salzbrunn Namibia 80 24.23S 18.00E
Salzburg Austria 39 47.48N 13.02E
Salzburg *d.* Austria 39 47.15N 13.00E
Salzgitter Germany 38 52.02N 10.22E
Salzkammergut *f.* Austria 39 47.38N 13.30E
Salzwedel Germany 38 52.51N 11.09E
Sam India 62 26.50N 70.31E
Sama Spain 26 43.18N 5.41W
Samalambo Angola 78 14.16S 17.53E
Samālūt Egypt 66 28.18N 30.43E
Samaná Dom. Rep. 117 19.14N 69.20W
Samana Cay *i.* Bahamas 117 23.05N 73.45W
Samanga Tanzania 79 8.24S 39.18E
Samannūd Egypt 66 30.58N 31.14E
Samar Jordan 67 32.41N 35.47E
Samar *i.* Phil. 59 11.45N125.15E
Samara *r.* U.S.S.R. 44 53.17N 50.42E
Samarai P.N.G. 90 10.37S150.40E
Samaria *see* As Sāmirah *f.* Jordan 67
Samarinda Indonesia 58 0.30S117.09E
Samarkand U.S.S.R. 9 39.40N 66.57E
Sāmarrā Iraq 65 34.13N 43.52E
Samāstipur India 63 25.51N 85.47E
Samawāri Pakistan 62 28.34N 66.46E
Samba Zaïre 78 0.14N 21.19E
Sambalpur India 63 21.27N 83.58E
Sambao *r.* Madagascar 81 16.40S 44.26E
Sambava Madagascar 81 14.16S 50.10E
Sambāza Pakistan 62 31.46N 69.20E
Sambhal India 63 28.35N 78.33E
Sāmbhar India 62 26.55N 75.12E
Sāmbhar L. India 62 26.58N 75.05E
Sambor U.S.S.R. 37 49.31N 23.10E
Samborombón, Bahía *b.* Argentina 125 36.00S 57.00W
Sambre *r.* Belgium 16 50.29N 4.52E
Samburu Kenya 79 3.46S 39.17E
Samch'ŏk S. Korea 53 37.30N129.10E
Samdari India 62 25.49N 72.35E
Same Tanzania 79 4.10S 37.43E
Samnū Libya 75 27.16N 14.54E
Samoa *is.* Pacific Oc. 84 14.20S170.00W
Samoa Is. Pacific Oc. 84 14.00S171.00W
Samobor Yugo. 36 45.48N 15.43E
Samokov Bulgaria 34 42.20N 23.33E
Samorogouan Burkina 76 11.21N 4.57W
Sámos *i.* Greece 35 37.45N 26.50E
Sámos *town* Greece 35 37.45N 27.00E
Samothráki *i.* Greece 34 40.30N 25.32E
Samothráki *town* Greece 34 40.28N 25.31E
Sampang Indonesia 59 7.13S113.15E
Sampit Indonesia 58 2.34S112.59E
Sampson U.S.A. 114 42.44N 76.54W
Sam Rayburn Resr. U.S.A. 111 31.27N 94.37W
Samsang China 63 30.22N 82.57E
Samsö Denmark 42 55.52N 10.37E
Sam Son Vietnam 55 19.44N105.53E
Samsun Turkey 64 41.17N 36.22E
Samtredia U.S.S.R. 45 42.10N 42.22E
Samui, Ko *i.* Thailand 56 9.30N100.00E
Samur *r.* U.S.S.R. 45 42.00N 48.20E
Samut Prakan Thailand 56 13.32N100.35E
Samut Sakhon Thailand 56 13.31N100.13E
San *r.* Cambodia 56 13.32N105.57E
San Mali 76 13.21N 4.57W
San *r.* Poland 37 50.25N 22.20E
Şan'ā' Yemen 71 15.23N 44.14E
Sana *see* Şan'ā' Yemen 71
Sana *r.* Yugo. 31 45.03N 16.23E
Sanaba Burkina 76 12.25N 3.47W
Sanaga *r.* Cameroon 77 3.35N 9.40E
San Ambrosio *i.* Chile 121 26.28S 79.53W
Sānand India 62 22.59N 72.23E
Sanandaj Iran 65 35.18N 47.01E
San Andreas U.S.A. 108 38.12N120.41W
San Andrés, Isla de *i.* Colombia 117 12.33N 81.42W
San Andrés Tuxtla Mexico 116 18.27N 95.13W
San Angelo U.S.A. 111 31.28N100.26W
San Antonio Chile 125 33.35S 71.38W
San Antonio N.Mex. U.S.A. 109 33.55N106.52W
San Antonio Tex. U.S.A. 111 29.28N 98.31W
San Antonio, C. Cuba 117 21.50N 84.57W
San Antonio, Cabo *c.* Argentina 125 36.40S 56.42W
San Antonio, Punta *c.* Mexico 109 29.45N115.41W
San Antonio, Sierra de *mts.* Mexico 109 30.00N110.10W
San Antonio Abad Spain 25 38.59N 1.18E
San Antonio de Areco Argentina 125 34.16S 59.30W
San Antonio Oeste Argentina 125 40.44S 64.57W
San Augustine U.S.A. 111 31.32N 94.07W
Sanāwad India 62 22.11N 76.04E
San Bartolomeo Italy 33 41.24N 15.01E
San Benedetto Italy 31 42.57N 13.53E
San Benedetto Po Italy 30 45.02N 10.55E
San Benito Guatemala 117 16.55N 89.54W
San Benito U.S.A. 111 26.08N 97.38W
San Bernardino U.S.A. 109 34.06N117.17W
San Bernardo Chile 125 33.36S 70.43W
San Blas, C. U.S.A. 113 29.40N 85.22W
San Bonifacio Italy 30 45.24N 11.16E
Sanbornville U.S.A. 115 43.30N 70.57W
San Candido Italy 30 46.44N 12.17E
San Carlos Chile 125 36.25S 71.58W
San Carlos Mexico 111 29.01N100.51W
San Carlos Nicaragua 117 11.07N 84.47W
San Carlos Phil. 59 15.59N120.22E
San Carlos Venezuela 122 1.55N 67.04W
San Carlos Venezuela 122 9.39N 68.35W
San Carlos de Bariloche Argentina 125 41.08S 71.15W
San Carlos del Zulia Venezuela 122 9.01N 71.55W
San Cataldo Italy 32 37.29N 14.00E
Sancergues France 19 47.09N 2.55E
Sancerre France 19 47.20N 2.51E
Sancerrois, Collines du *hills* France 19 47.25N 2.45E
Sancha He *r.* China 55 26.50N106.04E
San Clemente Spain 27 39.24N 2.26W
San Clemente U.S.A. 109 33.26N117.37W
San Clemente *i.* U.S.A. 109 32.54N118.29W
Sancoins France 19 46.50N 2.55E
San Cristóbal Argentina 124 30.20S 61.41W
San Cristóbal Dom. Rep. 117 18.27N 70.07W
San Cristóbal Venezuela 122 7.46N 72.15W
Sancti Spíritus Cuba 117 21.55N 79.28W
Sand Norway 42 59.29N 6.15E
Sanda *i.* U.K. 14 55.17N 5.34W
Sandakan Malaysia 58 5.52N118.04E
Sandanski Bulgaria 34 41.34N 23.17E
Sandaré Mali 76 14.40N 10.15W
Sandared Sweden 43 57.43N 12.47E
Sanday *i.* U.K. 14 59.15N 2.33W
Sandbach U.K. 12 53.09N 2.23W
Sandefjord Norway 42 59.08N 10.14E
Sanders U.S.A. 109 35.13N109.20W
Sanderson U.S.A. 111 30.09N102.24W
Sandersville U.S.A. 113 32.59N 82.49W
Sandgate Australia 93 27.18S153.00E
Sandhammaren *c.* Denmark 43 55.23N 14.12E
Sandhornöy *i.* Norway 40 67.05N 14.10E
Sāndi India 63 27.18N 79.57E
Sandia Peru 122 14.14S 69.25W
San Diego U.S.A. 109 32.43N117.09W
San Diego, C. Argentina 125 54.38S 65.05W
Sandīla India 63 27.05N 80.31E
Sand Lake *town* Canada 102 47.45N 84.30W
Sandnes Norway 42 58.51N 5.44E
Sandness U.K. 14 60.18N 1.38W
Sandö *i.* Faroe Is. 10 61.50N 6.45W
Sandoa Zaïre 78 9.41S 22.56E
Sandomierz Poland 37 50.41N 21.45E
San Donà di Piave Italy 30 45.38N 12.34E
Sandover *r.* Australia 90 21.43S136.32E
Sandoway Burma 56 18.28N 94.20E
Sandown U.K. 13 50.39N 1.09W
Sandpoint *town* U.S.A. 108 48.17N116.34W
Sandringham U.K. 12 52.50N 0.30E
Sandstone Australia 89 27.59S119.17E
Sandu Shuizu Zizhixian China 55 25.59N107.52E
Sandusky Mich. U.S.A. 114 43.25N 82.50W
Sandusky Ohio U.S.A. 114 41.27N 82.42W
Sandveld *f.* Namibia 80 21.25S 20.00E
Sandvika Norway 42 59.54N 10.31E
Sandviken Sweden 41 60.37N 16.46E
Sandwich B. Canada 103 53.35N 57.15W
Sandwīp I. Bangla. 63 22.29N 91.26E
Sandy U.S.A. 108 40.35N111.53W
Sandy B. St. Helena 127 16.02S 5.42W
Sandy Bight *b.* Australia 89 33.53S123.25E
Sandy C. Australia 90 24.42S153.17E
Sandy Creek *town* U.S.A. 115 43.39N 76.05W
Sandy Desert Pakistan 62 28.00N 65.00E
Sandy Hook *f.* U.S.A. 115 40.27N 74.00W
Sandy L. Nfld. Canada 103 49.16N 57.00W
Sandy L. Ont. Canada 102 53.00N 93.00W
Sandy Lake *town* Ont. Canada 102 53.00N 93.00W
Sandy Lake *town* Sask. Canada 101 57.00N107.15W
San Enrique Argentina 125 35.47S 60.22W
San Esteban, Isla *i.* Mexico 109 28.41N112.35W
San Esteban de Gormaz Spain 26 41.35N 3.12W
San Felipe Chile 125 32.45S 70.44W
San Felipe Colombia 122 1.55N 67.06W
San Felipe Mexico 109 31.00N114.52W
San Felipe Venezuela 122 10.25N 68.40W
San Félix *i.* Chile 121 26.23S 80.05W
San Fernando Argentina 125 34.26S 58.34W
San Fernando Chile 125 34.35S 71.00W
San Fernando *r.* Mexico 111 24.55N 97.40W
San Fernando Phil. 59 16.39N120.19E
San Fernando Spain 27 36.28N 6.12W
San Fernando Trinidad 122 10.16N 61.28W
San Fernando de Apure Venezuela 122 7.35N 67.15W
San Fernando de Atabapo Venezuela 122 4.03N 67.45W
Sanford *r.* Australia 88 27.22S115.53E
Sanford Fla. U.S.A. 113 28.49N 81.17W
Sanford Maine U.S.A. 115 43.26N 70.46W
Sanford N.C. U.S.A. 113 35.29N 79.10W
San Francisco Argentina 124 31.29S 62.06W
San Francisco Mexico 109 30.50N112.40W
San Francisco U.S.A. 108 37.48N122.24W
San Francisco *r.* U.S.A. 109 32.59N109.22W

San Francisco, C. to Sarzeau

San Francisco, C. Ecuador 122 0.50N 80.05W
San Francisco del Oro Mexico 109 26.52N105.51W
San Francisco de Macorís Dom. Rep. 117 19.19N 70.15W
San Fratelo Italy 33 38.01N 14.36E
Sanga Angola 78 11.09S 15.21E
Sanga-Tolon U.S.S.R. 51 61.44N149.30E
San Gavino Monreale Italy 32 39.33N 8.48E
Sang-e Māsheh Afghan. 62 33.08N 67.27E
Sangerhausen Germany 38 51.28N 11.17E
Sanggan He r. China 54 40.23N115.18E
Sangha r. Congo 78 1.10S 16.47E
Sanghar Pakistan 62 26.02N 68.57E
Sangihe i. Indonesia 59 3.30N125.30E
Sangihe, Kepulauan is. Indonesia 59 2.45N125.20E
San Gil Colombia 122 6.35N 73.08W
San Gimignano Italy 30 43.28N 11.02E
San Giovanni in Fiore Italy 33 39.16N 16.42E
San Giovanni in Persiceto Italy 30 44.38N 11.11E
San Giovanni Rotondo Italy 31 41.42N 15.44E
San Giovanni Valdarno Italy 30 43.34N 11.32E
Sangkulirang Indonesia 58 1.00N117.58E
Sāngli India 60 16.55N 74.37E
Sangmélima Cameroon 77 2.55N 12.01E
Sangonera r. Spain 25 37.59N 1.04W
San Gottardo, Passo del pass Switz. 39 46.33N 8.34E
Sangre de Cristo Mts. U.S.A. 108 37.30N105.15W
San Gregorio Uruguay 125 32.37S 55.40W
Sangri China 63 29.18N 92.05E
Sangro r. Italy 31 42.14N 14.32E
Sangrūr India 62 30.14N 75.51E
Sangsues, Lac aux l. Canada 105 46.29N 77.57W
Sangüesa Spain 25 42.35N 1.17W
Sangzhi China 55 29.24N110.09E
Sanhala Ivory Coast 76 10.01N 6.48W
San Ignacio Bolivia 124 16.23S 60.59W
San Ignacio Mexico 109 27.27N112.51W
San Ignacio Paraguay 124 26.52S 57.03W
San Ignacio, Laguna l. Mexico 109 26.50N113.11W
San Ildefonso o La Granja Spain 26 40.54N 4.00W
San Isidro Argentina 125 34.29S 58.31W
Sanīyah, Hawr as l. Iraq 65 31.52N 46.50E
San Javier Argentina 125 30.40S 59.55W
San Javier Bolivia 124 16.22S 62.38W
San Javier Chile 125 35.35S 71.45W
Sanjāwi Pakistan 62 30.17N 68.21E
Sanjō Japan 57 37.37N138.57E
San Joaquin r. U.S.A. 108 38.03N121.50W
San Jorge, Bahía de b. Mexico 109 31.08N113.15W
San Jorge, Golfo g. Argentina 125 46.00S 66.00W
San José Costa Rica 117 9.59N 84.04W
San José Guatemala 116 13.58N 90.50W
San José Mexico 109 27.32N110.09W
San Jose U.S.A. 108 37.20N121.53W
San José, Isla i. Mexico 109 25.00N110.38W
San José de Chiquitos Bolivia 124 17.53S 60.45W
San José de Feliciano Argentina 125 30.25S 58.45W
San José de Guanipa Venezuela 122 8.54N 64.09W
San José del Cabo town Mexico 109 23.03N109.41W
San José del Guaviare Colombia 122 2.35N 72.38W
San José de Mayo Uruguay 125 34.20S 56.42W
San José de Ocuné Colombia 122 4.15N 70.20W
San Juan Argentina 124 31.30S 68.30W
San Juan d. Argentina 124 31.00S 68.30W
San Juan r. Costa Rica 117 10.50N 83.40W
San Juan Dom. Rep. 117 18.40N 71.05W
San Juan Peru 124 15.20S 75.09W
San Juan Phil. 59 8.25N126.22E
San Juan Puerto Rico 117 18.29N 66.08W
San Juan r. U.S.A. 108 37.18N110.28W
San Juan, C. Argentina 125 54.45S 63.50W
San Juan, Embalse de resr. Spain 26 40.25N 4.25W
San Juan Bautista Spain 25 39.05N 1.30E
San Juan de Guadalupe Mexico 111 24.38N102.44W
San Juan del Norte Nicaragua 117 10.58N 83.40W
San Juan de los Morros Venezuela 122 9.53N 67.23W
San Juan del Río Durango Mexico 111 24.47N104.27W
San Juan del Río Querétaro Mexico 116 20.23N100.00W
San Juan Mts. U.S.A. 108 37.35N107.10W
San Julián Argentina 121 49.19S 67.40W
San Justo Argentina 125 30.47S 60.35W
Sankh r. India 63 22.15N 84.48E
Sankheda India 62 22.10N 73.35E
Sānkra India 63 20.18N 82.03E
Sankt Anton Austria 39 47.08N 10.16E
Sankt Gilgen Austria 39 47.46N 13.22E
Sankt Ingbert Germany 39 49.17N 7.06E
Sankt Johann im Pongau Austria 39 47.21N 13.12E
Sankt Johann in Tirol Austria 39 47.31N 12.26E
Sankt Niklaus Switz. 39 46.11N 7.48E
Sankt Paul Austria 31 46.42N 14.52E
Sankt Peter Germany 38 54.18N 8.38E
Sankt Veit an der Glan Austria 31 46.46N 14.21E
Sankt Wolfgang Austria 39 47.44N 13.27E
Sankuru r. Zaïre 78 4.20S 20.27E
San Lázaro, Cabo c. Mexico 109 24.50N112.18W
San Lázaro, Sierra de mts. Mexico 109 23.20N110.00W
San Leonardo Spain 26 41.51N 3.05W
San Leonardo in Passiria Italy 30 46.49N 11.15E
San Lorenzo Argentina 125 32.45S 60.44W
San Lorenzo mtn. Chile 125 47.37S 72.19W
San Lorenzo Ecuador 122 1.17N 78.50W
San Lorenzo r. Mexico 109 24.15N107.25W
San Lorenzo de El Escorial Spain 26 40.35N 4.09W
San Lorenzo de la Parrilla Spain 27 39.51N 2.22W
Sanlúcar de Barrameda Spain 27 36.47N 6.21W
Sanlúcar la Mayor Spain 27 37.23N 6.12W
San Lucas Bolivia 124 20.06S 65.07W
San Lucas, Cabo c. Mexico 109 22.50N109.55W
San Luis Argentina 125 33.20S 66.20W
San Luis d. Argentina 125 34.00S 66.00W
San Luis Cuba 117 20.13N 75.50W
San Luis Obispo U.S.A. 109 35.17N120.40W
San Luis Potosí Mexico 116 22.10N101.00W
San Luis Potosí d. Mexico 116 23.00N100.00W
San Luis Rio Colorado Mexico 109 32.29N114.48W
San Luis Valley f. U.S.A. 108 37.25N106.00W
Sanluri Italy 32 39.33N 8.54E
San Marco Spain 26 43.13N 8.17W
San Marcos U.S.A. 111 29.53N 97.57W
San Marino Europe 30 43.56N 12.25E
San Marino town San Marino 30 43.55N 12.26E
San Martin r. Bolivia 124 12.25S 64.25W
San Martin de Valdeiglesias Spain 26 40.21N 4.24W
San Mateo Spain 25 40.28N 0.11E
San Mateo U.S.A. 108 37.35N122.19W
San Matías Bolivia 122 16.22S 58.24W
San Matías, Golfo g. Argentina 125 41.30S 64.00W
Sanmenxia China 54 35.45N111.22E
Sanmenxia Shuiku resr. China 54 34.38N111.05E
San Miguel r. Bolivia 124 12.25S 64.25W
San Miguel El Salvador 117 13.28N 88.10W
San Miguel del Monte Argentina 125 35.25S 58.49W
San Miguel de Tucumán Argentina 124 26.49S 65.13W
San Miguelito Panama 117 9.02N 79.30W
Sanming China 55 26.25N117.35E
San Miniato Italy 30 43.41N 10.51E
Sannār Sudan 73 13.33N 33.38E
Sannicandro Italy 31 41.50N 15.34E
San Nicolas Argentina 125 33.20S 60.13W
Sanniquellie Liberia 76 7.24N 8.45W
Sanok Poland 37 49.35N 22.10E
San Pablo Phil. 59 13.58N121.10E
San Pedro Buenos Aires Argentina 125 33.40S 59.41W
San Pedro Jujuy Argentina 124 24.14S 64.50W
San Pedro Dom. Rep. 117 18.30N 69.18W
San Pedro Ivory Coast 76 4.45N 6.37W
San Pedro Sonora Mexico 109 27.00N109.53W
San Pedro Paraguay 126 24.08S 57.08W
San Pedro, Punta c. Costa Rica 117 8.38N 83.45W
San Pedro, Sierra de mts. Spain 27 39.20N 6.40W
San Pedro de las Colonais Mexico 111 25.45N102.59W
San Pedro Mártir, Sierra mts. Mexico 109 30.45N115.30W
San Pedro Sula Honduras 117 15.26N 88.01W
San Pellegrino Terme Italy 30 45.50N 9.40E
San Pietro i. Italy 28 39.09N 8.16E
Sanquhar U.K. 14 55.22N 3.56W
San Quintín Mexico 109 30.28N115.58W
San Rafael U.S.A. 108 37.59N122.31W
San Raphael Argentina 125 34.40S 68.21W
San Remo Italy 30 43.49N 7.46E
San Roque Spain 27 36.13N 5.24W
San Salvador Argentina 125 31.37S 58.30W
San Salvador i. Bahamas 117 24.00N 74.32W
San Salvador El Salvador 117 13.40N 89.10W
San Salvador de Jujuy Argentina 124 24.10S 65.20W
San Sebastián Argentina 125 53.15S 68.30W
San Sebastián Spain 26 43.19N 1.59W
Sansepolcro Italy 30 43.34N 12.08E
San Severino Marche Italy 30 43.13N 13.10E
San Severo Italy 31 41.41N 15.23E
Sanshui China 55 23.09N112.52E
San Simon U.S.A. 109 32.16N109.14W
Sanski Most Yugo. 31 44.46N 16.40E
Santa r. Peru 122 9.00S 78.35W
Santa Amalia Spain 26 39.01N 6.01W
Santa Ana Argentina 124 27.20S 65.35W
Santa Ana Bolivia 124 13.45S 65.35W
Santa Ana El Salvador 117 14.00N 89.31W
Santa Ana Mexico 109 30.33N111.07W
Santa Ana U.S.A. 109 33.44N117.54W
Santa Bárbara Mexico 109 26.48N105.49W
Santa Barbara U.S.A. 109 34.25N119.42W
Santa Catalina de Armara Spain 26 43.02N 8.49W
Santa Catarina d. Brazil 126 27.00S 52.00W
Santa Catarina Mexico 111 25.41N100.28W
Santa Cesarea Terme Italy 33 40.02N 18.29E
Santa Clara Cuba 117 22.25N 79.58W
Santa Clara Calif. U.S.A. 108 37.21N121.57W
Santa Clara Utah U.S.A. 108 37.08N113.39W
Santa Clotilde Peru 122 2.25S 73.35W
Santa Coloma de Farners Spain 25 41.52N 2.40E
Santa Comba Dão Portugal 26 40.24N 8.08W
Santa Cruz d. Argentina 125 48.00S 69.30W
Santa Cruz r. Argentina 125 50.03S 68.35W
Santa Cruz Bolivia 124 17.45S 63.14W
Santa Cruz d. Bolivia 124 17.45S 62.00W
Santa Cruz Madeira Is. 127 32.41N 16.48W
Santa Cruz U.S.A. 108 36.58N122.08W
Santa Cruz i. U.S.A. 109 34.01N119.45W
Santa Cruz de la Zarza Spain 27 39.58N 3.10W
Santa Cruz de Mudela Spain 26 38.38N 3.28W
Santa Cruz de Tenerife Canary Is. 74 28.28N 16.15W
Santa Cruz Is. Solomon Is. 84 10.30S166.00E
Santa Domingo Mexico 109 25.32N112.02W
Santa Elena Argentina 125 31.00S 59.50W
Santa Elena U.S.A. 111 26.46N 98.30W
Santa Elena, C. Costa Rica 117 10.54N 85.56W
Santa Eufemia Spain 26 38.36N 4.52W
Santa Eugenia Spain 26 42.33N 9.00W
Santa Eulalia Spain 25 40.34N 1.19W
Santa Eulalia del Río Spain 25 38.59N 1.31E
Santa Fé Argentina 125 31.40S 60.40W
Santa Fé d. Argentina 124 30.00S 61.00W
Santa Fe Spain 27 37.11N 3.43W
Santa Fe U.S.A. 109 35.42N106.57W
Santa Filomena Brazil 123 9.07S 45.56W
Sant'Agata di Militello Italy 33 38.04N 14.38E
Santai China 55 31.10N105.02E
Santa Inés, Isla i. Chile 125 53.40S 73.00W
Santa Isabel Argentina 125 36.15S 66.55W
Santa Isabel do Morro Brazil 123 11.36S 50.37W
Sāntalpur India 62 23.45N 71.10E
Santa Lucía Uruguay 125 34.27S 56.24W
Santa Lucía r. Uruguay 125 34.48S 56.22W
Santa Lucia Range mts. U.S.A. 109 36.00N121.20W
Santa Luzia Portugal 26 37.44N 8.24W
Santa Margarita, Isla de i. Mexico 109 24.25N111.50W
Santa Margarita, Sierra de mts. Mexico 109 30.00N110.00W
Santa Margherita Ligure Italy 30 44.20N 9.12E
Santa Maria Brazil 126 29.40S 53.47W
Santa Maria U.S.A. 109 34.57N120.26W
Santa Maria, Cabo de c. Portugal 27 36.58N 7.54W
Santa Maria, Laguna de l. Mexico 109 31.07N107.17W
Santa Maria Capua Vetere Italy 33 41.05N 14.15E
Santa Maria di Leuca, Capo c. Italy 33 39.47N 18.22E
Santa María la Real de Nieva Spain 26 41.04N 4.24W
Santa Maria Madalena Brazil 126 21.58S 42.02W
Santa-Maria-Siché France 30 41.52N 8.59E
Santa Marinella Italy 30 42.02N 11.51E
Santa Marta Colombia 122 11.18N 74.10W
Santa Marta, Sierra Nevada de mts. Colombia 122 11.20N 73.00W
Santa Monica U.S.A. 109 34.01N118.30W
Santana Madeira Is. 127 32.48N 16.54W
Santana do Livramento Brazil 125 30.53S 55.31W
Santander Colombia 122 3.00N 76.25W
Santander Spain 26 43.28N 3.48W
Sant'Angelo dei Lombardi Italy 33 40.56N 15.11E
Santanoni Pk. U.S.A. 105 44.08N 74.11W
Sant'Antioco Italy 32 39.02N 8.30E
Sant'Antioco, Isola di i. Italy 32 39.00N 8.25E
Santañy Spain 25 39.22N 3.07E
Santa Pola, Cabo de c. Spain 25 38.12N 0.31W
Sant'Arcangelo Italy 33 40.15N 16.17E
Santarém Brazil 123 2.26S 54.41W
Santarém Portugal 27 39.14N 8.41W
Santarém d. Portugal 27 39.10N 8.40W
Santa Rosa Argentina 125 36.00S 64.40W
Santa Rosa Bolivia 122 10.36S 67.25W
Santa Rosa Brazil 126 27.52S 54.29W
Santa Rosa Honduras 117 14.47N 88.46W
Santa Rosa i. U.S.A. 109 33.58N120.06W
Santa Rosa Calif. U.S.A. 108 38.26N122.34W
Santa Rosa N.Mex. U.S.A. 109 34.57N104.41W
Santa Rosa, Mt. Guam 84 13.32N144.55E
Santa Rosa de Cabal Colombia 122 4.52N 75.37W
Santa Rosalía Mexico 109 27.19N112.17W
Santa Rosa Range mts. U.S.A. 108 41.00N117.40W
Santa Teresa Mexico 111 25.19N 97.50W
Santa Teresa, Embalse de resr. Spain 26 40.40N 5.37W
Santa Teresa Gallura Italy 32 41.15N 9.12E
Santa Vitória do Palmar Brazil 126 33.31S 53.21W
Sant Boi de Llobregat Spain 25 41.21N 2.03E
Sant Carles de la Rapita Spain 25 40.37N 0.36E
San Telmo Mexico 109 31.00N116.06W
Sant'Eufemia, Golfo di g. Italy 33 38.50N 16.00E
Sant Feliu de Guíxols Spain 25 41.47N 3.02E
Santhià Italy 30 45.22N 8.10E
Santiago Chile 125 33.27S 70.40W
Santiago Dom. Rep. 117 19.30N 70.42W
Santiago Panama 117 8.08N 80.59W
Santiago r. Peru 122 4.30S 77.48W
Santiago de Compostela Spain 26 42.53N 8.33W
Santiago de Cuba Cuba 117 20.00N 75.49W
Santiago del Estero Argentina 124 27.50S 64.15W
Santiago del Estero d. Argentina 124 27.40S 63.30W
Santiago do Cacém Portugal 27 38.01N 8.42W
Santiago Vázquez Uruguay 125 34.48S 56.21W
Sāntipur India 63 23.15N 88.26E
Säntis mtn. Switz. 39 47.15N 9.21E
Santisteban del Puerto Spain 26 38.15N 3.12W
Santo Amaro Brazil 123 12.35S 38.41W
Santo André Brazil 126 23.39S 46.29W
Santo Angelo Brazil 126 28.18S 54.16W
Santo Antônio do Içá Brazil 122 3.05S 67.57W
Santo Domingo Dom. Rep. 117 18.30N 69.57W
Santo Domingo de la Calzada Spain 26 42.26N 2.57W
Santo Domingo Pueblo U.S.A. 109 35.31N106.22W
Santolea, Embalse de resr. Spain 25 40.47N 0.19W
Santoña Spain 26 43.27N 3.27W
Santos Brazil 126 23.56S 46.22W
Santos Dumont Brazil 126 21.30S 43.34W
Santo Tirso Portugal 26 41.21N 8.28W
Santo Tomás Peru 122 14.34S 72.30W
Santo Tomé Argentina 124 28.31S 56.03W
Santpoort Neth. 16 52.27N 4.38E
Şānūr Jordan 67 32.21N 35.15E
San Valentin, Cerro mtn. Chile 125 46.40S 73.25W
San Vicente El Salvador 117 13.38N 88.42W
San Vicente de Alcántara Spain 27 39.21N 7.08W
San Vicente de la Barquera Spain 26 43.23N 4.24W
San Vincenzo Italy 30 43.06N 10.32E
San Vito Italy 32 39.27N 9.32E
San Vito, Capo c. Italy 32 38.11N 12.43E
San Vito al Tagliamento Italy 30 45.54N 12.52E
San Vito dei Normanni Italy 33 40.39N 17.42E
Sanyuan China 54 34.30N108.52E
Sanza Pombo Angola 78 7.20S 16.12E
São Borja Brazil 126 28.35S 56.01W
São Bras de Alportel Portugal 27 37.08N 7.58W
São Caetano do Sul Brazil 126 23.36S 46.34W
São Carlos Brazil 126 22.01S 47.54W
São Domingos Guinea Bissau 76 12.22N 16.08W
São Francisco r. Brazil 123 10.20S 36.20W
São Francisco do Sul Brazil 126 26.17S 48.39W
São Gabriel Brazil 126 30.20S 54.19W
São Gonçalo do Sapucaí Brazil 126 21.54S 45.35W
Sao Hill town Tanzania 79 8.21S 35.10E
São João da Boa Vista Brazil 126 21.59S 46.45W
São João da Madeira Portugal 26 40.54N 8.30W
São João del Rei Brazil 126 21.08S 44.15W
São João do Piauí Brazil 123 8.21S 42.15W
São Joaquim da Barra Brazil 126 20.36S 47.51W
São José do Calçado Brazil 126 21.01S 41.37W
São José do Rio Prêto Brazil 126 20.50S 49.20W
São José dos Campos Brazil 126 23.07S 45.52W
São Leopoldo Brazil 126 29.46S 51.09W
São Lourenço Brazil 126 22.08S 45.05W
São Luís Brazil 123 2.34S 44.16W
São Manuel Brazil 126 22.40S 48.35W
São Manuel r. see Teles Pires r. Brazil 123
São Miguel d'Oeste Brazil 126 26.45S 53.34W
Saona i. Dom. Rep. 117 18.09N 68.42W
Saône r. France 21 45.44N 4.50E
Saône-et-Loire d. France 19 46.42N 4.45E
Saoner India 63 21.23N 78.54E
São Paulo Brazil 126 23.33S 46.39W
São Paulo d. Brazil 126 22.05S 48.00W
São Paulo de Olivença Brazil 122 3.34S 68.55W
São Pedro do Sul Portugal 26 40.45N 8.04W
São Roque Brazil 126 23.31S 47.09W
São Roque, Cabo de c. Brazil 121 5.00S 35.00W
São Sebastião Brazil 126 23.48S 45.26W
São Sebastião, Ilha de i. Brazil 126 23.53S 45.17W
São Sebastião do Paraíso Brazil 126 20.54S 46.59W
São Tiago Brazil 126 20.54S 44.30W
São Tomé & Príncipe Africa 70 0.19N 6.05E
Saoura, Oued wadi Algeria 74 28.48N 0.50W
São Vicente Brazil 126 23.57S 46.23W
São Vicente, Cabo de c. Portugal 27 37.01N 8.59W
São Vicente de Minas Brazil 126 21.40S 44.26W
Sápai Greece 34 41.02N 25.41E
Sapé Brazil 123 7.06S 35.13W
Sapele Nigeria 77 5.53N 5.41E
Sapelo I. U.S.A. 113 31.28N 81.15W
Sapporo Japan 57 43.05N141.21E
Sapri Italy 33 40.04N 15.38E
Sapt Kosi r. Nepal 63 26.30N 86.55E
Sapu Angola 78 12.28S 19.26E
Sapulpa U.S.A. 111 36.00N 96.06W
Saqin Sum China 54 42.06N111.03E
Saqqārah Egypt 66 29.51N 31.13E
Saqqez Iran 65 36.14N 46.15E
Sarāb Iran 65 37.56N 47.35E
Sarābiyūm Egypt 66 30.23N 32.17E
Sara Buri Thailand 56 14.30N100.59E
Sarāi Naurang Pakistan 62 32.50N 70.47E
Sarajevo Yugo. 31 43.52N 18.26E
Saranac L. U.S.A. 105 44.20N 74.10W
Saranac Lake town U.S.A. 105 44.20N 74.08W
Sarandë Albania 34 39.52N 20.00E
Sarandí del Yi Uruguay 125 33.21S 55.38W
Sarandí Grande Uruguay 125 33.44S 56.20W
Sārangarh India 63 21.36N 83.05E
Sārangpur India 62 23.34N 76.28E
Saranley Somali Rep. 73 2.28N 42.08E
Saranpaul U.S.S.R. 44 64.15N 60.58E
Saransk U.S.S.R. 44 54.12N 45.10E
Sarapul U.S.S.R. 44 56.30N 53.49E
Sarar Plain Somali Rep. 71 9.35N 46.15E
Sarasota U.S.A. 113 27.20N 82.32W
Sarata U.S.S.R. 37 46.00N 29.40E
Saratoga U.S.A. 108 37.16N122.02W
Saratoga Springs U.S.A. 115 43.05N 73.47W
Saratov U.S.S.R. 45 51.30N 45.55E
Saravan Laos 56 15.43N106.24E
Sarawak d. Malaysia 58 2.00N113.00E
Sarayakpinar Turkey 34 41.46N 26.29E
Saraychik U.S.S.R. 45 47.29N 51.42E
Sarbāz Iran 65 26.39N 61.20E
Sárbogárd Hungary 31 46.53N 18.38E
Sarcelles France 19 49.00N 2.23E
Sardār Chāh Pakistan 62 27.58N 64.50E
Sardārpur India 62 22.39N 74.59E
Sardārshahr India 62 28.26N 74.29E
Sardegna d. Italy 32 40.15N 9.00E
Sardegna i. Italy 32 40.00N 9.00E
Sardinia i. see Sardegna i. Italy 32
Sarek mtn. Sweden 40 67.25N 17.46E
Sareks Nat. Park Sweden 40 67.15N 17.30E
Sargasso Sea Atlantic Oc. 127 28.00N 60.00W
Sargodha Pakistan 60 32.01N 72.40E
Sarh Chad 77 9.08N 18.22E
Sarhro, Jbel mts. Morocco 74 31.00N 5.55W
Sarī Iran 65 36.33N 53.06E
Saría i. Greece 35 35.50N 27.15E
Sarikamiş Turkey 64 40.19N 42.35E
Sarikei Malaysia 58 2.07N111.31E
Sarina Australia 90 21.26S149.13E
Sariñena Spain 25 41.48N 0.10W
Sarita U.S.A. 111 37.13N 97.47W
Sark i. U.K. 13 49.26N 2.22W
Sarlat France 20 44.53N 1.13E
Sărmasu Romania 37 46.46N 24.11E
Sármellék Hungary 31 46.44N 17.10E
Sarmi Indonesia 59 1.51S138.45E
Sarmiento Argentina 125 45.35S 69.05W
Särna Sweden 41 61.41N 13.08E
Sarnen Switz. 39 46.54N 8.15E
Sarnia Canada 104 42.58N 82.23W
Sarno Italy 33 40.49N 14.37E
Sarny U.S.S.R. 37 51.21N 26.31E
Saronikós Kólpos g. Greece 35 37.54N 23.12E
Saronno Italy 30 45.38N 9.02E
Saros Körfezi g. Turkey 34 40.30N 26.20E
Sárospatak Hungary 37 48.19N 21.34E
Šar Planina mts. Yugo. 34 42.10N 21.00E
Sarpsborg Norway 42 59.17N 11.07E
Sarralbe France 19 49.00N 7.01E
Sarre r. see Saar r. France 19
Sarrebourg France 19 48.44N 7.03E
Sarreguemines France 19 49.06N 7.03E
Sarre-Union France 19 48.56N 7.05E
Sarria Spain 26 42.47N 7.24W
Sarro Mali 76 13.40N 5.05W
Sartène France 21 41.36N 8.59E
Sarthe d. France 18 48.00N 0.05E
Sarthe r. France 18 47.30N 0.32W
Sartilly France 18 48.45N 1.27W
Sartynya U.S.S.R. 50 63.22N 63.11E
Şarūr Oman 65 23.25N 58.10E
Sárvár Hungary 36 47.15N 16.57E
Sárvíz r. Hungary 31 46.24N 18.41E
Saryshagan U.S.S.R. 52 46.08N 73.32E
Sarzana Italy 30 44.07N 9.58E
Sarzeau France 18 47.32N 2.46W

Sasa Israel **67** 33.02N 35.24E
Sasabeneh Ethiopia **71** 7.55N 43.39E
Sasarām India **63** 24.57N 84.02E
Sasebo Japan **57** 33.10N129.42E
Saseginaga, L. Canada **104** 47.06N 78.35W
Saser *mtn.* Jammu & Kashmir **63** 34.50N 77.50E
Saskatchewan *d.* Canada **101** 55.00N106.00W
Saskatchewan *r.* Canada **101** 53.12N 99.16W
Saskatoon Canada **101** 52.07N106.38W
Sasovo U.S.S.R. **44** 54.21N 41.58E
Sassandra Ivory Coast **76** 4.58N 6.08W
Sassandra *r.* Ivory Coast **76** 5.00N 6.04W
Sassari Italy **32** 40.44N 8.33E
Sassnitz Germany **38** 54.31N 13.38E
Sassoferrato Italy **30** 43.26N 12.51E
Sasso Marconi Italy **30** 44.24N 11.15E
Sassuolo Italy **30** 44.33N 10.47E
Sastown Liberia **76** 4.44N 8.01W
Sasyk, Ozero *l.* U.S.S.R. **37** 45.38N 29.38E
Satadougou Mali **76** 12.30N 11.30W
Satāna India **62** 20.35N 74.12E
Satanta U.S.A. **111** 37.26N100.59W
Sátão Portugal **26** 40.44N 7.44W
Sātāra India **60** 17.43N 74.05E
Satit *r.* Sudan **72** 14.20N 35.50E
Satkānia Bangla. **63** 22.04N 92.03E
Satna India **63** 24.35N 80.50E
Sátoraljaújhely Hungary **37** 48.24N 21.39E
Sātpura Range *mts.* India **62** 21.30N 76.00E
Satu Mare Romania **37** 47.48N 22.52E
Satun Thailand **56** 6.38N100.05E
Sauce Argentina **125** 30.05S 58.45W
Sauda Norway **42** 59.39N 6.20E
Saudi Arabia Asia **64** 26.00N 44.00E
Sauerland *f.* Germany **38** 51.23N 8.20E
Saugeen *r.* Canada **104** 44.30N 81.22W
Saujon France **20** 45.40N 0.56W
Sauk Centre U.S.A. **110** 45.44N 94.57W
Saulgau Germany **39** 48.01N 9.30E
Saulieu France **19** 47.16N 4.14E
Sault-de-Vaucluse France **21** 44.05N 5.25E
Sault Sainte Marie Canada **104** 46.31N 84.20W
Sault Sainte Marie U.S.A. **104** 46.30N 84.21W
Saumarez Reef Australia **90** 21.50S153.40E
Saumlaki Indonesia **90** 7.59S131.22E
Saumur France **18** 47.16N 0.05W
Saurimo Angola **78** 9.38S 20.20E
Sausar India **63** 21.42N 78.52E
Sauveterre-de-Béarn France **20** 43.29N 0.56W
Sauveterre-en-Guyenne France **20** 44.42N 0.05W
Sava Italy **33** 40.24N 17.34E
Sava *r.* Yugo. **31** 44.50N 20.26E
Savage U.S.A. **108** 47.27N104.21W
Savai'i *i.* W. Samoa **84** 13.36S172.27W
Savalou Benin **77** 7.55N 1.59E
Savanna U.S.A. **110** 42.06N 90.07W
Savannah *r.* U.S.A. **113** 32.02N 80.53W
Savannah Ga. U.S.A. **113** 32.04N 81.05W
Savannah Tenn. U.S.A. **111** 35.14N 88.14W
Savannakhét Laos **56** 16.34N104.48E
Savant L. Canada **102** 50.48N 90.20W
Savant Lake *town* Canada **102** 50.20N 90.40W
Savé Benin **77** 8.04N 2.37E
Save *r.* France **20** 43.47N 1.17E
Save *r.* Mozambique **81** 20.59S 35.02E
Sāveh Iran **65** 35.00N 50.25E
Savelugu Ghana **76** 9.39N 0.48W
Savenay France **18** 47.22N 1.57W
Saverdun France **20** 43.14N 1.35E
Saverne France **19** 48.44N 7.22E
Savigliano Italy **30** 44.38N 7.40E
Savigny-sur-Braye France **18** 47.53N 0.49E
Šavnik Yugo. **31** 42.57N 19.05E
Savoie *d.* France **21** 45.30N 6.25E
Savona Italy **30** 44.17N 8.30E
Savonlinna Finland **44** 61.52N 28.51E
Savoonga U.S.A. **98** 63.42N170.27W
Sävsjö Sweden **43** 57.25N 14.40E
Savu Sea *see* Sawu, Laut *sea* Pacific Oc. **59**
Sawai Mādhopur India **62** 25.59N 76.22E
Sawākin Sudan **72** 19.07N 37.20E
Sawatch Range *mts.* U.S.A. **110** 39.10N106.25W
Sawbridgeworth U.K. **13** 51.50N 0.09W
Sawdā', Jabal as *hills* Libya **75** 28.40N 15.00E
Sawdā', Qurnat as *mtn.* Lebanon **66** 34.17N 36.04E
Sawdirī Sudan **72** 14.25N 29.05E
Sawfajjīn, Wādī Libya **75** 31.54N 15.07E
Sawhāj Egypt **64** 26.33N 31.42E
Şawqirah, Ghubbat *b.* Oman **71** 18.35N 57.00E
Sawston U.K. **13** 52.07N 0.11E
Sawtell Australia **93** 30.21S153.05E
Sawtooth Mts. U.S.A. **108** 44.03N114.35W
Sawu *i.* Indonesia **59** 10.30S121.50E
Sawu, Laut *sea* Pacific Oc. **59** 9.30S122.30E
Saxmundham U.K. **13** 52.13N 1.29E
Saxon Switz. **39** 46.09N 7.11E
Saxton U.S.A. **114** 40.13N 78.15W
Say Mali **76** 13.50N 4.57W
Say Niger **77** 13.08N 2.22E
Sayama Japan **57** 35.51N139.24E
Şaydā Lebanon **66** 33.32N 35.22E
Sayers Lake *town* Australia **92** 32.46S143.20E
Saylūn *site* Jordan **67** 32.03N 35.17E
Saynshand Mongolia **54** 44.58N110.12E
Sayre U.S.A. **115** 41.59N 76.32W
Sayula Mexico **116** 19.52N103.36W
Sayville U.S.A. **115** 40.44N 73.05W
Sazliyka *r.* Bulgaria **34** 42.15N 25.50E
Sázava *r.* Czech. **36** 49.53N 14.21E
Sbaa Algeria **74** 28.13N 0.10W
Scaër France **18** 48.02N 3.42W
Scafell Pike *mtn.* U.K. **12** 54.27N 3.12W
Scalea Italy **33** 39.49N 15.48E
Scalloway U.K. **14** 60.08N 1.17W
Scammon Bay *town* U.S.A. **98** 61.50N165.35W
Scansano Italy **30** 42.41N 11.20E
Scapa Flow *str.* U.K. **14** 58.53N 3.05W
Scarborough Canada **104** 43.44N 79.16W
Scarborough Tobago **122** 11.11N 60.45W
Scarborough U.K. **12** 54.17N 0.24W
Scenic U.S.A. **108** 43.46N102.32W
Schaalsee *l.* Germany **38** 53.35N 10.57E
Schaerbeek Belgium **16** 50.54N 4.20E
Schaffhausen Switz. **39** 47.42N 8.38E
Schaffhausen *d.* Switz. **39** 47.40N 8.36E
Schagen Neth. **16** 52.47N 4.47E
Schärding Austria **39** 48.27N 13.26E
Schefferville Canada **99** 54.50N 67.00W
Scheinfeld Germany **39** 49.40N 10.27E
Schelde *r.* Belgium **16** 51.13N 4.25E
Schell Creek Range *mts.* U.S.A. **108** 39.10N114.40W
Schenectady U.S.A. **115** 42.47N 73.53W
Schesslitz Germany **38** 49.59N 11.01E
Scheveningen Neth. **16** 52.07N 4.16E
Schiedam Neth. **16** 51.55N 4.25E
Schiermonnikoog *i.* Neth. **16** 53.28N 6.15E
Schiltigheim France **19** 48.36N 7.45E
Schio Italy **30** 45.43N 11.21E
Schkeuditz Germany **38** 51.24N 12.13E
Schladming Austria **39** 47.23N 13.41E
Schleiden Germany **38** 50.31N 6.28E
Schleswig Germany **38** 54.31N 9.33E
Schleswig-Holstein *d.* Germany **38** 54.39N 9.30E
Schleusingen Germany **39** 50.31N 10.45E
Schlitz Germany **38** 50.40N 9.33E
Schlüchtern Germany **39** 50.20N 9.31E
Schmalkalden Germany **38** 50.43N 10.26E
Schmidmühlen Germany **38** 49.16N 11.56E
Schmölln Germany **38** 50.53N 12.20E
Schmutter *r.* Germany **39** 48.43N 10.47E
Schneeberg *mtn.* Germany **38** 50.03N 11.51E
Schneverdingen Germany **38** 53.07N 9.47E
Schoharie U.S.A. **115** 42.40N 74.19W
Schoharie Creek *r.* U.S.A. **115** 42.57N 74.18W
Schönebeck Germany **38** 52.01N 11.45E
Schongau Germany **39** 47.49N 10.54E
Schopfheim Germany **39** 47.39N 7.49E
Schorndorf Germany **39** 48.48N 9.31E
Schouten, Kepulauan *is.* Indonesia **59** 0.45S135.50E
Schouwen *i.* Neth. **16** 51.42N 3.45E
Schramberg Germany **39** 48.13N 8.23E
Schreiber Canada **102** 48.45N 87.20W
Schrobenhausen Germany **39** 48.33N 11.17E
Schroon Lake *town* U.S.A. **105** 43.47N 73.46W
Schuler Canada **101** 50.22N110.05W
Schuylkill *r.* U.S.A. **115** 39.53N 75.12W
Schuylerville U.S.A. **115** 43.06N 73.35W
Schuylkill Haven U.S.A. **115** 40.38N 76.12W
Schwabach Germany **38** 49.20N 11.01E
Schwaben *f.* Germany **39** 48.10N 10.50E
Schwäbische Alb *mts.* Germany **39** 48.30N 9.38E
Schwäbisch Gmünd Germany **39** 48.48N 9.47E
Schwäbisch Hall Germany **39** 49.07N 9.44E
Schwabmünchen Germany **39** 48.11N 10.45E
Schwandorf Germany **39** 49.20N 12.08E
Schwaner, Pegunungan *mts.* Indonesia **58** 0.45S113.20E
Schwarze Elster *r.* Germany **38** 51.49N 12.51E
Schwarzenburg Switz. **39** 46.49N 7.21E
Schwarzrand *mts.* Namibia **80** 25.40S 16.53E
Schwarzwald *f.* Germany **36** 48.00N 7.45E
Schwaz Austria **39** 47.20N 11.42E
Schwedt Germany **38** 53.03N 14.17E
Schweich Germany **39** 49.49N 6.45E
Schweinfurt Germany **39** 50.03N 10.14E
Schweitzingen Germany **39** 49.23N 8.34E
Schwelm Germany **38** 51.17N 7.17E
Schwenningen Germany **39** 48.04N 8.32E
Schwerin Germany **38** 53.38N 11.25E
Schweriner See *l.* Germany **38** 53.45N 11.28E
Schwyz Switz. **39** 47.02N 8.40E
Schwyz *d.* Switz. **39** 47.00N 8.45E
Schyan Canada **105** 46.10N 77.00W
Sciacca Italy **32** 37.30N 13.06E
Scicli Italy **33** 36.47N 14.43E
Scilla Italy **33** 38.15N 15.44E
Scilly, Isles of U.K. **13** 49.55N 6.20W
Šćit *mtn.* Yugo. **31** 44.02N 17.47E
Scituate U.S.A. **115** 42.12N 70.44W
Scobey U.S.A. **108** 48.47N105.25W
Scone Australia **93** 32.01S150.53E
Scordia Italy **33** 37.18N 14.51E
Scorno, Punta di *c.* Italy **32** 41.07N 8.19E
Scotia Calif. U.S.A. **108** 40.26N123.31W
Scotia N.Y. U.S.A. **115** 42.47N 73.59W
Scotia Ridge *f.* Atlantic Oc. **127** 60.00S 35.00W
Scotia Sea Atlantic Oc. **127** 57.00S 45.00W
Scotland U.K. **14** 55.30N 4.00W
Scotsbluff U.S.A. **110** 41.52N103.40W
Scotstown Canada **105** 45.32N 71.17W
Scott Canada **105** 46.30N 71.04W
Scottburgh R.S.A. **80** 30.17S 30.45E
Scott City U.S.A. **110** 38.29N100.54W
Scottdale U.S.A. **114** 40.06N 79.35W
Scott Is. Canada **100** 50.48N128.40W
Scott L. Canada **101** 59.55N106.18W
Scott Reef Australia **88** 14.00S121.50E
Scottsbluff U.S.A. **108** 41.52N103.40W
Scottsboro U.S.A. **111** 34.40N 86.02W
Scottsdale Australia **91** 41.09S147.31E
Scottsdale U.S.A. **109** 33.30N111.56W
Scottsville U.S.A. **111** 36.45N 86.11W
Scranton U.S.A. **115** 41.24N 75.40W
Scugog, L. Canada **104** 44.10N 78.51W
Scunthorpe U.K. **12** 53.35N 0.38W
Scuol Switz. **39** 46.48N 10.18E
Scutari, L. Yugo./Albania **34** 42.17N 19.17E
Seabrook, L. Australia **89** 30.56S119.40E
Seaford U.S.A. **115** 38.39N 75.37W
Seaforth Canada **104** 43.33N 81.24W
Seagroves U.S.A. **111** 32.57N102.34W
Seahouses U.K. **12** 55.35N 1.38W
Sea Isle City U.S.A. **115** 39.09N 74.42W
Seal *r.* Canada **101** 59.04N 94.48W
Sea Lake *town* Australia **92** 35.31S142.54E
Seal Bight Canada **103** 52.27N 55.40W
Searchlight U.S.A. **109** 35.28N114.55W
Seascale U.K. **12** 54.24N 3.29W
Seaside Calif. U.S.A. **108** 36.37N121.50W
Seaside Oreg. U.S.A. **108** 46.02N123.55W
Seaton U.K. **13** 50.43N 3.05W
Seattle U.S.A. **108** 47.36N122.20W
Seaview Range *mts.* Australia **90** 18.56S146.00E
Sebastian U.S.A. **113** 27.50N 80.29W
Sebastián Vizcaíno, Bahía *b.* Mexico **109** 28.00N114.30W
Sebba Burkina **76** 13.27N 0.33E
Sebeş Romania **37** 45.58N 23.34E
Sebewaing U.S.A. **104** 43.44N 83.27W
Sebidiro P.N.G. **59** 9.00S142.15E
Sebinkarahisar Turkey **64** 40.19N 38.25E
Sebnitz Germany **38** 50.58N 14.16E
Sebou, Oued *r.* Morocco **74** 34.15N 6.40W
Sebring U.S.A. **113** 27.30N 81.28W
Sechura, Desierto de *des.* Peru **122** 6.00S 80.30W
Seclin France **16** 50.34N 3.01E
Sêda *r.* Portugal **27** 38.55N 8.01W
Sedalia U.S.A. **110** 38.42N 93.14W
Sedan France **19** 49.42N 4.57E
Sedan U.S.A. **111** 37.08N 96.11W
Sedano Spain **26** 42.43N 3.45W
Seddon New Zealand **86** 41.40S174.04E
Séderon France **21** 44.12N 5.32E
Sederot Israel **67** 31.31N 34.35E
Sedgewick Canada **101** 52.46N111.41W
Sédhiou Senegal **76** 12.44N 15.30W
Sedini Italy **32** 40.50N 8.49E
Sedom Israel **66** 31.04N 35.23E
Sedot Yam Israel **67** 32.29N 34.53E
Seefeld Austria **39** 47.20N 11.11E
Seehausen Germany **38** 52.53N 11.45E
Seeheim Namibia **80** 26.50S 17.45E
Seeleys Bay *town* Canada **105** 44.29N 76.14W
Seelow Germany **38** 52.32N 14.23E
Sées France **18** 48.36N 0.10E
Seesen Germany **38** 51.53N 10.10E
Seevetal Germany **38** 53.26N 9.58E
Sefrou Morocco **74** 33.50N 4.50W
Segbwema Sierra Leone **76** 8.00N 11.00W
Segesta *site* Italy **32** 37.56N 12.50E
Seggueur, Oued es *wadi* Algeria **75** 31.44N 2.18E
Segni Italy **30** 41.41N 13.01E
Ségou Mali **76** 13.28N 6.18W
Ségou *d.* Mali **76** 13.55N 6.20W
Segovia Spain **26** 40.57N 4.07W
Segovia *d.* Spain **26** 41.10N 4.00W
Segozero, Ozero *l.* U.S.S.R. **44** 63.15N 33.40E
Segré France **18** 47.41N 0.53W
Segre *r.* Spain **25** 41.40N 0.43E
Séguédine Niger **77** 20.12N 12.59E
Séguéla Ivory Coast **76** 7.58N 6.44W
Seguin U.S.A. **111** 29.34N 97.58W
Segura Portugal **27** 39.50N 6.59W
Segura *r.* Spain **25** 38.06N 0.38W
Segura, Sierra de *mts.* Spain **27** 38.15N 2.30W
Sehore India **62** 23.12N 77.05E
Sehwān Pakistan **62** 26.26N 67.52E
Seia Portugal **26** 40.25N 7.42W
Seiches-sur-le-Loir France **18** 47.35N 0.22W
Seiland *i.* Norway **40** 70.25N 23.10E
Seilhac France **20** 45.22N 1.42E
Seille *r.* France **19** 49.07N 6.11E
Seinäjoki Finland **40** 62.47N 22.50E
Seine *r.* France **18** 49.26N 0.26E
Seine, Baie de la *b.* France **18** 49.25N 0.15E
Seine-et-Marne *d.* France **19** 48.30N 3.00E
Seine-Maritime *d.* France **18** 49.45N 1.00E
Seixal Portugal **27** 38.38N 9.06W
Sejerö *i.* Denmark **42** 55.53N 11.09E
Sekayu Indonesia **58** 2.58S103.58E
Seki Japan **57** 35.29N136.55E
Sekoma Botswana **80** 24.41S 23.50E
Sekondi-Takoradi Ghana **76** 4.57N 1.44W
Sek'ot'a Ethiopia **73** 12.38N 39.03E
Sekūheh Iran **65** 30.45N 61.29E
Selaru *i.* Indonesia **90** 8.09S131.00E
Selatan, Tanjung *c.* Indonesia **58** 4.20S114.45E
Selatan Natuna, Kepulauan *is.* Indonesia **58** 3.00N108.50E
Selayar *i.* Indonesia **59** 6.07S120.28E
Selb Germany **39** 50.10N 12.08E
Selbu Norway **40** 63.14N 11.03E
Selby U.K. **12** 53.47N 1.05W
Selby U.S.A. **110** 45.31N100.02W
Selbyville U.S.A. **115** 38.28N 75.13W
Seldovia U.S.A. **98** 59.27N151.43W
Sele *r.* Italy **33** 40.27N 14.58E
Selenga *r.* U.S.S.R. **52** 52.20N106.20E
Selenge Mörön *r. see* Selenga Mongolia **52**
Selenicë Albania **34** 40.33N 19.39E
Sélestat France **19** 48.16N 7.27E
Seligman U.S.A. **109** 35.20N112.53W
Selimiye Turkey **35** 37.24N 27.40E
Sélingue, Lac de *l.* Mali **76** 11.25N 8.15W
Selinoús Greece **35** 37.35N 21.37E
Selinsgrove U.S.A. **114** 40.48N 76.52W
Selinunte *site* Italy **32** 37.35N 12.50E
Seljord Norway **42** 59.29N 8.37E
Selkirk Man. Canada **101** 50.09N 96.52W
Selkirk Ont. Canada **104** 42.49N 79.56W
Selkirk U.K. **14** 55.33N 2.51W
Selkirk Mts. Canada **100** 50.02N116.20W
Selles-sur-Cher France **19** 47.16N 1.33E
Sells U.S.A. **109** 31.55N111.53W
Selma Ala. U.S.A. **111** 32.25N 87.01W
Selma Calif. U.S.A. **109** 36.34N119.37W
Selmer U.S.A. **111** 35.11N 88.36W
Selseleh ye Safid Kūh *mts.* Afghan **65** 34.30N 63.30E
Selsey Bill *c.* U.K. **13** 50.44N 0.47W
Selty U.S.S.R. **44** 57.19N 52.12E
Sélune *r.* France **18** 48.35N 1.15W
Selva Argentina **126** 29.50S 62.02W
Selvas *f.* Brazil **122** 6.00S 65.00W
Selwyn L. Canada **101** 60.00N104.30W
Selwyn Mts. Canada **98** 63.00N130.00W
Selwyn Range *mts.* Australia **90** 21.35S140.35E
Seman *r.* Albania **34** 40.45N 19.50E
Semara W. Sahara **74** 26.44N 14.41W
Semarang Indonesia **59** 6.58S110.29E
Sembabule Uganda **79** 0.08S 31.27E
Semeru, Gunung *mtn.* Indonesia **59** 8.04S112.53E
Seminoe Resr. U.S.A. **108** 42.00N106.50W
Seminole U.S.A. **111** 32.43N102.39W
Semiozernoye U.S.S.R. **50** 52.22N 64.06E
Semipalatinsk U.S.S.R. **9** 50.26N 80.16E
Semīrom Iran **65** 31.31N 52.10E
Semiyarka U.S.S.R. **50** 50.52N 78.23E
Semliki *r.* Zaïre **79** 1.12N 30.27E
Semmering Pass Austria **36** 47.40N 16.00E
Semnān Iran **65** 35.31N 53.24E
Semois *r.* France **16** 49.53N 4.45E
Semporna Malaysia **58** 4.27N118.36E
Semu *r.* Tanzania **79** 3.57S 34.20E
Semur-en-Auxois France **19** 47.29N 4.20E
Sena Mozambique **79** 17.36S 35.00E
Senador Pompeu Brazil **123** 5.30S 39.25W
Senaja Malaysia **58** 6.49N117.02E
Sena Madureira Brazil **122** 9.04S 68.40W
Senanga Zambia **78** 15.52S 23.19E
Senatobia U.S.A. **111** 34.39N 89.58W
Sendai Kyushu Japan **57** 31.49N130.18E
Sendai Tofuku Japan **57** 38.20N140.50E
Sendenhorst Germany **38** 51.50N 7.49E
Sendhwa India **62** 21.41N 75.06E
Sendurjana India **63** 21.32N 78.17E
Seneca Oreg. U.S.A. **108** 44.08N118.58W
Seneca S.C. U.S.A. **113** 34.41N 82.59W
Seneca Falls *town* U.S.A. **114** 42.55N 76.48W
Seneca L. U.S.A. **114** 42.40N 76.57W
Senegal Africa **76** 14.30N 14.30W
Sénégal *r.* Senegal/Mauritania **76** 16.00N 16.28W
Senekal R.S.A. **80** 28.18S 27.37E
Senetosa, Punta di *c.* France **21** 41.33N 8.47E
Senftenberg Germany **38** 51.31N 14.00E
Senhor do Bonfim Brazil **123** 10.28S 40.11W
Senica Czech. **37** 48.41N 17.22E
Senigallia Italy **30** 43.43N 13.13E
Senise Italy **33** 40.09N 16.18E
Senj Yugo. **31** 44.59N 14.54E
Senja *i.* Norway **40** 69.15N 17.20E
Senlis France **19** 49.12N 2.35E
Senmonoron Vietnam **56** 12.27N107.12E
Sennan Japan **57** 34.22N135.17E
Sennen U.K. **13** 50.04N 5.42W
Sennestadt Germany **38** 51.57N 8.31E
Senneterre Canada **102** 48.25N 77.15W
Sennori Italy **32** 40.48N 8.34E
Sens France **19** 48.12N 3.17E
Senta Yugo. **31** 45.56N 20.04E
Sentinel U.S.A. **109** 32.53N113.12W
Šentjur Yugo. **31** 46.13N 15.24E
Seonāth *r.* India **63** 21.44N 82.28E
Seoni India **63** 22.05N 79.32E
Seoni Mālwa India **63** 22.27N 77.28E
Seorīnārāyan India **63** 21.44N 82.35E
Seoul *see* Sŏul S. Korea **53**
Sepik *r.* P.N.G. **59** 3.54S144.30E
Sepopa Botswana **80** 18.45S 22.11E
Sept Îles *town* Canada **103** 50.12N 66.23W
Sepúlveda Spain **26** 41.18N 3.45W
Sequeros Spain **26** 40.31N 6.01W
Seraing Belgium **16** 50.37N 5.33E
Seram *i.* Indonesia **59** 3.10S129.30E
Seram, Laut *sea* Pacific Oc. **59** 2.50S128.00E
Serang Indonesia **59** 6.07S106.09E
Serbia *d. see* Srbija *d.* Yugo. **31**
Serdo Ethiopia **73** 11.59N 41.30E
Seremban Malaysia **58** 2.42N101.54E
Serengeti Nat. Park Tanzania **79** 2.30S 35.00E
Serengeti Plain *f.* Tanzania **79** 3.00S 35.00E
Serenje Zambia **79** 13.12S 30.50E
Sergach U.S.S.R. **44** 55.32N 45.27E
Sergipe *d.* Brazil **123** 11.00S 37.00W
Sergiyevsk U.S.S.R. **44** 53.56N 50.01E
Seria Brunei **58** 4.39N114.23E
Serian Malaysia **58** 1.10N110.35E
Sericho Kenya **73** 1.05N 39.05E
Sérifos Greece **35** 37.09N 24.31E
Sérifos *i.* Greece **35** 37.11N 24.31E
Sérigny *r.* Canada **103** 55.59N 68.43W
Serkout, Djebel *mtn.* Algeria **75** 23.40N 6.48E
Serle, Mt Australia **92** 30.34S138.55E
Sermata *i.* Indonesia **59** 8.30S129.00E
Serodino Argentina **125** 32.37S 60.57W
Serov U.S.S.R. **44** 59.42N 60.32E
Serowe Botswana **80** 22.22S 26.42E
Serpa Portugal **27** 37.56N 7.36W
Serpeddi, Punta *mtn.* Italy **32** 39.22N 9.18E
Serpentine *r.* Australia **89** 32.33S115.46E
Serpent's Mouth *str.* Venezuela **122** 9.50N 61.00W
Serpis *r.* Spain **25** 38.59N 0.09W
Serpukhov U.S.S.R. **44** 54.53N 37.25E
Serra do Navio Brazil **123** 0.59N 52.03W
Sérrai Greece **34** 41.05N 23.32E
Serramanna Italy **32** 39.25N 8.54E
Serra San Bruno Italy **33** 38.35N 16.20E
Serrat, Cap *c.* Tunisia **32** 37.14N 9.13E
Serra Talhada Brazil **123** 8.01S 38.17W
Serravalle Scrivia Italy **30** 44.43N 8.51E
Serre *r.* France **16** 49.40N 3.22E
Serres France **21** 44.26N 5.43E
Serri Italy **32** 39.41N 9.09E
Serrières France **21** 45.19N 4.45E
Serrinha Brazil **123** 11.38S 38.56W
Sersale Italy **33** 39.01N 16.44E
Sertã Portugal **27** 39.48N 8.06W
Sēru Ethiopia **73** 7.50N 40.28E
Serui Indonesia **59** 1.53S136.15E
Serule Botswana **80** 21.54S 27.17E
Sérvia Greece **34** 40.09N 21.58E
Serviceton Australia **92** 36.22S141.02E
Şes, Munţii *mts.* Romania **37** 47.05N 22.30E

Seseganaga L. to Sidi-Kacem

Seseganaga L. Canada **102** 50.00N 90.10W
Sese Is. Uganda **79** 0.20S 32.30E
Sesepe Indonesia **59** 1.30S127.59E
Sesheke Zambia **78** 17.14S 24.22E
Sesia *r.* Italy **30** 45.05N 8.37E
Sesimbra Portugal **24** 38.26N 9.06W
Sessa Aurunca Italy **32** 41.14N 13.56E
Sestao Spain **26** 43.18N 3.00W
Sestri Levante Italy **30** 44.16N 9.24E
Setana Japan **57** 42.26N139.51E
Sète France **20** 43.24N 3.41E
Sete Lagoas Brazil **126** 19.29S 44.15W
Setesdal *f.* Norway **42** 59.25N 7.25E
Sétif Algeria **22** 36.10N 5.26E
Seto Japan **57** 35.14N137.06E
Settat Morocco **74** 33.04N 7.37W
Setté Cama Gabon **78** 2.32S 9.46E
Settimo Torinese Italy **30** 45.09N 7.46E
Settle U.K. **12** 54.05N 2.18W
Settlement of Edinburgh Tristan da Cunha **127** 37.03S 12.18W
Setúbal Portugal **27** 38.32N 8.54W
Setúbal *d.* Portugal **27** 38.15N 8.35W
Setúbal, Baía de *b.* Portugal **27** 38.20N 9.00W
Seugne *r.* France **20** 45.41N 0.34W
Seui Italy **32** 39.50N 9.20E
Seul, Lac *l.* Canada **102** 50.20N 92.30W
Seurre France **19** 47.00N 5.09E
Sevagram India **63** 20.45N 78.30E
Sevan, Ozero *l.* U.S.S.R. **65** 40.22N 45.20E
Sevastopol' U.S.S.R. **45** 44.36N 33.31E
Sevenoaks U.K. **13** 51.16N 0.12E
Seven Sisters Peaks *mts.* Canada **100** 54.56N128.10W
Sévérac France **20** 44.19N 3.04E
Severn *r.* Australia **93** 29.08S150.50E
Severn *r.* Canada **102** 56.00N 87.38W
Severn *r.* U.K. **13** 51.50N 2.21W
Severnaya Zemlya *is.* U.S.S.R. **51** 80.00N 96.00E
Severn Falls Canada **104** 44.51N 79.38W
Severnyy U.S.S.R. **44** 69.55N 49.01E
Severnyy Donets *r.* U.S.S.R. **45** 49.08N 37.28E
Severnyy Dvina *r.* U.S.S.R. **44** 57.03N 24.00E
Severočeský *d.* Czech. **39** 50.26N 13.45E
Severodvinsk U.S.S.R. **44** 64.35N 39.50E
Severomorsk U.S.S.R. **44** 69.05N 33.30E
Severskiy Donets *r.* U.S.S.R. **23** 47.35N 40.55E
Sevier *r.* U.S.A. **108** 39.04N113.06W
Sevier L. U.S.A. **108** 38.55N113.09W
Sevilla Spain **27** 37.23N 5.59W
Sevilla *d.* Spain **27** 37.35N 6.00W
Sevlievo Bulgaria **34** 43.01N 25.06E
Sèvre-Nantaise *r.* France **18** 47.08N 1.26W
Sèvre Niortaise *r.* France **20** 46.20N 1.09W
Sevrey Mongolia **54** 43.33N102.13E
Sewa *r.* Sierra Leone **76** 7.15N 12.08W
Seward *Alas.* U.S.A. **98** 60.05N149.34W
Seward Nebr. U.S.A. **110** 40.55N 97.06W
Seward Penn. U.S.A. **114** 40.25N 79.01W
Seward Pen. U.S.A. **98** 65.00N164.10W
Seychelles Indian Oc. **49** 5.00S 55.00E
Seydhisfjördhur *town* Iceland **40** 65.16N 14.02W
Seylac Somali Rep. **71** 11.21N 43.30E
Seym *r.* U.S.S.R. **45** 51.30N 32.30E
Seymour Australia **93** 37.01S145.10E
Seymour U.S.A. **111** 33.35N 99.16W
Seyne France **21** 44.21N 6.21E
Seyssel France **21** 45.57N 5.49E
Sežana Yugo. **31** 45.42N 13.52E
Sézanne France **19** 48.43N 3.43E
Sezimbra Portugal **27** 38.26N 9.06W
Sezze Italy **32** 41.30N 13.03E
Sfax Tunisia **22** 34.45N 10.43E
Sfîntu-Gheorghe Romania **37** 45.52N 25.50E
Sforströmmen *str.* Denmark **42** 54.58N 11.55E
'sGravenhage Neth. **16** 52.05N 4.16E
Shaanxi *d.* China **54** 35.00N108.30E
Shaba *d.* Zaïre **79** 8.00S 27.00E
Shabeelle *r.* Somali Rep. **79** 0.30N 43.10E
Shabunda Zaïre **79** 2.42S 27.20E
Shache China **52** 38.27N 77.16E
Shafter U.S.A. **109** 35.30N119.16W
Shaftesbury U.K. **13** 51.00N 2.12W
Shagamu *r.* Canada **102** 55.50N 86.48W
Shāhābād India **63** 27.39N 79.57E
Shāhāda India **62** 21.28N 74.18E
Shahbā' Syria **66** 32.51N 36.37E
Shāhbandar Pakistan **62** 24.10N 67.54E
Shāhbāz Kalāt Pakistan **62** 26.42N 63.58E
Shahdād Iran **65** 30.27N 57.44E
Shāhdādkot Pakistan **62** 27.51N 67.54E
Shāhdādpur Pakistan **62** 25.56N 68.37E
Shahdol India **63** 23.17N 81.21E
Shāhganj India **63** 26.03N 82.41E
Shāhgarh India **62** 27.07N 69.54E
Shaḥḥāt Libya **72** 32.50N 21.52E
Shāh Jahān, Kūh-e *mts.* Iran **65** 37.00N 58.00E
Shāhjahānpur India **63** 27.53N 79.55E
Shāh Jūy Afghan. **62** 32.31N 67.25E
Shāh Kot Pakistan **62** 31.34N 73.29E
Shāh Kūh *mtn.* Iran **65** 31.38N 59.16E
Shāhpur Pakistan **62** 28.43N 68.25E
Shāhpura India **62** 25.35N 75.00E
Shāhpur Chākar Pakistan **62** 26.09N 68.39E
Shahrak Afghan. **62** 34.06N 64.18E
Shahr-e Bābak Iran **65** 30.08N 55.04E
Shahrestān Afghan. **62** 34.22N 66.47E
Shahrezā Iran **65** 32.00N 51.52E
Shahr Kord Iran **65** 32.40N 50.52E
Sha'īb Abā al Qūr *wadi* Saudi Arabia **64** 31.02N 42.00E
Shaikhpura India **63** 25.09N 85.51E
Shājāpur India **62** 23.26N 76.16E
Shakawe Botswana **80** 18.22S 21.50E
Shaker Heights *town* U.S.A. **114** 41.29N 81.36W
Shakhty U.S.S.R. **23** 47.43N 40.16E
Shakhunya U.S.S.R. **44** 57.41N 46.46E
Shaki Nigeria **77** 8.41N 3.24E
Shakshūk Egypt **66** 29.28N 30.42E
Shala Hāyk' *l.* Ethiopia **73** 7.25N 38.30E
Shalingzi China **54** 40.42N114.55E
Shallotte U.S.A. **113** 33.58N 78.25W
Shalwa Israel **67** 31.34N 34.46E
Shām, Jabal ash *mtn.* Oman **65** 23.14N 57.17E
Shamāl Dārfūr *d.* Sudan **72** 17.15N 25.30E
Shamāl Kurdufān *d.* Sudan **72** 14.00N 29.00E
Shāmat al Akbād *des.* Saudi Arabia **64** 28.15N 43.05E
Shamir Israel **67** 33.10N 35.39E
Shāmli India **62** 29.27N 77.19E
Shamokin U.S.A. **115** 40.47N 76.34W
Shamrock U.S.A. **111** 35.13N100.15W
Shamva Zimbabwe **79** 17.20S 31.38E
Shan *d.* Burma **56** 22.00N 98.00E
Shandī Sudan **72** 16.42N 33.26E
Shandong *d.* China **54** 36.00N119.00E
Shandong Bandao *pen.* China **54** 37.00N121.30E
Shangcheng China **55** 31.48N115.24E
Shangdu China **54** 41.33N113.31E
Shanggao China **55** 28.15N114.55E
Shanghai China **55** 31.18N121.50E
Shanghai *d.* China **55** 31.00N121.30E
Shanglin China **55** 23.26N108.36E
Shangqiu China **54** 34.21N115.40E
Shangrao China **55** 28.24N117.56E
Shangshui China **54** 33.31N114.39E
Shang Xian China **54** 33.49N109.56E
Shangyi China **54** 41.06N114.00E
Shangyou Shuiku *resr.* China **55** 25.52N114.21E
Shangyu China **55** 30.01N120.52E
Shanhaiguan China **54** 39.58N119.45E
Shannon *r.* Rep. of Ire. **15** 52.39N 8.43W
Shannon, Mouth of the *est.* Rep. of Ire. **15** 52.29N 9.57W
Shan Plateau Burma **56** 18.50N 98.00E
Shanshan China **52** 42.52N 90.10E
Shantarskiy Ostrova *is.* U.S.S.R. **51** 55.00N138.00E
Shantou China **55** 23.22N116.39E
Shanwa Tanzania **79** 3.09S 33.48E
Shanxi *d.* China **54** 37.00N112.00E
Shanyin China **54** 39.30N112.50E
Shaoguan China **55** 24.53N113.31E
Shaoxing China **55** 30.01N120.40E
Shaoyang China **55** 27.10N111.14E
Shap U.K. **12** 54.32N 2.40W
Shapinsay *i.* U.K. **14** 59.03N 2.51W
Shapur *ruins* Iran **65** 29.42N 51.30E
Shaqrā Lebanon **67** 33.12N 35.28E
Shaqrā' Saudi Arabia **65** 25.17N 45.14E
Shaqrā' Syria **67** 32.54N 36.14E
Shaqrā' Yemen **71** 13.21N 45.42E
Sharan Jogīzai Pakistan **62** 31.02N 68.33E
Sharbot Lake *town* Canada **105** 44.46N 76.41W
Shark B. Australia **88** 25.30S113.30E
Sharlyk U.S.S.R. **44** 52.58N 54.46E
Sharm ash Shaykh Egypt **66** 27.51N 34.16E
Sharon U.S.A. **114** 41.14N 80.31W
Sharon Springs *town* U.S.A. **110** 38.54N101.45W
Sharq al Istiwā'īyah *d.* Sudan **73** 5.00N 33.00E
Sharqī, Al Jabal ash *mts.* Lebanon **66** 34.00N 36.25E
Sharqīyah, Aş Şaḩrā' ash *des.* Egypt **66** 27.40N 32.00E
Sharya U.S.S.R. **44** 58.22N 45.50E
Shashi *r.* Botswana / Zimbabwe **80** 22.10S 29.15E
Shashi China **55** 30.18N112.20E
Shasta, Mt. U.S.A. **108** 41.20N122.20W
Shatt al Arab *r.* Iraq **65** 30.00N 48.30E
Shaunavon Canada **101** 49.40N108.25W
Shawanaga Canada **104** 45.32N 80.24W
Shawangunk Mts. U.S.A. **115** 41.35N 74.30W
Shawano U.S.A. **102** 44.46N 88.38W
Shawbridge Canada **105** 45.52N 74.05W
Shaw I. Australia **90** 20.29S149.05E
Shawinigan Canada **105** 46.33N 72.45W
Shawinigan Sud Canada **105** 46.30N 72.45W
Shawnee Ohio U.S.A. **114** 39.36N 82.13W
Shawnee Okla. U.S.A. **111** 35.20N 96.55W
Shawville Canada **105** 45.36N 76.29W
Sha Xi *r.* China **55** 26.38N118.10E
Sha Xian China **55** 26.27N117.42E
Shayang China **55** 30.42N112.29E
Shay Gap *town* Australia **88** 20.28S120.05E
Shaykh, Jabal ash *mtn.* Lebanon **66** 33.24N 35.52E
Shaykh 'Uthmān Yemen **71** 12.52N 44.59E
Shchara *r.* U.S.S.R. **37** 53.27N 24.45E
Shchelyayur U.S.S.R. **44** 65.16N 53.17E
Shchors U.S.S.R. **37** 51.50N 31.59E
Sheboygan U.S.A. **110** 43.46N 87.36W
Shebshi Mts. Nigeria **77** 8.30N 11.45E
Shediac Canada **103** 46.13N 64.32W
Sheeffry Hills Rep. of Ire. **15** 53.41N 9.42W
Sheelin, Lough Rep. of Ire. **15** 53.48N 7.20W
Sheep Range *mts.* U.S.A. **109** 36.45N115.05W
Sheet Harbour Canada **103** 44.55N 62.32W
Shefar'am Israel **67** 32.48N 35.10E
Sheffield U.K. **12** 53.23N 1.28W
Sheffield Ala. U.S.A. **113** 34.46N 87.40W
Sheffield Penn. U.S.A. **114** 41.42N 79.02W
Sheffield Tex. U.S.A. **111** 30.41N101.49W
Shefford U.K. **13** 52.02N 0.20W
Shegaon India **62** 20.47N 76.41E
Sheguiandah Canada **104** 45.53N 81.57W
Shekatika Bay *town* Canada **103** 51.17N 58.20W
Shekhābād Afghan. **62** 34.05N 68.45E
Shek Hasan Ethiopia **73** 12.09N 35.54E
Shekhūpura Pakistan **62** 31.42N 73.59E
Sheki U.S.S.R. **45** 41.12N 47.10E
Sheksna *r.* U.S.S.R. **44** 60.00N 37.49E
Shelburne N.S. Canada **103** 43.46N 65.19W
Shelburne Ont. Canada **104** 44.04N 80.12W
Shelburne U.S.A. **105** 44.22N 73.15W
Shelburne B. Australia **90** 11.49S143.00E
Shelby Mich. U.S.A. **112** 43.36N 86.22W
Shelby Mont. U.S.A. **108** 48.30N111.51W
Shelby Ohio U.S.A. **114** 40.53N 82.40W
Shelbyville Ind. U.S.A. **112** 39.31N 85.46W
Shelbyville Tenn. U.S.A. **113** 35.29N 86.30W
Sheldon Iowa U.S.A. **110** 43.11N 95.51W
Sheldon N.Dak. U.S.A. **110** 46.35N 97.30W
Sheldrake Canada **103** 50.20N 64.51W
Shelikof Str. U.S.A. **98** 58.00N153.45W
Shelley U.S.A. **108** 43.23N112.07W
Shellharbour Australia **93** 34.35S150.52E
Shell Lake *town* Canada **101** 53.18N107.07W
Shelton U.S.A. **108** 47.13N123.06W
Shenandoah *r.* U.S.A. **114** 38.56N 78.12W
Shenandoah Iowa U.S.A. **110** 40.46N 95.22W
Shenandoah Penn. U.S.A. **115** 40.49N 76.12W
Shenandoah Va. U.S.A. **114** 38.29N 78.37W
Shenandoah, North Fork *r.* U.S.A. **114** 38.57N 78.12W
Shenandoah, South Fork *r.* U.S.A. **114** 38.57N 78.12W
Shenandoah Mts. U.S.A. **114** 38.55N 78.56W
Shenandoah Nat. Park U.S.A. **114** 38.48N 78.12W
Shenandoah Tower *mtn.* U.S.A. **114** 38.30N 79.09W
Shenandoah Valley *f.* U.S.A. **114** 38.42N 78.48W
Shenchi China **54** 39.08N112.10E
Shëngjin Albania **34** 41.50N 19.35E
Shengze China **55** 30.53N120.40E
Shenkursk U.S.S.R. **44** 62.05N 42.58E
Shenmu China **54** 38.54N110.24E
Shennongjia China **55** 31.44N110.44E
Shen Xian China **54** 36.15N115.40E
Shenyang China **54** 41.48N123.27E
Shenzhen China **55** 22.32N114.08E
Sheo India **62** 26.11N 71.15E
Sheoganj India **62** 25.09N 73.04E
Sheopur India **62** 25.40N 76.42E
Shepetovka U.S.S.R. **37** 50.12N 27.01E
Shepherd Is. Vanuatu **84** 16.55S168.36E
Shepparton Australia **93** 36.25S145.26E
Sheppey, Isle of U.K. **13** 51.24N 0.50E
Sherada Ethiopia **73** 7.21N 36.32E
Sherborne U.K. **13** 50.56N 2.31W
Sherbro I. Sierra Leone **76** 7.30N 12.50W
Sherbrooke Canada **105** 45.24N 71.54W
Sherburne U.S.A. **115** 42.41N 75.30W
Sheridan U.S.A. **108** 44.48N106.58W
Sheringa Australia **92** 33.51S135.15E
Sheringham U.K. **12** 52.56N 1.11E
Sherkin I. Rep. of Ire. **15** 51.28N 9.25W
Sherman N.Y. U.S.A. **114** 42.10N 79.36W
Sherman Tex. U.S.A. **111** 33.38N 96.36W
Sherman Mills U.S.A. **112** 45.52N 68.23W
Sherridon Canada **101** 55.07N101.05W
'sHertogenbosch Neth. **16** 51.42N 5.19E
Shesh Gāv Afghan. **62** 33.45N 68.33E
Shetland Is. *d.* U.K. **14** 60.20N 1.15W
Shetpe U.S.S.R. **45** 44.09N 52.06E
Shetrunji *r.* India **62** 21.20N 72.05E
Shevchenko U.S.S.R. **45** 43.37N 51.11E
Shewa *d.* Ethiopia **73** 8.40N 38.00E
Shewa Gīmīra Ethiopia **73** 7.00N 35.50E
Sheyang China **54** 33.47N120.19E
Sheyenne *r.* U.S.A. **110** 47.05N 96.50W
Shiawassee *r.* U.S.A. **104** 43.06N 84.10W
Shibām Yemen **71** 15.56N 48.38E
Shibecha Japan **57** 43.17N144.36E
Shibīn al Kawm Egypt **66** 30.33N 31.00E
Shibīn al Qanāṭir Egypt **66** 30.19N 31.19E
Shibogama L. Canada **102** 53.35N 88.10W
Shickshinny U.S.A. **115** 41.09N 76.09W
Shidao China **54** 36.52N122.26E
Shiel, Loch U.K. **14** 56.48N 5.33W
Shiga *d.* Japan **57** 34.55N136.00E
Shigaib Sudan **72** 15.01N 23.36E
Shihpao Shan *mts.* China **55** 30.00N112.00E
Shijak Albania **34** 41.21N 19.33E
Shijiazhuang China **54** 38.03N114.26E
Shijiu Hu *l.* China **55** 31.20N118.48E
Shikārpur Pakistan **62** 27.57N 68.38E
Shikohābād India **63** 27.06N 78.36E
Shikoku *d.* Japan **57** 33.30N133.00E
Shikoku *i.* Japan **57** 33.30N133.00E
Shikoku sanchi *mts.* Japan **57** 34.00N134.00E
Shikotsu ko *l.* Japan **57** 43.50N141.26E
Shilabo Ethiopia **71** 6.05N 44.48E
Shilka U.S.S.R. **53** 51.55N116.01E
Shilka *r.* U.S.S.R. **53** 53.20N121.10E
Shillington U.S.A. **115** 40.18N 75.58W
Shillo *r.* Israel **67** 32.07N 34.53E
Shillong India **63** 25.34N 91.53E
Shiloh *see* Saylūn Jordan **67**
Shilong China **55** 23.02N113.50E
Shima Japan **57** 34.13N136.51E
Shimada Japan **57** 34.49N138.11E
Shima-hantō *pen.* Japan **57** 34.25N136.45E
Shimizu Japan **57** 35.01N138.29E
Shimoda Japan **57** 34.40N138.57E
Shimoga India **60** 13.56N 75.31E
Shimo jima *i.* Japan **57** 32.10N130.30E
Shimo Koshiki jima *i.* Japan **57** 31.50N130.00E
Shimonoseki Japan **57** 34.02N130.58E
Shimpek U.S.S.R. **52** 44.50N 74.10E
Shin, Loch U.K. **14** 58.06N 4.32W
Shinano *r.* Japan **57** 37.58N139.02E
Shīndand Afghan. **62** 33.18N 62.08E
Shinglehouse U.S.A. **114** 41.58N 78.12W
Shingleton U.S.A. **112** 46.21N 86.28W
Shingū Japan **57** 33.44N135.59E
Shīnkay Afghan. **62** 31.57N 67.26E
Shīn Naray Afghan. **62** 31.19N 66.43E
Shinnston U.S.A. **114** 39.24N 80.18W
Shinshār Syria **66** 34.36N 36.45E
Shinshiro Japan **57** 34.54N137.30E
Shinyanga Tanzania **79** 3.40S 33.20E
Shinyanga *d.* Tanzania **79** 3.30S 33.00E
Shiono zaki *c.* Japan **57** 33.28N135.47E
Ship Bottom U.S.A. **115** 39.39N 74.11W
Shipka Pass Bulgaria **34** 42.46N 25.33E
Shippegan Canada **103** 47.45N 64.42W
Shippensburg U.S.A. **114** 40.03N 77.31W
Shiprock U.S.A. **108** 36.47N108.41W
Shipston on Stour U.K. **13** 52.04N 1.38W
Shiqian China **55** 27.20N108.10E
Shiqiao China **55** 31.19N111.59E
Shiqizhen China **55** 22.22N113.21E
Shiqma *r.* Israel **67** 31.36N 34.30E
Shiquan China **54** 33.03N108.17E
Shiquan He *r.* China **63** 32.30N 79.40E
Shirakawa Japan **57** 37.10N140.15E
Shirakskaya Step *f.* U.S.S.R. **65** 41.40N 46.20E
Shirane san *mtn.* Japan **57** 35.40N138.15E
Shīrāz Iran **65** 29.36N 52.33E
Shirbīn Egypt **66** 31.13N 31.31E
Shire *r.* Mozambique **79** 17.46S 35.20E
Shiriya saki *c.* Japan **57** 41.24N141.30E
Shīr Kūh *mtn.* Iran **65** 31.38N 54.07E
Shiroishi Japan **57** 38.00N140.37E
Shirpur India **62** 21.21N 74.53E
Shīrvān Iran **65** 37.24N 57.55E
Shivpuri India **63** 25.26N 77.39E
Shiwan Dashan *mts.* China **55** 21.48N107.50E
Shiyan Hubei China **54** 32.38N110.47E
Shizuishan China **54** 39.14N106.47E
Shizuoka Japan **57** 34.58N138.23E
Shizuoka *d.* Japan **57** 35.00N138.00E
Shklov U.S.S.R. **37** 54.16N 30.16E
Shkodër Albania **34** 42.05N 19.30E
Shkodër *d.* Albania **34** 42.10N 19.40E
Shkumbin *r.* Albania **34** 41.01N 19.26E
Shoal C. Australia **89** 33.51S121.10E
Shoalhaven *r.* Australia **93** 34.51S150.40E
Sholāpur India **60** 17.43N 75.56E
Shomera Israel **67** 33.05N 35.17E
Shonai *r.* Japan **57** 35.04N136.50E
Shoshone Calif. U.S.A. **109** 35.58N116.17W
Shoshone Idaho U.S.A. **108** 42.57N114.25W
Shoshone Mts. U.S.A. **108** 39.25N117.15W
Shoshoni U.S.A. **108** 43.14N108.07W
Shostka U.S.S.R. **44** 51.53N 33.30E
Shou Xian China **54** 32.30N116.35E
Shouyang China **54** 37.55N113.10E
Show Low U.S.A. **109** 34.15N110.02W
Shpola U.S.S.R. **37** 49.00N 31.25E
Shreve U.S.A. **114** 40.41N 82.01W
Shreveport U.S.A **111** 32.30N 93.45W
Shrewsbury U.K. **13** 52.42N 2.45W
Shropshire *d.* U.K. **13** 52.35N 2.40W
Shuangliao China **54** 43.28N123.27E
Shuangyashan China **53** 46.37N131.22E
Shu'ayb, Wādī Jordan **67** 31.54N 35.38E
Shubenacadie Canada **103** 45.05N 63.25W
Shubrā al Khaymah Egypt **66** 30.06N 31.15E
Shuicheng China **55** 26.36N104.51E
Shujāābād Pakistan **62** 29.53N 71.18E
Shujālpur India **62** 23.24N 76.43E
Shuksan U.S.A. **108** 48.55N121.43W
Shule China **52** 39.25N 76.06E
Shumagin Is. U.S.A. **98** 55.00N160.00W
Shumerlya U.S.S.R. **44** 55.30N 46.25E
Shumikha U.S.S.R. **50** 55.15N 63.14E
Shumyachi U.S.S.R. **37** 53.52N 32.25E
Shūnat Nimrīn Jordan **67** 31.54N 35.37E
Shunayn, Sabkhat *f.* Libya **72** 30.10N 21.00E
Shunchang China **55** 26.48N117.47E
Shunde China **55** 22.40N113.20E
Shuo Xian China **54** 39.19N112.25E
Shūr *r.* *Kermān* Iran **65** 30.45N 57.55E
Shūr *r.* *Kermān* Iran **65** 31.14N 55.29E
Shūr *r.* Khorāsān Iran **65** 34.11N 60.07E
Shūrāb Iran **65** 28.09N 60.18E
Shūrāb *r.* Iran **65** 31.30N 55.18E
Shurugwi Zimbabwe **80** 19.40S 30.00E
Shūshtar Iran **65** 32.04N 48.53E
Shuswap L. Canada **100** 50.55N119.03W
Shuwak Sudan **72** 14.23N 35.52E
Shuya U.S.S.R. **44** 56.49N 41.23E
Shwebo Burma **56** 22.35N 95.42E
Shyok Jammu & Kashmir **63** 34.11N 78.08E
Siāhān Range *mts.* Pakistan **62** 27.30N 64.30E
Siālkot Pakistan **62** 32.30N 74.31E
Sian *see* Xi'an China **54**
Siargao *i.* Phil. **59** 9.55N126.05E
Siari Jammu & Kashmir **62** 34.56N 76.44E
Siasconset U.S.A. **115** 41.16N 69.58W
Siátista Greece **34** 40.15N 21.33E
Siau *i.* Indonesia **59** 2.42N125.24E
Siauliai U.S.S.R. **41** 55.56N 23.19E
Sibasa R.S.A. **80** 22.56S 30.28E
Šibenik Yugo. **31** 43.44N 15.54E
Siberut *i.* Indonesia **58** 1.30S 99.00E
Sibi Pakistan **62** 29.33N 67.53E
Sibiti Congo **78** 3.40S 13.24E
Sibiti *r.* Tanzania **79** 3.47S 34.45E
Sibiu Romania **29** 45.47N 24.09E
Sibley U.S.A. **110** 43.25N 95.43W
Sibolga Indonesia **58** 1.42N 98.48E
Sibu Malaysia **58** 2.18N111.49E
Sibut C.A.R. **77** 5.46N 19.06E
Sicasica Bolivia **124** 17.22S 67.45W
Siccus *r.* Australia **92** 31.26S139.30E
Sichuan *d.* China **52** 30.30N103.00E
Sichuan Pendi *f.* China **55** 31.00N106.00E
Sicié, Cap *c.* France **21** 43.03N 5.51E
Sicilia *d.* Italy **33** 37.45N 14.00E
Sicilia *i.* Italy **33** 37.30N 14.00E
Sicily *i.* *see* Sicilia *i.* Italy **33**
Sicuani Peru **122** 14.21S 71.13W
Šid Yugo. **31** 45.08N 19.13E
Sidamo *d.* Ethiopia **73** 4.30N 39.00E
Sidaouet Niger **77** 18.34N 8.03E
Siderno Italy **33** 38.16N 16.18E
Sídheros, Ákra *c.* Greece **35** 35.19N 26.19E
Sidhi India **63** 24.25N 81.53E
Sidhirókastron Greece **34** 41.14N 23.22E
Sidhpur India **62** 23.55N 72.23E
Sīdī Barrānī Egypt **64** 31.38N 25.58E
Sidi bel Abbès Algeria **74** 35.12N 0.38W
Sidi Daoud Tunisia **32** 37.01N 10.55E
Sidi Ifni Morocco **74** 29.24N 10.12W
Sidi-Kacem Morocco **74** 34.15N 5.39W

Sīdī Sālim to Snowtown

Sīdī Sālim Egypt 66 31.16N 30.47E
Sidi Smaïl Morocco 74 32.49N 8.30W
Sidlaw Hills U.K. 14 56.31N 3.10W
Sidley, Mt. Antarctica 128 77.30S125.00W
Sidmouth U.K. 13 50.40N 3.13W
Sidney Canada 100 48.39N123.24W
Sidney Mont. U.S.A. 108 47.43N104.09W
Sidney Nebr. U.S.A. 110 41.09N102.59W
Sidney N.Y. U.S.A. 115 42.19N 75.24W
Sidney Ohio U.S.A. 112 40.16N 84.10W
Sidon see Şaydā Lebanon 66
Sidra, G. of see Surt, Khalīj g. Libya 75
Siedlce Poland 37 52.10N 22.18E
Sieg r. Germany 16 50.49N 7.11E
Siegburg Germany 38 50.47N 7.12E
Siegen Germany 38 50.52N 8.02E
Siemiatycze Poland 37 52.26N 22.53E
Siĕmréab Cambodia 56 13.21N103.50E
Siena Italy 30 43.19N 11.21E
Sieradz Poland 37 51.36N 18.45E
Sierck-les-Bains France 19 49.26N 6.21E
Sierpc Poland 37 52.52N 19.41E
Sierra Blanca town U.S.A. 109 31.11N105.12W
Sierra Colorada Argentina 125 40.35S 67.50W
Sierra de Outes town Spain 26 42.51N 8.54W
Sierra Leone Africa 76 9.00N 12.00W
Sierra Mojada town Mexico 111 27.17N103.42W
Sierra Nevada mts. U.S.A. 108 37.45N119.30W
Sierre Switz. 39 46.18N 7.32E
Sīfenī Ethiopia 73 12.20N 40.24E
Sífnos i. Greece 35 36.59N 24.40E
Sig Algeria 74 35.32N 0.11W
Sig U.S.S.R. 44 65.31N 34.16E
Sigean France 20 43.02N 2.59E
Sighetul Marmaţiei Romania 37 47.56N 23.54E
Sighişoara Romania 37 46.13N 24.49E
Sigli Indonesia 58 5.23N 95.57E
Siglufjördhur Iceland 40 66.12N 18.55W
Sigmaringen Germany 39 48.05N 9.13E
Signy France 19 49.42N 4.25E
Sigtuna Sweden 43 59.37N 17.43E
Sigüenza Spain 26 41.04N 2.38W
Sigües Spain 25 42.38N 1.00W
Siguiri Guinea 76 11.28N 9.07W
Sihor India 62 21.42N 71.58E
Sihorā India 63 23.29N 80.07E
Siika r. Finland 40 64.50N 24.44E
Si'īr Jordan 67 31.35N 35.09E
Siirt Turkey 64 37.56N 41.56E
Sikanni Chief r. Canada 100 58.20N121.50W
Sīkar India 62 27.37N 75.09E
Sikasso Mali 76 11.18N 5.38W
Sikasso d. Mali 76 11.20N 6.05W
Sikeston U.S.A. 111 36.53N 89.35W
Sikhote Alin mts. U.S.S.R. 53 44.00N135.00E
Sikiá Greece 34 40.02N 23.56E
Síkinos i. Greece 35 36.39N 25.06E
Sikión site Greece 35 37.59N 22.44E
Sikkim d. India 63 27.30N 88.30E
Sil r. Spain 26 42.27N 7.43W
Silandro Italy 30 46.38N 10.46E
Silba Yugo. 31 44.23N 14.42E
Silba i. Yugo. 31 44.23N 14.42E
Silchar India 61 24.49N 92.47E
Silcox Canada 101 57.12N 94.10W
Silet Algeria 75 22.39N 4.35E
Silgarhi-Doti Nepal 63 29.16N 80.58E
Silghāt India 63 26.37N 92.56E
Silifke Turkey 64 36.22N 33.57E
Silīguri India 63 26.42N 88.26E
Siliil Somali Rep. 71 10.59N 43.31E
Siling Co l. China 63 31.45N 88.50E
Silistra Bulgaria 29 44.07N 27.17E
Šiljak mtn. Yugo. 34 43.45N 21.50E
Siljan l. Sweden 41 60.50N 14.45E
Silkeborg Denmark 42 56.10N 9.34E
Sillé-le-Guillaume France 18 48.12N 0.08W
Sillian Austria 39 46.45N 12.25E
Sillian Italy 30 46.45N 12.25E
Sillon de Talbert c. France 18 48.53N 3.05W
Silloth U.K. 12 54.53N 3.25W
Silogui Indonesia 58 1.10S 98.46E
Silsbee U.S.A 111 30.21N 94.11W
Silvassa India 62 20.17N 73.00E
Silver Bow U.S.A. 108 46.00N112.40W
Silver City U.S.A. 109 32.46N108.17W
Silver Creek town U.S.A. 114 42.33N 79.10W
Silverdalen Sweden 43 57.32N 15.44E
Silver Lake town U.S.A. 108 43.08N120.56W
Silver Spring town U.S.A. 114 39.02N 77.03W
Silverstone U.K. 13 52.05N 1.03W
Silverthrone Mtn. Canada 100 51.31N126.06W
Silverton Australia 92 31.53S141.13E
Silverton U.S.A. 108 45.01N122.47W
Silves Portugal 27 37.11N 8.26W
Silvi Italy 31 42.34N 14.05E
Simanggang Malaysia 58 1.10N111.32E
Simàrd, Lac l. Canada 102 47.40N 78.40W
Simav r. Turkey 29 40.24N 28.31E
Simba Kenya 79 2.10S 37.37E
Simba Zaïre 78 0.36N 22.55E
Simbach Germany 39 48.34N 12.45E
Simcoe Canada 104 42.50N 80.18W
Simcoe, L. Canada 104 44.20N 79.20W
Simdega India 63 22.37N 84.31E
Simenga U.S.S.R. 51 62.42N108.25E
Simeria Romania 29 45.51N 23.01E
Simeto r. Italy 33 37.24N 15.06E
Simeulue i. Indonesia 58 2.30N 96.00E
Simferopol' U.S.S.R. 45 44.57N 34.05E
Sími Greece 35 36.35N 27.50E
Sími i. Greece 35 36.35N 27.50E
Simikot Nepal 63 29.58N 81.51E
Simitli Bulgaria 34 41.52N 23.07E
Simiyu r. Tanzania 79 2.32S 33.25E
Simla India 62 31.06N 77.09E
Simleul Silvaniei Romania 37 47.14N 22.48E
Simmern Germany 39 49.59N 7.31E
Simo r. Finland 40 65.37N 25.03E
Simojärvo l. Finland 40 66.06N 27.03E
Simon, Lac l. Canada 105 45.58N 75.05W
Simon's Town R.S.A. 80 34.12S 18.26E
Simoom Sound town Canada 98 50.45N126.45W
Simplon Pass Switz. 39 46.15N 8.02E
Simplon Tunnel Switz. 39 46.15N 8.10E
Simpson Desert Australia 90 25.00S136.50E
Simrishamn Sweden 43 55.33N 14.20E
Simuco Mozambique 79 14.00S 40.35E
Sīnā', Shibh Jazīrat pen. Egypt 66 29.00N 34.00E
Sinadhago Somali Rep. 71 5.22N 46.22E
Sinai see Sīnā', Shibh Jazīrat pen. Egypt 66
Sinaloa d. Mexico 109 25.00N107.30W
Sinaloa r. Mexico 109 25.18N108.30W
Sinalunga Italy 30 43.12N 11.44E
Sinan China 55 27.51N108.24E
Sīnāwin Libya 75 31.02N 10.36E
Sincelejo Colombia 122 9.17N 75.23W
Sinclair U.S.A. 108 41.47N107.07W
Sinclair Mills Canada 100 54.05N121.40W
Sind r. India 63 26.26N 79.13E
Sindal Denmark 42 57.28N 10.13E
Sindara Gabon 78 1.07S 10.41E
Sindari India 62 25.35N 71.55E
Sindelfingen Germany 39 48.42N 9.00E
Sindh d. Pakistan 62 26.45N 69.00E
Sindhūli Garhi Nepal 63 27.16N 85.58E
Sindri India 63 23.45N 86.42E
Sines Portugal 26 37.57N 8.52W
Sines, Cabo de c. Portugal 26 37.57N 8.53W
Sinfāis Portugal 26 41.04N 8.05W
Sinfra Ivory Coast 76 6.35N 5.56W
Singālila mtn. India 63 27.13N 88.01E
Singapore Asia 58 1.20N103.45E
Singapore town Singapore 58 1.20N103.45E
Singaraja Indonesia 59 8.06S115.07E
Singatoka Fiji 84 18.08S177.30E
Sing Buri Thailand 56 14.56N100.21E
Singida Tanzania 79 4.45S 34.42E
Singida d. Tanzania 79 6.00S 34.30E
Singing India 61 28.53N 94.47E
Singitikós Kólpos g. Greece 34 40.06N 24.00E
Singkaling Hkāmti Burma 61 26.00N 95.42E
Singkang Indonesia 59 4.09S120.02E
Singkawang Indonesia 58 0.57N108.57E
Singkep i. Indonesia 58 0.30S104.20E
Singleton Australia 93 32.33S151.11E
Singoli India 62 25.00N 75.25E
Singosan N. Korea 53 38.50N127.27E
Siniscola Italy 32 40.34N 9.41E
Sinj Yugo. 31 43.42N 16.38E
Sinjah Sudan 73 13.09N 33.56E
Sinjajevina mts. Yugo. 31 43.00N 19.15E
Sinjil Jordan 67 32.02N 35.16E
Sinkāt Sudan 72 18.50N 36.50E
Sinnai Italy 32 39.18N 9.12E
Sinnar India 62 19.51N 74.00E
Sinnemahoning r. U.S.A. 114 41.19N 78.06W
Sinnes Norway 42 58.56N 6.50E
Sinni r. Italy 33 40.09N 16.42E
Sînnicolau Mare Romania 29 46.05N 20.38E
Sinnūris Egypt 66 29.25N 30.52E
Sinop Turkey 64 42.02N 35.09E
Sinsheim Germany 39 49.16N 8.53E
Sintang Indonesia 58 0.03N111.31E
Sint Eustatius i. Leeward Is. 117 17.33N 63.00W
Sint Maarten i. see St. Martin i. Leeward Is. 117
Sinton U.S.A. 111 29.41N 95.58W
Sintra Portugal 27 38.48N 9.23W
Sinŭiju N. Korea 53 40.04N124.25E
Sinyavka U.S.S.R. 37 52.58N 26.30E
Sinyukha r. U.S.S.R. 37 48.03N 30.51E
Sió r. Hungary 31 46.20N 18.55E
Siocon Phil. 59 7.42N122.08E
Siófok Hungary 31 46.54N 18.04E
Sion Switz. 39 46.14N 7.21E
Sioux City U.S.A. 110 42.30N 96.23W
Sioux Falls town U.S.A. 110 43.32N 96.44W
Sioux Lookout town Canada 102 50.06N 91.55W
Siphaqeni R.S.A. 80 31.05S 29.29E
Siping Hubei China 55 31.58N111.10E
Siping Jilin China 54 43.10N124.24E
Sipiwesk L. Canada 101 55.05N 97.35W
Sipura i. Indonesia 58 2.10S 99.40E
Sira Norway 42 58.25N 6.38E
Sira r. Norway 42 58.17N 6.24E
Siracusa Italy 33 37.04N 15.17E
Sirājganj Bangla. 63 24.27N 89.43E
Sirakoro Mali 76 12.41N 9.14W
Sirasso Ivory Coast 76 9.16N 6.06W
Sirdalsvatn l. Norway 42 58.33N 6.41E
Sīrē Ethiopia 73 9.00N 36.55E
Sir Edward Pellew Group is. Australia 90 15.40S136.48E
Siret r. Romania 29 45.28N 27.56E
Sirevåg Norway 42 58.30N 5.47E
Sirha Nepal 63 26.39N 86.12E
Sirḩān, Wādī as f. Saudi Arabia 64 31.00N 37.30E
Sir James MacBrien, Mt. Canada 100 62.07N127.41W
Sir Joseph Banks Group is. Australia 92 34.35S136.12E
Sirohi India 62 24.53N 72.52E
Sironj India 63 24.06N 77.42E
Síros i. Greece 35 37.26N 24.54E
Sirrah, Wādī as r. Saudi Arabia 65 23.10N 44.22E
Sirsa India 62 29.32N 75.02E
Sir Wilfrid, Mt. Canada 105 46.41N 75.35W
Sisak Yugo. 31 45.29N 16.23E
Sisaket Thailand 56 15.08N104.18E
Sishen R.S.A. 80 27.46S 22.59E
Sisimiut see Holsteinsborg Greenland 99
Sisipuk L. Canada 101 55.45N101.50W
Sisŏphŏn Cambodia 56 13.37N102.58E
Sissach Switz. 39 47.28N 7.49E
Sisseton U.S.A. 110 45.40N 97.03W
Sissonne France 19 49.34N 3.54E
Sistema Central mts. Spain 26 41.00N 3.30W
Sistema Ibérico mts. Spain 26 41.00N 2.25W
Sistemas Béticos mts. Spain 27 37.20N 3.00W
Sisteron France 21 44.12N 5.56E
Sītāmarhi India 63 26.36N 85.29E
Sītāpur India 63 27.34N 80.41E
Sithonia pen. Greece 34 40.00N 23.45E
Sitía Greece 35 35.13N 26.06E
Sitka U.S.A. 100 57.05N135.20W
Sitnica r. Yugo. 34 42.45N 21.01E
Sittang r. Burma 56 17.25N 96.50E
Sittard Neth. 16 51.00N 5.52E
Sittensen Germany 38 53.17N 9.30E
Sittwe Burma 56 20.09N 92.50E
Situbondo Indonesia 59 7.40S114.01E
Siuruan r. Finland 40 65.20N 25.55E
Sīvan r. Iran 65 29.50N 52.47E
Sivas Turkey 64 39.44N 37.01E
Sivomaskinskiy U.S.S.R. 44 66.45N 62.44E
Sivrihisar Turkey 64 39.29N 31.32E
Sīwah Egypt 64 29.12N 25.31E
Sīwah, Wāḩat oasis Egypt 64 29.10N 25.40E
Siwalik Range mts. India 63 31.15N 77.45E
Siwān India 63 26.13N 84.22E
Siwa Oasis see Sīwah, Wāḩat oasis Egypt 64
Sixmilecross U.K. 15 54.34N 7.08W
Siya U.S.S.R. 44 63.38N 41.40E
Sizun France 18 48.24N 4.05W
Sjaelland i. Denmark 42 55.30N 11.45E
Sjaellands Odde c. Denmark 42 55.58N 11.22E
Sjenica Yugo. 31 43.16N 20.00E
Sjeništa mtn. Yugo. 31 43.42N 18.37E
Sjöbo Sweden 43 55.38N 13.42E
Sjötorp Sweden 43 58.50N 13.59E
Skaelskör Denmark 42 55.15N 11.19E
Skaerbaek Denmark 42 55.09N 8.46E
Skagafjördhur est. Iceland 40 65.55N 19.35W
Skagen Denmark 42 57.44N 10.36E
Skagern l. Sweden 43 58.59N 14.17E
Skagerrak str. Norway / Denmark 42 58.00N 9.30E
Skagway U.S.A. 100 59.23N135.20W
Skaill U.K. 14 58.56N 2.43W
Skala Greece 35 36.51N 22.40E
Skála Oropoú Greece 35 38.20N 23.46E
Skala Podolskaya U.S.S.R. 37 48.51N 26.11E
Skalat U.S.S.R. 37 49.20N 25.59E
Skalderviken b. Sweden 43 56.18N 12.38E
Skanderborg Denmark 42 56.02N 9.56E
Skåne f. Sweden 43 55.59N 13.30E
Skaneateles U.S.A. 115 42.57N 76.26W
Skånevik Norway 42 59.44N 5.59E
Skanör Sweden 43 55.25N 12.52E
Skara Sweden 43 58.22N 13.25E
Skaraborg d. Sweden 43 58.20N 13.30E
Skärhamn Sweden 42 58.00N 11.33E
Skarnes Norway 42 60.15N 11.41E
Skarżysko-Kamienna Poland 37 51.08N 20.53E
Skead Canada 104 46.40N 80.45W
Skeena r. Canada 100 54.09N130.02W
Skeena Mts. Canada 100 57.00N128.30W
Skegness U.K. 12 53.09N 0.20E
Skeleton L. Canada 104 45.15N 79.27W
Skellefte r. Sweden 40 64.42N 21.06E
Skellefteå Sweden 40 64.46N 20.57E
Skelleftehamn Sweden 40 64.41N 21.14E
Skelmersdale U.K. 12 53.34N 2.49W
Skene Sweden 43 57.29N 12.38E
Skerries Rep. of Ire. 15 53.35N 6.07W
Skhíza i. Greece 35 36.43N 21.46E
Ski Norway 42 59.43N 10.50E
Skíathos Greece 35 39.10N 23.29E
Skíathos i. Greece 35 39.12N 23.30E
Skiddaw mtn. U.K. 12 54.40N 3.09W
Skidel U.S.S.R. 37 53.37N 24.19E
Skien Norway 42 59.12N 9.36E
Skierniewice Poland 37 51.58N 20.08E
Skikda Algeria 75 36.53N 6.54E
Skillingaryd Sweden 43 57.26N 14.05E
Skinners Eddy U.S.A. 115 41.37N 76.08W
Skinnskatteberg Sweden 43 59.50N 15.41E
Skipness U.K. 14 56.45N 5.22W
Skipton U.K. 12 53.57N 2.01W
Skíros Greece 35 38.55N 24.34E
Skíros i. Greece 35 38.53N 24.32E
Skive Denmark 42 56.34N 9.02E
Skjálfanda Fljót r. Iceland 40 65.55N 17.30W
Skjálfandi est. Iceland 40 66.08N 17.38W
Skjern Denmark 42 55.57N 8.30E
Skjönsta Norway 40 67.12N 15.45E
Škofja Loka Yugo. 31 46.10N 14.18E
Skoghall Sweden 43 59.19N 13.26E
Skole U.S.S.R. 37 49.00N 23.30E
Skópelos Greece 35 39.07N 23.43E
Skópelos Greece 35 39.09N 26.47E
Skópelos i. Greece 35 39.10N 23.40E
Skopje Yugo. 34 42.01N 21.32E
Skörping Denmark 42 56.50N 9.53E
Skotfoss Norway 42 59.12N 9.30E
Skotterud Norway 43 59.59N 12.07E
Skövde Sweden 43 58.24N 13.50E
Skovorodino U.S.S.R. 51 54.00N123.53E
Skradin Yugo. 31 43.49N 15.56E
Skreia Norway 41 60.39N 10.56E
Skruv Sweden 43 56.41N 15.22E
Skudeneshavn Norway 42 59.09N 5.17E
Skull Rep. of Ire. 15 51.32N 9.33W
Skultorp Sweden 43 58.21N 13.49E
Skultuna Sweden 43 59.43N 16.25E
Skuodas U.S.S.R. 41 56.16N 21.32E
Skurup Sweden 43 55.28N 13.30E
Skutskär Sweden 41 60.38N 17.25E
Skvira U.S.S.R. 37 49.42N 29.40E
Skye i. U.K. 14 57.20N 6.15W
Slagelse Denmark 42 55.24N 11.22E
Sľalowa Wola Poland 37 50.40N 22.05E
Slamet mtn. Indonesia 59 7.14S109.10E
Slaney r. Rep. of Ire. 15 52.21N 6.30W
Slano Yugo. 31 42.47N 17.54E
Slantsy U.S.S.R. 44 59.09N 28.09E
Slaný Czech. 38 50.11N 14.04E
Slatina Romania 29 44.26N 24.23E
Slatina Yugo. 34 43.04N 20.58E
Slaton U.S.A. 111 33.26N101.39W
Slave r. Canada 100 61.18N113.39W
Slavgorod B.S.S.R. U.S.S.R. 37 53.25N 31.00E
Slavgorod R.S.F.S.R. U.S.S.R. 9 53.01N 78.37E
Slavonsko Požega Yugo. 31 45.20N 17.41E
Slavuta U.S.S.R. 37 50.20N 26.58E
Slavyansk U.S.S.R. 45 48.51N 37.36E
Sľawno Poland 36 54.22N 16.40E
Sleaford U.K. 12 53.00N 0.22W
Sleaford B. Australia 92 35.00S136.50E
Sleat, Sd. of str. U.K. 14 57.05N 5.48W
Sledge U.S.A. 111 34.26N 90.13W
Sledmere U.K. 12 54.04N 0.35W
Sleeper Is. Canada 102 56.50N 80.30W
Sleetmute U.S.A. 98 61.40N157.11W
Slide Mtn. U.S.A. 115 42.00N 74.23W
Sliedrecht Neth. 16 51.48N 4.46E
Slieve Aughty Mts. Rep. of Ire. 15 53.05N 8.31W
Slieve Bloom Mts. Rep. of Ire. 15 53.03N 7.35W
Slieve Callan mtn. Rep. of Ire. 15 52.51N 9.18W
Slieve Donard mtn. U.K. 15 54.11N 5.56W
Slieve Gamph mts. Rep. of Ire. 15 54.06N 8.52W
Slievekimalta mtn. Rep. of Ire. 15 52.45N 8.17W
Slieve Mish mts. Rep. of Ire. 15 52.48N 9.48W
Slieve Miskish mts. Rep. of Ire. 15 51.41N 9.56W
Slievenamon mtn. Rep. of Ire. 15 52.25N 7.34W
Slieve Snaght mtn. Donegal Rep. of Ire. 15 55.12N 7.20W
Sligo Rep. of Ire. 15 54.17N 8.28W
Sligo d. Rep. of Ire. 15 54.10N 8.35W
Sligo U.S.A. 114 41.07N 79.29W
Sligo B. Rep. of Ire. 15 54.18N 8.40W
Slippery Rock town U.S.A. 114 41.04N 80.03W
Slite Sweden 43 57.43N 18.48E
Sliven Bulgaria 34 42.42N 26.19E
Slivnitsa Bulgaria 34 42.50N 23.00E
Sloan U.S.A. 110 42.14N 96.14W
Slobodka U.S.S.R. 37 47.56N 29.18E
Slobodskoy U.S.S.R. 44 58.42N 50.10E
Slobozia Romania 34 43.52N 25.55E
Slonim U.S.S.R. 37 53.05N 25.21E
Slough U.K. 13 51.30N 0.35W
Slovechna r. U.S.S.R. 37 51.41N 29.41E
Slovechno U.S.S.R. 37 51.23N 28.20E
Slovenija d. Yugo. 31 46.00N 15.00E
Slovenjgradec Yugo. 31 46.31N 15.05E
Slovenska Bistrica Yugo. 31 46.23N 15.34E
Slovensko d. Czech. 37 48.25N 19.20E
Sľubice Poland 36 52.20N 14.32E
Sluch r. U.S.S.R. 37 52.08N 27.31E
Sluis Neth. 16 51.18N 3.23E
Slunj Yugo. 31 45.07N 15.35E
Sľupsk Poland 37 54.28N 17.01E
Slurry R.S.A. 80 25.48S 25.49E
Slutsk U.S.S.R. 37 53.02N 27.31E
Slyne Head Rep. of Ire. 15 53.25N 10.12W
Slyudyanka U.S.S.R. 52 51.40N103.40E
Småland f. Sweden 43 57.20N 15.00E
Smålandsfarvandet str. Denmark 42 55.05N 11.20E
Smålandsstenar Sweden 43 57.10N 13.24E
Smallwood Resr. Canada 103 54.00N 64.00W
Smeaton Canada 101 53.30N104.49W
Smederevo Yugo. 29 44.40N 20.56E
Smela U.S.S.R. 45 49.15N 31.54E
Smethport U.S.A. 114 41.49N 78.27W
Smilde Neth. 16 52.58N 6.28E
Smilovichi U.S.S.R. 37 53.45N 28.00E
Smith Canada 100 55.10N114.00W
Smith Arm b. Canada 98 66.15N124.00W
Smithers Canada 100 54.45N127.10W
Smithfield R.S.A. 80 30.11S 26.31E
Smiths Falls town Canada 105 44.54N 76.01W
Smithton Australia 91 40.52S145.07E
Smithtown Australia 93 31.03S152.53E
Smithville U.S.A. 114 39.04N 81.06W
Smoke Hole U.S.A. 114 38.52N 79.18W
Smoky r. Canada 100 56.10N117.21W
Smoky Bay town Australia 92 32.22S133.56E
Smoky C. Australia 93 30.55S153.05E
Smoky Hill r. U.S.A. 110 39.03N 96.48W
Smöla i. Norway 40 63.20N 8.00E
Smolensk U.S.S.R. 44 54.49N 32.04E
Smolevichi U.S.S.R. 37 54.00N 28.01E
Smólikas mtn. Greece 34 40.06N 20.52E
Smolyan Bulgaria 34 41.36N 24.38E
Smorgon U.S.S.R. 37 54.28N 26.20E
Smygehuk c. Sweden 43 55.21N 13.23E
Smyrna U.S.A. 115 39.18N 75.36W
Snaefell mtn. Iceland 40 64.48N 15.34W
Snaefell mtn. U.K. 12 54.16N 4.28W
Snake r. Idaho U.S.A. 106 43.50N117.05W
Snake r. Wash. U.S.A. 108 46.12N119.02W
Snake Range mts. U.S.A. 108 39.00N114.15W
Snake River town U.S.A. 108 44.10N110.40W
Snake River Plain f. U.S.A. 108 43.00N113.00W
Snåsa Norway 40 64.15N 12.23E
Snåsavatn l. Norway 40 64.05N 12.00E
Snedsted Denmark 42 56.54N 8.32E
Sneek Neth. 16 53.03N 5.40E
Sneem Rep. of Ire. 15 51.50N 9.54W
Sneeuwberg mtn. R.S.A. 80 32.30S 19.09E
Snežnik mtn. Yugo. 31 45.35N 14.27E
Śniardwy, Jezioro l. Poland 37 53.46N 21.44E
Snina Czech. 37 48.59N 22.07E
Snizort, Loch U.K. 14 57.35N 6.30W
Snöhetta mtn. Norway 41 62.20N 9.17E
Snov r. U.S.S.R. 37 51.45N 31.45E
Snowbird L. Canada 101 60.45N103.00W
Snowdon mtn. U.K. 12 53.05N 4.05W
Snowdrift Canada 101 62.24N110.44W
Snowdrift r. Canada 101 62.24N110.44W
Snowflake U.S.A. 109 34.30N110.05W
Snow Hill town U.S.A. 113 38.11N 75.23W
Snowtown Australia 92 33.47S138.13E

Tana to Ternopol

Tana *r.* Norway 40 69.45N 28.15E
Tana *i.* Vanuatu 84 19.30S169.20E
Tanacross U.S.A. 98 63.12N143.30W
Tanafjorden Norway 40 70.54N 28.40E
T'ana Hāyk' *l.* Ethiopia 73 12.00N 37.20E
Tanahgrogot Indonesia 58 1.55S116.12E
Tanahmerah Indonesia 59 6.08S140.18E
Tanakpur India 63 29.05N 80.07E
Tanami Desert Australia 88 19.50S130.50E
Tanana U.S.A. 98 65.11N152.10W
Tanana *r.* U.S.A. 98 65.09N151.55W
Tananarive *see* Antananarivo Madagascar 81
Tanaro *r.* Italy 30 45.01N 8.47E
Tanch'On N. Korea 57 40.27N128.54E
Tānda India 63 26.33N 82.39E
Tanda Ivory Coast 76 7.48N 3.10W
Tandaltī Sudan 73 13.01N 31.50E
Tăndărei Romania 37 44.38N 27.40E
Tandil Argentina 125 37.18S 59.10W
Tandjilé *d.* Chad 77 9.45N 16.28E
Tando Ādam Pakistan 62 25.46N 68.40E
Tando Allāhyār Pakistan 62 25.28N 68.43E
Tando Bāgo Pakistan 62 24.47N 68.58E
Tando Muhammad Khan Pakistan 62 25.08N 68.32E
Tandou L. Australia 92 32.38S142.05E
Tandula Tank *resr.* India 63 20.40N 81.12E
Tanega shima *i.* Japan 57 30.32N131.00E
Taneytown U.S.A. 114 39.40N 77.10W
Tanezrouft *des.* Algeria 74 22.25N 0.30E
Tanga Tanzania 79 5.07S 39.05E
Tanga *d.* Tanzania 79 5.20S 38.30E
Tangalla Sri Lanka 61 6.02N 80.47E
Tanganyika, L. Africa 79 6.00S 29.30E
Tanger Morocco 74 35.48N 5.45W
Tangerhütte Germany 38 52.26N 11.48E
Tangermünde Germany 38 52.32N 11.58E
Tanggo China 63 31.37N 93.18E
Tanggu China 54 39.01N117.43E
Tanggula Shan *mts.* China 63 33.00N 90.00E
Tanggula Shankou *pass* China 63 32.45N 92.24E
Tanggulashanqu China 63 34.10N 92.23E
Tanghe China 54 32.41N112.49E
Tāngi India 63 19.57N 85.30E
Tangi Pakistan 62 34.18N 71.40E
Tangier *see* Tanger Morocco 74
Tangmarg Jammu & Kashmir 62 34.02N 74.26E
Tangra Yumco *l.* China 63 31.00N 86.15E
Tangshan China 54 39.32N118.08E
Tangtse Jammu & Kashmir 63 34.02N 78.11E
Tanguiéta Benin 77 10.37N 1.18E
Tanimbar, Kepulauan *is.* Indonesia 59 7.50S131.30E
Taninges France 21 46.07N 6.36E
Tanishpa *mtn.* Pakistan 62 31.10N 68.24E
Tanjay Phil. 59 9.31N123.10E
Tanjona Ankaboa *c.* Madagascar 81 21.57S 43.16E
Tanjona Bobaomby *c.* Madagascar 81 11.57S 49.17E
Tanjona Masoala *c.* Madagascar 81 15.59S 50.13E
Tanjona Vilanandro *c.* Madagascar 81 16.11S 44.27E
Tanjona Vohimena *c.* Madagascar 81 25.36S 45.08E
Tanjung Indonesia 58 2.10S115.25E
Tanjungbalai Indonesia 58 2.59N 99.46E
Tanjungkarang Indonesia 58 5.28S105.16E
Tanjungpandan Indonesia 58 2.44S107.36E
Tanjungredeb Indonesia 58 2.09N117.29E
Tānk Pakistan 62 32.13N 70.23E
Tankapirtti Finland 40 68.16N 27.20E
Tännäs Sweden 41 62.27N 12.40E
Tannersville U.S.A. 115 42.12N 74.08W
Tannin Canada 102 49.40N 91.00W
Tannis Bugt *b.* Denmark 42 57.40N 10.15E
Tannu Ola *mts.* U.S.S.R. 51 51.00N 93.30E
Tannūrah, Ra's *c.* Saudi Arabia 71 26.39N 50.10E
Tano *r.* Ghana 76 5.07N 2.54W
Tanout Niger 77 14.55N 8.49E
Ţanţā Egypt 66 30.48N 31.00E
Tanumshede Sweden 42 58.44N 11.19E
Tanzania Africa 79 5.00S 35.00E
Tao'an China 54 45.20N122.48E
Taole China 54 38.50N106.40E
Taormina Italy 33 37.52N 15.17E
Taoudenni Mali 76 22.45N 4.00W
Tapachula Mexico 116 14.54N 92.15W
Tapajós *r.* Brazil 123 2.25S 54.40W
Tapaktuan Indonesia 58 3.30N 97.10E
Tapalquén Argentina 125 36.20S 60.02W
Tapanahoni *r.* Surinam 123 4.20N 54.25W
Tapanlieh Taiwan 55 21.58N120.47E
Tapanui New Zealand 86 45.57S169.16E
Tapauá *r.* Brazil 122 5.40S 64.20W
Tapeta Liberia 76 6.25N 8.47W
Tapirapecó, Serra *mts.* Venezuela/Brazil 122 1.00N 64.30W
Tāplejung Nepal 63 27.21N 87.40E
Tapolca Hungary 31 46.53N 17.27E
Tāpti *r.* India 62 21.05N 72.40E
Tapurucuara Brazil 122 0.24S 65.02W
Taquari *r.* Brazil 126 19.00S 57.27W
Taquaritinga Brazil 126 21.23S 48.33W
Tar *r.* U.S.A. 113 35.33N 77.05W
Tara Canada 104 44.28N 81.09W
Tara U.S.S.R. 9 56.55N 74.24E
Tara *r.* U.S.S.R. 50 56.30N 74.40E
Tara *r.* Yugo. 31 43.21N 18.51E
Tarabine, Oued Ti-n- *wadi* Algeria 75 21.16N 7.24E
Tarabuco Bolivia 124 19.10S 64.57W
Ţarābulus Lebanon 66 34.27N 35.50E
Ţarābulus *d.* Libya 75 32.40N 13.15E
Ţarābulus *f.* Libya 75 31.00N 13.30E
Ţarābulus *town* Libya 75 32.58N 13.12E
Tarago Australia 93 35.05S149.10E
Tarakan Indonesia 58 3.20N117.38E
Taranaki *d.* New Zealand 86 39.00S174.30E
Tarancón Spain 27 40.01N 3.01W
Taranto Italy 33 40.28N 17.15E
Taranto, Golfo di *g.* Italy 33 40.00N 17.10E
Tarapacá Colombia 122 2.52S 69.44W
Tarapoto Peru 122 6.31S 76.23W
Tarare France 21 45.54N 4.26E
Tarascon Ariège France 20 42.51N 1.36E
Tarascon Vaucluse France 21 43.48N 4.40E
Tarashcha U.S.S.R. 37 49.35N 30.20E
Tarasovo U.S.S.R. 44 66.14N 46.43E
Tarauacá Brazil 122 8.10S 70.46W
Tarauacá *r.* Brazil 122 6.42S 69.48W
Taravao, Isthme de Tahiti 85 17.43S149.19W
Taravo *r.* France 21 41.42N 8.49E
Tarawa *i.* Kiribati 84 1.25N173.00E
Tarawera New Zealand 86 39.02S176.36E
Tarazona Spain 25 41.54N 1.44W
Tarazona de la Mancha Spain 25 39.15N 1.55W
Tarbagatay, Khrebet *mts.* U.S.S.R. 52 47.00N 83.00E
Tarbat Ness *c.* U.K. 14 57.52N 3.46W
Tarbert Rep. of Ire. 15 52.34N 9.24W
Tarbert Strath. U.K. 14 55.51N 5.25W
Tarbert W. Isles U.K. 14 57.54N 6.49W
Tarbes France 20 43.14N 0.05E
Tarcento Italy 30 46.13N 13.13E
Tarcoola S.A. Australia 92 30.41S134.33E
Tarcoon Australia 93 30.19S146.43E
Tarcutta Australia 93 35.17S147.45E
Tardajos Spain 26 42.21N 3.49W
Taree Australia 93 31.54S152.26E
Tarella Australia 92 30.55S143.06E
Tärendö Sweden 40 67.10N 22.38E
Tarentum U.S.A. 114 40.36N 79.45W
Ţarfā, Wādī aţ *r.* Egypt 66 28.36N 30.50E
Tarfaya Morocco 74 27.58N 12.55W
Targon France 20 44.44N 0.16W
Tarhjicht Morocco 74 29.05N 9.24W
Tarifa Spain 27 36.01N 5.36W
Tarifa, Punta de *c.* Spain 27 36.00N 5.37W
Tarija Bolivia 124 21.31S 64.45W
Tarija *d.* Bolivia 124 21.40S 64.20W
Tarīm Yemen 71 16.03N 49.00E
Tarim He *r.* China 52 41.00N 83.30E
Tarīn Kowt Afghan. 62 32.52N 65.38E
Taritatu *r.* Indonesia 59 2.54S138.27E
Tarka La *mtn.* Bhutan 63 27.05N 89.40E
Tarkwa Ghana 76 5.16N 1.59W
Tarlac Phil. 59 15.29N120.35E
Tarm Denmark 42 55.55N 8.32E
Tarma Peru 122 11.28S 75.41W
Tarn *d.* France 20 43.50N 2.00E
Tarn *r.* France 20 44.05N 1.06E
Tärnaby Sweden 40 65.43N 15.16E
Tarnak *r.* Afghan. 62 31.26N 65.31E
Tarn-et-Garonne *d.* France 20 44.05N 1.20E
Tarnica *mtn.* Poland 37 49.05N 22.44E
Tarnobrzeg Poland 37 50.35N 21.41E
Tarnów Poland 37 50.01N 20.59E
Tärnsjö Sweden 43 60.09N 16.56E
Taro *r.* Italy 30 45.00N 10.15E
Taroom Australia 90 25.39S149.49E
Tarouca Portugal 26 41.00N 7.40W
Taroudannt Morocco 74 30.31N 8.55W
Tarpon Springs *town* U.S.A. 113 28.08N 82.45W
Tarquinia Italy 30 42.15N 11.45E
Tarqūmiyah Jordan 67 31.35N 35.01E
Tarragona Spain 25 41.07N 1.15E
Tarragona *d.* Spain 25 41.10N 0.40E
Tarran Hills Australia 93 32.27S146.27E
Tarrasa *see* Terrassa Spain 25
Tárrega Spain 25 41.39N 1.09E
Tarrytown U.S.A. 115 41.05N 73.52W
Tarso Ahon *mtn.* Chad 77 20.23N 18.18E
Tarso Ouri *mtn.* Chad 77 21.25N 18.56E
Tarsus Turkey 64 36.52N 34.52E
Tartagal Argentina 124 22.32S 63.50W
Tartas France 20 43.50N 0.48W
Tartu U.S.S.R. 44 58.20N 26.44E
Ţarţūs Syria 66 34.55N 35.52E
Tarutino U.S.S.R. 37 46.09N 29.04E
Tarutung Indonesia 58 2.01N 98.54E
Tarvisio Italy 31 46.30N 13.35E
Tashan China 54 40.51N120.56E
Tashauz U.S.S.R. 9 41.49N 59.58E
Tashi Gang Dzong Bhutan 63 27.19N 91.34E
Tashkent U.S.S.R. 9 41.16N 69.13E
Tasiilaq *see* Ammassalik Greenland 99
Tasikmalaya Indonesia 59 7.20S108.16E
Tasil Syria 67 32.50N 35.58E
Tåsinge *i.* Denmark 42 55.00N 10.36E
Tåsjön Sweden 40 64.15N 15.47E
Tasman B. New Zealand 86 41.00S173.15E
Tasmania *d.* Australia 91 42.00S147.00E
Tasman Mts. New Zealand 86 41.00S172.40E
Tasman Pen. Australia 91 43.08S147.51E
Tasman Sea Pacific Oc. 84 38.00S162.00E
Tassili-n-Ajjer *f.* Algeria 75 26.05N 7.00E
Tassili oua-n-Ahaggar *f.* Algeria 75 20.30N 5.00E
Tataa, Pt. Tahiti 85 17.33S149.36W
Tatabánya Hungary 37 47.34N 18.26E
Tatarsk U.S.S.R. 50 55.14N 76.00E
Tatarskiy Proliv *g.* U.S.S.R. 51 47.40N141.00E
Tateyama Japan 57 34.59N139.52E
Tathlina L. Canada 100 60.32N117.32W
Tathra Australia 93 36.44S149.58E
Tatinnai L. Canada 101 60.55N 97.40W
Tatnam, C. Canada 101 57.16N 91.00W
Tatong Australia 93 36.46S146.03E
Tatta Pakistan 62 24.45N 67.55E
Tatvan Turkey 64 38.31N 42.15E
Tau Norway 42 59.04N 5.54E
Tau *i.* Samoa 84 14.15S169.30W
Taubaté Brazil 126 23.00S 45.36W
Tauber *r.* Germany 39 49.46N 9.31E
Tauberbischofsheim Germany 39 49.37N 9.40E
Taulihawa Nepal 63 27.32N 83.05E
Taumarunui New Zealand 86 38.53S175.16E
Taumaturgo Brazil 122 8.57S 72.48W
Taung R.S.A. 80 27.32S 24.46E
Taungdwingyi Burma 56 20.00N 95.30E
Taung-gyi Burma 56 20.49N 97.01E
Taungup Burma 56 18.51N 94.14E
Taunoa Tahiti 85 17.45S149.21W
Taunsa Pakistan 62 30.42N 70.39E
Taunton U.K. 13 51.01N 3.07W
Taunton U.S.A. 115 41.54N 71.06W
Taunus *mts.* Germany 36 50.07N 7.48E
Taupo New Zealand 86 38.42S176.06E
Taupo, L. New Zealand 86 38.45S175.30E
Taurage U.S.S.R. 41 55.15N 22.17E
Tauranga New Zealand 86 37.42S176.11E
Taureau, Résr. Canada 105 46.46N 73.50W
Taurianova Italy 33 38.21N 16.01E
Taurus Mts. *see* Toros Dağlari *mts.* Turkey 64
Tauste Spain 25 41.55N 1.15W
Tautira Tahiti 85 17.45S149.10W
Tavani Canada 101 62.10N 93.30W
Tavda U.S.S.R. 50 58.04N 65.12E
Tavda *r.* U.S.S.R. 50 57.40N 67.00E
Taveta Kenya 79 3.23S 37.42E
Taveuni *i.* Fiji 84 16.56S179.58W
Tavira Portugal 27 37.07N 7.39W
Tavistock Canada 104 43.19N 80.50W
Tavistock U.K. 13 50.33N 4.09W
Tavor, Har *mtn.* Israel 67 32.41N 35.23E
Távora *r.* Portugal 26 41.08N 7.35W
Tavoy Burma 56 14.02N 98.12E
Tavropoú, Tekhnití Límni *l.* Greece 35 39.20N 21.45E
Taw *r.* U.K. 13 51.05N 4.05W
Tawas City U.S.A. 104 44.16N 83.31W
Tawau Malaysia 58 4.16N117.54E
Tawitawi *i.* Phil. 59 5.10N120.05E
Ţawkar Sudan 72 18.26N 37.44E
Tawu Taiwan 55 22.22N120.54E
Tāwurghā', Sabkhat *f.* Libya 22 31.10N 15.15E
Tay *r.* U.K. 14 56.21N 3.18W
Tay, L. Australia 89 33.00S120.52E
Tay, Loch U.K. 14 56.32N 4.08W
Tayabamba Peru 122 8.15S 77.15W
Tayan Indonesia 58 0.02S110.05E
Tayeegle Somali Rep. 71 4.02N 44.36E
Taylor Tex. U.S.A. 111 30.34N 97.25W
Taylor, Mt. U.S.A. 109 35.14N107.37W
Taylors Island *town* U.S.A. 115 38.28N 76.18W
Taymā' Saudi Arabia 64 27.37N 38.30E
Taymyr, Ozero *l.* U.S.S.R. 51 74.20N101.00E
Taymyr, Poluostrov *pen.* U.S.S.R. 51 75.30N 99.00E
Tay Ninh Vietnam 56 11.21N106.02E
Tayport U.K. 14 56.27N 2.53W
Tayshet U.S.S.R. 51 55.56N 98.01E
Tayside *d.* U.K. 14 56.35N 3.28W
Taytay Phil. 58 10.47N119.32E
Taz *r.* U.S.S.R. 50 67.30N 78.50E
Taza Morocco 74 34.16N 4.01W
Tazawa ko *l.* Japan 57 39.43N140.40E
Tazenakht Morocco 74 30.35N 7.12W
Tazin L. Canada 101 59.40N109.00W
Tāzirbū Libya 72 25.45N 21.00E
Tazovskiy U.S.S.R. 50 67.28N 78.43E
Tbilisi U.S.S.R. 65 41.43N 44.48E
Tchad, Lac *see* Chad, L. Africa 77
Tchamba Togo 77 9.05N 1.27E
Tchibanga Gabon 78 2.52S 11.07E
Tchien Liberia 76 6.00N 8.10W
Tchigaï, Plateau du *f.* Niger/Chad 77 21.30N 14.50E
Tcholliré Cameroon 77 8.25N 14.10E
Tczew Poland 37 54.06N 18.47E
Te Anau New Zealand 86 45.25S167.43E
Te Anau, L. New Zealand 86 45.10S167.15E
Teaneck U.S.A. 115 40.53N 74.01W
Teano Italy 33 41.15N 14.04E
Teapa Mexico 116 17.33N 92.57W
Te Araroa New Zealand 86 37.38S178.25E
Teba Spain 27 36.58N 4.56W
Tébessa Algeria 75 35.22N 8.08E
Tebingtinggi Indonesia 58 3.20N 99.08E
Tebingtinggi Indonesia 58 3.37S103.09E
Tébourba Tunisia 32 36.49N 9.51E
Teboursouk, Monts de *mts.* Tunisia 32 36.45N 9.20E
Tebulos Mta *mtn.* U.S.S.R. 45 42.34N 45.17E
Tech *r.* France 20 42.36N 3.03E
Techiman Ghana 76 7.36N 1.55W
Tecuci Romania 37 45.49N 27.27E
Tecumseh U.S.A. 104 42.00N 83.57W
Tedesa Ethiopia 73 5.07N 37.45E
Tees *r.* U.K. 12 54.35N 1.11W
Tefé Brazil 122 3.24S 64.45W
Tefé *r.* Brazil 122 3.35S 64.47W
Tegal Indonesia 59 6.52S109.07E
Tegelen Neth. 16 51.20N 6.08E
Tegernsee Germany 39 47.43N 11.45E
Tegina Nigeria 77 10.06N 6.11E
Tego Australia 93 28.48S146.47E
Tegouma *well* Niger 77 15.33N 9.19E
Tegucigalpa Honduras 117 14.05N 87.14W
Teguidda I-n-Tessoum Niger 77 17.21N 6.32E
Tehamiyam Sudan 72 18.20N 36.32E
Tehata Bangla. 63 23.43N 88.32E
Téhini Ivory Coast 76 9.39N 3.32W
Tehkummah Canada 104 45.39N 81.59W
Tehrān Iran 65 35.40N 51.26E
Tehri India 63 30.23N 78.29E
Tehuacán Mexico 116 18.30N 97.26W
Tehuantepec Mexico 116 16.21N 95.13W
Tehuantepec, Golfo de *g.* Mexico 116 16.00N 95.00W
Tehuantepec, Istmo de *f.* Mexico 116 17.00N 94.30W
Teifi *r.* U.K. 13 52.05N 4.41W
Teignmouth U.K. 13 50.33N 3.30W
Teixeiras Brazil 126 20.37S 42.52W
Tejakula Indonesia 59 8.09S115.19E
Tejo *r.* Portugal 27 38.40N 9.24W
Te Kaha New Zealand 86 37.44S177.52E
Tekamah U.S.A. 110 41.47N 96.13W
Tekapo, L. New Zealand 86 43.35S170.30E
Tekax Mexico 117 20.12N 89.17W
Teke Burnu *c.* Turkey 34 40.02N 26.10E
Tekezē *r.* Ethiopia *see* Satīt *r.* Sudan 72
Tekirdağ Turkey 29 40.59N 27.30E
Tekkali India 63 18.37N 84.14E
Tekouiat, Oued *wadi* Algeria 75 22.20N 2.30E
Tekro *well* Chad 72 19.30N 20.58E
Te Kuiti New Zealand 86 38.20S175.10E
Tel *r.* India 63 20.50N 83.54E
Tela Honduras 117 15.56N 87.25W
Tel 'Adashim Israel 67 32.39N 35.18E
Tel Arshaf *site* Israel 67 32.12N 34.48E
Tel Ashqelon *site* Israel 67 31.39N 34.32E
Telavåg Norway 42 60.16N 4.49E
Telavi U.S.S.R. 65 41.56N 45.30E
Tel Aviv *d.* Israel 67 32.05N 34.48E
Tel Aviv-Yafo Israel 67 32.05N 34.46E
Tele *r.* Zaïre 78 2.48N 24.00E
Telegraph Creek *town* Canada 100 57.55N131.10W
Telemark *d.* Norway 42 59.40N 8.45E
Teleneshty U.S.S.R. 37 47.35N 28.17E
Teles Pires *r.* Brazil 123 7.20S 57.30W
Telfer Australia 88 21.42S122.13E
Telford U.K. 13 52.42N 2.30W
Telfs Austria 39 47.18N 11.04E
Telgte Germany 38 51.59N 7.47E
Tel Hazor *site* Israel 67 33.01N 35.34E
Télimélé Guinea 76 10.54N 13.02W
Tel Lakhish *site* Israel 67 31.34N 34.51E
Tell Atlas *mts.* Algeria 75 36.00N 1.00E
Tell City U.S.A. 113 37.56N 86.46W
Teller U.S.A. 98 65.16N166.22N
Tel Mediggo *site* Israel 67 32.35N 35.11E
Tel Mond Israel 67 32.15N 34.56E
Telpos-Iz *mtn.* U.S.S.R. 44 63.56N 59.02E
Telsen Argentina 125 42.25S 67.00W
Telšiai U.S.S.R. 41 55.59N 22.15E
Telti Italy 32 40.52N 9.21E
Teltow Germany 38 52.23N 13.16E
Telukbetung Indonesia 58 5.28S105.16E
Teluk Intan Malaysia 58 4.00N101.00E
Tema Ghana 76 5.41N 0.01W
Temagami, L. Canada 104 47.00N 80.05W
Te Manga *mtn.* Rarotonga Cook Is. 84 21.13S159.45W
Temaverachi, Sierra *mts.* Mexico 109 29.30N109.30W
Tembleque Spain 27 39.42N 3.30W
Tembo Aluma Angola 78 7.42S 17.15E
Teme *r.* U.K. 13 52.10N 2.13W
Temerin Yugo. 31 45.24N 19.53E
Temir U.S.S.R. 45 49.09N 57.06E
Temirtau U.S.S.R. 9 50.05N 72.55E
Témiscaming Canada 104 46.43N 79.06W
Temora Australia 93 34.27S147.35E
Tempe U.S.A. 109 33.25N111.56W
Tempino Indonesia 58 1.55S103.23E
Tempio Italy 32 40.54N 9.07E
Temple U.S.A. 111 31.06N 97.21W
Temple B. Australia 90 12.15S143.04E
Templemore Rep. of Ire. 15 52.48N 7.51W
Templin Germany 38 53.07N 13.30E
Temuco Chile 125 38.44S 72.36W
Tenabo Mexico 116 20.03N 90.14W
Tenaha U.S.A. 111 31.57N 94.15W
Tenasserim Burma 56 12.05N 99.00E
Tenasserim *d.* Burma 56 13.00N 99.00E
Tenby U.K. 13 51.40N 4.42W
Tenby Bay *town* Canada 104 46.06N 83.56W
Tendaho Ethiopia 73 11.48N 40.52E
Tende France 21 44.05N 7.36E
Tende, Col de *pass* France/Italy 30 44.09N 7.34E
Ten Degree Channel Indian Oc. 56 10.00N 93.00E
Tendrara Morocco 74 33.04N 1.59W
Tenenkou Mali 76 14.25N 4.58W
Tenerife *i.* Canary Is. 74 28.10N 16.30W
Ténès Algeria 75 36.31N 1.18E
Teng *r.* Burma 56 19.50N 97.40E
Tengchong China 61 25.02N 98.28E
Tengger Shamo *des.* China 54 39.00N104.10E
Tengiz, Ozero *l.* U.S.S.R. 9 50.30N 69.00E
Teng Xian China 54 35.08N117.20E
Tenke Zaïre 78 10.34S 26.07E
Tenkodogo Burkina 76 11.47N 0.19W
Tenna *r.* Italy 31 43.14N 13.47E
Tennant Creek *town* Australia 90 19.31S134.15E
Tennessee *d.* U.S.A. 113 35.50N 85.30W
Tennessee *r.* U.S.A. 113 37.04N 88.33W
Tenosique Mexico 116 17.29N 91.26W
Tenryū Japan 57 34.52N137.49E
Tenryū *r.* Japan 57 34.39N137.47E
Tensift, Oued *r.* Morocco 74 32.02N 9.22W
Tenterfield Australia 93 29.01S152.04E
Teófilo Otoni Brazil 126 17.52S 41.31W
Tepa Indonesia 59 7.52S129.31E
Tepa Pt. Niue 84 19.07S169.56W
Tepelenë Albania 34 40.18N 20.01E
Tepic Mexico 116 21.30N104.51W
Teplice Czech. 38 50.39N 13.48E
Ter *r.* Spain 25 42.01N 3.12E
Téra Niger 76 14.01N 0.45E
Tera *r.* Portugal 27 38.55N 8.04W
Tera *r.* Spain 26 41.54N 5.44W
Teramo Italy 31 42.39N 13.42E
Terang Australia 92 38.13S142.56E
Tercan Turkey 64 39.47N 40.23E
Terebovlya U.S.S.R. 37 49.18N 25.44E
Terekhova U.S.S.R. 37 52.13N 31.28E
Teresina Brazil 123 5.09S 42.46W
Teresópolis Brazil 126 22.26S 42.59W
Terevaka *mtn.* I. de Pascua 85 27.05S109.23W
Tergnier France 19 49.39N 3.18E
Terhazza Mali 76 23.45N 4.59W
Termez U.S.S.R. 50 37.15N 67.15E
Termination I. Australia 89 34.25S121.53E
Termini Italy 28 37.59N 13.42E
Termini Imerese Italy 32 37.59N 13.42E
Termini Imerese, Golfo di *g.* Italy 32 38.05N 13.50E
Términos, Laguna de *b.* Mexico 116 18.30N 91.30W
Termoli Italy 33 41.58N 14.59E
Ternate Indonesia 59 0.48N127.23E
Terneuzen Neth. 16 51.20N 3.50E
Terney U.S.S.R. 57 45.05N136.36E
Terni Italy 30 42.34N 12.37E
Ternopol U.S.S.R. 37 49.35N 25.39E

Tocopilla to **Tropoja**

Tocopilla Chile **124** 22.05S 70.12W
Tocorpuri *mtn.* Bolivia/Chile **124** 22.26S 67.53W
Tocumwal Australia **93** 35.51S145.34E
Tocuyo *r.* Venezuela **122** 11.03N 68.23W
Todenyang Kenya **79** 4.34N 35.52E
Todi Italy **30** 42.47N 12.24E
Todos Santos Mexico **109** 23.27N110.13W
Todtnau Germany **39** 47.50N 7.56E
Tofte Norway **42** 59.33N 10.34E
Tofua *i.* Tonga **85** 19.45S175.05W
Togian, Kepulauan *is.* Indonesia **59** 0.20S122.00E
Togo Africa **76** 8.00N 1.00E
Tōhuku *d.* Japan **57** 35.00N137.00E
Toi Niue **84** 18.58S169.52W
Toijala Finland **41** 61.10N 23.52E
Toili Indonesia **59** 1.25S122.23E
Tojg Afghan. **62** 32.04N 61.48E
Tokaj Hungary **37** 48.08N 21.27E
Tokala *mtn.* Indonesia **59** 1.36S121.41E
Tokara kaikyō *str.* Japan **57** 30.10N130.10E
Tokat Turkey **64** 40.20N 36.35E
Tokelau Is. Pacific Oc. **84** 9.00S171.45W
Toki Japan **57** 35.21N137.11E
Toki *r.* Japan **57** 35.12N136.52E
Tokmak U.S.S.R. **52** 42.49N 75.15E
Tokoname Japan **57** 34.53N136.51E
Tokoroa New Zealand **86** 38.13S175.53E
Tokuno shima *i.* Japan **53** 27.40N129.00E
Tokushima Japan **57** 34.03N134.34E
Tokuyama Japan **57** 34.04N131.48E
Tōkyō Japan **57** 35.42N139.46E
Tōkyō-wan *b.* Japan **57** 35.25N139.45E
Tolaga Bay *town* New Zealand **86** 38.22S178.18E
Tolbukhin Bulgaria **29** 43.34N 27.52E
Toledo Spain **27** 39.52N 4.01W
Toledo *d.* Spain **27** 39.45N 4.10W
Toledo U.S.A. **112** 41.40N 83.35W
Toledo, Montes de *mts.* Spain **27** 39.33N 4.20W
Toledo Bend Resr. U.S.A. **111** 31.46N 93.25W
Tolentino Italy **30** 43.12N 13.17E
Toliara Madagascar **81** 23.21S 43.40E
Tolland U.S.A. **115** 41.52N 72.22W
Tollarp Sweden **43** 55.56N 13.59E
Tollense *r.* Germany **38** 53.54N 13.02E
Tolmezzo Italy **30** 46.24N 13.01E
Tolmin Yugo. **31** 46.11N 13.44E
Tolna Hungary **31** 46.26N 18.46E
Tolna *d.* Hungary **31** 46.35N 18.30E
Tolo, Teluk *g.* Indonesia **59** 2.00S122.30E
Tolosa Spain **26** 43.08N 2.04W
Tolstyy-Les U.S.S.R. **37** 51.24N 29.48E
Tolti Jammu & Kashmir **62** 35.02N 76.06E
Toluca Mexico **116** 19.20N 99.40W
Toluca *mtn.* Mexico **116** 19.10N 99.40W
Tol'yatti U.S.S.R. **44** 53.32N 49.24E
Tomah U.S.A. **110** 43.59N 90.30W
Tomakomai Japan **57** 42.39N141.33E
Tomar Portugal **27** 39.36N 8.25W
Tomás Gomensoro Uruguay **125** 30.26S 57.26W
Tomaszów Lubelski Poland **37** 50.28N 23.25E
Tomaszów Mazowiecki Poland **37** 51.32N 20.01E
Tombe Sudan **73** 5.49N 31.41E
Tombigbee *r.* U.S.A. **111** 31.04N 87.58W
Tombos Brazil **126** 20.53S 42.03W
Tombouctou Mali **76** 16.49N 2.59W
Tombouctou *d.* Mali **76** 19.35N 3.20W
Tombua Angola **78** 15.55S 11.51E
Tomé Chile **125** 36.37S 72.57W
Tomelilla Sweden **43** 55.33N 13.57E
Tomelloso Spain **27** 39.10N 3.01W
Tomiko Canada **104** 46.32N 79.49W
Tomingley Australia **93** 32.06S148.15E
Tomini Indonesia **59** 0.31N120.30E
Tomini, Teluk *g.* Indonesia **59** 0.30S120.45E
Tominian Mali **76** 13.17N 4.35W
Tomintoul U.K. **14** 57.15N 3.24W
Tomkinson Ranges *mts.* Australia **88** 26.11S129.05E
Tom Price Australia **88** 22.49S117.51E
Tomra China **63** 30.52N 87.30E
Tomra Norway **40** 62.34N 6.55E
Tomsk U.S.S.R. **50** 56.30N 85.05E
Toms River *town* U.S.A. **115** 39.57N 74.07W
Tomtabacken *hill* Sweden **43** 57.30N 14.28E
Tonalá Mexico **116** 16.08N 93.41W
Tonalea U.S.A. **109** 36.20N110.58W
Tonasket U.S.A. **108** 48.42N119.26W
Tonawanda U.S.A. **114** 43.01N 78.53W
Tonbridge U.K. **13** 51.12N 0.16E
Tondano Indonesia **59** 1.19N124.56E
Tönder Denmark **42** 54.56N 8.54E
Tondibi Mali **76** 16.39N 0.14W
Tondoro Namibia **80** 17.45S 18.50E
Tone *r.* Japan **57** 35.44N140.51E
Tonga Pacific Oc. **85** 20.00S175.00W
Tonga Sudan **73** 9.28N 31.03E
Tongaat R.S.A. **80** 29.34S 31.07E
Tong'an China **55** 24.44N118.09E
Tongatapu *i.* Tonga **85** 21.10S175.10W
Tongatapu Group *is.* Tonga **85** 21.10S175.10W
Tonga Trench *f.* Pacific Oc. **84** 20.00S173.00W
Tongchuan China **54** 35.05N109.10E
Tongeren Belgium **16** 50.47N 5.28E
Tongguan Hunan China **55** 28.27N112.48E
Tongguan Shaanxi China **54** 34.32N110.26E
Tonghai China **61** 24.07N102.45E
Tonghua China **53** 41.40N126.52E
Tongking, G. of China/Vietnam **56** 20.00N108.00E
Tongliao China **54** 43.40N122.20E
Tongling China **55** 30.55N117.42E
Tonglu China **55** 29.49N119.40E
Tongnae S. Korea **57** 35.12N129.05E
Tongo Australia **92** 30.30S143.47E
Tongoa *i.* Vanuatu **84** 16.54S168.34E
Tongobory Madagascar **81** 23.32S 44.20E
Tongoy Chile **124** 30.15S 71.30W
Tongren China **55** 27.41N109.08E
Tongsa Dzong Bhutan **63** 27.31N 90.30E
Tongtianheyan China **63** 33.50N 92.19E
Tongue U.K. **14** 58.28N 4.25W
Tongue *r.* U.S.A. **108** 46.24N105.25W
Tongwei China **54** 35.18N105.10E
Tong Xian China **54** 39.52N116.45E
Tongxin China **54** 36.59N105.50E
Tongyu China **54** 44.48N123.06E
Tongzi China **55** 28.08N106.49E
Tonj Sudan **73** 7.17N 28.45E
Tonk India **62** 26.10N 75.47E
Tonkābon Iran **65** 36.49N 50.54E
Tônlé Sap *l.* Cambodia **56** 12.50N104.15E
Tonnay-Boutonne France **20** 45.58N 0.42W
Tonneins France **20** 44.23N 0.19E
Tonnerre France **19** 47.51N 3.58E
Tönning Germany **38** 54.19N 8.56E
Tonopah U.S.A. **108** 38.04N117.14W
Tonota Botswana **80** 21.28S 27.24E
Tons *r.* India **63** 25.17N 82.04E
Tönsberg Norway **42** 59.17N 10.25E
Tonstad Norway **42** 58.40N 6.43E
Tonto Basin *town* U.S.A. **109** 33.55N111.18W
Toobeah Australia **93** 28.22S149.50E
Toodyay Australia **89** 31.35S116.26E
Tooele U.S.A. **108** 40.32N112.18W
Toolondo Australia **92** 36.55S142.00E
Toowoomba Australia **91** 27.35S151.54E
Topeka U.S.A. **110** 39.03N 95.41W
Topko *mtn.* U.S.S.R. **51** 57.20N138.10E
Topley Canada **100** 54.32N126.05W
Toplica *r.* Yugo. **34** 43.15N 21.30E
Toplița Romania **37** 46.55N 25.21E
Topock U.S.A. **109** 34.44N114.27W
Topolovgrad Bulgaria **34** 42.05N 26.20E
Topozero, Ozero *l.* U.S.S.R. **44** 65.45N 32.00E
Toppenish U.S.A. **108** 46.23N120.19W
Tor Ethiopia **73** 7.53N 33.40E
Tora-Khem U.S.S.R. **51** 52.31N 96.13E
Torbat-e Ḩeydarīyeh Iran **65** 35.16N 59.13E
Torbat-e Jām Iran **65** 35.15N 60.37E
Tördal Norway **42** 59.16N 8.49E
Tordera *r.* Spain **25** 41.39N 2.47E
Tordesillas Spain **26** 41.30N 5.00W
Tordino Italy **31** 42.44N 13.59E
Töre Sweden **40** 65.54N 22.39E
Töreboda Sweden **43** 58.43N 14.08E
Torekov Sweden **43** 56.26N 12.37E
Toreno Spain **26** 42.42N 6.30W
Torgau Germany **38** 51.34N 13.00E
Torhamn Sweden **43** 56.05N 15.50E
Torhout Belgium **16** 51.04N 3.06E
Toride Japan **57** 35.53N140.04E
Torino Italy **30** 45.03N 7.40E
Torio *r.* Spain **26** 42.35N 5.34W
Torit Sudan **73** 4.24N 32.34E
Tormes *r.* Spain **26** 41.18N 6.29W
Torne *r.* Sweden *see* Tornio *r.* Finland **40**
Torneträsk Sweden **40** 68.15N 19.30E
Torneträsk *l.* Sweden **40** 68.20N 19.10E
Tornio Finland **40** 65.52N 24.10E
Tornio *r.* Finland **40** 65.53N 24.07E
Tornquist Argentina **125** 38.06S 62.14W
Toro Spain **26** 41.31N 5.24W
Toronaíos Kólpos *g.* Greece **34** 40.05N 23.30E
Toronto Canada **104** 43.39N 79.23W
Toropets U.S.S.R. **44** 56.30N 31.40E
Tororo Uganda **79** 0.42N 34.13E
Toros Dağlari *mts.* Turkey **64** 37.15N 34.15E
Torquay Australia **92** 38.20S144.20E
Torquay U.K. **13** 50.27N 3.31W
Torquemada Spain **26** 42.02N 4.19W
Torrance U.S.A. **109** 33.50N118.19W
Torrão Portugal **27** 38.18N 8.13W
Torre Annunziata Italy **33** 40.45N 14.27E
Torre Baja Spain **25** 40.07N 1.15W
Torreblanca Spain **25** 40.13N 0.12E
Torrecilla *mtn.* Spain **27** 36.41N 4.59W
Torrecilla en Cameros Spain **26** 42.16N 2.37W
Torre del Campo Spain **27** 37.46N 3.53W
Torre de Moncorvo Portugal **26** 41.10N 7.03W
Torredonjimeno Spain **27** 37.46N 3.57W
Torrejón, Embalse de *resr.* Spain **27** 39.50N 5.50W
Torrejoncillo Spain **27** 39.54N 6.28W
Torrejón de Ardoz Spain **26** 40.27N 3.29W
Torrelaguna Spain **26** 40.50N 3.32W
Torrelavega Spain **26** 43.21N 4.03W
Torremaggiore Italy **33** 41.41N 15.17E
Torremolinos Spain **27** 36.37N 4.30W
Torrens, L. Australia **92** 31.00S137.50E
Torrens Creek *r.* Australia **90** 22.22S145.09E
Torrens Creek *town* Australia **90** 20.50S145.00E
Torrente Spain **25** 39.26N 0.28W
Torreón Mexico **111** 25.33N103.26W
Torre Pellice Italy **30** 44.49N 7.13E
Torreperogil Spain **26** 38.02N 3.17W
Torres Novas Portugal **27** 39.29N 8.32W
Torres Str. Australia **90** 10.00S142.20E
Torres Vedras Portugal **27** 39.06N 9.16W
Torrevieja Spain **25** 37.59N 0.41W
Torrey U.S.A. **108** 38.18N111.25W
Torridge *r.* U.K. **13** 51.01N 4.12W
Torridon U.K. **14** 57.23N 5.31W
Torridon, Loch U.K. **14** 57.35N 5.45W
Torriglia Italy **30** 44.31N 9.10E
Torrijos Spain **27** 39.59N 4.17W
Torrington Conn. U.S.A. **115** 41.48N 73.08W
Torrington Wyo. U.S.A. **108** 42.04N104.11W
Torrox Spain **27** 36.46N 3.58W
Torsås Sweden **43** 56.24N 16.00E
Torsby Sweden **43** 60.08N 13.00E
Torsö *i.* Sweden **43** 58.48N 13.50E
Tortola *i.* B.V.Is. **117** 18.28N 64.40W
Tortoli Italy **32** 39.55N 9.39E
Tortona Italy **30** 44.54N 8.52E
Tortorici Italy **33** 38.02N 14.39E
Tortosa Spain **25** 40.48N 0.31E
Tortosa, Cabo de *c.* Spain **25** 40.43N 0.55E
Tortue, Île de la *i.* Cuba **117** 20.05N 72.57W
Toruń Poland **37** 53.01N 18.35E
Torup Sweden **43** 56.58N 13.05E
Tory Hill *town* Canada **104** 44.58N 78.18W
Tory I. Rep. of Ire. **15** 55.16N 8.13W
Tory Sd. Rep. of Ire. **15** 55.14N 8.15W
Torzhok U.S.S.R. **44** 57.02N 34.51E
Tosas, Puerto de *pass* Spain **25** 42.19N 2.01E
Tosa wan *b.* Japan **57** 33.10N133.40E
Toscana *d.* Italy **30** 43.35N 11.00E
Tosen Norway **40** 65.16N 12.50E
Tosno U.S.S.R. **44** 59.38N 30.46E
Tostado Argentina **124** 29.15S 61.45W
Totak *l.* Norway **42** 59.42N 7.57E
Totana Spain **25** 37.46N 1.30W
Tôtes France **18** 49.41N 1.03E
Totma U.S.S.R. **44** 59.59N 42.44E
Totora Bolivia **124** 17.42S 65.09W
Tottenham Australia **93** 32.14S147.24E
Tottenham Canada **104** 44.01N 79.49W
Tottori Japan **57** 35.32N134.12E
Touba Ivory Coast **76** 8.22N 7.42W
Toubkal *mtn.* Morocco **74** 31.03N 7.57W
Toucy France **19** 47.44N 3.18E
Tougan Burkina **76** 13.05N 3.04W
Touggourt Algeria **75** 33.06N 6.04E
Tougué Guinea **76** 11.25N 11.50W
Toul France **19** 48.41N 5.54E
Toulnustouc *r.* Canada **103** 49.35N 68.25W
Toulon France **21** 43.07N 5.56E
Toulon-sur-Arroux France **19** 46.42N 4.08E
Toulouse France **20** 43.36N 1.26E
Toummo Niger **75** 22.45N 14.08E
Tounassine, Hamada *des.* Algeria **74** 28.36N 5.00W
Toungoo Burma **56** 18.57N 96.26E
Touques *r.* France **18** 49.22N 0.06E
Tourassine *well* Mauritania **74** 24.40N 11.20W
Tourcoing France **19** 50.43N 3.09E
Tourinan, Cabo *c.* Spain **26** 43.03N 9.18W
Tournai Belgium **16** 50.36N 3.23E
Tournon France **21** 45.04N 4.50E
Tournus France **19** 46.34N 4.54E
Tours France **18** 47.23N 0.41E
Toury France **19** 48.12N 1.56E
Toustain Algeria **32** 36.40N 8.15E
Touwsrivier *town* R.S.A. **80** 33.20S 20.02E
Toužim Czech. **39** 50.04N 13.00E
Tovdals *r.* Norway **42** 58.13N 8.08E
Towada ko *l.* Japan **57** 40.28N140.55E
Towanda U.S.A. **115** 41.46N 76.27W
Towcester U.K. **13** 52.07N 0.56W
Tower U.S.A. **110** 47.47N 92.19W
Towner U.S.A. **110** 48.21N100.25W
Townsend, Mt. Australia **93** 36.24S148.15E
Townshend I. Australia **90** 22.15S150.30E
Townsville Australia **90** 19.13S146.48E
Towrzī Afghan. **62** 30.11N 65.59E
Towson U.S.A. **115** 39.24N 76.36W
Towyn U.K. **13** 52.37N 4.08W
Toyah U.S.A. **111** 31.19N103.47W
Toyama Japan **57** 36.42N137.14E
Toyama wan *b.* Japan **57** 36.50N137.10E
Toyo *r.* Japan **57** 34.47N137.20E
Toyohashi Japan **57** 34.46N137.23E
Toyokawa Japan **57** 34.49N137.24E
Toyota Japan **57** 35.05N137.09E
Tozeur Tunisia **75** 33.55N 8.08E
Traben-Trarbach Germany **39** 49.57N 7.06E
Trabzon Turkey **64** 41.00N 39.43E
Tracadie Canada **103** 47.31N 64.54W
Tracy Canada **105** 46.01N 73.09W
Tracy U.S.A. **110** 44.14N 95.37W
Trade Town Liberia **76** 5.43N 9.56W
Trafalgar, Cabo *c.* Spain **27** 36.11N 6.02W
Tragacete Spain **25** 40.21N 1.51W
Traid Spain **25** 40.40N 1.49W
Traiguén Chile **125** 38.15S 72.41W
Trail Canada **100** 49.05N117.40W
Trajanova Vrata *pass* Bulgaria **34** 42.18N 23.58E
Trakt U.S.S.R. **44** 62.40N 51.26E
Tralee Rep. of Ire. **15** 52.16N 9.42W
Tralee B. Rep. of Ire. **15** 52.18N 9.55W
Tranås Sweden **43** 58.03N 14.59E
Tranco, Embalse del *resr.* Spain **26** 38.10N 2.45W
Trancoso Portugal **26** 40.47N 7.21W
Tranebjerg Denmark **42** 50.50N 10.36E
Trang Thailand **56** 7.35N 99.35E
Trangan *i.* Indonesia **59** 6.30S134.15E
Trangie Australia **93** 32.03S148.01E
Trani Italy **33** 41.17N 16.26E
Tranoroa Madagascar **81** 24.42S 45.04E
Tranqueras Uruguay **125** 31.12S 55.45W
Transkei Africa **80** 31.30S 29.00E
Transkei *f.* R.S.A. **80** 32.12S 28.20E
Transvaal *d.* R.S.A. **80** 24.30S 29.30E
Transylvanian Alps *see* Carpații Meridionali *mts.* Romania **29**
Trapani Italy **32** 38.01N 12.31E
Traralgon Australia **93** 38.12S146.32E
Traryd Sweden **43** 56.35N 13.45E
Trarza *d.* Mauritania **74** 18.00N 14.50W
Trarza *f.* Mauritania **74** 18.00N 15.00W
Trasacco Italy **31** 41.57N 13.32E
Trasimeno, Lago *l.* Italy **30** 43.08N 12.06E
Träslövsläge Sweden **43** 57.04N 12.16E
Trat Thailand **56** 12.14N102.33E
Traun Austria **39** 48.13N 14.14E
Traunsee *l.* Austria **39** 47.51N 13.48E
Traunstein Germany **39** 47.52N 12.38E
Trave *r.* Germany **38** 53.54N 10.50E
Travellers L. Australia **92** 33.18S142.00E
Travers, Mt. New Zealand **86** 42.05S172.45E
Traverse City U.S.A. **112** 44.46N 85.38W
Travnik Yugo. **31** 44.14N 17.40E
Trayning Australia **89** 31.09S117.46E
Trbovlje Yugo. **31** 46.10N 15.03E
Trebbia *r.* Italy **30** 45.04N 9.41E
Trebel *r.* Germany **38** 53.55N 13.01E
Třebíč Czech. **36** 49.13N 15.55E
Trebinje Yugo. **31** 42.43N 18.20E
Trebisacce Italy **33** 39.52N 16.32E
Trebišov Czech. **37** 48.40N 21.47E
Třeboň Czech. **36** 49.01N 14.50E
Trecate Italy **30** 45.26N 8.44E
Tredegar U.K. **13** 51.47N 3.16W
Treene *r.* Germany **38** 54.22N 9.05E
Tregaron U.K. **13** 52.14N 3.56W
Tregosse Islets and Reefs Australia **90** 17.41S150.43E
Tréguier France **18** 48.47N 3.14W
Treinta-y-Tres Uruguay **126** 33.16S 54.17W
Treis Germany **39** 50.10N 7.17E
Trélazé France **18** 47.27N 0.28W
Trelew Argentina **125** 43.15S 65.20W
Trelleborg Sweden **43** 55.22N 13.10E
Trélon France **19** 50.04N 4.06E
Tremadog B. U.K. **12** 52.52N 4.14W
Tremblant, Mont *mtn.* Canada **105** 46.16N 74.35W
Tremont U.S.A. **115** 40.38N 76.23W
Tremp Spain **25** 42.10N 0.54E
Trena Ethiopia **73** 10.45N 40.38E
Trenčín Czech. **37** 48.54N 18.04E
Trenggalek Indonesia **59** 8.01S111.38E
Trenque Lauquen Argentina **125** 35.56S 62.43W
Trent *r.* Canada **105** 44.06N 77.34W
Trent *r.* U.K. **12** 53.41N 0.41W
Trente-et un Milles, Lac des *l.* Canada **105** 46.12N 75.49W
Trentino-Alto Adige *d.* Italy **30** 46.35N 11.20E
Trento Italy **30** 46.04N 11.08E
Trenton Canada **105** 44.06N 77.35W
Trenton Mich. U.S.A. **104** 42.09N 83.11W
Trenton Mo. U.S.A. **110** 40.05N 93.37W
Trenton Nebr. U.S.A. **110** 40.11N101.01W
Trenton N.J. U.S.A. **115** 40.13N 74.45W
Trepassey Canada **99** 46.44N 53.22W
Trepuzzi Italy **33** 40.24N 18.05E
Tres Árboles Uruguay **125** 32.24S 56.43W
Tres Arroyos Argentina **125** 38.26S 60.17W
Três Corações Brazil **126** 21.44S 45.15W
Três Lagoas Brazil **126** 20.46S 51.43W
Três Marias, Represa *resr.* Brazil **126** 18.15S 45.15W
Três Pontas Brazil **126** 21.23S 45.29W
Três Rios Brazil **126** 22.07S 43.12W
Treuchtlingen Germany **39** 48.57N 10.54E
Treuenbrietzen Germany **38** 52.06N 12.52E
Treviglio Italy **30** 45.31N 9.35E
Treviño Spain **26** 42.44N 2.45W
Treviso Italy **30** 45.40N 12.15E
Trévoux France **21** 45.56N 4.46E
Trgovište Yugo. **34** 42.21N 22.05E
Triánda Greece **35** 36.25N 28.10E
Triberg Germany **39** 48.08N 8.13E
Tribsees Germany **38** 54.05N 12.45E
Tribulation, C. Australia **90** 16.03S145.30E
Tribune U.S.A. **110** 38.28N101.45W
Tricarico Italy **33** 40.37N 16.09E
Tricase Italy **33** 39.56N 18.22E
Trida Australia **93** 33.00S145.01E
Trier Germany **39** 49.45N 6.38E
Trieste Italy **31** 45.40N 13.46E
Trieux *r.* France **18** 48.47N 3.07W
Triglav *mtn.* Yugo. **31** 46.23N 13.50E
Trigno *r.* Italy **33** 42.04N 14.48E
Trigueros Spain **27** 37.23N 6.50W
Tríkala Greece **34** 39.34N 21.46E
Trikhonis, Limni *l.* Greece **35** 38.34N 21.28E
Tríkomon Cyprus **66** 35.17N 33.53E
Triman Pakistan **62** 29.38N 69.05E
Trincomalee Sri Lanka **61** 8.34N 81.13E
Trinidad Bolivia **124** 14.47S 64.47W
Trinidad Colombia **122** 5.25N 71.40W
Trinidad Cuba **117** 21.48N 80.00W
Trinidad Uruguay **125** 33.32S 56.54W
Trinidad U.S.A. **108** 37.10N104.31W
Trinidad & Tobago S. America **117** 10.30N 61.20W
Trinity *r.* U.S.A. **111** 29.55N 94.45W
Trinity B. Australia **90** 16.26S145.26E
Trinity B. Canada **103** 48.00N 53.40W
Trinity Range *mts.* U.S.A. **108** 40.13N119.12W
Trinkitat Sudan **72** 18.41N 37.43E
Trino Italy **30** 45.12N 8.18E
Tripoli *see* Ţarābulus Lebanon **66**
Tripoli *see* Ţarābulus Libya **75**
Trípolis Greece **35** 37.31N 22.21E
Tripolitania *f. see* Ţarābulus *f.* Libya **75**
Tripp U.S.A. **110** 43.13N 97.58W
Tripura *d.* India **63** 23.50N 92.00E
Tristan da Cunha *i.* Atlantic Oc. **127** 37.50S 12.30W
Triste Spain **25** 42.23N 0.43W
Trivandrum *see* Thiruvananthapuram India **60**
Trivento Italy **33** 41.47N 14.33E
Trnava Czech. **37** 48.23N 17.35E
Troarn France **18** 49.11N 0.11W
Trobriand Is. P.N.G. **90** 8.35S151.05E
Trogir Yugo. **31** 43.31N 16.15E
Troglav *mtn.* Yugo. **31** 43.57N 16.36E
Troia Italy **33** 41.22N 15.18E
Troina Italy **33** 37.47N 14.37E
Troisdorf Germany **38** 50.49N 7.08E
Trois-Rivières *town* Canada **105** 46.21N 72.33W
Troitsk U.S.S.R. **9** 54.08N 61.33E
Troitsko-Pechorsk U.S.S.R. **44** 62.40N 56.08E
Troitskoye R.S.F.S.R. U.S.S.R. **44** 52.18N 56.26E
Troitskoye UKr.S.S.R. U.S.S.R. **37** 47.38N 30.19E
Trölladyngja *mtn.* Iceland **40** 64.54N 17.16W
Trollhättan Sweden **43** 58.16N 12.18E
Trollheimen *mts.* Norway **40** 62.50N 9.15E
Tromelin *i.* Indian Oc. **49** 15.52S 54.25E
Troms *d.* Norway **40** 69.20N 19.30E
Tromsö Norway **40** 69.42N 19.00E
Trondheim Norway **40** 63.36N 10.23E
Trondheimsfjorden *est.* Norway **40** 63.40N 10.30E
Troödos *mts.* Cyprus **66** 34.57N 32.50E
Troon U.K. **14** 55.33N 4.40W
Tropea Italy **33** 38.41N 15.54E
Tropic U.S.A. **108** 37.37N112.05W
Tropoja Albania **34** 42.23N 20.10E

Trosa to Ultima

Trosa Sweden 43 58.54N 17.33E
Trosh U.S.S.R. 44 66.24N 56.08E
Trostan mtn. N. Ireland 15 55.03N 6.10W
Trostyanets U.S.S.R. 37 48.35N 29.10E
Trout r. Canada 100 61.19N119.51W
Trout Creek town Canada 104 45.59N 79.22W
Trout L. N.W.T. Canada 100 60.35N121.10W
Trout L. Ont. Canada 102 51.13N 93.20W
Trout River town Canada 103 49.29N 58.08W
Trout Run U.S.A. 114 41.23N 77.03W
Trouville France 18 49.22N 0.05E
Trowbridge U.K. 13 51.18N 2.12W
Troy site Turkey 34 39.57N 26.15E
Troy Ala. U.S.A. 113 31.49N 86.00W
Troy Mo. U.S.A. 110 38.59N 90.59W
Troy Mont. U.S.A. 108 48.28N115.53W
Troy N.H. U.S.A. 115 42.50N 72.11W
Troy N.Y. U.S.A. 115 42.43N 73.40W
Troy Ohio U.S.A. 112 40.02N 84.12W
Troy Penn. U.S.A. 114 41.47N 76.47W
Troyan Bulgaria 34 42.51N 24.43E
Troyes France 19 48.18N 4.05E
Troy Peak mtn. U.S.A. 108 38.19N115.30W
Trpanj Yugo. 31 43.00N 17.17E
Trstenik Yugo. 34 43.37N 21.00E
Truchas Peak mtn. U.S.A. 109 35.58N105.39W
Truckee U.S.A. 108 39.20N120.11W
Trujillo Honduras 117 15.55N 86.00W
Trujillo Peru 122 8.06S 79.00W
Trujillo Spain 27 39.28N 5.53W
Trujillo Venezuela 122 9.20N 70.37W
Trumansburg U.S.A. 115 42.33N 76.40W
Trûn Bulgaria 34 42.51N 22.38E
Trundle Australia 93 32.54S147.35E
Trung-Luong Vietnam 56 13.55N109.15E
Trunmore B. Canada 103 53.48N 57.10W
Truro Australia 92 34.23S139.09E
Truro Canada 103 45.22N 63.16W
Truro U.K. 13 50.17N 5.02W
Trûstenik Bulgaria 34 43.31N 24.28E
Trustrup Denmark 42 56.21N 10.47E
Truth or Consequences U.S.A. 109 33.08N107.15W
Truyère r. France 20 44.39N 2.34E
Tryavna Bulgaria 34 42.54N 25.25E
Trysil Norway 41 61.19N 12.16E
Trysil r. Norway 41 61.03N 12.30E
Trzemeszno Poland 37 52.35N 17.50E
Tržič Yugo. 31 46.22N 14.19E
Tsamandás Greece 34 39.46N 20.21E
Tsaratanana Madagascar 81 16.47S 47.39E
Tsaratanana, Massif de mts. Madagascar 81 14.00S 49.00E
Tsaritsáni Greece 34 39.53N 22.14E
Tsau Botswana 80 20.10S 22.29E
Tsavo Nat. Park Kenya 79 2.45S 38.45E
Tselinograd U.S.S.R. 9 51.10N 71.28E
Tsenovo Bulgaria 34 43.32N 25.39E
Tses Namibia 80 25.58S 18.08E
Tsévié Togo 77 6.28N 1.15E
Tshabong Botswana 80 26.03S 22.25E
Tshane Botswana 80 24.02S 21.54E
Tshela Zaïre 78 4.57S 12.57E
Tshesebe Botswana 80 20.45S 27.31E
Tshikapa Zaïre 78 6.28S 20.48E
Tshofa Zaïre 78 5.13S 25.20E
Tshopo r. Zaïre 78 0.30N 25.07E
Tshuapa r. Zaïre 78 0.14S 20.45E
Tsihombé Madagascar 81 25.18S 45.29E
Tsimlyansk U.S.S.R. 45 47.40N 42.06E
Tsimlyanskoye Vodokhranilishche resr. U.S.S.R. 45 48.00N 43.00E
Tsinan see Jinan China 54
Tsínga mtn. Greece 34 41.23N 24.44E
Tsingtao see Qingdao China 54
Tsiribihina Madagascar 81 19.42S 44.31E
Tsiroanomandidy Madagascar 81 18.46S 46.02E
Tsivilsk U.S.S.R. 44 55.50N 47.28E
Tsivory Madagascar 81 24.04S 46.05E
Tskhinvali U.S.S.R. 45 42.14N 43.58E
Tsna r. B.S.S.R. U.S.S.R. 37 52.10N 27.03E
Tsna r. R.S.F.S.R. U.S.S.R. 44 54.45N 41.54E
Tsobis Namibia 80 19.27S 17.30E
Tso Moriri l. Jammu & Kashmir 63 32.54N 78.20E
Tsu Japan 57 34.43N136.31E
Tsuchiura Japan 57 36.05N140.12E
Tsudakhar U.S.S.R. 45 42.20N 47.11E
Tsugaru kaikyō str. Japan 57 41.30N140.50E
Tsumeb Namibia 80 19.12S 17.43E
Tsuru Japan 57 35.30N138.56E
Tsuruga Japan 57 35.40N136.05E
Tsuruoka Japan 57 38.44N139.50E
Tsushima Japan 57 35.10N136.43E
Tsushima i. Japan 57 34.30N129.20E
Tsuyama Japan 57 35.04N134.01E
Tua r. Portugal 26 41.13N 7.26W
Tuam Rep. of Ire. 15 53.32N 8.52W
Tuamotu, Îles is. Pacific Oc. 85 17.00S142.00W
Tuapa Niue 84 18.59S169.54W
Tuapse U.S.S.R. 45 44.06N 39.05E
Tuatapere New Zealand 86 46.08S167.41E
Tubac U.S.A. 109 31.37N111.03W
Tuba City U.S.A. 109 36.08N111.14W
Tuban Indonesia 59 6.55S112.01E
Tubarão Brazil 126 28.30S 49.01W
Ţubās Jordan 67 32.19N 35.22E
Ţubayq, Jabal aţ mts. Saudi Arabia 66 29.30N 37.15E
Tubbercurry Rep. of Ire. 15 54.03N 8.45W
Tübingen Germany 39 48.31N 9.02E
Ţubjah, Wādī r. Saudi Arabia 64 25.35N 38.22E
Ţubruq Libya 72 32.06N 23.58E
Tubuai i. Pacific Oc. 85 23.23S149.27W
Tubuai Is. Pacific Oc. 85 23.00S150.00W
Tucacas Venezuela 122 10.48N 68.19W
Tuchola Poland 37 53.35N 17.50E
Tuckerton U.S.A. 115 39.36N 74.20W
Tucson U.S.A. 109 32.13N110.58W
Tucumán d. Argentina 124 26.30S 65.20W
Tucumcari U.S.A. 109 35.10N103.44W
Tucupita Venezuela 122 9.02N 62.04W
Tucuruí Brazil 123 3.42S 49.44W
Tucuruí, Reprêsa de resr. Brazil 123 4.35S 49.33W
Tudela Spain 25 42.05N 1.36W
Tudela de Duero Spain 26 41.35N 4.35W
Tuela r. Portugal 26 41.30N 7.12W
Tufi P.N.G. 90 9.05S149.20E
Tugela R.S.A. 80 29.10S 31.25E
Tug Hill mtn. U.S.A. 115 43.45N 75.39W
Tuguegarao Phil. 59 17.36N121.44E
Tugur U.S.S.R. 51 53.44N136.45E
Tuineje Canary Is. 127 28.18N 14.03W
Tukangbesi, Kepulauan is. Indonesia 59 5.30S124.00E
Tukayyid well Iraq 65 29.47N 45.36E
Ţūkh Egypt 66 30.21N 31.12E
Tūkrah Libya 75 32.32N 20.34E
Tuktoyaktuk Canada 98 69.27N133.00W
Tukums U.S.S.R. 41 57.00N 23.10E
Tukuyu Tanzania 79 9.20S 33.37E
Tula Mexico 116 23.00N 99.43W
Tula U.S.S.R. 44 54.11N 37.38E
Tūlāk Afghan. 62 33.58N 63.44E
Tulare U.S.A. 109 36.13N119.21W
Tulare L. resr. U.S.A. 109 36.03N119.49W
Tularosa U.S.A. 109 33.04N106.01W
Tulcan Ecuador 122 0.50N 77.48W
Tulcea Romania 29 45.10N 28.50E
Tulchin U.S.S.R. 37 48.40N 28.49E
Tulemalu L. Canada 101 62.58N 99.25W
Tuli Zimbabwe 80 21.50S 29.15E
Tuli r. Zimbabwe 80 21.49S 29.00E
Tulia U.S.A. 111 34.32N101.46W
Ţūlkarm Jordan 67 32.19N 35.02E
Tullahoma U.S.A. 113 35.21N 86.12W
Tullamore Australia 93 32.39S147.39E
Tullamore Rep. of Ire. 15 53.17N 7.31W
Tulle France 20 45.16N 1.46E
Tullins France 21 45.18N 5.29E
Tullow Rep. of Ire. 15 52.49N 6.45W
Tully Australia 90 17.55S145.59E
Tully U.S.A. 115 42.48N 76.07W
Tuloma r. U.S.S.R. 44 68.56N 33.00E
Tulsa U.S.A. 111 36.09N 95.58W
Tulsequah Canada 100 58.39N133.35W
Tuluá Colombia 122 4.05N 76.12W
Tulumbasy U.S.S.R. 44 57.27N 57.40E
Tulun U.S.S.R. 51 54.32N100.35E
Tulungagung Indonesia 59 8.03S111.54E
Tulu Welel mtn. Ethiopia 73 8.53N 34.47E
Tum Indonesia 59 3.28S130.21E
Tumaco Colombia 122 1.51N 78.46W
Tumba Sweden 43 59.12N 17.49E
Tumba, L. Zaïre 78 0.45S 18.00E
Tumbarumba Australia 93 35.49S148.01E
Tumbes Peru 122 3.37S 80.27W
Tumbler Ridge Canada 100 55.20N120.49W
Tumby Bay town Australia 92 34.20S136.05E
Tumd Youqi China 54 40.33N110.30E
Tumd Zuoqi China 54 40.42N111.08E
Tumeremo Venezuela 122 7.18N 61.30W
Tummel, Loch U.K. 14 56.43N 3.55W
Tump Pakistan 62 26.07N 62.22E
Tumsar India 63 21.23N 79.44E
Tumuc Humac Mts. S. America 123 2.20N 54.50W
Tumut Australia 93 35.20S148.14E
Tunari mtn. Bolivia 124 17.18S 66.22W
Tūnat al Jabal Egypt 66 27.46N 30.44E
Tunceli Turkey 64 39.07N 39.34E
Tuncurry Australia 93 32.17S152.29E
Tundubai well Sudan 72 18.31N 28.33E
Tunduma Tanzania 79 9.19S 32.47E
Tunduru Tanzania 79 11.08S 37.21E
Tundzha r. Bulgaria 34 42.00N 26.35E
Tungabhadra r. India 60 16.00N 78.15E
Tungaru Sudan 73 10.14N 30.42E
Tungchiang Taiwan 55 22.28N120.26E
Tungsten Canada 100 62.00N128.15W
Tungsten U.S.A. 108 40.48N118.08W
Tunica U.S.A. 111 34.41N 90.23W
Tunis Tunisia 32 36.48N 10.11E
Tunis, Golfe de g. Tunisia 32 37.00N 10.30E
Tunisia Africa 75 34.00N 9.00E
Tunja Colombia 122 5.33N 73.23W
Tunkhannock U.S.A. 115 41.32N 75.57W
Tunnsjöen l. Norway 40 64.45N 13.25E
Tunungayualok I. Canada 103 56.05N 61.05W
Tunuyán r. Argentina 125 33.33S 67.30W
Tunxi China 55 29.41N118.22E
Tuoy-Khaya U.S.S.R. 51 62.33N111.25E
Tupã Brazil 126 21.57S 50.28W
Tupelo U.S.A. 111 34.16N 88.43W
Tupinambaranas, Ilha f. Brazil 123 3.00S 58.00W
Tupiza Bolivia 124 21.27S 65.45W
Tupper Lake town U.S.A. 105 44.13N 74.29W
Tuquan China 54 45.22N121.41E
Túquerres Colombia 122 1.06N 77.37W
Tura India 63 25.31N 90.13E
Tura Tanzania 79 5.30S 33.50E
Tura U.S.S.R. 51 64.05N100.00E
Turabah Saudi Arabia 72 21.13N 41.39E
Turangi New Zealand 86 38.59S175.48E
Turano r. Italy 30 42.26N 12.47E
Turbaco Colombia 122 10.20N 75.25W
Turbanovo U.S.S.R. 44 60.05N 50.46E
Turbat Pakistan 62 25.59N 63.04E
Turbine Canada 104 46.22N 81.31W
Turbo Colombia 122 8.06N 76.44W
Turda Romania 37 46.34N 23.47E
Turek Poland 37 52.02N 18.30E
Turgay U.S.S.R. 9 49.38N 63.25E
Turgeon r. Canada 102 50.00N 78.54W
Tŭrgovishte Bulgaria 34 43.17N 26.38E
Turgutlu Turkey 29 38.30N 27.43E
Turhal Turkey 64 40.23N 36.05E
Türi U.S.S.R. 41 58.48N 25.26E
Turia r. Spain 25 39.27N 0.19W
Turiaçu Brazil 123 1.41S 45.21W
Turiaçu r. Brazil 123 1.36S 45.19W
Turin Canada 100 49.59N112.35W
Turin see Torino Italy 30
Turka U.S.S.R. 37 49.10N 23.02E
Turkana, L. Kenya 79 4.00N 36.00E
Turkestan U.S.S.R. 52 43.17N 68.16E
Turkey Asia 64 39.00N 35.00E
Turkey U.S.A. 111 34.23N100.54W
Turkey Creek town Australia 88 17.04S128.15E
Turkmenskaya S.S.R. d. U.S.S.R. 9 40.00N 60.00E
Turks Is. Turks & Caicos Is. 117 21.30N 71.10W
Turku Finland 41 60.27N 22.17E
Turku-Pori d. Finland 41 61.00N 22.35E
Turkwel r. Kenya 79 3.08N 35.39E
Turnagain r. Canada 100 59.06N127.35W
Turnberry Canada 101 53.25N101.45W
Turneffe Is. Belize 117 17.30N 87.45W
Turner U.S.A. 108 48.51N108.24W
Turnhout Belgium 16 51.19N 4.57E
Turnu Măgurele Romania 34 43.45N 24.53E
Turnu Roşu, Pasul pass Romania 29 45.37N 24.17E
Turnu-Severin Romania 29 44.37N 22.39E
Turon r. Australia 93 33.03S149.33E
Turon U.S.A. 111 37.48N 98.26W
Turopolje f. Yugo. 31 45.40N 16.00E
Turov U.S.S.R. 37 52.04N 27.40E
Turpan China 52 42.55N 89.06E
Turpan Pendi f. China 52 43.40N 89.00E
Turquino mtn. Cuba 117 20.05N 76.50W
Turriff U.K. 14 57.32N 2.28W
Turtkul U.S.S.R. 65 41.30N 61.00E
Turtle Lake town N.Dak. U.S.A. 110 47.31N100.53W
Turtle Lake town Wisc. U.S.A. 110 45.23N 92.09W
Turtle Mtn. Canada / U.S.A. 101 49.05N 99.45W
Turukhansk U.S.S.R. 51 65.21N 88.05E
Turya r. U.S.S.R. 37 51.48N 24.52E
Tuscaloosa U.S.A. 113 33.12N 87.33W
Tuscany see Toscana d. Italy 30
Tuscarawas r. U.S.A. 114 40.17N 81.52W
Tuscarora U.S.A. 108 41.19N116.14W
Tuscarora Mts. U.S.A. 114 40.10N 77.45W
Tuscola Ill. U.S.A. 110 39.48N 88.17W
Tuscola Tex. U.S.A. 111 32.12N 99.48W
Tutera see Tudela Spain 25
Tuticorin India 61 8.48N 78.10E
Tutin Yugo. 34 43.00N 20.20E
Tutóia Brazil 123 2.45S 42.16W
Tutrakan Bulgaria 29 44.02N 26.40E
Tuttle U.S.A. 110 47.09N100.00W
Tuttlingen Germany 39 47.59N 8.49E
Tutuala Indonesia 59 8.24S127.15E
Tutubu Tanzania 79 5.28S 32.43E
Tutuila i. Samoa 84 14.18S170.42W
Tuţūn Egypt 66 29.09N 30.46E
Tutzing Germany 39 47.54N 11.17E
Tuul Gol r. Mongolia 52 48.53N104.35E
Tuvalu Pacific Oc. 84 8.00S178.00E
Tuwayq, Jabal mts. Saudi Arabia 71 23.30N 46.20E
Tuxpan Mexico 116 21.00N 97.23W
Tuxtla Gutiérrez Mexico 116 16.45N 93.09W
Túy Spain 26 42.03N 8.38W
Tuyen Quang Vietnam 55 21.48N105.21E
Tuz Gölü l. Turkey 64 38.45N 33.24E
Ţūz Khurmātū Iraq 65 34.53N 44.38E
Tuzla Yugo. 31 44.32N 18.41E
Tvaerå Faroe Is. 10 61.34N 6.48W
Tvedestrand Norway 42 58.37N 8.55E
Tveitsund Norway 42 59.01N 8.32E
Tver U.S.S.R. 44 56.47N 35.57E
Tvŭrditsa Bulgaria 34 42.42N 25.52E
Tweed Canada 105 44.29N 77.19W
Tweed r. U.K. 14 55.46N 2.00W
Tweed Heads town Australia 93 28.13S153.33E
Tweedsmuir Prov. Park Canada 100 52.55N126.20W
Twentynine Palms U.S.A. 109 34.08N116.03W
Twin Bridges town U.S.A. 108 45.33N112.20W
Twin Falls town U.S.A. 108 42.34N114.28W
Twining U.S.A. 104 44.07N 83.48W
Twins Creek r. Australia 92 29.10S139.27E
Twin Valley town U.S.A. 110 47.16N 96.16W
Twizel New Zealand 86 44.15S170.06E
Twofold B. Australia 93 37.06S149.55E
Two Harbors town U.S.A. 110 47.02N 91.40W
Twyford U.K. 13 51.01N 1.19W
Tygart r. U.S.A. 114 38.30N 80.03W
Tyler Minn. U.S.A. 110 44.17N 96.08W
Tyler Tex. U.S.A. 111 32.21N 95.18W
Tylösand Sweden 43 56.39N 12.44E
Tylöskog hills Sweden 43 58.45N 15.20E
Tyndinskiy U.S.S.R. 51 55.11N124.34E
Tyne r. U.K. 12 55.00N 1.25W
Tyne and Wear d. U.K. 12 54.57N 1.35W
Tynemouth U.K. 12 55.01N 1.24W
Tynset Norway 41 62.17N 10.47E
Tyre see Şūr Lebanon 67
Tyrifjorden l. Norway 42 60.02N 10.08E
Tyringe Sweden 43 56.10N 13.35E
Tyron U.S.A. 113 35.13N 82.14W
Tyrone d. U.K. 15 54.35N 7.15W
Tyrone U.S.A. 114 40.40N 78.14W
Tyrrel Canada 101 54.35N 99.10W
Tyrrell r. Australia 92 35.28S142.55E
Tyrrell, L. Australia 92 35.22S142.50E
Tyrrhenian Sea Med. Sea 32 40.00N 12.00E
Tysnesöy i. Norway 42 60.00N 5.35E
Tyssedal Norway 42 60.07N 6.34E
Tyumen U.S.S.R. 9 57.11N 65.29E
Tywi r. U.K. 13 51.46N 4.22W
Tzaneen R.S.A. 80 23.49S 30.10E

U

Ua Huka i. Îs. Marquises 85 8.55S139.32W
Ua Pu i. Îs. Marquises 85 9.25S140.00W
Uatumã r. Brazil 123 2.30S 57.40W
Uaupés Brazil 122 0.07S 67.05W
Uaupés r. Brazil 122 0.00S 67.10W
Ubá Brazil 126 21.08S 42.59W
Ubangi r. Congo / Zaïre 78 0.25S 17.40E
Ubatuba Brazil 126 23.26S 45.05W
Ubauro Pakistan 62 28.10N 69.44E
Ubayyiḑ, Wādī al r. Iraq 64 32.04N 42.17E
Ube Japan 57 34.00N131.16E
Ubeda Spain 26 38.01N 3.22W
Uberaba Brazil 126 19.47S 47.57W
Uberlândia Brazil 126 18.57S 48.17W
Überlingen Germany 39 47.46N 9.10E
Ubombo R.S.A. 81 27.35S 32.05E
Ubort r. U.S.S.R. 37 52.06N 28.28E
Ubrique Spain 27 36.41N 5.27W
Ubundu Zaïre 78 0.24S 25.28E
Ucayali r. Peru 122 4.40S 73.20W
Uch Pakistan 62 29.14N 71.03E
Uchiura wan b. Japan 57 42.20N140.40E
Uckermark f. Germany 38 52.11N 13.50E
Udaipur India 62 24.35N 73.41E
Udalguri India 63 26.46N 92.08E
Udaquiola Argentina 125 36.35S 58.30W
Udaypur Nepal 63 26.54N 86.32E
Udbina Yugo. 31 44.32N 15.46E
Uddeholm Sweden 43 60.01N 13.37E
Uddevalla Sweden 42 58.21N 11.55E
Uddjaur l. Sweden 40 65.55N 17.49E
Udhampur Jammu & Kashmir 62 32.56N 75.08E
Udine Italy 30 46.03N 13.14E
Udipi India 60 13.21N 74.45E
údolní nádrž Lipno l. Czech. 39 48.43N 14.04E
Udon Thani Thailand 56 17.25N102.45E
Ueckermünde Germany 38 53.44N 14.03E
Uele r. Zaïre 73 4.09N 22.26E
Uelzen Germany 38 52.58N 10.33E
Ueno Japan 57 34.45N136.08E
Uere r. Zaïre 73 3.42N 25.24E
Uetersen Germany 38 53.41N 9.39E
Ufa U.S.S.R. 44 54.45N 55.58E
Ufa r. U.S.S.R. 44 54.45N 56.00E
Uffculme U.K. 13 50.45N 3.19W
Uffenheim Germany 39 49.32N 10.14E
Ugab r. Namibia 80 21.12S 13.37E
Ugalla r. Tanzania 79 5.43S 31.10E
Uganda Africa 79 2.00N 33.00E
Ugep Nigeria 77 5.48N 8.05E
Ughelli Nigeria 77 5.33N 6.00E
Ugijar Spain 27 36.57N 3.03W
Ugine France 21 45.45N 6.25E
Uglegorsk U.S.S.R. 51 49.01N142.04E
Ugljan i. Yugo. 31 44.05N 15.10E
Uglovka U.S.S.R. 44 58.13N 33.30E
Ugoma mtn. Zaïre 79 4.00S 28.45E
Ugra r. U.S.S.R. 44 54.30N 36.10E
Ugŭrchin Bulgaria 34 43.06N 24.26E
Uherske Hradiště Czech. 37 49.05N 17.28E
Uhrichsville U.S.A. 114 40.24N 81.20W
Uig U.K. 14 57.35N 6.22W
Uíge Angola 78 7.40S 15.09E
Uíge d. Angola 78 7.00S 15.30E
Uil U.S.S.R. 45 49.08N 54.43E
Uil r. U.S.S.R. 45 48.33N 52.25E
Uinta Mts. U.S.A. 108 40.45N110.05W
Uitenhage R.S.A. 80 33.46S 25.23E
Uithuizen Neth. 16 53.24N 6.41E
Uivlleq see Nanortalik Greenland 99
Ujhāni India 63 28.01N 79.01E
Uji r. Japan 57 34.53N135.48E
Ujiji Tanzania 79 4.55S 29.39E
Ujjain India 62 23.11N 75.46E
Ujpest Hungary 37 47.33N 19.05E
Ujście Poland 36 53.04N 16.43E
Ujung Pandang Indonesia 58 5.09S119.28E
Uka U.S.S.R. 51 57.50N162.02E
Ukerewe I. Tanzania 79 2.00S 33.00E
Ukhta U.S.S.R. 44 63.33N 53.44E
Ukiah U.S.A. 108 39.09N123.13W
Ukmerge U.S.S.R. 44 55.14N 24.49E
Ukrainskaya S.S.R. d. U.S.S.R. 37 49.45N 27.00E
Ukrina r. Yugo. 31 45.05N 17.56E
Uku Angola 78 11.24S 14.15E
Ukwi Botswana 80 23.22S 20.30E
Ulaanbaatar Mongolia 52 47.54N106.52E
Ulaangom Mongolia 52 49.59N 92.00E
Ulamba Zaïre 78 9.07S 23.40E
Ulan Bator see Ulaanbaatar Mongolia 52
Ulansuhai Nur l. China 54 40.56N108.49E
Ulan-Ude U.S.S.R. 52 51.55N107.40E
Ulan Ul Hu l. China 61 34.45N 90.25E
Ulcinj Yugo. 31 41.55N 19.11E
Ulefoss Norway 42 59.17N 9.16E
Ulenia, L. Australia 92 29.57S142.24E
Ulfborg Denmark 42 56.16N 8.20E
Ulhāsnagar India 62 19.13N 73.07E
Uliastay Mongolia 52 47.42N 96.52E
Ulindi r. Zaïre 78 1.38S 25.55E
Ulla r. Spain 26 42.40N 8.43W
Ulladulla Australia 93 35.21S150.25E
Ullånger Sweden 40 62.58N 18.16E
Ullapool U.K. 14 57.54N 5.10W
Ullswater l. U.K. 12 54.34N 2.52W
Ulm Germany 39 48.24N 10.00E
Ulongwé Mozambique 79 14.34S 34.21E
Ulricehamn Sweden 43 57.47N 13.25E
Ulsan S. Korea 57 35.34N129.19E
Ulsberg Norway 40 62.45N 9.59E
Ulster U.S.A. 115 41.51N 76.30W
Ultima Australia 92 35.30S143.20E

Ulu Sudan **73** 10.43N 33.29E
Ulúa *r.* Honduras **117** 15.50N 87.38W
Uluguru Mts. Tanzania **79** 7.05S 37.40E
Uluru *mtn.* Australia **90** 25.20S131.01E
Ulverston U.K. **12** 54.13N 3.07W
Ulverstone Australia **91** 41.09S146.10E
Ul'yanovsk U.S.S.R. **44** 54.19N 48.22E
Ulysses U.S.A. **111** 37.35N101.22W
Ulzë Albania **34** 41.41N 19.54E
Umag Yugo. **31** 45.25N 13.32E
Umaisha Nigeria **77** 8.01N 7.12E
Umala Bolivia **124** 17.21S 68.00W
Uman U.S.S.R. **37** 48.45N 30.10E
Umaria India **63** 23.32N 80.50E
Umarkot Pakistan **62** 25.22N 69.44E
Umbertide Italy **30** 43.18N 12.20E
Umbria *d.* Italy **30** 43.05N 12.30E
Ume *r.* Sweden **40** 63.47N 20.16E
Ume *r.* Zimbabwe **80** 17.00S 28.22E
Umeå Sweden **40** 63.45N 20.20E
Umfors Sweden **40** 65.56N 15.00E
Umfuli *r.* Zimbabwe **80** 17.32S 29.23E
Umiat U.S.A. **98** 69.25N152.20W
Umm-al-Qaywayn U.A.E. **65** 25.32N 55.34E
Umm Badr Sudan **72** 14.14N 27.57E
Umm Bel Sudan **73** 13.32N 28.04E
Umm Durmān Sudan **72** 15.37N 32.59E
Umm el Faḥm Israel **67** 32.31N 35.09E
Umm Kuwaykah Sudan **73** 12.49N 31.52E
Umm Lajj Saudi Arabia **64** 25.03N 37.17E
Umm Qays Jordan **67** 32.39N 35.41E
Umm Qurayn Sudan **73** 9.58N 28.55E
Umm Ruwābah Sudan **73** 12.54N 31.13E
Umm Shalīl Sudan **73** 10.51N 23.42E
Umm Shanqah Sudan **73** 13.14N 27.14E
Umniati Zimbabwe **80** 18.41S 29.45E
Umniati *r.* Zimbabwe **80** 17.32S 29.23E
Umrer India **63** 20.51N 79.20E
Umreth India **62** 22.42N 73.07E
Umtata R.S.A. **80** 31.35S 28.47E
Umuahia Nigeria **77** 5.31N 7.26E
Umzimkulu R.S.A. **80** 30.15S 29.56E
Umzimvubu R.S.A. **80** 31.37S 29.32E
Una India **62** 20.49N 71.02E
Una *r.* Yugo. **31** 45.16N 16.55E
Unac *r.* Yugo. **31** 44.30N 16.09E
Unadilla *r.* U.S.A. **115** 42.20N 75.19W
Unalakleet U.S.A. **98** 63.53N160.47W
'Unayzah Jordan **66** 30.29N 35.48E
'Unayzah Saudi Arabia **65** 26.05N 43.57E
'Unayzah, Jabal *mtn.* Iraq **64** 32.15N 39.19E
Uncia Bolivia **124** 18.27S 66.37W
Uncompahgre Peak U.S.A. **108** 38.04N107.28W
Uncompahgre Plateau *f.* U.S.A. **108** 38.30N108.25W
Unden *l.* Sweden **43** 58.47N 14.26E
Underberg R.S.A. **80** 29.46S 29.26E
Underbool Australia **92** 35.10S141.50E
Undu, C. Fiji **84** 16.08S179.57W
Unecha U.S.S.R. **37** 52.52N 32.42E
Ungarie Australia **93** 33.38S147.00E
Ungava, Péninsule d' *pen.* Canada **99** 60.00N 74.00W
Ungava B. Canada **99** 59.00N 67.30W
União Brazil **123** 4.35S 42.52W
União da Vitória Brazil **126** 26.13S 51.05W
Unije *i.* Yugo. **31** 44.38N 14.15E
Unimak I. U.S.A. **98** 54.50N164.00W
Unini Peru **122** 10.41S 73.59W
Union Miss U.S.A. **111** 32.34N 89.14W
Union S.C. U.S.A. **113** 34.42N 81.37W
Union City Penn. U.S.A. **114** 41.54N 79.51W
Union City Tenn. U.S.A. **111** 36.26N 89.03W
Uniondale R.S.A. **80** 33.39S 23.07E
Union Gap U.S.A. **108** 46.34N120.34W
Union of Soviet Socialist Republics Europe / Asia **37** 50.00N 28.00E
Union Springs *town* U.S.A. **113** 32.08N 85.44W
Uniontown U.S.A. **114** 39.54N 79.44W
Unionville U.S.A. **110** 40.29N 93.01W
United Arab Emirates Asia **65** 24.00N 54.00E
United Kingdom Europe **11** 55.00N 2.00W
United States of America N. America **106** 39.00N100.00W
Unity Canada **101** 52.27N109.10W
Universales, Montes *mts.* Spain **25** 40.20N 1.30W
University Park *town* U.S.A. **109** 32.17N106.45W
Unjha India **62** 23.48N 72.24E
Unna Germany **38** 51.32N 7.41E
Unnão India **63** 26.32N 80.30E
Unst *i.* U.K. **14** 60.45N 0.55W
Unstrut *r.* Germany **38** 51.10N 11.48E
Unterwalden *d.* Switz. **39** 46.55N 8.17E
Ünye Turkey **64** 41.09N 37.15E
Upata Venezuela **122** 8.02N 62.25W
Upemba, L. Zaïre **78** 8.35S 26.28E
Upemba Nat. Park Zaïre **78** 9.00S 26.30E
Upernavik Greenland **99** 72.50N 56.00W
Upington R.S.A. **80** 28.26S 21.12E
Upleta India **62** 21.44N 70.17E
Upolu *i.* W. Samoa **84** 13.55S171.45W
Upolu Pt. Hawaiian Is. **85** 20.16N155.51W
Upper Arrow L. Canada **100** 50.30N117.50W
Upper East *d.* Ghana **76** 10.40N 0.20W
Upper Egypt *see* Aş Şa'īd *f.* Egypt **64**
Upper Hutt New Zealand **86** 41.07S175.04E
Upper Klamath L. U.S.A. **108** 42.23N122.55W
Upper Laberge Canada **100** 60.54N135.12W
Upper Lough Erne N. Ireland **15** 54.13N 7.32W
Upper Pen. *f.* U.S.A. **104** 46.12N 84.32W
Upper Red L. U.S.A. **110** 48.05N 94.50W
Upper Tean U.K. **12** 52.57N 1.59W
Upper Volta *see* Burkina Africa **76**
Upper West *d.* Ghana **76** 10.25N 2.00W
Upper Yarra Resr. Australia **93** 37.43S145.56E
Uppland *f.* Sweden **43** 59.59N 17.48E
Upplands-Väsby Sweden **43** 59.31N 17.54E
Uppsala Sweden **43** 59.52N 17.38E
Uppsala *d.* Sweden **41** 60.10N 17.50E
Upshi Jammu & Kashmir **63** 33.50N 77.49E
Upton Canada **105** 45.39N 72.41W
Upton U.S.A. **108** 44.06N104.38W
Uqlat aş Şuqūr Saudi Arabia **64** 25.50N 42.12E
Ur *ruins* Iraq **65** 30.55N 46.07E
Uracoa Venezuela **122** 9.03N 62.27W
Uraga-suido *str.* Japan **57** 35.10N139.42E
Urahoro Japan **57** 42.48N143.39E
Urakawa Japan **57** 42.09N142.47E
Ural *r.* U.S.S.R. **45** 47.00N 52.00E
Uralla Australia **93** 30.40S151.31E
Ural Mts. *see* Ural'skiye Gory *mts.* U.S.S.R. **44**
Ural'sk U.S.S.R. **45** 51.19N 51.20E
Ural'skiye Gory *mts.* U.S.S.R. **44** 60.00N 59.00E
Urana Australia **93** 35.21S146.19E
Urana, L. Australia **93** 35.21S146.19E
Urandangi Australia **90** 21.36S138.18E
Uranium City Canada **101** 59.28N108.40W
Urapunga Australia **90** 14.41S134.34E
Uraricoera *r.* Brazil **122** 3.10N 60.30W
Urawa Japan **57** 35.51N139.39E
Uray U.S.S.R. **50** 60.11N 65.00E
Urbana U.S.A. **110** 40.07N 88.12W
Urbania Italy **30** 43.40N 12.31E
Urbino Italy **30** 43.43N 12.38E
Urcos Peru **122** 13.40S 71.38W
Urda U.S.S.R. **45** 48.44N 47.30E
Urdzhar U.S.S.R. **50** 47.06N 81.33E
Ure *r.* U.K. **12** 54.05N 1.20W
Urechye U.S.S.R. **37** 52.59N 27.50E
Uren U.S.S.R. **44** 57.30N 45.50E
Urengoy U.S.S.R. **50** 65.59N 78.30E
Ures Mexico **116** 29.26N110.24W
Urfa Turkey **64** 37.08N 38.45E
Ürgüp Turkey **64** 38.39N 34.55E
Uri *d.* Switz. **39** 46.45N 8.35E
Uribia Colombia **122** 11.43N 72.16W
Urim Israel **67** 31.18N 34.31E
Urisino Australia **92** 29.44S143.49E
Urjala Finland **41** 61.05N 23.32E
Urk Neth. **16** 52.40N 5.36E
Urlingford Rep. of Ire. **15** 52.44N 7.35W
Urmia, L. *see* Daryācheh-ye Orūmīyeh *l.* Iran **65**
Uroševac Yugo. **34** 42.22N 21.09E
Ursus Poland **37** 52.12N 20.53E
Uruaçu Brazil **123** 14.30S 49.10W
Uruapan Mexico **116** 19.26N102.04W
Urubamba Peru **122** 13.20S 72.07W
Urubamba *r.* Peru **122** 10.43S 73.55W
Urucará Brazil **123** 2.32S 57.45W
Uruçui Brazil **123** 7.14S 44.33W
Uruguaiana Brazil **125** 29.45S 57.05W
Uruguay *r.* Argentina / Uruguay **125** 34.00S 58.30W
Uruguay S. America **126** 33.15S 56.00W
Ürümqi China **52** 43.43N 87.38E
Urun P.N.G. **90** 8.36S147.15E
Urunga Australia **93** 30.30S152.28E
Urup *r.* U.S.S.R. **45** 44.59N 41.12E
Uryu ko *l.* Japan **57** 44.22N142.15E
Urzhum U.S.S.R. **44** 57.08N 50.00E
Urziceni Romania **29** 44.43N 26.38E
Usa *r.* U.S.S.R. **44** 65.58N 56.35E
Uşak Turkey **64** 38.42N 29.25E
Usakos Namibia **80** 22.02S 15.35E
Usambara Mts. Tanzania **79** 4.45S 38.25E
Ušće Yugo. **34** 43.28N 20.37E
Usedom *i.* Germany **38** 54.00N 14.00E
Ushant *i.* *see* Ouessant, Île d' *i.* France **18**
Ush-Tobe U.S.S.R. **52** 45.15N 77.59E
Ushuaia Argentina **125** 54.47S 68.20W
Ushumun U.S.S.R. **51** 52.48N126.27E
Usisya Malaŵi **79** 11.10S 34.12E
Usk *r.* U.K. **13** 51.34N 2.59W
Uskedal Norway **42** 59.56N 5.52E
Üsküdar Turkey **29** 41.00N 29.03E
Uslar Germany **38** 51.39N 9.38E
Usman U.S.S.R. **45** 52.02N 39.43E
Usovo U.S.S.R. **37** 51.20N 28.01E
Uspenskiy U.S.S.R. **50** 48.41N 72.43E
Ussel France **20** 45.33N 2.18E
Ussuriysk U.S.S.R. **53** 43.48N131.59E
Ustaoset Norway **41** 60.30N 8.04E
Ustaritz France **20** 43.24N 1.27W
Ustica *i.* Italy **32** 38.42N 13.10E
Ust'-Ilga U.S.S.R. **51** 54.59N105.00E
Ústí nad Labem Czech. **38** 50.40N 14.02E
Ust Ishim U.S.S.R. **50** 57.45N 71.05E
Ustka Poland **36** 54.35N 16.50E
Ust'kamchatsk U.S.S.R. **51** 56.14N162.28E
Ust-Kamenogorsk U.S.S.R. **50** 50.00N 82.40E
Ust Kulom U.S.S.R. **44** 61.34N 53.40E
Ust Kut U.S.S.R. **51** 56.40N105.50E
Ust Lyzha U.S.S.R. **44** 65.45N 56.38E
Ust'Maya U.S.S.R. **51** 60.25N134.28E
Ust Nem U.S.S.R. **44** 61.38N 54.50E
Ust Olenëk U.S.S.R. **51** 72.59N120.00E
Ust-Omchug U.S.S.R. **51** 61.08N149.38E
Ust Port U.S.S.R. **50** 69.44N 84.23E
Ust Tapsuy U.S.S.R. **44** 62.25N 61.42E
Ust'Tsilma U.S.S.R. **44** 65.28N 53.09E
Ust-Tungir U.S.S.R. **51** 55.25N120.15E
Ust Ura U.S.S.R. **44** 63.06N 44.41E
Ust Vaga U.S.S.R. **44** 62.42N 42.45E
Ust Vym U.S.S.R. **44** 62.15N 50.25E
Ustyurt, Plato *f.* U.S.S.R. **45** 43.30N 55.00E
Usu China **52** 44.27N 84.37E
Usumacinta *r.* Mexico **116** 18.22N 92.40W
U.S. Virgin Is. C. America **117** 18.30N 65.00W
Ut U.S.S.R. **37** 52.18N 31.10E
Utah *d.* U.S.A. **108** 39.37N112.28W
Utah L. U.S.A. **108** 40.13N111.49W
'Uta Vava'u Tonga **85** 18.35S174.00W
'Utaybah, Buḩayrat al *l.* Syria **66** 33.31N 36.37E
Utembo *r.* Angola **78** 17.03S 22.00E
Utengule Tanzania **79** 8.55S 35.43E
Utersum Germany **38** 54.43N 8.24E
Utete Tanzania **79** 8.00S 38.49E
Uthal Pakistan **62** 25.48N 66.37E
Utiariti Brazil **122** 13.02S 58.17W
Utica Kans. U.S.A. **110** 38.39N100.10W
Utica Mich. U.S.A. **114** 42.38N 83.02W
Utica N.Y. U.S.A. **115** 43.05N 75.14W
Utica Ohio U.S.A. **114** 40.14N 82.27W
Utiel Spain **25** 39.34N 1.12W
Utikuma L. Canada **100** 55.50N115.30W
Utique Tunisia **32** 37.03N 10.03E
Utö *i.* Sweden **43** 58.56N 18.16E
Utopia Australia **90** 22.14S134.33E
Utraula India **63** 27.19N 82.25E
Utrecht Neth. **16** 52.04N 5.07E
Utrecht *d.* Neth. **16** 52.04N 5.10E
Utrecht R.S.A. **80** 27.38S 30.19E
Utrera Spain **27** 37.11N 5.47W
Utsira Norway **42** 59.18N 4.54E
Utsjoki Finland **40** 69.53N 27.00E
Utsunomiya Japan **57** 36.40N139.52E
Utta U.S.S.R. **45** 46.24N 46.01E
Uttaradit Thailand **56** 17.38N100.05E
Uttarkāshi India **63** 30.44N 78.27E
Uttar Pradesh *d.* India **63** 26.30N 81.30E
Utterson Canada **104** 45.13N 79.20W
Uturoà Îs. de la Société **85** 16.44S151.25W
Uummanarsuaq *see* Farvel, K. *c.* Greenland **99**
Uusikaupunki Finland **41** 60.48N 21.25E
Uusimaa *d.* Finland **41** 60.30N 25.00E
Uvalde U.S.A. **111** 29.13N 99.47W
Uvarovichi U.S.S.R. **37** 52.35N 30.44E
Uvat U.S.S.R. **50** 59.10N 68.49E
Uvdal Norway **42** 60.16N 8.44E
Uvéa, Île *i.* N. Cal. **84** 20.30S166.35E
Uvinza Tanzania **79** 5.08S 30.23E
Uvira Zaïre **79** 3.22S 29.06E
Uvs Nuur *l.* Mongolia **52** 50.30N 92.30E
Uwajima Japan **57** 33.13N132.32E
Uwayl Sudan **73** 8.46N 27.24E
'Uwaynāt, Jabal al *mtn.* Libya / Sudan **72** 21.54N 24.58E
Uxbridge Canada **104** 44.06N 79.07W
Uxin Qi China **54** 38.30N108.53E
Uyo Nigeria **77** 5.01N 7.56E
Uyuni Bolivia **124** 20.28S 66.50W
Uyuni, Salar de *f.* Bolivia **124** 20.20S 67.42W
Uzbekskaya S.S.R. *d.* U.S.S.R. **9** 42.00N 63.00E
Uzda U.S.S.R. **37** 53.28N 27.11E
Uzerche France **20** 45.26N 1.34E
Uzès France **21** 44.01N 4.25E
Uzh *r.* U.S.S.R. **37** 51.15N 30.12E
Uzhgorod U.S.S.R. **37** 48.38N 22.15E
Uzunköpru Turkey **34** 41.16N 26.41E

Vä Sweden **43** 55.59N 14.05E
Vaagö *i.* Faroe Is. **10** 62.03N 7.14W
Vaal *r.* R.S.A. **80** 29.04S 23.37E
Vaala Finland **40** 64.26N 26.48E
Vaal Dam R.S.A. **80** 26.51S 28.08E
Vaasa Finland **40** 63.06N 21.36E
Vaasa *d.* Finland **40** 62.50N 22.50E
Vác Hungary **37** 47.49N 19.10E
Vaccarès, Étang de *b.* France **21** 43.32N 4.34E
Vadodara India **60** 22.19N 73.14E
Vado Ligure Italy **30** 44.17N 8.27E
Vadsö Norway **40** 70.05N 29.46E
Vadstena Sweden **43** 58.27N 14.54E
Vaduz Liech. **39** 47.09N 9.31E
Vaeröy *i.* Norway **40** 67.40N 12.40E
Vaga *r.* U.S.S.R. **44** 62.45N 42.48E
Vågåmo Norway **41** 61.53N 9.06E
Vaganski Vrh *mtn.* Yugo. **31** 44.22N 15.31E
Vaggeryd Sweden **43** 57.30N 14.07E
Váh *r.* Czech. **37** 47.40N 17.50E
Vahsel B. Antarctica **128** 77.00S 38.00W
Vaiea Niue **84** 19.08S169.53W
Vaihu I. de Pascua **85** 27.10S109.22W
Vaijāpur India **62** 19.55N 74.44E
Vailly-sur-Aisne France **19** 49.25N 3.31E
Vairao Tahiti **85** 17.48S149.17W
Vaison-la-Romaine France **21** 44.14N 5.04E
Vaitupu *i.* Tuvalu **84** 7.28S178.41E
Vakaga C.A.R. **73** 9.50N 22.30E
Vakarai Sri Lanka **61** 8.08N 81.26E
Vålådalen Sweden **40** 63.09N 13.00E
Valais *d.* Switz. **39** 46.00N 7.20E
Valandovo Yugo. **34** 41.19N 22.34E
Valatie U.S.A. **115** 42.25N 73.41W
Valavsk U.S.S.R. **37** 51.40N 28.38E
Val Barrette Canada **105** 46.31N 75.22W
Välberg Sweden **43** 59.24N 13.12E
Valcartier Canada **105** 46.56N 71.27W
Valcheta Argentina **125** 40.40S 66.10W
Valdagno Italy **30** 45.39N 11.18E
Valdavia *r.* Spain **26** 42.24N 4.16W
Valday U.S.S.R. **44** 57.59N 33.10E
Valdayskaya Vozvyshennost *mts.* U.S.S.R. **44** 57.10N 33.00E
Valdecañas, Embalse de *resr.* Spain **27** 39.45N 5.30W
Valdemārpils U.S.S.R. **41** 57.22N 22.35E
Valdemarsvik Sweden **43** 58.12N 16.36E
Valdepeñas Spain **26** 38.46N 3.23W
Valderaduey *r.* Spain **26** 41.31N 5.42W
Valderas Spain **26** 42.05N 5.27W
Valderrobres Spain **25** 40.53N 0.09W
Valdés, Pen. Argentina **125** 42.30S 64.00W
Val des Bois Canada **105** 45.54N 75.35W
Valdez U.S.A. **98** 61.07N146.17W
Val di Mazara *f.* Italy **32** 37.50N 13.00E
Val di Noto *f.* Italy **33** 36.54N 14.45E
Val d'Isère France **21** 45.27N 6.59E
Valdivia Chile **125** 39.46S 73.15W
Val d'Oise *d.* France **19** 49.10N 2.10E
Val d'Or *town* Canada **102** 48.07N 77.47W
Valdosta U.S.A. **113** 30.51N 83.51W
Valdoviño Spain **26** 43.36N 8.08W
Valença Bahia Brazil **123** 13.22S 39.06W
Valença R. de Janeiro Brazil **126** 22.14S 43.45W
Valença Portugal **26** 42.02N 8.38W
Valençay France **19** 47.09N 1.34E
Valence France **21** 44.56N 4.54E
Valencia Spain **25** 39.28N 0.22W
Valencia *d.* Spain **25** 39.20N 0.45W
Valencia Venezuela **122** 10.14N 67.59W
Valencia, Golfo de *g.* Spain **25** 39.30N 0.20W
Valencia de Alcántara Spain **27** 39.25N 7.14W
Valencia de Don Juan Spain **26** 42.18N 5.31W
Valenciennes France **19** 50.21N 3.32E
Valentin U.S.S.R. **57** 43.09N134.15E
Valentine Nebr. U.S.A. **110** 42.52N100.30W
Valentine N.Mex. U.S.A. **109** 30.34N104.29W
Vale of Evesham *f.* U.K. **13** 52.05N 1.55W
Vale of Pewsey *f.* U.K. **13** 51.21N 1.45W
Vale of York *f.* U.K. **12** 54.12N 1.25W
Valera Venezuela **122** 9.21N 70.38W
Valga U.S.S.R. **44** 57.44N 26.00E
Valguarnera Caropepe Italy **33** 37.30N 14.24E
Valinco, Golfe de *g.* France **21** 41.40N 8.50E
Valjevo Yugo. **31** 44.16N 19.53E
Valkeakoski Finland **41** 61.16N 24.02E
Valkenswaard Neth. **16** 51.21N 5.27E
Valladolid Mexico **117** 20.41N 88.12W
Valladolid Spain **26** 41.39N 4.43W
Valladolid *d.* Spain **26** 41.45N 4.50W
Vall de Uxó Spain **25** 39.49N 0.14W
Valle Norway **42** 59.12N 7.32E
Valle d'Aosta *d.* Italy **30** 45.50N 7.25E
Valle de Cabuérniga Spain **26** 43.14N 4.18W
Valle de la Pascua Venezuela **122** 9.15N 66.00W
Valledupar Colombia **122** 10.31N 73.16W
Valle Edén Uruguay **125** 31.50S 56.09W
Vallegrande Bolivia **124** 18.29S 64.06W
Valle Hermoso Mexico **111** 25.39N 97.52W
Vallenar Chile **124** 28.35S 70.46W
Vallentuna Sweden **43** 59.32N 18.05E
Vallet France **18** 47.10N 1.16W
Valletta Malta **28** 35.53N 14.31E
Valley City U.S.A. **110** 46.57N 97.58W
Valley Falls *town* U.S.A. **108** 42.29N120.16W
Valleyfield Canada **105** 45.15N 74.08W
Valley Head *town* U.S.A. **114** 38.33N 80.02W
Valley Stream *town* U.S.A. **115** 40.40N 73.42W
Valleyview Canada **100** 55.04N117.17W
Vallgrund *i.* Finland **40** 63.12N 21.14E
Vallo della Lucania Italy **33** 40.14N 15.17E
Vallon France **21** 44.24N 4.24E
Vallorbe Switz. **19** 46.43N 6.22E
Valls Spain **25** 41.17N 1.15E
Val Marie Canada **101** 49.14N107.44W
Valmiera U.S.S.R. **44** 57.32N 25.29E
Valnera *mtn.* Spain **26** 43.09N 3.40W
Valognes France **18** 49.31N 1.28W
Valongo Portugal **26** 41.11N 8.30W
Valoria la Buena Spain **26** 41.48N 4.32W
Valparaíso Chile **125** 33.02S 71.38W
Valparaíso Mexico **116** 22.46N103.34W
Valparaiso U.S.A. **113** 30.30N 86.31W
Valpovo Yugo. **31** 45.39N 18.25E
Valréas France **21** 44.23N 4.59E
Vals, Tanjung *c.* Indonesia **59** 8.30S137.30E
Valverde Dom. Rep. **117** 19.37N 71.04W
Valverde del Camino Spain **27** 37.34N 6.45W
Vammala Finland **41** 61.20N 22.54E
Vamsadhāra *r.* India **63** 18.21N 84.08E
Van Turkey **64** 38.28N 43.20E
Van Blommestein Meer, W.J. *resr.* Surinam **123** 4.45N 55.05W
Van Buren Ark. U.S.A. **111** 35.26N 94.21W
Van Buren Mo. U.S.A. **111** 37.00N 91.01W
Vancouver Canada **100** 49.20N123.10W
Vancouver U.S.A. **108** 45.39N122.40W
Vancouver I. Canada **100** 49.45N126.00W
Vandalia Ill. U.S.A. **110** 38.58N 89.06W
Vandalia Mo. U.S.A. **110** 39.19N 91.29W
Vanderbilt U.S.A. **104** 45.09N 84.40W
Vandergrift U.S.A. **114** 40.36N 79.34W
Vanderlin I. Australia **90** 15.44S137.02E
Van Diemen, C. Australia **90** 16.31S139.41E
Van Diemen G. Australia **90** 11.50S132.00E
Vandry Canada **103** 47.50N 73.34W
Vänern *l.* Sweden **43** 58.55N 13.30E
Vänersborg Sweden **43** 58.22N 12.19E
Vang Norway **41** 61.10N 8.40E
Vanga Kenya **79** 4.37S 39.13E
Vangaindrano Madagascar **81** 23.21S 47.36E
Van Gölü *l.* Turkey **64** 38.35N 42.52E
Vanier Canada **105** 45.26N 75.40W
Vanimo P.N.G. **59** 2.40S141.17E
Vankarem U.S.S.R. **51** 67.50N175.51E
Vankleek Hill *town* Canada **105** 45.31N 74.39W
Vanna *i.* Norway **40** 70.10N 19.40E
Vännäs Sweden **40** 63.58N 19.48E
Vannes France **18** 47.39N 2.46W
Vanoise, Massif de la *mts.* France **21** 45.20N 6.40E
Vanrhynsdorp R.S.A. **80** 31.37S 18.42E
Vansbro Sweden **41** 60.31N 14.13E
Vantaa Finland **41** 60.13N 25.01E
Van Tassell U.S.A. **108** 42.40N104.02W
Vanthali India **62** 21.29N 70.20E
Vanua Levu *i.* Fiji **84** 16.33S179.15E
Vanua Mbalavu *i.* Fiji **84** 17.40S178.57W
Vanuatu Pacific Oc. **84** 16.00S167.00E
Van Wert U.S.A. **112** 40.53N 84.36W

Vanzylsrus to **Villé**

Vanzylsrus R.S.A. **80** 26.51S 22.03E
Vapnyarka U.S.S.R. **37** 48.31N 28.44E
Var d. France **21** 43.30N 6.20E
Var r. France **21** 43.39N 7.11E
Vara Sweden **43** 58.16N 12.57E
Varades France **18** 47.23N 1.02W
Varallo Italy **30** 45.49N 8.15E
Varāmīn Iran **65** 35.20N 51.39E
Vārānasi India **63** 25.20N 83.00E
Varangerfjorden est. Norway **40** 70.00N 30.00E
Varangerhalvöya pen. Norway **40** 70.25N 29.30E
Varano, Lago di l. Italy **33** 41.53N 15.45E
Varaždin Yugo. **31** 46.19N 16.20E
Varazze Italy **30** 44.22N 8.34E
Varberg Sweden **43** 57.06N 12.15E
Vardak d. Afghan. **62** 34.15N 68.30E
Vardar r. Yugo. see Axios r. Greece **34**
Varde Denmark **42** 55.38N 8.29E
Vardhoúsia Óri mts. Greece **35** 38.44N 22.07E
Varel Germany **38** 53.24N 8.08E
Varennes Canada **105** 45.41N 73.26W
Varennes France **20** 46.19N 3.24E
Vareš Yugo. **31** 44.09N 18.19E
Varese Italy **30** 45.48N 8.48E
Varese Ligure Italy **30** 44.22N 9.37E
Vårgårda Sweden **43** 58.02N 12.48E
Varginha Brazil **126** 21.33S 45.25W
Vargön Sweden **43** 58.22N 12.22E
Varkhān r. Afghan. **62** 32.55N 65.30E
Varley Australia **89** 32.48S119.31E
Värmeln l. Sweden **43** 59.32N 12.54E
Värmland d. Sweden **43** 59.45N 13.15E
Värmland f. Sweden **43** 60.05N 13.25E
Värmlandsnäs c. Sweden **43** 59.00N 13.10E
Varna Bulgaria **37** 43.13N 27.57E
Värnamo Sweden **43** 57.11N 14.02E
Varnsdorf Germany **38** 50.52N 14.40E
Värö Sweden **43** 57.16N 12.11E
Várpalota Hungary **37** 47.12N 18.09E
Vartofta Sweden **43** 58.06N 13.40E
Varvarin Yugo. **34** 43.43N 21.19E
Varzo Italy **30** 46.12N 8.15E
Varzy France **19** 47.22N 3.23E
Vasa see Vaasa Finland **40**
Vasai India **62** 19.21N 72.48E
Vascão r. Portugal **27** 37.31N 7.31W
Vashka r. U.S.S.R. **44** 64.55N 45.50E
Vasilika Greece **34** 40.28N 23.08E
Vasilkov U.S.S.R. **37** 50.12N 30.15E
Vaslui Romania **37** 46.38N 27.44E
Väsman l. Sweden **43** 60.11N 15.04E
Vassar U.S.A. **104** 43.22N 83.35W
Västerås Sweden **43** 59.37N 16.33E
Västerbotten d. Sweden **40** 64.50N 18.10E
Västerdal r. Sweden **41** 60.33N 15.08E
Västergötland Sweden **43** 58.01N 13.03E
Västerhaninge Sweden **43** 59.07N 18.06E
Västernorrland d. Sweden **40** 63.20N 17.30E
Västervik Sweden **43** 57.45N 16.38E
Västmanland d. Sweden **43** 59.53N 16.20E
Västmanland f. Sweden **43** 59.47N 15.45E
Vasto Italy **33** 42.07N 14.42E
Vasvár Hungary **31** 47.03N 16.49E
Vatan France **19** 47.05N 1.48E
Váthia Greece **35** 36.29N 22.29E
Vatican City Europe **32** 41.54N 12.27E
Vaticano, Capo c. Italy **33** 38.38N 15.50E
Vatnajökull mts. Iceland **40** 64.20N 17.00W
Vatneyri Iceland **40** 65.36N 23.59W
Vatomandry Madagascar **81** 19.20S 48.59E
Vatra Dornei Romania **37** 47.21N 25.21E
Vättern l. Sweden **43** 58.24N 14.36E
Vaucluse d. France **21** 44.00N 5.20E
Vaucouleurs France **19** 48.36N 5.40E
Vaud d. Switz. **39** 46.38N 6.30E
Vaughan Canada **104** 43.50N 79.32W
Vaughn Mont. U.S.A. **108** 47.35N111.34W
Vaughn N.Mex. U.S.A. **109** 34.36N105.13W
Vaupés r. Colombia **122** 0.20N 69.00W
Vauvert France **21** 43.42N 4.17E
Vava'u Group is. Tonga **85** 18.40S174.00W
Vavuniya Sri Lanka **61** 8.45N 80.30E
Växjö Sweden **43** 56.52N 14.49E
Vaygach U.S.S.R. **50** 70.28N 58.59E
Vaygach, Ostrov i. U.S.S.R. **44** 70.00N 59.00E
Vecht r. Neth. **16** 52.39N 6.01E
Vechta Germany **38** 52.43N 8.16E
Vecsés Hungary **37** 47.26N 19.19E
Veddige Sweden **43** 57.16N 12.19E
Vedea r. Romania **34** 44.00N 25.20E
Veendam Neth. **16** 53.08N 6.52E
Veenendaal Neth. **16** 52.03N 5.32E
Vega i. Norway **40** 65.39N 11.50E
Vega U.S.A. **111** 35.15N102.26W
Vegarsvatn l. Norway **42** 58.50N 8.50E
Veghel Neth. **16** 51.37N 5.35E
Vegreville Canada **100** 53.30N112.05W
Veinticinco de Mayo Argentina **125** 35.25S 60.11W
Vejen Denmark **42** 55.29N 9.09E
Vejer Spain **27** 36.15N 5.58W
Vejle Denmark **42** 55.42N 9.32E
Vela Luka Yugo. **31** 42.58N 16.43E
Velddrif R.S.A. **80** 32.47S 18.09E
Velebit Planina mts. Yugo. **31** 44.35N 15.00E
Velebitski Kanal str. Yugo. **31** 44.40N 14.55E
Velenje Yugo. **31** 46.21N 15.06E
Velestínon Greece **35** 39.23N 22.45E
Vélez-Málaga Spain **27** 36.47N 4.06W
Vélez Rubio Spain **25** 37.39N 2.04W
Velhas r. Brazil **126** 17.20S 44.55W
Velika Gorica Yugo. **31** 45.43N 16.05E
Velika Kapela mts. Yugo. **31** 45.20N 15.00E
Velike Lašče Yugo. **31** 45.50N 14.38E
Veliki Canal Yugo. **31** 45.45N 19.07E
Veliki Vitorog mtn. Yugo. **31** 44.07N 17.03E
Velikiye-Luki U.S.S.R. **44** 56.19N 30.31E
Velikiy Ustyug U.S.S.R. **44** 60.48N 45.15E
Veliko Tŭrnovo Bulgaria **34** 43.05N 25.41E
Veli Lošinj Yugo. **31** 44.31N 14.30E
Velingrad Bulgaria **34** 42.04N 23.58E
Velino, Monte mtn. Italy **30** 42.09N 13.23E
Velizh U.S.S.R. **44** 55.36N 31.13E
Velletri Italy **30** 41.41N 12.47E
Vellinge Sweden **43** 55.28N 13.01E
Vellore India **61** 12.56N 79.09E
Velsen Neth. **16** 52.28N 4.39E
Velsk U.S.S.R. **44** 61.05N 42.06E
Velten Germany **38** 52.41N 13.10E
Veluwe f. Neth. **16** 52.17N 5.45E
Velvendós Greece **34** 40.15N 22.06E
Vemdalen Sweden **40** 62.29N 13.55E
Ven i. Sweden **43** 55.54N 12.41E
Venaco France **21** 42.14N 9.10E
Venado Tuerto Argentina **125** 33.45S 61.56W
Venafro Italy **33** 41.29N 14.02E
Venaria Italy **30** 45.08N 7.38E
Vence France **21** 43.43N 7.07E
Venda Africa **80** 22.40S 30.40E
Venda Nova Portugal **26** 41.40N 7.58W
Vendas Novas Portugal **27** 38.41N 8.28W
Vendée d. France **18** 46.40N 1.20W
Vendée f. France **18** 46.40N 1.10W
Vendée r. France **18** 46.30N 0.45W
Vendeuvre-sur-Barse France **19** 48.14N 4.28E
Vendôme France **18** 47.48N 1.04E
Vendsyssel f. Denmark **42** 57.20N 10.00E
Veneto d. Italy **30** 45.50N 12.00E
Venev U.S.S.R. **44** 54.22N 38.15E
Venezia Italy **30** 45.26N 12.20E
Venezuela S. America **122** 7.00N 65.20W
Venezuela, Golfo de g. Venezuela **122** 11.30N 71.00W
Venezuelan Basin f. Carib. Sea. **127** 14.30N 68.00W
Vengurla India **60** 15.52N 73.38E
Veniaminof Mtn. U.S.A. **98** 56.05N159.20W
Venice see Venezia Italy **30**
Venice U.S.A. **113** 27.05N 82.26W
Venice, G. of Med. Sea **30** 45.20N 13.00E
Vénissieux France **21** 45.41N 4.53E
Venlo Neth. **16** 51.22N 6.10E
Vennesla Norway **42** 58.17N 7.59E
Venosa Italy **33** 40.57N 15.49E
Venraij Neth. **16** 51.32N 5.58E
Vent Austria **30** 46.52N 10.55E
Vent, Îles du is. Îs. de la Société **85** 17.30S149.30W
Venta r. U.S.S.R. **41** 57.24N 21.33E
Ventersdorp R.S.A. **80** 26.19S 26.48E
Ventimiglia Italy **30** 43.47N 7.36E
Ventnor U.K. **13** 50.35N 1.12W
Ventspils U.S.S.R. **41** 57.24N 21.36E
Ventuari r. Venezuela **122** 4.00N 67.35W
Venus B. Australia **93** 38.40S145.43E
Vera Argentina **126** 29.31S 60.30W
Vera Spain **27** 37.15N 1.51W
Veracruz Mexico **116** 19.11N 96.10W
Veracruz d. Mexico **116** 18.00N 95.00W
Verāval India **62** 20.54N 70.22E
Verbania Italy **30** 45.56N 8.33E
Vercel France **19** 47.11N 6.23E
Vercelli Italy **30** 45.19N 8.25E
Vercors d. France **21** 44.57N 5.25E
Verde r. Argentina **125** 42.10S 65.03W
Verde r. Brazil **124** 19.11S 50.44W
Verden Germany **38** 52.55N 9.13E
Verdhikoúsa Greece **34** 39.47N 21.59E
Verdon r. France **21** 43.43N 5.46E
Verdun Canada **105** 45.27N 73.34W
Verdun Meuse France **19** 49.10N 5.23E
Verdun T.G. France **20** 43.52N 1.14E
Verdun-sur-le-Doubs France **19** 46.54N 5.01E
Vereeniging R.S.A. **80** 26.40S 27.55E
Vergara Spain **26** 43.07N 2.25W
Vergelee R.S.A. **80** 25.46S 24.09E
Vergennes U.S.A. **105** 44.10N 73.15W
Vergoritis, Límni l. Greece **34** 40.45N 21.49E
Vergt France **20** 45.02N 0.43E
Verín Spain **26** 41.56N 7.26W
Verkhniy Baskunchak U.S.S.R. **45** 48.14N 46.44E
Verkhniy Lyulyukary U.S.S.R. **44** 65.45N 64.28E
Verkhniy Shar U.S.S.R. **44** 68.21N 50.45E
Verkhniy Ufaley U.S.S.R. **44** 56.05N 60.14E
Verkhnyaya Taymyra r. U.S.S.R. **51** 74.10N 99.50E
Verkhnyaya Tura U.S.S.R. **44** 58.22N 59.50E
Verkhovye U.S.S.R. **44** 52.49N 37.14E
Verkhoyansk U.S.S.R. **51** 67.25N133.25E
Verkhoyanskiy Khrebet mts. U.S.S.R. **51** 66.00N130.00E
Vermenton France **19** 47.40N 3.44E
Vermilion Canada **101** 53.22N110.51W
Vermilion r. Canada **104** 46.16N 81.41W
Vermilion U.S.A. **114** 41.25N 82.22W
Vermilion Bay town Canada **102** 49.51N 93.24W
Vermilion Chutes Canada **100** 58.22N114.51W
Vermillion U.S.A. **110** 42.48N 96.55W
Vermont d. U.S.A. **105** 43.50N 72.45W
Vernal U.S.A. **108** 40.27N109.32W
Verner Canada **104** 46.25N 80.07W
Verneuil France **18** 48.44N 0.56E
Vernon Canada **100** 50.20N119.15W
Vernon France **18** 49.05N 1.29E
Vernon U.S.A. **111** 34.09N 99.17W
Verny France **19** 49.01N 6.12E
Vero r. Spain **25** 42.00N 0.10E
Vero Beach town U.S.A. **113** 27.39N 80.24W
Véroia Greece **34** 40.31N 22.12E
Verona Italy **30** 45.27N 11.00E
Verónica Argentina **125** 35.24S 57.22W
Verrès Italy **30** 45.40N 7.42E
Versailles France **19** 48.48N 2.08E
Versailles U.S.A. **113** 38.02N 84.45W
Vert, Cap c. Senegal **76** 14.45N 17.25W
Verteillac France **20** 45.21N 0.22E
Vertou France **18** 47.10N 1.29W
Vertus France **19** 48.54N 4.00E
Vervey Switz. **39** 46.28N 6.51E
Verviers Belgium **16** 50.36N 5.52E
Vervins France **19** 49.50N 3.54E
Vesanto Finland **40** 62.56N 26.25E
Vescovato France **21** 42.30N 9.26E
Veselí nad Lužnicí Czech. **36** 49.11N 14.43E
Vesle r. France **19** 49.23N 3.38E
Vesoul France **19** 47.38N 6.10E
Vest-Agder d. Norway **42** 58.45N 7.00E
Vestbygd Norway **42** 58.06N 6.35E
Vesterö Havn Denmark **42** 57.18N 10.56E
Vestfjorden est. Norway **40** 68.10N 15.00E
Vestfold d. Norway **42** 59.20N 10.10E
Vestmanhavn Faroe Is. **10** 62.09N 7.11W
Vestmannaeyjar is. Iceland **40** 63.30N 20.20W
Vestvågöy i. Norway **40** 68.10N 13.50E
Vesuvio mtn. Italy **33** 40.49N 14.26E
Vesyegonsk U.S.S.R. **44** 58.38N 37.19E
Veszprém Hungary **37** 47.06N 17.55E
Vésztö Hungary **37** 46.55N 21.16E
Vetka U.S.S.R. **37** 52.35N 31.13E
Vetlanda Sweden **43** 57.26N 15.04E
Vetluga U.S.S.R. **44** 57.50N 45.42E
Vetluga r. U.S.S.R. **44** 56.18N 46.19E
Vetovo Bulgaria **34** 43.42N 26.16E
Vetralla Italy **30** 42.19N 12.03E
Vetren Bulgaria **34** 42.15N 24.03E
Vetschau Germany **38** 51.47N 14.04E
Vettore, Monte mtn. Italy **30** 42.49N 13.16E
Veurne Belgium **16** 51.04N 2.40E
Vevelstad Norway **40** 65.43N 12.30E
Vevey Switz. **19** 46.28N 6.51E
Vévi Greece **34** 40.47N 21.38E
Veynes France **21** 44.32N 5.49E
Vézelise France **19** 48.29N 6.05E
Vézère r. France **20** 44.53N 0.53E
Vezhen mtn. Bulgaria **34** 42.50N 24.20E
Viacha Bolivia **122** 16.40S 68.17W
Viadana Italy **30** 44.56N 10.31E
Viana Brazil **123** 3.13S 45.00W
Viana Portugal **27** 38.20N 8.00W
Viana del Bollo Spain **26** 42.11N 7.06W
Viana do Castelo Portugal **26** 41.42N 8.50W
Viana do Castelo d. Portugal **26** 41.55N 8.30W
Viangchan see Vientiane Laos **56**
Viar r. Spain **27** 37.36N 5.50W
Viareggio Italy **30** 43.52N 10.14E
Viaur r. France **20** 44.08N 2.23E
Viborg Denmark **42** 56.26N 9.24E
Vibo Valentia Italy **33** 38.40N 16.06E
Vibraye France **18** 48.03N 0.44E
Vic Spain **25** 41.56N 2.15E
Vic-en-Bigorre France **20** 43.06N 0.05E
Vicente López Argentina **125** 34.32S 58.29W
Vicenza Italy **30** 45.33N 11.33E
Vich see Vic Spain **25**
Vichada r. Colombia **122** 4.58N 67.35W
Vichuga U.S.S.R. **44** 57.12N 41.50E
Vichy France **20** 46.08N 3.26E
Vicksburg U.S.A. **111** 32.14N 90.56W
Vico France **21** 42.10N 8.48E
Viçosa Alagoas Brazil **123** 9.22S 36.10W
Viçosa Minas Gerais Brazil **126** 20.45S 42.53W
Vic-sur-Cère France **20** 44.59N 2.37E
Victor U.S.A. **114** 42.59N 77.24W
Victor Harbor Australia **92** 35.36S138.35E
Victoria Argentina **125** 32.40S 60.10W
Victoria d. Australia **93** 37.20S145.00E
Victoria r. Australia **88** 15.12S129.43E
Victoria Canada **100** 48.30N123.25W
Victoria Chile **125** 38.13S 72.20W
Victoria Guinea **76** 10.50N 14.32W
Victoria Hong Kong **48** 22.16N114.15E
Victoria U.S.A. **111** 28.48N 97.00W
Victoria, L. Africa **79** 1.00S 33.00E
Victoria, L. Australia **92** 34.00S141.15E
Victoria, Mt. Burma **56** 21.12N 93.55E
Victoria, Mt. P.N.G. **90** 8.55S147.35E
Victoria Beach town Canada **101** 50.43N 96.33W
Victoria de las Tunas Cuba **117** 20.58N 76.59W
Victoria Falls f. Zimbabwe / Zambia **80** 17.58S 25.45E
Victoria Harbour Canada **104** 44.45N 79.46W
Victoria I. Canada **98** 71.00N110.00W
Victoria L. Australia **92** 32.29S143.22E
Victoria Nile r. Uganda **79** 2.14N 31.20E
Victoria River town Australia **88** 15.36S131.06E
Victoria River Downs town Australia **90** 16.24S131.00E
Victoriaville Canada **105** 46.03N 71.57W
Victoria West R.S.A. **80** 31.24S 23.07E
Victorica Argentina **125** 36.15S 65.25W
Vidalia U.S.A. **113** 32.14N 82.24W
Vidauban France **21** 43.26N 6.26E
Videbaek Denmark **42** 56.05N 8.38E
Videle Romania **37** 44.16N 25.31E
Viderö i. Faroe Is. **10** 62.21N 6.30W
Vidigueira Portugal **27** 38.13N 7.48W
Vidin Bulgaria **34** 43.59N 22.52E
Vidisha India **63** 23.32N 77.49E
Vidöstern l. Sweden **43** 57.04N 14.01E
Viechtach Germany **39** 49.05N 12.53E
Viedma Argentina **125** 40.50S 63.00W
Viedma, L. Argentina **125** 49.40S 72.30W
Vieira do Minho Portugal **26** 41.39N 8.09W
Viella Spain **25** 42.42N 0.48E
Vienna see Wien Austria **36**
Vienna Md. U.S.A. **115** 38.29N 75.49W
Vienna S.Dak. U.S.A. **110** 44.42N 97.30W
Vienna Va. U.S.A. **114** 38.54N 77.16W
Vienne d. France **18** 46.35N 0.30E
Vienne r. France **18** 47.13N 0.05E
Vientiane Laos **56** 17.59N102.38E
Vieques i. Puerto Rico **117** 18.08N 65.30W
Viernheim Germany **39** 49.33N 8.39E
Viersen Germany **38** 51.15N 6.23E
Vierwaldstätter See l. Switz. **39** 47.00N 8.28E
Vierzon France **19** 47.13N 2.05E
Vieste Italy **31** 41.53N 16.10E
Vietnam Asia **56** 15.00N108.30E
Viet Tri Vietnam **55** 21.20N105.26E
Vieux-Condé France **16** 50.29N 3.31E
Vif France **21** 45.03N 5.40E
Vigan France **20** 43.59N 3.35E
Vigan Phil. **59** 17.35N120.23E
Vigeland Norway **42** 58.05N 7.18E
Vigevano Italy **30** 45.19N 8.51E
Vignemale, Pic de mtn. France **20** 42.46N 0.08W
Vigneulles-lès-Hattonchâtel France **19** 48.59N 5.43E
Vigo Spain **26** 42.14N 8.43W
Vigo, Ría de est. Spain **26** 42.15N 8.45W
Vigrestad Norway **42** 58.34N 5.42E
Vihāri Pakistan **62** 30.02N 72.21E
Vihiers France **18** 47.09N 0.32W
Vihowa Pakistan **62** 31.08N 70.30E
Vijāpur India **62** 23.35N 72.45E
Vijayawāda India **61** 16.34N 80.40E
Vik Norway **40** 65.19N 12.10E
Vikajärvi Finland **40** 66.37N 26.12E
Vikeke Indonesia **59** 8.42S126.30E
Viken Sweden **43** 56.09N 12.34E
Viken l. Sweden **43** 58.39N 14.20E
Vikersund Norway **42** 59.59N 10.02E
Vikmanshyttan Sweden **43** 60.17N 15.49E
Vikna i. Norway **40** 64.52N 10.57E
Vikulovo U.S.S.R. **50** 56.51N 70.30E
Vila Vanuatu **84** 17.44S168.19E
Vila da Maganja Mozambique **79** 17.25S 37.32E
Vila de Rei Portugal **27** 39.40N 8.09W
Vila do Bispo Portugal **27** 37.05N 8.55W
Vila do Conde Portugal **26** 41.21N 8.45W
Vila Flor Portugal **26** 41.18N 7.09W
Vila Franca Portugal **27** 38.57N 8.59W
Vilafranca del Penedès Spain **25** 41.21N 1.42E
Vilaine r. France **18** 47.30N 2.27W
Vilanculos Mozambique **81** 21.59S 35.16E
Vila Nova de Famalicão Portugal **26** 41.25N 8.32W
Vila Nova de Fozcoa Portugal **26** 41.05N 7.12W
Vila Nova de Gaia Portugal **26** 41.45N 8.34W
Vila Nova de Ourém Portugal **27** 39.39N 8.35W
Vilanova i La Geltrú Spain **25** 41.14N 1.44E
Vila Real Portugal **26** 41.18N 7.45W
Vila Real d. Portugal **26** 41.35N 7.35W
Vila Real de Santo António Portugal **27** 37.12N 7.25W
Vilar Formoso Portugal **26** 40.35N 6.53W
Vila Velha Brazil **126** 20.20S 40.17W
Vila Velha de Ródão Portugal **27** 39.38N 7.40W
Vila Verde Portugal **26** 41.39N 8.26W
Vila Verissimo Sarmento Angola **78** 8.08S 20.38E
Vila Viçosa Portugal **27** 38.47N 7.25W
Vildbjerg Denmark **42** 56.12N 8.46E
Vileyka U.S.S.R. **37** 54.30N 26.50E
Vilhelmina Sweden **40** 64.37N 16.39E
Vilhena Brazil **122** 12.40S 60.08W
Viliga Kushka U.S.S.R. **51** 61.35N156.55E
Viljandi U.S.S.R. **44** 58.22N 25.30E
Vilkavišhkis U.S.S.R. **37** 54.39N 23.02E
Vil'kitskogo, Proliv str. U.S.S.R. **51** 77.57N102.30E
Vilkovo U.S.S.R. **37** 45.28N 29.32E
Villa Adriana site Italy **30** 41.56N 12.45E
Villa Angela Argentina **124** 27.34S 60.45W
Villa Bella Bolivia **124** 10.23S 65.24W
Villablino Spain **26** 42.56N 6.19W
Villacañas Spain **27** 39.38N 3.20W
Villacarriedo Spain **26** 43.14N 3.48W
Villacarrillo Spain **26** 38.07N 3.05W
Villacastín Spain **26** 40.47N 4.25W
Villach Austria **31** 46.36N 13.50E
Villa Clara Argentina **125** 31.46S 58.50W
Villa Constitución Argentina **125** 33.14S 60.21W
Villada Spain **26** 42.15N 4.59W
Villa del Río Spain **27** 37.59N 4.17W
Villa de Santiago Mexico **111** 25.26N100.09W
Villadiego Spain **26** 42.31N 4.00W
Villa Dolores Argentina **124** 31.58S 65.12W
Villafranca del Bierzo Spain **26** 42.36N 6.48W
Villafranca de los Barros Spain **27** 38.34N 6.20W
Villafranca di Verona Italy **30** 45.21N 10.50E
Villagarcía Spain **26** 42.36N 8.45W
Villaguay Argentina **125** 31.55S 59.00W
Villahermosa Mexico **116** 18.00N 92.53W
Villa Hernandarias Argentina **125** 31.15S 59.58W
Villa Huidobro Argentina **125** 34.50S 64.34W
Villaines-la-Juhel France **18** 48.21N 0.17W
Villajoyosa Spain **25** 38.30N 0.14W
Villalba Spain **26** 43.18N 7.41W
Villalón de Campos Spain **26** 42.06N 5.02W
Villalpando Spain **26** 41.52N 5.24W
Villa María Argentina **124** 32.25S 63.15W
Villamartín Spain **27** 36.52N 5.38W
Villa Montes Bolivia **124** 21.15S 63.30W
Villandraut France **20** 44.28N 0.23W
Villanova Monteleone Italy **32** 40.30N 8.28E
Villanueva de Córdoba Spain **26** 38.20N 4.37W
Villanueva de la Serena Spain **26** 38.58N 5.48W
Villanueva de los Infantes Spain **27** 38.45N 3.01W
Villanueva del Río y Minas Spain **27** 37.39N 5.42W
Villaputzu Italy **32** 39.28N 9.33E
Villarcayo Spain **26** 42.56N 3.34W
Villard-de-Lans France **21** 45.04N 5.33E
Villardefrades Spain **26** 41.43N 5.15W
Villar del Arzobispo Spain **25** 39.44N 0.49W
Villarobledo Spain **27** 39.16N 2.36W
Villarreal Spain **25** 39.56N 0.06W
Villarrica Chile **125** 39.15S 72.15W
Villarrica Paraguay **126** 25.45S 56.28W
Villarrobledo Spain **24** 39.16N 2.36W
Villarrubia de los Ojos Spain **27** 39.13N 3.36W
Villa San Giovanni Italy **33** 38.13N 15.39E
Villa San José Argentina **125** 32.12S 58.15W
Villasayas Spain **26** 41.21N 2.37W
Villasimius Italy **32** 39.09N 9.31E
Villasor Italy **32** 39.22N 8.57E
Villavicencio Colombia **122** 4.09N 73.38W
Villaviciosa Spain **26** 43.29N 5.26W
Villaviciosa de Córdoba Spain **26** 38.05N 5.01W
Villazón Bolivia **124** 22.06S 65.36W
Villé France **19** 48.20N 7.18E

Villedieu France 18 48.50N 1.13W
Villefort France 20 44.26N 3.56E
Villefranche France 21 45.59N 4.43E
Villefranche-de-Rouergue France 20 44.21N 2.02E
Ville Marie Canada 104 47.19N 79.26W
Villena Spain 25 38.38N 0.51W
Villenauxe-la-Grande France 19 48.35N 3.33E
Villeneuve France 20 44.25N 0.42E
Villeneuve-d'Ascq France 19 50.37N 3.10E
Villeneuve-d'Aveyron France 20 44.26N 2.02E
Villeneuve-de-Berg France 21 44.33N 4.30E
Villeneuve-St. Georges France 19 48.44N 2.27E
Villeneuve-sur-Yonne France 19 48.05N 3.18E
Villeroy Canada 105 46.23N 71.53W
Villers Bocage France 18 49.05N 0.39W
Villers-Cotterêts France 19 49.15N 3.05E
Villersexel France 19 47.33N 6.26E
Villers sur Mer France 18 49.21N 0.02W
Villeurbanne France 21 45.46N 4.53E
Villingen Germany 39 48.03N 8.27E
Vilnius U.S.S.R. 37 54.40N 25.19E
Vils r. Germany 39 48.39N 13.11E
Vilsbiburg Germany 39 48.27N 12.12E
Vilshofen Germany 39 48.39N 13.12E
Vilvoorde Belgium 16 50.56N 4.25E
Vilyuy r. U.S.S.R. 51 64.20N126.55E
Vilyuysk U.S.S.R. 51 63.46N121.35E
Vimianzo Spain 26 43.07N 9.02W
Vimmerby Sweden 43 57.40N 15.51E
Vimoutiers France 18 48.55N 0.12E
Vimperk Czech. 38 49.03N 13.47E
Vina r. Chad 77 7.43N 15.30E
Viña del Mar Chile 125 33.02S 71.34W
Vinaroz Spain 25 40.28N 0.29E
Vincennes France 19 48.51N 2.26E
Vincennes U.S.A. 110 38.41N 87.32W
Vincent U.S.A. 114 39.23N 81.40W
Vindel r. Sweden 40 63.54N 19.52E
Vindeln Sweden 40 64.12N 19.44E
Vinderup Denmark 42 56.29N 8.47E
Vindhya Range mts. India 62 22.45N 75.30E
Vineland U.S.A. 115 39.29N 75.02W
Vineyard Haven U.S.A. 115 41.27N 70.36W
Vineyard Sd. U.S.A. 115 41.25N 70.46W
Vingåker Sweden 43 59.02N 15.52E
Vinh Vietnam 56 18.42N105.41E
Vinhais Portugal 26 41.50N 7.00W
Vinh Long Vietnam 56 10.15N105.59E
Vinica Yugo. 31 45.28N 15.15E
Vinita U.S.A. 111 36.39N 95.09W
Vinju Mare Romania 37 44.26N 22.52E
Vinkovci Yugo. 31 45.17N 18.49E
Vinnitsa U.S.S.R. 37 49.11N 28.30E
Vinson Massif Antarctica 128 78.00S 85.00W
Vintar Phil. 55 18.16N120.40E
Vinton U.S.A. 110 42.10N 92.01W
Vioolsdrif R.S.A. 80 28.45S 17.33E
Vipava Yugo. 31 45.51N 13.58E
Vipiteno Italy 30 46.54N 11.26E
Vir i. Yugo. 31 44.18N 15.04E
Virac Phil. 59 13.35N124.15E
Viramgam India 62 23.07N 72.02E
Viranşehir Turkey 64 37.13N 39.45E
Virden Canada 101 49.51N100.55W
Vire France 18 48.50N 0.53W
Vire r. France 18 49.20N 1.07W
Vírgenes, C. Argentina 125 52.00S 68.50W
Virgin Gorda i. B.V.Is. 117 18.30N 64.26W
Virginia U.S.A. 110 47.31N 92.32W
Virginia d. U.S.A. 113 37.30N 78.45W
Virginia Beach town U.S.A. 113 36.51N 75.59W
Virginia City Mont. U.S.A. 108 45.18N111.56W
Virginia City Nev. U.S.A. 108 39.19N119.39W
Virieu-le-Grand France 21 45.51N 5.39E
Virje Yugo. 31 46.04N 16.59E
Virovitica Yugo. 31 45.50N 17.23E
Virpazar Yugo. 31 42.15N 19.05E
Virrat Finland 40 62.14N 23.47E
Virserum Sweden 41 57.19N 15.35E
Virton Belgium 16 49.35N 5.32E
Virtsu U.S.S.R. 41 58.34N 23.31E
Virunga Nat. Park Zaïre 79 0.30S 29.15E
Vis Yugo. 31 43.03N 16.12E
Vis i. Yugo. 31 43.02N 16.11E
Visalia U.S.A. 109 36.20N119.18W
Visayan Sea Phil. 59 11.35N123.51E
Visby Sweden 43 57.38N 18.18E
Visconde do Rio Branco Brazil 126 21.00S 42.51W
Viscount Melville Sd. Canada 98 74.30N104.00W
Visé Belgium 16 50.44N 5.42E
Višegrad Yugo. 31 43.47N 19.17E
Viserum Sweden 43 57.21N 15.34E
Viseu Brazil 123 1.12S 46.07W
Viseu Portugal 26 40.39N 7.55W
Viseu d. Portugal 26 40.47N 7.55W
Viseu de Sus Romania 37 47.44N 24.22E
Vishākhapatnam India 61 17.42N 83.24E
Viskafors Sweden 43 57.37N 12.50E
Viskan r. Sweden 43 57.14N 12.12E
Visnagar India 62 23.42N 72.33E
Viso, Monte mtn. Italy 30 44.40N 7.07E
Visoko Yugo. 31 43.59N 18.11E
Visp Switz. 39 46.18N 7.53E
Vissefjärda Sweden 43 56.32N 15.35E
Visselhövede Germany 38 52.59N 9.35E
Vista U.S.A. 109 33.12N117.15W
Vistula r. see Wisła r. Poland 37
Vit r. Bulgaria 34 43.30N 24.30E
Vitanje Yugo. 31 46.23N 15.18E
Vitarte Peru 122 12.03S 76.51W
Vitebsk U.S.S.R. 44 55.10N 30.14E
Viterbo Italy 30 42.25N 12.06E
Viti Levu i. Fiji 84 18.00S158.00E
Vitim U.S.S.R. 51 59.28N112.35E
Vitim r. U.S.S.R. 51 59.30N112.11E
Vitória Espírito Santo Brazil 126 20.19S 40.21W
Vitoria Spain 26 42.51N 2.40W

Vitré France 18 48.08N 1.12W
Vitry-le-François France 19 48.44N 4.35E
Vitteaux France 19 47.24N 4.32E
Vittel France 19 48.12N 5.57E
Vittoria Italy 33 36.57N 14.32E
Vittorio Veneto Italy 32 45.59N 12.18E
Vittsjö Sweden 43 56.20N 13.40E
Viver Spain 25 39.55N 0.36W
Vivero Spain 26 43.38N 7.35W
Viviers France 21 44.29N 4.41E
Vivonne France 18 46.26N 0.16E
Vivonne Bay town Australia 92 35.58S137.10E
Vizcaíno, Desierto de des. Mexico 109 27.40N114.40W
Vizcaíno, Sierra mts. Mexico 109 27.20N114.30W
Vizcaya d. Spain 26 43.25N 2.45W
Vizianagaram India 61 18.07N 83.30E
Vizille France 21 45.05N 5.46E
Vižinad Yugo. 31 45.20N 13.46E
Vizzini Italy 33 37.09N 14.46E
Vjosë r. Albania 34 40.37N 19.20E
Vlaardingen Neth. 16 51.55N 4.20E
Vladičin Han Yugo. 34 42.42N 22.04E
Vladikavkaz U.S.S.R. 45 43.02N 44.43E
Vladimir U.S.S.R. 44 56.08N 40.25E
Vladimirets U.S.S.R. 37 51.28N 26.03E
Vladimir Volynskiy U.S.S.R. 37 50.51N 24.19E
Vladivostok U.S.S.R. 53 43.09N131.53E
Vlasenica Yugo. 31 44.11N 18.56E
Vlieland i. Neth. 16 53.15N 5.00E
Vlissingen Neth. 16 51.27N 3.35E
Vlorë Albania 34 40.01N 19.30E
Vlorë d. Albania 34 40.29N 19.29E
Vltava r. Czech. 39 50.21N 14.30E
Vočin Yugo. 31 45.37N 17.32E
Vöcklabruck Austria 39 48.01N 13.39E
Vodňany Czech. 39 49.09N 14.11E
Vodnjan Yugo. 31 44.57N 13.51E
Voerde Germany 16 51.37N 6.39E
Vogelkop f. see Jazirah Doberai f. Indonesia 59
Vogelsberg mts. Germany 38 50.30N 9.15E
Voghera Italy 30 44.59N 9.01E
Voh N. Cal. 84 20.58S164.42E
Vohibinany Madagascar 81 18.49S 49.04E
Vohimarina Madagascar 81 13.21S 50.02E
Vohipeno Madagascar 81 22.22S 47.51E
Voi Kenya 79 3.23S 38.35E
Void France 19 48.41N 5.37E
Voiron France 21 45.22N 5.35E
Voitsberg Austria 31 47.03N 15.10E
Vojens Denmark 42 55.15N 9.19E
Vojnić Yugo. 31 45.19N 15.43E
Volary Czech. 38 48.55N 13.54E
Volborg U.S.A. 108 45.50N105.40W
Volcano Is. Japan 84 25.00N141.00E
Volda Norway 41 62.09N 6.06E
Volga r. U.S.S.R. 45 45.45N 47.50E
Volgograd U.S.S.R. 45 48.45N 44.30E
Volgogradskoye Vodokhranilishche resr. U.S.S.R. 45 51.00N 46.05E
Volissós Greece 35 38.29N 25.58E
Volkach Germany 39 49.52N 10.13E
Volkhov U.S.S.R. 44 59.54N 32.47E
Volkhov r. U.S.S.R. 44 60.15N 32.15E
Völklingen Germany 39 49.15N 6.50E
Volkovysk U.S.S.R. 37 53.10N 24.28E
Vollenhove Neth. 16 52.41N 5.59E
Volnovakha U.S.S.R. 45 47.36N 37.32E
Volochanka U.S.S.R. 51 70.59N 94.18E
Volochisk U.S.S.R. 37 49.34N 26.10E
Volodarsk U.S.S.R. 44 56.14N 43.10E
Vologda U.S.S.R. 44 59.10N 39.55E
Volokolamsk U.S.S.R. 44 56.02N 35.56E
Volonne France 21 44.07N 6.01E
Vólos Greece 35 39.21N 22.56E
Volovets U.S.S.R. 37 48.44N 23.14E
Volsk U.S.S.R. 44 52.04N 47.22E
Volta d. Ghana 76 7.03N 0.25E
Volta r. Ghana 76 5.50N 0.41E
Volta, L. Ghana 76 7.00N 0.00
Volta-Noire d. Burkina 76 12.30N 3.25W
Volta Redonda Brazil 126 22.31S 44.05W
Volterra Italy 30 43.24N 10.51E
Voltri Italy 30 44.26N 8.45E
Volturno r. Italy 33 41.01N 13.55E
Volvi, Límni i. Greece 34 40.41N 23.23E
Volyně Czech. 38 49.10N 13.53E
Volzhskiy U.S.S.R. 45 48.48N 44.45E
Vondrozo Madagascar 81 22.49S 47.20E
Vónitsa Greece 35 38.53N 20.58E
Voorburg Neth. 16 52.05N 4.22E
Vopnafjördhur isd. Iceland 40 65.50N 14.30W
Vopnafjördhur town Iceland 40 65.46N 14.50W
Vorarlberg d. Austria 39 47.13N 9.55E
Vorderrhein r. Switz. 39 46.49N 9.25E
Vordingborg Denmark 42 55.01N 11.55E
Voríai Sporádhes is. Greece 35 39.17N 23.23E
Vórios-Evvoïkós Kólpos b. Greece 35 38.45N 23.15E
Vorkuta U.S.S.R. 44 67.27N 64.00E
Vorma r. Norway 42 60.09N 11.27E
Vormsi i. U.S.S.R. 41 59.00N 23.20E
Voronezh U.S.S.R. 45 51.40N 39.13E
Voronovo U.S.S.R. 37 54.09N 25.19E
Vosges d. France 19 48.10N 6.20E
Vosges mts. France 19 48.30N 7.10E
Voss Norway 41 60.39N 6.26E
Vostochno Sibirskoye More sea U.S.S.R. 51 73.00N160.00E
Vostochnyy Sayan mts. U.S.S.R. 52 51.30N102.00E
Vostok I. Kiribati 85 10.05S152.23W
Votkinsk U.S.S.R. 44 57.02N 53.59E
Votkinskoye Vodokhranilishche resr. U.S.S.R. 44 57.00N 55.00E
Votuporanga Brazil 124 20.26S 49.53W
Vouga r. Portugal 26 40.41N 8.40W
Vouillé France 18 46.39N 0.10E

Voulou C.A.R. 73 8.33N 22.36E
Vouziers France 19 49.24N 4.42E
Voves France 19 48.16N 1.38E
Voxna Sweden 41 61.20N 15.30E
Voxna r. Sweden 41 61.17N 16.26E
Voyvozh U.S.S.R. 44 64.19N 55.12E
Vozhega U.S.S.R. 44 60.25N 40.11E
Voznesensk U.S.S.R. 23 47.34N 31.21E
Vrå Denmark 42 57.21N 9.57E
Vrådal Norway 42 59.20N 8.25E
Vrakhnéïka Greece 35 38.10N 21.40E
Vrangelya, Ostrov i. U.S.S.R. 51 71.00N180.00
Vranje Yugo. 34 42.34N 21.54E
Vratsa Bulgaria 34 43.13N 23.30E
Vrbas Yugo. 31 45.35N 19.39E
Vrbas r. Yugo. 31 45.06N 17.31E
Vrbovec Yugo. 31 45.53N 16.25E
Vrbovsko Yugo. 31 45.23N 15.05E
Vrede R.S.A. 80 27.24S 29.09E
Vredendal R.S.A. 80 31.40S 18.28E
Vrena Sweden 43 58.52N 16.41E
Vresse Belgium 16 49.53N 4.57E
Vrgnmost Yugo. 31 45.21N 15.52E
Vrhnika Yugo. 31 45.58N 14.18E
Vries Neth. 16 53.06N 6.35E
Vrigstad Sweden 43 57.21N 14.28E
Vrindāvan India 63 27.35N 77.42E
Vrlika Yugo. 31 43.55N 16.24E
Vrnograč Yugo. 31 45.10N 15.57E
Vrondádhes Greece 35 38.25N 26.08E
Vršac Yugo. 37 45.08N 21.18E
Vryburg R.S.A. 80 26.57S 24.42E
Vučitrn Yugo. 34 42.49N 20.59E
Vught Neth. 16 51.39N 5.18E
Vukovar Yugo. 31 45.21N 19.00E
Vulcano, Isola i. Italy 33 38.27N 14.58E
Vûlchedruma Bulgaria 34 43.42N 23.16E
Vung Tau Vietnam 56 10.21N107.04E
Vurshets Bulgaria 34 43.12N 23.17E
Vyara India 62 21.07N 73.24E
Vyatka r. U.S.S.R. 50 55.40N 51.40E
Vyatskiye Polyany U.S.S.R. 44 56.14N 51.08E
Vyazma U.S.S.R. 44 55.12N 34.17E
Vyazniki U.S.S.R. 44 56.14N 42.08E
Vyborg U.S.S.R. 44 60.45N 28.41E
Vychegda r. U.S.S.R. 44 61.15N 46.28E
Vychodné Beskydy mts. Europe 37 49.30N 22.00E
Vygozero, Ozero l. U.S.S.R. 44 63.30N 34.30E
Vyrnwy, L. U.K. 12 52.46N 3.30W
Vyshka U.S.S.R. 65 39.19N 54.10E
Vyshniy-Volochek U.S.S.R. 44 57.34N 34.23E
Vyšší Brod Czech. 39 48.37N 14.19E
Vytegra U.S.S.R. 44 61.04N 36.27E

W

Wa Ghana 76 10.07N 2.28W
Waal r. Neth. 16 51.45N 4.40E
Waalwijk Neth. 16 51.42N 5.04E
Wabag P.N.G. 59 5.28S143.40E
Wabasca r. Canada 100 58.22N115.20W
Wabash U.S.A. 110 40.47N 85.48W
Wabash r. U.S.A. 110 37.46N 88.02W
Wabe Mena r. Ethiopia 73 6.20N 40.41E
Wabeno U.S.A. 110 45.27N 88.38W
Wabera Ethiopia 73 6.25N 40.45E
Wabē Shebelē r. Ethiopia see Shabeelle r. Somali Rep. 71
Wabrzeźno Poland 37 53.17N 18.57E
Wabush City Canada 103 52.53N 66.50W
Waco U.S.A. 111 31.55N 97.08W
Wacouno r. Canada 103 50.50N 65.58W
Wad Pakistan 62 27.21N 66.22E
Wad Bandah Sudan 73 13.06N 27.57E
Waddān Libya 75 29.10N 16.08E
Waddeneilanden is. Neth. 16 53.20N 5.00E
Waddenzee b. Neth. 16 53.15N 5.05E
Waddikee Australia 92 33.18S136.12E
Waddington U.S.A. 105 44.52N 75.12W
Waddington, Mt. Canada 100 51.23N125.15W
Wadena U.S.A. 110 46.26N 95.08W
Wädenswil Switz. 39 47.14N 8.40E
Wad Hāmid Sudan 72 16.30N 32.48E
Wadhurst U.K. 13 51.03N 0.21E
Wādi as Sir town Jordan 67 31.57N 35.49E
Wādi Halfa' Sudan 64 21.56N 31.20E
Wādi Mūsa town Jordan 66 30.19N 35.29E
Wad Madani Sudan 72 14.24N 33.32E
Wad Nimr Sudan 72 14.32N 32.08E
Wadsworth U.S.A. 114 41.02N 81.44W
Wafrah Kuwait 65 28.39N 47.56E
Wageningen Neth. 16 51.58N 5.39E
Wager B. Canada 99 65.26N 88.40W
Wager Bay town Canada 99 65.50N 90.40W
Wagga Wagga Australia 93 35.07S147.24E
Wagin Australia 89 33.18S117.21E
Wagon Mound town U.S.A. 109 36.01N104.42W
Wagrien f. Germany 38 54.15N 10.45E
Wāh Pakistan 62 33.48N 72.42E
Wahai Indonesia 59 2.48S129.30E
Wāhat Salimah Sudan 72 21.22N 29.19E
Wahiawa Hawaiian Is. 85 21.30N158.01W
Wahiba Sands des. Oman 65 21.56N 58.55E
Wahpeton U.S.A. 110 46.16N 96.36W
Waiau New Zealand 86 42.39S173.03E

Waiblingen Germany 39 48.50N 9.19E
Waidhān India 63 24.04N 82.20E
Waidhofen Austria 36 47.58N 14.47E
Waigeo i. Indonesia 59 0.05S130.30E
Waihi New Zealand 86 37.24S175.50E
Waikato d. New Zealand 86 38.15S175.10E
Waikato r. New Zealand 86 37.19S174.50E
Waikerie Australia 92 34.11S139.59E
Waikokopu New Zealand 86 39.05S177.50E
Waikouaiti New Zealand 86 45.36S170.41E
Wailuku Hawaiian Is. 85 20.53N156.30W
Waimakariri r. New Zealand 86 43.23S172.40E
Waimate New Zealand 86 44.45S171.03E
Waimea Hawaiian Is. 85 20.01N155.41W
Wainganga r. India 63 18.50N 79.55E
Waingapu Indonesia 59 9.30S120.10E
Wainwright Canada 101 52.49N110.52W
Wainwright U.S.A. 98 70.39N160.00W
Waiouru New Zealand 86 39.38S175.40E
Waipara New Zealand 86 43.03S172.45E
Waipawa New Zealand 86 39.56S176.35E
Waipiro New Zealand 86 38.02S178.21E
Waipu New Zealand 86 35.59S174.26E
Waipukurau New Zealand 86 40.00S176.33E
Wairau r. New Zealand 86 41.32S174.08E
Wairoa New Zealand 86 39.03S177.25E
Waitaki r. New Zealand 86 44.56S171.10E
Waitara New Zealand 86 38.59S174.13E
Waiuku New Zealand 86 37.15S174.44E
Wajima Japan 57 37.24N136.54E
Wajir Kenya 79 1.46N 40.05E
Waka Ethiopia 73 7.07N 37.26E
Waka Zaïre 78 0.48S 20.10E
Wakasa wan b. Japan 57 35.50N135.40E
Wakatipu, L. New Zealand 86 45.10S168.30E
Wakayama Japan 57 34.13N135.11E
Wakefield Canada 105 45.38N 75.56W
Wakefield d. New Zealand 86 37.19S176.00E
Wakefield U.K. 12 53.41N 1.31W
Wakefield U.S.A. 115 41.26N 71.30W
Wake I. Pacific Oc. 84 19.17N166.36E
Wakema Burma 56 16.36N 95.11E
Wakkanai Japan 57 45.26N141.43E
Wakonassin r. Canada 104 46.28N 81.51W
Wakre Indonesia 59 0.30S131.05E
Wakuach, L. Canada 103 55.37N 67.40W
Walamba Zambia 79 13.27S 28.44E
Wałbrzych Poland 36 50.48N 16.19E
Walcha Australia 93 31.00S151.36E
Walcheren f. Neth. 16 51.32N 3.35E
Wałcz Poland 36 53.17N 16.28E
Waldbröl Germany 16 50.52N 7.34E
Waldeck Germany 38 51.12N 9.04E
Walden U.S.A. 108 40.34N106.11W
Waldkirch Germany 39 48.06N 7.57E
Waldorf U.S.A. 114 38.37N 76.54W
Waldport U.S.A. 108 44.26N124.04W
Waldron U.S.A. 111 34.54N 94.05W
Waldshut Germany 39 47.37N 8.13E
Wales d. U.K. 13 52.30N 3.45W
Wales U.S.A. 110 47.13N 91.41W
Walgett Australia 93 30.03S148.10E
Walhonding r. U.S.A. 114 40.18N 81.53W
Walikale U.S.S.R. 79 1.29S 28.05E
Walker U.S.A. 110 47.06N 94.35W
Walker L. U.S.A. 108 38.44N118.43W
Walkerton Canada 104 44.07N 81.09W
Wall U.S.A. 108 43.59N102.14W
Wallace Canada 104 45.23N 78.05W
Wallace Idaho U.S.A. 108 47.28N115.55W
Wallace Nebr. U.S.A. 110 40.50N101.10W
Wallaceburg Canada 104 42.36N 82.23W
Wallachia f. Romania 37 44.35N 25.00E
Wallambin, L. Australia 89 30.58S117.30E
Wallaroo Australia 92 33.57S137.36E
Walla Walla Australia 93 35.48S146.52E
Walla Walla U.S.A. 108 46.08N118.20W
Wallenpaupack, L. U.S.A. 115 41.25N 75.12W
Wallingford U.S.A. 115 41.27N 72.50W
Wallis, Îles is. Pacific Oc. 84 13.16S176.15W
Wallkill r. U.S.A. 115 41.51N 74.03W
Wallowa U.S.A. 108 45.34N117.32W
Wallowa Mts. U.S.A. 108 45.10N117.30W
Wallsend Australia 93 32.55S151.40E
Walpole Australia 89 34.57S116.44E
Walsall U.K. 13 52.36N 1.59W
Walsenburg U.S.A. 108 37.37N104.47W
Walsrode Germany 38 52.52N 9.35E
Walterboro U.S.A. 113 32.54N 80.21W
Waltershausen Germany 38 50.53N 10.33E
Waltham Canada 105 45.55N 76.57W
Walton U.N.Y. U.S.A. 115 42.10N 75.08W
Walton W.Va. U.S.A. 114 38.40N 81.26W
Walton on the Naze U.K. 13 51.52N 1.17E
Walton on the Wolds U.K. 12 52.49N 0.49W
Walvis B. R.S.A. 80 22.55S 14.30E
Walvisbaai R.S.A. 80 22.57S 14.30E
Walvis Bay r. R.S.A. 80 22.56S 14.35E
Walvis Bay town see Walvisbaai R.S.A. 80
Walvis Ridge f. Atlantic Oc. 127 28.00S 4.00E
Wamanfo Ghana 76 7.16N 2.44W
Wamba Kenya 79 0.58N 37.19E
Wamba Nigeria 77 8.57N 8.42E
Wamba r. Zaïre 78 4.35S 17.15E
Wami r. Tanzania 79 6.10S 38.50E
Wampsville U.S.A. 115 43.05N 75.42W
Wamsasi Indonesia 59 3.27S126.07E
Wan Indonesia 90 8.23S137.55E
Wāna Pakistan 62 32.17N 69.35E
Wanaaring Australia 92 29.42S144.14E
Wanaka New Zealand 86 44.42S169.08E
Wanaka, L. New Zealand 86 44.30S169.10E
Wan'an China 55 26.27N114.46E
Wanapiri Indonesia 59 4.30S135.50E
Wanapitei r. Canada 104 46.02N 80.51W
Wanapitei L. Canada 104 46.45N 80.45W

219

Wanbi to Whakatane

Wanbi Australia **92** 34.46S140.19E
Wandana Australia **92** 32.04S133.45E
Wandoan Australia **90** 26.09S149.51E
Wanganella Australia **93** 35.13S144.53E
Wanganui New Zealand **86** 39.56S175.00E
Wangaratta Australia **93** 36.22S146.20E
Wangary Australia **92** 34.30S135.26E
Wangdu China **54** 38.43N115.09E
Wangdu Phodrang Bhutan **63** 27.29N 89.54E
Wangen Germany **39** 47.42N 9.50E
Wangerooge *i.* Germany **38** 53.46N 7.55E
Wanghai Shan *mtn.* China **54** 41.40N121.43E
Wangianna Australia **92** 29.42S137.32E
Wangjiang China **55** 30.07N116.41E
Wangpan Yang *b.* China **55** 30.30N121.30E
Wangqing China **57** 43.20N129.48E
Wangyuanqiao China **54** 38.24N106.16E
Wani India **63** 20.04N 78.57E
Wānkāner India **62** 22.37N 70.56E
Wanle Weyne Somali Rep. **71** 2.38N 44.55E
Wannian China **55** 28.42N117.03E
Wanning China **55** 18.48N110.22E
Wānow Afghan. **62** 32.38N 65.54E
Wantage U.K. **13** 51.35N 1.25W
Wanup Canada **104** 46.24N 80.49W
Wanxian China **55** 30.52N108.20E
Wanyang Shan *mts.* China **55** 26.01N113.48E
Wanyuan China **54** 32.04N108.02E
Wanzai China **55** 28.06N114.27E
Wanzleben Germany **38** 52.03N 11.26E
Wāpi India **62** 20.22N 72.54E
Wapiti *r.* Canada **100** 55.05N118.18W
Wappingers Falls U.S.A. **115** 41.36N 73.55W
Waqqāş Jordan **67** 32.33N 35.36E
Wārāh Pakistan **62** 27.27N 67.48E
Warangal India **61** 18.00N 79.35E
Waranga Resr. Australia **93** 36.32S145.04E
Wārāseoni India **63** 21.45N 80.02E
Waratah B. Australia **91** 38.55S146.04E
Warburg Germany **38** 51.29N 9.08E
Warburton *r.* Australia **91** 27.55S137.15E
Warburton Range *mts.* S.A. Australia **92** 30.30S134.32E
Warburton Range *mts.* W.A. Australia **88** 26.09S126.38E
Ward Rep. of Ire. **15** 53.26N 6.20W
Warden R.S.A. **80** 27.49S 28.57E
Wardenburg Germany **38** 53.04N 8.11E
Wardha India **63** 20.45N 78.37E
Wardha *r.* India **63** 19.38N 79.48E
Ward Hill U.K. **10** 58.54N 3.20W
Wardlow Canada **101** 50.54N111.33W
Ware U.S.A. **115** 42.16N 72.15W
Wareham U.S.A. **115** 41.46N 70.43W
Waren Germany **38** 53.31N 12.40E
Warendorf Germany **38** 51.57N 7.59E
Warfordsburg U.S.A. **114** 39.44N 78.15W
Warialda Australia **93** 29.33S150.36E
Wark Forest *hills* U.K. **12** 55.06N 2.24W
Warkopi Indonesia **59** 1.12S134.09E
Warkworth New Zealand **86** 36.24S174.40E
Warley U.K. **13** 52.29N 2.02W
Warmbad Namibia **80** 28.26S 18.41E
Warminster U.K. **13** 51.12N 2.11W
Warm Springs *town* U.S.A. **108** 39.39N114.49W
Warnemünde Germany **38** 54.10N 12.04E
Warner U.S.A. **115** 43.17N 71.49W
Warner Robins U.S.A. **113** 32.35N 83.37W
Warnow *r.* Germany **38** 54.06N 12.09E
Waroona Australia **89** 32.51S115.50E
Warracknabeal Australia **92** 36.15S142.28E
Warragul Australia **93** 38.11S145.55E
Warrakalanna, L. Australia **92** 28.13S139.23E
Warrambool *r.* Australia **93** 30.04S147.38E
Warrego *r.* Australia **93** 30.25S145.18E
Warrego Range *mts.* Australia **90** 24.55S146.20E
Warren Australia **93** 31.44S147.53E
Warren Ont. Canada **104** 46.27N 80.20W
Warren Ark. U.S.A. **111** 33.37N 92.04W
Warren Mich. U.S.A. **114** 42.28N 83.01W
Warren Minn. U.S.A. **110** 48.12N 96.46W
Warren N.H. U.S.A. **105** 43.56N 71.54W
Warren Ohio U.S.A. **114** 41.14N 80.52W
Warren Penn. U.S.A. **114** 41.51N 79.08W
Warren R.I. U.S.A. **115** 41.43N 71.17W
Warren Vt. U.S.A. **105** 44.06N 72.52W
Warrenpoint U.K. **15** 54.06N 6.15W
Warrensburg Mo. U.S.A. **110** 38.46N 93.44W
Warrensburg N.Y. U.S.A. **115** 43.30N 73.46W
Warrenton R.S.A. **80** 28.07S 24.49E
Warrenton U.S.A. **114** 38.43N 77.48W
Warri Nigeria **77** 5.36N 5.46E
Warrina Australia **92** 28.10S135.49E
Warriner Creek *r.* Australia **92** 29.15S137.03E
Warrington U.K. **12** 53.25N 2.38W
Warrington U.S.A. **111** 30.23N 87.16W
Warrnambool Australia **92** 38.23S142.03E
Warroad U.S.A. **110** 48.54N 95.19W
Warrumbungle Range *mts.* Australia **93** 31.20S149.00E
Warsaw *see* Warszawa Poland **37**
Warsaw Ind. U.S.A. **112** 41.13N 85.52W
Warsaw N.Y. U.S.A. **114** 42.44N 78.08W
Warsaw Ohio U.S.A. **114** 40.20N 82.00W
Warshiikh Somali Rep. **71** 2.19N 45.50E
Warszawa Poland **37** 52.15N 21.00E
Warta *r.* Poland **36** 52.45N 15.09E
Warud India **63** 21.28N 78.16E
Warwick Australia **93** 28.12S152.00E
Warwick Canada **105** 45.56N 71.59W
Warwick U.K. **13** 52.17N 1.36W
Warwick N.Y. U.S.A. **115** 41.16N 74.22W
Warwick R.I. U.S.A. **115** 41.43N 71.28W
Warwickshire *d.* U.K. **13** 52.13N 1.30W
Wasaga Beach Canada **104** 44.31N 80.01W
Wasatch Plateau *f.* U.S.A. **108** 39.20N111.30W
Wasco Calif. U.S.A. **109** 35.36N119.20W
Wasco Oreg. U.S.A. **108** 45.35N120.42W
Washago Canada **104** 44.45N 79.20W
Washburn N.Dak. U.S.A. **110** 47.17N101.02W
Washburn Wisc. U.S.A. **110** 46.41N 90.52W
Washburn L. Canada **98** 70.03N106.50W
Wāshim India **62** 20.06N 77.09E
Washington U.K. **12** 54.55N 1.30W
Washington *d.* U.S.A. **108** 47.43N120.00W
Washington D.C. U.S.A. **114** 38.55N 77.00W
Washington Ga. U.S.A. **113** 33.43N 82.46W
Washington Ind. U.S.A. **112** 38.40N 87.10W
Washington Iowa U.S.A. **110** 41.18N 91.42W
Washington N.C. U.S.A. **113** 35.33N 77.04W
Washington Penn. U.S.A. **114** 40.10N 80.15W
Washington Utah U.S.A. **108** 37.08N113.30W
Washington Va. U.S.A. **114** 38.43N 78.10W
Washington Crossing U.S.A. **115** 40.18N 74.52W
Wāshuk Pakistan **62** 27.44N 64.48E
Wasian Indonesia **59** 1.51S133.21E
Wasior Indonesia **59** 2.38S134.27E
Wasiri Indonesia **59** 7.30S126.30E
Waskaganish Canada **102** 51.29N 78.45W
Waskesiu L. Canada **101** 53.56N106.10W
Waskigomog L. Canada **104** 46.00N 78.59W
Wassen Switz. **39** 46.42N 8.36E
Wassenaar Neth. **16** 52.10N 4.26E
Wasseralfingen Germany **39** 48.52N 10.06E
Wasserburg Germany **39** 48.04N 12.13E
Wasserkuppe *mtn.* Germany **38** 50.30N 9.56E
Wassy France **19** 48.30N 4.57E
Waswanipi Lac *l.* Canada **102** 49.35N 76.40W
Watampone Indonesia **59** 4.33S120.20E
Watchet U.K. **13** 51.10N 3.20W
Waterbury U.S.A. **115** 41.33N 73.02W
Waterbury L. Canada **101** 58.16N105.00W
Waterford Canada **104** 42.56N 80.17W
Waterford Rep. of Ire. **15** 52.16N 7.08W
Waterford *d.* Rep. of Ire. **15** 52.10N 7.40W
Waterford U.S.A. **114** 41.57N 79.59W
Waterford Harbour *est.* Rep. of Ire. **15** 52.12N 6.56W
Waterloo Belgium **16** 50.44N 4.24E
Waterloo Ont. Canada **104** 43.28N 80.31W
Waterloo Que. Canada **105** 45.21N 72.31W
Waterloo Iowa U.S.A. **110** 42.30N 92.20W
Waterloo N.Y. U.S.A. **114** 42.54N 76.52W
Waterton Glacier International Peace Park U.S.A. / Canada **108** 48.47N113.45W
Watertown N.Y. U.S.A. **105** 43.59N 75.55W
Watertown S.Dak. U.S.A. **110** 44.54N 97.07W
Watervale Australia **92** 33.58S138.39E
Water Valley *town* U.S.A. **111** 34.09N 89.38W
Waterville Canada **105** 45.16N 71.54W
Waterville Rep. of Ire. **15** 51.50N 10.11W
Waterville Maine U.S.A. **112** 44.33N 69.38W
Waterville N.Y. U.S.A. **115** 42.56N 75.23W
Waterville Wash. U.S.A. **108** 47.39N120.04W
Watervliet U.S.A. **115** 42.44N 73.42W
Watford Canada **104** 42.57N 81.53W
Watford U.K. **13** 51.40N 0.25W
Watford City U.S.A. **110** 47.48N103.17W
Wa'th Sudan **73** 7.24N 28.58E
Wathaman L. Canada **101** 56.55N103.43W
Watkins Glen U.S.A. **114** 42.23N 76.52W
Watonga U.S.A. **111** 35.51N 98.25W
Watrous Canada **101** 51.40N105.28W
Watsa Zaïre **79** 3.03N 29.29E
Watson Canada **101** 52.07N104.31W
Watson Lake *town* Canada **100** 60.06N128.49W
Watsontown U.S.A. **114** 41.05N 76.52W
Watsonville U.S.A. **108** 36.55N121.45W
Wattiwarriganna Creek *r.* Australia **92** 28.57S136.10E
Wattwil Switz. **39** 47.18N 9.06E
Watzmann *mtn.* Germany **39** 47.33N 12.55E
Wau P.N.G. **59** 7.22S146.40E
Wauchope N.S.W. Australia **93** 31.27S152.43E
Wauchope N.T. Australia **90** 20.39S134.13E
Waukaringa Australia **92** 32.18S139.27E
Waukegan U.S.A. **110** 42.22N 87.50W
Waukesha U.S.A. **110** 43.01N 88.14W
Waukon U.S.A. **110** 43.16N 91.29W
Wauneta U.S.A. **110** 40.25N101.23W
Waurika U.S.A. **111** 34.10N 98.00W
Wausau U.S.A. **110** 44.58N 89.40W
Wautoma U.S.A. **110** 44.05N 89.17W
Wauwatosa U.S.A. **110** 43.04N 88.02W
Wave Hill *town* Australia **88** 17.29S130.57E
Waveney *r.* U.K. **13** 52.29N 1.46E
Waverly Ill. U.S.A. **110** 39.36N 89.57W
Waverly Iowa U.S.A. **110** 42.44N 92.29W
Waverly N.Y. U.S.A. **115** 42.00N 76.32W
Wavre Belgium **16** 50.43N 4.37E
Wāw Sudan **73** 7.42N 28.00E
Wāw al Kabīr Libya **75** 25.20N 16.43E
Waxahachie U.S.A. **111** 32.24N 96.51W
Waxweiler Germany **39** 50.05N 6.22E
Way, L. Australia **88** 26.47S120.21E
Waycross U.S.A. **113** 31.12N 82.22W
Wayland U.S.A. **114** 42.34N 77.35W
Wayne N.J. U.S.A. **115** 40.03N 75.23W
Wayne W.Va. U.S.A. **114** 38.13N 82.27W
Waynesboro Ga. U.S.A. **113** 33.04N 82.01W
Waynesboro Penn. U.S.A. **114** 39.45N 77.35W
Waynesboro Va. U.S.A. **113** 38.04N 78.53W
Waynesburg Ohio U.S.A. **114** 40.40N 81.16W
Waynesburg Penn. U.S.A. **114** 39.54N 80.11W
Waynesville U.S.A. **113** 35.30N 82.58W
Waynoka U.S.A. **111** 36.35N 98.53W
Wazay Afghan. **62** 33.22N 69.26E
Waziers France **19** 50.23N 3.07E
Wazīrābād Pakistan **62** 32.27N 74.07E
Wear *r.* U.K. **12** 54.55N 1.21W
Weatherford Okla. U.S.A. **111** 35.32N 98.42W
Weatherford Tex. U.S.A. **111** 32.46N 97.48W
Webbwood Canada **104** 46.16N 81.53W
Webster Mass. U.S.A. **115** 42.03N 71.53W
Webster N.Y. U.S.A. **114** 43.13N 77.26W
Webster Wisc. U.S.A. **110** 45.53N 92.22W
Webster City U.S.A. **110** 42.28N 93.49W
Webster Groves U.S.A. **110** 38.35N 90.21W
Webster Springs *town* U.S.A. **114** 38.29N 80.25W
Weda Indonesia **59** 0.30N127.52E
Weddell Sea Antarctica **128** 70.00S 40.00W
Wedderburn Australia **92** 36.26S143.39E
Wedgeport Canada **103** 43.44N 65.59W
Wedmore U.K. **13** 51.14N 2.50W
Wedza Zimbabwe **81** 18.37S 31.33E
Weedon Canada **105** 45.42N 71.28W
Weedsport U.S.A. **115** 43.03N 76.34W
Weeho *r.* Canada **100** 63.20N115.10W
Weelde Belgium **16** 51.25N 5.00E
Weemelah Australia **93** 29.02S149.15E
Weert Neth. **16** 51.14N 5.40E
Wee Waa Australia **93** 30.34S149.27E
Wegorzyno Poland **36** 53.32N 15.33E
Węgrów Poland **37** 52.25N 22.01E
Wegscheid Germany **39** 48.36N 13.48E
Weichang China **54** 41.56N117.34E
Weida Germany **38** 50.45N 12.04E
Weiden in der Oberpfalz Germany **39** 49.41N 12.10E
Weifang China **54** 36.40N119.10E
Weihai China **54** 37.28N122.05E
Wei He *r.* Shaanxi China **54** 34.27N109.30E
Wei He *r.* Shandong China **54** 36.47N115.42E
Weilburg Germany **38** 50.29N 8.15E
Weilheim Germany **39** 47.50N 11.08E
Weilmoringle Australia **93** 29.16S146.55E
Weimar Germany **38** 50.59N 11.19E
Weinan China **54** 34.25N109.30E
Weinheim Germany **39** 49.32N 8.39E
Weipa Australia **90** 12.41S141.52E
Weir *r.* Australia **93** 29.10S149.06E
Weirton U.S.A. **114** 40.25N 80.35W
Weiser U.S.A. **108** 44.37N116.58W
Weishan Hu *l.* China **54** 34.40N117.25E
Weishi China **54** 34.24N114.14E
Weisse Elster *r.* Germany **38** 51.26N 11.57E
Weissenburg in Bayern Germany **38** 49.01N 10.58E
Weissenfels Germany **38** 51.12N 11.58E
Weisswasser Germany **38** 51.30N 14.38E
Wei Xian China **54** 36.21N114.56E
Weixin China **55** 27.48N105.05E
Weiya China **52** 41.50N 94.24E
Weizhou *i.* China **55** 21.01N109.03E
Wejherowo Poland **37** 54.37N 18.15E
Wekusko Canada **101** 54.45N 99.45W
Weldiya Ethiopia **73** 11.50N 39.36E
Weldon U.S.A. **109** 35.40N118.20W
Welega *d.* Ethiopia **73** 9.40N 35.50E
Welkom R.S.A. **80** 27.59S 26.42E
Welland Canada **104** 42.59N 79.14W
Welland *r.* U.K. **12** 52.53N 0.00
Wellesley Is. Australia **90** 16.42S139.30E
Wellfleet U.S.A. **115** 41.56N 70.02W
Wellin Belgium **16** 50.05N 5.07E
Wellingborough U.K. **13** 52.18N 0.41W
Wellington N.S.W. Australia **93** 32.33S148.59E
Wellington S.A. Australia **92** 35.21S139.23E
Wellington Canada **105** 43.57N 77.21W
Wellington New Zealand **86** 41.17S174.47E
Wellington *d.* New Zealand **86** 40.00S175.30E
Wellington Shrops. U.K. **13** 52.42N 2.31W
Wellington Somerset U.K. **13** 50.58N 3.13W
Wellington Kans. U.S.A. **111** 37.16N 97.24W
Wellington Nev. U.S.A. **108** 38.45N119.22W
Wellington Ohio U.S.A. **114** 41.10N 82.13W
Wellington, Isla *i.* Chile **125** 49.30S 75.00W
Wells U.K. **13** 51.12N 2.39W
Wells Maine U.S.A. **115** 43.20N 70.35W
Wells Nev. U.S.A. **108** 41.07N114.58W
Wells N.Y. U.S.A. **115** 43.24N 74.17W
Wellsboro U.S.A. **114** 41.45N 77.18W
Wellsburg U.S.A. **114** 40.16N 80.37W
Wells Gray Prov. Park Canada **100** 52.30N120.15W
Wells L. Canada **101** 57.15N101.00W
Wells-next-the-Sea U.K. **12** 52.57N 0.51E
Wells River *town* U.S.A. **105** 44.09N 72.06W
Wellston U.S.A. **114** 39.07N 82.32W
Wellsville Mo. U.S.A. **110** 39.04N 91.34W
Wellsville N.Y. U.S.A. **114** 42.07N 77.57W
Wellton U.S.A. **109** 32.40N114.08W
Welmel *r.* Ethiopia **73** 6.00N 40.20E
Welo *d.* Ethiopia **73** 11.30N 40.00E
Wels Austria **39** 48.10N 14.02E
Welshpool U.K. **13** 52.40N 3.09W
Welwyn Garden City U.K. **13** 51.48N 0.13W
Wem U.K. **12** 52.52N 2.45W
Wembere *r.* Tanzania **79** 4.07S 34.15E
Wenatchee U.S.A. **108** 47.25N120.19W
Wenchang China **55** 19.37N110.43E
Wenchi Ghana **76** 7.40N 2.06W
Wendel U.S.A. **108** 40.20N120.14W
Wendo Ethiopia **73** 6.40N 38.27E
Wendover U.S.A. **108** 40.44N114.02W
Wenebegon L. Canada **102** 47.25N 83.05W
Wengfengzhen China **54** 34.56N104.38E
Wenlock *r.* Australia **90** 12.02S141.55E
Wenquan China **63** 33.13N 91.50E
Wenshan China **55** 23.20N104.11E
Wensleydale *f.* U.K. **12** 54.19N 2.04W
Wentworth Australia **92** 34.06S141.56E
Wen Xian China **54** 32.52N104.40E
Wenzhou China **53** 28.02N120.40E
Weott U.S.A. **108** 40.19N123.54W
Wepener R.S.A. **80** 29.43S 27.01E
Werda Botswana **80** 25.15S 23.16E
Werdau Germany **38** 50.44N 12.22E
Werdēr *well* Ethiopia **71** 6.58N 45.21E
Werder Germany **38** 52.23N 12.56E
Werdohl Germany **38** 51.15N 7.45E
Were Īlu Ethiopia **73** 10.37N 39.28E
Weri Indonesia **59** 3.10S132.30E
Werne Germany **16** 51.39N 7.36E
Wernigerode Germany **38** 51.50N 10.47E
Werra *r.* Germany **38** 51.26N 9.39E
Werribee Australia **93** 37.54S144.40E
Werris Creek *town* Australia **93** 31.20S150.41E
Wertheim Germany **39** 49.46N 9.31E
Wertingen Germany **39** 48.34N 10.41E
Wesel Germany **38** 51.40N 6.38E
Weser *r.* Germany **38** 53.15N 8.34E
Weslaco U.S.A. **111** 26.09N 97.59W
Weslemkoon L. Canada **105** 45.02N 77.25W
Wesleyville Canada **103** 49.09N 53.34W
Wesleyville U.S.A. **114** 42.08N 80.01W
Wessel, C. Australia **90** 10.59S136.46E
Wessel Is. Australia **90** 11.30S136.25E
Wessington U.S.A. **110** 44.27N 98.42W
Wessington Springs *town* U.S.A. **110** 44.05N 98.34W
West U.S.A. **111** 31.48N 97.06W
West *r.* U.S.A. **115** 42.52N 72.33W
West Australian Basin *f.* Indian Oc. **49** 15.00S100.00E
West B. U.S.A. **111** 29.15N 94.57W
West Bank Jordan **67** 32.00N 35.15E
West Bend U.S.A. **110** 43.25N 88.11W
West Bengal *d.* India **63** 23.00N 88.00E
West Branch U.S.A. **104** 44.17N 84.14W
West Bromwich U.K. **13** 52.32N 2.01W
Westbrook U.S.A. **112** 43.41N 70.21W
West Burke U.S.A. **105** 44.38N 71.59W
West Burra *i.* U.K. **10** 60.05N 1.21W
West Canada Creek *r.* U.S.A. **115** 43.01N 74.58W
West Caroline Basin Pacific Oc. **84** 5.00N139.00E
West Chester U.S.A. **115** 39.58N 75.36W
West Coast *d.* New Zealand **86** 43.15S170.10E
West Des Moines U.S.A. **110** 41.35N 93.43W
Westende Belgium **16** 51.10N 2.46E
Westerland Germany **38** 54.54N 8.18E
Westerly U.S.A. **115** 41.22N 71.50W
Western *d.* Ghana **76** 6.00N 2.40W
Western *d.* Kenya **79** 0.30N 34.30E
Western *d.* Zambia **80** 16.00S 23.45E
Western Australia *d.* Australia **88** 24.20S122.30E
Western Duck I. Canada **104** 45.45N 83.00W
Western Ghāts *mts.* India **60** 15.30N 74.30E
Western Isles *d.* U.K. **14** 57.40N 7.10W
Westernport U.S.A. **114** 39.29N 79.03W
Western Sahara Africa **74** 25.00N 13.30W
Western Samoa Pacific Oc. **84** 13.55S172.00W
Westerschelde *est.* Neth. **16** 51.25N 3.40E
Westerstede Germany **38** 53.15N 7.55E
Westerville U.S.A. **114** 40.08N 82.56W
Westerwald *f.* Germany **38** 50.40N 7.45E
West Falkland *i.* Falkland Is. **125** 51.40W 60.00W
West Felton U.K. **12** 52.49N 2.58W
Westfield *r.* U.S.A. **115** 42.05N 72.35W
Westfield Mass. U.S.A. **115** 42.08N 72.45W
Westfield N.J. U.S.A. **115** 40.39N 74.21W
Westfield N.Y. U.S.A. **114** 42.19N 79.35W
Westfield Penn. U.S.A. **114** 41.55N 77.32W
West Fork *r.* U.S.A. **114** 39.28N 80.09W
West Frankfort U.S.A. **111** 37.54N 88.55W
West Frisian Is. *see* Waddeneilanden Neth. **36**
West Glamorgan *d.* U.K. **13** 51.42N 3.47W
Westhampton U.S.A. **115** 40.49N 72.39W
West Haven U.S.A. **115** 41.16N 72.57W
Westhope U.S.A. **110** 48.55N101.01W
West Indies *is.* C. America **127** 21.00N 74.00W
West Lafayette U.S.A. **112** 40.26N 86.56W
West Leyden U.S.A. **115** 43.28N 75.28W
West Linton U.K. **14** 55.45N 3.21W
Westlock Canada **100** 54.09N113.55W
West Lorne Canada **104** 42.36N 81.36W
Westmeath Canada **105** 45.49N 76.54W
Westmeath *d.* Rep. of Ire. **15** 53.30N 7.30W
West Memphis U.S.A. **111** 35.08N 90.11W
West Middlesex U.S.A. **114** 41.10N 80.27W
West Midlands *d.* U.K. **13** 52.28N 1.50W
Westminster U.S.A. **114** 39.35N 77.00W
Westmoreland Australia **90** 17.18S138.12E
Westmoreland U.S.A. **115** 42.59N 72.25W
West Nicholson Zimbabwe **80** 21.06S 29.25E
Weston Malaysia **58** 5.14N115.35E
Weston U.S.A. **114** 39.02N 80.28W
Weston-Super-Mare U.K. **13** 51.20N 2.59W
West Palm Beach *town* U.S.A. **113** 26.42N 80.05W
West Plains *town* U.S.A. **111** 36.44N 91.51W
West Point *town* U.S.A. **111** 33.36N 88.39W
Westport Canada **105** 44.41N 76.26W
Westport New Zealand **86** 41.46S171.38E
Westport Rep. of Ire. **15** 53.48N 9.32W
Westport Conn. U.S.A. **115** 41.09N 73.22W
Westport N.Y. U.S.A. **105** 44.13N 73.39W
Westport Wash. U.S.A. **108** 46.53N124.06W
Westray Canada **101** 53.36N101.24W
Westray *i.* U.K. **14** 59.18N 2.58W
Westree Canada **104** 47.26N 81.34W
West Road *r.* Canada **100** 53.18N122.53W
West Siberian Plain *f. see* Zapadno-Sibirskaya Ravnina *f.* U.S.S.R. **9**
West Springfield U.S.A. **115** 42.06N 72.38W
West Sussex *d.* U.K. **13** 50.58N 0.30W
West Terschelling Neth. **16** 53.22N 5.13E
West Union U.S.A. **114** 39.18N 80.47W
West Virginia *d.* U.S.A. **114** 38.45N 80.30W
West Vlaanderen *d.* Belgium **16** 51.00N 3.00E
West Wyalong Australia **93** 33.54S147.12E
West Yellowstone U.S.A. **108** 44.30N111.05W
West York U.S.A. **114** 39.57N 76.46W
West Yorkshire *d.* U.K. **12** 53.45N 1.40W
Wetar *i.* Indonesia **59** 7.45S126.00E
Wetaskiwin Canada **100** 52.55N113.24W
Wetteren Belgium **16** 51.00N 3.51E
Wetzlar Germany **38** 50.33N 8.29E
Wewak P.N.G. **59** 3.35S143.35E
Wewoka U.S.A. **111** 35.09N 96.30W
Wexford Rep. of Ire. **15** 52.20N 6.28W
Wexford *d.* Rep. of Ire. **15** 52.20N 6.25W
Wexford B. Rep. of Ire. **15** 52.27N 6.18W
Weyburn Canada **101** 49.41N103.52W
Weyīb *r.* Ethiopia **73** 4.11N 42.09E
Weymouth U.K. **13** 50.36N 2.28W
Weymouth, C. Australia **90** 12.32S143.36E
Whakatane New Zealand **86** 37.56S177.00E

Whalan to **Wuyuan**

Whalan *r.* Australia **93** 29.10S148.42E
Whale Cove *town* Canada **101** 62.11N 92.36W
Whalsay *i.* U.K. **14** 60.22N 0.59W
Whangarei New Zealand **86** 35.43S174.20E
Wharfe *r.* U.K. **12** 53.50N 1.07W
Wharfedale *f.* U.K. **12** 54.00N 1.55W
Wharton U.S.A. **111** 29.19N 96.06W
Whataroa New Zealand **86** 43.16S170.22E
Wheatland U.S.A. **108** 42.03N104.57W
Wheatley Canada **104** 42.06N 82.27W
Wheaton Md. U.S.A. **114** 39.03N 77.03W
Wheaton Minn. U.S.A. **110** 45.48N 96.30W
Wheeler *r.* Que. Canada **103** 58.05N 67.12W
Wheeler *r.* Sask. Canada **101** 57.25N105.30W
Wheeler Peak *mtn.* Nev. U.S.A. **108** 38.59N114.19W
Wheeler Peak *mtn.* N.Mex. U.S.A. **108** 36.34N105.25W
Wheeler Ridge *town* U.S.A. **109** 35.06N119.01W
Wheeler Springs *town* U.S.A. **109** 34.30N119.18W
Wheeling U.S.A. **114** 40.05N 80.42W
Whernside *mtn.* U.K. **12** 54.14N 2.25W
Whidbey Is. Australia **92** 34.50S135.00E
Whiskey Gap *town* Canada **100** 49.00N113.03W
Whitburn U.K. **14** 55.52N 3.41W
Whitby Canada **104** 43.52N 78.56W
Whitby U.K. **12** 54.29N 0.37W
Whitchurch Shrops. U.K. **12** 52.58N 2.42W
White *r.* Ark. U.S.A. **111** 33.53N 91.10W
White *r.* Ind. U.S.A. **112** 38.29N 87.45W
White *r.* S.Dak. U.S.A. **110** 43.48N 99.22W
White *r.* Utah U.S.A. **106** 40.04N109.41W
White *r.* Vt. U.S.A. **105** 43.37N 72.20W
White, L. Australia **88** 21.05S129.00E
White B. Canada **103** 50.00N 56.30W
White Cliffs *town* Australia **92** 30.51S143.05E
Whiteface, Mt. U.S.A. **105** 44.22N 73.54W
Whitefield U.S.A. **105** 44.22N 71.36W
Whitefish Canada **104** 46.23N 81.20W
Whitefish U.S.A. **108** 48.25N114.20W
Whitefish B. U.S.A. **104** 46.40N 84.50W
Whitefish Falls *town* Canada **104** 46.07N 81.44W
Whitefish L. Canada **101** 62.41N106.48W
Whitefish Point *town* U.S.A. **104** 46.45N 84.59W
Whitefish Pt. U.S.A. **104** 46.45N 85.00W
Whitehall Mont. U.S.A. **108** 45.52N112.06W
Whitehall N.Y. U.S.A. **115** 43.33N 73.25W
Whitehall Ohio U.S.A. **114** 39.58N 82.54W
Whitehall Wisc. U.S.A. **110** 44.22N 91.19W
Whitehaven U.K. **12** 54.33N 3.35W
White Haven U.S.A. **115** 41.04N 75.47W
Whitehorse Canada **100** 60.43N135.03W
White L. Canada **105** 45.18N 76.31W
White L. U.S.A. **111** 29.45N 92.30W
Whitemark Australia **91** 40.07S148.00E
White Mountain Peak U.S.A. **108** 37.38N118.15W
White Mts. Calif. U.S.A. **108** 37.30N118.15W
White Mts. N.H. U.S.A. **105** 44.10N 71.35W
Whitemud *r.* Canada **100** 56.41N117.15W
White Nile *r. see* Abyaḍ, Al Baḥr al *r.* Sudan **72**
White Otter L. Canada **102** 49.09N 91.50W
White Plains *town* Liberia **76** 6.28N 10.40W
White Plains *town* U.S.A. **115** 41.02N 73.46W
Whitesand *r.* Canada **101** 51.34N101.55W
Whitesboro U.S.A. **115** 43.07N 75.18W
White Sea *see* Beloye More *sea* U.S.S.R. **44**
Whiteshell Prov. Park. Canada **101** 50.00N 95.25W
Whitetail U.S.A. **108** 48.54N105.10W
White Volta *r.* Ghana **76** 9.13N 1.15W
Whitewater Baldy *mtn.* U.S.A. **109** 33.20N108.39W
Whitfield Australia **93** 36.49S146.22E
Whithorn U.K. **14** 54.44N 4.25W
Whitianga New Zealand **86** 36.50S175.42E
Whiting U.S.A. **115** 39.57N 74.23W
Whitley Bay *town* U.K. **12** 55.03N 1.25W
Whitney Canada **104** 45.30N 78.14W
Whitney, Mt. U.S.A. **109** 36.35N118.18W
Whitney Point *town* U.S.A. **115** 42.20N 75.58W
Whitstable U.K. **13** 51.21N 1.02E
Whitsunday I. Australia **90** 20.17S148.59E
Whittemore U.S.A. **104** 44.14N 83.48W
Whittier U.S.A. **98** 60.46N148.41W
Whittlesea Australia **93** 37.31S145.08E
Whitton U.K. **12** 53.42N 0.39W
Wholdaia L. Canada **101** 60.43N104.20W
Whyalla Australia **92** 33.02S137.35E
Wiarton Canada **104** 44.45N 81.09W
Wichita U.S.A. **111** 37.41N 97.20W
Wichita Falls *town* U.S.A. **111** 33.54N 98.30W
Wick U.K. **14** 58.26N 3.06W
Wickenburg U.S.A. **109** 33.58N112.44W
Wickepin Australia **89** 32.45S117.31E
Wickliffe U.S.A. **114** 41.36N 81.28W
Wicklow Rep. of Ire. **15** 52.59N 6.03W
Wicklow *d.* Rep. of Ire. **15** 52.59N 6.25W
Wicklow Head Rep. of Ire. **15** 52.58N 6.00W
Wicklow Mts. Rep. of Ire. **15** 53.06N 6.20W
Widdifield Canada **104** 46.25N 79.20W
Widen U.S.A. **114** 38.28N 80.52W
Widgiemooltha Australia **89** 31.30S121.34E
Widnes U.K. **12** 53.22N 2.44W
Wiehl Germany **38** 50.57N 7.31E
Wiek Germany **38** 54.37N 13.17E
Wieluń Poland **37** 51.14N 18.34E
Wien Austria **36** 48.13N 16.22E
Wiener Neustadt Austria **36** 47.49N 16.15E
Wieprz *r.* Poland **37** 51.34N 21.49E
Wiesbaden Germany **39** 50.05N 8.14E
Wiesloch Germany **39** 49.17N 8.42E
Wietze Germany **38** 52.39N 9.50E
Wigan U.K. **12** 53.33N 2.38W
Wight, Isle of U.K. **11** 50.40N 1.17W
Wigton U.K. **12** 54.50N 3.09W
Wigtown U.K. **14** 54.47N 4.26W
Wigtown B. U.K. **14** 54.47N 4.15W
Wikwemikong Canada **104** 45.48N 81.44W
Wil Switz. **39** 47.27N 9.03E
Wilber U.S.A. **110** 40.29N 96.58W
Wilberforce Canada **104** 45.03N 78.15W
Wilcannia Australia **92** 31.33S143.24E
Wilcox U.S.A. **114** 41.35N 78.41W
Wilderness U.S.A. **114** 38.19N 77.48W
Wildhorn *mtn.* Switz. **38** 46.22N 7.22E
Wildon Austria **31** 46.53N 15.31E
Wildrose U.S.A. **110** 48.38N103.11W
Wildspitze *mtn.* Austria **39** 46.53N 10.52E
Wildwood U.S.A. **115** 38.59N 74.49W
Wilgena Australia **92** 30.46S134.44E
Wilhelm, Mt. P.N.G. **59** 6.00S144.55E
Wilhelm II Land Antarctica **128** 68.00S 89.00E
Wilhelm-Pieck-Stadt Guben Germany **38** 51.57N 14.43E
Wilhelmshaven Germany **38** 53.31N 8.08E
Wilkes-Barre U.S.A. **115** 41.14N 75.53W
Wilkesboro U.S.A. **113** 36.08N 81.09W
Wilkes Land *f.* Antarctica **128** 69.00S120.00E
Wilkie Canada **101** 52.25N108.43W
Wilkinsburg U.S.A. **114** 40.27N 79.53W
Wilkinson Lakes Australia **91** 29.40S132.39E
Willandra Billabong *r.* Australia **92** 33.08S144.06E
Willard N.Mex. U.S.A. **109** 34.36N106.02W
Willard Ohio U.S.A. **114** 41.03N 82.44W
Willemstad Neth. Antilles **122** 12.12N 68.56W
Willeroo Australia **88** 15.17S131.35E
William, Mt. Australia **92** 37.20S142.41E
William Creek *town* Australia **92** 28.52S136.18E
Williams Australia **89** 33.01S116.45E
Williams *r.* Australia **89** 32.59S116.24E
Williamsburg U.S.A. **113** 37.17N 76.43W
Williams Lake *town* Canada **100** 52.08N122.10W
Williamson U.S.A. **113** 37.42N 82.16W
Williamsport Md. U.S.A. **114** 39.32N 77.50W
Williamsport Penn. U.S.A. **114** 41.14N 77.00W
Williamston U.S.A. **113** 35.53N 77.05W
Williamstown N.J. U.S.A. **115** 39.41N 75.00W
Williamstown N.Y. U.S.A. **115** 43.26N 75.55W
Williamstown W.Va. U.S.A. **114** 39.24N 81.27W
Willimantic U.S.A. **115** 41.43N 72.12W
Willis Group *is.* Australia **90** 16.18S150.00E
Williston R.S.A. **80** 31.21S 20.53E
Williston U.S.A. **110** 48.09N103.37W
Williston L. Canada **100** 55.40N123.40W
Willits U.S.A. **108** 39.25N123.21W
Willmar U.S.A. **110** 45.07N 95.03W
Willmore Wilderness Park Canada **100** 53.45N119.00W
Willochra Australia **92** 32.12S138.10E
Willochra *r.* Australia **92** 31.57S137.52E
Willoughby U.S.A. **114** 41.38N 81.25W
Willow U.S.A. **98** 61.42N150.08W
Willow Grove U.S.A. **115** 40.08N 75.06W
Willow Hill *town* U.S.A. **114** 40.06N 77.48W
Willow L. Canada **100** 62.10N119.08W
Willowmore R.S.A. **80** 33.18S 23.28E
Willow Ranch U.S.A. **108** 41.55N120.21W
Willow River *town* Canada **100** 54.06N122.28W
Willsboro U.S.A. **105** 44.22N 73.26W
Willunga Australia **92** 35.18S138.33E
Wilmette U.S.A. **110** 42.04N 87.43W
Wilmington Del. U.S.A. **115** 39.44N 75.33W
Wilmington N.C. U.S.A. **113** 34.14N 77.55W
Wilmington Vt. U.S.A. **115** 42.52N 72.52W
Wilmslow U.K. **12** 53.19N 2.14W
Wilpena *r.* Australia **92** 31.13S139.25E
Wilson N.C. U.S.A. **113** 35.43N 77.56W
Wilson N.Y. U.S.A. **114** 43.19N 78.50W
Wilson's Promontory *c.* Australia **93** 39.06S146.23E
Wilton *r.* Australia **90** 14.45S134.33E
Wilton U.K. **13** 51.05N 1.52W
Wilton N.Dak. U.S.A. **110** 47.10N100.47W
Wilton N.H. U.S.A. **115** 42.51N 71.44W
Wiltshire *d.* U.K. **13** 51.20N 0.34W
Wiltz Lux. **16** 49.59N 5.53E
Wiluna Australia **88** 26.36S120.13E
Wimmera *r.* Australia **92** 36.05S141.56E
Winam *b.* Kenya **79** 0.15S 34.30E
Winburg R.S.A. **80** 28.30S 27.01E
Wincanton U.K. **13** 51.03N 2.24W
Winchendon U.S.A. **115** 42.41N 72.03W
Winchester Canada **105** 45.06N 75.21W
Winchester U.K. **13** 51.04N 1.19W
Winchester Ky. U.S.A. **113** 38.00N 84.10W
Winchester N.H. U.S.A. **115** 42.46N 72.23W
Winchester Va. U.S.A. **114** 39.11N 78.10W
Winchester Wyo. U.S.A. **108** 43.51N108.10W
Windber U.S.A. **114** 40.14N 78.50W
Windermere *l.* U.K. **12** 54.20N 2.56W
Windfall Canada **100** 54.12N116.13W
Windham U.S.A. **114** 41.14N 81.03W
Windhoek Namibia **80** 22.34S 17.06E
Windom U.S.A. **110** 43.52N 95.07W
Windorah Australia **90** 25.26S142.39E
Wind River Range *mts.* U.S.A. **108** 43.05N109.25W
Windsor Australia **93** 33.38S150.47E
Windsor Nfld. Canada **103** 48.58N 55.40W
Windsor N.S. Canada **103** 44.59N 64.08W
Windsor Ont. Canada **104** 42.18N 83.01W
Windsor Que. Canada **105** 45.34N 72.00W
Windsor U.K. **13** 51.29N 0.38W
Windsor Conn. U.S.A. **115** 41.51N 72.39W
Windsor N.Y. U.S.A. **115** 42.05N 75.39W
Windsor Vt. U.S.A. **115** 43.29N 72.23W
Windsor Locks U.S.A. **115** 41.56N 72.38W
Windward Is. C. America **117** 13.00N 60.00W
Windward Passage *str.* Carib. Sea **117** 20.00N 74.00W
Winfield Kans. U.S.A. **111** 37.15N 96.59W
Winfield W.Va. U.S.A. **114** 38.32N 81.53W
Wingen Australia **93** 31.43S150.54E
Wingham Australia **93** 31.50S152.20E
Wingham Canada **104** 43.53N 81.19W
Winifred U.S.A. **108** 47.34N109.23W
Winisk Canada **102** 55.20N 85.15W
Winisk *r.* Canada **102** 55.00N 85.20W
Winisk L. Canada **102** 53.00N 88.00W
Winkler Canada **101** 49.11N 97.56W
Winklern Austria **39** 46.52N 12.52E
Winneba Ghana **76** 5.22N 0.38W
Winnebago, L. U.S.A. **110** 44.00N 88.25W
Winnemucca U.S.A. **106** 40.58N117.45W
Winnemucca L. U.S.A. **108** 40.09N119.20W
Winner U.S.A. **110** 43.22N 99.51W
Winnfield U.S.A. **111** 31.55N 92.38W
Winnipeg Canada **101** 49.53N 97.09W
Winnipeg *r.* Canada **101** 50.38N 96.19W
Winnipeg, L. Canada **101** 52.00N 97.00W
Winnipegosis, L. Canada **101** 52.30N100.00W
Winnipesaukee, L. U.S.A. **115** 43.35N 71.20W
Winnsboro La. U.S.A. **111** 32.10N 91.43W
Winnsboro S.C. U.S.A. **113** 34.22N 81.05W
Winona Kans. U.S.A. **110** 39.04N101.15W
Winona Minn. U.S.A. **110** 44.03N 91.39W
Winona Miss. U.S.A. **111** 33.29N 89.44W
Winooski U.S.A. **105** 44.29N 73.11W
Winooski *r.* U.S.A. **105** 44.30N 73.15W
Winschoten Neth. **16** 53.07N 7.02E
Winsen Germany **38** 53.22N 10.12E
Winsford U.K. **12** 53.12N 2.31W
Winslow Ariz. U.S.A. **109** 35.01N110.42W
Winslow Maine U.S.A. **112** 44.32N 69.38W
Winsted U.S.A. **115** 41.55N 73.04W
Winston U.S.A. **108** 46.28N111.38W
Winston-Salem U.S.A. **113** 36.05N 80.18W
Winsum Neth. **16** 53.20N 6.31E
Winter Haven U.S.A. **113** 28.02N 81.46W
Winterset U.S.A. **110** 41.20N 94.01W
Winterswijk Neth. **16** 51.58N 6.44E
Winterthur Switz. **39** 47.30N 8.43E
Winthrop Minn. U.S.A. **110** 44.32N 94.22W
Winthrop Wash. U.S.A. **108** 48.29N120.11W
Winton Australia **90** 22.22S143.00E
Winton New Zealand **86** 46.10S168.20E
Winton U.S.A. **108** 41.45N109.10W
Wipper *r.* Germany **38** 51.47N 11.42E
Wirrabara Australia **92** 33.03S138.18E
Wirraminna Australia **92** 31.11S136.04E
Wirrappa Australia **92** 31.28S137.00E
Wirrega Australia **92** 36.11S140.37E
Wirrida, L. Australia **92** 29.45S134.39E
Wirulla Australia **92** 32.24S134.33E
Wisbech U.K. **13** 52.39N 0.10E
Wisconsin *d.* U.S.A. **110** 44.30N 90.00W
Wisconsin *r.* U.S.A. **110** 43.00N 91.15W
Wisconsin Dells U.S.A. **110** 43.38N 89.46W
Wisconsin Rapids *town* U.S.A. **110** 44.24N 89.50W
Wisdom U.S.A. **108** 45.37N113.27W
Wisła *r.* Poland **37** 54.23N 18.52E
Wismar Germany **38** 53.53N 11.28E
Wisner U.S.A. **110** 41.59N 96.55W
Wissembourg France **19** 49.02N 7.57E
Wissen Germany **38** 50.47N 7.43E
Wissmar Germany **38** 50.38N 8.41E
Wisznice Poland **37** 51.48N 23.12E
Witchekan L. Canada **101** 53.25N107.35W
Witham *r.* U.K. **12** 52.56N 0.04E
Witherbee U.S.A. **105** 44.05N 73.32W
Withernsea U.K. **12** 53.43N 0.02E
Witkowo Poland **37** 52.27N 17.47E
Witney U.K. **13** 51.47N 1.29W
Witsand R.S.A. **80** 34.23S 20.49E
Witten Germany **16** 51.26N 7.19E
Wittenberg Germany **38** 51.53N 12.39E
Wittenberge Germany **38** 53.00N 11.44E
Wittenburg Germany **38** 53.31N 11.04E
Wittenoom Australia **88** 22.19S118.21E
Wittingen Germany **38** 52.43N 10.44E
Wittlich Germany **39** 49.59N 6.53E
Wittstock Germany **38** 53.10N 12.29E
Witu Kenya **79** 2.22S 40.20E
Witvlei Namibia **80** 22.25S 18.29E
Witzenhausen Germany **38** 51.20N 9.51E
Wiveliscombe U.K. **13** 51.02N 3.20W
Wkra *r.* Poland **37** 52.27N 20.44E
Władysławowo Poland **37** 54.49N 18.25E
Włocławek Poland **37** 52.39N 19.01E
Włodawa Poland **37** 51.33N 23.31E
Wodonga Australia **93** 36.08S146.09E
Woerden Neth. **16** 52.07N 4.55E
Wohutun China **54** 43.40N123.30E
Wokam *i.* Indonesia **59** 5.45S134.30E
Woking Canada **100** 55.35N118.50W
Woking U.K. **13** 51.20N 0.34W
Wolcott U.S.A. **114** 43.13N 76.49W
Woleai *i.* Pacific Oc. **84** 7.21N143.52E
Wolf *r.* U.S.A. **110** 44.07N 88.43W
Wolfach Germany **39** 48.17N 8.13E
Wolfboro U.S.A. **115** 43.35N 71.12W
Wolf Creek *town* U.S.A. **108** 46.50N112.20W
Wolfe Island *town* Canada **105** 44.12N 76.26W
Wolfen Germany **38** 51.40N 12.16E
Wolfenbüttel Germany **38** 52.10N 10.32E
Wolfhagen Germany **38** 51.19N 9.10E
Wolf Point *town* U.S.A. **108** 48.05N105.39W
Wolfratshausen Germany **39** 47.54N 11.25E
Wolfsberg Austria **31** 46.51N 14.51E
Wolfsburg Germany **38** 52.25N 10.47E
Wolgast Germany **38** 54.03N 13.46E
Wolin Poland **36** 53.51N 14.38E
Wollaston L. Canada **101** 58.15N103.20W
Wollaston Pen. Canada **98** 70.00N115.00W
Wollongong Australia **93** 34.25S150.52E
Wolmaransstad R.S.A. **80** 27.11S 25.58E
Wołomin Poland **37** 52.21N 21.14E
Wolseley Australia **92** 36.21S140.55E
Wolseley Bay *town* Canada **104** 46.07N 80.22W
Wolvega Neth. **16** 52.53N 6.00E
Wolverhampton U.K. **13** 52.35N 2.06W
Wolverine U.S.A. **104** 45.16N 84.36W
Womelsdorf U.S.A. **115** 40.22N 76.11W
Wondai Australia **90** 26.19S151.52E
Wongan Hills *town* Australia **89** 30.55S116.41E
Wonogiri Indonesia **59** 7.48S110.52E
Wonosari Indonesia **59** 7.55S110.39E
Wonosobo Indonesia **59** 7.21S109.56E
Wŏnsan N. Korea **53** 39.07N127.26E
Wonthaggi Australia **93** 38.38S145.37E
Woocalla Australia **92** 31.44S137.10E
Woodbine U.S.A. **115** 39.14N 74.49W
Woodbridge U.K. **13** 52.06N 1.19E
Woodbridge U.S.A. **114** 38.39N 77.15W
Wood Buffalo Nat. Park Canada **100** 59.00N113.41W
Woodburn Australia **93** 29.04S153.21E
Woodbury U.S.A. **115** 39.50N 75.10W
Wooded Bluff *f.* Australia **93** 29.22S153.22E
Woodenbong Australia **93** 28.28S152.35E
Woodgate U.S.A. **115** 43.32N 75.12W
Woodland U.S.A. **108** 38.41N121.46W
Woodlark I. P.N.G. **90** 9.05S152.50E
Wood Mts. Canada **101** 49.14N106.20W
Woodroffe, Mt. Australia **90** 26.20S131.45E
Woods, L. Australia **90** 17.50S133.30E
Woods, L. of the Canada/U.S.A. **102** 49.15N 94.45W
Woodsfield U.S.A. **114** 39.46N 81.07W
Woods Hole U.S.A. **115** 41.31N 70.40W
Woodside Australia **93** 38.31S146.52E
Woods L. Canada **103** 54.40N 64.21W
Woodstock Canada **104** 43.08N 80.45W
Woodstock U.K. **13** 51.51N 1.20W
Woodstock U.S.A. **115** 43.37N 72.31W
Woodstown U.S.A. **115** 39.39N 75.20W
Woodsville U.S.A. **105** 44.09N 72.02W
Woodville New Zealand **86** 40.20S175.52E
Woodward U.S.A. **111** 36.26N 99.24W
Wooler U.K. **12** 55.33N 2.01W
Woolgoolga Australia **93** 30.07S153.12E
Wooltana Australia **92** 30.28S139.26E
Woomera Australia **92** 31.11S136.54E
Woonsocket U.S.A. **115** 42.00N 71.31W
Wooramel Australia **88** 25.42S114.20E
Wooramel *r.* Australia **88** 25.47S114.10E
Woorong, L. Australia **92** 29.24S134.06E
Wooster U.S.A. **114** 40.48N 81.56W
Worb Switz. **19** 46.56N 7.34E
Worcester R.S.A. **80** 33.39S 19.25E
Worcester U.K. **13** 52.12N 2.12W
Worcester U.S.A. **115** 42.16N 71.48W
Wörgl Austria **39** 47.29N 12.04E
Workington U.K. **12** 54.39N 3.34W
Worksop U.K. **12** 53.19N 1.09W
Workum Neth. **16** 53.00N 5.26E
Worland U.S.A. **108** 44.01N107.57W
Worms Germany **39** 49.38N 8.22E
Wörnitz *r.* Germany **39** 48.42N 10.45E
Wörrstadt Germany **39** 49.50N 8.07E
Wörther See *l.* Austria **31** 46.37N 14.10E
Worthing U.K. **13** 50.49N 0.21W
Worthington Minn. U.S.A. **110** 43.37N 95.36W
Worthington Ohio U.S.A. **112** 40.03N 83.03W
Worthville U.S.A. **112** 38.38N 85.05W
Wosi Indonesia **59** 0.15S128.00E
Wour Chad **77** 21.21N 15.57E
Wowtchaba Cameroon **77** 5.13N 13.05E
Wowoni *i.* Indonesia **59** 4.10S123.10E
Wragby U.K. **12** 53.17N 0.18E
Wrangel I. *see* Vrangelya, Ostrov *i.* U.S.S.R. **51**
Wrangell U.S.A. **100** 56.28N132.23W
Wrangell Mts. U.S.A. **98** 62.00N143.00W
Wrangle U.K. **12** 53.03N 0.09E
Wrath, C. U.K. **14** 58.37N 5.01W
Wray U.S.A. **110** 40.05N102.13W
Wrecks, B. of Kiribati **85** 1.52N157.17W
Wrexham U.K. **12** 53.05N 3.00W
Wrigley Canada **98** 63.16N123.39W
Wrocław Poland **37** 51.05N 17.00E
Wronki Poland **36** 52.43N 16.23E
Wroxeter Canada **104** 43.50N 81.07W
Września Poland **37** 52.20N 17.34E
Wubin Australia **89** 30.06S116.38E
Wuchang China **55** 30.21N114.19E
Wucheng China **54** 37.12N116.04E
Wuchuan Guangdong China **55** 21.21N110.40E
Wuchuan Nei Monggol China **54** 41.08N111.24E
Wuda China **54** 39.40N106.40E
Wuday'ah Saudi Arabia **71** 16.05N 47.05E
Wudham 'Alwā' Oman **65** 23.48N 57.33E
Wudinna Australia **92** 33.03S135.28E
Wudu China **54** 33.24N104.50E
Wufeng China **55** 30.12N110.36E
Wugang China **55** 26.42N110.31E
Wugong Shan *mts.* China **55** 27.15N114.00E
Wuhai China **54** 39.50N106.40E
Wuhan China **55** 30.37N114.19E
Wuhu China **55** 31.25N118.25E
Wūjang China **63** 33.38N 79.55E
Wu Jiang *r.* China **55** 29.41N107.24E
Wukari Nigeria **77** 7.57N 9.42E
Wulian China **54** 35.45N119.12E
Wuliang Shan *mts.* China **52** 24.27N100.43E
Wum Cameroon **77** 6.25N 10.03E
Wumbulgal Australia **93** 34.25S146.16E
Wuming China **55** 23.10N108.16E
Wuning China **55** 29.17N115.05E
Wunnummin L. Canada **102** 52.50N 89.20W
Wun Rog Sudan **73** 9.00N 28.21E
Wunstorf Germany **38** 52.25N 9.26E
Wuppertal Germany **38** 51.16N 7.11E
Wuppertal R.S.A. **80** 32.16S 19.12E
Wuqi China **54** 37.03N108.14E
Wuqiao China **54** 37.38N116.22E
Wuqing China **54** 39.19N117.05E
Wurno Nigeria **77** 13.20N 5.28E
Wurtsboro U.S.A. **115** 41.35N 74.29W
Würzburg Germany **39** 49.48N 9.56E
Wurzen Germany **38** 51.22N 12.44E
Wusong China **55** 31.20N121.30E
Wutach *r.* Germany **39** 47.37N 8.15E
Wutongqiao China **55** 29.20N103.48E
Wuwei China **54** 38.00N102.59E
Wuxi Jiangsu China **55** 31.34N120.20E
Wuxi Sichuan China **55** 31.28N109.36E
Wuxing China **55** 30.59N120.04E
Wuyi Shan *mts.* China **55** 27.00N117.00E
Wuyuan China **54** 41.06N108.16E

Wuzhan to **Yirga' Alem**

Wuzhan China 53 50.14N125.18E
Wuzhi Shan *mts.* China 55 18.50N109.30E
Wuzhou China 55 23.28N111.21E
Wyalkatchem Australia 89 31.21S117.22E
Wyalong Australia 93 33.55S147.17E
Wyandotte U.S.A. 114 42.12N 83.10W
Wyandra Australia 91 27.15S146.00E
Wyangala Resr. Australia 93 33.58S148.55E
Wyara, L. Australia 92 28.42S144.16E
Wycheproof Australia 92 36.04S143.14E
Wye U.K. 13 51.11N 0.56E
Wye *r.* U.K. 13 51.37N 2.40W
Wyk Germany 38 54.42N 8.34E
Wymondham U.K. 13 52.34N 1.07E
Wynbring Australia 91 30.33S133.32E
Wyndham Australia 88 15.29S128.05E
Wynne U.S.A. 111 35.14N 90.47W
Wyoming Canada 104 42.57N 82.07W
Wyoming *d.* U.S.A. 108 43.10N107.36W
Wyong Australia 93 33.17S151.25E
Wyszków Poland 37 52.36N 21.28E
Wytheville U.S.A. 113 36.57N 81.07W

Xa Cassau Angola 78 9.02S 20.17E
Xagquka China 63 31.50N 92.46E
Xainza China 63 30.56N 88.40E
Xaitongmoin China 63 29.22N 88.15E
Xai-Xai Mozambique 81 25.05S 33.38E
Xalin *well* Somali Rep. 71 9.08N 48.47E
Xam Nua Laos 56 20.25N104.10E
Xangdoring China 63 32.06N 82.02E
Xangongo Angola 78 16.31S 15.00E
Xanten Germany 38 51.39N 6.26E
Xánthi Greece 34 41.08N 24.53E
Xarardheere Somali Rep. 71 4.32N 47.53E
Xar Hudag China 54 45.07N114.28E
Xar Moron He *r.* China 54 43.30N120.42E
Xarrama *r.* Portugal 27 38.14N 8.20W
Xassengue Angola 78 10.26S 18.32E
Xau, L. Botswana 80 21.15S 24.50E
Xebert China 54 44.02N122.00E
Xenia U.S.A. 112 39.41N 83.56W
Xequessa Angola 78 16.47S 19.05E
Xertigny France 19 48.03N 6.24E
Xhora R.S.A. 80 31.58S 28.40E
Xiachuan *i.* China 55 21.40N112.37E
Xiaguan China 52 25.33N100.09E
Xiamen China 55 24.30N118.08E
Xi'an China 54 34.11N108.55E
Xianfeng China 55 29.41N109.02E
Xiangcheng China 54 33.50N113.29E
Xiangfan China 55 32.04N112.05E
Xiangfen China 54 35.52N111.24E
Xiang Jiang *r.* China 55 28.49N112.30E
Xiangkhoang Laos 56 19.21N103.23E
Xiangquan He *r.* China 63 31.45N 78.40E
Xiangshan China 55 29.29N121.51E
Xiangtan China 55 27.50N112.49E
Xiangtang China 55 28.26N115.58E
Xiangyin China 55 28.40N112.53E
Xiangyuan China 54 36.32N113.02E
Xiangzhou China 55 23.58N109.41E
Xianju China 55 28.51N120.44E
Xianning China 55 29.53N114.13E
Xian Xian China 54 38.12N116.07E
Xianyang China 54 34.20N108.40E
Xianyou China 55 25.28N118.50E
Xiao Hinggan Ling *mts.* China 53 48.40N128.30E
Xiaojiang China 55 27.34N120.27E
Xiaojiao China 54 38.24N113.42E
Xiaowutai Shan *mtn.* China 54 39.57N114.59E
Xiapu China 55 26.58N119.57E
Xiayang China 55 26.45N117.58E
Xichang China 52 27.53N102.18E
Xichou China 55 23.27N104.40E
Xichuan China 54 33.15N111.27E
Xifeng China 55 27.06N106.44E
Xigazê China 52 29.18N 88.50E
Xiheying China 54 39.53N114.42E
Xiji China 54 35.52N105.35E
Xi Jiang *r.* China 55 22.23N113.20E
Xiliao He *r.* China 54 43.48N123.00E
Xilin China 55 24.30N105.03E
Xilókastron Greece 35 38.04N 22.43E
Ximeng China 61 22.45N 99.29E
Xin'anjiang China 55 29.27N119.14E
Xin'anjiang Shuiku *resr.* China 55 29.32N119.00E
Xincheng Guang. Zhuang. China 55 24.04N108.40E
Xincheng Ningxia Huizu China 54 38.33N106.10E
Xincheng Shanxi China 54 37.57N112.35E
Xindu China 55 30.50N104.12E
Xinfeng Guangdong China 55 24.04N114.12E
Xinfeng Jiangxi China 55 25.27N114.58E
Xing'an China 55 25.35N110.32E
Xingcheng China 54 40.37N120.43E
Xinghua China 54 32.51N119.50E
Xingkai Hu *l.* *see* Khanka, Ozero U.S.S.R./China 53
Xingren China 55 25.26N105.14E
Xingshan China 55 31.10N110.51E
Xingtai China 54 37.04N114.26E
Xingu *r.* Brazil 123 1.40S 52.15W
Xing Xian China 54 38.31N111.04E
Xingyi China 55 25.00N104.59E
Xinhe Hebei China 54 37.22N115.14E
Xinhe Xin. Uygur China 52 41.34N 82.38E
Xinhua China 55 27.45N111.18E
Xining China 52 36.35N101.55E
Xinji China 54 35.17N115.35E
Xinjiang-Uygur *d.* China 52 41.15N 87.00E
Xinjie China 54 39.15N109.36E
Xinjin Liaoning China 54 39.27N121.48E
Xinjin Sichuan China 55 30.30N103.47E
Xinle China 54 38.15N114.40E
Xinlitun China 54 42.00N122.09E
Xinmin China 54 42.01N122.48E
Xinning China 55 26.31N110.48E
Xinshao China 55 27.20N111.26E
Xin Xian China 54 38.24N112.47E
Xinxiang China 54 35.12N113.57E
Xinyang China 54 32.08N114.04E
Xinyi Guangdong China 55 22.21N110.57E
Xinyi Jiangsu China 54 34.20N118.30E
Xinyu China 55 27.50N114.55E
Xinzheng China 54 34.25N113.46E
Xinzhu Taiwan 55 24.50N120.58E
Xiping Henan China 54 33.23N114.02E
Xiping Zhejiang China 55 28.27N119.29E
Xique Xique Brazil 123 10.47S 42.44W
Xi Ujimqin Qi China 54 44.32N117.40E
Xiuning China 55 29.48N118.20E
Xiushan China 55 28.27N108.59E
Xiushui China 55 29.01N114.37E
Xixabangma Feng *mtn.* China 63 28.21N 85.47E
Xixia China 54 33.30N111.30E
Xizang *d.* China 63 31.45N 87.00E
Xorkol China 52 39.04N 91.05E
Xuancheng China 55 30.59N118.40E
Xuang *r.* Laos 56 19.59N102.20E
Xuanhan China 55 31.25N107.38E
Xuanhua China 54 40.30N115.00E
Xuanwei China 55 26.16N104.01E
Xuchang China 54 34.02N113.50E
Xuddur Somali Rep. 71 4.10N 43.53E
Xuefeng Shan *mts.* China 55 27.30N111.00E
Xueshuiwen China 53 49.15N129.39E
Xugou China 54 34.40N119.26E
Xunyang China 54 32.48N109.27E
Xupu China 55 27.54N110.35E
Xushui China 54 39.01N115.39E
Xuwen China 55 20.25N110.20E
Xuyong China 55 28.17N105.21E
Xuzhou China 54 34.14N117.20E

Ya Gabon 78 1.17S 14.14E
Ya'an China 61 30.00N102.59E
Yaapeet Australia 92 35.48S142.07E
Ya'bad Jordan 67 32.27N 35.10E
Yabassi Cameroon 77 4.30N 9.55E
Yabēlo Ethiopia 73 4.54N 38.05E
Yābis, Wādī al Jordan 67 32.24N 35.35E
Yablonovyy Khrebet *mts.* U.S.S.R. 51 53.20N115.00E
Yabrai Shan *mts.* China 54 39.50N103.30E
Yabrai Yanchang China 54 39.24N102.43E
Yabrūd Syria 66 33.58N 36.40E
Yacheng China 55 18.35N109.13E
Yacuiba Bolivia 124 22.00S 63.25W
Yādgīr India 60 16.46N 77.08E
Yadong China 63 27.29N 88.54E
Yagaba Ghana 76 10.13N 1.14W
Yagoua Cameroon 77 10.23N 15.13E
Yagra China 63 31.32N 82.27E
Yagur Israel 67 32.44N 35.04E
Yahagi *r.* Japan 57 34.50N136.59E
Yahisuli Zaïre 78 0.08S 24.04E
Yahuma Zaïre 78 1.06N 23.10E
Yaizu Japan 57 34.52N138.20E
Yajua Nigeria 77 11.27N 12.49E
Yakchāl Afghan. 62 31.47N 64.41E
Yakima U.S.A. 108 46.36N120.31W
Yakmach Pakistan 62 28.45N 63.51E
Yaksha U.S.S.R. 44 61.51N 56.59E
Yaku shima *i.* Japan 57 30.20N130.40E
Yakutat U.S.A. 100 59.29N139.49W
Yakutat B. U.S.A. 100 59.29N139.49W
Yakutsk U.S.S.R. 51 62.10N129.20E
Yala Thailand 56 6.32N101.19E
Yale U.S.A. 114 43.08N 82.48W
Yalgoo Australia 89 28.20S116.41E
Yalinga C.A.R. 73 6.31N 23.15E
Yallourn Australia 93 38.09S146.22E
Yalong Jiang *r.* China 52 26.35N101.44E
Yalta U.S.S.R. 45 44.30N 34.09E
Yalu Jiang *r.* China 54 40.10N124.25E
Yalutorovsk U.S.S.R. 50 56.41N 66.12E
Yamagata Japan 57 38.16N140.19E
Yamaguchi Japan 57 34.10N131.28E
Yamal, Poluostrov *pen.* U.S.S.R. 50 70.20N 70.00E
Yamanashi Japan 57 35.40N138.40E
Yamanashi *d.* Japan 57 35.30N138.35E
Yamandjo Zaïre 78 1.38N 23.27E
Yaman Tau *mtn.* U.S.S.R. 44 54.20N 58.10E
Yamaska Canada 105 46.01N 72.55W
Yamaska *r.* Canada 105 46.06N 72.56W
Yamato Japan 57 35.29N139.29E
Yamato-takada Japan 57 34.31N135.45E
Yamba N.S.W. Australia 93 29.26S153.22E
Yamba S.A. Australia 92 34.15S140.54E
Yambéring Guinea 76 11.49N 12.18W
Yambio Sudan 73 4.34N 28.23E
Yambol Bulgaria 34 42.30N 26.30E
Yamdena *i.* Indonesia 59 7.30S131.00E
Yamenyingzi China 54 42.23N121.03E
Yamethin Burma 56 20.24N 96.08E
Yam HaMelah *see* Dead Sea Jordan 67
Yam Kinneret *l.* Israel 67 32.49N 35.36E
Yamma Yamma, L. Australia 90 26.20S141.25E
Yamoussoukro Ivory Coast 76 6.51N 5.18W
Yampi Sound Australia 88 16.11S123.30E
Yampol U.S.S.R. 37 48.13N 28.12E
Yamuna *r.* India 63 25.25N 81.50E
Yamzho Yumco *l.* China 63 29.00N 90.40E
Yan Nigeria 77 10.05N 12.11E
Yana *r.* U.S.S.R. 51 71.30N135.00E
Yanac Australia 92 36.09S141.29E
Yan'an China 54 36.45N109.22E
Yanbu'al Baḩr Saudi Arabia 64 24.07N 38.04E
Yancannia Australia 92 30.16S142.50E
Yancheng China 54 33.22N120.05E
Yanchep Australia 89 31.32S115.33E
Yanchi China 54 37.47N107.24E
Yanchuan China 54 36.51N110.05E
Yanco Australia 93 34.36S146.25E
Yanco Glen *town* Australia 92 31.43S141.39E
Yanda *r.* Australia 93 30.22S145.38E
Yandong China 55 24.02N107.09E
Yandoon Burma 56 17.02N 95.39E
Yanfolila Mali 76 11.11N 8.09W
Yangarey U.S.S.R. 44 68.46N 61.29E
Yangchun China 55 22.03N111.46E
Yangcun China 55 23.26N114.30E
Yangjiang China 55 21.50N111.54E
Yangmingshan Taiwan 55 25.18N121.35E
Yangon *see* Rangoon Burma 56
Yangqu China 54 38.03N112.36E
Yangquan China 54 37.49N113.28E
Yangshan Guangdong China 55 24.29N112.38E
Yangshan Liaoning China 54 41.15N120.18E
Yangshuo China 55 24.47N110.30E
Yangtze *r.* *see* Chang Jiang *r.* China 55
Yang Xian China 54 33.10N107.35E
Yangxin China 55 29.50N115.10E
Yangze China 55 26.59N118.19E
Yangzhou China 54 32.22N119.26E
Yanhuqu China 63 32.32N 82.44E
Yanji China 53 42.45N129.25E
Yanko Creek *r.* Australia 93 35.25S145.27E
Yankton U.S.A. 110 42.53N 97.23W
Yanqi China 52 42.00N 86.30E
Yanshan China 61 23.36N104.20E
Yanshiping China 63 33.35N 92.04E
Yanskiy Zaliv *g.* U.S.S.R. 51 72.00N136.10E
Yantabulla Australia 93 29.13S145.01E
Yantai China 54 37.27N121.26E
Yantra *r.* Bulgaria 34 43.35N 25.37E
Yanxi China 55 28.11N110.58E
Yanzhou China 54 35.35N116.52E
Yao Chad 77 12.52N 17.34E
Yao Japan 57 34.37N135.36E
Yaopu China 55 26.05N105.42E
Yaoundé Cameroon 77 3.51N 11.31E
Yao Xian China 54 34.52N109.01E
Yap *i.* Caroline Is. 59 9.30N138.09E
Yapehe Zaïre 78 0.10S 24.20E
Yapen *i.* Indonesia 59 1.45S136.10E
Yaqui *r.* Mexico 109 27.37N110.39W
Yar U.S.S.R. 44 58.13N 52.08E
Yaraka Australia 90 24.53S144.04E
Yaransk U.S.S.R. 44 57.22N 47.49E
Yardea Australia 92 32.23S135.32E
Yare *r.* U.K. 13 52.34N 1.45E
Yaremcha U.S.S.R. 37 48.26N 24.29E
Yarensk U.S.S.R. 44 62.10N 49.07E
Yargora U.S.S.R. 37 46.25N 28.20E
Yariga take *mtn.* Japan 57 36.21N137.39E
Yārīn Lebanon 67 33.06N 35.14E
Yaritagua Venezuela 122 10.05N 69.07W
Yarkant He *r.* China 52 40.30N 80.55E
Yarker Canada 105 44.22N 76.46W
Yarlung Zangbo Jiang *r.* China *see* Brahmaputra *r.* Asia 63
Yarmouth Canada 103 43.50N 66.07W
Yarmūk *r.* Jordan/Syria 67 32.38N 35.34E
Yaroslavl U.S.S.R. 44 57.34N 39.52E
Yarqon *r.* Israel 67 32.06N 34.47E
Yarra *r.* Australia 93 37.51S144.54E
Yarram Australia 93 38.30S146.41E
Yarrawonga Australia 93 36.02S145.59E
Yarrow *r.* U.K. 14 55.32N 2.51W
Yar Sale U.S.S.R. 50 66.50N 70.48E
Yartsevo R.S.F.S.R. U.S.S.R. 51 60.17N 90.02E
Yartsevo R.S.F.S.R. U.S.S.R. 44 55.06N 32.43E
Yarumal Colombia 122 6.59N 75.25W
Yasanyama Zaïre 73 4.18N 21.11E
Yaselda *r.* U.S.S.R. 37 52.07N 26.28E
Yasen U.S.S.R. 37 53.10N 28.55E
Yashi Nigeria 77 12.23N 7.54E
Yashkul U.S.S.R. 45 46.10N 45.20E
Yasinya U.S.S.R. 37 48.12N 24.20E
Yasothon Thailand 56 15.46N104.12E
Yass Australia 93 34.51S148.55E
Yas'ur Israel 67 32.54N 35.10E
Yatakala Niger 76 14.52N 0.22E
Yaté N. Cal. 84 22.09S166.57E
Yates Center U.S.A. 111 37.53N 95.44W
Yathkyed L. Canada 101 62.40N 98.00W
Yatsuo Japan 57 36.35N137.10E
Yatsushiro Japan 57 32.32N130.35E
Yaţţah Jordan 67 31.27N 35.05E
Yāval India 62 21.10N 75.42E
Yavatmāl India 63 20.24N 78.08E
Yaví, Cerro *mtn.* Venezuela 122 5.32N 65.59W
Yavne Israel 67 31.53N 34.45E
Yavne'el Israel 67 32.42N 35.30E
Yavorov U.S.S.R. 37 49.59N 23.20E
Yawng-hwe Burma 56 20.35N 96.58E
Yaxi China 55 27.35N106.40E
Ya Xian China 55 18.19N109.32E
Yazd Iran 65 31.54N 54.22E
Yazmān Pakistan 62 29.08N 71.45E
Yazoo *r.* U.S.A. 111 32.22N 91.00W
Yazoo City U.S.A. 111 32.51N 90.28W
Ybbs Austria 36 48.11N 15.05E
Yding Skovhöj *hill* Denmark 42 56.00N 9.48E
Ydsteböhavn Norway 42 59.08N 5.15E
Ye Burma 56 15.15N 97.50E
Yea Australia 93 37.12S145.25E
Yecla Spain 25 38.37N 1.07W
Yedintsy U.S.S.R. 45 48.09N 27.18E
Yeeda Australia 88 17.36S123.39E
Yefremov U.S.S.R. 44 53.08N 38.08E
Yegorlyk *r.* U.S.S.R. 45 46.30N 41.52E
Yegoryevsk U.S.S.R. 44 55.21N 39.01E
Yegros Paraguay 126 26.24S 56.25W
Yei Sudan 73 4.05N 30.40E
Yei *r.* Sudan 73 7.20N 30.39E
Yeji China 55 31.51N115.01E
Yelets U.S.S.R. 44 52.36N 38.30E
Yeletskiy U.S.S.R. 44 67.04N 64.00E
Yélimané Mali 76 15.08N 10.34W
Yell *i.* U.K. 14 60.35N 1.05W
Yellowdine Australia 89 31.19S119.36E
Yellowhead Pass Canada 100 52.53N118.25W
Yellowknife Canada 100 62.27N114.21W
Yellowknife *r.* Canada 100 62.27N114.19W
Yellow Mt. Australia 93 32.19S146.50E
Yellow Sea Asia 53 35.00N123.00E
Yellowstone *r.* U.S.A. 106 47.55N103.45W
Yellowstone L. U.S.A. 108 44.25N110.38W
Yellowstone Nat. Park U.S.A. 108 44.30N110.35W
Yell Sd. U.K. 14 60.30N 1.11W
Yelma Australia 88 26.30S121.40E
Yelsk U.S.S.R. 37 51.50N 29.10E
Yelwa Nigeria 77 10.48N 4.42E
Yemen Asia 71 14.00N 47.00E
Yemilchino U.S.S.R. 37 50.58N 27.40E
Yenagoa Nigeria 77 4.59N 6.15E
Yenangyaung Burma 56 20.28N 94.54E
Yen Bai Vietnam 56 21.43N104.44E
Yenda Australia 93 34.15S146.13E
Yendi Ghana 76 9.29N 0.01W
Yengan Burma 56 21.06N 96.30E
Yenisey *r.* U.S.S.R. 51 69.00N 86.00E
Yeniseysk U.S.S.R. 51 58.27N 92.13E
Yeniseyskiy Zaliv *g.* U.S.S.R. 50 73.00N 79.00E
Yenshui Taiwan 55 23.20N120.16E
Yenyuka U.S.S.R. 51 57.57N121.15E
Yeo *l.* Canada 104 45.24N 81.49W
Yeo L. Australia 89 28.04S124.23E
Yeola India 62 20.02N 74.29E
Yeoval Australia 93 32.44S148.39E
Yeovil U.K. 13 50.57N 2.38W
Yepáchic U.S.A. 109 28.27N108.25W
Yeppoon Australia 90 23.08S150.45E
Yeráki Greece 35 37.00N 22.42E
Yerbent U.S.S.R. 65 39.23N 58.35E
Yercha U.S.S.R. 51 69.34N147.30E
Yerda Australia 92 31.05S135.04E
Yerepol U.S.S.R. 51 65.15N168.43E
Yerevan U.S.S.R. 65 40.10N 44.31E
Yerington U.S.A. 108 38.59N119.10W
Yermak U.S.S.R. 50 52.03N 76.55E
Yermitsa U.S.S.R. 44 66.56N 52.20E
Yermo Mexico 111 26.23N104.01W
Yermo U.S.A. 109 34.54N116.50W
Yerolimin Greece 35 36.28N 22.24E
Yershov U.S.S.R. 45 51.22N 48.16E
Yertom U.S.S.R. 44 63.31N 47.51E
Yerushalayim *d.* Israel 67 31.45N 35.00E
Yerushalayim Israel/Jordan 67 31.47N 35.13E
Yesa, Embalse de *resr.* Spain 25 42.36N 1.09W
Yeşil *r.* Turkey 64 41.22N 36.37E
Yeso U.S.A. 109 34.26N104.37W
Yessey U.S.S.R. 51 68.29N102.15E
Yeste Spain 26 38.22N 2.18W
Yetman Australia 93 28.55S150.49E
Yeu Burma 56 22.49N 95.26E
Yeu, Île d' *i.* France 18 46.42N 2.20W
Yevpatoriya U.S.S.R. 45 45.12N 33.20E
Yevstratovskiy U.S.S.R. 45 50.07N 39.45E
Yew Mtn. U.S.A. 114 38.05N 80.16W
Ye Xian China 54 37.10N119.56E
Yeysk U.S.S.R. 45 46.43N 38.17E
Yi *r.* Uruguay 125 33.17S 58.08W
Yiannitsá Greece 34 40.46N 22.24E
Yíaros *i.* Greece 35 37.36N 24.40E
Yibin China 55 28.42N104.34E
Yibug Caka *l.* China 63 33.50N 87.00E
Yichang China 55 30.21N111.21E
Yichuan China 54 34.25N112.26E
Yidu China 54 36.45N118.24E
Yifag Ethiopia 73 12.02N 37.44E
Yiftah Israel 67 33.07N 35.33E
Yijun China 54 35.23N109.07E
Yilan China 53 46.22N129.31E
Yilehuli Shan *mts.* China 53 51.20N124.20E
Yilliminning Australia 89 32.54S117.22E
Yilong China 55 31.34N106.24E
Yimen China 54 34.21N107.07E
Yinan China 54 35.33N118.27E
Yinchuan China 54 38.27N106.18E
Yindarlgooda, L. Australia 89 30.45S121.55E
Yingcheng China 55 30.57N113.33E
Yingde China 55 24.07N113.20E
Yinggehai China 55 18.31N108.40E
Yingkou China 54 40.39N122.18E
Yingshan China 55 31.06N116.35E
Yingshang China 54 32.42N116.20E
Yingtan China 55 28.11N116.55E
Yinkanie Australia 92 34.21S140.20E
Yinning China 52 43.57N 81.23E
Yin Shan *mts.* China 54 41.30N109.00E
Yirga' Alem Ethiopia 73 6.52N 38.22E

Yirol to **Zomba**

Yirol Sudan **73** 6.33N 30.30E
Yirwa Sudan **73** 7.47N 27.15E
Yishan China **55** 24.37N108.32E
Yíthion Greece **35** 36.45N 22.34E
Yiwu China **55** 29.18N120.04E
Yi Xian China **54** 41.30N121.14E
Yiyang Henan China **54** 34.30N112.10E
Yiyang Hunan China **55** 28.20N112.30E
Yiyuan China **54** 36.12N118.08E
Yizhang China **55** 25.24N112.57E
Yizre'el Israel **67** 32.33N 35.20E
Ylitornio Finland **40** 66.19N 23.40E
Ylivieska Finland **40** 64.05N 24.33E
Yngaren *l.* Sweden **43** 58.52N 16.35E
Yoakum U.S.A. **111** 29.17N 97.09W
Yodo *r.* Japan **57** 34.41N135.25E
Yogyakarta Indonesia **59** 7.48S110.24E
Yogyakarta *d.* Indonesia **59** 7.48S110.22E
Yokadouma Cameroon **77** 3.26N 15.06E
Yokkaichi Japan **57** 34.58N136.37E
Yoko Cameroon **77** 5.29N 12.19E
Yokohama Japan **57** 35.27N139.39E
Yokosuka Japan **57** 35.18N139.40E
Yola Nigeria **77** 9.14N 12.32E
Yom *r.* Thailand **56** 15.47N100.05E
Yona Guam **84** 13.25N144.47E
Yonago Japan **57** 35.27N133.20E
Yondŏk S. Korea **57** 36.26N129.23E
Yongcheng China **54** 33.56N116.22E
Yongchuan China **55** 29.19N105.55E
Yongchun China **55** 25.19N118.17E
Yongdeng China **54** 36.44N103.24E
Yonghe China **54** 36.44N110.39E
Yongnian China **54** 36.47N114.30E
Yongring China **55** 22.45N108.29E
Yongshou China **54** 34.40N108.04E
Yongxiu China **55** 28.58N115.43E
Yonkers U.S.A. **115** 40.56N 73.52W
Yonne *d.* France **19** 47.55N 3.45E
Yonne *r.* France **19** 48.23N 2.58E
York Australia **89** 31.55S116.45E
York Canada **104** 43.41N 79.29W
York U.K. **12** 53.58N 1.07W
York *r.* U.S.A. **113** 37.15N 76.23W
York Nebr. U.S.A. **110** 40.52N 97.36W
York Penn. U.S.A. **114** 39.58N 76.44W
York, C. Australia **90** 10.42S142.31E
Yorke Pen. Australia **92** 35.00S137.30E
Yorketown Australia **92** 35.02S137.35E
York Factory *town* Canada **101** 57.00N 92.18W
York Haven U.S.A. **114** 40.07N 76.43W
Yorkshire Wolds *hills* U.K. **12** 54.00N 0.39W
Yorkton Canada **101** 51.13N102.28W
York Village U.S.A. **115** 43.08N 70.38W
Yoro Honduras **117** 15.09N 87.07W
Yōrō Japan **57** 35.32N140.04E
Yosemite Nat. Park U.S.A. **108** 37.45N119.35W
Yoshino *r.* Japan **57** 34.22N135.40E
Yoshkar Ola U.S.S.R. **44** 56.38N 47.52E
Yos Sudarsa, Pulau *i.* Indonesia **59** 8.00S138.30E
Yŏsu S. Korea **53** 34.46N127.45E
Youghal Rep. of Ire. **15** 51.58N 7.51W
You Jiang *r.* Guang. Zhuang. China **55** 23.28N111.18E
Youkou Ivory Coast **76** 5.16N 7.16W
Youkounkoun Guinea **76** 12.35N 13.11W
Young Australia **93** 34.19S148.20E
Young *r.* Australia **89** 33.45S121.12E
Young Uruguay **125** 32.41S 57.38W
Young U.S.A. **109** 34.06N110.57W
Younghusband, L. Australia **92** 30.51S136.05E
Younghusband Pen. Australia **92** 36.00S139.15E
Youngstown Canada **101** 51.32N111.13W
Youngstown U.S.A. **114** 41.06N 80.39W
Youngsville U.S.A. **114** 41.48N 74.54W
You Xian China **55** 26.59N113.12E
Youyang China **55** 28.52N108.45E
Youyu China **54** 39.59N112.27E
Yoxford U.K. **13** 52.16N 1.30E
Yozgat Turkey **64** 39.50N 34.48E
Ypsilanti U.S.A. **104** 42.15N 83.36W
Yreka U.S.A. **108** 41.44N122.38W
Yssingeaux France **21** 45.08N 4.07E
Ystad Sweden **43** 55.25N 13.49E
Ythan *r.* U.K. **14** 57.21N 2.01W
Ytterhogdal Sweden **41** 62.12N 14.51E
Yu'alliq, Jabal *mtn.* Egypt **66** 30.21N 33.31E
Yuanbaoshan China **54** 42.15N119.14E
Yuan Jiang *r.* Hunan China **55** 29.00N111.55E
Yuan Jiang *r.* Yunnan China *see* Hong Hàr. *r.* Vietnam **52**
Yuanling China **55** 28.28N110.15E
Yuanping China **54** 38.42N112.46E
Yuba City U.S.A. **108** 39.08N121.27W
Yūbari Japan **57** 43.04N141.59E
Yubdo Ethiopia **73** 9.00N 35.22E
Yucatán *d.* Mexico **117** 19.30N 89.00W
Yucatan Channel Carib. Sea **117** 21.30N 86.00W
Yucatan Pen. Mexico **116** 19.00N 90.00W
Yucca U.S.A. **109** 34.52N114.09W
Yuci China **54** 37.37N112.47E
Yudino U.S.S.R. **50** 55.49N 48.54E
Yudu China **55** 25.57N115.16E
Yuendumu Australia **90** 22.14S131.47E
Yueqing China **55** 28.08N120.57E
Yuexi China **52** 28.36N102.35E
Yueyang China **55** 29.22N113.10E
Yugan China **55** 28.41N116.41E
Yugorskiy Poluostrov *pen.* U.S.S.R. **44** 69.00N 62.30E
Yugoslavia Europe **34** 44.00N 20.00E
Yuhang China **55** 30.25N120.18E
Yuhebu China **54** 37.59N109.51E
Yukon *r.* U.S.A. **98** 62.35N164.20W
Yukon Territory *d.* Canada **98** 65.00N135.00W
Yulara Australia **90** 25.14S131.02E
Yule *r.* Australia **88** 20.19S118.08E
Yuleba Australia **90** 26.37S149.20E
Yulin Guang. Zhuang. China **55** 22.38N110.10E
Yulin Shaanxi China **54** 38.11N109.33E
Yuma Ariz. U.S.A. **109** 32.43N114.37W
Yuma Colo. U.S.A. **108** 40.08N102.43W
Yumen China **52** 40.19N 97.12E
Yunan China **55** 23.14N111.35E
Yuncheng China **54** 35.02N111.00E
Yungas *f.* Bolivia **124** 16.20S 65.00W
Yungera Australia **92** 34.48S143.10E
Yungxiao China **55** 23.59N117.27E
Yunkai Dashan *mts.* China **55** 22.30N111.05E
Yunnan *d.* China **52** 24.30N101.30E
Yunta Australia **92** 32.37S139.34E
Yunxi China **54** 33.00N110.22E
Yun Xian China **54** 32.48N110.50E
Yunyang China **55** 30.55N108.56E
Yuqing China **55** 27.12N107.56E
Yuribey U.S.S.R. **50** 71.02N 77.02E
Yurimaguas Peru **122** 5.54S 76.07W
Yuryuzan U.S.S.R. **44** 54.51N 58.25E
Yu Shan *mtn.* Taiwan **55** 23.20N121.03E
Yushkozero U.S.S.R. **44** 64.45N 32.03E
Yushu China **52** 33.06N 96.48E
Yūtō Japan **57** 34.42N137.38E
Yu Xian China **54** 34.10N113.28E
Yuxikou China **55** 31.29N118.16E
Yuyao China **55** 30.03N120.11E
Yuzhno Sakhalinsk U.S.S.R. **53** 46.58N142.45E
Yuzhnyy Bug *r.* U.S.S.R. **37** 46.55N 31.59E
Yuzhong China **54** 35.52N104.02E
Yvelines *d.* France **19** 48.50N 1.50E
Yverdon Switz. **39** 46.47N 6.39E
Yvetot France **18** 49.37N 0.46E

Z

Zaandam Neth. **16** 52.27N 4.49E
Zabid Yemen **72** 14.12N 43.19E
Žabljak Yugo. **31** 43.09N 19.07E
Zābol *d.* Afghan. **62** 32.00N 67.00E
Zābol Iran **65** 31.00N 61.32E
Zāboli Iran **65** 27.08N 61.36E
Zabqung China **63** 31.38N 87.20E
Zabrze Poland **37** 50.18N 18.47E
Zacapa Guatemala **117** 15.00N 89.30W
Zacatecas Mexico **116** 22.48N102.33W
Zacatecas *d.* Mexico **116** 24.00N103.00W
Zadar Yugo. **31** 44.07N 15.14E
Zafra Spain **27** 38.25N 6.25W
Zafriyya Israel **67** 32.00N 34.51E
Zaglivérion Greece **34** 40.36N 23.15E
Zagorá Greece **34** 39.27N 23.06E
Zagorsk U.S.S.R. **44** 56.20N 38.10E
Zagreb Yugo. **31** 45.48N 15.58E
Zāgros, Kūhhā-ye *mts.* Iran **65** 32.00N 51.00E
Zagros Mts. *see* Zāgros, Kūhhā-ye *mts.* Iran **65**
Zāhedān Iran **65** 29.32N 60.54E
Zaḩlah Lebanon **66** 33.50N 35.55E
Zahrān Saudi Arabia **71** 17.40N 43.30E
Zaindeh *r.* Iran **65** 32.40N 52.50E
Zaïre Africa **78** 2.00S 22.00E
Zaire *d.* Angola **78** 6.30S 13.30E
Zaïre *r.* Zaïre **78** 6.00S 12.30E
Zaječar Yugo. **34** 43.53N 22.18E
Zákas Greece **34** 40.02N 21.16E
Zakataly U.S.S.R. **65** 41.39N 46.40E
Zákinthos *i.* Greece **35** 37.52N 20.44E
Zákinthos *town* Greece **35** 37.47N 20.54E
Zákinthou, Porthmós *str.* Greece **35** 37.50N 21.00E
Zakopane Poland **37** 49.19N 19.57E
Zala *d.* Hungary **31** 46.35N 16.40E
Zalaegerszeg Hungary **31** 46.51N 16.51E
Zalalövö Hungary **31** 46.51N 16.35E
Zalamea de la Serena Spain **26** 38.39N 5.39W
Zalaszentgrót Hungary **31** 46.59N 17.02E
Zalău Romania **37** 47.11N 23.03E
Žalec Yugo. **31** 46.15N 15.10E
Zaleshchiki U.S.S.R. **37** 48.39N 25.50E
Zalim Saudi Arabia **64** 22.43N 42.11E
Zalingei Sudan **73** 12.54N 23.29E
Zambezi *r.* Mozambique / Zambia **81** 18.15S 35.55E
Zambezi Zambia **78** 13.30S 23.12E
Zambezia *d.* Mozambique **81** 16.30S 37.30E
Zambia Africa **79** 14.00S 28.00E
Zamboanga Phil. **59** 6.55N122.05E
Zambrów Poland **37** 53.00N 22.15E
Zambue Mozambique **80** 15.09S 30.47E
Zamfara *r.* Nigeria **77** 12.04N 4.00E
Zamora Mexico **116** 20.00N102.18W
Zamora Spain **26** 41.30N 5.45W
Zamora *d.* Spain **26** 41.45N 6.00W
Zamość Poland **37** 50.43N 23.15E
Zamtang China **61** 32.26N101.06E
Zaña Peru **122** 7.00S 79.30W
Záncara *r.* Spain **27** 39.18N 3.18W
Zanda China **63** 31.29N 79.50E
Zanesville U.S.A. **114** 39.56N 82.01W
Zangoza *see* Sangüesa Spain **25**
Zanjān Iran **65** 36.40N 48.30E
Zanthus Australia **89** 31.02S123.34E
Zanzibar Tanzania **79** 6.10S 39.16E
Zanzibar I. Tanzania **79** 6.00S 39.20E
Zaouatallaz Algeria **75** 24.52N 8.26E
Zaouiet Azmour Tunisia **32** 36.55N 11.01E
Zaouiet el Mgaïz Tunisia **32** 36.56N 10.50E
Zaozhuang China **54** 34.48N117.50E
Zapadna Morava *r.* Yugo. **34** 43.50N 20.15E
Zapadni Rodopi *mts.* Bulgaria **34** 41.49N 23.58E
Zapadno-Sibirskaya Ravnina *f.* U.S.S.R. **9** 60.00N 75.00E
Zapadnyy Sayan *mts.* U.S.S.R. **51** 53.00N 92.00E
Západočeský *d.* Czech. **38** 49.40N 13.00E
Zapala Argentina **125** 38.55S 70.05W
Zapardiel *r.* Spain **26** 41.29N 5.02W
Zapata U.S.A. **111** 26.52N 99.19W
Zaporozhye U.S.S.R. **45** 47.50N 35.10E
Zapug China **63** 33.17N 80.50E
Zara Turkey **64** 39.55N 37.44E
Zaragoza Spain **25** 41.38N 0.53W
Zaragoza *d.* Spain **25** 41.40N 1.10W
Zarand Iran **65** 30.50N 56.35E
Zaranj Afghan. **62** 31.06N 61.53E
Zárate Argentina **125** 34.05S 59.02W
Zarauz Spain **26** 43.17N 2.10W
Zaraza Venezuela **122** 9.23N 65.20W
Zard Kūh *mtn.* Iran **65** 32.21N 50.04E
Zarembo I. U.S.A. **100** 56.20N132.50W
Zarghūn Shahr Afghan. **60** 32.51N 68.25E
Zari Nigeria **77** 13.03N 12.46E
Zaria Nigeria **77** 11.01N 7.44E
Zárkon Greece **34** 39.37N 22.07E
Zaruma Ecuador **122** 3.40S 79.30W
Żary Poland **36** 51.40N 15.10E
Zarzal Colombia **122** 4.24N 76.01W
Zāskār *r.* Jammu & Kashmir **62** 34.10N 77.20E
Zāskār Mts. Jammu & Kashmir **63** 33.15N 78.00E
Zaslavl U.S.S.R. **37** 54.00N 27.15E
Za'tarī, Wādī az Jordan **67** 32.09N 36.15E
Žatec Czech. **39** 50.18N 13.32E
Zatishye U.S.S.R. **37** 47.20N 29.58E
Zave Zimbabwe **80** 17.14S 30.02E
Zavet Bulgaria **34** 43.46N 26.40E
Zavidovići Yugo. **31** 44.27N 18.09E
Zavitinsk U.S.S.R. **53** 50.08N129.24E
Zāwa Pakistan **62** 28.04N 66.23E
Zawīlah Libya **75** 26.10N 15.07E
Zāwiyat al Amwāt Egypt **66** 28.04N 30.50E
Zāwiyat al Mukhaylá Libya **72** 32.10N 22.17E
Zāyandeh *r.* Iran **65** 32.40N 52.50E
Zaydābād Afghan. **62** 34.17N 69.07E
Zaydī, Wādī az Syria **67** 32.45N 35.50E
Zaysan U.S.S.R. **52** 47.30N 84.57E
Zaysan, Ozero *l.* U.S.S.R. **52** 48.00N 83.30E
Zayzūn Syria **67** 32.43N 35.56E
Zbarazh U.S.S.R. **37** 49.40N 25.49E
Zborov U.S.S.R. **37** 49.40N 25.09E
Zbraslav Czech. **38** 49.59N 14.24E
Zdolbunov U.S.S.R. **37** 50.30N 26.10E
Zduńska Wola Poland **37** 51.36N 18.57E
Zeballos Canada **100** 49.59N126.50W
Zebediela R.S.A. **80** 24.19S 29.17E
Zeebrugge Belgium **16** 51.20N 3.13E
Zeehan Australia **91** 41.55S145.21E
Zeeland *d.* Neth. **16** 51.30N 3.45E
Ze'elim Israel **67** 31.12N 34.32E
Zeerust R.S.A. **80** 25.32S 26.04E
Zefa' Israel **67** 31.07N 35.12E
Zefat Israel **67** 32.57N 35.27E
Zehdenick Germany **38** 52.59N 13.20E
Zeist Neth. **16** 52.03N 5.16E
Zeitz Germany **38** 51.03N 12.08E
Zelechów Poland **37** 51.49N 21.54E
Zelengora *mts.* Yugo. **31** 43.20N 18.30E
Zelenodolsk U.S.S.R. **44** 55.50N 48.30E
Zelenogorsk U.S.S.R. **44** 60.15N 29.31E
Zelenokumsk U.S.S.R. **45** 44.25N 43.54E
Zelentsovo U.S.S.R. **44** 59.51N 44.59E
Zelina Yugo. **31** 45.58N 16.15E
Zell Germany **39** 50.01N 7.10E
Zella-Mehlis Germany **38** 50.39N 10.39E
Zell am Ziller Austria **39** 47.14N 11.53E
Zelts U.S.S.R. **37** 46.38N 30.00E
Zelzate Belgium **16** 51.12N 3.49E
Zembra, Île *i.* Tunisia **32** 37.08N 10.48E
Zemio C.A.R. **73** 5.02N 25.08E
Zemoul, Oued *wadi* Morocco **74** 29.12N 7.52W
Zemun Yugo. **29** 44.51N 20.23E
Zendeh Jān Afghan. **62** 34.21N 61.45E
Zenica Yugo. **31** 44.12N 17.55E
Zenn *r.* Germany **39** 49.31N 10.58E
Zenne *r.* Belgium **16** 51.04N 4.25E
Zerbst Germany **38** 51.58N 12.04E
Zereh, Gowd-e *l.* Afghan. **62** 29.45N 61.50E
Zergan Albania **34** 41.30N 20.21E
Zetel Germany **38** 53.25N 7.58E
Zeulenroda Germany **38** 50.39N 11.58E
Zeven Germany **38** 53.18N 9.16E
Zevenaar Neth. **16** 51.57N 6.04E
Zevenbergen Neth. **16** 51.41N 4.42E
Zeya U.S.S.R. **51** 53.48N127.14E
Zeya *r.* U.S.S.R. **51** 50.20N127.30E
Zêzere *r.* Portugal **27** 39.28N 8.20W
Zgierz Poland **37** 51.52N 19.25E
Zgorzelec Poland **36** 51.12N 15.01E
Zhailma U.S.S.R. **50** 51.37N 61.33E
Zhanatas U.S.S.R. **52** 43.11N 69.35E
Zhangbei China **54** 41.08N114.44E
Zhanghua Taiwan **55** 24.05N120.30E
Zhangjiakou China **54** 40.47N114.56E
Zhangping China **55** 25.25N117.28E
Zhangpu China **55** 24.06N117.37E
Zhangwu China **54** 42.22N122.31E
Zhang Xian China **54** 34.48N104.27E
Zhangye China **52** 38.56N100.27E
Zhangzhou China **55** 24.57N118.32E
Zhanjiang China **55** 21.08N110.22E
Zhanyu China **54** 44.31N122.40E
Zhao'an China **55** 23.45N117.14E
Zhaoping China **55** 24.06N110.48E
Zhaoqing China **55** 23.02N112.29E
Zhari Namco *l.* China **63** 31.00N 85.30E
Zhashkov U.S.S.R. **37** 49.12N 30.05E
Zhashui China **54** 33.41N109.06E
Zhaxi Co *l.* China **63** 32.10N 85.00E
Zhaxigang China **63** 32.31N 79.33E
Zhejiang *d.* China **55** 29.00N120.00E
Zheleznodorozhnyy R.S.F.S.R. U.S.S.R. **44** 62.39N 50.59E
Zheleznodorozhnyy R.S.F.S.R. U.S.S.R. **44** 67.59N 64.47E
Zhen'an China **54** 33.24N109.12E
Zhenba China **54** 32.34N107.58E
Zheng'an China **55** 28.30N107.30E
Zhenghe China **55** 27.23N118.51E
Zhengyang China **54** 32.36N114.23E
Zhengzhou China **54** 34.40N113.38E
Zhenhai China **55** 29.58N121.45E
Zhenjiang China **54** 32.09N119.30E
Zhenxiong China **55** 27.27N104.50E
Zhenyuan China **54** 35.42N106.58E
Zherdnoye U.S.S.R. **37** 51.40N 30.11E
Zherong China **55** 27.13N119.52E
Zhidachov U.S.S.R. **37** 49.20N 24.22E
Zhigansk U.S.S.R. **51** 66.48N123.27E
Zhijiang China **55** 27.27N109.41E
Zhitkovichi U.S.S.R. **37** 52.12N 27.49E
Zhitomir U.S.S.R. **37** 50.18N 28.40E
Zhlobin U.S.S.R. **37** 52.50N 30.00E
Zhmerinka U.S.S.R. **37** 49.00N 28.02E
Zhob *r.* Pakistan **62** 32.04N 69.50E
Zhongba China **63** 29.40N 84.07E
Zhongdian China **61** 28.00N 99.30E
Zhongli Taiwan **55** 24.54N121.09E
Zhongning China **54** 37.28N105.41E
Zhongshan Guangdong China **55** 22.31N113.22E
Zhongtiao Shan China **54** 36.00N113.30E
Zhongwei China **54** 37.30N105.15E
Zhoucun China **54** 36.49N117.49E
Zhoushan *i.* China **55** 30.05N122.15E
Zhouzhi China **54** 34.08N108.14E
Zhuanghe China **54** 39.41N123.02E
Zhucheng China **54** 36.00N119.24E
Zhugqu China **54** 33.46N104.18E
Zhuji China **55** 29.43N120.14E
Zhumadian China **54** 32.58N114.02E
Zhuo Xian China **54** 39.30N116.55E
Zhuozi China **54** 40.52N112.33E
Zhuozi Shan *mtn.* China **54** 39.36N107.00E
Zhupanovo U.S.S.R. **51** 53.40N159.52E
Zhuxi China **54** 32.19N109.52E
Zhuzhou China **55** 27.49N113.07E
Ziārat Pakistan **62** 30.23N 67.43E
Ziārat-e Shāh Maqsūd Afghan. **62** 31.59N 65.30E
Žiar nad Hronom Czech. **37** 48.36N 18.52E
Zibo China **54** 36.50N118.00E
Zicavo France **21** 41.54N 9.08E
Ziegenhain Germany **38** 50.50N 9.07E
Ziel, Mt. Australia **88** 23.24S132.23E
Zielona Góra Poland **36** 51.57N 15.30E
Ziesar Germany **38** 52.16N 12.17E
Ziftá Egypt **66** 30.43N 31.14E
Zigey Chad **77** 14.43N 15.47E
Zigong China **55** 29.18N104.45E
Zigui China **55** 31.01N110.35E
Ziguinchor Senegal **76** 12.35N 16.20W
Zikhron Ya'aqov Israel **67** 32.34N 34.57E
Zile Turkey **64** 40.18N 35.52E
Žilina Czech. **37** 49.14N 18.46E
Zillah Libya **75** 28.33N 17.35E
Zillertaler Alpen *mts.* Austria / Italy **30** 47.00N 11.55E
Zima U.S.S.R. **51** 53.58N102.02E
Zimatlán Mexico **116** 16.52N 96.45W
Zimba Zambia **78** 17.20S 26.25E
Zimbabwe Africa **80** 18.55S 30.00E
Zimbor Romania **37** 47.00N 23.16E
Zimi Sierra Leone **76** 7.22N 11.21W
Zimnicea Romania **34** 43.39N 25.21E
Zimniy Bereg *f.* U.S.S.R. **44** 65.50N 41.30E
Zinder Niger **77** 13.46N 8.58E
Zinder *d.* Niger **77** 14.20N 9.30E
Zinga Mtwara Tanzania **79** 9.01S 38.47E
Ziniaré Burkina **76** 12.34N 1.12W
Zinkgruvan Sweden **43** 58.49N 15.05E
Zinnowitz Germany **38** 54.04N 13.55E
Zion Grove U.S.A. **115** 40.54N 76.13W
Zippori Israel **67** 32.45N 35.17E
Žirje *i.* Yugo. **31** 43.40N 15.39E
Ziro India **61** 27.38N 93.42E
Zi Shui *r.* China **55** 28.38N112.30E
Zitong China **55** 31.38N105.11E
Zitsa Greece **34** 39.47N 20.40E
Zittau Germany **38** 50.54N 14.47E
Zitundo Mozambique **81** 26.45S 32.49E
Ziway Hāyk' *l.* Ethiopia **73** 8.00N 38.50E
Zixi China **55** 27.42N117.05E
Ziyang China **55** 30.02N104.42E
Zizhong China **55** 29.48N104.51E
Zlarin Yugo. **31** 43.42N 15.50E
Zlatar Yugo. **31** 46.06N 16.05E
Zlatograd Bulgaria **34** 41.22N 25.07E
Zlatoust U.S.S.R. **44** 55.10N 59.38E
Zletovo Yugo. **34** 41.59N 22.17E
Zlín Czech. **37** 49.13N 17.41E
Zlīṭan Libya **75** 32.28N 14.34E
Złoczew Poland **37** 51.25N 18.36E
Złotów Poland **37** 53.22N 17.02E
Žlutice Czech. **39** 50.03N 13.10E
Zlynka U.S.S.R. **37** 52.24N 31.45E
Zmeinogorsk U.S.S.R. **50** 51.11N 82.14E
Žminj Yugo. **31** 45.09N 13.55E
Zmiyevka U.S.S.R. **44** 52.40N 36.22E
Znamenka U.S.S.R. **45** 48.42N 32.40E
Żnin Poland **37** 52.52N 17.43E
Znojmo Czech. **36** 48.52N 16.05E
Zobia Zaïre **78** 2.58N 25.56E
Zobue Mozambique **81** 15.35S 34.26E
Zoétélé Cameroon **77** 3.17N 11.54E
Zogno Italy **30** 45.48N 9.40E
Zohreh *r.* Iran **65** 30.04N 49.32E
Zolochev U.S.S.R. **37** 49.48N 24.51E
Zolotonosha U.S.S.R. **45** 49.39N 32.05E
Zomba Malaŵi **79** 15.22S 35.22E

Zonguldak Turkey **64** 41.26N 31.47E
Zong Xian China **55** 30.16N 108.01E
Zorita Spain **27** 39.17N 5.42W
Zorzor Liberia **76** 7.46N 9.28W
Zouar Chad **77** 20.27N 16.32E
Zouîrât Mauritania **74** 22.35N 12.20W
Zoutkamp Neth. **16** 53.21N 6.18E
Zrenjanin Yugo. **29** 45.22N 20.23E
Zrmanja r. Yugo. **31** 44.15N 15.32E
Zuckerhütl mtn. Austria **30** 46.58N 11.09E
Zuénoula Ivory Coast **76** 7.34N 6.03W
Zuera Spain **25** 41.52N 0.47W
Zug Switz. **39** 47.10N 8.31E

Zug d. Switz. **39** 47.10N 8.40E
Zugspitze mtn. Germany **39** 47.25N 10.59E
Zuid Beveland f. Neth. **16** 51.30N 3.50E
Zuidelijk-Flevoland f. Neth. **16** 52.22N 5.22E
Zuid Holland d. Neth. **16** 52.00N 4.30E
Zuidhorn Neth. **16** 53.16N 6.25E
Zújar r. Spain **26** 39.01N 5.47W
Zújar, Embalse del resr. Spain **26** 38.50N 5.20W
Zülpich Germany **38** 50.41N 6.39E
Zululand see Kwa Zulu f. R.S.A. **80**
Zumbo Mozambique **80** 15.36S 30.24E
Zungeru Nigeria **77** 9.48N 6.03E
Zunyi China **55** 27.39N 106.48E

Županja Yugo. **31** 45.04N 18.42E
Zurich Neth. **16** 53.08N 5.25E
Zürich Switz. **39** 47.23N 8.32E
Zürich d. Switz. **39** 47.25N 8.45E
Zürichsee l. Switz. **39** 47.13N 8.45E
Zuru Nigeria **77** 11.26N 5.16E
Zushi Japan **57** 35.18N 139.35E
Žut i. Yugo. **31** 43.52N 15.19E
Zutphen Neth. **16** 52.08N 6.12E
Zuwârah Libya **75** 32.56N 12.06E
Zuwayzā Jordan **67** 31.42N 35.55E
Žužemberk Yugo. **31** 45.50N 14.56E
Zvenigorodka U.S.S.R. **37** 49.05N 30.58E

Zverinogolovskoye U.S.S.R. **50** 48.01N 40.09E
Zvishavane Zimbabwe **80** 20.20S 30.05E
Zvolen Czech. **37** 48.35N 19.08E
Zweibrücken Germany **39** 49.15N 7.21E
Zweisimmen Switz. **39** 46.33N 7.22E
Zwettl Austria **36** 48.37N 15.10E
Zwickau Germany **38** 50.44N 12.29E
Zwiesel Germany **39** 49.01N 13.14E
Zwischenahn Germany **38** 53.12N 8.00E
Zwoleń Poland **37** 51.22N 21.35E
Zwolle Neth. **16** 52.31N 6.06E
Zyryanovsk U.S.S.R. **50** 49.45N 84.16E
Zywiec Poland **37** 49.41N 19.12E

OCEANIA
MAPS 82 – 93

NORTH AMERICA
MAPS 94 – 117

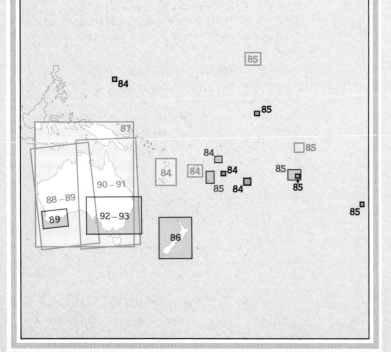

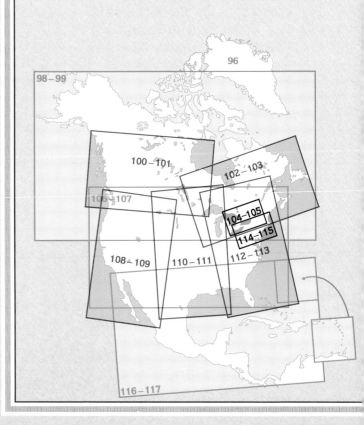

Continuation from Front Endpaper

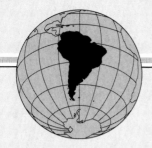

SOUTH AMERICA
MAPS 118 – 126

118–119 **SOUTH AMERICA Political**
Global View
120–121 **SOUTH AMERICA** 1:25M
122–123 **SOUTH AMERICA – NORTH** 1:12½M
124–125 **SOUTH AMERICA – SOUTH** 1:12½M
River Plate 1:7½M
126 **SOUTH AMERICA – EAST** 1:12½M
Rio – São Paulo 1:7½M

ATLANTIC & POLAR
MAPS 127 – 128

127 **ATLANTIC OCEAN** 1:60M
Bermuda 1:1M
Ascension 1:1M
St. Helena 1:1M
Canary Islands 1:10M
Madeira Islands 1:1M
Tristan da Cunha 1:1M
128 **POLAR REGIONS** 1:50M

By reference to this Key to Maps, and its continuation on the front endpaper, the most suitable map of a required area can be found.

The map pages of the core World Atlas section are keyed according to their continental subsections and scale category. There are three scale categories, as indicated below. All scales are quoted as representative ratios expressed in millions (as denoted by the abbreviation M).

Large scale: between 1:1M and 2½M

Medium scale: between 1:2½M and 1:7½M

Small scale: smaller than 1:7½M

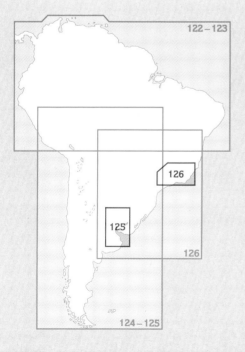